Encyclopedia of

American Poetry

THE NINETEENTH CENTURY

Encyclopedia of
American Poetry

THE NINETEENTH CENTURY

EDITED BY ERIC L. HARALSON

JOHN HOLLANDER, ADVISORY EDITOR

FITZROY DEARBORN PUBLISHERS

Chicago ❧ London

For information write to:

FITZROY DEARBORN PUBLISHERS
919 N. Michigan Avenue, Suite 760
Chicago, Illinois 60611
USA

or

FITZROY DEARBORN PUBLISHERS
310 Regent Street
London W1R 5AJ
England

Cataloging-in-Publication Data is available from the Library of Congress and the British Library

ISBN 1-57958-008-4

 # 39285700

First published in the USA and UK 1998

Typeset and Printed by Sheridan Books, Inc., Ann Arbor, Michigan
Cover design by Peter Aristedes

For Howard, of course –
who loved to recite "Buffalo Bill's / defunct" –
and for Kathryn the great

CONTENTS

EDITOR'S NOTE
AND GUIDE TO USAGE

"Stop this day and night with me and you shall possess the origin of all poems," beckons the irresistible Walt Whitman in "Song of Myself": "You shall no longer take things at second or third hand / . . . nor feed on the spectres in books, // You shall listen to all sides and filter them from yourself." Sound advice for approaching verse, surely, and please do read every bit contained in the fine two-volume anthology *American Poetry: The Nineteenth Century*, published in 1993 by The Library of America under the editorship of the distinguished poet and critic John Hollander. Then, if you should desire further guidance in possessing the origins of all those poems – or many of them, rather, for more than a thousand appear there – the book you are holding now in hand will be of great use.

As you will have discovered, the Library of America anthology presents selections not only from the usual suspects, such as Whitman and Emily Dickinson, but from numerous other poets – nearly 150 in all – whose contributions are vital to our understanding of the emerging culture – literary, social, and political – of the United States. This reference "companion" – dreamed up some years ago while I was serving as a textual researcher for The Library of America – offers insightful, in-depth accounts of the lives, writings, and other achievements of more than 100 of the authors anthologized, while many of the rest come in for treatment in the topical essays **Nineteenth-Century Versions of American Indian Poetry, Popular Poetry, Songs and Ballads,** and **Spirituals.**

As suggested by these four headings, entries are arranged alphabetically, and words or names in **bold** indicate cross-references, directing the reader's attention to related essays and marking either important conjunctions among verse forms or (more often) intersections in the careers of individual poets. This encyclopedia is keyed to *American Poetry: The Nineteenth Century* in a more intimate way as well: contributors have focused their essays, as much as possible, on the works representing their respective poets (or topics) in that collection, and each instance of such a correlation is signaled by a parenthetical citation of the volume and page where the reader can find the verses under discussion. Upon first mention in a given essay, for example, Dickinson's "Wild Nights – Wild Nights!" will be followed by a cue to consult page 233 of volume 2 of the Library of America anthology (LOA, 2: 233), where that poem begins.

Although best read alongside *American Poetry: The Nineteenth Century*, the *Encyclopedia of American Poetry: The Nineteenth Century* stands as a comprehensive reference resource in its own right, well suited to the diverse needs of students, teachers, and scholars. For apart from the obligation to coordinate entries with the Library of America anthology, contributors were given a free hand, on the editorial hunch that an excellent corps of authors, left to their own devices, would know how to construct an excellent group of essays. As you will see, besides furnishing useful facts and dates, biographical background, and information on the provenance of the poetry – as one would expect from any reference volume of this title – each entry amounts to an incisive *critical* essay, delving into the formal features, literary-historical significance, and cultural relevance of the verses being addressed. The larger scope of the entries also permitted contributors to *extend* the Library of America edition by covering many more works per author or verse category than could reasonably have been anthologized. Moreover, readers who become enthusiastic about a particular poet or topic will be steered toward other pertinent sources by the list of Selected Works at the end of each entry. Those who study the Further Reading portion of enough of these bibliographies will also learn, before long, which broad surveys of the American poetic tradition promise to be most rewarding to their subsequent research.

In its range, then, the *Encyclopedia of American Poetry* participates in the ongoing effort to recuperate "lost" or submerged parts of the cultural heritage of the United States. In content and organization, the book demonstrates the dividends of reading works by relatively well-known poets – William Cullen Bryant, Stephen Crane, Ralph Waldo Emerson, Henry Wadsworth Longfellow, Herman Melville, Edgar Allan Poe, Edwin Arlington Robinson, and John Greenleaf Whittier – in the context of works by less familiar and frequently undervalued figures of the nineteenth-century literary scene. Without detriment to others treated here, these figures include overlooked women poets such as Maria Gowen Brooks, Alice and Phoebe Cary, Sarah Morgan Bryan Piatt, and Lizette Woodworth Reese; African American poets like Paul Laurence Dunbar and Frances E. W. Harper, and Native American poets such as Alexander Posey and John Rollin Ridge; neglected Southern poets, notably Sidney Lanier and Henry Timrod; underappreciated talents like Trumbull Stickney, Frederick Goddard Tuckerman, and Jones Very, or fading "fireside" poets such as Oliver Wendell Holmes and James Russell Lowell; poets who are more famous as writers in other genres (Margaret Fuller, Nathaniel Hawthorne, Henry David Thoreau, Edith Wharton), as painters (Washington Allston, Thomas Cole), as sculptors (William Wetmore Story), as actors (Frances Kemble), or as politicians (John Quincy Adams); and finally, those authors who have vanished, as it were, in the very popularity of their productions, such as "Casey at the Bat," "The Man with the Hoe," "The Purple Cow," and "Curfew Must Not Ring To-Night." Not all of the poetry encountered here will make you feel as if the top of your head were being taken off – to borrow Dickinson's formula for the real, right thing in verse – but all of it, as we are about to prove, will repay your interest.

Acknowledgments

In a project of this scope and duration, the debts incurred are many, but let me try to count the ways. At The Library of America (wonderful enterprise), early endorsements came from Cheryl Hurley and Hannah (Gila) Bercovitch; leads on several invaluable contributors, from Richard Poirier; and periodic enlightenment on textual matters, from Cameron McDonald, Geoffrey O'Brien, Max Rudin, and Derick Schilling. Joan Zseleczsky, Phyllis Korper, and Audrey Leung – three of the finest people in publishing – each gave this book a big push at (respectively) the beginning, middle, and end of the process; and Chuck Bartelt, Jason Goldfarb, Elizabeth Manus, Justin Brent, and Jay McRoy, in their bountiful technical expertise, coaxed it along as well. Lawrence Buell and Tom Bechtle offered timely moral support. My old friend Patrick Cheung knows just what his essential role in the saga was, and how much I appreciate it.

As for Fitzroy Dearborn Publishers, my very great gratitude to George Walsh, for believing in this book when it badly needed such faith; to Carol Burwash, for her perfect and always pleasant handling of the product as commissioning editor; and to William Weaver, for his intrepid copyediting. A very special thanks to my advisory editor, John Hollander, for unexampled generosity and steadfast support. To my terrific (and very patient) contributors, who made the whole thing possible, my heartfelt thanks. And to my dear (and even more patient) family – Susan Notkin, who sustains my life and labor, Sara and Lucas, who brighten every day – my love.

ERIC HARALSON
State University of New York at Stony Brook

LIST OF ENTRIES AND CONTRIBUTORS

Henry Adams

(1838–1918)

In his autobiographical sketch for the Life-Book of Harvard's Class of 1858, Henry Adams expressed his desire to lead "a quiet and a literary life." He spent his remaining 60 years pursuing these two somewhat contradictory goals. Naturally reticent, Adams sought to preserve the privacy that would guarantee him a "quiet" life. The tenacity with which he pursued his literary occupation, however, demonstrated an equally compelling desire to reach the very public from which he held himself aloof. In his later years, Adams created his own private "public," the coterie of friends and relatives who were allowed to read his privately printed works such as *Mont Saint Michel and Chartres* (1904) and *The Education of Henry Adams* (1907). The privacy of a printing that ran to 100 or so copies became rather tenuously artificial: when word got out, people beyond Adams's circle of friends clamored for copies. *The Education* became Adams's best known work, and even *Chartres* overshadowed Adams's *History of the United States of America During the Administrations of Thomas Jefferson and James Madison* (1889–91), which some regard as the finest history ever written by an American.

By contrast to his coy but unmistakably published prose, Adams's poetry remained relatively private and confidential. Only one poem was published in his lifetime: "Buddha and Brahma" (LOA, 2: 383). Composed in 1891, this poem did not appear in print until 1915 (in the *Yale Review*). Adams had previously given a copy to his close friend John **Hay** with the injunction that the lines go no further. Another well-known poem, "Prayer to the Virgin of Chartres," written in the winter of 1900–01, went to Elizabeth Cameron, who became the emotional center of Adams's life after his wife's death and who, it is assumed, inspired his idealization of the Virgin. His niece Mabel La Farge published the poem along with his letters to her in 1920.

Although it is impossible to read even Adams's correspondence without sensing that he imagined posterity looking over his shoulder as he wrote, these two poems seem to have served a more personal function for him. They lack the ironic tone used to such effect in both *The Education* and the correspondence. The fruit of contemplation, "Buddha and Brahma" and "Prayer" bear the same relation to Adams's philosophy of life that any liturgy has to the faith of those who repeat it. These private poems, however, reveal not an obscure personal iconography, but a keen intellect grappling with philosophical concerns that speak directly to a late-nineteenth-century context. "Buddha and Brahma" describes the necessity of resigning oneself to an intellectual appreciation of Nirvana rather than its attainment. "Prayer" is less a profession of faith than a lamenting of the desolation caused by the way in which people replace the worship of a recognizably human deity (the Virgin) with an intellectual construct of the universe as an inhuman and indifferent, although manipulable, field of atomic energy. In neither poem can a direct connection to the transcendent realm, whether the Nirvana of Buddha or the Heaven of the Virgin Mary, be taken for granted. The nostalgia for religious experience in these poems, however, belongs neither to a Brah-

man of the sixth century B.C., nor to a Christian of the thirteenth century, but to an atheistic, or at best an agnostic American of the nineteenth. Both poems are also shaped by intellectual fashions. Buddhism was in vogue among certain American intellectuals, including some friends of Adams. The nineteenth century also saw a revival of interest in medieval architecture and culture – from Scott to Ruskin and the Pre-Raphaelites – stimulated by authors such as the French architectural historian Eugène Viollet-le-Duc.

Adams's poetry constitutes only a tiny fraction of his prodigious literary output. Besides "Buddha and Brahma" and "Prayer" scholars only know about a handful of poems, mostly sonnets, that he shared only with Elizabeth Cameron or other close friends. He also translated poems by Petrarch for his novel *Esther* and medieval chansons and poems by Adam de Saint Victor and Chretien de Troyes for *Chartres*. Adams's other prose works include three biographies, another novel, newspaper pieces, political essays, book reviews, scholarly articles, and a volume of ethnography and Tahitian family history. An inveterate letter writer, Adams left behind a massive correspondence.

Within the Adams family, writing was as much a tradition as political service. Born in Boston, the fourth of seven children of Charles Francis Adams and Abigail Brooks Adams, Henry Brooks Adams was the grandson and great-grandson of two presidents: John Quincy **Adams** and John Adams. As a child, Henry witnessed and perhaps assisted in the editing and publishing of his great-grandparents' (John's and Abigail's) letters and papers, with which his father busied himself from 1840 to 1856. John Quincy Adams, despite six decades of nearly continuous public service, also was a diarist, essayist, and poet. Henry's brothers, Charles Francis II and Brooks, also wrote essays, biographies, and works of history.

Adams entered Harvard in the fall of 1854. During his undergraduate literary apprenticeship, he contributed essays and book reviews to the *Harvard Magazine*, took second place in competition for the Bowdoin Prize, and was elected class orator. The bawdy doggerel he composed to fulfill his duties as "Krokodeilos" of the Hasty Pudding Club was some of his earliest poetry. Among his professors was the poet James Russell **Lowell**. Upon graduation in 1858, Adams traveled to Europe. He spent most of two years in Berlin and Dresden, studying German and attending lectures on the civil law. He toured Germany, Austria, Italy, and Sicily, and visited Paris before returning to the United States in 1860. It was the first long period of travel in a life filled with trips to the Continent and other, more exotic locales. Out of this particular trip came a series of travel letters that recount, among other things, Adams's interview with Garibaldi, the Italian patriot who had just triumphed at Palermo. Although they affect a familiar tone, these letters were self-consciously literary and written for publication in the Boston *Daily Courier*.

Shortly after his return, Adams's father pressed him into service as his private secretary, first in Washington, D.C., on the eve of the Civil War, and then for seven years in London, where Charles Francis Adams served as U.S. minister to Great Britain.

Thus Henry (like Mark Twain, William Dean **Howells**, and the James brothers, Henry and William) experienced the event that defined his generation – the Civil War – at second hand. The years of hobnobbing in London gave Adams cosmopolitan polish. He became acquainted with many notables, including Robert Browning, Edward Bulwer-Lytton, Charles Dickens, Charles Lyell, John Stuart Mill, Algernon Swinburne, John Forster, Richard Monckton Milnes (Lord Houghton), Francis Turner Palgrave, Henry Reeve, and Thomas Woolner, and he began lifelong friendships with Charles Milnes Gaskell and Sir Robert Cunliffe.

Adams honed his writing skills during this period, first by serving as a newspaper correspondent and then by writing scholarly pieces for the *North American Review*, which debunked John Smith's Pocahontas story, treated British finance, and reviewed Lyell's *Principles of Geology*. In general, Adams sought to use these writings to shape public opinion. As "The Great Secession Winter 1860–1861" (not published until nearly 50 years later) demonstrates, however, Adams preferred to take the long view, to interject historical references and philosophical speculation rather than simply to report events. This tendency was also apparent in his articles on current politics, which he produced after he returning to Washington, D.C., in 1868.

In 1870, Adams accepted a joint appointment as editor of the *North American Review* and assistant professor of medieval history at Harvard. In preparation, he immersed himself in the history of institutions, a forerunner of the new discipline of anthropology. The notions about primitive society and social evolution he encountered as a professor influenced later works such as *Memoirs of Arii Taimai* and even *Chartres* and "Prayer to the Virgin of Chartres." As editor of the *North American Review*, Adams wrote numerous reviews of historical works and provided a forum for liberal and reform politics.

In June 1872, Adams married Marian ("Clover") Hooper, an intelligent, well-educated woman from a wealthy Boston family. Through her, he became friends with Henry James. Henry and Marian Adams had no children. The thirteen years they had together before she committed suicide in December 1885 after a long period of depression were, according to Adams, the happiest of his life. They were certainly some of the most productive. Some scholars have regarded the curious gap between the first and second parts of *The Education*, a gap that leaves out Adams's marriage and the writing of his *History*, as a symptom of the guilt and devastation he felt even decades after Marian's death. One can also see this omission as part of Adams's continuing attempt to keep his private life private. The display of emotions he did not allow himself in his ostensibly autobiographical work, however, can sometimes be found in his poetry, which he kept carefully unpublished.

In 1877, Adams resigned from Harvard, and he and Marian moved to Washington, D.C., where she established an exclusive salon and he pursued his researches into American political history. He edited *Documents Relating to New England Federalism* (1877) and *The Writings of Albert Gallatin* (1879) and published biographies of Gallatin (1879) and the Virginia statesman John Randolph (1882). Gallatin, who served as secretary of the treasury under Presidents Jefferson and Madison, is portrayed as a hero, often at the expense of Adams's own grandfather, John Quincy Adams. But in the venomous portrait of John Randolph, family prejudices have full rein. Adams published *Democracy: An American Novel* anonymously in 1880, and *Esther* under the pseudonym Frances Snow Compton in 1884. The protagonist of each is an intelligent, strongwilled woman compelled by conscience to reject the marriage that both plot and convention seem to dictate. *Democracy* satirizes Washington politics and skewers in particular those politicians who sacrifice morality and the public good to party allegiance. *Esther* dramatizes the difficulty of religious unbelief, and thus addresses the same philosophical dilemmas Adams later treated in both "Buddha and Brahma" and "Prayer to the Virgin of Chartres." In this novel, the game of translating and reciting Petrarch's sonnets to his beloved Laura becomes a central element in Reverend Stephen Hazard's courtship of Esther Dudley.

All extant poetry by Adams, excepting the Hasty Pudding doggerel, was written after his wife's death. Unlike the *History*, the poems were not intended for posterity. Moreover, the sonnets written to Elizabeth Cameron, wife of Senator Donald Cameron, have perhaps more value as windows into Adams's emotional life than as literature. Sonneteering was a game he and his friends John Hay and Cecil Spring Rice engaged in to amuse themselves. The poems also served as a decorous, discreet way to "make love" to a married woman. One of these works, "The Capitol by Moonlight," recalls an evening stroll taken in the company of Hay, Cameron, and another woman. The poem evokes an atmosphere of quiet unrest: "Peace broods." Personification and classical allusion abound. The dome of the Capitol is "Endymion, dreaming still that on his Latmian height / He feels Helene's breath warm on his eyes and hair." The "fire of Mars," possibly an allusion to a military installation, flashes in the West, and the Washington monument "mocks us." The poem is sprinkled liberally with exclamation points, which contrast with the understatement characteristic of many of Adams's best prose passages.

Another sonnet consists of an extended metaphor in which the speaker is a musician and his "mistress" the "viol that he chanced upon." Under the musician's touch, the instrument's "notes grow deeper and more sure; / Its scope more ample with each ripening year." The couplet, which concludes the simile, sounds a Shakespearean note: "So I, who, all these years, my mistress task, / Find more and richer charm, the more I ask." The poem seems a veiled commentary on the relationship between the much younger Cameron and the poet, which was, in many ways, that of pupil and mentor. Adams sent the poem "Eagle Head" to Cameron on the eve of his departure for the South Seas in 1890. (Eagle Head is a promontory near Adams's summer house in Beverly Farms, Massachusetts, where Cameron and her young daughter Martha were spending the summer.) With unusually inflated language, the speaker describes the eternal restlessness of the ocean as it beats against Eagle Head, a restlessness echoed in the scream of the eagles that nest there. The sonnet laments an impossible love: the heart "Beats against fate." But it ends by asking the loved one to join the speaker at Eagle Head and share the pain of this impossible love: " – Here let us lie and watch the wave-vexed shore, / Repeating, heart to heart, the eagles' strain, / The ocean's cry of passion and of pain."

Homesickness informs a poem Adams sent to Cameron from Samoa a few months later. The speaker of the poem looks out upon a Samoan village at dawn but imagines his friends in Washington. The first five stanzas are unaffected and familiar, although somewhat trite (he actually resorts to the "moon"/"June" rhyme). The abrupt shift in the last stanza to a philosophical summation also seems forced and unnatural:

> Death is not hard when once you feel its measure;
> One learns to know that Paradise is gain;
> One bids farewell to all that gave one pleasure;
> One bids farewell to all that gave one pain.

As in "Eagle Head," pleasure and pain are inextricably linked. Adams characteristically seeks philosophical import even in his own longings for friends back home, but in this instance, the intellectualization is awkward.

Another sonnet, "The Slaves of Michael Angelo," compares the struggle evident in the slave figures to the suffering of a Christian martyr, and both struggles are compared to Michelangelo's own agony. Adams apparently shared this poem with his friend the sculptor Augustus Saint-Gaudens sometime before April 1902. It voices a theme that Adams sounded repeatedly during his later years, most memorably in *Chartres*: the decline not only of spirituality but also of artistic sensibility in the post-Renaissance West. "Beauty like this no more to earth descends; / Strength such as his no more with life contends."

"Buddha and Brahma" is a narrative poem written in blank verse. The tone reminds one of Ralph Waldo **Emerson**. The poem dramatizes the search for an answer to the question "Is the world eternal?" Malunka, the young Buddhist disciple who poses the question, receives no verbal response from Buddha and thus seeks out his more voluble Brahman father. The Brahman's response sets forth conclusions similar to those that Adams himself had reached regarding the two Eastern religions: namely, that they are two paths to the same end (union with the Universal) and that Brahmanism (Hinduism) encompasses Buddhism. The silence of the Buddha, although venerated as somehow more pure than speech (his response to Malunka's question is to raise the lotus in his hand – "a mystic sign, / The symbol of a symbol"), is imitated neither by the Brahman nor by Adams. The Brahman represents Adams's nineteenth-century man, who is caught up in a life that requires action and speech and bereft of the "perfect union with the single Spirit" that Buddha achieves through contemplation and silence.

"Prayer to the Virgin of Chartres" seems to have been inspired partly by the appreciation of the figure of the Virgin Mary that Adams acquired through his studies and partly by his visit to the Hall of Dynamos at the Paris Exposition of 1900. The speaker penitently presents himself before the Virgin as the representative of Western humanity, past and present. Although the speaker's tone is earnest, the history lesson he recites belies the preoccupation of the historian-poet. The speaker confesses to having dethroned first the Mother, a metaphor for the Protestant Reformation, and then the Father, a metaphor for the ascendancy of scientific explanation. Nostalgia, not religious belief, thus sets the tone of the poem, and it is a nostalgia rooted in Adams's theories about history. One senses that the Virgin of Chartres was no less an intellectual construct to Adams than the theories of electromagnetic force that, when applied, resulted in dynamos.

The central portion of this poem is the "Prayer to the Dynamo," which expresses a desperate defiance of the "Mysterious Power," the "Primal Force" behind the dynamos. The poem also evinces an intention to control this force and a fear of being controlled by it.

> What are we then? the lords of space?
> The master-mind whose tasks you do?
> Jockey who rides you in the race?
> Or are we atoms whirled apace,
> Shaped and controlled by you?

The "Prayer to the Dynamo" is offered up as evidence of how far the nineteenth-century American, descendant of Protestants, has strayed from the more natural and more comforting worship of the Virgin Mother. In the final section, the narrator addresses the Virgin:

> A curious prayer, dear lady! is it not?
> Strangely unlike the prayers I prayed to you!
> Stranger because you find me at this spot,
> Here, at your feet, asking your help anew.
> . . . .
> What immortality our strength shall wring
> From Time and Space, we may – or may not – care;
> But years, or ages, or eternity,
> Will find me still in thought before your throne,
> Pondering the mystery of Maternity,
> Soul within Soul, – Mother and Child in One!

The speaker concludes by begging the Virgin not to intercede on his behalf for divine forgiveness – as a twelfth-century penitent would have – but to help him to see, to know, to feel, and to bear the "futile folly of the Infinite!" The poem must not be mistaken for an attempt to rediscover religious belief. Rather, Adams laments the deadening of sensibility that he sees as the peculiar ailment of turn-of-the-century humanity. The loss of religious belief is a metaphor for, not necessarily a cause of, this loss of sensibility.

The emotion that prompted Adams's poems may have been genuine, but he uses conventional tropes and stilted language. Indeed, the conventionality of the expression serves to render the emotion innocuous. "Buddha and Brahma" and "Prayer" succeed somewhat better than the others. For Adams's best writing, one must turn to his more polished prose works. Passages in *Chartres*, for example, like that in which the Gothic cathedral becomes a metonym for the theology of St. Thomas Aquinas, or in *The Education*, where his eldest sister's death by tetanus is described, display a pared-down elegance, carefully measured phrases, and an adroit use of metaphor.

Restlessness characterized Adams's later years. He may not have been among the best-selling but he was certainly among the best-traveled of American authors. With the artist John La Farge as a companion, Adams traveled to Japan in 1886 and four years later to Hawaii, Samoa, Tahiti, Fiji, Australia, and Ceylon (now Sri Lanka). He also toured the American West, Canada, Mexico, Cuba, and the Caribbean. Adams journeyed repeatedly to Europe, visiting many countries, and from 1899 to 1911, he spent part of every year in Paris. He visited the World's Fairs in Chicago (1893) and St. Louis (1904), as well as the Paris Exhibition of 1900.

Adams's travel experiences may have provided the impetus

for his writings, but these experiences were themselves always mediated by the vast knowledge he obtained through his reading. His travel literature is unmistakably "bookish." For instance, "Buddha and Brahma," written after his visit to Anuradhapura, Ceylon, the ancient Buddhist capital, is based loosely upon an anecdote from *Questions of King Milinda*. Adams's poem thus does not respond to Anuradhapura but to the anecdote – discovered in a Buddhist temple library before his visit – and to all he had previously read about Buddhism and Brahmanism.

Adams's reintroduction to Gothic architecture during a trip through Normandy in 1895 prompted him to resume his studies of medieval history and culture. This time he immersed himself not in law and institutions but in twelfth- and thirteenth-century architecture, literature, and theology. Nearly a decade later (1904), he privately printed *Mont Saint Michel and Chartres*, a work too impressionistic to be called history but too scholarly to pass as a guidebook. Theories of history, both as a discipline and as a phenomenon, were another late preoccupation. His "Dynamic Theory of History" assumed an ever accelerating pace of change in human knowledge that threatened to outstrip the adaptive capabilities of the human animal. Variations of this theory appeared in two essays – "The Rule of Phase Applied to History" (written 1909) and *A Letter to American Teachers of History* (1910) – that proceed with a curious confidence in the ability of figurative language to bridge the gap between the increasingly distinct disciplines of science and history.

A stroke put an end to Adams's literary activity in 1912, but he lived several years more, dying on March 27, 1918 in Washington, D.C. The first trade edition of *The Education*, published in September 1918, received the Pulitzer Prize for biography in 1919. Indisputably a master of prose style, Henry Adams remained a dilettante, although not an untalented one, when it came to poetry. The few poems he left behind, however, are good enough to suggest that he could have been an accomplished poet, had he chosen to be. More importantly, they provide us with a glimpse into the inner life of a major American intellectual of the late-nineteenth century.

JANE REMUS

Selected Works
Democracy, Esther, Mont Saint Michel and Chartres, The Education of Henry Adams, edited by Ernest Samuels and Jayne N. Samuels, New York: Library of America, 1983
History of the United States of America During the Administrations of Thomas Jefferson and James Madison, edited by Earl N. Harbert, New York: Library of America, 1986
The Letters of Henry Adams, edited by J. C. Levenson, et al., 6 vols., Cambridge, Massachusetts: Harvard University Press, 1982–88; London: Belknap, 1982–88

Further Reading
Decker, William Merrill, *The Literary Vocation of Henry Adams*, Chapel Hill and London: University of North Carolina Press, 1990
Dusinberre, William, *Henry Adams: The Myth of Failure*, Charlottesville: University Press of Virginia, 1980
Jacobson, Joanne, *Authority and Alliance in the Letters of Henry Adams*, Madison: University of Wisconsin Press, 1992
Levenson, J. C., *The Mind and Art of Henry Adams*, Boston: Houghton Mifflin, 1957
Lyon, Melvin, *Symbol and Idea in Henry Adams*, Lincoln: University of Nebraska Press, 1970
Mane, Robert, *Henry Adams on the Road to Chartres*, Cambridge, Massachusetts: Belknap/Harvard University Press, 1971
Nagel, Paul C., *Descent from Glory: Four Generations of the John Adams Family*, New York and Oxford: Oxford University Press, 1983
O'Toole, Patricia, *The Five of Hearts: An Intimate Portrait of Henry Adams and His Friends 1880–1918*, New York: Clarkson Potter, 1990
Porter, Carolyn, *Seeing and Being: The Plight of the Participant Observer in Emerson, James, Adams, and Faulkner*, Middletown, Connecticut: Wesleyan University Press, 1981
Rowe, John Carlos, *Henry Adams and Henry James: The Emergence of a Modern Consciousness*, Ithaca, New York, and London: Cornell University Press, 1976
Samuels, Ernest, *Henry Adams*, Cambridge, Massachusetts, and London: Belknap/Harvard University Press, 1989
———, *Henry Adams: The Middle Years*, Cambridge, Massachusetts: Belknap/Harvard University Press, 1958
Sayre, Robert F., *The Examined Self: Benjamin Franklin, Henry Adams, Henry James*, Princeton, New Jersey: Princeton University Press, 1964
Tehan, Arline Boucher, *Henry Adams in Love: The Pursuit of Elizabeth Sherman Cameron*, New York: Universe Books, 1983
Wagner, Vern, *The Suspension of Henry Adams*, Detroit, Michigan: Wayne State University Press, 1969

John Quincy Adams

(1767–1848)

John Quincy Adams maintained a love for writing poetry throughout his long and active career in law and public service for the state of Massachusetts and the federal government. Early in life, he was far more interested in pursuing a literary career than in becoming a lawyer or public servant, but the strong influence of his famous father, John Adams, and the political exigencies of the young republic compelled him to give up his first love. While on a diplomatic tour in Europe in 1796, he longed to return to America and a mode of life that would allow him the leisure to follow his "favorite pursuits and literary studies." Clearly motivated by a spirit of nationalism, he wrote his father from The Hague: "But the Americans have in Europe a sad reputation on the article of literature, and I shall propose to render a service to my country by devoting to it the remainder of my life." To his regret, he was never able to fulfill his ambition. As he wrote in his diary on Christmas day in 1820: "The summit of my ambition would have been by some great work of literature to have done honor to my age and country, and to have lived in the gratitude of future ages. This consummation of happiness has been denied me."

Between 1778 and 1785, Adams was on his second trip abroad, attending school in Paris and Leyden, serving as the private secretary to Francis Dana, the U.S. minister to Russia, and helping his father with diplomatic matters in Holland and England. Adams followed an exacting course of studies in the classics and mastered English and French poetry to prepare himself for his formal studies at Harvard College, a vocation in law and politics, and an avocation in letters. Almost unremitting subsequent studies earned him a widespread reputation as a classical scholar of the highest order. Of the ancient authors, it was Horace, whose *Epistula ad Pisones* (*Ars Poetica*) he had twice translated before 1784, who influenced Adams's aesthetics most. He found appealing Horace's dicta that poetry should be serious, moral, instructive, inspired, and subjected to outside criticism. In his composition of poetry, therefore, Adams never abandoned the classical requisites of order, regularity in meter, common sense, and didacticism that he learned in his early years. Well prepared, he entered Harvard with advanced standing in 1786 and graduated one year later.

As a 15-year-old student abroad, Adams first began to keep composition books in which he wrote verses, translations, and miscellaneous literary matters. He continued the practice until he died at age 81. He wrote poems (about 350 of which survive) regularly over the years, and he often kept duplicates and variant versions in his commonplace books (kept in the Adams Papers at the Massachusetts Historical Society and available on microfilm). Versatile in the genres, Adams wrote short lyrics, odes, sonnets, pastorals, narratives, ballads, epigrams, fables, elegies, prayers, hymns, translations, versifications of the Psalms, and epics. Not uncommon for a poet rooted in neoclassical soil, Adams used a wide range of subjects (although often with much overlapping): fables ("The Eagle and the Worm," "The Crow Playing the Eagle," and "The Plague in the Forest"); science and industry ("To a Magnet," "A Theory of Comets," and "Solar Eclipse"); family ("To Louisa [Catherine Adams]," "On the Birth of a Son," and "An Epistle to My Mother"); Native Americans ("Indian Marriages," "War Song of the Osages"); classics ("The Corinthian Brass," "Paris to Helen," and "Tibullus Elegy II"); historical figures and events ("Our Country," "Charles the Fifth's Clocks," and "Nero, the Reformer"); aesthetics and criticism ("Art," "Proem," and "Song of the Critic"); patriotic ("Our Country," "On Becoming Secretary of State," and "To the Muse of History over the Clock in the House of Representatives"); nature ("The Rising Sun," "To Spring," and "Sonnet to Evening"); and religion ("The Death of Children," "To Chaunticleer" ["Watch and Pray"], and "A Sunday Hymn").

Adams was scarcely influenced by the Romantic trends toward originality, natural rhythms, common diction, and the creation of art for art's sake. Many of his poems were written for his own amusement, for the pleasure and instruction of family and friends, as a diversion from his political labors, and as album gifts for the wives, daughters, and friends of fellow politicians. Many were printed in local newspapers, periodicals, giftbooks, and hymnals. Early in his career Adams wrote anonymously or used pseudonyms to protect his identity and to avoid the stigma of being an idler. In time, however, Adams's avocation as a poet became widely known. Nonetheless, no collection of his poetry was made until shortly after his death, when two of his congressional colleagues, John Davis and Thomas Hart Benton, published the small unauthorized edition *Poems of Religion and Society* (1848). The first edition contained 36 poems, which the editors had collected from periodicals and miscellanies; the 1850 edition added excerpts of his long poem "A Vision."

Back in New York in July 1785 after a six-year stay abroad, Adams read a satirical poem entitled "Receipt [i.e., Recipe] for a Wife." Soon after, he wrote in his diary that the poem had nothing to recommend it, "yet it turn'd me poetaster. I am trying to see if I can say something not so bad in the same way." In the autumn, when he began to write more light poetry in imitation of "Receipt for a Wife," he found that it was not as easy: "The hill [Parnassus] I fear is by far too slippery for me." In December, he completed "An Epistle to Delia," the first of several poems that dealt playfully with the battle of the sexes, love, courtship, and the search for the ideal female. Speaking of one of these poems, which he had written to give away, he remarked: "If it is but insipid flattery, it is no more than what every young Lady expects from Gentlemen; and what few of the Gentlemen refuse them." Between 1786 and 1789, while Adams was a student at Harvard and a law clerk in the office of Theophilus Parsons in Newburyport, he labored to develop his skills as a poet. Referring to the 16-stanza "A Ballad Founded on Fact," he wrote (in January 1788) of his difficulty in completing poems: "I have I suppose begun an hundred times to write poetry. I have tried every measure and every kind of strophe but of the whole, I never finish'd but one of any length, and that was in fact but the work of a day. . . . I fear I shall end this Time, as I always do."

During this period, the Boston newspapers and periodicals

burgeoned with poems by and about beaux and belles; the latter bore such conventional cant names as Belinda, Vanessa, Corinna, Statira, Almira, and Lucinda. These poems were often in the form of acrostics, puzzles, and rebuses. Adams joined in the craze of writing witty verses. Some of his efforts appeared under the names of "Scipio Africanus" in the *Boston Herald* (February 1789); and "Celadon," "Corydon," and "Alcander" were his pseudonyms in the *Massachusetts Magazine* (March and September, 1789). In the latter number of the *Massachusetts Magazine*, Adams also published a pastoral ode, "To Emma: or the Rose." These "fugitive" poems, as he called them, later became parts of "A Vision," a satirical criticism of several belles in fashionable Boston, Cambridge, and Newburyport society, which he began in early 1788 and completed by June 1790. Typical of the regular couplets in "A Vision" are the following on Miss Lucy Knight, first written in Adams's diary in March 1788:

> With all the charms of beauty richly fraught,
> Lucinda's form my fond attention caught.
> A faultless person and a lovely mind,
> I found with wonder, were in her combin'd
> Deficient only in a single part,
> She wanted nothing but a feeling heart.
> Calm and unruffled as a Summer Sea,
> From Passion's gale's Lucinda's breast is free,
> A faithless lover she may well defy,
> Recall her heart nor breathe a single sigh
> And should a second prove inconstant too
> She changes on till she can find one true.

Although circulated by the summer of 1790, "A Vision" was not published until December 1839, when it appeared, printed from a long lost manuscript without Adams's knowledge, in the New York weekly *Brother Jonathan*. Upon seeing it in print, Adams said that "as a poet I have never surpassed it."

By the fall of 1790, Adams was trying to settle down to a serious law practice in Boston and resolved to stop writing light verse for publication. In April 1791, he wrote to Thomas Boylston Adams, his brother, and said that he had given up writing rebuses, elegies, and acrostics about "juvenile Misses"; for the time being, he did so. Years later, he recalled that he had once been "a Volunteer Laureate for the News Carriers" and wistfully added, "But my verses are among the most forgotten things of this world, where I do not know that a copy of them yet exists." In September 1794, Adams was sent abroad by President Washington as a minister to the Netherlands, but finding the country occupied by the French, he went elsewhere in Europe to study, observe, and attend to miscellaneous diplomatic assignments. While in Berlin on this trip (1797–99), he helped himself learn German and translated Christoph Wieland's popular poetic romance *Oberon* (1780), rewriting his English version three times. It remained in manuscript until 1940, when it was printed with an introduction and scholarly notes by A. B. Faust, who described it as "a complete metrical translation of unusual scholarly merit, remarkable for fidelity to the original and its genuine artistry."

Adams returned to America in 1801 to resume his law practice in Boston and to begin his career as a Massachusetts state senator (1802) and U.S. senator (1803). But even before he returned, he was writing for Joseph Dennie's newly begun *Port Folio* in Philadelphia. He wrote his brother Thomas in March 1801: "I am not solicitous of poetical fame, tho' I would like to contribute what I can to excite a taste for poetry among my countrymen." Between January 1801 and May 1805, he contributed to the *Port Folio* a great deal of prose, poetry translations, and original poetry. For the opening number, January 3, 1801, he translated "The Thirteenth Satire of Juvenal," and in May 1805, he produced "The Seventh Satire of Juvenal"; both were praised and often reprinted. He also contributed the rhymed fables "The Ram and the Bull" (May 1801) and "The Dancing Bear" (March 1803). Under the pseudonym of "Batisto," he published the light polemic "The Address" (March 1803). All of these works were invested with political satire. Many years later, when thinking about his early political career and "The Thirteenth Satire of Juvenal," Adams said: "One satirical song, overlooked when first published, was dragged into light nearly twenty years afterward, for political effect against me, because it laughed at the political Lama – Jefferson." In the *Port Folio*, he momentarily lapsed back into his old ways of writing about "juvenile Misses" in "Ballad" (February 1802), a formulaic and saccharine 80-line poem on "Phillida's beauty." As "Batisto," he wrote two light love poems: "The Lucky Fall" (March 1803) and "The Test: To Lucy" (May 1803). He stopped writing for the *Port Folio* about the time he was appointed Boylston Professor of Rhetoric at Harvard in 1806, a position he filled with distinction until 1809. Due to popular demand, his lectures were published in 1810.

In the summer of 1809, Adams entered upon a long period of uninterrupted government service as minister to Russia (1809–14), minister to Great Britain (1815–16), secretary of state (1817–25), president of the United States (1825–29), and (after a three-year respite) U.S. representative (1831–48). Many poems written during these years of federal service survive in his notebooks and in periodicals. One species of poetry very dear to Adams and valued by his contemporaries was his religious verse, which took the form of hymns, prayers, and versifications of the Psalms and other passages from the Old Testament. Citing the admirable hymns and verse paraphrases of Alexander Pope, Joseph Addison, Jean Jacques Rousseau, Philip Doddridge, and Isaac Watts, Adams disagreed with Samuel Johnson, who proscribed such religious poetry. Reverend William P. Lunt included 36 of Adams's religious poems in his popular *The Christian Psalter* (1841). Twenty of the poems in Davis and Benton's collection are Adams's hymns and versified Psalms. One of Adams's popular original hymn was "The Hour Glass" (1829–35), the first stanza of which reads:

> Alas! how swift the moments fly!
> How flash the years along!
> Scarce here, yet gone already by,
> The burden of a song.
> See childhood, youth, and manhood pass,
> And age, with furrowed brow;
> Time was – Time shall be – drain the glass –
> But where is Time *now*?

Written on his deceased father's birthday in 1827, when John Quincy was in the White House, the sonnet praising his father's love of freedom remains a good example of a poem that combines domestic and national themes:

Day of my father's birth, I hail thee yet.
  What though his body moulders in the grave,
  Yet shall not Death th' immortal soul enslave;
The sun is not extinct – his orb has set.
And where on wide earth shall man be met,
  While time shall run, but from the spirit brave
  Shall learn to grasp the boon his Maker gave,
And spurn the terror of a tyrant's threat?
Who but shall learn that freedom is the prize
  Man still is bound to rescue or maintain;
That nature's God commands the slave to rise,
  And on the oppressor's head to break his chain.
Roll, years of promise, rapidly roll round,
Till not a slave shall on this earth be found.

Biographer Samuel Flagg Bemis finds this to be the best poem Adams ever wrote. Adams wrote it in shorthand so that it would be legible only to himself or someone who would take the trouble to decipher it. In his old age, however, he made a transcription, which someone inserted in the diary. His son, Charles Francis Adams, published it in his father's *Memoirs* under the date of October 30, 1826.

Adams left the presidency in 1829, but his Massachusetts constituency returned him to the House of Representatives in 1831. Between late September 1830, when some supporters urged him to run for office, and mid-October, when he decided to enter the race, he wrote the sonnet "To the Sun-Dial" (LOA, 1: 36). The poem indicates his state of mind about seizing the moment and acting for the public good, whether by running for office or by doing some other useful work. The version below, from *Poems of Religion and Society* (1850), differs only slightly from the 1830 version:

> *Under the Window of the Hall of the House of*
> *Representatives of the United States*
> Thou silent herald of Time's silent flight!
>   Say, could'st thou speak, what warning voice were
>   thine?
>   Shade, who canst only show how others shine!
> Dark, sullen witness of resplendent light
> In day's broad glare, and when the noontide bright
>   Of laughing fortune sheds the ray divine,
>   Thy ready favors cheer us – but decline
> The clouds of morning and the gloom of night.
> Yet are thy counsels faithful, just, and wise;
>   They bid us seize the moments as they pass –
> Snatch the retrieveless sunbeam as it flies,
>   Nor lose one sand of life's revolving glass –
> Aspiring still, with energy sublime,
> By virtuous deeds to give eternity to Time.

In February 1831, shortly before Adams entered Congress, he undertook his most ambitious attempt in writing poetry when he began the epic *Dermot MacMorrogh; or the Conquest of Ireland*. The poem related the twelfth-century story (drawn from Hume) of the intrigues between Henry II, king of England, and the immoral Dermot MacMorrogh, king of Leinster, which resulted in Henry II's conquest of Ireland. Probably prompted by his perceptions of his antagonist Andrew Jackson, who had succeeded him as president, Adams announced in the preface that the poem was intended as a moral piece,

"teaching the citizens of these States of both sexes, the virtues of conjugal fidelity, of genuine piety, and devotion to their country." Just as importantly, however, Adams also wanted once and for all to test his ability to write a serious poem of national importance; clearly he felt he had not fulfilled his potential as a poet. In March 1831, he wrote in his diary that his poems sometimes seemed at first to have merit, but when reviewed later they seemed good for nothing: "In a few instances, I have suffered the publication of my effusions, and am accredited as one of the smallest poets of my country." Imitating Byron (whose prosody but not morals he admired), Adams chose ottava rima as his form. He labored over the poem for two months and finished it in mid-April. Viewing his handiwork upon completion, he said: "Beyond this I shall never attain, and now it is an important question whether I shall throw this, and all other verses I have written in the fire."

Adams was not, however, seriously tempted to consign *Dermot* to the flames, but rather saw three editions through the press within three years. Although he was proud of his epic, he resolved not to undertake anything so serious again, saying in his diary in October 1833: "I have pushed my experiment on the public temper far enough." The poem was not well reviewed. A critic in *The Christian Examiner* said that it was "not very good, nor very bad, but . . . very indifferent. . . . But if the reader looks for . . . signs of what is called poetical inspiration he will look in vain" (March 1833). Upon reading his father's poem, Charles Francis Adams expressed in his diary (November 1832) similarly unflattering sentiments: "But as a whole the work wants invention and imagination. It is totally deficient in descriptive imagery and leans as almost all my father's poetry does, too much to the didactic style. . . . My opinion is that he would have done better not to publish it." When the aged poet confronted his son for his opinion, Charles Francis muddled through a candid reply about its defects and later recorded in his diary: "How I got out of the scrape God knows, but I meant well" (October 1833).

Despite his disappointment in not gaining more fame as a poet with *Dermot*, Adams continued to write poems regularly while he was a member of the House. One popular poem that occupied a great deal of his time was "The Wants of Man" (LOA, 1: 29), which he wrote during May and June of 1840. Adams composed much of this poem, as was his habit, while out walking or riding as a relief from the strenuous congressional debates. The wife of William H. Stewart, governor of New York, secured Adams's permission to publish it in Thurlow Weed's Albany *Evening Journal* in September 1841, and the poem was widely reprinted. Stanza I takes the first two lines from Oliver Goldsmith's "The Hermit" (from *The Vicar of Wakefield*). Adams says:

> "Man wants but little here below,
>   Nor wants that little long."
> 'Tis not with ME exactly so,
>   But 'tis so in the song.
> MY wants are many, and if told
>   Would muster many a score;
> And were each wish a mint of gold,
>   I still should long for more.

And then in two hundred lines of iambic tetrameter cross rhyme, the poet catalogs his (mostly temporal) wants. Toward the end of the poem, however, his consummate want is commensurate with the higher desires expressed so many times previously in his religious poems:

These are the wants of mortal man;
    I cannot want them long,
For life itself is but a span,
    And earthly bliss a song.
My last great want, absorbing all,
    Is, when beneath the sod,
And summon'd to my final call,
    The mercy of my God.

In August 1841, when a House of Representatives colleague from Maryland asked Adams to write some verses for the albums of two young women in his district, Ellen and Sally Bruce, Adams gratified him by writing "To Miss Ellen Bruce" and "A Canzonet to Sally. Imitated from Horace. For Miss Sally B – ." The poems first appeared in the *Southern Literary Messenger* in October 1841, and then in the *Quincy Patriot* in November 1841. Davis and Benton included the canzonet in their collection under the title "To Sally" (LOA, 1: 36). They also added an epigraph from Horace, "Integer vitæ sclerisque purus / Non eget Mauris jaculis, neque arcu" ("He who is upright in his life and pure of guilt, needs not Moorish arrows, nor bow"). In the first three stanzas, the poet moralizes that a righteous man will be directed and protected by virtue, and then playfully illustrates his point:

Else wherefore was it, Thursday last,
    While strolling down the valley
Defenceless, musing as I pass'd
    A canzonet to Sally;
A wolf, with mouth protruding snout,
    Forth from the thicket bounded –
I clapped my hands and raised a shout –
    He heard – and fled – confounded.

Tangier nor Tunis never bred
    An animal more crabbed;
Nor Fez, dry nurse of lions, fed
    A monster half so rabid.
Nor Ararat so fierce a beast
    Has seen, since days of Noah;
Nor strong, more eager for a feast,
    The fell constrictor boa.

Oh! place me where the solar beam
    Has scorch'd all verdure vernal;
Or on the polar verge extreme,
    Block'd up with ice eternal –
Still shall my voice's tender lays
    Of love remain unbroken;
And still my charming SALLY praise,
    Sweet smiling and sweet spoken.

After the young Bruces acknowledged the poems with thanks, Adams wrote his House of Representatives colleague: "I cannot hold [the verses] altogether worthless if they succeed in giving a moment of pleasure to those ladies and to you. . . . Should any of the effusions of my mind in poetical numbers

ever be thought worthy of collection and publication in one volume, the names of the two ladies shall certainly be given at full length, to serve as the best passport to them for the acceptance of readers of a future age." Here is one of the few hints that Adams thought someone might someday collect and circulate his poems. Verse of this kind was undoubtedly what Adams had in mind when he wrote in his diary in June 1839 that he had kept copies of all his contributions to albums and sickened at the sight of them; nonetheless, he continued almost to his dying day to write such poems. On February 20, 1848, he penned some lines for a Miss Caroline Edwards of Springfield, Massachusetts. His last day on the floor of the House, February 21, 1848, was a busy one, but he found time to autograph as gifts some stanzas of his poem "To the Muse of History Perched on Her Wheeled and Winged Car Over the Front Door of the Hall of Representatives." That same day, while still at the House, Adams collapsed from a paralyzing stroke; he died two days later.

Adams never deluded himself that he was a great or even a good poet, but he had a passion for poetry, and he could not stop writing. To his credit, he sought honest criticism and strove to improve. In February 1829, he wrote to the influential editor Robert Walsh of Philadelphia, admitting that "I know well enough that the star of my birth did not make me a poet." He further asked Walsh "as a philosopher, critic, and poet," to help him get a correct estimation of himself. Walsh replied: "Whether you were born a poet, I will not pretend to decide; but certain it is that productions like the Stanzas on Fortitude & 13th Satire of Juvenile [*sic*] prove you to be an adept in metre." Among the wants that Adams listed in "The Wants of Man" were "the genius to conceive / The talents to unfold" and "the voice of honest praise / To follow me behind," but all these were denied him as a poet. He moralized to a fault, was never able to distance himself from excessive nationalistic and political sentiment, and could not escape the ossifying influences of the classics in an age when winds of Romantic vitality were beginning to stir. Nevertheless, his poetry deserves to be preserved and read for its abundance of good humor, wit, and satire, nobility of moral and patriotic thought, commentary on important contemporaries and events, and insights into the literary habits of one of America's political and cultural patriarchs.

GUY R. WOODALL

Selected Works

Lectures on Rhetoric and Oratory, Cambridge: Hilliard and Metcalf, 1810

Dermot MacMorrogh, or the Conquest of Ireland, Boston: Carter and Hendee, 1832

The Wants of Man, Lowell, Massachusetts: Amos Upton, 1842; reprinted, with an introduction by Lyman H. Butterfield, Worcester, Massachusetts: Achille J. St. Onge, 1962; reprinted, Barre, Massachusetts: Imprint Society, 1972

Poems of Religion and Society, edited by John Davis and Thomas Hart Benton, New York: William H. Graham, 1848

Memoirs of John Quincy Adams, edited by Charles Francis Adams, 12 vols., Philadelphia: Lippincott, 1874–77

The Writings of John Quincy Adams, edited by Worthington C. Ford, 7 vols., New York: Macmillan, 1913–17

Oberon, A Poetical Romance in Twelve Books, edited by A. B. Faust, New York: F. S. Crofts, 1940

The Diary of John Quincy Adams, 1794–1845, edited by Allan Nevins, New York: Unger, 1951

Microfilm of the Adams Papers, Owned by the Adams Manuscript Trust, Boston: Massachusetts Historical Society, 1954– (the writer acknowledges with gratitude the permission of the Adams Papers to quote directly from the microfilm)

Adams Family Correspondence, edited by L. H. Butterfield, et al., 4 vols., Cambridge, Massachusetts: Harvard University Press, 1963–73

The Diary of Charles Francis Adams, edited by Aida and David Donald, et al., 8 vols., Cambridge, Massachusetts: Harvard University Press, 1964–

Further Reading

Bemis, Samuel F., *John Quincy Adams and the Foundations of American Foreign Policy*, New York: Knopf, 1949

———, *John Quincy Adams and the Union*, New York: Knopf, 1956

East, Robert A., *John Quincy Adams: The Critical Years 1785–1794*, New York: Bookman Associates, 1962

Amos Bronson Alcott

(1799–1888)

A self-educated philosopher, essayist, and poet, Bronson Alcott has been the subject of several biographies, the best of which are written by Franklin Benjamin Sanborn and William Torrey Harris (1893), Odell Shepard (1937), and Frederick Dalhstrand (1982). These works tell of Alcott's salient experiences as a youth on the Connecticut frontier, farmer, Yankee peddler, innovative educator, reformer, conversationalist, and miscellaneous author.

Although Alcott produced a significant number of poems, literary historians, critics, and anthologists have given him short shrift as a poet. The reason is not that he failed to write some poems of high quality, but that he was simply overshadowed by friends among the Transcendentalists: Ralph Waldo **Emerson**, Henry **Thoreau**, William Ellery **Channing**, and Jones **Very**. Alcott's relative anonymity may also be attributed to his choice of "the conversation" as his chief métier in art and communication. He frequently employed verse in his conversations, but he was more proud of the conversation itself, which he felt was a distinctively American art and pedagogical form that he himself had helped construct. Alcott, further, has not been duly considered as a poet because much of his poetry has remained ungathered and unedited in letters, periodicals, and more than fifty volumes of unpublished manuscript journals. The journals attest to his lifetime passion for poetry.

In *Nature* (1836), the manifesto of New England Transcendentalism, Emerson paid tribute to Alcott, calling him an "Orphic poet"; viewing Alcott as a true seer, he later persuaded Margaret **Fuller** to include Alcott's "Orphic Sayings," a series of 50 philosophical epigrams, in the first number of *The Dial* (July 1840). The recondite and mystical nature of the "Orphic Sayings" drew ridicule from the Boston community and even from some within the Transcendentalist circle. The "Orphic Sayings" long militated against Alcott's reputation by stigmatizing him as a misty-brained poet-philosopher, but Alcott was undaunted and continued to speak and write orphically. Although always his most supportive friend, Emerson came in time to realize that Alcott's ability to write poetry or prose would never measure up to his ability as an original thinker. In 1843, Emerson said that Alcott had been writing poetry all winter, but noted with regret that his friend's "overpowering personality destroys all poetic faculty." Alcott once recalled that Emerson was candid with him about his lack of talent: "I ought perhaps to distrust the having of poetic gifts after Emerson telling me I had neither ear nor eye for melody or metre. At any rate, I have written too little verse to claim the poet's inspiration." In "A Fable for Critics" (see LOA, 1: 684), James Russell **Lowell** spoke with humor for most who knew Alcott when he allowed that he was a good talker but a bad writer:

> While he talks he is great, but goes out like a taper,
> If you shut him up closely with pen, ink, and paper;
> Yet his fingers itch for 'em from morning till night,
> And he thinks he does wrong if he don't always write;
> In this, as in all things, a lamb among men,
> He goes to sure death when he goes to the pen.

In the end Emerson, Lowell, and others were not correct, for Alcott continued to write and improve his art, and in his old age produced a body of highly respectable prose and poetry. Alcott's first book, *Conversations with Children on the Gospels* (2 vols., 1836–37), which grew out of his experiences at the Temple School in Boston (1834–37), contains no original poetry. The book incurred the wrath of the Boston community because it recounted Alcott's having involved the schoolchildren in discussions of the socially proscribed subjects of sex and procreation. Following the devastating failure of the Temple School, he published no more books until 1868. But prompted by the successes of his daughter Louisa May Alcott, who became a celebrity with *Hospital Sketches* (1863) and *Little Women* (1868–69), he began to publish increasingly out of his journals. Upon comparing some of his essays with Emerson's, moreover, he was encouraged to reappraise his own abilities as a writer and press on. One outlet that he chose for his poetry was the public journals. In 1863, he published "The Goblet," "The Return," "The Chase," "The Reaper," and "The Patriot" in the *Commonwealth*. In 1866, he published in *The Radical* new versions of "The Patriot" and "The Chase," and "Misrule." Twenty-two of his "Philosophemes" (short philosophical poems) appeared in the *Journal of Speculative Philosophy* in January 1881, followed by the sonnets "Childhood" (January 1882), "R. W. E." (April 1884; read at Emerson's funeral), "Love" (January 1885), "Immortality" (April 1885), and "Ion: A Monody" (on the death of Emerson) in April 1885.

In September 1868, Alcott published *Tablets*, a collection of philosophical essays in which he interspersed some of his best poems: "The Seer's Rations," "Lonely My Dwelling Here," "Tasked Days," "Rise in the Morning," "Friendship," "Man" (also called "Adam"), and variants of "The Return," "The Chase," and "The Goblet." Encouraged by a favorable reception, in 1869 he began his third book, *Concord Days* (1872). It contained less philosophical and speculative matter than his previous books, and more material on his friends, his reading, and his beloved Concord. The poems in the book are "Sing, Sing the Immortals," "'T Is Clear," "Mind Omnipotent Is," "The Patriot" (first published in the *Commonwealth*), "Our Spirits," "Whose the Decree," and "The Path of Felicity."

Alcott's fourth book, *Table Talk* (1877), included more than 100 brief paragraph essays on subjects that he categorized under "Practical" and "Speculative." The pages are filled with verse, but only two poems are Alcott's: "Matter" and "The Heart." His next book was an autobiographical epic poem entitled *New Connecticut* (1881). Published with the help of his friend Frank Sanborn, editor of the Boston *Commonwealth*, the poem dealt only with Alcott's early life. In the first of two sections, Alcott writes of his rural upbringing and formative experiences on Spindle Hill near Wolcott, Connecticut. In the second section, he writes of leaving Spindle Hill to seek his fortune as a Yankee peddler on five trips to Virginia and South Carolina (1817–23). After Sanborn reviewed it favorably, Alcott wrote in his journal: "He seems better satisfied with the poetic significance of the verses than I am, though I read these with a certain pleasure, sometimes deceived as if they were the work of another." Lawrence Buell is correct when he speaks of *New Connecticut* as being "vapid" and imitative of William Wordsworth's *The Prelude*; read in light of the author's extensive notes, however, the poem gives good insights into rural New England life at the beginning of the nineteenth century (e.g., flax growing and linen making, regional dialect, the business of peddling). At the time Alcott wrote *New Connecticut* in the winter of 1880, he was lamenting the death of his daughter, May, and writing a threnody on her death entitled "Love's Morrow," which he later included in *Sonnets and Canzonets*.

Alcott wrote most of his poems in traditional rhymes and meters; they also exemplify conventions of the neoclassical age: artificial diction, rhetorical flights, questions and exclamations, personifications, references and allusions to the classics, didactic intent, imitative genre structures, and moral tone. Although he greatly admired much of Wordsworth's and Coleridge's thinking, Alcott paid little attention to their call for modern diction, originality, natural sounds, and organic structuring. In the unpublished poems in his journals for 1832–34, however, there are two blank verse poems. Alcott had a restricted range of subjects: philosophical speculations, autobiographical matters, religion, and portraits of family and friends. He rarely attempted to write purely lyrical, descriptive, or entertaining narrative verse for publication.

In his poems, Alcott demonstrates the Transcendental faith that he cultivated between 1831 and 1834 when he plunged into the works of Samuel Taylor Coleridge, Plato, Bishop Berkeley, Immanuel Kant, Thomas Carlyle, Johann Wolfgang von Goethe, Victor Cousin, and Proclus. The upshot of his intense reading program was that he discarded the sensual philosophy of Aristotle, Francis Bacon, and John Locke, and the mechanism of Isaac Newton, and became a thoroughgoing Transcendentalist, believing that the highest order of reality was the spiritual or the ideal; that the material universe is but the dress of the spirit; and that God is immanent in humanity and matter, unifying all, and making all partake of divinity. Alcott firmly placed his faith in intuition, holding it superior to experience. He believed that the universe was moral, well ordered, and alive. He never doubted the doctrine of pre-existence and innate ideas. His Transcendentalism made him oracular, optimistic, didactic, and idealistic in his verse.

In a poem included in the essay "Ideal Culture," from *Concord Days*, Alcott plays a favorite tune – that the ideal is superior to the material:

> 'T is clear
> Mind's sphere
> Is not here;
> The Ideal guest
> In ceaseless quest
> Pursues the Best;
> The very Better
> The while her fetter,
> Her desire
> Higher, still higher;
> Ever is fleeing
> Past Seeming to Being;

> Nor doth the sight content itself with seeing,
>   As forms emerge they fast from sense are fleeing,
> Things but appear to vanish into Being.

For Alcott, humanity is a part of the divine Whole or One, and the mind gives form and meaning to the surrounding universe. In "Man" ("Adam") from an essay of the same name in *Tablets*, Alcott writes:

> He omnipresent is;
> All around himself he lies,
> Osiris spread abroad,
> Upstarting in all eyes:
> Nature his globed thought,
> Without him she were not,
> Cosmos from Chaos were not spoken,
> And God bereft of visible token.

The idealism here is much like that of Emerson's "Brahma" (LOA, 1: 319), which held that all is *maya* or illusion. In "Matter" Alcott says, "Nature is the eyeball of the Mind / The fleeting pageant tells for nought / Till shaped in Mind's created thought." In the beautiful "The Chase," moreover, Alcott postulates that beauty is to be found only in the ideal and that the search for the ideal finally ends within one's self. In this poem, the soul reaches the absolute mind by chasing the beautiful in bodily forms.

Alcott's poetry represents nature as efficacious, instructive, and curative; nature ministers to the spirit and the body. In 1847, he wrote in his journal: "I for my part seem always puny and insignificant, a meanness and pretence, when caught in towns, and lose that command of my powers that Nature finds for me whenever I court her presence." Unlike his friend Thoreau, however, Alcott was not a primitivist. As much as he loved external nature, Alcott never abandoned the neoclassical sentiment that humanity should enter into a partnership with nature and improve it by producing gardens, orchards, and idyllic villages. But Alcott also was quite responsive to nature without such improvements. In an aubade in *Tablets* that would have pleased Thoreau, he said:

> Rise in the morning, rise
> While yet the streaming tide
> Flames o'er the blue acclivities,
> And pours its splendors wide;
> Kindling its high intent
> Along the firmament,
> Silence and sleep to break,
> Imaginations wake,
> Ideas insphere
> And bring them here.
> Loiter nor play
> In soft delay;
> Speed glad thy course along
> The orbs and globes among,
> And as yon toiling sun
> Attain thy high meridian:
> Radiant and round the day; –
> Speed, speed thee on thy way.

Nature had recreative powers for Alcott. Written in the wake of one of Alcott's fits of despair (probably after a breakdown following the failure of the Temple School, or, some say, after his ill-fated Fruitlands experiment in 1843–44), "The Return" tells of fleeing to nature and healing: "Recovered, / Himself again / Over his threshold led, / Peace fills his breast, / He finds his rest." Alcott wrote other poems about despair, such as "Lonely My Dwelling Here," but it was not in the optimistic philosopher to live too much in shadows. He was a part of the divine whole, and he could also find happiness by losing himself in labor.

Perhaps Alcott's finest achievement in poetry was his final book, *Sonnets and Canzonets* (1882). This work consisted mainly of poetic portraits and estimates of his family and beloved friends, most of whom he had outlived. Frank Sanborn, who assisted in editing the volume, said that Alcott's genius resulted from his not being familiar with the "accustomed movement in poetry in our time" and from his lifelong sense of brotherhood with the noble souls about him. Sanborn also stated (quite accurately) that Alcott had written "with little order and number of his rhymes, but with much regard to the spirit of the sonnet as a high form of verse"; Sanborn thus warned readers that the poems were highly suggestive and that they should not expect great definiteness in them. Alcott generously acknowledged Sanborn's help in "The Proem."

Among those pictured in the sonnets are Alcott's wife, Abby May Alcott, his four daughters, an infant granddaughter, a cousin, and friends and public figures, notably Dr. William Ellery Channing, Elizabeth Palmer Peabody, Emerson, Lidian Emerson, Margaret Fuller, William H. Channing, Thoreau, William Ellery Channing (the poet), Nathaniel **Hawthorne**, Wendell Phillips, John Brown (of Harpers Ferry), Theodore Parker, William Lloyd Garrison, and James A. Garfield. The book also included an idyllic poem on Concord ("Calm vale of comfort, peace, and industry").

In Sonnet XIV, from Part I (LOA, 1: 226), Alcott could not escape philosophizing. The poem was first entitled "Childhood" when it was inserted in *Journal of Speculative Philosophy* in January 1882.

> Not Wordsworth's genius, Pestalozzi's love,
> The stream have sounded of clear infancy.
> Baptismal waters from the Head above
> These babes I foster daily are to me;
> I dip my pitcher in these living springs
> And draw, from depths below, sincerity;
> Unsealed, mine eyes behold all outward things
> Arrayed in splendors of divinity.
> What mount of vision can with mine compare?
> Not Roman Jove nor yet Olympian Zeus
> Darted from loftier ether through bright air
> One spark of holier fire for human use.
> Glad tidings thence these angels downward bring,
> As at their birth the heavenly choirs do sing.

The reference to Pestalozzi relates to Alcott's early faith in the empiricism of educator Johann Heinrich Pestalozzi (1746–1827), which gave way later to his interest in the idealistic doctrines of Plato on the spiritual purity of children, pre-existence, and innate ideas. Alcott, however, also found the latter ideas in Wordsworth, particularly in his "Immortality Ode." But it was more from his own intuition and the life of Christ that he learned about the divinity, innocence, and purity of children.

The "babes" could refer to any of the students in Alcott's several schools, but in the context of the family portraits in the volume, they also stood in for his own four daughters, whose education he directed himself.

Alcott's most highly esteemed Concord friend was Emerson, to whom he devoted four sonnets and a reprinting of "Ion." After Alcott and Emerson met in July 1835 and became associated in the Transcendental Club, there followed the closest of friendships for almost 50 years. Alcott was Emerson's "Orphic poet" and "God-made priest." Emerson was Alcott's "Hierophant of the soul" and "Ion." Emerson's patience with and moral and material support of the often impractical and impecunious Alcott were little short of heroic; but Alcott's well of affection for Emerson was bottomless. Praises of Emerson abound in Alcott's journals, and likewise for Alcott in Emerson's journals. Emerson wrote: "It were too much to say that the Platonic world I might have learned to treat as cloud-land, had I not known Alcott, who is a native of that country, yet I will say he makes it as solid as Massachusetts to me." The friendship inspired Alcott to write his best piece of prose, *Ralph Waldo Emerson* (1882), to which he attached his excellent monody "Ion." Emerson is the subject of Sonnet II (Part II).

> Misfortune to have lived not knowing thee!
> 'T were not high living, nor to noblest end,
> Who, dwelling near, learned not sincerity,
> Rich friendship's ornament that still doth lend
> To life its consequence and propriety.
> Thy fellowship was my culture, noble friend:
> By the hand thou took'st me, and didst condescend
> To bring me straightway into thy fair guild;
> And life-long hath it been high compliment
> By that to have been known, and thy friend styled,
> Given to rare thought and learning bent;
> Whilst in my straits an angel on me smiled.
> Permit me, then, thus honored, still to be
> A scholar in thy university.

Next to Emerson, Alcott's most highly regarded Concord friend was Thoreau, to whom he devoted Sonnets XIII and XIV (Part II). Their lifelong friendship began when Alcott met Thoreau in April 1839 on one of his frequent visits to Concord before he moved there. Alcott's journals are rich in praise of Thoreau. At a time when not many were speaking for Thoreau, Alcott recognized and published his merits in "The Forester" in *The Atlantic Monthly* (1862). In Sonnet XIII, Alcott depicts Thoreau as a "Concord Pan" (Thoreau indeed loved to play his flute) who holds up nature as a mirror to his fellows to make them wiser. In March 1847, Alcott entered a thought in his journal that he was to repeat in Sonnet XIV: "Thoreau took his position in Nature, where he was in deed and in spirit – a genius of the natural world, a savage mind amidst savage faculties, yet adorned with the graces of a civilization which he disowned, but celebrating thereby Nature still." In Sonnet XIV, Alcott becomes Thoreau's apologist and sides with his idealism and humanitarianism.

> Much do they wrong our Henry, wise and kind,
> Morose who name thee, cynical to men,
> Forsaking manners civil and refined

To build thyself in Walden woods a den, —
Then flout society, flatter the rude hind.
We better knew thee, loyal citizen!
Thou, friendship's all-adventuring pioneer,
Civility itself didst civilize:
Whilst braggart boors, wavering 'twixt rage and fear
Slave hearths lay waste, and Indian huts surprise,
And swift the Martyr's gibbet would uprear:
Thou hail'dst him great whose valorous emprise
Orion's blazing belt dimmed in the sky, —
Then bowed thy unrepining head to die.

In lines 6–14, Alcott recognizes Thoreau's disdain for the institution of slavery and for his fellow citizens who gave comfort to slavery by their vacillating conduct. Lines 11–14 refer to Captain John Brown. After Brown's capture following his raid at Harpers Ferry, Thoreau delivered an impassioned defense of Brown before his Concord townsmen on October 30, 1859. Few Concordians, however, were sympathetic to either Thoreau or Brown. Alcott was himself to praise Brown as a "prophet of God, Messias of the slave" in Sonnet XXIV (Part II).

Another Concord friend whom Alcott pictured in the sonnets was William Ellery Channing, often called "Ellery." A Harvard dropout, Ellery early dedicated himself to being a poet and, somewhat like Thoreau, resisted a commitment to the ordinary trades and professions by spending much time walking in the woods, boating, and writing poetry. One biographer has characterized him as being "fractious and incalculable as he was brilliant." Alcott felt the same way, but he counted Channing a friend. He often entertained him in his home and boated and walked (Alcott preferred to talk) with him; he held Channing to be a person of subtle thought and wit. In Sonnet XVIII, from Part II (LOA, 1: 226), Alcott says of his friend:

Adventurous mariner! in whose gray skiff,
Dashing disastrous o'er the fretful wave,
The steersman, subject to each breeze's whiff,
Or blast capricious that o'er seas doth rave,
Scarce turns his rudder from the fatal cliff, –
Scorning his craft or e'en himself to save.
Ye Powers of air, that shift the seaman's grave,
Adjust the tackle of his right intent,
And bring him to safely to the port he meant!
Long musing there on that divinity
Who to his hazard had assistance lent,
He verses cons, oft taken by surprise
In diverse meanings, and shrewd subtlety,
That pass quaint Donne, and even Shakespeare wise.

Channing was literally an "adventurous mariner" in that he explored all of the waters about Concord in a skiff. To Alcott, however, he was an "adventurous mariner" because of the remarkable intransigence with which he spurned the conventional and kept on a steady course of doing just what he wanted to do in life: choosing friends and company on his own terms and writing poetry. Lines 7–11 probably refer to Channing's "atomic atheism," which Alcott deplored. In lines 12–14, Alcott, as always, gives unsparing praise to Channing's poetry. "Channing," observed Alcott in his journal in 1871, "writes better lines of verse than any contemporary, if subtlety and ex-

quisiteness of sense and melody are considered." Alcott's journals and published essays are filled with Channing's verses.

In Sonnet XIX, from Part II (LOA, 1: 227), Alcott pictures Hawthorne, whom he came to know well after 1842, when the newly married Salemite and his young bride, Sophia Peabody, moved to Concord to live at the Old Manse. In 1852 before Hawthorne went abroad on a consular tour, he purchased Alcott's house, Hillside, and renamed it The Wayside. In line three, the "baronial keep" refers to an obtrusive study room that Hawthorne had built atop The Wayside as a place for solitude and writing; the reference to the Muse's vexing and teasing Hawthorne recalls his admitted inability to regain his imaginative and creative powers after returning from abroad in 1860. Hawthorne and Alcott lived as next-door neighbors and occasionally visited and walked together; but Hawthorne, to Alcott's disappointment, kept him (and all others) at a distance. Sonnet XIX catches precisely the features that Alcott and most others found in Hawthorne: his feminine reticence, his ability to weave spellbinding dark and mysterious tales in poetic prose, and his fascination with guilt, evil, and retribution.

Romancer, far more coy than that coy sex!
Perchance some stroke of magic thee befell,
Ere thy baronial keep the Muse did vex,
Nor grant deliverance from enchanted spell,
But tease thee all the while and sore perplex.
Till thou that wizard tale shouldst fairly tell,
Better than poets in thy own clear prose.
Painter of sin in its deep scarlet dyes,
Thy doomsday pencil Justice doth expose,
Hearing and judging at the dread assize;
New England's guilt blazoning before all eyes,
No other chronicler than thee she chose.
Magician deathless! dost thou vigil keep,
Whilst 'neath our pines thou feignest deathlike sleep?

In a journal entry in June 1870, Alcott spoke at length of Hawthorne's morbid, gloomy, solitary nature. And then in an essay in *Concord Days*, he wrote sympathetically of Hawthorne's sensitiveness, his love of solitude, and his being coy "as a maiden." The last two lines of the sonnet refer to Hawthorne's keeping a vigil in Concord's Sleepy Hollow cemetery, where he had been buried in May 1864, with Alcott as one of the distinguished pallbearers.

Sonnets and Canzonets appeared in February 1882 to few, but favorable, reviews. Several presentation copies were illustrated with pictures. In mid-April, Alcott gave the aged and ailing Emerson a copy of the poems, several of which Emerson read with "emphasis and delight." Alcott celebrated the memory of Emerson's death (April 27, 1882) at the summer session of the School of Philosophy in July 1882, by reading "Ion." The work on this poem was Alcott's last; he was proofreading it when he had a stroke in October 1882 that virtually ended his physical activities. He died in Boston on March 4, 1888.

Alcott the poet still needs full scholarly treatment by textual and documentary editors. There lie in his journals unedited poems about his family, friends, philosophy, events, and his own life that need to be explicated and put more exactly into the context of his life and milieu. While not always of the highest quality, his poetry and poetic prose (for example, "The Goblet,"

"Matter," and "Orphic Sayings") were now and then good enough in his own time to be mistaken for Emerson's, and some even thought that Emerson's *Nature* was his. Alcott's stature as a poet will never rise to rival that of his Transcendentalist friends Emerson, Thoreau, Channing, or Jones Very (to say nothing of his Brahmin friends Henry Wadsworth **Longfellow**, Lowell, and Oliver Wendell **Holmes**), but scrutiny by scholars will support the conclusion that he was more than a loquacious conversationalist and inept communicator. Upon close inspection, he emerges as a writer who produced a respectable body of philosophical and autobiographical poems and insightful vignettes of the principal New England Transcendentalists.

GUY R. WOODALL

Selected Works

Tablets, Boston: Roberts Brothers, 1868; reprinted, Philadelphia: Albert Saifer, 1969

Concord Days, Boston: Roberts, 1872; reprinted, West Orange, New Jersey: Albert Saifer, n.d.

New Connecticut: An Autobiographical Poem, Boston: privately printed, 1881; 2nd ed., F. B. Sanborn: Boston, 1887; reprinted, Philadelphia: Albert Saifer, 1970

Ralph Waldo Emerson, An Estimate of His Life and Character and Genius in Prose and Verse, Boston: Stanley and Usher, 1882

Sonnets and Canzonets, Boston: Roberts Brothers, 1882

The Journals of Bronson Alcott, edited by Odell Shepard, Boston: Little Brown, 1938; reprinted, 2 vols., Port Washington, New York: Kennikat Press, 1966

Orphic Sayings, edited by William Pierce Randel, Mt. Vernon, N.Y.: Golden Eagle Press, 1939

The Letters of A. Bronson Alcott, edited by Richard L. Herrnstadt, Ames: Iowa State University Press, 1969

Further Reading

Albanese, Catherine L., *Corresponding Motion: Transcendental Religion and the New America*, Philadelphia: Temple University Press, 1977

Alcott, Louisa May, *Transcendental Wild Oats*, Boston: Harvard Common Press, 1975

Bedell, Madelon, *The Alcotts*, New York: Clarkson N. Potter, 1980

Buell, Lawrence, *Literary Transcendentalism*, Ithaca, New York: Cornell University Press, 1973

Cooke, George Willis, *The Poets of Transcendentalism*, Boston: Houghton Mifflin, 1903

Dahlstrand, Frederick C., *Amos Bronson Alcott: An Intellectual Biography*, Rutherford, New Jersey: Fairleigh Dickinson University Press, 1982

Hoeltje, Hubert H., *Sheltering Tree: A Story of the Friendship of Ralph Waldo Emerson and Amos Bronson Alcott*, Durham, North Carolina: Duke University Press, 1943

McCuskey, Dorothy, *Bronson Alcott, Teacher*, New York: Macmillan, 1940

Morrow, Honore Willsie, *The Father of Little Women*, Boston: Little, Brown, 1927

Sanborn Franklin Benjamin, and William Torrey Harris, *A. Bronson Alcott: His Life and Philosophy*, 2 vols., Boston: Roberts Brothers, 1893

Sears, Clara Endicott, *Bronson Alcott and Fruitlands*, Boston: Houghton Mifflin, 1915

Shepard, Odell, *Pedlar's Progress: The Life of Bronson Alcott*, Boston: Little, Brown, 1937

Washington Allston

(1779–1843)

"I read the other day some verses written by an eminent painter which were original and not conventional. The soul always hears an admonition in such lines. . . ." These are the first sentences in Ralph Waldo **Emerson's** "Self-Reliance" (1841); the artist was Washington Allston, one of the nineteenth century's most persistent admonishing ghosts. Like many eminent painters, Allston had some notable bad luck. When he first arrived in London in 1801, fresh out of Harvard College, he came with a little training in portraiture (America had little to offer), a limited patrimony, and a letter of introduction to Sir Joshua Reynolds, the founder of the Royal Academy and the author of *Discourses on Art*, the young Allston's bible of art theory. Along with these assets, Allston brought a determination to learn the allegorical style of history – more literally, story – painting, the "grand manner" that Reynolds had helped to glorify above all other styles.

The training served Allston well: he was accepted as a student at the Academy. His patrimony, however, ran out fast. Not only that, Reynolds had just died by the time Allston disembarked, and so the days of the grand manner were already numbered. Moreover, Reynolds's successor as president of the Academy, Benjamin West, was on the way out of favor with the critics and the court and, worst, with many of the Academy's younger painters. Allston, who described West to a friend as the best painter in London, grew up in the rear guard. His paintings were not unpopular or stuffy: in fact, they were universally admired, even within the factious Academy. And the paintings wore their passion fashionably on their sleeve: from an early age, Allston devoted himself to scenes of eighteenth-century romance, Salvator Rosa–style banditti in particular. In his maturity, Allston was not only Emerson's but William Wordsworth's favorite living painter. Yet, Allston painted with an eye to the old distinctions: if (as E. P. Richardson has argued) he was America's first Romantic painter, he was also the last American Romantic to stake his reputation on religious and literary subjects – and to paint these for the connoisseur instead of the admission-paying public.

The choice may have been noble, but it may have been crippling as well. History painting had never paid much, even in its glory days, and it paid still less in America, where Allston returned for good in 1818. Despite his relative fame and the subsequent success of his career, Allston became best known in the years after his death for the failure of his most cherished effort, the monumental *Belshazzar's Feast*. He started work on the painting in 1817 and boasted a few months later to a friend that it was near completion. Ten years later, the unfinished *Feast* lifted him temporarily out of debt; promising to produce the painting soon, he in effect mortgaged it to 12 rich subscribers for the extraordinary amount of 10 thousand dollars. The deal made news; several unscrupulous journalists published made-up accounts of the finished work, and the weight of expectation (together with a series of physical ailments) overwhelmed Allston. He would lock himself up with the *Feast* for days only to abandon it for months and years, promising a speedy completion all the while. Sixteen years later, at his

death, his friends found the canvas defaced with false starts and second thoughts. Allston the painter would live on in the American imagination less for his own images than for Henry James's image of him – as that type of the artist obsessed, Theobald, in "The Madonna of the Future."

As a poet, Allston enjoyed better luck. Even in youth he had a talent for verse, and he published a number of poems as an undergraduate. Then in 1806, on his first trip to Rome, he met Coleridge. At 33, Coleridge was already an old man. His best poetry was behind him; he was poor, ill, addicted to laudanum, estranged from his wife, and terribly lonely, having already begun to drift apart from the Wordsworths. Allston was a much younger, happier 26, as eager for a mentor as Coleridge was for a disciple. The two became fast friends, with Washington Irving for an occasional third companion. Coleridge in essence finished Allston's education and helped to make him one of the best educated, most refined Americans of his day. Readers recognized Allston's polish; his one volume of verse, *The Sylphs of the Seasons* (1813), was a great success, and poems from this volume were anthologized well into the nineteenth century.

Still, the aims of Allston's poetry often seem more foreign to us than those of his English contemporaries, and Allston sounds surprisingly conservative when we compare him to American poets who were only a little younger than him. As his poem "America to Great Britain" (LOA, 1: 57) shows, he defined himself as a poet in the same way that he defined himself as a painter, by looking back at England, and, more specifically, at the England of his older teachers. In the *Cambridge History of American Literature*, Barbara L. Packer speculates that Allston's poetic conservatism has often put him (and much of his generation) out of the reach of twentieth-century readers. This generation displayed poetic convention proudly, Packer writes, as a sign of cultural maturity:

> Most of [their] exercises in pure invention now seem slight, though the constant distinction they draw between their own world and the world of "Mammon's slaves" [a reference to "Sylphs of the Seasons"] leads one to suspect that what looks to us like dilettantism had strong ideological appeal. Foreign critics loved to sneer that the mercantile spirit of the Americans was hostile to the production of poetry; American poets reacted by trying to create things whose uselessness vouched for their beauty. The result is a kind of innocent decadence, differing from the late nineteenth-century sort chiefly in its ignorance of its own sexual motives.

Allston's most "decadent" mode leans heavily on Coleridge; and yet, Allston's decadence is by far a paler, tamer thing than "Kubla Kahn," "Christabel," or "The Rime of the Ancient Mariner." Sometimes we hear little echoes of particular lines, as in the "Mariner"-like "Mad Lover":

Thine eyes are glazed, thy cheeks are pale,
   Thy lips are livid, and thy breath

Too truly tells the dreadful tale, –
    Thou comest from the house of death!

More often – as exemplified in "The Sylphs of the Seasons" (LOA, 1: 48) – Allston looks to Coleridge for a general model. Allston wrote poems of sheer fancy, in which an ostensible (but muted) allegory lets the poet wander and describe. The poems, however, lack the visionary intensity of John Keats or Percy Bysshe Shelley – and eschew the traditional georgic vehicle of witty, sentimental vignettes used by poets like James Thomson, William Cowper, or, most important, Wordsworth. In longer verse romances like "The Paint-King" and "The Angel and the Nightingale," in his satires, "Eccentricity" and "The Two Painters," and in many short poems like the one quoted above, Allston repeatedly shows his distance from these most enduring strands of Romanticism. His choice of immediate precursor – Coleridge, at his most fanciful, over Wordsworth – also sets Allston apart from most American poets after him. Although he helped introduce both Coleridge and Wordsworth to Boston literary circles, Allston never wrote the kind of nature poetry that would, under Wordsworth's influence, become the standard American mode of serious verse.

What he does learn from Wordsworth – most obviously, to use the Petrarchan sonnet as a record of looking – Allston uses for subjects all his own. And even at his most Wordsworthian, in later poems like "Art" (LOA, 1: 59) or "To the Author of 'The Diary of an Ennuyé'" (which inspired the opening of "Self-Reliance"), Allston takes his subjects from the world of representation rather than from untouched nature. The vices and virtues of artists, the relation of tradition to originality, the experience of looking at a painting: these topics are finally what interest Allston most.

Even when Allston treats subjects outside the world of painting, his interests incline toward problems of artistic representation. It must have come naturally to him to consider these problems of a piece; he insisted that his painting students read widely and that poetry, and even novels, could teach ways of picturing scenes and characters. Allston himself loved to experiment with all kinds of writing. In 1821, he published a short humorous story, "The Hypochondriac," and in 1822, he wrote *Monaldi*, a gothic romance (unpublished until 1841). As an old man, he wrote a short series entitled *Lectures on Art*, America's first such treatise. In his youth, he even dabbled in drama. Although Allston seems never to have had his scripts performed, he loved the theater all his life and maintained close friendships with several actors. As the late poem "On Kean's Hamlet" (LOA, 1: 60) shows, he also remained a shrewd judge of stagecraft. Emerson remarked in his journals that Allston's "merit" was "like that of Kean's recitation merely outlinear, strictly emptied of all obtrusive individuality, but a vase to receive & not a fountain to impart *character*."

Allston's shrewdness and receptivity make "On Kean's Hamlet" one of the most accessible of his poems of looking. He begins by complaining that Shakespeare's characters seem to defy representation. Doomed forever to private readings by individual readers, they seem to move best "as in some necromantic glass" across the forgiving magic mirror of the page. Not even Michelangelo or Raphael could paint them satisfactorily:

And vainer still, methought, by mimic tone,
    And feignèd look, and attitude, and air,

The Actor's toil; for self will have its share
    With nicest mimicry, and, though it spare
To others largely, gives not all its own.
    So did I deem . . .

It is not until the poet sees Charles Kemble's Coriolanus and George Cooke's Shylock that he believes "self" can be momentarily overcome by something besides purely literary study:

. . . these were beings tangible in vice,
    Their purpose searchable, their every thought
Indexed in living men; yet only sought,
    Plain as they seem, by genius, – only bought
By genius even with laborious price.

Each character comes to life because he is "tangible in vice," compounded of particular desires and actions. The task, Allston discovers, is not after all to mimic "look, and attitude, and air," but to take on purpose and thought and let the look of the thing take care of itself.

But what, Allston now asks, can any actor do with Hamlet, a character entirely familiar in his charismatic outward show – and altogether mysterious underneath? Allston may well have heard Coleridge's lectures on Shakespeare; certainly, his Hamlet is Coleridge's "man who cannot make up his mind," a character defined by conflicted purposes. This makes him almost impossible to play without lame "mimicry" and requires the greatest actor, Edmund Kean, to bring to life the "princely Denmark's form" by playing the purposes as they conflict:

If this be Kean, then Hamlet lived indeed!
    Look! how his purpose hurries him apace,
    Seeking a fitful rest from place to place!
    And yet his trouble fits him with a grace,
As if his heart did love what makes it bleed.

Kean plays the purpose without playing, as it were, the purpose of the purpose, without playing the character. He concerns himself with small actions and leaves these outlines to be filled in by the poet.

The poem ends boldly, even baldly: "Or Kean or Hamlet, – what I see is real!" But we accept Allston's admiration because it comes so thoroughly tempered by fine observation and questioning, because the reality of representation is not so much at issue as the "what." Allston asks: "what starts before me?" It is this curiosity – what combination of need and method makes for successful, real representation? – that animates the poem.

In *Lectures on Art*, Allston defined *line* as "the course or medium through which the eye is led from one part of the picture to another. The indication of this course is various and multiform, appertaining equally to shape, to color, and to light and dark; in a word, to whatever attracts and keeps the eye in motion." Suitably enough, his greatest poetic achievement is a series of five ecphrastic sonnets, each one tracing the eye in motion over the work of a different painter. To these pieces Allston attaches a sixth sonnet, dedicated to Benjamin West ("To My Venerable Friend, the President of the Royal Academy" [LOA, 1: 56]). This celebration of a painter in his official role as a teacher is not at all out of place. Like Allston's *Lectures* at their best, these sonnets teach how to pay attention to the particulars of pictures and then how to look past these particulars for the character of the whole. They also form the best possible introduction to Allston's short lyrics: they help teach what to listen for in his other sonnets and sonnet fragments.

The first of the five, "On a Falling Group in the Last Judgement of Michael Angelo, in the Cappella Sistina" (LOA, 1: 54), limits its look to one detail, which can be found at the lower right corner of the fresco:

> How vast, how dread, o'erwhelming is the thought
> Of Space interminable! to the soul
> A circling weight that crushes into nought
> Her mighty faculties! a wond'rous whole,
> Without or parts, beginning, or an end!
> How fearful then on desp'rate wings to send
> The fancy e'en amid the waste profound!
> Yet, born as if all daring to astound,
> Thy giant hand, oh Angelo, hath hurl'd
> E'en human forms, with all their mortal weight,
> Down the dread void – fall endless as their fate!
> Already now they seem from world to world
> For ages thrown; yet doom'd, another past,
> Another still to reach, nor e'er to reach the last!

Although the detail will be familiar to many readers, few will have seen its horrors so distinctly – or return to it without some inkling of Allston's dread. If we read the sonnet without having the picture before us, it is easy to forget that "the thought / Of Space interminable" is just that, a thought. The fresco itself is packed with figures and full of light, and the "waste profound" is a matter of draftsmanship and lives only in the outlines that separate one figure from another.

What happens when we look again at the fresco, when we see it under Allston's tutelage? As before, we see the falling group in the first split second of its fall. Some figures teeter and clutch at the angels who shove them down (the ether seems just to have given way under them). Others topple over or away from each other, abandoning themselves to gravity like dreamers in a nightmare. Now, these details hold the eye in a new way. We see the damned no longer as a group, but as a collection of solitudes. By the strangeness of their poses (we watch them from what should be beneath, behind, or above), by the outward gazes of the peripheral figures, by the central figure's haunting self-contemplation, and by every possible device except the use of actual blank space, Michelangelo has set the crowded figures apart from each other and from us. Like the rose and blue lovers of Edvard Munch's *Encounter in Space*, who sail past each other without contact or recognition, Michelangelo's figures give the feeling, more than the sight, of falling (they are nothing like, say, the views revealed to us by stop photography). In his discussion of the sublime, Edmund Burke compares the effect of "vacuities" in painting to the experience of sitting in a chair and finding it lower than we expect, or to waking "with a most violent start . . . preceded by a sort of dream of our falling down a precipice." Allston's sonnet reverses the analogy: from the shock and imbalance in Michelangelo's figures, Allston lets us extrapolate the void, the actual fall. (It would come as no surprise if the strange, later sonnet "A Word: Man" [LOA, 1: 61] took its inspiration from the same terrible figures.)

Like Reynolds, Allston was in the habit of referring to Michelangelo as the Milton of the visual arts. Although Michelangelo never painted the Fall of the Rebel Angels that he planned for the entry of the Sistine Chapel, Allston suggests that the *Last Judgment* gives us a scene of damnation comparable to Milton's: in it Michelangelo has realized the paradox of "darkness visible," not by making it dark (as a theorist like Burke would prescribe), but by making it clearly, intensely visible.

As always in painting, making the figures visible means holding them still. In this case, the feat is especially remarkable. For Allston, it is the unfulfilled sense that the heels of the main figure are about to tumble forward that makes thought "A circling weight that crushes into nought / [The soul's] mighty faculties": it is the actual stasis of the figure that gets eyes and thought rolling in the first place. In itself, this emphasis on movement, as a mark of sublimity, is not new: contemporary critics had grown up on Longinus's dictum that "It is the nature of the Pathetic and Sublime, to run rapidly along, and carry all before them." Burke, for example, explains the effect of sublimity in paintings as a kind of eyestrain.

But for Allston, the feeling of rapid, helpless circling is part of looking at any great painting; it has as much to do with grace and beauty as with the strainings of sublimity. In the second sonnet, "On the Group of the Three Angels Before the Tent of Abraham, by Raffaelle, in the Vatican" (LOA, 1: 54), Allston also describes his kind of active looking as a purely pleasurable, purely beautiful enchantment:

> Oh, now I feel as though another sense
> From Heaven descending had inform'd my soul;
> I feel the pleasurable, full control
> Of Grace, harmonious, boundless, and intense.
> In thee, celestial Group, embodied lives
> The subtle mystery; that speaking gives
> Itself resolv'd; the essences combin'd
> Of Motion ceaseless, Unity complete.
> Borne like a leaf by some soft eddying wind,
> Mine eyes, impell'd as by enchantment sweet,
> From part to part with circling motion rove,
> Yet seem unconscious of the power to move;
> From line to line through endless changes run,
> O'er countless shapes, yet seem to gaze on One.

As John Hollander has noted, Allston's aesthetic interest in the painting governs and finally overwhelms the sonnet's Trinitarian allegory. Allston is too fascinated by the way in which the angels look to insist on what they mean; in the end, the mystery of the Trinity becomes a figure for his own response to the painting, a figure for his own willing captivation. From the beginning, Allston receives the sight of the angels as a gift of imminent creative power; this sight constitutes "another sense" that informs (teaches and reshapes) his soul. He feels "the pleasurable, full control / Of Grace" as a control over him and, at the same time, as a control available to him. If this is rapture, the rapture entices without sublimity's violence: Allston joins in his own transport. He is the one who lets himself get swept away.

Reynolds's *Discourses* held up Raphael and Michelangelo as the highest examples of the beautiful and sublime, respectively; as the representative of the sublime, Michelangelo was considered the greater of the two. Allston would replay the contest in his own lectures – with a less definitive outcome: "If any man may be said to have reigned over the hearts of his fellows, it was Raffaelle Sanzio. . . . In this the greatest names in Art fall before him; in this he has no rival." In Allston's sonnet, therefore, we might say that the three dynamic, muscular youths stand in for Raphael himself; they reign over and rejuvenate the viewer's heart at the same time that they enchant Abraham and Sarah's unfaithful, barren marriage.

In both cases, the enchantment attends on a scene of informing. The angels are there to tell Abraham and Sarah something at first unbelievable about themselves – that they will desire each other again and make love – and Raphael reduces this information to the three gestures that organize the painting, so that his angels come, like Eros, to be embodiments of creative power. As often in Allston's poems (see, for instance, the sonnets "Art" or "On the Statue of an Angel, by Bienaimé in the Possession of J.S. Copley Greene, Esq." [LOA, 1: 59]), artistic inspiration feels like divine redemption, if only because it intrudes from outside to inform the self. The episode of the angels gripped Allston in later life as a symbol of young inspiration: in the introduction to his lectures he asks, "Could we read the annals scored on every human heart . . . who will doubt that their darkest passages are those made visible by the distant gleams from those angelic Forms [Beauty, Truth, and Goodness], that, like the Three which stood before the tent of Abraham, once looked upon his youth?" Allston recognizes that the angels' first miracle is not Sarah's conception, but the fact that Sarah and Abraham desire each other anew. In Allston's account, even Raphael's old couple (whose unimportant bodies seem hardly to belong in the same painting with the angels) might be reconciled to love and work in a world that received such visitations.

The third sonnet, "On Seeing the Picture of Æolus by Pelegrino Tibaldi, in the Institute at Bologna" (LOA, 1: 55), follows up Allston's interest in paintings as stories of their own inspiration – in this case, inspiration by the kind of awesome sublimity, or *terribilità*, that frightened Allston in the *Last Judgment*. At first, Allston imagines "the mighty spell of Bonarotti" (i.e., Michelangelo) as a kind of magic writing, born on the winds that accompany Pellegrino's Aeolus; then the tribute to both painters grows more complex. The giant Aeolus, glaring down from his ceiling at Allston, provokes (and finally dismisses) the question of how much of Aeolus, or of Michelangelo, Pellegrino actually understands:

> Full well, Tibaldi, did thy kindred mind
> The mighty spell of Bonarotti own.
> Like one who, reading magick words, receives
> The gift of intercourse with worlds unknown,
> 'Twas thine, decyph'ring Nature's mystick leaves,
> To hold strange converse with the viewless wind;
> To see the Spirits, in embodied forms,
> Of gales and whirlwinds, hurricanes and storms.
> For, lo! obedient to thy bidding, teems
> Fierce into shape their stern relentless Lord:
> His form of motion ever-restless seems;
> Or, if to rest inclin'd his turbid soul,
> On Hecla's top to stretch, and give the word
> To subject Winds that sweep the desert pole.

In the first four lines, we are told that Pellegrino's mind owns Michelangelo's spell: Pellegrino reads the spell, and he conjures up interlocutors from "worlds unknown." And yet, Allston never lets us guess how well Pellegrino knows these worlds, or whether he holds his "intercourse" purely by rote, through words that belonged, and still belong, to Michelangelo. The next two lines only thicken the mystery. If Pellegrino deciphers nature's mystic leaves, are these the leaves penned and scattered by Michelangelo? Or are they new leaves, dictated to Pellegrino by Michelangelo's source? And if this source is "Nature," who is she, if not the worlds unknown? The figures in Pellegrino's Large Ulysses Room, where Aeolus appears, have long been said to owe especially much to Michelangelo's Sibyls and Prophets, but if Michelangelo's scenes of prophecy have their source in natural inspiration, does this mean that a true reading of the prophetic scenes can return the later painter to this source?

Allston turns from these riddles in lines six through eight. Pellegrino's "strange converse" with the viewless, or invisible, wind is to be measured in sights, not words: the fact of artistic mastery (not exactly originality) is what counts here, what explains Pellegrino's ownership, and what makes Pellegrino a force to be obeyed. Although "Lord" in the tenth line refers primarily to Aeolus, we can hardly rule out Michelangelo as a secondary referent: the "form of motion" belongs to them equally. For Allston this ambiguity finds a kind of mirror in the Michelangelesque ambiguity of Aeolus's pose (is he springing into action or lapsing into relaxation?). Allston notes the ambiguity and heightens it by a twist of syntax: "His form of motion ever-restless seems / Or . . . [seems] to stretch." The spirits that Pellegrino has tamed are not just the monstrous, puff-cheeked putti behind Aeolus; they stand for every power that Pellegrino owns without understanding or originating, without making fully his.

By glorifying Pellegrino – as a good student of Michelangelo – Allston defends both the minor painter and his task. When we study the strangeness of great paintings, Allston suggests, we learn new powers, new spells bigger than we can understand or originate ourselves. Even a derivative painting, if it is good, distinguishes the hand that painted it, if only by lifting a painter like Pellegrino to heights where he cannot feel quite at home. (So, in the first lines of "On Michael Angelo" [LOA, 1: 62] Allston claims a ray of Michelangelo's light for himself without pretending to benefit the source: "'T is not to honor thee by verse of mine / I bear a record of thy wondrous power.")

In the fourth sonnet, "On Rembrant[*sic*]; Occasioned by His Picture of Jacob's Dream" (LOA, 1: 55), Allston extends the claim. According to Allston, the powers of strange paintings change our minds. Even if we never understand them, we think new things because of them. They seem to talk back to us:

> As in that twilight, superstitious age
> When all beyond the narrow grasp of mind
> Seem'd fraught with meanings of supernal kind,
> When e'en the learned philosophic sage,
> Wont with the stars thro' boundless space to range,
> Listen'd with rev'rence to the changeling's tale;
> E'en so, thou strangest of all beings strange!
> E'en so thy visionary scenes I hail;
> That like the rambling of an idiot's speech,
> No image giving of a thing on earth,

Nor thought significant in Reason's reach,
Yet in their random shadowings give birth
To thoughts and things from other worlds that come,
And fill the soul, and strike the reason dumb.

In his *Lectures,* Allston would defend the Dutch masters (from critics like Reynolds who attacked the "meanness of their characters"). For instance, he concludes his praise of a "coarse" Dutch cottage scene with an appeal to artists: "They, we are sure, will be the last to question the character of the feeling because of the ingredients which worked the spell, and, if true to themselves, they must call it poetry." Here, Allston is not afraid to associate earthy detail with a mysterious spell. It is worth noting that the sonnet is dedicated to Rembrandt as a comment on his work in general; in this dark painting (now thought to have been executed by a pupil, Aert de Gelder, from Rembrandt's sketch), the lighted figures make a kind of foil to their shadows, to the enveloping blackness. And this effect is typical of Rembrandt: the familiarity, the coarseness, the recognizable humanness of what we see turns the eye all the more forcefully back to what we cannot see, what lies hidden in the dark, unfamiliar surrounding.

De Gelder's portly angel (so human that he must lift up his robe to step down to earth) and the heaven hovering only a foot or two above the angel's head strike Allston as "visionary" because they compete for actuality with the black night and the forest billowing around them. If there is something mad in the competition ("like the rambling of an idiot's speech"), it is no less compelling for its madness. The closeness of de Gelder's heaven – in general, the intrusion of dream light on night – startles Allston (as one of his favorite contemporaries, Fuseli, must also have done). He thus cannot help but peer into the "random shadowings" that exemplify motives and wisdoms nonsensical to the reason of his own age and temperament. For Allston, there can be no crossing the gulf that lies between him and Rembrandt; it begs nevertheless to be crossed, and Allston must satisfy himself with this, his own communication (however randomly shadowed) "from other worlds."

In the fifth sonnet, "On the Luxembourg Gallery" (LOA, 1: 56), Allston's subject is once again a painter who is hard for the Age of Reason to accept. The difficulty with Rembrandt is that he tells an unreasonable truth; the trouble with Rubens is that he refuses to tell the truth at all. His art is passionately politic; it mocks every moral and critical system, including Allston's. "The fact is," Allston once told a friend, "Rubens was a liar, a splendid liar":

and I would rather lie like Rubens than to tell the truth in the poor, tame manner in which some painters do. His pictures are like the sophistical reasonings of a liar, to whom you have only to grant his premises and he will thereon erect a gorgeous fabric, but deny these premises and it all falls to the ground.

This talent for dissimulation shines forth most brilliantly in the cycle that Rubens painted for the gallery of Maria de Medicis's Luxembourg Palace. In these 23 allegorical paintings, commissioned to represent Maria's "very illustrious life and heroic deeds," Rubens had his work cut out for him. He was expected to glorify Maria's rocky political career (her marriage to her fa-

ther's philandering debtor Henri IV and her notably corrupt reign after his death); to satirize the son, Louis XIII, who in a coup d'état had displaced and imprisoned her; and to offend no one (least of all Louis) in the process.

Even without these political complications, the cycle required extraordinary feats of good taste. How to make a courtship that took two years of papal engineering look like love at first sight – particularly when both principals were remarkably ugly? How to paint a marriage by proxy? How to paint the queen's arrival in France, when the king was too busy (with a second, less fortunate fiancée) to meet her? How to paint, of all things, *The Marriage Consummated in Lyons*? Every subject demanded a new delicacy, a new kind of flattery; nonetheless, each painting must flirt with absurdity. And yet, Allston argues, if we miss the cycle's charm, the fault lies with us:

There is a Charm no vulgar mind can reach,
No critick thwart, no mighty master teach;
A Charm how mingled of the good and ill!
Yet still so mingled that the mystick whole
Shall captive hold the struggling Gazer's will,
'Till vanquish'd reason own its full control.
And such, oh Rubens, thy mysterious art,
The charm that vexes, yet enslaves the heart!
Thy lawless style, from timid systems free,
Impetuous rolling like a troubled sea,
High o'er the rocks of reason's lofty verge
Impending hangs; yet, ere the foamy surge
Breaks o'er the bound, the refluent ebb of taste
Back from the shore impels the wat'ry waste.

Allston answers Rubens's sophistication with what we might call a fiction of imitative form: the verse is unusually tricky. The three strongly significant enjambments, the subtle vowel shifts in lines three through six, the continual suggestiveness of the rhymes, and the complexity of the sonnet's last image, itself suggested by the sea gods that dominate Rubens's *Arrival at Marseilles* (see the poem's shorter version, "Rubens" [LOA, 1: 62]) – all of these complexities make the poem sound modern, all invite close reading.

Allston relies on this fiction of imitation not just to versify, but to sketch Rubens himself. In the casual aristocratic pose that he perfected, the master stands before the cycle like one of his own portraits: charming, lawless, and impetuous all at once. In Allston's sketch, it is as if Rubens's pictures of command were somehow bound up with Rubens's command of pictures. (Allston might well reply that Rubens suggested the lie himself in his later self-portraits.) Confronted with so much mastery, the strongest possible response for Allston is to acknowledge himself beaten.

With this humble gesture of appreciation, Allston draws the series of ecphrastic sonnets to a close. The sonnet to West celebrates another kind of strong humility: the true artist's devotion to work over self. This ideal, "E'en for itself to love thy soul-ennobling art," returns again and again in Allston's letters, in the *Lectures,* and in the aphorisms (published with the *Lectures*) that he pinned to his studio walls. This ideal also constitutes the tragic paradox of *Monaldi,* in which Allston divides the artist's soul between two friends, a self-seeking poet and a self-forgetting painter. Whereas Reynolds could encourage his students to strive after lasting fame (rather than passing popularity), Allston preaches what we might call a more thoroughly Protestant idealism: art must be its own reward, a reward untainted by worldly considerations. True fame – which, for Allston as well as Reynolds, always means posterity – must come on its own and cannot be of any concern to the artist: "I cannot believe that any man who deserved fame ever labored for it; that is, *directly*." In the sonnet that follows Allston's best poems, therefore, West stands in for an underlying ideal of the cycle: "the manly race / Of one who felt the purifying grace / Of honest fame."

LORIN STEIN

Selected Works

Lectures on Art, and Poems (1850) and Monaldi (1842), edited by Nathalia Wright, Gainesville, Florida: Scholars' Facsimiles and Reprints, 1967

The Correspondence of Washington Allston, edited by Nathalia Wright, Lexington: University Press of Kentucky, 1993

Further Reading

Flagg, Jared B., *Life and Letters of Washington Allston*, 1892; reprinted, New York: Kennedy Galleries, n.d.

Hollander, John, *The Gazer's Spirit*, University of Chicago Press, 1995

Kasson, Joy S., *Artistic Voyagers: Europe and the American Imagination in the Works of Irving, Allston, Cole, Cooper, and Hawthorne*, Westport, Connecticut: Greenwood, 1982

Packer, Barbara, introduction, *The Oxford Anthology of American Literature*, vol. 1

Richardson, E. P., *Washington Allston: A Study of the Romantic Artist in America*, 1948; reprinted, New York: Apollo Editions, n.d.

Joel Barlow

(1754–1812)

In "The Poetic Principle" (1848), Edgar Allan **Poe** writes: "That the extent of a poetical work is, *caeteris paribus*, the measure of its merit seems undoubtedly, when we state it, a proposition sufficiently absurd. . . . A mountain, to be sure, by the mere sentiment of physical magnitude which it conveys, *does* impress us with a sense of the sublime – but no man is impressed after *this* fashion by the material grandeur of even 'The Columbiad.'" As the quotation illustrates, Joel Barlow's most ambitious work, *The Columbiad* (LOA, 1: 12), was much maligned by the literati and the populace alike in the nineteenth century, a critical disparagement that has remained unrevised. Indeed, most present-day criticism dismisses the epic as a ponderous historical curiosity at best. Generally perceived as an epic poem whose vision exceeds the talents of its creator, *The Columbiad* has become synonymous with works of immense physical magnitude – and meager artistic proficiency.

To judge Barlow's poetry by current aesthetic or critical standards that ignore its historical and political context and its aesthetic milieu, however, is unfair. Twentieth-century readers must examine the prevalent beliefs, issues, and temper of the time in which Barlow's poetry was written. Although it was abruptly terminated by his untimely death, Barlow's poetic and political career (1778–1812) spanned a period characterized by events of great turmoil: the American and French Revolutions, the establishment of the early American republic, and the commencement of the Napoleonic wars.

The American Revolution was not only a political revisionary movement, but a moral and philosophical one as well. For the embattled American colonists, the Revolution became the first viable testing of Enlightenment ideals of benevolence and rationalism, especially the philosophies of John Locke and Jean-Jacques Rousseau, and galvanized exponents of a new Augustan Age on this side of the Atlantic. These self-proclaimed New World Augustans believed that the Revolution would usher in a new age of political and artistic felicity – and, most importantly, an age founded upon democratic ideals.

Despite the fervor and positivism of various politicians and artists, however, the fledgling nation's transformation from a wilderness to a New Athenian order was impeded by postwar worries. In the early years the nation was inauspiciously afflicted with severe economic, political, and social problems. Beset by tenuous relations with Great Britain and increasingly belligerent ones with its former ally France, the new nation faced internal ills as well. Although Alexander Hamilton worked to stabilize the nation's financial situation through the establishment of a national bank and protective tariffs, the monetary system was shaky and commerce was waning. Farmers and other rural inhabitants suffered great economic hardships, and many moved into the cities looking for work. Urban areas rapidly became overcrowded, leading to substandard sanitation, disease, and a marked rise in crime.

During this tumultuous period, the notion of republican virtue surfaced – that is, that the private interests of the individual, no matter how noble, must be subsumed for the good of the republic. Many Americans, especially those who es-poused Thomas Jefferson's republican philosophy, viewed the propensity to perpetuate the British way of life – seen as self-indulgent, corrupt, and obsessed with luxury – as a dangerous course. Therefore, they emphasized Lockean and Newtonian ideas of order and discipline, that freedom must be circumscribed by civic obligations. As a result of these ideas, members of the period's two main ideological camps became embroiled in a particularly divisive dispute: the Federalists' fear of the populace spawned an emphasis on the need for governmental constraints, whereas the Jeffersonian republicans championed the idea that reason could emancipate humanity and thus edify the personal and the civic. In addition, after the Revolution public opinion became divided over the role of the arts in society; some saw the arts as an indication of societal degeneration, but others thought they exemplified American progress.

Nevertheless, for many artists in the early republic, such as Barlow, the Revolutionary War and its aftermath were worthy of artistic celebration. And like many of his peers, Barlow adhered to and, through his poetry, promulgated the classical and Renaissance concept of *translatio studii* (or *translatio imperii*). Ostensibly, *translatio studii* is the tenet that the progress of civilization emulates solar movement; like celestial bodies, civilization, too, moves from east to west. Consequently, to those who postulated this idea, North America was the natural future residence of the arts and sciences, a new Athens, and its culture and art would eventually supersede that of the British.

As products of the Enlightenment, Barlow and his Yale classmates were trained in poetic and oratorical imitation of classical and British literary forms. In fact, Barlow was one of the most well-read American citizens of the early republic. His erudition served him well as a poet, but also as a scholar and a diplomat, for Barlow became a judicious and savvy political official of the Jefferson and James Madison administrations. Although Barlow is better remembered for his political adroitness and enlightened philosophical stance than for his art, his poetic opus is worthy of greater scrutiny, especially in relation to his political involvements.

Barlow's beginnings, although not unpropitious, were not providential either. He was born March 24, 1754, the son of Samuel Barlow, a prosperous Connecticut farmer whose forebear, John Barlow, had emigrated to Connecticut one hundred years before, and Esther Hull, Samuel's second wife. As the eighth of nine children (the elder four were from Samuel Barlow's first marriage), young Joel was provided with the most rigorous liberal education the elder Barlow could afford. As a special student under Parson Bartlett's tutelage, in one year Barlow successfully prepared for entrance into Moor's Indian School in Hanover, New Hampshire. After completing his course of study there, he entered Dartmouth in 1774, but left after three months for Yale upon the death of his father. When Yale was temporarily closed because of a potential typhoid epidemic in New Haven, Barlow joined the militia, but he then returned to Yale to complete his baccalaureate degree.

Upon graduation in 1778, Barlow as class poet read "The Prospect of Peace" at commencement. This early work anticipates the Commencement Poem of 1781, *The Vision of Columbus*, and *The Columbiad* in both theme and form. Written in heroic couplets (a form Barlow used extensively), "The Prospect of Peace" opens with a grandiose description of the American struggle for independence and optimistically ends with a millennial vision of the United States where "Love shall rule, and Tyrants be no more." Typical of commencement poems of the period, it employs a newly popular poetic form: the prospect poem. Notable examples of this subgenre include John Trumbull's "Prospect of the Future Glory of America" (1770) and Philip **Freneau** and Hugh Henry Brackenridge's "The Rising Glory of America" (1771). The prospect poem subgenre reached its zenith in Francis Scott Key's "The Star-Spangled Banner" (1814; LOA, 1: 46), a foreshortened variant that employed anapestic couplets to emblazon its vision of glory and sovereignty. In general, the prospect poem was patterned after the last two books of Milton's *Paradise Lost*, which deal with the archangel Michael's prophesy. American variants, which primarily used prophesy as a means to praise republican ideals, were typically composed of approximately two hundred to six hundred lines of blank verse or heroic couplets. According to John McWilliams, the "crisis of America's self-definition led patriotic poets to cherish one particular poetic subgenre – an oratorical prophesy"; hence the popularity of the prospect poem (*Columbia History of the United States*, ed. Emory Elliott, 1988).

As a new college graduate, Barlow found few occupations open to him. He briefly settled on a career as a schoolmaster (1778–79), but he always heard the Muse's seductive call. Determined to launch a career as a poet, Barlow convinced his older brother Nathaniel to subsidize his graduate studies at Yale. At this time, Barlow hit upon his idea for the epic that would dominate his poetic efforts: Columbus and the discovery of America. In a letter to his former tutor and friend Joseph Buckminster, Barlow explained: "The discovery of America made an important revolution in the history of mankind. It served the purpose of displaying knowledge, liberty, and religion." Barlow's graduate Commencement Poem of 1781 is of interest because it offers excerpts from the work in progress *The Vision of Columbus*. This abbreviated form of his grand epic opens with laudatory descriptions of Yale and then shifts to a postwar prophesy concerning the millennium. Reverberating with the concept of *translatio studii*, the poem augurs that the literature of the new republic will ultimately fashion a new world.

Unfortunately, although Barlow was respected by his Yale colleagues as a promising poet, he found himself floundering in his search for a profession that would provide a viable income while allowing him to pursue his art. Finally, after acquiescing to friends' entreaties and relying on their influence, Barlow was ordained a minister and became a chaplain in the army. But even though he had enjoyed the study of theology as an undergraduate, his brief ministerial career could be described, at best, as lackluster. Upon his discharge, Barlow embarked on a successful career as a diplomat and served his country in various offices, most notably as minister to France. (Like Washington, Hamilton, and Thomas Paine, Barlow was elected to French citizenship; this award testifies to his skill and success as a politician.)

Despite his political achievements, Barlow never would for-

sake his Muse, and was constantly honing his craft. For a brief period, he became affiliated with a group of conservative Federalist poets, known as the Connecticut Wits (or the Hartford Wits). A group of Yale graduates, including Barlow, John Trumbull, David Humphreys, and Timothy Dwight, launched a political satire entitled *The Anarchiad* (ominously subtitled "A Poem on the Restoration of Chaos and Substantial Night"), which they published in thirteen installments in the *New Haven Gazette* (1786–87). *The Anarchiad* primarily served as a conservative response to Shays's Rebellion, a series of armed conflicts that grew out of an economic crisis on the Massachusetts frontier and that could not be quelled by the militia until February 1787.

Published soon after Barlow's involvement with the "wicked wits," *The Vision of Columbus* (1787) was a more patriotic poem than his previous ones and espoused a more moderate view. Of course, Barlow's moderate ideas in this poem registered his pre–French Revolution views. Heavy publicity and an impressive subscription list made the poem a financial success. The poem opens with a prose summary of the life of Columbus, which leads into Book I, where an aged, imprisoned Columbus is elaborately and despairingly pondering his fate. An angel mercifully appears and whisks him off to the Mount of Vision so that he can see the future of the New World he has discovered. Over the next three books, the vision chronicles the history of the Incan Empire and its remarkable founder, Manco Capac. (Barlow even inserts a prosaic 15-page essay, "On the Genius and Institutions of Manco Capac.") Book IV concludes with the colonization of the North American continent, and then Books V–VI describe both the French and Indian Wars and the Revolutionary War. Lastly, Book VII commences the hymn to peace. Here the poet glorifies American progress in the arts and sciences, while interjecting diverse philosophical "treatises" on such subjects as the relationship between the Creator and humanity, the problems of extreme passion or extreme reason, and the ultimate union of reason and passion, which the poem claims will result in a future of peace and humanity. The poem concludes with Columbus joyfully musing on a vision of a peaceful millennium.

The Vision of Columbus is ostensibly a summation of Barlow's early conservative beliefs – that is, his New England–influenced faith in progress, his belief in the unchanging constant of the human condition, and his affirmation of spiritual revelation. According to these beliefs, false religion led to excess passion, and reason carried to excess led to error.

After 1788, Barlow broke with such conservative thought. His poetics and politics, which originated from the rather rustic confines of New Haven, expanded to the more global proportions that the views from the drawing rooms of Washington, London, and Paris afforded. Instead of pursuing his friendships and political alliances with conservatives such as Dwight, he aligned himself with proponents of English radicalism, the Girondists of the French Revolution, and American republicans such as Jefferson and Madison.

Between composing the moderate *Vision of Columbus* and its revision, the republican *The Columbiad*, Barlow wrote what is generally considered to be his finest poetic effort, the parodic "The Hasty Pudding" (composed in 1793; published in 1796). This engaging mock-epic paean to cornmeal mush was written in Europe during a fit of homesickness. In brief, the narrator gleefully discovers the homey dish in the Alps, which causes him to reflect on the recipe. The recipe is an unusual one, for it opens with the planting of the corn, details the harvesting and concocting of the mush, and ends with advice on the type of bowls and utensils one should use when serving this "purest of all food" and a mock treatise on table etiquette. Interspersed within the four cantos is an apostrophe to the corn and a delightful description of the Connecticut countryside.

But Barlow chose to forsake humor for a more serious agenda. *The Columbiad* (1807) is his valiant attempt to use old poetic forms to establish a republican vision. Celebratory in tone, the epic venerates commerce, nature, and the triumph of the common people over the corrupt aristocracy. Although criticized for its loosely episodic construction and its ponderous rhythm (the heroic couplets attempt to emulate the more skillful Alexander Pope), the work has merits other than its magnificent scope. We can more accurately assess these merits by contextualizing the poem in relation to Barlow's own outline of his poetics in the poem's preface. According to the preface, epic poems should be judged according to "the importance of the action, the disposition of the parts, the invention and application of incidents, the propriety of the illustrations, the liveliness and chastity of the images, the suitable intervention of machinery, the moral tendency of the manners, the strength and sublimity of the sentiments; the whole being clothed in language whose energy, harmony, and elegance shall constitute a style every where suited to the matter they have to treat." Also in the preface, Barlow espouses the view that past epics (notably, the *Iliad* and the *Aeneid*) had a pernicious influence on their audiences inasmuch as they promoted the notion of the divine right of kings. One of his purposes in writing *The Columbiad* is to recontextualize the epic, and thereby celebrate republicanism.

A complex, ambitious work, *The Columbiad* is structured as follows:

Books I–V: The various visions of Columbus (very similar to the structure Barlow utilized in the earlier *Vision of Columbus*).

Books VI–VII: An expansion of Barlow's visions, which incorporates American Revolutionary heroes. These heroes, particularly Washington, are depicted as larger than life, and the action within these books is on a grander scale (and therefore more "epic"). The subject matter in these books is also more detailed.

Book VIII: A paean of peace and discourse directed toward Revolutionary War patriots.

Book IX: Barlow's scientific and philosophical ideas (basically, utilitarianism and Lockean rationalism).

Book X: A culmination of the previous books, which ends in a representation of the union of humanity (an historical evolution).

The Christopher Columbus of *The Columbiad* diverges from the popular early-nineteenth-century conception of an explorer whose courage and skill were of mythic proportions. Barlow's Columbus is frail and aged, and wrongfully imprisoned by his former patron (as in *The Vision of Columbus*). The Seraph of the West, Hesper, appears and offers him a series of visions that culminate in the vision of the future glory of America. Hesper ultimately usurps the role of narrator and presents Columbus with vignettes that center on the discovery of America, the founding of the English colonies, and their successful struggle for independence. When the more recent visions are shown, especially those focusing on the Revolution and the surrender of the British at Yorktown, the narrative voice becomes more personal. Hesper's subsequent prophetic pictures evince a utopian concept of a prodigious assemblage of all nations in which political accord and tranquillity prevail. Despite his frailty, Columbus unflaggingly makes the proper republican response to the visions Hesper puts before him. He becomes ecstatic while witnessing republican progress, but despondent at displays of aristocratic and theological corruption. In all, *The Columbiad* is a significant reworking of the *translatio studii* and republican vision.

Barlow's last poem, "Advice to a Raven in Russia" (LOA, 1: 24), was written in 1812, approximately one month before his death. It is a scathing and reasonably skillful criticism of the Napoleonic wars, and of Napoleon's overriding ambition in particular. Beginning on a plaintive note, the narrator confronts a raven scavenging for food. "Black fool, why winter here," the narrator says, when fresh carnage is available in warmer climates? The poem chronicles Napoleon's bloody march across Europe, and as James Woodress has asserted, the final lines provide the most damning indictment of Napoleon's ruthless ambition that ever appeared poetic form:

> War after war his hungry soul requires,
> State after state shall sink beneath his fires,
> . . . .
> Each land lie reeking with its people's slain
> And not a stream run bloodless to the main.
> Till men resume their souls, and dare to shed
> Earth's total vengeance on the monster's head . . .

Barlow's poetic passion was cut short when he died of pneumonia in Zarnowiec, Poland, while in the diplomatic service of his country. A marble marker on the parish church commemorates his passing and his life:

> JOEL BARLOW
> Plentipotens Minister
> a Statibus unitis America
> ad Imp. Gallorum & Reg. Italia
> Itinerando hicce obiit
> 26 December 1812

Oddly, there is no reference to his poetry.

ANITA M. VICKERS

Selected Works

The Prospect of Peace, New Haven, Connecticut: Thomas and Samuel Green, 1778

A Poem, Spoken at the Public Commencement at Yale College, New Haven, Connecticut: Hudson and Goodwin, 1781

An Elegy on the Late Honorable Titus Hosmer, Hartford, Connecticut: Hudson and Goodwin, 1782

The Vision of Columbus, Hartford, Connecticut: Hudson and Goodwin, 1787

The Conspiracy of Kings, London: J. Johnson, St. Paul's Churchyard, 1792

The Hasty Pudding, New Haven, Connecticut: T. and S. Green, 1796

The Columbiad, ca. 1807, Washington, D.C.: Joseph Milligan, 1825

"Advice to a Raven in Russia," ca. 1812, reprinted in Woodress

Further Reading

Dowling, William C., *Poetry and Ideology in Revolutionary Connecticut*, Athens: University of Georgia Press, 1990

Howard, Leon, *The Connecticut Wits*, Chicago: University of Chicago Press, 1943

Todd, Charles Burr, *The Life and Letters of Joel Barlow: Poet, Statesman, Philosopher*, New York: Da Capo, 1970

Woodress, James, *A Yankee's Odyssey: The Life of Joel Barlow*, Philadelphia and New York: Lippincott, 1958

Zunder, Theodore Albert, *The Early Days of Joel Barlow: A Connecticut Wit*, New Haven, Connecticut: Yale University Press, 1934

Ambrose Bierce

(1842–1914)

Despite being a dead white male, Ambrose Bierce has always hovered on the margins of the canon. And even there, his place has been secured by his short stories and the epigrammatic definitions in his *Devil's Dictionary*. Most readers will be startled to learn that he wrote any poetry at all. It is not surprising, therefore, that the selections in the Library of America anthology are, for the most part, drawn from the verses appended to the mordant entries in *The Devil's Dictionary*. Yet Bierce, despite his own disclaimers, *was* a poet, one who occupies a unique niche in nineteenth-century American verse. As the sole modern commentator on his poetry, Donald Sidney-Fryer, has observed, "Bierce has remained almost unknown as a poet, qua poet," although he "clearly merits the attention of the discriminating lover and student of poetry."

Born on a farm in Meigs County, Ohio, on June 24, 1842, Bierce moved with his family to northern Indiana in 1846. In 1861, when national tensions exploded in the Civil War, he enlisted while still a teenager in the Ninth Indiana Infantry Regiment and was discharged a first lieutenant in 1865. He was later breveted to the rank of major after he participated in a military expedition through Indian country from Omaha, Nebraska, to San Francisco, California. There, in 1867, he began training himself to be a writer, publishing poems and prose in various publications. In 1872, accompanied by a new bride, Mary Ellen Day, he sailed for England, where his first three books were published and his two sons were born. In 1875, he returned to San Francisco and resumed his journalistic career. His career took a giant leap into security and prominence when he was hired by William Randolph Hearst in 1887 to write for the *San Francisco Examiner*, where almost all of his most famous work appeared initially.

The years from 1887 to 1899 were the most significant in Bierce's life. His anguish over the separation from his wife and the death of his older son in a gun duel over a woman was transmuted into the writing of some of his greatest stories, collected in *Tales of Soldiers and Civilians* (1892; title in England: *In the Midst of Life*) and *Can Such Things Be?* (1893). Moreover, he composed numerous satirical verses against California rogues and fools that were assembled in *Black Beetles in Amber* (1892). He left California permanently for the East in 1899, settling in Washington, D.C. In 1903, he published a second book of poems, *Shapes of Clay*, and in 1906 *The Cynic's Word Book*, as *The Devil's Dictionary* was initially titled.

Bierce continued to write for Hearst's newspapers and *Cosmopolitan* until 1909, when he resigned and began to prepare his 12-volume *Collected Works*. It was completed in 1912, and the next year he left Washington, D.C., in October on the first stage of a trip that he planned would take him through Mexico to South America. After revisiting the battlefields of his Civil War days, he crossed the Texas border at El Paso into Mexico, where at Juarez, he was given credentials to join the revolutionary army of Pancho Villa as an observer. Villa had occupied Chihuahua on December 8. Bierce wrote from Chihuahua, on December 26, 1913, that he intended to join the Villista forces in Ojinaga the next day. On January 11, 1914,

there was a fierce battle in Ojinaga during which, the circumstantial evidence convinces me, Bierce was killed (see also *Benét's Reader's Encyclopedia of American Literature*).

Although Bierce regarded great poetry as the "highest, ripest, richest fruit" of all endeavors, his disarmingly modest little verse "Humility" indicates the place he assigned himself:

Great poets fire the world with fagots big
   That make a crackling racket,
But I'm content with but a whispering twig
   To warm some single jacket.

He regarded poetry as a complex amalgam of emotion, thought, and imagination. A poet as poet may have a profound thought but must express it so as to produce an emotion: "It is the philosopher's trade to make us think, the poet's to make us feel." Nevertheless, although thought is not essential to poetry, "no elevated composition has the right to be called great if the message that it delivers is neither true nor just. All poets, even the little ones, are feelers, for poetry is emotional; but all the great poets are thinkers as well." In order to achieve the poetic effect on the reader, the poet must have the supreme literary endowment of imagination, which in the poem takes the form of imagery.

Thought, emotion, and imagination have in their turn an intricate relation to the diction through which they are made manifest. Diction is to poetry, Bierce wrote, "what color is to painting. The thought is the outline drawing, which, if it be great, no dauber who stops short of actually painting it out can make wholly mean, but to which the true artist with his pigments can add a higher glory and a new significance." Since the best poetry, like the best prose, is "severely simple in diction," no one "who knows how to write prose can hold in light esteem an art so nearly allied to his own as that of poetic expression." Sidney-Fryer has pointed out that Bierce, in his own poetry, has "a good ear for colloquial speech" and "a good eye for the unexpected and homely detail," anticipating the "modern poetic temper at once ironical and colloquial." Although "a master of the grand manner, . . . in most of his poems he simply uses his own conversational style."

One aspect of diction is verse. And although all poetry is good, not all verse is good, for "poetry is a thing apart from the metrical form in which it is most acceptable," and "some of the finest poetry extant . . . is neither metric nor rhythmic." Still, meter and rhyme induce a sensual pleasure in readers because sounds in harmony with the physical organism that perceives them, including its sense of time, have a natural charm. Versification is thus an intricate art embracing "a multitude of dainty wisdoms."

The age in which poets live has much to do with the practice of their art. Bierce was very much a man of his time in being concerned about the impact of science on contemporary culture, sapping as it did the substructure not only of religion but of art. "I do not regret the substitution of knowledge for conjecture," he wrote, "and doubt for faith; I only say that it has its disadvantages, and among them we reckon the decay of poesy. . . . The world's greatest poets have lived in rude ages, when their races were not long emerged from the night of barbarism." He voiced the same idea in the concluding stanza of "Geotheos":

Barbaric, O Man, was thy runing
    When mountains were stained as with wine
    By the dawning of Time, and as wine
Were the seas, yet its echoes are crooning,
    Achant in the gusty pine
    And the pulse of the poet's line.

But science has revealed nature's secrets and "found them uninteresting to the last degree," narrowing the unknown "to such mean dimensions that imagination has lost her free, exultant stride, and moves with mincing step and hesitating heart."

Nevertheless, poets cannot ignore the epoch in which they live; despite its drawbacks, the poet must assume the mental attitude of doubt and speculation. Joaquin **Miller's** problem was that, being "a rude individual intelligence," he would have been in full sympathy with the barbarism of the ancients. But he was an isolated voice in an age of polish. Alfred Lloyd Tennyson, on the other hand, "the man of culture," full of the disposition of his less-than-vital time, loyally accepted its hard conditions, touching "with a valid hand the harp which the other beats in vain": "As inspiration grows weak and acceptance disobedient, form of delivery becomes of greater moment; in so far as it can, the munificence of manner must mitigate the poverty of matter; so it occurs that the poets of later life excel their predecessors in the delicate and difficult arts and artifices of versification as much as they fall below them in imagination and power."

These views sound astonishingly modern when read in the light of observations by the Nobel prizewinning poet Joseph Brodsky. In "Poetry as a Form of Resistance to Reality," Brodsky dismisses free verse as a "low-calorie diet," arguing that "only content can be innovative and . . . formal innovation can occur only within the limits of form. Rejection of form is a rejection of innovation." He adds: "Form is appealing not because of its inherited nobility but because it is a sign of restraint and a sign of strength."

A knowledge of Bierce's theory of poetry contributes greatly to an understanding of his own output. If he was not by his own standards a great poet, he was nevertheless a good one. And just as he was versatile in the kinds of literature he wrote, so was he versatile in the kinds of poetry he wrote. His subjects ranged from the cosmic to the particular and local. Representative of the former is "The Passing Show" (LOA, 2: 439), and it bears comparison with another poem, "A Vision of Doom," which deserves to be quoted in full:

I stood upon a hill. The setting sun
Was crimson with a curse and a portent,
And scarce his angry ray lit up the land
That lay below, whose lurid gloom appeared
Freaked with a moving mist, which, reeking up
From dim tarns hateful with some horrid ban,
Took shapes forbidden and without a name.
Gigantic night-birds, rising from the reeds

With cries discordant, startled all the air,
And bodiless voices babbled in the gloom –
The ghosts of blasphemies long ages stilled,
And shrieks of women, and men's curses. All
These visible shapes, and sounds no mortal ear
Had ever heard, some spiritual sense
Interpreted, though brokenly; for I
Was haunted by a consciousness of crime,
Some giant guilt, but whose I knew not. All
These things malign, by sight and sound revealed,
Were sin-begotten; that I knew – no more –
And that but dimly, as in dreadful dreams
The sleepy senses babble to the brain
Imperfect witness. As I stood, a voice,
But whence it came I knew not, cried aloud
Some words to me in a forgotten tongue,
Yet straight I knew me for a ghost forlorn,
Returned from the illimited inane.
Again, but in a language that I knew,
As in reply to something which in me
Had shaped itself a thought, but found no words,
It spake from the dread mystery about:

"Immortal shadow of a mortal soul
That perished with eternity, attend.
What thou beholdest is as void as thou:
The shadow of a poet's dream – himself
As thou, his soul as thine, long dead,
But not like thine outlasted by its shade.
His dreams alone survive eternity
As pictures in the unsubstantial void.
Excepting thee and me (and we because
The poet wove us in his thought) remains
Of nature and the universe no part
Nor vestige but the poet's dreams. This dread,
Unspeakable land about thy feet, with all
Its desolation and its terrors – lo!
'Tis but a phantom world. So long ago
That God and all the angels since have died
That poet lived – yourself long dead – his mind
Filled with the light of a prophetic fire,
And standing by the Western sea, above
The youngest, fairest city in the world,
Named in another tongue than his for one
Ensainted, saw its populous domain
Plague-smitten with a nameless shame. For there
Red-handed murder rioted; and there
The people gathered gold, nor cared to loose
The assassin's fingers from the victim's throat,
But said, each in his vile pursuit engrossed:
'Am I my brother's keeper? Let the Law
Look to the matter.' But the Law did not.
And there, O pitiful! The babe was slain
Within its mother's breast and the same grave
Held babe and mother; and the people smiled,
Still gathering gold, and said: 'The Law, the Law.'
Then the great poet, touched upon the lips
With a live coal from Truth's high altar, raised
His arms to heaven and sang a song of doom –

Sang of the time to be, when God should lean
Indignant from the Throne and lift His hand,
And that foul city be no more! – a tale,
A dream, a desolation and a curse!
No vestige of its glory should survive
In fact or memory: its people dead,
Its site forgotten, and its very name
Disputed."
   "Was the prophecy fulfilled?"

The sullen disc of the declining sun
Was crimson with a curse and a portent,
And scarce his angry ray lit up the land
Freaked with a moving mist, which, reeking up
From dim tarns hateful with a horrid ban,
Took shapes forbidden and without a name.
And bodiless voices babbled in the gloom.
But not to me came any voice again;
And, covering my face with thin, dead hands,
I wept, and woke, and cried aloud to God!

Metrically the two poems are different, yet the four-line iambic pentameter stanzas of "The Passing Show" (rhyming *aaba*) and the blank verse of "A Vision of Doom" are both appropriate to serious verse. What the poet sees is chilling in its bleak despair, for these poems portray not merely the devolution of a degenerating society, but that of a dying universe. Today, we can see that Bierce is grappling with the concept of entropy, or, according to one dictionary definition, "the degradation of the matter and energy in the universe to an ultimate state of inert uniformity." But he is also presenting an equally abstruse *philosophical* concept: metaphysical idealism. In other words, the dying universe itself has no ontological being; it is a "phantom world" that exists only as "the shadow of a poet's dream."

  Other serious poems by Bierce are not on this cosmic scale but deal with his concern over his country's future. His stance was diametrically opposed to the exuberant optimism of Walt **Whitman**, but it was no less the expression of a deeply felt patriotism. His most famous poem in this vein – probably his most famous poem – was "Invocation," composed for a San Francisco Fourth of July celebration in 1888:

    Goddess of Liberty! O thou
      Whose tearless eyes behold the chain,
      And look unmoved upon the slain,
    Eternal peace upon thy brow, –

    Before thy shrine the races press,
      Thy perfect favor to implore –
      The proudest tyrant asks no more,
    The ironed anarchist no less.

    Thine altar-coals that touch the lips
      Of prophets kindle, too, the brand
      By Discord flung with wanton hand
    Among the houses and the ships.

    Upon thy tranquil front the star
      Burns bleak and passionless and white,

      Its cold inclemency of light
    More dreadful than the shadows are.

    Thy name we do not here invoke
      Our civic rites to sanctify:
      Enthroned in thy remoter sky,
    Thou heedest not our broken yoke.
. . . .
    The light that fills the patriot's tomb
      Is not of thee. The shining crown
      Compassionately offered down
    To those who falter in the gloom,

    And fall, and call upon thy name,
      And die desiring – 'tis the sign
      Of a diviner love than thine,
    Rewarding with a richer fame.

    To him alone let freemen cry
      Who hears alike the victor's shout,
      The song of faith, the moan of doubt,
    And bends him from his nearer sky.
. . . .
    God of my country and my race!
      So greater than the gods of old –
      So fairer than the prophets told
    Who dimly saw and feared thy face, –

    Who didst but half reveal thy will
      And gracious ends to their desire,
      Behind the dawn's advancing fire
    Thy tender day-beam veiling still, –
. . . .
    Whose laws, imperfect and unjust,
      Thy just and perfect purpose serve:
      The needle, howsoe'er it swerve,
    Still warranting the sailor's trust, –

    God, lift thy hand and make us free
      To crown the work thou hast designed.
      O, strike away the chains that bind
    Our souls to one idolatry!

    The liberty thy love hath given
      We thank thee for. We thank thee for
      Our great dead fathers' holy war
    Wherein our manacles were riven.

    We thank thee for the stronger stroke
      Ourselves delivered and incurred
      When – thine incitement half unheard –
    The chains we riveted we broke.
. . . .
    Let Man salute the rising day
      Of Liberty, but not adore.
      'Tis Opportunity – no more –
    A useful, not a sacred, ray.
. . . .
    Give thou more or less, as we

Shall serve the right or serve the wrong.
  Confirm our freedom but so long
As we are worthy to be free.

But when (O, distant be the time!)
  Majorities in passion draw
  Insurgent swords to murder Law,
And all the land is red with crime;

Or – nearer menace! – when the band
  Of feeble spirits cringe and plead
  To the gigantic strength of Greed,
And fawn upon his iron hand; –

Nay, when the steps to state are worn
  In hollows by the feet of thieves,
  And Mammon sits among the sheaves
And chuckles while the reapers mourn:

Then stay thy miracle! – replace
  The broken throne, repair the chain,
  Restore the interrupted reign
And veil again thy patient face.

Lo! here upon the world's extreme
  We stand with lifted arms and dare
  By thine eternal name to swear
Our country, which so fair we deem –

Upon whose hills, a bannered throng,
  The spirits of the sun display
  Their flashing lances day by day
And hear the sea's pacific song –

Shall be so ruled in right and grace
  That men shall say: "O, drive afield
  The lawless eagle from the shield,
And call an angel to the place!"

This poem, like "Freedom" (LOA, 2: 434) and "To the Bartholdi Statue" (LOA, 2: 441), embodies a recurrent theme in Bierce's thinking: that liberty was a means, not an end to be pursued for its own sake. This in turn was but one aspect of his adherence to what today we call "situational ethics." He was no ideologue, holding fast to principles through thick and thin. He maintained, rather, that principles should always be considered in the light of circumstances of time and place.

  Like "To the Bartholdi Statue," "Invocation" touches on the threat of anarchism, which with its turn toward violence at the end of the nineteenth century had drawn the attention of Henry James and Joseph Conrad as well as Bierce. He also mentions the Civil War ("The chains we riveted we broke"), to which he devoted a number of other poems. Whereas his short stories about the war deal with the immediacies of its horrors – soldiers in the midst of battle – his poetry reflects the contemplative wisdom of an older man looking back on the fiery passages of his youth; it exhibits a serene magnanimity toward a respected fallen foe and expresses doubts about the wisdom of the fratricidal war. Some verses of "The Hesitating Veteran" reveal his mature opinion:

When I was young and full of faith
  And other fads that youngsters cherish
A cry rose as of one that saith
  With emphasis: "Help or I perish!"
'Twas heard in all the land, and men
  The sound were each to each repeating.
It made my heart beat faster then
  Than any heart can now be beating.
. . . .
Besides, the melancholy cry
  Was that of one, 'tis now conceded,
Whose plight no one beneath the sky
  Felt half so poignantly as he did.

Moreover, he was black. And yet
  That sentimental generation
With an austere compassion set
  Its face and faith to the occasion.
. . . .
That all is over now – the reign
  Of love and trade stills all dissensions,
And the clear heavens arch again
  Above a land of peace and pensions.
The black chap – at the last we gave
  Him everything that he had cried for,
Though many white chaps in the grave
  'Twould puzzle to say what they died for.

I hope he's better off – I trust
  That his society and his master's
Are worth the price we paid, and must
  Continue paying, in disasters;
But sometimes doubts press thronging round
  ('Tis mostly when my hurts are aching)
If war for Union was a sound
  And profitable undertaking.
. . . .
No mortal man can Truth restore,
  Or say where she is to be sought for.
I know what uniform I wore –
  O, that I knew which side I fought for!

  "A Year's 'Casualties'" concludes: "O Father of Battles, pray give us release / From the horrors of peace, the horrors of peace!" These two poems and "At a 'National Encampment'" refer to the speaker's own old wounds. His magnanimity toward the South is presented in both "The Confederate Flags" and "To E. S. Salomon." In the former, he argues for returning the Confederate colors to the troops who had fought under them:

Among the rebels when we made a breach
  Was it to get their banners?
was but incidental – 'twas to teach
  Them better manners.

They know the lesson well enough to-day;
  Now, let us try to show them
That we're not only stronger far than they,
  (How we did mow them!)

But more magnanimous. My lads, 'tis plain
   'Twas an uncommon riot;
The warlike tribes of Europe fight for gain;
   We fought for quiet.

If we were victors, then we all must live
   With the same flag above us;
'Twas all in vain unless we now forgive
   And make them love us.
. . . .
All human governments must take the chance
   And hazard of sedition.
O wretch! to pledge your manhood in advance
   To blind submission.

It may be wrong, it may be right, to rise
   In warlike insurrection:
The loyalty that fools so dearly prize
   May mean subjection.

Be loyal to your country, yes – but how
   If tyrants hold dominion?
The South believed they did; can't you allow
   For that opinion?
. . . .
Give back the foolish flags whose bearers fell,
   Too valiant to forsake them.
Is it presumptuous, this counsel? Well,
   I helped to take them.

And he attacks an orator who protested against decorating the graves of the Confederate dead in "To E. S. Salomon":

The brave respect the brave. The brave
   Respect the dead; . . .
. . . .
What if the dead whom still you hate
   Were wrong? Are you so surely right?
. . . .
Men live and die, and other men
   Arise with knowledges diverse:
What seemed a blessing seems a curse,
   And Now is still at odds with Then.

The years go on, the old comes back
   To mock the new – beneath the sun
Is *nothing* new; ideas run
   Recurrent in an endless track.

What most we censure, men as wise
   Have reverently practised; nor
Will future wisdom fail to war
   On principles we dearly prize.
. . . .
The broken light, the shadows wide –
   Behold the battle-field displayed!
God save the vanquished from the blade,
   The victor from the victor's pride!
. . . .
Remember how the flood of years
   Has rolled across the erring slain;

Remember, too, the cleansing rain
   Of widows' and of orphans' tears.

The dead are dead – let that atone:
   And though with equal hand we strew
The blooms on saint and sinner too,
   Yet God will know to choose his own.

The wretch, whate'er his life and lot,
   Who does not love the harmless dead
With all his heart and all his head –
   May God forgive him, *I* shall not.

Related to his poems on the Civil War are those about the Union's commander-in-chief, and later United States president, Ulysses S. Grant. "The Death of Grant" characterizes him as "For anything but duty's deed / Too simply wise, too humbly great." In "Contentment" the Voice of Posterity asks of Grant:

Why do no statues celebrate thy name,
   No monuments thy services proclaim?
Why did not thy contemporaries rear
   To thee some schoolhouse or memorial college?

The voice of Grant's shade replies: "I'd rather you would question why, in park / And street, my monuments were not erected / Than why they were."

Among the shorter serious poems Bierce wrote were a number of elegiac lyrics, despite the fact that "Elegy" (LOA, 2: 434) parodies Thomas Gray's "Elegy Written in a Country Churchyard." But it was typical of Bierce to poke fun at practices he himself followed. His elegies, in fact, are among the most charming lyrics he ever wrote. His impressionistic "A Study in Gray" is a kind of verbal equivalent to Whistler's portrait of his mother. To give a sampling of other poems in this vein:

William F. Smith
Light lie the earth upon his dear dead heart,
   And dreams disturb him never.
Be deeper peace than Paradise his part
   Forever and forever.

Another Way
I lay in silence, dead. A woman came
   And laid a rose upon my breast and said:
"May God be merciful." She spoke my name,
   And added: "It is strange to think him dead.

He loved me well enough, but 'twas his way
   To speak it lightly." Then, beneath her breath:
"Besides" – I knew what further she would say,
   But then a footfall broke my dream of death.

To-day the words are mine. I lay the rose
   Upon her breast, and speak her name, and deem
It strange indeed that she is dead. God knows
   I had more pleasure in the other dream.

Presentiment
With saintly grace and reverent tread,
   She walked among the graves with me;

Her every foot-fall seemed to be
A benediction on the dead.

The guardian spirit of the place
  She seemed, and I some ghost forlorn
  Surprised in the untimely morn
She made with her resplendent face.

Moved by some waywardness of will,
  Three paces from the path apart
  She stepped and stood – my prescient heart
Was stricken with a passing chill.

The folk-lore of the years agone
  Remembering, I smiled and thought:
  "Who shudders suddenly at naught,
His grave is being trod upon."

But now I know that it was more
  Than idle fancy. O, my sweet,
  I did not think so little feet
Could make a buried heart so sore!

In quite a different vein was his epitaph on the Englishman T. Arundel Harcourt, who assisted the historian H. H. Bancroft, wrote accomplished verses, and translated Emile Zola. He had been a coauthor with Bierce of a little book called *The Dance of Death*, a best-selling literary hoax purporting to attack the obscene appeal of the waltz. After his wife ran away with another man, Harcourt turned to alcohol, then jumped from a window to his death. In the *Examiner* for February 5, 1888 (quoted in Fatout's *Devil's Lexicographer*), Bierce wrote of him that he "went to the everlasting bad through domestic infelicity and foreign brandy, dying in poverty's last ditch upon a golden couch." Bierce had memorialized him in verse:

T. A. H.

Yes, he was that, or that, as you prefer –
Did so and so, though, faith, it wasn't all;
Lived like a fool, or a philosopher,
And had whatever's needful to a fall.
As rough inflections on a planet merge
In the true bend of the gigantic sphere,
Nor mar the perfect circle of its verge,
So in the survey of his worth the small
Asperities of spirit disappear,
Lost in the grander curves of character.
He lately was hit hard: none knew but I
The strength and terror of that ghastly stroke –
Not even herself. He uttered not a cry,
But set his teeth and made a revelry;
Drank like a devil – staining sometimes red
The goblet's edge; diced with his conscience; spread,
Like Sisyphus, a feast for Death and spoke
His welcome in a tongue so long forgot
That even his ancient guest remembered not
What race had cursed him in it. Thus my friend,
Still conjugating with each failing sense

The verb "to die" in every mood and tense,
Pursued his awful humor to the end.
When like a stormy dawn the crimson broke
From his white lips he smiled and mutely bled,
And, having meanly lived, is grandly dead.

By far the greatest part of Bierce's output in verse, however, was satire. The theory it embodied was based on three principles. First, satire should criticize specific individuals, not abstractions. Second, it was a form of punishment, a lashing of rascals. And third, it was the satire itself that would have lasting significance, not its objects. In other words, even if the persons named were obscure, they would achieve a kind of permanence if the verse in which they were pilloried had literary merit. Bierce derived these principles of "applied satire" and its "laws, liberties, and limitations," he said, from "reverent study of the masters." And, indeed, the influence of Alexander Pope and Jonathan Swift, among others, is easy to track in his satirical verses. Characterizing himself as a satirist "who does not accept the remarkable doctrine that while condemning a sin he should spare the sinner," he wrote in "Substance or Shadow":

So, gentle critics, you would have me tilt,
Not at the guilty, only at their guilt! –
Spare the offender and condemn Offense,
And make life miserable to Pretense!
"Whip Vice and Folly – that is satire's use –
But be not personal, for *that's* abuse;
Nor e'er forget what, 'like a razor keen,
Wounds with a touch that's scarcely felt or seen.'"
Well, friends, I venture, destitute of awe,
To think that razor but an old, old saw,
A trifle rusty; and a wound, I'm sure,
That's felt not, seen not, one can well endure.

And in "To a Censor" he scorns those who attack, not specific rascals, but the abstraction Rascality, fearlessly affirming "That wickedness is wrong and sin a vice, / That wrong's not right, nor foulness ever nice," smiting the offense while sparing the offender:

We know that judges are corrupt. We know
That crimes are lively and that laws are slow.
We know that lawyers lie and doctors slay;
That priests and preachers are but birds of pray;
That merchants cheat and journalists for gold
Flatter the vicious while at vice they scold.
. . . .
But since, while some are wicked some are good
(As trees may differ though they all are wood),
Names here and there, to show whose head is hit,
The bad would sentence and the good acquit.
In sparing everybody none you spare:
Rebukes most personal are least unfair.

Nevertheless, Bierce did write a few satires on general subjects. Among his favorite targets were Christmas (he was a veritable Scrooge), theosophy, politics (e.g., "The Statesmen" [LOA, 2: 434] and "Egotist" [LOA, 2: 442]), religion, dogs (the only animals he disliked), science, and law. "Unexpounded" deserves special note:

On Evidence, on Deeds, on Bills,
On Copyhold, on Loans, on Wills,
Lawyers great books indite.
The creaking of their busy quills
    I never heard on Right.

And he satirizes spelling reformers in "Orthography" (LOA, 2: 436).

The great preponderance of Bierce's satire, however, was directed against particular figures: William Jennings Bryan in "Safety-Clutch" (LOA, 2: 437), James Whitcomb **Riley** in "A Literary Method," and California's Governor George Stoneman in "Matter for Gratitude." He was vituperative against judges ("Judex Judicatus," "A Growler") and above all lawyers ("To a Bully"), and his satires against them should be read in the light of his long essay "Some Features of the Law." In "To an Insolent Attorney," he apostrophizes:

To you 'tis one, to challenge or defend;
Clients are means, their money is an end.
. . . .
Happy the lawyer! – at his favored hands
Nor truth nor decency the world demands.
. . . .
His brains for sale, morality for hire,
In every land and century a licensed liar!

He criticized Charles Crocker and Collis P. Huntington, "railrogues" who maneuvered legislators into passing bills to further their own commercial interests at the expense of the public weal in what modern economists call "rent-seeking." But his favorite victim was their colleague "£eland $tanford." Typical of his numerous appearances in Bierce's satirical verses is the following in "Substance and Shadow":

Behold advances in dignity and state –
Grave, smug, serene, indubitably great –
Stanford, philanthropist! One hand bestows
In alms what t'other one to justice owes.
. . . .
The fellow's self invites assault; his crimes
Will each bear killing twenty thousand times!

One of Bierce's untitled epitaphs is also devoted to him:

Here Stanford lies, who thought it odd
That he should go to meet his God.
He looked, until his eyes grew dim,
For God to hasten to meet him.

Sidney-Fryer characterizes Bierce's satires as "agreeably nasty cast-iron thorns in the Victorian rose-garden." Probably their most significant characteristic is that they embody wit, not humor. Bierce expounded this basic distinction at length in his essay "Wit and Humor," as well as elsewhere. Pitilessly sharp and "as bleak as steel," wit is "a serious matter. To laugh at it is to confess that you do not understand." It "stabs, begs pardon – and turns the weapon in the wound." Bierce also makes frequent use of puns in his satire: a razor is a rusty saw,

preachers are "birds of pray," legislators vote "I," and hypochondriasis is the Dumps.

Finally, when we turn to Bierce's poetry as a whole, certain features stand out. Although an autodidact, he was a learned man, and the reader who fails to detect the tracks of other writers in his poetry will miss some of its appeal. Sidney-Fryer has indicated "the line of general poetic descent" in Bierce as running from "Edmund Spenser and the Elizabethans to William Blake and the English Romantics," and then to Tennyson, Edgar Allan **Poe**, and Algernon Charles Swinburne. More specifically, echoes of the Bible and Shakespeare abound, as do those of Greek and Latin writers, notably in his remarkable translation of "Dies Irae," which itself finds an echo in "Matter for Gratitude." Omar Khayyám's *Rubáiyát* in Edward FitzGerald's translation can be traced in some of his verses; and stanza 82 furnished the title, *Shapes of Clay*, for one collection.

He parodied Joaquin Miller in "The Mormon Question," a sly hit at Miller's marital irregularities, and Oliver Goldsmith in "The Perverted Village." Tennyson, Poe, William Wordsworth, Samuel Taylor Coleridge, and Oliver Wendell **Holmes**, as well as François Rabelais, Ernest Renan, and Victor Hugo can also be traced in his poetry. Poe's influence is a rather special one, since it nearly always takes the form of a borrowed metrical pattern and rhyme scheme. But his attitude toward writers who influenced him was not uncritical adoration. Tennyson's "The Northern Farmer" was dismissed as a mere "thing," and his "Charge of the Light Brigade" as "resonant patriotic lines" devoid of poetry; Poe's "The Bells" (LOA, 1: 543) was "rubbishy stuff."

As might be expected given his theory of poetry, Bierce paid a great deal of attention to the arts of versification. He relied heavily on iambic pentameter couplets in his satires, but he essayed blank verse in his serious poems. He made frequent use of the Petrarchan sonnet in apostrophizing women, and one has only to read a number of his poems to discover the variety and extent of the stanzaic forms he employed. Sidney-Fryer, noting that he is "a master of the run-over line" and that his handling of rhyme, meter, consonance, and assonance "is assured and often ingenious," has called him "an adroit and facile versifier" who is "able to make his poetic statement move through difficult and demanding traditional forms with singular ease."

Bierce's poetic voice was a distinctive one and deserves far more attention than it has received. Interestingly enough, it was recognized in his own time by a fellow poet and critic, Edmund Clarence **Stedman**, who, with tact and taste, included seven poems by Bierce in *An American Anthology*: "The Death of Grant," "The Bride," "Another Way," "Montefiore," "Presentiment," "Creation," and "T. A. H." By and large, however, Bierce's poetry was ignored until the appearance in 1980 of Sidney-Fryer's excellent selection, *A Vision of Doom*. A thoughtful introductory essay describes Bierce's best poems as "compact, imaginative, and powerful, or – quite unexpectedly – tender." In deference to the two lonely voices who appreciated Bierce's abilities as a poet, it seems fitting to conclude by turning once again to his own work, a little tercet called "Creation" that they both included in their anthologies. Sidney-Fryer indeed thought it was probably Bierce's greatest poem, a "little masterpiece of boldness and compression": "God dreamed – the suns sprang flaming into place, / And sailing worlds with many a venturous race! / He woke – His smile alone illumined space."

M. E. GRENANDER

Selected Works

The Dance of Death, by Ambrose Bierce and Thomas A. Harcourt, as William Herman, San Francisco: privately printed, 1877; corrected and enlarged edition, San Francisco: Henry Keller, 1877

Black Beetles in Amber, San Francisco: Western Authors Publishing, 1892; revised and enlarged as vol. 5 of *Collected Works*

An American Anthology, 1787–1900, edited by Edmund Clarence Stedman, Boston: Houghton Mifflin, 1900

Shapes of Clay, San Francisco: W. E. Wood, 1903; revised and enlarged as vol. 4 of *Collected Works*

The Cynic's Word Book, New York: Doubleday, Page, 1906; enlarged as *The Devil's Dictionary*, vol. 7 of *Collected Works*

The Collected Works of Ambrose Bierce, 12 vols., New York and Washington, D.C.: Neale, 1909–12

The Sardonic Humor of Ambrose Bierce, edited by George Barkin, New York: Dover, 1963

A Vision of Doom: Poems by Ambrose Bierce, edited and introduced by Donald Sidney-Fryer, West Kingston, Rhode Island: Donald M. Grant, 1980

Further Reading

Davidson, Cathy N., ed., *Critical Essays on Ambrose Bierce*, Boston: G. K. Hall, 1982

Fatout, Paul, *Ambrose Bierce, the Devil's Lexicographer*, Norman: University of Oklahoma Press, 1951

_____, *Ambrose Bierce and the Black Hills,* Norman: University of Oklahoma Press, 1956

Grenander, M. E., *Ambrose Bierce*, New York: Twayne, 1971

Hall, Carroll C., *Bierce and the Poe Hoax*, San Francisco: Book Club of California, 1934

McWilliams, Carey, introduction, *The Devil's Dictionary*, New York: Sagamore/American Century, 1957; California, 1945

Benjamin Paul Blood

(1832–1919)

Benjamin Blood can best be described as a bardic philosopher-poet, whose independent mind and spirit typify the Emersonian age. Little known today, he was, in his prime, lavishly praised by his intellectual cohorts, among them, the philosopher William James. Perhaps more daring than the established men of letters who admired his work, Blood as a young man refused to compromise his innate desire for self-fulfillment to worldly ambition. In his foreword to the posthumously published 1924 collection of Blood's poems, John Edmund Willoughby portrays Blood as a man who "lived life to the full, during his eighty-six years, and savored it as few men do." A self-professed "healthy mystic," whose health of mind and body "was still notable in advanced age," Blood was, according to Willoughby, a man among men; one who "never lost touch with earth and with the common things of life. He knew ordinary men and their ways; he enjoyed mingling with them and drawing them out."

At the same time, Blood's intellectual prowess and extensive learning, specifically his brilliance in the area of speculative philosophy, set him somewhat apart from "ordinary men." In his temperament, Blood resembled Romantic iconoclasts such as William Blake, Percy Bysshe Shelley, and Lord Byron. By his own confession, Blood disdained public opinion and professed to have led his life to his own satisfaction. He knew that he "could never value things at others' rates – never was respectable or conforming."

His rebellion, however, did not take the shape of a restless, journeying quest. A man of considerable means, Blood saw no need to leave the comfort of his home on the south bank of the Mohawk river, in east-central New York, where he lived until his death. His independence revealed itself in his freedom of thought and expression and in his steadfast resolution to live his life on his own terms. During his lifetime he was an inventor, a gambler, a gymnast, a poet, and a metaphysician.

A survey of his published works and lectures reveals the multifaceted nature of Blood's talents. His essays in the *Journal of Speculative Philosophy* were erudite and provocative and garnered him respect from such men as Ralph Waldo **Emerson**, Alfred, Lord Tennyson, and Robert Louis Stevenson. William James also was profoundly moved late in his life by Blood's recounting of an experience he had while under anesthesia, an experience he referred to as *The Anaesthetic Revelation* (1874). Blood's experience under anesthesia occurred 14 years prior to his published account of it. His explanation for delayed publication was that at 40 he could better withstand the risk of being "called a mad one" than he could have when he was a youthful 24. Blood's discovery was, as he put it, "unutterable," and his portrayal of it, by necessity, turns on the philosophical dilemma of the identity and difference of the same and the other, of being and knowing. The philosophical "The Gist of Philosophy" serves as a preface to *The Anaesthetic Revelation* and thus provides a contextual envelope for Blood's account. Citing the words of Fichte, Blood observes that most men vainly strive to bring the divine or the infinite into perceived human form. "For of God [Fichte] said: '*Thou*

art,' etc. – 'but I now and ever must conceive of being *Thou art not*.' This sort of confession cost [Fichte] his professional chair; for to his wise censors, who fancied God as some shape with ideas, this was atheism."

Blood's description of faith, which helps to explain his revelation and his subsequent philosophical interpretation of it, mirrors the Puritan concept of divine grace. "It arrests us rather than is assumed by us . . . [it is] 'the gift of God.'. . . For Him who has done his best there is an honest ignorance that shall face the highest inquisition." Having established this framework, Blood goes on to describe the "anaesthetic revelation" as a tool that helps us understand the "genius of being." According to Blood, the "anaesthetic revelation" is an *un*condition that remains formless and forgotten until we return to it: "As here we find in trances, men / Forget the dream that happens then, / Until they fall in trance again." Blood confesses that he is able to attain this trance-like state only through the "use of anaesthetic agents" and that it is during that period of "coming to" or crossing the threshold from stupor to sensibility that "the genius of being is revealed." Blood admits, however, that once consciousness is fully regained, the revelation is then irretrievable.

For Blood, this experience substantiates the eternal mystery of Christianity while confirming a pluralistic, relative solution to the crux of being and knowing. After conferring with dentists and surgeons about this strange experience, Blood claimed that many patients at the moment of recall seem to have discovered something in their own natures but that when attempting to speak of it, they invariably fail in a lost mood of introspection. Having moved from philosophy through religious mysticism to end up, at last, in the realm of the imagination, Blood concludes his revelation by quoting Shakespeare's Prospero:

> We are such stuff
> As dreams are made of, and our little life
> Is rounded with a sleep

Blood clearly belongs to that tribe of Romantic philosopher-poets for whom the transition from conventional thought into the ranges of speculation and experimental form meant nothing less than a spiritual awakening or moral conversion. Whether as in William Wordsworth's Immortality Ode, Coleridge's "Kubla Khan," or John Keats's expression of "negative capability," each experience brings with it the insights that creative inspiration is dream-given or surreal and that the boundaries between self and other for that brief moment of encounter are virtually dissolved. Keats's definition of the poet remains the best starting point for an understanding of Blood's concept of the poet. As Philip Levine explains of Keats, "he rejects the conventional notion of the world as a 'vale of tears' . . . and prefers to conceive of the world as 'The Vale of Soul Making.' . . . His notion of what is required of a poet, that is of a person who lives fully and morally, is surprisingly contemporary." For Keats, the poet must possess the capability "of being in uncertainties, mysteries, doubts, without any irritable reaching after fact and reason." In what is perhaps Benjamin Blood's most Keatsian poem, *The Bride of the Iconoclast* (LOA, 2: 318), the spiritual quest of the heroic bard is recounted in Spenserian stanzas that echo the sensuous, surreal quality of Keats's masterpiece, "The Eve of St. Agnes."

Published when Blood was only twenty-two, *The Bride of the Iconoclast* exhibits a remarkable skill with metrical romance. In the preface, Blood recommends that his poem be perused "where the grim hills bristle in the sunshine": "Where truth dwells in nature's nakedness rough hewn and wild, would I hang these visions on the vacant walls of imagination." He goes on to apologize "for many points whereat this poem is faulty. . . . Be the work good or bad, it is from the hand of a minor."

The poem, which consists of five cantos with a varying number of segments, dramatizes the love between the bardic hero, Barron, and his virgin bride Hermia, who suffers a tragic fate at the hands of ruffian pirates. Their story is also an allegory of the human spirit, the soul quest of Barron, Blood's "iconoclast." The opening canto describes a stagnant, joyless city, whose aged king lies dying in his tomb.

> There was a city on whose sultry domes
> Stood bright the dazzle of the tropic blaze,
> 'Bove streets deserted, courts, and haunted homes,
> Luring the ocean from his reckless ways.
> An autumn, sober stillness, and a haze
> Sabbath and dreamy as life's buried years,
> Was th' atmosphere. The gold sun's muffled gaze
> Sent light, but little joy; and thoughtful tears
> Stole up the cool, sad eyes that looked, not void of fears.

The second section introduces the beautiful Hermia, gliding inland in her sumptuous shallop on "the orange morning": "A bauble shallop was it, bulging wide / Of shell-shaped bow with velvets lined of rose." Hermia, "In mist-light robes all gauzily bedight / . . . Did look a seraph wafted from the sight." Blood introduces Barron in the third section of the first canto, "Proud, daring, generous, a god in face, / With brain of energy, and heart untamed." Barron, the iconoclast, son of the dying king, "did greet / One Power alone – one Deity adored." Before dying, his father bid him "Bring / The virgin Hermia to this clay shore's side: / I wed these linked hands: be blessed!" Hermia's love for Barron is limitless: "As thou dost trust thy formless God and mine, / So shall I trust thee, Barron. . . / . . . 'round thee are these arms – I have no god but thee!" At the conclusion of the first long canto, Barron and Hermia, pledging eternal troth, fall into a deep sleep, from which they awaken to a new world.

> They slept, and ocean, like a lethean lake
> Bedrowzed with slumbrous, opiate influences
> Of stars dream-smothered – nodding half awake
> In downy mist ethereal, did confess
> Himself was sleepy; and a damp'ning stress
> Did blear his weltry eye. Fitful and low
> The Wind, faint-breath'd in silent wakefulness,
> Moved not the boom hung o'er the shallop's bow
> With muffled sail – so soft on tip-toe crept she now.

Canto II opens to a "soft dawning light. . . / Warm, red, and sultry in the leaden east." The lovers "Stood up alone in that wide universe / Large souled and calm, true nature-worshipers." Barron invokes the blessing of his "Power Ubiquitous," as he and Hermia begin their quest for a new life, a life in which "death shall end not all," where "We two, made seraphs, winging far away / From Heaven's serene and ancient battlements / May poise our snowy vans of purest light, / And say, 'the Earth – lost emerald – was here.'" The shallop is borne to a strange island teeming with eerie natural presences: "A cold, white flower, with red and pimply spots – / Like milk-faced maiden budding crimson sores, / Would not look up." On the island live a wise man, known as the Ancient, and a boy of twelve, and it is here that Hermia and Barron dally.

Throughout the romance, the narrative voice of the poet intrudes, giving the poem its storylike atmosphere, distancing the action and controlling the tone. A vivid example of this strategy can be found toward the end of Canto II. "Leave we yon pair to wander where they will," the narrator advises us, as he invites us to "belounge the turret-tops." At this point in the romance, the story takes an ominous turn that is truly reminiscent of Keats's "silver, snarling trumpets" and "carved angels, ever eager-eyed" in "The Eve of St. Agnes." The poet commands us, "Stop! – Gaze thro' this hushed gallery! The air / Is beat by wild-limbed statues: how they glow / with life and action!" In the gallery hangs a solemn portrait with deep gazing eyes that seem to pierce the souls of all who look upon it. The warning is clear:

> WITH EVERY CONSCIENCE DEALETH DEITY.
> BUT ONE EXPERIENCE DOTH ONE SOUL
>   AVAIL.
> THOU FEEL'ST THE EYE ON THEE. THOU CANST
>   PROVE
>   NO MAN'S TALE. –

The poet offers us a vision of life in which human souls, like barks on a tossing sea, "Life-vessels" on "the Pool of Death," are drawn to their destruction: "with few flags half-mast, the fated barks go down."

The third canto initiates the tragic conclusion to Blood's romance, when a band of drunken pirates plot to abduct Hermia. With names like Hyena and Turtle, they epitomize a fatal brutishness in nature that strikes without warning. In Canto IV, the Barron is taken unawares and comes too late to save his bride, who even in death "was beautiful": "The taper chin upthrown, revealed the curvings of a throat / Of grained marble." Hermia's body is cast into the sea, where she is received by a "golden Siren":

> Come to the last in my ocean hold
> Thou bride of a hapless day!
> . . . .
> A royal grave is the ocean wave, –
> And white sails the grave-stones be!
> For the wise and the simple, the dastard, the brave,
> The jewels of beauty, the chains of the slave,
> Were lost in the deep, deep sea.

In the final canto, Barron suffers a last encounter with the pirates, who are given the death blow by a storm at sea. Barron's crew survives the storm, and the words of the poet offer a final warning to all humanity; in the voyage of life, humankind has only conscience as its guide: "Be brave, for thou art watching thee; be kind, / Thou ever shalt keep company thyself." Or, as Emerson admonished, "Trust thyself: every heart vibrates to that iron string."

Another long poem, more sophisticated in its intent, is *The Colonnades* (1868). It consists of a "Proem" and nine sections and again uses a classical mythical framework. In this poem, the poet embarks on a spiritual journey through history. With the aid of Charon, he speaks with the dead, with Socrates, Aesop, Praxiteles, Plato, Emanuel Swedenborg, James Thomson, Shakespeare, Robert Burns, Byron, Alexander Pope, William Cowper, and Abraham Lincoln. The influence of Swedenborg and the ideas of Henry James Sr. are apparent in this poem. Blood opens the "Proem" with the following proclamation:

> Welcome as Christ into his father's house,
> To hands divine soothing the sobbing locks
> Which the dews drenched upon Judean hills,
> Should bard be to the world.

One can easily perceive the Christ/poet of Walt **Whitman** and Henry James Sr.'s poet as divine man in Blood's scheme. Blood's poet, as redeemer, "climbs downward into failures for success. / Man's justice pays him not." The final section is devoted to a controversy concerning the comparative happiness of Hell and Heaven. Loyola, an Angel, debates Gladiola, Champion of the Damned. The poet concludes by proposing a visit to the kingdom of Lucifer.

Collected in the posthumous volume *Heirlooms,* Blood's shorter poems display the poet's skill with dialect and the ballad form. "The Broken Spear" tells the story of a wounded soldier who returns to the farm to work the land with his one remaining arm. "'Come, lively now!' cried Farmer Buck, / And donned his harvest frock, / 'Let's have that fifteen-acre field / All in by six o'clock!'" "Late" (LOA, 2: 317), also from *Heirlooms,* is reminiscent of Wordsworth's odes. In this work, the poet longs for that innocent youthful joy when "title-pages opened into Heaven," and when, as a boy, the poet's "days lay open to the universe" and he "saw the One of all things. . . / . . . and saw, beyond, / The field transcend the One." Feeling no need to relinquish his despairing tone, the poet laments, "Late, oh, late! / The westering pathos glooms the fervent hours. / Again my gray gull lifts against the nightfall, / And takes the damp leagues with a shoreless eye."

In his intellectual diversity and in his extraordinary energy, Benjamin Blood typified his age. Not content to be merely a philosopher or merely a poet, he set out to investigate many areas of thought and action, coming into contact, as he did so, with the great thinkers and artists of his time. His volumes of poetry are matched by his lectures and published speculations – *The Anaesthetic Revelation, Pluriverse: An Essay in the Philosophy of Pluralism* (1920), and a historical lecture, *Napoleon I* (1863). He was, like all poets, fascinated by the power of language, and in his speculations concerning the psychological effect of sounds and the prospects for a universal language, Blood shares an affinity with Edgar Allan **Poe**, George Bernard Shaw, Ezra Pound, Wallace Stevens, and, of course, Ferdinand de Saussure. In *Suggestions Toward the Mechanical Art of Poetry* (1854), Blood maintains that each letter of the alphabet "has in some sense a suggestive character of its own": "O, which is the letter of wonder and loftiness, is the sound most fit and easy to the facial muscles of a wondering man." He quotes, for illustration, lines from Poe's "The Raven" (LOA, 1: 535):

> Ah! distinctly I remember it was in the bleak
>   December,
> And each separate dying ember wrought its ghost
>   upon the floor.

Blood might well have quoted from his own poetry, from what many considered to be his most magnificent poem, "The Lion of the Nile":

> Whelped in the desert sands, and desert-bred
> From dugs whose sustenance was blood alone –
> A life translated out of other lives,
> I grew the king of beasts. . . .

LYNDA S. BOREN

Selected Works

The Bride of the Iconoclast, Boston and Cambridge, Massachusetts: James Munroe, 1854
The Colonnades, Amsterdam, New York: private ed., 1868
Heirlooms, Albany, New York: Frederick S. Hills, 1924
The Poetical Alphabet, introduced by Stephen Schwartz, Radical America, The Surrealist Group, 1972; Arno Press, 1976

Further Reading

James, William, *Writings 1902–1910*, New York: Library of America, 1987
Perry, Ralph Barton, *The Thought and Character of William James*, Boston: Little, Brown, 1935

Manoah Bodman

(1765–1850)

The eldest of seven children of Joseph and Esther (Field) Bodman, Manoah (or Noah) Bodman was born on January 28, 1765 in Sunderland, Massachusetts. His family moved to the recently incorporated town of Williamsburg, Massachusetts, when he was 14, and this village remained his home for the rest of his life. Located in the Hampshire Hills seven miles west of the Connecticut River, the village was still surrounded largely by wilderness. When the Bodmans arrived, the only route to the next settlement was a bridle-path through what Josiah Gilbert **Holland** described as "dark, dismal, swampy ground, known as 'The Cellars.'"

His uncles, William and Samuel Bodman, had settled in Williamsburg earlier. William, who served for many years as a selectman and state representative, was considered the town's "most influential man," according to Alason Nash's account (*Hampshire Gazette*, February 1861). "Distinguished for his eloquence," William Bodman was Williamsburg's delegate to the Massachusetts convention that was called to ratify the federal constitution. In a speech at this convention that gave him considerable local fame, he argued that by giving unlimited power to Congress to raise taxes, the constitution posed a grave threat to state sovereignty.

Manoah Bodman was a lawyer and, like his celebrated uncle, an orator, but while his uncle was greatly respected, Bodman was a village oddity. The editor of a local newspaper recalled that when he was boy, he heard Bodman speak: "He used good language, and an abundance of it, but whether his reasoning and appeals were convincing, I never could comprehend, as the flood of words always eclipsed the force of his logic."

Bodman did not marry until he was almost thirty-five, and his wife, Theodocia Green, died within a year. He never remarried, living instead with his brother Joseph Jr., an austere Calvinist and staunch Federalist, who became as powerful in the community as his uncle had been. Joseph served as selectman, state representative, justice of the peace, and deacon; in the latter capacity, he was known for the vigor and doctrinal rectitude with which he managed church affairs. Manoah was once jailed for bankruptcy, and Joseph posted the bail.

Bodman published one book, *An Oration on Death, and the Happiness of the Separate State, or the Pleasures of Paradise* (1817; reprinted 1818; see LOA, 1: 27), and three pamphlets, *An Oration Delivered at Williamsburgh, July 4, 1803*, *Washington's Birth Day, An Oration* (as by "Noah" Bodman, 1814), and *Oration on the Birth of Our Savior* (1826). A broadside privately printed in 1837 contains two poems, which the poet Lewis Turco believes may be Bodman's, although neither poem has the rough energy and linguistic invention of his other work. Turco has also suggested that the 1803 oration may be a parody of Bodman; this idea has some plausibility since this oration is much less accomplished than the other orations. The differences in accomplishment could also exist, however, because the 1803 oration was written much earlier than the others, before Bodman had mastered the diction and cadences that characterize his work at its best.

The pamphlets are quite brief (four, 17, and 26 pages, respectively), but the *Oration on Death* (printed on a press in his uncle Samuel's tannery) is a substantial volume of 300 pages, including preface, introduction, poems, and two long orations – "An Oration on Death" and "An Oration, on the Outpourings of the Spirit of God." The book also includes "Four Poems, on Solemn and Divine Subjects," printed together at the end of the book, and four short poems quoted in the orations themselves.

Aside from two early orations on patriotic subjects, all of Bodman's writings are concerned with spiritual and theological matters. During his youth, the churches in his and surrounding towns were all Calvinist, and the influence of Jonathan Edwards, who had been the minister in the neighboring community of Northampton, remained strong. Edwards left his pastorate in 1750 because of a doctrinal dispute, but he left behind a strong revivalist temper. Williamsburg, like other towns in the area, was periodically swept by revivals that were part of the Second Great Awakening. During one of these revivals in 1779, Bodman "supposed" that he received divine grace.

Ten years later, while suffering under a "great outward trouble," he experienced the first of many mystical visitations. "All at once," he wrote in the *Oration on Death*, "I perceived an invisible being, that seemed to be coming to comfort and console me, with a language that was sweet and endearing." Bodman never identified this "great outward trouble," but in that year, 1789, his 19-year-old brother Samuel died. In later visitations, the "invisible being" assumed the shape of "one of my deceased friends." At other times, Bodman believed that he was visited by God Himself. The visitations eventually ceased but suddenly resumed in 1799 during his wife's final illness. After her death, she supposedly came to Bodman repeatedly, assuring him "that she had arrived at glory."

Bodman wrote that he had many spiritual visitors. They supposedly told him that the millennium was coming, that heavenly hosts would be descending to earth, and that they would "carry on a perfect correspondence with its inhabitants." In these visions, God, or the being Bodman had until this time identified as God, told him that he would be party to remarkable truths, which he should publish, and which "would pass through the world like a shock of electricity." At this point, according to Bodman, God Himself intervened, telling Bodman – by means "not now necessary to relate" – that the visitations had all been the work of Satan. Although Bodman immediately resolved "to defy all the powers of darkness," it seemed at first a struggle he would lose. The visitor Bodman now called Satan then supposedly tried to convince him that he had committed the unpardonable sin and on one occasion Bodman went into convulsions during which Satan supposedly told him that "he would [be shaken] . . . into hell the next time."

The minister and the doctor were called: the former to pray and the latter to bleed the distraught man. Another violent seizure followed, and although Bodman survived it and other torments, he concluded at last that he would "never do any thing but sin, and blaspheme against God." Deciding, therefore, "to shut [his] mouth, lest it should be so," he felt "immediate relief," realizing that he had never in fact committed the unpardonable sin and "could go unto God, as a child unto his father." It is possible, as some have conjectured, that Bodman suffered from epilepsy or that he was schizophrenic. Whatever the organic origins of his visions, they were as real to him as his family; the critical problem for Bodman was to place them, like his writings, within a theologically approved context.

Experiences like Bodman's were not altogether unknown in his part of the world. Charles Grandison Finney's vision of Christ on the streets of Adams, New York, in 1821, for example, was widely reported and accepted as fact. Indeed Bodman himself indicates that "in the view and opinion of all candid and substantial people, [his visitations] were perfectly supernatural." Bodman's spiritual visitors were clearly important to him for they offered comforting proof of salvation. He also said that they became his special guardians. However astonishing they may have sounded to his fellow townspeople, his experiences certainly posed no threat to the order of the community, but when he began believing that God would soon make him His prophet, Bodman effectively claimed for himself a role far above the church and the town's leaders. Another person in his situation might have been simply dismissed as a crank, but Bodman belonged to a respected, influential family, and he was the brother of the town's foremost citizen.

What were the means "not now necessary to relate" by which God informed Bodman that he had been deluded by Satan? Bodman says only that "no supernatural voices, or communications" were involved. Was he in fact "reasoned" out of his "delusions" by family members, townspeople, or the local minister (felicitously named Henry Lord), a man of such tenacity in the refinements of theological disputation that he once preached forty Sundays in a row on the doctrine of election? And if Bodman was argued into believing that God did not chose him as His prophet, what could the troubled man do – since his visions had certainly seemed real – other than reconceive them as diabolical?

But if Bodman was denied the mantle of a prophet, he was still able to use his beliefs and experiences to transcend the isolation and provinciality that life in his community necessarily entailed. He could not announce the millennium, but he could powerfully affirm his convictions and beliefs as long as they remained orthodox. Stated another way, he could not be a prophet, but he could be a writer and a very compelling one as well. Given the consummate importance that religion conferred on every Christian in matters of salvation, Bodman could still consider an account of his struggle with the powers of darkness as potentially beneficial to "the whole world," and it was with this conviction that he recorded his experiences.

In this account, Bodman pictures himself at one moment as "a worm of the dust" and at another as the center of a moral crisis of momentous import. Both characterizations permitted him to project a powerful, agonized presence; his works never retreat to the cool theological refinements one finds in the published sermons of Henry Lord and other local ministers. Nevertheless, Bodman remained acutely sensitive to the more liberal manifestations of orthodox Calvinist theology. He accepted the fundamental doctrines of election and reprobation, but only in the modified form promoted by the "New Divinity." According-

ing to this interpretation, God was a "Moral Governor," and humans were His "moral agents" in a cosmic drama exemplifying His authority. At the least, such a role conferred on the individual a spiritual function of supreme importance. Bodman, as he argued in one of the orations, could not accept the doctrine of election in "every preconceived notion of it": individuals, he asserted, were "moral agents," not "eternal machines."

In Cummington, a few miles west of Williamsburg, William Cullen **Bryant** grappled with problems much like Bodman's. Bryant, too, was obsessed with death as seen through the Calvinist lens, but he resolved the problem by adopting the deistic view expressed in "Thanatopsis" (published in 1817, the same year as Bodman's *Oration on Death*; see LOA, 1: 122) – and then by leaving the Calvinist hilltowns and settling in New York City. Bodman took the more conservative route, remaining at home and writing poems and orations that hewed to theological and social norms, yet he achieved in language an expressive intensity that his contemporaries, including Bryant, rarely equaled.

Aside from the broadside of 1837, if it is indeed his, Bodman's only known poems are the eight works he published in his *Oration on Death*. The orations themselves, however, frequently use poetic analogies to illustrate their arguments. "The holiness of all the saints in heaven" is compared, for example, to the sun reflected "on a piece of polished metal," and "the notices that we obtain by the light of grace, or the gospel here on earth" are likened to "the moon at midnight shining upon a dark world." Sinners, he says, flock to Christ like "doves to their windows."

The orations also anticipate the kind of poetry Walt **Whitman** developed two generations later. Bodman used an "abrupt method," arguing, that is, more through assertion than logic. He said that "An Oration on Death" and "An Oration, on the Outpourings of the Spirit of God" were delivered extemporaneously and recorded by a clerk; statements in other orations, as well as internal evidence in all of them, suggest that they, too, were composed in this manner. At its best, this method encouraged a fervently cadenced diction: "Ah! grim messenger! rightly art thou named King of Terrors! Dost thou indeed transmit to regions of woe, as well as of bliss; and open the gates of the infernal prison, to receive the poor, guilty, trembling fugitive from our earth, and fast lock the adamantine bars upon him?" Whitman never approximates this tone, but when his rhetorical techniques draw on political oratory and the cadences of the King James Bible, he can sound very much like Bodman. In "A Song of the Rolling Earth," for example, Whitman wrote, "Say on, sayers! sing on, singers! / Delve! Mould! pile the words of the earth! / Work on, age after age, nothing is to be lost."

Although Bodman's orations use rhetorical techniques with which Whitman devised a transformative poetry, he did not himself make that leap; yet he came near it and, in the process, discovered a language of conviction that at times reaches toward poetic rapture and religious transport. In any case, Bodman found in oratory a vehicle for the immediate, and seemingly unmediated, expression of his convictions. His orations have the force of personal testimony – a value not to be lost on a lawyer like himself.

Bodman's verse appears at first to be less inventive than the orations. Superficially, Bodman seems a latter-day Augustan poet, and a very imitative one at that, who describes his spiritual insights and feelings in traditional poetic forms. His model was Isaac Watts (1674–1748), whose hymns, collected in *Christian Psalmody* and *The Psalms, Hymns, and Spiritual Songs*, were common throughout New England at that time. Bodman thought Watts had been the world's supreme poet and was surely now in heaven, "elucidating the grand theme of poetry in the face of heavenly day." As a consequence, Bodman never ventured beyond the types of metrical and stanzaic conventions seen in the following lines from Watts's "The Penitent Pardoned."

> Black heavy thoughts, like mountains, roll
> O'er my poor breast, with boding fears,
> And crushing hard my tortured soul,
> Wring through my eyes the briny tears.

Here, for comparison, is the opening stanza from Bodman's "A Soliloquy, or Rather Conference, Between the Divine Attributes of Mercy and Justice, Relative to the State of Fallen Man":

> The spirit of the gospel comes,
> To call dead sinners from their tombs;
> Then hear and see and taste and feel,
> The grace that vanquishes all hell.

Bodman seems to be imitating Watts, but the copy is not exact. His stanzas are less neatly groomed than his mentor's, and this roughness gives them their peculiar strength. That effect does not by any means result from carelessness or happy accident, however; Bodman was an exceedingly painstaking craftsman. The spondees in the second and fourth lines in the opening stanza from "A Soliloquy," for example, emphasize "dead" and "all" – words central to the argument. The spondees also interrupt the tripping rhythm that the iambic tetrameter easily establishes but that would obviously be inappropriate here. The off-rhymes further slow the rhythm ("comes"/"tombs," "feels"/"hell"), which in turn helps to give the stanza a rugged and serious tone.

If Bodman's orations have the virtues of their extemporaneousness, his poems have the virtues of this careful and inventive construction, and their difference from Watts's canon can be seen as partly owing to differences of setting and culture. Bodman's verse is never genteel, like that of his mentor from London, but employs a diction more appropriate to a hometown that was largely wilderness during his lifetime. In his search for suitable expression, he turned, as Turco has pointed out in "Poet of the Second Awakening" (*Costerus* 8 [1973]), to "standard, non-literary contractions, a natural speech, and such . . . techniques as slant-rhyme long before anyone else of consequence had attempted them [on] his side of the Atlantic Ocean." (In "Manoah Bodman: Poet of the Second Awakening," Turco reprints "A Soliloquy" and four poems he identifies as being by Isaac Watts, which Bodman wove into the text of his *Oration on Death*.) The result is a poetry as intimately of its region and time as Robert Frost's a century later.

Although Bodman did make some poetic innovations, verse also offered him the advantages of precedent; if Watts or another admired poet had written in a given way, could it be wrong to do it again? In the note preceding "A Soliloquy," for example, Bodman observes that "somewhat in conformity to the usages of ancient poets and orators," the speakers in his poem include "invisible beings or things . . . from the animate, inanimate, or intellectual worlds." Perhaps recalling the spiritual confusions into which he had been led by his visitations, he added that in personifying "divine attributes" he meant "nothing more, than that this would probably be their language, should they appear and consult in person."

Bodman's anguished battle with the powers of darkness, the defining episode in his imaginative life, began when he was 24. The *Oration on Death* was published when he was 52. In between passed almost 30 years of a life lived more intensely than his neighbors may have imagined, and which culminated in one of the most accomplished works to emerge in the literature of the early republic. After the publication of his *Oration on Death*, however, Bodman almost disappeared from literature and history. He announced in that book that he would be writing and publishing a work to be called *A Brief of the Author's Life* (a good title, certainly, for a lawyer's autobiography), and in the prefatory note to his *Oration on the Birth of Our Savior*, he said that this particular work was not the one (under the same title) to which readers had subscribed but rather a continuation of it. He further stated that "the other work shall be published as soon as may be." He also said that he also hoped to write a work proving Christ's divinity on the basis the Old Testament, thereby demonstrating to those who believed otherwise "and the world, that they are wrong, totally wrong; and that the doctrine if it be wrong carries death in its train." We know nothing further of these works, if indeed they were written.

On January 15, 1850, the *Hampshire Courier*, a local newspaper, carried the following notice: "In Williamsburg, Jan 1, Manoah Bodman, Esq., age 83 [he was in fact 84]. He was usually [*sic*] well at 3 o'clock in the morning when he arose and dressed himself, mistaking the bright moonlight for the approach of day; but on discovering his error he again retired, without undressing, and at daybreak was found a corpse." This was the totality of the obituary and the only one of any substance to appear that recorded the fact that one had passed from the earth whose struggle with the powers of evil was of such weight that, in the words of the *Oration on Death*, "the whole world ought to be benefited by the relation."

EDWARD HALSEY FOSTER

Selected Works

An Oration, Delivered at Williamsburgh, July 4, 1803, Northampton, Massachusetts: n.p., 1803
Washington's Birth Day, An Oration, Northampton, Massachusetts: n.p., 1814 (as by "Noah" Bodman)
An Oration on Death, and the Happiness of the Separate State, or the Pleasures of Paradise, Williamsburgh, Massassachusetts: Ephraim Whitman, 1817
Oration on the Birth of Our Savior, Northampton, Massachusetts: n.p., 1826

Further Reading

Bodman, Ellen-Fairbanks Diggs, et al., *A Bodman Chronicle*, Evansville, Indiana: Unigraphic, 1979
Conforti, Joseph A., *Samuel Hopkins and the New Divinity Movement*, Washington, D.C.: Christian University Press, 1981

Deming, Phyllis Baker, *A History of Williamsburg in Massachusetts*, Northampton, Massachusetts: Hampshire Bookshop, 1946

Everts, Louis H., *History of the Connecticut River Valley*, Philadelphia: Louis H. Everts, 1879

Holland, Josiah Gilbert, *History of Western Massachusetts*, Springfield, Massachusetts: Samuel Bowles, 1855

Kuklick, Bruce, *Churchmen and Philosophers: From Jonathan Edwards to John Dewey*, New Haven, Connecticut, and London: Yale University Press, 1985

O'Connor, James P., ed., *Williamsburg: Fact and Fable*, Northampton, Massachusetts: Gazette, 1971

Turco, Lewis, *Visions and Revisions of American Poetry*, Fayetteville: University of Arkansas Press, 1986

George Henry Boker

(1823–1890)

George Henry Boker himself best described the figure he has cut in American literary history. In the sonnet "If history, that feeds upon the past," he proposed a design for his own memorial monument:

> A radiant form, almost sustained in air,
> . . . Another form, mere man in shape and mind,
> Turning his churlish back against mankind,
> Forever kneeling to that lady fair.

And so posterity has remembered him, the devoted servant of a timeless ideal of beauty, a champion – against the tide of his own times – of poetry for poetry's sake. Modern readers, schooled to equate nineteenth-century American poetry with the formally and topically radical verse of Walt **Whitman** and Emily **Dickinson**, are baffled and even embarrassed by Boker's consistent conventionalism in form and subjects.

Current definitions of nineteenth-century American poetic style and substance derive from Whitman's poetics, as put forth in the preface to *Leaves of Grass* (1855). Whitman's disdain, in *Democratic Vistas* (1871), for those his generation called "American poets" – "flood[ing] us with their thin sentiment of parlors, . . . the five-hundredth importation, . . . chasing one aborted conceit after another, and forever occupied in dyspeptic amours with dyspeptic women" – might well express a modern student's response to Boker's life and work. Reacting against these "dandies and ennuyees," Whitman boldly marketed himself, the author of a "great psalm of the republic" with a form as "unerring" and "loose" as "lilacs or roses on a bush," as the answer to Ralph Waldo **Emerson's** call for American poets who would dare to let their argument, "like the spirit of a plant or animal," make the meter of their poems.

Boker's poetics are directly opposed to Whitman's: his meter always determines his argument. Instead of breaking open the poetic line to accommodate what Emerson termed the "barbarism and materialism of the times," Boker conformed his song to the most hallowed forms and set meters of the English poetic tradition: odes, elegies, blank verse, ballads, and, most of all, sonnets. In a letter of August 1865, he boasted to Bayard **Taylor** that he had "written more sonnets . . . than any poet in the language, except Wordsworth, and I shall outnumber him if I keep on." Boker wrote, in fact, the type of poetry *against* which Whitman defined his poetics in "Song of Myself"; he produced the sort of verse that the nineteenth-century American public had "practiced so long to learn to read." Today, American readers practice to read Whitman, and Boker, in comparison, seems unreadable, alien, and un-American.

Neither Boker nor Whitman secured the contemporary fame that he sought. Neither figures significantly in poetry anthologies published in the nineteenth century; neither ascended to Emerson's *Parnassus* (1874). Their responses to the world's neglect, however, were very different. In 1856, the year after Whitman published *Leaves of Grass*, Boker compiled the two-volume *Plays and Poems* and called it his "last dash at the laurel," "a life's venture on the cast." Having set such stakes on the work's success, the 33-year-old poet was crushed by the

lack of critical enthusiasm. Much later, in 1882, he claimed he was "choked off and silenced" by the reading public's indifference. Whitman, by contrast, understood why fame was not his. His *Leaves of Grass* offended aesthetic and moral convention – he *meant* them to offend – and he consoled himself in "A Backward Glance O'er Travel'd Roads" (1888) by saying that his song of insurrection was his "*carte de visite* [visiting card] to future generations."

Boker imagined the poet's role differently, not as the prophet of the future, or even the singer of the present, but as the preserver of past traditions and truths. In January 1850 he advised Richard Henry Stoddard, his friend and fellow poet, "Get out of your own age as much as you can"; he further argued in "The Lesson of Life" (1848) that the poet must not "pander to the present time." Resenting European critics who "bid us work within ourselves," he countered that America's "grandest regions" were "all bare of legendary lore, / . . . the scenery, not the play" ("Ad Criticum," in *Königsmark* [1869]). Even the pastoralized scenery of Boker's poems – like the dewy "glades" and "yon dreary yew" of "The leaden eyelids of wan twilight close" (Sonnet XXV, *Sequence on Profane Love*, dated 1858) – is thus more specific to Arcadia than to the eastern United States.

Whitman's judgment of his rival poets, "those *genteel* little creatures," does, however, suggest the proper context for understanding Boker's poetic career, which constituted part of the "genteel endeavor" (the phrase is John Tomsich's) of a close-knit group of upper-class literary men, including Boker and Taylor, who were attempting, in the words of one member, Edmund Clarence **Stedman**, to "creat[e] a civic Arcadia of our own." Born in Philadelphia on October 6, 1823, to what Rufus Griswold has called "a life of opulent leisure," Boker was tutored at home until age seven. He then attended Sears Walker's and John Seely Hart's Edge Hill schools between 1830 and 1838, when he matriculated at Princeton. According to his lifelong friend, the poet and scholar Charles Godfrey **Leland**, Boker became the Princeton campus "swell." Tall and graced with "the form of an Apollo," and a head like "the bust of Byron," Boker was "quite familiar, in a refined and gentlemanly way, with all the dissipation of Philadelphia and New York." Outwardly, he "trained himself . . . to self-restraint, calmness, and the *nil admirari* air"; privately, however, he played the libertine.

The contrasts between public conformity and private transgression, public calm and private turmoil, pervade Boker's life and art. Two years after graduating from Princeton in 1842, he married Julia Riggs, who came from a wealthy Washington family, and settled down in the house provided by his businessman-banker father, Charles. By 1851, however, he was involved in the first of the series of love affairs that continued into his sixties. Elizabeth Barstow Stoddard, the novelist and wife of his friend R. H. Stoddard, wrote Stedman that Boker was "the sort of man that would have taken the Virgin Mary from the Ass, before Joseph, and helped her kindly into an adjoining hedge."

During the first years of his marriage, Boker halfheartedly studied law to please his father, but soon gave it up to pursue the glorious vocational course he had laid out in "The Pre-eminence of the Man of Letters" (1843). He completed eight plays and two books of verse between 1848 and 1856, and the productions of six of his plays in Philadelphia and New York between 1850 and 1855 brought him some renown. This fame did not satisfy Boker, however. He felt the playwright's authority was too compromised in the move from text to stage. He insisted to Taylor in October 1855: "My theatrical success I never valued. . . . If I could not be acknowledged as a poet I had no further desire, and no further active concern in literature."

Two circumstances forced Boker's attention away from his belletristic pursuits to the real world of money, law, and politics that he had sought to avoid. First, after his father's death in 1858, Charles Boker's employer, Girard Bank, brought a suit against the estate, charging fraud. Although he eventually succeeded in vindicating his father, the suit dominated Boker's life for the next fifteen years. The second determining event was the Civil War. Emphatically pro-Union, Boker cofounded the Union League of Philadelphia in 1862. He served as the league's secretary for the next nine years and turned his pen to the service of the state, writing a pro-Lincoln pamphlet, "The Will of the People," and a book of verse, *Poems of the War* (both 1864). These poems, most of them circulated on broadsides or printed first in newspapers, commemorate specific military engagements ("On Board the Cumberland," "The Ballad of New Orleans") and honor characters both generic ("The Sword-Bearer," "The Black Regiment") and specific (General Joseph Hooker in "Hooker's Across," General William T. Sherman in "Before Vicksburg").

After his play *Francesca da Rimini* (first produced in 1855), Boker's exhortations and memorials comprise his best-known contribution to American letters. He figures prominently in actor James Murdoch's wartime lecture series, *Patriotism in Poetry and Prose* (1865), and Boker's "Dirge for a Soldier" is his most anthologized poem. These poems are uncharacteristically occasional, but it is not simply that, as Murdoch claims, "when our flag was assailed, [Boker] threw off his indifference to national subjects." Rather, as Boker himself implies in "Our Heroic Themes" (1865), American materials had finally become worthy of his song:

Find me in history, since Adam fell,
This story's rival or its parallel:
A nation rising to undo a wrong
Forged by itself, and to its mind made strong
By every word its angry tongue had hurled
In stout defiance at a sneering world.

Emphasizing the high tragic irony of the conflict – the United States' own boasts of freedom and equality have lent symbolic force to the nation's failure – Boker sees here the richest epic subject since Milton sang *Paradise Lost*. Boker thus calls upon his fellow poets to "strike the sounding lyre, / To touch the heroes of our holy-cause / Heart-deep with ancient fire" ("Ad Poetas"). His high-flown language here confirms that it was not his poetics but the world that had changed.

In three of the four sonnets in *Poems of the War* – placed toward the end and spoken by a nonparticipant observer – Boker expresses a more clearly personal and dissenting view of the war. (The fourth sonnet, "Grant," casts the Union general as the nation's "Moses" and helped secure Boker's postwar commission as minister to Turkey from 1871 to 1875.) For instance, "Blood! Blood! The lines of every printed sheet" protests that the war has imposed a bloody preoccupation upon the nation's writers, himself included: all "printed sheet[s]," like the "dark arteries" of the body politic, "reek with running gore"; the speaker further resents how "gory Death" has displaced "our very Love." The lover-speaker of "Oh! craven, craven! while my brothers fall," an "easy vassal to [his] own delight," feels "shamed in [his] manhood," but he still resists giving up his suitor's pen for the soldier's sword.

In the third sonnet, "Brave comrade, answer! When you joined the war," the speaker interrogates a soldier in his effort to understand "that simple duty, conscience-plain and clear / To dullest minds" ("Oh! craven, craven!"). Even as the rhythm and breaks of their dialogue strain the sonnet's flow – Oliver Evans notes that, in all his sonnets, Boker "limits his liberties to the placement of the turn" – the poem moves steadily toward the soldier's paean to

Duty! Something more than life.
That which made Abraham bare the priestly knife,
And Isaac kneel, or that young Hebrew girl
Who sought her father coming from the strife.

Boker's second allusion here sounds a subtle note of protest. The reference to Jephthah's daughter (Judges 11:34–39) is neither syntactically nor sensibly parallel to the first allusion. Abraham consciously strove to prove his faith by sacrificing his son, and God, impressed, spared Isaac (Genesis 22). Jephthah, however, obliviously pursued his dreams of military glory; his virgin daughter's sacrifice is the accidental result of his prideful promise and her own innocent devotion. The poem leaves the reader awaiting the verb that describes her action; the silence inclines us to compare her situation to the soldier's.

An earlier poem, "Lear and Cordelia! 't was an ancient tale," likewise conjoins the sonnet and the articulation of a complex attitude toward authorities, both paternal and political. In this first sonnet of his 1852–54 "To England" sequence, written to declare America's support of England as the parent country moved toward the Crimean War, Boker casts America as daughter Cordelia to England's father Lear: America/Cordelia,

. . . an outcast, dowerless, and pale,
. . . in a foreign gale
Spread her young banner, till its sway became
A wonder to the nations.

Now that England's "destiny / Storms on thy straw-crowned head, and thou dost stand / Weak, helpless, mad, a by-word in the land," the poet prays, "God grant thy daughter a Cordelia be!"

Boker's figure of America as Cordelia also provides a context for understanding his lifelong devotion to the sonnet. In *The Book of the Sonnet* (1867), S. Adams Lee claims that Boker did not "pursu[e] a conventional system of versification from any blind reverence for authority." His sonnets are not thus merely symptomatic of the "vassalage of opinion and style" of which Rufus Griswold complained in *Poets and Poetry of America* (1842). Boker's poetry is, to quote Shakespeare's

Cordelia, no "glib and oily art." Instead, like Cordelia, who models virtue to her too-proud father, Boker pointedly reminds England of the true meaning of her legend, noting, "'t was an ancient tale / *Before* thy Shakespeare gave it deathless fame." There is something here of the original reforming puritanical impulse associated with the American settlement: the parent country is seen as deranged and has become, like Lear, the child to his child. In this context, the American poet's sonnet writing advances his larger "genteel endeavor," to reform American *and* English poetry. As his contemporary Lee describes, the period's writers assumed that the sonnet was the best means of purifying prevailing tastes in poetry, "of bringing certain classes of the literary public to a clear perception of what is true and beautiful in poetic art."

Another group of sonnets reveals a more private significance to Boker's restorationist generic choice. The poets of Boker and Taylor's circle habitually wrote each other Christmas and birthday sonnets. In his birthday sonnet to Taylor (1865), Stoddard parenthetically distinguishes his own love from that of the poet's "troops" of friends: "(How deeply *one*, it suits not now to tell)". In a sonnet for Stedman, sent with a volume of Shakespeare's sonnets, Stoddard further connects this sotto voce confession of an illicit love to his choice of verse form:

> Had we been living in the antique days,
>   With him whose young but cunning fingers penned
>   These sugared sonnets to his strange-sweet friend,
> I dare be sworn we would have won the bays.
> Why not? We could have twined with amorous phrase
>   Sonnets like these, where love and friendship blend,
>   (Or were they writ for some more private end?)
> And this, we see, remembered is with praise.

For these poets, the textual space of the sonnet figures a now-lost world, Stedman's "civic Arcadia," to which they desire to belong, not only because this imaginary world values the "true and beautiful in poetic art" over all else, but also for "some more private end." In this world, the love between men, like that of Shakespeare and his "strange-sweet friend," can be openly expressed; there they can "twine in amorous phrase."

In two sonnets addressed to Taylor (1856), Boker evokes their own more freely intimate and poetically fruitful youth together. Moreover, Boker's prewar letters to Taylor (see, e.g., Evans, 114–18) are intensely passionate. Although it is unlikely, as Robert K. Martin provocatively suggests, that Taylor is the "Dark Lady" of the *Sequence on Profane Love* (the 313 love sonnets Boker secretly wrote between 1857 and 1887), he may still have had a role in their erotic economy. In August 1865, Boker told Taylor of the existence of the sequence, concluding, "I judiciously, and out of regard to my reputation, keep all these to myself, designing them to form a portion of my 'remains' to be edited by you with bawdy notes and illustrations to match." Boker's playful appointment of Taylor's editorial role reconfigures and perpetuates the triangulated address of Shakespeare's sonnets. This letter, together with Boker's nigh-pornographic letters to Stoddard about their extramarital affairs (quoted in Tomsich, 158–161), illustrates what Eve Kosofsky Sedgwick calls the "heterosexual detour of male homosocial desire," men's transaction of their mutual desire through the exchange of a woman.

This woman may be of flesh or of fancy. Remembering that Boker and his fellow Arcadians conceived of poetry as a mistress to be wooed ("The Spirit of Poesy"), the reader detects another desire being transacted in the *Sequence on Profane Love*: the desire for fame. The bulk of the sonnets, I–CCLXXXII, Sculley Bradley has argued, are addressed to Angie Hicks, the wife of portraitist Thomas Hicks (*American Literature*, 1936). Hicks's own copy – which she carefully bound in book covers and titled "An Old Story, by George H. Boker" – contains only 88 sonnets, dated between March 1861 and June 1864, and ends with sonnet CXIV. Bradley speculates that sonnets CXV–CCLXXXII, dated between 1864 and 1871, were "written in a mood of recollection." Sonnet CLXXXVIII ("My darling's features, painted by the light," dated March 4, 1866) addresses a painting, a "fraud," and CCLXXXII ("Ah, lute, how well I know each tone of thee," dated October 14, 1871), a lute, a mere "shell of my fancy" that the poet would happily exchange for the "vivid smart / Of sentient life."

If sonnets CXV–CCLXXXII were indeed not sent, the reader must ask what desire sustains the sequence throughout its considerable length. Evans argues that Boker, like Wordsworth's Dante, exchanges the "laurel for the myrtle," thus substituting "his love affair for his earlier search for poetic fame." The reverse, however, is equally true: as the lady herself recedes from the scene of writing, she becomes a term in Boker's ongoing imagination of his poetic vocation, his subject, and his relation to his readers. In the absence of the beloved, the sonnets, what Boker calls the "records of my complex case" (sonnet I), become the ultimate test of his poetic powers. The beloved incarnates the high ideal of beauty for which he has shunned the world's regard; his love for her, like "a statue on its pedestal," sustains him "amidst the storms of civil mutiny" (CLXV, dated March 17, 1865).

The beloved also stands in for Boker's genteel circle, his Miltonic audience of "fit though few": her "sacred tear" is the poet's only hope that a "spray of green" might start from the "dust" of his previous poetic sowing (CXLVIII, dated February 6, 1865). Worrying, however, that she is unworthy of his faith, he rages: "Hast thou hung / Among thy trophies, that which I have flung / Beside my heart – a poet's budding crown?" (XIX, undated). By placing his hopes for fame with her, he has in fact risked infamy; in sonnet XC (February 5, 1863) he frets that

> . . . our secret love's poor cheer,
> . . . will reach the common ear,
> . . . Be cried about like any public thing; –
> Made the gross jest of street and marketplace.

Thanks to Bradley's editorial labors, this secret love did indeed reach the common ear – and if it had not, Boker might have been wholly forgotten in this century. The revelation of Boker's fleshly fallibility – thirty-nine years after his death on January 2, 1890 – has actually made him more interesting to modern readers and complicated our initial view of his self-designed memorial. The image of the poet kneeling to his "lady fair" figures both his belletristic pursuit and his carnal desire. If Bradley *had* edited the poems in the manner Boker specified to Taylor, what "bawdy illustration" might he have provided here?

LUCY RINEHART

Selected Works

The Lesson of Life and Other Poems, Philadelphia: Appleton, 1848

Calaynos, Philadelphia: Butler, 1848

"The Spirit of Poesy," in *The Snowflake*, Philadelphia: Butler, 1848

Anne Boleyn, Philadelphia: Hart, 1850

The Podesta's Daughter and Other Poems, Philadelphia: Hart, 1852

Plays and Poems, 2 vols., Boston: Ticknor and Fields, 1856; reprinted, New York: AMS, 1967

Poems of the War, Boston: Ticknor & Fields, 1864; reprinted, Arno Press, 1972

Königsmark, The Legend of the Hounds, and Other Poems, Philadelphia: Lippincott, 1869

The Book of the Dead, Philadelphia: Lippincott, 1882

Nydia, edited by Edward Sculley Bradley, Philadelphia: University of Pennsylvania Press, 1929

Sonnets: A Sequence on Profane Love, edited by Edward Sculley Bradley, Philadelphia: University of Pennsylvania Press, 1929

Glaucus and Other Plays, edited by Edward Sculley Bradley, Princeton, New Jersey: Princeton University Press, 1940

Further Reading

Bradley, Edward Sculley, *George Henry Boker: Poet and Patriot*, Philadelphia: University of Pennsylvania Press, 1927; reprinted, New York: AMS, 1969

Evans, Oliver, *George Henry Boker*, Boston: Twayne, 1984

Hunt, Leigh, and S. Adams Lee, eds., *The Book of the Sonnet*, 2 vols. Boston: Roberts Brothers, 1867

Kitts, Thomas, *The Theatrical Life of George Henry Boker*, New York: Peter Lang, 1994

Leland, Charles Godfrey, *Memoirs*, New York: Appleton, 1893; reprinted, Detroit: Gale, 1968

Martin, Robert K., *The Homosexual Tradition in American Poetry*, Austin: University of Texas Press, 1979

Stoddard, Richard Henry, *Recollections*, edited by Ripley Hitchcock, New York: Barnes, 1893

Tomsich, John, *A Genteel Endeavour: American Culture and Politics in the Gilded Age*, Stanford, California: Stanford University Press, 1971

Augusta Cooper Bristol

(1835–1910)

Like Verena Tarrant in Henry James's *The Bostonians* (1886), Augusta Cooper Bristol attracted considerable attention as an orator. She began her career, like Tarrant, out west and in modest circumstances – talking to neighbors in the frontier town of Carbondale, Illinois, on "enlightened motherhood" – but she ended up a popular speaker in cities throughout the United States and Europe. Her choice of topics would probably have pleased Olive Chancellor, Tarrant's radical patron: collected after her death in *The Present Phase of Woman's Advancement, and Other Addresses* (1916), her speeches included "Woman, the New Factor in Economics," "Labor and Capital," and "The Relation of the Maternal Function to the Woman's Intellect." Even unsympathetic auditors found reason to praise her. A writer in the *Journal de Bruxelles*, who reviewed a speech she made in Brussels in August 1880, sounds rather like James's Basil Ransom, the archconservative Mississippian who falls for Tarrant's charm in spite of her feminist ideas.

> The principles of Madame Bristol's discourse repose upon the philosophy of Comte and Spencer. We discuss not these principles; we disapprove them. We speak only of her oratory. Madame Augusta Cooper Bristol is really the Rachel, the Ristori, the Sarah Bernhardt of eloquent lecturers. The calm gesture, the picturesque inflection of the voice, the majesty of attitude, the complete possession of herself, mingle in this artist with a sweetness and a feminine propriety which is astonishing. Madame Bristol spoke in English, but she held equally well that large majority of the audience who could not comprehend her.

Bristol's poetry – which has survived into the late twentieth century almost entirely without a history of reception – is as susceptible to misconstruction as her oratory. Although Bristol seems to have found her public voice in her oratory, she had more difficulty finding a public voice as a poet. A latter-day Olive Chancellor might draw out her poetry's occasionally strident political voice, a voice that would "sweep up the echoes of all former time / Into diviner fullness" and see "a new kingdom" ("The New Time," from *The Web of Life* [1895]). An iconoclast like Ransom, out of step with his age, might just as surely savor the delicacies of Bristol's diction – even her sentimentalities. This essay will borrow a little from the mode of each, but will also attend to the ways in which the poems represent themselves – as social texts and as works of art.

There is no recent secondary literature on Bristol, and the details of her contemporary reviews await scholarly treatment. Her books themselves are scarce: *The Web of Life* was issued in a limited edition of six hundred copies, and her first book, *Poems* (1868), is extant today in only a dozen or so American libraries. (*A Spray of Cosmos* [1904] is equally scarce and merely selects older material.) Born in Croydon, New Hampshire, in 1835, Bristol has yet to find a thorough biographer, but the best available source – Bessie Bristol Mason's preface to *The Present Phase* – tells of an early teaching career; a failed first marriage and a successful second one, which began in cor-

respondence about a poem; a son's early death; much lecturing and reading of Herbert Spencer and Auguste Comte; and involvement with the Greenback Party and the Women's Christian Temperance Union. "The output of my poetry has been comparatively small," Bristol wrote late in her career; "I never followed literature as a profession, writing only when impelled to expression by the pressure of the ideal life within."

In choosing among the works of less well-known poets, editors of anthologies can have an unusual degree of influence. Small acts of recognition not only may mean the difference between a literary afterlife of sorts and continuing oblivion, but may shape the terms on which this afterlife is lived. In picking Bristol's poem "The Pyxidanthera" from *The Web of Life* to represent her in *An American Anthology* (1900), Edmund Clarence **Stedman** cast Bristol as a certain type of poet. He printed the poem alongside Constance Fenimore **Woolson's** "Yellow Jessamine" and Mary Bolles Branch's "The Petrified Fern," so he seems to have been attracted to Bristol's lyrical handling of natural imagery:

> Sweet child of April, I have found thy place
> Of deep retirement. Where the low swamp ferns
> Curl upward from their sheathes, and lichens creep
> Upon the fallen branch, and mosses dark
> Deepen and brighten, where the ardent sun
> Doth enter with restrained and chastened beam,
> And the light cadence of the blue-bird[']s song
> Doth falter in the cedar, – there the Spring,
> In gratitude hath wrought the sweet surprise
> And marvel of thy unobtrusive bloom.

Basil Ransom also would have liked this "unobtrusive bloom" of a poem. Yet "surprise" and "marvel" tend not to be modest terms in American poetry: they work as tropes of power. Unremarked upon in her own lifetime as a poet, Bristol may covertly be refusing here to have her poetry blush unseen. Aware of her relative lowliness in the literary cosmos, she wants nonetheless to claim for her poetic position a particular charm.

That she has a kinship with the Pyxidanthera, at least, is explicitly thematized as the poem continues:

> Most perfect symbol of my purest thought, –
> A thought so close and warm within my heart
> No words can shape its secret, and no prayer
> Can breathe its sacredness – be thou my type,
> And breathe to one who wanders here at dawn,
> The deep devotion, which transcending speech,
> Lights all the folded silence of my heart
> As thy sweet beauty doth the shadow here.
>
> So let thy clusters brighten, star on star
> Of pink and white about his lingering feet,
> Till, dreaming and enchanted, there shall pass
> Into his life the story that my soul
> Hath given thee. So shall his will be stirred

To purest purpose and divinest deed,
And every hour be touched with grace and light.

Just as Bristol finds a detaining power in this symbolic bloom, she hopes the anonymous passerby – a reader? – will be forced to stop and marvel at her "unobtrusive" poem. Addressing the flower, she sounds oddly like Shelley shouting to the west wind: "Be thou my type" is her version of "Be thou me, impetuous one!" While the flower is as small and silent as the wind is large and loud, however, both are capable of "transcending speech" – of bearing and transmitting meanings above the limiting mediation of the poets' particular words. In this sense, "The Pyxidanthera" seems almost as ambitious as "Ode to the West Wind," but its tone conceals the similarity. The difference may partly mark Bristol's mature and self-conscious recognition of her lesser fame and skill. The "story" she gives the flower is a story about her position on the literary margins. Publishing in editions of six hundred, she was unobtrusive, whereas Shelley really did scatter his "words among mankind."

As a woman, though, Bristol would also have felt pressure to couch whatever ambition she may have had in a quiet, sentimental language. Introducing Bristol's first book, A. A. Livermore, the editor of *Newspaper Poets; or, Waifs and Their Authors* (1876), condescendingly describes the tonal quality that many would expect her to have: "While, then, the great organs thunder forth in Dantean or Miltonic strains the sublime ecstasies that shake the soul, we will not disdain to listen to the gentle lute, which with heavenly melody . . . tells us of that love of God which is in all things, least and greatest. The voice of the Sisterhood as well as that of the Brotherhood, is needed to complete the gamut."

Up to a point, Bristol fulfills the terms of these relatively low expectations in clichéd and saccharine poems about Christian piety, babies, and *tristesses* (woes). Yet other poems take on a strident, public voice at odds with these too-heavenly melodies and thus hint at Bristol's dissatisfaction with the tyrannies of social convention. The Civil War especially seems to have brought out a declamatory strength in her; its exigencies perhaps made such strength acceptable for the woman writer at the time. "The Crime of the Ages" (1861; LOA, 2: 333), which opens the "Poems of the War" section of *Poems*, begins commandingly, and in a verse form suited to exhortation:

Poet, write!
Not of a purpose dark and dire,
That souls of evil fashion,
Nor the power that nerves the assassin's hand,
In the white heat of his passion:
    But let thy rhyme,
    Through every clime,
A burthen bear of this one crime:
Let the world draw in a shuddering breath,
O'er the crime that aims at a nation's death!

Repeating this urgent formula in subsequent stanzas – "Minstrel, sing!"; "Soldier, fight!"; "Prophet, speak!" – Bristol envisions a nation of laborers-in-their-vocation united equally against a common foe, each performing his or her share.

In part, the confidence with which she feels the poet can contribute to the war effort simply attests to the vital currency of poetry in mid-nineteenth-century public discourse (compare Wallace Stevens's defensive overconfidence about the poet's war role in the coda to "Notes Toward a Supreme Fiction" [1942]). Yet, this confidence also reveals an impatience with those who would limit her speech to its more delicate registers. In "The Union Soldier" (1861), a poem that praises the rough strength of the common fighting man over the refinements of the aristocrat, Bristol at once describes and imitates the kind of thunder Livermore would deny her:

The voice that joins
In dulcet melody, or learns to speak
In courtly tones, can never be so dear
As that whose proud command, in danger's hour,
Has gained us victory; a voice attuned
To the retorting guns; a sound of strength
To friends, and dread to foes. So do I prize
An accent or a word from patriot tongues.

The attainment of such a voice would free Bristol from the poetic sweetness otherwise imposed on her, and she seems to revel in the rehearsal of it. Yet, this voice, too, could become monotonous – a party line, intolerant of deviation. A third voice, neither sweet nor strident – really the voice of chaste self-withholding from both sensual and social incursions – keeps Bristol from turning completely in either direction:

The riddle of my life
Is folded up, and fastened with a seal,
The world can never break. The curious
Will peck with sharpened guessings, but will tire,
And leave it as I left it, – unrevealed.
        ("Another Love")

The violence of "sharpened guessings" might reveal Bristol definitively, as Olive Chancellor and Basil Ransom both would reveal Verena Tarrant. But the poet will not be exposed; and the curious have indeed, until very recently, left her poems as she left them.

MATTHEW PARR

Selected Works
Poems, Boston: Adams, 1868
Discours sur la science comme base de morale, Paris: n.p., 1880
The Web of Life, Buffalo, New York: C. W. Moulton, 1895
A Spray of Cosmos, Boston: R. G. Badger, 1904
The Present Phase of Woman's Advancement and Other Addresses, Boston: Christopher, 1916

Charles Timothy Brooks

(1813–1883)

According to Henry Pochmann, Charles Timothy Brooks was "the most assiduous translator of German literature ever to appear on the American scene." In Stanley Vogel's terms, Brooks demonstrated an "unflagging zeal and . . . complete devotion to the beauties of German literature [that] profoundly influenced the men of his time." Brooks was born in Salem, Massachusetts, in 1813, and was securely grounded in Puritan stock. Both paternal and maternal ancestors – including the Reverend Francis Higginson, whose vocation Brooks would follow – can be traced to mid-seventeenth-century Massachusetts. He began his translating career in 1838, with Friederich Schiller's *William Tell*, which his friend John Sullivan Dwight reviewed favorably in the *Christian Examiner*. Four years later, Brooks's translations of German lyric poetry, *Songs and Ballads: Translated from Uhland, Körner, Bürger, and Other German Lyric Poets*, appeared in George Ripley's *Specimens of Foreign Standard Literature*. His most successful translation appears to have been Johann Wolfgang von Goethe's *Faust, Part I*, first published in 1856. Its popularity demanded 14 more editions by 1880, and Vogel deems it "superior to all previous translations." Thomas Carlyle commended Brooks's version of Jean Paul Richter's *Titan* in 1864: "You have been wonderfully successful: have caught a good deal of the tune of Jean Paul, and have unwinded his meaning, in general, with perfect accuracy, into comfortable clearness, out of those coils he involves it in. I did not keep the original open all the way, but had a feeling that I was safe in your hands." His adeptness in translating abstruse works is again revealed in his incomplete translation of Friedrich Rückert's *Die Weisheit des Brahmanen*. As Vogel remarks: this work provided "perhaps the most difficult literary task of [Brooks's] career, but in spite of its mystical nature, Oriental imagery, and involved construction, Brooks reproduced it with remarkable accuracy and skill." Vogel also lauds Brooks's pioneering attempts to introduce German humorous literature to America, but generally deems Brooks's translations uneven and laments a lack of aesthetic judgment in his selections of German poetry, which indiscriminately span the best and the worst.

Little attention has been paid to Brooks's own poetry, but it is perhaps best examined in light of his ministerial career rather than in light of the translations that brought him such contemporary notice. Brooks's studies at Harvard College and Cambridge Divinity School coincided with the height of Unitarianism and the dawning of Transcendentalism. He entered Cambridge in 1832, the same year that Ralph Waldo **Emerson** resigned from the Second Church. Despite Brooks's allegiances to certain Transcendentalists, including Dwight, Theodore Parker, Christopher Pearse **Cranch**, William Ellery Channing, and Emerson – who apparently recommended him to Margaret **Fuller** as a possible contributor to *The Dial* – critics have suggested that Brooks's tone of piety and sentiment place him more firmly within the genteel tradition of poetry, which emphasized literature's sentimental and moral uses. Charles W. Wendte, however, considered Brooks a natural Transcendentalist, and Brooks's own poetry, which voices Transcendental themes such as the concern over the relationship of man to nature and the correspondences between the visible and invisible realms, reveals a philosophical affiliation with Transcendentalism.

Brooks most clearly embraces Transcendentalist philosophy in his memorial poem "Channing." The poet depicts his subject "Communing . . . with Nature's word, / Beside the vast and solemn sea." Encountering "a Spirit everywhere," Brooks's Channing feels a physiological connection with nature: "His bosom, heaving with the sea, / Exulted in the glorious din; / The elemental energy / Woke answering energy within." Here, as in "Our Island Home" (LOA, 1: 626), Brooks explores the notion that correspondences exist between the natural and the spiritual spheres: "human thoughts, that come and go – / Whence – whither – no man knoweth" are likened to stars rising and setting in the heavens. The ocean and sky, emblematic of "God's vast being," serve as a conduit, "a broad highway," by which souls can reach "endless realms." Similarly, Channing's solitary "rapturous self-communion" in the midst of nature offers him inner "peace and power." His spirit survives his death; listeners whose souls have been aroused by Channing's preaching become his "living monument."

Brooks's wonder at the power of words seems to be at the heart of both his literary and ministerial vocations. Brooks was ordained by Channing at Newport, Rhode Island, in May 1837. Despite periodic absences due to respiratory illnesses, Brooks served as a Unitarian minister in Newport for 37 years. Not until late in his service did he encounter hostile opposition from his congregation, but in his 1861 Fast Day sermon, Brooks made patently clear his stand on the issue of slavery: "No laws or institutions should oppress any class of God's children. The oppressor should cease from his oppression, and the enslaved go free. Such is the fast that God hath chosen." This sermon was not the first suggestion of Brooks's abolitionist sentiments in the pulpit, and opposing members of the congregation threatened, without success, to have him dismissed. His sermon on Thanksgiving Day, 1864, echoes, perhaps more eloquently, many of the motifs of his poems:

> Our text is written on the soil of a land reconsecrated by the blood of a new army of martyrs; in is written on the sky into which the smoke of a nation's sacrifice for freedom and righteousness and humanity is still ascending; . . . and whoso will pause and listen to the still small voice of the inner witness shall hear the Holy Spirit interpreting, expounding, and applying the text I speak of to every freeman's conscience.

These few lines reveal Brooks's love of the American landscape (as do the titles of his two collections of poetry, *Aquidneck* [1848] and *Songs of Field and Flood* [1853]) as well as the concept that nature speaks to us if only we "will pause and listen."

It comes as no surprise that Brooks's first sermon upon graduating from Cambridge Divinity School was entitled "The Voice of the Spirit" and referred to Hebrews 3.15, "Today, when you hear his voice, do not harden your hearts." So many of Brooks's poems deal precisely with the issue of listening to the spiritual realm through nature. The Calvinist belief that "faith comes by hearing" is also manifest in much of Brooks's poetry. For Brooks, humanity must harken to the sounds of nature – or to those who, like Channing, preach "the gospel, large and free." The Atlantic Ocean bellows, in "Our Island Home," "with trumpet-swell, / The hymn of Law and Liberty!" Moreover, the title of his second collection, *Songs of Field and Flood*, underscores the importance of the voice of nature in the Transcendental experience. In "To Samuel G. Howe," the speaker experiences a Transcendental moment that is both visual and aural. Preceded by "a momentary hush,"

> a thrill of awe
> Rang through the silent vale: for, lo!
> That spectral mountain-chain I saw
> Lit with a preternatural glow.

The spectacular sight remains with and permanently transforms the speaker: "Who that has seen those evening shows / Their look and voice can e'er forget?" In "Pascagoula," one of Brooks's most melodic poems, the speaker is haunted by the "witching, wild music" of a port in southeastern Mississippi.

> O Nature! thy Sabbath – I spent it with thee,
> In the still, solemn woods, by the silent, glad sea.
> As sweet to my ear was the hymn of that morn
> As if angels were singing creation just born.

For Brooks, the absence of "human priest's accents" does not preclude the presence of God's spirit. In "Pascagoula," the "winds and waves chant" and the "trembling leaves bow" to God, and "that green, old, moss-garlanded tree" is "Arrayed in its robes as priest unto Thee." Epiphanies are available in less exotic locations as well. Closer to home, the sounds of nature, "often at noon, when the birds and the bees / Hum a drowsy, sweet tune in the grass and the trees," evoke the same ecstasy as the mysterious sounds of Pascagoula.

Echoes of Wordsworth's notion of poetry as "the spontaneous overflow of powerful feelings . . . recollected in tranquility" also ring in "Pascagoula," and in many of Brooks's other poems that rely on the combination of memory and solitude. For instance, Brooks's "The Prophecy of Youth" recalls Wordsworth:

> The morning visions fair, that hovered round
> Our wayward steps on youth's enchanted ground,
> Come back again, and stand revealed anew
> In clearer light to manhood's calmer view.

In this poem, one must pass beyond "the din and dust of earth's bewildering strife" in order to hear and see what is real. Here, the "din" of earthly strife precludes hearing "the thrill of awe." "The glorious din" of the elements described in "Channing," however, offers an auditory parallel to unimpaired vision, which in turn becomes the prominent metaphor of "The Prophecy of Youth":

> the clearer eye,
> Purged from ambition's fire
> And fever-heat of passionate desire,
> Looks back, with wistful gaze,
> To the fair hours and haunts of youthful days.

The "roseate glow" of youth, however, is not merely illusory; it "prophesies / A morning yet to rise / Upon the soul in these immortal skies": "The visionary gleam . . . / On the dew-spangled landscape of our youth / . . . come[s] from a land within." Here, Brooks complicates the Transcendental correspondence between the material and the spiritual. By making the material world a metaphor of youth, he connects nature, time, and spirit. Brooks also uses memory as a steppingstone to transcend the present moment. Through the past, he connects with an unimaginable future. Furthermore, memory is a conduit to revelation because it exemplifies the omnipresence of the dead:

> And memory's holy moonlight glow,
> How sweet along life's landscape shed;
> Transfiguring forms of long ago,
> And summoning to life the dead!

Through memory, as through nature, the evanescence of the material world is revealed for Brooks. Memory inspires a similar epiphany in "The Past," which renders "The living shapes that bustle at our side" mere "phantoms":

> So with the things of time, – like dreams they glide;
> The eternal things are ever at our side.
> The present moments sparkle, fade, and flee;
> The Past is part of God's eternity.

In "Salem," the speaker returns to the town of his birth, eager to find the memories of his youth: "the old green Gibraltar-cart," "the midnight blaze of wood-wax on Witch Hill" and "the cheering beam of Baker's Island Light." What he finds instead are "the old town pastures," "delectable mountains," and "the barberry and the columbine." The human works have passed, but "Mother Nature" has remain unchanged. Here, as in "Channing," Brooks derogates art in relation to nature and spirit: "the broad and chainless sea, / The blue sky" express Channing's spirit "As neither stone nor canvas can." Similarly, in "A Last Flying Glance at Mount Washington," the revelations granted by nature and recorded in one's soul are "Beyond the reach of human art," and in "Lines: Composed at the Old Temples of Maralipoor" (LOA, 1: 627), the speaker is awed by nature's power: "And still their course the waters hold, / While man and all his works decay."

The imperfect vision of youth described in "A Prophecy of Youth" finds its analogy in the skewed vision of humanity contained in Emerson's description of myopia in "Nature" (1836): "To speak truly, few adult persons can see nature. Most persons do not see the sun. At least they have a very superficial seeing. . . . The lover of nature is he whose inward and outward senses are still truly adjusted to each other." In Brooks's poem "A Dark Morning," the speaker is bewildered by the change of scenery effected by a storm: "Where is the world that, yesterday, / With tranquil beauty tranced my sight . . . ?" The speaker's vision is confounded by the desolation:

> Where'er I turn my straining sight,
> I see no living, moving form,
> Save black-winged clouds in heavy flight,
> And trees that tremble in the storm.

The poem's eventual consolation for life's grief and sorrow is celestial bliss, which must be seen "with unbeclouded eye."

Clearly, for Brooks, as for Emerson, the sight of nature is not a sufficient catalyst for the Transcendental moment: one's spirit must be attuned. As Emerson notes, "Nature is made to conspire with spirit to emancipate us. Certain mechanical changes, a small alteration in our local position, apprizes us of a dualism. We are strangely affected by seeing the shore from a moving ship, from a balloon, or through the tints of an unusual sky. The least change in our point of view gives the whole world a pictorial air." Coincidentally, all three of the changes of perspective described by Emerson become metaphors in Brooks's poetry.

In "The Past," Brooks makes an analogy between the broadened perspective offered as a boat sails away from a coast, which allows the viewer to see the inland hills, and the clearer vision of age, which enables us to view the past as "not all passed." The shift in point of view engenders a metaphysical response. "A Last Flying Glance at Mount Washington" describes an aerial view of the snow-capped mountain against a "crimson, gold and flaming red" valley, which symbolizes, for the speaker, the meeting of winter and summer. This "soul-entrancing sight," however, is "Perchance for mortal eye too bright": "But pictured on the inner eye, / These revelations from on high / Shall last when earthly shadows fly." For Brooks, the Transcendental moment is an instance of unaccustomed perspective that alters the viewer's relationship with the universe and, unavoidably, with himself. Similarly, "Sunrise on the Sea-Coast" places the speaker "alone upon a rock" at the "holy hour of dawn." Like the meeting of winter and summer in the previous poem, gladness and sorrow meet as the sun and clouds compete to illuminate or shade the ocean. Here, the speaker's joy at the sunrise, his shout of exaltation that is the poem, is met with a corresponding "shout on high / Of exaltation" from "foaming waves."

"The deep, expectant hush" that this speaker encounters in his Transcendental moment has its parallel in Brooks's poem about the setting sun, "To Samuel G. Howe." In the latter poem, the speaker looks to a sunset in order to understand the concept of human death. Immediately prior to the intuition, which registers as a sudden "thrill of awe," the speaker remarks "a momentary hush." The poem evinces the unforgettable effect by an inversion of the natural drama: "Can the pure world that then arose / On the soul's vision ever set?" The speaker's change of perspective, likened to a sunrise, is permanent, and correspondingly he realizes that spiritual life is eternal:

> Though death's pale mountains hide the sun
> Of noble lives from mortal eyes,
> Oh deem not then their day is done!
> They sank, in higher heavens to rise.

Like the "inland hills" of "The Past," the "boundary hills are they that rise" and "Veil and reveal to mortal eyes / The land of everlasting light." In all three instances, the speaker realizes that the physical realm is phenomenal, a metaphor for his own state of being.

Certainly, a shift in perspective is what Brooks also tried to accomplish in translating German literature for the American public: "Of all the German writers and men, Richter is the one whom we are most eager that our countrymen should appreciate and understand. . . . He is to us by far the most suggestive, soul-stirring, improving of German minds . . . the Shakespeare of Germany." The influence that many of his translations had upon sophisticated readers indicates that he might have succeeded. Shortly after Brooks's death in 1883, E. P. Whipple wrote in a letter to Dwight: "What good that man has done, considered simply as a translator of Goethe and Richter! Yet his patriotism in making us familiar with great works of the German mind is hardly yet appreciated – except by men like you."

LAURA BARRETT

Selected Works
Poems, Original and Translated, by Charles T. Brooks, edited by W. P. Andrews, with memoir by Charles W. Wendte, New York: Arno, 1972

Further Reading
Myerson, Joel, *The New England Transcendentalists and the Dial*, Rutherford, New Jersey: Fairleigh Dickenson University Press, 1980
Pochmann, Henry A., *German Culture in America*, Madison: University of Wisconsin Press, 1961
Vogel, Stanley M., *German Literary Influences on the American Transcendentalists*, New Haven, Connecticut: Yale University Press, 1955

Maria Gowen Brooks

(1794?–1845)

In a time of reticence, when a woman of artistic genius was not wanted, Maria Gowen Brooks, better known as "Maria del Occidente," demonstrated her knowledge and intellect in the form of poetry. Her female contemporaries Emily **Dickinson**, Elizabeth Barrett Browning, Margaret **Fuller**, and Letitia Landon were also pushing the boundaries of a society that discouraged writers, especially women writers, from having a "sincere, bold and natural expression of strong emotion." In that age of modesty and restraint, Brooks's poetry raised eyebrows because of its passion and sensuality. Staunch supporter Rufus Wilmot Griswold described her as "the poet of passion" and stated that her writings were "fearless in thought and expression" and gave the heart its "true voice." According to Stanley Kunitz and Howard Haycroft, less enthusiastic critics referred to her poetry as "lush, syrupy, feminine – in the worst meaning of the term." Yet Brooks spoke frankly of the passionate side of women and illuminated their desire not only for love but for knowledge as well.

Born around 1794, in Medford, Massachusetts, into an influential family, Abigail Gowen (her given name) received the best life then had to offer. Her father, William Gowen, was a goldsmith and a man of cultivation, who was on familiar terms with Harvard professors. By the age of nine, Abigail had committed to memory works by William Shakespeare, John Milton, Alexander Pope, and Robert Southey, and could recite Milton's *Comus* and Southey's *Madoc*. Abigail flourished under her father's guidance, attaining fluency in several languages, including French and Italian, and displaying proficiency in music and painting. In 1809, however, her father died and left the family in financial ruin. Through the support of her widowed brother-in-law, the Boston merchant John Brooks, Abigail was able to continue her education, but she later felt obliged to accept his proposal of marriage. In August 1810, Abigail, then fifteen or sixteen, married Brooks, who was nearly fifty, and became the stepmother of his two sons. For a brief period, Abigail enjoyed a life of affluence and high culture; she also had her name legally changed to Mary Abigail Brooks and gave birth to a child, Edgar, in November 1811. Because of poor investments and the market effects of the War of 1812, however, Brooks filed for bankruptcy in 1812 and moved his family to the provincial town of Portland, Maine. There Mary became bored and even more conscious of her loveless marriage. The notes to her best work, *Zophiël, or The Bride of Seven* (1833; LOA, 1: 175), reveal her mental sufferings and her consequent opinions on premature marriage. In August 1813, a second son, Horace, was born. Although she accepted her role as mother, Mary battled against the restrictive view that women were the appointed guardians of the home and its inhabitants.

Attempting to escape the censure of her close-minded peers, who often displayed a puritanical mistrust of the arts, Mary turned to sewing and reading. She became an avid reader of Far Eastern literature and the Bible. During this time, she fell in love with a young Canadian army officer – known to us only by the initials E.W.R.A. Since she was married, however, Mary

did not act on her intense feelings, and the officer departed without discerning his impact upon her. In frustration, and for consolation, she turned to poetry. Her first volume, *Judith, Esther, and Other Poems*, "by a Lover of the Fine Arts" (1820), was based on the Apocrypha.

Three years later, John Brooks died, and Mary was forced to provide for the family. Her writing became her only source of income. Fortunately, she and her four sons were soon invited to live with her uncle, William Cutter, on his coffee plantation in Matanzas, Cuba. Cutter died within months of her arrival and left her the estate and its holdings, so Mary never had to worry about her financial condition again. Accompanied by her brother, she immediately proceeded to Quebec to find the army officer who had evoked such powerful emotions in her. They became engaged, but in less than a year, they were estranged, and Mary subsequently attempted to commit suicide twice by drinking laudanum. After the second attempt, a friend intervened and made her promise never to attempt suicide again. He presented her with a small cross on a ribbon as a reminder of her vow, and the necklace can be seen in all of her portraits.

After recovering from her bouts of depression, at least physically, Brooks turned her complete attention to writing poetry. In the coffee plantation's tropical garden, she had a replica of a Greek temple constructed. In this lush, sensual setting, she wrote the first canto of her epic *Zophiël* and published it in Boston in 1825 to an indifferent reception. Around 1826, she began corresponding with the English poet laureate, Southey. Intrigued by the tragic nature of her poetry, Southey encouraged her to continue writing. Initially, he was wary of meeting her, but she soon had the entire Southey household charmed during an 1830 visit. During that time, she worked on the remaining cantos of *Zophiël*, completing them in Paris. With Southey's guidance and influence, *Zophiël* was published in London in 1833 under the pseudonym "Maria del Occidente" – a name reportedly created by Southey. Because of her close association with Southey and her Welsh ancestry, she was thought of as a sort of "honorary" Lake Poet.

Zophiël, a name borrowed from Milton's *Paradise Lost*, is composed of six cantos: "Grove of Acacias," "Death of Altheetor," "Palace of Gnomes," "The Storm," "Zameia," and "Bridal of Helon." As in *Paradise Lost*, each canto is preceded by an "argument," and the main character, Zophiël, is a fallen angel. The work is based on the sixth, seventh, and eighth chapters of the Apocryphal book of Tobit, in which the evil demon Asmodeus has fallen in love with Sara, a Hebrew virgin. After being falsely accused of murder, Sara attempts to commit suicide by hanging herself (recalling Brooks's own attempts at suicide) and pleads with God to save her, if that is His will. In response, God sends the angel Raphael to cure her troubles. Tobias, the son of Tobit, is destined to marry Sara, and, on Raphael's advice, he uses the heart and liver of a fish to vanquish Asmodeus. The marriage is accomplished.

In Brooks's version, Zophiël is not depicted as an evil

spirit like Asmodeus. In fact, as other scholars have noted, Zophiël has redeeming qualities and hopes one day to be reunited with God. He is also identified with the Greek god Apollo. According to Zadel B. Gustafson, "the plot of the poem clearly indicates its purpose – to show how the passion of love affects individual fate, moulding and swaying both human and angelic nature." Zophiël is so consumed by his love for Egla, Brooks's equivalent of the apocryphal Sara (even though Egla had a first husband), that he attempts to locate an elixir that will immortalize her youth and beauty. His efforts are thwarted by a tempest created by Lucifer, which, by means of the implied contrast, reinforces the notion that Zophiël is not diabolical. When Zophiël is defeated by Helon (Brooks's version of Tobias) in the last canto, Hariph (or Raphael) gives the impression that Zophiël may be restored to his original position in heaven by encouraging him to have hope.

In the sixth canto, Egla's life is threatened by a jealous lover, Zameia. The intensity of Zameia's love for Meles, Egla's first husband, recalls Brooks's volatile love for the unidentified Canadian officer. In her rage, Zameia attempts to murder Egla, but Zophiël intervenes, and Egla witnesses Zameia's death. This canto is the most evocative of Brooks's own life. Although Zameia loves Meles, she is trapped in a loveless marriage to Imlec. As Thomas O. Mabbott observes, Egla's loneliness is also similar to the loneliness Brooks experienced during her stay in Portland (*American Collector*, 1926). Perhaps the most revealing and certainly the most passionate section of the entire work is Egla's "Twilight Song." Southey claimed that it was better than Sappho's "Ode to Aphrodite," and it caused Charles Lamb to exclaim, in a rather backhanded compliment, "Southey says it is written by some Yankee woman: as if there had ever been a woman capable of anything so great." The *London Quarterly* remarked, in surprise, "And all this out of a coffee plantation in Cuba!"

In the "Twilight Song," Egla expresses her desire to love completely and her decision to yield to Zophiël. The song, composed in Brooks's Grecian temple, is suitably sensual. From Egla's "inmost core / . . . feelings gushed / . . . As never had her lip expressed before." She eloquently voices both her loneliness and her rapture. In Mabbott's terms, the song ends in "utter abandonment" of everything else for a "consuming flame of unselfish love." Nevertheless, before she completely succumbs to Zophiël, Helon intervenes and saves her.

Overall, the reception of Brooks's epic was lukewarm at best. As Brooks stated in her preface, the first edition was published to benefit Polish refugees in wake of revolution. Unfortunately, neither her wonderful writing nor her charitable spirit assisted *Zophiël*'s popularity. In fact, after mediocre sales, Brooks eventually removed it from the market altogether. Despite the overwhelming support of Southey, Lamb, Griswold, and John Quincy **Adams**, both English and American readers ignored the book. Most of those who opposed the work cited the extensive notes as a basis of their dislike. The running type was in fact littered with daggers and asterisks. Yet, Brooks's notes are extremely informative and clearly display the depth of her knowledge, especially about ancient cultures. Gustafson describes the notes as "a groundwork of erudition, as thickly sprinkled with occult bits of thought, research, and profound study, as the tunic and tresses of an oda-lisque with gems." In the preface, Brooks defended her notes and also offered the following advice: "It will be better to read the story as it was composed, without reference to explanations or comments till the whole is finished." According to Brooks, reading in that manner would make the work as comprehensible as the *Arabian Nights* or any "common novel." In the 1879 edition, Gustafson placed the notes at the end of the poem to avoid confusion.

Undaunted by *Zophiël*'s lack of popularity, the "gifted and impassioned poet" (Southey's words) continued to write. Brooks began working almost immediately on a prose tale, *Idomen: or, The Vale of Yumuri*. Serialized in Boston's *Saturday Evening Gazette* between February and September 1838, *Idomen* created a sensation unlike any of her previous works. It was considered one of the most candid documents ever written because it addressed the nature of a woman's passions and emotional trials. It is also regarded as the most autobiographical of her works. Under the guise of fiction, Brooks disclosed her relationship with the Canadian officer in addition to other personal details of her life. Desiring to have all of her works published in one volume, Brooks authorized Griswold to find a publisher. Although she was not surprised that her offer was refused, she was outraged when the reason for the rejection was divulged. Harper's informed her that her poetry was "of too elevated a character to sell." In a letter to Griswold, she retorted, "I do not think any thing from my humble imagination can be too elevated, or elevated enough." As a result, in 1843, she financed a limited edition of the prose tale.

In that same year, tragedy revisited. She received news that her son, Edgar, and one of her stepsons had succumbed to tropical fever. As with other events in her life, Brooks used poetry to give voice to her emotions by creating the stirring tribute "Ode to the Departed." Brooks returned to the plantation to mourn her loss and began working on another epic of passion, *Beatriz, the Beloved of Columbus*. Unfortunately, two years later, she died of tropical fever before it could be finished. Her remaining stepson died on the same day. Throughout her life and works, Maria Gowen Brooks gave voice to woman's passion. In the face of adversity, she questioned the traditional roles of women and challenged convention. She was a passion flower – an educated and highly artistic passion flower.

GEOFRILYN M. WALKER

Selected Works

Judith, Esther, and Other Poems, Boston: Cummings and Hillard, 1820
Zophiël, or The Bride of Seven, London: 1833; Boston: Hilliard, Gray, 1834
Idomen: or The Vale of Yumuri, New York: S. Colman, 1843
Zophiël, or The Bride of Seven, edited by Zadel Barnes Gustafson, Boston: Lee and Shepard, 1879

Further Reading

Granniss, Ruth W., *An American Friend of Southey*, New York: DeVinne, 1913
Griswold, Rufus W., *The Female Poets of America*, Philadelphia: Carey and Hart, 1848

_____, *The Poets and Poetry of America*, Philadelphia: Carey and Hart, 1842

Kane, Paul, ed., *Poetry of the American Renaissance*, New York: Braziller, 1995

Kunitz, Stanley J., and Howard Haycroft, eds., *American Authors 1600–1900*, New York: Wilson, 1938

Ostriker, Alicia, *Stealing the Language: The Emergence of Women's Poetry in America*, Boston: Beach, 1986

Walker, Cheryl, *American Women Poets of the Nineteenth Century: An Anthology*, New Brunswick, New Jersey: Rutgers University Press, 1992

Henry Howard Brownell

(1820–1872)

Walt **Whitman** once complained that "the real war," by which he meant the Civil War, "will never get in the books." Bayard **Taylor**, a contemporary of Whitman's, lamented in similar fashion that "the sword of Mars chop[ped] in two the strings of Apollo's lyre!" Whitman and Taylor were not alone in their complaint. Many others agreed not only that it was difficult to write about the Civil War, but that the conflict made it difficult to write at all. It was not just that the war's rush of events violated the repose necessary for the composition of poetry (though that is probably what Taylor had in mind). This first "modern war" was, in every way, distinctly antipoetic.

To begin with, the prosecution of the war required a systematic, wholesale destruction of life and property that was almost unimaginable. "It seems to me like a great slaughter-house [with] men mutually butchering each other," observed Whitman. In addition, the size and scope of the conflict made it difficult to get any sort of meaningful perspective on the war at all. "Man no longer has an individual existence but is counted in thousands and is measured in miles," said Clara Barton, founder of the American Red Cross. Ultimately, the war transformed America in ways that few at the time either understood or were prepared to accept. The vast mobilization of men and material needed to mount years of extensive military campaigns required a prosaic, albeit important, reorganization of American life that included innovations in logistics, production, distribution, financing, transportation, and communication – all of which was made possible by the emergence of a powerful national government in partnership with American business.

Needless to say, the genteel conventions of antebellum poetry – symbolized tellingly in Taylor's archaic allusion to "the strings of Apollo's lyre" – were hardly equipped to assimilate this new and startling range of experience. Apollo's lyre was far more effective in celebrating individual acts of heroism or in mourning over a "fallen soldier" than it was in wresting significance from the anonymity and ambiguity of modern warfare. The alternative to the lyre was, of course, the fife and drum. Many patriotic verses certainly sped the soldiers on their way – among them, Whitman's own "Beat! Beat! Drums!" But here, too, the same limitations prevailed. In the end, neither the lyre nor the fife and drum proved adequate to deal with the complexities of the conflict. Despite the vast outpouring of literature it provoked, the Civil War remained, in some fundamental respects, an "unwritten war" (in Daniel Aaron's phrase).

This does not mean that those literary figures who attempted to write about the Civil War are without interest. On the contrary, the limitations – and the surprising strengths – of their responses are revealing for what they tell us about an antebellum *mentalité* that fomented the Civil War, but that looked conspicuously anachronistic with the initiation of hostilities. Faced with their inability to imagine the war and the absolute necessity of doing so, poets struggled with what might be called a crisis of representation. For the most part, the his-

torical tensions secreted within this crisis have been obscured by the tendency of literature and literary criticism to place an undue value on what Cary Nelson – in *Repression and Recovery* – has called "the heroism of individual achievement or the equally romantic tragedy of individual failure." Instead, Nelson argues that critics should pay greater attention to the discursive possibilities available to poetry within a particular historical moment:

> Most poets work within a contextualized sense of what is possible rhetorically: what innovations are made available to them by the work of their contemporaries; what tendencies are to be emulated, transformed, resisted; what issues it seems necessary (or unimaginable) to address; what cultural roles have been won over or lost for poetry.

The poetry of the Civil War is interesting precisely because it allows us to witness this complicated rhetorical struggle at work within a volatile historical milieu, a milieu in which the success or failure of a particular mode of representation was of immense practical, social, and moral consequence for Americans who sought to understand not only the war but, to some extent, their own future.

Anyone proposing to undertake an investigation of this sort immediately confronts a certain degree of cultural amnesia. Today, the poetry of the Civil War is remembered, if at all, in a handful of poems – most of them written by Whitman. Beyond Whitman's *Drum-Taps* (LOA, 1: 887) and its sequel – which includes his magnificent elegy for President Lincoln, "When Lilacs Last in the Dooryard Bloom'd" (LOA, 1: 895) – the poetry of this period has been largely forgotten. Julia Ward **Howe's** "Battle Hymn of the Republic" (LOA, 1: 709) is still sung, but it is doubtful that most people know the origin of the words. And Herman **Melville's** *Battle-Pieces* continues to receive attention, although it is generally relegated to the critical vacuum of his "silent" period.

Among those forgotten is a poet by the name of Henry Howard Brownell. Although he may be obscure to us now, in the 1860s there was probably no one more closely associated with the Civil War than Brownell himself. John Greenleaf **Whittier's** body of antislavery poetry may have been more extensive, and James Russell **Lowell's** Harvard Commemoration Ode (LOA, 1: 696) was thought by his generation to be the most eloquent summation of the war. For many, however, Brownell was, in the words of Oliver Wendell **Holmes**, "Our Battle Laureate" (*Atlantic Monthly*, May 1865). A passionate partisan, Brownell was to the Union what Henry **Timrod** was to the Confederacy. And it is through Brownell that we understand the assumptions, confusions, and passions of the North's most idealistic supporters.

Judged solely on the basis of his technical gifts, Brownell's obscurity is well deserved. He is, in many ways, a poor poet. His verse is by turns leaden and overwrought; his diction is hackneyed, his rhymes predictable, and his metrics awkward and frequently forced. But the fault lines caused by the tremors of the Civil War run through his work with a striking clarity. In both his poetry and its reception, there is a tension between a still dominant genteel culture and an emerging realist aesthetic. Moreover, Brownell's inability to surmount this division allows us to see more clearly the cultural roles and concomitant modes of representation available to poetry in the third quarter of the nineteenth century. In this respect, at least, the poet's weakness constitutes the critic's boon.

Brownell was born in Providence, Rhode Island, and raised in East Hartford, Connecticut. He graduated from Washington (now Trinity) College in 1841, and three years later, he was admitted to the bar. But Brownell preferred poetry to the law. In fact, a story is told about the poet in his youth – the sort of story that is always told about genteel poets in their youth – "walking two miles every day at the age of six to a neighbor's house that he might read a translation of Homer." Whether this is true or not, Brownell managed to accommodate both his love for poetry and the demands of the law for some time. Ultimately, however, they proved to be less easily reconciled than the following poem – "A Lawyer's Invocation to Spring" – would seem to suggest:

> Whereas, on certain boughs and sprays,
> Now divers birds are heard to sing,
> And sundry flowers their heads upraise,
> Hail to the coming on of Spring!
> . . . .
> The birds aforesaid – happy pairs! –
> Love, 'mid the aforesaid boughs, inshines
> In freehold nests; themselves, their heirs,
> Administrators, and assigns.

Brownell, himself an heir to a modest inheritance, eventually gave up his career as a lawyer in order to write poetry full-time. His first volume of poems was published in 1847, and another volume followed in 1855. Most of his early poetry, which Daniel Aaron has called "more earnest than artful," is indistinguishable from the poetry of the day. As such, it is largely preoccupied with mortality, loss, and the vanity of human wishes. In addition to these early volumes of poetry, Brownell also wrote popular histories for subscription publishers, such as *The People's Book of Ancient and Modern History* (1851) and *The Discoverers, Pioneers, and Settlers of North and South America* (1853), later reissued as *The New World: Embracing American History* (1856). The latter attempts to account for the triumph of the Anglo-American empire in the New World in contradistinction to the relative "failures" of the Spanish, French, and Dutch. The volume makes for interesting reading, largely due to Brownell's attempt to make a case for the "genius" of Anglo-American political and social institutions in the face of what appeared to be their likely demise just a few years afterwards.

During the 1850s Brownell also published several editorials in the local Hartford newspapers in which he inveighed against slavery. While he was capable of adopting a conciliatory tone toward Southerners, he would have no truck with their peculiar institution and those (North or South) who supported it either by deed or by tacit consent. Given a choice between slavery and the Union, Brownell could contemplate the dissolution of the latter with equanimity: "Time hath its revolutions," he wrote in his history of the New World. "There must be a pe-riod and an end to all temporal things – *finis rerum*. . . . Let the name and dignity of [the United States] stand so long as it pleaseth God." In the midst of war, he subsequently urged his country to finish what it had begun:

> It is now these many years that we have held an uncommonly large Candle . . . to the Devil. It is going out, and the snuff and smoke come under our noses pretty strongly – but he won't let us drop it, as long as a spark remains to light his work withal. Let us bear it as we may, and not make matters worse by trying to puff it alight again.

The poetry that emerged out of this fierce conviction was collected in *Lyrics of a Day* (1864), later expanded as *War Lyrics* (1866). Edmund Wilson dismissed the work as "partisan hatred" filled with "vehement animus," but such criticism does not do justice to the moral and spiritual vision that animated Brownell's best poems. Nor does it do justice to the limited but resolute vision of genteel culture, which served as Brownell's point of departure, and which ultimately gave meaning to an otherwise senseless, grisly conflict. To be sure, this vision can, on occasion, take on a "vehement animus," but that animus is filled less with "partisan hatred" than with legitimate moral outrage. This is particularly evident in Brownell's "Bury Them," a poem that recalls the slaughter of Colonel Robert Gould Shaw and his African-American soldiers at Fort Wagner. "Bury the Dragon's Teeth!" the poem's Confederate speaker begins, "Trample them, clod by clod / . . . [the teeth] that the Monster, Freedom, shed / On the sacred, strong Slave-Sod." But the South's hoped-for liberation from the "Monster Freedom" does not materialize. Instead, the speaker of the poem gives voice to a dark prophecy in which the dragon's teeth yield "a crop of steel . . . / Spike . . . anther, and blade, / . . . from the bloody shade." As the poem continues, the South is forced to confront the nightmarish harvest it has sown:

> There are tassels of blood-red maize –
> How the horrible Harvest grows!
> 'Tis sabres that glint and daze –
> 'Tis bayonets all ablaze
> Uprearing in dreadful rows!

On other occasions, Brownell attempts to contain and spiritualize the conflict within the typology of the church militant – more often than not, in imagery borrowed from the Book of Revelations. "This is not a war of men," Brownell proclaims in "Annus Memorabilis," "but of Angels Good and Ill." Accordingly, the poet's "Apocalyptic Pen" figures the North as an avenging archangel that scourges the sins of "the Serpent and his crew."

It is hard to appreciate the cultural work accomplished by these uncompromising representations of the war. But they played an important role in imbuing the conflict with a potent symbology that helped motivate a dubious populace. When, on occasion, this moral vision is absent in Brownell's work, as it is in "Sumter," the poet succumbs to a mindless cant of his own, thereby allowing us to see what otherwise distinguishes his poetry from the easy patriotism of many of his Unionist contemporaries:

> Forward my hearties!
> Shoulder to shoulder

Sight o'er the trunnion –
  Send home the rammer –
  Linstock and hammer!
Speak for the Union!
  Tones that won't stammer!

At his best, however, Brownell tempers his unswerving moral vision with an awareness of the tremendous human cost of the conflict. This effort results in the elegiac turn of poems like "The Battle Summers" (LOA, 2: 87), which commemorates the Union war dead. The title recalls those fierce and bloody encounters – such as Manassas, Shiloh, Chancellorsville – when the warm weather of summer permitted the stalled military campaigns to resume their carnage in earnest. Here as elsewhere, the same aesthetic limitations prevail. But the poem also possesses a certain stateliness. This is derived, in part, from an elegant modulation of voice that meditates over the accumulating pastoral imagery, which the poem carefully builds up in a slow, unhurried manner. As such, "The Battle Summers" remains one of the more moving elegies of the Civil War – all the more so as it was written in the aftermath of some of the war's bloodiest fighting, during the difficult days of 1863 when, despite recent successes at Vicksburg and Gettysburg, Union skepticism about the conflict had reached its apogee.

The poem begins as a paean to a natural world "touched with autumn's tenderest glow." Brownell describes that world extensively and provides details of various woodland creatures – crows, quail, woodcock, partridge, and a gray squirrel – as they go about the business of "seek[ing] their winter store." Despite the lateness of the season, it is "Indian Summer." And the "dreamy sunshine" of that anomalous weather is filled with the troublesome memories of those "Battle Summers" that disturb the pastoral scene:

The haze of Indian Summer seemed
  Borne from far fields of sulphury breath –
  A subtle atmosphere of death
Was ever round us as we dreamed.

"Et in arcadia ego?" (Have I, too, lived in Arcadia?) Brownell asks in the classic refrain of the pastoral tradition. Following the conventions of that tradition, one would expect Brownell to find a way to transmute death's presence within this pastoral Eden. But the nostalgic, elegizing mode of Brownell's pastoral is troubled by a natural world that seems to resist, if only gently, the bucolic construction the poem's conventions require. Indian summer is, after all, a false summer. And as such, it becomes a figure for nature's doubleness and capricious play. The haze of this false summer is all too reminiscent of the "sulphury breath" of gunpowder and decaying bodies, while the stormy weather mimes the sights and sounds of battle:

The horizon's dim heat-lightning played
  Like small-arms, still, through nights of drouth,
  And the low thunder of the south
Was dull and distant cannonade.

Despite this subtle parody, Brownell eventually finds a way to reconcile nature and human event. "Death," to borrow Wallace Stevens's phrase, becomes "the mother of beauty." The natural world takes "color from the dread Unseen" and weaves a "braver green" and a "lovelier blue" than it could

have achieved on its own. As such, "a fuller life informs the fall" – a fullness that derives from the human events (awful and awesome) that have transpired in nature's midst.

The consolation offered here, however, is not as satisfying as it would appear. "Behold, thy summer days are o'er," the poem's speaker laments, as much for himself as for the dead soldiers. But the end of summer does not engender a corresponding fullness in the speaker. Instead, that fullness parodies the speaker's lack. We do not need to seek far to find the reason for this parody. The speaker stands outside the cycle of nature because he stands outside the cycle of human events as a nonparticipant in the war:

'Twas well to sing by stream and sod
  And they there were that loved thy lays –
  But lo, where, 'neath yon battle-haze,
Thy brothers bare the breast for God!

It may be that Brownell's doubts about his own contribution to the war effort (in comparison to those who "bare[d] the breast for God") have prompted comparable doubts about the capacity of his verse to represent the conflict. Whatever the case, just a few weeks after Brownell penned these lines, the war would give him a radically new poetic opportunity.

The catalyst for this change in fortune was a poem Brownell published several months before, in which he versified Captain David Farragut's orders to his fleet on the eve of the Union's assault on New Orleans. The poem caused a minor stir and led to an exchange of letters between Farragut and Brownell in which the latter expressed his desire to see the war firsthand. Farragut obliged Brownell by securing an appointment for him as his secretary on board his flagship, the *Hartford*. In that capacity, Brownell became legendary for his coolness and fortitude; he often transcribed the events of the battle – sometimes in verse form – in the very midst of the fray. "I did not want any of you picking up my manuscript in case I was shot and saying I was afraid," Brownell is reputed to have said (or so the story goes).

This experience resulted in Brownell's book of war poems, *Lyrics of a Day*, to which the author gave the revealing subtitle *Newspaper-Poetry*. The subtitle intrigues for what it implies about Brownell's intentions, if not his results. For the most part, the poems alternate between Apollo's lyre and the fife and drum. But the journalistic metaphor in his subtitle signals an attempt to find an alternative to these more traditional approaches. On the most basic level, some of these poems qualify as "newspaper poetry" because they were first published in newspapers. In a few cases, moreover, they were the most authoritative account of a particular battle published up to that point. But beyond that, the designation indicates a desire to associate these poems with the ordinary, matter-of-fact accounts found in the daily newspaper. Hence, the poems are, as Brownell tells us forthrightly and without apology in his preface, "trivial . . . ephemeral expressions . . . penned for the most part, on occasion, from day to day, (and often literally *currente calamo* [in the midst of battle])."

The subtitle and preface, however, frame the volume's contents in a misleading manner. At the very least, the closed verse forms deployed in *Lyrics of a Day* militate against the openness implicit in the idea of newspaper poetry. Moreover, few of the poems seem directly concerned with the sort of everyday experience that the title and preface might lead one to expect. As we have seen, they concern themselves more with otherworldly (apocalyptic and pastoral) characterizations of that experience. This contradiction between Brownell's putative intentions for the volume and the poetry it contains, can only be explained by the poet's genuine but misguided attempt to ground a realistic content within the constraints that defined and delimited the genteel conventions of antebellum poetry. The resulting confusion tells us a great deal about the assumptions and expectations associated with these two conflicting modes of representation.

Nowhere is this more evident than in Brownell's response to the events surrounding the Battle of Mobile Bay. The battle was significant because it enabled the North to extend its blockade of the South's seaborne supply lines, and it provided a base of operations for Union incursions into the interior of Alabama. Brownell was not only an eyewitness to this crucial Northern victory, but as Farragut's secretary, he was responsible for furnishing the notes upon which the official report of the battle was based. Thus, he was in a position to record the battle's events firsthand, and one might expect his poem, "The Bay Fight," to reflect this unique opportunity. To some extent it does. As Aaron puts it, "Nothing of importance mentioned in the official report escaped his attention: the deployment of vessels against the forts, the perilous passage through the mine fields and the explosion of the ironclad *Tecumseh*, and the final assault on the monstrous Confederate ram, the *Tennessee*, when 'Half the fleet in an angry ring / Closed round the hideous Thing.'" Despite a general fidelity to the events themselves, however, Brownell's depiction distinctly lacks journalistic realism.

Perhaps the best way to appreciate this is to contrast "The Bay Fight" with another poem inspired by the Battle of Mobile Bay, Melville's "A Utilitarian View of the Monitor's Fight" (LOA, 2: 8). Although the poems share a similar subject matter, each takes a very different tack. For Melville, the war's antipoetic modernity – symbolized by new military technology like the ironclad – precipitates an ominous sea change: the "old display / [of] garniture, emblazonment, / And heraldry" that once characterized the great sea battles like Trafalgar ("The Temeraire" [LOA, 2: 6]) has been transformed into a "Deadlier, closer" encounter in which the theatrics of battle have been reduced to "crank, / Pivot, and screw." In this brave new world, heroism is similarly reduced: the "war-paint shows the streaks of weather" and "warriors / Are now but operatives." The reductive terms upon which navies conduct modern warfare clearly place new demands upon representation as well. Accordingly, Melville casts about for a more muted, "utilitarian" aesthetic:

Plain be the phrase, yet apt the verse,
    More ponderous than nimble;
For since grimed War here laid aside
His orient pomp, 'twould ill befit
        Overmuch to ply
    The rhyme's barbaric cymbal.

In "The Bay Fight," meanwhile, the "painted pomp" of battle continues unabated. Brownell's "warriors" are anything but "operatives," and his approach to the problem of representation is anything but utilitarian. Instead of submitting to the reduced terms of modern warfare (its "crank, / Pivot, and

screw"), Brownell seeks to overcome them by making the Battle of Mobile Bay the equal of Trafalgar. And he gives no hint that he is anything but successful in his designs. Eschewing Melville's utilitarian aesthetic, he plies "rhyme's barbaric cymbal" in the high romantic mode:

Trust me, our berth was hot,
Ah, wickedly well they shot;
How their death-bolts howled and stung!
And their water-batteries played
With their deadly cannonade
Till the air around us rung;
So the battle raged and roared –
Ah, had you been aboard
To have seen the fight we made!

It is hard to believe that, in an age familiar with the candor of Matthew Brady's Civil War photographs, passages like these could have earned Brownell a reputation as a reliable observer of the war. And yet, in review after review, the "Battle Laureate" was celebrated on precisely these grounds. Holmes burbled, for example, "If Drayton had fought at Agincourt . . . if Scott had been in the saddle with Marmion, if Tennyson had charged with the six hundred at Balaklava," they could not have recreated scenes of battle "as faithfully and as fearfully as Mr. Brownell has painted the sea-fights in which he took part as a combatant." More than half a century later that reputation was still intact. No less an authority than the *Cambridge History of American Literature* (1931) would continue to praise Brownell in a similar vein:

His power lay in combining vivid detail with lyric exultation. No other Northern poet reported real warfare so accurately. Some of Brownell's lines read like rhymed journalism, but he had everywhere such intensity of visualization, such fiery passion, and such natural racy language dignified by sincerity that he rarely suffered any descent into prose.

Brownell's poetry, to be sure, exhibits a certain "vivid" quality in its details, which, when combined with the poet's "lyric exultation," can make for exciting reading. But it is hardly "rhymed journalism" (although it occasionally reads like yellow journalism). Brownell's "realism" – if that is the appropriate term – is a rather meager affair. His much-praised attention to the specifics of individual engagements is largely superficial and often consists of an occasional homely reference to the pitch and tar used to caulk the ship in between heroic accounts of battle related in the high romantic mode. Consequently, his realism devolves into nothing more than a form of onomatopoeia in which words like "clinking," "rattling," and "roaring" create an atmospherics of battle, which hides a scandalous lack of substance.

Ironically, much of what Holmes praised in Brownell's "vigorous pictures . . . fresh from the terrible original" was not "fresh" at all. In fact, Brownell wrote many of his battle poems long before he left Connecticut for the front. Indeed, his whole reputation as "battle laureate," as a man intimate with war, rests on no more than five poems written during his nine-month sojourn with Farragut: "Suspiria Ensis" (January 1864), "A War Study" (March 1864), "The River Fight" (March 1864), "Night Quarters" (May 1864), and "The Bay

Fight" (August 1864). Brownell derived his other war poems from newspaper articles or official reports that he versified much the way he did with Farragut's general orders. It is, in fact, impossible to tell the poems Brownell composed in the heat of battle from those he composed after reading newspapers.

It hardly matters. Even on those occasions where Brownell was an "eyewitness" to a particular conflict, he literally could not see it, or at least could not see beyond the theatrics of battle. The romantic conventions in which he imagined the war, together with his own moral absolutism, filtered out much of its real-life significance. This process resulted in a poetry that is anything but a "realistic" account, much less one that satisfies a desire to understand the war's magnitude and complexity.

Brownell was not alone in this conundrum. Nor was he particularly obtuse. He merely remained indebted to genteel poetic conventions that did not allow him to explore the possibilities of realism his firsthand experience had opened up to him. These limitations prevented Brownell from representing certain aspects of the Civil War, but they also enabled him to represent others. What Brownell's poetry lost in realistic representation, it more than made up in its passionate conviction – one that helped frame the issues of the Civil War in such a way that the abolition of slavery eventually became the only alter-native. A generation later, when realism was in its heyday and the typical author was proclaiming his (rarely her) "objectivity," this sort of moral fervor would be looked upon with condescension, if not outright disdain.

JONATHAN VEITCH

Selected Works
Poems, New York: D. Appleton, 1847
Ephemeron, New York: D. Appleton, 1855
Lyrics of a Day: or Newspaper-Poetry, Hartford, Connecticut: Lockwood, 1864
War Lyrics, Boston: Ticknor and Fields, 1866
Lines of Battle and Other Poems, edited by M. A. De Wolfe Howe, Boston: Riverside, 1912

Further Reading
Aaron, Daniel, *The Unwritten War: American Writers and the Civil War*, Oxford: Oxford University Press, 1973; reprinted, Madison: University of Wisconsin Press, 1987
Frederickson, George M., *The Inner Civil War: Northern Intellectuals and the Crisis of the Union*, Urbana: University of Illinois Press, 1993
Wilson, Edmund, *Patriotic Gore*, Boston: Northeastern University Press, 1984

William Cullen Bryant

(1794–1878)

It is difficult today to bear in mind that for a long time Bryant was widely held to be the greatest poet America had yet produced. During his lifetime and for a considerable period after his death, no one could have predicted his eventual critical eclipse by Walt **Whitman** and, of course, by Emily **Dickinson**. Another explanation not so much for the decline of his critical reputation as for the general amnesia about him is that he lacks the badness we sometimes encounter in poets like James Russell **Lowell** and Oliver Wendell **Holmes**; Bryant is forgettable to the extent that he is not egregious. While rarely great, his work is never clumsy, stupid, or crass. One would be hard-pressed to find a single awful line in the entirety of Bryant's oeuvre. Read alongside that of his contemporaries, his work is remarkable for a certain refinement in its diction, its eschewal of bombast and sentimentality, and its mastery of meter and overall poetic craftsmanship. Harold Bloom refers to Bryant as "a superb poet, always and still undervalued," and if he be regarded qua poet, that is to say in the older sense of a maker in words rather than as an inspired genius, this assessment is certainly just. Of poets who write in English, his greatest affinities are with an aspect of William Wordsworth, yet his poems lack the radicalism with which Wordsworth's early work broke with its eighteenth-century predecessors; Bryant's poetry has qualities that seem at times to place him nearer to pre-Romantics such as James Thomson or Thomas Gray. His closest American antecedents are Timothy Dwight and Philip **Freneau**, the latter being by far the happier of the two influences. Whatever interest Bryant now has for us lies largely in his having been an American, so that we can see what an American Wordsworthian looks like and how such a model differs from its British counterparts.

Bryant was born in 1794 in Cummington, Massachusetts, where he spent his boyhood in the rural surroundings of his maternal grandfather's farm. The area was strongly Federalist and Congregational, although his father, Dr. Peter Bryant, had liberal Unitarian leanings that were to impart to his son a life-long progressive and egalitarian bias. Peter Bryant also had an extensive library with whose books his son acquired an early familiarity. He assisted the young poet in translations of Virgil and helped him publish his first poem, an anti-Jeffersonian satire on the shipping embargo, at the age of 14.

Bryant was trained for the law and opened a legal practice in 1815, although he continued to write poetry. In 1817, the *North American Review* published the first version of "Thanatopsis" (LOA, 1: 122), which had been found at his desk in manuscript by his father and submitted to the editors. His reputation was established by this, still his most famous poem, written at the age of 17 and revised several times throughout his life. In 1821, he published his first collection of poems. By 1825, his legal practice was effectively over, and in 1827, he joined the *New York Evening Post*, becoming editor-in-chief and part owner in 1829, a position he would hold until his death in 1878. As the head of the *Evening Post,* he became a powerful and influential player in the public life of his time; Bryant was courted, admired, and reviled by politi-cians including Presidents Andrew Jackson, Abraham Lincoln, and Ulysses S. Grant. At one point he even had to publicly refuse his own Presidential nomination when rumors spread that dissidents of the Grant administration preferred him for their choice of candidate. Flags were flown at half-mast at New York City Hall and Union Square when he died, and huge crowds attended his funeral. He was vehemently and polemically antislavery and pro-Union, but his main legacy as public figure survives in the establishment of Central Park, the idea for which he was largely responsible. His statue stands in Bryant Park behind the New York Public Library.

Bryant was frequently characterized by his contemporaries as cold and unemotional, but this was also a man who once administered the public chastisement of a rival editor with a cowskin whip he had concealed in his hat. His letters to his wife and family show him to have been capable of great warmth and tenderness; something of this depth of feeling can be seen in the love poem to his wife, "'Oh Fairest of the Rural Maids'" (LOA, 1: 132):

> The twilight of the trees and rocks
> Is in the light shade of thy locks;
> Thy step is as the wind, that weaves
> Its playful way among the leaves.

Bryant had a deep appreciation of the visual arts and numbered some of the greatest American painters of his day among his friends, including Thomas **Cole**, with whose work his poems have affinities. The painting *Kindred Spirits* by Asher B. Durand shows Bryant and Cole standing on Table Rock in the Catskills and contemplating the natural beauty of the valley three thousand feet below. As a poet Bryant was admired by Ralph Waldo **Emerson**, Whitman, and Edgar Allan **Poe**, something that may now strike us as unlikely. This perception is a superficial one, however, and by reviewing the remarks of his fellow poets we can recapture qualities of his verse that might otherwise have been lost with the passage of time and with changes in critical climate.

"I found him always original," Emerson wrote, " – a true painter of the face of this country, and of the sentiment of his own people. When I read the verses of popular American and English poets, I often think that they appear to have gone into the art galleries and to have seen pictures of mountains, but this man to have seen mountains. . . . He renders Berkshire to me in verse, with the sober coloring, too, to which my nature cleaves, only now and then permitting herself the scarlet and gold of the prism. It is his proper praise that he first, and he only made known to mankind our northern landscape – its summer splendor, its autumn russets, its winter lights and glooms." Bryant had indeed an eye for naturalistic detail rivaled in America only by Henry David **Thoreau** and in England only by Dorothy Wordsworth. And it is not the least of his distinctions from his British counterparts that this eye was enlisted in the service of describing a new world; historical novelty also allowed him to treat Native American themes, as had been done previously by Freneau and by his contemporary and friend James Fenimore Cooper. Bryant also had a lifelong interest in botany, having early learned the nomenclature of Linnaeus from the books in his father's office, and this interest is exemplified with unusual precision in his poetry. A good example is the opening stanzas of "The Fountain" (LOA, 1: 165):

> . . . There the spice-bush lifts
> Her leafy lances; the viburnum there,
> Paler of foliage, to the sun holds up
> Her circlet of green berries. In and out
> The chipping sparrow, in her coat of brown,
> Steals silently, lest I should mark her nest.

(This botanical specificity may owe something to stanzas 10 through 15 of Freneau's "A Vision" from *The House of Night*.)

Whitman defended Bryant when he was attacked by what the former termed "literary quacks" and wrote that "there will come a time when the writings of this beautiful poet shall attain their proper rank – a rank far higher than has been accorded to them by many accomplished men, who think of them by no means disparagingly." He also called him "one of the best poets in the world." Obscured though they may be by surface differences, there actually are some affinities between Bryant's and Whitman's poems. One might detect a model for the Whitmanian catalog in the lines of "Thanatopsis" that enumerate the "decorations all / Of the great tomb of man" and that list the different sorts of people who "shall come, / And make their bed with thee." Like Whitman, Bryant often took as his theme the westward expansion of the American people. In the poem "Hymn to the City," he elaborated the idea that evidence of the Deity is present in urban crowds as well as in rural scenes, an idea that, although atypical of Bryant, was expanded upon in numerous poems by Whitman, such as "Crossing Brooklyn Ferry" (LOA, 1: 864). There are also parallels between the two poets in both their political tendencies and their commitment to journalism.

Poe, always the technician, had great admiration for Bryant as a craftsman and defended his use of the trisyllabic foot and his occasional substitution of a trochaic foot for an iambic one. He called Bryant the first poet of America, as well as a poet of "uncommon strength and genius." In spite of this high praise, he felt Bryant fell short of the genius of the British poets Percy Bysshe Shelley, Samuel Taylor Coleridge, Wordsworth, and John Keats. As an American working within a tradition established by the English Romantics, it is easy to see why Poe would have both a sympathy for and an interest in Bryant's work, although Poe is closer in sensibility to Coleridge and Lord Byron than he is to Wordsworth and may have felt Bryant's poetry was lacking both Coleridgean phantasmagoria and Byronic élan. We nevertheless see him appreciative of Bryant's feel for narrative, a quality of his verse that usually goes unremarked.

It is in some ways unfortunate that Bryant is still best known for "Thanatopsis," for it is far from being his best poem. A certain decorous stiffness make it seem to be struggling unsuccessfully to free itself from neoclassical constraints, and there is a kind of heavy-handedness as well as superficiality to its consolations, as if the poet's point of departure had been Wordsworth's old age rather than his youth. It nevertheless seems that, despite unmistakable echoes from Robert Blair and Gray, the strongest precursor poem, here as throughout

Bryant's canon, is Wordsworth's "Tintern Abbey." Bryant was to rewrite "Thanatopsis" in various poems throughout his life and with greater poetic success, yet it is the rhythm, tonality, and thematic of "Tintern Abbey" that we keep hearing throughout his poetry, even as late as "The Night Journey of a River" (LOA, 1: 169), where the sounds of an American river substitute for the murmuring of the river Wye.

A look at the relationship between the Wordsworth and Bryant poems reveals those essential differences and similarities that illuminate Bryant's entire poetic output. We could begin by observing that "Thanatopsis" has both a greater and a lesser degree of seclusion, depending on how we view this term. For Wordsworth the past involves a recollection of his own past selves; for Bryant the past is basically a matter of the transitory ages of humankind, of great but fleeting epochs of history, with all their ceremonial pomp and splendor. Already at 17, there seems to be little or no distance between the public and private Bryant; hence we get almost no sense of a particular individual speaking. Bryant had neither the talent nor the inclination for self-dramatization; this becomes even clearer when we consider a poem like "The Ages" (LOA, 1: 133). Parts of this poem evidently owe something to "Childe Harold's Pilgrimage," but we feel an keen absence of dramatic persona in the contrast between Bryant and Byron. "Thanatopsis" serves to ameliorate a condition – mortality – that all humans share, while "Tintern Abbey," though taken up with a concern many will recognize, is really about Wordsworth's own very personal relationship with nature. There is an epiphanic quality to this interaction; we can really believe that Wordsworth has "felt / A presence that disturbs me with the joy / Of elevated thoughts." Bryant lacks this quality; nature may provide access to a moral insight but never to a cosmic experience. While "Tintern Abbey" culminates in the poet's turning to his sister Dorothy, whom he addresses directly and passionately ("My dear, dear Friend"), in "Thanatopsis" it is "no friend" who will "Take note of thy departure." Rather than by a single companion, the seclusion in "Thanatopsis" is relieved by the company of "the wise, the good" with whom the reader shall lie down at life's close. Wordsworth also invokes "a good man's life," but the reference is to a living man and the part nature plays in urging that man to "little, nameless, unremembered, acts / Of kindness and of love." It is as if Bryant's far-reaching magnanimity toward humanity in general substitutes imperfectly for an inability to achieve one-on-one rapport.

Bryant's concern with the passing of ages and civilizations is probably due in part to the influence of Timothy Dwight, and there are clear analogies in the paintings of Thomas Cole, especially in the *Course of Empire* series. Harold Bloom has pointed to Bryant's frequent use of the word "wild" – or variations thereon, as in the line from the poem to Cole (LOA, 1: 160): "But keep that earlier, wilder image bright" – as evidence of his distinctive Americanness, but if "Tintern Abbey," which uses the word five times, is the precursor poem I take it to be, one might just as easily point to it as a source. It is true that the word occurs again and again throughout Bryant's verse, and perhaps it would be accurate to say that, seeing the new world through a Wordsworthian lens, he was naturally led to emphasize those aspects of his native environment that lent themselves to Wordsworthian treatment. Here we should pause and consider Bryant's own account of his first scene of instruction when he discovered Wordsworth and Coleridge's *Lyrical Ballads* in 1815. He told Richard Henry **Dana** that, upon opening the book, "a thousand springs seemed to gush up into his heart, and the face of Nature, of a sudden, to change into a strange freshness and life."

Nature as consolation – this is the theme Bryant borrows from Wordsworth repeatedly. And yet he lacks Wordsworth's philosophical depth. One way of pinpointing the difference would be to say that Bryant did not have a Coleridgean bone in his body, but this would not be entirely accurate, for we occasionally see him venturing upon phantasmagoria, especially in his narrative poems. This is an aspect of his work that may owe as much to Freneau as it does to Coleridge. As Bryant's work develops from "Thanatopsis" on, we see it gaining in vividness, specificity, and force.

"The Ages" is a panoramic treatment of the coming and going of civilizations. In this poem, Bryant takes a certain pride in the wildness and savagery of the new world as opposed to the more structured world of Europe; America is the place where "The savage urged his skiff like wild bird on the wing." The coming of the European settlers heralds the rise of freedom.

> Here the free spirit of mankind, at length,
> Throws its last fetters off; and who shall place
> A limit to the giant's unchained strength,
> Or curb his swiftness in the forward race?
> Far, like the comet's way through infinite space,
> Stretches the long untravelled path of light
> Into the depths of ages: we may trace,
> Distant, the brightening glory of its flight,
> Till the receding rays are lost to human sight.

America is compared favorably to Europe, which is still "given a prey to sterner fates, / And writhes in shackles." The new world is a beacon to other countries in their struggle for liberty.

In "Inscription for the Entrance to a Wood" (LOA, 1: 126), we have a reference to the Fall and the exemption of nature from this fall in "The primal curse / Fell, it is true, upon the unsinning earth, / But not in vengeance." Bryant is not ready to dispense with the Fall, like Emerson, but he rejects the doctrine of apocatastasis (i.e., that nature is involved in the Fall and stands, like humanity, in need of divine restitution) embraced by Milton and Blake. It would be interesting to speculate to what extent Bryant was both bound to and in conflict with the Calvinism of the region of his childhood. In Bryant's poetry, while nature has the power to console, there are limits to its capacity to transform; there seems to be little danger of the poet's ever becoming an Emersonian transparent eyeball. But we can see already in this poem, with its minute naturalistic detail, the great strides taken away from the abstractness and generality of "Thanatopsis." There is no "Presence" in these woods, but there *are* birds, squirrels, insects, and winds. Nature is never as problematic for Bryant as it is for Wordsworth; in place of ontology we get loving attention to detail.

"To a Waterfowl" (LOA, 1: 125) amounts to a simple declaration of faith in the rightness of the power that guides bird and human alike. "Green River" (LOA, 1: 127) has some of the simple decorum one associates with Thomson; at times it has, like "The Rivulet" (LOA, 1: 143), a seeming naïveté reminiscent of Clare. But the last two lines, especially, echo "Tintern Abbey": "An image of that calm life appears, / That won my heart in my greener years." There are even clearer echoes of "Tintern Abbey" in "A Winter Piece" (LOA, 1: 129), which is a more personal poem than "Thanatopsis" and exhibits some of Bryant's fine gift for naturalistic description. A slight tone of regret seems to characterize the opening lines, as the poet recalls a time when these "wild solitudes" "were trod by me / Oftener than now." Yet this tone of mourning for the passing of a lost self more attuned to nature is never really developed; the poem goes on to describe the beauty of the woods in winter and finally both invites and commands the reader to participate in the scenes it renders.

The memory of past selves – as well as the anticipation of future ones – is treated in "The Rivulet," but it is only "the world" that "wears no more / The coloring of romance it wore"; nature has kept faith in the form of the rivulet that "changest not." The concern with past and future selves does not prevent the poet from taking up his by now familiar theme of the passing of the ages. "Summer Wind" (LOA, 1: 146) is interesting in that it has no moral to impart: it is sufficient at this point for Bryant to engage in pure description. As if to atone for this absence of moral edification, "After a Tempest" (LOA, 1: 149), published three months after "Summer Wind," is a particularly emphatic presentation of nature as emblem of progress and peace. A polarity we see again and again in Bryant is that between nature and human ambition. "Autumn Woods" (LOA, 1: 151) is an especially eloquent example. The sonnets to the seasons, such as "October" (LOA, 1: 159) and "November" (LOA, 1: 153), show his skill at fleshing out ready-made themes.

"I Cannot Forget With What Fervid Devotion" (LOA, 1: 124) mourns the loss of sympathy with nature and to that extent echoes "Tintern Abbey." But this loss is attributed to the poet's having "mixed with the world," whereas Wordsworth is sustained while pent "in lonely rooms, and 'mid the din / Of towns and cities" by his memories of natural beauty. "The Damsel of Peru" (LOA, 1: 159) exhibits Bryant's talent for narrative; its rhythms suggest the "wilder rhyme" and "livelier note" of the damsel's song. In "The Conjunction of Jupiter and Venus" (LOA, 1: 156), he becomes an outspoken apologist for Romanticism as he makes the case for the spirit's needing "Impulses from a deeper source" than reason. Yet, significantly, reason is not surrendered in the contest between it and these impulses: "She should be my counsellor, / But not my tyrant." Reason is still a force, and the neoclassical pressure, somehow always more palpable in Bryant than in (early) Wordsworth, can be felt in the poem's title and in the characterization of the stars as "Emblems of Power and Beauty!" But "Tintern Abbey" is still being echoed in "And there are motions, in the mind of man: / That she must look upon with awe" (compare "and in the mind of man / A motion and a spirit"). The progress of American freedom and westward expansion, and the idea of America as a harbinger of European freedom, are also themes that distinguish this poem from anything a British Wordsworthian might produce. "To an American Painter Departing for Europe" (LOA, 1: 160) continues to contrast America favorably with Europe in its previously noted depiction of the vision of the new world as "earlier" and "wilder." This is a familiar theme in early American poetry, going back at least as far as Anne Bradstreet's "A Dialogue Between Old England and New."

Freneau's influence can be seen in this aspect of Bryant's work; we occasionally notice more subtle shades of this influence, as in "To the Fringed Gentian" (LOA, 1: 161), which seems to descend fairly directly from "The Wild Honey Suckle." (Harold Bloom has traced this lineage further, from Bryant to Dickinson all the way to Hart Crane.) Bryant also takes up Freneau's handling of Native American themes with considerable success; a poem like Freneau's "The Indian Burying Ground" with its vivid imagery and anthropological verisimilitude can be seen to have had a beneficial impact on the battle sequence in Bryant's "The Fountain." Like his friend James Fenimore Cooper and like many early American authors, including the Gothic novelist Charles Brockden Brown, Bryant was concerned that American literature distinguish itself by its choice of authentically American subject matter; this led naturally to literary treatment of the Indian. Although Cooper's *The Last of the Mohicans* and Henry Wadsworth **Longfellow's** *Hiawatha* (see LOA, 1: 399) are better known, Bryant's numerous poems about America's aboriginal people, such as "The Indian Girl's Lament" and "An Indian at the Burying-Place of His Fathers" (LOA, 1: 147), are well worth reading. Bryant's interest in Indians was an early preoccupation, and he returned to it in his old age with "Tree-Burial" and "A Legend of the Delawares." In "The Prairies" (LOA, 1: 162), the Indian is mentioned as part of the larger panoramic sweep, but the word "wilder" reminds us that it is the new world versus the old that is being sung. The poem ends on a note of seclusion deeper than that of any other poem by Bryant.

"The Painted Cup" (LOA, 1: 168) is another poem that wishes to underscore the differences between new world and old. This work even seems to anticipate the antipoetics of William Carlos Williams in such lines as: "Call not up, / Amid this fresh and virgin solitude, / The faded fancies of an elder world." The reader, if a poet, is told to eschew the claim that the flowers of the poem's title "were tinted thus / To hold the dew for fairies." Botanical specificity is preferable to a neo-Elizabethan dreamscape. Bryant's love of botany is also evident in "The Fountain," a poem that treats of the Indians and the passing of ages with a violence unusual for Bryant and indeed for any other poet of the period. "The Constellations" (LOA, 1: 172), like "The Conjunction of Jupiter and Venus," has both neoclassical *and* Romantic qualities. A late poem, it returns to the coming and going of the good and the great with which the poet began in "Thanatopsis."

Bryant, like Longfellow, had a considerable flair for languages and traveled extensively in Europe, learning the language of each country he visited. He did regular translations from Provençal, Spanish, Portuguese, Italian, and German. Toward the end of his life he translated *The Iliad* and *The Odyssey*. Some of his reverence for great poetry in a language not his own is captured in "Dante" (LOA, 1: 174; Longfellow, another conduit for European literature, translated Michelangelo's sonnet of the same title). "Oh Fairest of the Rural Maids," the love poem to his wife, was held in great esteem by Poe, who called it "a gem, of which we cannot sufficiently express our admiration." Poe went on to say that a "rich simplicity is a main feature in this poem" and that the "original conception is of the very loftiest order of true Poesy." Poe based this second opinion on Bryant's having made the poem's heroine imbibe "in her physical as well as moral being, the

traits, the very features of the delicious scenery around her" rather than simply drawing analogies between her and her rural surroundings.

More than with most poets, appreciation of Bryant entails appreciation of the milieu from which he arose. While death in this milieu was not seen as the unspeakable obscenity that it is today, it was not something to be fully encountered and grappled with as it was in the age of Shakespeare and Donne. Thus, while we hear echoes of Hamlet's famous soliloquy ("For who would bear the whips and scorns of time") in "Tintern Abbey" –

> that neither evil tongues,
> Rash judgements, nor the sneers of selfish men,
> Nor greetings where no kindness is, nor all
> The dreary intercourse of daily life

– and while "Tintern Abbey" resounds all through Bryant's work, neither Bryant nor Wordsworth would follow Hamlet's train of thought to deeply explore "The undiscover'd country, from whose bourn / No traveler returns." With Bryant especially one feels that the subject is broached only to be dropped before the reader really grasps how little consolation it is, after all, to be told that he will "lie down / With patriarchs of the infant world – with kings, / The powerful of the earth – the wise, the good. . . ." Indeed, the whole notion of the vocation of poetry as primarily one of consolation comes out of a society with little time or interest left for the more profound capabilities of poetry, and those poets who refused to console (or merely to console) – Poe, Whitman, Dickinson – suffered the consequences of relative obscurity or poverty.

Bryant had, as Roy Harvey Pearce has written, a "patriarchal significance for the Fireside Poets" – Longfellow, Lowell, Holmes, John Greenleaf **Whittier**. Pearce goes on to observe: "Elite art of the past, as it were, reaches out to us and pulls us back (if we know how to be pulled) into its historical ambiance, judges us and so teaches us how to judge ourselves; whereas we must reach back to popular art and reconstruct its ambiance so as to take the art as seriously as it deserves, only then to appreciate and judge it." This was an ambiance in which a special conception of wildness coexisted with a special kind of gentility; we must be open to both to receive what Bryant has to offer.

Bryant's treatment of nature is similar to his treatment of death in being ultimately unsatisfying for those with some awareness of the full range of poetic possibility. His belief in the correspondences between the moral and natural orders is so unproblematic as to be drearily predictable. There is nothing of the conflict between imagination and nature that we find in Wordsworth, or of Emerson's cataclysmic absorption in nature. Typically, Bryant observes some natural fact and then goes on to draw from it a conclusion in the form of some safe and reassuring homily: from the waterfowl he learns that the same force that guides its flight will lead him safely through life; from the fringed gentian he learns the value of hope as life draws to its close. There are no hard lessons here, either in the sense of hard to learn or hard to bear, for to teach such lessons would be to violate what Bryant may have perceived as the unwritten contract between poet and reader: between a wise parent and a frightened child in need of comfort. As with Longfellow, Bryant's Unitarian sympathies had a softening effect on his religious outlook, and another source of potentially fructifying poetic conflict, the differences between the residual Calvinism of his boyhood surroundings and the more liberal views of his father, are diffused in a rational and optimistic orthodoxy so general as to preclude any trace of religious tension. He is neither as radical as Emerson nor as Bible-haunted as Dickinson.

Yet in the little-known poem "Rizpah," we catch a glimpse of the road not taken by Bryant, which could have conceivably led to the emergence of a very different poet, one perhaps more congenial to the modern temperament. The poem was not liked in its own day (Poe wrote that "we like it less than any poem yet mentioned"), nor is it much appreciated in ours (biographer Charles H. Brown writes that "'Rizpah' is not one of Bryant's better poems"), but it has a kind of sparse toughness that bears comparison with late Yeats.

The poem is prefaced with a quotation from II Samuel that recounts the story of Rizpah's grieving for her sons, who had been handed over to the Gibeonites to be hanged as recompense for Saul's blood guilt. A concubine of Saul's who is stolen by Abner, Rizpah is mentioned somewhat parenthetically, and her grief can only be inferred from her actions. From a perspective like that of Vico, we might say Bryant is retelling a story from the theocratic age in terms of the democratic age; one of the little people, previously in the shadow of the heroic figures surrounding her, is here foregrounded, allowed to have a voice for the first time:

> I have wept till I could not weep, and the pain
> Of the burning eyeballs went to my brain.
>   Seven blackened corpses before me lie,
>   In the blaze of the sun and the winds of the sky.
>   I have watched them through the burning day,
>   And driven the vulture and raven away;
>   And the cormorant wheeled in circles round,
>   Yet feared to alight on the guarded ground.

This is the poet who took a cowskin whip to his enemy, the man who was a fierce opponent of slavery, and the voice which had to be repressed in order for the genteel patriarch of the fireside poets to emerge. A more atypical Bryant poem would be hard to find, yet its choice of biblical subject matter and, to some extent, its form go back even earlier than "Thanatopsis," to the period before his tenth birthday and to the earliest verse he is known to have written, an 88-line paraphrase of the first chapter of the Book of Job. This was a time when Bryant was more affected by the hymns of Isaac Watts and the sermons heard in a rural church than by his father's taste for Horace and Pope or by his own later discovery of Wordsworth and Coleridge. Something primal and untainted is visible in these lines; perhaps they afford access to the real individual simmering beneath the public persona.

Bryant is important for having set the tone of all subsequent American poetry, which, despite the manifestos of Pound and his followers, is and probably always will be fundamentally in the Romantic tradition. One should recall that at the time Bryant first wrote, neoclassicism was the reigning taste; its practitioners enjoyed a hegemony not unlike that of the practitioners of free verse in our own day. His friends Richard Henry Dana and Willard Phillips were thrown out of the *North American Review* for defending those "perverters of litera-

ture," the Lake School of English poets. By bending the Wordsworthian style to his own needs and making it respectable, Bryant had an incalculable influence in shaping the further course of American poetry. Bryant is fortunate in having a thorough, sympathetic, and exemplary biographer in Charles H. Brown. Much critical work remains to be done, however, especially regarding the religious and philosophical subtleties of the poetry as they reflect nineteenth-century American society as a whole.

PAUL BRAY

Selected Works

Poems, Cambridge, Massachusetts: Hilliard and Metcalf, 1821

Poems, New York: Elam Bliss, 1832; revised editions through 1871

The Fountain and Other Poems, New York: Wiley and Putnam, 1842

The White-Footed Deer and Other Poems, New York: I. S. Platt, 1844

Thirty Poems, New York: D. Appleton, 1864

Hymns, n.p.: n.p., 1864

Poems, New York: D. Appleton, 1876

The Poetical Works of William Cullen Bryant, edited by Parke Godwin, 2 vols., New York: D. Appleton, 1883; reprinted, Russell and Russell, 1967

The Letters of William Cullen Bryant, edited by William Cullen Bryant II and Thomas G. Voss, vol. 1: 1809–1836, New York: Fordham University Press, 1975

Further Reading

Allen, Gay Wilson, *American Prosody*, New York: American Book, 1935

Arms, George W., *The Fields Were Green*, Stanford, California: Stanford University Press, 1953

Bloom, Harold, *The Ringers in the Tower*, Chicago: University of Chicago Press, 1971

Brodwin, Stanley, et al., eds., *William Cullen Bryant and His America*, New York: AMS, 1983

Brown, Charles H., *William Cullen Bryant*, New York: Scribner's, 1971

Buell, Lawrence, *New England Literary Culture: From Revolution Through Renaissance*, Cambridge: Cambridge University Press, 1986

Callow, James T., *Kindred Spirits: Knickerbocker Writers and American Artists, 1807–1855*, Chapel Hill: University of North Carolina Press, 1967

Johnson, Curtiss S., *Politics and a Belly-Full*, New York: Vantage, 1962

Krapf, Norbert, ed., *Under Open Sky: Poets on William Cullen Bryant*, New York: Fordham University Press, 1986

McLean, Albert F., Jr., *William Cullen Bryant*, New York: Twayne, 1964

Pearce, Roy Harvey, *The Continuity of American Poetry*, Princeton, New Jersey: Princeton University Press, 1961

Ringe, Donald A., *The Pictorial Mode: Space and Time in the Art of Bryant, Irving and Cooper*, Lexington: University Press of Kentucky, 1971

Josiah D. Canning

(1816–1892)

Josiah Canning was born Josiah Dean Cannon on August 31, 1816, in Gill, Massachusetts, the third of five sons of the Reverend Josiah Weeks Cannon and Almira Smith Cannon. Josiah Weeks Cannon, a native of New Braintree, Massachusetts, graduated from Williams College in Williamstown, Massachusetts in 1803 and was called to pastor the First Congregational Church of Gill in June 1806. Owing to conflicts within the parish, he resigned from the pastorate in 1827. For five years afterward, he taught at his alma mater, then at Canajoharie, New York. Cannon returned to Gill in 1832, where he preached at the Congregational church from 1832 until he was officially resettled in 1839. According to Josiah Gilbert **Holland**, the elder Canning (the name was changed in 1831) was "a fine scholar, and, in former years, was accustomed to have his study filled with young men fitting for college, or the various professions, many of whom have risen to eminence." His own sons, at least the younger four, were among them.

Josiah D. Canning was educated first in the Gill public schools and then by his father. Although his older brothers, Ebenezer and Edward, benefited from a Williams College education, Josiah did not, but letters written by his father to Ebenezer at Williams in 1826 indicate that Josiah was "making some proficiency in English grammar" and making "Latin Grammar his evening study." Josiah also took an early interest in American antiquities and natural history, subjects that would occupy him, and his poetry, for the rest of his life.

At 15, Canning built a printing press and made his first attempt to record local history in a weekly newspaper, the *Village Post*, beginning in May 1831. The miniature sheet – four pages' worth – was sold to subscribers at the rate of five cents for six months. The first issue featured on its front page "The Execution of the Pirates," which Canning took from a New York City paper, with a hand-drawn illustration of the hanging tipped in. The second number, in a column headed "Foreign News," featured a similarly gruesome front-page story: the murder of seven inhabitants of Lisbon by the tyrant Don Miguel, complete with an account of their death throes. News of insurrections in Poland and Ireland, the wreck of the steamboat *Washington*, a riot in Providence, the food eaten by Arabs, and the bizarre death of a child struck by an eagle bearing a sickle all filled the tiny pages of the *Village Post* for its first six months.

The first series ceased in October 1831, but a new series in a larger octavo format began in May 1833. Canning adopted as the paper's slogan "The Tyrant's Foe, the People's Friend." The new series reflected many of the same interests: travel, foreign news, and local items. But increased space gave Canning the opportunity to include more poetry (at least one column of text was devoted to poetry in each issue); "original communications" from readers on various subjects including weather and crops, the origin and purpose of the decimal point, and the education of women; excerpts taken from newspapers like the *Nantucket Inquirer* and journals like the *Edinburgh Review*; and selections from books like Richard Lander's *Travels in Africa* and John D. Godman's *American Natural History*. The poetry selections give some clues about Canning's literary influences and tastes. Brief poems by Lord Byron, James Thomson, William Collins, Robert Burns, Thomas Moore, and Felicia Hemans were reprinted, alongside original poetry written by Josiah Canning and his brothers.

In April 1834, Canning took out the following advertisement in the *Post*: "The subscriber intending to leave New England for the Far West, earnestly requests All Persons indebted to him for papers, printing, or advertising, to make immediate payment – before the 1st of May." In the paper's final number, on April 29, 1834, Canning published an original poem, "The Village Post's Finale," which bid farewell to his "good patrons" in 76 lines of blank verse. After first commenting on the quick passage of time, he thanked subscribers for supporting his "youthful enterprise" and the "Press" more generally, "without whose 'Light' / The world were dark, tho' thousand suns should blaze." Canning expressed his gratitude for their tolerance and hoped that, in spite of its faults, his work may have done some "partial good" by rescuing "from oblivion / The passing tidings of the time." But humility did not prevent him from beseeching his subscribers to pay up on their debts so that he could finance his travels:

> To our list we look
> For the good wherewithal to jog us on.
> Against each name we wish anon to write
> That honest word and welcome – 'PAID.' Our thanks
> To those ere this who have remembered us,
> Would that a few more might remember – then
> The POST should 'post' its book with joy, and die
> Without a debt to call its spirit back.

Whether or not his subscribers settled their debts, Canning traveled to Detroit that spring to join his brother Ebenezer on the staff of the *Detroit Courier* as a journeyman printer (beginning in June 1834). Only two months after his arrival, however, a cholera epidemic ravaged Detroit, claiming Ebenezer's life in early August despite Josiah's diligent nursing.

A week later, Canning traveled home to Gill, noting in his journal that the steam packet on which he traveled and all the ports at which it stopped along the Erie Canal had been affected by cholera. In October, Canning again found work as a journeyman printer at the *Franklin Mercury* in neighboring Greenfield. He remained there several months, but when invited to enter into a partnership, buy out the paper, and "publish a sheet upon our own responsibility," he rejected the offer, "being young & desirous of seeing more of the world – and lastly not wholly decided in continuing a printer." An opportunity to see more of the world came in the form of an invitation to work at the *Gazette* in Wheeling, Virginia (now West Virginia), where his brother Edward was teaching at the Wheeling Institute. Canning arrived in September 1835, and began work as a foreman. Publishing a triweekly and a weekly version of the paper made for a heavy workload, and Canning began to dream of other pursuits: "My labors were constant and irksome, but I found it of little use to complain or be down-hearted: so I looked ahead to the time when, perhaps, I should have done with printing offices, and be settled upon a pretty, fertile farm." Yet Canning was successful at printing, and when the paper was sold, the new owner appointed him foreman over three journeymen and "three or four boys": "His reason for so doing was, the good report he had received of me during my stay with Mr. D [Davis, the original owner]. I considered myself perfect in all branches of my calling; and took the responsibility of executing all fine jobs; and superintending the mechanical, &c. appearance of the paper." Upon returning from the Wisconsin Territory, Davis invited Canning to join him as the government printer for the territory. Eager to leave Wheeling, Canning made the long journey with Davis in the fall of 1837, only to return to Gill the following year when printing equipment and supplies failed to arrive.

There Canning turned to farming. At this time, farming was still the major occupation in the Connecticut River Valley, although light industry was developing: sawmills, a pail factory, a cotton batting factory, manufacturers of cutlery, doeskins, and baby carriages, and a mill where "female industry" turned out 36,000 palm leaf hats annually. But Canning felt called to the land, and thus began his relationship with the storied landscape and his chosen persona as a versifying plowman. In 1838, *Poems* was published by Phelps & Ingersoll, printers in Greenfield, and Canning's introduction to this volume spoke of the pastoral origins of his poetry: "my muse sprang from the green turf, and is clad in the rustic garb of the plough." Above all he presented himself as simple, sincere, and honest: "mine is an oaten reed. – I have blown thereon the artless airs of simplicity." The collection is permeated by a love for New England, particularly for the landscape and his town, which he celebrates in "The Return," "Autumn," "Massachusetts," and "Apostrophe to New-England." Canning also took up the patriotism of his maternal grandfather, Revolutionary War soldier Ebenezer Smith, in "Elegy." His travels inspired some poems, including "The Wisconsin Moon," "Farewell to the Valley!" and "Lines written beneath an Indian moon west of the Mississippi." The collection clearly demonstrates his reading of Burns, Ossian, and James Beattie. In the "Vision of Poesy," he describes a dream in which the muse calls him to be the poet of New England; this poem also makes explicit his kinship with Burns, "Scotia's ancient bard."

The publication of *Poems* brought Canning his first national recognition when Louis Gaylord Clark of the *Knickerbocker* announced in the "Editor's Table": "Make way, . . . ye intellectual dapperlings, and literary exquisites, who beat the coverts of the imagination for hard-wrought similes, make way for a farmer's boy, from a sequestered vale of the Connecticut, who draws his figures from ever-glorious nature!" From this moment Canning's identity as the "Peasant Bard," as Clark later called him, was sealed. Clark quoted an introductory letter from Canning and then concluded, "Verily, MAGA [in this case, the *Knickerbocker*] shall go 'sans charge' to the writer, for many a long year; and although we are compelled, from the use we have made of his letter, to suppress his name, it will yet be made widely known to the American public, through these pages, or we are no literary seer." Indeed, over the next decade and a half, the *Knickerbocker* published several of Canning's poems and noticed two more volumes of his poetry, *Thanksgiving Eve* (1847) and *The Harp and Plow* (1852).

The poem Canning appended to his first letter to "Old Knick" was entitled "Lament of the Cherokee"; it was intended to be sung to the tune, appropriately enough, of "Exile of Erin." The poem was prompted by the removal by U.S. troops of the Cherokee nation from their land in Georgia to the Oklahoma Territory. The forced march along the Trail of Tears was begun in the summer of 1838. In the poem, Canning speaks for the Cherokee who is preparing to leave his homeland:

> Can a tree that is torn from its root by the fountain,
>   The pride of the valley, green-spreading and fair,
> Can it flourish, removed to the rock of the mountain,
>   Unwarmed by the sun, and unwatered by care?

The spiritual tie that links the Cherokee to the land of his ancestors is made clear in the natural images Canning chooses: the Cherokee is like a tree, his homeland a fertile and nourishing place. The distant land is a desert, not only because it is dry and desolate, but also because the speaker has no ancient ties to it. The white man's God and also the "Great Spirit of Good" seem to have abandoned the Cherokee:

> O'er the ruins of home, o'er my heart's desolation,
>   No more shalt thou hear my unblest lamentation;
> For death's dark encounter I make preparation,
>   He hears the last groan of the wild Cherokee!

Canning had been interested in Indian activities all his life and was steeped in the lore of Indian raids and massacres of the Connecticut River Valley. The area around Greenfield was the site of two famous Indian battles: the Turners Falls Fight during King Philip's War in 1676 and the Battle of Bloody Brook in 1704. Josiah Holland notes that Gill was renowned for Indian relics, which farmers regularly turned up in their fields. But Canning's travels to Detroit in 1834 had developed his interests more fully. His journal records his impressions of Indian encounters on the shores of Lake Erie in Michigan: "A tribe of Potawatamic Indians were holding a *powwow* there, beneath a long tent. . . . At Detroit I saw hundreds of the 'red brothers' who came in after their government presents. I took much interest in them, being a particular friend of the 'poor Indian.'" Later, as he traveled to Wheeling in 1835, he again wrote of his feelings toward Native Americans:

> One moonlit night in particular, the canal lay close to the waters of the Susquehanna studded with numerous woody islets. My busy imagination pictured the red native dipping the 'feathery oar,' or the yellow light of his council fire gleaming on the opposite shore – and I thought of the justness of his struggle to maintain a home so clearly romantic, so nobly grand, – the home of his fathers, the resting place of their ashes. But where, reasoned I, is he now? The long canal and the labors of art contrast strangely with the lone stream, butting crag, and primeval forest upon whose wild solitudes they are intruding. The red man is not here! – The blighting ruin of [extremity] has swept over him, and he has departed like the sere and rusty leaf!

"The Indian Gone!" (LOA, 1: 658), published in the 1838 *Poems*, captures much of the spirit of this passage. Under a brilliant moon that seems to be shining for a native hunter to string his bow, the poet is made aware of the Indians' disappearance, and he wonders where they have gone. While wandering along a riverbank, thinking about the ancient rituals that had taken place there, he hears "a mournful voice deplore / The perfidy that slew his race." The poet then tells of finding an Indian relic while plowing his field, realizing that someone's hands had made it long ago and again wondering where that race has gone. In the final stanza, while the poet pursues pheasants in the woods and hears the rustling of dead leaves, Nature itself answers his query with "a wailing funeral cry, / For Nature mourned her children dear."

The poet never tells us nature's "answer": we don't discover where the Indian has gone. We only know that he has disappeared, conspicuous by his absence – under the moon, along the shore, in the woods – and by what he has left behind, "a relic of the chase," dug up by a plow. This general sense of loss pervades Canning's poems about Native Americans, as does his sympathetic view of their plight and his acknowledgment of "the perfidy that slew [their] race." He thus participated fully in the nineteenth-century romanticization of the Indians, but he also managed to give the Native Americans he romanticizes an identity of their own; they are human beings, not merely savage foils to white people's humanity. Canning's poems about the native inhabitants of the land to which he himself was deeply attached were attempts to rescue the past from oblivion, as was his collecting of Native American artifacts and stories about the region.

In his later life, these interests found a natural outgrowth in the Pocumtuck Valley Memorial Association, an organization founded in 1870 for commemorating those who died in the Bloody Brook massacre of 1704 and "for collecting and preserving such memorials, books, papers and curiosities, as may tend to illustrate and perpetuate the history of the early settlers of this region, and of the race which vanished before them" (the association's library, at Historic Deerfield, also holds the Canning family papers). Canning served as the organization's vice president for its first year, and served it in other capacities for several years afterward. PVMA meetings also provided occasions for Canning's verse: "Here, on this storied shore," later published in *Connecticut River Reeds*, was read there at the bicentennial celebration of the Turners Falls Fight of 1676; "None may the future read correctly" was written for the annual meeting in 1881; and "To-day is all that we can call our own" was written for an 1891 field meeting. Each of these poems expressed Canning's antiquarianism, which by the time he had reached middle age had become dark, almost despairing. Not only had the native inhabitants passed away, but the agricultural way of life was in danger of disappearing, too. To navigate the future properly, he wrote, meant to "fix the Present and restore the Past" – an expression of the mission of the PVMA. But Canning's ambivalence about the present creeps in at the conclusion of "None may the future read correctly":

> Has our fond regard
> For human progress warped our mental view
> Of the great Future? Can it come to pass
> That when a few more wonders of our time,
> Marvels of science and of art, are found,
> Till we become as gods in knowledges, –
> A mighty, jealous power shall supervene,
> Revulsion, revolution dire occur;
> Forgetfulness, impenetrable gloom,
> Blotting the brilliant science of the age,
> Shall fall on man and cast his status back
> To Babel's lost, disintegrated base?

Canning here expresses concern not about the disappearance of Native Americans and their history, but about the ultimate outcome of arrogant white expansionism: self-destruction.

Fear of this destruction also led to Canning's involvement in local affairs. As with more prominent figures known for their poetry – William Cullen **Bryant**, John Greenleaf **Whittier**, James Russell **Lowell**, and Oliver Wendell **Holmes** – the worth of Canning's life must be measured by his other pursuits as well. He served as Gill town clerk for many years, and in 1866, he was elected to the Massachusetts legislature. In 1872, he was instrumental in founding the library in Gill, eventually becoming the first librarian. The small collection was housed in the building that served as the post office at which Canning himself was the postmaster. Canning was remembered by his contemporaries as an active citizen and an antiquarian, but mainly as a poet. For us, he may serve as an example of the many "peasant bards" who proliferated in towns across America in the nineteenth century and whose verse rescued from oblivion the history they helped preserve and create.

CHRISTINE A. MODEY

Selected Works

Poems, Greenfield, Massachusetts: Phelps & Ingersoll, 1838

Thanksgiving Eve, Greenfield, Massachusetts: Merriam and Mirick, 1847

The Harp and Plow, Greenfield, Massachusetts: M. H. Tyler, 1852

The Shad-Fishers, Greenfield, Massachusetts: R. C. Graves, 1854

Connecticut River Reeds, Blown by the "Peasant bard", Boston: J. C. Cupples, 1892

Further Reading

Holland, Josiah Gilbert, *History of Western Massachusetts*, 2 vols., Springfield, Massachusetts: Samuel Bowles, 1855

Stoughton, Ralph M., *History of the Town of Gill, Franklin County, Massachusetts, 1793–1943*, Gill, 1978

Alice Cary

(1820–1871)

Phoebe Cary

(1824–1871)

The poetry of Alice and Phoebe Cary has been pretty much forgotten by now, although Alice's fiction, especially her two series of *Clovernook* sketches (1852–53), has lately received some attention as part of the general revival of interest in women's fiction of the mid-nineteenth century. The Carys were extravagantly praised – and also sharply criticized – during their lifetimes by male reviewers who promoted a prescriptive definition of feminine literary duty. They also each produced a popular religious poem that ranks among the best-loved poems of the nineteenth century. Less daringly experimental in the portrayal of passion than Frances Sargent Osgood, and less overtly political than Elizabeth Oakes-Smith, Alice and Phoebe Cary nevertheless provide a particularly interesting case study in the structure of sentimental poetic response, and in the ambivalent life and work of the "female poet."

The lives of these two poetic sisters are readily divisible into two discrete periods that embody the extremes of nineteenth-century American experience: the harsh isolation of the Western frontier was theirs by inheritance, while the chaotic claustrophobia of the industrializing urban East became theirs by choice. The facts of their biography seem almost mythic, an American and female real-life version of a bildungsroman. Born in the Ohio Valley, then considered part of the "West," these two self-educated sisters, armed (the legend goes) with only a modicum of talent and a determination to work hard, moved to New York City in 1851. Not only did they succeed in supporting themselves by their pens in Manhattan's competitive environment, but they also established their home on East 20th Street as the closest equivalent to the Parisian literary salon that American life could offer at the time. Although the work of these "frontier" poets has been considered as the first literary fruit of the westward expansion, their own geographical movement was in exactly the opposite direction. Thus, their lives can be used to reinforce American pieties about the virtues of self-reliance and self-discipline, but the Carys can also be seen as early feminist exemplars of self-supporting women in the big city.

Alice Cary entered into puberty – and into poetry – in an atmosphere of death. When she was 12, she lost two sisters to disease within a month, including an older sister to whom she had been extremely close; when she was 15, her mother died of consumption; when she was seventeen, her father remarried, choosing a new wife with whom Alice was never able to establish much sympathy; and when she was eighteen, she published her first poem in a Cincinnati newspaper. If we are seeking a psychoanalytic explanation for the "morbid" tendencies that reviewers were later to complain of in her poems – which repeatedly associate love with feelings of loss, abandonment, and

dislocation – there is obviously ample material to be found in the turbulent psychosexual dynamics of Alice's death-scarred adolesence.

Although Alice lived the first 30 years of her life in the cultural isolation of Mount Healthy, Ohio, she was to spend the last 20 at the heart of New York's cosmopolitan literary society. Certainly, an important impetus for this transformation was the sheer need for money. As early as 1845, the Cary sisters were writing to a local poet, seeking to find ways to make money out of their writing. By 1848, they had begun writing for – and being paid by – *The National Era*, an abolitionist paper that would become famous for serializing *Uncle Tom's Cabin*. Once she got her first taste of financial independence and literary success, Alice would never look back: after a brief East Coast visit in 1850, she decided within months on a permanent relocation. For the rest of her life she would toil ceaselessly with her pen, despite chronic ill health, and she managed to make both a name and a paycheck for herself in a time when this was no common achievement for a middle-class woman.

Like so many mid-nineteenth-century women writers, especially poets, Alice and Phoebe Cary launched their careers largely through the patronage of a handful of powerful literary men who served as critical gatekeepers. The first of these was John Greenleaf **Whittier**, who, among his many other activities, was a contributing editor of *The National Era*. When the Carys traveled east in the spring of 1850, they visited the ailing poet at his home in Massachusetts, an event that Whittier memorialized years later, after Alice's death, in "The Singer." Their second patron was the famous newspaper editor Horace Greeley, who had visited them in Ohio before they achieved any notable reputation – and who later denied having given them any advice to "Go East, young women." The third, and the most helpful in a practical way, was Rufus Griswold, who was perhaps the most important figure of the period for helping to define a preliminary American literary canon. Griswold's influential 1848 anthology, *The Female Poets of America*, first exposed the Carys' work was first exposed to a large audience; the editor himself added words of praise about their poetic potential. Griswold then helped to arrange the publication of their first, joint volume of poetry in 1849 (*Poems of Alice and Phoebe Cary*), serving, as he did with many other "female poets," as the editor who selected the contents from among the sisters' 350 extant poems.

The fourth male figure – and the one who had perhaps the greatest effect on Alice's long-term reputation, although he died before he could meet her in person – was Edgar Allan **Poe**, who was second only to Griswold as a promoter of "female poets." Although Alice Cary wrote hundreds of poems, her reputation as a poet rested to a large extent on a single early poem, "Pictures of Memory." Griswold chose it for his anthology, and Poe, in a review, wrote that, "in all the higher elements of poetry – in true imagination – in the power of exciting the only real poetical effect – elevation of *the soul*, in contradistinction from mere excitement of the intellect or heart – the poem . . . is the noblest in the book." This judgment was highly influential: the poem was frequently mentioned, praised, and quoted more than twenty years later in eulogies for Alice – often in conjunction with Poe's quotation – and it continued to appear in anthologies well into the twentieth century.

"Pictures of Memory" deals with an extremely painful subject, one that many nineteenth-century readers would have directly experienced: the death of a younger brother in childhood. Or, to be more precise, it portrays a particular attitude that the speaker has attained toward that death many years later:

> I once had a little brother,
>   With eyes that were dark and deep –
> In the lap of that old dim forest
>   He lieth in peace asleep:
> Light as the down of the thistle,
>   Free as the winds that blow,
> We roved there the beautiful summers,
>   The summers of long ago;
> But his feet on the hills grew weary,
>   And, one of the autumn eves,
> I made for my little brother
>   A bed of the yellow leaves.

The poem presents the dying brother as fading seamlessly from human life and becoming part of a natural world controlled by a beneficent God. The work describes a heightened state of consciousness from which the boy's death now appears not as a painful memory, as the modern reader might expect, but as a pleasant one, in fact the *most* pleasant of all memories, the one that "of all the pictures / That hang on Memory's wall . . . / Seemeth the best of all."

This translucent spiritual consciousness cannot be easily or quickly achieved, and a reviewer in *Graham's* called it "a mood of mind rarely experienced in its purity by any intellect." Thus, nineteenth-century reviewers, from Poe forward, immediately understood that Cary was imagining an ideal spiritual state: not mere detachment, but rather a moment when personal will dissolves and coalesces with God's will, when what once appeared horrible now is transfigured as not only inevitable but also beautiful and even desirable.

Reviews of Alice's early poetry mostly took their cue from Griswold's portrait of a promising young poet of the West and from Poe's remarkable praise. Poe had rated Alice the "most imaginative" poet in Griswold's anthology. *Graham's* and *American Review* quickly echoed this emphasis on her strong "imagination." In her 1848 anthology of "female poets," Caroline May wrote of Alice's possessing "a nobility and independence of thought, . . . a breadth of sympathy, . . . [and] a fervour of imagination." But the sisters themselves did not agree with this unanimous chorus of approval. In her 1871 eulogy for her sister, Phoebe tells us that Alice disliked all of her early poems, including "Pictures of Memory," and goes on to describe the 1849 volume in her own astringent manner as "but the feeble echoes of well-known poets, or at best senti-

mental fancies or morbid plaints of sorrow more imaginary than real." Certainly these first efforts, like those of many antebellum women poets, are heavily indebted to previous generations of Romantic writers: the works echo writings by Lord Byron, Samuel Taylor Coleridge, Percy Bysshe Shelley, and (especially) John Keats. They also recall Felicia Hemans's influential feminization of Romantic themes and American adaptations of Romantic material by William Cullen **Bryant**, Henry Wadsworth **Longfellow**, and Lydia **Sigourney**. Indeed, as Katharine Lee Bates pointed out, Alice Cary frequently appropriated whole lines and image clusters from her predecessors, especially in her poem "Keats," which functions as part eulogy and part pastiche, and which opens Alice's section of the 1849 volume. Another indication of the sisters' influences (whether positive or negative) may be the list of Phoebe's victims in *Poems and Parodies* (1854): William Shakespeare, Oliver Goldsmith, Robert Burns, William Wordsworth, Byron, Hemans (the only woman so honored), Poe (see "Samuel Brown," LOA, 2: 154), Thomas Hood, Thomas Moore, Nathaniel Parker **Willis**, Longfellow ("'The Day Is Done,'" LOA, 2: 159), and Alfred, Lord Tennyson ("Granny's House," LOA, 2: 155).

A *Graham's* reviewer of the sisters' first volume described the poetry as evoking the "chivalric rather than the critical sentiment," and indeed the Carys, like many women poets in the 1840s and early 1850s, were forced to accept condescending praise in place of serious critiques of their work. This began to change around 1855, when Alice brought out a volume that collected much of her earlier verse and added some new poems. Perhaps the amazing commercial success achieved by novelists such as Susan Warner and Harriet Beecher Stowe in the early 1850s, which threatened to overwhelm the works of male writers, had produced a backlash among male reviewers, a determination to be more severe and less chivalrous toward women authors, or perhaps critical standards were beginning to change for other reasons. In any case, although she continued to be praised by some reviewers, sometimes hyperbolically ("the first poetess of the New World"), a new critical line on Alice Cary began to emerge at this time: *Poems* was described as "a sob in three hundred and ninety-nine parts" and "a parish register of funerals rendered into doleful rhyme." According to W. H. Venable, this acerbic opinion wounded Alice deeply, even though the same critic went on to say that "Miss Cary writes much better verse than most women who publish poetry." Of the 141 poems in her 1855 volume, a *Putnam's* reviewer asserted, "nearly seventy culminate in a death, or in the expression of a desire to die, usually on account of the unfaithfulness of a lover. And almost all the remainder of the book is melancholy in sentiment." Similarly, the *North American Review* complained that "they are all in the minor key, – a prolonged and varied dirge-note, – a wail, under a great diversity of titles, of disappointed love, desertion, betrayal, and bereavement."

Taking a "female poet" such as Alice Cary to task for her supposed "morbid" tendencies, as many of these male reviewers of the 1850s and 1860s did, is a bit like a twentieth-century white person asking Robert Johnson why his blues songs contain so many images of suffering: both corpora of work need to be placed in the context of a particular history of oppression. Mary Clemmer Ames's biography attempts to explain Alice's fascination with mortality in personal terms; she traces a disappointed love affair in Alice's youth and makes reference to Alice's years of grinding deskwork and ill health in New York. But a similar count of poems about death by Alice's contemporaries, from the highly visible Lydia Sigourney to the reclusive Emily **Dickinson**, would come up with percentages comparable to those used to mock Alice Cary. This circumstance suggests that the explanation for Alice's "morbidity" ought to be sought first in the common social condition and shared experience of women, rather than in the poet's individual sufferings. Alice's preoccupation with themes of death and grieving were not unusual for a period that faced not only the universal problems of infant mortality and the adult epidemic of tuberculosis, but also the special tragedies of the protracted and bloody Civil War. Like the blues, nineteenth-century American women's poetry was a stylized manner of singing the funky facts of women's lives.

Perhaps stung by this critical hostility, Alice did not publish another volume of poetry for 10 years, although she did publish some individual poems in magazines and managed to turn out three books of fiction despite ill health. One of these, *Pictures of Country Life*, was highly successful. It won critical praise in England and at home, was translated into several foreign languages, and garnered favorable comparisons with the earlier *Clovernook* sketches, with which it shares an affinity in tone and subject matter. By the time Alice published her next book of poems, however, her style had evolved considerably. Her later poems are more emotionally restrained, and fewer of them are death-centered.

Alice's self-conscious poetic progression may conveniently be charted by comparing two different poems with the same title, "To the Spirit of Song," the first published in *Lyra* (1852) and the second, subtitled "Apology," included as a prelude to *Ballads, Lyrics, and Hymns* (1866). The earlier poem addresses the "sweet spirit" as an absent lover, inviting him "in the dreamland light, / [To] keep with me a tryst tonight." The male muse appears as a force with the power to dispel demons, quell dark fears, and reassure the speaker that death is not in control. And yet, he is himself associated with fantasy, passion, and clandestine nocturnal meetings. Alice's early poetry flirts with death, even as she calls on poetry itself to preserve her from it. By 1866, poetry is no longer figured as a young, sexy dark lover, but has been transformed into a more familiar, husbandly relation: "O ever true and comfortable mate, / For whom my love outwore the fleeting red / Of my young cheeks, nor did one jot abate." In other later poems about poetry, Alice seems more self-confident as well. In "The Blackbird" she declares: "I shall be wise, if I ever am wise, / Out of my own ears, and of my own eyes," and goes on to take the bird as an exemplar of natural poetic self-expression: "Do you think, if he said, 'I'm ashamed to be black!!' / That he could have shaken the sassafras-tree / As he does with the song he was born to? not he!"

This new Alice Cary is less histrionic than the earlier one, more in control – a hard-won poetic conquest fought through physical pain and clouds of self-doubt. Her mature poetic persona is less passionately unhappy than the deserted girl of yesteryear, but this is partly because she no longer expects as much from life and has resigned herself to making the most of what it has brought her. Like the speaker of "To Solitude"

(LOA, 2: 93), Cary seeks to make her peace with a world that has made her "weary," and in which "my trusts but torments prove." She attempts to remedy this condition not by finding trustworthy human companionship but by embracing the inhuman "spirit sweet" of Solitude as "my true and tender love." Many of these later poems – "Autumn," for example (LOA, 2: 94) – have a wistful quality to them, a yearning for a gentler, vanished world.

A casual reader would never guess from a perusal of these poems that their author had lived in Manhattan for nearly 20 years, or that her drawing room was at the center of metropolitan literary life. One notable fact about the poetry of both Cary sisters is the nearly entire absence of imagery drawn from observation of their urban milieu, or themes distilled from their own lives as city women. Instead, their characteristic settings are pastoral or attempts to recreate their rural childhood. In "The West Country" (LOA, 2: 96), Alice uses her knowledge of the region to focus on the experience of tired women in isolated cabins who "forget their [spinning] wheels" in order to ask a passing traveler, with a mixture of curiosity and desperation, for

> . . . news of the villages
> Where they were used to be,
> Gay girls at work in the factories
> With their lovers gone to sea!

Alice clearly knew those bleak plains and those weary women from her own youth – and had determined at the age of 30 that she was not going to remain in the West to become one of them. Her idealization of the "gay girls in the factories" might come as a surprise to the urban women who actually worked there (not so far from the Carys' parlor) for low wages in bad conditions, but it does reflect Alice's mature understanding that the growing industrial cities, with their nascent literary infrastructure, were the best place for an intelligent woman, all things considered. Certainly Alice's pervasive invocation of natural images recalls her Western girlhood, but neither her poetry nor her fiction sugarcoats the lives of the people who live in the "West country." All that the women in this poem have to look forward to, in exchange for their prolonged sacrifice and endurance of privation, is the possible success of their sons:

> . . . for many a lad
> Born to rough work and ways,
> Strips off his ragged coat, and makes
> Men clothe him with their praise.

In "Katrina on the Porch" (LOA, 2: 95), subtitled "A Bit of Turner Put into Words," Alice attempts to synthesize the rural world of her childhood, evoked by her detailed description of natural surroundings, with her later and more cosmopolitan New York consciousness. She does so by alluding to one of her favorite painters, Joseph M. W. Turner:

> Only a study for homely eyes,
> And never a picture poet would paint;
> But I hold the woman above the saint,
> And the light of the humblest hearth I prize
> O'er the luminous air-built castle.

The young Thackeray, in response to Turner's *The "Fighting Temeraire"* (1838), had envisioned a day "when the art of translating colours into music or poetry shall be discovered," and Turner's painting would then be seen as "a magnificent national ode" (see also **Melville's** "The Temeraire," LOA, 2: 6). Alice Cary seems also to desire a translation of Turner's vision into poetry, but she envisions a less nationalistic and more domestic landscape, which focuses on the "woman" and the "hearth," the traditional materials of the "female poet." Turner himself showed little interest in domestic scenes, and indeed Turner and Cary seem a rather odd aesthetic couple, his proto-Impressionistic innovations clashing with her more conventional post-Romantic poetic modes. Yet a copy of a "Venetian scene" by Turner hung, Ames tells us, on the Carys' New York wall for many years, and perhaps its oblique influence may be traced not only in this poem but in some of Alice's other vivid landscape descriptions.

By 1867, *Catholic World* regarded Alice with something akin to pity, insisting that "there is nothing to read twice in the book [*Ballads, Lyrics and Hymns*]. It is not poetry." This review does concede that "there are gleams amid the commonplace that make it, to our mind, one of the saddest books we ever opened – sad with the unfulfilled promise of a busy yet wasted life." This reviewer traces Alice's failure as a poet to the demands of writing in order to support herself: "But the woman never had a chance. As fast as an idea budded, it was contracted for in advance and plucked long before ripeness." The *Catholic World* reviewer concludes that "we think better of her than of her book," and many of the later comments on Alice took up the same tone and idea. Even Phoebe's eulogy agrees that Alice was a better woman than she was a poet: "for her plans and desires were so much greater than her performance, and her life so much better than her words, that those who did not know her here can never now know her at all."

Phoebe Cary's work has always languished in the shadow of her more famous – and far more productive – sister. But if Alice was the literary leader, Phoebe was the center of attention at the Carys' famous Sunday evening salons, which attracted a wide cross section of New York literati to the sisters' modest flat for tea and sprightly conversation. Regulars included Elizabeth Stoddard, whose innovative novel *The Morgesons* has now been rediscovered, and her poet husband, Richard Henry Stoddard; progressive political activists such as Elizabeth Cady Stanton and Oliver Johnson; and journalists like Greeley, Kate Field, Mary L. Booth, and Robert Bonner, the flamboyant, free-spending editor of the *New York Ledger*. Whittier would drop by when he was in town, and other poets such as Bayard **Taylor** were also to be found there, along with prose writers such as Mary E. Dodge and Robert Dale Owen, and assorted clergymen, including Phoebe's pastor, Reverend Charles Deems, who wrote a sketch of these gatherings for *Packard's Monthly*.

Another frequent guest at the Cary soirees was P. T. Barnum, who, with his flair for the superlative, nominated Phoebe "the wittiest woman in America." Indeed, Phoebe developed a reputation for lightning-quick repartee. Unlike her more reserved and earnest older sister, Phoebe was a vivacious, extroverted woman who sought the spotlight in social situations and attracted the notice of numerous suitors, whose marriage proposals she had on occasion to turn down. Ames calls her a "disenchanter": "Hold up to her, in her literal, every-day mood, your most precious dream, and in an instant, by a single rapier of a sentence, she would thrust it through, and strip it of the last vestige of glamour, and you see nothing before you but a cold, staring fact, ridiculous or dismal."

Aside from a few random anecdotes preserved by Ames and others, the most tangible remaining specimens of Phoebe's literalizing wit appear in the "Parodies" portion of her *Poems and Parodies* (1854), which has never met with great favor, although it achieved some notoriety in its time. Reviewers of the 1850s seemed to think that Longfellow's "A Psalm of Life" (LOA, 1: 370) got what it deserved (Phoebe's version begins: "Tell me not, in idle jingle / Marriage is an empty dream, / For the girl is dead that's single . . ."), but her other frivolous treatments of serious subjects apparently crossed over some invisible boundary of Victorian earnestness and into the realm of the offensive. A *Graham's* reviewer, while praising some parodies, found her treatment of James Aldrich's "A Death-Bed" to be "in wretched taste" and saw her burlesque of Bryant's "The Future Life" as "a profanation. In all poetry these are the last lines which we could imagine a woman of sentiment selecting for the exercise of her humor." But of course, this is exactly the point: Phoebe's puncturing wit is calling into question the very definition of "a woman of sentiment" by transposing pious pseudo-profundities into lighthearted romps. She also reverses the genders of speaker and object as a means of commenting playfully on the masculine bias inherent in extant poetic conventions. Wordworth's pastoral "Lucy," for example, becomes in Phoebe's urbanized "Jacob" (LOA, 2: 160) a mocking portrait of an unattractive man –

> He dwelt among "apartments let,"
>   About five stories high;
> A man I thought that none would get,
>   And very few would try

– whom the speaker ends up marrying because no one else is available ("But he has got a wife, – and O! / The difference to me!"). Even more subversively, her rewriting of Goldsmith's "Stanzas on Women" ("When lovely woman stoops to folly") dares to mock the assertion that a fallen woman's impermissible exercise of her sexuality can only end in death:

> When lovely woman wants a favor
>   And finds, too late, that man wont bend,
> What earthly circumstance can save her
>   From disappointment in the end?
>
> The only way to bring him over,
>   The last experiment to try,
> Whether a husband or a lover,
>   If he have feeling, is, to cry!
>   (LOA, 2: 161)

Where Goldsmith's poem marches inexorably from "folly" to death, Phoebe insists on remaining at the level of folly, and the tragic portrait of a fallen woman becomes a comic exercise in coquettish manipulation and sexual gamesmanship. Whatever else we may say of her poetry generally, Phoebe's wicked wit in these parodies is not afraid of overturning cherished pieties (momentarily) or of bending genders (gently) in the service of a quick, broad laugh – although one that is not without its political overtones.

Yet Phoebe was best known during her lifetime not for these

irreverent reversals, but for an earnest hymn she wrote at about the same time:

> One sweetly solemn thought
>   Comes to me o'er and o'er;
> I am nearer home to-day
>   Than I have ever been before;
>
> Nearer my Father's house,
>   Where the many mansions be . . .

"Nearer Home" was Phoebe's equivalent to Alice's "Pictures of Memory," another hugely popular piece of unironic piety that was widely reprinted, preserved in private scrapbooks, set to music, and taught to children in Sunday schools; it was even reputed to have led to the reformation of two prodigiously sinful men in a Chinese gambling den.

Refusing to "plead the 'urgent request of friends'" – the conventional women's excuse for publishing – Phoebe admitted in a letter to Whittier, regarding her *Poems of Faith, Hope and Love* (1868), that she held her later poems in some esteem: "I had some poems scattered about which I was vain enough to think were worth at least being put in a volume and hoped there might be found some others who would agree with me." Some justification for this belief may be found in a few of these poems, but the glaringly pious title of the volume invites one to speculate about what Phoebe Cary the parodist might have done had she turned her biting wit against Phoebe Cary the earnest sentimental poet.

Both Cary sisters are poets of faith, but also of resignation; their love poems tend to be poems of absence and loss. In Alice's early poems, this resignation takes the form of an exaggerated tragical melancholy, while in her later poems the passionate despair is transmuted into a more subdued, almost nostalgic wistfulness. For Phoebe's early poems, love is a topic for a lighthearted joke, while the most interesting of the later poems are the not-quite-love poems, in which the speaker stands back and contemplates with a sort of amused abstraction an emotion that perhaps she *might* have felt had circumstances been a little different. In "Wooed and Won," for example, when the "maiden" has accepted her true lover, she finds "she would almost hide the truth":

> For the spell of enchantment is broken now,
> And all the future is seen so clear,
> That she longs for the very longing gone,
> For the restless pleasure of hope and fear.

Single by choice, Phoebe for the most part stayed outside that "spell of enchantment," that turbulent cycle of "hope and fear." Although Phoebe was once tempted, Ames suggests, to accept a suitor, she refrained because she would not leave Alice. Phoebe's love poems generally approach their topic with a tone of detached amusement. "Believe me," she told Alice once in a similar vein, "I never loved any man well enough to lie awake half an hour, to be miserable about him."

Phoebe's ironic stance in relation to human emotions may have made her less skillful as a pure lyric singer than Alice, but it sometimes led her to write poems that are stronger in dramatic flair and psychological insight. Among her later poems, "Up and Down" stands out as a subtle study in sentimental irony. A young man takes the speaker's hand in his own and tells her that

> . . . I resembled his sweetheart
>   Sometimes in my words and my ways,
> That I had the same womanly feelings,
>   My thoughts were as noble and high;
> But that she was a trifle, say, fairer,
>   And a year or two younger, than I.

The speaker goes on to protest that "my kindness is disinterested," but advises young men nevertheless not to speak of the absent perfect love "to the lady that's present." Other love poems attempt with varying degrees of success to walk the line between sentimental earnestness and puckish cynicism. "Somebody's Lovers" coolly catalogs the shortcomings of various types of men who present themselves as candidates for affection, while "Dead Love" presents mournful lovers examining the corpse of their relationship. "Amy's Love-Letter" portrays a woman musing over an old love letter and wondering what has happened to its author: "I wish I could only remember what – / But he's either married or dead."

Griswold's introduction to the Cary sisters in his 1848 anthology contends that Phoebe "refers more than Alice to the common experience, and has perhaps a deeper sympathy with that philosophy and those movements of the day, which look for a nearer approach to equality, in culture, fortune, and social relations." One might support this distinction, among the early poems, by comparing Alice's "The Homeless" with Phoebe's "Homes for All" (later retitled "Plea for the Homeless"). Alice's poem, in her characteristic early mode, ends with a lament:

> One word of the commonest kindness
> Could make all around me seem bright . . .
> But lacking that word, on my spirit
> There settles the heaviest gloom
> And I sit with the midnight around me
> And long for the peace of the tomb.

Any political agitation for alleviation of this condition is left implicit, and, indeed, the only relief envisioned is a "word" from a concerned individual rather than a stronger collective action. Phoebe's poem, on the other hand, invokes the natural advantages and agricultural might of the American continent in the first half of the poem, and then moves on to condemn the continuing deprivation of those who "ask the blessing of a home in vain" in the "populous cities." Phoebe ends with a call to America to be a better mother to her children:

> Turn not, Columbia! from their pleading eyes;
> Give to thy sons that ask of thee a home;
> So shall they gather round thee, not with sighs,
> But as young children to their mother come . . .

Phoebe's image of America as a neglectful maternal figure turns the domestic rhetoric of sentimental poetry toward an avowedly political end – a strategy similar to that Stowe would employ a few years later with the conventions of the sentimental novel.

Such overt political content is relatively rare in both Phoebe's and Alice's work; their more characteristic modes are religious, psychological, or humorous. This is certainly not to say, however, that the Carys did not have strong political convictions. They began their writing careers, after all, in the pages of an abolitionist journal. And both sisters later considered themselves very sympathetic with the women's rights movement, although in both cases their active political involvement was minimal. Phoebe's most explicit feminist statement came in a poem published in the *New York Tribune*, "Advice Gratis to Certain Women: By a Woman" (LOA 2: 161):

> O, my strong-minded sisters, aspiring to vote,
> And to row with your brothers, all in the same boat,
> When you come out to speak to the public your mind,
> Leave your tricks, and your airs, and your graces
>   behind!
> . . . .
> Don't mistake me; I mean that the public's not home,
> You must do as the Romans do, when you're in Rome;
> I would have you be womanly, while you are wise;
> 'Tis the weak and the womanish tricks I despise.
> . . . .
> 'T is a good thing to write, and to rule in the state,
> But to be a true, womanly woman is great:
> And if you ever come to be that, 'twill be when
> You can cease to be babies, nor try to be men!

Here, Phoebe's fabled wit is enlisted in a simultaneous exhortation and admonition to the New Women aspiring to suffrage and to the professions, especially the writing professions. Clearly, she associates herself with these new aspirations, even while she pokes fun at the excesses of "female" writing as it had been conventionally conceived and practiced. In her distinction between the "womanly" and the "womanish," Phoebe takes pains to differentiate her vision both from radicals who saw no essential difference between women and men and from conservative definitions of the "woman's sphere."

Phoebe served for a brief period as assistant editor of Susan B. Anthony's *Revolution*, and Alice was similarly enticed – or bullied – into becoming the first president of Sorosis, a New York women's literary club. Her inaugural address marked her first and last public appearance as a speaker. In this lecture (reprinted in Ames), Alice makes a strong statement placing herself among those who

> proposed the inculcation of deeper and broader ideas among women, proposed to teach them to think for themselves, and to get their opinions at first hand, not so much because it is their right as because it is their duty. We have also proposed to open out new avenues of employment to women, to make them less dependent and less burdensome, to lift them out of unwomanly self-distrust [and] disqualifying diffidence, into womanly self-respect and self-knowledge.

Readers of Alice's poetry will search in vain for a feminist expression approaching the explicitness of this prose one. Perhaps the nineteenth-century definition of poetry as the noble pursuit of a shadowy spiritual ideal precluded for Alice the idea of using poetic rhetoric for overtly political ends. Phoebe's "Advice Gratis," partaking of a more public tradition of satirical newspaper verse, seems less constrained in this way. There is some evidence that late in her life Alice was beginning to take up a more expressly political stance on women's issues. At the time of her death, she had been at work on a new novel, *The Born Thrall* (the opening chapters of which were serialized in *Revolution*); this book was projected to address, according to Ames, "her deepest thoughts and maturest convictions concerning the sorrows and wrongs of women."

After Alice's death, the *Woman's Journal* reprinted her poem "Work," which perhaps stands as well as anything as her lasting contribution to the cause of women's rights and women's poetry. Certainly it embodies her own credo of industrious self-reliance: "I hold that a man had better be dead / Than alive, when his work is done!" And that goes – as her own lifelong example asserted implicitly and more controversially – for a woman, too, for nobody worked harder, right up to the last moment of her capacity, than Alice Cary. Through weary years of churning out word after word, she had proved that it was possible for a single woman in mid-nineteenth-century America to make her living by her writing alone. She even supported another person, for Phoebe's far more sporadic pen never brought in a reliable stream of cash. Judged from a purely literary point of view, Phoebe's poems may arguably be the superior achievement. She shows a tart wit in the parodies and greater psychological range and a greater dramatic complexity than Alice in some of her later poems. But the sheer volume of Alice's writings in poetry and prose testify to the dogged tenacity of this near-invalid's determination to live independently as a woman writer, and it was in this role – and not in that of a poet of the "West" – that she most decisively demonstrated her pioneering spirit.

JONATHAN HALL

Selected Works

The Poetical Works of Alice and Phoebe Cary, New York: Hurd and Houghton, 1876; reprinted, Houghton Mifflin, "Household Edition," 1898

The Poems of Alice and Phoebe Cary, edited by Katharine Lee Bates, New York: Crowell, 1903

Alice Cary, *Clovernook Sketches and Other Stories*, edited by and introduced by Judith Fetterley, Brunswick, New Jersey: Rutgers University Press, 1987

Phoebe Cary, "Alice Cary," *The Ladies' Repository* (July 1871)

Further Reading

Ames, Mary Clemmer, *A Memorial of Alice and Phoebe Cary*, New York, 1873; reprinted, in *The Poetical Works*

Coggeshall, William T., *The Poets and Poetry of the West*, Columbus, 1860

Derby, James C., *Fifty Years Among Authors, Books, and Publishers*, New York, 1884

Kolodny, Annette, *The Land Before Her*, Chapel Hill: University of North Carolina Press, 1984

Long, Laura, *Singing Sisters*, New York: Longmans, Green, 1941

Reynolds, David S., *Beneath the American Renaissance*, Cambridge, Massachusetts: Harvard University Press, 1989

Venable, Emerson, ed., *Poets of Ohio*, Cincinnati, Ohio, 1899

Venable, W. H., *Beginnings of Literary Culture in the Ohio Valley*, Cincinnati, Ohio, 1891

Whittier, John Greenleaf, *Whittier on Writers and Writing: The Uncollected Critical Writings of John Greenleaf Whittier*, edited by E. H. Cady and H. H. Clark, Ithaca, New York, 1950

Madison Cawein

(1865–1914)

While T. S. Eliot, Ezra Pound, and Harriet **Monroe** were inciting each other to revolution during the first decade and a half of the twentieth century, Madison Cawein was publishing as many as a hundred poems a year, all after the manner of the English Romantics and Victorians. In the *South Atlantic Quarterly* in 1915, Professor H. Houston Peckham of Purdue wrote in a rapture of prophetic criticism:

> Long after erudite students shall have ceased to worry their brains about the conceits of Donne and Herbert and Crashaw; long after most of Walt Whitman's "Leaves of Grass" have grown sear and have returned unto dust; long, long after men have forgotten that some flowing-haired, horn-spectacled critic once pronounced Ezra Pound wonderful, or that Ezra Pound ever lived and moved and had his being, a grateful public will rejoice that Madison Cawein sat at the feet of Milton the stately, and Keats the lovely, and hearkened not to the clanging cymbals of some freakish innovator, some stridently clamorous mountebank outside the gates of the sacred temple of Poesy.

Such perspicacity indicates as much about why Professor Peckham was teaching English at an engineering school as it does about middle America's genteel literary tastes during this period.

Largely derivative, Cawein's poetry was, from about 1892 to 1912, popular enough to support him and, after 1904, a wife and child, with some supplement from his investments in real estate and the stock market. Shaped by his cultural isolation in Louisville, Kentucky, still something of a frontier city, his prodigious gift for versifying produced a poetry firmly grounded in the American genteel tradition that never broke from its English models. Ripening in this climate, and producing 36 volumes in a lifetime of only 49 years, he published and republished much inferior work.

Born in Louisville in 1865, Cawein spent his life there except for 18 months in 1874–75 when his father managed a resort in Brownsville, Kentucky, and three years (1875–78) when the family lived on a farm in southern Indiana. His sensibility was shaped by his German immigrant father, a confectioner who gathered herbs and compounded patent medicines as a sideline, and by his mother, a noted spiritualist whose parents had come from Germany. Cawein spent many evenings listening to his mother discuss the supernatural, and long days with his father, rambling the fields and woods, learning plant and animal lore. Admirers like Peckham had to defend Cawein's focus on specific natural phenomena even as they tried to praise it:

> No one denies Cawein's love for the little things of nature, his marvelously close observation, his minute accuracy of description. Indeed some have charged that he peered too closely, that he crowded his canvas too full of rank undergrowth, that he made his picture as bewilderingly prolix and as wearisomely prosey as the index to a treatise on botany or ornithology.

When he was 21, he graduated as class poet from Louisville Male High School, where he had fallen under the spell of Spenser, Coleridge, Scott, Keats, Shelley, Browning, and Tennyson and had steeped himself in the mythologies of Greece and Rome. His friend Anna B. McGill recalled that when he, as a teenager, finished reading *The Faerie Queene* for the first time, he wrote to the publisher asking if more books were available. When he learned that Spenser died before the work was completed, he simply read the existing books over again. She quotes his own description of his literary apprenticeship:

> I used to burn the midnight oil in my teens, writing long narrative poems modelled first on one [poet] and then on the other; I remember one in the manner of "Christabel" and another in the manner of "The Ancient Mariner" that I wrote sitting up till two or three o'clock in the morning to finish, one or two thousand lines in length.

He burned many of these early poems, but enough survived to form his first volume, *Blooms of the Berry* (1887), published when he was a 22-year-old assistant cashier in the Newmarket Pool Room.

Cawein wanted to to go to college, but his family was unable to send him. During the six years he worked at the Newmarket, where his main duty was to make book on horse races, he parlayed his salary into a considerable fortune in real estate and stocks. When he was finally able to leave this job, he spent his mornings watching stock reports and his afternoons rambling and writing in the forest that eventually became Cherokee Park, a few miles south of Louisville. He lived with his parents until he married Gertrude McKelvey when he was 38 and moved into a grand house on St. James Court in Old Louisville. In 1904, his one child, Preston Hamilton, was born. After Cawein died when his son was 10, the boy's name was legally changed to Madison Cawein II.

The San Francisco earthquake of 1906 sent tremors through Cawein's hard-won financial security, and he was forced to move his family from their comfortable house into a nearby apartment. He struggled against this return of poverty and felt some bitterness that he could not support himself with his poetry. In 1913 his stocks again lost value. His health waned as his worries waxed, and he took on the appearance of a prematurely stooped, balding, aged man. He died at age 49 after a fall in his bathroom, possibly the result of a stroke.

His literary fortunes, too, waxed early and ended disappointingly. *Blooms of the Berry* fell into the hands of William Dean **Howells's** daughter Winifred, who brought it to her father's attention. He wrote a guarded appreciation of it for *Harper's Magazine* in 1888. Acknowledging the derivativeness of Cawein's poetry, Howells still heard in it the poet's own voice and saw evidence of a rich sensitivity to place and nature and of a gift for color and metaphor. Cawein dedicated his second book, *The Triumph of Music* (1888), to Howells.

From his early 20s until his death, Cawein lived the life of a man of letters, feeling fairly successful for the first 15 years, but becoming bitter at the fading of his star. His second major triumph came in 1902 when Sir Edmund Gosse, the foremost London critic of the day, selected the verses for and wrote the introduction to *Kentucky Poems.* Five years later, Gosse's introduction (which praised Cawein's depictions of Kentucky's history and flora and fauna, and remarked on his making Dionysus and Artemis at home in the Kentucky landscape) was reprinted in an American five-volume selection of his work, illustrated with 17 photogravures of paintings by the popular illustrator Eric Pape.

Along with these successes came friendship with other writers such as James Whitcomb **Riley,** Henry Van Dyke, Kate Chopin, Edwin Arlington **Robinson,** Joaquin **Miller,** and Oliver Wendell **Holmes.** During the five years following the publication of *Kentucky Poems,* the wave of his fame crested; he was inducted in absentia into the Authors' Club of London and into the National Institute of Arts and Letters; he was praised by President Theodore Roosevelt in an article in *The Outlook* and invited to the White House in November 1905. In 1907 he was invited to compose a commemorative ode to celebrate the founding of the Massachusetts Bay Colony in 1623. Oglethorpe University in Georgia asked him, as the premier Southern poet, to write an ode for the occasion of the laying of its cornerstone. He died before completing this poem.

These honors came at long intervals and were never accompanied by the steady income that he longed for. Although, according to David A. Perkins, Cawein told the *Louisville Courier-Journal* that he earned from "magazine verse from the year 1900 . . . about $100 per month," and this was "at a time when the salary of university professors was likely to be $1500 to $2000 per year," this income was not consistent and did not last long for Cawein. American magazine editors of the time complained that little good poetry was submitted to them and that consequently they did not publish much poetry (Perkins quotes Bliss Perry, editor of *The Atlantic,* to this effect). Consequently the market for poets like Cawein, who were competent mainly at framing American scenes and experience in traditional European forms, provided fewer and fewer remunerative outlets. Sometime after the turn of the century, Cawein began to feel aggrieved that his efforts brought so little reward, and the honors that gradually came to him felt hollow in light of his meager sales and deteriorating financial condition.

Almost half the 2,700 poems appearing in his 36 volumes were reprints or revisions. Most of his work draws its imagery from the homes, farmyards, fields, and forests of Kentucky, but, in spite of the seeming earthiness of his subjects, his poems are full of fairies, sprites, and creatures from classical mythology, which give them an air of unreality and emotional remoteness. His gifts as a poet, his fluency and melody, were also his curse because they enabled his easy production of many glib verses, along with his rarer moments of clear insight into human emotion and its connection with the natural world. Louis Untermeyer aptly characterized Cawein's writing:

> Cawein's work divides itself into two distinct veins. In the realistic one he dealt with the scenes and incidents of his mountain environment: the sag of an old house, the echoes of a feud, rumblings of the Ku Klux Klan, the ghastly details of a lynching. In his other mood (the one which unfortunately possessed him the greater part of the time) he spent page after page romanticizing Nature,

gilding his already painted lilies, polishing his thinly plated artificialities until the base metal showed through. He pictured all outdoors with painstaking detail; and yet it is somehow unreal, prettified, remote.

"The Lynchers" and "Ku Klux" from *Kentucky Poems* (1902) typify the first kind of poems, which Untermeyer mistakenly characterizes as mountain. Cawein's native culture of north-central Kentucky and southern Indiana, where the poems are often set, although certainly rural, is midwestern rather than mountain (the closest mountains are 150 miles east of Louisville). "The Lynchers" paints a stark picture, simple in its outline, of the violence of a white mob murdering a black man assumed to have killed a woman (presumably white). Chillingly, the persona who speaks the poem identifies with the lynchers: "The sumac high and the elder thick, / Where we found the stone and the ragged stick." The iambic tetrameter couplets, exactly rhymed fairly naturally, march the short poem (22 lines) to its inexorable conclusion, which ominously echoes the first stanza:

> A word, a curse, and a shape that swings;
> The lonely night and a bat's black wings.

> At the moon's down-going let it be
> On the quarry hill with its one gnarled tree.

Similarly, "Ku Klux" and "The Man Hunt" use homespun diction, regular rhyme and meter, and a simple set of images to create a romanticized, yet still terror-ridden, sense of racist violence. The detail of the watermelon seeds that begins "Ku Klux" typifies the close observation that gives these poems some reality of emotion: "We have sent him seeds of the melon's core, / And nailed a warning upon his door: / By the Ku Klux laws we can do no more."

Most of Cawein's poems, however, are without these saving touches of realism. "Wood Dreams," in *Minions of the Moon* (1913), begins, as most of his poems do, with a heavy overlay of references to classical mythology and to his favorite geography, that of the fairy world:

> About the time when bluebells swing
>   Their elfin belfries for the bee
> And in the fragrant House of Spring
>   Wild Music moves; and Fantasy
>   Sits weaving webs of witchery. . . .

Yet a third type of Cawein poem has aged better than either the local-color or the romantic-mythological ones. When his genteel defenses are down, he can express a strong sexual energy, particularly in the figure of archetypal femmes fatale. In such poems, his imagery transcends the quaintness of nature as scenery and connects the darknesses of the self to the powerful rhythms of the natural world. In "The Purple Valleys" (LOA, 2: 569), "Caverns" (LOA, 2: 570), "Orgie" (LOA, 2: 570), and "Dead Cities" (LOA, 2: 572), all published between 1899 and 1902, Cawein evokes a landscape, creates a strong sense of a particular place, and, by means of this setting, invokes the presence of the Great Goddess, the archetypal femme fatale, woman as both destroyer and creator. Rigidified as he often was, he could break free when his lavish rhetoric fit his emotions for his subject. In these poems, the chaotic, chthonic processes that argue for a connection between the psyche and nature burst through the romantic-mythic vision of nature that otherwise dominates his poetry.

In "The Purple Valleys" Cawein evokes most explicitly the femme fatale, that resilient figure who, according to Camille Paglia's *Sexual Personae*, emerges as a by-product of Apollonian attempts to transcend messy, death-ridden Dionysian experience and who reappears "the more nature is beaten back . . . as a return of the repressed." Writing to his friend R. E. Lee Gibson in May 1899, just after *Myth and Romance* was published, Cawein described this poem as "steeped in the very blood of my heart and full of myself and my soul's most terrible experience." By his own lights, then, it required a "terrible" access of the maelstrom of sexuality to convert this usually self-conscious poeticizing into convincing, energetic dramatization.

The gigantic body of the goddess fills the landscape, and the "purple valleys" suggest female genitalia. Primal in her inarticulateness, like the "soul of music," she unites opposites – "shadow and fire," "sweeter than Arabian storax, / . . . bitterer than myrrh," inspiring in the male persona "the horror and the rapture / The utterless awe, the joy akin to anguish, / The terror and the worship of the spirit." Over the scene presides the moon, "night's . . . / White queen of love and tragedy and madness," the ethereal, removed aspect of the goddess. She compels him through the power of her eyes to surrender his own will and rationality and to acquiesce to her sexuality:

> Again I feel her eyes pierce through and through me;
> Her deep eyes, lovelier than imperial pansies,
> Velvet and flame, through which her fierce will holds
>   me,
> Powerless and tame, and draws me on and onward
> To sad, unsatisfied and animal yearnings,
> Wild and unrestrained – the brute within the human –
> To fling me panting on her mouth and bosom.

She renders him passive, powerless, and makes him know his repressed body's hungers, which come at him with all the irrationality of obsessive sexuality.

He cannot, does not, resist her, although her embrace defeats all the prettiness of orderly Apollonian spirituality:

> Again I feel her lips like ice and fire,
> Her red lips . . .
> . . . within whose kiss destruction
> Lies serpent-like.

Simultaneously, as these repressed parts of himself come to life, he dies to himself as he has known himself. The old persona deflated and empty, "soul and body," the male persona drifts with the laughing goddess into the abysm of pagan bodiliness, and out of the limited jurisdiction of the male Judeo-Christian "God." This one reality that Cawein confronts in his poetry, like Gorgon, of whom she is a version, mortally threatens the man who confronts her.

In "Dionysia," the poem Cawein thought the best in *Myth and Romance*, the speaker, as in "Purple Valleys," experiences a primal sexuality that unites him with the body of nature. But in this lesser poem, the incident is removed from speaker and reader because it is merely a dream, which the ending suggests might have some reality in a past life. The poem begins with the flat assertion, "The day is dead," and then, like all Cawein's femme fatale poems, it invokes the moon, Diana's "crystal-kindled crest," and through the madness of the moonlight, enters the frenzy of the maenads, their passionate dance of life and death, in which participate all the spirits of nature: the dryads (tree spirits), naiads (stream and spring spirits), oreads (mountain spirits), and so on. Amid this lush animism, "she" finally appears, enchanting "Night with sensuous nudity":

> Lo! again I hear her pant
> Breasting through the dewy glooms. . . .
> Lo, like love, she comes again,
> Through the pale, voluptuous dusk,
> Sweet of limb with breasts of musk.
> With her lips, like blossoms, breathing
> Honeyed pungence of her kiss. . . .

Uniting opposites as always, her "delicious body," "like fire and snow," expresses to the speaker's mind "all / the allurements of the world." Here the experience remains "in the mind," does not become actual, as it does in "Purple Valleys." He only dreams that he lifts his "wine-stained hand" over his "tumultuous hair" and joins in the "Phallic orgies," drunk with "Bacchus lusting in each vein." With "her pagan lips" on his, he dances "like a god," in the vision of "the splendor of her limbs."

The last stanza begins with a statement as flat as that which begins the poem: "So it seems." And we are told that the woods are really empty and that the speaker has been asleep. These revels are only "the rush / of nightwinds through bough and brush." The poem concludes with a series of limp questions:

> . . . is it more
> Than mere dreaming? Is some door
> Opened in my soul? a curtain
> Raised: to let me see for certain
> I have lived before?

The Dionysian negation of civilized values is prettified by its transmutation into dream, and the bone-deep knowledge that one lives in a dying body is reduced to the feelings of an imagined drunken orgy in a previous life as a Greek. With its regular rhyme and sing-along diction, "Dionysia" is more typical of Cawein's work than the naked confrontations of the unrhymed, emotionally immediate "Purple Valleys."

"Caverns: Written of Colossal Cave, Kentucky," a sonnet in *Weeds By the Wall* (1901), looks unflinchingly at the realities of chthonic nature. The poem describes Mammoth Cave as hell, as a conjunction of human consciousness and the destructiveness of nature in the form of Gorgon, whose stare turns all life to stone while she laughs. The cave is "Aisles and abysses; leagues" of rock and night, all "domes" and "pits" with "earthquake-builded floors." The forms of three women ("silence", "echo," and "Gorgon") are incarnate in the archaic night, in the "rock that labyrinths," and in the tortures of the subterranean torrents that emblematize dark functions of the female body. The underside of nature, repressed so fervidly in most of Cawein's poetry, erupts in this imagery. Paglia describes the dilemma that haunts Cawein:

> We say that nature is beautiful. But this aesthetic judgment, which not all peoples have shared, is another de-

fense formation, woefully inadequate for encompassing nature's totality. What is pretty in nature is confined to the thin skin of the globe upon which we huddle. Scratch that skin, and nature's daemonic ugliness will erupt.

Cawein in "Caverns" scratches away the pretty surface of nature's "scenery" to expose nature's bowels. The eternal night within the cave is the chaos out of which all came and into which all will ultimately dissolve. The cave-womb, the female nature principle as both creator and destroyer, the vagina dentata, eats its creatures. In Christian culture this became the realm of evil demons, but for the Greeks the daimonic, like nature neither good nor evil, was simply the reality of existence: to live is to be constantly dying. Thus nature is Gorgon, woman who embodies this truth, whose stare turns the denying Apollonian man to stone and thus embodies his most deeply repressed fears. The unspeakable repulsiveness of Gorgon with her many heads and her snake hair symbolizes the Great Mother's rejection and repression by culture generally. Like the Furies in *The Oresteia*, who are also vestigial incarnations of the goddess, Gorgon is made ugly by general neglect and disrespect. All that is left of her are these frightening, invisible dark organs, "wrecks terrific of the ruined Earth, – / An ancient causeway of forgotten Hell," the birth canal that delivers all into the maelstrom of nature.

"Orgie" and "Dead Cities" (*Kentucky Poems,* 1902) also dramatize the dangerous mystery of female presence. In the first, the goddess as Great Mother dances the speaker to his death in a sort of frenzy that Isadora Duncan called "the final convulsion and sinking down into nothingness that often leads to the gravest disasters – for the intelligence and the spirit." Again, the moon presides over the landscape:

On nights like this, when bayou and lagoon
　　Dream in the moonlight's mystic radiance,
　　I seem to walk like one deep in a trance
With old-world myths born of the mist and moon.

The regularly rhyming iambic pentameter quatrains mesmerize with the rhythms of the dance, and the repeated "oo" sounds in the first two lines are chilling. The glow of the lunar goddess induces the speaker to an altered consciousness, a body awareness of compelling sexuality:

Lascivious eyes and mouths of sensual rose
　　Smile into mine; and breasts of luring light,
　　And tresses streaming golden to the night,
Persuade me onward where the forest glows.

The maenads come in "troops," drinking and shouting like soldiers, and destined to "have their wills." Nothing pretty or traditionally feminine about them, they presage the speaker's vision of the goddess herself:

And then I feel her limbs will be revealed
　　Like some great snow-white moth among the trees;
　　Her vampire beauty, waiting there to seize
And dance me downward where my doom is sealed.

As in "Dead Cities," the man becomes the sacrifice demanded by the naked sight of female nature's undiluted and ecstatic presence.

In "Dead Cities," about the discovery of a ruined Toltec city in the wilds of southeastern Mexico, the human sacrifice to the forces of nature has already been consummated, and those forces have overwhelmed puny human attempts to keep them in check. The city's distance in time ("So old the moon can only know / How old") and isolation in place ("Weeks – / And then a city that no man / Had ever seen") signify its fragile reality in the face of inexorable nature: "Volcanic rock walled in the whole, / Lost in the woods as in some sea."

Like Shelley's "Ozymandias," this poem contemplates the tenuousness of the works of human builders. But here the Apollonian, male, sun-worshiping attempts at stopping in stone the ineluctable processes of growth and decay (cycles associated with the female, the goddess, the moon) are overthrown not just by the passage of time but also by the superior force of these processes, particularly by the jungle trees that have taken over the terraces and the temples:

. . . ancient forests grow
On mighty wall and pyramid.
Huge ceïbas, whose trunks were scarred
With ages, and dense yuccas, hid
Fanes 'mid the cacti, scarlet-starred.

With only the feminine moon left to witness, the priests survive as angry monkeys, cursing the discoverer of their defeat:

. . . while in hate
Mad monkeys cursed me, as if dead
Priests of its past had taken form
To guard its ruined shrines from harm.

"Dead Cities" suggests that these shrines honored an incomplete deity, the masculine sun, leaving out the complementary femaleness of the moon.

A poem akin in imagery, "Wasteland" (*Minions of the Moon,* 1913), makes a lifeless landscape a metaphor for emotional sterility, as does T. S. Eliot's "The Waste Land" (1922). The complexity, richness, and inventiveness of Eliot's poem compared to the one-dimensionality of Cawein's indicate the differences between the two contemporaries. Cawein's poem explicitly and literally lays out the parallel:

Briar and fennel and chinquapin
　　And rue and ragweed everywhere;
The field seemed sick as a soul with sin,
　　Or dead of an old despair,
　　Born of an ancient care.

When an old man appears in the landscape, the speaker is not sure if he is real or a phantasm:

I looked at the man. I saw him plain.
　　Like a dead weed, gray and wan,
Or a breath of dust. – I looked again –
　　And man and dog were gone –
　　Like wisps o' the graying dawn. . . .

Since Eliot read voraciously in contemporary poetry, it is likely he knew Cawein's poem and that it was one of many seeds from which his own poem grew.

Another strength of Cawein's is the quatrain, in which he could be explicitly philosophical, and which is too short to become seriously mired in faery. A series, "Quatrains" (*Kentucky Poems,* 1902), collects some of the best of these, all characterized by impacted allusiveness and direct statement of meanings in which metaphor is usually mere adornment. In "Poetry" (LOA, 2: 567), the muse's beauty strikes the worshiper blind and compels him to climb always "towards her temple's place," never reaching it, but "Weighed with song's sweet, inexorable woe." Like Sappho's relation to her lovers and to Aphrodite, the poet's relation to the goddess here is at once creative and destructive.

"The Unimaginative" (LOA, 2: 567) specifies the plight of the "unanointed," those who look upon the world without imagination: they will never see the "wild fairy-dance" of the Earth because they cannot perceive that beauty is "but the new disguise / Of thought more beautiful than forms can be." In "Music" (LOA, 2: 567), the primordial energy of being, the goddess Music, born before the male gods, creates the universe out of the pure emotion of music:

> . . . she hurled,
> With awful symphonies of flood and fire,
> God's name on rocking Chaos – world by world
> Flamed as the universe rolled from her lyre.

In spite of Cawein's patriarchal assumptions, the goddess Music is the actual creator as she violently hurls God's name on "rocking Chaos" and transforms it in the fire of creation. "The Three Elements" (LOA, 2: 567) also explores, but in a more abstract and conventional way, the cosmic forces that lie behind being. As "foam and wind and heat," these elements carry the power of "God's wrath and law," the principles of the universe that make it what it is.

"On Reading the Life of Haroun Er Reshid" (LOA, 2: 568) takes us back to the less comforting vision cruelty as a principle of nature and of human life. Haroun, an Arabic Robin Hood, represents an ideal we can believe in when we are young and innocent. When one gets inside his palace, however, violent surprises and death await:

> Down all the lanterned Bagdad of our youth
> He steals, with golden justice for the poor:
> Within his palace – you shall know the truth –
> A blood-smeared headsman hides behind each door.

Perversion and violence are part of existence, as much as the morally acceptable idea of stealing for the poor.

Four last quatrains are also honest visions of chthonic nature. "Mnemosyne" (LOA, 2: 569) sees the goddess of memory (briefly Zeus's wife, and mother of the nine Muses) as "cold, immaculate" sculpture, "stern and still." Yet "deep-chiselled" on her brow are love and hate, both of which "sorrow o'er dead roses in her hands." The roses, associated with the Muses because they grew at the Pierian spring where the Muses lived, are dead because art cannot transform potent memory. Art is neutral Apollonian energy, undone by remembered passions.

Similarly, in "Beauty" (LOA, 2: 568), appearances give the slip to reality. Beauty in its mystery, unknown in "Earth's . . . masquerade," pervades all levels of experience and can reside in lowly as well as in exalted places:

> High as a star, yet lowly as a flower,
> Unknown she takes her unassuming place
> At Earth's proud masquerade – the appointed hour
> Strikes, and, behold, the marvel of her face.

Searing like a lightning bolt, beauty manifests as revelation, a penetration of everyday illusion. The run-on lines, without Cawein's customary end-stops, imitate the flow of experience, into which the goddess' energies once again strike in an awful way.

Two last quatrains consider two modes in which reality "speaks" itself. "The Stars" (LOA, 2: 568) sees these "bright symbols of man's hope and fame" as "syllables with which God speaks His name / In the vast utterance of the universe." The stars, discreet articulations, comprise the name of God in the whole of the Word, the Logos, which comprises the Universe. Like the other quatrains, this one directly signifies its meaning, relegating metaphor to decorativeness.

In contrast and atypically, "Echo" (LOA, 2: 568) comments metaphorically on poetry and other attempts at imposing Apollonian order on Dionysian nature. Echo, cursed by Hera because she helped Zeus betray her, could say only the last syllables of words spoken in her presence. Echo fell in love with Narcissus but could not win him because she could not converse with him. When he rejected her, she withdrew into a cave and died. Her bones turned to stone, and all that was left of her was her voice saying last syllables. Zeus punished Narcissus for rejecting her by making him fall in love with his own image. Both would-be lovers, then, are trapped in their solipsistic universe. Her plight, in one of Cawein's strongest quatrains, becomes a metaphor for all failure of communication:

> Dweller in hollow places, hills and rocks,
> Daughter of Silence and old Solitude,
> Tip-toe she stands within her cave or wood,
> Her only life the noises that she mocks.

Isolated, alienated from the world of human love and comfort, her anxiety is reflected in her tip-toe posture, straining to hear some sound, the source of her only life, derivative as that is.

A fitting metaphor for Cawein's opus, "Echo" dramatizes the stance of the derivative poet, whose work is about sound and sense, but who can muster little of either that is truly his own. A few of Cawein's poems effectively dramatize sexualized energy transformed metaphorically into archetypal woman as destroyer and creator. The rest, except for a handful of local-color poems and a few philosophical quatrains, appear to derive from emotion that Cawein either would not or could not follow to its source, and address there. Instead, his poems haunt the fringes of the spirit's landscape, finding there the ghosts of sprites, fairies, and gods long dead. Only through the figure of the goddess did he manage to confront the cruelty, perversity, and death that are part of human experience. The comet of his reputation flared only briefly in the black sky as the nineteenth century gave way to the twentieth and the traditional modes of Romanticism and Victorianism gave way to modernism, so foreign to his imagination and sensibility. In 1899, he wrote to poet R. E. Lee Gibson:

> I . . . persuade myself that it is all true and that, perhaps, I am a pretty good poet. After awhile then it is borne in upon me that I am a writer with great limitations, and one who has happily done his best, not up to the average juvenile work of the great poets of literature.

These limitations rendered him unable to understand why he was a second-rate poet, and he died fifteen years later, puzzled, hurt, and and as close to embittered as such a gentle soul could be.

JANE GENTRY VANCE

Selected Works

Blooms of the Berry, Louisville, Kentucky: John P. Morton, 1887

The Triumph of Music and Other Lyrics, Louisville, Kentucky: John P. Morton, 1888

Accolon of Gaul, with Other Poems, Louisville, Kentucky: John P. Morton, 1889

Lyrics and Idyls, Louisville, Kentucky: John P. Morton, 1890

Days and Dreams, New York: Putnam's, 1891

Moods and Memories, New York: Putnam's, 1892

Red Leaves and Roses, New York: Putnam's, 1893

Poems of Nature and Love, New York: Putnam's, 1893

Intimations of the Beautiful and Other Poems, New York: Putnam's, 1894

The White Snake and Other Poems, Louisville, Kentucky: John P. Morton, 1895

Undertones, Boston: Copeland & Day, 1896

The Garden of Dreams, Louisville, Kentucky: John P. Morton, 1896

Shapes and Shadows, New York: R. H. Russell, 1898

Idyllic Monologues: Old and New World Verses, Louisville, Kentucky: John P. Morton, 1898

Myth and Romance: A Book of Verses, New York: Putnam's, 1899

One Day and Another: A Lyrical Eclogue, Boston: Richard G. Badger, 1901

Weeds by the Wall, Louisville, Kentucky: John P. Morton, 1901

Kentucky Poems, introduction by Edmund Gosse, London: Grant Richards, 1902; New York: Dutton, 1903

A Voice on the Wind and Other Poems, Louisville, Kentucky: John P. Morton, 1902

The Vale of Tempe, New York: Dutton, 1905

Nature Notes and Impressions in Prose and Verse, New York: Dutton, 1906

The Poems of Madison Cawein, 5 vols., Indianapolis, Indiana: Bobbs-Merrill, 1907; Boston: Small, Maynard, 1907

An Ode, Louisville, Kentucky: John P. Morton, 1908

New Poems, London: Grant Richards, 1909

The Giant and the Star: Little Annals in Rhyme, Boston: Small, Maynard, 1909

The Shadow Garden and Other Plays, New York: Putnam's, 1910

Poems by Madison Cawein, foreword by William Dean Howells, New York: Macmillan, 1911

The Poet, the Fool and the Faeries, Boston: Small, Maynard, 1912

The Republic: A Little Book of Homespun Verse, Cincinnati, Ohio: Stewart & Kidd, 1913

Minions of the Moon: A Little Book of Song and Story, Cincinnati, Ohio: Stewart & Kidd, 1913

The Poet and Nature and the Morning Road, Louisville, Kentucky: John P. Morton, 1914

The Cup of Comus: Fact and Fancy, New York: Cameo, 1915

Further Reading

Kerr, Charles, *History of Kentucky*, Chicago and New York: American Historical Society, 1922, 4:653–646

Perkins, David A., *A History of Modern Poetry*, Cambridge, Massachusetts: Harvard University Press, Belknap Press, 1976

Rothert, Otto A., *The Story of a Poet: Madison Cawein*, Louisville, Kentucky: Filson Club, vol. 30, John P. Morton, 1921

Untermeyer, Louis, ed., *Modern American Poetry: A Critical Anthology*, New York: Harcourt, Brace, 1936

Ward, William G., *A Literary History of Kentucky*, Knoxville: University of Tennessee Press, 1988

William Ellery Channing

(1818–1901)

Concord poet William Ellery Channing II was best known in his own time as Henry **Thoreau's** walking companion and biographer. As a poet, however, he was never very popular, and today he is rarely remembered. Occasionally, anthologists and literary historians still confuse him with his uncle, Dr. William Ellery Channing, the celebrated spokesman for Unitarian theology, committed abolitionist, and member of the New England intelligentsia. To an extent, this confusion is understandable, not only because of the shared name, but also because at different times both uncle and nephew were associated with Ralph Waldo **Emerson**, Margaret **Fuller**, and other members of the Transcendentalist movement. Adding to this confusion, the younger Channing also was a cousin to Reverend William Henry Channing, another Unitarian theologian and Transcendentalist who supported American Fourierism and the Brook Farm experiment, contributed to the movement's famous periodical, the *Dial*, and edited Fuller's *Memoirs*. Because they swam in the same waters, one might easily assume that these three Channings held similar values or practiced similar vocations, but beyond his connections to these Concord luminaries and Transcendentalism in general, Channing the poet shared little in common with his more famous relatives. In fact, he was something of a failure in life and in letters – a failure, that is, by his own standards and those of a few of his critics.

The second of four children born to Dr. Walter Channing and Barbara Perkins Channing, the young poet experienced little in the way of a secure or happy family life. Having lost his mother to sudden death when he was a small child, Channing was passed from relative to relative during his youth. As a young man, he grew increasingly despondent and rebellious; he probably performed poorly during his first term at Harvard in 1834 because he cut so many of his classes. Before his low marks could be formally registered, Channing had packed his bags and departed, choosing to reside with family friends in the country rather than return to his father's house in Boston. He did eventually return to Boston, where he began to write poetry, but he made no further effort to decide upon a profession for himself, as his family hoped he would. To their even greater disappointment, Channing borrowed money to purchase some farmland on the Illinois frontier and moved west in 1839. Oddly enough, it was during his brief stint as a farmer that Channing received his first recognition as a poet from Emerson. Channing soon abandoned his project as pioneer and returned to New England to write poetry. But en route, in Cincinnati, he met and married Ellen Fuller, Margaret Fuller's sister.

Both the Fuller and Channing families expressed concern about the union; the groom had few prospects for a career to support his new family and had yet to prove that he could commit himself to anything, least of all a marriage. As it turned out, the couple spent the duration of their relationship struggling to make ends meet on a meager allowance provided by Channing's father and the poet's sporadic but resentful bouts of employment. In fact, Channing retreated from the working world and its social obligations and took refuge in a life of excursions through the woods and in his friendship with Thoreau. Eventu-

ally, Channing all but abandoned his growing family, who depended on him for financial support at the very least. By the time he had two children, Channing had achieved a reputation (comparable in kind to Thoreau's) as a brooding, enigmatic woodsman and ne'er-do-well. In 1853, exhausted and frustrated, Ellen took the children and left her aloof husband. She did agree to a reunion two years later against the strong advice of friends and family. In 1856, however, Ellen became ill after giving birth to their fourth child and died. The Channing children were distributed among relatives, much as Channing himself had been, and saw little of their estranged father thereafter. Channing continued to roam the countryside and write poetry, outliving most of his friends. He died in 1901.

But the sad facts of this poet's life do not explain his lack of popularity as a poet in his own time, nor do they account for his frequent omission from the roll call of Transcendentalist poets in ours. A writer's personal misfortunes or supposed lapses in character seldom deter scholars; on the contrary, such factors often serve to heighten scholarly interest by allowing us to imagine the artist surrounded by an aura of emotional suffering – an ostensible prerequisite for inspiration. So the question arises: what is it exactly that makes Channing of so little interest to past and present readers and to scholars of nineteenth-century verse? After all, in addition to hundreds of poems and essays that were either unpublished or uncollected during his lifetime, he produced seven books of poetry: *Poems* (1843), *Conversations in Rome* (1847), *Poems: Second Series* (1847), *The Woodman, and Other Poems* (1849), *Near Home* (1858), *The Wanderer* (1871), and *Eliot, A Poem* (1885). He also wrote one long dramatic poem, *John Brown and the Heroes of Harpers Ferry* (1886); and a biography, *Thoreau, the Poet-Naturalist* (1873). In 1902, F. B. Sanborn collected and edited a volume of Channing's poems entitled *Poems of Sixty-Five Years*. In 1965, Walter Harding edited and published *The Collected Poems* from facsimile reproductions; this edition restores Channing's works to their original condition by excising Sanborn's emendations.

Given this sizable body of work, it seems a bit puzzling that since the time of his death, only two major critical works devoted to Channing have been published: Frederick T. McGill Jr.'s *Channing of Concord* (1967) and Robert Hudspeth's *Ellery Channing* (1973). Moreover, some of his correspondence has begun to surface only very recently. Many of his writings, including the early autobiographical essay "Major Leviticus," either remain unpublished or can be read only in the nineteenth-century papers and periodicals in which they originally appeared. Again, we must ask why, even now, when scholars are in the process of re-evaluating the inclusions and exclusions of the American literary canon, Channing's works receive so little attention.

Undoubtedly there are a number of factors. None of Channing's books was a financial success, nor was his work well-received by reviewers, many of whom were highly successful writers in their own right. James Russell **Lowell** criticized Channing for too closely imitating Emerson. Nathaniel **Haw-**

thorne referred to him as a poor substitute for Thoreau. Channing's cousin, William Henry, likewise faulted him for not being true to himself or the Transcendentalist ethos. In a review of Channing's first book, he advised: "Your daily thoughts are better poems than you can write. . . . Never shall you know the full music of your shell, and thread the strings of your lyre with the grateful tears of your brothers, your countrymen, till you own yourself to be one beating pulse of this wonderful mankind, struggling as it is towards symmetry and perfectness." From his cousin's perspective, Channing's choice of nature for his subject matter resulted in his neglect of "mankind" and, consequently, his neglect of those important political and ethical issues – abolition in particular – indicative of the human struggle toward perfection.

But perhaps the most devastating critique came from Edgar Allan **Poe** in his review of Channing's first book for *Graham's Monthly*: "His book contains about sixty three things, which he calls poems, and which he no doubt seriously supposes so to be. They are full of all kinds of mistakes, of which the most important is that of their having been written at all. They are not precisely English – nor will we insult a great nation by calling them Kickapoo; perhaps they are Channingese." Such virulence is characteristic of Poe; his distaste for what he perceived as naive Romanticism and parochialism among Transcendentalists led him to lambaste writers associated with the movement, which he dubbed "frogpondism." But this review goes beyond an attack on Channing's philosophical outlook to cite numerous grammatical errors, awkward rhymes, and oblique metaphors; the review results in a thorough argument for the rejection of Channing as a poet.

Even Channing's friends and supporters felt compelled to acknowledge his technical inadequacies. Out of an editor's respect for the word as written, Fuller had to dissuade Emerson from correcting misspellings and grammatical errors in the poems Channing submitted to the *Dial* in the early 1840s. Decades later, in his preface to Channing's *The Wanderer*, Emerson confessed his impatience for "a needless or even willful neglect of rhythm in a poet who has sometimes shown a facility and grace in his art which promised to outdo his rivals, and now risks offense by harshness." But the risk, Emerson concluded, was worth taking, for Channing's artistic imperfections signified what Emerson most valued: a break with convention and a disregard for traditional canons and popular opinion. "Here is Hamlet in the fields," Emerson continued, "with never a thought to waste even on Horatio's opinion of his sallies." For Emerson, much of Channing's brilliance had to do with his defiance of his reader's expectations and with his ability to write to himself and for himself in his attempt to discover nature's truths. But perhaps such brilliance was necessarily lost on most readers, since only other self-reliant philosophers could fully appreciate individualism in this form. Many other readers saw Channing as a more tragic Hamlet, who was mired in conventional rhythms and clichés and unable to communicate his vision successfully.

But aside from Emerson, who, despite his criticisms, was his most ardent admirer, Channing had other fans. Sanborn depicted the poet as an undiscovered if unpredictable genius. Bronson **Alcott** declared that Channing wrote "better lines of verse than any contemporary, if subtlety and exquisiteness of sense and melody are considered." In her journal, Fuller wrote:

"The dignity of Ellery's aspiration astounds me. It makes my own seem low and external. . . . Truly the life of soul is all to him. May he keep it inviolate as hitherto." Yet, it was Thoreau who perhaps best understood Channing, even though he also considered him an enigma. In his journal, Thoreau prophetically described Channing as "one who will not stoop to rise. He wants something for which he will not pay the going price. He will learn slowly by failure, – not a noble, but disgraceful, failure."

What was the going price? Perhaps it was conformity to the aesthetic and intellectual standards set by the urban literary community. Several critics mistakenly insist that Channing was the most "casual" of adherents to the movement as Emerson defined it. This assessment comes as no surprise. Out of his deep suspicion for any socially sanctioned art form or way of thinking, Channing himself rejected the label "Transcendentalist." Channing, however, was steeped in Transcendentalism, even if he did not live up to everyone's expectations, or even his own. Like Emerson, Thoreau, and Fuller, he valued originality over artificiality and convention, spontaneity over imitation, contradiction over consistency, the private over the public self, the present over the past, and nature above all. He rebelled against material culture and institutions because he associated urban life with spiritual stagnation and the loss of imaginative power. In "The Youth of the Poet and Painter," Channing's poet declares in the most Emersonian of tones: "I have no conception of anything which has a right to be called poetry, unless it come living out of the poet's nature, like the stream gushing from the rock, free and clear. It demands life from the depths of character, and must be written necessarily." Like Samuel Taylor Coleridge and the German idealists whose philosophies strongly influenced American Transcendentalists, Channing believed that the particulars of nature had to be interpreted as a hieroglyphics of universal spirit. He also believed in the Romantic idealization of the poet as the individual most sensitive to the unity or totality of nature. For Channing, therefore, the poetic process was indistinguishable from the processes of nature.

His poem "Hymn of the Earth" (LOA, 1: 672) remains one of the best expressions of Channing's adherence to this philosophy. Here the natural, transpersonal perspective is that of "Mother Earth" herself. Like other Romantic poets, William Wordsworth and William Cullen **Bryant** in particular, Channing anthropomorphizes nature in order to use it as a vehicle for the expression of transcendent truths. "The Earth," a figure for the supreme poet, sings her own celestial praises here, but because she is one with humankind, her song is echoed by the "Chorus" of her "pleasant Company" of human offspring. "The issues of the general Soul" are reflected in even the most minute natural processes – falling leaves, rolling pebbles. The poem thus frames the earth as both a principle of organic unity and an ideal model for the naturalist poet.

For William Henry Channing, Fuller, Emerson, Walt **Whitman**, and Thoreau, however, Transcendentalism was not merely a philosophy of the self in its relation to nature; it demanded one's political and artistic engagement to one of the greatest liberation movements of America's history. This belief in the equal participation of nature and humanity in a transcendental, spiritual world was radically democratic. If everyone participated equally in the realm of the divine, then everyone, including women, Native Americans, and African-Americans, ought to have equal access to the rights and privileges of citizenship. In a sense, Transcendentalism spiritualized the republican philosophy of the Revolutionary period, and thus threatened the status quo of a new nation that disguised its oppressive practices behind the rhetoric of liberty and equality. While Channing agreed in principle with abolition and universal suffrage, however, he chose to support the abolitionist movement at a distance and took no clear position on the rights of women and Native Americans. Apparently, it was his vehement distaste for modern society that prevented him from participating in any social or political activity. But one did not have to attend meetings or go to Boston to fight slavery: Concord was a stop on the Underground Railroad. Given his deep admiration for Thoreau, moreover, it is surprising that Channing chose not to emulate his actions. In *Thoreau, the Poet-Naturalist*, Channing writes: "The institution of American slavery was a filthy and rotten shed which Thoreau used his utmost strength to cut away and burn up. From first to last he loved and honored abolitionism. Not one slave alone was expedited to Canada by Thoreau's personal assistance."

Writing was also a form of action. The abolitionist movement depended on the public support of articulate writers from all over the Northern states. Still, the extent of Channing's public contribution to the abolitionist cause consists of several poems he was persuaded to write in 1852 for the American Anti-Slavery Society's *Letter to Louis Kossuth, Concerning Freedom and Slavery in the United States*. While he may have met with John Brown, who visited Concord in 1857 and 1859, it was not until 1878 that Channing saw fit to pay him homage in *John Brown and the Heroes of Harpers Ferry*. In this blank-verse drama, Channing depicts Brown as a fellow Transcendentalist, naturalist, and visionary who despised oppressive institutions and acted gloriously on his own moral principles. Had it been written and published 20 or 30 years earlier, this work might have had a profound impact on many more readers. But coming, as it did, so long after the fact, it seems more an expression of Channing's philosophy than Brown's.

Privately, however, Channing expressed his opinions on slavery at some length. In a letter to his friend Mary Watson in October 1862, Channing used the fiery rhetoric reminiscent of such abolitionist orators as Frederick Douglass to condemn the North's economic complicity in the slaveholding system:

> We have trifled too long with the immutable rules of right. Our merchants have grown rich on the blood and stripes of the negro. Behold the result. War, in which the side pretendedly fails, – for we are truly the real slaveholders. Look at Lowell, New York, Boston, and their towers built on the foundation of negro bones, glued together with the tears of sundered families, the dying groans of murdered innocents, the prayers for mercy of four millions [of] wretches. Is that nothing? Shall we pay no forfeit? Yes! when wrong is unpunished, when crime is unwhipt of justice, when the Devil reigns?

Even if Channing was an abolitionist only in spirit, he did not follow other Northerners in attempting to conceal his passivity behind a facade of moral superiority or innocence; on the contrary, he honorably implicated himself (along with all Northerners) in the nation's crimes against Africans and African Americans, even as he tried to withdraw from the nation into a private, natural world.

Channing hoped that his detachment from social life would put him in closer touch with the truth within himself and in nature and that his poetry would express his communion with spirit. He thus sought his own emancipation – the emancipation of the soul, the individual – from the corrupting, oppressive forces of an industrial economy and its materialistic values. Unfortunately, he could not reconcile his personal struggle for freedom with an overt commitment to freeing slaves. Nor would he compromise his philosophy by competing in the world of commerce, where, he felt, the ambition demanded by the market economy inevitably led to greed and conformity. In place of a capitalist work ethic, Channing substituted his own version of Emersonian self-reliance: he isolated himself from other people altogether.

For Channing, poetic creation required solitude, a mind uncluttered by the detritus of society. And yet, in many of his poems, self-reliance and solitude give way to alienation and isolation. Despite their idiosyncrasies, these works throw into relief a contradictory tendency in Transcendentalism toward self-absorption, perhaps even solipsism. In "The Poet's Dejection," for example, Channing's poet mourns his detachment from a "gay" yet "remorseless crowd":

> The path he treads must be by them untrod;
> His destiny a veil, his heart – unsealed;
> While all around him swims dancing in joy,
> And smiling faces and soft azure skies,
> Tantalus-like that he shall never touch,
> Look in across the dead sea of his life,
> Like goblin masks, fleshless and cold and pale.

What separates Channing's poet from the crowd is the lonesome, seemingly lifeless path he has chosen for himself, but he perceives it as a necessary separation. As Channing suggests in "Murillo's Magdalen" (LOA, 1: 675), the poet's life is one of "eternal sacrifice." Ironically, the speaker's redemption, like that of the frozen, repentant figure of Mary, depends upon his union with another solitary soul "Who may renew my light in me, / And both shall thus the past forget." Renewal, in this case, requires companionship, something Channing himself rejected yet longed for. His poems convey a tension between a desire for friendship, on the one hand, and a lack of faith or trust in people, on the other. They alternate between affirming self-reliance as a first principle and lamenting the loneliness or dissatisfaction that result from service to this principle.

Many of Channing's poems also express – perhaps inadvertently – the difficulties of achieving the Transcendental vision or understanding he so desires. In "The Harbor" (LOA, 1: 672), for example, Channing uses the extended metaphor of a ship reaching a harbor after a rough voyage (metaphors of ships and sailing are ubiquitous in his verse) to explore the "treacherous" process of composing a poem. The "prize," poetic inspiration, is found only at the end of the voyage, at which time "sound" is transformed into "song." But the second stanza underscores the inherent artifice of poetic inspiration. The natural beauty of the harbor is not enough, so the speaker decides to "steal" from his past – perhaps his previous efforts to create an inspired poem – in order to "throw more beauty" around this imagined refuge. The poet/sailor persona thus gives way momentarily to that of a poet/metallurgist or prospector who purifies "the gold" and forges from this experience a meaningful coin stamped "with thy every-day." Contrary to what we might expect from the Transcendentalist's perspective, inspiration in this poem does not erupt spontaneously or naturally, but is manufactured by the poet figure. Still, inspiration somehow comes as a surprise: "I did not dream to welcome thee; / Like all I have thou camest unknown." Interestingly, in the last stanza the speaker abandons the harbor metaphor in favor of the figure of a desert oasis and the well-worn image of a natural spring. Paradoxically, the poem represents inspiration in terms of the most conventional metaphor imaginable, but one that nevertheless unites the speaker's senses and allows him to "drink the sound" he "hoped to hear." These long excursions to the harbor and well suggest the poet's own long bouts of searching and self-doubt, but the success of such struggling remains uncertain. Perhaps like John Keats's "Ode to a Nightingale," Channing's "The Harbor" expresses a wish as yet unfulfilled.

In "The Barren Moors" (LOA, 1: 673), the speaker finds silence and isolation salutary. Resembling Shakespeare's King Lear, he celebrates rather than bemoans his isolation on the moors, a natural place "distinct from all" and far removed from the social relationships that vexed him. "Like desert Islands far at sea / Where not a ship can ever land," the barren moors satisfy him because they suggest "something veritable." And yet, likened to unapproachable islands – islands without inspirational harbors – this truthful "something" might very well be the unattainability of his wished for communion with nature. After all, in the last half of the poem the natural imagery once again gives way to the artificial in the form of a metaphor of an abandoned hall. The speaker concludes by taking refuge not in a natural haven but in a "dreamy home." Upheld by "A single pensive thought," this desolate structure signifies the poet's imagination. The poem concludes with the image of the speaker standing alone like a kind of living pillar between "two silent floors," and thus suggests his inability to think outside of the conventional intellectual structures of modern urban life that he seeks to abandon.

While many of his poems self-reflexively explore the limitations of the poetic process, Channing's journals and letters reveal his more adamant sense of failure that he has not achieved a unique vision. In his unpublished journal of 1867, he portrays himself as a would-be poet:

Dull I came upon the planet, untalented, the one talent still in that tremendous napkin, out of which I have never been able to unwrap it and where it is still like to be for all I can discern thro[ugh] its folds. Still, I shall seek a little longer before I shut up the magic lens called opportunity and utterly hibernate, like the woodchuck whose tracks I do not see all the long winter thro[ugh]. But every animal makes tracks, only some do not come into view. Why even I succeed in making tracks in the snow, and others in walking in them. Methinks, this is the greatest success I ever had in life.

Although he never felt that he succeeded in his efforts to "unwrap" his talent, Channing spent a lifetime leaving his poetic "tracks" on the pages of many volumes. He left his mark on the work of others, particularly Emerson, who quotes the closing line from Channing's "The Poet's Hope" at the end of his essay on Montaigne ("If my bark sinks, 'tis to another sea"). Critics have also noted that Channing's "Hymn of the Earth" and "Spider" are clearly sources for Emerson's "Brahma" (LOA, 1: 319) and "The Humble-Bee" (LOA, 1: 272). Such achievements, however, were of little comfort to Channing.

As for some of his more personal "tracks," Channing chose to erase all evidence of them, for he burned any letters he received and requested that the recipients of his correspondence do the same. Fortunately, some did not comply. Francis P. Dedmond has recently edited and published a selection of the surviving letters that illuminates the poet's perception of himself. Among these letters, one finds long, sometimes passionate, often philosophical love letters to unattainable women, letters that contrast sharply with the rather cold and detached little notes Channing sent to his children after the death of their mother. Taken together, these letters reveal a man deeply frustrated in his search for acceptance and understanding, a lonely man who both craves and fears intimacy. They too speak of sacrifice, loss, and wished for inspiration, and thus provide a key to a fuller understanding of Channing's poetic themes.

In another letter to Mary Watson, who was considering a writing career, Channing used himself as an example of what might lie ahead:

Nothing demands more unflinching perseverance than writing as a business. . . . But I have passed ten, more long years of my life in its best estate, writing and publishing; five distinct volumes have been printed under my name, besides this I have written much else and have failed utterly and entirely in my own estimate and that of all others to justify myself in their or my own light as a writer at all more (most) especially as a poet. I am telling this to you soberly and sincerely to show you what I have *done* and accomplished *nothing*. Are you willing to do so much? to throw away (if you fail) ten years, the least you can hope to test the "speriment" in? Are you willing to come fainly to the sacrifice and give yourself up on the altar of scribbling, a lamb of literary hope, possibly to be chopped into hero's meat?

He believed he had given himself up to the poet's endeavor, but he had been outdone by others whom he both admired and resented.

In a letter of 1864, Channing bitterly discloses what he feels is the real reason for his failure: "Mediocre poetry is worse than nothing & mine is not even mediocre. It is a jingle, a catch-penny. . . . Nearly a quarter-century of experience as a writer, has taught me many things. These need not be revealed. If I had been a Waldo Emerson or a Russell Lowell, if I had been the pet of fortune & society, the idol of clubs & young ladies, and a contributor to the 'Atlantic Monthly,' I might have written my experiences. As it is they are useless." Still unwilling to "unwrap" himself entirely, he suggests here that his failure is at least in part the result of being judged by readers or critics who prefer the written experiences of a more social, more cosmopolitan, or perhaps even more wealthy poet, as Thoreau had intimated.

Channing's resentment is understandable. He worked hard to maintain a relationship with Emerson, from whom he derived many of his ideas, but he was continually frustrated by what he perceived as Emerson's lack of interest. (In the early years of their acquaintance, the impoverished Channing chopped wood and did odd jobs for the Emersons.) Moreover, Channing could never have imagined himself the fellow traveler of a "pet of society," or an "idol" of "young ladies." It may be that, apart from his more personal motives for resentment, Channing felt that Emerson's popularity among the urban literati implicated the latter in the commercial, materialistic culture both claimed to reject. If so, Lowell, who began editing the *Atlantic Monthly* in 1857, was no better; he claimed affinities with Transcendentalist thought, yet criticized Thoreau for being reclusive, a criticism that most certainly would have extended to Channing. (In 1870, Channing wrote an imaginary dialogue involving Emerson, Lowell, and himself entitled "Critics of Literature," his own version of Lowell's *A Fable for Critics*, in which he satirizes the inabilities of his fellow critics to comprehend either his or Thoreau's writing.) Because he felt he had been true to his ideals, even if he was seldom satisfied with his poetry, Channing resented the overshadowing popularity of poets and writers who succeeded without similar sacrifices.

Channing both identified and resisted identification with Emerson. Thoreau was the only writer who consistently embodied Channing's ideals, for, unlike other Transcendentalists, he made no distinction between his art, his philosophy, and the manner in which he lived his life. For Channing, Thoreau appeared to have fulfilled his destiny by renouncing materialism and living a life of self-reliance, moral conviction, and blissful communion with nature. Thoreau had found the meaning of his existence in a life of solitude. In "Walden" (LOA, 1: 674), Channing honors his companion through the personification of Walden Pond:

> Thrice happy art thou, Walden! in thyself,
> Such purity is in thy limpid springs;
> In those green shores which do reflect in thee,
> And in this man who dwells upon thy edge,
> A holy man within a Hermitage.

Just as the water reflects the trees along the shore, so Thoreau's virtuous principles are reflected in nature, and vice versa. (Among Channing's many memorial verses in *Thoreau*, we find similar passages and metaphors in which Thoreau is depicted as nature's virtuous offspring or even the embodiment of nature itself.) His holiness derives from his seclusion, his refusal to participate in the corrupt processes of material culture; Thoreau resembles a "faithful Merchant" only in that he "does account / To God for what he spends, and in what way."

It is through his recounting of the lives of others that Channing tells the story of a life he himself wanted to live. One can read *Thoreau*, which is also filled with anecdotes about Emerson, as a series of the biographer's self-reflections, much like the reflections in his poem "Walden." But not all of these reflections take the form of positive ideals; as much as he wanted to emulate his peers, Channing also projected some of himself onto his companions. For example, in this passage from Thoreau (the chapter "Walks and Talks"), the biographer might just as well have been referring to himself: "Emerson was never in the least contented. This made walking or company to him a penance. The Future – that was the terrible Gorgon face that turned the present into 'a thousand belly-aches.' 'When shall I be perfect? When shall I be moral? When shall I be this and that? When will the really good rhyme get written?' Here is the Emerson colic. Thoreau had a like disease. Men are said never to be satisfied." Channing surely had the same affliction. As he saw it, dissatisfaction was part and parcel of the Transcendentalist's enterprise. (Although he refers only to "men" here, he might just as well have included Fuller.) One had to struggle perpetually to improve and evolve; the content and complacent individual could never hope to sense or experience his or her place in the moral universe. This individual might have taken a little pride in the fact that he had earned the right to feel the least satisfied of all.

Channing's long life of excursions was marked by this struggle, or, as he put it this "disease." But even if this dissatisfaction rendered him a failure in his own eyes, it need not prevent the late twentieth-century reader from exploring his poetry. Although he might have preferred that we consider his poems apart from any specific social or historical context, Channing's verse is nonetheless best understood in light of the politics as well as the philosophy of Transcendentalism. Whether or not they measure up to our standards for "good" poetry, his works are significant because they alter the common view of this movement by revealing some of the limitations and effects of a philosophy of self-reliance. In a culture that continues to promote individualism – an ideology that often discourages positive social interaction and political engagement – Channing's poetic excursions can be taken as a warning to those who would seek solutions to social crises in isolation.

KRISTA WALTER

Selected Works

Poems, Boston: Little and Brown, 1843

Poems: Second Series, Boston: James Munroe, 1847

The Woodman, and Other Poems, Boston: James Munroe, 1849

Near Home; A Poem, Boston: James Munroe, 1858

The Wanderer: A Colloquial Poem, Boston: James R. Osgood, 1871

Thoreau, the Poet-Naturalist, Boston: Roberts Brothers, 1873; revised and enlarged, edited by F. B. Sanborn, Boston: Goodspeed, 1902

Eliot; A Poem, Boston: Cupples, Uppham, 1885

John Brown and the Heroes of Harpers Ferry; A Poem, Boston: Cupples, Uppham, 1886

Poems of Sixty-Five Years, edited by F. B. Sanborn, Philadelphia and Concord, Massachusetts: James H. Bentley, 1902

The Collected Poems of William Ellery Channing the Younger, edited by Walter Harding, Gainesville, Florida: Scholars' Facsimiles, 1967

"The Selected Letters of William Ellery Channing the Younger," parts 1–3, edited by Francis B. Dedmond, *Studies in the American Renaissance*, edited by Joel Myerson, Charlottesville: Virginia University Press, 1989–91: pp. 115–218 (1989), pp. 159–142 (1990), pp. 257–344 (1991)

Further Reading
Buell, Lawrence, *Literary Transcendentalism*, Ithaca, New York, and London: Cornell University Press, 1973
Ellis, Charles Mayo, *An Essay on Transcendentalism*, edited by Walter Harding, Gainesville, Florida: Scholars' Facsimiles, 1954
Hudspeth, Robert N., *Ellery Channing*, New York: Twayne, 1973
McGill, Frederick T., Jr., *Channing of Concord*, New Brunswick, New Jersey: Rutgers University Press, 1967
Sanborn, Franklin Benjamin, *Sixty Years of Concord, 1855–1915*, edited by Kenneth Walter Cameron, Hartford, Connecticut: Transcendental Books, 1976

John Jay Chapman

(1862–1933)

Chapman was at various times a lawyer, reformer, poet, playwright, and essayist. Regardless of the genre in which he wrote, his work may perhaps be best described as cultural criticism. His dedication to Emersonian individualism, his intense involvement with social and political issues, and his dislike of dogma all inform his work. His poetry, in particular, is deeply engaged with its cultural context. Chapman wrote verse throughout his life, but he published only one volume, *Songs and Poems* (1919). His other poems are scattered throughout magazines and journals and have never been collected. Although Chapman's renown today rests largely upon his essays, his poetry provides valuable insights into the cultural moods of the late nineteenth and early twentieth centuries through the way in which it merges poetic and political discourse.

Chapman was born in New York City on March 2, 1862 to Eleanor Jay and Henry Grafton Chapman. From both sides of his family, Chapman inherited a legacy of public service and political activism. His father was a founder of the Knickerbocker Club and president of the New York Stock Exchange. His mother's side of the family was equally distinguished, most notably by Chapman's great-great-grandfather, John Jay, president of the Continental Congress, twice governor of New York, and chief justice of the Supreme Court. This legacy of public service influenced Chapman throughout his life.

In 1876, Chapman entered St. Paul's School in Concord, New Hampshire, but left after less than two years, when the strenuous regimen and oppressive religious atmosphere of the school precipitated a physical and mental breakdown. He returned home, where for the next several years private tutors helped him prepare for Harvard, which he entered in 1880. After graduating in 1884, Chapman traveled throughout Europe for over a year. In 1885, he returned to the United States and entered Harvard Law School. While in law school, he was involved in a bizarre incident. According to his autobiographical fragment, "Retrospections," Chapman was deeply in love with Minna Timmins, a young Italian American woman, in 1887. Convinced that she had been mistreated by Percival Lowell (of the prominent line of Boston Lowells), the enraged Chapman violently beat Lowell with a cane. Several days later, Chapman deliberately thrust his left hand into an open fire, burning it so severely that it had to be amputated the next day. Richard B. Hovey, one of Chapman's biographers, claims that Chapman's account of the incident glosses over several important facts. According to Hovey, Chapman was unsure of Timmins's feelings toward him; wrongly convincing himself that Lowell had seduced her, Chapman flew into the rage that prompted the beating. Further, Hovey proposes that the self-mutilation was prompted by a letter that Chapman received from Timmins, in which she asked him to apologize to Lowell. Although her family insisted that after this event the couple separate for over a year, Timmins and Chapman were married on July 2, 1889.

Chapman reluctantly turned to law for financial support and was admitted to the New York Bar in 1888. Subsequently, he became interested in politics and political reform and joined the City Reform Club and the Good Government Club. The

Chapmans soon had two children, Victor Emmanuel and John Jay, Jr. Minna Chapman died in January 1897, a month after giving birth to their third son, Conrad. On April 23, 1898, Chapman married Elizabeth Chanler, a close family friend. They had a son, Chanler, in 1901.

In March 1897, Chapman founded one of the more interesting periodicals of the late nineteenth century. Originally entitled *The Nursery* (later changed to *The Political Nursery*), this journal was edited by Chapman, who was also the principal writer. The running masthead read: "The object of *The Nursery* is to tell the truth. There is no publication at present which seems to cover this exact field. Truth is best seen by the light of example, hence *The Nursery* does not shun personalities when they are in the point." In order to "tell the truth," Chapman targeted the "moral cowardice" that he thought was undermining American democracy and employed satire in devastating attacks on politicians and the machine politics of New York. He also wrote philosophical and literary essays for *The Nursery*, but these comprised a relatively small portion of the journal.

The Nursery is important not only for its scathing indictments of political corruption, but also because it first published virtually all of Chapman's political poetry. The sentiments expressed in his poetry resemble those expressed in his prose – primarily disgust with the machine politics that ruled New York. His political verse is clever, satirical, and witty, but the knowledge of post–Gilded Age politics that it presupposes renders some of it obscure to today's readers. Its humor, however, is readily apparent; Chapman fills the skeltonic verses with tumbling rhymes that keep the lines moving at a fast pace. "Hurly Burly" (January 1899), for example, which attacks New York politicians including Theodore Roosevelt, is loaded with double and triple rhymes:

> Tell with impunity
> Careless of unity
> Just what I think of this seething community?
> Certainly, willingly,
> Though it is killingly
> Odious ever to utter disdainingly
> What you believe, though you talk entertainingly.

"The Heavy Brigade" (1897), a parody of Alfred, Lord Tennyson's "The Charge of the Light Brigade," also attacks machine politics, chanting, "Half a deal, half a deal, half a deal onward." Still satirical, but more serious, is "The Choir Invisible" (March 1898), which speaks of Chapman's frustrations as a reformer. Businessmen clamor for reforms of the municipal government, yet when asked to help, they respond, "I can't go myself – I should never live through it – / My business would suffer, you see, there's the rub."

Perhaps the most important poem published in *The Nursery* is "Bismarck" (July 1898; LOA, 2: 543), retitled and shortened considerably in *Songs and Poems* as "Lines on the Death of Bismarck." "Bismarck," which presciently foresees the rise of Nazism, reflects Chapman's passionate political beliefs and reveals his understanding of the legacy of German nationalism. The poem identifies Otto von Bismarck, first chancellor of the German Empire, as the personal driving force behind the movement toward German nationalism. Bismarck's policy to unify the various German principalities was, for Chapman, based largely on campaigns of fear and hatred: "One race, one tongue, one instinct. Unify / By banking prejudice and, gaining power, / Attract by vanity, compel by fear." What Bismarck set in motion survives him: "strong as dynamite, / An empire and a whirlwind, on it moves, / While he that set it rolling lies so still." The penultimate stanza, which forms the crux of the poem, reflects Chapman's Emersonian belief in the individual and his frustration with international politics:

> The only force that can improve the world,
> Enlightened public thought in private men,
> Is minimized in Europe, till The Powers
> Stand over Crete to watch a butchery
> And diplomats decide the fate of men.

According to the poem, Bismarck's policy of "Organized hatred" and unity at any cost crushed the individual in Germany; as Chapman accurately prophesied, moreover, it was the failure of the "Enlightened" individual in Europe to speak out that allowed German nationalism to grow unchecked until it threatened the rest of Europe.

Chapman produced other important works during this decade, including *Emerson and Other Essays* (1898), *Causes and Consequences* (1898), and *Practical Agitation* (1900). *Emerson and Other Essays* includes a number of literary essays, most notably discussions of Dante, Robert Browning, Ralph Waldo **Emerson**, and Walt **Whitman**. *Causes and Consequences* attacks the selfishness resulting from post–Civil War industrialism and commercialism, claiming that business interests have taken control of politics and the government. *Practical Agitation* argues for a third political party that will offer a moral vision to voters tired of greed and corruption in the two party system. Taken together, these three works represent the culmination of Chapman's thought during the 1890s.

In 1901, however, Chapman suffered a series of devastating disappointments. *The Nursery* failed at the same time that he was overexerting himself with his political reform efforts, and he succumbed to a serious case of influenza. Following this illness, he suffered a mental and physical breakdown that required bed rest for nearly a year, and from which he took 10 years to recover fully. Chapman was writing during this period, however, and produced a number of plays for children, some in blank verse. In 1913, he also published *William Lloyd Garrison*, a study of the life of the famous abolitionist.

In 1919, Chapman published *Songs and Poems*, a collection of 35 new and previously published works. This volume excludes his satirical political verse, concentrating instead on his lyrical nature and war poems. In this volume, these poems are linked thematically rather than formally. Chapman in fact eschewed a formal poetic theory, arguing in his essay "Walt Whitman" (reprinted in *Emerson and Other Essays*) that the attempt to conform to a poetic theory betrays damaging self-consciousness even in work by the best poets. Although most reviewers faulted Chapman for the conventionality of his verse, contemporary reviews of *Songs and Poems* were generally favorable. The reviewer for the *Boston Transcript*, for example,

explains that "At a first glance these verses seem . . . the expression of a writer who is entirely oblivious to the very modern currents of poetic thoughts and feelings." Later critics, like Hovey, agreed with this assessment, arguing that

> what was poetic in him Chapman expressed in his prose. He had developed a prose style unique and his own – in its rhythms, its tone, its diction and imagery. . . . In contrast, Chapman's voice in his poetry is often so muffled and disguised that one can scarcely recognize it. Another man – a considerable number of other versemakers – could have written these poems. In them is a voice of the past, of the Victorian romantic tradition. In his verse, Chapman's wit is dulled; his images are mostly those tried and made safe by the centuries; and too often his diction is artificially, sometimes curiously Old World, occasionally antiquated.

Although Hovey's assessment is harsh, the verse form and expression of *Songs and Poems* show that his work is a product of nineteenth-century poetic expectations. Further, the dates of composition for these poems range over two decades, so some of the poems indeed date back to the nineteenth century. Despite the conventionality of much of Chapman's verse, however, *Songs and Poems* is not without merit. A number of poems demonstrate fine poetic insight and interesting use of images and metaphors.

Songs and Poems falls naturally into two halves. The first section includes classically inspired verse, occasional poems, and nature poetry. Chapman's nature poetry, which focuses on depictions of autumn, comprises the largest portion of this section. "Moonlight" chiefly interests for its personification of the moon as a passionate woman, and for its use of Spenserian stanzas. "Harvest Time" personifies autumn as an emperor bearing gifts. The six-stanza "October" describes the fulfillment of autumn, when

> Something Elysian, – a faint tang of joy, –
>   Breathes from the moisture of the open field,
> Recalling Spring, yet Spring with no alloy
>   Of heartache, such as hovers on the view
> Of things in promise.

The enjambment of lines in the middle of each stanza prevents the meter and rhyme scheme from becoming mechanical. It is Chapman's interesting use of similes and metaphors, however, that makes "October" the best of his nature poems. He likens the peculiar clarity of the autumn air to "the lens of a vast telescope," while cropped fields become "A text that all may understand / With margins where wild vines expand / In crimson revelry."

"Taps at West Point" and "Lines on the Death of Bismarck" act as a bridge to the second half of *Songs and Poems*, which concentrates on Chapman's verse occasioned by World War I. The loosely chronological arrangement of these poems allows them to be read as a poetic journal of the war years that documents Chapman's alternating emotions of despondency and elation. Thus, we see the wild despair of a poem like "May, 1917":

> Would I had perished with the past!
>   Would I had shared the fate

Of those who heard the trumpet-call
And rode upon the blast, –

Songs and Poems juxtaposes this poem against the heavily nationalistic and romantic "Ode on the Sailing of Our Troops for France," in which Chapman, inflamed by the ravages France was experiencing in the war, could make the epic benediction:

Go, Western Warriors! Take the place
The ages have assigned you in a strife
Which to have died in were enough of life;
For you there awaits a quest
    Such as no paladin or hero knew
Of all who lifted sword or wielded mace
Since George the Dragon slew. . . .

Perhaps the best of Chapman's war poems is "Augustus Peabody Gardner." It is certainly one of his more balanced works; it is free of stilted diction and frenzied emotion. Exploring a sense of loss from the death of friends, the speaker says,

I SEE – within my spirit – mystic walls,
    And slender windows casting hallowed light
Along dim aisles where many a shadow falls
On text and trophy, effigy and tomb . . .

This "chapel" within the speaker memorializes the dead "companions I have known, / Whose hands I clasped but yesterday, / Whose voices ring within my ear." Although mechanical meter and rhyme mar many individual poems, the cumulative, contrapuntal effect of this series of war poems on the whole is greater than the sum of its parts.

The war's end marked a number of changes in Chapman's life. He continued to write and publish poetry, but apparently never made any effort to collect it. His interest in municipal politics also waned. Chapman's unpublished "Sonnet on Middle Life" (found in Howe) seems to express some of the exhaustion he felt; in this poem, the waves speak to the poet: "'Trouble thyself no more. The time is brief. / Thy mind is harvested: its little sheaf / Stands in the granary of yesterday.'" Instead, Chapman's interests turned to education and he attacked the increasing commercialization that he saw in American universities. It was also during the 1920s that Chapman began his most unpopular agitations. Alarmed by the uneasy global political situation, rumors of conspiracy theories, and mass immigration into the United States, Chapman became fearful of the potential political power of the Jewish and Catholic religions. In particular, he disliked the Catholic church's allegiance to dogma and worried that its powerful hierarchical structure might negatively influence the democratic process. His views reflect the political climate of his times, but nonetheless they are difficult to reconcile with those of the earlier reformer who argued that education was the key to eliminating racism and cultural prejudices, and who in the same decade spoke of the need for unity among the human race.

Chapman continued to write poetry throughout the 1920s, publishing in such journals as *Scribner's*, the *Sewanee Review*, the *Atlantic Monthly*, and *Harper's*. The autobiographical poem "Last Words," published in *Scribner's* in July 1929, marks the end of his life as a public agitator. It also expresses his continued doubts about the efficacy of his reform efforts:

In fact – I say it in your ear –
It was a grand mistake, I fear,
    To try to better you.
The more I probed, the more I found
    The Evil's deeper source.
I digged: – the truth was underground;
Star-gazed: – 'twas cosmic force.
And as the baffling years slipped by
The streams of hope were running dry
    In their meandering course.

Yet, the doubt that Chapman expresses here seems to be directed not toward his own ideas, but rather toward the whole idea of reform; the frustration that he experiences is not with himself, but with the world for failing to recognize his ideas. Although he suffered from continued ill health during the last three years of his life, Chapman published two more poems, "Souls in Prison" in the *New York Herald Tribune Books* and "Fulfillment" in the *Atlantic*, and two volumes of essays. Diagnosed with cancer of the liver, he had surgery to treat the disease, but died at age 71 on November 4, 1933.

Although Chapman has chiefly been remembered as an essayist, his poetry provides us with valuable insight into American culture in the late nineteenth and early twentieth centuries. His political satire in *The Nursery* is clever and witty. And while parts of *Songs and Poems* reflect Chapman's passionate desire for justice, sometimes at the cost of aesthetic effect, the volume nonetheless contains a number of fine poems.

KAREN A. WEYLER

Selected Works

The Selected Writings of John Jay Chapman, edited by Jacques Barzun, New York: Farrar, Straus & Cudahy, 1957
The Collected Works of John Jay Chapman, edited by Melvin H. Bernstein, 12 vols., Weston, Massachusetts: M & S Press, 1970

Further Reading

Bernstein, Melvin H., *John Jay Chapman*, New York: Twayne, 1964
Hovey, Richard B., *John Jay Chapman – An American Mind*, New York: Columbia University Press, 1959
Howe, M. A. DeWolfe, *John Jay Chapman and His Letters*, Boston and New York: Houghton Mifflin, 1937
Wilson, Edmund, *The Triple Thinkers*, New York: Oxford University Press, 1948

Thomas Holley Chivers

(1809–1858)

The eldest of seven children, Thomas Holley Chivers was born in 1809 and enjoyed a comfortable childhood at Digby Manor, a plantation near Washington, Georgia. In S. Foster Damon's words, "he was a boy in a virgin country, living close to nature in a handsome 'cottage' surrounded by oaks and pines." Nevertheless, at an early age, Chivers was profoundly convinced that the bliss of heaven far outweighed the "trials" of mortal life. When he was still a boy, Chivers's sister died, and he tried to express in poetry his vision of her union with God and her ascendance into heaven. Damon cites Chivers's "On the Death of Adaline":

> Oh, dying sister!
> How can I emblem that I never saw? how
> Can a brother's words depict that which he
> Only saw reflected from a mirror
> Of your infant soul?
> . . . .
> An Iris ever varient – ever
> New, converging all its rays in focus
> Of eternity.

This effort marks the beginning of Chivers's determination to articulate his visions through poetry.

Having grown up in the security of a loving, wealthy family, Chivers was devastated by the failure of his youthful marriage to his cousin, Frances, who left him during the first year of their marriage and never let him see the child of their union. Distraught, Chivers left his hometown to travel and then to attend medical school in Kentucky; he graduated with distinction in 1830, but did not return to Georgia until 1835. During his self-imposed "exile," he continued to write as a way to compensate for the profound disappointments of his young adult life. Although he consistently signed his literary efforts Thomas Holley Chivers, M.D., he practiced medicine only briefly.

He published his early work himself – *The Path of Sorrow* (1832) and *Conrad and Eudora* (1834) – but in 1837, *Nacoochee* was published by W. E. Dean of New York, and in 1839, Chivers began to sell his poems to magazines such as *The New Yorker* and the *National Magazine and Republican Review*. In 1837 he remarried, and his personal and professional life seemed to change from despair and disappointment to love and promise.

In 1839, his wife, Harriette Hunt, gave birth to their first child, Allegra Florence. Damon concludes that for Chivers "it was no ordinary birth"; he cites Chivers's essay in the December 9, 1848 issue of *Univercoelum*: "Eight years before [Allegra] was born, she came down to me from Heaven in the form of an Angel. She bore a golden harp in her hand . . . she played most ravishingly – entrancing my soul." In the next year, their son Eugene was born. In that same year, Chivers began an epistolary relationship with Edgar Allan **Poe**, who would later praise Chivers's *The Lost Pleiad* in *The Broadway Journal*: "We consider many of the pieces in the volume before us as possessing merit of a very lofty – if not of the very loftiest order."

This time of happiness and promise, however, was cut short by Allegra's sudden death from typhoid at age three, coincidentally on Chivers's birthday, in October 1842. At her death, Chivers records in *Univercoelum*, the same song he had heard in his prophetic vision of her birth recurred:

> then did I hear the same sorrowful, imploring wail of the song that she sang to me when she came down to me in spirit with the golden harp in her hand . . . fading away into an echo of the song of the soul of him whose hope is full of immortality.

Chivers's sorrow continued, because he lost three other children to typhoid as well. In "Avalon" (LOA, 1: 574), he writes:

> Four little Angels killed by one cold Death
> To make God glad!
> Four Cherubs gone to God, the best he hath –
> And all I had!
> . . . .
> Can any thing that Christ has ever said,
> Make my heart whole?

Much of Chivers's poetry despairs over the death of loved ones, anticipates the solace of life after death, and describes angelic presences in the beauty of the world we see. *The Lost Pleiad*, Chivers's third book of poetry, is full of his sorrow at Allegra's death. In fact, the elegy to Allegra, "To Allegra Florence in Heaven," is the poem that caused so much controversy between Chivers and Poe. Chivers alleged that Poe "borrowed" heavily from it to write "The Raven" (LOA, 1: 535), the poem that pushed Poe's work into the literary spotlight while Chivers remained an outsider to the literary scene. It is intriguing that Poe did not publish excerpts from this poem in his article praising *The Lost Pleiad*. Instead, Poe chose excerpts from four others: "Shelley," "The Lost Pleiad: An Elegy on the Death of My First-Born," "The Son's Destiny," and "Sonnet: To Isa Sleeping" (LOA, 1: 574).

Unlike Poe, Chivers was independently wealthy, and much of the correspondence between Poe and Chivers revolved around Poe's requests for money. Chivers never fulfilled these requests because Poe never fulfilled Chivers's entreaties for philosophical exchanges. The last reference to Chivers in Poe's correspondence suggests a certain bitterness on Poe's part – "received another sneaking letter from Chivers" – yet Chivers felt so strongly about his friendship with Poe that he offered to house and take care of him; Poe never responded to the invitation.

Critics have made much of the Poe-Chivers controversy (see Damon, Benton, Lombard, and Watts), yet as Watts suggests, "not once in any of their letters is there a hint of the plagiarism which after Poe's death became the central issue." Chivers in fact held Poe's work in high regard and wrote an exoneration of Poe, "A New Life of Edgar A. Poe," to dispute Rufus Griswold's efforts to malign Poe's character. Chivers's manuscript was never accepted in entirety by a publisher, but excerpts were printed after his death in *Century Magazine* (1903). Watts contends, however, that Chivers's "high-flying charges of plagiarism" in defense of his own work during the *Waverly Magazine* feud undermined any critical estimation of Chivers's poetry until 1930.

Clearly, Chivers admired Poe's genius, and many similarities exist between Chivers's ideas about poetry and Poe's. This is especially evident in Chivers's preface to *Atlanta*, published in 1853, four years after Poe's death. Agreeing with Poe's statement in "The Poetic Principle" that "a long poem does not exist . . . [it] is simply a flat contradiction in terms," Chivers says: "no poem of any considerable length, from the very nature of the relations subsisting between the power of the soul to receive, and the impressions to be made, can be pleasing." He then goes on to "quote" Bacon: *"There is no exquisite beauty without some strangeness in proportion"*; however, he actually seems to take this misquotation from Poe's "Ligeia." It seems not merely coincidental that Chivers quotes Poe's misquotation rather than Bacon ("There is no excellent beauty that hath not some strangeness in proportion") and then goes on to argue that Bacon's contention "cannot be truth."

Chivers immediately turns to another of Poe's concerns found in "Philosophy of Composition." Like Poe, he exonerates novelty: "the novel suddenness or rare unexpectedness of those impressions before named, will confer delight, because, at every appeal made, there will be something new – something the memory of which will not crowd out of the soul succeeding impressions. This is what constitutes delight." Chivers's preface ends with his recognition that the poem that follows, "Atlanta," like his other work, will be appreciated only by "the *Chosen Few*," thereby suggesting the ignorance of the "general public," as Poe often implied if not openly asserted.

Altogether, Chivers published nine volumes of poetry. Watts suggests that Chivers strove for "the effect of sound for its own sake, beauty to evoke beauty with the belief that its creation is a deliberate emotional experience worthy of expression." In fact, Chivers often made up words to suit the sound and feeling he desired. Lombard quotes Chivers's article in the June 28, 1851 *Georgia Citizen*, which describes how he derived the title *Eonchs of Ruby*:

> The Word *Eonch* is the same as *Concha Marina – Shell of the Sea. Eonch* is used instead of *Concha*, merely for its euphony. It is the same as the Kaur Gaur of the Hebrews. Ruby signifies, in the language of correspondence, *Divine Love*. The word Eonch is used, as a title, by metonymy, for *Songs*. The meaning of the title is, therefore, apparent: namely, *Songs of Divine Love*. The clouds, I hope, are now dispelled; and the mystery, I presume, evaporates.

These "experiments with forms of expression," Watts observes, "go far beyond anything that Poe attempted." Damon suggests that Chivers's technical transgressions were based in the belief that "the melody of verse outweighs both the literal meaning and the moral." Damon also argues that "the richness of open vowels, of luxuriant alliteration; the possibilities of returns and varied repetitions; the elaborately-built stanza-forms" were of great concern to Chivers's craft. Chivers's poetry, critics claim, anticipated the French symbolists.

Poe, too, seems to praise Chivers's work for its "originality," suggesting that it has *"no* taint – absolutely none – of either [Lord] Byron, or [Percy Bysshe] Shelley, or [William] Wordsworth, or [Samuel Taylor] Coleridge, or [Alfred, Lord] Tennyson." But we can only assume that Poe is again playing with his audience. Chivers's poetry not only uses many quotations from these poets (Shelley in particular) as epigraphs, he goes so far as to write "Mary's Lament for Shelley Lost at Sea," along with other poems that praise Shelley as the epitome of the poet. Lombard also suggests that Chivers was heavily influenced by Swedenborgian principles:

> Chivers had been a fervent Baptist and he retained his evangelical zeal after embracing the tenets of the New Church. Through the theory of correspondence Swedenborg opened to Chivers fresh poetic vistas. The universe was alive with symbols, not mere abstractions but reminders of a higher order of truths in the World of Spirits . . . [His] poems abound with references to angelic presences in man's midst, a reminder of the Swedenborgian precept that the next life is just a step away.

As for inspiration, Lombard concludes that Chivers held that writing poetry was "a mystic and supernatural experience in which the poet received directly from God a revelation of a particular aspect of the beautiful." Watts suggests that Chivers believed that poetry provided "another world in which he could create all that this one . . . had failed to supply him with. . . . His understanding of that world came from within himself; so there was no need to square it with the reality he saw about him." Watts cites Chivers's "The Poet of Love" to support this contention:

> From the inflorescence of his own high soul
>   The incense of his Eden-song doth rise,
> Whose golden river of pure redolence doth roll
>   Down the dark vistas of all time in melodies.

Although many may read Chivers's work and question its excesses, Watts believes that this very excess produces for the reader an experience equivalent to the ecstasy of the poet who claims to be in the process of writing divinely inspired work. This, Watts concludes, "explain[s] Chivers's statement that all true poetry is dramatic . . . that the true poet describes not the scene before him, but his experience in reacting to it." In the preface to *Nacoochee*, Chivers cites the poet's charge:

> from communing with the beauties of this earth, he is capable of giving birth to other beings brighter than himself; and of lifting up his spirit to the presence of those things which he shall enjoy in another state; and which he manifests to *this* through the instrumentality of certain words and sentences melodiously concatenated.

In this way, Chivers's poetry performs its content, much as Shelley's "The Triumph of Life" not only describes a state of *dejá vu* but involves the reader in a similar extra-ordinary experience in its very iteration. In Chivers's poetry, sounds are meant to mesmerize in an incantatory way through repetition and excessiveness; they enfold the cognitive into the intuitive and lead the reader to a plane of otherworldliness. As Damon suggests, Chivers "endeavored to express subtle states of mind by a series of words (often his own invention) and of images, the surface meanings of which are subordinate to the general hypnotic effect."

"Avalon," with its repetitive refrain, echoing rhyme, and unrelenting rhythm, draws the reader further and further into an incantatory dirge that bemoans the fate of living "beneath Death's iron rod!" Even when appealing to God for "refreshment" from this mourning pain, for His "heavenly Word" to heal him, the poet remembers his son, "A living Lyre of God who charmed me so," and angrily rises to demand:

> Can less than bringing back the early dead,
>   Restore my soul?
> No! this alone can make my Heavenly bread –
> Christ's Bread of Life brought down from Heaven,
>   instead
> Of this sad Song.

Yet, "this sad Song" continues and finally becomes a desperate hope that "battering down God's Golden Gates on high, / With my complaint" could bring his son back or cause him, too, to die. Like the epigraph from Psalms that precedes his poem, however, the poet remains sunk "in deep mire where there is no standing." His poem becomes only one more effort to cajole his sorrow.

Like many of Chivers's poems, "The Lost Pleiad: An Elegy on the Death of My First-Born" (1845) speaks of this despair:

> Until my death, or soon or late
> My heart shall be disconsolate!
> Shall grieve for thee forever more!
> Forever more still grieves for thee!

"To Allegra Florence in Heaven" repeats this theme:

> . . . this dark heart of mine!
> Which, though broken, is still breaking,
> And shall never more cease aching
> For the sleep which has no waking –
> For the sleep which now is thine!

This theme is prevalent throughout Chivers's poetry, but others express his sensuous praise of his wife ("Sonnet: To Isa Sleeping," "Song to Isa," "Song to Isa Singing"), his joy in nature's renewal ("Spring," "The Voice of My Delight"), or his delight in God's inspiration ("Apollo," "The Beautiful Silence").

"Apollo" (LOA, 1: 581), with its regular rhyme (*ababcd-cdd*), nevertheless departs from regular form with nine line stanzas. The last line of each, which echoes both the sound and the meaning of the line that precedes them, accentuates the poet's resignation to the "truth" of "mortal" life: that "Life . . . *cannot* be immortal" and that "stars, which are the echoes of the shining of the sun," are "forever blooming." Likened to the "hieroglyphics of God's glory," these stars nonetheless echo that glory, just as the words of poetry merely echo divine inspiration. Yet, Chivers upholds this task of "reflecting" God's meanings and affirming that the poet is "the inheritor here, on earth, of the joys which are 'undefiled and that fadeth not away' in Heaven – holding within the hollow of his hand not only the Rod of Hermes, but the Keys of the doors of the Kingdom of Heaven."

Despite the slight critical attention his work received, Chivers continued to write throughout his lifetime, secure in his self-acknowledged satisfaction that "poetry was not only the highest attainment of man; but the revelation of the inspiration of the pre-destined influx of the Divine Life of God into the soul"; for Chivers, this was a greater reward than the "fleeting" satisfaction of contemporary recognition.

BARBARA CANTALUPO

Selected Works

The Path of Sorrow, or, The Lament of Youth: A Poem, Franklin, Tennessee: *Western Weekly Review,* 1832

Conrad and Eudora; or, The Death of Alonzo, Philadelphia: Chivers, 1834

Nacoochee; or, The Beautiful Star, with Other Poems, New York: W. E. Dean, 1837

The Lost Pleiad; and Other Poems, New York: Edward O. Jenkins, 1845

Search After Truth; or, A New Revelation of the Psycho-physiological Nature of Man, New York: Cobb & Yallalee, 1848

Eonchs of Ruby, A Gift of Love, New York: Spalding and Shepard, 1851

Atlanta; or, The True Blessed Island of Poesy, A Paul Epic – In Three Lustra, Macon, Georgia: *Georgia Citizen,* 1853

Memoralia; or, Phials of Amber Full of the Tears of Love. A Gift for the Beautiful, Philadelphia: Lippincott, 1853

Virginalia; or, Songs of My Summer Nights. A Gift of Love for the Beautiful, Philadelphia: Lippincott, 1853

Birth-Day Song of Liberty, A Paean of Glory for the Heroes of Freedom, Atlanta, Georgia: C. R. Hanleiter, 1856

The Sons of Usna: A Tragi-Apotheosis, in Five Acts, Philadelphia: Sherman & Son, 1858

Chivers' Life of Poe, edited by Richard Beale Davis, New York: Dutton, 1952

The Correspondence of Thomas Holley Chivers, edited by Emma Chase and Lois Parks, Providence, Rhode Island: Brown University Press, 1957

Further Reading

Bell, Landon, *Poe and Chivers,* Columbus, Ohio: Trowbridge, 1931

Benton, Joel, *In the Poe Circle,* New York: Mansfield & Wessels, 1899

Damon, S. Foster, *Thomas Holley Chivers, Friend of Poe,* New York: Harper, 1930

Lombard, Charles, *Thomas Holley Chivers,* Boston: Twayne, 1979

Parks, Edd Winfield, *Southern Poets,* New York: American Book, 1936

Poe, Edgar Allan, *Complete Works of Edgar Allan Poe,* edited by James Harrison, New York: T. Y. Crowell, 1902

Watts, Charles Henry, *Thomas Holley Chivers: His Literary Career and His Poetry,* Athens: Georgia University Press, 1956

Thomas Cole

(1801–1848)

As one of nineteenth-century America's best-known painters, Thomas Cole helped to shape the visual representation of American nature. For almost a quarter of a century, his vivid, lively landscape paintings spearheaded the movement that came to be known as the Hudson River School, and his elaborate allegorical works, such as the five-part *Course of Empire* (1834–36), brought him praise for their qualities of poetic spirituality. The fact that this well-known painter wrote poetry and short stories, as well as explanatory texts to accompany many of his paintings, emphasizes the intimate relationship between written literature and the visual arts during the nineteenth century. Like his friends James Fenimore Cooper and William Cullen **Bryant**, Cole brought a Romantic aesthetic to bear on native American materials. As we shall see, this aesthetic not only informed Cole's poetry but helped him created visual art for an audience of patrons and exhibition-goers in the fast-changing climate of Jacksonian America.

Born in 1801 in Bolton-le-Moors, a town in Lancashire, England, known for its tradition of religious dissent, Cole grew up in a middle-class family on the margins of the Industrial Revolution. Cole subsequently migrated to America in 1818 with his parents and three sisters. With a smattering of education and some training as an engraver, he picked up instruction in painting and drawing from books and from an itinerant painter in Steubenville, Ohio, where he had settled with his family. By 1823, he had arrived in Philadelphia, where the Pennsylvania Academy of Fine Arts offered contact with other artists and models for study. In 1825, he moved to New York, where sale of his early paintings financed sketching trips up the Hudson River. The resulting landscape paintings were bought and acclaimed by leaders of the New York art world, including painters John Trumbull and Asher B. Durand, as well as painter, playwright, and historian William Dunlap. Trumbull, a Revolutionary War veteran and president of the American Academy of Art, gave Cole an important endorsement, exclaiming (according to Cole's friend and biographer Louis Legrand Noble), "You have already done what I, with all my years and experience, am yet unable to do." Dunlap wrote a review of Cole's work in the *New-York Evening Post* (November 1825), which introduced readers to this young artist in terms that reflect the artistic nationalism that was then in full force: this "American boy," Dunlap insists, "has equaled those works which have been the boast of Europe and the admiration of ages." Never mind the fact that Cole had been born in England and was now nearly twenty-five; New York's cultural leaders were eagerly looking for confirmation that American artists and writers could refute the famous taunt of Sydney Smith: "In the four quarters of the globe, who reads an American book? or goes to an American play? or looks at an American picture or statue?" Dunlap would later feature Cole in his *History of the Rise and Progress of the Arts of Design in the United States* (1834) as an inspirational American success story, stressing Cole's early difficulties and his struggles to learn his craft. Like Benjamin Franklin's entry into Philadelphia, Thomas Cole's arrival in New York became part of the story of American artistic nationalism.

Over the next few years, Cole established himself as a leading member of the New York art world. He painted landscape views based on his trips to upstate New York and New Hampshire, received commissions from prosperous merchants from New York to Baltimore, and exhibited allegorical and religious paintings. He socialized with other painters and writers, and helped to found the Sketch Club, which held its organizational meeting in his rooms in 1829. While many of his landscapes were based solely on topographical sketches, Cole introduced narrative elements into some paintings, such as the British soldiers in *Gelyna, or View Near Fort Ticonderoga* (1826 and 1829) or the American Indians in *Kaaterskill Falls* (1826). In *Scene from "The Last of the Mohicans"* (1827), Cole used small figures and a dramatic landscape to represent a scene from a novel written by his friend and patron Cooper. A similar blending of literary reference and landscape representation marked his religious paintings such as *Landscape, Composition, St. John in the Wilderness* (1827) and *Expulsion from the Garden of Eden* (1828). While one of his most important patrons, Robert Gilmor of Baltimore, urged Cole to paint more closely from nature, the young painter insisted that "compositions" were more poetic, and therefore of a higher order of the imagination.

At this transitional point in his career, Cole raised money to go abroad; like other American artists, he felt a need to see firsthand examples of the art of the Old Masters and to enrich his repertoire of scenery with that of the Old World. The significance of travel for an American artist was not lost on Cole or his friends; Bryant marked the occasion by writing a poem, "To Cole, the Painter, Departing for Europe" (LOA, 1: 160), in which he urged his friend to carry with him "a living image of thy native land" and, in spite of the pleasures of the European scene, to "keep that earlier, wilder image bright." Echoing the thought, Cole wrote in his sketch book:

Let not the ostentatious gaud of art,
That tempts the eye, but touches not the heart,
Lure me from nature's purer love divine:
But, like a pilgrim, at some holy shrine,
Bow down to her devotedly, and learn,
In her most sacred features, to discern
That truth is beauty.

Cole sailed for England, the country he had left only 11 years earlier, affirming not only his American nationality, but his allegiance to a Romantic aesthetic and a commitment to what he described as "a higher style of landscape."

Travel to England and Italy in 1829–32 brought Cole into contact with European artists, aroused his interest in history and architecture, and inspired a number of paintings of Italian landscapes. Upon his return, he held an exhibition of recently completed works that included a biblical scene, *The Dead Abel* (1831–32), as well as depictions of Roman aqueducts and *Landscape Composition, Italian Scenery* (1832). A friendly review described him as ranking "with the most favored ornaments of an art, which, with poetry and music, is the loveliest embellishment of civilization" (*New-York Mirror*, January 12, 1833). Between 1833 and 1836, Cole worked on a five-painting series, *The Course of Empire*, which traced the rise and fall of a fictional civilization from a wilderness scene to a landscape of vine-covered ruins. In each painting, an identifiable rock outcropping marks the scene; the five canvases progress from dawn through morning, noon, evening, and moonrise. The first painting of the series, *The Savage State*, envisions the dawn of civilization: as the morning mists lift, a wilderness landscape is peopled by hunters wearing skins, while in the distance teepee-like huts circle a fire and canoes float in the bay. The second canvas, *The Pastoral or Arcadian State*, shows shepherds, farmers, a woman with a spindle, a circular temple, a man drawing geometrical figures in the sand, and the beginnings of a commercial settlement on the bay. In *The Consummation of Empire*, the noontime sun shines on an elaborate architectural fantasy, based on the cities of Greece and Rome, as a conqueror leads a procession across the bridge to the heart of the city. This civilization has turned corrupt in the fourth painting, *Destruction*, in which a warlike statue has replaced the goddess Minerva as the city's emblem. Amid a swirling storm, the city is being attacked by barbarians who burn, kill, and destroy. Finally, in the fifth painting, *Desolation*, the moon rises over a ruined column, bridge, and colonnade. As Cole wrote in a published description of the series, "Though man and his works have perished, the steep promontory, with its insulated rock, still rears against the sky unmoved, unchanged. Violence and time have crumbled the works of man, and art is again resolving into elemental nature" (*American Monthly Magazine*, November 1836). Exhibition of the paintings in New York, before their delivery to patron Luman Reed, yielded over 1,000 dollars in profit and many favorable reviews.

A popular and successful painter by the late 1830s, Cole continued to paint both landscape compositions like *View from Mount Holyoke, Northampton, Massachusetts, after a Thunderstorm (The Oxbow)* (1836) and historical fantasies such as *The Departure* and *The Return* (1836), and *The Past and The Present* (1837). *The Voyage of Life* (1839–40), a four-part series with a religious theme, marked a turn toward more religious subjects. Hoping to imitate his success with *The Course of Empire*, Cole painted the series on commission from a patron, Samuel Ward, and exhibited it accompanied by a prose description that spelled out the symbolism and iconography: human life as a journey down a river, through a landscape that seems lush and inviting in childhood and youth, but becomes rough, threatening, and treacherous before the battered boat reaches its destination and the now aged traveler is welcomed by angels streaming from heaven. The paintings were enthusiastically received when exhibited in New York in 1841, and a reviewer described them as "a moral poem" and praised Cole as a "pictorial poet" (*New-York Mirror*, January 2, 1841).

After a second trip to Europe in 1841–42, Cole continued to work on European and allegorical subjects together with landscape compositions. Exhibitions of his painting in Boston and New York drew good reviews but disappointing revenues; during the 1840s, he struggled to interest patrons in the "poetical" compositions he preferred to paint. In February 1848, he died suddenly after a short illness; eulogized by fellow painters and writers like Bryant, Cole was considered at his death one of the leading American painters.

Verbal expression was important to Cole throughout his career. His journals include observations of nature, sketches, fiction, and poetry, and long before he gained recognition as a painter, he had already published a fictional tale, "Emma Moreton, A West Indian Tale," in the *Saturday Evening Post*, May 14, 1825. After he had become established as a painter, he delivered a number of lectures on art, scenery, and European antiquities, some of which were later published. Three poems, "The Summer Days Are Ended," "The Lament of the Forest" (LOA, 1: 230), and "Winds," appeared in *The Knickerbocker* in 1840–41. Like the most renowned American painter of the previous generation, Washington **Allston**, to whom the younger artist paid a courtesy call in 1828, Cole envisioned a professional life in which painters also participated in a larger field of philosophical and poetic expression.

Nature poetry predominates in Cole's written work; like his friend Bryant (who may have helped him revise some of his poetry for publication), Cole celebrates nature's beauty while reflecting on the transience of life. Echoes of William Wordsworth ("the earth with light is filled, my heart with pleasure") and John Keats ("Thine early Hopes are fading one by one") invigorate his often conventional diction ("fleecy clouds," "sunny hours," "the glory of the forest"). Most of his poetry appeared as part of the journals that he kept throughout most of his creative life. Some have a particular, occasional quality, such as "Lines Written after a Walk on [a] Beautiful Morning in November" (1833) or "On seeing that a favorite tree of the Author's had been cut down" (1834), and suggest hasty composition. Others, such as "The Summer Days Are Ended" (1840) or "Autumn" (1842), exist in several drafts that indicate revision and attention to issues of literary craftsmanship. In some poems, short, concrete images evoke a particular place – such as "O Cedar Grove!" – but Cole also wrote sonnets, two versions of an elegy on the death of his patron Luman Reed, love poetry, and narrative poetry ("The night was calm," 1825).

Cole's poetic works illustrate the same duality that can be found in his paintings: on the one hand, a recognition that his fame rested on his special gift for the depiction of vivid, concrete scenes from nature; on the other, a desire to participate in what his culture valued as a "higher" aesthetic discourse. Like his friends and contemporaries, Bryant and Cooper, Cole grounded his aesthetic thinking in eighteenth-century philosophy and was influenced by concepts of the sublime and the picturesque that were drawn originally from Edmund Burke's *A Philosophical Enquiry into the Origin of Our Ideas of the Sublime and Beautiful* (1757) and the British theorists of picturesque landscape. As Ellwood C. Parry III has pointed out, these concepts had a common currency among travel writers in Europe and the United States by the early decades of the nineteenth century. Cole's application of these aesthetic categories to landscape was also shaped by the notion of "associationism" formulated within the philosophical writings of Archibald Alison. When Cole wrote the "Essay on American Scenery" in 1835, he assumed his readers placed the highest value on scenery that was "hallowed" by the "footsteps and immortal verse" of writers such as Milton and Petrarch and by the memory of "the gigantic associations of the storied past."

In his Italian landscapes and the allegorical series paintings like *The Course of Empire*, as well as in his poems such as

"Mt. Etna," Cole worked within associationist conventions: "Beneath thy gaze / Nations have birth and death." However, as he argues in "Essay on American Scenery," an associationist reading of the American landscape would have to chart new territory. "American associations are not so much of the past as of the present and future," he claims, and he goes on to sketch in words a scene that matches very closely a painting on which he was then working, *View from Mount Holyoke*:

> Seated on a pleasant knoll, look down into the bosom of that secluded valley, begirt with wooded hills – through those enameled meadows and wide waving fields of grain, a silver stream winds lingeringly along – here, seeking the green shade of trees – there, glancing in the sunshine: on its banks are rural dwellings shaded by elms and garlanded by flowers – from yonder dark mass of foliage the village spire beams like a star. You see no ruined tower to tell of outrage – no gorgeous temple to speak of ostentation; but freedom's offspring – peace, security, and happiness, dwell there, the spirits of the scene.

In his poem that addresses Mount Washington as the "Vast monument of power that God hath reared / Upon the lowly earth to conquer time" ("To Mount Washington," 1828) or the poem that exclaims, "A holy calm pervades / The rural earth" ("Again the wreathed snow," 1834), Cole tries similarly to interpret American nature as a hieroglyphic expression of spiritual truths. Thus, American nature, like the more familiar European scene, can represent for an American painter or poet "the exhaustless mine from which the poet and the painter have brought such wondrous treasures – an unfailing fountain of intellectual enjoyment, where all may drink, and be awakened to a deeper feeling of the works of genius, and a keener perception of the beauty of our existence" ("Essay on American Scenery").

Cole's poetry also anticipates the religious turn of his later painting. His writing often combines a Wordsworthian theme of memory ("O! let me fill my soul with this bright scene / And garner up its beauty" ["Lines Written after a Walk . . ."]) with an elegiac note most fully expressed by his friend Bryant in "Thanatopsis" (1817, 1821; LOA, 1: 122). In "Evening Thoughts" (1835), for example, Cole meditates on the contrast between nature's continuity and the fragility of human life:

> But whence the shade of sadness o'er us thrown
> When thoughts are purest in the quiet hour?
> From sense of sin arises that sad tone?
> Knowing that we alone feel passion's power
> That touches not the mountain far and lone?
>   Or is it that the fading light reminds
>   That we are mortal and the latter day
>   Steals onward swiftly, like the unseen winds
>   And all our years are clouds that quickly pass away.

The image he would later place at the heart of *The Voyage of Life* began appearing in his poetry by 1833, when he wrote "Lines Written after a Walk":

>   Thus we
> Upon the winding stream of human life,
> In its calm, happier days, when wo[e] and strife
> Are far; live all within ourselves – forget

> The ebbing tide of time, is swiftly set
> Towards eternity; nor think that storm
> May soon o'ertake us, and our course deform –
> E'en now upon yon distant bark a change
> Is come . . .

Images such as a guardian spirit ("Hope and Trust Spring from the Contemplation of the Works of God," 1835), a deep cavern ("I saw a Cave of sable depth profound," 1838 [LOA, 1: 228]), a river flowing toward eternity ("Vain is my fondest hope!" 1833), a "sea-worn bark / Strained by a thousand storms" ("The eager vessel flies the broken surge," 1832), and "A lasting Day [that] shall dawn in the resplendent East" ("Thine early hopes are fading, one by one," 1838), all suggest that Cole's poetry served as a workshop to develop the imagery of his best-known and most successful series of paintings and that his poetry charts his increasing tendency to cast spiritual issues in Christian terms.

Cole's poetry also traces his increasing uneasiness over the impact of American "progress" on the natural environment. Like Cooper, who as early as 1823 had registered in *The Pioneers* his criticism of the "wasty ways" of the settlements as they encroached upon the wilderness, Cole was by the mid-1830s raging at the "dollar-godded utilitarians" who were "cutting down all the trees in the beautiful valley on which I have looked so often with a loving eye." From that time onward, Cole's paintings often contain an allusion to the destruction of the forests, symbolized by tree stumps with ax marks, like those in *Notch of the White Mountains (Crawford Notch)* (1839). The short poem "On seeing that a favorite tree of the Author's had been cut down" chastised "destroying man" for the work of his "unpitying axe." More dramatically, the longer poem "The Lament of the Forest" predicts "doom" for the nation that was turning "each hill and every valley" into "an altar unto Mammon":

> "A few short years! – these valleys, greenly clad,
> These slumbering mountains, resting in our arms,
> Shall naked glare beneath the scorching sun,
> And all their wimpling rivulets be dry.
> No more the deer shall haunt these bosky glens,
> Nor the pert squirrel chatter near his store.
> A few short years! – our ancient race shall be,
> Like Israel's, scattered 'mong the tribes of men."

Working at the height of Jacksonian democracy, but temperamentally allied to the rising merchant class who purchased his paintings, Cole expressed in his poetry and his paintings the concern that, like the mythical nation he had portrayed in *The Course of Empire*, the United States was headed toward self-destruction. As Alan Wallach and other recent scholars have shown, Cole's celebration of wilderness, his immersion in the details of romantic nature, and his insistence on the spirituality available to those who contemplated nature either directly or through the artist's mediation represented both a protest against the vigorous commercial culture of his time and a nostalgic reassurance that those who benefited from America's commercial development could capture and preserve an image of the world their technological progress had displaced.

Cole's sudden and unexpected death provoked an outpouring of tribute from his friends and colleagues in the literary and artistic world. The terms in which Cole was eulogized reinforce his own dual calling to represent nature in vivid and concrete terms and to insist on its redeeming spirituality for a rapidly commercializing society. In his *Funeral Oration* for Cole, Bryant remembered his "delight" in viewing Cole's pictures:

> which carried the eye over scenes of wild grandeur peculiar to our country, over our aerial mountain-tops with their mighty growth of forest never touched by the axe, along the banks of streams never deformed by culture, and into the depth of skies bright with the hues of our own climate; skies such as few but Cole could ever paint, and through the transparent abysses of which it seemed that you might send an arrow out of sight.

This verbal evocation of Cole's impact on his contemporaries was matched in another medium by his fellow painter, Asher B. Durand, who was commissioned by a patron, Jonathan Sturges, to paint a tribute to the friendship between Bryant and Cole. Durand's *Kindred Spirits* (1849), one of the best-known of the Hudson River School paintings, depicts Cole and Bryant standing on a rocky outcropping above a stream in the midst of a mountain range. Silvery-green tree branches connect above them like a Gothic arch, while the rock on which they stand resembles a pulpit. In the church of nature, painter and poet contemplate life, death, and immortality. Splintered trees in the dark foreground suggest the theme of mortality, while a soaring bird, to which Cole points with his cane, suggests the immortality of the spirit. The legacy implied by these tributes was one of kinship between the visual and literary arts, and harmony between man and nature. By contrast, Cole's poems, like his paintings, suggest the fragility of that harmony and undercut the serene assurance of Durand's tribute.

In his paintings, Cole presented vivid and dramatic depiction of natural objects – colorful autumn foliage, dramatically positioned trees, distant lakes, clear skies – in the service of what he called "the pleasures of the imagination." His career as a painter thus always was inflected by his need to seek a balance between concreteness and spirituality, and to convince patrons and reviewers to view his art in the same way. "I am not the painter I should have been had there been a higher taste," he complained in his notebooks. These conflicts, as well as his equivocal relationship to his culture's contradictory reverence for progress and nature, can be traced in his poetry, which, unlike his painting, was never intended as a commercial product. His poetry served as private meditation and, on a few occasions, public expression of his intellectual and spiritual aims and struggles.

JOY S. KASSON

Selected Works

"Essay on American Scenery," in *American Art 1700–1960: Sources and Documents*, edited by John W. McCoubrey, Englewood Cliffs, New Jersey: Prentice-Hall, 1965

Thomas Cole's Poetry, edited by Marshall B. Tymn, York, Pennsylvania: Liberty Cap, 1972

Thomas Cole: The Collected Essays and Prose Sketches, edited by Marshall B. Tymn, St. Paul, Minnesota: John Colet, 1980

Further Reading

Baigell, Matthew, *Thomas Cole*, New York: Watson-Guptill, 1981

Callow, James T., *Kindred Spirits: Knickerbocker Writers and American Artists, 1807–1855*, Chapel Hill: University of North Carolina Press, 1967

Noble, Louis Legrand, *The Life and Works of Thomas Cole*, edited by Elliot S. Vessell, Cambridge: Harvard University Press, 1964

Parry, Ellwood C., III, *The Art of Thomas Cole: Ambition and Imagination*, Newark: University of Delaware Press, 1988

Truettner, William, and Alan Wallach, eds. *Thomas Cole: Landscape into History*, New Haven, Connecticut: Yale University Press, 1994

Philip Pendleton Cooke

(1816–1850)

The verse that Cooke produced in his brief and colorful life consists of only some 5,000 lines, but it nonetheless constitutes a distinctive and durable achievement. Cooke is virtually unique among southern authors in embodying both the Tidewater aristocracy and the mountain frontier traditions and giving artistic expression to this melded experience. Born in Martinsburg, Virginia (now West Virginia), he spent all but four of his 33 years in that section of the Shenandoah Valley. Removed from burgeoning cultural centers of the Tidewater such as Richmond, Norfolk, and Petersburg, Cooke maintained a self-conscious pride in being a scion of what he called "the old families of the land," and he enjoyed this gentrified life to the full.

In a letter to Edgar Allan **Poe** in the summer of 1839, Cooke apologized for being remiss in responding to the latter's solicitation of contributions for *Burton's Gentleman's Magazine* by explaining that he had been involved in a whirl of dinners, barbecues, riding parties, and the like. Having seen more of guns, horses, and dogs than of pens and paper, he continued, he could simply not write for Poe or anyone else at the moment. While it is tempting to regard this confession as merely the excuse of a dilettante, such a charge is only partially accurate. Contemporary critics ranked Cooke's achievement in both the lyric and the narrative modes with that of the most accomplished poets of his generation. What his admission to Poe indicates more clearly is that the planter class in the antebellum South did not always make literary endeavor a top priority. In a later correspondence to Poe, Cooke confesses: "The 'Valdemar Case' I read in a number of your *Broadway Journal* last winter – as I lay in a Turkey blind, muffled to the eyes in overcoats, etc."

Reviewing *Froissart Ballads and Other Poems*, Cooke's only published collection, for the *Southern Literary Messenger* in 1847, Nathaniel Beverley Tucker correctly labeled the author's tastes and feelings as "at once refined and manly." This is particularly true of the lyrics. Two notable examples are "The Mountains" and "Life in the Autumn Woods," both of which directly respond to a natural milieu that Cooke knew intimately and to which he responded with a fervor tempered by a rather self-conscious literary frame of reference. A typical stanza of "Life in the Autumn Woods" begins: "What a brave splendour / Is in the October air! How rich and clear – / How life-full, and all joyous!" A later stanza incorporates a familiar indigenous image, while affirming the Romantic belief in the nurturing power of nature:

> Urge your swift horse
> After the crying hounds in this fresh hour –
> Vanquish high hills – stem perilous streams perforce –
> Where the glades ope give free wings to your course –
> And you will know the power
> Of the brave chase – and how of griefs, the sorest,
> A cure is in the forest.

Although such responses to natural splendors and vigorous sport indicate an unabashed pleasure, there is frequently a reflective dimension to that pleasure's expression. Exploring the woods gives way to "melancholy moods"; "every natural wonder" offers "strange lessons." Moreover, Cooke intersperses the stanzas with references to Shakespeare and Sir William Wortley.

Cooke's work reflects the training in the classics and English literature that he received at Princeton College. Upon graduation in 1835, at age 19, he began reading law in the office of his father, John Rogers Cooke, a noted Virginia attorney. Although he had already published a number of successful lyrics, Cooke recognized that the figure of the professional author, by now a commonplace in the north, was rarely found in the south. Owing to the dearth of regional publishers, the southern author, no matter how talented or prolific, typically looked upon literature as an avocation. For Cooke, as for many of these talented literati – William Wirt, William Gilmore **Simms**, Augustus B. Longstreet, John Pendleton Kennedy, Henry **Timrod**, Paul Hamilton **Hayne**, and Richard Henry **Wilde** – law was the primary profession of choice. Some attained prominence in the field (Wirt served as attorney general of the United States for more than a decade), but for most it was a necessary regimen that, although unwelcome, allowed for avocational literary pursuits.

For Cooke, the law proved neither remunerative nor fulfilling. Possessing a free, spontaneous nature, and a devotion to his native style of living, he came to regard the law as so much drudgery. On one occasion he effused: "I detest the law. On the other hand, I love the fever-fits of composition." He was admitted to the bar before his 21st birthday, but shortly thereafter he and his family suffered financial reverses that were to have serious and long-ranging consequences, especially for his creative efforts. From the mid-1830s – by which time he had published several lyrics in the *Knickerbocker* and the *Southern Literary Messenger* – until 1840, he apparently produced little verse. As he confessed to Poe, "The 'madness of scribbling' which once itched and tingled at my fingers-ends has been considerably cured by a profession and matrimony [in 1837] – money-cares and domestic squabbles – buying beef and mutton, and curing my child's croup, collicks, etc. . . . The fever with which I was afflicted has given way to a chill." Cooke's home region was one of many areas that suffered monetary problems resulting from the panic of 1837. Having married, and having assumed partial obligation for his father's debts, Cooke in fact lived in straits so severe that he was forced into bankruptcy. Nonetheless, in 1840, in response to the invitation from Poe, he submitted to *Burton's* two lyrics, one of which was "Florence Vane" (LOA, 1: 650).

There are many reasons, both timely and aesthetic, why "Florence Vane" became one of the most popular lyrics written in nineteenth-century America. First and foremost, however, it should be seen as reflecting Cooke at his most characteristic. The poem was inspired by his courtship of a cousin, Mary Evelina Dandridge. This was a quixotic, if typically cavalier, quest that involved riding 20 miles on horseback to throw bouquets into her window. Although ardent and flamboyant (at least on Cooke's part), the romance had ended years before the poem was composed. Mary Evelina was now happily married, as was Cooke. He nevertheless enhances these events by having the eponymous subject die prematurely after she rejects her suitor. Thus, the lament of the poetic persona combines the angst of the rejected lover with the anguish of bereavement:

> Thou wast lovelier than the roses
>   In their prime;
> Thy voice excelled the closes
>   Of sweetest rhyme;
> Thy heart was as a river
>   Without a main.
> Would I had loved thee never,
>   Florence Vane!

Both the short-lived lily of the valley and the pansy are used as symbolic embellishments for the grave of the young woman. But the pansy also functions as a symbol of memory that itself constitutes, broadly speaking, the theme of the poem. Despite the pain of rejection, the remembered beauty of the subject, fragile but undimmed, remains with the poet. Thus, the lyric ends:

> May [the flowers'] bloom in beauty vying,
>   Never wane,
> Where thine earthly part is lying,
>   Florence Vane!

At the end of each stanza, the name is repeated, leaving the reader with the fading sound of a long open vowel. This device, used later with similar effectiveness and greater notoriety by Poe in "Ulalume" (LOA, 1: 540) and "Annabel Lee" (LOA, 1: 550), functions as a subtle onomatopoeia; the tone suggests a lingering, plaintive wail. Moreover, the repeated surname resonates with suggestions of homonymic variations ("vain," as in "hopeless" and "conceited") that enhance the connotative meaning.

Following its March 1840 publication in *Burton's*, the poem started to gain the popularity that would assure it a place in the canon of nineteenth-century verse. It was reprinted in numerous contemporary newspapers and in gift books and anthologies (including Rufus Griswold's *Poets and Poetry of America*). Several composers set the poem to music, a would-be poet in Ohio named his infant daughter Florence Vane Hunt and asked Cooke for an autograph text, and Poe recited the poem in his lecture "The Poets and Poetry of America" in February 1845 in New York and remarked upon its pathos in his correspondence.

Although richly enhanced by an active poetic imagination, the emotion to which Cooke gave voice was essentially heartfelt. However, the central motif of youthful feminine beauty, dying untimely and being reabsorbed into the harmonious natural order, also was a staple of Romantic lyric poetry in England and America. For the poetic fancy of the antebellum South, this motif in fact became a defining characteristic. The pervasive use of this and other popular devices, however, also gave rise to various charges of plagiarism. For instance, Poe and Thomas Holley **Chivers** were both accused of appropriating from one another (Poe's "Annabel Lee" and Chivers's "Rosalie Lee" being a particular point of contention). But in 1835 – long before either of these poets had produced the lyrics in question – Cooke had published "Young Rosalie Lee,"

which both in title and theme bears marked resemblance to the two subsequent works.

Cooke embodied the maturing influence of the Romantic aesthetic in America in a variety of ways; indeed, the tradition in its many literary manifestations dominates the entire body of his poetry and prose. (After *Froissart Ballads*, he devoted the remainder of his life to prose fiction.) After having expressed concern that Cooke had hopelessly succumbed to the Romantic influence, Poe reassured him: "You need not attempt to shake off or to banter Romance. It is an evil you will never get rid of to the end of your days. It is a part of yourself – a portion of your soul. Age will only mellow it a little, and give it a holier tone."

As a Romantic poet, Cooke showed as strong a penchant for the narrative as for the lyric mode. Well over two-thirds of the pages of *Froissart Ballads* are given over to "ballad" stories. The title is somewhat misleading, however, in that it suggests a heavy reliance upon Froissart. In reality, the influence is much more selective. As Cooke notes in the preface, even when he borrows from the medieval chronicler, he does so "with a difference." Moreover, rather than attempting lengthy metrical narratives that copy the originals in Froissart, Cooke adapts the popular ballad form (and stanza), which traditionally treats briefer, more tightly compressed subjects. Of the five such "ballads" included in the collection, only three derive from Froissart.

One of these is "Orthone" (LOA, 1: 651), a singular incident that Froissart says was told to him by a courtier of Earl Gaston of Foix, at Ortaise. It concerns a Lord Corasse, who has been feuding with a Catalonian clerk over the latter's right to tithe his lands. Fearing for his safety, the clerk flees, but not before vowing revenge. Sometime later, Lord Corasse is awakened by loud knocking on the door of his bed chamber. In answer to the lord's questioning, the intruder identifies himself as Orthone and claims to have been sent by the clerk. The events that follow are set forth with the simple directness that characterizes Cooke's narrative style:

> "Orthone," said on the baron stout,
>   "A beggar like the clerk
> Will give you little thanks, or wage
>   For moiling at his work:
> I pray you be my servant!" –
>   With this the clamour ceased,
> And Orthone said, "So let it be –
>   I weary of the priest."

In the service of Lord Corasse, Orthone fills his master's ear nightly with "news of distant lands, / Of battle-field, and court"; however, he has never shown his face. One day Lord Corasse, inebriated, lets slip the secret of his amazing servant and is challenged by another nobleman to determine his appearance. Put off by Corasse's request that he reveal himself, Orthone promises that he will be the first thing the lord sees upon arising in the morning. What Corasse sees is a dancing, talking stalk of broomstraw, which states that it is Orthone. When Orthone speaks into his ear that night, Corasse expresses disbelief that the straw could have been the disguised servant and asks him to assume a form "of greater bulk and stature." The following morning, Corasse's eyes alight upon a large sow, which disappears when approached by the house mastiffs. Corasse now realizes that Orthone had fulfilled his promise, and he regrets having asked to see him in the flesh. Orthone never returns. We know from later correspondence that Cooke's wife thought the talking broomstraw and sow to be crude devices, but he found them consistent with "the rude Gothic images of the north, where Froissart had put them."

Cooke's interest in medieval materials reinforces his identification with the multifaceted Romantic tradition. More particularly, it identifies him with the redactive methods of Samuel Taylor Coleridge and John Keats, and, most especially, those of Sir Walter Scott. As with these predecessors, Cooke's intention was to create the semblance of a medieval genre, whether that meant endowing an idea of his own invention with seemingly authentic trappings or taking liberties with an original source. These British hybridizations enjoyed a contemporary vogue in nineteenth-century America and surely influenced Cooke. But he also established a more direct connection with the Middle Ages by reading period authors such as Froissart and Chaucer. Although his interest in things medieval seems to have been genuine, Cooke also was emulating a vogue that was becoming pandemic in the South. In addition to literature, this influence – thanks in large measure to the immense popularity of Scott's medieval romances – was found in a range of tangible manifestations that included architecture, furniture, interior design, place names, and mock jousting tournaments at popular spas.

While Cooke's tastes inclined toward a European sense of antiquity, many of his contemporaries such as James Fenimore Cooper, Washington Irving, Simms, and Wirt looked more to native materials and discovered a usable past in the American Revolution and other segments of American history. Cooke was by no means indifferent to this heritage. For instance, Native American subjects are featured in several of his poems (e.g., "Song of the Sioux Lovers," "The Murder of Cornstalk," and "The Last Indian"). His prose romances, to which he devoted the last years of his life, expand upon this interest and involve subjects derived from the American Revolution and the frontier of the lower Shenandoah.

Cooke's fecund sphere of existence offered unusual raw materials for artistic treatment. Although he was attracted to frontier traditions as well as to those of the aristocratic class, Cooke customarily assessed his hybrid world from the viewpoint of a gentleman of cultivation and taste. Like many American artists before and since, he decried a widespread philistinism in the country. On one occasion, he wrote to Griswold: "What do you think of a good friend of mine, a most valuable and worthy, and hard-working one, saying to me a short time ago, 'I wouldn't waste time on a damned thing like poetry; you might make yourself, with all your sense and judgment, a useful man in settling neighborhood disputes and difficulties.'" Similar sentiments had been expressed but a few years before by Alexis de Tocqueville. That astute critic of American culture might have felt a particular empathy with a subsequent passage in the same letter, in which Cooke observes that the very people who denounce cultural pursuits are the first to praise authors whose works become popular and to buy (but probably not read) their books.

That image had come to count for more than substance in nineteenth-century America was a concept alien to Cooke. Fame held little interest for him, and he became concerned about pay only when personal finances demanded. He seems, moreover, to have known little of the workings of the publishing world. *Froissart Ballads* was prepared at the urging of Griswold and Cooke's first cousin, John Pendleton Kennedy. Cooke's awkward reaction to their suggestion that he collect his fugitive pieces indicates that he found the idea novel, and not something that he would have contemplated on his own. "I am quite as ignorant as any country gentleman ever was of the business part of literature," he admitted. Thus, in an era when publishing was becoming a burgeoning American industry, Cooke appears as something of an ingenue.

Creativity was spontaneous for Cooke, and his work habits reveal that he emphasized inspiration over the discipline of planning and revision. According to his younger sibling, John Esten Cooke, "Literature with my brother was a recreation – and he would never write unless he felt the desire and could take pleasure in embodying his thoughts." To appreciate Philip Pendleton's poetic achievement, therefore, one must acknowledge that while the contemporary literary establishment might rightly deny him professional status, a majority of its members regarded him as a remarkably gifted amateur. Of the few dozen poems he authored several are marked with brilliance. Along with most of the Froissart pieces, "Florence Vane," "Life in the Autumn Woods," and "The Mountains" proved mainstays for critics and anthologists for more than a century.

Many of Cooke's contemporaries expressed admiration for his talent and accomplishments. For instance, John Esten Cooke, while observing that his brother's poetic creativity was a recreation, maintained that Philip Pendleton's talent was superior to his own. (This was high praise, as John Esten himself became a respected novelist and historian in the post–Civil War era.) Even Poe, whose quarrels and critical attacks were legion, told Cooke that he "valued [his] opinion more highly than that of any man in America." Northern as well as southern reviewers were generous in their praise of *Froissart Ballads*. And following Cooke's untimely death in 1850, Griswold (admittedly no stranger to hyperbole) called him "the finest poet that ever lived in Virginia – one of the finest that have written in our day."

In reviewing *Froissart*, Nathaniel Beverley Tucker was slightly more guarded. Calling the volume "the harbinger of better things," his assessment acknowledges that despite its highlights of proven brilliance, Cooke's poetry was more the product of an evolving, as opposed to a mature, talent. Cooke freely acknowledged this criticism. After the review appeared, he corresponded with Tucker on the relative strengths and weaknesses in the volume. In these discussions and in several published essays, Cooke reveals a more mature critical understanding of poetry than might be supposed in a poet who considered writing recreational rather than professional. For instance, he reveals to Tucker that the ballads in the volume were very carefully constructed, with consideration given to various contemporary and ancient models for guidance. He also speaks of prosody, which suggests that this, too, was more studied in his verse than might be imagined from its apparent effortlessness. In particular, he discusses the matter of feminine endings, which he employs rather freely. He does so by way of responding to Tucker's protest against the "modern device" of "introducing studied harshness in verse." Cooke defended the feminine endings as a desirable means of "making poetic measure sound rough without becoming unmusical." Even in what is perhaps his earliest statement on poetic criticism – an 1835 letter to the *Southern Literary Messenger* in defense of "A Song of the Seasons" – he reveals a finely developed sense of word choice, a well-tuned ear, and a liberal range of poetic tastes. Still, Cooke maintained a concern that his work needed revision if it were going to be well received by the public and by his peers. His worry, expressed to John Pendleton Kennedy, about the "alternation of half desponding, half-loathing after-feeling which has cut off so many of my pieces . . . in the middle" is more than modest self-effacement.

Cooke's biographers and critics have expressed regret that he did not live to realize the full promise of his talent and tastes. The same has been said of Keats, Percy Bysshe Shelley, and other Romantics whose intense lives and evolving talents were cut short. But to reinvent these figures by means of academic surmise runs the risk of obscuring who they truly were and what they actually did accomplish. Wading into the icy waters of the Shenandoah River in January 1850 to retrieve a wood duck he had wounded was far more characteristic of Cooke – and of the order that had shaped his poetic sensibility – than what his future literary efforts might have produced. What is certain is that his resulting death did not dim either the indelible imprint he left upon a small but vivid body of poems or that spirited past of which he is an enduring emblem.

WELFORD DUNAWAY TAYLOR

Selected Works
Froissart Ballads and Other Poems, 1847; reprinted, New York: Arno Press, 1972

Further Reading
Allen, John Daniel, *Philip Pendleton Cooke*, Chapel Hill: University of North Carolina Press, 1942
_____, *Philip Pendleton Cooke: Poet, Critic, Novelist*, Johnson City: East Tennessee State University Advisory Council, 1969
Beaty, John O., *John Esten Cooke, Virginian*, New York: Columbia University Press, 1922
Harrison, James A., ed., *Life and Letters of Edgar Allan Poe*, New York: Crowell, 1903
Jackson, David K., comp., *The Contributors and Contributions to The Southern Literary Messenger (1834–1864)*, Charlottesville, Virginia: Historical Publishing, 1936
_____, *Poe and The Southern Literary Messenger*, Richmond, Virginia: Dietz Press, 1934
Ostrom, John Ward, *The Letters of Edgar Allan Poe*, Cambridge, Massachusetts: Harvard University Press, 1948

Rose Terry Cooke

(1827–1892)

How can we understand a writer who begins a poem: "I wear a rose in my hair, / Because I feel like a weed" ("Truths")? A poet who ends another:

What care I for your tedious love,
    For tender word or fond caress?
I die for one free flight above,
    One rapture of the wilderness!
        ("Captive")

From one perspective, these poems reiterate some conventions of women's poetry in the nineteenth century. "Truths," for example, focuses on the narrator's experience of "despair" and concludes with the commonplace idea of Jesus' championship of the poor and downcast. Similarly, "Captive" is ostensibly a poem about a bird, part of the nineteenth-century female poet's domain of nature, spirit, home, and children.

But as in the work of many of her contemporaries, Rose Terry Cooke's work has an excess, a residue of significance that places it outside the circumscribed realms assigned to the nineteenth-century "poetess" by the culture, and in particular, by its literary men. Hence in "Captive," Cooke's real subject is women's cultural imprisonment; in "Truths," she juxtaposes the incongruous images of "rose" and "weed" just as her contemporary, Emily **Dickinson**, conjoins those of "Pearl" and "Weed" in her poem about female renunciation, "She rose to his requirement – dropt." Like the woman in Dickinson's poem, Cooke's narrator also speaks about renunciation, but her voice has a willed quality. Cooke's poetry, too, has a demonic element that modern readers so often admire in Dickinson.

It is difficult to think about any nineteenth-century poet without recourse to Dickinson – the "Queen," to use one of her favorite words, of American literary scholarship. Although Cooke probably never met Dickinson, in spite of each woman's receiving support from Thomas Wentworth Higginson, she has many poems that resonate for us the way that Dickinson's do. She also has many that echo and exceed the voices of other poets whom we consider canonical, such as Alfred, Lord Tennyson, Edgar Allan **Poe**, William Wordsworth, John Keats, Charles Baudelaire, Edwin Arlington **Robinson**, and Robert Frost. Like them, Cooke addresses themes common in the Western poetic tradition: heroism, unrequited love, and death. She often writes in traditional ballad meter. But she also enters forbidden ground for women poets, exploring female self-sufficiency, desire, passion, and fear more directly than many of her poetic peers. Central among these groundbreaking poems are "Arachne" and "Blue-Beard's Closet."

How these poems emerge from Cooke's life experiences is unclear. She was born near Hartford, Connecticut, on February 17, 1827. Like many of her contemporaries among women poets, she was brought up in a well-to-do family and given an excellent education, not only attending the Hartford Female Seminary but also receiving demanding lessons from a stern mother. Nevertheless, her mother, Anne Hurlbut Terry, may have been the inspiration for Cooke's departures from orthodoxy in the women characters of her short fiction or in the voice of her poems. Cooke describes her mother to the short-story writer Harriet Prescott Spofford as having "a favorable wildness about her, a passion for getting out of doors, and in just as little covering as possible." Of Cooke herself, Spofford writes, "She loved her gardens, but she loved wild nature more." Wildness and passion are two of the recurring themes of Cooke's two volumes of poetry, both titled simply *Poems*, the first published in 1861 and the second in 1888.

Like many of her peers, Cooke also suffered from a serious illness as a child. This illness left her somewhat frail, and she profited, as Sarah Orne **Jewett** would in later years, from the extra attention of her father. The reversal in fortune suffered by her family when she was in her mid-teens also was important in her development; like many women with the same experience, she turned to writing to earn a living. During her long career, Cooke received encouragement from such important literary men as Higginson, William Dean **Howells**, and John Greenleaf **Whittier**. By age 30, she was established enough to merit an invitation to appear in 1857 (with the story "Sally Parson's Duty") in the first issue of what would become one of the most influential literary outlets of its time, the *Atlantic Monthly*. She was in good company; the other contributors included Henry Wadsworth **Longfellow**, Oliver Wendell **Holmes**, Ralph Waldo **Emerson**, Whittier, and Harriet Beecher Stowe. Although she published widely in magazines from the 1850s until her death, Cooke also acknowledged, in "A Letter to Mary Ann," the sexism that dictated male writers be paid more (and often more promptly) than their female counterparts.

Although in her teens Cooke became a member of the Congregational church, she was at times a harsh critic of the institution of marriage and of the Calvinism that frequently supported its inequities and even its abuses. Not surprisingly, she married later in life; she was 46 at the time of her union to Rollin H. Cooke, who was 16 years her junior. The marriage occurred, perhaps not coincidentally, in the year following her mother's death (1873); another reason for the delay may have been the writer's greater willingness to marry when the possibility of having children, with its physical and financial worries, was likely past. Given Cooke's complex understanding of the institution of marriage, it is ironic that her husband, through his father, became a financial drain and wasted the modest savings that she had accumulated; this made her need for income through writing even more imperative, until her death on July 18, 1892.

Cooke would not be alone in this imperative; the later fiction-writer Mary E. Wilkins Freeman and the poet-essayist Celia Thaxter both labored long and hard to surmount the burden of improvident husbands. Cooke, however, seems to have been the happiest of the three in her selection, for her husband was supportive of her creative work. In her last two decades, she not only published many new poems and sketches, she also collected earlier magazine work in *Somebody's Neighbors* (1881), *Root-Bound and Other Sketches* (1885), and *Huckleberries Gathered from New England Hills* (1891).

With Jewett, Freeman, and others, Cooke has become more widely known in recent years. Assessment of her writing has most often focused on her fiction, however, even though, as her recent editor Elizabeth Ammons points out, Cooke's "first love was as a writer of poetry, the most prestigious literary form of her era, and it was as a writer of verse that she hoped to make her way in the late 1840s and early 1850s." According to Donald R. Makosky, Cooke was "in early adolescence a protégée of Lydia **Sigourney**." Because American literary scholarship often pigeonholes writers into a single genre and because of the frequent overlay, in Cooke's work, of traditionally female values, concerns, and styles, she has not been taken all that seriously as a poet. This neglect has occurred in spite of her having published more than 200 poems in various periodicals, as well as her two collections of poetry, and having been anthologized often and as recently (before the LOA anthology) as 1949. Even Makosky, in writing about Cooke's extraordinary verse drama *Matred and Tamar*, observes, "Her published verse is all stanzaic and quite conventional in its diction as well as its subject matter" (*Resources for Literary Study*, 1984). More recently, however, writers like Cheryl Walker, Paula Bennett, Joanne Dobson, and Emily Stipes Watts have provided us with new frameworks within which to study nineteenth-century women poets.

A quick survey of Cooke's poetry shows both range and depth. In addition to *Matred and Tamar*, which is not only a Christian parable but a Romantic drama of strong womanhood and sisterhood, she published on the "women's subjects" mentioned earlier: flowers ("Trailing Arbutus," "Columbine,"), the seasons ("Latter Spring," "The Snow-Filled Nest"), and children ("Valentines – for my two"). Religion was another popular topic, and Cooke's Christian perspective is evident in such poems as "Rest" and "Mary, the Mother of the Lord." But Cooke's art often transforms her traditional subject matter. In "Monotropa," which focuses on the flower known as Indian pipe, Cooke transmogrifies our vision. Cooke depicts the Indian pipe as a flower unlike any other: more fungal than floral, it is a "pale alabaster" growth in "the black untrodden earth," whose "frosted chalices" hold "no sweetness." Imagining a flower that is pure yet poisonous and suggesting by the title and diction a solitary virgin, Cooke creates a poem in which conventional religious language clashes with a perspective of awe-fulness and "dread." The poem evokes the gothicism and Romanticism of Poe, Herman **Melville**, Keats, and Tennyson and anticipates Frost's out-of-kilter realism.

Cooke's work not only entered into dialogue with the literary norms of her time, it also engaged with such tremendous upheavals in United States culture as the abolitionist movement and the Civil War, the reservation movement and the Indian wars, and the Seneca Falls convention and the women's suffrage movement. Some ballads, like "After the Camanches" and "Done For," reflect racist stereotypes of Native Americans, figuring them as "brute Camanche[s]," "thieving wolves," and "Digger Squaw[s]." But others, like "John Brown" (also known as "Samson Agonistes"), celebrate African-Americans' heroic struggle against slavery. By comparing him to Samson, Cooke makes Brown a strong, trans-human figure, while white America becomes his cruel torturer who will soon lose power. The concluding stanza celebrates Brown's resurrection and predicts his ultimate triumph:

Oh, fools! his arms are round your temple-pillars;
  Oh, blind! his strength divine begins to wake; –
Hark! the great roof-tree trembles from its centre,
  Hark! how the rafters bend and swerve and shake!

Similarly, the movement for women's rights may have spun the thread of a feminist sensibility. Poems like "In the Hammock" and "Captive" underscore women's desire for freedom; "A Story," through its conventional imagery of flower and bee, provides a biting comment on men's exploitation of women; and "La Coquette" criticizes women's acceptance of false social norms.

In "Arachne" (LOA, 2: 179), Cooke does some of her finest work in this vein; in this poem, she subversively celebrates female self-sufficiency while seeming to applaud conventional female domesticity. The opening stanza condenses this tension:

I watch her in the corner there,
  As, restless, bold, and unafraid,
She slips and floats along the air
  Till all her subtile house is made.

The spider-housekeeper seems at first diminished by the size of her domain, the "corner"; perhaps Cooke also underscores here how "cornered" some women feel by domestic duties. While we might wonder if "restless" could refer to her circumscription in a narrow space and her exhausting duties – "a woman's work is never done" – it could also emphasize her strength and tirelessness, for Cooke quickly undercuts the first portrait by affirming the spider's energy and courage.

In the last two lines of the stanza, the spider transcends her corner realm as she "slips and floats" like a bird or like the wind. Her creative work, the work of *making* – not just keeping – a "house" transforms her from an ordinary to an extraordinary being not bound by the laws of gravity. "Subtile" underscores her achievement, for only those of delicate perceptions can see it. Cooke emphasizes the spider's self-sufficiency in the next stanzas: "her home, her bed, her daily food / All from that hidden store she draws." Unlike a bird, the spider creates her home from within, according to "instinct's strong and sacred laws."

Comparing herself to the spider in the next few stanzas, the narrator elaborates a clever, politically charged pun: "Poor sister of the *spin*ster clan (my emphasis)"; this comparison points not only to the spinster's obscurity, but to the self-sufficiency and creativity of her own domestic duties, which Cooke also depicts explicitly in the sketch "Miss Lucinda." In addition, Cooke intimates that even childless women, "spinsters," can be happy, useful, and "peace[ful]"; this suggestion, echoed in her short fiction, conflicts with the mid-nineteenth-century ideology of mothering as the highest and best goal for women. Cooke also points indirectly here to the tension between humans and nature, a theme that American writers found, and continue to find, compelling.

The poem ends on an apparently conventional gesture, that is, a reference to the "soul." Contrary to expectation, however, Cooke omits a reference to God and salvation and ends in a manner that presages a modernist sensibility: "I know . . . / That not for life I spin, alone. / But day by day I spin my shroud." With its evocation of the loss of hope and the pain of self-awareness, the poem echoes such Dickinson poems such as

"We grow accustomed to the dark," and "I'm 'wife' – I've finished that," and it anticipates such poems as Edna St. Vincent Millay's "Spring" and Adrienne Rich's "Power." At the same time, the regular iambic tetrameter ballad meter, echoing that of the hymn, suggests Christian faith and constancy; this meter also underscores the poem's potential criticism of the unexamined conscience that sometimes undergirds that faith.

"Arachne" needs one last look in the context of classical mythology. In Ovid's famous recounting, Arachne is a mortal whose weaving skill threatens to equal that of her teacher, Minerva (Athena). When the younger woman refuses to bow to the goddess, Minerva visits Arachne in the guise of an old woman, and a weaving contest ensues. Minerva cannot find a flaw in her protégée's cloth and, angry, transforms her into a spider.

This myth resonates in Cooke's poem in the skill of the spider and, by extension, of the housekeeper; Cooke makes the humble spider and the equally humble spinster divinely taught. Classical Arachne's pride thus appears, but it is muted by the narrator's knowledge of her own mortality. In addition, knowledge of the myth suggests that Cooke's spider is not merely a housekeeper but an artist in her own right, and a subversive one at that. In the myth, Minerva weaves into her cloth cautionary tales about mortals who challenged gods, while Arachne depicts scenes of the gods' deceptions of mortal women. Thus, Arachne criticizes those who are in power over her. As such, she and the spider are worthy symbols for Cooke herself. For in spite of claims like that by *Notable American Women* (1971) that "her poetry . . . is derivative, except for the frontier ballads," Cooke often transforms the expected into the new.

In particular, Cooke often makes of the "domestic poem" a challenge to male authority. The stories that intervene so include "Freedom Wheeler's Controversy with Providence" and "Mrs. Flint's Married Experience," but the poems, somehow, add a new dimension to this challenge. In "He and She," for example, Cooke focuses on women's faithfulness and men's self-centeredness in love. Depicting the constancy of women, she asks, "How does a woman love? Once, no more: / Though life forever its loss deplore." Of men, by contrast, she observes: "Though souls may madden or frail hearts break: / Better than wife, or child, or pelf, / Once and forever, he loves – himself!" In Cooke's bitter and explicit criticism, neither family nor money can compete with man's self-love.

This critical voice emerges at its most acerbic, perhaps, in "Blue-Beard's Castle" (LOA, 2: 178–179). The poem derives from a French folktale that has several versions. Bluebeard (a king, merchant, or sorcerer) has married his seventh (or third) wife. When he takes her home, he warns her not to open the door of a certain room. During an absence when he has given her his keys, she defies his warning, opens the door, and discovers the bodies of his previous wives, who have disobeyed him as she has (or, alternatively, she finds a bowl of blood). Bluebeard returns and, discovering her disobedience, tells her to prepare for death. In the various versions of the tale, either the wife outwits and kills Bluebeard or she is saved by her brothers (or a young man).

"Blue-Beard's Closet" reinvents, from a woman writer's perspective, the claustrophobia and hidden violence in a married woman's world. Cooke's Bluebeard conjoins the images of king, merchant, and sorcerer; her depiction of the events of the story is murky and suggestive. The poem's opening forecasts hidden threat: "Fasten the chamber! / Hide the red key." Is Bluebeard fastening the door, or is his last wife doing so, having seen the bloody vision of her predecessors? Why does the key need to be hidden? Its redness suggests the murders, but it also intimates that the sorority of the wives, their shameful femaleness, and their affiliation with and of blood, all need to be hidden.

Bluebeard's last wife seems to attempt to suppress her knowledge, which the poem embodies, literally and metaphorically, in the figure of (and in) the chamber: "*The chamber is there!*" Reiterated, it becomes a haunting, inescapable inner refrain. The "chamber" reverberates in any number of ways. Identified with the "closet" of the title, it suggests repression and enclosure; coupled with the idea of knowledge (in its fullest sense), it gestures toward the traditional linking of sexuality, love, death, and birth. We must wonder: could these women have died in childbirth? Is that end, too, a form of murder?

Enclosed in the domain of blood, madness threatens Bluebeard's wife. We are told that the castle once was "open / As shore to the sea," yet the poet gives us only an intimation of when and why it has become closed. Is it because of "wedding and prayer"? Or because of the "pale" "monarch"? We cannot know for certain; we can know only that escape is futile. Whether the wife stays or goes, "Flying or staying, / *The chamber is there!*" Ineluctable, the chamber invades the wife's mind and becomes a metaphor for consciousness itself. With chilling restraint and a blend of Romantic unworldliness and modernist suggestiveness, Cooke underscores the terrors women feel in marriage: men dominate women not only by cohabiting with but by inhabiting them. In voicing these ideas, Cooke echoes poems like Dickinson's "He fumbles at your soul" and "He put the belt around my life" and she anticipates Charlotte Perkins Gilman's "The Yellow Wallpaper" and Frost's "Home Burial" and "The Witch of Coös."

With its use of repetition, incomplete images, and insistent rhyme, Cooke's "Blue-Beard," like much of her work, has all the echo and weirdness of Poe's "Annabel Lee" or Tennyson's "Mariana," but it is augmented by the writer's knowledge of women's enclosure in a patriarchal world. Cooke unearths the reality that undergirds male-authored poetry's ideologies of love and fantasies of female being, from Wordsworth's "She Was a Phantom of Delight" to Poe's "To Helen." "Blue-Beard's Closet" not only echoes the gothic terror of Cooke's sketch "The Ring Fetter," it amplifies that terror to an almost unendurable pitch. That we now hear her uncanny poetic voice after an absence of many years does not diminish its power and authority.

KAREN L. KILCUP

Selected Works

Poems (as Rose Terry), Boston: Ticknor and Fields, 1860
"A Letter to Mary Ann," *Sunday Afternoon* 3 (January 1879), pp. 79–83
"One More Letter to Mary Ann," *Sunday Afternoon* 3 (August 1879), pp. 752–755
Somebody's Neighbors, Boston: Osgood, 1881
Root-Bound and Other Sketches, Boston: Congregational Sunday School and Publishing Society, 1885

Poems, New York: William S. Gottsberger, 1888

Huckleberries Gathered from New England Hills, Boston: Houghton Mifflin, 1891

"The Memorial of A. B., or Matilda Muffin" (as Rose Terry), *Legacy* 2 (1985), pp. 80–82

"How Celia Changed Her Mind" and Selected Stories, edited by Elizabeth Ammons, New Brunswick, New Jersey: Rutgers University Press, 1986

Further Reading

Dobson, Joanne, *Dickinson and the Strategies of Reticence*, Bloomington: Indiana University Press, 1989

Donovan, Josephine, *New England Local Color Literature: A Woman's Tradition*, New York: Ungar, 1983

James, Edward T., et al., eds., *Notable American Women 1607–1950, A Biographical Dictionary*, 3 vols., Cambridge, Massachusetts: Belknap-Harvard University Press, 1971

Spofford, Harriet Prescott, *A Little Book of Friends*, Boston: Little, Brown, 1916

Stedman, Edmund Clarence, *Poets of America*, Boston: Houghton Mifflin, 1885

Stevenson, Burton Egbert, ed., *The Home Book of Verse*, 2 vols., 8th ed., New York: Henry Holt, 1949

Walker, Cheryl, ed., *American Women Poets of the Nineteenth Century*, New Brunswick, New Jersey: Rutgers University Press, 1992

Watts, Emily Stipes, *The Poetry of American Women from 1632 to 1943*, Austin: University of Texas Press, 1977

Christopher Pearse Cranch

(1813–1892)

Like the diffident youth who had to choose a destiny from among Music, Art, and Poetry in his poem "The Three Muses," Christopher Pearse Cranch struggled with a "divided worship." During his lifetime, he achieved recognition as a poet, painter, musician, children's author, translator, and caricaturist. Residents of Brook Farm remembered his visits there as "events," citing his good baritone; facility on piano, guitar, flute, and violin; imaginative readings of his own poems and "travesties" (complete with imitations of barnyard animals and locomotives); and "picturesque type of beauty." His caricatures of New England Transcendentalism – the most famous treating Ralph Waldo **Emerson**'s "bolder metaphors" – are said to have delighted even those whose utterances or personalities provided their subjects. His landscape paintings were exhibited in salons in Paris and New York. His scenes of Venice, of which William Dean **Howells** thought highly, secured him full membership in the National Academy. His early poetry was so esteemed by Emerson and Margaret **Fuller** that he was *The Dial*'s most frequent verse contributor for its first two volumes.

According to his more famous contemporaries, however, Cranch's accomplishments in these several arts only drew attention to his failure to achieve greatness in any one of them. Despite his early enthusiasm for Cranch's poetry, Emerson politely begs the question of Cranch's poetic talent in an 1874 letter: "I have always understood that you are the victim of your own various gifts; that all the muses, jealous each of the other, haunt your brain." Others echo this assessment. James Russell **Lowell** wrote that "Cranch had gifts enough for three – only his foolish fairy left out the *brass* when she brought her gifts to his cradle." Henry James described Cranch as someone who "produced pictures that the American traveler sometimes acquired and left verses that the American compiler sometimes includes. Pictures and verses had alike, in any case, the mark of his great, his refined personal modesty; it was not in them at least, for good or for ill, to emphasize or insist."

Born on March 8, 1813, in Alexandria, District of Columbia, Cranch, the youngest son in a family of 13 children (only seven of whom survived well into adulthood), could claim kinship to and acquaintance with some of the most influential people of the age. Cranch's grandfather, Richard Cranch, a watchmaker who became both a Massachusetts state senator and a judge, was a lifelong friend of John Adams, and also Adams's brother-in-law upon his marriage to Abigail Adams's sister. Cranch's father, William, who was close to (and attended Harvard with) his cousin John Quincy **Adams**, was also appointed to a judgeship in the District of Columbia by John Adams, and made chief judge of the District Circuit Court by Thomas Jefferson. Cranch's mother, the former Nancy Greenleaf, counted Noah Webster and Judge Thomas Dawes as brothers-in-law. Cranch himself married his cousin, Elizabeth DeWindt, John Adams's granddaughter. His sister, Elizabeth, married poet Rufus Dawes; his sister Abby, who married cousin William Greenleaf Eliot, was T. S. Eliot's grandmother.

Artistic ability ran strong in the Cranch family. Cranch's older brother John became a portrait painter in Italy. His brother Edward, despite a life spent practicing law in Cincinnati, designed and decorated pottery. Cranch's reminiscences of his childhood in Alexandria, while replete with romps in orchards and gardens, also take particular note of flute duets with Edward, of their "copy[ing] pictures in India ink out of Rees's Cyclopaedia," and of his own "first versification, a paraphrase from Ossian." Throughout his life, Cranch would refer to this idyllic and artistic boyhood in order to urge Edward to give up the law and follow his artistic gifts.

This advice to Edward was not lightly given. Although remarking that his father's recreations included music and that "he repeated old poems to himself in his walks," Cranch also notes that Judge Cranch saw the arts only as pastimes. Upon Cranch's graduation from Columbian College in Washington, his father advised him to follow one of the three learned professions: law, medicine, or the ministry. Since he felt one lawyer in the family was enough and had little inclination toward medicine, Cranch chose the ministry as the profession most suited to his temperament.

This choice was fraught with difficulties from the first. Packed off to Harvard Divinity School in 1832, Cranch immediately fell in with a crowd of nascent Transcendentalists – Samuel Osgood, John Sullivan Dwight, and Theodore Parker – who, in subsequent years, would challenge the Unitarian orthodoxy preached by the Divinity School faculty. Cranch seems to have had little interest in his studies. Edward Emerson recalled that Cranch and his roommate, Dwight, devoted so much of their time to playing duets that Parker, who did not care for music, would take his revenge by sawing wood outside of their door.

Cranch's experiences as a Unitarian minister constituted the logical outcome of his philosophical and temperamental difficulties with his career choice. During his eight years in the ministry, Cranch remained an ambivalent and itinerant "supply [substitute] preacher." He described his first assignment, supplying for a large church in Providence, as having "frightened me not a little." In Andover, Maine, he complained of cold and loneliness, finding "inhabitants and parishioners few and far between" and "entirely ignorant of Unitarianism," but also "more or less disgusted with the orthodox preaching they have had . . . and willing and glad to hear something more liberal and rational from the pulpit." Conversely, in Richmond, he tried to introduce Transcendental ideas to his congregation, but he complained that the "Virginians will not read and inquire for themselves. . . . They depend very much on what they hear from the pulpit, but more persons depend entirely upon hearsay."

Encouraged by his future brother-in-law, William Greenleaf Eliot, to pursue his career in the West, Cranch supplied pulpits in St. Louis, Cincinnati, Peoria, and Louisville. Although no more settled, Cranch's Western experience apparently was more agreeable to him. He became quite close to his congregation in Peoria and fell in with sympathetic and musical company in Louisville. Among this company was James Freeman

Clarke, for and with whom Cranch drew his infamous caricatures – the most well-known being his rendering of Emerson's "transparent eyeball." He also contributed several articles and religious poems to Clarke's *Western Messenger*, a forebear to *The Dial* in its philosophical and literary sympathies. The *Messenger* was among the first publications to print Emerson's poetry, and Cranch himself favorably reviewed Emerson's "Phi Beta Kappa address" in its pages. Cranch also took over as the journal's editor during two of Clarke's annual visits to the East.

Although Cranch testified in an 1836 letter to Dwight to having had "some most glorious moments in the pulpit, moments which have carried with them an excitement I do not remember ever to have experienced elsewhere, or ever so deeply," his usual attitude toward his ministerial duties was less enthusiastic. His journals and letters from various posts reveal loneliness and a felt need to keep duty and action always in mind. In a journal entry of 1839, written while he was being considered for a position in Cincinnati, he imagines a friend of his as better suited: "He will make the most efficient minister to the poor, that could be found in the country. He is already fitted for it. I am not. The time that *I* shd spend in learning, he would spend in acting – and acting on the broadest foundation, & with the most earnest & devoted spirit."

Cranch's struggles continued. In 1840, his father, an eminent lay Unitarian, wrote to express his concern for his son's faith. While affirming that faith, Cranch also asserted that "men will never agree about the fundamentals of Christianity as long as they are possessed with the idea that Christ came to teach a system of doctrines. The only steadfast ground to be taken is that Christ came as a spiritual reformer, not as an institutor of new doctrines." This rejection of doctrine turns up in a poem he was invited to deliver at the two hundredth anniversary of the incorporation of Quincy, Massachusetts. Cranch pays tribute to the town's Pilgrim settlers, who sought religious freedom in America. Defending them against charges that their goal was actually political power, he declares that "our forefathers sought / These cold, inhospitable coasts for aught / But Truth and Freedom." Yet, in an effort to emulate their commitment to truth, he also cites their own persecution of the Merrymount revelers. In attempting to justify the Pilgrims' removal of Thomas Wollaston, the Merrymount leader who armed the local Indians with firearms, Cranch can only excuse their resolve "to look on difference of faith as crime" as part of "the general error of the time." He insists that "few had reached the creed, / That all good men are Christ's in truth and deed." In treating the Pilgrims as victims of a benighted age, Cranch establishes his own age as a more progressive one, in which religious and political leaders have a chance to build on the Puritan legacy by avoiding their mistakes. Decrying international religious and political persecution, he moves beyond the occasion to challenge America to make good on its heritage:

> The scholar, priest, and statesman still must see
> More truth and freedom for the true and free.
> Truth that outlives all visionary dreams,
> Freedom which *is* – and not which only *seems* –

This denunciation of creed in favor of a more inclusive and constructive view of religious difference would remain a feature of much of Cranch's poetry throughout the years.

Cranch's contemporaneous poems in *The Dial* reveal his devotion to Emerson and the progressive ideals of the "New School." One work, "Correspondences" (LOA, 1: 590), has been read as a direct poetic translation of Emerson's essay by the same name. The poem, which has long lines that recall Emerson's aphoristic prose, presents the Emersonian view of nature as the site of truth and divinity with which "man" may connect. Nature is a "scroll" with "God's handwriting thereon" that man was able to read before its "key" was "stolen away by sin." The glimpses of truth that man gets when he looks on nature's visible symbols are reinforced by his unconscious use of certain figures of speech. Man's project, then, is to recover that meaning and to direct his attention to those correspondences of which he already has an inkling so that he sees "in all things around, types of the Infinite Mind." When Cranch wrote to Emerson in 1840 to express his "deep gratitude for the instruction and delight [he had] derived from all [Emerson's] productions, published and spoken," Emerson responded, "If my thoughts have interested you, it only shows how much they were already yours."

Having absorbed Emersonian ideas and having established a literary relationship with the man he considered "the master mind of New England," Cranch turned to Emerson with his doubts about his own career. In an 1841 letter, he describes to Emerson having "lately taken very vigorously to landscape painting, which I am strongly tempted to follow in future instead of sermon writing." Emerson responded by congratulating Cranch's discovery that "the beauty of natural forms will not let you rest, but you must serve and celebrate them with your pencil" and his decision to "quit the pulpit as a profession." Yet, even Emerson's approval was quite not enough to turn Cranch from the ministry. In 1842, he wrote to Dwight that he was "determined not to give up preaching unless compelled to by health, and by want of sympathy and encouragement from without. I like my profession in many respects, and have grown accustomed to it. I should never get my bread in any other way." Presumably his engagement to Elizabeth DeWindt, whom he fell in love with when hired by her father as her German tutor, had something to do with the measured tone of appreciation Cranch displays here. A man who was anticipating supporting a wife and family needed to know that he could "get [his] bread" somehow. Just over a year later, however, Cranch wrote to his brother Edward that his fiancée had had an active part in his final change of heart: "So far from my lady love's thinking it a descent from pulpitdom to any otherdom, she rejoices infinitely over the chance, and would indeed have me be anything but a minister"; indeed she wished him to devote himself to "landscape painting and illustrations; also to authorship. But her own taste in painting encourages me particularly towards that path." Thus, in late 1843, Cranch and his new bride, in a move financed primarily by Cranch's father-in-law, set up housekeeping in New York. Their new abode had a room in which Cranch could paint and extra rooms for a few boarders, which in turn gave the Cranches some extra income.

Still, the most significant artistic product Cranch produced in the next few years was the volume *Poems*, issued by Carey and Hart in 1844. This volume, dedicated to Emerson, contained all of *The Dial* poems, two of which Rufus Griswold had seen fit to publish in *Poets and Poetry of America* two years earlier. Focusing on the search for individual transcendence, the poems put the New School's philosophy and goals in more personal terms. Adopting the view of nature described in "Correspondences," the poems consider the roles and the interplay of feeling, thought, and speech in the effort to connect with and interpret nature. Yet, if "Correspondences" outlines the project and its goals, other poems detail the struggle such a project entails. The feelings and thoughts most often apparent in these poems are those of loneliness, with speech proving inadequate to express the truths that nature exhibits fleetingly or at some remove.

Isolation and separation either provide the necessary and unsettling precondition for connection or become the condition to which one returns when connection is fleeting. The speakers of these poems are often alone, speaking from or looking into "deeps" they cannot fathom. In "The Ocean," the speaker describes himself and his "brother" as "Half afloat and half on land, / Wishing much to leave the strand, – / Standing, gazing with devotion, / Yet afraid to trust the Ocean – ." Yet the ocean – "Symbol of the Infinite" – exerts its pull, luring even those who have retreated from it down to its verge, where "we stand with vague distress, / Yearning for the measureless." The poem ends with the speaker asking the "Holy One" to grant him the courage to plunge in, "And in thee, thou Parent-Sea / Live and love eternally."

"Niagara" presents a similarly spellbinding glimpse of the infinite. Although no longer physically present at the falls, Cranch attempts a correspondence with nature through language and sees "down, down for ever, / Something falling, falling, falling / Up, up for ever – up, up for ever, / Resting never, / Boiling up for ever." This vision speaks "a word that since the world began, / And waters ran / Hath spoken still to man, – / Of God and of Eternity hath spoken." "To a Humming Bird" calls the very project of interpretation into question. The poet dreams of having his boyish questions about the hummingbird cleared up, particularly why "unto the flowers thou hummest, / And dost never sing"; however, a "sober spirit" tells him that "Thou canst seldom track THE SPIRIT, / Whence or how or why it is; / In its unseen deeps for ever / Are there mysteries" and that one should be grateful simply to be able to *see* the emblems nature provides.

In "Gnosis" (LOA, 1: 591), the volume's most famous poem and the one most frequently anthologized, Cranch locates human identity in feeling, which he calls "deeper than all thought." In terming thought, in turn, "deeper than all speech," Cranch describes both the desire for human fellowship and the insufficiency of words and ideas to establish it. Moving from the already familiar image of human beings as "spirits clad in veils," he focuses on their inability to reach each other despite their proximity to one another. They are "columns left alone, / Of a temple once complete" and "stars that gem the sky, / Far apart, though seeming near"; these images embrace the desire for connection and completion even as they establish and increase the distance to be overcome. This distance is one that neither speech nor thought may bridge. Cranch portrays "social company" as inconsequential, "a babbling summer stream," and "wise philosophy" as illusory, "the glancing of a dream." All that is left is human feeling, the desire for connection that is both deeper, truer, and more inspirational than earthly expressions will allow. Cranch then turns to

"the sun of love" to provide the heat that can dissolve the boundaries the poem's imagery has thus far established. This sun, indeed, liquifies the poem's remaining images. When it "melts the scattered stars of thought," the "columns left alone" are replaced by "the Fount" that feeds these souls, and the poet forecasts that "parted drops of rain / Swelling till they meet and run, / Shall be all absorbed again, / Melting, flowing into one." Thus, feeling has a reality and a power that may not only affect, but actually overcome, the exigencies with which the world makes humanity struggle.

In its preoccupation with the interplay of interior and exterior reality, *Poems* is an apt translation of Cranch's struggle with his career, philosophy, and temperament. It embraces Transcendental views of nature, the individual, and the role of the poet and makes use of imagery made familiar by Transcendentalists to do so. While Cranch's friend, Dwight, gave it a glowing review in Brook Farm's *Harbinger*, most reviewers avoided the volume or used it to mock the "New School." A reviewer for *Graham's Magazine*, which had heretofore published many of Cranch's poems, chastises him for his uncritical use of images that form "a kind of jargon now worn almost threadbare." Cranch's own view of the volume was hardly more positive. In a letter of April 1844, he describes its poems as seeming "hardly to do justice to what I might say and sing now. . . . [They] are of the past, in a great degree."

For the Cranch who might sing now was no longer alone and no longer shackled to a profession for which he thought himself unfit. His remarks on his new profession display a sense of communion that he did not find as a clergyman. They fulfill the search that *Poems* describes:

> I feel, while painting, as if I were amid the very scenes which my inexperienced brush attempts to portray. It is living with nature. It is more, for I feel the joy of a creator, as if I were the spring, – making the trees put out leaves and unloosing the purling streams, and rolling them down their rocky beds, calling up clouds, and lighting them with sunset glories.

His new profession so pleases him that he admits to "welcome poverty . . . if it wears such a jewel as this – if I can so brighten my days with the delights and fascinations of an artist's life." Landscape painting was to him "a perpetual spiritual joy and satisfaction. It is its own reward. Besides I have some hopes that in a year or two it may bring something to me in the way of vulgar dollars and cents, which I by no means affect to despise." Some positive notice in the press and a couple of sales and commissions encouraged Cranch, but also convinced him that he needed to go to Europe to further his career. For in addition to suffering a certain lack of prestige because he had not been abroad, Cranch had been told that it was easier for an American to sell another American a painting if they were both in Italy or France at the time. Thus, in 1846, vowing to keep "Nature and nothing but nature [as his] guide," Cranch, his wife, and his friend George William Curtis set sail for Europe, with plans to settle into the artist's life in Italy.

Aside from Curtis, William Wetmore **Story**, Margaret Fuller, and sculptor Hiram Powers were among the Cranches' American friends in Italy. Their life in Rome was both inexpensive and eventful. It involved sightseeing and study, rounds of meals, concerts, operas, religious and civic fairs and festivals, and excursions to the countryside. Cranch's journal is full of descriptions of the pictorial possibilities that the surrounding towns offered the artist. The Cranches also traveled to Naples, where he climbed Mt. Vesuvius, and to Pompeii, the Isle of Capri, Amalfi, and Sorrento, where they made their summer home. Their son, George William, was born during their first winter in Rome; their daughter, Leonora, was born in Sorrento in 1848. During a trip to Florence in December of that year, the Cranches used Fuller's introduction to establish an enduring friendship with Robert and Elizabeth Barrett Browning, both of whom not only showed an interest in Cranch's paintings and drawings but also read and commented on his poetry.

Despite Cranch's intention to take nature as his guide in his painting, this period marked a return to history in his poetry, in part because the Cranches' three year stay in Italy coincided with revolutions in Austria, Italy, and France. Cranch writes in his journal of a civil war in Naples, which broke out only days after his family's removal to Sorrento. On his trip to Vesuvius, Cranch went aboard an American frigate, where he discussed the state of Europe with a "hard, practical, shrewd old" American commodore, who vowed that "no one would ever have predicted the Viennese Revolution." Several poems written during this time and several years later address these European political realities. This attention to history gives the volume *The Bird and the Bell and Other Poems*, which did not appear until 1874, a tone very different from that of *Poems*. Yet Cranch saw political and social revolution as an extension and fulfillment of Transcendental ideas. The poems in this volume forego neither the attitudes toward nature and creed, nor the sort of oppositional strategies that Cranch favored in *Poems*. "The Bird and the Bell" (LOA, 1: 592), a poem about Italy just before, during, and after the Italian Revolution, uses images of clanging bells and birdsong to compare the freedom inherent in nature to the tyranny of the Roman Catholic church.

The birdsong, which Cranch characterizes as a "fresh message from the Beauty Infinite," calls up nature in all its variety: "breeze-swept banks of bloom," "the pine-grove's gloom," "home-gardens," and "apple-orchards." These images then give way to visions of freedom and peace, but the song and its accompanying vision are then both drowned out and dispelled by the "brazen bell." At this point in the poem, "Nature's improvisations" give way to "weird tones" that recall dark visions of Florence – with its "towers like chanting priests," palaces, a "great ghost-organ," and "dark channelled streets." Cranch uses the several contrasts that accompany birdsong and bell to embody and justify a social, political, and decidedly Transcendental revolution in Italy. The church, which Cranch portrays in images of darkness and inhuman sound, is far from offering access to the infinite through its symbols and creeds; it in fact has become an obstacle to such communion. It celebrates not God but itself, and has both coopted and diminished the work and ideas of those who sought to express more than its creed would allow. Its symbols, then, and the language they speak are both dead and deadening. Thus, Cranch gives us the church as "a wrinkled bride / Affianced to the blind," whose "gay-robed priest" presides over "an empty feast . . . at his tin-selled altar." The "gloomy cloisters" voice "croaking chants," and the church's organ music issues as "penitential groans." Good has come from the church's long-standing tyranny, however, for it has created the circumstances for the political revo-

lution, in which Italy (which Cranch personifies) rises up – with France's help – to do battle with its "royal despots." Victorious, yet far from vengeful, this newly invigorated Italy "asks no boon, except to stand enrolled / Among the nations," who "greet her as some lovely guest / Arriving late, where friends pour out the wine" to toast to her great future.

Having carried out a revolution against the royal despots, Italy is now ready, according to Cranch, to take on the church. Invoking images from "Gnosis," he portrays the church as "moth-eaten draperies round the columns tall." Our "heavenly Architect," he maintains, "wills a temple beautiful and wide / As man and nature, – not a cloister dim, / Nor strange pagoda of barbaric pride / Scrawled o'er with hieroglyph and picture grim / Of saint and fiend." Humanity and nature – vital and blooming, as they were at the poem's beginning – provide the images of the hope and vigor that must finally overmaster the dead forms and creeds. For humanity and God, Cranch insists, cannot be kept from each other. A single bird may be silenced, but at poem's end, a flock of birds return. Their

> . . . entrancing voices in the spring
> Of primal Truth and Beauty, were the chime
> Of heaven and earth! still we may hear you sing.
> No clang of hierarchal bells shall ring,
> To drown your carol, in the airs that move
> And stir the dawning age of Liberty and Love!

Hopes for Europe notwithstanding, the Cranches returned to America during the summer of 1849. After his three years abroad, life in America "seemed strange" to Cranch. While he had fulfilled his purpose in going to Europe, cultivating his art and selling two thousand dollars' worth of paintings, he did not find his fortune made on his return. Living in New York, in the more picturesque Lenox, Massachusetts (in the house where **Hawthorne** had written *The House of the Seven Gables*), and in Fishkill, New York, he painted landscapes that earned him a place in the Hudson River School but little mention in the press. Although he sold another two thousand dollars' worth of paintings between 1849 and 1853, this income was still insufficient to his family's needs, and he still had to count on his relatives for money. He had hoped to come out with another volume of poetry in these years, but found, upon his return from Europe, that he had no public. Finally, in the spring of 1853, Cranch decided anew that an artist belonged in Europe and moved his family to Paris, where they remained for ten years. The Cranches' daughter Carrie was born in May 1853, just prior to their departure; their son Quincy was born during their residence abroad.

Life in Paris resembled the Cranches' first sojourn in Italy. Surrounded by artist friends – mostly American – Cranch studied, attended concerts, and made painting and sketching trips to Barbizon, the forest of Fontainebleau, Switzerland, Rome, and Venice. (With Lowell, a close friend from this time forward, he also made a literary visit to London, where he saw Robert Browning and met William Makepeace Thackeray.) In a letter to his brother Edward, Cranch details the advantages Paris offered the artist, calling it "the very place, at least for study" and citing the better and cheaper materials available there, "from a studio down to engravings, colors, and drawing pencils." He also extolled the virtues of the Louvre, "which [a man] can enter at any time, and if he chooses study and copy in," and the "good specimens of contemporary art," architecture, gardens, and fountains in Paris. Cranch benefited from his surroundings, contributing work to the great Universal Exhibition of 1855 and exhibiting two or three times at the Salon.

Yet, Cranch found he could not support his family through his painting alone. Thus, for two years, he worked as a correspondent for the New York *Evening Post* and wrote two children's books. *The Last of the Huggermuggers* was a story of an American discovery of the two remaining members of a race of giants, the gentle Huggermugger and his wife, and *Kobboltozo* was the sequel, which traces the adventures of Kobboltozo, the spiteful dwarf out to discover the secret of the lately departed Huggermuggers' growth so that he may rule the island in their place. Although the books were successful – friends in America arranged terms with publishers and hoped that "children will [soon] think of Santa Claus and Cranch as brothers" – Cranch published no more children's books. He did, however, contribute a number of poems to American children's periodicals and left behind an unpublished collection, "Father Gander's Rhymes."

Cranch's struggles to support his family may account for the more earthbound artists who populate the poems of this period. In "Luna Through a Lorgnette," "Cornucopia" (LOA, 1: 611), and "The American Pantheon," Cranch concerns himself more with the realities than with the aspirations of artists. In "Luna," he mocks the poet whose romantic vision of the moon has been undone by the invention of the telescope. Where he had seen an "orb that shone Elysian" and a "crescent boat which lightly / Tilted o'er the cloud-rack nightly," the poet now sees that "the moon's constructed queerly, / Full of wrinkles, warts, and freckles, / Gilded cracks and spots and speckles." "Cornucopia," the rhyming tale of a trumpeter who tortures his neighbors with his bad and indefatigable blowing, reminds one that art is not merely the province of great or even promising talents, but also of untalented amateurs. "The American Pantheon" ultimately argues that the poet must follow his muse and forego fame or the world's appreciation, but also factors the limits of talent into this vision; Cranch also reflects here on his own status as one of the hundred poets in Griswold's *Poets and Poetry of America*, and his subsequent failure to achieve further recognition. Disappointed in their hopes of fame, lesser talents must ultimately recognize that "few are the world's great singers. Far apart." Although he argues that "each in turn has sung some lay / The world will not be willing to forget," and further suggests that no one would have put in the "costly hours the muse alone should claim / Did not some finer thought, some nobler end, / Breathe ardors sweeter than poetic fame," disappointment, if not futility, nonetheless dominates the tone of these lines.

Cranch's personal disappointments during this time did not, however, undermine his faith in political and social progress. He saw Transcendental ideals being fulfilled not only through political revolution but through technological advancement. Although "Luna" comically opposes the poet and the scientist, Cranch comes down on the scientist's side, advising the poet to change the way he conducts his art. "The Spirit of the Age" (LOA, 1: 613) reflects that change, with Cranch using "mighty electricity" as the metaphor by which one might comprehend the spread of truths made apparent through revolution. A series of sonnets, "Seven Wonders of the World," which Cranch

published in the 1887 volume *Ariel and Caliban and Other Poems*, takes technology and its revolutionary quality as its subject. Looking to the past, Cranch supposes in "The Printing-Press" (LOA, 1: 624) that just as Aladdin had "rubbed his lamp and raised / The towering Djin whose form his soul amazed," so Gutenberg harnessed a "giant sprite / Of vaster power" that "hand in hand with Faith and Science wrought / To free the struggling spirit's limèd wings, / And guard the ancestral throne of sovereign Thought." Cranch similarly mythologizes "The Photograph" (LOA, 1: 625), "The Spectroscope," and "The Locomotive" (LOA, 1: 624). He portrays this last wonder as a "roaring monster, blazing through the land . . . / Like those weird bulls Medea learned to tame / By sorcery" and finds its material progress through the land a "gain far more divine / Than when the daring Argonauts from far / Came for the golden fleece."

Cranch's optimism about political and technological progress was tested upon his return to America in the midst of the Civil War. Although not a reformer himself, Cranch, like other Transcendentalists, vehemently supported the Northern cause. While still in Paris, Cranch wrote to Curtis that he has "long believed there was no hope for the Nation but in striking directly at the heart and brain and spinal marrow of the rebellion. If we are to compromise and settle the union on the old slavery basis, I for one, should like to turn my back forever on my country." The fervor displayed here makes its way into a number of poems. Both anger and anguish inform those taking up the cause of the conflict, its violence, and the assassination of Lincoln. Although a call to battle is nothing new in Cranch, his poems addressing the assassination display a bitterness that goes beyond even that he leveled against the Italian church. "The Martyr" even urges a return to war:

No, not in vain he dies, not all in vain, –
Our good, great President. This people's hands
Are linked together in one mighty chain,
Knit tighter now in triple woven bands,
To crush the fiends in human mask, whose might
We suffer, O, too long! No league or truce
Save *men* with *men*. The devils we must fight
With fire. God wills it in this deed. This use
We draw from the most impious murder done
Since Calvary. Rise, then, O countrymen!
Scatter these marsh-light hopes of union won
Through pardoning clemency. Strike, strike again!
Draw closer round the foe a girdling flame!
We are stabbed whene'er we spare. Strike, in God's
    name!

The virulence of the language and the position, unleavened by optimism or the suggestion of an ultimate reconciliation, is unfamiliar. Coming so immediately after the apparent triumph of right, however, the assassination has temporarily fulfilled Cranch's fears of the defeat of progress. But Cranch, the lifelong Transcendentalist, cannot sustain the gloom or anger this poem describes. In "Our Country," the last of the war poems, and the last poem in *The Bird and the Bell*, Cranch, although shaken, returns to a more familiar position, portraying the nation as a "Ship of State," "sound at the core, though tossed by storms but late" and finally "nearing our port."

The Cranches remained in America for 17 years, living variously in New York, Staten Island, and Cambridge. During the early part of this period, Cranch had his greatest success as a painter. His *Venice in Tricolors* earned him full membership in the National Academy in 1864, and he exhibited there regularly until 1871. After that time, he shifted his interest and energy from painting to literature and published two volumes of poetry and a verse translation of the *Aeneid* in the 1870s. Begun as an amusement in 1869, this translation, published in 1872, not only was critically well-received but also sold well; new editions were issued periodically until 1928. In 1873, Cranch published a book-length poem, *Satan: A Libretto*, which follows Emersonian thought on the privative nature of evil. As Satan himself puts it:

> Naught evil, though it were the Prince of evil,
> Hath being in itself. For God alone
> Existeth in Himself, and good, which lives
> As sunshine lives, born of the parent Sun.
> I am the finite shadow of that Sun,
> Opposite, not opposing, only seen
> Upon the nether side.

The volume's "dangerous title," according to Emerson, guaranteed its failure with the public. Although Howells, then editor of the influential *Atlantic Monthly*, was among a number of reviewers who gave the volume good notices, not one copy was sold. (Cranch later reworked and renamed the poem; it appeared as "Ormuzd and Ahriman: A Cantata" in his final collection of poetry.)

Cranch had little more luck with *The Bird and Bell* (1874). Considering that the volume contained, according to his introductory sonnet, "the hoarded flasks of many a varying year," it is no surprise that readers generally found the volume's variety of styles and subjects disconcerting. According to F. DeWolfe Miller, however, most of the reviews were favorable; some critics even assigned Cranch a status as "a minor poet with a finished style." In addition to this veritable publishing explosion in the 1870s, Cranch also lectured and socialized. He spoke often at the Radical Club and read tributes to both Oliver Wendell **Holmes** and John Greenleaf **Whittier** at their birthday celebrations. A newspaperman at the Whittier dinner described him as "the most poetic looking man" there.

This period was one marked by tragedy and change for the Cranch family. In 1867, George Cranch died. Having enlisted in the war, he had managed to make it home to enroll in medical school, but died when a severe cold developed into "lung fever" with complications. In November 1875, Quincy Cranch was killed when he fell from the mast of a ship sailing around the Cape of Good Hope. The Cranches did not find out about his death until his father's birthday nearly four months later. While Leonora married during this time, Carrie was still at home and had taken up portrait painting. To further her education, the Cranches made their third trip to Europe in 1880 and stopped in Paris, London, Rome, and Florence during their two-year stay. This trip was marked by nostalgia. Writing in his journal of visiting the Pincio in Rome, Cranch describes finding the place "more beautiful than ever," but adds, "as the music went on, and the people promenaded up and down under the green palms and pines, the vague memories of the old days came over me with a saddening sweep. . . . I don't much like these ghosts of the buried past."

Such feelings mark Cranch's final volume, *Ariel and Caliban* (1887). Age, its poems declare, brings its satisfactions and disappointments. Cranch describes the homely comforts of "My Studio," "where labor is but joy and peace supreme" in the "too short" days of autumn. Several other poems show his appreciation for good books and good friends. The volume includes tributes to Henry Wadsworth **Longfellow**, whose "treasured books / Suggest the visions rarer than themselves," to Emerson, whose "keen, clear intuition knit the threads / Of truths disjoined in one symmetric whole," and to Lowell, Holmes, Whittier, Alfred, Lord Tennyson, Bayard **Taylor**, and others. Sonnets to "G.W.C." (George W. Curtis) commemorate the anniversary of their trip to Europe together.

The volume also contains tributes to the nation's maturity. "The Centennial Year" celebrates America's hundred years as a republic, portraying the country as a commanding "Titan mother queen," around whose feet "the flattering world crowds," "one half to see the gifts the other half / Has laid before her." Then "The Centennial Year" (subtitled "A Hope") goes on to express the wish that America can "turn the century's fears / To heralds of a cloudless light." "The Victories of Peace" specifies some of those fears, while expressing the certainty that the nation has put behind it the "dark desolation" of the Civil War and can spread that "cloudless light" to other nations.

Cranch's temperament and history guarantee his attention to the thornier issues of age as well. He wonders in "A Question" whether the "riper wisdom" that "age has earned" or the "early faith" that "boyhood gained" is the best guide to truth. He reassesses "Talent and Genius," describing the former as "on the high road travelling steady," "radiant in his day and season / With the world's reflected reason," while describing the latter as "swooping capricious to faults and to errors" and "opening through chaos fresh pathways forever" with a voice "only heard when no hand can restore him." In "Broken Wings," he asks "gray-headed poets, whom the full years bless / With life and health and chance still multiplied" to "give a thought for those who died too young – dropped – their visions half conceived – / Their lays unsung."

The theme of reconciliation – to one's old age and personal circumstances or in the aftermath of war, of seemingly opposing elements – marks the volume from start to finish. It begins with the title poem, an epilogue of sorts to Shakespeare's *The Tempest*, in which Cranch has the ethereal Ariel overcome his enmity toward the base Caliban and recognize the latter as both worthy and capable of improving his nature with a little spiritual guidance. In turn, Caliban accepts Ariel's contention that Prospero's actions toward him were just and gives up thoughts of revenge and despair and his lonely sovereignty over the island. The two agree to form a fellowship, working together to free themselves from the island and to move in the direction of even greater human fellowship. The volume's final poem, "A Poet's Soliloquy," suggests the act of reconciliation most meaningful to Cranch. Its poet-speaker recovers his soul as he "turn[s] from the crowd" and is finally able to "sing as [he] please[s]." As the final line has it: "what need of applause from the world, when Art is its own reward?"

According to Leonora Cranch Scott, her father's health began to fail in 1889. He began to suffer what he described in a letter to his brother Edward as "horrid dyspepsia with complications." He died peacefully on January 20, 1992. Shortly his death, in *Harper's Monthly*, George W. Curtis put a more positive spin on a familiar charge when he paid tribute to his friend as "an artist in various kinds. The diamond which the good genius brought to his cradle, it broke into many parts."

LISA HONAKER

Selected Works

A Poem Delivered in the First Congregational Church in the Town of Quincy, May 25, 1840, Boston: James Munroe, 1840

Poems, Philadelphia: Carey & Hart, 1844

The Aeneid of Virgil, translator, Boston: James R. Osgood, 1872

Satan: A Libretto, Boston: Roberts Brothers, 1874

The Bird and the Bell, with Other Poems, Boston: James R. Osgood, 1875

Ariel and Caliban with Other Poems, Boston: Houghton, Mifflin, 1887

Collected Poems of Christopher Pearse Cranch, introduction by Joseph M. DeFalco, Gainesville, Florida: Scholar's Facsimiles & Reprints, 1971

Further Reading

Brooks, Van Wyck, *The Flowering of New England*, New York: Dutton, 1952

Miller, F. DeWolfe, *Christopher Pearse Cranch and His Caricatures of New England Transcendentalism*, Cambridge, Massachusetts: Harvard University Press, 1951

Myerson, Joel, *The New England Transcendentalists and the Dial*, Rutherford, New Jersey: Fairleigh Dickinson University Press, 1980

———, ed., *The Transcendentalists: A Review of Research and Criticism*, New York: Modern Language Association, 1984

Scott, Leonora Cranch, *The Life and Letters of Christopher Pearse Cranch*, Boston: Houghton Mifflin, 1917

Stephen Crane

(1871–1900)

"I suppose I ought to be thankful to 'The Red Badge,' but I am much fonder of my little book of poems, 'The Black Riders,'" Crane wrote to an editor of *Leslie's Weekly* in 1895. In October of that year *The Red Badge of Courage* appeared and made him instantly famous, but "the reason, perhaps," for his preferring his book of verses, his first commercially published book which had come out on May 11, "is that it was a more ambitious effort. My aim was to comprehend in it the thoughts I have had about life in general, while 'The Red Badge' is a mere episode in life, an amplification."

In the ensuing century critical opinion has disposed otherwise: Crane's "mere episode" is acknowledged as his masterpiece, an unrivaled treatment of man's emotions under fire, a forerunner of the stream-of-consciousness fictional method. Each of his other fictions is, like *The Red Badge*, "a mere episode in life," presented in such a variety of stylistic means that Crane appears to have been an experimental writer. Few authors of the 1890s had lived, or in their fiction depicted, such a range of experiences as his: boyhood in a small town in *Whilomville Stories*; the cruel hypocrisies of adults in the same community in *The Monster*; the humor, loneliness, and terror of frontier experience in *Sullivan County Sketches*, "The Bride Comes to Yellow Sky," and "The Blue Hotel"; the degradation of life in a city slum in *Maggie: A Girl of the Streets*, and of alcoholism in *George's Mother*. If his poems meant more to him than his fiction, why did Crane, whose collected works include further war tales and distinguished journalism covering city life, the West, and Mexico, as well as reportage from three wars – Cuban independence, the Spanish-American War, and the Greco-Turkish War of 1897 – write only one more brief volume of verse, *War Is Kind* (1899)?

We must begin with the fact that Stephen Crane was a preacher's kid. Born on November 1, 1871, he was the fourteenth and youngest child of the Reverend Jonathan Townley Crane and Mary Helen Peck, daughter of a prominent Methodist minister, George Peck, and niece of the bishop of Syracuse, Jesse Peck. Stephen grew up in a busy household of religious authorship and disputation. All of the aforementioned Cranes and Pecks were writers: Mary was an assiduous correspondent for Methodist newspapers, her father wrote travel books on the American West, and her uncle produced brimstone-burning tracts. Crane's father, a much more moderate Methodist than his in-laws, proposed a God of forgiveness and mercy rather than, like them, a deity of vengeance. The other relevant strain in Crane's ancestry is the military heritage of the antecedent Cranes, including the Stephen for whom he was named, a founder of the city of Newark, New Jersey, where Crane was born. Other early Cranes included a revolutionary hero and settlers who battled Indians. Familial precedents may thus explain Stephen Crane's fascination with war (and with other perilous situations) and his recurrent deep skepticism about God's purposes and the notion of redemption through sacrifice. In Crane, the usual adolescent rebellion by which a boy declares independence from his family to establish his own identity was expressed through his rejections of famil-

ial piety and respectability. A dissenter from belief, a rebellious poet, and a stylistic innovator in prose, he early became a bohemian – indeed, he lived a life of scandal.

His boyhood was spent in Port Jervis, New York, the site of his father's ministry, with summers at the Jersey shore, where his mother covered Methodist meetings for the religious press and his older brother Townley reported social and political events for the New York *Herald*. Early on, Stephen, too, became a contributor in this newspaper; one of his earliest publications was a news story in 1892 describing a trade union parade in Asbury Park, filed under his brother's name. Already Stephen's writing was tinged with irony, imagery, and satire; in this case, the story's tone was so embarrassing to the publisher of the *Herald*, Whitelaw Reid, Republican candidate for vice president, that Townley was sacked. Stephen had attended Claverack College–Hudson River Institute (1888–90), a military boarding school where he became captain of the corps of cadets. He later referred to this as the happiest period of his life. In 1890, he enrolled as an engineering student at Lafayette College, but with a record of "academic delinquencies," he lasted only one term. In January 1891, he transferred as a special student to Syracuse University, admitted, no doubt, because of his family connection to Bishop Peck, its founder. At Syracuse, Crane took a course in English literature, but his heart was clearly with the baseball team, on which he played shortstop and catcher. He became a college reporter for the New York *Tribune*, sending in sketches and stories, and here – in a fraternity house – he drafted his first novella, *Maggie: A Girl of the Streets,* which was based on his explorations of the Syracuse tenement district and his interviews with prostitutes in police court. He left Syracuse after one semester for New York City, earning a precarious living as a free-lancer for various newspapers and becoming friends with young illustrators at the Art Students League who put him up in their studio flats. He reported on the underside of metropolitan life – the Bowery, prostitution – as well as the vivid sights of the city. When he defended a woman arrested in his presence for solicitation, he ran afoul of the police department and had to leave town.

The acclaim of *The Red Badge of Courage* led to Crane's being hired as a correspondent by the Hearst and Bachellor news syndicates. He was sent to the West, to Mexico, and then, in 1896, to Florida to cover the rebellion of the Caribbean colonies against Spain. He shipped aboard a tug running guns to the rebels; the vessel foundered, and Crane and the crew were set adrift in lifeboats – an experience leading to his tale "The Open Boat." During the Spanish-American War, Crane covered frontline action by marines in Cuba. In Jacksonville, he met a cultivated woman, the abandoned wife of a British officer; Cora Taylor was proprietress of a high-class brothel, the Hotel de Dream. She and Crane lived together, moving to England in 1897, and they both covered the Greco-Turkish War; she was the first American woman war correspondent. Living beyond their means in a large manor house in Surrey, Crane became acquainted with Joseph Conrad, H. G. Wells, Henry James, and Harold Frederic. Suffering from consumption (probably acquired while living rough in Cuba), Crane undertook hack work while striving to finish several novels. His condition worsened, and Cora sent him to a sanitarium in the Black Forest in Germany, where, on June 5, 1900, he died. He was not yet 29 years old. He is buried in Hillside, New Jersey.

It is evident that however important his poems seemed to Crane, they occupied only a minor portion of his time, energy, and creative concentration. What is there in them that makes them "more ambitious" than *The Red Badge* or his other fiction? The title poem (LOA, 2: 600) of his first book of verse suggests some reasons for their author's commitment to his "little book of poems":

Black riders came from the sea.
There was clang and clang of spear and shield,
And clash and clash of hoof and heel,
Wild shouts and the wave of hair
In the rush upon the wind:
Thus the ride of sin.

The full title of the book is *The Black Riders and Other Lines*. Crane is determined to call his verses something other than poems, for he does not wish to be considered a poet. Writing in a decade when the leading magazines featured such facile versifiers as Richard Watson **Gilder** and Edmund Clarence **Stedman**, Crane rebels against the gentility of their themes and the conventionality of their expression. His unmetered, unrhymed lines appeared shocking, as did his manhandling of conventional religious themes. His "lines" set their first readers' teeth on edge: they were attacked for their apparent barbarism, for their want of art, and for the author's nerve in trying to pass off as poetry such "disjointed effusions." In fact, however, his lines are by no means as artless as their first reviewers found them. The poem just quoted, for example, is knitted together by alliterations and onomatopoeia: the recurrences, in only six lines, of sound in *sea*, *spear*, *shield*, *shouts*, *sin*; *hoof*, *heel*, *hair*; *wild*, *wave*, *wind*; *shield*, *shouts*, *rush*; *rush*, *ride*; the assonantal line-endings *shield* and *heel*; and *wind* and *sin*, all make aurally vivid the description of an action whose significance is withheld until the last word of the last line. The imagery evokes warfare, a scene of savage abandon. It is an uncanny anticipation of James Joyce's more complex "I hear an army charging upon the land" in *Chamber Music* 22 years later; but where Joyce's oneiric vision of horsemen rising from the foam offers images of despair to an abandoned lover (as it were, a mere episode), Crane's black warriors represent "the ride of sin."

Writing during a decade when the Darwinian challenge to literal readings of the Bible was widely felt, Crane nonetheless remains Calvinist in his conviction that men share the common fate of original sin, as in poem IX (LOA, 2: 600) from *The Black Riders* (hereafter abbreviated as *BR*):

I stood upon a high place,
And saw, below, many devils
Running, leaping,
And carousing in sin.
One looked up, grinning,
And said, "Comrade! Brother!"

No sin in particular is adduced – like many of Crane's attempts to state large truths (whereas his fiction deals only with specific instances), this little set of lines suffers from abstraction. By 1895, Crane had observed and written about, perhaps had participated in, the seamy side of Bowery life, and could readily have provided relevant "episodes" were that his intention. One form of sin he does in another poem specify interestingly, internalizing the hell witnessed in the last poem:

Many red devils ran from my heart
And out upon the page.
They were so tiny
The pen could mash them
And many struggled in the ink.
It was strange
To write in this red muck
Of things from my heart.
            (*BR*:XLVI)

Crane cannot abandon the conception of human nature as inherently flawed and sinful, as proposed by, among others, his great-uncle Jesse Peck in *What Must I Do to Be Saved?* (1858). As will be seen, however, he defiantly rejects the God who condemns men's souls to the lake of fire. No doubt the guilt Crane felt in his rebellion made him think of writing itself as a ride of sin.

The flaw of abstraction in his poems is mitigated by his use of allegory and parable, as in *BR*:III (LOA, 2: 600):

In the desert
I saw a creature, naked, bestial,
Who, squatting upon the ground,
Held his heart in his hands,
And ate of it.
I said, "Is it good, friend?"
"It is bitter – bitter," he answered;
"But I like it
"Because it is bitter,
"And because it is my heart."

Although condemned to savor such bitter fare, Crane can defy the vengeful deity who speaks in thunder:

Blustering god,
Stamping across the sky
With loud swagger,
I fear you not. . . .
            (*BR*:LIII)

Fortunately, man has an alternative –

The god of his inner thoughts.
And this one looked at him
With soft eyes
Lit with infinite comprehension,
And said, "My poor child!"
            (*BR*:LI)

This compassionate God is the deity proposed by Jonathan Townley Crane, Stephen's father, author of *Holiness the Birthright of All God's Children* (1874), who was ostracized by more orthodox and influential members of the Methodist hierarchy for his liberal beliefs. (On the religious differences within Crane's family and their effect on his work, see Hoffman, 43–99, and Benfey, 21–38.)

Among Crane's "thoughts about life in general" are those of

the iconoclast who can doubt that God exists, as in *BR*:LXVI (LOA, 2: 603).

> If I should cast off this tattered coat,
> And go free into the mighty sky;
> If I should find nothing there
> But a vast blue,
> Echoless, ignorant, –
> What then?

Scornful of religiosity, Crane tells with irony of the persistence of belief (or idealism) in the face of experience to the contrary:

> A man saw a ball of gold in the sky;
> He climbed for it,
> And eventually he achieved it –
> It was clay.
>
> Now this is the strange part:
> When the man went to the earth
> And looked again,
> Lo, there was the ball of gold.
> Now this is the strange part:
> It was a ball of gold.
> Ay, by the heavens, it was a ball of gold.
> (*BR*:XXXV)

If God does exist, according to Crane, regard for us may not figure among His purposes.

> God fashioned the ship of the world carefully.
> With the infinite skill of an all-master
> Made He the hull and the sails. . . .
> . . . .
> Then – at fateful time – a wrong called,
> And God turned, heeding.
> Lo, the ship, at this opportunity, slipped slyly,
> Making cunning noiseless travel down the ways.
> So that, for ever rudderless, it went upon the seas
> Going ridiculous voyages.
> . . . .
> And there were many in the sky
> Who laughed at this thing.
> (*BR*:VI)

Not all of *The Black Riders* deals with Crane's arm-wrestling an oppressive God. Take, for instance, *BR*:XXVII (LOA, 2: 602):

> A youth in apparel that glittered
> Went to walk in a grim forest.
> There he met an assassin
> Attired all in garb of old days;
> He, scowling through the thickets,
> And dagger poised quivering,
> Rushed upon the youth.
> "Sir," said this latter,
> "I am enchanted, believe me,
> "To die, thus,
> "In this medieval fashion,
> "According to the best legends;
> "Ah, what joy!"

> Then took he the wound, smiling,
> And died, content.

Here, the violence and aggression that Crane elsewhere attributes to the "Blustering God" is directed inward and is welcomed by the youth whose glittering apparel and love of "the best legends" represent his subjection to convention. Medievalism was much in vogue in Crane's period, from the fashion of Gothic churches and college campuses to literary works as disparate as Mark Twain's *The Prince and the Pauper* and Henry **Adams's** *Mont St. Michel and Chartres*. Perhaps the only American poem like "A youth in apparel that glittered" is Edwin Arlington **Robinson's** "Miniver Cheevy," whose title character "missed the medieval grace / Of iron clothing." Crane's poem, with its nine adjectival and adverbial modifiers, is more elaborately appareled than most of his lines. (The inversion at the end, "Then took he the wound," embodies the young masochist's fixation on archaic convention.) In *Stephen Crane: An Omnibus*, R. W. Stallman notes this youth's resemblance to Henry Fleming in *The Red Badge of Courage*, with his notions of a glorious death in battle.

We might compare to "A youth . . ." the absolute concision of this next poem (LOA, 2: 602), which shares with the last one the recurrence of one of Crane's most violent nouns:

> A man feared that he might find an assassin;
> Another that he might find a victim.
> One was more wise than the other.
> (*BR*:LVI)

That's it – there is no more. These gnomic lines, frightening in their intensity, seem an anticipatory précis of Crane's fear-striated tale "The Blue Hotel" (1898). Such plainness of diction – all the words are monosyllables except the four key terms, *assassin*, *Another*, *victim*, *other* – strips the action down to bare archetype. Most of Crane's poems, in fact, are barren of metaphor. In them, the action of the allegory or parable is itself the governing metaphor for the meaning of the poem. Nothing could be further from the decorative similes and metaphors of conventional period verse. The purposive lack of musicality in Crane's lines declared his independence from whatever the poetry-reading public might have been expected to welcome. In a later poem (from *War Is Kind*), Crane even says as much:

> There was a man with tongue of wood
> Who essayed to sing
> And in truth it was lamentable
> But there was one who heard
> The clip-clapper of this tongue of wood
> And knew what the man
> Wished to sing
> And with that the singer was content.

While Crane may intimate that one particular person, a lover, would understand his lines no matter what scorn the world might heap upon them, we can take this poem to say that he will be content with whatever comprehending reader his lines may find.

Nothing like Crane's lines had appeared in the *Century*, *Scribner's*, *Harper's*, or the *Atlantic*. After so many decades of free versing in American poetry it may not be immediately evident how little like poetry Crane's lines appeared to his first readers. Their appearance startled. *The Black Riders* arrived with an orchid design (which Crane approved) trailing across its cover and suggesting affinity with the Decadent movement. Its contents were untitled and were printed all in capital letters. A recent biographer, Christopher Benfey, argues that this layout reflected the aesthetic of the Arts and Crafts movement (with which Crane had some affiliation through Elbert Hubbard, who published several of his poems in *The Philistine*). The upper-case format, Benfey suggests, made the poems resemble telegrams or headlines in newspapers, while at the same time giving the lines a rough-hewn look consonant with the handcrafted furniture made by Hubbard's Roycrofters.

If the poems' appearance startled, the language of the lines was conspicuously unadorned, in contrast to the violent and colorful animistic imagery of Crane's prose. Their direct treatment of subject and lack of conventional craft removed these minimalist strophes from the known categories of poetry. In his second term at Syracuse University, Crane took only one course, in English literature, and so he must have read in the canonical poets. At 22, however, he had met no poets; the only allusion in his collected verse is a quatrain that parodies Henry Wadsworth **Longfellow's** "A Psalm of Life" (LOA, 1: 370) by proposing that the "sublime" would never be reached by "Dabbling much in rhyme." In a notebook, Crane copied this defiant sentence of **Emerson's**: "Congratulate yourself if you have done something strange and extravagant and have broken the monotony of a decorous age." Crane's lines indeed succeed in this respect. By the end of his life, he owned volumes of numerous standard poets (William Ernest Henley, Rudyard Kipling, William Shakespeare, Robert Burns, John Dryden, George Meredith, Longfellow, and Robert Browning among them), but it is impossible to tell whether he had read any of these before writing *The Black Riders*. Its lines show no trace of indebtedness to, or influence of, such poets.

Since not even a book as iconoclastic in style and subject as this one springs from its author's hand without any precedents at all, what is most likely is that the antecedents of Crane's lines were in prose rather than in the received canon of verse. As noted above, his best poems are saved from the abstractness of their general statements about God or sin by being cast in the form of parables and allegories. The son of a preacher would have heard parables in his father's sermons throughout a boyhood of Sundays; in his pious home, Stephen must have been immersed in the Bible. Freeing himself from hypocritical religiosity, he came upon a popular work by the South African writer Olive Schreiner and appropriated from her *Dreams* (1891) parabolic structures that he used ironically – her dreams were all sentimental – to attack the pretensions of sages, the smug, and the self-righteous.

Hamlin **Garland**, whom Crane met while in New York, claimed that Crane composed his lines in his presence – that the poems came out in their final form, as though by automatic writing. More likely, Crane wrote out for Garland poems he had already formulated and knew by heart. His prose manuscripts, as well as those of his verse, show Crane to have clearly conceptualized his style – whether metaphorical in prose or plain in verse – before writing it down in his clear hand, trained to make copy legible for newspaper compositors. He made few corrections and emendations. But this, no more than the unpoetic language and lineation, does not mean that Crane wrote without premeditation or art. He knew very well what he was about, and he did it in ways unprecedented in our poetry.

In the volume *War Is Kind* (1899), the title poem again opens the book. In appearance, however, the only element in Frederic Gordon's design for *The Black Riders* that suggests the design Will Bradley imposed on Crane's second volume is the orchid on the cover of the first. *War Is Kind* takes its visual aesthetic not from the imagery of its title poem but from the spirit of the suite of love poems that close the volume. One poem in this suite, "Intrigue: I," has little indeed of the structural muscularity or aggressive diction of Crane's other poems, nor the cosmic sense of abandonment seen in the earlier *BR:X* (LOA, 2: 601):

> Should the wide world roll away
> Leaving black terror
> Limitless night,
> Nor God, nor man, nor place to stand
> Would be to me essential
> If thou and thy white arms were there
> And the fall to doom a long way.

Now, in "Intrigue: I," Crane himself seems to speak as a "youth in apparel that glittered" who welcomes his own doom.

> Thou art my love
> And thou art death
> Ay, thou art death
> Black and yet black
> But I love thee
> I love thee
> Woe, welcome woe, to me.

These eight poems, sentimental, self-pitying, and only occasionally flickering into strength ("I thought of the thunders that lived in my head"), unfortunately set the mood for the book's format. Bradley's Beardsleyesque illustrations and decorations include flowing depictions of long-tressed women and such conventional motifs as a lyre, birds, candles, and flowers. The poems are set with only a few lines at the top of each page, curiously perched above deep white space that is occasionally broken by the stylized images.

This Decadent, arty appearance is belied by the rest of the contents of *War Is Kind*. This volume extends Crane's range of themes, and several of the poems are structurally more complex than hitherto. Some poems continue his argument with, or about, God; however, Crane's distrust of divine purpose, as in the earlier "God fashioned the ship of the world," is now differently phrased. In this poem, Crane has moved away from fin de siècle iconoclasm to a naturalistic view of man's fate:

> A man said to the universe:
> "Sir, I exist!"
> "However," replied the universe,
> "The fact has not created in me
> A sense of obligation."
> (LOA, 2: 606)

This little fable anticipates the modern view of the universe as a field of force, and the consequent dissociation of its physical laws from our moral imperatives. Crane develops the theme analogously in chapter six of "The Open Boat" (1897).

When it occurs to a man that nature does not regard him as important, and that she feels she would not maim the universe by disposing of him, he at first wishes to throw bricks at the temple, and he hates deeply the fact that there are no bricks and no temples. Any visible expression of nature would surely be pelleted with his jeers. . . .

A high cold star on a winter's night is the word he feels that she says to him. Thereafter he knows the pathos of his situation.

One is struck by the utter absence in the poem of the complex imagery seen in the prose passage. This poem, like many of Crane's, is made dramatic by its dialogic structure. A speaker makes an utterance and another replies; this conceptualization permits a variety of tones, since the response can either reinforce, contradict, or puncture the pretensions of the first speaker's avowal.

In fact, this dialogic structure does not depend on a conversation; it can embody contrasting views of reality:

> To the maiden
> The sea was blue meadow
> Alive with little froth-people
> Singing.
>
> To the sailor, wrecked,
> The sea was dead grey walls
> Superlative in vacancy
> Upon which nevertheless at fateful time,
> Was written
> The grim hatred of nature.

In a posthumously published poem, Crane again deals with the theme and scene of the foregoing (as in "The Open Boat"). Here, the poem's structure is much more complex, and it uses some of the verse conventions Crane earlier had so conspicuously spurned. In this poem, two sets of two quatrains, each with a refrain, are separated by a nine-line passage without refrain. The quatrain stanzas describe the scene, and the interpolated longer passage comments upon it. The texture of the language is richer; its lines are filled with arresting images.

> A man adrift on a slim spar
> A horizon smaller than the rim of a bottle
> Tented waves rearing lashy dark points
> The near whine of froth in circles.
> God is cold.
>
> The incessant raise and swing of the sea
> And growl after growl of crest
> The sinkings, green, seething, endless
> The upheaval half-completed.
> God is cold.
>
> The seas are in the hollow of The Hand;
> Oceans may be turned to a spray
> Raining down through the stars
> Because of a gesture of pity toward a babe.
> Oceans may become grey ashes,
> Die with a long moan and a roar
> Amid the tumult of the fishes

> And the cries of the ships,
> Because The Hand beckons the mice.
>
> A horizon smaller than a doomed assassin's cap,
> Inky, surging tumults
> A reeling, drunken sky and no sky
> A pale hand sliding from a polished spar.
> God is cold.
>
> The puff of a coat imprisoning air.
> A face kissing the water-death
> A weary slow sway of a lost hand
> And the sea, the moving sea, the sea.
> God is cold.
> (LOA, 2: 608)

The poem's sophisticated structure suggests that Crane had learned a thing or two from his readings among the poets whose books he owned; his style, his point of view, and the intensity of his imagery, however, are completely his own.

Although Crane's first published novel, *Maggie*, was a vivid depiction – at once naturalistic and impressionistic – of the degradation of life in a city slum, his lines in his two books of poems avoid such criticism or comment on specific social problems, which Crane would consider episodes subsumed under his more general condemnations of sin and hypocrisy. Still, in a couple of late poems he does get down to cases. The following poem epitomizes the yellow journalism practiced in New York when Crane eked out a living as a journalist, sometimes being paid as much as 15 dollars for a feature:

> A newspaper is a collection of half-injustices
> Which, bawled by boys from mile to mile,
> Spreads its curious opinion
> To a million merciful and sneering men,
> While families cuddle the joys of the fireside
> When spurred by tale of dire lone agony.
> A newspaper is a court
> Where every one is kindly and unfairly tried
> By a squalor of honest men.
> . . . .
> It is fetless [feckless] life's chronicle,
> A collection of loud tales
> Concentrating eternal stupidities,
> That in remote ages lived unhaltered,
> Roaming through a fenceless world.
> (LOA, 2: 605)

Crane's irony spares neither subjects, readers, nor writers of the chronicles of half-injustices. In its structure, which is based on repetitions, and its profusion of accurate and surprising images, this, like other poems in *War Is Kind*, shows how Crane was developing his craft. In diction, phrasing, and lineation it reads, nearly a century after being written, as though it was just published in a contemporary magazine. These qualities, a seemingly prosaic language intensified in striking images and a structure stanzaic with refrain, characterize the first poem in *War Is Kind* (LOA, 2: 604), from which the volume takes its title. Its subject is that of his most famous fiction, *The Red Badge of Courage*, and his tales in *The Little Regiment*; but where his fiction explores the mystery of heroism, Crane's poem contrasts that vainglorious pursuit to its tragic cost, which the slain soldier's survivors must bear.

> Do not weep, maiden, for war is kind.
> Because your lover threw wild hands toward the sky
> And the affrighted steed ran on alone,
> Do not weep.
> War is kind.
>
> Hoarse, booming drums of the regiment
> Little souls who thirst for fight,
> These men were born to drill and die
> The unexplained glory flies above them
> Great is the battle-god, great, and his kingdom –
> A field where a thousand corpses lie.
>
> Do not weep, babe, for war is kind.
> Because your father tumbled in the yellow trenches,
> Raged at his breast, gulped and died,
> Do not weep.
> War is kind.
>
> Swift, blazing flag of the regiment
> Eagle with crest of red and gold,
> These men were born to drill and die
> Point for them the virtue of slaughter
> Make plain to them the excellence of killing
> And a field where a thousand corpses lie.
>
> Mother whose heart hung humble as a button
> On the bright splendid shroud of your son,
> Do not weep.
> War is kind.

Although the irony of the refrain (and book title) may be too self-evident, this does not vitiate the compassion of the three stanzas, nor diminish their understated yet powerful cutting down of the rhetoric of the interleaved passages that glorify the "Hoarse, booming drums of the regiment." John Berryman has pointed out that this poem "is based on the letter *i* in the word 'kind.'"

There are rhymes "die" and "lie" in the set-in stanzas; wild, sky, affrighted, flies, bright; just these, and they ought to make a high lament. But of course they do nothing of the sort. . . . The poem takes place in the successful war of the *prose* ("unexplained," "gulped," and so on) *against* the poetic appearance of lament. It takes some readers a while to hear this poem. Once heard, it is passionately moving . . . not at all in the "bright splendid shroud" line, but in the beautiful and i-less line before it. A domestic, terrible poem, what it whispers is: "I would console you, how I would console you! *If I honestly could.*"

To this appreciation, one may add a word on the stylistic and structural sophistication of the poem. Whereas in Crane's earlier, shorter poems there seems a reckless absence of craft, his later work embodies an impressive poetic technique. Crane dramatizes his alternation of viewpoint and feeling by using, in the stanzas addressed to lover, child, and mother, a two- or three-line strophe followed by a brief two-line refrain. In the interpolated passages that invoke pomp and glory only to undercut them, however, the strophes are six lines long, in tetrameter, with the only rhyme-endings in the poem, in refrains that emphasize the *i* sounds on which Berryman commented. Thus, the conflict within the poem is expressed in the appearance, rhythm, sound, and structure of the alternating stanzas, which in turn dramatize grief and the cost of glory. It is as though the first set of stanzas anticipates Wilfred Owen or Isaac Rosenberg, and the second, Rupert Brooke – to cite poets of another country and a later war. In American poetry, Crane's poem is worthy to stand beside those in Walt **Whitman's** *Drum-Taps*, such as "Come Up from the Fields Father" (LOA, 1: 887), and Herman **Melville's** *Battle Pieces*, such as "The Portent" (LOA, 2: 2) and "Shiloh" (LOA, 2: 9). Despite the nation's experience of two world wars, the Korean War, and the Vietnam War, no twentieth-century American poet has written of war's illusions and sufferings with like authority. Crane, as well as our poets of the Civil War and England's of World War I, prove Yeats wrong in his famous assertion that "the poetry is not in the pity."

Had Stephen Crane lived into the twentieth century, he would have joined his contemporaries Robert Frost and Robinson, Ezra Pound, Wallace Stevens, and T. S. Eliot in further developing the modernism that, in prose as well as verse, he anticipated without directly influencing. Stevens, attending Crane's funeral in New York (he was then a reporter for the same paper, the *Tribune*, for which Crane had written in 1891–92), wrote in his diary that "the hearse rattled . . . over the cobbles . . . with not a single person paying the least attention to it." Crane seemed forgotten as soon as dead. His verse certainly faded from view. A dozen years later the Imagist movement appeared, heralded by Pound and publicized by Amy Lowell. Looking for poetic ancestors, in 1916 Carl Sandburg addressed a flat poem, "Letter to Dead Imagists," to Emily **Dickinson** and "Stevie" Crane; but Crane received little serious attention until the appearance in 1923 of Thomas Beer's idiosyncratic biography, which, despite inaccuracies and fabrications, presented Crane as a major writer. At this moment in history, Crane was deemed worthy of a collected edition, which Knopf published in twelve volumes between 1925 and 1927, edited by Wilson Follett with introductions by such luminaries as Willa Cather, Joseph Hergesheimer, and H. L. Mencken. The volume of verse was introduced by Amy Lowell, who in effect disowned Crane as a pre-Imagist; she presented him as a poet without a period or context, "A boy, spiritually killed by neglect," as though his consumption was caused by the neglect of the literati. Collections of Crane's fiction appeared in the 1930s and 1940s, and the war, of course, rekindled interest in his work. The major author most evidently influenced by Crane is Hemingway, both in his early book of verse and in the themes and style of his fiction.

Crane was no longer neglected, and by 1950 he was firmly established in the American canon. In that year, John Berryman's intensely appreciative and keenly analytical study of Crane's life and work appeared, as did the first of many subsequent college text editions of Crane's writings. Robert W. Stallman's *Stephen Crane: An Omnibus* (1952) presented a generous selection of the writings, with introductions combining biographical background with interpretations applying principles of the New Criticism to the texts. The trickle of scholarly studies of Crane swelled thereafter into a large bibliography.

Until the rise of confessional and autobiographical poetry since the 1960s, modernist American verse for the most part shunned narrative, allegory, and parable. Still, in *The Black Riders* and later, Crane anticipated the abandonment of received forms and meters so characteristic of one aspect of modernism, the vers libre movement from 1912 on. If in its iconoclasm *The Black Riders* now seems a product of the 1890s, Crane's later poems, in which paradox and irony are voiced in intense, dreamlike images apparently summoned from inexplicable sources, express the sensibility of the century he did not live to experience. His prose, as in "The Blue Hotel," "The Open Boat," and his tales of war, is more complex than most of his verse, but his poems were developing toward a richly metaphoric language and a dialogic structure of stanzaic and rhythmic patterns and refrains that embodied their contrasting themes. Had Crane lived and continued to develop as a poet, his work would doubtlessly have participated in the modernism that the best poems he has left us so tellingly anticipate. His major achievement is in his novels and tales, but the best of his poems are inimitable and well deserve their permanent place in American literature.

DANIEL HOFFMAN

Selected Works

The Black Riders, Boston: Copeland & Day, 1895

War Is Kind, New York: Frederick A. Stokes, 1899

The Black Riders and Other Lines, vol. 6 in *The Work of Stephen Crane*, edited by Wilson Follett, introduction by Amy Lowell, 12 vols., New York: Knopf, 1926

The Collected Poems of Stephen Crane, edited by Wilson Follett, New York: Knopf, 1930

Stephen Crane: An Omnibus, edited by Robert Wooster Stallman, New York: Knopf, 1952

The University of Virginia Edition of the Works of Stephen Crane, edited by Fredson Bowers, vol. 10, *Poems and Literary Remains*, Charlottesville: University Press of Virginia, 1969

The Complete Poems of Stephen Crane, edited by Joseph Katz, Ithaca, New York: Cornell University Press, 1972

Stephen Crane: Prose and Poetry, edited by J. C. Levenson, New York: Library of America, 1984

The Correspondence of Stephen Crane, edited by Stanley Wertheim and Paul Sorrentino, 2 vols., New York: Columbia University Press, 1988

Further Reading

Baron, Herman, *A Concordance to the Poems of Stephen Crane*, Boston: G. K. Hall, 1974

Bassan, Maurice, ed., *Stephen Crane: A Collection of Critical Essays*, Englewood Cliffs, New Jersey: Prentice-Hall, 1967

Beer, Thomas, *Stephen Crane: A Study in American Letters*, New York: Knopf, 1923

Benfey, Christopher, *The Double Life of Stephen Crane*, New York: Knopf, 1992

Berryman, John, *Stephen Crane: A Critical Biography*, rev. ed., New York: Farrar, Straus & Giroux, 1962

Bloom, Harold, *Stephen Crane: Modern Critical Views*, New York: Chelsea House, 1987

Cady, Edwin H., *Stephen Crane*, Boston: Twayne, 1980

Dooley, Patrick K., *The Pluralistic Philosophy of Stephen Crane*, Urbana: University of Illinois Press, 1993

Gullason, Thomas Y., ed., *Stephen Crane's Career: Perspectives and Evaluations*, New York: New York University Press, 1972

Haliburton, David, *The Color of the Sky: A Study of Stephen Crane*, Cambridge: Cambridge University Press, 1989

Hoffman, Daniel, *The Poetry of Stephen Crane*, New York: Columbia University Press, 1957

LaFrance, Marston, *A Reading of Stephen Crane*, Oxford: Clarendon, 1971

Stallman, Robert Wooster, *Stephen Crane: A Biography*, New York: Braziller, 1968

_____, *Stephen Crane: A Critical Bibliography*, Ames: Iowa State University Press, 1972

Weatherford, Richard M., ed., *Stephen Crane: The Critical Heritage*, London: Routledge & Kegan Paul, 1973

Wertheim, Stanley, and Paul Sorrentino, eds., *The Crane Log*, Boston: G. K. Hall, 1994

Richard Henry Dana Sr.

(1787–1879)

Dana was a poet, essayist, writer of short fiction, and literary and cultural critic. He was less well-known and, perhaps, less talented than his contemporaries William Cullen **Bryant**, Washington Irving, and James Fenimore Cooper. But Dana is nonetheless important for having written interesting and prescient psychological, aesthetic, and philosophical explorations of Romantic ideas. He was an early rebel against neoclassicism and a lifelong advocate of the literary possibilities of Romanticism. In his own way, he anticipated the psychological tales of Edgar Allan **Poe** and the metaphysical speculations of Herman **Melville** and Ralph Waldo **Emerson**. His work posed the issues and explored the literary strategies that engaged writers of the subsequent generation.

Dana was born in Boston on November 15, 1787, the youngest son of the Federalist judge Francis Dana and a descendant of influential merchants, lawyers, and Revolutionary War patriots. After a lonely and gloomy childhood, he attended Harvard College, where he conceived a lifelong revulsion against Locke's psychological theories. In a December 1834 letter, explaining to a friend his particular brand of speculative writing, Dana said: "Could a hog, when his viscera have been appropriated for a harslet dinner & stuffed sausages, be endowed with sensation, in his empty condition, he would feel much as I used to feel after reading Locke. Thus you see how I was kept from being a prodigious philosopher & led to writing reviews, & tales, & verses." From that moment forward, he was attracted to philosophical idealism. He was the first American literary critic to draw inspiration and insight from the Romantic aesthetics of Archibald Alison, William Wordsworth, and Samuel Taylor Coleridge. Unlike poets of the eighteenth century whose views of the mind were based on the ideas of John Locke and David Hartley and who thought of the imagination as the faculty of the mind responsible only for amusing fancies, these English writers viewed the imagination as a power capable of bringing the poet and the reader to truths unavailable to reason, logic, and fact. An admirer of Coleridge's *Biographia Literaria* (1817), Dana believed that the inspired poet had godlike powers analogous to those possessed by the divine mind. (He was probably told about the *Biographia Literaria* by his future brother-in-law, the painter Washington **Allston,** who was in London during the year of its publication.)

For some time after his older brother lost the family fortune in disastrous land speculations, Dana was forced, against all his desires, to pursue a career in the law. In 1817, he found an outlet for his literary views as a contributor to and editorial assistant for the *North American Review*. The four reviews he wrote for the periodical are notable for the clarity and vigor of his writing style and for his unusual sensitivity to the important philosophical issues then dividing Augustan writers from younger writers and critics who were wedded to Romantic aesthetics. In his reviews, Dana questioned the conventional literary wisdom of his time. He argued that writers should emphasize the subjective when representing human experience. Rejecting the neoclassical belief in timeless literary conventions, Dana claimed that a reviewer must have wide tastes, "be trammeled by no narrow systems or schools," and, above all else, possess in his own right the imagination to be caught up in the author's act of creation.

In a review of Allston's *The Sylphs of the Seasons* (1813; see LOA, 1: 48), Dana proclaimed the coming of a new age in poetry. According to Dana, popular poets of the eighteenth century such as Alexander Pope, William Cowper, and Thomas Campbell had engaged in altogether too much finger-wagging morality and sly drawing-room artificiality. Dana believed that the new poets would put aside narrow social distinctions and demonstrate the poetic possibilities associated with depictions of nature and the lives of ordinary women and men. Dissatisfied with Allston's "weak amiableness," Dana expressed a preference for Lord Byron's explorations of the dark side of the soul and Wordsworth's evocations of the spiritual significance of nature.

Dana was at his best in a review of English critic William Hazlitt's *Lectures on the English Poets* (1818). The two men shared several convictions associated with the Romantic aesthetics. Both believed that the mind is an active agent in the creation of an individual's impressions of the world. Both believed that passions are sources of cognitive truths. As Romanticists, they also shared a common enemy in the prestige accorded to the empirical method and to science. Hazlitt worried that the advances of science threatened to demystify the world, while Dana feared that the arrogance of scientific utilitarianism inspired contempt for those powers of the heart, mind, and imagination that he presumed defied quantification.

Despite these similarities, Dana found himself at odds with Hazlitt over the merits of particular poets. Hazlitt admired Pope as a "great writer of some sort." Convinced that Americans would never write great poetry until they got beyond their veneration of Pope, however, Dana complained of the poet's conceits, "unmeaning words," false sentimentality, and misplaced passions. Hazlitt preferred James Thomson to Cowper. By contrast, Dana thought Thomson's descriptions of nature were little better than "meteorological tables," while Cowper seemed to him an accomplished poet who could infuse nature with religious and domestic associations. It was Hazlitt's cool appraisal of the poetry of Wordsworth and Coleridge that most troubled Dana, however. He found it hard to reconcile Hazlitt's Romantic aesthetics with his lack of enthusiasm for the Lake Poets. He concluded that Hazlitt was too "envious and Spleeny, . . . too full of himself to have a sincere love and interest for what is abstractly good and great."

Dana's reviews did not sit well with the people who mattered in Boston. In the course of these reviews, he had raised questions about the adequacy of Scottish Common Sense philosophy, accused Harvard of smothering genius, and urged a form of metaphysical idealism. To suggest, as he had, that the private visions of poets were truer than the conventions of the community and more important than social solidarity was unacceptable to Boston's establishment. In 1843, the literary arbiter Rufus Griswold recorded that Dana had "the whole influence of the university, of the literary and fashionable society of the city, and of the press to contend against." Their opposition eventually cost Dana the editorship of the *North American Review*. When the association of contributors chose Edward Everett as editor instead of Dana, they opted for the Augustan values of detachment and rationality over the Romanticist commitment to originality and daring. Bryant commented that if the *Review* had "remained in Dana's hands he would have imparted a character of originality and decision to its critical articles which no literary man of the country was at that time qualified to give it." Dana had thought he was in the vanguard of a new literary movement, but discovered that no one was following him.

Although discouraged by the criticism that denied him the editorship of the *North American Review*, Dana took heart from the apparent popularity of Washington Irving's *Sketch Book*. In 1821, he published the first issue of his own literary miscellany, ironically titled *The Idle Man*. The six issues, published over a period of fifteen months, contained essays, fiction ("Edward and Mary," "Thomas Thornton," and "Paul Felton"), a review of Edmund Kean's performance of *Richard III*, and poems by Allston and Bryant.

It was while writing for *The Idle Man* that personal tragedy and growing doubts about the Romantic vision brought about a deep crisis in Dana's life. In the spring of 1822, his wife Ruth Charlotte died of tuberculosis and his youngest daughter perished from injuries received during a fall. These events brought on a grief that, according to his son, "no description of agony short of madness has equaled." Dana's conviction that the mind plays an active role in shaping one's experience of the world may have intensified this crisis. On the one hand, he believed that the transforming power of the imagination could reveal to the poet a higher order of spiritual truth. On the other hand, it seemed increasingly clear to him that there was another possibility: under the influence of grief and the darker forces of the unconscious mind, the imagination might just as easily lead the poet to nihilism and madness.

Dana explained the first possibility in a short essay entitled "Musings," published in *The Idle Man* in 1821. In this essay, Dana sets up a contrast between the metaphysical idealist, this "man of feeling and imagination," and the commonsense realist favored by the new commercial order. In the latter's eyes, forests, marshes, and lakes are the raw material of fortunes. But for the poet, Dana claimed, everything leaves aside "its particular and short-lived and irregular nature, and puts on the garments of spiritual beings, and takes the everlasting nature of the soul." In the earlier sentimental stories published in *The Idle Man*, he had made few metaphysical claims for the imagination and was contented simply to show how nature heals the wounded spirit and consoles those who suffer poverty and the world's neglect. But in "Musings," he joined Coleridge in claiming that the imagination, because it arises out of the soul and shares with nature an identical origin in the one transcendent spiritual reality, can reveal divine truths.

According to Dana, the truth known to the imagination is that the world and the self are one. The imagination thus transcends the old historical dualities dividing mind and feeling and subject from object. In "Musings," Dana explains that "soul and body are blending into one; the senses and thoughts mix in one delight; [the poet] sees a universe of order and beauty, and joy and life, of which he becomes a part, and finds

himself carried along in the eternal going-on of nature." "Musings" was the first declaration of what would become the Transcendentalist position by an American writer. It spurred William H. Prescott, the reviewer for the *North American Review*, to protest Dana's "mystical, fine-spun, indefinite phraseology." Few things so aroused the scorn of the men of the *North American Review* as ideas that smacked of mysticism.

Dana also published his only efforts at fiction in *The Idle Man*. Intrigued by the outlaw-hero figure made popular by Byron, Dana wrote several short stories featuring such characters. The figure of the outlaw-hero allowed Dana to explore the darker, unconscious sources of the imagination. During the period of intellectual and psychological crisis brought on by the death of his wife, for example, Dana wrote a short story entitled "Paul Felton." The hero of the story combines the qualities of the Romantic poet and the moral outlaw. Paul Felton is a loner, an "isolato," who is filled with self-doubts and suspicions. He spends much of his time outdoors, where his imagination reveals that nature is a

grand and beautiful mystery, – in his better moments, a holy one. It was power, and intellect, and love, made visible, calling out the sympathies of his being, and causing him to feel the living Presence throughout the whole. Material became intellectual beauty with him; he was as a part of the great universe, and all he looked upon, or thought on, was in some way connected with his own mind and heart.

But this vision, so reminiscent of "Musings," is only a fleeting one. More often Felton feels cut off from nature and distracted by his loneliness and fears. His marriage fills him with insane jealousy and moves him to murder and madness. "Paul Felton" suggests that Dana had become convinced that the imagination was not a trustworthy guide. Dana had discovered that minds of the "highest intellectual order," when governed by the imagination, are as likely to experience "visitants from hell" as "hours of bright and holy aspirations."

Four years later, when Dana began to publish poetry for the first time, his most important theme was again the imagination, but his views about this subject were beginning to change. (His first poems – including "The Dying Raven," "Fragments from an Epistle," "Little Beach Bird," and "The Husband and Wife's Grave" – were published in 1825 in the *New York Review and Athenaeum Magazine*, edited by his friend Bryant.) In the years following his agonizing personal crisis in 1821, he had begun to work toward an explicitly Christian metaphysics and poetics. In the winter of 1826, during an evangelical campaign conducted in Cambridge by Lyman Beecher, Dana converted to Congregationalism. In 1843 he joined the Church of the Advent, a gathering of high church Episcopalians. This ongoing religious pilgrimage was an inseparable part of his philosophical struggle to come to terms with literary Romanticism. He became convinced that in Christianity he had discovered a higher ground for the Romantic vision.

The despair aroused by Dana's personal crisis and the inability of the Romantic vision to cure this despair pervades one of his earliest poems. In "Changes of Home," grief and disappointment overwhelm the narrator, cutting him off from the healing power of nature. Hoping to recover the joy he once knew before the blasting of his boyish dreams and the death of his wife, the narrator returns to the scenes of his childhood. Echoing the language of Coleridge's "Dejection," however, the narrator admits that his imagination is powerless: "I cannot feel, though lovely all I see; / A void is in my soul; my heart is dry; / They touch me not – these things of earth and sky." Among the conventions of literary Romanticism, nothing signifies alienation from the spiritual meaning of life so completely as this indifference to the beauty of nature. The poem offers no solace; the narrator leaves his boyhood haunts to take a berth aboard a ship, a choice that, through associations already established in the poem, hints of his death.

In several of his early poems, Dana also suggests a Christianized version of the transcendental idealism first discussed in "Musings." In "The Dying Raven" (LOA, 1: 71), for example, he links God, nature, and the individual in one harmonious spiritual whole. The raven is addressed as "Priest of Nature, Priest of God, to man!" Its presence even in the harshest winter signifies to the poet the promise of spring and spiritual resurrection. The divinity that pervades nature thus also guides the poet's imagination. To those who might reject such a suggestion, Dana warns:

> Who scoffs these sympathies,
> Makes mock of the divinity within;
> Nor feels he gently breathing through his soul
> The universal spirit. – Hear it cry,
> "How does thy pride abase thee, man, vain man!
> How deaden thee to universal love,
> And joy of kindred, with all humble things, –
> God's creatures all!"

This same theme appears again in "The Little Beach Bird." In this, perhaps the best of his lyric poems, Dana successfully links the poem's mood and theme with haunting and beautifully observed imagery of the sea and the sandpiper. He describes the ocean as singing a requiem, mourning "man's woe and fall, / His sinless glory fled." The sandpiper's "flitting form . . . ghostly dim and pale" moves "in strange accord" with the "motion and the roar" of the surging surf, its "melancholy piping cry" a priestly commentary on the human condition. The poet urges the little beach bird to flee the "complaining sea" and take its place "on meadows light / Where birds for gladness sing." Like the dying raven, the beach bird plays a redemptive role: its message is "One spirit . . . The mystery, – the Word." Although a reader might question the poem's contrived solution (do sandpipers find their way to inland meadows?), Dana may have wished to suggest, as he had in "The Dying Raven," the hope of redemption.

In "Fragment of an Epistle," a poem written at about the same time, Dana again asserts a harmony between God, nature, and the imagination of the poet. Although the Christian framework is still more pronounced in this poem than in "The Dying Raven," Dana preserves the transcendental belief that all experience is unified through the identity that mind and nature share with the divine source of all creation. Writing to a friend to announce his recovery from a long illness, the poet states that he has come through his affliction because God has touched his heart with peace and armed his imagination with the power to render nature in consoling and delightful ways. From his window vantage point, the poet joins, in his imagina-

tion, boys sledding down wintery slopes and then sees the scene transformed into the city of "Revelation." Suddenly the sun goes down, and the path of light that appeared to lead to the heavenly city vanishes. Although these events seem to raise the question of the value of such fanciful imaginings, the poet defends the imagination:

> Are holy thoughts but happy dreams
> Chased by despair, as starry gleams
> By clouds? – Nay, turn, and read thy mind;
> Nay, look on Nature's face, and find
> Kind, gentle graces, thoughts to raise
> The tired spirit, – hope and praise.

Most of Dana's poetry reflects this Christianized Romanticism. While writing the poems that appeared in Bryant's *New York Review*, Dana seems to have been feeling his way toward an increasingly explicit Christian metaphysics and poetics. In "The Dying Raven," remnants of his faith in what looks like a radical transcendental idealism persisted. But more typical is the vision expressed in "Daybreak" (LOA, 1: 77). Here, the poet's search for spiritual consolation is not found in nature or in the insights of the imagination but in the redemptive power of grace. Awakened at dawn and invited by the morning star to share in the sweetness of nature at that hour, the poet at first resists, declaring that nature seems to him to share in his own sorrow. In an epiphanic moment, however, his despair is swept away. Symbolized by the rising sun, Christ banishes the poet's "pining discontent." The poem concludes: "Be call'd my chamber, PEACE, when ends the day; / And let me with the dawn, like PILGRIM, sing and pray!"

Dana struck a more popular vein in "The Pleasure Boat" (LOA, 1: 74). In this work, two women sail upon a tranquil bay, their adventure heightened when they are momentarily becalmed. The language and the iambic meter of the poem suggest the swooping, darting motions of the little sailboat. Images of dipping ducks, darting gulls, glancing sunlight, and glassy reflections set a mood that highlights the pleasure and physical exhilaration involved in the outing.

For a time after his conversion experience, a gloomy sort of neo-Calvinism settled down over Dana and cast dark shadows over his family. He felt remorse for his previous contempt of evangelical views, blaming himself for having substituted vague thoughts of some sentimental ideal for the "revealed God" (as he wrote to Bryant in June 1825). He also criticized his friends and urged his sons to give up their lighthearted ways with the warning, "Be ye also ready." In the end, however, it was Platonism more than Beecher's religious views that determined the outlines of Dana's Christianized Romanticism and enabled him to disassociate the idea of the creative imagination from his fears of nihilism.

Although familiar from his youth with the poetry of the Cambridge Platonists, Dana found in Coleridge's *Aids to Reflection*, which is an extended commentary on Platonists Henry More and Bishop Leighton, a way to reclaim the Romantic theory of the imagination. According to the Platonists, God gives order to the cosmos by projecting his ideas into material form. Through the work of the imagination, humans share in God's creative power. But this forming power of the imagination is likely to go astray without the guidance of divine grace.

In the opening stanza of his poem "Thoughts on the Soul,"

Dana describes in Platonist terms the soul's creative power and the possible consequences of man's otherness.

> It is the Soul's prerogative, its fate,
> To shape the outward to its own estate.
> If right itself, then, all around is well;
> If wrong, it makes of all without a hell.

Later in the same poem, he tells again of the spiritual turmoil of the person gifted with the transforming power of the imagination, such as himself, all his tormented heroes from Paul Felton and Thomas Thornton, and the narrator of "Changes of Home."

> Who has no inward beauty, none perceives,
> Though all around is beautiful . . .
> He makes a turmoil of a quiet world;
> And fiends of his own bosom people air
> With kindred fiends, that hunt him to despair.

By the 1830s, Dana believed that the Holy Spirit could take possession of the imagination, which in turn enabled the poet to perceive the spiritual meaning that lies at the heart of things. In "Factitious Life," written during this period in 1832, Dana tried to give his readers a sense of the true vision made possible in the conversion experience.

> On thy transformed soul celestial light
> Bursts; and the earth, transfigured, on thy sight
> Breaks, a new sphere! Ay, stand in glad amaze
> While all its figures, opening on thy gaze,
> Unfold new meanings. Thou shalt understand
> Its mystic hierograph, thy God's own hand.
> . . . .
> "From nature up to nature's God," no more
> Grope out his way through parts, nor place before
> The Former the thing formed: Man yet shall learn
> The outward by the inward to discern, –
> The inward by the spirit.

In this poem, Dana celebrates the self-reliance born of reliance upon God. He further claims that believers live free of the dualisms that separate humanity from nature and the poet's imagination from both the divine spirit and the subconscious sources of its own intuitions. The Christian poet, he claims, experiences a new kind of freedom:

> Now all is thine; nor need'st thou longer fear
> To take thy share in all. The far, the near
> To thee, are God's, – so, thine; and all things live
> To higher ends than earth; and thou dost give
> That life which God gives thee.

The poem that most attractively presents Dana's version of Christian Platonism is "The Chanting Cherubs" (LOA, 1: 83). In this tribute to sculptor Horatio Greenough's piece of the same name, Dana represents the sculptor as capturing in marble the pure and eternal forms that exist in God's own mind. At first, the admiring poet wonders where the cherubs – such creatures "pure and bright" – might have come from if not from the heavens. The cherubs reply that they do not come from the moon or the stars since the moon wanes and the stars pale. Instead, they claim immortality – not the immortality of a divine birth, but rather the immortality bestowed by the sculptor who shares with the Creator a common ground. Inspired by the pure forms that exist in "heaven above," the sculptor immortalizes his winged thoughts in the creations of his own hands.

The first collected edition of Dana's short fiction and poetry was published in 1833. The critical response to his poetry was not particularly encouraging, but no one knew better than Dana his limitations as a poet. He admitted to Bryant that he came to poetry a raw and ignorant recruit. But when Bryant gently tried to teach him the rules of poetic versification, Dana protested that he had an affection for his way of expressing his thoughts, and so he would "hardly be willing to have thrust aside to humour that idle company, the public." When critics complimented him on the originality of his ideas but observed that he was not much of a versifier, therefore, their complaint did not trouble Dana very much. **Longfellow**, writing in the *American Monthly Review*, most accurately assessed Dana's place in American letters. He wrote that upon encountering Dana's work for the first time, one felt oneself "in the presence of a highly gifted intellect. As a poetical thinker, Mr. Dana has no superior, – hardly an equal in the country; as a mere versifier, we could point out several who are his superiors."

At a time when most American writers were content to beat the drums of national patriotism or to give voice to the homilies of the Unitarian Enlightenment, Dana dared to explore the more uncertain terrain of Romantic psychology and epistemology. He lived to be 92, but published little after the mid-1830s, although he delivered several lectures assessing the impact of democracy on American culture. In the midst of the Jacksonian era, a period during which only the most foolhardy would risk so outrageously defying the public taste, Dana deplored the effects of majoritarianism on the quality of American politics and cultural life. Driven by poverty and recognizing that he could earn more from lectures than from writing, he also began a series of lecture tours in 1838. His lectures on Shakespeare were notable primarily for their Romantic interpretations of the characters of Macbeth and Hamlet. A second, two-volume edition of his complete works was published in 1850. After his son Richard Henry Dana Jr. finally managed to put the family on a secure financial basis, Dana ceased to write entirely, certain that no audience existed for views as anachronistic or as iconoclastic as his.

DOREEN M. HUNTER

Selected Works
Poems and Prose Writings, 2 vols., New York: Baker & Scribner, 1850

Further Reading
Buell, Lawrence, *New England Literary Culture: From Revolution Through Renaissance*, Cambridge: Cambridge University Press, 1986

Boller, Paul F., *American Transcendentalism, 1830–1860*, New York: Putnam's, 1974

Charvat, Willam, *The Origins of American Critical Thought, 1810–1835*, New York: A. S. Barnes, 1961

Dana, Richard Henry, Jr., *The Journal of Richard Henry*

Dana, Jr., edited by Robert F. Lucid, 3 vols., Cambridge, Massachusetts: Harvard University Press, 1968

Ferguson, Robert A., *Law and Letters in American Culture*, Cambridge, Massachusetts: Harvard University Press, 1984

Howe, Daniel Walker, *The Unitarian Conscience: Harvard Moral Philosophy, 1805–1861*, Cambridge, Massachusetts: Harvard University Press, 1970

Hunter, Doreen M., *Richard Henry Dana, Sr.*, Boston: Twayne, 1987

Pearce, Roy Harvey, *The Continuity of American Poetry*, Princeton, New Jersey: Princeton University Press, 1967

Emily Dickinson

(1830–1886)

No nineteenth-century American poet – indeed, no American poet – has captivated the general imagination more decidedly than Emily Dickinson. *Poems* (1890), a small selection of her works published four years after her death, almost immediately went into a second printing. Its warm reception focused attention on a reclusive spinster whom reviewers described as a brilliant, but fastidious daughter of an Amherst lawyer. To her was attributed as well a pattern of mysterious behavior.

Emily Dickinson was born on December 10, 1830, in Amherst, Massachusetts, and died there on May 15, 1886. The significant events of her life were private: the writing of poems and the experience(s) of rewarding but probably unfulfilled love. To the small public who knew her – friends, neighbors, relatives – her conduct became unusual only after her thirties, when she avoided visitors and kept to her father's grounds. At Amherst Academy and Mary Lyon's Female Seminary in Mount Holyoke, she received a superior education, including lessons in botany, chemistry, languages, and drawing. She liked music and dancing, had a sprightly sense of humor, and acquired a reputation for candor and intellectual courage. Always shy, she spoke of herself in maturity as a rustic "Backwoodsman" for whom drawing room society was a trial. But her life, although secluded, was rich, she insisted, with "ecstasy." Certainly, her days were full. As a gardener, she was inventive and expert. (The Dickinson gardens interested Frederick Law Olmsted, who designed New York's Central Park.) She baked, sewed, canned, eventually nursed her paralyzed mother, and – in addition to her poems – wrote unique letters that often seemed to her correspondents "Bulletins" from "Immortality" (*Poems*, #827; LOA, 2: 294). Her personal attachments were deep, her fondness for children was well-known, and her learning and cultivation were considerable. After her death, the degree of Dickinson's quiet commitment to writing surprised even her family. More than 700 poems were discovered hidden in her bedroom. Almost three times that number were eventually collected.

Edited by her brother's mistress, Mabel Loomis Todd, and by the notable poet-critic Thomas Wentworth Higginson, a selection of Dickinson's poetry was reluctantly brought before the public on November 12, 1890. Her publishers, Roberts Brothers of Boston, acted at the behest of Dickinson's sister Lavinia. They never expected the slim, silver-gilt volume – embossed with the poet's favorite flower, Indian pipes, and priced at $1.50 – to sell. But while some reviewers scorned what they judged her parochialism and unconventionality, others such as Charles Goodrich Whiting of the *Springfield Republican* responded with praise of Dickinson's "delicate sensibility," "spiritual insight," and originality. Her astonished publishers were forced to repay her sister for the cost of the printers' plates. Fame, toward which the poet had been ambivalent, began to attach itself to her name. (This was a curious irony, since Dickinson had often hidden even her signature from public view.) It was agreed that for better or worse Dickinson's poems seemed, as Higginson put it in the preface to *Poems*, "woven out of the heart's own atoms." Fascinated readers were determined to know and understand that heart. Thus, the career of Emily Dickinson as both writer and legend began.

Dickinson's imaginative vision is inclusive, her subjects various, and her attitude toward them intricate and intense. Since her life is known to have been outwardly restricted, the sophistication of her perceptions, which she expressed in a highly individualistic style, has seemed to many readers marvelous. In addition, her public is drawn to the Dickinson mysterium – questions about her life – which her poems appear to construct and to which they provocatively allude. Both her art and the artist herself, therefore, make Emily Dickinson the subject of profound interest, incessant study, and lively controversy.

Dickinson's poetry concerns itself, as great verse does, with urgent and essential matters. Her poetic subjects include: the role of the persona, more particularly the consciousness, in this world; the possible fortunes of that personality in another, subsequent universe; the drama, inevitability, usefulness, and pain of deep feeling – whether it be love, hope, remorse, joy, grief in loss (a favorite theme), or any of the considerable number of sensations she studies and clarifies; the immense problem that is death; questions of sex and marriage; the function and aspiration of art; the limits of religious faith; and, fundamental to each set of issues, the seen world with its birds, trees, mountains, rivers, clouds, sun, moon, and faces of all kinds (human and nonhuman, ghostly or living).

The expansiveness and humanity of this subject matter commend Dickinson's verse to the serious and casual reader alike. For the first type of reader explores and is rewarded by her inventive approach to classically poetic themes, while the second typically enjoys the aphoristic justice of her insights and carries away a few lines to hoard as incitement, explanation, or comfort. Thus, like the major writers to whom she was early compared – William Blake, Ralph Waldo **Emerson**, and even the Shakespeare of the sonnets – Dickinson has always appeared, in her admired Alfred Tennyson's words, to see "through life and death" and "through [her] own soul." Such is an historic activity of poets.

At the same time, Dickinson's verse is stylistically ingenious, even in the texts that Todd and Higginson altered (and, we might say, marred) to suit contemporary conventions about diction and rhyme. Walt **Whitman**, also admired for his bold address to great subjects, declared in the preface to *Leaves of Grass* (1855) that "the greatest poet has less a marked style" and that he wanted no "originality" to "hang in the way between me and the rest." Whitman himself – Dickinson reports in a letter of April 1862 that she hears he is "disgraceful" – was a powerful original. The commonplace representation of these mid-Victorian American poets (unknown to each other) as violent opposites, however, is a distortion. For when Whitman says that the poet is "the free channel of himself," who, "if he breathes into any thing that was before thought small it dilates with the grandeur and life of the universe," his phrase aptly describes Dickinson and her work.

It is true, however, that Whitman's prescriptions against

"effect" or an aesthetic aim to "startle" might condemn Dickinson's poetry; for she had the art to "stun" with "Bolts of Melody" (#505; LOA, 2: 265). To surprise was among her manifest aims. The characteristic play of her mind – witty, mordant, and concerned with perplexing oddities or persuasive and evocative realities – could only represent itself finally in an idiom that seemed even to her earliest readers singular. The large canvas of Whitman's *Leaves*, with its grand terrain of the United States as reflection of the poet's eye, was struck off mostly in free verse and long lines. In writing about her major theme, the intersection of "Eternity" with "Time," Dickinson attempts a subject equally, or even more, superb. In so doing, though, she selects brief, acute forms: the quatrain, chiefly, or the tercet, or (very occasionally) iconoclastic versions of the sonnet or rime royale. These forms she frames with restraint; her melodic embellishments are rare or often composed of off-rhyme, consonance, or assonance, in order to achieve an incisive and meditative obliquity.

Like Whitman's, her poetry emphasizes the apprehensions of a vivid self. "I" is her most frequent word: it is used nearly 1700 times in the verse as Thomas H. Johnson's *Complete Poems* (1957) orders it. The tension between the brevity and compactness of her poetic forms and the expressiveness and vitality of that self is what generates the unmistakable effect of the Dickinson lyrics. Introspective, clever, and charged, their subtle ambience is as daring as the spacious and handsome ease of Whitman; but her work voices a romantic exuberance tempered by the Puritan tone. There is always implicit restraint, even in her most incandescent poems. Dickinson's public is also challenged by her distinctive punctuation and orthography and by her special speech: a partly private vocabulary in which words like "Eden," "wife," and "Czar" and phrases such as "white election" clearly (or unclearly) seem imbued with enigmatic meaning.

The combination of Dickinson's august themes – "Love and Death," as she frugally described them in a letter – with her antitraditional techniques, and her arresting vocabulary did not immediately secure for her a reputation as a major poet. Despite a largely continuous popularity as a maiden sage, who was deemed lovable for her puzzling and oddly magical eloquence, Dickinson achieved her present poetic eminence only after Johnson published her restored texts. During the 1920s and 1930s, when Dickinson's niece Martha Bianchi and Todd's daughter Millicent Bingham brought out rival collections of edited verses, the poet's competency seemed uncertain. How to justify the logic of one who likened a "cornice" to a "mound" of dirt, as her editors rendered "Cornice – in the Ground" in the poem "Because I could not stop for Death –" (LOA, 2: 288)? In addition, there were the distractions of biographical embellishment and dispute. Who was the secret lover of her erotic poems? Was Dickinson a "perverse little person / Without an idea," as Amy Lowell's "old gentleman" objects in *A Critical Fable*, or was she a genius?

With the establishment of her own wordings in Johnson's *Complete Poems* (1957) and *Letters* (1958), with the increased understanding of her life furnished especially by George Whicher, Richard Sewall, and Jay Leyda, and with the ministrations first of the New Critics and now of textual and cultural critics of varied approaches, Dickinson's art has come to be regarded with high seriousness. John Crowe Ransom once excused her unorthodox punctuation and orthography by saying, "Emily Dickinson was a little home-keeping person." Such a comment seems to most today to be a grave blunder, as the fond vision of "Our Emily" has given way to the person who called herself "Dickinson": a determined poet whose verse may have been carefully planned even in its most irregular aspects. Recent criticism puts old questions in new ways. For instance, of what specific importance is it to the form and content of Dickinson's poems that she is a *woman* writer (a persona not captured in Ransom's epithet)? How did her gender contribute to her habit of "publishing" only in letters?

Today, we return after 100 years by different paths and with enriched conception to some of the earliest concerns about the poetry of Emily Dickinson. The image of the sibyl and her sayings retains some of its power. But while new issues have arisen – determining the exact number of her poems, for example, or even how she intended them to be arranged – there is no longer any doubt that "This was a Poet –" (#448; LOA, 2: 260).

In the 1890 volume, Dickinson's poems were collected under four headings: "Life," "Love," "Nature," and "Time and Eternity." As the vast generality of each heading predicts, the categories almost entirely overlap. Dickinson rarely gave her poems titles. She labeled only a few cursorily. Presently, the poems are usually cited either by first line or by the numbers Johnson assigned them. Since she was from the first considered a difficult poet, the titles that her editors gave her poems were intended, like the categories, to facilitate approaches to her work. Although it is not especially elusive, "Success is counted sweetest" (#67; LOA, 2: 227), which opens both *Poems* (1890) and the Library of America selection, exhibits some of the verbal complexity that prompted their efforts. It also shows how her rich poetry resists even such modest simplifications.

"Success is counted sweetest" has as its central event a dying soldier's recognition of the enemy's victory. It may be said in passing that Dickinson is often accused of showing inadequate concern about, or even indifference to, the Civil War; yet this poem – like "Bless God, he went as soldiers" (#147), "It feels a shame to be Alive –" (#444), "My Portion is Defeat – today" (#639; LOA, 2: 280), or "My Triumph lasted till the Drums" (#1227; LOA, 2: 304) – reveals her keen awareness of the horrors of battle. Dickinson begins, as she frequently does, with a thesis: "Success is counted sweetest / By those who ne'er succeed." Like many of her initial theses – "I cannot live with You – / It would be Life –" (#640; LOA, 2: 281), "Peril as a Possession / 'Tis Good to bear" (#1678), or "The Show is not the Show / But they that go –" (#1206) – it is developed and tested by the remainder of the poem.

The poem's thesis, furthermore, is quintessentially Dickinsonian, for it affirms that to lack is to have and that true possession – in this case, the possession of knowledge – is the result of loss or deprivation. Many of the major Dickinson lyrics are built around this type of supposition or conceit. For instance, "A *Wounded* Deer – leaps highest" (#165; LOA, 2: 230) argues that the greatest powers of performance are attained by the loss of power; the speaker of "The Tint I cannot take – is best" (#627; LOA, 2: 278) is most thrilled by what she finds intolerable or inexplicable. (Dickinson dotes on such paradoxes, which some critics believe reveal an Elizabethan quality in her work attributable in part to her relish for Shakespeare.) That "success is counted sweetest" by those who never experience it is also an assumption that wins ready credence; the phrase has a tough aptness, earned, it seems, from experience. This experiential quality, too, characterizes Dickinson's best work.

The next couplet contains one of the poet's challenging and subtly radical uses of language. By saying "To *comprehend* a nectar" (my emphasis), she means "to understand" but also "to take in" – since one drinks nectar. Possibly, she also means to include the undercurrent of the Latin *comprehendere*, "seize," which seems appropriate for Dickinson, who knew Latin, and appropriate to a poem in which victors "took the Flag" and seized the day while the "dying" take in only the significance of their defeat and the others' success. Dickinson's first quatrain ends, rhyming "need" with "succeed." Since rhyme enforces connections, she thus underscores the assumption that need or lack helps one to understand "success." This use of full rhyme – less frequent in Dickinson than her iconoclastic, crypto-modern slant rhymes – establishes the equation between unfulfilled desire and perfect understanding that the poem's next two quatrains continue to explore in the example of the soldier.

The sweep of these quatrains, which builds to the word "Burst," is passionate but exacting. The victorious enemy is a "purple Host," perhaps because for Dickinson purple is a royal color and the victorious are like kings enjoying conquest; perhaps because with her keen appreciation of purple sunsets, she associated purple with the culmination and therefore triumph of the day; or perhaps because to the poet who spoke of dropping her hallowed life "into the purple well," purple also meant both sacred and "mystic" (#271). Certainly, this poet who spoke of the muses as the "Hosts [that] do visit me –" (#298) also counted on her nineteenth-century reader, who was incomparably more familiar than present-day readers with the King James Bible, to regard the hosts of #67 as both battalions of men and agents of the eternal, angels of destiny. The soldier, "defeated – dying –" (her sympathy manifests itself in the force of alliteration), is set apart from the living world. He is one of the many isolatos, which include her own soul and even consciousness, that Dickinson selects in order to examine. We imagine him prone on the field and helpless. The word "agonized" is descriptive both of his reaction to the victorious trumpets and of his death agony. To him, to whom success is "forbidden," the meaning of success is "clear" – as certain as the shell that kills him, the shell Dickinson manages to imply by her use of the word "Burst." (Disliking the word's robustness, Todd and Higginson printed in its place the polite and enervated "Break" first used by Thomas Niles when the poem appeared in *A Masque of Poets* [1874], one of the few occasions on which Dickinson was published during her lifetime.)

To which of Higginson's categories does poem #67 belong? To all, certainly. It comments on "Life"; concerns love of country, honor, duty; suggests the natural world; and finally focuses on the revelation in time that immediately precedes the soldier's entrance into the timeless world, eternity. Like most of Dickinson's poems, it is brief and, by its brevity, achieves nearly epigrammatic consequence. She once rebuked Higginson for writing a long, flaccid elegy for a soldier by sending him the four-line "Lay this Laurel on the One" (#1393). In it, the single word "intrinsic" does the work of much of his poem. With severe clarity, "intrinsic" expressed the idea that the buried hero had possessed a sense of honor, integrity, and duty, which Higginson's poem took seven stanzas to list and describe.

Dickinson's preference for compression and her zeal to capture experience with fresh acuity are related, and contribute to the difficulties her verse often presents to the new reader. With the exception of certain mysterious love and marriage poems, whose language was (perhaps) utterly transparent only to the people for whom she composed them, her subject matter is traditionally "poetical." Yet her public has sometimes experienced feelings of inadequacy in reading her work, and understandably so. Her ardor for accuracy without wastefulness – and for her, wastefulness often included the pleasantly musical and seductive developments of traditional verse – led to Dickinson's lean but complex poetic directness, which includes syntactical omissions, elisions, and truncations or variations of accepted usage. The reader is frequently obliged to retrieve buried connections in a lyric or to become accustomed to a quaintly original habit of mind and speech that results in a blade of grass being called "a Hay" (#333) or the regalia of nobility being labeled "Pelf" (#551). As in the cases of other idiosyncratic poets like Blake or William Butler Yeats, however, Dickinson becomes easier to read with experience.

She is a meticulous and empathetic poet of nature. Although her "Compound Manner" (#830) and "Compound Vision" (#906) relate her to the metaphysical poets, of whom (especially George Herbert) she had some knowledge, Dickinson's approach to nature is both typically Romantic and mid-Victorian. Like most nineteenth-century American writers and painters, she knew Emerson's groundbreaking essay "Nature" (1836) and evidently valued its injunctions to "learn [from nature] the lesson of worship," to study its "sea of forms," and to acquire the adequacy of "eye" that enables a poet "to see the miraculous in the common." Besides, her favorite reading included John Ruskin's *Modern Painters* (1843–46). With its celebration of J. M. W. Turner and the Pre-Raphaelites and with its conviction that nature was the source of art, *Modern Painters* helped to turn Dickinson's attention to subject matter she would share with the great painters of her age.

Throughout her life, Dickinson enjoyed drawing and sometimes accompanied her poems with sketches. She twice signed herself "Cole" in a comical note about landscape painting, thus showing her acquaintance with the founder of the Hudson River school, Thomas **Cole**. Like Cole and his fellows – such as Frederic E. Church, Jasper Cropsey, Martin Johnson Heade, and Sanford Gifford – Dickinson practiced what Ruskin, echoing John Constable, called "skying." To "sky" was to gaze at the heavens and clouds in order to find and replicate the meaningful shapes there. She wrote lyrics about sunrise and sunset, the seasons, the anatomy and symbolism of planets, flowers, insects, animals, and birds. Like the Hudson River and the Luminist painters, she sought to reveal these subjects' inner spirit and spirituality. Like the American Pre-Raphaelites, she did so with an economy of means and with sharp outlines and striking specificity. Ruskin's belief that one must draw nature "with great botanical precision" reinforced Dickinson's youthful interest in cataloging and pressing flowers and enabled what she called her "measur[ing]" eye (#561).

Dickinson's interest in painting derived in part from her family's tastes. Her brother Austin collected both Hudson Riv-

er and Pre-Raphaelite paintings; the Dickinsons read magazines such as *The Crayon, Harper's, Scribner's,* and the *Century,* which continually featured developments in the art world;
and all this, together with internal evidence furnished by her
poems themselves, suggests that the methods and subject matter of the contemporary visual arts were of the highest importance to Emily Dickinson. In fact, her poems about nature
choose a variety of perspectives, moreover, each of which finds
analogues among nineteenth-century artists. She usually provides faithful description, as in "Four Trees – upon a solitary
Acre –" (#742; LOA, 2: 290) or "The Wind begun to rock the
Grass" (#824; LOA, 2: 293); this habit of minute and vigorous attention to detail is also observable in the canvases of
such painters as Church and Heade. But Dickinson's descriptions of nature often become the means of examining human
nature. What she sees is the stimulus, explanation, or celebration of what she feels. Thus, "A Light exists in Spring" that
"speaks to [her]" (#812; LOA, 2: 293); another kind of
"Light" that she "knew . . . before" (#692) becomes the moment of her death; and the "eager look[s]" on landscapes as
seasons change give her a glimpse of infinity, or, as she calls it,
"Moments of Dominion" (#627; LOA, 2: 278). This sort of
introspection for which nature acts as a catalyst is found in the
Symbolist painters, like Odilon Redon, or the more symbolic
works of Dante Gabriel Rossetti (probably known to Dickinson).

So unique is Dickinson's genius, however, that to consider
one of her poems about nature is often to encounter qualities
that associate her with her own time as well as characteristics
that, for some, act to separate her from it. Thus, the "metaphysical" attributes of her imagination and diction and her
fondness for paradox and for scenes that include distortion,
deformity, or unreality have been said to be both Jacobean and
modern. Such lyrics as "I watched the Moon around the
House" (#629; LOA, 2: 278), "The Moon upon her fluent
Route" (#1528; LOA, 2: 308), and "The Moon was but a Chin
of Gold" (#737) have essentially the same subject. Yet the
speaker conceives and presents that subject distinctively in each
poem. Moonlight was a favorite Romantic theme; scenes of
"nocturnal Luminism" were favorites among mid-Victorian
painters. In two cases, however, Dickinson approaches the lunar poem with a desire to explore the mid-Victorian precept of
nature's complete relevancy to human life. In a third, she manifests the common view of the moon's charm as picturesque.

"I watched the Moon around the House" presents the stu-
dious Ruskinian "I" that eagerly notes its subject. Yet her description is not especially painterly but conceptual. The moon
is a "Traveller" to the speaker's grounds; indeed, it travels to
her world of "Life – and Death / And Afterwards – or Nay – ."
That is, unlike the speaker, the moon has nothing to do with
living, dying, and the question of whether or not there is immortality. She is "engrossed to Absolute" (one of Dickinson's
economical shorthand phrases) and absorbed totally in her
own identity and purpose: "shining – and the Sky – ." On one
hand, therefore, the moon is inhuman and not like the usual
traveler, who wants food, lodging, and a bath, or who might
play or ponder:

No Hunger – had she – nor an Inn –
Her Toilette – to suffice –

Nor Avocation – nor Concern
For little Mysteries
As harass us –

On the other hand, the moon does take "Rest" momentarily
upon a windowpane, the poet's fairy-tale way of describing its
steady light outside her window. The speaker's curiosity is like
that of a woman who lifts her lorgnette to study a stranger's
face. But this stranger truly "justifie[s]" curiosity, because unlike travelers who have plans or "Formula[s]," as well as ap-
pendages ("a Foot," a "Hand"), the moon is nothing but a
head. Furthermore, her head is like a head on "a Guillotine /
Slid carelessly away – ." It is "independent" in the sky and
moves without a body. (Did tales of aristocrats whose lips
twitched on severed heads inspire this macabre image? Was T.
S. Eliot – with his witless moon, smiling in corners, in "Rhapsody on a Windy Night" – familiar with this Dickinsonian image? Her poems about emptiness, black corridors of the brain,
and the terrors of solitude and of memory seem to have influenced not only Eliot but a number of modern poets, male and
female.) More lyrically but still oddly, the moon is a "Stemless
Flower," mysteriously upheld.

This combination of the intimate and aloof is finally emphasized when, like an acrobat or a god, the moon "vault[s] out of
Gaze – ." Too grotesque and fey to resemble the classical
Artemis, she nevertheless "follow[s] her superior Road – ." At
this point in the poem, the speaker must recognize herself "far
below" the moon with her "Blue" "advantage," that is, her
heavenly ascendancy. As is almost always the case in reading
Dickinson, who declared her dictionary her constant companion, one profits by knowing the etymology or multiple signifi-
cances of her words in poem #629. Thus, *advantage* means both
the moon's height and her precedence (*avantage* in Middle English) over the humble speaker. Dickinson uses off-rhymes in
poem #629 (only the third quatrain rhymes regularly) to convey
the differences she observes between the celestial body and the
persona. This poem does not actually philosophize upon these
differences but sets them out with wary irony.

The moon's distance, real and symbolic, from the speaker
engages her attention once more in poem #1528, a work probably written 20 years later. (Dickinson's poems are dated hypo-
thetically by her handwriting, of which three distinctive kinds
appear on letters that bear dates. Furthermore, she often included poems in dated letters, indicating approximately when
they were written.) In "The Moon upon her fluent Route," the
speaker is again impressed by the ease with which the moon
transcends constraints that afflict human beings. Her route, unlike their roads, is not fixed (a subsidiary connotation of "fluent"). Acknowledging this, the poet moves to draw the sort of
dignified general inference that she likes to take from particular
circumstances: "The Star's Etruscan Argument / Substantiate a
God – ." The Etruscans, the ancient non-Italic race that settled
in northern Italy around 800 B.C., are associated here with
mystery. No one knows where they came from and no one has
deciphered their language. Thus, for Dickinson, the "argument" or light of a star, which radiates from far off in space
and time and is therefore mysterious or "Etruscan," supports
the idea that God exists. And she says "substantiate[s]"; that
is, the very *substance* of the star shapes its argument. Furthermore, by dropping the *s* from the third-person form of the verb

substantiate, she establishes the hortatory mode: *let* or *may* "the Star's Etruscan Argument / Substantiate a God – ." These lines are more conclusive than those of poem #629. And here, she is entertaining the idea associated with William Wordsworth, Emerson, and Ruskin, that the accurate study of landscape leads to the divine.

In the second quatrain of this poem, she once again considers whether astral bodies like the moon have any purpose. By using the Emersonian term "Aim," she underscores the moral ingredient in purpose. Dickinson's age was, after all, the age of Charles Darwin (whom one of her letters mentions), in which the natural sciences challenged faith. She debates the advantages of each in several poems such as "By my Window have I for Scenery" (#797). Never an orthodox Christian, although the Bible was, with Shakespeare, her chief reading, Dickinson customarily forms her own opinion of divine revelation. It is always skeptical to some extent. In poem #1528, she declares that "the ones allowed to know" these secrets of the heavens – the dead who have acquired superior knowledge, presumably – also understand "that which makes [all aims] forgot"; that is, they understand infinitude. Like the moon, they participate in God's plan completely and so have transcended all human routes, arguments, and aims. She ends the poem with the image of dawn, an image associated in most of her poems and letters with immortality. Even as the finite dawn makes one forget the stars, the life of eternity makes the dead forget earth. Nevertheless, her second quatrain begins with the word "If." Therefore, like most of her poems about nature and belief, poem #1528 avoids linking these two concepts as cause and effect.

Since she accomplishes so much in a mere eight lines, one can understand Dickinson's equation of her artistic methods with the compression that produces perfume in poem #675, "Essential Oils – are wrung –" (LOA, 2: 285). Like poem #629, "The Moon upon her fluent Route" may ostensibly concern the natural scene. But, fundamentally, the latter poem moves away from the natural scene in order to consider Dickinson's chief theme: the nature of time and eternity. Not all her nature poems, however, have such a serious mission. In poem #737, she writes with a mannerist cuteness governed by playful pictorial conceits:

The Moon was but a Chin of Gold
A Night or two ago –
And now she turns Her perfect Face
Upon the World below

Her Forehead is of Amplest Blonde –
Her Cheek – a Beryl hewn –
Her Eye unto the Summer Dew
The likest I have known –

Her Bonnet is the Firmament –
The Universe – Her Shoe –
The Stars – the Trinkets at Her Belt –
Her Dimities – of Blue –

This poem is a nursery cutout and has none of the thoughtful richness of Dickinson's lunar portraits discussed earlier. That she attempted such a variety of effects throughout her life, however, only illustrates the breadth of her ambition. She could fling her energies even into such a poem as this one,

which is not so distantly related both to the sweet singing of Lydia **Sigourney** and to the nonsense verse of Lewis Carroll.

One need not deplore such playfulness, for in its own way it explicates the connections Dickinson conceived and savored between everything grand and riddlesome and all things simple and comforting. The landscapes she draws are often such as a child might enjoy. The great becomes ordinary. Twilight is just a boy "With hat in hand" (#1104), the wind is a "Bugle" (#1593; LOA, 2: 311), and the earth is a "Drum" (#888).

Noon – is the Hinge of Day –
Evening – the Tissue Door –
Morning – the East compelling the sill
Till all the World is ajar –
       (#931)

The world – terrifying elsewhere – is in this poem only a house entered by morning light. In bad weather, "Shadows walk / Upon the Hills" "Like Men and Women" and can be greeted like "Neighbors" (#1105). Night can be frightening in Dickinson's poetry; in her great poems about death and mental breakdown, she faithfully renders the terror of "Darknesses – / Those Evenings of the Brain" (#419) and obliteration: the black hand that "disembodies" (#860). In playful moods, however, she could observe dark arriving, like the moon, as just another visitor to her house of life. This was a confident mood similar to Whitman's when he addresses Death as "great deliveress," and we find it expressed in poem #1104:

A Vastness, as a Neighbor, came,
A Wisdom, without Face, or Name,
A Peace, as Hemispheres at Home
And so the Night became.

Among Emily Dickinson's most persuasive and beautiful nature poems are her celebrations of sunrise and sunset. Ruskin's *Modern Painters* urged nineteenth-century artists (who were often poets, too – consider D. G. Rossetti, Cole, Albert Pinkham Ryder, and Washington **Allston**) to paint morning as "of all visible things the least material" or as "the farthest . . . from the earth prison-house." Dickinson's familiarity with dawn is the subject of many letters. Her poems suggest that she composed at night and far into the early morning. A poem like "The Birds begun at Four o'clock" (#783) regards the birth of day as a "Miracle" that is nonetheless forgotten as soon as it is "fulfilled." This poem abounds in precise observations: for example, it suggests that since the song of birds comes spontaneously from so many throats, it cannot be counted like notes of sheet music, even as space cannot be counted. Furthermore, the poem indicates that birdsong ends abruptly. The work also draws conclusions. The birds (like beauty itself) exist in an ecstasy independent of both God and humanity. Similarly, the "Morn" is its own justification.

Nature appealed to Dickinson most in movement, and she describes the sunrise, in one of her most famous poems, as light in motion:

I'll tell you how the Sun rose –
A Ribbon at a time –
The Steeples swam in Amethyst –
The news, like Squirrels, ran –
       (#318; LOA, 2: 243)

Sunrise had religious associations: the resurrection of the sun and the Son. Similarly, sunset, which Dickinson whimsically calls "the largest Fire ever known" (#1114), was seen as a sublime event, the sun's death and burial; the event also assembled a plethora of connotations. To take a related example from painting, Frederic E. Church's magnificent *Twilight in the Wilderness* (1860), which could almost be described by Dickinson's lines about "Whole Gulfs – of Red, and Fleets – of Red – / And Crews – of solid Blood –" (#658), was also read by his public as a work about the impending Civil War, about the threat posed by industry to the American wilderness, and about Church's religious reverence for Christ's passion. In Dickinson's lyrics, sunset could inspire anxiety, resignation, rapture, or hope. Some of her sunrise and sunset poems also suggest that, however apolitical she claimed to be, she was caught up, like most, in the Civil War crisis.

When she writes about "Bronze – and Blaze –" in poem #290 (LOA, 2: 239), what absorbs her is nature's own self-absorption. It is "preconcerted with itself": that is, it has long ago determined that it will fulfill its own plan. "Preconcert" is a legal term often found in Blackstone's *Commentaries,* alluding to prior agreements. Since both her father and her brother were lawyers, Dickinson had ample exposure to legal language. Like Shakespeare, she thus often employs its cold exactitude to measure phenomena that are not concrete – love or, in this case, nature as a vast conceit. Nature is "distant – to alarms –" whether they be personal to the speaker, or of a public character: those that in 1861 beset the nation, possibly. Indeed, the sunset "forms"

> An Unconcern so sovereign
> To Universe, or me –
> Infects my simple spirit
> With Taints of Majesty –
> Till I take vaster attitudes –

Dickinson enjoyed punning. Here "taints" (since nature is painting a sunset) plays on the more usual "tints." But in poem #290, the word also alludes to the infection of "Arrogance," because the speaker's rapture at sunset so ennobles her that she feels superior to everything, even to the air or "Oxygen" she breathes. Thus, sunset belongs to her ("My Splendors") and – like Dickinson's favorite spectacle, the circus – is a "Show" beyond compare, "Competeless."

Often nature's "show" is so beautiful – she sees it as a theater with "Mighty Foot Lights," which has God as its noblest audience (#595) – that Dickinson's speakers shrink from the thought of leaving the "Menagerie" of this world. (A menagerie may be a zoo, of course, so the word is wryly charged.) Similarly, "Of Bronze – and Blaze – " is an exercise in what mid-Victorians deemed the "beautiful sublime," a mode wherein beauty evokes awe. And the poem concludes on an awful, homely truth: that nature will go on making sunsets after the poet's death and burial in a narrow, untended plot, visited only by insects that feed on her: "When I, am long ago, / An Island in dishonored Grass – / Whom none but Beetles – know."

Since Dickinson's major themes are interrelated, it is moving to set this stoic observation against another in poem #307, wherein she suggests that the poet/painter of sunsets is superior to the "day" "itself." For her, the arts of the "Martyr Poet" and the "Martyr Painter" (#544; LOA, 2: 269) were nearly synonymous. In poem #307, she celebrates the fame of artists who can permanently duplicate in art the sunsets nature must make again daily. "One who could repeat the Summer day / Were greater than itself," she declares; when the east and west no longer exist, "His name [will] remain." Probably because Dickinson was modest, she always imagines herself small. She is "the slightest in the House" (#486), "minute" (*Letters*, 2: 316), and even a "minute landscape" (#1105). The artist of poem #307 will be immortal, she declares, although that artist were the "minutest" of creatures. It is thus tempting to hope that she is speaking of herself.

Although Emily Dickinson said she despised fame – "a fickle food / Upon a shifting plate" (#1659) – she dreamt and wrote repeatedly about immortality. It was "Slow Gold – but Everlasting"; it was "the Mine" (also one of her words for eros) compared with mere money (#406). As an artist she thus worked for immortality, "that Great Water in the West –" (#726). She pictures herself in poem #486 with her little lamp and book: "So stationed I could catch the Mint / That never ceased to fall." Her poems about art regard it, like love, as impervious to death; according to Dickinson, art is related to passion in its deathlessness. Furthermore, poems such as "Essential Oils – are wrung" conceive of art in terms that her own art fulfills. When she writes, "The Attar from the Rose / Be not expressed by Suns – alone – / It is the gift of Screws – ," Dickinson might be speaking of the techniques of compression and condensation that we find richly illustrated in her verse. For Dickinson, it is not only imagination or "Suns" that make a work of art, but the disciplines of selection and analysis. Paradoxically, the screws also immortalize the suns; for while all roses, summers, and ladies die, poems remind us of them, just as in a dead lady's bureau drawer, sachets made by the arts of the perfumer recall summer's scents of roses. Thus, art preserves memory, even personality, in "Ceaseless Rosemary" (#675); for rosemary signifies remembrance, as *Hamlet*'s Ophelia (or the Victorian language of flowers) would have informed Emily Dickinson.

Art is to Dickinson a form of truth, an "amazing sense" distilled from ordinary meanings (#448; LOA, 2: 260). True poems "arrest" the fleeting forms of beauty and disclose their hidden nature. Poetry is recognizable because, as she told T. W. Higginson in 1870, it makes you "feel physically as if the top of [your] head were taken off." All these concepts, especially the last, frame an aesthetic that relates her work to that of John Keats and other Romantic poets whom she read and quoted. "Circumference," her expression for the significance of life as poetry discovers it, is the "Bride of Awe" (#1620). For her, as for Wordsworth, this significance is born of wonder, even fear. Finally, poetry sums up everything: the sun (often an image for love in Dickinson), the summer (nature), and heaven (meaning) itself (#569; LOA, 2: 272). This was so because what Emily Dickinson valued even above beauty, perhaps, was permanence. Art provides for it. "Just as He spoke it from his Hands," a building – architecture is also synonymous for her with poetry – preserves the design of its architect. It is an ornament to his "absent character" (#848; LOA, 2: 295). So poetry preserves the dead.

About death and the dead, Emily Dickinson thought, dreamt, and wrote even more than about what one of her letters calls the "Flood subject": immortality. Nature, eternity, life, and death were intermingled themes in her poetry, but death was the subject she said she never penetrated. "Without any body," she mused with anguish when her father died, "what kind can that be?" Death, "striking sharp and early," gave her "awe for friends" (as another letter says) and made her shrewd with the "God of Flint" (#1076) who stole them away. Again and again, she essayed the theme of death from various perspectives. Like most Victorian women, she had often been present at a deathwatch. She describes "the Stillness in the Room" (#465; LOA, 2: 261), the mourners who long for notice (#482) and, especially, the behavior of the dying, who are about to put off the "Option Gown" of the body (#1462) in order to experience what a letter calls "that great Romance," eternity. "I measure every Grief I meet," she writes, "With narrow, probing, Eyes –" (#561); it is the eyes of those about to forfeit the knowledge gained by "measuring" that often perturb her. She watches them "obscure," darken:

> I've seen a Dying Eye
> Run round and round a Room –
> In search of Something – as it seemed –
> Then Cloudier become –
> And then – obscure with Fog –
> And then – be soldered down
> (#547; LOA, 2: 270)

To her who spoke of writing as painting and who depicted life as landscape, the body was a canvas on which the spirit configures "scenes" and expressions that dissipate in death. She studies a corpse:

> 'Twas warm – at first – like Us –
> Until there crept upon
> A Chill – like frost upon a Glass –
> Till all the scene – be gone
> (#519; LOA, 2: 267)

The man or woman "Around [a] fireside" (#521), warm with life, becomes a stone-cold package the sexton drops into a hole. That even babies were forced into that "ice nest," the grave, pained and amazed her. Therefore, her descriptions of the effects of death upon the living are among her most brilliant, forming documentary vignettes of great yet thrifty power:

> There's been a Death, in the Opposite House,
> As lately as Today –
> I know it, by the numb look
> Such Houses have – alway –
>
> The Neighbors rustle in and out –
> The Doctor – drives away –
> A Window opens like a Pod –
> Abrupt – mechanically –
>
> Somebody flings a Mattress out –

In this poem, as in others, the dead person, being nullified, becomes an "it," and the speaker, as in other poems, alludes to herself as "a Boy." The boy Dickinson, the poet's adventurous creative self, free of the sexual/intellectual restraints imposed on Victorian women, is well able to contemplate all mysteries,

especially the carnal: death and passion, dissolution and procreation. But like the author she called "dear Dickens," Dickinson contemplates these mysteries with a grotesquely cheerful sense of humor: the undertaker ("of the Appalling Trade" – he horrifies, and he makes palls) takes "the measure of the House" (all the occupants, not just the dead). For, of course, all experience grief and all will die and at last be measured for their shrouds. She concludes: "There'll be that Dark Parade – / Of Tassels – and of Coaches – soon – ." The reader knows that this funeral procession of which the poet speaks includes everyone; for the word "parade" alludes not only to the mourners of poem #389 but to all of us destined for the grave.

Dickinson's imagination was especially absorbed by the transition from life to death – she often describes it as a journey – and by where the dead "went": "What did they do since I saw them" (#900). As a skeptic, she found the sentimental, pretty heaven of harps and cherubs adequate only for whimsical or cynical verse. She preferred an austere infinity, sometimes (and sometimes not) inhabited by God and his saints. Although some have found her studies of death and dying morbid, they are really energetic efforts to extend her consciousness beyond the grave; the survival of the soul – her thinking, feeling self – was essential to her. Repeatedly, she confronts the miracle of translation from this world, hoping to discover even in the posture of a corpse some irony that shows that death is temporary. She made at least four efforts, for example, to convey a vision of the torpor of the dead as mere sleep. This Romantic euphemism had its roots in her favorite Bible verse (1 Cor. xv), with its account of the resurrection of "them that slept." Dickinson's various renderings of "Safe in their Alabaster Chambers –" (#216; LOA, 2: 232) all preserve the next two lines: "Untouched by Morning – / And untouched by Noon – ." Following upon the word "safe," they make death seem fortunate, an escape from alarms. But her attitude toward the finality of death is inevitably disposed by the grave at which she looks. Although she says in version one of this poem in 1859, "Sleep the meek members of the Resurrection" (emphasis mine), in version two of 1861 they merely "Lie." Her stress shifts from the dead's security in Christ's promise of renewed life to the precincts in which the dead find themselves: coffins lined with satin, which lie under that "Roof," their headstones. In every version of the second verse, she illustrates the separation of the dead from all cosmic activity, whether it be the song of birds (version one), the motions of the firmament (version two), or the progress of the ages (discarded versions three and four in Johnson's Complete Poems, I, 153). The rigor and candor of her analyses frequently cause Dickinson to stop at what she named the masked bed in the marble house, and her proviso "Safe" is just that: a proviso, and not truly affirmative.

When Dickinson achieves a vision of death as constructive, she most often employs one of three poetic modes. In one mode, apparent in her love poetry, she regards dying (by a trope relevant to traditional ones in works from Shakespeare to the Brownings, Tennyson, Charlotte Brontë, and D. G. Rossetti) as the means of final union with a forbidden beloved. In a related mode, she is able to pass over her terrified (and terrifying) obsession with being divorced from the living self by imagining her passage into a future world. In this second mode, she is either suspended beyond time and its confinements, or enraptured by the experience of union with the universe. Her great poems "Because I could not stop for Death –" and "Behind Me – dips Eternity –" (#721; LOA, 2: 288–89) present such approaches to the problem of disembodiment. Ironically, they are narratives, and thus they earn their grandeur in part by alluding to the circumstances of human life that are being given up. Finally, in the third mode, some poems present death as the means of acquiring ultimate knowledge ("I shall know why – when time is over –" [#193]) or lasting importance as a writer. To Dickinson, whose contempt for the fame "that does not stay" (#1475) was matched by a thirst for immortal stature, death provided honor and, as she said, "a Name" (#382): "'Tis Honor – though I die – / For that no Man obtain / Till He be justified by Death –" (#522).

With a theologizing skill that revealed her Puritan roots (like Jonathan Edwards, she was a Connecticut River Valley writer), Emily Dickinson enjoyed characterizing Shame, Doom, Faith, Despair, Delight, Hope, Gratitude, and, of course, Love, in addition to other emotions, virtues, and vices. Austin Warren and other critics of the 1930s insisted that unlike Nathaniel **Hawthorne** and Herman **Melville**, Dickinson did not understand evil. But about all forms of falsehood and dishonesty and about infidelity, both sexual and intellectual, she is eloquent. Furthermore, murder and violent crime interested her as poetic topics! They described the explosion of the self and the rupture of control.

Able to imagine Love as a boyish "Guard" (#924), Dickinson spent years characterizing Death. He is "the postponeless Creature – ," an "it" that overtakes the one who cannot escape: "'You know Me – Sir'?" (#390). He is also a neighbor, although mysterious: "the only one / You cannot find out all about / In his native town –" (#153). But her most striking characterization of Death was one with which the nineteenth century, with its passion for depicting beautiful women's corpses or the Angel of Death with a woman in his arms, could wholly sympathize. In several compelling lyrics, she regards Death as "the supple Suitor / that wins at last" (#1445), a cavalier akin to the "Master" of her love poems, although more ferociously attentive than he.

"Because I could not stop for Death –" is one of the great poems in English and is entirely characteristic of Dickinson's approach to a major theme. Although keenly visualized, the settings and simple arrangements of the poem – the carriage, the speaker's clothing – are both plain and mysterious. The journey she undergoes from/through time to a place that is out-of-time, yet not precisely eternity, has stages. The whole action of the poem moves to a disclosure of the infinite importance of this journey, which is nevertheless commonplace, even as the tetrameters commonly associated with Isaac Watts's hymns are both ordinary and ordinal. The speaker, like nearly all of Dickinson's dying women, is a busy person. Civil, "kindly," Death calls for her, thus sparing her effort. Nevertheless, he interrupts her life. Instead of the medieval scythe, his emblem is the waiting buggy. He is a beau who will take her for a momentous drive, yet they are not alone. For, perhaps in recognition of her own artistry, Dickinson includes her desired Immortality as the third passenger.

The drive is slow, and as in so many literary death scenes, the dying speaker surveys the course of her life. She observes childhood, where even children must strive, even at recess. She gazes at the spacious fields of maturity. She confronts old age with its setting sun. She sees all of these things as real and ordered by time. But when in the fourth quatrain the sun passes the carriage in which she and Death drive, she realizes that she no longer belongs in the temporal world. The carriage moves because, as we are told in the penultimate quatrain, "We paused." Yet its motion is conceptual; we never know whether it "stops" or "continues," even when the poem ends. The speaker is both unprepared for the journey – she wears what appears to be a morning gown of gossamer and tulle – and weirdly prepared for it, since such materials were also used for shrouds and bridal dresses. The speaker says she is cold in the fourth quatrain, having died at that point precisely. Death does not hurry; he is a ceremonial force outside time. In the courtship of Death and the speaker, time and the timeless fuse.

The final quatrains are both surreal and bluntly specific. The speaker is brought to her own grave, which, being new, is "a Swelling of the Ground – ." Yet in the very next line, years have passed, since the tombstone is "scarcely visible," covered (one supposes) with moss. The following line explains that the cornice has sunk, which suggests a lapse of decades. Meanwhile, her gallant companion has disappeared, and the final quatrain leaves the speaker nowhere in particular. Using perfect rhyme with bravery and aplomb, Dickinson repeats the designated placeless place: "the Ground." But the speaker of poem #712 is distinct from her own body. She remains in meditation upon the central mystery of Dickinson's house of art: "Eternity," toward which the carriage once drove and in which the bodiless speaker may now be suspended. Like all of Dickinson's great poems, this one seeks to expand the limits of consciousness and comprehension. It expresses the inchoate, the terrifying, and the sublime with a homely alertness and simplicity.

If she was unafraid to imagine death, Emily Dickinson was similarly unembarrassed to write of love. For its supreme importance, she was a convinced apologist. She observes in poem #1731 that a metaphor of infinity and an emblem of art, love, "can do all but raise the Dead"; moreover, even that is possible, since "Love – is that later Thing than Death –" (#924). Dickinson's letters and poems alike celebrate love in several forms, among them friendship, kinship, parental (especially maternal) feeling, students' pious affection for teachers, the wife's gratitude to and pride in a kind husband, God's possessiveness of his own creation, Christ's redemptive tenderness, and the devotion of the poet to her muse. Piquing curiosity for decades, her writing includes a profound investigation of romantic love and physical passion. Although her baffled preceptor T. W. Higginson received striking examples of her love poetry, he nevertheless declared in the *Atlantic Monthly* (1870) that "the American poet of passion is yet to come." When he read Dickinson's wittily sensual "Wild Nights" (#249; LOA, 2: 233), however, he recognized the candor of her sensuality. Before admitting the work into the first edition of *Poems* (1890), he worried that such lines as "Might I but moor – Tonight – / In Thee!" might cause her life and character to be misinterpreted. Or, rather, that she might be *rightly* interpreted as one who understood the satisfactions offered by the sexual act: the rapturous violence, described in the first stanza, that leads to consummation and tranquillity, the "moor[ing]" of the second.

Although her intricate imagination could fully envision lovemaking, Dickinson's erotic poems are constructed, like the rest, on her fundamental conception that lacking is having. To her, failure to possess the beloved is the highest form of possession and clarifies and intensifies an appetite that can only be appeased in paradise. One group of poems displays a narrative structure wherein a small, deprived woman who "had been hungry, all the Years –" (#579) finally feels herself fed (or a plain girl is dowered and adorned as a bride [#473]). In this group, the spouse who rescues Dickinson's speaker from what she deems the fatigue of frustration is named "Master" and has a set of characteristics such as superior physical and spiritual stature, irascibility, generosity, handsomeness, and playfulness. These characteristics are also repeatedly portrayed in the famous letters Dickinson wrote between 1858 and 1861 to someone also called "Master." So suasive and emotionally gripped are Dickinson's accents in these poems and letters that from their earliest publication, the possible identity of a real Master has come under discussion. Various male candidates have been proposed from among Dickinson's beloved friends or even acquaintants. Most recently, and despite the masculine terminology of the Master materials, a few feminist critics have suggested that "Master" is really a woman, probably the poet's sister-in-law, Susan Gilbert Dickinson.

Certain it is that, as Austin Dickinson said of his sister, she had loved more than once. Judge Otis Lord was her known suitor when she was 50, while the Master literature was written in her thirties. In refusing Lord, Dickinson summoned her traditional, classical imagery of food as sexuality, writing, "You ask the divine Crust and that would doom the Bread." In her presentation to Master, Dickinson's speaker imagines wifehood as well as mystic marriage. But she is more content and more eloquent when she conceives of satisfaction that is either postponed or forever denied. There is abundant justification for concluding that the poet's preference was for the solitary state that, however painful, gave her both the freedom and the stimulus to create poems.

Nevertheless, her readers marvel at the glamour and specificity of Dickinson's erotic imagination, whether it be devoted to physical experience or to its sublimation. Some poems, like "He was my host – he was my guest," seem to summarize a woman's experience with a man:

I never to this day
If I invited him could tell,
Or he invited me.

So infinite our intercourse
So intimate, indeed.
Analysis as capsule seemed
To keeper of the seed.
(#1721)

A whole cycle of poems that contemplate the brilliance and strength of a godlike lover focus on a face reminiscent of that of Jane Eyre's Mr. Rochester, whom Brontë also called "Master." These poems never avoid acknowledgment of the physical. "Struck, was I, not yet by Lightning" (#925), for example, describes a woman's orgasmic loss of virginity before it shifts to Dickinson's frequent image of the resurrection and communion of blighted lovers beyond the grave. At the same time,

many poems like "I live with Him – I see His face –" (#463) remind us that Thomas à Kempis's *Imitation of Christ* was among Dickinson's favorite books. They describe the rapture of a sequestered soul experiencing love for God and so offer the possibility that the divine face fuses with Master's face in some instances.

The kingly Master, although responsive, is the speaker's forbidden lover because, according to a Dickinson letter, "the Queen's place" next to him is already taken. Complicating and enlarging the compass of Dickinson's love poetry, however, is another group of poems, apparently written about and directed to a beloved woman. Both the speaker and this woman are "Queens" to each other and are also "wed one summer." But the woman's future is sunny and fortunate, while Dickinson's is "sown" "in Frost" (#631). A number of poems about lost pearls and jewels (#245, #452) and the rape of a woman by a "Malay" (#424, #452) substantiate a narrative akin to that of the speaker and Master because envy and desire attend the speaker's frustrated passion. Dickinson's attachment to her sister-in-law Susan, which endured – not without angry altercation – over 40 years, was openly expressed in poems like "One Sister have I in our house" (#14). It is voiced as well, however, in hundreds of letters like #393 in which such lines as "We remind her we love her – Unimportant fact, though Dante did'nt think so" profess attachment in wording that depicts the two as a romantic pair. This wording has come to be taken seriously by some recent crit-ics, although most accept the probability that in the case of the beloved woman, as with Master, Dickinson's poem #568 (LOA, 2: 271) summarized her experience – knowledge through "Ignorance":

We learned the Whole of Love –
The Alphabet – the Words –
A Chapter – then the mighty Book –
Then – Revelation closed –

Impatient with theories about her life and possible lovers; fascinated by Dickinson's style, which seems to them both seventeenth-century and modern; and subscribing to views of Victorian art as both verbose and effete, some scholars are dismissive of the passional literature. Or, engaging it, a few regard it as based upon fictions the poet read or made up. Some prefer to see Emily Dickinson as a kind of premonitory Wallace Stevens. According to this view, she was born before her time, wrote with most interest about art as in such (uncharacteristic) poems as "Dare you see a Soul *at the White Heat*?" (#365; LOA, 2: 251), and at the end of her life, triumphed over personal emotions and other links to her own experiences and century. These representations of the poet are problematic, however. Even more than Robert Browning's, Dickinson's style was unique and idiosyncratically formed; but her subject matter strongly emphasizes human feeling, especially personal love, to the last. Indeed, since "Love is all there is" (#1765), she chooses marital passion as her emblem for the poetic act (#1620). Her Victorian critics, including Higginson, did not find Dickinson's style untimely so much as they claimed that her work resembled that of the "Spasmodics," the contemporary poetic school noted for complex thought and jagged meters. Assuredly, her style was not precisely like any other Victorian's, although her subject matter is that of the best – and worst – poets of the age. It is possible that, as in the case of

Gerard Manley Hopkins (so often cited with her in this connection), the fact that Dickinson indisputably *was* a nineteenth-century poet may finally modify our conception of that century's artistic products.

Since the early 1980s, Dickinson's style has attracted increasing consideration, because a number of textual critics, not necessarily indifferent to biography, have proposed the inadequacy of Johnson's *Poems* (1955) as a definitive text. A poet of the portfolio who never prepared her own verse for publication, Dickinson copied it from about 1858 to 1864 into little booklets, which she fashioned from stationery and bound with thread. After this period of greatest activity, she jotted her poems on any handy materials – from paper bags to bargain flyers. Johnson presented the poems in the booklets, which Todd called "fascicles," and the "scraps" chronologically and restored their wording and punctuation (especially the frequent dashes), but he did not indicate the order of their appearance in the fascicles. Johnson thus represented Dickinson's intentions far more faithfully than did her earlier editors. But he, too, was forced to make decisions about the arrangement and punctuation of the poems and to choose from among Dickinson's variant wordings, to which she called attention by using asterisks and by listing alternates at the base of a poem.

After the publication of a facsimile text, *The Manuscript Books of Emily Dickinson* (1981), edited by R. W. Franklin, a number of questions have arisen about the poet's original intentions as to form and language. If the manuscript books were really her private "publications" rather than merely her method of copying and assembling the poems after she wrote them, did Dickinson intend the fascicles to be read in sequence, or as distinctly related, or even as specific commentaries on one another? Furthermore, would Dickinson have concurred in Johnson's choice of traditional verse forms like the quatrain for some poems in which, judging by her handwriting, she appears to be experimenting with arbitrary patterns of lineation? (This last issue has been raised especially by feminist critics who regard the quatrain, like the sonnet and other classical forms, as "patriarchal" and who consider Dickinson subversive of her own culture and part of an alternative tradition of *écriture féminine,* or feminine writing.) Moreover, with respect to the texts, there is the fact that even Dickinson's dashes are not always dashes precisely but dots or lines of varying lengths. What effect does that have for interpreting the sense of the poems?

An example of the challenges presented to the reader of a Dickinson facsimile is furnished by her manuscript entry of "Because I could not stop for Death – ." Johnson arranged this poem in quatrains, although each stanza takes six lines in manuscript. He did so not only because the quatrain was traditional to mid-Victorian verse, especially in tetrameters like Dickinson's, but because Dickinson herself observed the quatrain formation in recopying her verses in letters. Johnson knew, too, that, in Dickinson's time, "turnover lines" – the remainders of lines for which there is no space – were set out flush against the left margin of the subsequent line. Dickinson seems to copy many of her poems in this way so that, to avoid cramping her script, she must extend one line into the space below and conclude it against the left margin. "Deprived of other Banquet" (#773) appears in manuscript as "Deprived of other Ban- / quet –"; the syllable *quet* takes up the whole of the second line. Understandably, Johnson printed both of these lines

as one. Yet it is true that the manuscript of "Because I could not stop for Death –" reveals the first line of the second stanza (which Johnson printed as "We slowly drove – He knew no haste") as "We slowly drove – He" and the next line as "knew no haste," with the *k* looking like a capital letter.

The possible complications and enrichments a fact such as this suggests to readers used to the works of e. e. cummings, Ezra Pound, and Marianne Moore feed the present debate about the Dickinson texts. In this matter of the formal aspects of her poems, as in that of the poems' relation to her life, Dickinson's readers must encounter an uncommon degree of speculation. Most scholars agree, however, that what is needed today is a representative printed text of the fascicle poems in their proper order.

Shortly after Dickinson's *Poems* (1890) were first published, the Reverend Dr. E. Winchester Donald, an 1869 graduate of Amherst College, wrote about them to Mabel Loomis Todd and marveled that "A fever in these pages burns / Beneath the calm they feign." Even then and thus, the mysterious relation between the poet and her art seized the imagination, and Dickinson's intensity as a writer challenged the tame conventions of print. Continued study of the manuscripts and increased reflection on what has been called Dickinson's "coding" – private emblematic uses of language, especially in the love poems – are only likely to fortify our conviction that she is a major poet. Dickinson herself observed that "Legends grow" slowly (#1697); but in her case the many legends about her private life fashioned by her family and friends grew quickly, even while she lived. Together with the disarray of her manuscripts and their division among the feuding Dickinsons, the legends have helped to obscure her genius. More than 100 years since her nineteenth-century readers encountered her measured words about "Success," however, Emily Dickinson has been accorded the stature that always belonged to her.

JUDITH FARR

Selected Works

Emily Dickinson Face to Face: Unpublished Letters with Notes and Reminiscences, edited by Martha Dickinson Bianchi, Boston: Houghton Mifflin, 1932
The Poems of Emily Dickinson, Including Variant Readings Critically Compared with All Known Manuscripts, 3 vols., edited by Thomas H. Johnson, Cambridge, Massachusetts: Harvard University Press, 1955
The Letters of Emily Dickinson, 3 vols., edited by Thomas H. Johnson and Theodora Ward, Cambridge, Massachusetts: Harvard University Press, 1958
The Manuscript Books of Emily Dickinson, 2 vols., edited by R. W. Franklin, Cambridge, Massachusetts: Belknap, 1980
The Master Letters of Emily Dickinson, edited by R. W. Franklin, Amherst, Massachusetts: Amherst College Press, 1986

Further Reading

Anderson, Charles R., *Emily Dickinson's Poetry: Stairway of Surprise*, New York: Holt, Rinehart and Winston, 1960
Bingham, Millicent, *Ancestor's Brocades: The Literary Debut of Emily Dickinson*, New York: Harper, 1945
_____, *Emily Dickinson's Home*, New York: Harper, 1955
Blake, Caesar R., and Carlton F. Wells, eds., *The Recognition*

of Emily Dickinson, Ann Arbor: University of Michigan Press, 1964

Buckingham, Willis J., ed., *Emily Dickinson's Reception in the 1890s: A Documentary History*, Pittsburgh, Pennsylvania, University of Pittsburgh Press, 1989

Cady, Edwin H., and Louis J. Budd, eds., *Dickinson: The Best from American Literature,* Durham, North Carolina: Duke University Press, 1990

Cameron, Sharon, *Choosing, Not Choosing: Dickinson's Fascicles*, Chicago: University of Chicago Press, 1993

Capp, Jack L., *Emily Dickinson's Reading*, Cambridge, Massachusetts: Harvard University Press, 1966

Cody, John, *After Great Pain: The Inner Life of Emily Dickinson*, Cambridge, Massachusetts: Harvard University Press, 1971

Diehl, Joanne Feit, *Dickinson and the Romantic Imagination*, Princeton, New Jersey: Princeton University Press, 1981

Duchac, Joseph, *The Poems of Emily Dickinson: An Annotated Guide to Commentary Published in English, 1890–1977*, Boston: G. K. Hall, 1979

Eberwein, Jane Donahue, *Dickinson: Strategies of Limitation*, Amherst: University of Massachusetts Press, 1985

Farr, Judith, *The Passion of Emily Dickinson*, Cambridge, Massachusetts: Harvard University Press, 1992

Farr, Judith, ed., *Emily Dickinson: A Collection of Critical Essays*, Englewood Cliffs, New Jersey: Prentice-Hall, 1996

Franklin, R. W., *The Editing of Emily Dickinson*, Madison: University of Wisconsin Press, 1967

Gelpi, Albert, *Emily Dickinson: The Mind of the Poet*, Cambridge, Massachusetts: Harvard University Press, 1966

Juhasz, Suzanne, ed., *Feminist Critics Read Emily Dickinson*, Bloomington: University of Indiana Press, 1983

Leyda, Jay, *The Years and Hours of Emily Dickinson*, 2 vols., New Haven, Connecticut: Yale University Press, 1960

Lindberg-Seyersted, Brita, *The Voice of the Poet*, Cambridge, Massachusetts: Harvard University Press, 1968

Longsworth, Polly, *Austin and Mabel*, New York: Farrar, Straus and Giroux, 1984

Pollak, Vivian R., *Dickinson: The Anxiety of Gender*, Ithaca, New York: Cornell University Press, 1984

Porter, David T., *The Art of Emily Dickinson's Early Poetry*, Cambridge, Massachusetts: Harvard University Press, 1966

Rosenbaum, S. P., ed., *A Concordance to the Poems of Emily Dickinson*, Ithaca, New York: Cornell University Press, 1964

St. Armand, Barton Levi, *Emily Dickinson and Her Culture: The Soul's Society*, London: Cambridge University Press, 1984

Sewall, Richard B., *The Life of Emily Dickinson*, 2 vols., New York: Farrar, Straus and Giroux, 1974

———, *The Lyman Letters*, Amherst: University of Massachusetts Press, 1965

Smith, Martha Nell, *Rowing in Eden: Rereading Emily Dickinson*, Austin: University of Texas Press, 1992

Wolff, Cynthia Griffin, *Emily Dickinson*, New York: Knopf, 1986

Samuel Henry Dickson

(1798–1872)

Born on September 20, 1798, in Charleston, South Carolina, Dickson was a physician, educator, and poet. He was the second son of Scottish descendants who had emigrated to America from Belfast, Ireland, prior to the American Revolution. Both of his parents were Presbyterians, and his father was a schoolmaster. Dickson's early education was acquired at the College of Charleston. In 1814, shortly before his sixteenth birthday, he received his bachelor's degree from Yale. Following a three-year apprenticeship to a Dr. P. G. Prioleau, under whom he studied medicine in Charleston, Dickson once again traveled north, where in 1819 he received his medical degree from the University of Pennsylvania.

A vigorous proponent of reforms in medical education, Dickson early in his career encouraged the establishment of a medical college in Charleston. His dream was realized with the opening of the Medical College of South Carolina, of which he was both a founder and a faculty member. Except for brief intervals such as 1847–50, when he was at the University of New York, Dickson taught medicine in the city of his birth from 1824 until 1858. Threatened by phthisis – a lung condition – Dickson traveled North in 1825. Suffering with hemoptysis the next year, he toured Europe in the hope of hastening his recovery. During this trip, he also collected for the medical school in Charleston an anatomical cabinet of preparations from the best sources in France and Italy. Primarily for health reasons, Dickson purchased plots of land in 1837 and in 1843 on the Swanannoa River near Asheville, North Carolina. In poor health and still in search of a suitable climate, Dickson accepted a position in 1858 at Jefferson Medical College, Philadelphia, a position he held until his death on March 31, 1872.

During his distinguished medical career, Dickson was a polished and charismatic speaker who was much in demand. His varied interests can be read from the topics of his surviving orations: insanity, cholera, slavery, physical and mental hygiene, malaria, grief, women physicians and healers, yellow fever, dueling, temperance, horticulture, the history of the Masonic Lodge in South Carolina, advancing civilization, heat, alcoholism, smallpox, and suicide. Dickson's civic-mindedness and meliorist spirit are well evident in these speeches: "Let there be every where parks and gardens, and public walks and baths, accessible reading rooms, concerts of music, shows and games, and gymnastic exercises in the bright sunlight and beneath the open sky; and for the evenings, lyceums, and scientific and miscellaneous lectures, debates, oratory, and recitations."

Dickson's only literary work is *Poems* (1844), a collection of 34 verses written between the ages of 18 and 45. The order of the entries is chronological, and most of the verses had already been "circulated either in manuscript or on the pages of some of our periodicals." Since many of his poems were published anonymously, this slim volume also has value for establishing that Dickson's wrote specific poems. His manuscripts, now kept at the South Caroliniana Library (University of South Carolina), include another 15 poems. *Poems* was re-viewed in the year of publication in the *Southern Literary Messenger*:

> Professor Dickson, of the Medical College of South Carolina, is . . . well known to the whole country . . . as a scientific man, . . . a polished and skillful reviewer and a graceful essayist. There are few subjects of interest upon which his mind cannot throw light and to which his taste could not impart grace and beauty. As an orator, he has honored some of the most venerable desks in the Union. At home, he is deservedly recognized as the urbane and accomplished gentleman. It is not so well known, however, that he engages in frequent and fortunate dalliance with the muses.

The review notes the "sometimes plaintive, sometimes mournful" and "frequently gloomy" tone of Dickson's verse and deems *Poems* an occasional, although worthy, performance presented "only for his personal friends" by an "amiable" gentleman-scientist.

Dickson lived the poet's life in his leisure time, a life he found relaxing, refreshing, and pleasurable. There is little doubt that he saw poetry as a means of alleviating the weight of his scientific and medical endeavors. In "An Oration Delivered at New Haven, Before the Phi Beta Kappa Society" (1842), Dickson asserts, "The progress of man in civilization, his advancement in knowledge, will be found as distinctly impressed upon the character of his recreations, his favorite amusements, as upon his occupations and serious pursuits." He further declares that cultured physical and mental pleasures renew the enjoyment of life and force us to "relax for an occasional interval the iron grasp of care." In his numerous speeches, Dickson invariably expounded upon this theme of the balanced life when speaking of the working masses and, especially, the proletarian poor of the north. These workers' lives, he observed, were often as short as they were miserable.

In an 1859 lecture on pain and death that he delivered in Philadelphia, for example, Dickson boldly discusses the plight of the person born into poverty in large and flourishing cities:

> Being poor, the atmosphere he breathes is poisonous; the food he eats is garbage; the water with which he quenches his thirst is saturated with abominations; his clothing is rags; he earns his foul morsel through vice and humiliation; throughout the whole of his existence of sorrow and discomfort – this living death – he is watched by those who live around him in ease and comfort, and enjoyment, as dangerous to them, both morally and physically; and if he does not fall into the hands of an executioner, may consider himself fortunate to be permitted to expire in the ward of some hospital.

In his many articles, pamphlets, and medical books, Dickson advocated temperance, chided those who saw suicide as a sign of mental depravity, defended the free press, and applauded the benefits of good hygiene. He also argued for the education of black slaves, while contending that their overall condition was healthier than that of the proletariat in northern cities. Dickson confessed that he saw the potential for evil in slavery, but maintained it was not as great an evil as the poverty that resulted from the northern free labor system.

Dickson's poetry, by contrast, is characterized by an almost total absence of social and medical subjects. Instead, his verse concentrates on love, home, family, friends, and nature and underscores his dedication to the philosophy of a well-balanced, cultivated human existence. Dickson's search for balance is also obvious from his choice of friends. Rather than confine himself to the company of fellow physicians and scientists, he became a regular visitor to Russell's Book Shop on King Street, Charleston, where, for many years, the city's literati met. The undisputed leader of this group was William Gilmore **Simms**, who encouraged Dickson's literary interests. Much of Dickson's poetry was published anonymously in the group's periodical, *Russell's Magazine*.

Although Dickson was some nine years Simms's senior, the two became close friends. Dickson lent Simms money and provided emotional support when he was at a low point in his remarkable career. Simms honored the friendship by dedicating *The Yemassee* (1835), one of his most successful novels, to Dickson. He also visited Dickson at his mountain property in Asheville – the stretch of land celebrated in Dickson's 1842 poem "The Mountains! the Mountains! amidst them is my home" – and Simms's first version of "Sonnet – By The Swannannoa" (see LOA, 1: 365), published in the *Magnolia* (March 1843), refers to "the gentle slope, the Grace's seat, / Where Dickson muses in his calm retreat." In 1845, Simms printed Dickson's "I Sigh for the Land of the Cypress and Pine" ("Song – Written at the North," LOA, 1: 225) and two eloquent excerpts from the New Haven Phi Beta Kappa oration in the miscellany *The Charleston Book*. He also persuaded Evert Duyckinck to include an entry on Dickson's poetry in the important *Cyclopaedia of American Literature* (1854). After the war, Simms included "South Carolina," Dickson's poem on secession, in his *War Poetry of The South* (1866).

In his poetry, Dickson grapples with the issues of death and dying. He does not do so as a doctor who faced it in his daily work, however, but as a son who lost parents, as a father who lost children, and as a husband who outlived two of his three wives. Dickson occasionally used his poetry as a means for emptying himself of pain in order that he might continue to function rather than sink into depression. Many of his orations and several of his best poems, in fact, were composed near the time of a loved one's death. Included in these poems, which express the rhythm of pain, the swelling and sinking of suffering, is the especially memorable "On Seeing the Portrait of a Dear Child."

Dickson was praised by his fellow Southerners for his war songs and odes, which poked fun at the enemy and employed catchy rhythms that were uplifting and easy to remember. The martial lyric "South Carolina," written in December 1860 before the beginning of hostilities, reflected Dickson's passion for the land and people of his home state, and established him as a staunch supporter of the culture and society of antebellum Carolina.

Several of Dickson's earlier poems were composed during his courting days. Addressed to his beloved's and, later, his wives, they lead one to surmise that he had a good sense of humor. Although some are trite and sentimental – the kind of verse only the person receiving it could appreciate – others are good, but perhaps would be more admired if the reader knows what personal trauma Dickson is enduring.

Dickson's nature poetry constitutes some of his best work. Not only "I Long for the Land of the Cypress and the Pine," but also "Japonica" ("Thou art welcome every where, / Charming flower!") and "Harper's Ferry" deserve to be remembered. Dickson wrote "Harper's Ferry" to commemorate the beautiful natural scene and the "Philosophic Sage" Thomas Jefferson, "who after a glowing description in his *Notes on Virginia* of the passage of the Shenandoah and Potomac through the Blue Ridge, declares that one view of it is worth a voyage across the Atlantic." As Dickson writes:

Innum'rous islets gay with shrubs and flowers,
Moistened with rainbow spray and sparkling showers,
Smile as they lie 'midst the loud rapids spread,
While frowning rocks hang darkly overhead.
The Philosophic Sage whose kindling eyes,
First viewed this vale with rapture and surprise,
Painted the landscape with faithful touch,
Nor though entranced, expressed one grace too much.

Dickson's "The Whip-poor-Will" uses a cadence that recalls the song of the night bird – a mournful, lost, and lonely sound. "Sullivan's Island Retreat" is a good poem, as is "Green Be the Turf Beneath My Head," in which the speaker asks to be buried not in a city but rather beneath a cypress where the leaves will become his canopy. The poem expresses a total retreat into the bosom of nature away from a crass man-made world.

"I Long for the Land" (or "Song – Written at the North") is not Dickson's best poem, but it is his most accessible. Dickson spent much time traveling in the north, attending medical conventions, supervising publication of his medical books, doing medical research, and convalescing. Demonstrating his strong emotional attachment to his home, this 1830 poem was published in the *Songs of the South* series and is known today largely because it was set to music and distributed widely. Dickson loved the south as a place of natural beauty and fertility. With the eye of a scientist, the social concern of a medical doctor, and the heart of a poet, he embraced the civilization of his native state. He also defended that state and its people against what he deemed capricious and tumultuous attacks. According to Dickson's view, the agricultural civilization of South Carolina was worth preserving even if it meant seceding from the Union. For Dickson, the struggle was not over slavery, but for "the land of the cypress and the pine" and its right to self-government.

Much of Dickson's poetry was written in moments of passion – the birth or death of children, the love and loss of wives, wartime, and instances of intense aesthetic appreciation and feelings about the deep tranquillity within nature. One also perceives that Dickson often had fun with his poetry, for much of it is charming and light. Although he was not a professional poet, Dickson was a worthy amateur. His verse gives us a fuller appreciation of the sophisticated intellectual culture that existed in Charleston before the war.

DAVID AIKEN

Selected Works

Poems, Charleston, South Carolina: privately printed, 1844

The Charleston Book: A Miscellany in Prose and Verse, edited by William Gilmore Simms, Charleston, South Carolina: Samuel Hart, 1845

Russell's Magazine, 6 vols., Charleston, South Carolina: Walker, Evans, 1857–60

Writing of S. H. Dickson, 3 vols., Columbia: South Caroliniana Library, n.d.

Further Reading

Knight, Lucian Lamar, *Library of Southern Literature*, vol. 15, Atlanta, Georgia: Martin & Hoyt, 1907

Waring, Joseph Ioor, *A History of Medicine in S.C. 1825–1900*, South Carolina Medical Association, 1967

Joseph Rodman Drake

(1795–1820)

Joseph Rodman Drake was born in New York City on August 7, 1795, the fourth child and only son of Jonathan and Hannah Drake. His father died when Joseph was two, leaving his penniless widow to support herself and her children by keeping a boardinghouse. In 1809, she married a New Orleans merchant and followed him to Louisiana with her two elder daughters. Drake and his sister Caroline were left with an aunt and uncle in New York, where Drake was intended for a business career. But he was unhappy working as a clerk in his uncle's store, and felt (as he wrote to his sister in New Orleans) "alone, forlorn, and cheerless." This feeling only intensified when he received word of his mother's death in 1811. "There is nothing so desolate as the heart without home or stay," he later remembered, and added that the gloom of a prison or a cavern was nothing beside the "dreadful feeling of abandonment and isolation" that afflicts someone alone in the world. His happiest hours were spent with some older cousins at a family estate called "The Grange" on Hunt's Point in the Bronx, where Drake would wander for hours along the shores of the Bronx River and enjoy the rural scenery or the view across the Sound to Long Island (see "Bronx," LOA, 1: 217). A small family burying ground on the estate held his father's grave.

In the spring of 1813, when he was 17, Drake decided to leave his uncle's shop and take up the study of medicine. The three-year course of study in one of the city's newer medical schools required apprenticeship to a medical practitioner as well as attendance at formal lectures and at clinical lectures given in the city's almshouses and hospitals. Drake completed his course of study and was awarded his degree in the spring of 1816, a few months short of his twenty-first birthday. After some months spent hoping to secure an academic position, Drake opened a medical practice in New York City.

Despite his lack of formal schooling, Drake had been an avid reader from an early age and had quickly progressed from reading children's stories to reading serious literature and history. He began writing verse when he was five years old (so family tradition has it) and wrote his first publishable poem when he was 14. "The Mocking-bird" (LOA, 1: 204) was published in the Philadelphia *Port Folio* three years later, in 1812. It is remarkable not only for its fluency and charm but for its calm acknowledgment that all poets must imitate before they can sing their own song. As the poem implies, the mockingbird's song, a medley of snatches stolen from other birds' songs, is in fact more beautiful than any of them, and the listener stands astonished before an originality fabricated wholly of thefts.

Drake shared a passion for the poetry of William Shakespeare, Sir Walter Scott, Robert Burns, Tom Moore, and Thomas Campbell with Fitz-Greene **Halleck**, whom he met in 1813 and who became his close friend and poetic collaborator. When Drake married Sarah Eckford in the fall of 1816, Halleck was best man at the wedding. When the couple went abroad in 1818, Halleck was the recipient of one of Drake's best comic poems, "Poetic Epistle to Fitz-Greene Halleck, May 1, 1818," which is a mocking description of the Scottish landscape in a bristling pseudo-Scots dialect. The collaboration that made them famous in New York began in 1819, when they amused themselves by writing comic poems and decided to send samples anonymously to the New York *Evening Post* in hopes that the editor might publish them. Drake had signed the poems with the pen name "Croaker," after a character in Goldsmith's comedy "The Good-Natured Man." To their delight the *Post* ran a notice the next day promising to run the poems and pronouncing them "productions of superior taste and genius." From March 19 to July 24, 1819, New York readers were titillated by a series of "Croaker" poems, some written by Drake, some by Halleck, and some in collaboration. The short poems were irreverent and personal, mocking everything from ludicrous poetry and bad painting to the pomposities of Governor Clinton and the hapless surgeon general of New York, whose attempt to define "militia" and "grog" in his annual report led him into the morasses of bureaucratic redundancy. Some of the poems abandoned satire for literary burlesque; the best of these is surely "Ode to Impudence," Drake's parody of Horace's famous ode *Integer vitæ*. In a modern twist on the theme of innocence triumphing over menace, Drake's penniless but unabashed diner, the "man who wears a brazen face," simply shouts "*Charge it*" to the waiter who advances on him with a bill – and the amazed waiter bows and complies.

Drake's lyrical poems are largely conventional; his patriotic poems like "Niagara" (LOA, 1: 211) and "The American Flag" (LOA, 1: 209) – in which Freedom tears "the azure robe of night" for the blue field and sets in it the "stars of glory" – were once popular as recitation poems, but today seem like fustian. It is worth noting, however, that "The American Flag" has been set to music by Vincenzo Bellini and by Antonín Dvořák. Drake's long narrative poem, *The Culprit Fay* (LOA, 1: 207), written in 1816, concerns the trials of a "fay," or fairy, who has disgraced himself by loving a mortal woman, although one chaste and fair, and who must survive a series of trials set by the monarch of the fairies, headquartered in the vicinity of Crow's Neck on the Hudson. The poem owes a good deal to Shakespeare's *A Midsummer Night's Dream* and Alexander Pope's *The Rape of the Lock* – yet the flora and fauna are all American, and Drake clearly enjoys showing that he can enlist local species of insects and flowers in his fiction as easily as English and Scottish poets did. The poem (like most of his work) was not published until after his death, but it quickly became popular and went through many editions in both England and America. Although critics are right to call it more a poem of the fancy than of the imagination, its imagery and lightness still make it attractive.

After several bouts of illness, Drake's health began to decline dramatically in the autumn of 1819, when his symptoms of advanced tuberculosis led him to seek a warmer climate. A trip to New Orleans allowed him to see his sisters once more but failed to arrest his disease. In the spring of 1820, he returned to New York City, where he died on September 21. He was buried in the family cemetery at Hunt's Point. Two lines from the famous elegy written by his friend Halleck grace Drake's monument (LOA, 1: 97): "None knew thee but to love thee / Nor named thee but to praise."

BARBARA PACKER

Selected Works

The Culprit Fay, and Other Poems, New York: G. Dearborn, 1835

Further Reading

Pleadwell, Frank Lester, *The Life and Works of Joseph Rodman Drake (1795–1820)*, Boston: Merrymount, 1935

Paul Laurence Dunbar

(1872–1906)

Dunbar has received much attention as one of the first African American writers to achieve professional success. During his short life, he produced over 400 poems, four collections of short stories, uncollected stories equivalent to another volume, four novels, a number of social commentaries, and a variety of lyrics and libretti for the theater. In 1893, Frederick Douglass said, "I regard Paul Dunbar as the most promising young colored man in America," and that articulation of Dunbar's "promise" certainly held more than personal significance: he was to become America's *black* poet, the representative man who would transform the social and intellectual possibilities of an entire race. Historians of African American literature have noted the poet's legacy for writers such as James Weldon Johnson, Countee Cullen, and Langston Hughes. And although African American poets such as Lucy Terry, Jupiter Hammon, and Phillis Wheatley had written prior to Dunbar, it is his accomplishment that inaugurated what many critics refer to as an African American poetic tradition. As Henry Louis Gates Jr. explains, this tradition came to have more than artistic relevance; it became "proof" of black humanity and black intellect. Besides the way in which it places emphasis on writing as evidence of equality, the notion of such a specific tradition claims to distinguish the common features of writing produced by African Americans. Consequently, many have read Dunbar's poems as literary commentary on black life and sentiment. Following the publication of *Lyrics of Lowly Life* (1896), moreover, particularized notions of blackness gained a widely recognizable cultural meaning. About the poet, one critic wrote:

> The whole civilized world has greater respect for that race which some have the ignorance to underestimate and others the hardihood to despise, because of this black man, through whose veins not a drop of Caucasian blood was known to flow, [and who] has given such a splendid and striking proof of its capacity for high intellectual achievement.

Indeed, Dunbar became a symbol of the future of black accomplishment, and as such his legacy acquires a racial meaning that defines the terms according to which many read writing by African Americans.

If Dunbar became a symbol and a prospect for black accomplishment, however, he himself was ambivalent about the requirements of his professional success and about the literary and cultural role he was to occupy. This ambivalence can be seen most clearly in his poetry. Dunbar wrote both vernacular and standard Victorian English poems; taken together, they help characterize a significant poetic moment at the turn of the century. Authors as diverse as Mark Twain, Kate Chopin, and James Whitcomb **Riley** established careers in both dialect and "standard" forms. But if "standard" language was the poetic discourse of high culture, with the claim that the artistic judgments of an educated elite were universal, dialect poetry imitating the spoken language of a region constituted a "low" art movement that celebrated the authority of a specific con-

stituency. Most turn-of-the-century readers and critics preferred Dunbar's "negro" dialect verse, and this preference reflects an insistence on racially distinct categories that render the poet and his poems "black." The presumption that Dunbar's corpus represents an unambiguously "black" cultural project, however, denies an intercultural dialogue about American literature. Moreover, it ignores the poet's intentions. Dunbar the poet possesses a dual identity, and while it is not unique to him, this duality nuanced by racial discourse offers an important insight into the reception of his work.

Paul Laurence Dunbar was born on June 27, 1872, in Dayton, Ohio. His parents, Joshua Dunbar and Matilda Murphy, were married in Dayton in 1871 and were divorced in 1876. Paul's younger sister, Elizabeth, died at two years of age, and although he had two older siblings from his mother's previous marriage, he was raised as an only child. Both of his parents had been slaves in Kentucky, and his father had escaped via the Underground Railroad and later served in the Civil War; the poet celebrates his father's heroism in "Our Martyred Soldiers" and "Emancipation." Matilda Murphy not only taught her son to read but made many sacrifices so that he could receive the best education available. He was the only black student in his class at Central High School, where he was editor-in-chief of the school newspaper, president of the literary Philomathean Society, and author of the class song performed at his graduation at the Dayton Opera House in June 1891. He married Alice Ruth Moore, a teacher and writer (now anthologized as Alice Dunbar Nelson) from New Orleans, in 1898. They separated in 1902, four years before his death by tuberculosis.

In 1888, he published his first poems, including "Our Martyred Soldiers," in the *Dayton Herald*. Despite this early success and his aspiration to earn a law degree at Harvard, Dunbar found upon graduation that menial labor was his only option, so he took a job as an elevator boy in downtown Dayton. He continued to write poetry, and in 1892, he borrowed the money to publish his first volume, *Oak and Ivy*, which is dedicated to his mother, "who has ever been my guide, teacher, and inspiration." With several copies of *Oak and Ivy* in his possession, he left his job and attended the World's Columbian Exposition in Chicago (1893). At this exposition, he met Frederick Douglass, who was serving as the U.S. minister to Haiti and as the commissioner of the Haitian exhibition. Impressed by Dunbar, Douglass hired him as a clerk in the Haitian building, arranged for him to read at the Colored American Day celebration, and introduced him to other black artists and writers, including Ida B. Wells and Mary Church Terrell. Dunbar also met Will Marion Cook and Harry Burleigh, with whom he would later collaborate in writing musicals for black theater companies. Although Douglass died in 1895, he left a lasting impression on Dunbar, as the poem "Frederick Douglass" attests. Among other important Dunbar patrons were two white men, Charles A. Thatcher and Dr. Henry A. Tobey, who not only arranged public readings and secured critical endorsements for him but also financed the publication of his second collection, *Majors and Minors* (1895). The book, which reprinted the best of *Oak and Ivy* and added new material, included a frontispiece portrait of the author that, as an unmistakable authenticator, declared to the reader the fact of the poet's race. Dr. Tobey encouraged Dunbar to deliver a copy of *Majors and Minors* to a well-known actor, who enthusiastically sent it to the influential editor and novelist William Dean **Howells**. It was Howells's review of *Majors and Minors* in the June 27, 1896 issue of *Harper's Weekly* that introduced Dunbar's poetry to readers across the nation.

While the Howells review helped secure a commercial publisher as well as national recognition, it also created a curious dilemma for the poet. Like most readers, Howells preferred the verse that Dunbar wrote in black vernacular. The poems in *Majors and Minors*, however, were primarily composed in standard English in the tradition of Henry Wadsworth **Longfellow**, William Wordsworth, and John Keats; Dunbar imagined these works as his "major" poems. The "minor" poems, written in a variety of dialects (including the Hoosier dialect popularized by Riley and German dialect), were conceived as regional sketches that would participate in the local-color movement in American literary realism. As a local-color realist, Dunbar, like Twain, Chopin, Sarah Orne **Jewett**, and Willa Cather, sought accurately to represent a particular place. But unlike the dialect poems and short stories of his white contemporaries, Dunbar's black dialect poems came to be seen as something more than a realistic depiction of a region; they were read as embodying the "reality" of a race.

Thus, the Howells review (reprinted as the introduction to *Lyrics of Lowly Life*) characterizes Dunbar as a poet whose gift was in articulating the "truth" about African American life and feeling. Howells writes that the poet's "brilliant and unique achievement was to have studied the American negro objectively, and to represent him as he found him to be, with humor, with sympathy, and yet with what the reader must instinctively feel to be the entire truthfulness." That "truthfulness" instinctively felt by the reader is the racial authenticity imagined by a primarily white audience and apparently affirmed by what Howells calls "the only man of pure African blood and of American civilization to feel the negro life aesthetically and express it lyrically." Howells's words not only launched Dunbar's professional career, they inaugurated his reception as a definitively *black* poet and author. Dunbar's parents, wrote Howells, were "negroes without admixture of white blood" and had been slaves, while the poet himself had been forced to work as an elevator boy. This biographical information also insists on a reading of Dunbar's poetry that is inextricably bound to the history of the poet's social and racial status. While Howells imagined himself as an advocate of the "essential unity of the human race," he did not reject the imposition of the color line in life or in literature: "There is a precious difference of temperament between the races which it would be a great pity ever to lose, and . . . this is best preserved and most charmingly suggested by Mr. Dunbar in those pieces of his where he studies the moods and traits of his race in its own accent of our English." This reception of Dunbar's black vernacular poems brings racial discourse to life. Howells's articulated conception of a recognizably black language that he distinguishes from "our," presumably white, English, insists on inscribing racial difference in literature, establishes Dunbar's literary identity as a black poet, and typifies the era's more general and urgent desire to see and know the difference between being black and being white.

Unlike versions of black dialect produced by white authors such as Thomas Nelson Page and Joel Chandler Harris, Dunbar's representation was understood as "real." This imposition of racial authenticity transformed the specific representation of regional dialect into a universalized embodiment of black American life. Similarly, the seeming universality of standard English came to specify the distinction of whiteness; as a consequence of the author's race Dunbar's standard language Victorian verse, regardless of its content, could not achieve "universal" significance. The poet was aware of this predicament and spent much of his career in an ambiguous relationship to his art. As he commented, "my position is most unfortunate. I am a black white man." His words not only illustrate the tension of his dual poetic identity, they also suggest an interpretive coherence to his work as well as a powerful critique of the supply-and-demand nature of the turn-of-the-century interest in an authentic black voice.

Poems such as "Accountability" (LOA, 2: 610), "The Deserted Plantation," "An Ante-Bellum Sermon" (LOA, 2: 622), and "When Malindy Sings" (LOA, 2: 613) appear to authenticate recognizable black "types" whose particular speech and habits romanticize the antebellum past. Harris and Page had already produced minstrel versions of African American characters whose singing, banjo-playing, dancing, religious emotionalism, and affinity for chicken sought to justify racial distinction and hierarchy. When, in "A Banjo Song," Dunbar's slave speaker says, "oh, dere's lots o' keer an' trouble / in dis world to swaller down / An' it's when I tek at ebenin' / My ol' banjo f'om de wall," a preexisting "type" became "real" for contemporary readers; coupled with the poet's blackness, the speaker's language and his habits suggest the absence of both the blackface minstrel mask and the artifice generally inherent in representation. Similarly, in "The Deserted Plantation," a former slave laments the disappearance of plantation life: "could n't one o' dem dat see it in its glory / Stay to watch it in de hour of decay." The comment seems to affirm the past and present social structure in what has become an identifiable black voice. In his dialect poems, Dunbar apparently reported black sentiment and black life from the depths of his experience. This strategy, however, not only lends credibility to black "types" but also, as in "When Malindy Sings," gently applauds the difference between black and white. In celebrating Malindy's vocal skill, the speaker offers a primitive version of blackness that satisfies a particular racial fantasy:

> G'way an' quit dat noise, Miss Lucy –
> Put dat music book away;
> What's de use to keep on tryin'?
> Ef you practise twell you 're gray,
> You cain't sta't no notes a-flyin'
> Lak de ones dat rants and rings
> F'om de kitchen to de big woods
> When Malindy sings.

Regardless of Miss Lucy's ability to read music, the speaker warns that her literate intelligence cannot equal Malindy's intuitive achievement. Unlike her white mistress, who "ain't got de nachel o'gans / Fu' to make de soun' come right," Malindy possesses an innate instinct. Her temperament is authentic:

Easy 'nough fu' folks to hollah,
   Lookin' at de lines an' dots,
. . . .
But fu' real melojous music,
   Dat jes' strikes yo' hea't and clings,
Jes' you stan' an' listen wif me
   When Malindy sings.

According to the narrator, this black woman's voice cannot be rivaled or copied, so that upon hearing Malindy sing even the "Mockin'-bird quit tryin' to whistle, / 'Cause he jes' so shamed hisse'f." Here, Dunbar utilizes existing assumptions about the qualities of a distinctly African American temperament to illustrate the depth of Malindy's skill. In this way he manipulates stereotypes to give his local-color realism a heightened effect that renders the poem "black."

Some of Dunbar's dialect poems, however, resist the impulse to make black types "real." If, in their submission to a white supremacist status quo, stereotypical African American characters embody and validate a hierarchical difference between "black" and "white," many of Dunbar's types perform versions of blackness designed to emphasize precisely that those versions are performances. These characters demonstrate rhetorical cunning that implicitly rejects the desire for the poem to stand in for the real thing. In "An Ante-Bellum Sermon," a slave preacher manipulates a "black" rhetorical form to invalidate hierarchical notions of difference and to expose the hypocrisy present in "white" standards of civilization. In his rendering of an Old Testament story, the preacher allegorizes his contemporary social structure:

Now ole Pher'oh, down in Egypt,
   Was de wuss man evah bo'n,
An' he had de Hebrew chillun
   Down dah wukin' in his co'n;
'T well de Lawd got tiahed o' his foolin',
   An' sez he: "I'll let him know –
Look hyeah, Moses, go tell Pher'oh
   Fu' to let dem chillun go."

He describes Moses' mission to Pharaoh as one that, despite the preacher's disclaimer ("I will pause right hyeah to say, / Dat I'm still a-preachin' ancient, / I ain't talkin' 'bout to-day"), obviously parallels the problem of slavery in the United States. The speaker's glaringly insistent message of social indictment, and perhaps even of insurrection, is most clearly articulated in his disclaimer, so that the story of Moses leading the Israelites from Egypt becomes an undeniable metaphor for emancipation:

So you see de Lawd's intention,
   Evah sence de worl' began,
Was dat His almighty freedom
   Should belong to evah man.

The preacher in "An Ante-Bellum Sermon" deploys assumptions concerning "black" humility and religious emotionalism to satirize and critique institutional slavery and racism.

If the dialect verse in "An Ante-Bellum Sermon" questions the legitimacy of white privilege, "Accountability," which initially seems to read as a genuine articulation of blackness, becomes a critique of imposing the color line on literature. Early

in the poem, a slave confirms the ideology of difference: "We is all constructed diff'rent, d'ain't no two of us de same; / We can't he'p ouah likes an' dislikes, ef we'se bad we ain't to blame." He informs his audience of the fact of individual identities and fixed dispositions and suggests that the relevant personal distinction – racial distinction, as the dialect makes clear – is beyond our control. "Folks aint got no right to censuah uthah folks about dey habits," he says, and his grammar and phonetically spelled version of "censure" call to mind the difference that, in Howells's terms, is "their" accent of "our English." The speaker thus seemingly offers the "truth" about his character and condition by acknowledging the "natural" order – "We gits into su'ttain channels dat we jes caint he'p pu'suin'" – and by claiming that every individual's place has been preordained: "Him dat made de streets an' driveways wasn't shamed to make de alleys." Seemingly passive and content, the slave "reveals" his "negro" type just as the language naturalizes "black" actions under the plantation regime: "Don't keer whut you does, you has to, an' hit sholy beats de dickens, – / Viney go put on de kittle, I got one o' mastah's chickens." This revelation at the end reinforces a racialized explanation for variety in human temperament and brings to life what Howells called "the precious difference . . . between the races."

At the moment the slave speaker asserts the "truth" about racial identity, however, Dunbar calls it into question by violating the dialect with a line of standard English: "When you come to think about it, how it's all planned out it's splendid." Here, "white" English enters the "black" rhetorical form and draws attention to a "flaw" in the speaker's seemingly pure authenticity as well as to the artifice inherent in poetic representation. It also focuses critical attention upon the prevalent literary aesthetic that demanded a "black" voice. In "Accountability," then, the speaker is only acting; his direct address in standard English necessitates a brief, but conscious, recognition of the artfulness inherent in emblematizing race in language. While one could read this momentary integration of standard English as a gesture toward a third, hybrid category that is simultaneously "black" and "white," this revelatory moment altogether denies racialization by refusing any answer to the question of authenticity. The presence of standard English in what Howells calls Dunbar's "black poems" indicates the fallacy of identifying race in language.

What then is the meaning of Dunbar's language in the standard English poems? By insisting on the poet's race, the frontispiece portrait accompanying *Majors and Minors* introduces the risk that the poems will be read as more and less than art. But when Dunbar's work was taken as a depiction of authentic experience, his attempt at a particular version of local color was transformed into a statement concerning the whole truth of black life. In 1895, Dunbar wrote that his project was to "be able to interpret my own people through song and story, and to prove to the many that after all we are more human than African." He had hoped to create a poetry that would render black feeling and sentiment in a manner that would appeal to a general human experience rather than to embody a more specific racial condition. As Dr. Tobey intimates, however, "Thank God, he's black! . . . whatever genius he may have cannot be attributed to the white blood he may have in him." Dunbar could not escape the constant racialization of his achievement, and thus reception of his standard English poems as "more human than African" became difficult. One of his earliest poems, "Ere Sleep Comes Down to Soothe the Weary Eyes" (LOA, 2: 617), seeks the "universal":

> Ere sleep comes down to soothe the weary eyes,
>   Which all the day with ceaseless care have sought
> The magic gold which from the seeker flies;
>   Ere dreams put on the gown and cap of thought,
> And make the waking world a world of lies, –
>   Of lies most palpable, uncouth, forlorn,
> That say life's full of aches and tears and sighs, –
>   Oh, how with more than dreams the soul is torn,
> Ere sleep comes down to soothe the weary eyes.

The description of everyday hardships that only sleep can relieve claims an appeal to a general human experience. The poem's standard Victorian language, moreover, invokes a "high" European tradition that, for poets like Alfred Tennyson and John Keats, permitted "universal" reference. For Dunbar, also the *black* poet, to have access to standard English implies access to the "universal." This possibility, however, paradoxically endangers the authenticity of his race as well as the authenticity of his "black" poems, but it also threatens the distinctions made between "our English" and "their" English.

In writing standard English, Dunbar's challenge was to offer his version of black experience in a broadly accepted medium. His theory of art resists the imposition of a racially specified form and seeks the limitless possibility of an "unraced" artist. When asked about the difference between poems written by blacks and by whites, he said, "we must write like white men. I do not mean to imitate them; but our life is now the same." Because Dunbar imagines black lives and white lives as having equal stake in America, he believes that writing by black people could have the same cultural effects upon American literature and American discourse. It would thus be a mistake to interpret Dunbar's position as a desire to be white; rather, he is challenging the preeminence of racial discourse, especially its influence on African American writers. In referring to himself as a "black white man," it may be that Dunbar is claiming a humanity beyond race, with "black" indicating a recognition of the prejudicial market limitations that race imposes and "white" indicating a privileged status free from social and aesthetic restrictions. To prove that his people were "more human than African," Dunbar would in fact strive to prove that they were beyond the culturally depreciating specificity of race. In his "major" poems, therefore, Dunbar employs the formal language of English verse to elevate his people to a new status. The first poem in *Oak and Ivy*, "Ode to Ethiopia," pays tribute to the race:

> O Mother Race! to thee I bring
> This pledge of faith unwavering,
>   This tribute to thy glory.
> I know the pangs which thou didst feel,
> When slavery crushed thee with its heel,
>   With thy dear blood all gory.
> . . . .
> Be proud, my Race, in mind and soul;
> Thy name is writ on Glory's scroll
>   In characters of fire.
> High 'mid the clouds of Fame's bright sky

> Thy banner's blazoned folds now fly,
>   And truth shall lift them higher.

The ode utilizes the formal *rime couèe* to deliver black American experience into another class. By defining a particularized racial experience as heroic, the poet can make it more generally recognizable and therefore "more human than African." Peter Revell explains that the "choice of form asserts a claim that the race and its sufferings and achievements merit the language usually accorded to heroic events in the nation's history"; thus for Dunbar, standard English makes possible black humanity, and perhaps even the audibility of his own voice.

"The Colored Soldiers" (LOA, 2: 619) – a Tennysonian battle poem describing African American participation in the Civil War – similarly employs "white" language and poetics in an effort to translate "black" into "human" accomplishment.

> If the muse were mine to tempt it
>   And my feeble voice were strong,
> If my tongue were trained to measures,
>   I would sing a stirring song.
> I would sing a song heroic
>   Of those noble sons of Ham,
> Of the gallant colored soldiers
>   Who fought for Uncle Sam!

The essential objective here is to demonstrate black men's right to full citizenship and respect – a status universally known to white men. The speaker suggests that the freedom to make such claims is not quite within his reach: "If the muse *were* mine," he says, "I *would* sing a stirring song" (emphasis added). The muse that enables this kind of poetry is not his; it is *theirs*, the "white" language and "white" tradition in which an articulation of "universal" humanity is possible. Consequently, "The Colored Soldiers" must access the rhetorical space of whiteness in order to establish for its subjects a meritorious place in the life of the nation. And, despite the recognition of racially determined constraints, the speaker manages to produce a heroic ballad and simultaneously substantiate his own claim to a new status and identity beyond racial specificity.

For Dunbar, however, blackness is ultimately inescapable; as a black poet, race always specifies his art. As a "black white man," color informs his existential possibilities. Hence the dilemma: "black white" poems cannot claim universal humanity because such a claim relies on an unqualified status that "black" does not allow. "Black" negates the possibility of "white," and poems written by a black poet, in standard English or in dialect, are equally "colored" and equally specified. Dunbar's poetry can be read as the literal evidence of this racial discourse, which in turn produces a tension vividly evident in both poetic languages. As he writes in "We Wear the Mask" (LOA, 2: 613):

> We wear the mask that grins and lies,
> It hides our cheeks and shades our eyes –
> This debt we pay to human guile;
> With torn and bleeding hearts we smile
> And mouth with myriad subtleties.

Here, the poet uses standard English to articulate the predicament that characterizes all of his verse. The "mask that grins and lies" is the black whiteness that insists on shaping his self-perception as well as his poetry. As simultaneously black and white, Dunbar's poems cannot claim truth or general reference: "it hides our cheeks and shades our eyes"; rather, in a "mouth with myriad subtleties," the poet articulates the gambit of racial discourse. His words precede W. E. B. Du Bois and Frantz Fanon, and, most importantly, they reflect the fraught concept of authenticity that informs how we read black writing.

SHELLY EVERSLEY

Selected Works

Oak and Ivy, Dayton, Ohio: Press of the United Brethren Publishing House, 1893

Majors and Minors, Toledo, Ohio: Hadley and Hadley, 1895

Lyrics of Lowly Life, introduction by William Dean Howells, New York: Dodd, Mead, 1896

Lyrics of the Hearthside, New York: Dodd, Mead, 1899

Poems of Cabin and Field, New York: Dodd, Mead, 1899

Candle-Lightin' Time, New York: Dodd, Mead, 1901

Lyrics of Love and Laughter, New York: Dodd, Mead, 1903

When Malindy Sings, New York: Dodd, Mead, 1903

Li'l' Gal, New York: Dodd, Mead, 1904

Chris'mus Is A-Comin' and Other Poems, New York: Dodd, Mead, 1905

Howdy, Honey, Howdy, New York: Dodd, Mead, 1905

Lyrics of Sunshine and Shadow, New York: Dodd, Mead, 1905

A Plantation Portrait, New York: Dodd, Mead, 1905

Joggin' Erlong, New York: Dodd, Mead, 1906

Life and Works, Naperville, Illinois, and Memphis, Tennessee: J. L. Nichols, 1907

The Collected Poetry of Paul Laurence Dunbar, edited by Joanne M. Braxton, Charlottesville: University of Virginia Press, 1993

Further Reading

Brawley, Benjamin, *Paul Laurence Dunbar*, Port Washington, New York: Kennikat Press, 1936

Gates, Henry Louis, Jr., *"Race," Writing, and Difference*, Chicago: University of Chicago Press, 1986

Revell, Peter, *Paul Laurence Dunbar*, Boston: Twayne, 1979

Ralph Waldo Emerson

(1803–1882)

Writing in his journal in 1846, a year of sudden poetic efflorescence for him, Emerson addresses one of his many Muse figures:

> O Bacchus, make them drunk, drive them mad, this multitude of vagabonds, hungry for eloquence, hungry for poetry, starving for symbols, perishing for want of electricity to vitalize this too much pasture; &, in the long delay, indemnifying themselves with the false wine of alcohol, of politics, or of money. Pour for them, o Bacchus, the wine of wine. Give them, at last, Poetry.

This exorbitant exhortation typifies Emerson's exalted conception of poetry's power to move, and of the concomitant role of the true poet in society. That visionary strain also marks one of the characteristic features of Emerson's verse, although it is by no means the only note that he seeks to strike. Indeed (and this comes as a surprise to some), he is a poet of considerable range, a poet of many moods and many modes, and it takes some time for the reader to come to terms with the full scope of his accomplishment.

Emerson, although best known for his essays, is first and foremost a poet. He began writing verses as a young child and continued until well into his declining years. As he puts it, with characteristic diffidence, in a letter to his fiancée, Lydia Jackson:

> I am born a poet, of a low class without doubt, yet a poet. This is my nature and vocation. My singing, be sure, is very "husky," and is for the most part in prose. Still am I a poet in the sense of a perceiver and dear lover of the harmonies that are in the soul and in matter.

Like Percy Bysshe Shelley's, Emerson's notion of poetry is broad and embraces the realm of prose. Indeed, critics of Emerson's essays often proceed as if they were reading prose poems, so dense and rhetorically sophisticated is his writing. But in addition to his many essays, lectures, and sermons, Emerson was also a prolific writer of verse and composed in his notebooks and journals almost 1,500 pages of poetry, including numerous translations of Italian, German, and Persian poetry. Besides publishing individual poems in the *Dial* and other journals and newspapers, Emerson brought out two collections – *Poems* (1847) and *May-Day and Other Pieces* (1867). In 1876, he published *Selected Poems*, which contained some new verse. These books, which sold well and went through many printings, evoked a wide range of responses, from the hostile to the adulatory. But regardless of how the critics felt, it was clear that Emerson was a poet to be reckoned with, and *Poems* in particular remains one of the most original books of verse published by an American poet.

After his death in 1882, Emerson's work was collected into two multivolume sets; the first, known as the Riverside edition (1883–93), was edited by his literary executor, James Elliot Cabot, and the second, the Centenary edition (1903–04), was edited by Emerson's son, Edward Emerson. Both editors devoted a separate volume to the poetry, and each included unpublished material from the notebooks and journals, although the selection and the editing of these texts are, by modern standards, unreliable and intrusive. The Centenary edition of the poems had functioned as the standard, but has now been superseded by a fuller and more scrupulous edition in the Library of America series, *Ralph Waldo Emerson: Collected Poems and Translations.* Harvard University Press plans a more limited edition of the poetry in its multivolume *Collected Works.* In addition to these collections, almost all of Emerson's published and unpublished verse can be found, in draft form and in various versions, in his notebooks and journals. The *Journals and Miscellaneous Notebooks* (in 16 volumes) and the *Poetry Notebooks* (one volume) allow us to see Emerson at work on his verse. Successive drafts of poems often wander from one notebook to another over a period of years until they are abandoned or published, and it is instructive to see just how particular Emerson could be about a word, a line, or a rhyme. Although many of the poems in these notebooks were never finished to Emerson's satisfaction, much of the poetry found there is among his most striking; moreover, these notebooks reveal the process of development from Emerson's early verse to his more mature and experimental style.

Given this wealth of material, relatively little work has been done on the poetry – especially when compared to the prose – and any consideration of Emerson's poetry should take into account the fact that he remains, along with Herman **Melville**, our least-read major poet. As with Melville, this neglect – or in Emerson's case, misapprehension – stems in part from the overwhelming achievement of the prose. Emerson's essays continue to dazzle and provoke us, but the poems are often mistakenly read as pale versions of the prose. Another perhaps equally potent reason for Emerson's one-sided reputation is the nature of the verse itself: it has struck readers and critics as both peculiar and conventional, as too poetical and yet somehow not poetic enough. There is a certain confusion about Emerson's verse; many even suspect that – technically – it is slightly inept. Compared to the eloquent cascades of the essays, the poems feel cramped, terse, and odd. It is, of course, not unusual to find a writer who is gifted in one genre to be less so in another, but when we attribute so much artistry and genius to the prose writer, we should be wary about an assumption that those same qualities disappear when the same writer turns his hand to verse. Eventually, we might wonder why is it that so many critics do not read the poetry with the same generosity and attention that they do the prose? The answer, again, may be largely because of the nature of the verse – which is to say, because of the decisions Emerson made about the kind of poetry that he wished to write. Those decisions are enormously important in determining the quality of his verse, and, in approaching Emerson's poetry, it is worth our while to inquire into his sense of his own poetic project.

We can start by looking first at an early and untitled manuscript poem that Emerson wrote in June 1827, when he was 24 (LOA, 1: 344). It begins:

Awed I behold once more
My old familiar haunts; here the blue river
The same blue wonder that my infant eye
Admired, sage doubting whence the traveller came, –
Whence brought his sunny bubbles ere he washed
The fragrant flag roots in my father's fields,
And where thereafter in the world he went.
Look, here he is unaltered, save that now
He hath broke his banks & flooded all the vales
With his redundant waves.

The river here is the Concord River, which he elsewhere refers to by its original name, Musketaquid. But the accents of the blank verse recall another river, William Wordsworth's Wye in Monmouthshire, England, the setting of the "Tintern Abbey" ode. Emerson's poem is clearly indebted to Wordsworthian themes of recollected youth and natural piety. Where Wordsworth claims that "other gifts / Have followed; for such loss, I would believe, / Abundant recompense," Emerson echoes:

These are the same, but I am not the same
But wiser than I was, & wise enough
Not to regret the changes, tho' they cost
Me many a sigh.

In addition to Wordsworth, one hears the blank verse and the often melancholy and elegiac tone of earlier sensibility poets such as James Thomson, Thomas Gray, and William Cowper, as in the final stanza of this poem:

I feel as I were welcome to these trees
After long months of weary wandering,
Acknowledged by their hospitable boughs;
They know me as their son, for side by side,
They were coeval with my ancestors,
Adorned with them my country's primitive times,
And soon may give my dust their funeral shade.

After noting the Wordsworthian parallels, Harold Bloom claims that had Emerson continued in this vein, he would have become a better poet. It is certainly likely that if he had so continued that Emerson would have become a more popular poet, more in tune with the "fireside poets" – William Cullen **Bryant**, Henry Wadsworth **Longfellow**, James Russell **Lowell**, and Oliver Wendell **Holmes**. But although Emerson would subsequently write a good many poems in iambic pentameter, he moved away from the easy cadences of the blank verse that he mastered early on, and it is not clear that he was a worse poet for it. This conscious decision by Emerson to eschew the dominant meter of his time results in a far more distinct, idiosyncratic, and original line. This is exemplified by a poem such as "Give All to Love" (LOA, 1: 288), which opens:

Give all to love;
Obey thy heart;
Friends, kindred, days,
Estate, good-fame,
Plans, credit, and the Muse, –
Nothing refuse.

The short lines, the erratic rhyming, and the staccato delivery are all hallmarks of a new style that Emerson cultivated. It is not calculated to strike us as mellifluous or urbane, or even particularly accomplished. But as exemplified in this poem, which turns away from conventional consolations for the loss of love, the deliberate paring down creates striking effects:

Though thou loved her as thyself,
As a self of purer clay,
Though her parting dims the day,
Stealing grace from all alive;
Heartily know,
When half-gods go,
The gods arrive.

Emerson here turns from the great "half-gods" of canonical poetry (whom he nevertheless continues to regard as semi-divine) in order to invite in the "gods" themselves – that is, the uncompromising resonance of a bardic and prophetic voice that sounds in his strongest poems. Once we realize that the effects of Emerson's poems are, by and large, precisely the ones that he intends, we can readjust our focus and begin to see the poems for what they are, and not for what they fail to do conventionally. What Samuel Taylor Coleridge said of criticisms of William Shakespeare applies equally to Emerson, that it would be "the mere dreams of a pedantry that arraigned the eagle because it had not the dimensions of the swan." Indeed, as the composer Charles Ives once put it, "If Emerson's manner is not always beautiful in accordance with accepted standards, why not accept a few other standards?" The real proof of the matter, however, will come from the results of our reading Emerson's poems carefully and with a full sense of their design upon us.

Ralph Waldo Emerson was born in Boston, Massachusetts, on May 25, 1803, Election Day, into a family distinguished by a long line of Protestant ministers. Of the 10 children (eight boys and two girls) born to his parents, William and Ruth Haskins Emerson, only five brothers survived childhood, and Emerson, one of the weakest children initially, outlived them all. The family was scourged by tuberculosis, and there is good reason to believe that Emerson himself was ill with it at various times. Consumption was responsible for the death of his father (in Emerson's eighth year); of at least three of his brothers, John, Edward, and Charles; and, most tragically for Emerson, of his first wife, Ellen Tucker, after little more than a year of marriage in 1831. Ellen's death seemed to precipitate a crisis in Emerson's affairs, bringing to a head his misgivings about his ministry at the South Church in Boston (which he soon resigned) and propelling him, through the sheer force of his inconsolable grief, into a new mode of verse.

Up to 1831, Emerson (who began writing poetry at the age of nine) composed verses on eighteenth-century models or on earlier Renaissance forms. We find poems in heroic couplets, blank verse, hymn meters, and ballad measures, as well as the frequent use of fixed forms such as sonnets or tail-rhyme and *Venus and Adonis* stanzas. It is good to keep this early training in mind when confronting Emerson's later poetry because it foregrounds his unconventional intentions. The opening sextet of "Good-Bye" is characteristic of this early period:

Good-bye, proud world! I'm going home:
Thou art not my friend, and I'm not thine.
Long through thy weary crowds I roam;

A river-ark on the ocean brine,
Long I've been tossed like the driven foam;
But now, proud world! I'm going home.

Equally typical of this early style are the love poems that Emerson wrote to his fiancée and young wife, Ellen, all of which deploy traditional tropes and forms. That mode, however, shifted dramatically in 1831 when Ellen died. Subsequent to her death, we find in manuscript numerous elegies written in what might be termed "broken forms," unusual poems having passages that range from pathetic outpourings –

And now I am alone
Unheard I moan
She never comes to me
Sits never by my side
I never hear her voice
She comes not even to my dreams
O Ellen
> ("She never comes to me")

– to surprisingly bitter and caustic complaints:

Teach me I am forgotten by the dead
And that the dead is by herself forgot
And I no longer would keep terms with me.
I would not murder, steal, or fornicate,
Nor with ambition break the peace of towns
But I would bury my ambition
The hope & action of my sovereign soul
In miserable ruin.
> ("What avails it me")

A more measured but equally disconsolate expression is found in another unpublished poem, addressed to William Emerson in 1831, "Dear brother, would you know the life" (LOA, 1: 345). After announcing that he would rather go off and live in the woods by himself than stay in "this weary town," Emerson says,

There will I bring my books, my household gods,
The reliquaries of my dead saint, & dwell
In the sweet odor of her memory.
There, in the uncouth solitude, unlock
My stock of art, plant dials, in the grass,
Hang in the air a bright thermometer,
And aim a telescope at the inviolate Sun.

The odd juxtaposition of "uncouth solitude" with scientific items (dial, thermometer, and telescope) bespeaks a double desire to dwell upon a human inner past and to reach out toward an objectified nature, something other than oneself. This dual impulse is something Emerson soon abandons in the light of vision, when the "transparent eyeball" invoked in his book *Nature* apparently subsumes both self and nature into a transcendental unity. But here his grief is the overwhelming fact of his existence.

Taken together, the "Ellen Poems" show the transition in Emerson's poetry from an adherence to traditional form to a far more experimental and heterodox style. In the crucible of his mourning, he works new forms that afterward mark the range of possibilities in his poetry. From 1831 on, Emerson has at his disposal not only conventional forms, which he contin-

ues to use in his own way, but idiosyncratic and ad hoc forms that allow him a new freedom and that become the vehicle for his often stark originality.

The year 1834 has been termed by one scholar Emerson's "year of poetic maturity." There is some merit to this notion, since a cluster of fine poems was written that year: "The Rhodora" (LOA, 1: 272), "Each and All" (LOA, 1: 258), "Compensation" (LOA, 1: 287), and "The Snow-Storm" (LOA, 1: 274) – all among his best-known and most accessible works. But there is one poem, "Grace" (LOA, 1: 336), written the year before, that is remarkable for its apparent disjunction from the ideas of self-reliance and the soul that Emerson was then working out for his first book, *Nature*. "Grace" is surprisingly Calvinist in orientation:

How much, Preventing God! how much I owe
To the defences thou hast round me set:
Example, custom, fear, occasion slow; –
These scorned bondmen were my parapet.
I dare not peep over this parapet,
To gauge with glance the roaring gulf below,
The depths of sin to which I had descended,
Had not these me against myself defended.

The first draft of this poem was found on the inside front cover of a volume of Milton's prose works, so the occasion of the poem may owe something to the effect of Milton's stern Puritanism. But the real influence here is George Herbert, a poet Emerson greatly admired. In fact, when the poem was included anonymously as an epigraph to Emerson's chapter of the *Memoirs of Margaret Fuller Ossoli* in 1852, it was attributed to Herbert by William Ellery **Channing**, much to Emerson's bemused gratification. The poem is clearly modeled after Herbert's poem "Sinne," which begins, "Lord, with what care hast thou begirt us round!" Although "Grace" may have been something of an exercise for Emerson – imaginatively entering into a mode of piety not his own – it is also probably a genuine expression of the Calvinist schooling that he received as a boy, particularly at the hands of his strong-willed aunt, Mary Moody Emerson, who firmly urged the revivalist "New Light" Calvinism associated with the Great Awakening. Every item in "Grace," each one of those "scorned bondmen" ("Example, custom, fear, occasion slow"), will soon be rejected and overturned by Emerson. Hereafter, it is not a "Preventing God" that he turns to but an enabling one, whose divine grace is made identical with oneself.

Emerson left the ministry in 1832 and spent most of the next year abroad, where he met, and was largely unimpressed with, Walter Savage Landor, John Stuart Mill, Wordsworth, and Coleridge. When Emerson eventually returned to Boston, he continued to preach most Sundays. Emerson's preaching was gradually replaced or secularized by his lecturing, from whence came his published essays; thus, his break with the Unitarian church was not itself a break in the continuity of his religious interests. A transvaluation of ideas takes place for Emerson during this period, but with this basic continuum functioning as a transcendental ground. Years later, in "The Problem" (partially written one day in church in 1839; LOA, 1: 259), Emerson reflects upon the problematic attraction of the ministry:

I like a church; I like a cowl;
I love a prophet of the soul;
And on my heart monastic aisles
Fall like sweet strains, or pensive smiles;
Yet not for all his faith can see
Would I that cowled churchman be.

Why should the vest on him allure,
Which I could not on me endure?

This poem has its beginnings, typically, in a prose passage in Emerson's journals, a source that he mined for both poems and essays. The journal entry makes an interesting gloss on "The Problem" and illustrates how Emerson later reworked such passages into verse. The entry is dated August 28, 1838:

> It is very grateful to me to go into an English Church [Anglican] & hear the liturgy read. Yet nothing would induce me to be the English priest. I find an unpleasant dilemma in this, nearer home. I dislike to be a clergyman & refuse to be one. Yet how rich a music would be to me a holy clergyman in my town. It seems to me he cannot be a man, quite & whole. Yet how plain is the need of one, & how high yes highest is the function. Here is Division of labor that I like not. A man must sacrifice his manhood for the social good. Something is wrong I see not what.

By the time Emerson comes to write "Uriel" (1845; LOA, 1: 264), this sense of dilemma is resolved. Following the uproar over Emerson's "Divinity School Address" at Harvard University, which enraged his old teachers and galvanized the Unitarian elite against him (Emerson was banned from Harvard for almost 30 years), the only course open to him was that of a "fallen angel" espousing an ironic and defiant self-knowledge. Before turning to the major poems of the 1840s, however, we need to look at two more of his "mature" poems and some of the characteristic features and themes of that verse.

"Each and All" works Emerson's dialectic of unity and multiplicity, and it does so through the agency of the senses of sight and hearing. As with so many of Emerson's poems, it is concerned with the way in which a moment of perception alters one's sense of reality. It opens with an image of distant and unapprehended vision: "Little thinks, in the field, yon red-cloaked clown, / Of thee from the hill-top looking down." The farmboy does not know that he is being watched or seen, and is therefore part of a larger scene; but the perspective is not simply voyeuristic here, since the "all" of vision would take in the seer in the process of seeing as well. This perspective recalls the "transparent eyeball" passage in *Nature*, where Emerson states, "I am nothing; I see all." But the poem proceeds to shift away from this problematic to consider the natural ground of perception – the way in which beauty is a holistic sensory phenomenon. No image of beauty – the sparrow's song, the seashells, or the maiden – can be abstracted from the whole of its context and still delight us in the same way. The disappointment attendant upon this discovery leads the speaker to turn away from the pursuit of beauty in order to pursue the more ascetic way of knowledge: "Then I said, 'I covet truth; / Beauty is unripe childhood's cheat; / I leave it behind with the games of youth.'"

In a romantic reprise, we discover that there can be no truth without beauty, and no beauty without the senses. Despite himself, the speaker sees the ground-pine curling over club moss, smells the violets at his feet, hears the morning songbird, and becomes aware of the context of forest and sky and river: "Beauty through my senses stole; / I yielded myself to the perfect whole." The perfect whole here would seem to be a unity of thought and impression, of the individual with the universal, and of each and all: "All are needed by each one; / Nothing is fair or good alone." But the whole is also the poem itself, since it is only by means of the poem that one comes to the perception (or perfection) of the opening vision or perspective. We find that the "red-cloaked clown," the lowing heifer, the sexton, and we ourselves (in relation to our neighbors) are all implicated in an ignorance: none is aware of the whole picture. Even in yielding to a sense of wholeness, the speaker – by implication – must still undergo a moment of negation whereby he suddenly sees that he is ignorant of the implications of that moment. It is the poem, and the process of poetry itself, that provides this perspective. The seductive close of the poem, where we yield to the pretty perfection of the whole, is subtly complicated by the ever-widening perspectivism that inheres in the opening lines. "Each and All" is a good example of how Emerson's poems can be very quirky and cunning – much like Emily **Dickinson's** poetry, which seems indebted to this aspect of Emerson's style.

In "The Snow-Storm," Emerson once again turns to nature to find a structure for transcendence. The poem divides nicely into two sections: the first presents the outward phenomenon of the storm and culminates in the lines that inspired John Greenleaf **Whittier** to write his famous poem "Snow-Bound" (LOA, 1: 476):

> The sled and traveller stopped, the courier's feet
> Delayed, all friends shut out, the housemates sit
> Around the radiant fireplace, enclosed
> In a tumultuous privacy of storm.

The second section then turns inward and begins to reflect upon the first. We are asked to "Come see the north wind's masonry," which is "wild work." Here, nature – that "fierce artificer" in the guise of the north wind – seems to mock human enterprise. Emerson's poems often enact a correspondence between nature and consciousness, but here we find the snowstorm astonishing art, which can only patiently and laboriously "mimic in slow structures, stone by stone" the swiftness of "the mad wind's night-work, / The frolic architecture of the snow." What correspondence there is seems to work to the disadvantage of humanity, and it is often the case that the way of nature is – in Emerson's phrase – "a little rude." But the analogy at work here is also an opposition between genius and talent, between the inspiration of the bard and the artfulness of the versifier. Transposed to another key, it is the opposition between divine intuitive reason and the discursive diurnal faculty of the understanding (a distinction Emerson derives from Coleridge's account of Kantian philosophy). What Emerson says of the north wind he says equally of the bardic poet, the "fierce artificer" whose work is "So fanciful, so savage, nought cares he / For number or proportion." This is the figure that Emerson celebrates in his essay "The Poet":

The poets are thus liberating gods. The ancient British bards had for the title of their order, "Those who are free throughout the world." They are free, and they make free. An imaginative book renders us much more service at first, by stimulating us through its tropes, than afterward when we arrive at the precise sense of the author. I think nothing is of any value in books excepting the transcendental and extraordinary.

Such sentiments, "transcendental and extraordinary" in themselves, are what propel Emerson into his runic and bardic mode. Although traces of each of Emerson's various styles can be found throughout his entire career, concentrations of poems during specific periods seem to indicate long-term shifts in his poetic activity. We see it in the Ellen poems of the early 1830s; again in the "mature poems" of 1834; and once again in the poems of the 1840s, especially those written around 1845–46 – "Hamatreya" (LOA, 1: 270), "Ode, Inscribed to W. H. Channing" (LOA, 1: 282), "Merlin I" and "Merlin II" (LOA, 1: 294, 297), and "Bacchus" (LOA, 1: 298) – which testify to a renewed intensity of visionary purpose.

Emerson found in the bardic literature of the early Welsh poets and in the runic lines of the Anglo-Saxon poets models for some of the effects that he was trying to attain. Although he was influenced in part by the subject matter of the eighteenth-century "bardic revival" of Gray, James Macpherson, and others, who emphasized a vatic romance element, it is really the free form of the Welsh fragments and the short lines of the Anglo-Saxon poems that underwrite Emerson's formal experimentation in such poems as "Merlin I" and "Merlin II," "Hamatreya," the Channing "Ode," "Bacchus," "Ode to Beauty," "The Past," "Terminus" (LOA, 1: 331), and a number of others. Emerson thus arrived at another expedient form with which to augment the repertoire of his poetic practice. It gave him the opportunity to put the "artful thunder" of strong-stress metrical lines into combination with the symmetrical and, for him, metaphysical necessities of rhyme. That potent combination suggests for Emerson an extraordinary possibility for poetry; as he puts it in one journal entry:

Rhyme; not tinkling rhyme but grand Pindaric strokes as firm as the tread of a horse. Rhyme that vindicates itself as an art, the stroke of the bell of a cathedral. Rhyme which knocks at prose & dulness with the stroke of a cannon ball. Rhyme which builds out of Chaos & Old night a splendid architecture to bridge the impassable, & call aloud on all the children of morning that the Creation is recommencing. I wish to write such rhymes as shall not suggest a restraint but contrariwise the wildest freedom.

This sense of the power of poetry informs the "Merlin" poems of 1846.

Although "Merlin I" and "Merlin II" can be taken as separate and distinct poems, they are directly related. The second part of "Merlin" was written first, and it begins with an apparent allusion to the Arthurian court. However, Emerson's Merlin is a composite of two Merlins, the sixth-century Welsh bard (Myrddhin) and the more familiar legendary Merlin. Although Emerson's version remains a mixture of these two throughout, in "Merlin I" the bardic figure predominates, while in "Merlin II" the court magician is preeminent.

At the beginning of "Merlin I," Emerson, in the bardic guise of Merlin/Myrddhin, presents us with an *ars poetica* and a critique of contemporary practice. Here are the opening quatrains of the first stanza:

Thy trivial harp will never please
Or fill my craving ear;
Its chords should ring as blows the breeze,
Free, peremptory, clear.
No jingling serenader's art,
Nor tinkle of piano strings,
Can make the wild blood start
In its mystic springs.

The famous first quatrain opposes the "trivial harp" of closeted convention to the organic urgency of ringing chords. The figure suggests that most Romantic of tropes, the Aeolian harp. That instrument – through which "blows the breeze, / Free, peremptory, clear" – is the very opposite of the piano, where the strings are enclosed and the action mechanical. The point is the familiar one, that the poet is to be a denizen of natural inspiration, not a mere designer of cultural artifacts. The second quatrain ends with a call for an art that moves the "wild blood" suddenly in its "mystic springs." We are then told that the "kingly bard" (he who can modulate the king's affairs in "Merlin II") must strike the chords hard and with authority (since the "mace" refers both to the war club and to the symbol of power) in order to "render back / Artful thunder." The poem goes on to present images of inward or outward power that reveal the strength implicit in opposition and violence. These are representations of "Power" seeking release or expression. But we should not mistake these images of correspondence or "Chiming" for a poetic program of mimetic form. Merlin's blows chime with these phenomena (wind, thunder) in the sense that they partake of the same essential power. It is not, however, thereby a call for a poetry that gasps and moans and is full of din. That is a later *ars poetica* based on a misreading of Emerson's poetics. Artful thunder is intended to bring about flashes of insight; on its own and for itself, such thunder is of no use.

The bard's "great art" is the result of his leaving behind "rule and pale forethought," for "He shall aye climb / For his rhyme." The play here on "aye" is dense: it reads as an affirmation that, indeed, "I climb," which is echoed at the same time by a "yes." That process is almost always expressed by Emerson as a matter of perception, hence of the "eye," which is echoed now by the sense of "aye" as "ever" or "always." Hence, in unpacking the trope, we get something like, "I am the ever onward eye of yes," the affirming principle of poetry. The rhythmic pattern of the line underscores the density, since each of the three adjacent stresses ("shall aye climb") enforces a steplike pause, and as a sequence they move the performance of the sounds from the back of the mouth to the front, as if climbing up and out into space.

The next line, spoken by the angels, shifts the locale of the poem and suggests a present reality: "'Pass in, pass in,' the angels say, / 'In to the upper doors'." The poet is then advised not to be distracted by the compartments or the rooms on the floors (something a poet like Edmund Spenser would have lavished cantos on), but rather to "mount" directly "to paradise / By the stairway of surprise.'" The rhyming here is indicative of the necessity, the instrumentality, of "surprise" in its relation to "paradise." This is the Emersonian procedure of "surprise," that uplifting, discontinuous leap into sudden transcendence, the transparent seeing that comes with a moment of paradisaical awareness. This is what artful thunder is intended to convey, although the experience is difficult to define in other than Emersonian terms. It is clearly meant to be something other than just an epistemological category, since it involves matters of being as well as knowing.

At the end of the poem we find that the doors of perception close as mystifyingly as they open: they are "Self-moved," in that they seem to close by themselves. But we are also to read "Self-moved" as self-motivated, that we ourselves are somehow responsible for this closure. This is a dark suggestion, since it summons forth (or foreshadows) the idea of Nemesis in "Merlin II" – a self-correcting fate of constant alternation, a goddess of corresponding retribution for each godlike moment of transcendence. (This is borne out in the original manuscript version, which reads: "Then suddenly the hours shut / Nor word of angels could reveal / What they conceal.") The substitution of "doors" for "hours" and the reappearance of "angels" create an ironic resonance here with the paradise of the second stanza. That Edenic vision is now over; at the end of the poem we are driven from the Garden, and the "sword/word" of the penultimate line suggests the figure of the Archangel Michael and his "brandisht Sword of God" at the close of *Paradise Lost*. Yet even that "flaming Brand" could not "reveal," or unveil, what is now hidden. Merlin's power is unlimited while it flows, but when it stops he is powerless to command it. He must "climb / For his rhyme," but the angels must be there to allow him to pass in. The poem ends in similar fashion to "Merlin II," where "the two twilights of the day / Fold us music-drunken in." The closure is complete, fatal. "Merlin I" ends with the word "conceal," marking a mysterious thwarting of vision. In a very literal and iconic sense, the word also marks the end of the inspiration that drives the poem. Both parts of "Merlin" conclude on somber notes, in contrast to the heights each probes. And yet, the vision of each is neither elided nor altogether compromised; it is qualified by that portion of the truth it first represses. Emerson, in his horror of partiality, is always, in the end, willing to embrace horror itself, literally "dread" (*horrere*) – the aspect of awareness that stands at "the brink of fear." The method and "metaphysics" of rhyme require it.

The progression in "Merlin II" from nature to thought to fate is meant to be precisely the "rhyme" that "Modulates the king's affairs." The trajectory of ultimate justice demands of the poet this cautionary tale of correspondence and compensation. Merlin is, after all, the king's adviser and soothsayer, and all that ever can be predicted is the truth of reality. That it may seem ruthless is perhaps accounted for by the rhyming presence of "ruth" within "truth."

In addition to his numerous prophetic and meditative lyrics, Emerson also published six long poems: "Woodnotes I," "Woodnotes II" (LOA, 1: 275), "Monadnoc" (LOA, 1: 280), "Initial, Dæmonic, and Celestial Love" (LOA, 1: 290), "May-Day," and "The Adirondacs." One critic has referred to some of these long poems as "rambles," and that is a good term for

their "sociable" and loose construction. But to give a better sense of the range of Emerson's poetry, it might be useful to note the various categories of poems that he could be said to have composed. The following dozen groupings are not exact or rigorously delineated, but they do suggest a spectrum of poetic activity:

(1) *philosophic*: here, we would include "The Problem," "The World-Soul" (LOA, 1: 265), "The Sphinx" (LOA, 1: 254), "Brahma" (LOA, 1: 319), "Nemesis," "Fate" (LOA, 1: 341), "Una," "Love and Thought," and "The Past";

(2) *political and public poems*: "Ode, Inscribed to W. H. Channing," the Concord "Hymn" (LOA, 1: 318), "Boston Hymn," "Voluntaries" (LOA, 1: 320), "Boston," and the epigrams on Daniel Webster;

(3) *prophetic or bardic poems*: "Uriel" (LOA, 1: 264), both "Merlin" poems, "Bacchus," and "Saadi" (LOA, 1: 300);

(4) *meditative poems*: "Each and All," "Hamatreya," "The Rhodora," "The Humble-Bee" (LOA, 1: 272), "The Snow-Storm," "Musketaquid" (LOA, 1: 308), "Days" (LOA, 1: 324), "My Garden," "The Titmouse," "Two Rivers" (LOA, 1: 329), and "Waldeinsamkeit" (LOA, 1: 329);

(5) *elegiac poems*: the unpublished poems to Ellen, "Blight" (LOA, 1: 307), "Dirge," "Threnody" (LOA, 1: 311), "Terminus," and "In Memoriam E. B. E.";

(6) *didactic poems*: "The Visit" (LOA, 1: 263), "Give All To Love" (LOA, 1: 288), "Sursum Corda" (LOA, 1: 288), "Initial, Dæmonic and Celestial Love," "The Apology," "Xenophanes" (LOA, 1: 305), "Merlin's Song," "Sea-Shore" (LOA, 1: 324), and "Song of Nature" (LOA, 1: 326);

(7) *rambles*: "Woodnotes" (I and II), "Monadnoc," "May-Day," and "The Adirondacs";

(8) *gnomic poems*: here we would find most of the "mottos" and "elements," and various of the "quatrains";

(9) *dramatic monologues* (or personae poems): "The Nun's Aspiration," "The Chartist's Complaint," "The Romany Girl," "Maiden Speech of the Æolian Harp," and portions of several other poems (such as "Monadnoc" and "Woodnotes");

(10) *love poems*: almost exclusively those from among the early poems to Ellen, but also including some of the translations;

(11) *translations*: the many poems from Persian authors (including Omar Khayyám and Hafiz), poems of Michelangelo and others, and Emerson's translation of Dante's *Vita Nuova*;

(12) *squibs*: short, often satiric verses (mostly found in the journals and notebooks).

Although this list does not account for all of Emerson's poems and does not do justice to the often mixed generic modes that he employed, it does help us to see the breadth of his poetry in the formal terms of genre. This is important to keep in mind, since we only have space here to look at a few poems, and this may limit or distort our sense of what Emerson actually accomplished. An extended discussion of one poem may be of help, however, in establishing the kinds of poetic concerns that Emerson had in general. There are a number of excellent readings of Emerson poems, so we will close our discussion of his poetry by looking in detail at one poem that has received relatively less attention, "Hamatreya."

The title, "Hamatreya," is a deformation of a person's name (Maitreye) that Emerson encountered in his reading of the Hindu sacred text, the *Vishnu Purána*. By substituting the Greek prefix *hama*, meaning "at the same time" or "all together," Emerson expanded the audience and the implication of the poem (as we will see). As a title, this strange word acts as a foil to the opening lines of the poem by juxtaposing a Hindu name with the parochial names of Concord, Massachusetts. This disparity of locale is the first of several deliberate surprises in the poem.

The six names in the opening line comprise an honor roll of the early settlers of Concord, and we are told that they "Possessed the land," which in turn yielded them the eight commodities listed in the third line. But the insistent parallelism should alert us to the possible irony of equating men with things, as if both "merely" partake of the same nature. As we will see, possession becomes an increasingly problematic term in the poem, but here at the beginning everything seems straightforward enough. The men, "these landlords," then speak (line 5), claiming their land as not only theirs and their children's, but their "name's" as well. This brings forward a central concern in the poem about the relation between property and the proper name, as to whether the act of naming is itself an act of appropriation. The poem will go on to question the notion of ownership, but for now the landlords (in line 7) continue to declaim about their holdings, each one admiring the shadows that climb his hill and fancying that the waters and the "flags" (both stones and cattails) "Know me, as does my dog: we sympathize; / And, I affirm, my actions smack of the soil." At this point, the language of the poem, which has bordered on the ironic, is finally revealed to be so when the poet turns and asks, "Where are these men?" The answer is: "Asleep beneath their grounds; / And strangers, fond as they, their furrows plough." The shadows they so admired, it turns out, were harbingers of death, which gracefully climbed the hill toward them; the "sympathy" they felt with water and "flags" and their dogs was not identification with something transcendental but corresponded with the lower and grosser elements of the natural world. Their actions did indeed "smack of the soil," since soil has become their milieu. Their grounds are no longer theirs, since others, equally fond of the land (and equally "foolish," as "fond" still meant), plow "their" furrows. Ownership, it seems, is a superfluous ambition.

This sudden shift of perspective in the poem is meant to shock. It is a disruptive crossing from one frame of reference to another, from the retrospective calm of a loco-descriptive meditation to the ironic mode of a satire. What we have is a reversal of the *ubi sunt* tradition, where the transitoriness of life is affirmed but not actually lamented. The initial list of names is not of "makars" (as in William Dunbar) but of presumptuous farmers undone by Nemesis. We detect, in the insufficient ground of their stance, what Emerson called in his essay "Circles" the "slight dislocations, which apprize us that this surface on which we now stand is not fixed, but sliding." Once this perspective is broached, Emerson drives home the point:

Earth laughs in flowers, to see her boastful boys
Earth-proud, proud of the earth which is not theirs;
Who steer the plough, but cannot steer their feet
Clear of the grave.

The men have been reduced to "boastful boys" who are unaware of their own hubris, and (in line 16) they are brought up short. The truncated line, "Clear of the grave," is an instance of iconic form acting as ironic form, where the blank space after the line is a literal absence. The revealing enjambment in line 15 and the dense repetition of "earth" and "steer" and "proud" compress the thought into a grim disdain. The remainder of this section of the poem is an accretion of mockery. The avarice of the landlords causes them to sigh "for all that bounded their domain," not realizing that death is what actually bounded it. They call for more dirt ("clay, lime, gravel, granite-ledge"), as if in sympathy with it, and look for a lowland "where to go for peat," the decomposed vegetal matter for which they are destined. They cross the sea and back and appreciate their "sitfast acres," but in the crossing to come, it will be they who will sit fast. The colloquial diction that Emerson uses here for their speech becomes a parody of Yankee practicality and self-satisfaction; it has a sort of deadly charm. He ends this section with an apostrophe, "Ah! the hot owner sees not Death, who adds / Him to his land, a lump of mould the more," which equates the landlord with a lump of dirt and completes the reversal of ownership (whereby Death, in collusion with the Earth, adds the landlord to the property of cold nature). The heroic names of the first line are thus crossed out. The poet then turns once again and asks us to "Hear what the Earth says." The "Earth-Song" opens:

'Mine and yours;
Mine, not yours.
Earth endures;
Stars abide –
Shine down in the old sea;
Old are the shores;
But where are old men?
I who have seen much,
Such have I never seen.'

In the "Earth-Song," we move from the blank verse of the first section to a highly condensed runic line, where the irregular rhymes and the strong-stress metric continually disconcert us with an unpredictable patterning. It is as if everything has been stripped away, the early charm and countenance of the opening excoriated, which leaves us with a chant of unnaming. The entirety of the section is contained in miniature in the first two lines, "'Mine and yours; / Mine, not yours.'" The first affirms a co-ownership, the second negates it; a man's history is thus encapsulated, his loud boast cut short by a radical decrescendo. Humanity does not have the substantiality of the natural world, which "endures" and can "abide"; whatever sympathetic and anthropomorphic sense we may have of nature, it is an alien Other. The Earth speaks of a temporal realm beyond the ken of humankind, of old seas and old shores. "But where are old men?" the Earth asks; "I who have seen much, / Such have I never seen."

There is something of complaint or perplexity in that last statement. In the second stanza, the Earth points to the "lawyer's deed," the legal and binding contract that entailed the land and restricted it to the lineal descendants of the owners. In the poem, it comes across as a parody of legal language, where the sense of the terms gets reversed such that "Who shall succeed, / Without fail, / Forevermore" might as well read "Who shall fail, / Without success, / Forevermore." Despite the legal agreement, the actual result – in the next stanza – is that the land ("Shaggy with wood, / With its old valley") remains but is without any of its "heritors." Indeed, not only they but (in progressively larger categories) the lawyers, the laws, and the kingdom itself are "Clean swept herefrom," like mere foam on the surface of a stream. The contract, it would seem, has been broken, the "understanding" not carried through.

In its last stanza, the Earth speaks in a displaced vocabulary of freedom and slavery, where ownership, control, and desire are ironized by a naming that is a failed appropriation ("'They called me theirs'" – but they are gone). And then the critical question is asked: "'How am I theirs, / If they cannot hold me, / But I hold them?'" We now read this in the context of the severe irony of the poem's first section, and so it seems entirely a rhetorical question. When we recall how "Earth laughs in flowers" (line 13), this last flourish becomes an even grimmer joke. And yet, when taken on its own, the tone of the "Earth-Song" is not so easily ascertained. After all, it is only on the basis of the speaker's perspective that we read the second section as deliberately ironic. It is equally possible to read the last question as a grammatical proposition, a genuine question, which would drain the "Earth-Song" of its ironic and dissembling aspect, and thus leave us with a tone of naive incomprehension. If that is the case, then the Earth truly does not understand humanity and has no capacity for ridicule. Depending on how we read it, the "Earth-Song" is either the cynical chant of a powerful rhetor or the credulous dirge of an artless grammarian. The tone, once we set aside the framing or hermeneutic imposition of the initial speaker, hovers between the two possibilities. The question of interpretation now becomes paramount, since the last stanza of the poem presents us with the speaker or poet reading this section of his own poem:

> When I heard the Earth-song,
> I was no longer brave;
> My avarice cooled
> Like lust in the chill of the grave.

Having heard the foregoing "song," the poet responds not only with a loss of bravery and a cooling of avarice, but presumably with an act of writing. That is to say, the external impingement upon the self by a sublime Other (the Earth) brings forth the poem "Hamatreya" itself. Thus, the entire first section and the final quatrain together embrace the "Earth-Song" and offer an interpretative response to it, one based on a rhetorical reading of the song. The crux of the entire poem is in the poet's reaction, which is presented here in the litotes of the last two lines, where the question of avarice or desire (paralleling that of the early settlers') is related to bravery or self-sufficiency, to whatever it is that drives someone toward a founding moment. The poet's avarice is "cooled / Like lust in the chill of the grave," but lust (whether thought of as pleasure, craving, or lasciviousness) does not cool down in the grave, it is utterly extinguished. The image is deliberately unsettling, particularly in its subtle equation of avarice and lust (and the Pauline allusion to the wages of sin). This mode of surprising the reader, which is meant to instill fear and awe before a chilling reality, is nonetheless a "descendentalized" sublime: there is no transcendental perspective offered – the entire passage reeks of mortality. Such surprises, in taking us unawares, make us aware and wary of the fact that we are always threatened by death, an aspect of nature's power. In this instance, the poet yields to that power, and, if we take into account the later revi-

sion of the first line ("Bulkeley, Hunt, Willard, Hosmer, Meriam, Flint"), it appears that Emerson ironically aligns himself with the "landlords," since Bulkeley was one of Emerson's own ancestors. In the end, then, the poem seems at odds with the transcendentalist version of nature so often celebrated in Emerson's early essays. The poet's response to the "Earth-Song" indicates a chastisement. But, we may ask, what is the status of the poet's interpretation of the "Earth-Song"? How are we to interpret his interpretation?

At this point, once we have grasped the hermeneutic impulse of the poem, it is important to see that the temporal order of the sections has been reversed and that the poem is an inversion of the usual pattern of the negative sublime (that is, possession, resistance, and then recuperation). The "Earth-Song" is meant to have occurred prior to the rest of the poem as a sublime revelation to the poet, followed not so much by resistance as by a collapse into the over-mastered withdrawal of the final quatrain. This collapse determines the "new attitude" that the poem adopts in the opening section leading up to the "Earth-Song." The sublime encounter does not result in the mind recognizing its own power in the face of the Other since there is no recuperation, only a diminishment of the self into a defensive, ironic, and critical stance meant to accommodate the negativity of a surprising reversal. Men had thought that they possessed the land but are instead themselves possessed, like the poet, by a sublime power, death. This is the very opposite of the Romantic or egotistical sublime and represents a failed apocalypse for the poetic imagination. At the same time, it is still based on a rhetorical reading of the "Earth-Song" that forecloses the possibility of a transcendental dialectic, since the Earth is seen in ironic, almost malevolent, terms. Were the "Earth-Song" to be read "grammatically" – as a genuine perplexity – the poet would have the possibility of identifying, metonymically, with the power revealed to him because it would remain more as an available force of power than as an agent of fate (or Nemesis, as in "Merlin II"). Put in these Emersonian terms, the verse represents the old antagonism between power and fate, or of the power that can be said to inhere in fate:

> For, if Fate is so prevailing, man also is part of it, and can confront fate with fate. If the Universe have these savage accidents, our atoms are as savage in resistance. We should be crushed by the atmosphere, but for the reaction of the air within the body. A tube made of a film of glass can resist the shock of the ocean, if filled with the same water. If there be omnipotence in the stroke, there is omnipotence of recoil. ("Fate")

This response, this sublime resistance, is apparently evaded or eviscerated in the poem; it is the other side of a poetics that we saw manifest in "Merlin I," where the poet "shall aye climb / For his rhyme" in order to receive the imparadising insight and in-flowing of power – a response that, as Emerson puts it, "throws us on the party and interest of the Universe, against all and sundry; against ourselves as much as others" ("Fate"). As a poem, "Hamatreya" appears to represent the voice of fate; as a title, however, "Hamatreya" points to a dialectic of fate and power (similar to Hegel's *Aufhebung*, a simultaneous negation and elevation), inasmuch as we must rise to the perception of "all together" (*hama*) in order to cross over into sublimity. This approach would invoke the alternative interpretation or counter-text of "Hamatreya," the other reading of the Other. In this version, we are asked to transcend the limited perspective of the poet's response to the "Earth-Song" and reject the imaginative defeat that it records. Or, working more directly through the poem's perspective, it asks us to abandon the avarice of worldly ownership in order to own up to our real inheritance, which is "part or particle of God" (*Nature*). Such a reading involves a radical act of interpretation, since it undoes the poet's own interpretation, or so it would seem. The fact that the poem foregrounds interpretation by constituting itself as an interpretation suggests that Emerson is once again bent on forcing us out of any easy complacency. This alternate interpretation, however, does not necessarily present a more correct perception. Depending on whether we read with the grain, as it were, or against it, we have two versions of the poem that the poem supports. To put this in more theoretical terms, although these alternating interpretations of "Hamatreya" are ultimately incompatible, it is not therefore *undecidability* itself that we should look for in Emerson, but rather the instrumental necessity of it as the means of "shooting the gulf," or attaining to sublime power. This is one way of inducing a sort of self-reliance in the reader, an unsettling of meaning that opens up new possibilities of insight and understanding. "Hamatreya," we could say, is therefore built on the platform of "Emersonian surprise," his own peculiar mechanism of the poetic sublime, which is intended to bring on new shocks of recognition.

In the end, almost all of Emerson's important poems require and yield to what Nietzsche termed "slow reading." The simplicity and ease of surface in Emerson's poetry can mislead us into a superficial apprehension of what is going on in a poem. Emerson plays a deep game, and if we do not attend to both his boldness and his subtlety, we are apt to lose our way and be the poorer for it. As he says in "The Sphinx," "'Profounder, profounder, / Man's spirit must dive," but lest we think we understand too quickly, we might keep in mind the Sphinx's closing words, "'Who telleth one of my meanings, / Is master of all I am." Emerson – a masterful writer, to be sure – is as oracular and prophetic a poet as we have had in our American, our visionary, literature.

PAUL KANE

Selected Works

The Complete Works of Ralph Waldo Emerson, edited by Edward Waldo Emerson, 12 vols., Centenary Edition, Boston: Houghton Mifflin, 1903–04

The Letters of Ralph Waldo Emerson, edited by Ralph L. Rusk, New York: Columbia University Press, 1939

The Journals and Miscellaneous Notebooks of Ralph Waldo Emerson, edited by William Gilman, et al., Cambridge, Massachusetts: Belknap/Harvard University Press, 1960

The Collected Works of Ralph Waldo Emerson, edited by Robert Spiller, Alfred Ferguson, et al., Cambridge: Belknap/Harvard University Press, 1971–

Essays and Lectures, edited by Joel Porte, New York: Library of America, 1983

The Poetry Notebooks of Ralph Waldo Emerson, edited by Ralph H. Orth, et. al., Columbia: University of Missouri Press, 1986

Collected Poems and Translations, edited by Harold Bloom and Paul Kane, New York: Library of America, 1994

Further Reading

Allen, Gay Wilson, *Waldo Emerson: A Biography*, New York: Viking, 1981

Anderson, John Q., *The Liberating Gods: Emerson on Poets and Poetry*, Coral Gables, Florida: University of Miami Press, 1971

Barish, Evelyn, *Emerson: The Roots of Prophecy*, Princeton, New Jersey: Princeton University Press, 1989

Benton, Joel E., *Emerson as a Poet*, New York: M. L. Holbrook, 1883

Bishop, Jonathan, *Emerson on the Soul*, Cambridge, Massachusetts: Harvard University Press, 1964

Bloom, Harold, *Ringers in the Tower*, Chicago: University of Chicago Press, 1971

_____, ed., *Emerson: Modern Critical Views*, New York: Chelsea House, 1985

Buell, Lawrence, *New England Literary Culture*, New York: Cambridge University Press, 1986

Burkholder, Robert E., and Joel Myerson, eds., *Critical Essays on Ralph Waldo Emerson*, Boston: G. K. Hall, 1983

Carpenter, Frederic Ives, *Emerson Handbook*, New York: Hendricks House, 1953

Cavell, Stanley, *This New Yet Unapproachable America*, Albuquerque, New Mexico: Living Batch, 1989

Cayton, Mary Kupiec, *Emerson's Emergence*, Chapel Hill: University of North Carolina Press, 1989

Cheyfitz, Eric, *The Trans-Parent: Sexual Politics in the Language of Emerson*, Baltimore, Maryland: Johns Hopkins University Press, 1981

Ellison, Julie, *Emerson's Romantic Style*, Princeton, New Jersey: Princeton University Press, 1984

Foster, C. H., *Emerson's Theory of Poetry*, Iowa City, Iowa: Midland House, 1939

Gregg, Edith W., ed., *One First Love: The Letters of Ellen Louisa Tucker to Ralph Waldo Emerson*, Cambridge, Massachusetts: Belknap/Harvard University Press, 1962

Hopkins, Vivian, *Spires of Form: A Study of Emerson's Aesthetic Theory*, Cambridge, Massachusetts: Harvard University Press, 1951

Hughes, Gertrude, *Emerson's Demanding Optimism*, Baton Rouge: Louisiana State University Press, 1984

Konvitz, Milton R., and Stephen E. Whicher, eds., *Emerson: A Collection of Critical Essays*, Englewood Cliffs, New Jersey: Prentice-Hall, 1962

Kronick, Joseph G., *American Poetics of History: From Emerson to the Moderns*, Baton Rouge: Louisiana State University Press, 1984

Levin, David, ed., *Emerson: Prophecy, Metamorphosis, and Influence*, New York: Columbia University Press, 1975

Loving, Jerome, *Emerson, Whitman, and the American Muse*, Chapel Hill: University of North Carolina Press, 1982

Matthiessen, F. O., *American Renaissance*, New York: Oxford University Press, 1941

McAleer, John, *Ralph Waldo Emerson: Days of Encounter*, Boston: Little, Brown, 1984

Myerson, Joel, ed., *Emerson Centenary Essays*, Carbondale: Southern Illinois University Press, 1982

Packer, Barbara L., *Emerson's Fall*, New York: Continuum, 1982

Paul, Sherman, *Emerson's Angle of Vision*, Cambridge, Massachusetts: Harvard University Press, 1952

Pearce, Roy Harvey, *The Continuity of American Poetry*, Princeton, New Jersey: Princeton University Press, 1961

Poirier, Richard, *The Renewal of Literature*, New York: Random House, 1987

Porte, Joel, ed., *Emerson: Prospect and Retrospect*, Cambridge, Massachusetts: Harvard University Press, 1982
_____, *Representative Man: Ralph Waldo Emerson in His Time*, New York: Oxford University Press, 1967

Porter, Carolyn, *Seeing and Being: The Plight of the Participant-Observer in Emerson, James, Adams, Faulkner*, Middletown, Connecticut: Wesleyan University Press, 1981

Porter, David, *Emerson and Literary Change*, Cambridge, Massachusetts: Harvard University Press, 1978

Reynolds, David S., *Beneath the American Renaissance*, Cambridge, Massachusetts: Harvard University Press, 1989

Richardson, Robert D., Jr., *Emerson: The Mind on Fire*, Berkeley and Los Angeles: University of California Press, 1995

Robinson, David, *Apostle of Culture: Emerson as Preacher and Lecturer*, Philadelphia: University of Pennsylvania Press, 1982

Rusk, Ralph L., *The Life of Ralph Waldo Emerson*, New York: Scribners, 1949

Waggoner, Hyatt H., *Emerson as Poet*, Princeton: Princeton University Press, 1974

Whicher, Stephen, *Freedom and Fate*, Philadelphia: University of Pennsylvania Press, 1943

Yoder, R. A., *Emerson and the Orphic Poet in America*, Berkeley: University of California Press, 1978

Ernest Fenollosa

(1853–1908)

A full assessment of Ernest Fenollosa's place in American intellectual history awaits the gathering and publication of his works. Novels, plays, essays, lectures, and doubtless much else linger in the archives of this late–nineteenth-century polymath, who is remembered more for one stray essay than for his several books and impressive cultural achievements. Fenollosa's contribution to modernism has long been recognized. His posthumously published *The Chinese Written Character as a Medium for Poetry*, happened upon and promoted by his executor Ezra Pound, became a central document in a variety of modernist and postmodern concerns. Its author, however vanished from critical view in a puff of fin de siècle orientalism. Like a number of contemporary American figures, Fenollosa crossed disciplinary and cultural boundaries in pursuit of some underlying narrative that he believed shaped our experience. If his achievement as an intellectual, scholar, and culture prophet lacks a full measure, his achievement as a poet is without measure. A consideration of Fenollosa's poetry alters the received sense of American poetry on the eve of modernism.

As the Harvard class poet of 1874 and first in his class, Fenollosa was poised for entry into the literary elite of Boston. His rhetorical flair and his taste for idealist philosophy would have earned him a niche in the dying orders of New England literary culture, and the fellowship to Cambridge he received upon graduating might well have proved a step toward his return to Harvard as a faculty member in philosophy. But Fenollosa's interests moved in the late 1870s to visual arts. A teaching appointment in Japan brought him into extensive contact with Japanese art and sculpture. His deep fascination with Asian visual arts brought him both as a poet and as a scholar and intellectual to his grand theme: the mystic marriage of the hemispheres.

As Lawrence Chisolm's indispensable study of Fenollosa makes clear, the traditional arts of Japan were of little interest to late–nineteenth-century Japanese artists and arbiters of culture. In the rush to westernize that followed upon the opening up of Japan to western commerce, the old styles of artwork were ignored by the younger generation of artists, who were busy emulating European styles. By contrast, Fenollosa found in these failing traditions the answer to his own dissatisfaction with contemporary western styles of representation. For Fenollosa, the literary and visual art of his day seemed to be in bondage to realism. Thus, in accordance with this view, Fenollosa convinced leading Japanese cultural figures to restore prestige to traditional art forms, arguing with an Emersonian twist (as Chisolm notes) that the Japanese would become more truly themselves by emulating their own past. The poet soon found himself in charge of a national campaign to collect and catalog the treasures of hundreds of years of Japanese art; this position provided him with an overview no previous scholar had ever achieved.

Those works of Fenollosa most familiar to students of modernism were not his most characteristic or complete. The essays on and translations of Noh plays and the notes that Pound shaped into the Cathay poems are primarily literary and seem to be the fruit of Fenollosa's second stay in Japan. His central effort was the two-volume *Epochs of Chinese and Japanese Art* (1911), which his wife, Mary, struggled in the years after his death to have published. The period in which he wrote this work was, after all, the age of the great synthesizing and summary works of anthropologists and historians of culture. Fenollosa was clearly aware of how archaeologists in Greece were transforming the past, and he felt himself uniquely situated to perform similar acts of visionary scholarship. In this work, he sought to present to the west and the Japanese a vast cultural history that gave an account of the origins of form and documented its progress from ancient Greece and India to modern Japan. Fenollosa also desired to make the case for the existence of a unified prehistoric Pacific Basin culture that linked North American prehistoric artifacts with those found in China and Malaysia. As a student of Herbert Spencer and Hegel, Fenollosa believed that epochs could be delineated even in the face of such daunting materials. Combined with his scholarly zeal, his training in evolutionary thought and idealist dialectics provided the foundation for a series of visionary poetic suites. Fenollosa the poet trumpeted what he promoted as an unprecedented transformation in human nature, one brought about through the synthesis of east and west.

The late nineteenth century saw a surge of interest in Asian art and life among poets, particularly those touched by Symbolist and Decadent rhetoric. In the work of George Cabot **Lodge**, Henry **Adams**, and Trumbull **Stickney**, and for that matter in the work of Mallarmé's American pupil Stuart **Merrill**, Asia embodied the qualities of asceticism, voluptuous enervation, and fervid nihilism that made the idiom such a powerful alternative to realism. While Fenollosa deserves a place in the annals of American neo-symbolism, he enjoys a certain distinction, apart from that conferred by his residence abroad and his scholarship. Unlike these other writers, Fenollosa actually converted to Buddhism, a religion he described as "an evolutionary religion, never content with old formalisms, but, filled with spiritual ardor, continually re-adapting itself to the needs of the human nature with which it finds itself in contact." Fenollosa belonged to a particular sect called Tendai, and some of the most speculative and intriguing chapters of *Epochs* are devoted to the influence of this mystical esoteric branch of Buddhist belief. This lifelong commitment to Buddhism would greatly influence his crowning poetic effort, the "Ode on Reincarnation" (see LOA, 2: 513).

Fenollosa found himself in an era inhospitable to his conception of poetic art. He felt the lack of idealistic and abstract High Romantic imagining in his age and saw it, as he notes in *The Classic Noh Theater of Japan*, as a "weak, transitional period of our Western poetic life." In explaining the history and intention of a Japanese literary form, Fenollosa offers an intriguing glimpse of how he construed western poetic tradition:

> It can be shown that the freedom of the Elizabethan mind, and its power to range over all planes of human experience, as in Shakespeare, was, in part, an aftermath

of Oriental contacts – in the Crusades, in an intimacy with the Mongols such as Marco Polo's, in the discovery of a double sea passage to Persia and India, and in the first gleanings of the Jesuit mission to Asia. . . . The romantic movement in English poetry . . . was influenced and enriched, though often in a subtle and hidden way, by the beginnings of scholarly study and translation of Oriental literature. Bishop Percy, who afterwards revived our knowledge of the mediaeval ballad, published early in the 1760's the first appreciative English account of Chinese poetry; and Bishop Hood wrote an essay on the Chinese theater, seriously comparing it with the Greek. A few years later Voltaire published his first Chinese tragedy, modified from a Jesuit translation; and an independent version held the London stage till 1824. Moore, Byron, Shelley, and Coleridge were influenced by the spirit, and often by the very subject, of Persian translation; and Wordsworth's Intimations of Immortality verges on the Hindoo doctrine of reincarnation.

Here, Fenollosa is clearly making a case for his own translations and researches into Japanese literary forms, but one can also see Fenollosa the poet offering a historical justification for his life and art. In fact, he has very neatly established his poetics as the proper descendant of the most significant European writing since the Renaissance.

Poetry, in this view, requires constant encounters with other cultures. Fenollosa here constructs the poetic tradition as one that requires hybridization. Western writers from William Shakespeare to William Wordsworth, he argues, have achieved their supreme moments by looking east. What is significant about this theory, aside from its interest in correlating style and the cultural poetics of otherness, is that it is evolutionary. The contact between cultures, while often admitted to be conflictual or destructive, points toward an as yet unknown culture coming into being. As Fenollosa suggests, the sum of his poetry also offers a significant correlative to discussions of race and culture in late–nineteenth-century America. While many were pointing to the presence of immigrants and descendants of slaves in the American scene, lamenting the "race suicide" of white Anglo-Saxon Protestants, and fearfully pondering such issues as miscegenation and cultural degeneracy, Fenollosa, himself the son of an immigrant, had found in Asia what was needed for the final transfiguration of humankind. For Fenollosa, America is in essence deferred, only rising into view once our westernmost edge has fallen back.

East and West (1893; LOA, 2: 500), Fenollosa's only volume of poetry, wastes no time in establishing a cosmological drama within which the poems occur. His introduction, in effect a manifesto for a visionary cross-cultural poetics, links the poet's ambition to the grand forces that he believed underlie and direct events. His focus is on the relation of eastern and western cultures: "the synthesis of two continental civilizations, matured apart through fifteen hundred years, will mark the close of our century as an unique dramatic epoch in human affairs. At the end of a great cycle the two halves of the world come together for the final creation of man." Like his contemporary Yeats, Fenollosa sees himself as the prophet who witnesses the end of a great cycle. For Fenollosa, however, the apocalypse arrives without dragons and mayhem. The title poem will describe this "final creation of man," but long before we get there the poet will complicate an already complex theme: the interaction of east and west. While keeping to traditional characterizations of the east as feminine and the west as masculine, the poet argues that each culture contains the antithesis of its own dominant traits within itself. The femininity of the east, therefore, is offset by its own militarism. The west's masculine and scientific disposition is modified by "the feminine faith of love, renunciation, obedience, salvation from without." Fenollosa foresees in the meeting of these cultural extremes "a stupendous double antithesis [that] seems to me the most significant fact in all history."

For Fenollosa, the merging of east and west required an adventurous kind of poet, a spiritual Columbus, to establish the coordinates of the final empire of the ideal. By the time of East and West, Fenollosa had made himself expert in a tradition of image-making spanning the prehistory to the present, which he could summon against the prevailing realism in American art and literature. Fenollosa the prophet of culture had thus worked for almost two decades to transform the world that Fenollosa the poet could inherit. By the mid-1890s, he no doubt saw himself as the only suitable nuptial singer for the final creation of humanity. According to Fenollosa, the principals of realism could not serve, nor could the poetic vision of Walt **Whitman**, who in his most emphatic and excitable strophes bears resemblance to Fenollosa's. Yet Fenollosa's work is more frankly apocalyptic than that of Whitman. The major poetic efforts in East and West describe the moment when one world ceases and another begins.

The poem "East and West" is a visionary account of world history from classical times forward. Fenollosa's researches into the history of Eastern art had led him to what he believed was an original point of contact between east and west. Greek and Indian culture had at one time influenced each other. According to Fenollosa, however, a catastrophic severance had occurred, and rendering this severance made him rewrite the war in heaven as it had been imagined by Milton in Paradise Lost. As the poem opens, in the first of its five parts, two winged spirits are discoursing above a panorama of two armies on the brink of war in classical times. The spirits sadly anticipate the destruction below dictated by "universal law" and speak of the promised fruit of the struggle below, which in turn is in part the suffering of incarnation itself. The poem then descends to the fateful confrontation between the armies of Alexander the Great and Darius, King of Persia. After a battle recounted with epic pretensions, the Greeks triumph. As a consequence of this clash, the "germ of art" is transmitted from west to east. With the death of Alexander, however, the historical and the spiritual worlds are split in two. As compensation for the lost wholeness of culture, the west embraces Christianity, while the east develops art.

The second section of the poem summons the spirit of Fenollosa's teacher and mentor during the extraordinary years of Fenollosa's initiation into and discovery of Japanese art and Buddhist belief. Kano Hogai was himself an artist, "the greatest Japanese painter of recent times." He died, a note tells us, in 1888, and his death was "a national calamity." Hogai would become the subject of what is perhaps Fenollosa's most enduring poem, the "Ode on Reincarnation." Here, Hogai rises up as a prophet and spirit guide, taking us through the development of Chinese and Japanese art. This section is elegiac and stands in pointed contrast to the abstract and disembodied perspectives of the opening. Unfamiliar and recalcitrant material is conveyed with fervor and anguish, which draws the reader into the splendors of Asian art and mystical belief as the poem mourns the passing of a master. Attesting to the integration of art, culture, and the divine, Hogai sanctions the qualities in Asian art that Fenollosa found most appealing. Through his mentor's ghost, Fenollosa extends the varieties of religious thought that his poem embraces and introduces the notion of reincarnation as both a playful homage to a revered teacher and a variation on the eschatology of the poem. A second and more frankly spiritual teacher presides over the conclusion of this section, as ritual mourning gives way to ritual practice and as the reader joins in the group prayer of the Tendai sect. The speaker cedes his role to the head of Fenollosa's Buddhist sect, who concludes the chronicle of the separation of the east from the west by announcing that the next stage in the spiritual evolution of the world is at hand:

> "Antagony
> Of untold agony!
> On no external god relying,
> Self-armed, heaven and hell alike defying,
> Lonely,
> With bare will only,
> Biting his bitter blood-stained sod; –
> This for the *world*, as for Japan,
> This is to be a man!
> This is to be a god!"

The third section, "The Separated West," surveys the course of western culture since the cataclysmic sundering of the ancient world. The west has fared far less well than the east and is mired in self-aggrandizement, war, and rampant masculinity. An almost apocalyptic landscape forms a backdrop to Fenollosa's depictions of the transgressions of western mania. At the close of the first part of this section, Christianity has come to the Roman world. Now, fresh disasters arise: the Teutons, "a flood of human fiends, by furies driven / To quaff the wine of life from lipless skulls." The third part of this section sweeps onward, through Nordic mythology, the Middle Ages, and the Reformation, and builds its indictment against western progress. The catalog of western vices concludes with the imperialism of Fenollosa's own day, a parodic or demonic version of the spiritualized commerce that Fenollosa prophesies will be transacted between east and west.

> Now on high noon of hot commercial tides
> See thy ripe products borne to Eastern spheres;
> Threatening the world with thy belligerent types,
> Threatening thyself with thine excess of zeal.
> The very lust and greed by which is spun
> The knitting tissue of these cruel wounds,
> The very curse which whips our naked crews
> To span the world with steel-bound leap of trade.

The malaise laid bare, the two interlocutory spirits return. The spirit of the east chides that of the west: so much failure in the 2,000 years since they parted. The east, it seems, had lent the west the "gem / Of broken souled contrition, / The victory of submission," from her "Eastern diadem," but the west

seems to have wrought no true profit from it. At this point in the poem, Fenollosa addresses Christianity, which the poem has already criticized for its persecutorial zeal in the Reformation and implicated for its role in constructing the brutal shape of Western selfhood. As an idealist, however, Fenollosa still finds value in Christianity. The spirit of the west responds, presenting the achievements of Christian spirituality as, paradoxically, the fruits of the east. The angel of the west cites the power of prayer to curb "brutal passion," and the power of the central Christian sacrifice to allay despair and speak to human suffering on a large scale. But perhaps the truest flowering of Christianity is the inspired art of the Renaissance:

> Hast thou not seen
> The tenderest human loves which Raphael paints,
> Transport of saints
> The angelic brother limned
> Kneeling in ecstasy with eyes tear-dimmed?

The current relation of east and west – evidenced by the misunderstandings of each in regard to the other – is the subject of the poem's fourth section. In this section, Fenollosa adds satire to his mixture of ecstatic hymn and invective. The broad comic swipes at spiritual pretensions raise the poetry, at times, to a doggerel pitch. And yet this strategy helps set the tone for the mysterious "double nuptial" announced at the conclusion of the marriage song in the previous section. This "double nupital" is itself an allusion to the cultural theorizing set out in the preface, in which each partner stands revealed as already containing aspects of the other. Each hemisphere must recognize and repudiate its mimicry of the other before the marriage can occur. For instance, the east is taken to task for its desire to westernize: "O you West in the East like the slime of a beast, / Why must you devour that exquisite flower?"

Here, Fenollosa casts in poetic form the situation of Japan as it was when he arrived in the 1880s, when traditional Japanese arts had been repudiated, and Western styles were the rage. Having arrived in Japan at an extraordinarily propitious moment and having been granted access to temples and archival collections, Fenollosa the consummate outsider was, paradoxically, able to speak with a special cultural authority about Japan to Japan. The fourth section, then, draws upon the poet's work as a scholar and culture critic to focus particularly upon the aesthetic education of the young – a concern that would later become a central part of his plans to reform American education.

> And here come art-students with honors!
> They graduate strictly in marble madonnas . . .
> Improving the mighty Napoleon
> With phrenology slightly Mongolian.
> Child of some blind bewildered bard
> Learning Sunday-school tunes by the yard!
> Sons of earth's supplest dancers
> To graduate in the Lancers!

Conversely, Fenollosa sees the western world as caught up in faddish imitations of the east. He also lampoons the western culture of belief of the late nineteenth century, especially the vogue of spiritualism that was the larger response to evolutionary science, with its mahatmas and psychical science, vegetarianism, health cures, astrology, cabala, reincarnation, and demonism. Then the poet speaks to the west in the east and the east in the west, an address that now encompasses both the actual cultural contact between the two hemispheres, and the desires of those living within each to imitate the other. According to Fenollosa, since each severed culture contains aspects of the other, the encounter of east and west is a recognition of a past and a potential unity. To assure that the satiric particularity of the section will not make the unification of east and west seem impossible or absurd and to break the spell of intractable folly cast upon the poem by corrupt spiritual discourses, Fenollosa closes with an even more emphatic trope of union – that of harmony in music. The achievement of the west in advanced harmony and composition is called forth by the names of Beethoven and Brahms. While Fenollosa's main concern was visual culture, here he clearly subordinates the visual to the aural. The as yet unfelt "chromatic powers" that will inform our life and art once the marriage of east and west has been consummated are foreshadowed by Music, "our fairest, latest daughter, / Diamond of perfect water," whom the poet beseeches to "Plead for the West before the throne of Truth, / Pledge of our unripe youth!"

The last section, "The Future Union of East and West," is divided into four parts. The first draws attention to the poet himself, who like the angelic presences who provided the perspective from which history is viewed, has occasionally commented upon himself but has for the most part remained elusive. Here, the poet repeats the soliloquy from the third section, "Soul of my inner face, face of my race." Previously, this invocation lead to the long elaboration of the idea of mask, the mask of the west. Fenollosa now problematizes the interrelationship of the poem's three key terms – *soul, race,* and *mask* – since the third term quickly subsumes the possible meanings of the other terms. Now the mask is to be removed:

> The play is o'er. Remove thy tragic mask,
> And show that hidden feature which no god
> Hath e'er divined; till she, thy counterpart,
> Bent o'er thy heart when listening to thy sleep.
>   Then in thine own true dream she saw thee smile
> With sunlike manhood; and she said, "Tis well.
> The world has waited.
> With my kiss he wakes!"

The vast historical narrative of separation, degeneration, and strident longing for reintegration that, Fenollosa argues, informs all of history reveals itself here to touch the life of the individual as well. Questions about the nature of self-consciousness have never been far from the center of this ostensibly historical poem; the poet quite naturally concludes with the drama of a single self coming to awareness of its nature. The only plausible solution to a divided self and a fallen world, the poem argues, is ecstasy, an intense and overpowering absolution of distinction. In the most striking and convincing passage of the entire work, Fenollosa turns on the careful dialectics that have moved his poem through time and events and supplants the poem's historical vision with an anagogical one. The poem that has so carefully delineated the hemispheres, dramatized their history, and speculated about the manner and means of their reunion now calls upon an annihilation of these distinctions. The pace of the ending is insistent yet measured:

> Not a crushing code of rules
> For a paradise of fools;
> But fresh joy of leaping fountains
> Mid the broken shafts of schools.
>
> Faith incredulous of creeds,
> Love is full of bursting seeds;
> Scatters showers of living flowers
> Through a wilderness of weeds.

Here, with rhymed quatrains at midsection, the poet imagines a balanced and harmonious existence, but this vision cannot stand as a conclusion. It is insufficiently apocalyptic. To rest in a balanced relation between the contrary forces that move through the poem would be to submit to a vision of the world as purely cyclical. For Fenollosa, time and history will soon be abolished in the birth of a new world. His prophetic role depends on it. What the "final Creation of Man" might look like as it gathers in a superabundant void is beyond the terms of the poem:

> As when some saint is lifted up and hurled
> Out of this mortal world,
> This temple transitory
> For Nature's inemancipated priest,
> Into the silence of Nirwana's glory,
> Where there is no more West and no more East.

In January 1973, Akiko Murakata published in the *Harvard Library Bulletin* a substantial poetic work that he had come upon in the Fenollosa collection of Houghton Library. The "Ode on Reincarnation " is Fenollosa's finest poetic work. More meditative than dramatic, the poem draws upon his life and scholarship in its attempt to expound a vision of the secret order of the cosmos. In "East and West" this order was found largely in historical processes; here, the poet takes up the matter in terms of the fate of the individual soul. The voice of the cultural prophet and reformer still reverberates through these stanzas, touching in its calmest moments upon a Whitmanian exuberance. In keeping with the theme of individual incarnation, however, the poem begins upon and returns to a note of personal loss. The opening lines show the poet grieving the loss of both his first wife and his teacher. This commitment to particular lives and places challenges the apocalyptic argument of Fenollosa's historical poems. The memories of wife and teacher require the poet to reflect upon their lives' meaning, and so he takes up the question of how "nirwana" will be reached. In the poem, the cycles that govern all history, east and west, operate as well within the life of each of us, and like an ancient *Book of the Dead,* the work lays out before readers the soul's adventures after death.

According to Murakata, the poem was composed during Fenollosa's second stay in Japan, from 1896 to 1900. This is the period in which Fenollosa investigated Eastern literary art, composing the notes and essays that would find their way to Ezra Pound. There is a further biographical significance to this second stay. Fenollosa had returned to Japan after the scandal of his divorce and remarriage had driven him from Boston in 1895. The life of curator and genteel scholar was no longer in his grasp. The rejection by Boston society no doubt intensified Fenollosa's desire to preach about the new age that was coming. The poet in fact takes revenge on his native land in several places in the "Ode on Reincarnation," although the poet chooses not to sound the vexation brought upon him by a protracted divorce settlement.

The poem begins calmly. The poet associates his dead wife with the highest cultural achievements of the west. As he lays an olive bough on her grave, however, he begins his attack upon the "Western view of life and death." Fenollosa finds this western view – that we live only once and long for a heaven that offers little more than rest – unacceptable. For Fenollosa, it in fact offers a nightmare of injustice; social inequities, in this view, are only the joke of sadistic Creator. The doctrine of reincarnation that Fenollosa will propose as an alternative to the western vision does not rectify this apparent injustice, but it does complicate the picture. According to this doctrine, the soul's journey takes place in this world. Each instance of our life conforms to some large plan in which we take our current shape based on our actions in a previous life. Turning from the west, and the buried wife, the speaker in section III proclaims his conviction, derived from eastern art and culture: "Yet is this moment before my death but as the links of sleep which bind the jewelled beads of my days. / I feel, – I know – I have lived here, and shall live again!"

We have already seen how this poet finds likeness in things opposed; not surprisingly, then, Fenollosa believes that western thought should have an equivalent doctrine of reincarnation, and he argues that western reincarnation is not to be found in theosophy or occultism or folklore, but in evolution. Here, Fenollosa the poet-aesthetician brings the scientific theory so often seen as the theoretical justification for the realism that he detested to the defense of idealism. Moreover, evolution is characterized as an Eastern doctrine: "Re-incarnation! / Chief gift of modern East to ancient West! / Corollary of Evolution, itself Eastern!" As the very strain of the assertion reminds us, the greatest fear in the poet's world is that things are no more than what they seem. The Christian heaven, where the soul comes to an end of its trials and simply exists, is Fenollosa's hell. For the poet, identity can only be permutation. In "East and West," the races of the earth are constantly mirroring aspects of each other and preparing for a final transformation; here, the poet takes pains to establish an idea of freedom that coincides with his elaboration of fatedness: "I the sage of occidental universities, thank God that I have become an oriental. / How shall I not sing one word that shall pierce with light to the heart of that ignorant West?" While the poem does not take up in any systematic way a discussion of evolution and its relation to reincarnation, an awareness of evolutionary science informs its spiritual meditations. The obvious analogy between evolution and reincarnation would be that, just as the species of the earth are constantly improving themselves, so each incarnation of an individual soul would be the equivalent of untold generations and would represent new stages in a spiritual progress. The poet verges on a kind of race mysticism here, since he finds the similarities between successive types of the same species to be as significant as evolutionary changes. Yet Fenollosa does not seem interested in conserving some ancient racial essence.

What is at stake for the poet and for his poetic task – to sing the joys of rebirth while commemorating particular lives – is whether or not the soul has access to memories of previous incarnations. To answer this query, Fenollosa recapitulates some of the oldest questions associated with the elegiac imagination. For reincarnation to be an event worth celebrating, an intimate relation to a past life must be possible, or else existence is again conceded to tragedy. What does it matter if we are reborn if, as in stoic philosophy, our souls are purged of us, and no individual memory survives the fire of the upper regions? While he retains a progressive narrative derived from evolution, therefore, Fenollosa spiritualizes nature in order to transform the notion of heredity. As soon as the poet evokes evolution, he begins to transform it, preferring the immortality bestowed by "personal love" to "the scientific continuity of the race only" and making this personal love a part of the evolutionary process.

In his attempt to hold ancient religious doctrine and contemporary science firmly in mind without contradiction, Fenollosa also adds a startling revision to the doctrine of reincarnation. Science has been skeptical of reincarnation, he argues, because of the vast stretch of time generally held to pass between incarnations: "The interposition of so many strange bodies, – the long slim thread of moral nexus only across the ages! / No wonder the sages of Science reject the far tale." In Fenollosa's more scientific formulation, reincarnation is continuous. We are each reborn in the next generation or two, in fact, just as our children or grandchildren have come into maturity. Thus, in the poet's phrase, we can enter right into the harvest of our own labors. It is at this point in the poem that the poet gives us a glimpse of his own situation, of the frustration and despair of a writer with Fenollosa's breadth of interests who has not, and did not, achieve quite the level of mastery that his gifts seemed to promise. While Fenollosa was an energetic poet and a considerable intellectual and scholar, one does not find sufficient grounds to rank him with the best of his contemporaries. The bleak grandeur he achieves in the expression of his own hope for a fuller poetic life suggest that he seems to have sensed the judgment of the future: "The poem that tortured you for the hopelessness of expression / Shall have summoned winged words to itself with your fresh blood."

The beginning of a deeper imagining of the phenomenological life of the reincarnated begins with section VIII, where the poet meditates on a figure in a Chinese painting seen in a Buddhist temple in Kyoto. Here, Fenollosa depicts the ecstatic moment, emblematized in the painting, when heredity is seen as freedom. The actions of a previous life have determined the parents of this one. The old man, the "dead saint," is allowed to watch his new incarnation as the self that he will be is delivered to his new parents:

A simply clad pair, a Chinese husband and wife, stood
  reverently with frames bent slightly forward
Hands clasped, faces sweetly lifted in gladness, but in
  absence of wonder at the miracle
Stood ready to receive the soul for which they had
  prayed.
And lo, walking down the path of the clouds,
A figure like a Chinese nurse, in cap and wadded
  garment,
But gleaming with unearthly brightness,
Bears to them with careful step on a golden dish, and
  wrapped in a crystal globe
A little naked crouching babe, the soft casket of the
  new-old soul

> While back of all stands a master spirit, whose very
>   fingers are like knots with the currents of power.

The parents have in some sense chosen the child. The child has chosen the parents. A master spirit regulates, presumably, the commerce of the living and the dead. As the poet continues his elaboration of Karma, which argues its superiority to Christian and Greek notions of incarnation and the fate of the soul, certain issues become crucial. Given that incarnations are almost continuous – each man is born again into his own community, becomes his own descendants, and maintains friendships and marriages over many lifetimes – the question arises concerning what kind of choice is really operative here. Those who die content might well choose more of the same, but what of those who suffer or are miserable? Do they choose better versions of the life they have known, or the same one again? And those who promote unhappiness in one life, do they wreak misery for all time? An inquiry into the nature of justice in this model of reincarnation is inevitable. The poet must reconcile the choices of each individual soul with the one law that he sees underlying existence.

Again, the key term here is heredity. According to Fenollosa, heredity without reincarnation is an outrage. Poverty and madness are without justification. Men and women, in the poet's figure, are no more than worms who have been writhing in a sewer for 2,000 years since the death of Christ. According to Fenollosa, therefore, the chief delusion of Christianity is the doctrine of "vicarious atonement." Although we might expect Fenollosa to repudiate the sacrificial core of Christian thought, however, he does not quite do this. The poet argues that the "gospel of reincarnation" replaces "vicarious atonement" with a notion of individual atonement. In this alternate model, each person held accountable in one life for his or her shortcomings in a previous life, and so heredity is transformed from fatedness to justice. Moreover, there remains the veneration of the sacrificial act. Among those spiritually superior souls who have completed their incarnations and are ready to enter Nirvana are some of unsurpassed nobility, and these souls choose incarnation and return to help others.

Fenollosa's teacher is such a soul. In order to trace the progress of the teacher's soul in the afterlife, the poem describes a complex scheme of reincarnation that leads the poet from the fields of realism and evolution to the newly emerging science of psychology. With the tools of this science, he begins to make his case, which asserts that the poet is the reincarnation of the master. His first step is to procure for his argument the psychological concept of the uncanny. Section IX of the poem, addressed to his new wife, links a series of moments that leads from the scent of the beloved's hair to a vision of divine justice. The beauty and repetitions of nature brought to mind by the thought of erotic love suggest that all has existed before. We have already seen how Fenollosa has revamped ancient notions of reincarnation, dispensed with the temporal abyss that separates discrete incarnations, and shaped to his view a more scientific version of a religious hope. "Most men are born again and again into the self-same villages," he tells us, and so in visiting the city of Florence the poet has intimations of a previous life that take the form of foreknowledge. Here is certainly one of the more extreme instances of the late–nineteenth-century theme of the American innocent abroad:

> On first visiting Florence I know just where I shall find
>   the old familiar tower
> Yes, even around the dark corner I almost know that I
>   shall see an old red kerchiefed woman with a flower-
>   stand.
> The ghosts of heart-beats seem to jump at me from
>   every stone and window ledge.
> A little boy on the Ponte Vecchio greets the foreign
>   stranger by moonlight;
> He whispers sweet silvery confidences to me, and shows
>   me the treasures of old rusty buttons in his pockets.
> Why do his liquid black eyes seem to jet up soul-
>   warmth into me, like those of a lost son?
> Why does some hooded face I pass in the street drag me
>   into an old icy current of fear? . . .
> Tis but the continuity of the soul's drama . . .

Fenollosa finds in the uncanny an authentic link between past and present, an experience that is not merely biology ("blood-memory") or merely religion ("the daily food to the gods of the household") but a fact of consciousness itself. These moments of recognition when we find our own features in an unfamiliar face constitute our karma. Once all history reveals itself to be no more than the occasion for acts of self-knowing, the poet argues, freedom can be restored to us even as the world described in the process of coming to this revelation shows itself to be more a prison than a paradise of the poetic will.

Through a celebration of wedded love, the poet attacks the fatalism that haunts these assertions of freedom. Fenollosa had already concluded his annunciation of the uncanny with an unsettling celebration (at least to modern readers) of aristocratic privilege and the divine right of kings. While this no doubt spoke to the Fenollosa's desire to revere the past, it only inhibited his equally strong desire to be the prophet of radical social transformation. Although he ostensibly distances his work from the Western cult of love – attacking John Keats, among others, for lamenting the loss of the beloved – Fenollosa also powerfully asserts the value of erotic love. Perhaps because the "Western poets" sing the praises of consorts rather than wives, obsessions rather than choices (or so the poet would have it), they sing of despair rather than of consummation. The poem claims, by contrast, that the beloved can never be lost. Each dies with the image of the other in his or her heart, and this constitutes a talisman by which the two can find each other in the next life. "The perfect union shall not be taken from us," the poem promises; in pursuing this union and in searching each incarnation and recovering the eternal spouse, we will discover that the lesser miseries that wreck an individual life can be overcome in succeeding lives.

Having described a version of reincarnation, meditated on issues of fatedness and choice, and established the primacy of love within each incarnation, the poet demonstrates his argument by offering his own experience as evidence. The penultimate section of the poem outlines the mechanics of the poet's cosmos and the manner in which souls get from one life to the next: "the bewildered soul, / Loosed at death from the bonds of customary sense-pulses, / Having for the moment no organ for self expression, / Drifts like a cloud in the direction of what was its habitual love through life, or special desire at death."

The dead thus enter the living who loved them as they wait to return to the flesh. The effect is something like inspiration: "The keen thought of the dead one pulses through and enkindles his thoughts." Originality, although the poet does not say this outright, comes to look more like a spiritual possession. Moreover, this liminal state where the soul hovers between lives becomes the basis for cultural authority. The order of the invisible world confirms the inheritance of power, not as a matter of divinely sanctioned judgment and tradition but as a fact of life. Dead teachers live for a while within the bodies of their pupils. Thus, hierarchies are preserved from politics. So, too, does the poet justify his prophetic stance and, further, announce his ambition to bring enlightenment to the world through the help of his teacher, who through his worthiness has freed himself from the "chain of rebirths." With this choice, the reincarnations would seem, for a moment, to be completed. Now the chastened soul enters bliss. But some extraordinary souls decline eternal joy, return to the world, voluntarily take up incarnation in order to help others progress, and thus, become a Bodisatva.

Ernest Fenollosa ended his life as a lecturer and promoter of eastern culture and values in America. His journal *The Golden Age* promoted a broader cultural awareness. Through his influence on the American painter and pedagogue James Dow, Fenollosa's interest in abstract design entered the curricula of American aesthetic education. As a collector, he established significant holdings in Eastern art in both Boston and Washington. As a poet, Fenollosa occupies a fascinating place in American literature. Along with Lodge and Stickney, he can be seen as constituting a neo-symbolist American moment. One can see in his works, in varying degrees, a dissatisfaction with the condition of the given world, and a desire for a world too pure or imprecise to provide evidence of itself. This is the hour before Imagism, when for a generation or more the problem would be solved through an idealized materiality. Ernest Fenollosa died in London in 1908, as his daughter read to him a favorite poem, Gabriel Rosetti's "The Blessed Damosel."

JOSEPH DONAHUE

Selected Works

Catalogue of the Exhibition of Paintings of Hokusai, Tokyo: Bunshichi Kobayashi, 1901
Epochs of Chinese and Japanese Art, 2 vols., New York: Dover, 1963
The Chinese Written Character as a Medium for Poetry, San Francisco: City Lights, 1968
East and West: The Discovery of America and Other Poems, Upper Saddle River, New Jersey: Literature House/Gregg, 1970
"Ode on Reincarnation," edited by Akiko Murakata, *Harvard Library Bulletin*, January 1973
The Classic Noh Theatre of Japan, with Ezra Pound, Westport, Connecticut: Greenwood, 1977

Further Reading

Brooks, Van Wyck, *Fenollosa and His Circle*, New York: Dutton, 1962
Chisholm, Lawrence W., *Fenollosa: The Far East and American Culture*, New Haven, Connecticut: Yale University Press, 1963

Philip Freneau

(1752–1832)

On December 18, 1832, Philip Freneau, the "Poet of the Revolution," left the Davis-Lippincott Store in the midst of a snowstorm and began the two-mile walk to his farmhouse in Freehold, New Jersey. He never made it home and was found the following day dead of exposure. Based on the account provided by one of his biographers, we might be tempted to see his death as an apt culmination of his literary career. As Lewis Leary's *That Rascal Freneau: A Study in Literary Failure* begins:

> Philip Freneau failed in almost everything he attempted. It was partly his own fault and partly the restless spirit of his time. . . . He was not a political philosopher: he was a poet, and too sensitive to personal hurt, too quick to turn in anger on an opponent, to be taken seriously as a measure of the philosophical content of his time. Through all his life Freneau was the young radical who never forgets his quarrel with a world which makes no room for him. As such, he belongs to the twentieth century as well as to the eighteenth, and represents a type of literary failure familiar in almost any age.

Leary qualifies this judgment by stating that even with these concerns, "Freneau shall not be forgotten"; while scholars after Leary have certainly not forgotten Freneau, however, they have also rarely moved beyond this early assessment. Freneau has been viewed as a man who felt deeply the tensions of his era, but who never quite discovered his calling or quite reached self-fulfillment. Only recently have a handful of scholars like Richard C. Vitzhum attempted to dissuade us from this view. Still, we must travel a long way before Freneau receives the recognition he deserves.

Freneau was one of the first poets to describe the new nation, and, as many critics have noted, he described it in all its diversity, from "The Indian Burying Ground" to "On Mr. Paine's Rights of Man" to "To a New England Poet." This role as the nation's first poet is one reason that his achievement is a lasting one. In addition, Freneau's dramatization of the uniqueness of the American mission and the tensions involved in that mission helps account for his literary success. His poetry and prose aided his new nation in legitimizing itself in its exciting but tumultuous first 50 years. Yet, in spite of the overwhelming nationalism, Freneau also realized the dangers of progress for the United States. In this chaotic time he created art out of the chaos and celebrated both the achievements and the possible concerns of the new nation.

Philip Morin Freneau was born in New York City to Pierre and Agnes Watson Fresneau in 1752. Pierre Fresneau, a wine merchant of French Huguenot descent, moved with his family to Mount Pleasant, New Jersey, and his son was educated at home and at one or more private schools in preparation for study at a university. In 1767, Freneau's father died and left the family in dire financial straits; yet they still sent him to the Presbyterian College of New Jersey, now Princeton. His classmates at Princeton included Hugh Henry Brackenridge and James Madison, and with Brackenridge, Freneau wrote the poem that would serve as their commencement address, "A Poem, on the Rising Glory of America." Already, Freneau had begun to defend his country.

Freneau attempted to ascertain his calling in the years after his graduation. He taught school for a short time, studied for the ministry, and also published a collection of his poems. The start of hostilities between the British and the colonies prompted him to compose the poetry that later gave him the title "Poet of the Revolution." During the war, he sailed to the West Indies and remained there as the secretary for a wealthy painter. He returned to New Jersey in 1778 and enlisted in the militia for a short time. He then traveled back and forth between the United States and the Caribbean as the master of a ship. While Freneau traveled as a passenger on a ship in 1780, the British took him and held him as a prisoner for six weeks, an episode that weakened his health and exacerbated his hatred of the British.

Upon his release, he worked in Philadelphia at a variety of jobs, including assistant editor and contributor to Francis Bailey's *Freeman's Journal*. Freneau continued to publish poems in journals throughout this period, and at the conclusion of the War in 1784, he again went to sea. During the five years he spent at sea, Bailey published a collection of his poems and miscellaneous works. After his marriage to Eleanor Forman in 1790, Freneau worked in New York as a journalist until 1791, when he began to publish the *National Gazette* in Philadelphia. In this enterprise, he received the support of Thomas Jefferson and Madison, who feared the mouthpiece for Hamiltonian Federalism, John Fenno's *Gazette of the United States*. Freneau's writings in the newspaper did much in fact to promote the cause of the Republicans. Freneau's lively prose made him many enemies among the Federalists – Washington termed him "that rascal Freneau" – but also bolstered his reputation as a champion of democracy. For instance, Jefferson stood Freneau a defender of the Constitution against monarchical impulses in the new nation.

Freneau was not discouraged from publishing by the demise of the *National Gazette* in 1793; he returned to his Mount Pleasant home, a place where he often retired after his projects failed. He established his own press and published two journals and an edition of his own poems. After these enterprises failed, he tried his hand at editing and publishing in New York. He collaborated on *The Time Piece* for a year and then submitted a series of essays to the Philadelphia *Aurora* (signed with the pen name "Robert Slender") that had appeared in his earlier collected miscellaneous works.

After a stay at his farm, Freneau, still contributing to the *Aurora*, returned to sea. In 1807, Jefferson passed the Embargo Act, and Freneau returned to his farm. He oversaw the publication of two more volumes of his poems, one in 1809 and another in 1815. He continued to produce prose and poetry on philosophical issues and current events during those years, including the War of 1812, the conflict during which his college friend, James Madison, served as president.

The last years of Freneau's life were difficult ones. After his home was burned in 1818, his family moved to a smaller farm in Freehold, New Jersey. He was still producing essays and poems, but these words did not supply enough money to support the family. He was forced to sell large portions of the land he had inherited from his family and, in the last years of his life, applied for a government pension for Revolutionary War veterans. He died in 1832 at the age of 80.

Although Freneau has not received very favorable treatment at the hands of critics, his constant presence in anthologies testifies to his importance as one of the first American poets. Most often, students read poems like "The Wild Honey Suckle" and "The Indian Burying Ground." However, a large body of Freneau's work, particularly his later pieces from the nineteenth century, remains unread, perhaps because his earlier role as a "poet of nature" causes that sort of poetry to be looked upon as his best, or because critics often view his eighteenth-century works as more powerful. This essay will concentrate upon Freneau's later works. Four of these poems, "On the Conflagrations at Washington" (LOA, 1: 8), "To Mr. Blanchard, the Celebrated Aeronaut in America" (LOA, 1: 6), "On the Great Western Canal of the State of New York" (LOA, 1: 3), and "On the Civilization of the Western Aboriginal Country" (LOA, 1: 1), remain interesting for Freneau's description of tensions in the American idea of progress. His late poetry thus provides us with information about his mindset as well as an index to the events and the temper of the early–nineteenth-century United States.

Two years into the "Second War of Independence," British troops, under the leadership of General Robert Ross, marched on Washington and burned parts of the city, including the Capitol and the White House. As Madison was forced to flee the city, Freneau countered with "On the Conflagrations at Washington," a poem structured in tercets that suggests the public mood of outrage at the event. The poem attempts to instill confidence in the American people, who, less than 40 years earlier, had declared their independence from the British throne. It also chronicles the shift in Freneau's view of the British. According to Mary W. Bowden, "Freneau's treatment of the British in his poetry of the War of 1812 is less radical than that of the revolutionary war." Indeed, he tempers his intense hatred of the British in the later poems; while it still vents anger, "On the Conflagrations at Washington," dated August 24, 1814, also portrays the British as cowards who have, in a way, done the United States a service by countering some of the detrimental aspects of American progress.

Although this poem indicates Freneau's debt to earlier English poets like Alexander Pope, it has a distinctly "American" tone. He represents the English as fainthearted soldiers who are to be ridiculed for their shoddy attempt to emulate Julius Caesar's armies: "They came – they saw – they burnt – and fled." The Americans, meanwhile, stand as the arbiters of freedom who realize the dangers of the attack but also are strengthened by an awareness of the consequences of the war: "The warfare, now, th' invaders make / Must surely keep us all awake, / Or life is lost for freedom's sake." Thus the poet pits American democracy against the British monarchy and the divine right of kings and relates his confidence in the superiority of the American system of government: "A doctrine has prevail'd too long; / A king, they hold, *can do no wrong* – / Merely a pitch-fork, without prong."

Freneau also attacks the reasoning behind the British government and, more specifically, its strategy in the burning of Washington. He writes:

> The mode is this, now acted on;
> In conflagrating *Washington*,
> They held our independence gone!
>
> Supposing *George's* house at Kew
> Were burnt, (as we intend to do,)
> Would that be burning England too?

The American reasoning, by contrast, is that of the new world order, as evidenced by what Freneau saw as a divine retribution against the English: "But not unpunish'd they retired; / They something paid, for all they fired, / In soldiers kill'd, and chiefs expired." This "chief expired" is General Robert Ross, head of the forces that burned Washington. According to Leary, Ross's death "seemed to Freneau an omen that freedom would triumph over ambition and avarice, and he rejoiced in the brave defense which the citizens of Baltimore made against the naval attack against their city." In these writings, Freneau defines an American definition of freedom that emphasizes strength, confidence, and perseverance.

Despite Freneau's somewhat softened view of the British, however, he feels that the United States is justified in avenging itself, particularly in an attack on Canada in response to the illogical and dishonorable British attack: "An idiot only would require / Such war – the worst they could desire – / The felon's war – the war of fire." He compares the brutal tactics of the British to these of their Anglo-Saxon forbears, describing George III as a "vandal" and George IV as a "goth": "Like danes, of old, their fleet they man / And rove from *Beersheba* to *Dan*, / To burn, and beard us – where they can." In this manner, Freneau defends any retaliatory measures the United States might entertain.

Interestingly, amid this nationalism, Freneau returns to a favorite theme of his earlier years, the folly of human ambition:

> They left our congress naked walls –
> Farewell to towers and capitols!
> To lofty roots and splendid halls!
>
> To courtly domes and glittering things,
> To folly, that too near us clings,
> To courtiers who – tis well – had wings.

For Freneau, America has the potential to fulfill what would later be called its "manifest destiny," but movement away from its pristine innocence, as evidenced by "courtly domes and glittering things," too easily allows "folly" and "courtiers." According to William D. Andrews, Freneau here presents "a vision of future glory, yet qualified by the awareness of man's capacity to debase his own high ideals" (see *American Literature 1764–1789*, edited by Everett Emerson, 1977). While "On the Conflagrations" certainly promotes the idea of American legitimacy as a nation, therefore, it does not completely justify the actions of the American people. In essence, Freneau is questioning the idea of progress. How, exactly, do we define the term? Is it always a good? Apparently, the United States has progressed; according to Freneau, however, but it has also corrupted itself in its desire for the Old World trappings. The later poetry seems to represent his awareness of the precarious nature of the idea of progress and constitute his attempt to counsel his country on the problem.

Can progress in the scientific realm be justified in the pursuit of high ideals? Freneau seems to have mixed views on this question, if we judge by "To Mr. Blanchard, the Celebrated Aeronaut in America," published in the *New-York Weekly Museum* on September 21, 1816. Freneau dedicates the poem to Jean-Pierre Blanchard, a French balloonist who crossed the English Channel in 1785 and, when visiting Philadelphia in 1793, made the first aerial flight in America. The poet, whose sympathies had always been with the French rather than the English, had composed a number of poems and prose pieces describing Blanchard's efforts. In this poem, he muses on the wonders of the universe that are revealed to those who dare to venture above the earth. He counterbalances his praise of the balloonist by questioning the human desire to exceed earthly boundaries. Freneau sees dangers in the balloonist's ambitious mission and uses the Frenchman to warn Americans about their own ambition.

The poem sets up a contrast between the earth and the sky, as symbolized by the earthly silk that Blanchard uses for other worldly reasons. Although "no *Weaver* meant [it] should trail above / The surface of the earth we tread," Blanchard has used it to create a balloon, a symbol of the soul:

But *you* ambitious, have design'd
With silk to soar above mankind: –
On silk you hang your splendid car
And mount towards the morning star

Although Freneau clearly admires Blanchard, he also compares the balloonist with Phaeton, who, in his mortality and his ignorance, tried to do the job of his immortal father and almost destroyed the earth.

Freneau creates a series of dichotomies to illustrate the dangers of Blanchard's mission. Besides the earth and the sky, he also sets images of the land and the sea against one another. According to Richard C. Vitzhum, much of Freneau's lyric poetry is organized around this latter opposition, with the sea representing strength and vitality but also destruction and chaos. The poet queries:

Where would you rove? amidst the storms,
Departed Ghosts, and shadowy forms,
Vast tracts of æther, and, what's more,
A sea of space without a shore! –

This passage creates an eerie atmosphere, populated by foreign and perilous objects, where there is no shelter. Even for Freneau, an expert mariner, a "sea of space without a shore" must have seemed the most intimidating of experiences.

The poet then takes Blanchard and the reader on a journey through the solar system, musing about the spectacular things the balloonist might witness and mixing the science of his day with classical mythology. Implying that he has no right to make these attempts, the poet banters with Blanchard in an accusatory tone about possible stops in his travels: "Would you the lunar mountains trace, / Or in her fair flight Venus chase." The poet concludes with a tour of the sun:

Attracted by so huge a sphere
You might become a stranger here:

There you might be, if there you fly,
A giant sixty fathoms high.

May heaven preserve you from that fate!
Here, men are men of little weight:
There, Polypheme, it might be shown,
Is but a middle sized baboon. –

Here, the poet speaks against scientific progress if it prompts individuals to move beyond the human condition. Freneau is obviously influenced by one of the dominant philosophies of his day, the neoclassical notion of the Great Chain of Being, and urged that humans should accept their present place.

The poet concludes that "this little world of things" is indeed problematic, but it is the true home for humanity, even for ambitious men like Blanchard:

Your silken project is too great;
Stay here, Blanchard, 'till death or fate
To which, yourself, like us, must bow,
Shall send you where you want to go.

Yes – wait, and let the heav'ns decide; –
Your wishes may be gratified.

Freneau here expresses a traditional concept of heavenly judgment that stands in opposition to a confidence that humans will achieve ultimate wisdom. He counsels Blanchard to let a higher power decide if he will ever reach the "Chrystal spheres" of the other realm. We also notice hints of Freneau's sobering acceptance of death and fate, which must have hit closer to home as he approached old age.

Freneau's earlier comments on Blanchard also help to indicate a change in his viewpoint over the decades after the Revolution. In the *National Gazette*, in August 1793, he published an article signed by "An old ALMANAC-MAKER," in which he engaged in lighthearted discussion with Blanchard:

Tell Mars, our good and potent ally, to display his flag and hurl his thunder bolts on the heads of the combined despots; tell him there's almost an universal combination of the sons of gun-powder in this terraqueous globe against France and liberty; tell him that in spite of them, France will still hold up her head and be triumphant! . . . Avoid Venus; she is a coaxing slut and exceedingly fond of silk petticoats.

With the need for support for France, Freneau here humorously rises to the call. Although his earlier writings show less seriousness than the later poem, although he grapples with some similar issues in another poem entitled "To Mr. Blanchard," published in the *Time Piece and Literary Companion* in May 1797. He begins, "By science taught, on silken wings / Beyond our grovelling race you rise," but concludes by admonishing Blanchard not to travel too high "for human ken: / Reflect, our humble safe abode / Is all that Nature meant for men."

Freneau often wrote a variety of pieces on the same subject, and often published revised versions of his poems in newspapers or collections. "On the Great Western Canal of the State of New York," an enthusiastic review of the construction of the Erie Canal, is one of these poems. An earlier version of this poem appeared as "Stanzas Written on the Grand Western Canal of the State of New York, contemplated to connect the Atlantic Ocean with the Interior Lakes of North America," was published in *True American* in June 1821. With relatively minor changes, Freneau published "Stanzas on the Great Western Canal of the State of New York," in the *Fredonian* in August 1822. He appended a brief passage at the conclusion:

On June 1st 1822 the Canal had an uninterrupted navigation of two hundred and twenty eight miles. Then there remained to be finished, about 122 miles to Buffalo, at which place the canal will be connected with Lake Erie. The whole will be completed, it is said, by October 1825 – It is calculated it will then produce an annual revenue of ten million dollars! A sum almost exceeding the credibility and transcending the most reasonable computation – as well as the sanguine expectation.

In the poem, "On the Great Western Canal," Freneau's enthusiastic reception of progress links successful commerce to democracy and to improved nature, arts, and human action. At the close of the age of despots, humankind will engage in "works of peace," arts will flourish, and, most incredibly, "*Nature*, herself, will change her face." Freneau credits the wonder of the canal to the rise of an honorable system of government formed on "reason's plan" and "the *Rights of Man*." His use of the word "reason" strengthens his argument for democracy and also harks back to his neoclassical philosophical beliefs.

Although Freneau hints at the destructive capacity of progress, he seems convinced that nature, along with the United States, will be fortified by the construction of the canal: "Before the task is finished, all, / What rocks must yield, what forests fall?" He continues by praising the artistry of the canal and the speed with which it was built, calling it a "Work from Nature's *chaos* won." Nature is strong, but not as strong as the builders: "Where Nature toiled to bar the way / You mark'd her steps, but changed her sway."

According to Freneau, if the canal alters nature, it actually frees the natural world to realize its potential for itself and, more importantly, for the American people: the waterway "awakes / Imprisoned seas and bounded lakes." The canal thus stands as a monument to the vital, future-oriented, and vigorous Americans. The Native Americans are not present: we only hear of their former hunting grounds and the "rude abodes of savage man." In this poem, Freneau does not measure the consequences of the destruction to the environment or to the homes of the natives, or, if he does, nonetheless comes out in favor of the canal. Perhaps this is because Freneau views those who built the canal as creators like himself. Just as the poet creates art from words, these "Artists" also produce order from chaos, and he gives them full license to proceed, hoping, of course, that their projects will be as fruitful: "And in your bold career / May every Plan as wise appear, / As *this*, which joins to *Hudson's wave* / What Nature to *St. Lawrence* gave." Despite its costs, the progress is justified by the creative, rejuvenative act.

Is it because Freneau was caught up in the nationalistic spirit of the time that "bold" men, the American canal builders, are sanctioned, while "ambitious" men like Blanchard are admonished? If this is true, how do we reconcile this viewpoint with the opposing opinion of American progress that Freneau promoted in another occasional poem published just one year later? In "On the Civilization of the Western Aboriginal Coun-

try," published in *True American* in July 1822 and signed "A," Freneau struggles with a number of conflicting ideas, including nature versus nurture and civilization, and progress versus primitive existence.

"On the Civilization" harks back to "To Mr. Blanchard" in its cautions, but while Blanchard cannot harm the heavens, Freneau is seriously concerned with the problems that Americans can create in the accessible and vulnerable Western lands. The personified Nature is stronger and nobler here than in Freneau's earlier treatment, and he introduces "her" by describing her role in the cycle of birth and death:

Two wheels has Nature constantly in play,
She turns them both, but turns a different way;
What one creates, subsists a year, an hour,
Then, by destruction's wheel is crushed once more.
No art, no strength this wheel of fate restrains,
While matter, deathless matter, still remains,
Again, perhaps, now modelled, to revive.
Again to perish, and again to live!

In this poem, Freneau toys with the medieval idea of the wheel of fortune and depicts two wheels, one that creates and another that destroys, as parts of a mill that contains the grist of human experience. Nature appears all-powerful and unprejudiced, as she continually recreates the process of birth, death, and rebirth. Unfortunately, though, Nature and the more natural aborigines cannot protect themselves against "civilized" encroachment.

Freneau addresses those "who shalt rove the trackless western waste, / Tribes to reform, or have new *breeds* embraced" to warn them of the dangers of "civilizing" the Native Americans. He takes a condescending, but not a negative, view of Native Americans, claiming that "the native of the wild / If wrong, is only Nature's ruder child." He belittles the "arts" of the reformers, which they perceive as welcome gifts: "The arts you teach, perhaps not ALL amiss, / Are arts destructive of domestic bliss." The domestic bliss that concerns Freneau is that of the Native Americans, and he carefully weighs the virtues of civilization against the perceived happiness of primitive cultures.

Freneau's depiction of the Native Americans as uncultured souls who heed neither past nor future is, of course, misguided, but his sympathetic portrait of the Native American farmer, who is despondent over the loss of his land, is interesting and surprising in a period when public sympathy for the plight of the Native American was uncommon. Freneau applies cultural relativism to compare favorably the Native American to the white settlers:

All moral virtue, joined in one vast frame,
In 'forms though varying, still endures the same;
Draws to one point, finds but one general end,
As bodies to one common centre tend.

As opposed to those who posited that the Native Americans' prospects for salvation were worthless, Freneau provisionally contends that religion is immaterial, provided that "moral virtue" exists in both societies.

The poet continues by reacting against westward expansion, claiming that changing the religious beliefs of the Native Americans, seeking personal profit through land speculation, or transforming "simple Nature" leads to an abundance of vice. He thus admonishes the settlers to "plow the soil at home" rather than interfere with the wilderness. Then, as if remembering his heritage, Freneau compromises his argument for his American readers. He claims that those "devoid of subterfuge, or art" should "Go, and convince the natives of the west / That *christian* morals are the first, the best." It appears that Freneau has significantly altered his argument. Or has he? At the poem's conclusion, he seems to appeal to a natural law above and beyond all culturally relative moral laws and ends the poem with this injunction to those who would convert the Native Americans:

> Go, teach what Reason dictates should be taught,
> And learn from *Indians* one great Truth you ought,
> That, though the world, wherever man exists,
> Involved in darkness, or obscured in mists,
> The *Negro*, scorching on *Angola's* coasts,
> Or *Tartar*, shivering in *Siberian* frosts;
> Take all, through all, through nation, tribe, or clan,
> The child of Nature is the *better* man.

In this passage, Freneau returns to his old romanticism concerning the Native Americans, as in his 1787 poem "The Indian Burying Ground," with its "ruder race" repressented by a "painted chief," a "restless Indian queen," and "children of the forest." The relationship between the Native Americans and the settlers is depicted as a reciprocal exchange of truth between two cultures.

Freneau's caution that humanity not exceed its bounds, prevalent in much of his poetry, confronts his concerns about the expansion not only of the United States, but also of the human spirit. This paradoxical conjunction of two disparate ideas gives his poetry an energy that makes it rise above the fare offered by his contemporaries. By combining these ideas, Freneau illuminated the psyche of a fledgling nation, for he demonstrated not only the self-doubt that comes to any rational individual in the face of such sweeping and life changing national transformations, but also the confidence and pride that such changes would bring.

JULIE NORKO

Selected Works

The Last Poems of Philip Freneau, edited by Lewis Leary, New Brunswick, New Jersey: Rutgers University Press, 1945

Poems of Freneau, edited by Harry Hayden Clark, New York: Hafner, 1960

A Freneau Sampler, edited by Philip M. Marsh, New York: Scarecrow, 1963

Poems of Philip Freneau, edited by Fred Lewis Pattee, 3 vols., New York: Russell and Russell, 1963

The Final Poems of Philip Freneau (1827–1828), edited by Judith Hiltner, Delmar, New York: Scholars' Facsimiles and Reprints, 1976

The Poems (1786) and Miscellaneous Works of Philip Freneau, edited by Lewis Leary, Delmar, New York: Scholars' Facsimiles and Reprints, 1976

Poems on American Affairs, edited by Lewis Leary, Delmar, New York: Scholars' Facsimiles and Reprints, 1976

The Newspaper Verse of Philip Freneau, edited by Judith R. Hiltner, Troy, New York: Whitston, 1986

Further Reading

Axelrad, Jacob, *Philip Freneau: Champion of Democracy*, Austin: University of Texas Press, 1967

Bowden, Mary Weatherspoon, *Philip Freneau*, Boston: Twayne, 1976

Clark, Harry Hayden, *The Literary Influences of Philip Freneau*, Chapel Hill, North Carolina: n.p., 1925

Leary, Lewis, *That Rascal Freneau: A Study in Literary Failure*, New Brunswick, New Jersey: Rutgers University Press, 1941

Marsh, Philip M., *Philip Freneau: Poet and Journalist*, Minneapolis, Minnesota: Dillon, 1967

Silverman, Kenneth, *A Cultural History of the American Revolution*, New York: Columbia University Press, 1987

Vitzhum, Richard C., *Land and Sea: The Lyric Poetry of Philip Freneau*, Minneapolis: University of Minnesota Press, 1978

Margaret Fuller

(1810–1850)

The first child of Timothy and Margarett Crane Fuller, Margaret Fuller was born in Cambridgeport, Massachusetts, on May 23, 1810. During her youth, her father – a four-term congressman – played the central role in her emotional and intellectual life. By the time she was nine, he was training her to recite Latin classics and to study political histories and biographies. Such an education was not unusual for a boy in the opening decades of the nineteenth century; as the education of a girl, however, it clashed with the gender roles of the time. At an age when most young women of Fuller's generation were being trained for a life of marriage and raising children, Fuller was developing a voracious appetite for books and a critical temperament that later led her to become one of the most distinguished literary and social critics of her day. In Fuller's upbringing, qualities of domesticity and submissiveness (expected of the "true woman") often took second place to attributes like literary ambition and intellectual pride – attributes more often expected of nineteenth-century men. She sewed for her family and helped care for her six younger siblings, yet she also found time to read many of the masterpieces of European literature, often in their original languages.

Fuller's mother also had a profound influence on her daughter's development. Her mother's garden provided a welcome refuge from the strain of academic recitation in her father's study; in later years, flowers became powerful maternal symbols in Fuller's essays and poetry. Unlike many women of her day, however, Fuller did not fit easily into woman's "separate sphere." Instead, Fuller attempted to balance in herself qualities that had been coded both male and female in her culture, as *both* her father and mother provided models of being that she attempted to emulate. In her most famous work, *Woman in the Nineteenth Century* (1845), she eventually argued that women (as well as men) should exhibit both "masculine" and "feminine" qualities such as harmony and energy, beauty and power, and love and intellect. In a revision of the theory of "self-reliance" popularized by her friend Ralph Waldo **Emerson**, she created a model of personal independence that took into account gender difference.

In many ways, Fuller's unique position as literary critic, social observer, and gender theorist resulted from the unusual circumstances of her upbringing. Having been taught by her father standards of (in her words) "clear judgment," "courage," and "honor and fidelity," she expected a similar integrity in others. But around her she found men who seemed most concerned with their personal aggrandizement and domesticated women who seemed to enjoy lives of ornamental passivity. Her most famous writings addressed such a gender division, as well as other social issues. In *Summer on the Lakes* (1844), a travel narrative that also contains some of Fuller's poetry, she analyzed the various ways in which the American landscape, women, and racial minorities had been treated as exploitable commodities. *Woman in the Nineteenth Century* radically remapped the gender roles of American men and women. Her 1844–46 articles for Horace Greeley's *New-York Tribune* promoted a number of reform causes and the expansion of cultur-

al literacy. Her European dispatches (published in the *Tribune* in 1846–50) exposed her American readers to the revolutionary movements that were transforming the landscape of Europe.

Fuller's final years were spent in Italy with Giovanni Ossoli (it is a matter of debate whether they ever married) and their son, Angelo. As a member of the Civic Guard in Rome, Giovanni was directly involved in the Italian revolutionary movement of 1848. When Rome (like a number of other Italian states) declared its independent existence as a republic, he fought against the French troops that invaded Italy in order to restore the papacy. As the director of the Hospital of the Fate Bene Fratelli, Fuller saw firsthand the agonies of wounded and dying soldiers. Her dispatches during this period convey a sense of historical immediacy and revolutionary fervor that have impressed many readers, who have felt that her history of the Italian revolution (if it had survived) would have had a momentous impact. But Fuller's last book was lost because she and her family were drowned. On their return voyage from Italy to America, their vessel, the *Elizabeth*, sank in a storm off Fire Island, New York, on July 19, 1850.

After her death, her friends and relatives reshaped Fuller's literary reputation. In *The Memoirs of Margaret Fuller Ossoli*, Emerson, James Freeman Clarke, and William Henry Channing glossed over the circumstances of her relationship with Ossoli while emphasizing her more conventional female attributes. In a succession of volumes, Fuller's brother Arthur reprinted her works; he also corrected and regularized them. In *Life Without and Life Within* (1859), for example, he published 44 poems written by his sister. While Arthur did include a handful of Fuller's more important poems, he excluded her most personal texts and revised a number of others, eliminating lines that seemed too controversial (such as those that criticized the institution of marriage). As a result of her brother's censorship, most of her best poetry remained unpublished for more than 140 years. In 1992, 18 of Fuller's lost poems, edited from her manuscripts, were included in *The Essential Margaret Fuller*.

Constructing a kind of verse autobiography, Fuller consistently wrote poetry in response to specific circumstances in her personal life. For instance, among her earliest poems are several striking verse epistles addressed to her friend Anna Barker. "To A. H. B. On our meeting, on my return from New York to Boston, August 1835" provides a familiar nineteenth-century vision of female friendship, as Fuller imagines that the two of them might retreat from the world's ills to a sanctuary, "far from the haunts of men," where they could live in peace. But the most striking of Fuller's early poems, also addressed to Barker, is the imperfect sonnet "To the Same. A Feverish Vision":

After a day of wearying, wasting pain,
  At last my aching eyes I think to close; –
  Hoping to win some moments of repose,
Though I must wake to suffering again.

But what delirious horrors haunt my brain!
  In a deep ghastly pit, bound down I lie, –
  About me flows a stream of crimson dye,
Amid its burning waves I strive in vain;
  Upward I stretch my arms, – aloud I cry
  In frantic anguish, – "raise me, or I die!"
When with soft eyes, beaming the tenderest love,
I see thy dear face, Anna! far above, –
By magnet drawn up to thee I seem,
And for some moments was dispelled the fever's
    frightful dream! –

Written in September 1835, this poem introduces one of the most important patterns in Fuller's writing: the intercession of a godlike woman who reaches down from above and lifts the poet up from a region of blood and pain. When she later recreated her "earliest recollection" (the death of her infant sister Julia), Fuller later commented upon this pattern, which was first defined for her when she returned home to look up into the consoling face of their nursery-maid: "it has often seemed since that . . . I have looked up just so, at times of threatening, of doubt, and distress, and . . . just so has some being of the next order of existences looked down, aware of a law unknown to me, and tenderly commiserating the pain I must endure in emerging from my ignorance."

In the poem to Barker, the poet is lifted up from a region of *blood*. A powerful symbol of female being, blood recurred in Fuller's nightmares. In one dream, for example, she was rescued from a debilitating headache by "a sweet female form," a moment that she linked to her poem to Anna: "the feeling I had was the same when Anna in the fever drew me up out of the pit of blood. It is the true feeling of feminine influence. . . . As I have masculine traits, I am naturally often relieved by the women in my imaginary distresses." In Fuller's personal mythology, a mythologized "feminine influence" often elevated her from pain, grief, and physical suffering to a region of transcendence.

In some versions of this recurring nightmare, the pit of blood echoed a scene Fuller describes herself as having "read in her Virgil" – Aeneas's account of the sack of Troy. In Book II of the *Aeneid*, Virgil graphically dramatizes the ruthless slaughter of scores of people, who pour out their lives in streams of blood. Horror-struck by the carnage, Aeneas remembers how he was about to throw himself blindly into the battle until he was stopped short by a vision of his mother, the goddess Venus, who "came before my eyes, in pure radiance gleaming through the night" (trans. H. Rushton Fairclough). Barker's rescue of Fuller from the pit of blood (in the latter's dream) thus parallels Aeneas's rescue from the carnage at Troy by the goddess. In both narratives, an embattled figure is rescued from the turmoil of material existence by a mythologized image of a saving "feminine influence." Significantly, Fuller's "masculine" side (her identification with Aeneas) cannot save her; just as Aeneas must be pulled from uncontrollable passion (his lust for vengeance) by the goddess, she needs to be rescued from the abyss of pain by a maternalized female power associated with her closest female friends.

This rhythm of emotional entrapment and divine rescue became even more pronounced in Fuller's poetry of 1840 and 1841, as she faced a new crisis in her life – the engagement and marriage of Anna Barker and Samuel Ward, both of whom she loved. As the Barker-Ward wedding approached and passed in October 1840 (near the anniversary of her father's death), Fuller entered a period of ecstatic solitude that she later characterized as "the era of illumination in my mental life." Experiencing a state of deep mystical seclusion, she felt herself transfused by an overwhelming power – a mood that lasted well into the new year. I have shown elsewhere, in "The Call of Eurydice" (see *Influence and Intertextuality in Literary History*, edited by Eric Rothstein and Jay Clayton, 1991), that this identity crisis was shaped by a delayed process of disordered mourning dating back to the death of Fuller's father in October 1835. Combined with self-conscious grief at her own inexplicable psychological changes, the double echo of losing both Barker and Ward impelled Fuller toward narrative moments that echoed processes of mourning. Driven by personal circumstances into an unwonted isolation, Fuller was forced to attune the self to its inner spiritual resources. From this point on, her poetry became the place where she most directly confronted the demands of self-reliance. "Yet is the spirit lone, its problem deep," she observed in an 1840 poem, "No other may work out, its mystic way / No other wing may try"; for "The soul," she realized, "must do its own immortal work."

In the middle of this crisis on New Year's Day 1841, Fuller composed what is probably the most remarkable of all her poems – a 136-line, rhapsodic psychological allegory, "River of beauty flowing through the life." In this work, she traces the course of her life's "river of beauty," which had once flowed smoothly through "plain and vale," but which now "plunged . . . astonished" down a "chasm" through a "wild cleft" into a region of dark caverns. Portraying herself as cut off from love, she dramatizes her descent into a landscape that lacks any "look of love" or "mute caress" – a place of dull repetition and "weariness," where she imagines herself communicating the "glorious secrets of sad love." By the third stanza, a suffering alter ego, "Melodia," enters the poem. Overwhelmed by her solitude, Melodia wanders, weeping, through a grove in which "none had ear" for her sad song. Capturing both the pain and the ecstasy of her spiritual crisis of 1840–41, Fuller used the figure of Melodia to diagnose her solitude and to dramatize the insight that emerged from her mourning.

This double emotional valence is captured perfectly at the moment when Melodia, overwhelmed by loneliness, sings to herself and is startled by the appearance of a familiar figure, "her angel and her friend." Reminiscent of Samuel Ward, who relinquished his painting to marry Anna Barker, this figure evokes the pain of that emotional loss but also suggests the triumph of compensatory artistic creation. For Fuller's alter ego, Melodia, is a sculptor whose "keen voice" has had the power to release this masculine figure "from the rock." Once again, she draws him forth from his imprisonment:

  But now the hour had come; –
And, through the skilful wounds and splintering blows
  Which Nature uses most, loving the most,
Slowly he had come forth, of godlike mould.
  The Paria, from Paros' whiteness named
Sepulchral whiteness of the holiest tomb.

Here, from the depths of the psyche, Fuller draws a profound image of the Muse. Rising from its "cradle tomb," the figure of

Paria bears a powerful psychological resonance; for the outlines of Ward and the Muse resolve, as well, into the shape of Fuller's dead father.

There ensues a brief moment of ecstatic union between Melodia and Paria, a moment of harmony that seems to resolve the discords of Fuller's complex imaginative life:

> They lived the multiple of Unity,
> Revolved, the all-embracing Sun and Moon,
>   Shed forth in that one look of mutual love,
> All stars, flowers, rivers, Angels, Gods and Thoughts,
>   And brooding, trembling, hovered into life;
> Such was the smile of God which these two angels
>   meant,
>   The fullest utterance One has ever made,
> The much that calls for more, the light of final shade.

Fuller's fondest dream was to balance the antinomies splitting her being. Father and mother, library and garden, sun and moon, Paria and Melodia, and Minerva and Muse (in *Woman in the Nineteenth Century*) – the terms proliferate as poles of a psychological process that impels Fuller toward her dream of harmony, the "sacred marriage" she eventually defined in her poem of that title. The union of Melodia and Paria seems to offer a point of balance in this search. But this moment of harmony fails, partly because it does not offer a lasting alternative to the conventional roles held by male and female lovers. In 1841, Fuller's poetic figures also still remain too closely entwined with her biography. Melodia exhibits briefly an artistic strength – the capacity to call her muse, Paria, from his imprisonment. However, the moment passes: Paria returns "into the secret caves," and Melodia resumes her solitude. Fuller's rhapsody concludes with a lament; Melodia sees herself as "a wandering vestal of herself bereft" and waits again for the "voice" that will give her "life."

During the next three years, Fuller's poems reflect the emergence of a new note of wisdom. As she matured, she was able to control the image of loss within poetic contexts that enabled more stable models of personal transformation. In her 1843 essay "The Great Lawsuit" (later expanded into *Woman in the Nineteenth Century*), she included the memorable poem that begins:

> Each Orpheus must to the depths descend,
> For only thus the Poet can be wise,
>   Must make the sad Persephone his friend,
> And buried love to second life arise . . .

Imagining the role of the poet to be the excavation of buried powers (the dead carried within), Fuller then proceeds to revise that male model with the striking assertion "that the time is come when Euridice is to call for an Orpheus, rather than Orpheus for Euridice" (*The Dial*, July 1843). Journeying into the underworld after the death of his beloved wife Eurydice, Orpheus exhibits a bravado celebrated by male Romantic artists. But in Fuller's hands, this figure takes on a complexity and irony lacking in the more celebratory allusions of her male contemporaries. In the classical myth, Orpheus was told by Death that he could rescue Eurydice only if he did not look back until after they returned to the world of the living. But he succumbs to curiosity, and loses her once again. Interpreting Orpheus as a symbol of man's lack of faith in woman, Fuller suggests that

he fails to trust Eurydice (woman) enough to raise her up to his level. Instead, he leaves her in the underworld of a half-completed psychological process. According to Fuller, man has failed to rescue woman, and it is time to reverse the process and allow woman to rescue man and raise him to a higher level of self-realization.

As Fuller knew well from her study of Ovid's *Metamorphoses*, the call of Orpheus and the discovery of his poetic vocation resulted from the loss of Eurydice to Hades. (In her "Autobiographical Romance," Fuller remarks that "Ovid gave me not Rome, nor himself, but a view into the enchanted gardens of the Greek mythology. This path I . . . have been following ever since.") Silenced and objectified by male discourse, Eurydice became the occasion of male artistic production. By reversing the equation, Fuller disrupts one of the dominant traditions of male discourse. In place of a passive and mute Eurydice, Orpheus's muse who occasioned an endless cycle of mourning, she imagines a female agent who escapes from an economy of grief in which woman remains the most evocative signifier. By calling Orpheus, Eurydice inaugurates a new vocation – one in which woman finds a role as the agent of artistic production, not just its object. This act transfigures the familiar nineteenth-century myth of female influence by giving woman an active power. It also prefigures the role Fuller herself adopted in her most important poetry.

According to Fuller, however, Eurydice must face both his absence and her own paralyzing grief, the "death" she carries within before she can call Orpheus. Fuller suggests that only by facing the part of her being that has been paralyzed and killed can she begin the long journey back toward life. Mourning herself, Eurydice recuperates that part of her self that is trapped with Orpheus in the underworld. In Fuller's hands, this revised narrative of mourning takes on an important political dimension. The tone of Eurydice's sorrow remains, but it is subordinated to an increasing faith that woman's pain can be transcended through a transformation of the self. Echoing Emerson's principle of "Compensation," Fuller here dramatizes the metamorphosis of suffering into insight by focusing upon mourning as the female equivalent to male melancholia. Traditionally, as Juliana Schiesari has shown, male writers were provided with "the most privileged access to the display of loss"; representations of female suffering, such as discourses of female mourning, failed to achieve the stature of male representations of grief. In her poetry, by contrast, Fuller begins to provide the terms for a proto-feminist rethinking of mourning: she represents the personal deprivations arising from women's existence within patriarchal culture, while at the same time constructing personae able to escape from this region of loss.

One can easily see this new process of mourning and psychological recovery in the poems that Fuller wrote during 1844. An early poem that year, "I wish I were where Helen lies," appeared in *Summer on the Lakes*. The poem depicts the utterances of another grieving persona, "Mariana." Lamenting her loveless solitude, Mariana portrays herself as a homeless child doomed to wander in a forbidding world. A "lost lover," she becomes the "prey and spoil" of others who use her rather than comforting her. Cut off from the world of human love, her only hope is the promise of divine charity: perhaps "the angel" of her life might return and "soothe" her "to Eternity." With its allusion to a rescuing "angel," this poem recalls the imagery of Fuller's early poems to Anna Barker. But by 1844, there is a significant shift in Fuller's viewpoint. Instead of focusing solely on her personal losses, she sees that suffering as representative of what the narrator of *Summer on the Lakes* calls a "defect in the position of woman."

As the year progressed, Fuller's poetic analysis of the "position of woman" shifted: instead of identifying with suffering victims (Melodia or Mariana), she began to adopt the persona of the rescuing goddess. This change is evident in a poem Fuller addressed to her friend Caroline Sturgis. No longer seeing herself as a bereft and abandoned lover, the poet offers a talismanic power that might protect her friend from danger:

> Now wandering on a tangled way –
> Is their lost child pure spirits say
> The diamond marshal thee by day,
> By night the carbuncle defend
> Hearts-blood of a bosom friend . . .

In Fuller's usage, the blood-red carbuncle is a symbol of mystical power, which she associates with the philosopher's stone at the end of the alchemist's spiritual quest. This mystical symbol helps Fuller appropriate agency to her self-image, which has shifted from that of a passive sufferer who has to be rescued by another. A similar change is exemplified in a poem Fuller composed on May 5, which contains the memorable lines:

> I had walked forth alone, seeking in vain
> After dull days of many petty cares,
> Of petty, seemingly of useless cares,
> To find again my nobler life, – again
> To weave the web which, from the frosty ground,
> Should keep the tender feet of prisoned Queen,
> Or wrap the breast of weeping beggar child,
> Or curtain from the saint a wicked world,
> Or, – if but rightly woven were this web
> For any, for all uses it were fit:
> But I had lost the shuttle from my hand . . .

Again, the image of the lost child appears; but here, the poet imagines herself as capable of achieving a "nobler life" of creative expression that might protect her from such vulnerability. Like Alfred, Lord Tennyson's cloistered weaver in "The Lady of Shalott," she has woven the protecting "web"; she might do so again, if she can find the lost "shuttle."

As Fuller explored in her poetry what she depicted as transformative powers, she also attended to the external forces that threatened personal freedom. In one of her most unusual poems, "On the boundless plain careering," she created a striking allegory of the ways in which a free being (a wild horse named Konic) can be captured and emotionally shackled by the "tyrant" – man. Opening with a vista of the "untamed" Konic galloping on the "boundless plain," this poem portrays his transformation from a creature who knows "no servile moment" to one whose spirit has been broken. Then "Centaur forms" appear: broken horses bearing riders who hasten to "make new captives as forlorn." When they rope and release the terrified Konic, his psyche is marked as indelibly as the brand that he now carries; he now bears both the "mark of man" and the "fear of man" (mirroring the psychological position of any dominated group, whether American slaves or American women). After a number of intervening years, the

"captor re-appears" to find Konic with "broken pride." At that moment, the poet comments, "Thou'rt *wedded* to the sad estate" (emphasis added). And then, in lines that Fuller's brother later suppressed, she makes the connection explicit:

> Sometime, on a fairer plain
> May those captives live again
> Where no tyrant stigmas stain.
> Marriage will then have broke the rod
> Where wicked foot has never trod
> The verdure sacred to a God.

Someday, the poet hopes, free and untyrannical relationships will be possible in a world where marriage will no longer be modeled upon a pattern of domination.

During the remainder of June and early July of 1844, Fuller dramatized the transformation of pain into vision in a series of striking, mythical poems. A sense of divine illumination fills "Leila in the Arabian Zone," a poem that celebrates the power of Leila and her avatars – the classical goddesses Io, Isis, Diana, Hecate, and Phoebe. Fuller's description of Isis is particularly significant:

> The magic Sistrum arms her hand
> And at her deep eye's command
> Brutes are raised to thinking men
> Soul growing to her soul filled ken.

Fuller chose as her personal talisman the sistrum of Isis, which – in Plutarch's myth – was a rattle used to frighten away the serpent Typhon. In *The Memoirs of Margaret Fuller Ossoli*, she is recorded as saying, "I have a great share of Typhon to the Osiris [the consort of Isis], wild rush and leap, blind force for the sake of force." In these terms, the sistrum is a talisman of the psychic control that tames otherwise unruly moods. As in the call of Eurydice, Fuller also imagines here an active power of female agency able to transform men. In many ways, this is an early version of the "sentimental power" discussed by Jane Tompkins: like Harriet Beecher Stowe after her, Fuller portrays her female characters as embodying a "sacred drama of redemption" that might reform American values.

Fuller's next poem, "Double Triangle, Serpent and Rays," symbolizes the transfiguration of destructive serpent energies into a powerful symbol of androgynous union (significantly, this design – interlocking triangles, surrounded by a serpent swallowing its tail, and rays – was used by Fuller as a frontispiece to *Woman in the Nineteenth Century*):

> Patient serpent, circle round,
> Till in death thy life is found;
> Double form of godly prime
> Holding the whole thought of time,
> When the perfect two embrace,
> Male & female, black & white,
> Soul is justified in space,
> Dark made fruitful by the light;
> And, centred in the diamond Sun,
> Time & Eternity are one.

"Male and female represent the two sides of the great radical dualism. . . . There is no wholly masculine man, no purely feminine woman," Fuller had written in "The Great Lawsuit." Now, as she expanded that essay into *Woman in the Nine-*

teenth Century, she returned to an even more profound vision of androgyny. Praying for a wholeness that had eluded her, she defined a mandala that might resolve for her the contradictions of her existence.

"Winged Sphynx" maintains the image of the spiritual quest as a progression through renunciation (the position of Mariana, for example) to fulfillment. The imagery of this poem connects Fuller's spiritual awakening of 1844 with her crisis during the winter of 1840–41. But now, that earlier crisis is interpreted as a necessary station on the poet's journey. In Fuller's new model, the fragments of her life cohere into a pattern of spiritual progression that leads toward insight and the assumption of a queenly power. "My Seal Ring" continues this argument. Following the lead of Mercury, the poet "cast[s] aside . . . intellectual pride" in order to accept "the soul." Only in this way can one become "wholly human," a "spotless radiant ruby heart" who has learned to tame each "serpent thought." In similar terms, Fuller's next poem, "Sistrum" (LOA, 1: 587), celebrates the rattle of Isis. Only through maintaining the "ceaseless motion" of the sistrum, the poet argues, can one escape from the petrifaction of "dead devotion." By controlling serpent instincts, one can preserve an image of purity and spiritual fulfillment.

During the second half of 1844, Fuller wrote four poems that celebrated the quest for that harmony of spirit she termed a "sacred marriage." Weaving a rich blend of Christian, alchemical, and mystical symbols, these poems came closest to defining the private mythology that oriented much of Fuller's life and writing. In "Sub Rosa-Crux," she uses Rosicrucian imagery to evoke a private spiritual discipline. We have lost, the poet laments, the strict devotion of the "Knights of the Rosy Cross," who wore "within the heart" a secret fire corresponding to the "glistening ruby" they bore without. Although we "wear the cross of ebony and gold," we lack the capacity to "feed an undying lamp." Yet the poet holds forth the promise that spiritual aspiration, the faithful mining of "the vein of gold," might lead to transfiguration. Happiness, the poet asserts, is the reward of those who maintain this vision even in the face of adversity. In contrast to Fuller's poems of despair and solitude, these works sublimate pain into an illumination arising from spiritual discipline.

In her finest poem, "Raphael's Deposition from the Cross," Fuller expands the meditation upon Christian symbolism by evoking Mary's grief at the moment of Christ's death. As in Fuller's spiritual crisis of 1840–41, a grieving process prepares the way for vision. Only by accepting and working through her sense of loss – her grief for "the heavenly child, / Crucified within my heart" – can the poet rediscover her deepest spiritual and creative energies. "Let me to the tomb repair," she prays, "Find the angel watching there, / Ask his aid to walk again. . . ." The goal she longs for is purification and apotheosis – her old self dying "in a Phenix [*sic*] birth" into a renewed being. Returning in the second part of this poem to the image of the mourning Virgin, the poet realizes that "power" is only reached through the "deepest of distress," because the resurrection of the self depends upon the acceptance – not the avoidance – of pain. Only by working through the "blight" hidden in the "coffin," Fuller asserts, can one "escape and bathe in God."

The concluding stanzas evoke the accession of spiritual power in the shape of a "muselike form" (Leila), who appears "new-born in primal light." Written in the same year, both "Leila in the Arabian zone" and "Raphael's Deposition from the Cross" feature the figure of Leila. The return of this figure after a three-year absence from Fuller's poetry is highly significant, for Leila appears in Fuller's writing when the disruptive power of grief is contained and transformed into creative power. Significantly, death in this poem ceases to be a specter – the hiding place of either a father or a muse – but becomes rather a source of release:

> Fate that in the cradle bound thee,
> In the coffin hides thy blight;
>   All transfused the orb now glowing,
> Full-voiced and free the music growing
>   Planted in a senseless sod
> The life is risen to flower a God.

At this triumphant moment, all sense of entrapment and enclosure falls away. Resurrected from the ashes of her former existence, the poet rises with a godlike power. Fulfilling the Transcendentalist dream of the "God within," she manifests the essential divinity of the self.

Despite its triumphant conclusion, however, "Raphael's Deposition from the Cross" only depicts a moment of *potential* atonement. Two other poems written in the autumn of 1844 strike this note of spiritual desire, but deploy radically different terms in the process. Rather than using the familiar imagery of Christianity, they analyze the healing of the self as a harmonizing of the masculine and feminine sides of the personality. "To the Face seen in the Moon" opens by evoking a solace familiar from Fuller's other poems – the "soft Mother's smile" of the consoling moon. But as she meditates, the poet realizes that her maternal strength is matched by another side of her personality:

> But, if I stedfast gaze upon thy face
> A human secret, like my own, I trace,
>   For through the woman's smile looks the male eye
> So mildly, stedfastly but mournfully
>   He holds the bush to point us to his cave,
> Teaching anew the truth so bright, so grave
>   Escape not from the middle of the earth
> Through mortal pangs to win immortal birth,
>   Both man and woman, from the natural womb,
> Must slowly win the secrets of the tomb . . .

In order to realize the androgynous union in which man and woman are seen as "the two-fold expression of one thought," the poet must allow the "Man from the Moon" side of her personality to express his "secret heart." This process is portrayed as winning "the secrets of the tomb." Having released herself from the burden of mourning, she depicts her heart as a crypt that can be reopened to reveal both masculine and feminine power. At this moment of release, both "Moon and Sun" rise from their grave. In order to achieve that consummation, however, the poet must wed the "Man from the Moon," her "Apollo," in an act that expresses both her masculinity and her femininity. Only when the man hidden inside her is released can the "union" of the self be realized – a moment of ecstatic communion from which shall arise a kingly power that might win his own "Juno."

Fuller achieves her most direct expression of this ideal in the poem "The Sacred Marriage," which she placed at the conclusion of *Woman in the Nineteenth Century*. If this position in the book emphasizes the significance of the poem, its importance for Fuller is underscored by the existence in her journals of a draft of 19 stanzas that are not included in the published version. Although these lines lack the polish of Fuller's finished verse, they maintain a resonance, especially in the light of the poems Fuller had been writing in 1844. For example, the image of the tomb recurs, as the poet longs for "Each thought" to "be planted in a fruitful grave." Paired with this release from the burden of mourning is the poet's realization that her self is constellated of disparate powers that must be balanced and harmonized. The published version of the poem emphasizes the need to maintain both an inner and an outer balance. The harmonizing of self and other, "Twin stars," will release a corresponding harmony within, leading ultimately to "A Home in Heaven, – the Union in the Soul."

In her best poems, Margaret Fuller realized a vision of personal transcendence that rivaled the poetic visions produced by her friends Emerson and Henry David **Thoreau**. Expressing Transcendentalist spiritual aspirations, these works add to the equation a profound recognition of gender difference. The achievement of personal security and inner harmony, they also suggest, may be more difficult for the woman poet, for she must extricate herself from culturally-inscribed, gendered narratives of loss (such as those of the bereaved lover) that emphasize female passivity. First through the image of the female savior and, then, through that of a divine power she perceived within, Fuller's poetry transforms the expression of grief into an assertion of power. Like Emily **Dickinson** after her, she found in the process of mourning the avenue to poetic agency.

JEFFREY STEELE

Selected Works

The Memoirs of Margaret Fuller Ossoli, edited by Ralph Waldo Emerson, James Freeman Clarke, and William Henry Channing, 2 vols., Boston: Phillips, Sampson, 1852

The Letters of Margaret Fuller, edited by Robert N. Hudspeth, 6 vols., Ithaca, New York: Cornell University Press, 1983–

"'The Impulses of Human Nature': Margaret Fuller's Journal from June through October 1844," edited by Martha Berg and Alice de V. Perry, *Proceedings of the Massachusetts Historical Society* 102 (1990), pp. 38–126

The Essential Margaret Fuller, edited by Jeffrey Steele, New Brunswick, New Jersey: Rutgers University Press, 1992

Further Reading

Allen, Margaret Vanderhaar, *The Achievement of Margaret Fuller*, University Park: Pennsylvania State University Press, 1979

Berg, Barbara J., *The Remembered Gate: Origins of American Feminism*, Oxford and New York: Oxford University Press, 1978

Blanchard, Paula, *Margaret Fuller: From Transcendentalism to Revolution*, New York: Dell, 1979

Buell, Lawrence, *Literary Transcendentalism*, Ithaca, New York, and London: Cornell University Press, 1973

Capper, Charles, *Margaret Fuller, An American Romantic Life*, New York and Oxford: Oxford University Press, 1992

Ellison, Julie, *Delicate Subjects: Romanticism, Gender, and the Ethics of Understanding*, Ithaca, New York, and London: Cornell University Press, 1990

Higginson, Thomas Wentworth, *Margaret Fuller Ossoli*, 1884; reprinted, New York: Confucian Press, 1980

Myerson, Joel, ed., *Critical Essays on Margaret Fuller*, Boston: G. K. Hall, 1980

———, *Margaret Fuller: A Descriptive Biobibliography*, Pittsburgh: University of Pittsburgh Press, 1978

Reynolds, Larry J., *European Revolutions and the American Literary Renaissance*, New Haven, Connecticut, and London: Yale University Press, 1988

Richardson, Robert D., Jr., *Myth and Literature in the American Renaissance*, Bloomington and London: Indiana University Press, 1978

Schiesari, Juliana, *The Gendering of Melancholia*, Ithaca, New York, and London: Cornell University Press, 1992

Schorsch, Anita, *Mourning Becomes America*, Clinton, New Jersey: Main Street, 1976

Smith-Rosenberg, Carroll, *Disorderly Conduct: Visions of Gender in Victorian America*, New York: Knopf, 1985

Tompkins, Jane, *Sensational Designs: The Cultural Work of American Fiction, 1790–1860*, New York and Oxford: Oxford University Press, 1985

Welter, Barbara, *Dimity Convictions: The American Woman in the Nineteenth Century*, Athens: Ohio University Press, 1976

Hamlin Garland

(1860–1940)

From his birth in West Salem, Wisconsin, on September 14, 1860, to his death in Los Angeles, California, on March 4, 1940, Hamlin Garland enjoyed a productive and varied literary career in which he published nearly 50 volumes. But his reputation rests principally on his short fiction written before 1895, especially his volume of short stories, *Main-Travelled Roads* (1891), and his autobiographies, *A Son of the Middle Border* (1917) and his Pulitzer Prize–winning *A Daughter of the Middle Border* (1921). In these volumes, Garland demonstrated that it had at last become possible to deal realistically with the American farmer in literature instead of seeing him simply through the veil of literary convention. By creating new types of characters, Garland hoped not only to inform readers about the realities of western farm life but to touch the deeper feelings of the nation.

After his formative years growing up on family farms in Wisconsin, Iowa, and the Dakota Territory, Garland made the most crucial decision in both his personal life and his artistic career in the fall of 1884 when he journeyed to Boston, then the intellectual and literary center of the country. While in Boston, he eagerly read Walt **Whitman's** poetry and absorbed the poet's view of the spiritual brotherhood of workers, as well as much of his nationalistic feeling. He also studied Charles Darwin and Herbert Spencer in an effort to understand how evolutionary and biological processes could be applied to society. His reading of Henry George's *Progress and Poverty* (1879) confirmed his own experiences of farm life, quickly converted him into an advocate of the single tax, and filled him with enthusiasm for the Populist movement.

But it was not until his meeting with William Dean **Howells** in 1887 (the start of a long, fruitful friendship) and a trip back to the west the same year that Garland began to consider an artistic career. After having spent three years in the east, the barrenness of farm life made a deeper impression on Garland than ever before. He later recalled in *A Son of the Middle Border* that

> something deep and resonant vibrated within my brain as I looked out upon this monotonous landscape. I realized for the first time that the east had surfeited me with picturesqueness. It appeared that I had been living for six years amid painted, neatly arranged pasteboard scenery. Now I dropped to the level of nature unadorned down to the ugly unkempt lanes I knew so well, back to the pungent realities of the streamless plain.

Garland's associations with Richard Watson **Gilder**, editor of the prestigious *Century*, and Benjamin Orange Flower, editor of the radical *Arena*, gave impetus to his publishing career. However, it soon became evident that the contrasting positions on the value of literary art espoused by Gilder and Flower provided a tension within Garland, one that he never fully reconciled. He not only wanted to tell the truth about life on the middle border and, perhaps, to change conditions through his art, as Flower urged, but he also desired the recognition and success as an artist that Gilder's praise and respect would give

him. Fundamentally, Garland's struggle to identify his artistic mission troubled him in one form or another for the rest of his life.

One of America's foremost local colorists, Garland graphically depicted the countryside of his native Middle West in verse, fiction, and powerful autobiographical narratives in which he memorably portrays the hardships and futility of farm life. His literary career includes his early realistic and propagandistic novels and short stories (1888–95), a period in which he wrote Rocky Mountain romances (1896–1916), and a final phase of literary autobiography (1917–40). He also published a major volume of poetry, a biography of Ulysses S. Grant, a book of literary criticism, and several books on spiritualism. He also wrote about the struggle for women's rights in the 1890s and about problems facing Native Americans, and he was a leading advocate of Impressionism at the turn of the century.

Without question, Garland's short fiction before 1895 portrays more vividly than any other work of its time the conditions that led to the Populist revolt. In praising *Main-Travelled Roads*, Howells observed, "These stories are full of the bitter and burning dust, the foul and trampled slush, of the common avenues of life, the life of the men who hopelessly and cheerlessly make the wealth that enriches the alien and the idler, and impoverishes the producer." Garland himself later remarked that he "put in the storm as well as the sun. I included the mud and manure as well as the wild roses and the clover." Although Garland's stories in this period emphasize that farm life is sometimes tragic and generally desolate and monotonous, and although they constantly express outrage at the social injustices suffered by the farmer, however, they also contain exhilarating moments. Indeed, even at its grimmest, the stories present a persistent, although perhaps muted, strain of romantic optimism, which reaffirms Garland's compassionate view of human nature and his love of the land, and which contradicts the stories' diffused pessimism.

This romantic strain is evident in the majority of Garland's poems, most of which were produced during two bursts of inspiration. The first occurred between 1885 and 1887, when he was living in Boston and taking refuge in the remembered west of his boyhood. The second occurred on two summer trips to Colorado in 1892 and 1893, during which he rediscovered his romantic inspiration and contemplated a move away from the polemical and social themes that had dominated his fiction in favor of more purely "artistic" material. To be sure, although Garland dabbled in poetry throughout his life, his best work is not to be found in his verse. Even he privately felt that his own poetry was not especially important. In the foreword to his one major book of poetry, *Prairie Songs* (1893), he is even more explicit:

> Most modern men, I fancy, find it rather difficult to take verse (not poetry) seriously. It is so restrictive and so monotonous in comparison with the flexibility of prose, that it forever hampers and binds in man's larger feel-

ings. Prose seems to be drawing off all that is most modern and freest and most characteristic of our American civilization. I do not expect, therefore, to have these verses taken to represent my larger work.

When Garland began preparing *Prairie Songs* for publication, he decided to exclude poems that were incompatible with the overall mood and theme he was trying to achieve, especially those dealing with the single tax and Populism. As a consequence, except for a grouping of poems toward the end of the volume, the poems seem to depict a different world from the one represented in his fiction. In fact, the remembered past of Garland's boyhood on the prairies of Iowa dominates most of these more than 80 "songs." Many of these songs nostalgically depict a nature unspoiled by humanity and uninterrupted by the often painful current affairs of the farmer – a past, in other words, that no longer existed.

Garland made his overall purpose clear in the foreword, where he speaks of the "rich and splendid meadows" of northern Iowa that "had swarmed with herbivora for ages of undisturbed possession." From these hills, Garland says, he was able to construct some idea of "the grandeur of the flocks which once peopled these green vistas. . . . I have lived many phases of life, but those few years among the colts and cattle of the prairies, before settlement closed the cows' wild pasture and stabled the horses, are among my happiest recollections." In an attempt to provide a unity of material and mood to the volume, he concludes:

> The prairies are gone. I held one of the ripping, snarling, braking plows that rolled the hazelbushes and the wild sunflowers under. I saw the wild steers come into pasture and the wild colts come under harness. I saw the wild fowl scatter and turn aside; I saw the black sod burst into gold and lavender harvests of wheat and corn – and so there comes into my reminiscences an unmistakable note of sadness. I do not excuse or conceal it. I set it down as it comes to me. I have designedly excluded all things alien to the book and its title. I make no further claim than this; – it is composed of prairie songs.

When *Prairie Songs* finally appeared, it was clear that its primary subject was nature. In the poems, Garland focused on many of the same subjects that he had already treated in a series of articles, "Boy-Life on a Prairie," written in 1887 (and reissued as *Boy Life on the Prairie* in 1899). Within the articles, which describe a year's cycle of farm activities from the point of view of a boy in the 1870s, however, Garland included both accounts of the painful realities of western farm life and a nostalgic attempt to dwell on the world of his boyhood. By contrast, the poems are largely idyllic and tender, often ecstatic and celebratory, with few hints of the accompanying pain. The primary pain felt in the poems does not stem from the harsh life on the farm, but rather from the loss of that world. In fact, as in *Boy Life on the Prairie*, Garland suggests that the loss of youth corresponds with the passing of the prairie. In *Boy Life*, he makes this correspondence explicit by inserting one of his favorite poems, "Ladrone," which he published earlier in *Prairie Songs*. At the end of this poem's narrative, the poet returns to the prairie when no longer a boy. Reflecting on his earlier freedom, the poet concludes:

> O magic west wind of the mountains
> O steed with the stinging mane,
> In sleep I draw rein at the fountain,
> And wake with a shiver of pain;
> For the heart and heat of the city
> Are walls and prison and chain.
> Lost my Ladrone – gone the wild living –
> I dream, but my dreaming is vain.

Beyond specific subjects, however, was the question of what emotion Garland wanted to communicate in his poetry. About 1886, in his copy of Eugene Véron's *Aesthetics*, Garland annotated a passage that praised the Impressionists' coloring, and then went on to note that "poetry is less the result of versification than [of] the intervention of the personality in a state of emotion." The poetic emotion for Garland himself was clearly expressed in his reminiscences. Indeed, there is almost a passion for memory in his poetry; Garland seems to recognize that only through his recollections can the past remain alive and vital, even if rendered nostalgically. Thus, the uses of memory, or rather memory itself, occasionally becomes the subject of Garland's poetry. In "Meadow Memories," he begins with this theme: "O Memory, what conjury is thine!" Then, using the most common thematic device in the collection, he provides the city man's recollection of his youth on the prairie:

> From iron pavements ceaseless clank,
> From grinding hooves and jar of car
> I flee, and lave my boyish feet
> Where bee-lodged clover blossoms are!

More than bucolic, an unmistakable note of sadness enters many of the poems, and the works become elegiac and quietly plaintive. Poems such as "Indian Summer" (LOA, 2: 526), "In August" (LOA, 2: 526), or "On the Mississippi" (LOA, 2: 527) express that one can only hope to recapture the passing moment. And sometimes, as in "Boyish Sleep" (LOA, 2: 528) or "Midnight Snows," Garland's recollections take on a dreamlike quality. But nearly always the past is pleasant and idyllic. And even when the poet confronts a harsher nature, as in "Lost in a Norther," it is clear that Garland's depiction is closer to the romantic treatments by Whitman or Henry David **Thoreau** than to more naturalistic treatments by Jack London or Stephen **Crane**.

At the end of *Prairie Songs*, Garland includes several poems written in dialect that, at first glance, seem to be written in the same sentimental vein as the other poems, but merely with a different voice. And certainly some of these poems, such as "Then It's Spring," one of the best lyric pieces, continue this mood. Many of the memories found here, however, are more painful, and Garland renders them with what seem like more immediacy, perhaps because they are told with a vernacular voice. "Across the Picket Line" and "Logan at Peach Tree Creek," for example, are memories of the Civil War, also inspired perhaps by Whitman's war poems, which retell stories Garland heard when he was a boy. The voices heard in "Paid His Way" and "Growing Old" add a painful note to the collection. And, in one of perhaps the strongest and most moving poems, "A Farmer's Wife," a note of bitterness is heard, as Garland treats the farmer's wife in verse whose tone recalls that of his prose:

"Born an' scrubbed, suffered and died."
That's all you need to say, elder.
  Never mind sayin' "made a bride,"
Nor when her hair got gray.
  Jes' say, born 'n worked t' death;
  That fits it – save y'r breath.
. . . .
  Worked to death. Starved to death.
Died f'r lack of air an' sun –
  Dyin' f'r rest, and f'r jest a breath
O' simple praise fer what she'd done.
  An' many 's the woman this very day
  Elder, dyin' slow in that same way.

It is in these dialect poems that Garland attempts to put into practice some of his deeply felt literary theories. Before 1895, he was preoccupied with advancing the cause of western literature. He regularly expressed local-color theories and called upon western writers and critics to abandon their allegiance to the standards of the past and of the east and to produce and evaluate an indigenous literature. Garland believed that the dialect poems of James Whitcomb **Riley** not only attempted to break with obsolete literary traditions, but exemplified some of the best tendencies in American literature. In the unpublished essay "Riley and the Question of Dialect," he was critical of earlier poets and novelists in America; in particular, he viewed the absence of the vernacular in their work as a serious shortcoming:

> The strongest characteristic of the early history of American literature is the aloofness of fiction and poetry from the realities of colonial life. For two centuries our poets wrote as if in violent distaste of their surroundings, as if poetic exaltation could be derived only from the memories of their old world homes, or in the books which they had brought from there. Nothing worthy their singing, nothing like literature was in their task of building an empire. Later, when they did begin to write, they put skylarks and nightingales into their verse, and lords and ladies rode through the pages of such pale and feeble novels as they were able to compose. The bobolink, the partridge, the mocking-bird, the home-spun events of the villager were too vulgar and common to be worthy a rhyme – just as the speech of the hunters, carpenters, drivers and servant-girls of Virginia was considered beneath the notice of the literary man of the South. . . . In short, literature was an aristocratic exercise, something far above the common life and common speech.

It is somewhat ironic, and surprising as well, that Garland spent so little time exploring and developing the use of the vernacular in his poetry.

Except for the few dialect poems in *Prairie Songs* and a few social poems excluded from the collection, Garland's poetry has, for the most part, a consistent mood and tone. The forms of these poems, however, are exceedingly diverse, ranging from the simple lyric to longer narratives, from rhyme and meter to free verse. Appreciative of Sidney **Lanier's** theories of the relationship between music and poetry, and influenced by the narrative style of Joaquin **Miller** and the dialect poetry of Riley, as well as by both the forms and contents of Whitman's work, Garland attempted to shape the poem as the subject demanded. But having abandoned the traditional forms of English prosody, he was seldom able to achieve the powerful rhythmic effects or subtle nuances of Whitman's or Lanier's verse.

Garland's best poetic work is almost always in the short descriptive poems, in which, guided by his impressionistic beliefs, he achieves a unity of tone and effect. As in his short fiction, he writes most strongly when he captures isolated scenes and incidents or when he focuses upon descriptive details from a strictly limited point of view. By exploiting his strong sense of color and using images of nature, especially the wind and the grass, he gives a genuine feeling for the prairies and the plains as he remembered them. When he ranges beyond this, he often becomes preachy and, not trusting his art to speak for itself, overwrites and editorializes. When Garland stuck to what he could do best, the results were often successful, as can perhaps be seen most dramatically in the stark and quietly powerful "Fighting Fire" (LOA, 2: 527) – one of the few poems in *Prairie Songs*, incidentally, that focuses upon human beings stoically going about their business in spite of, or indifferent to, nature's beauty.

Finally, one must conclude that Hamlin Garland's poetry, as a whole, does not merit lengthy consideration. He will continue to be best known for his realistic short fiction written before 1895. Scattered throughout his small poetic output, totaling perhaps no more than 200 published pieces, however, can be found some poems of remarkable strength and poignancy.

JOSEPH B. MCCULLOUGH

Selected Works

Prairie Songs, Cambridge and Chicago: Stone & Kimball, 1893
Boy Life on the Prairie, New York: Macmillan, 1899
The Trail of the Goldseekers, New York: Macmillan, 1899
Iowa, O Iowa, Iowa City, Iowa: Clio Press, 1935

Further Reading
Holloway, Jean, *Hamlin Garland: A Biography*, Austin: University of Texas Press, 1956
Mane, Robert, *Hamlin Garland: L'homme et l'oeuvre (1860–1940)*, Paris: Didier, 1968
McCullough, Joseph B., *Hamlin Garland*, Boston: Twayne, 1978
Pizer, Donald, *Hamlin Garland's Early Work and Career*, Berkeley: University of California Press, 1960

Richard Watson Gilder

(1844–1909)

The twentieth century has been unkind to the self-appointed "squire of poesy," Richard Watson Gilder. Once revered as a poetic genius, Gilder seemed destined at the turn of the century to occupy a place after William Cullen **Bryant**, Henry Wadsworth **Longfellow**, James Russell **Lowell**, and John Greenleaf **Whittier** in the cavalcade of American literary giants. Certain that his literary stock would continue to rise, Houghton Mifflin planned in 1908 to make Gilder the first living writer in the firm's series on "American Household Poets," a distinction that seemed warranted by brisk sales of his verse and uncritical outpourings of praise from admirers. James Onderdonk spoke for most of Gilder's contemporaries when he crooned over the squire's "translucent" strains, noting that Gilder's "Dantean mysticism" ascends to "the highest realms of spiritual poetry, whither in these days not many care to follow."

Sadly for this extremely modest – and, it should be said, modestly talented – poet, these days even fewer readers care to follow his lyrical wanderings into the upper atmosphere, and Gilder's poetry is now almost entirely forgotten. In the revisionary hindsight of the 1930s, his name became synonymous with the dreaded "genteel tradition," and his work as editor of *The Century* magazine from 1881 to 1909 came to be viewed as part of a reactionary effort to impede the "New Realism" of writers like Stephen **Crane** and Theodore Dreiser. More recently, Gilder has been vilified for his conservative editorial policy toward the un-Reconstructed south, a policy that favored the plantation fiction of Thomas Nelson Page and Joel Chandler Harris over the social protest work of writers like George Washington Cable and Charles Chesnutt.

Both of these images, Gilder as a New World Dante and Gilder as a genteel reactionary, are exaggerated. As a poet, Gilder was prone to Victorian excesses, and his verse is marked – some would say cursed – by the same virulent strain of aesthetic idealism that characterizes most late–nineteenth-century American poetry. "I am a stickler for form in literature," he admitted unapologetically, and, indeed, most of Gilder's poetry drones on predictably in outworn cadences and regular rhyme schemes. Certainly, he also was handicapped by having selected Edmund Clarence **Stedman**, another highly influential editor-critic-poet of the era, as his "master" in lyrical composition, but Gilder's formalism seems to have required little encouragement. Stedman, whose aesthetic opinions were neatly expressed in his habit of referring to poetry as "ideal effort," helped to nurture Gilder's love of form, his aversion to flesh, and his sense of responsibility as an official custodian of beauty and truth. Yet for all his tutelage under the doyen of genteel opinion, Gilder's formalism was more expansive than Stedman would have liked. His verse, moreover, was more complex than most of the twentieth-century critics who castigate the genteel tradition care to remember.

Gilder's meditation on "The Sonnet" (LOA, 2: 445), his favorite form, is characteristic of the best and the worst in his poetry. An explanatory note, "In Answer to a Question," establishes the poem's occasion and underscores the authoritative tone with which Gilder and his well-placed colleagues were apt to address "the public" about literary matters. "What is a sonnet?" the sonnet begins, and the poet, qua specialist on ineffable aesthetic questions, answers with a catalog of trite Victorianisms:

> What is a sonnet? 'T is the pearly shell
>   That murmurs of the far-off murmuring sea;
>   A precious jewel carved most curiously;
>   It is a little picture painted well.

As this list appears to be headed nowhere, the question is raised again, this time evoking an even more bathetic set of images and a nod to European literary tradition:

> What is a sonnet? 'T is the tear that fell
>   From a great poet's hidden ecstasy;
>   A two-edged sword, a star, a song – ah me!
>   Sometimes a heavy-tolling funeral bell.
> This was the flame that shook with Dante's breath;
>   The solemn organ whereon Milton played,
>   And the clear glass where Shakespeare's shadow falls.

There is little here to suggest that Gilder possessed talent, and much to suggest that he did not. The forced emotion of "a star, a song – ah me" would be downright comical if the speaker weren't so obviously straining for profundity. Yet such inauspicious preparation lends striking freshness to the final lines, which almost rescue the poem by offering a compelling simile: "A sea this is – beware who ventureth! / For like a fjord the narrow floor is laid / Deep as mid-ocean to the sheer mountain walls." With its relatively stark, clipped diction and hard imagery, the final lines seem a long way from the trite opening images of the "murmuring sea," and the dissonance created by these two images is characteristic of Gilder's uneven art. Whether the effect was intended or not, Gilder often gives the most precious Victorian platitudes their comeuppance within the concentrated space of a short poem or a single line. He seems almost capable of self-parody in the manner of Edwin Arlington **Robinson** or Robert Frost, two younger poets with whom Gilder wielded considerable, and not entirely negative, influence.

There is a degree of irony in this grouping, for it was the editorial oligarchy of men like Gilder and Thomas Bailey Aldrich of the *Atlantic* that compelled Frost to publish his first book of verse in England and that delayed American recognition of Robinson's genius. Nevertheless, a just reading of Gilder's poetry cannot ignore its occasional moments of Frostian irony and compression, qualities that made Gilder's verse "not only interesting but exciting" to readers like Robinson, who praised Gilder's "willingness to look life in the face without resorting to the nauseating evasions of the uncompromising 'optimist.'" Perhaps it would be fair to say that Gilder was a compromising optimist, committed to the language of idealism but ambivalent or agnostic about the capacity of art to deliver on its ultimate promises.

At its best, his poetry registers this ambivalence self-consciously, as in the deceptively moving "An Hour in a Studio" (LOA, 2: 446). The speaker of this poem is an easterner with romantic sensibilities, who meditates on a series of painted images of the southwestern landscape. From his remote vantage in a tidy studio, ruined Native American cities appear "weird, mystical, dark, inarticulate," and he is struck by the astonishing distance that separates him from the "enchanted Mesa" with its "fated wall." The poem at this point seems to be working up to a sentimental apology for manifest destiny, but the speaker's purpose in evoking a past civilization emerges in the effective final stanza. Stimulated by the images before him, the speaker recalls a story told by the artist about Native American shepherds who sang through the night to comfort their herds, circling them with music instead of the white man's fences.

> But I remember better than all else
> One night he told of in that land of fright, –
> The love-songs swarthy men sang to their herds
> On the high plains to keep the beasts in heart;
> Piercing the silence one keen tenor voice
> Singing "Ai nostri monti" clear and high:
> Instead of stakes and fences round about
> They circled them with music in the night.

The notion of shepherds tending their flocks on an American landscape is admittedly perverse, and perhaps Gilder had no more in mind than to kidnap a favorite Wordsworthian motif. But Gilder's image of "swarthy men" who pierce the silence with their pagan song eerily anticipates Wallace Stevens's "Sunday Morning." Like the "supple and turbulent" ring of men who "chant in orgy . . . / Their boisterous devotion to the sun" in Stevens's modernist classic, these imaginary Native Americans offer a devastating rebuke to polite conceptions of art, including the speaker's own effete romanticism. More masculine than mystical, their intangible songs literally frame the landscape as neither paintings nor fences; the effect maintains what Frost would call a "stay against confusion." Indeed, as an argument for the formal dimension in poetry, the poem's final two lines are worthy of comparison with Frost's own memorable treatment of this theme in "Mending Wall."

If such poetic moments were too infrequent to establish Gilder's permanent place in the annals of American literature, he will at least be remembered by admirers and detractors for his monumental editorial work in the pages of *Scribner's Monthly* and *Century*. As an editor for this magazine for nearly 40 years, he lorded over the American literary scene with an influence second only to that of William Dean **Howells**. In fact, Gilder's unlikely rise to editorial prominence paralleled Howells's own, as both men were swept from intellectually humble origins into positions of great influence by the remarkable expansion of magazine readership during the postwar era.

Born on February 8, 1844, in Bordentown, New Jersey, Gilder received a somewhat unconventional education at Long Island's Flushing Female Academy, where his father served as proprietor and headmaster. After brief service in a Union militia during the Civil War, he returned home to support his family, editing a volume of Ellen Howarth's poems while working as paymaster for the Camden and Amboy Railroad. In 1869, Gilder joined Robert Newton Crane, an uncle of Stephen Crane's, in founding the Newark *Morning Register*. He also took a second job as assistant editor for Charles Scribner's monthly magazine, *Hours at Home*.

Within a few months, Gilder was appointed editor in chief of Scribner's modest, unillustrated publication, but he was afforded little time to enjoy his newfound position of authority. By the time of Gilder's appointment, Scribner had already begun making plans to replace *Hours at Home* with a new venture, the much more glamorous and ambitious *Scribner's Monthly Magazine*, which he launched under the editorship of Josiah Gilbert **Holland** in 1870, with Gilder serving as assistant editor. After guiding the magazine's miraculous growth for ten years, Holland died in 1881. Gilder became editor of the magazine, which was renamed the *Century Illustrated Monthly Magazine* to reflect a change in corporate structure. At this point in time, this magazine was well established as a monthly journal and was equal in prestige and circulation to its principal rivals, *Harper's* and the *Atlantic*. The *Century* continued to thrive under Gilder's editorship, introducing some of the period's finest American writing to a large reading audience. A single issue in February 1885, arguably the best 25 cents' worth in the history of American publishing, included selections from Howells's *The Rise of Silas Lapham*, Mark Twain's *Adventures of Huckleberry Finn*, and Henry James's *The Bostonians*. An unapologetic nationalist in editorial policy and a Howellsian realist in aesthetic principle, Gilder sought out and published most of the important American writers of his day, including Hamlin **Garland**, Walt **Whitman**, Herman **Melville**, Edward Eggleston, Cable, Harris, Bret **Harte**, Joaquin **Miller**, and Robinson, to name only a few.

Although he managed his professional relationships with extraordinary tact and deference, Gilder's somewhat squeamish sense of propriety and conservative estimates of reader tolerance occasionally brought him into conflict with contributors. In fact, his dubious reputation today owes more to his celebrated concern over Howells's use of the word "dynamite" in *The Rise of Silas Lapham* and his bowdlerization of *Huckleberry Finn* than to the mediocrity of his own poetry. The charge of excessive squeamishness is legitimate, but all the evidence suggests that Gilder acted as any prudent editor would have done; his editorial policies and social views were actually relatively liberal. He did reject Crane's manuscript for *Maggie: A Girl of the Streets* on the grounds that it was "too honest." He also did dismiss Cable's recommendation to publish Chesnutt's "The Negro's Answer to the Negro Question," because it was "so timely and so political . . . that we cannot handle it." Regrettable as these decisions appear in hindsight, it should be pointed out in Gilder's defense that no editor of the period would touch Crane's manuscript and that Gilder took the courageous step of denying the *Century*'s pages to opponents of southern Reconstruction, while making space for important polemical works such as Cable's "The Freedman's Case in Equity." Envisioning his magazine as a vehicle for national reconciliation, Gilder actively solicited works that might appease sectional, class, and racial tensions. If his commitment to an editorial policy of appeasement appears irresponsible today, as critics have recently charged, perhaps that is because we underestimate the intensity of social debates during the last decades of the nineteenth century.

It seems likely, and not altogether unfair, that Gilder's 19 books of poetry will continue to molder in rare book shops and on library shelves, and just as likely that his editorial reputation will never fully recover from the charge that he perpetuated genteel standards of value into the early twentieth century, where those standards had no place. Perhaps his most important service to American literature, then, was his unstinting work in support of international copyright legislation. Not only did Gilder go out of his way to make the *Century* a showcase for American writing at a time when many editors preferred to feature popular British authors, but he was also a founder of the American Copyright League and led the fight in Washington, D.C., for the reform of existing copyright laws. For 100 years before an international treaty was signed in 1891, American writers struggled at an enormous disadvantage to convince publishers that contemporary fiction and poetry by Americans might be worth printing, despite the fact that popular British works could be pirated for little or no cost. Moreover, when those authors did succeed in wooing a publisher, they often saw their own works pirated abroad in cheap editions, for which they received no compensation. As one of a handful of literary men who could depend on a regular salary, Gilder was somewhat insulated from the problem, yet he brought his considerable influence directly to bear on the issue of copyright reform and played an instrumental role in seeing the 1891 treaty bill through Congress.

By the time of Gilder's death in 1909, the *Century* was in decline, and the era of the great literary monthlies was drawing rapidly to a close. His poetry had been published in a collected edition the previous year, and immortality looked secure until the early 1920s, when the first scathing reports of his complicity in the genteel tradition's rearguard actions against the "New Realism" began to circulate among young critics like James L. Ford. Whatever the literary sins of Gilder's generation, it seems vindictive to continue the assault at this late date. Without apologizing for his idealist conceptions of art and his old-fashioned social liberalism, it seems possible to appreciate Gilder's centrality to the literary culture of late–nineteenth-century America, an era deemed by one tongue-in-cheek biographer "The Gilder Age."

Henry B. Wonham

Selected Works

Poems of Richard Watson Gilder, Boston: Houghton, Mifflin, 1908

Letters of Richard Watson Gilder, edited by Rosamond Gilder, Boston: Houghton, Mifflin, 1916

Further Reading

Ford, James L., *Forty-Odd Years in the Literary Shop*, New York: Dutton, 1921

Onderdonk, James L., *History of American Verse (1610–1897)*, Chicago: McClurg, 1901

Smith, Herbert F., *Richard Watson Gilder*, New York: Twayne, 1970

Warren, Kenneth W., *Black and White Strangers: Race and American Literary Realism*, Chicago: University of Chicago Press, 1993

Louise Imogen Guiney

(1861–1920)

Born while the Fireside Poets were admired and dying the year T. S. Eliot published "Gerontion," Guiney has not fit easily into Americanist canons. As quirkily individualist as Emily **Dickinson**, Guiney was no modernist, nor a bohemian, nor yet a sentimentalist. After Guiney's death, Harriet **Monroe**, an architect of modernist taste, commented on her "courage and spiritual integrity," as well as on the "fine high quality" of her verse. Although she grants that Guiney's work had a certain period charm, what she called the "flavor of the nineties," however, Monroe found the deceased poet's oeuvre regrettably "imperfect and incomplete" (*Poetry*, January 1921). Monroe's judgment characterizes the modernist response to Guiney's work: as essayist Agnes Repplier, writing only five years later, shrewdly observed: "no one shows less tolerance for the poet of yesterday than does the poet of to-day."

Yet Guiney was not as far from the modernists as they might have liked to think. Like those modernists who rejected her verse, she loved John Donne, Henry Vaughan, and Andrew Marvell. "I know most seventeenth-century English writers," Guiney wrote to a friend, "and I know nothing else." Like T. E. Hulme, she deeply admired the classics: "several very learned fish" (in her words) even believed her "Alexandriana" to be translations instead of original works. Like Eliot, she explored an eerily quiet London; like Hart Crane, she packed a line densely, overwhelming readers with imagery, allusion, and muscled force.

At the same time, Guiney can be seen as antimodernist. T. J. Jackson **Lears** presents persuasive evidence of her stand as a "romantic activist." This view emphasizes Guiney's convictions that individual's strivings could militate against perceived determinism and anomie. In accordance with these convictions, she appreciated William Butler Yeats most during the 1890s, when he still had some sense of distant isles; moreover, she boosted A. E. Housman (long before most Americans knew his work), a classicist whose grave doubts were tinged with a stoic's resignation. More characteristically, Guiney admired many poets we have forgotten: she thought Helen Gray Cone's verse particularly fine and Alice Meynell's work "ever lovely."

Criticism, especially self-criticism, was probably the single greatest obstacle to Guiney's poetic growth: after her death, a sheaf of poems were found worthy of publication even though she had rejected them as unfinished. To those who did not know of her ceaseless writing and self-silencing, she may have appeared a mere dilettante. Monroe, for example, thought that Guiney demonstrated great "love of the art" of poetry, but "practised [it] too fitfully" to gain a place in the contemporary pantheon. Guiney would have agreed: after 1894, her letters make frequent reference to an unreliable muse. She wrote, with wry self-deprecation, "I knew what I was up to when I called [my last collection] *Happy Ending*." Judging by her continued poetic output, however, her poetic silence was not a literal end. By the mid-1890s, moreover, Guiney also endured a punishing schedule of prose. After a decade of being one of Boston's most celebrated young poets, she turned to freelance research, bi-ographies, historical studies, magazine and journal articles, occasional essays, and translations.

In attempting to explain this truncated career, Guiney scholars have emphasized three facets of her life story. For some, she is the stalwart daughter of a Union general who passed on his stiff upper lip and fierce military pride; this is the poet, "soldierhood's most ardent minstrel," who, in the words of short story writer Harriet Prescott Spofford, had "drum-beat and sword-flash" for "part of her being." Other writers recall Guiney as the toast of a disappearing world. She was presented at the home of Annie Fields, admired by Henry Wadsworth **Longfellow** and Thomas Bailey Aldrich, and called "[my] little Golden Guinea" by poet Oliver Wendell **Holmes**. For a few more, Guiney has proved of interest as a Roman Catholic, one of the first Catholic writers to gain acceptance among Protestant Boston litterateurs. Unfortunately, none of these frames fully explains her decision to forego her poetic gifts; instead, each accepts and affirms her own explanation that the source was dry. Reading Guiney's career in relation to the looming shadow of modernism, moreover, has caused her work to fit uneasily alongside that of her poetic compatriots. For instance, few realize that her admirers were those who also enjoyed "discovering" Dickinson in the 1890s. Unlike Dickinson, however, Guiney was alive to be feted and criticized; furthermore, she was in full public view as she felt her poetic powers wane. Yet at the start, the poet thought to be "one of the bright lights in Boston literature" seemed destined to take up the mantle of Brahminism. Nor was she simply the gifted darling of a Beacon Hill elite: Hamlin **Garland** enjoyed her verses, and Willa Cather remembered that Guiney manuscripts "passed from hand to hand" among the cognoscenti. How, then, did her work dwindle into a sepia memory? Henry Fairbanks notes the irony of Guiney's penchant for the near-great figures of Western history and literature: that was the ground she herself would come to occupy.

The standard biography begins in Roxbury, Massachusetts, a fashionable suburb in 1861, and jumps immediately to the poet's father, Patrick Robert Guiney. When she was a teenager, he died of a wound that he received during the Civil War. This death has seemed important to those who admire Guiney's "Memorial Day" ("O day of roses and regrets") and her versified tributes to Generals U. S. Grant and William Tecumseh Sherman. And it is true that Guiney, who had dearly loved her dashing father, also upheld a lifelong passion for the romantic Stuarts, Charles and James. Yet her interests were too broad to confine her imagination to one theme or topic. Educated at some of the finest Catholic schools in Massachusetts and Rhode Island, she graduated in 1879, aware that her training did not prepare her to earn a living. If, as one biographer suggests, Guiney planned to become a nun, she shelved the idea when she took on the task of supporting her widowed mother and dependent aunt. But there was little this convent-bred lady could turn her hand to – except the uncertain career of professional writer.

So it must have been a joy for Guiney, in the early 1880s, to find that by some stroke of luck or talent, literary Boston adored her work. Beginning with anonymous verses in Boston and New York periodicals, Guiney soon progressed to poetry and prose signed with her own initials. Then, in 1884, she published *Songs at the Start* and entered what one biographer calls "the most enchanting years of her life." During the period between *Songs at the Start* and *A Roadside Harp* (1893), Guiney enjoyed adulation, critical success, and the flattering sense that she merited a place among the northeast's most important writers. This recognition is now somewhat difficult to fathom: *Songs* is a pleasant collection of fresh and winning poems, but its somewhat jejune worldview is everywhere apparent.

To situate Guiney's popularity, we must recall where American verse then found itself. Although Walt **Whitman** was still writing, and Mabel Loomis Todd was preparing the first collection of Dickinson's work, the important poets in Boston were such now-marginal figures as Edith Thomas and Louise Chandler Moulton, as well as a few novelist-poets such as Sarah Orne **Jewett**. Not many would have known that new sap was rising in poems by Stephen **Crane** and Edwin Arlington **Robinson**, for a handful of people controlled Boston's literary marketplace, and magazines like the *Atlantic Monthly* determined who would be published under the Brahmin imprimatur. Thus, if a young poet could please the few powerful tastemakers, she could catapult to fame with one brief collection. It must have been heady to dazzle critics with little effort; yet at the same time, so tailor-made was Guiney's talent to prevailing Bostonian literary demands that she was destined to fall when those tastes – or tastemakers – disappeared almost overnight. After her death, her friend Alice Brown deplored the modern editor's thirst for "magazinable" verse, a criterion that left Guiney's poetry behind.

In her halcyon decade, however, Guiney was critically acclaimed for her charm, classicism, and bright wit. She must have seemed excitingly modern, too, for like Dickinson, she used a jagged line and staccato rhythm, and like Gerard Manley Hopkins, she could make certain words spring off the page, especially when the poem was a prayer. There was little of the sentimentalist about her. Eva Mabel Tenison points out that "were it not for the feminine Christian names on the title page [of *Songs*], the poems might just as well have been those of a young man." Indeed, all Boston knew of her sassy confidence: when Thomas Bailey Aldrich was the city's leading literary gatekeeper, Guiney published a parody of his poetic style in a prominent newspaper. While literary Boston tittered, Aldrich acknowledged the "hit." All her life, Guiney's friends commented on her innocent mischief and sparkling sense of fun.

Befitting her convent training, however, much of *Songs* was serious and reverent. "Deo Optimo Maximo" exhibits her dramatic rhythms and somber confidence; recall that when this book was published, the poet had just turned 23. Here is the first stanza:

> All else for use, One only for desire;
> Thanksgiving for the good, but thirst for Thee:
> Up from the best, whereof no man need tire,
> Impel Thou me.

In more playful poems, the poet's youth is apparent; indeed, it sounds as though another writer has taken over. "Private Theatricals" is one of the more girlish:

> You were a haughty beauty, Polly,
>   (That was in the play,)
> I was the lover melancholy;
>   (That was in the play.)
> And when your fan and you receded,
> And all my passion lay unheeded,
> If still with tender words I pleaded,
>   That was in the play!
>
> I met my rival at the gateway,
>   (That was in the play,)
> And so we fought a duel straightway;
>   (That was in the play.)
> But when Jack hurt my arm unduly,
> And you rushed over, softened newly,
> And kissed me, Polly! truly, truly,
>   Was that in the play?

If this has a peekaboo archness, note that Guiney would soon publish lyrics for both sheet music and the Boston stage.

That "popular" ear and sprightly playfulness did not appear in Guiney's next collection, *The White Sail* (1887). Here, her themes are more arcane, her diction is difficult, and her syntax is twisted. Only one poem, "Wild Ride," might ring a bell with late–twentieth-century readers. This poem echoes galloping horses: "I hear in my heart, I hear in its ominous pulses / All day, on the road, the hoofs of invisible horses, / All night, in their stalls the importunate pawing and neighing." This tone was a far cry from the eerie whispers of Yeats's Innisfree, and Guiney was often compared to Robert Browning. She said she first thought of this poem in a dream.

The White Sail contains some of Guiney's most difficult poetry. Densely compacted imagery and sometimes faltering syntax suggest the coterie. But Fairbanks is too harsh when he accuses *The White Sail* of "aesthetic jargon . . . a mandarin tongue spoken by the esoterics of a mutual admiration society." As "A Salutation" (LOA, 2: 530) and "At a Symphony" (LOA, 2: 530) demonstrate, delights of meter, imagery, and tone can be found within the poems' complex language. Still, readers of "At a Symphony" may initially feel befuddled by the gnarled lines and thrusting rhythm. The first four lines are straightforward enough, as the sharp accents and short clauses build excitement:

> Oh, I would have these tongues oracular
> Dip into silence, tease no more, let be!
> They madden, like some choral of the free
> Gusty and sweet against a prison-bar.

But the next five lines are not so easy or intelligible, and the exclamation points feel strained and ultimately fall flat.

> To earth the boast that her gold empires are,
> The menace of delicious death to me,
> Great Undesign, strong as by God's decree,
> Piercing the heart with beauty from afar!
> Music too winning to the sense forlorn!

Horace Scudder, who admired Guiney, cautioned her against this poetic path. "She is so ambitious to be terse and sinewy," he wrote in an 1888 review; "she evidently holds in such disdain the smooth ways of fluent versifiers, that she allows herself to tie knots in her sentences." He thought Guiney would overcome this misguided tendency in more polished work: "So much strength can well afford to expend itself in the perfection of form." Guiney heeded the advice: she would soon repudiate *The White Sail* and look for new ways to voice her thoughts. After a short time, she even begged friends not to read the book.

E. M. Tenison, however, judged that *The White Sail* demonstrates "swift-rushing movement, force, fire, and 'grip,' contrasted with an exquisite tranquillity." Tenison particularly admired Guiney's blending of classical and Romantic elements, which Jessie Rittenhouse noted, too: "Some critic has said of Miss Guiney's work that to come suddenly upon it among other volumes of modern poetry is like coming upon a Greek temple in an American woodland; and the comparison is an apt one." Rittenhouse included Guiney in *Younger American Poets* (1906), but hinted that her interests were somewhat estranged from the everyday – "Miss Guiney has little to do with the times and conditions in which she finds herself" – and that certain readers "may require more warmth, more abandon." Edmund Clarence **Stedman**, a good friend of Guiney's, thought her work worthy of a place in his important compendium of American poets (1900). Both Rittenhouse and Stedman favored "The Wild Ride," "Sanctuary," and "A Footnote to a Famous Lyric." The last is an addendum to Richard Lovelace's "To Lucasta, Going to the Wars" (1649); Guiney was devoted to the Cavalier poets. These choices indicate the two anthologists' preference for her more straightforward verse. Rittenhouse, whose thoughts on Guiney's poetry are more judicious than laudatory, observed that her "work is sometimes lacking in that clear, swiftly communicative quality which poetry should possess," but added that "in her lyric inspirations, where the form and melody condition the diction, one may note the perfect clarity and flexibility which she attains. There is sinew and brawn in Miss Guiney's work; she is not dallying in the scented gardens of poesy, but entering the tourney in valorous emprise."

Guiney would have enjoyed the masculine imagery. In "Salutation," she expressed her admiration for a warrior-poet. There is much to like in the "imperious bent" of this heavily accented sonnet and much to enjoy, as well, in the drama she builds with forceful sweep and gusty rush. If this line is "sweet," it is also autocratic and "Venturous, frank, romantic, vehement" at its heart. Her next collection, *A Roadside Harp*, exhibits little of the militaresque, yet remains "sinew and brawn." Explanations for the new tone sometimes cite Guiney's nature poems such as "When on the Marge of Evening," "Cobwebs," and "An Outdoor Litany" to argue the influence of her Catholic faith upon her work. Another argument focuses on her Celtic heritage, noting the "saving earthiness" of the two "songs" she writes about Irish scenes. A third explanation proposes Guiney's love of animals as an antidote to salon longueurs. The last point is worth a little clarification. Especially fond of Saint Bernards, such as the ones she named "Brontë" (after Emily) and "Wendell Phillips" (after the American reformer), Guiney wrote both essays and poems on pets that she mourned years after their deaths. The essay "The Puppy: A Portrait" grants a glimpse of the qualities her circle found endearing:

He is the twenty-sixth in direct descent, and his coat is like amber damask, and his blue eyes are the most winning that you ever saw. They seem to proclaim him as much too good for the vulgar world, and worthy of such zeal and devotion as you, only you, could give to his helpless infancy. . . . When you are told that he has eaten a yard and a quarter of the new stair-carpet, you look into those dreamy eyes again; no reproach shall reach him, you swear, because you stand forevermore between.

Guiney also loved cats. When one "dear little [feline] fellow" died, she wrote to a friend, "His going cost us . . . a lot of grief. . . . We buried some purple pansies with him, and this on a card: 'G.C.G. and L.I.G. thank God for you, Wee-One, and for much joy in you now taken away.'" Because the day was too icy for a horse-drawn cab, the poet and her cousin Grace Guiney carried the 13-pound corpse two miles to be buried beside a dog that the cat "used to love very much."

But love of nature or domestic animals does not explain how Guiney pulled herself away from the intricacies of *The White Sail* to produce the beguiling charm of *A Roadside Harp*. Perhaps part of the answer *does* lie in her love of Irish heroes, Scottish princes, and the British Isles, to which she traveled in 1889. But more important were the financial responsibilities that confronted the young breadwinner when she returned to America in 1891. Responsible for the support of her mother and aunt, Guiney turned to essays and biographical prose; more surprisingly, perhaps, she also translated French drama for the Boston and New York stage. At the same time, she was laboring to complete *A Roadside Harp* (1893). It seems likely that the discipline helped her poetry, for the vigor, confidence, and youthful feel of the volume might indicate that Guiney had insufficient leisure to frequent ingrown literary circles. But if so, her crowded hours exacted a price as well: after *A Roadside Harp*, Guiney complained increasingly that her muse had become a treacherous jade.

Nonetheless, this lovely book was and is considered her best; it exhibits a freshness of tone and clarity of diction far removed from the complexities of *The White Sail*. The Library of America anthology highlights Guiney's maturity by focusing on poems that first appeared in *A Roadside Harp*, including five of the 12 sonnets to the city she called her "early and only love." Before turning to these particular "London Sonnets," it is enlightening to look at the first sonnet in the series, which depicts Guiney's seemingly willed rebirth as an Anglican and a royalist. "On First Entering Westminster Abbey" commemorates her deep reverence for the melding of church, state, and poetry. She attended Robert Browning's funeral at the Abbey in 1889, an experience that may explain the awe that permeates this sonnet:

Holy of England! since my light is short
And faint, Oh, rather by the sun anew
Of timeless passion set my dial true,
That with thy saints and thee I may consort.

Guiney also was deeply moved by the shrine of Saint Edward the Confessor: "To an English-speaking Catholic there can hardly be a more touching and attractive spot, bound up as it is, by visible and invisible links, with the poetry of human history and surcharged with 'the imperishable aroma of the Catholic past.'" Like many tourists, she also admired the Abbey as "the cool enshadowed port / Of poets." But this sonnet turns on a more spiritual allegiance: "Receive my soul, who . . . / Hath broken tryst with transitory things."

What Guiney most loved about England, London, the Abbey, and Oxford's Bodleian Library was their un-American quiet. "One day when I am free," she told a friend, "I am going to emigrate to some hamlet which smells strong of the Middle Ages, and put cotton wool in my ears, and swing out clear from this very smart century." Guiney would end her days in a cottage in Chipping Camden, doing research at the British Museum and her beloved Bodleian. Such tastes, however, were already developed when she published her "London Sonnets." In the scholarly atmosphere of the British Museum Reading Room, Karl Marx had researched his theories that would change the world, and Virginia Woolf would use this scene to stage a feminist inquiry into the past. Speaking of this same haven, and cornucopia, of academic labor, by contrast, Guiney praised the "moon of books!" that stands in awe before "the fallen Past" she dearly loved ("In the Reading-Room of the British Museum," LOA 2: 534). Indeed, the "very heaven" of literature is her version of William Wordsworth's paean, in *The Prelude*, to revolution, young love, and the boundless enthusiasm for human potential. Wordsworth's first flush of optimism would fall away; Guiney's love of books, especially obscure ones, endured a lifetime. This poem does partake a bit of the faults that plague *The White Sail*: it has a difficult structure, uncertain antecedents, and agreement problems. Its fervor, although, is unmistakable, and the language is liquid and the homage meek.

Still lovelier is the subtle imagery of "Fog" (LOA, 2: 532), an evocation of dim, misty atmospheres as effective, in compressed form, as the opening paragraph of Charles Dickens's *Bleak House*. Describing fog as a sort of "bodiless water passing in a sigh," Guiney makes the everyday half-sensuous and quite uncanny: fog is a thing of gloom plastered against the sun, a miasma that drowns a once fair city in "disastrous undertow." "Fog" follows "On First Entering Westminster Abbey" in Guiney's 12 sonnets to the "City of Stains." Its mood is therefore sharpened by contrast to the lofty silence, and hallowed certainty, of the church that was founded to ensure that religious faith would underwrite a smoothly functioning monarchy. "Fog" is quiet, too, but this is a silence of muffled work, at a distance; of echoing footsteps, surprisingly close; and perhaps, under it all, of the love of humanity still discernible. In "Fog," brightness is shrouded and greatness is obscured; like "The Lights of London" (LOA, 2: 533), "Fog" shows the dusk as well as the fitful gleams. Guiney seems more certain in "Fog" that good lies hidden beneath the dark visor; in "Lights of London," that good is uncertain, evanescent.

"Dover Beach" seems to hover in the echoes of these poems, and Guiney in fact would edit a collection of Matthew Arnold's poetry in 1899. Near the end of her life, she also edited Lionel Johnson's work (he is best remembered for the line "All is gone, gone, Cynara! Gone with the wind"). Guiney shared these two poets' interest in loss, in ephemeral beauties,

and in the decay of hopes and dreams, bright futures, and "timeless" love. A great admirer of Philip Savage and Robert Louis Stevenson, Guiney would be pushed aside by those who measured lives with coffee spoons. For where modernists tried to write out their measurings of pat answers and personal experience with clinical suspicion, Guiney held onto faith and belief in individual achievement.

"Sunday Chimes in the City" (LOA, 2: 534) lingers near the river this poet loved. The poem creates a scene of sabbath calm, in which the Thames is almost motionless, devoid of human life or meaning. The "wrinkled tide" drags the black anchor chain; otherwise, there is no sound and no bustle until low church bells ring out across "dispeopled ways." The sound echoes; no one answers. But where some would hear despair, Guiney asserts that the lone voice is still perceived, if unheeded; that one voice signifies and that faith endures. At the same time, the somber control of imagery demonstrates her growth as a poet. In *Songs at the Start*, her lines to a seagull had settled for a hackneyed prototype:

> Beautiful is thy coming,
>   Light is thy wing as it goes:
> And O! but to leap and follow this hour
>   Thy perfect flight to the close.
>
> O but to leap and follow
>   Where freedom and rest may be;
> Where the soul that I loved in surpassing love
>   Hath vanished away, with thee!

This is a pretty image, but the sentiment is rather stale. By contrast, "Sunday Chimes" digs deeper into the evocations of a lone bird's flight. "A subtle beauty on the empty hour," Guiney says of the tolling bells,

> From all their dark throats aching and outblown;
> Aye in the prayerless places welcome most,
> Like the last gull that up a naked coast
> Deploys her white and steady wing, alone.

Comparison of the two poems suggests Guiney's maturing talents and highlights the effective pathos in the descriptions offered in "Sunday Chimes." Just as important, the sonnet concludes with greater solace, that quality notably lacking in modernist icons such as Robinson's frost-bitten villages and Pound's despairing cry: "I cannot make it cohere."

Trained as we are today in cynicism, it can be difficult to appreciate Guiney's optimism. But she was too deeply steeped in the classics to offer readers fatuous solutions. Her "Strikers in Hyde Park" (LOA, 2: 533) is as strong, in its way, as Stephen Crane's *Maggie*: "Come men bereft of time and scant of bread, / Loud, who were dumb, immortal, who were dead, / Thro' the cowed world their kingdom to retrieve." Indeed, the energy driving this sonnet when Guiney conjures up her fear of angry voices and pushing bodies recalls J. M. W. Turner's swirling oils. "What ails thee, England? Altar, mart, and grange / Dream of the knife by night; not so, not so." Guiney finds – or imposes – closure in the image of a republic's "noonday mountains' open range," a clear evocation of the freedoms she thought American opportunity could provide. Yet as long as they are trapped within the confines of Hyde Park, the British workers can only grow more enraged, so Guiney aptly ends this poem with an uncertain prayer.

Although Guiney did not know it during her trip to England, she would find herself a trapped worker, too, when she returned to America in 1891. By 1893, she was exploring official channels in search of a steady job; in 1894, President Grover Cleveland named her postmistress of Auburndale, Massachusetts. She accepted the job with a self-deprecating glance at her poetry. "It occurs to me," she wrote to a friend, "in these my final hours of liberty and loafing, that if the Muse stays where I mean for a while to put her, behind me, it will harm neither herself, me, nor current civilization." But she follows this remark with, "I wish I were atop of the Heath, with a woolly yellow fog afloat," and with great poets for companions. She winced a bit under her contemporaries' good-natured jibes: puns on "woman of letters" flew thick and fast. More galling was the loss of both poetic inspiration and the time to write. "Post-officing," she told an editor who wanted to see recent work, "has put an end to that mood in me." In 1896, she admitted she had lost faith in her work: "The trail of the P.O. is over it all." Soon, she would add, "My Muse, poor lass! is scared off utterly" – a loss that she met with public resignation and private grief. After *A Roadside Harp*, she printed only gift editions of her poetry, until *Happy Ending*, a compilation of revised, already published, verse.

Besides long hours on the job, Guiney also faced the virulent reaction of Yankee Auburndale to a Roman Catholic postmistress. When the townspeople made a concerted effort to drive her out, she resolutely resisted, at least at first. "I was so like a fish swimming the wind," she told a friend in 1895, "with the stress and novelty and difficulty of a business life [but] I am somewhat broken in, now, and somewhat broken up, too!" But she disdained pity: "one reason why I approve of you," she told a clerical friend in 1896, "is that you don't 'poor' me, as almost everybody does, on the subject of P.O. It is hateful, of course, but it is also humorous; and the discipline is mighty good for me, to wake me up, and call me down." When the boycott became too much for her, Guiney chose, characteristically, to go off on a walking tour of England and Wales. Her energies restored, she led a campaign to refurbish the gravesites of Henry Vaughan and Emily Brontë.

Back in America again, she accepted a reappointment at the post office in 1897; within a matter of months, she was ill with what her doctors labeled "meningitis" but what we might consider a nervous breakdown. After recovering, she left the post office for a cottage (named "Shack Guiney") in Maine, where she tried to write, translate, and otherwise live the literary life. "I am even as I was four years agone," she told a friend, "only with the po'try carefully drained out, and some character, let us hope, screwed in." The character may have been fixed, but the "po'try" did not return. By 1898, Guiney's finances forced her to accept a job in the catalog room of the Boston Public Library. "It is as beautiful a prison house as can be imagined," she wrote to a friend in 1899, "Post Office is a bad dream, to look back upon." She concluded this determinedly optimistic letter with her usual love of London: "My head is always full of London, and of the things I could do if I were only there." But those "things," for the first time, did not include poetry:

her heart was set on "nice biographical seventeenth-century things." When she returned to England to stay, in 1901, poetry dropped to the status of an unfulfilled wish, and scholarly prose works filled her final years.

Guiney's next career, as a biographer, concentrated on short-lived heroes, near-great warriors, and lost poets. She was attracted to those given a brief, limited, or underappreciated gift. Some were patriots, labeled "rebels" by the march of history; some were keepers of an unpopular flame; and some were cherishers of values her contemporaries were apt to scorn. All, that is, were marginal figures that Guiney thought were worth recovering; one of the better-known was William Hazlitt. T. W. Parsons had dubbed Guiney "Hazlitt's child" when her career dawned bright in Boston. In *A Roadside Harp*, she printed a tribute to this predecessor's work, "W.H., 1778–1830" (LOA, 2: 531), which sets out her view of him as a great but neglected forebear. For the insufficiently understood figures, she thought, the real obstacle was being born out of time. Their one hope, she believed, were eternal standards that would aid future readers in discovering their artistry. She thought that beauty, at least contemporaries' evaluations of it, was an ignis fatuus (will o' the wisp), but also that truth could be relied on to reclaim its own: according to Guiney, "the stars are shining," the great artists live, and "the People march."

From her invocation in "W.H." to "Keep, Time" to the poem "Open, Time" (LOA, 2: 531), Guiney associated temporal passages with death. She denied that "Open, Time" was a tribute to Whitman, saying that it was "written for no concrete man or reason, but [because] it came out as Walt lay dying, the clever newspapers immediately applied it to him. I wrote it for anybody dead tired of labor and the stuffy room." Was Guiney tired? Biographies, translations, critical prefaces, collections of neglected poets, and a host of essays filled her life in England, which she much preferred to "the noise, the publicity, the icicles, the mosquitoes, the extreme climatic conditions" of America. Her nickname for her homeland, "Hustlerium Tremens sive Americanitis" (trembling American hustler-itis), contrasts to what she called "Quiet London," the title of an essay published in *Patrins* in 1897. As Guiney remarks, "A certain subdued mighty hum London lacks not; but a crass explosion never breaks it. The imponderable quiet of the vast capital completes her inscrutable charm. She has the effect of a muted orchestra on ears driven mad with the horrible din of new America." In this tranquil setting, Guiney settled herself to become (as her best biographer dubbed her) "the laureate of the lost." "Apollo," she wrote, "has a class of might-have-beens whom he loves: poets bred in melancholy places, under disabilities, with thwarted growth and thinned voices; poets compounded of everything magical and fair . . . [but] which wants, in the end . . . the essence of immortality."

This was the poet who also wrote in the voice of Saint George (in "The Knight Errant"): "A short life in the saddle, Lord! / Not long life by the fire." The poem may constitute, as Harriet Monroe suggests, a "keenly personal confession": Guiney knew, by the time she published *Happy Ending*, that her poetic life had been short. On the other hand, she knew, too, as Alice Brown asserts, that she had "her own small public always. To these, her books were cool colonnades with the sea at the end." These few would have understood this poet's call to "Open, Time." Guiney, like those to whom she wrote, aspired to standards beyond mortal ken.

BARBARA RYAN

Selected Works

Songs at the Start, Boston, 1884
The White Sail and Other Poems, Boston, 1887
A Roadside Harp, Boston and New York, 1893
Nine Sonnets Written at Oxford, Cambridge, 1895
England and Yesterday, London, 1898
The Martyr's Idyl and Shorter Poems, Boston, 1900
Happy Ending, Boston, 1909, revised 1927
Letters of Louise Imogen Guiney, edited by Grace Guiney, preface by Agnes Repplier, New York and London: Harper, 1926
Recusant Poets, London and New York, 1938

Further Reading

Brown, Alice, *Louise Imogen Guiney*, New York: Macmillan, 1921
Fairbanks, Henry G., *Louise Imogen Guiney*, New York: Twayne, 1973
———, *Louise Imogen Guiney: Laureate of the Lost*, Albany, New York: Magi Books, 1972
Hart, Mary Adorita, Sister, *Soul Ordained to Fail*, New York: Pageant, 1962
Lears, T. J. Jackson, *No Place of Grace*, New York: Pantheon, 1981
Tenison, E. M., *Louise Imogen Guiney: Her Life and Works 1861–1920*, London: Macmillan, 1923

Fitz-Greene Halleck

(1790–1867)

Halleck was one of the first Americans whose fame rested principally on his being a poet. Universally respected during his lifetime (with the exception of a few dissenters such as Edgar Allan **Poe**), he was just as universally scorned after his death, which in turn has precipitated a neglect that endures today, even though he has always been accorded a brief mention in the standard literary histories. Properly regarded, Halleck emerges as having possessed a talent that produced exciting poetry in widely differing genres. His work epitomizes a time and a place – New York City and environs in the 1820s – as completely as has been achieved by any American poet. It is only a purist ideology that takes the Emersonian poetic line as a synecdoche for national identity that has removed Halleck from critical consideration for so long.

Ironically, Halleck, who was long considered the éminence grise of the "Knickerbocker School," was not born in New York State at all, but in Guilford, Connecticut, on July 8, 1790. Here, he impressed his local community as an introverted and bookish boy, before heading off to the already burgeoning metropolis. Hardly one who derived his income mainly from poetry, Halleck worked in various business positions: chief among them was his position as superintendent of most of the commercial interests of the famous millionaire John Jacob Astor. Halleck was a poet of the self-made, upper-middle class, and shared many of the assumptions of the audience for which he wrote. Most of his poetry was written in his youth, although he continued to write through the last decade of his life. Upon retirement, he returned to Guilford, where he died on November 19, 1867.

Halleck's poetic career began when he collaborated with his close friend Joseph Rodman **Drake** to produce the "Croaker" series in the *New York Evening Post* in 1819. These newspaper poems were, as to be expected, satiric and topical in nature. Their quality was so far above that of the usual fare, however, that the young men behind the pseudonymous persona of "Croaker" shot to sudden fame. In many ways, Halleck and Drake became famous because a newly assertive, expanding America was looking for young talent to celebrate the "era of good feelings." But this should not lead us to denigrate their talent. A look at the "new literatures in English" will show us that the same phenomenon has occurred in many later postcolonial societies such as Australia or Nigeria and that, despite some temporarily overrated reputations, many good writers have been recognized who otherwise would have been slighted because of their nations' perceived cultural marginality. Halleck and Drake may not have been world-class authors, but they were among the most talented poets America produced at the time, and their role in bringing the idea of an "American literature" to world prominence was an honorable one. Moreover, their collaboration – along with the presence in New York City of Washington Irving, James Fenimore Cooper, William Cullen **Bryant**, and James Kirke **Paulding** – helped create a civic culture, an urbanity that could appreciate great writing even if it did not always produce it.

"Marco Bozzaris" (LOA, 1: 101), one of Halleck's first poems not written in the "Croaker" persona, became his most famous lyric. As he put it in a letter to his sister, the poem was "the keystone of the arch of my renown." Part of this appeal had to do with its subject, the independence movement in Greece, which also made it the first American poem to be translated into modern Greek. Halleck's salute to the Greek rebel hero emanated from his Romantic philhellenism; but the poet's American perspective also suggests why this work redefines the tensions between tradition and modernity evident in work such as Percy Bysshe Shelley's Greek poems. As cultural heirs of classical learning and as members of a country that provided a contemporary exemplar for the fountainhead of democracy itself, early-century Americans felt a special fondness for Greece, which in part manifested in the modern Greek names such as "Ypsilanti" that are scattered among the Athenses and Corinths of the American Midwest. "Marco Bozzaris" is conscious of this kinship throughout, especially in terms of the way in which it presents the Greek struggle to an American readership. The first character encountered is not Bozzaris himself but a Turkish adversary, who dreams of conquest, of impressing his sovereign, and finally of a time when he would have "pressed that monarch's throne – a king." Note that the word "king" is used here and not "Sultan" – we are meant to think of some ambitious Redcoat officer standing stymied before Breed's Hill. As compared to the frivolous pomp of the Turk, Bozzaris the Greek is frugal and austere and leads a small "Suliote band" of guerrillas. Yet compared to classical warriors, Bozzaris's band is more reminiscent of a backwoods militia. This can be glimpsed in Bozzaris's cheers to his soldiers:

> "Strike – till the last armed foe expires;
> Strike – for your altars and your fires;
> Strike – for the green graves of your sires;
>   God – and your native land!"

This vigorous exhortation is quite reminiscent of the cry at the Revolutionary battle of Bennington, "For we must beat them, boys, ere set of sun / OR MARY STARK's a widow," which Halleck quotes in his poem "Connecticut." This allusion does not imply parochialism on Halleck's part, however; it is part of his effort to look beneath the historical trappings and see that the real significance of the Greek revolt went beyond classical nostalgia: for Halleck, the revolt's vision of freedom was not bound by ethnic or geographical limits. Bozzaris's summons to his men is compared to the cry that told Columbus that he had reached landfall. The martyred Bozzaris is at one with previous liberators whose death was but transfiguration: "For thou art Freedom's now, and Fame's; / One of the few, the immortal names, / That were not born to die." This transnational doctrine of liberation renders Bozzaris's significance as more than historical or political; he is a symbol of imaginative freedom that can endure as an example even while his heroism is, as a gesture, transitory.

The burden of the past is much more noticeable in Halleck's other famous poem on a European subject, "Alnwick Castle"

(LOA, 1: 98). This poem on the Northumbrian home of the aristocratic Percys describes and chronicles the house and its history in light, almost singsong stanzas. The point, however, is not to praise Alnwick Castle as such but to demonstrate how out of place it is in the modern world, which has surrendered to workaday commerce. But if Halleck does not particularly denounce commerce, neither does he lament the aristocracy. He is drawing a contrast that he wants the reader to recognize without necessarily taking sides or perceiving the contrast itself in hyperbolic terms. (A glance at Halleck's "The Poet's Daughter," which similarly questions the viability of the muse in the post-aristocratic, post-revolutionary world of the 1820s, shows that this poem is also aware of its own problematic at an immediate level: the very existence of a poem chronicling the fall of poetry in beautiful stanzas means there is obviously poetry after the death of Poetry as such.)

As an American, Halleck was alive to the contradictions of his still Europe-dominated world. His American perspective, moreover, is as much the key to the neutrality in "Alnwick Castle" as it is to the partisanship in "Marco Bozzaris." As an American, Halleck can look at the Northumbrian scene with a kind of wry bemusement and describe the way in which a past that he has never culturally "known" is buffeted by the same modernity that the American poet has imbibed from birth. The poem closes with the American observer cheerfully buying his way into Alnwick Castle for "ten-and-sixpence sterling" – not exactly a note of genteel regret. Much as in Henry Wadsworth **Longfellow's** "Belfry of Bruges," the celebration of the European past in "Alnwick Castle" emanates from an outside position that, although lacking a blatantly self-conscious nationalism, is nonetheless indelibly American in perspective. There is no way Sir Walter Scott could have written this poem, whatever affinity he might have felt for the subject.

Because Halleck does not adopt a tub-thumping nationalist rhetoric, critics have attacked him as derivative, particularly in regard to his narrative poem *Fanny* (1819), where he is accused of aping Lord Byron. This poem, of course, could be seen now as an act of postcolonial mimicry, with Halleck's seeming imitation constituting an act of dialogic subversion. A similar argument could be made about "Wyoming," which Halleck in part wrote as a response to the British poet Thomas Campbell's "Gertrude of Wyoming." The dynamic here, however, is even simpler. Halleck is poking fun at Campbell for writing a long poem about a place where he had never been. (The "Wyoming" here is not the later-named state but the county in Pennsylvania famed for Native American-settler warfare in the Revolutionary era.) Halleck made a point of actually visiting the Wyoming valley and demonstrating in his poem what Campbell had gotten right (not much) and gotten wrong (far more). In a friendlier, more jocose way, Halleck is making the same rejoinder to Campbell that African writers have made to Conrad's portrait of the continent in *Heart of Darkness*. Halleck did not mean to rival Campbell, whom he revered; indeed, he would be amazed to find both himself and the British poet in equal oblivion a century and a half later. Halleck is merely asserting his locality and, in a genial way, making as much of an advantage of it as possible.

Halleck's interest in local history is also seen in "Red Jacket" (LOA, 1: 104). Red Jacket, or Sagoyewetha, was a prominent Seneca chief during the late eighteenth and early nineteenth century who played a key role in relations between the previously powerful Iroquois confederacy and the federal government. In this poem, Halleck starts out by surveying the American national confidence that Cooper had already pictured in his "Leatherstocking" novels and by predicting that "in fifty years . . . / We shall export our poetry and wine; / And our brave fleet . . . / Will sweep the seas from Zembla to the Line" – predictions that were off by at most a few decades. Halleck starts out by surveying just this American national confidence, as pictured by Cooper and exemplified by predictions that "in fifty years . . . / We shall export our poetry and wine / And our brave fleet . . . / Will sweep the seas from Zembla to the Line" – predictions that were off by at most a few decades. But Halleck also calls attention to Red Jacket as a figure at once neglected by this triumphalism and peculiarly expressive of it: "we, the Democratic, / Outrival Europe, even in our Kings!" Comparing the Iroquois chieftain with European romantic-nationalist heroes such as Rob Roy or Robin Hood, Halleck admires Red Jacket's leadership skills, personal integrity, and spiritual convictions.

It is true, as Lucy Maddox has written in *Removals*, that much of the commonplace American literary praise of the Indian, however generous and admiring, was founded upon the Indians' having been politically and culturally wiped out or exiled westward. Halleck's praise of Red Jacket is admittedly in the mannered and rhetorical vein that is premised upon a general European victory in the continent's race wars. "Red Jacket" does not seek a full emotional reconciliation between natives and Europeans. Halleck's treatment thus differs from that of novelists such as Lydia Maria Child and Catherine Maria Sedgwick, who interrogated the possible harmony between white and native far more thoroughly. But our awareness of the racial self-interest contained in Halleck's poem should not blind us to his genuine reverence for the Native American leader or his noteworthy interest in claiming the Indian heritage for the cultural history of the entire nation.

Although only an adopted New Yorker, Halleck became a vigorous regional patriot, and part of Red Jacket's appeal for him must have been that he lived in western New York State. Halleck's adult allegiances are well displayed in a long poem he wrote about the state of his birth and childhood. "Connecticut" (LOA, 1: 107) evokes a regional rivalry between New York and its neighbor. The poem praises the ingenuity and conviction of the Connecticut Yankee, even as it mocks Puritan intolerance and witch-burning. Halleck is particularly scathing on the historical writings of Cotton Mather, whom he accuses of being as big a liar as Herodotus or Geoffrey of Monmouth. Implicitly, Halleck chastises Puritan New Englanders for being cruel to the Indians, and thus corroborates the sense of local pride in New York State's relative leniency. Although he prefers New York's easygoing pluralism to Connecticut's sometimes excessive probity, however, Halleck retains a wry and unsentimental affection for his homeland; he is capable of praising Mather a couple of stanzas after rebuking him, and the poem ends with an ode to the peace and plenty that Connecticut's brave soldiers had helped win in the rebellion against the British.

Fanny is Halleck's longest poem, and the most resistant to latter-day literary taste. Its failure to achieve Byron's quality of Byronism is often mentioned, but we should pay attention to what Halleck *does* achieve as a poet. Composed in six-line narrative stanzas with many interpolated "songs," *Fanny* chronicles a very American story of the loss and gain of wealth. In the poem, Fanny's beauty is celebrated by the young men of New York after her middle-class father makes enough money to smooth his entrance into high society. In the end, however, the money is lost as speedily as it was gained, and the grace and charm Fanny has afforded New York society prove ephemeral. Hoping at the end for redemption, the father hears music and fancies that it is "the music of the spheres." Instead, it is "Yankee Doodle played by Scudder's band," which in turn associates quick reverses in financial fortune with American nationhood. In the New York of *Fanny*, money makes or breaks everything; the poem anticipates later chroniclers of metropolitan manners such as Edith **Wharton**. *Fanny* is a very social poem because it concerns itself with economics and class mobility, but also because it is concerned with social mores and interpersonal relations. The poem's social emphasis has troubled readers apt to filter lyric poetry through a "romantic ideology" and to hold poetic utterance to a high lyrical standard. But the point may be moot now that poets such as George Crabbe and Charlotte Smith, whose view of the imagination is far less "esemplastic" than Samuel Taylor Coleridge's, have been admitted to the previously arch-visionary English Romantic canon.

The social orientation of *Fanny*, however, may prove less an obstacle to the contemporary reader than its intense localism. Halleck's description of 1820s New York is so specific to its time and place that it required footnotes even when the poem was republished late in his own lifetime. Even a New Yorker of much later vintage will find many of Halleck's references obscure or will sense that they have taken on a different connotation (his praise of the wild, forested beauty of Weehawken is particularly hilarious). The metropolitan area's exponential rate of growth rather than Halleck's verse is responsible for these incongruities; his description of the Hudson Highlands in "The Rhyme of the Ancient Coaster," for example, is much more recognizable. Halleck actually even articulates a credo of specificity in the course of the poem:

> Since that wise pedant, Johnson, was in fashion,
>   Manners have changed as well as moons; and he
> Would fret himself once more into a passion
>   Should he return (which Heaven forbid!) and see
> How strangely from his standard dictionary
> The meaning of some words is made to vary.

Halleck's transient mode of reference argues against the sort of general referentiality promoted by Dr. Johnson's dictionary and advocates the importance of specific terms, however time-bound the poet may acknowledge them to be. Once its haze of references to long-gone people, restaurants, social clubs, and shops is either penetrated or just taken as a given, moreover, *Fanny* does have its own drama and pathos. The perspective of the implied narrator and the tone of his resigned yet empathetic reaction to Fanny's rise and fall is interesting. And the song that closes the poem stays in the reader's mind, and, indeed, was one of the most treasured and quoted stanzas of Halleck's poetry:

> The moonlight music of the waves
> In storms is heard no more

> When the living lightning mocks the wreck
>   At midnight on the shore;
> And the mariner's song of home has ceased,
>   His corse is on the sea –
> And music ceases when it rains
>   In Scudder's balcony.

The music is Fanny's gaiety, and the rain is the economic distress into which her father falls. But Halleck's closing image, with its aura of sweet yet realistic melancholy and its characteristically particular reference to "Scudder's balcony," succeeds in capturing an emotional tone that is at once frolicsome and sensitively mature.

Fanny represented the peak of Halleck's poetic energy; after this point, he turned his attention more to the business and social worlds. One reason for this shift may have been the death of Drake. Halleck always claimed that Drake was the more talented of the two friends, a status inevitably accorded Drake by literary history because of his untimely death at age 25 in 1820. Halleck, who survived Drake by nearly a half-century, assumed the role of the less inspired but hardier of the pair, which has more to do with the traditional role of the mourner in elegy than with any noticeable inferiority in Halleck's skills. The death of Drake put Halleck in the elegiac position represented by Milton in "Lycidas" and Shelley in "Adonais." In these poems, both poets mourn the death of colleagues their age yet simultaneously define their own very much ongoing careers. Surprisingly, however, Halleck's elegy for Drake (LOA, 1: 97) is totally free of poetic posturing. Posed in stark, laconic quatrains, Halleck speaks simply to the subject of the loss of his friend and refrains from any self-indulgent rhetoric or any jostling for position within a crowded elegiac tradition.

> Green be the turf above thee,
>   Friend of my better days!
> None knew thee but to love thee,
> Nor named thee but to praise.

Revealingly, Halleck never once mentions that Drake is a poet; he is mourned entirely as a friend, which lends an unusually personal and honest note to the poem.

Most of Halleck's poetry, however, is quite the opposite of this almost blank straightforwardness. Poems such as "An Epistle to ****" depict a more characteristically bustling scene of current social interaction and establish conclusively that the 1820s was Halleck's decade and that he was its most thorough chronicler. Poised between the Jeffersonian and Jacksonian eras, the 1820s were an odd island in American history; at this moment in time, the accent seemed to be on national expansion and self-realization rather than the divisive issues of slavery and regionalism that would dominate the political discourse of succeeding decades. The atmosphere of this time remains strikingly vivid in Halleck's verse.

Halleck wrote far less during the remainder of his long life; however, one very late poem deserves mention. "Young America," written in the midst of the Civil War, although without direct reference to that conflict, is an allegory that depicts a 14-year-old boy who drowses off in a forest and ambles through a pastoral idyll. Although this idyll is replete with nymphs and fairies, it also expresses a genuine aesthetic and natural beauty. This prolonged reverie abruptly ends when the boy wakes up and realizes that he will soon turn 15 and that he therefore needs to dedicate himself to wooing a rich wife. The implication is clear: for all of America's lofty aspirations and the inner and outer beauty of its national self-conception, the threat, as well as the reality, of an uglier and more expedient ethic is always close at hand. This conclusion, at once a more realistic and a more imaginative view of the interaction of money and imagination than the one that Halleck represented at the end of "Alnwick Castle," reveals that even in his old age, the poet's acute social observation still complemented his truly individual creative spirit.

NICHOLAS BIRNS

Selected Works

The Poetical Writings of Fitz-Greene Halleck, edited by James Grant Wilson, New York: Appleton, 1901

Further Reading

Adkins, Nelson, *Fitz-Greene Halleck*, New Haven, Connecticut: Yale University Press, 1930

Bender, Thomas, *New York Intellect*, New York: Knopf, 1987

Callow, James T., *Kindred Spirits: Knickerbocker Writers and American Artists, 1807–1855*, Chapel Hill: University of North Carolina Press, 1967

Duyckinck, Evert A., *A Memorial of Fitz-Greene Halleck*, New York: Amerman & Wilson, 1877

Hows, John Augustus, *In the Woods with Bryant, Longfellow, and Halleck*, New York: J. G. Gregory, 1863

Mabie, Hamilton Wright, *The Writers of Knickerbocker New York*, New York, Grolier, 1912

Maddox, Lucy, *Removals: Nineteenth-Century American Literature and the Politics of Indian Affairs*, New York: Oxford University Press, 1991

Miller, Perry, *The Raven and the Whale*, New York: Harcourt, 1956

Poe, Edgar Allan, "Fitz-Greene Halleck," in "The Literati of New York City," *Complete Works of Edgar Allan Poe*, vol. 15, New York: AMS, 1965

Wilson, James Grant, *The Life and Letters of Fitz-Greene Halleck*, New York: Appleton, 1869

———, *The Memorial History of the City of New York*, New York: New York History, 1893

Frances Ellen Watkins Harper

(1825–1911)

When Frances E. W. Harper's Philadelphia home was restored in 1988, her poem "Bury Me in a Free Land" was engraved on a bronze plaque and mounted next to the front door. For the "bronze muse" of the abolitionist movement, this work was the most prominent of her antislavery poems. First published in the *Liberator* in 1864, it endured beyond Harper's life and has assured her position in African American literature. The origin of the poem was found in an 1858 letter to William Still, a black Philadelphia "stationmaster" for the underground railroad and a lifelong friend of Harper's:

> Well, perhaps it is my lot to die from home and be buried among strangers; and yet I do not regret that I espoused this cause; perhaps I have been of some service to the cause of human rights, and I hope the consciousness that I have not lived in vain, will be a halo of peace around my dying bed, a heavenly sunshine lighting up the dark valley and shadow of death.

> Make me a grave where'er you will,
> In a lowly plain, or a lofty hill,
> Make it among earth's humblest graves,
> But not in a land where men are slaves.

> I have lived in the midst of oppression and wrong, and I am saddened by every captured fugitive in the North [i.e., under the federal Fugitive Slave Law of 1850]; a blow has been struck at my freedom; North and South have both been guilty, and they that sin must suffer.

Harper was born free on September 24, 1825; there is no record of who her father was, and her mother's early death left her orphaned before she was three. On a primal level, the death of her mother haunted the imagery of her poetry, and an undercurrent of loneliness resided in her steadfast embrace of human suffering. In another letter to Still, Harper explains: "Oh, is it not a privilege, if you are sisterless and lonely, to be a sister to the human race, and to place your heart where it may throb close to downtrodden humanity." Her early losses infused her poetry with empathetic appeal; for instance, she compared the selling of slave children away from their mothers to the death of loved ones. Written in the first person, "Bury Me in a Free Land" is perhaps as much the poet's epitaph as it is a protest poem. Her other abolitionist poems are tales of escaping slaves who brave death for freedom or sacrifice their lives, but in this poem she reveals her political commitment in a personal voice and projects slavery as the hell that will haunt her grave. This is the consciousness of a nineteenth-century woman whose life was beleaguered by the social curses of caste and class.

In late September 1854, Harper delivered her first lecture on behalf of the antislavery cause in New Bedford. One month later, her second book of poetry, *Poems on Miscellaneous Subjects*, was published in Boston, with an introduction by the abolitionist William Lloyd Garrison. Many of these poems were reprinted from her first book, *Forest Leaves* (1846), as well as from abolitionist periodicals. She had already accrued a modest literary reputation, which this second book dramatically expanded. Its thematic range challenges the philosophical foundation of the "free republic"; confronts American social, political, and cultural repression; and exposes contradictions to the democratic ideal. Harper's religious poetry, in particular, opposes popular biblical misinterpretations used to validate slavery and repress women. More broadly, the topics pivot around human suffering and the "miscellaneous" format of the book shows the poet's farsighted radical vision, which takes in lower-class oppression, Charles Dickens's England, the temperance crusade, male-female relationships and gender attitudes. The recent republication of her poetry and prose has not only reestablished her prominence in African American literature but demonstrated the relevance of her class-conscious feminism to contemporary history.

When her poetry engages the perspective of the slave woman, it reveals how racism and sexism converge to preserve a classist society. Many of her abolitionist poems depict the destruction of the slave family. Her works represent the way in which slave mothers are physically and emotionally abused and their children become destined for debasing servitude. Other poems about enslaved men describe heroic acts of resistance and escape, and thus contradict propaganda about the "contented slave" and the stereotype of the "docile Negro."

Harper's class-consciousness is evident in such poems as "Died of Starvation" and "The Slave Mother" (see LOA, 2: 167 for an earlier version). Even though the first poem, which was inspired by scenes in Charles Dickens's *Oliver Twist*, deals with the underclass in Victorian England and the second poem charts the slave experience in America, there is a striking similarity between the poems' disenfranchised "characters" and their perspectives of desperation and defeat.

> But the embers were too feeble,
>   She could not see each face,
> So she clasped her arms around them –
>   'Twas their mother's last embrace.
>   ("Died of Starvation")

> They tear him from her circling arms,
>   Her vast and fond embrace.
> Oh! never more may her sad eyes
>   Gaze on his mournful face.

> No marvel, then, these bitter shrieks
>   Disturb the listening air:
> She is the mother, and her heart
>   Is breaking in despair.
>   ("The Slave Mother")

Harper's preference for the ballad form had direct bearing on the practicality of her art, and she frequently incorporated dialogue in her poems, thereby personalizing and dramatizing her point of view. Her poetry was integrally related to her activism – her lectures and political writing. Her overriding purpose was to challenge the white male supremacist view in social, political, and cultural terms, and the ballad form helped Harper embrace the natural lyrical patterns of nineteenth-century mass culture; the form's flexible meter also coincided well with the elocutionary format.

Moreover, Harper's activism intensified her creative efforts. She wove her poems into the context of her lectures, and the abolitionist platform enhanced her national stature as an intellectual and artist. Her imagery was intended to disturb audiences by focusing on individual slave experiences, and thus personalizing the appeal for justice. Harper suffused the audience's thoughts with these subjective experiences, which she reinforced with subliminal poetic devices and the power of rhyme. The physical and cultural distance that contributed to northern indifference to southern slavery was bridged by such storytelling.

"The Slave Auction" (LOA, 2: 169), one of Harper's most famous poems, begins with stanzas that present slavery as an extension of an inhumane economic institution. She emphasizes the moral disgrace of dealing in human life by directing attention to the emotional humiliation and devastation of those being bartered, which she contrasts to the abstract insensitivity of the slave dealers:

> The sale began – young girls were there,
>   Defenceless in their wretchedness,
> Whose stifled sobs of deep despair
>   Revealed their anguish and distress.
>
> And mothers stood, with streaming eyes,
>   And saw their dearest children sold;
> Unheeded rose their bitter cries,
>   While tyrants barter'd them for gold.

The poem evokes an emotional response by means of a graphic description of the trauma of being a slave on the block. A complex interplay between low pitch and slow syllabic duration underscores these dehumanizing dynamics. The poem opens with the African women internalizing the shame of their nakedness in the human marketplace. The second stanza expands the picture, with children being severed from their screaming mothers. This terrorizing destruction of the family is further dramatized as the power of the slave market divorces these women from their husbands. The fourth stanza crystallizes the composition with a shift in perspective, as "shrinking children" foreshadow the subjugation of "that mournful band." The ultimate gesture of the poem is a direct appeal to the audience's empathy, which references familial grief at the death of loved ones. Slavery is depicted as an agonizing existence, grimmer than such grief and crueler than death.

> Ye who have laid your lov'd to rest,
>   And wept above their lifeless clay,
> Know not the anguish of that breast,
>   Whose lov'd are rudely torn away.
>
> Ye may not know how desolate
>   Are bosoms rudely forced to part,
> And how a dull and heavy weight
>   Will press the life-drops from the heart.

"The Slave Mother (A Tale of the Ohio)" is based on a true story of a runaway slave who was tracked down by slave catchers after reaching Ohio (the story is retold in Toni Morrison's *Beloved* [1988]). In despair, the mother kills one of her children and attempts to slay the others rather than see them enslaved again:

> I will save my precious children
>   From their darkly threatened doom,
> I will hew their path to freedom
>   Through the portals of the tomb.

The mother is restrained from killing all of her children by the captors. Rather than leave things to the audience's logic, the poet describes the mother's action as a "deed of fearful daring" and raises the rhetorical question: "Do the icy hands of slavery / Every pure emotion chill?" The last stanza, like that of "The Slave Auction," rallies for the antislavery cause and appeals to the moral responsibility of the audience:

> Oh! if there is any honor,
>   Truth or justice in the land,
> Will ye not, as men and Christians,
>   On the side of freedom stand?

"The Tennessee Hero" is another poem based on "an actual incident in 1856," and it invokes the voice of a dead slave, an unheralded hero. The poem's epigraph reads: "He had heard his comrades plotting to obtain their liberty, and rather than betray them he received 750 lashes and died." "The Tennessee Hero" champions one man's resistance against sanctioned tyranny; at the same time, it counters the racist assumption that black men do not "inherently" possess ethical principles. The dramatic tension of the poem takes the form of a confrontational dialogue between the slave and his assailants. The hero's defiance defines resistance to tyranny as natural, necessary, and spiritual:

> Like storms of wrath, of hate and pain,
>   The blows rained thick and fast;
> But the monarch soul kept true
>   Till the gates of life were past.
>
> And the martyr spirit fled
>   To the throne of God on high,
> And showed his gaping wounds
>   Before unslumbering eye.

"Free Produce" refers to a form of abolitionism that advocated the boycott of products generated from slave labor. In an October 1854 letter to William Still, Harper explains that her commitment to this movement resulted from reading the slave narrative of Solomon Northrup: "Oh, how can we pamper our appetites upon luxuries drawn from reluctant fingers? Oh, could slavery exist long if it did not sit on a commercial throne? I have reason to be thankful that I am able to give a little more for a Free Labor dress, if it is coarser. I can thank God that upon its warf and woof I see no stain of blood and tears." The poem develops around the image of the poet's dress, and, as in much of her writing, Harper uses language directly from her correspondence:

> And from its ample folds
> Shall rise no cry to God,
> Upon its warp and woof shall be
> No stain of tears and blood.

Thus, the dress becomes a symbol of freedom, as the aspects of its design are contrasted with the horrors of slavery.

"Lines" (see LOA, 2: 170 for a later revision) first appeared in the *National Anti-Slavery Standard* in November 1856. Unlike "The Slave Auction," "The Tennessee Hero," or "The Slave Mother," which focus on specific people and events, this poem is more general and personifies slavery itself as an evil force. In particular, the poem addresses the expansion of slavery and envisions this force kidnapping babies, spreading hatred, and causing pain and suffering. In the poem, Harper appeals for justice and for the audience to join in the fight against slavery – a struggle inspired by God's will to free His children.

> If ye strive for Truth and Justice,
>   If ye battle for the Right,
> Ye shall lay your hands all strengthened
>   On God's robe of love and light;
>
> But if ye trample on His children,
>   To His ear will float each groan,
> Jar the cords that bind them to Him,
>   And they'll vibrate at his throne.

The imagery of another poem, "Bury Me in a Free Land," reverses the common association of death with peaceful slumber and depicts criminal violations against the enslaved, including murder, kidnapping, and rape:

> I could not sleep if I saw the lash
> Drinking her blood at each fearful gash,
> And I saw her babes torn from her breast,
> Like trembling doves from their parent nest.
>
> I'd shudder and start if I heard the bay
> Of bloodhounds seizing their human prey,
> And I heard the captive plead in vain
> As they bound afresh his galling chain.
>
> If I saw young girls from their mothers' arms
> Bartered and sold for their youthful charms,
> My eye would flash with a mournful flame,
> My death-paled cheek glow red with shame.

The poem's tone and themes may allude to the death of William Watkins, the most influential person in Harper's early life. Harper's maternal uncle, Watkins raised and educated his niece. He died in Toronto in 1858, the year the poem appeared. He had moved to Canada shortly before, because he wanted to spend the last years of his life on "free land." Harper also sent this poem to Aaron A. Stevens, who was convicted for treason for his participation in John Brown's raid on Harpers Ferry in 1859. After Stevens was hanged, the poem, which he had hand copied, was found in his trunk.

Harper's dedication to freedom also included her interest in the plight of women in "free" society. "The Contrast" criticizes the hypocrisy of gender values by telling the story of a woman who is disgraced for her involvement in a love affair, while the man, a person of position and wealth, is assured impunity and marries another in a proper ceremony.

> None scorned him for his sinning,
>   Few saw it through his gold;

> His crimes were only foibles,
>   And these were gently told.

The poem, however, provides a typical Victorian twist to this all too common scenario. In the poem's second part, the man stands undaunted at the altar, but a vision of "the other woman's" funeral flashes before his shocked consciousness: the "scorned" woman is dead. The superimposition of the funeral over the wedding creates a contrast that emphasizes the tragic consequences of an endorsed double standard in society.

Harper revives this theme but revises the plot in "A Double Standard" (1895), which transforms tragic resignation into feminist resistance and a transcendent consciousness. Instead of committing suicide, the shunned woman testifies against the privileged position of the man, repudiates social condemnation, and chooses a life that has been renewed through spiritual redemption. Like Eve, she was tempted by the "adder's hiss," and like the Samaritan woman, her lips were pressed to stone. But like Jesus, who defended the Samaritan woman condemned for alleged infidelity, Harper becomes the shunned woman's advocate. The poem promotes forgiveness and transcendence in order to reverse Victorian patriarchal and religious persecution.

Harper's radical Christianity underlined and facilitated her feminist and abolitionist convictions. Seeing conventional Christianity as largely corrupted by the economic and social designs of white patriarchal culture, the poet sought to reveal the contradictions in orthodox theological interpretations and their impact on everyday experience. The poem "Bible Defence of Slavery" (LOA, 2: 168) highlights the difference between "Mount Zion, the city of the living God," and the "New Egypt" in the United States. The poem attacks an 1851 book of the same title that distorts biblical texts to support the institution of slavery, employs pseudoscientific logic to prove Caucasian supremacy, and promotes "a plan of national colonization for the entire removal of the free blacks."

The poem aptly indicts this racist religious appeal by identifying its contradictions and by explaining how it endangers the moral and social integrity of the country. Harper refers to Sodom and Gomorrah (Genesis 13:10), whose wicked citizens were destroyed by God (Matthew 10:15), and concludes that such denigration will be answered on Judgment Day. The poem forewarns against the treachery of church and state:

> A "reverend" man, whose light should be
>   The guide of age and youth,
> Brings to the shrine of Slavery
>   The sacrifice of truth!
>
> For the direst wrong by men imposed,
>   Since Sodom's fearful cry,
> The word of life has been unclos'd,
>   To give your God the lie.
>
> Oh! when ye pray for heathen lands,
>   And plead for their dark shores,
> Remember Slavery's cruel hands
>   Make heathens at your doors!

"Vashti," from *Poems* (1871), one of Harper's later and most exemplary religious poems, deserves attention. Characteristic of her feminist revisions of biblical interpretations, the poem focuses on the banishment of a queen of Persia who refuses to be disgraced by her king's demand that she unveil before a crowd of drunken men. The king wants to display her beauty as his prize possession. Defending her self-respect, she exclaims:

> "I'll take the crown from off my head
>   And tread it 'neath my feet
> Before their rude and careless gaze
>   My shrinking eyes shall meet.
>
> A queen unveil'd before the crowd! –
>   Upon each lip my name! –
> Why, Persia's women all would blush
>   And weep for Vashti's shame!"

This act of resistance is met with a patriarchal protest by the king's counselors:

> "The women, restive 'neath our rule,
>   Would learn to scorn our name,
> And from her deed to us would come
>   Reproach and burning shame."

The king is encouraged to dethrone and banish the queen from his vast kingdom, which stretches "From distant Jud to Ethiop." In addition to Harper's portrayal of this repressive act, which the poem also associates with intemperance, the geographic detail invokes a black African historical presence that contrasts to the exclusion of Africa from orthodox religious teachings and from some versions of the Bible.

Temperance was also a key issue for Christian abolitionists and radical feminists, and it found favor in Harper's poetry. As in her class-conscious Dickens poem, "Died of Starvation," her dedication to the temperance movement indicates a far-reaching progressive vision. Alcoholism was one of the most destructive forces in oppressed communities and families during the nineteenth century, and "The Drunkard's Child" dramatizes the pathos of its devastating impact. As in "Died of Starvation" and "The Slave Mother (A Tale of the Ohio)," this poem ends with death. It also provokes the audience's imagination, empathy, and moral outrage when the father acknowledges the fatal consequence of his parental negligence. In "The Revel," Harper equates drink with death and counters the illusion of gaiety and mirth with a warning:

> The wine cup's sparkling glow
>   Blends with the viands rare,
> There's revelry and show,
>   But still, the dead are there!

Death figures as the ultimate deliverer in these poems because an indifferent society rules. The grave becomes the cistern for human resignation and the only way to end grief. Twentieth-century resistance to sentimentality is a common critical excuse for the aesthetic dismissal of such poems. But as evidenced in the work of Elizabeth Barrett Browning and many other nineteenth-century women poets, the purpose of such poetry is to instigate a passionate response. Harper conveyed this same sentimental charge from the lectern to heighten the subjective receptivity of her audience. She intended to effect others' feelings, and thereby, to alter their actions.

By 1858, *Poems on Miscellaneous Subjects* had reached 12,000 copies in print, and by 1874, it had been reprinted seven times. Harper's perspective in this volume is holistic and transcendent; she addresses the compounded forms of injustice in American society and reiterates the need for spiritual clarity. Poems written after 1854 were collected in *Poems* (1871), an elegant hardcover, which was reprinted in different colors, and which added and deleted poems until its final edition in 1901. *Poems* contains inspirational verses such as "Words for the Home," which recruits for the Civil War; "The Freedom Bill," which pronounces all the nation free; and the salutatory "President Lincoln's Proclamation of Freedom," which anticipates "the glorious dawn of freedom," and which was also collected in Lydia Maria Child's *The Freedmen's Book* (1865). As in "Lines" – where the subject is the expansion of slavery, subjectified as a force of oppression – "President Lincoln's Proclamation" represents the force of freedom as a beacon that overcomes and that leads the way out of oppressive darkness:

> Like the dim and ancient chaos,
>   Shrinking from the dawn of light,
> Oppression, grim and hoary,
>   Shall cower at the light.

Frances Ellen Watkins was married in 1860, to Fenton Harper of Ohio, but the brief marriage ended abruptly when he died in 1864, leaving the poet with their daughter and his three children from a previous marriage. In January 1865, Harper returned to her birthplace of Baltimore after 11 years away. En route, in November 1864, she celebrated the new status of Maryland as a slave-free state with the black abolitionist and journalist Henry Highland Garnett at the Cooper Institute in New York City. In Baltimore, she was reunited with the Watkinses and Frederick Douglass, a former Maryland slave who was visiting with his newly emancipated sister for the first time in 30 years. Thereafter, Harper made her home in Philadelphia, securing a house on Bainbridge Street, which was situated within walking distance of her friend William Still and the old underground railroad network.

Her poetry continued to flourish and expand with the demands of her activism. According to Still, 50,000 copies of her first four books were in print by 1872. *Moses, A Story of the Nile* (1869) demonstrates her most accomplished work, and *Sketches of Southern Life* (1872) stands as her most innovative performance. The title poem, "Sketches of Southern Life," which is voiced in the first person and written in the ballad form for its musicality and compatibility with dialect, is a sort of poetic slave narrative that advocates Harper's religious, educational, feminist, and political convictions. "Learning to Read," a part of the long title poem, addresses the quest for literacy during and after slavery. Aunt Chloe, this poem's speaker, conveys the historical connection between African American education and racial repression: "Our masters always tried to hide / Book learning from our eyes." The popular belief of the slaveholding class was that an educated slave was a discontented slave; earlier in the century, in fact, the impact of David Walker's *Appeal to the Colored Citizens of the World* (1829), which advocated violent resistance to slavery, and Nat Turner's rebellion in 1830 had both encouraged the enactment of antiliteracy legislation.

Aunt Chloe relays the tales of Uncle Caldwell and Ben Turner, who pursued reading during slavery despite the threat of punishment. Caldwell "took pot liquor fat / and greased the pages of his book / and hid it in his hat." This maneuver fooled his overseers, who would not suspect these "greasy papers" were part of a library. Ben Turner, a character in Harper's 1892 novel *Iola Leroy* (and possibly an allusion to Nat Turner), "heard the children spell," memorized their words, and learned to read by aural association. Chloe also tells that earlier she "longed to read [her] Bible," but because she was "rising sixty," most folks said it was too late. But Chloe considered her age an incentive and did not stop studying until she could read the "hymns and Testament." Afterward, she acquired her own place, which allows the poem to connect literacy to self-sufficiency and autonomy, as well as to spiritual independence:

> Then I got a little cabin
>   A place to call my own –
> And I felt as independent
>   As a queen upon her throne.

"Aunt Chloe's Politics" – the third and shortest part of the poem – attacks the diabolical motives of politicians, white and black, with sardonic similes:

> I've seen 'em honey-fugle round,
>   And talk so awful sweet,
> That you'd think them full of kindness,
>   As an egg is full of meat.

Harper's political concern, shared by the freedwomen whom she deals with in her letters and essays, is for the future of the race; in particular, "we want to school our children." Likewise, Chloe's politics do not exempt responsibility according to color:

> If money isn't there,
> Whether black or white have took it,
>   The loss we all must share.
>
> And this buying up each other
>   Is something worse than mean,
> Though I thinks a heap of voting,
>   I go for voting clean.

As Harper makes clear, black women (like white women) did not have the vote, but they realized the value of electoral politics to the race. In fact, Harper was a leader in the women's movement, working with Susan B. Anthony and Elizabeth Cady Stanton, speaking at the Woman's Rights Convention in 1866 in New York, and holding office in various women's organizations. "An Appeal to My Country Women" was published in 1900, when the lynching of black men, women, and children was at a critical high. And at a time when one of the major differences between white and black feminists was the issue of race, the poem explicitly addresses lynching as a woman's issue by indicting white women for their silent complicity with their male counterparts and by warning them that their privileged position will not protect their descendants against the legacy of racist crimes:

> Oh, people sin-laden and guilty,
>   So lusty and proud in your prime,
> The sharp sickles of God's retribution
>   Will gather your harvest of crime.

> Weep not, oh my well-sheltered sisters,
>   Weep not for the Negro alone,
> But weep for your sons who must gather
>   The crops which their fathers have sown.

> Go read on the tombstones of nations
>   Of chieftains who masterful trod,
> The sentence which time has engraven,
>   That they had forgotten their God.

> 'Tis the judgment of God that men reap
>   The tares which in madness they sow,
> Sorrow follows the footsteps of crime,
>   And Sin is the consort of Woe.

Frances E. W. Harper's presence profoundly effected and furthered the human rights struggle carried on during Reconstruction by the Colored Women's Clubs and by the temperance and suffrage movements, and her poetry became even more politically pronounced in the process. The educational and cultural needs of the "free communities" were central to her vision of creative expression: "If our talents are to be recognized we must write less of issues that are particular and more of feelings that are general. We are blessed with hearts and brains that encompass more than ourselves in our present plight. . . . We must look to the future which, God willing, will be better than the present or the past, and delve into the heart of the world."

MELBA JOYCE BOYD

Selected Works

Forest Leaves, Baltimore, Maryland: n.p., 1846
Poems on Miscellaneous Subjects, Boston: J. B. Yerrinton and Sons, 1854
Poems on Miscellaneous Subjects, Philadelphia, Pennsylvania: Merrihew & Thompson, 1857
Moses: A Story of the Nile, Philadelphia, Pennsylvania: Merrihew and Son, 1869
Poems, Philadelphia, Pennsylvania: Merrihew and Son, 1871
Sketches of Southern Life, Philadelphia, Pennsylvania: Merrihew and Son, 1872
Poems, Providence, Rhode Island: A. Crawford Greene and Son, 1880
Iola Leroy or Shadows Uplifted, Boston: James H. Earle, 1892; reprinted, New York: Oxford University Press, 1988
Complete Poems of Frances E. W. Harper, edited by Maryemma Graham, New York: Oxford University Press, 1988

Further Reading

Aptheker, Bettina, *Woman's Legacy*, Amherst: University of Massachusetts Press, 1982
Boyd, Melba Joyce, *Discarded Legacy: Politics and Poetics in the Life of Frances Ellen Watkins Harper 1825–1911*, Detroit, Michigan: Wayne State University Press, 1994
Foster, Frances Smith, *A Brighter Coming Day*, New York: Feminist Press, 1990
Giddings, Paula, *When and Where I Enter*, New York: William Morrow, 1984

Redding, Jay Saunders, *To Make A Poet Black*, Chapel Hill: University of North Carolina Press, 1939

Redmond, Eugene B., ed., *Drumvoices: The Mission of Afro-American Poetry*, Garden City, Nee York: Anchor Press/Doubleday, 1976

Sherman, Joan R., *Invisible Poets*, Urbana: University of Illinois Press, 1974

Sterling, Dorothy, *We Are Your Sisters*, New York: Norton, 1984

Stetson, Erlene, *Black Sister: Poetry by Black American Women, 1746–1980*, Bloomington: Indiana University Press, 1981

Still, William, *The Underground Rail Road*, Philadelphia, Pennsylvania: Porter & Coates, 1872

Washington, Mary Helen, *Invented Lives: Narratives of Black Women 1860–1960*, New York: Anchor Press/Doubleday, 1987

Francis Brett (Bret) Harte

(1836–1902)

Bret Harte is best known for his popular stories about the mining camps of northern California during the Gold Rush years. American literature anthologies usually include his tales to demonstrate the transition that bridges a dying romanticism with a developing realism. Some authorities point to Harte's depiction of character, setting, and plot, and to his use of the vernacular to support including him in the realistic movement. His fiction, moreover, is often classified among local-color prose works of the nineteenth century. Harte's stories are frequently noted for his combined use of pathos and humor, and his treatment of the paradoxical in human nature. His fiction is sometimes praised for its originality and directness, but it must be said that, in all of its characteristics, Harte's work is just as often criticized.

While the merits of Harte's short fiction have continued to be a subject of critical commentary and controversy, his plays, novels, literary criticism, and poetry have all but been ignored in this century. Along with many volumes of postbellum verse, his poetry, especially, has been condemned as "sentimental." This is unfortunate because, like much other verse written after the Civil War, Harte's poetry not only sheds light on the social conditions out of which it grew but also becomes more engaging itself as we more fully understand its historical context.

Harte was born in Albany, New York, to Henry Harte, a schoolmaster, and Elizabeth Rebecca (Ostrander) Harte. Although he left school at the age of 14 and supported himself by working first in a lawyer's office and then later in a counting-house, Harte read widely. He especially enjoyed Charles Dickens, from whom he learned to depict the foibles and virtues of common people with the realism and pathos. This strategy won both authors accolades from contemporary readers. In 1845, Harte's father died, and in 1854, his eighteenth year, Harte and his sister sailed to San Francisco to join their recently remarried mother. There, he taught school and clerked in a drugstore. Harte also probably rode a pony express route and mined the mother lode near Stanislaus.

Although Harte had published his first poem at age 11 and the collection *The Lost Galleon and Other Tales* in 1867, it was not until the success of his story "The Luck of Roaring Camp" (1868) and his enormously popular verse narrative, "Plain Language from Truthful James" (1870; LOA, 2: 340), that Harte's abilities to spin an entertaining tale in the vein of other vernacular humorists became apparent to the public. Although critics often consider his efforts second-rate, Harte's work continues to be included in anthologies and enjoyed by students. For many authorities, however, Harte's local color and realism fail to explain his continued popularity. Rather, it is his humor that keeps his fiction, at least, in the modern critical limelight. It is the humor of his poetry, too, that obliges us to take another look. For the humor that has kept his fiction alive is even more unmistakable in the concentrated form of his verses.

To fully appreciate Harte's poetry, one must be acquainted with the genres of nineteenth-century humorous verse. After the Civil War, two types of humorous verse reacted to the failed dreams of prewar idealism. These two otherwise different types shared two characteristics. Both popular vernacular humorists and elitist society poets wrote to discredit romantic individualism, and both partook of an element of sentimentalism that had its roots in the eighteenth century and that remained a major philosophical force throughout the nineteenth century. Both local-color humorists and vers-de-société wits thus continued to value the sentimental ideal of expressing "genuine sympathy" with humanity. Both types of verse have been misunderstood in our century – in part because of our failure to understand Victorian culture in general.

As recent research is beginning to demonstrate, however, the eighteenth-century philosophy of moral sentiments and its definitions of human nature influenced much of Victorian literature on both sides of the Atlantic. Believing that – in Fred Kaplan's words – "human beings are innately good, that the source of evil is malignant social conditioning, and that the spontaneous, uninhibited expression of the natural feelings . . . is admirable and the basis for successful human relationships," Victorian authors such as Dickens and William Makepeace Thackeray wrote literature that defended against the devaluing of human potential, which seemed threatened both by scientific positivism and by traditional religious notions of fallen nature. Further, unlike the romantic prophet/poet, who isolated himself in a self-sufficient, imaginative flight into the joy and misery of the spiritual realm, the Victorian poet who was influenced by this sentimentalist moral sense expressed community values of optimism and benevolence toward humanity. "Sentimentalists," those who adhered to this philosophy, believed in "the universal potential for moral reformation of the human community through an appeal to the moral sentiments." In this model, therefore, our innately good feelings make us naturally and genuinely sympathetic with our neighbors; when we feel sorrow or happiness in concert with the human community and when we act on those feelings, all humanity benefits. According to sentimentalists, genuine sympathy was a necessary feature in the inevitable progress of humankind, and they opposed it to individualism and self-reliance.

Like other early realists, including Dickens, Harte might with accuracy be called a "sentimental realist." Rejecting the idealization of the common individual, sentimental realists embraced a sympathetic optimism for humanity and yet described the very real conditions and characters they witnessed. Harte, along with Will Carleton, John Hay, and other American poets, used a sympathetic backwoods humor to paint the unrefined scenes around them. Although Harry Hayden Clark has marked 1871 as the beginning of "The Rise of Realism," he and other modern critics have paid little attention to the significant movement of realism impelled by sentiment. The year of Clark's assigned watershed, Hay's humorously sentimental *Pike County Ballads* and Carleton's first volume of humorous poems about midwestern farm life made record sales. Just the year before, Harte's hugely popular "Truthful James" had been published.

The tender sentiments of Carleton's *Farm Ballads* (1873),

although practically unknown today, share elements of both the sweet, romanticized, eastern humor of Henry Wadsworth **Longfellow** and the raucous revelry of the western local colorists. A contributor to the *Ladies Repository* applauded Carleton's "homeliness," testifying that "we know of nothing more natural, quaintly humorous and touching, than these ballad-like productions. They enter right into the loves and hates and prejudices of the masses, and express them in their own language." Like Harte, Carleton was praised by reviewers for his "blend of sentimentality, rustic humor, and dialect." As a whole, his *Farm Ballads* and *Farm Legends* (1876) and eight additional volumes sold 500,000 copies during Carleton's lifetime. He treated his characters, like the popular favorite "Uncle Sammy," with the sympathy required by sentimentalist philosophy. In *Farm Ballads*, "Uncle Sammy" is introduced by a sympathetically amused narrator:

> Some men were born for great things,
>   Some were born for small;
> Some – it is not recorded
>   Why they were born at all;
> But Uncle Sammy was certain he had a legitimate call.
>
> Some were born with a talent,
>   Some with scrip and land;
> Some with a spoon of silver,
>   And some with a different brand;
> But Uncle Sammy came holding an argument in each
>   hand.

Uncle Sammy's adventures in arguing his way through life and marriage pleased Carleton's readers. Although relegating Carleton to the status of poet of the populace, reviewers found the sentiment of his humor genuine and touching. His sympathetic treatment of men and women fit perfectly with the sentimental ideal of goodwill toward one's friends and neighbors; at the same time, he realistically depicted people both familiar and authentic.

The verses of another humorist, John Hay, also did well in the marketplace. But Hay's poetry, like Harte's, was often panned by reviewers who felt his ironic sympathy extended too far toward characters who were undeserving of compassion or understanding. One critic called Hay's *Pike County Ballads* "blasphemous" and denounced his "vulgarity"; this criticism also was often leveled at Harte's vernacular verses. For instance, Hay's riverboat hero, Jim Bludso (LOA, 2: 381), who had "One wife in Natchez-under-the-Hill / And another one here, in Pike," was considered "offensive to decency." Because nineteenth-century doctrines of moral sentiments continued to emphasize eighteenth-century notions of good works and benevolence, however, Hay's riverboat captain, despite a lifetime of wild conduct, is counted a hero when he saves a group of people. Although some reviewers objected, America's poetry reading public eagerly looked for humor and sympathy in the less-than-perfect world they saw during the years of disillusionment following the Civil War. Hay, like Harte, found he could sell his poems by creating characters who, if they had no other virtues, at least followed the sentiments of the moral doctrine of benevolence toward their fellow backwoods rascals.

Even more than Carleton's or Hay's verses, Bret Harte's po-

etry pleased popular and critical readers. And even more than Hay, Harte satirized the society in which he lived. He lampooned love, the western hero, manifest destiny, war, racial stereotypes, and other sacred cows of his day. Several of Harte's poems, for example, mock his culture's fascination with science. Poems entitled "To the Pliocene Skull: A Geological Address," "A Geological Madrigal: After Shenstone," and "The Society upon the Stanislaus" parody the seriousness with which the nineteenth-century scientific community took itself and its discoveries.

In "The Society upon the Stanislaus," Harte burlesques scientific "societies" of his day. When a group of backwoods characters put on eastern airs and form a society, the results mock the pretensions of both the cultured elitists and their country cousins. In addition, when the "natural and innate emotions" of the California miners erupt into violence, the very tenets of sentimentalism are humorously called into question. As was customary in Harte's poetry, the narrator is Truthful James. James's ostensible role is as an unbiased, educated, and moral-thinking observer of the behaviors of his less enlightened companions. The poem begins:

> I reside at Table Mountain, and my name is Truthful
>   James;
> I am not up to small deceit, or any sinful games;
> And I'll tell in simple language what I know about the
>   row
> That broke up our society upon the Stanislow.

All seems to go well in the first six months of the scientific meetings: "Till Brown of Calaveras brought a lot of fossil bones / That he found within a tunnel near the tenement of Jones."

> Then Brown he read a paper, and he reconstructed
>   there,
> From those same bones, an animal that was extremely
>   rare:
> And Jones then asked the Chair for a suspension of the
>   rules,
> Till he could prove "if" those same bones was one of
>   his lost mules.
>
> Then Brown he smiled a bitter smile, and said he was at
>   fault.
> It seemed he had been trespassing on Jones's family
>   vault.

Truthful James then makes one of his habitual ironic editorial comments on the action of his excitable colleagues.

> Now I hold it is not decent for a scientific gent
> To say another is an ass, – at least, to all intent;
> Nor should the individual who happens to be meant
> Reply by heaving rocks at him to any great extent.

A fight breaks out and worsens until James, with characteristic understatement, records of one of the unconscious academics that "the subsequent proceedings interested him no more." James concludes the "proceedings of the scientific society" with the following summation, including the protestation of his own guileless participation as a neutral and clearheaded observer:

... in less time than I write it, every member did engage
In a warfare with the remnants of a paleozoic age;
And the way they heaved those fossils in their anger was
   a sin,
Till the skull of an old mammoth caved the head of
   Thompson in.

And this is all I have to say of these improper games,
For I live at Table Mountain, and my name is Truthful
   James;
And I've told in simple language what I know about the
   row
That broke up our society upon the Stanislow.

Critics of the sentimentalist philosophy argued that unrestrained emotion often led to immoral rather than virtuous behavior. It seems Harte agreed that, at least in California, it might.

Harte's satiric verses unquestionably reveal his true feelings for the west that he left as soon as his fame would allow. In "California Madrigal" (LOA, 2: 342), for example, Harte parodies a springtime ode. The poem begins with the clichéd "Oh come, my beloved! from thy winter abode," which signals his humorous intent. It ends:

Once more glares the sunlight on awning and roof,
Once more the red clay's pulverized by the hoof,
Once more the dust powders the "outsides" with red,
Once more at the station the whiskey is spread.

Then fly with me, love, ere the summer's begun,
And the mercury mounts to one hundred and one;
Ere the grass now so green shall be withered and sear,
In the spring that obtains but one month in the year.

Harte often parodied contemporary verse forms. His careful burlesques of Edgar Allan **Poe**, Longfellow, and other popular writers have been valued as a measure of his critical genius.

But his penchant for parodying fashionable poetic styles also places Harte among a group of society writers who, in his home state of New York and in Philadelphia, were gently ridiculing nineteenth-century extremes. While some of these vers-de-société writers mocked the eastern pretentiousness of the genteel effete, Harte debunked romanticized accounts of the west's reputedly rugged individualists. While society poets melodramatically ridiculed sentimental notions of sacrificial love, Harte lampooned the racial prejudice and manifest destiny philosophies that he had encountered in America's west.

A host of vers-de-société volumes were written by such postbellum authors as Edmund Clarence **Stedman**, Thomas Bailey Aldrich, Eugene Field, Richard Henry Stoddard, Mary Mapes Dodge, and Nora Perry. A single example of American vers de société will serve. In "A Mourner À La Mode," John Godfrey Saxe compares a new widow's preoccupation with fashion to the sham of emotion that sometimes takes the place of genuine moral sentiment. The poet depicts a widow who is dressed to the hilt at her husband's funeral and states that "devotion / Performed at so vast an expense / Betrayed an excess of emotion" and that often "sorrow" seems to go "by the yard." After several verses that describe her voguish attire, he concludes:

Ah well! it were idle to quarrel
   With Fashion, or aught she may do;
And so I conclude with a moral
   And metaphor – warranted new: –
When *measles* come handsomely out,
   The patient is safest, they say;
And the *Sorrow* is mildest, no doubt,
   That works in a similar way!

Since Harte spent time both in the east and in the west, he could use his humor to ridicule both regions. His companion poems "Her Letter" and "His Answer" show him jeering at both eastern pretense and western naïveté. In "Her Letter," a young woman whose father has struck it rich in the gold fields has gone east. She writes the boyfriend she left behind at "Poverty Flat":

I'm sitting alone by the fire,
   Dressed just as I came from the dance,
In a robe even *you* would admire, –
   It cost a cool thousand in France;
I'm be-diamonded out of all reason,
   My hair is done up in a cue:
In short, sir, "the belle of the season"
   Is wasting an hour on you.

Throughout the poem, she callously lists all the advantages she now has thanks to her father's recently acquired fortune, but she also admits that her "taste is still low," because she wishes that instead of being "'finished' by travel," she could be with her old, but poor, beau. In this poem, Harte unquestionably holds no sympathy for the poor little rich girl, and in the companion poem, he just as plainly criticizes the gullibility of his western characters. In "His Answer," Truthful James helps his bedridden, sentimental, and forsaken friend write a reply. Truthful James begins by explaining that Joseph cannot write for himself as "his arm it was broken quite recent, / And [he] has something gone wrong with his lung." Harte goes on in imitation of immoderately sentimental contemporary love poetry:

And he says that the mountains are fairer
   For once being held in your thought;
That each rock holds a wealth that is rarer
   Than ever by gold-seeker sought.

In a postscript, Truthful James lets the lady know that if "it's just empty pockets as lies / Betwixt you and Joseph," then he, the friend, is willing to offer his 600 dollars in life savings as a solution. The incongruities between true love and greed, between artificiality and gullibility, and between pragmatism and the sentimental moral code are often represented by James in incongruous epilogues such as this, which in turn also portray Harte's satiric and stinging views.

Harte's most biting criticism of America comes in his poems that illustrate racial prejudice in California. His "Plain Language from Truthful James," popularly known as "The Heathen Chinee," for example, satirizes the rationalizations and bigotry involved when Caucasian miners and Chinese immigrants struggle to live side by side. Truthful James, again posing as an innocent observer, tells of a round of poker in which a Chinese launderer, quaintly named Ah Sin, plays against Bill Nye, Harte's consistently corrupt ironic hero. Truthful James announces that as far as he and Bill knew, the "Chinee" ostensibly "didn't understand" the game. James characteristically appears innocent of the crooked intentions of his friend, Bill, and says, feigning moral indignation:

> Yet the cards they were stocked
>   In a way that I grieve,
> And my feelings were shocked
>   At the state of Nye's sleeve:
> Which was stuffed full of aces and bowers,
>   And the same with intent to deceive.

Both James and his cheating friend have misjudged their opponent, however, and are swindled themselves. It seems the "Chinee" hid 20 packs of cards in his long sleeves. The game ends in a fight and Nye's judgment that they are "ruined by Chinese cheap labor." In making both parties guilty, Harte avoided the polemics that might have been charged to him had he depicted the Chinese as innocent victims.

Another poem, even more contemptuous of white injustice to the Chinese in northern California, is "The Latest Chinese Outrage." In this poem, Truthful James witnesses a brawl between miners and Chinese launderers. When the miners refuse time after time to pay for their cleaned clothing, the Chinese loot the miners' belongings and make off wearing the unpaid-for wash. A man named Johnson calls out chauvinistically to the others to fight:

> Shall we stand here as idle, and let Asia pour
> Her barbaric hordes on this civilized shore?
> Has the White Man no country? are we left in the
>   lurch?
> And likewise what's gone of the Established Church?
>
> And he sprang up the hillside – to stop him none dare –
> Till a yell from the top told a "White Man was there!"
>   A White Man was there!
>   We prayed he might spare
>   Those misguided heathens
>   The few clothes they wear.

When the noise dies down and the other miners go to see what has resulted from Johnson's lone attack, they find the Chinese have put him in a bamboo cage, drugged him with opium, and dressed him to look like themselves, including tacking a cue on his head. As usual, Harte's epilogue is a paradoxically stated rhetorical question put by an unreliable character: in this case, a questionable politician stumping for a democracy that is safe for the white man.

> And the man from our District that goes up next year
> Goes up on one issue – that's patent and clear:
>   "Can the work of a mean,
>   Degraded, unclean
>   Believer in Buddha
>   Be held as a lien?"

Harte's message is clear, if hidden by incongruity. His ironic treatment of racial prejudice was nonetheless an accepted way of dealing with social problems. The same strategy allowed Dickens to write humorously of the heartrending conditions of London's orphans and Mark Twain to write about the treatment of blacks in the South.

Harte's accuracy in depicting conditions in the west has been called into question, but it is apparent that if much of Harte's western poems were fabrications, his verses concerning racial injustices were based on experiences he had, indeed, witnessed. As a young man, for example, Harte had been released from his assistant editorship of the *Northern Californian* in 1851 shortly after he wrote an article criticizing the callous attitude of Californians toward the fashion of casually murdering Native Americans. Twenty-two years later, in 1873, when Harte was a successful and popular poet, he ventured again, this time in verse, to protest the unfair treatment of Indians in the west. Following the notorious execution of four members of the Modoc tribe, Harte wrote his satirical "Truthful James to the Editor" (LOA, 2: 345).

History relates that a peaceful group of Modocs had left their reservation in Oregon to avoid being killed by the warring Klamaths. The U. S. Army attempted to return them to their reservation forcibly. The endeavor, costly in both lives and resources, ended when the Modocs were removed to a reservation in Oklahoma. Harte's fictionalized version of the events includes the scalping of Truthful James's unscrupulous friend William Nye, but the Captain Long Jack invoked in the poem was a real-life Modoc chief. The narrator, subject to Harte's irony, begins by asking whether the United States belongs to the white man or not:

> Which it is not my style
>   To produce needless pain
> By statements that rile,
>   Or that go 'gin the grain,
> But here's Captain Jack still a livin', and Nye
> has no skelp on his brain!
>
> On that Caucasian head
>   There is no crown of hair.
> It has gone, it has fled!
>   And Echo sez "where?"
> And I asks, "Is this Nation a White Man's,
> and is generally things on the square?"

Nye's Indian wife had told him where the Modoc tribe was camped. Unauthorized, he goes there on a dubious and violent errand and is captured. He protests that he "looks to be treated . . . as a pris'ner, a pris'ner of war!" But he is found guilty by the tribe of stealing another man's "squaw," attempting to murder Long Jack, and successfully burning Nasty Jim's wives and children to death. He is further condemned for selling the tribe the guns that they used on the white settlers. The Modoc judge announces that Nye's pleas should go unheeded in the face of the "indictment" against him.

> "But you're tried and condemned,
>   And skelping's your doom,"
> And he paused and he hemmed, –
>   But why this resume?
> He was skelped 'gainst the custom of Nations,
> and cut off like a rose in its bloom.
>
> So I asks without guile,
>   And I trusts not in vain,
> If this is the style

That is going to obtain, –
If here's Captain Jack still a livin, and Nye
with no skelp on his brain?

Like his fiction, Harte's poetry satirized nearly every aspect of the life he witnessed. Like Twain and Ambrose **Bierce**, Harte pointed out to postwar audiences the incongruities of their culture. Harte's poetry has shared the ignominious fate of most other nineteenth-century verse. Another reason for the current lack of interest in Harte's poetry, perhaps, lies in its early reception. Harte's popular poems about the adventures of the characters upon the Stanislow received mixed reviews. His eastern seaboard reviewers preferred Harte's humorous short stories to his poetry. *Scribner's*, for example, complained that it was unfortunate "the world" knew Harte best for his "queer, quaint poems in dialect," "doggerel," and the "unworthiness of the pun," and suggested, "may we not hope that he will hereafter use his rare poetic powers to better purpose than writing verse?" While *Scribner's* kindly encouraged Harte to keep his humor in prose, the *Catholic World* condemned his poetry across the board, saying, "The author is not sufficiently aware of the distinction between coarseness and originality, or else prefers notoriety to fame." For many nineteenth-century literary journalists, poetry was supposed to help readers contemplate the ideal. Anything less than this, they considered vulgar.

But when reviewers read Harte's works and found that they and their readership enjoyed them, they were faced with a critical dilemma. While true poetry was to concern itself with the highest aims of humanity, the *Atlantic Monthly* admitted in 1872, "You laugh, and reproach yourself for laughing." Three years later, the same magazine observed in Harte's rhymes the quality that counted for more than any other in postwar poetry. "Somehow you are coaxed into enjoyment against which your criteria and principles severally and collectively protest," wrote a reviewer, who stated that he found "warmth," "charm," and "pathos in it all, before which you cannot continue unmoved." For a time, at least, Harte had found a combination irresistible to nineteenth-century American audiences – humor with pathos. When lesser poets attempted to imitate him, *Harper's* expressed dismay that they "sprang up" to imitate Harte with "a nauseating realism unredeemed by the genuine humor and sentiment which had saved [Harte] from vulgarity." The sympathy for humanity that both readers and critics appreciated in Harte's humorous verses represented the best of their nineteenth-century sentimental attitude toward life.

Harte left the United States in 1878 to become United States consul to Krefeld, Prussia (Germany). Later, he moved to England where, although in poor health, he continued to write to support himself and his family. He died in Surrey, England, in 1902.

ALLENE COOPER

Selected Works

The Complete Poetical Works, 2 vols., Boston: Houghton Mifflin, 1912

Further Reading

Barnett, Linda Diz, *Bret Harte: A Reference Guide*, Boston: G. K. Hall, 1980

Kaplan, Fred, *Sacred Tears: Sentimentality in Victorian Literature*, Princeton, New Jersey: Princeton University Press, 1987

Knowles, Frederic L., *The Poetry of American Wit and Humor*, Boston: Page, 1899

_____, *Library of Wit and Humor: American*, New York: Review of Reviews, 1917

Matthews, Brander, *American Familiar Verse: Vers de Société*, New York: Longmans, Green, 1904

Merwin, Henry Childs, *The Life of Bret Harte*, Boston: Houghton Mifflin, 1911

Pemberton, T. Edgar, *The Life of Bret Harte*, London: C. Arthur Pearson, 1903

Nathaniel Hawthorne

(1804–1864)

"I am full of scraps of poetry," the 15-year-old Nathaniel Hawthorne wrote to his younger sister, Louisa, in September 1819. He punctuated his letter with verses, remarking that "though those are my rhymes, yet they are not exactly my thoughts" and that "I could vomit up a dozen pages more if I was a mind to." Nineteen poems survive from Hawthorne's teens and early 20s. Although his rhymes would never become an important vessel for his thoughts, some of these efforts transcend their seemingly autonomic composition, and verse writing played a significant part in Hawthorne's apprenticeship as a writer.

In the hierarchy of genres, lyric poetry held an honored place in the early nineteenth century and drew the aspirations of many ambitious young literary persons. But at the same time, verse also was a parlor and a newspaper genre; verse writing in Hawthorne's milieu was less a sign of a literary vocation than a marker of middle-class refinement and a part of the education of a college man. Typical assignments at Bowdoin College, which Hawthorne attended from 1821 to 1824, included translations from classical poets, at which he excelled; with his classmate Henry Wadsworth **Longfellow**, Hawthorne belonged to the Potato Club, whose members regularly composed and recited verse (or risked forfeiting potatoes, according to the bylaws). By the time the writer was 25, however, he had virtually abandoned poetry. Even the poetic character type, a figure of romantic possibility in his apprentice novel, *Fanshawe* (1828), becomes an object of burlesque in his later work. And yet, despite this renunciation, Hawthorne critics have, with marked consistency across the years, discerned in him the poetry that, as he lamented to his sister, he couldn't "keep . . . out of my brain."

To his contemporaries, Hawthorne was "the greatest poet . . . that America has given to the world" (James Russell **Lowell**), "in the highest sense a poet" (R. H. Stoddard), and a "true poet" (Longfellow); "prose like his was poesy's high tone" (Edmund Clarence **Stedman**). His chief literary heir, Henry James, considered Hawthorne's search "for images which shall place themselves in picturesque correspondence with the spiritual facts . . . the very essence of poetry." Closer to our own time, Q. D. Leavis's "Hawthorne as Poet" (which does not treat Hawthorne's verse writing) suggests that Hawthorne modeled himself on Shakespeare, for his tales were "essentially dramatic" and their "use of language . . . poetic" (*Sewanee Review* 59 [1951]). It is known that Hawthorne relied on poetry for many of his themes and devices; he even named a daughter Una after the heroine of *The Faerie Queene*. Dante, William Shakespeare, Edmund Spenser, Andrew Marvell, John Milton, William Wordsworth, Samuel Taylor Coleridge, Lord Byron, John Keats, and Percy Bysshe Shelley – works by all of these poets echo within Hawthorne's prose.

If Hawthorne's fans have knighted him with the title of "poet" and critics warrant that his literary masters were at least as likely to be poets as novelists, his own poems might have a tale to tell. Of the 29 poems ascribed to Nathaniel Hawthorne in *Poems* (1967), edited by Richard Peck, 17 first appeared in his adolescent letters and home-produced "newspaper"; two, although printed over the name "Hawthorne" in 1845, may well not be his, as their uncharacteristic length and piety suggests; two are drinking songs from his first novel, *Fanshawe*; one appeared in the magazine printing of his tale "The Threefold Destiny," but was dropped from the book printing; four are light verse written toward the end of his life; and one was, according to his daughter Una, a "Verse that Papa and I composed together for fun," although it has a somber Civil War theme. The two remaining poems appeared anonymously in Boston area newspapers when the writer was in his early 20s. Other poems from his teens may have seen print – "Tell Ebe [the elder sister] she's not the only one of the family whose works have appeared in the papers," he also wrote in the letter to Louisa cited above – but they have never turned up.

Hawthorne repudiated his Gothic romance, *Fanshawe*, the later and more famous product of his apprenticeship, a few years after subsidizing its printing. By contrast, he never explicitly disowned his first publication, "The Ocean" (1825; LOA, 1: 350), or any of his other poems; no one seems to have much noticed them, and they faded effortlessly. Once he was an established figure, Hawthorne may nonetheless have wished to disclaim them as well; in a letter of January 1851 to his publisher, James T. Fields, who was sleuthing around for Hawthorne's lost first novel, Hawthorne wrote of "the literary or other follies of my nonage," asked Fields "not to brush away the dust that may have gathered over them," and enjoined him "not to read any unacknowledged page which you may suppose to be mine." At the present, however, "The Ocean" and three other verses are available in two anthologies: the Library of America Anthology and *Poetry of the American Renaissance* (ed. Paul Kane). Two of these newly available poems – "I left my low and humble home" (LOA, 1: 349) and "Oh could I raise the darken'd veil" (LOA, 1: 350) – saw print, strictly speaking, for the first time in Peck's collection; they originally shared column space with such news items as the birth announcement "Mrs. Hawthorne's Cat SEVEN KITTENS" in the 16-year-old Hawthorne's homemade newspaper, whose eight issues circulated within the family during August and September of 1820 and in early 1822.

The career this apprenticeship was preparing him for is well-known. Nathaniel Hawthorne's fame rests on his four novels – *The Scarlet Letter* (1850), *The House of the Seven Gables* (1851), *The Blithedale Romance* (1852), and *The Marble Faun* (1860) – and more than 100 tales. Hawthorne's stature was recognized early and confirmed with the publication of *The Scarlet Letter*. In America, his canonicity has so far survived every fashion; a 1994 College Board survey cites *The Scarlet Letter* as the most frequently recommended book for American high school seniors and beginning college students. Hawthorne's first successes, however, came from his tales, which he began to publish when he was 26, and which soon included masterpieces of the genre: "My Kinsman, Major Molineux," "Roger Malvin's Burial," and "The Wives of the Dead" (all in 1832); "The Minister's Black Veil," "The May-

Pole of Merry Mount," and "Young Goodman Brown" (all in 1835). His first collection, *Twice-Told Tales*, came out in 1837, and although his uncertain finances required that he accept the patronage jobs that came his way – in the Boston and Salem custom houses (1839–40 and 1846–49, respectively) and as a Liverpool consul (1853–57) – his literary reputation was now secure.

The tales represent a wedding of talent to opportunity, for these works were well suited to the burgeoning periodical and gift annual trade of the 1830s and 1840s. Although some biographers have seen Hawthorne's youth and the decade he spent in Salem after graduating from college as marked by morbid seclusion, he nonetheless had a keen sense of the new American profession of authorship; he trained for it and, with some canniness, made his way in the commercial landscape. Aside from his tales, his other work-for-hire literary labors and products included a children's geography book, *Peter Parley's Universal History* (1837), which he compiled with his sister Elizabeth, and the editorship, during 1836, of the *American Magazine of Useful and Entertaining Knowledge*. The professionalized writer had to have a try at any genre that presented itself – from newspaper verse to sketches for gift annuals to schoolbooks to children's stories. The worldliness that is one consequence of such exposure to the marketplace, however, uneasily coexists with the constant menace of mere hackdom, and it is perhaps this tension that helped create Hawthorne's self-protective tone of self-deprecating cosmopolitanism.

In his first literary enterprise, Hawthorne displayed a witty mastery of the motley tones and genres seen in the newspapers of his day. Questioning the picture of Hawthorne's "morbid, solitary, dangerously introspective youth," Elizabeth L. Chandler points to the "dry, satirical humor" in his hand-lettered newspaper, titled, with Augustan ambition and literary self-consciousness, "The Spectator," presumably after Addison and Steele (*New England Quarterly* 4 [1931]). "The Spectator" seamlessly melds tone, content, and appearance into an only slightly twisted replica, on a reduced scale, of local papers like the *Salem Gazette*. Hawthorne himself wrote all the copy (with occasional assistance from his younger sister) and placed it under such headings as "Poetry," "Editor's Address," "Foreign Intelligence," "Domestic News," and "Advertisements." He also was, in his own words, "our own Printers, Printing-Press and Types." His writing carefully imitated newspaper type and layout, and he seemed struck by the notion of being the very means by which his work was produced – even to the extreme of *being* himself the press and types – even while he inserted sly advertisements for job printing.

"The Spectator" might be thought of as an example of what Joan Hedrick calls "parlor literature," which she sees as "an integral part of polite society and domestic culture" in the antebellum middle class (*Signs* 17 [1992]). Hawthorne's "newspaper" does share in the sometimes mock-heroic tone and in the sociable function that Hedrick identifies for parlor literature and, like parlor literature, blurs distinctions between public and private – even distinctions of what constitutes publication. "The Spectator" seems to have provided Hawthorne with a means to socialize in a teasing and, no doubt, sometimes piquing way with his extended family. But it also provided him with an apprentice job of work.

This apprentice task entailed an exploration of the restric-tions and opportunities of genre and tone, as well as a consciousness of the boundaries between public and private, which in turn shift even within the anomalous category of a "home-manufactured publication," as Hawthorne called his paper. While learning to be an author – that is, a writer for publication – Hawthorne adopted a world-weary Grub Street voice. Under "Deaths," he notes "that of the Publisher of this Paper, who died of starvation"; he also advertises "a NEW EDITION of the MISERIES OF AUTHORS," with "REMARKS drawn from his own experience." Here, from the outset, is the familiar tone of mild self-mockery that Hawthorne later reserves for narrators such as Miles Coverdale in *The Blithedale Romance* and the narrators of his prefaces and introductions, who transparently function as authors.

With near-perfect pitch, "The Spectator" recreates the many-voiced world of the newspaper, a subset of the universe of print, with its technical terms and business details. Among these newspaper voices is that of the poet, a fixture of the early American newspaper. "I left my low and humble home" appeared in the first number of "The Spectator" in August 1820. Leaving his "peaceful cot," the soldier-speaker heads off, "Far from my Father's fields to roam." Desire for glory points to a "path which led / O'er heaps of dying and of dead," and although the poem's hero "gain'd the envied height," the victory has been won in gore, and he longs for home. Here, Hawthorne also uses the conventional topos of the prodigal to invert the biographical facts of his own family: it was his sea captain father who left (he died of yellow fever in Surinam in 1808), and the son who stayed. Thus, the inaugural issue of his newspaper constituted a kind of announcement that Hawthorne *was* to leave his father's metaphoric home and to seek his arena of glory in literature, not war, and, more pointedly, not the sea, as it had been for many Hawthornes. In its air of Wordsworthian pastoral and nostalgia, which colors the speaker's memories of "youthful ecstacy," this poem suits the newspaper-verse genre. And yet it is also a young writer's reflection on success, in whatever quarter: on the one hand, glory frees one from the menace – or the influence – of "slaughter'd foes" (he ascends over "heaps" of them with "eager feet"), but on the other hand, the threat exists that "Glory's ray, / Could never bring one happy day." These "crosscurrents of aspiration and dismay," which T. Walter Herbert identifies as a central paradox of Hawthorne's young manhood, appear to be enmeshed in his relationship to his father.

A few days before he produced this issue of "The Spectator," Hawthorne had tried his hand at another manuscript genre, not of the parlor but of the sea: the logbook. Logbooks of four of his father's sea voyages survive, and (as Luther Luedtke has discussed) Hawthorne's annotations in them suggest that the lost father was an object of fascination during his apprentice years. Hawthorne's father inscribed in his log two quatrains of verse, which the son copied over and amended the spelling and punctuation, as though working a schoolroom exercise. Along with other graffiti in the logs, these notations seem an effort to open a conversation. On the title page of a log, the father had written repeatedly, "Let this auspicious day be ever sacred"; the son responds: "For what?" One can only speculate at the tone – laconic, exasperated, plangent – with which the son tried to hold up his side of the dialogue. Through these associations and by retracing in his own handwriting and his own words the father's only traces, Hawthorne seems at once to identify with the young officer's apprenticeship, to resist the mythic father, to reclaim the father's poetic voice, and to internalize his father.

The evidence of the logbooks, "The Spectator," and the poetry shows that the young Hawthorne had a keen sense of beginning on his journey of life. And while his apprentice labors, from "The Spectator" to his college work to *Fanshawe* to his early professional tasks, tell us that his vocational choice had its practical aspects, it had also, of course, emerged from Hawthorne's intense desire, ambition, and sense of destiny. He wrote in the "Editor's Address" with which he launched his paper that "Our feelings upon sending into the World the first No. of the Spectator, may be compared to those of a fond Parent, when he beholds a beloved child about to embark on the troubled Ocean of public Life." A nice imitation of editorial cant, Hawthorne's choice of trope nonetheless carries more weight with the knowledge that during this same week he had been contemplating his own parent's ultimately fatal voyage on real oceans.

Hawthorne's first known publication is "The Ocean," in the Salem *Gazette* for August 16, 1825. Written when he was 21 and printed anonymously soon after his graduation from Bowdoin, the poem's apparent theme of consolation for those with loved ones lost at sea struck a chord, for it was reprinted in *The Mariner's Library or Voyager's Companion* (1833). The poem contrasts the ocean's "silent caves" and the "purity" of its "solitudes" both with the "fury" of the ocean surface and with the care and guilt of earth and earth's unquiet graves. "The young, the bright, the fair" who have died have found nothing more or less than "peaceful sleep." "The Ocean" may not so much console as smooth over and placate; these dead seem not to have achieved spiritual dispensation so much as they have been simply dispensed with. And although beneath its turbulent surface, the ocean promises quietude, it is also there that "The awful spirits of the deep / Hold their communion." Like the dead of this poem, these spirits are left unidentified and faceless; but they disturb the poem's efforts to define an undersea world remote from care. The poem's subtext may well be the son's effort to rebury – or resubmerge – the dead father in an endlessly unturbulent ocean; but he keeps resurfacing.

"Oh could I raise the darken'd veil," one of Hawthorne's most "Hawthornian" verses, was written for the third "Spectator" (September 1820) and dilates on the dread possibility that life's journey might come to worse than nothing:

Oh could I raise the darken'd veil,
Which hides my future life from me,
Could unborn ages slowly sail,
Before my view – and could I see
My every action painted there,
To cast one look I would not dare.
There poverty and grief might stand,
And dark Despair's corroding hand,
Would make me seek the lonely tomb
To slumber in its endless gloom.
Then let me never cast a look,
Within Fate's fix'd mysterious book.

Among the most frequently recurring icons in Hawthorne's

writings, the veil is precisely the kind of charged, ambiguous, yet emblematic image that marks his writing as "poetic." The veil stands between Reverend Hooper and ordinary sociability in "The Minister's Black Veil" and between Reuben Bourne and the son he is unknowingly about to kill in "Roger Malvin's Burial." Furthermore, in a letter to Sophia Peabody, then his fiancée, Hawthorne writes in May 1840: "words may be a thick a darksome veil of mystery between the soul and the truth which it seeks." In these examples, and in the "Veiled Lady" of *The Blithedale Romance*, the veil radically disrupts the continuity of social life.

But the earliest use of the image somewhat shifts its etymology; Hawthorne has embedded in the veil an element of destiny and inevitability. In "Oh could I raise the darken'd veil," the veil does not thwart communion between individuals but falls between two aspects of one self at separate moments on a time line. This poem weaves together two recognizably Hawthornian themes: the divided self and the treachery of destiny. Here, the veil assists in what the young Hawthorne saw as a *desirable* discontinuity between present and future identities. When he began to have success as an author in his late 20s, he marked what he may have perceived as a shift in his own destiny by changing the spelling of his name from the inherited "Hathorne." But fatedness and its links to catastrophe continued to enthrall Hawthorne. If "la gloire" is one of the Old World's most powerful icons, failure is America's, and it haunted Hawthorne in its constant nearness.

His first full novel, and the last of his apprentice works, the Gothic romance *Fanshawe*, may be read as a meditation on romantic failure through the study of the types of poetic personality. Its chapters carry poetic epigraphs – from Sir Walter Scott, James Thomson, Robert Southey, and Shakespeare – as though establishing credentials for a genealogy. (Hawthorne refrains from epigraphs in the later novels.) The novel is, in part, a study of three poetic character types that could be loosely aligned with the contemporary reputations of Robert Burns, Wordsworth, and Keats. The innkeeper Hugh Crombie, a drinker with a checkered past, is a Burnsian figure whose "effusions, tavern-haunter and vagrant though he was, have gained a continuance of fame . . . which many, who called themselves poets then, and would have scorned such a brother, have failed to equal." The conventional hero, Edward Walcott, "the poet of his class," gives up the poetry of his youth in exchange for getting the girl. Fanshawe, of the three the most conventionally "poetic" type, frail and scholarly, is also the only one of the three cursed with ambition; although he seems not to care for things of the world, nonetheless if "his inmost heart could have been laid open, there would have been discovered that dream of undying fame, which, dream as it is, is more powerful than a thousand realities." After giving up the girl, he gives up the ghost, apparently as a result of reading too much. Alcoholism and local renown, conventional success but forfeit of literary passion, and early death – these are the options the reputations of Burns, Wordsworth, and Keats held out for the young writer.

In later works, this early skepticism about poetic promise evolves into repudiation. For Hawthorne, the poet becomes a stock comic character who is shaped by the bathos of thwarted literary ambition, and whose high ideals contrast absurdly with his circumstances and capacities. In "The Great Carbuncle" (1837), a poet, along with a feckless crew of other character types, hunts for a magical gem reputedly hidden in the White Mountains. A Grub Street dreamer, he at last mistakes a piece of ice for the jewel: "The critics say, that, if his poetry lacked the splendor of the gem, it retained all the coldness of the ice." A later sketch, "P.'s Correspondence" (1845), brilliantly illustrates Hawthorne's demotion of poets from the world-historical company of Thomas Carlyle's *On Heroes, Hero-Worship, and the Heroic in History* (1841). The narrator's correspondent, P., in a delusionary fantasy that he is in London visiting the literati, depicts, in the place of Carlyle's "wide, placid, far-seeing" Shakespeare and "deep, fierce" Dante, a parade of comically broken-down, emasculated romantic figures.

Hawthorne's inverted literary history kills off the current competition, while imagining a reputation-corroding old age for the Romantics. In this imaginary London, an "enormously fat," gouty Byron, religiously Methodist and politically conservative and reconciled to Lady Byron, edits an expurgated version of his complete works; "his passions . . . burnt out," Byron "no longer understands his own poetry." An aged Burns has ascended from poverty to live in "perfect comfort," but is "no longer capable of pathos." As for the others, Sir Walter Scott is paralytic, Charles Dickens and Wordsworth are dead, Coleridge is dying of a "troublesome affection of the tongue," and Shelley is an "unbound . . . upholder of the Established Church"; Keats is worse off than dead – he is composing an epic. As for Americans, William Cullen **Bryant** is dead, John Greenleaf **Whittier** has been "lynched . . . in South Carolina," and Longfellow has "perished . . . of intense application, at the University of Göttingen." Of course, these three Hawthorne contemporaries (and Dickens and Wordsworth) were alive and thriving in 1845, five years before *The Scarlet Letter*. The tale telegraphs its satiric strategy in P.'s encounter with the wreck of Napoleon – another of Carlyle's heroes, who in fact died in 1821 – on Pall Mall, escorted by two nursemaiding policemen:

> There is no surer method of annihilating the magic influence of a great renown, than by exhibiting the possessor of it in the decline, the overthrow, the utter degradation of his powers – buried beneath his own mortality. . . . This is the state to which disease, aggravated by long endurance of a tropical climate, and assisted by old age – for he is now above seventy – has reduced Bonaparte.

Hawthorne's satire annihilates the Carlylean hero by letting long life exhaust the hero's fund of valor. It is worth noting that Napoleon's generation, and that of most of the Romantic poets in this sketch, is also that of Hawthorne's father, whose swift decline and death occurred in Surinam's "tropical climate."

Around 1830, when Hawthorne began to publish tales anonymously and apparently stopped writing verse, he amended the spelling of the family name; as early as 1827, when he was 23, he inscribed a copy of *The Beauties of the Spectator* several times using both spellings, as though "feeling along the line" of both names. As he abandoned the poetry of his youth, Hawthorne thus abandoned his father's name. Once firmly launched on what he later called "the sea of literature," Hawthorne seems to have wished to bury not only his early works but his early influences as well. If these abandonments had a cost, they were in the service of establishing his authorial identity, which was at least in part constructed through the negation and denial of his father and of the romantic literary figures that towered over his apprentice years.

PATRICIA CRAIN

Selected Works

Poems, edited by Richard E. Peck, Bibliographical Society of the University of Virginia, 1967
The Letters, 1813–1843, edited by Thomas Woodson, L. Neal Smith, and Norman Holmes Pearson, Centenary Edition, vol. 15, Columbus: Ohio State University Press, 1984
Miscellaneous Prose and Verse, edited by Thomas Woodson, Claude M. Simpson, and L. Neal Smith, Centenary Edition, vol. 23, Columbus: Ohio State University Press, 1994

Further Reading

Baym, Nina, *The Shape of Hawthorne's Career*, Ithaca, New York: Cornell University Press, 1976
Brodhead, Richard, *The School of Hawthorne*, New York: Oxford University Press, 1986
Chai, Leonard, *The Romantic Foundations of the American Renaissance*, Ithaca, New York: Cornell University Press, 1987
Charvat, William, *The Profession of Authorship in America, 1800–1870*, 1968; edited by Matthew J. Bruccoli, New York: Columbia University Press, 1992
Crews, Frederick, *The Sins of the Fathers: Hawthorne's Psychological Themes*, 1966, Berkeley: University of California Press, 1989
Herbert, T. Walter, *Dearest Beloved: The Hawthornes and the Making of the Middle-Class Family*, Berkeley: University of California Press, 1993
Kane, Paul, ed., *Poetry of the American Renaissance*, New York: Braziller, 1995
Luedtke, Luther S., *Nathaniel Hawthorne and the Romance of the Orient*, Bloomington: Indiana University Press, 1989
Miller, Edwin Haviland, *Salem Is My Dwelling Place: A Life of Nathaniel Hawthorne*, Iowa City: University of Iowa Press, 1991
Turner, Arlin, *Nathaniel Hawthorne: A Biography*, New York: Oxford University Press, 1980

John Hay

(1838–1905)

John Hay secured a small but enduring niche for himself in American poetry when, as a young editorial writer for the *New York Tribune*, he wrote a series of ballads in western dialect that reflected the life that he knew growing up on the Mississippi River in western Illinois. This was hardly the kind of poetic fame that Hay, who had been writing verse since his days as an undergraduate at Brown University, would have liked to claim. Even at the time of the publication of *Pike County Ballads and Other Pieces* (1871), he professed a certain degree of embarrassment at the widespread popularity of his dialect verse. In 1897, when Hay was appointed ambassador to the Court of St. James, he was chagrined to see his ballads republished in Great Britain. As secretary of state under Presidents William McKinley and Theodore Roosevelt, John Hay was hailed around the world for his successes in international diplomacy. That he was also a pioneer in shaping a distinctly new nativist voice in American poetry is easily forgotten in the light of his later career as a statesman.

Poetry was only one of several areas in which the versatile John Hay made his mark. Born in 1838 in Salem, Indiana, he grew up in Warsaw, Illinois. In 1855, he was sent east to study at Brown University, where he became class poet. While in Providence, Hay became enchanted with the literary life and was a welcome guest in the Providence literary circles led by Sarah Helen **Whitman**. The harshness of the western life to which he returned after graduation in 1858, however, contrasted with the more sophisticated world of the East. Hay thought of himself as "a poet in exile," but he resolved to make the best of his lot and studied law with his uncle in Springfield, Illinois.

As luck would have it, Hay's uncle's law office was next door to that of Abraham Lincoln, and when Lincoln was elected president in 1860, young John Hay was invited to Washington, D.C., as the new president's assistant secretary. He continued to write poetry during his four years in the White House, but he also tried his hand at essays and short stories. Hay's service to Lincoln led to a series of diplomatic appointments from 1865 to 1870 in Paris, Vienna, and Madrid. Fired with republican ideals that were made even more ardent by his experiences in Washington, D.C., during the Civil War, Hay reacted strongly to the antidemocratic monarchical traditions he encountered in Europe. These European experiences also inspired several poems and essays.

In September 1870, Hay returned to the United States and accepted a position with the *New York Tribune*, the leading journalistic voice of the Republican Party. According to *Tribune* editor Horace Greeley, Hay was the best editorial writer that he ever knew. Hay had been with the *Tribune* only a few months when his dialect poems brought him instant fame, but he also enjoyed critical acclaim in 1871 for *Castilian Days*, a volume of essays based on impressions of Spain.

Having achieved a measure of renown in diplomacy, journalism, and poetry, Hay's career took another turn in 1874 when he married Clara Stone, the daughter of the wealthy Cleveland industrialist Amasa Stone. Hay abandoned journalism and moved to Cleveland, where he assisted in managing his father-in-law's business enterprises and began to work seriously on the monumental *Abraham Lincoln: A History*, which he coauthored with John G. Nicolay, Hay's friend and Lincoln's secretary. Except for a brief sojourn in Washington, D.C., as an assistant secretary of state in 1880–81 and a six-month stint as editor of the *New York Tribune*, filling in for Whitelaw Reid, work on the Lincoln history occupied Hay throughout the 1880s. He largely abandoned poetry, but he did find time to write a novel, *The Bread-Winners*, which generated considerable interest because of its anonymous authorship and its dim view of the emerging labor movement.

When the complete *Abraham Lincoln: A History* was finally published in 10 volumes in 1890, Hay was without a major preoccupation. He felt that his days as a poet were past and he was apparently not inclined to pursue the writing of fiction, even though his success with *The Bread-Winners* clearly demonstrated a talent in that field as well. As a consequence, he occupied himself with his family, traveled in Europe, and labored behind the scenes in Ohio Republican circles. His political efforts eventually won for him diplomatic appointments by President McKinley that were the crowning glory of his career.

Of Hay's many callings, that of poetry was the oldest and it continued to manifest itself, albeit sporadically, throughout his life. As affairs of state consumed his time in later years, he turned to poetry only rarely. Among his last poems was a sonnet to Theodore Roosevelt written when he was secretary of state. Hay was given to disparaging his achievements in all areas, and so his feelings toward his poetry in general and his western ballads in particular must be understood in the light of his customary self-deprecation.

The history of the composition of the Pike County ballads is somewhat uncertain, and from time to time there has been a debate over whether John Hay or Bret **Harte** was the first to give poetic voice to the western pioneers. Mark Twain was convinced that Hay had been first in the field, but the weight of the evidence would seem to favor Harte. The one clear fact is that in the expansive mood of post–Civil War America, the time was right to render the voice of the western pioneer in verse, much as James Russell **Lowell** had depicted the voice of the native New England Yankee in *The Biglow Papers* two decades earlier.

The first of Hay's ballads, "Little Breeches," appeared in the *New York Weekly Tribune* on December 2, 1870. Ten days later Hay wrote to John Nicolay that it "has had a ridiculous run" and "has been published in nearly the whole country press from here to the Rocky Mountains." "Jim Bludso" (LOA, 2: 381) appeared in the *Tribune* on January 6, 1871, and had an equally sensational renown. The poem was both widely praised and widely denounced. Two more ballads, "Banty Tim" and "The Mystery of Gilgal," quickly followed. By April 1871, James R. Osgood and Co. had published *Pike County Ballads and Other Pieces*, which contained the four ballads and a gathering of Hay's other, more traditional verse. A new collection of Hay's poems published in 1890 added two more ballads.

The appeal of Hay's Pike County ballads was twofold. First,

they are all marked by the freshness of the poetic narrator's dialect. This dialect is distinguished not just by its renderings of local pronunciation such as "whar" for "where," "terbacker" for "tobacco," and "j'int" for "joint." The narratives also constitute a treasure trove of native colloquialisms. Jim Bludso didn't just die on the Prairie Belle, he "passed in his checks." The narrator of "Banty Tim" describes going to hell as "He kin check his trunks to a warmer clime / than he'll find in Illanoy." Such verse is prone to picturesque imagery as well. After the brawl at Tom Taggart's bar in "The Mystery of Gilgal," for example, "They piled the stiffs outside the door; / They made, I reckon, a cord or more." In "The Pledge at Spunky Point," a humorous account of a failed attempt to keep the temperance pledge for a year, Hay writes:

> And along in March the Golyers
> Got so drunk that a fresh-biled owl
> Would 'a' looked 'long-side o' them two young men,
> Like a sober temperance fowl.

Hay's dialect was realistic rather than invented, a point which William Dean **Howells** made in 1890. Howells thus found Hay's work in this genre superior to other dialect poets "who were so creative that they created even the vernacular employed by their rude sons of the soil."

As important as his innovative use of native western dialect in the Pike County ballads was Hay's democratic point of view, his ready identification with the common man. This is perhaps most evident in "Jim Bludso." The hero of this poem is hardly a paragon of virtue by mid-Victorian standards. "He were n't no saint," Hay writes, and like other steamboat engineers, Bludso has two wives at different stops along the Mississippi River. Furthermore, he is "a keerless man in his talk," and the only kind of religion he has is

> To treat his engine well;
> Never be passed on the river
> To mind the pilot's bell;
> And if ever the Prairie Belle took fire, –
> A thousand times he swore,
> He'd hold her nozzle agin the bank
> Till the last soul got ashore.

Jim's true character is shown, however, the night that the Prairie Belle bursts into flames and he manages to maintain his position "Till the last galoot's ashore." His devotion to duty brings his death, which Hay celebrates in the ballad's final stanza.

> He were n't no saint, – but at jedgment
> I'd run my chance with Jim,
> 'Longside of some pious gentlemen
> That would n't shook hands with him.
> He seen his duty, a dead-sure thing, –
> And went for it thar and then;
> And Christ ain't a going to be too hard
> On a man that died for men.

The theme of the ballad relates to the ancient argument over justification by works or justification by faith. Hay obviously sides with good works, even to the point of making Jim into a Christ figure in the last line. To make a hero out of a character like Jim Bludso and to suggest that his life was morally superior to that of many outwardly pious Christians was too much

for many people to swallow. Much to Hay's bewilderment, the religious and moral lessons of "Jim Bludso" were hotly debated and often condemned in both the religious and secular press across the country.

Hay's other Pike County ballads are tinged with some of the same religious iconoclasm. The rescue of "Little Breeches," who is four years old and chews tobacco, is attributed to the work of angels. Such an effort is deemed to be "a derned sight better business / Than loafing around the Throne." This image of heavenly life struck some people as particularly blasphemous. In "Golyer," a pale imitation of "Jim Bludso," the stagecoach driver Ben Golyer, who "wa'n't the best man that ever you seen," gives his own life to save the life of a little boy during an Apache Indian attack. "The Pledge at Spunky Point" mocks the greatest moral and religious crusade of the time, the temperance movement.

Hay's ballads, therefore, were innovative in both their realistic use of language and their idealization of the democratic ethos that characterized the frontier. Hay even treated the subject of racial tolerance in "Banty Tim," in which Sergeant Tilmon Joy stands up to the "White Man's Committee of Spunky Point" that seeks to run a young black man out of the area they regard as "white man's country." Threatening the life of any villager who harms this man, Sergeant Joy relates how Tim saved his life at the battle of Vicksburg Heights by carrying him off the battlefield under a hail of Confederate bullets.

Although Hay's reputation as a poet rests chiefly on the Pike County ballads, they represent only a small portion of his poetic output. Among his other poems, some of the verses written in reaction to his European experiences are useful for the insight they give into Hay's early political thought. "Sunrise in the Place de la Concorde," for example, laments the return to power in France of Louis Napoleon and the crushing of the ideals of the revolution of 1848 but ends with a hopeful vision of the future restoration of liberty during a new dawn of freedom. "A Triumph of Order" portrays an incident near the close of the Paris Commune in which a young boy is murdered by the infantry. With its ironic title and conclusion, the poem suggests that social order achieved at the cost of armed brutality is no order worth having.

Some of Hay's more memorable lyrics revolve around the themes of death or aging. In "The Stirrup Cup," he uses the biblical image of death as a pale horse:

> My short and happy day is done,
> The long and dreary night comes on;
> And at my door the Pale Horse stands,
> To carry me to unknown lands.

In a late sonnet, "Thanatos Athanatos (Deathless Death)," the poet, "conscious of wrinkling face and whitening hair," muses on "the immortal youthfulness of the early dead." He ponders the lots of Raphael, John Keats, Percy Bysshe Shelley,

> And soldier boys who snatched death's starry prize,
> With sweet life radiant in their fearless eyes,
> The dreams of love upon their beardless lips,
> Bartering dull age for immortality;

By dying young, Hay suggests, these men have somehow achieved a kind of deathless death because their memory is frozen in the time of their youth. In "The Crows at Washington,"

Hay uses the ominous image of "dim battalions" of crows flying over the capital to provoke memories "Of days when life and hope were strong, / When love was prompt and wit was gay."

Despite the intelligence and skill that some of Hay's other poems display, however, it is the Pike County ballads that have endured, and "Jim Bludso" is the most memorable of them all. Despite his inclination to have the ballads forgotten, even Hay himself in 1889 expressed a fondness for Jim. Clearly, the poem has had an impact. The story is told that George Eliot pronounced "Jim Bludso" "one of the finest gems of the English language" and then proceeded to recite it out loud, "the tears flowing from her eyes as she spoke the closing lines." Jim even gets a mention in James Joyce's *Ulysses*, when Leopold Bloom muses, "I did all a white man could . . . Jim Bludso. Hold her nozzle again the bank."

Hay's skillful use of realistic dialect and his ability to render the drama of the ballad so vividly and concisely make Jim's sacrifice a noble one without sentimentalizing it too much. Compared to "Jim Bludso," the other Pike County ballads, however clever, seem a bit lightweight. This should not be too surprising, since it seems likely that Hay merely dashed them off quite casually. It is perhaps a measure of John Hay's literary instincts and talent that he could produce with relatively little effort a few ballads that not only tapped a new vein in American poetry in the 1870s but can still be read with pleasure today.

PHILIP B. EPPARD

Selected Works

Pike County Ballads and Other Pieces, Boston: James R. Osgood, 1871
Poems, Boston and New York: Houghton Mifflin, 1890
The Complete Poetical Works of John Hay, Boston and New York: Houghton Mifflin, 1916
John Hay's Pike County: Two Tales and Seven Ballads, edited by George Monteiro, Western Illinois Monograph Series, no. 3, Macomb: Western Illinois University Press, 1984

Further Reading

Clymer, Kenton J., *John Hay: The Gentleman as Diplomat*, Ann Arbor: University of Michigan Press, 1975
Dennett, Tyler, *John Hay: From Poetry to Politics*, New York: Dodd, Mead, 1933
Gale, Robert L., *John Hay*, Boston: Twayne, 1978
Kushner, Howard I., and Anne Hummel Sherrill, *John Milton Hay: The Union of Poetry and Politics*, Boston: Twayne, 1977
Monteiro, George, *Henry James and John Hay: The Record of a Friendship*, Providence, Rhode Island: Brown University Press, 1965
Thayer, William Roscoe, *The Life and Letters of John Hay*, 2 vols., Boston and New York: Houghton Mifflin, 1915
Ward, Saint Ignatius, Sister, *The Poetry of John Hay*, Washington, D.C.: Catholic University of America, 1930

Paul Hamilton Hayne

(1830–1886)

Hayne belonged to a prominent South Carolina family, several members of which had made important contributions to the history of the state. One of these, Robert Y. Hayne, a proponent of states' rights in the famous Senate debate on nullification in 1830–31, was Paul Hayne's uncle and guardian. Born in the year of the great debate, reared in Charleston, and educated in a well-known private school and at the College of Charleston (1847–50), Hayne also read law with James Louis Petigru, another notable South Carolinian. Early in his 20s, however, he began contributing to the *Southern Literary Messenger*, *Graham's Magazine*, and other periodicals. He also edited the *Southern Literary Gazette* (1852–54) and *Russell's Magazine* (1857–60). With the help of subsidies in the 1850s, he published three slim volumes of poetry: *Poems* (c. 1854), *Sonnets, and Other Poems* (1857), and *Avolio; A Legend of the Island of Cos* (c. 1859). When war came in 1861, he fervently supported his state and the Confederacy, although poor health limited him to a four-month tour of active duty as aide-de-camp to Governor Francis Pickens. After the spring of 1862, he contributed to the cause with his pen. Ruined financially by the war and depressed by its outcome, Hayne bought on credit a small tract of land near Augusta, Georgia, which he later called Copse Hill, moved there in 1866, and spent the last 20 years of his life contributing verse and prose to magazines and newspapers, corresponding with other writers throughout the nation and in Britain, promoting southern letters and political causes, and bringing out three more volumes of poetry: *Legends and Lyrics* (1872), *The Mountain of the Lovers* (1875), and *Poems* ("Complete Edition," 1882).

After the death of William Gilmore **Simms** in 1870 and the publication of *Legends and Lyrics* in 1872, Hayne was considered by many throughout the country as the poet laureate of the south, the "representative" southern poet and man of letters, and the chief southern literary spokesman to both regional and national audiences. He took himself seriously in this role, and few political or cultural occasions passed without some sort of poetic comment or tribute from his pen. His literary contemporaries – Henry Wadsworth **Longfellow**, Oliver Wendell **Holmes**, William Cullen **Bryant**, Edwin Percy Whipple, Edmund Clarence **Stedman**, Simms, Henry **Timrod**, and Sidney **Lanier**, among them, to say nothing of British authors like Jean Ingelow, Philip Bourke Marston, R. D. Blackmore, and Wilkie Collins – thought well of him and his poetry. On Hayne's death in 1886, John Greenleaf **Whittier** wrote that Hayne was assured a place in the "Valhalla of the country" along with Longfellow, Bryant, and Bayard **Taylor**.

During the past century, however, Hayne's reputation has declined, and he is now usually dealt with in a page or two in literary histories (*LHUS* [1963], for instance) and frequently omitted in anthologies of American verse like Edwin H. Cady's *The American Poets: 1800–1900* (1966). Nor is he represented in such avowedly inclusive recent collections as the *Harper American Literature* (1987) or the *Heath Anthology* (1990), although he is included in several others: Leon Howard, et al., eds., *American Heritage* (1955), Walter Blair, et al., eds., *The*

Literature of the United States (3rd ed., 1966), and Louis D. Rubin, Jr., *The Literary South* (1979), to mention a few. Scholarly activity has followed certain lines. Selections of Hayne's correspondence have been edited by D. M. McKeithan (1944), Charles Duffy (1945, 1951–52), and Rayburn S. Moore (1982). His work as poet and man of letters has been assessed by Jay B. Hubbell (1954) and Moore (1972), and Edd W. Parks has considered his criticism (1962). Moore has also dealt with a number of topics in articles and essays, but a full-scale biography and a scholarly edition of the poems remain desiderata. On the whole, then, Hayne's poetry has not been fully evaluated in the twentieth century.

Let it be granted immediately that his poetry's weaknesses – its derivative nature, frequent lack of intellectual force and vigor, and occasional failure to express the substance of life adequately – are significant and, perhaps, even damning. Let it also be admitted that the absence of a critical or selective edition of his poems enlarges the task of criticism and makes the achievement of critical focus more difficult. But Hayne's work is not unique either in these faults or in the want of a scholarly edition. The former are characteristic of much nineteenth-century poetry and, certainly, of much poetry written by Hayne's contemporaries, southern or otherwise. The latter is a common need among American writers that until recently has failed to receive proper attention. Despite these strictures and difficulties, however, a case for Hayne may be made.

In the first place, some of the strengths of Hayne's poetry are closely related to its weaknesses. His work does derive nourishment from its sources. Geoffrey Chaucer, Edmund Spenser, William Wordsworth, John Keats, and Alfred, Lord Tennyson are worthy models and offer the lesser artist much in the way of precept and technique, as is clear in "The Wife of Brittany" (1870), a redaction of "The Franklin's Tale" that is Hayne's best sustained piece of narrative verse, or in "Unveiled" (1878), an irregular, Wordsworth-like ode whose tone and view of nature suggest a philosophical kinship with "Tintern Abbey" and whose diction at times has a Tennysonian cast.

I pass with reverent thought,
Attuned to every tiniest trill of sound,
    Whether by brook or bird
    The perfumed air be stirred.
But most, because the unwearied strains are fraught
With Nature's freedom in her happiest moods,
I love the mock-bird's, and brown thrush's lay,
    The melted soul of May.
    Beneath those matchless notes,
From jocund hearts upwelled to fervid throats,
    In gushes of clear harmony,
    I seem, oft-times I seem
To find remoter meanings; the far tone
Of ante-natal music faintly blown
From out the misted realms of memory;
The pathos and the passion of a dream;

Or, broken fugues of a diviner tongue
That e'er hath chanted, since our earth was young,
And o'er her peace-enamored solitudes
    The stars of morning sung!

There are times, assuredly, when Hayne's poems smack too much of the lamp rather than of life, but on occasion he treats his locality and situation with an authenticity of detail and observation, as in a number of lyrics that focus upon the natural world of Copse Hill. Furthermore, "South Carolina to the States of the North," a *cri de coeur* (cry from the heart) that was written in late 1876 when political strife over Reconstruction had reached a climax, exudes an intense emotion charged with bitter experience, which in turn reflects Hayne's passionate concern for his state. In an address to others of the "original thirteen":

I lift these hands with iron fetters banded:
    Beneath the scornful sunlight and cold stars
I rear my once imperial forehead branded
    By alien shame's immedicable scars;
Like some pale captive, shunned by all the nations,
    I crouch unpitied, quivering and apart –
Laden with countless woes and desolations,
    The life-blood freezing round a broken heart!

Although not so urgent with passion, the Copse Hill poems are no less instinct with feeling for the life immediately around him and his home in Georgia. These pieces – "Aspects of the Pines," "The Voice in the Pines," "The Pine's Mystery," "Forest Pictures," "Midsummer in the South," and "The Mocking-Bird," among others – were written mostly in the 1870s and contributed chiefly to the *Atlantic Monthly*. "Midsummer in the South," although it did not appear in the *Atlantic* and has since been less-frequently reprinted than the pine lyrics, is nevertheless typical.

I love midsummer uplands, free
To the bold raids of breeze and bee,
Where, nested warm in yellowing grass,
I hear the swift-winged partridge pass,
With whirr and boom of gusty flight,
Across the broad heath's treeless height:
Or, just where, elbow-poised, I lift
Above the wild flower's careless drift
My half-closed eyes, I see and hear
The blithe field-sparrow twittering near
Quick ditties to his tiny love;
While, from afar, the timid dove,
With faint, voluptuous murmur, wakes
The silence of the pastoral brakes.

In addition to his appropriation of the British poetic tradition and his treatment of the life surrounding him, Hayne is a versatile versifier. He employs competently a wide range of forms, metrical schemes, and techniques. He is at his best in short poems, in sonnets – "October" (LOA, 2: 220) and "On the Occurrence of a Spell of Arctic Weather in May, 1858" (LOA, 2: 220) are examples – and in lyrics like those on "Charlotte Brontë" (LOA, 2: 221) and on the Copse Hill country and in later lyrics like "In Harbor" (1882) and "Face to Face" (1866). A sonnet addressed to Swinburne even

brought forth the English poet's "cordial thanks" in a letter of May 2, 1880.

Not since proud Marlowe poured his potent song
Through fadeless meadows to a marvellous main,
Has England hearkened to so sweet a strain –
So sweet as thine, and ah! so subtly strong!
Whether sad love it mourns, or wreaks on wrong
The rhythmic rage of measureless disdain,
Dallies with joy, or swells in fiery pain,
What ravished souls the entrancing notes prolong!
At thy charmed breath pale histories blush once more;
See! Rosamond's smile! drink love from Mary's eyes;
Quail at the foul Medici's midnight frown.
Or hark to black Bartholomew's anguished cries!
Blent with far horns of Calydon widely blown
O'er the grim death-growl of the ensanguined boar!

The valedictories pronounced in "In Harbor" and "Face to Face," moreover, advance and demonstrate Hayne's simple faith and his serene acceptance of the coming of death, the latest expression of which, "Face to Face," appeared in *Harper's New Monthly Magazine* only six weeks before his death.

But beyond the stars and the sun
    I can follow him still on his way,
Till the pearl-white gates are won
    In the calm of the central day.
Far voices of fond acclaim
    Thrill down from the place of souls,
As Death, with a touch like flame,
    Uncloses the goal of goals;
And from heaven of heavens above
    God speaketh with bateless breath –
My angel of perfect love
    Is the angel men call Death!

Hayne can also write longer poems, odes, and narratives of the quality of the already-mentioned "Unveiled" and "The Wife of Brittany." Such works include: dramatic and meditative verse like "Vicksburg" (1862), his best-known ballad on the Civil War; "Fire Pictures" (1867; rev., 1871), a tour de force in the style and meter of Edgar Allan **Poe**; "Cambyses and the Macrobian Bow" (1872), a stark and grim retelling in blank verse of an incident from Herodotus (Hayne's own favorite among his shorter narratives); "By the Grave of Henry Timrod" (1874), a moving elegy in memory of his late friend and fellow poet; and "Muscadines" (1876), a sensuous ode whose verbal melody derives from the "liquid magic" of the southern grape and also suggests Keats's influence.

Ah! how the ripened wild fruit of the South
    Melted upon my mouth!
Its magic juices through each captured vein
    Rose to the yielding brain,
Till, like the hero of an old romance,
Caught by the fays, my spirit lapsed away,
Lost to the sights and sounds of mortal day.

Even late in his career, Hayne continued to write long pieces, frequently in response to requests from organizations and institutions for occasional poems to celebrate or commemorate events such as the centennials of the battles of King's Mountain and Yorktown in 1881, the inauguration of the International Cotton Exposition in Atlanta in 1882, or the sesquicentennial of the founding of Georgia in 1883.

Representative of the quality of these longer poems is "The Return of Peace," a prophetic tribute to an Atlanta that rises from the ashes of "war-wasted lands" and shakes off the "lotus-languishment of grief" to establish the "fresh foundations of a nobler sway" based on art and commerce, industry and agriculture.

> Now throned above the half-forgotten pain
>   Of dreadful war, and war's remorseless blight,
>   Thy heart-throbs glad and great,
> Sending through all thy Titan-statured state,
> Fresh life and gathering tides of grander power
>   From glorious hour to hour,
>   Thousands thy deeds shall bless
> With strenuous pride, toned down to tenderness:
> Shall bless thy deeds, exalt thy name;
> Till every breeze that sweeps from hill to lea,
> And every wind that furrows the deep sea,
> Shall waft the fragrance of the soul abroad
> The sweetness and the splendor of thy fame: –
> For thou, midmost a large and opulent store,
> Of all things wrought to meet a nation's need,
>   Thou, nobly pure,
> Of any darkening taint of selfish greed, –
>   Wert pre-ordained to be
> Purveyor of divinest charity, –
> The love-commissioned almoner of God.

Indeed, in the scope, versatility, and bulk of his production, Hayne is one of the most substantial southern poets of the nineteenth century, a judgment no less true despite the fact that a sizable proportion of his output is mere magazine verse and, by its very nature, ephemeral. Admittedly, he did not write any one poem that comes near the perfection of Poe's "To Helen" (LOA, 1: 522) or Timrod's "Ode," but he wrote more passably good verse than Poe, Timrod, or Lanier, although it should also be remembered that his career lasted half a generation longer than theirs. He lacked Poe's sense of art and critical acumen, Simms's facility and vitality, Timrod's theme and control, and Lanier's inventiveness and fertility, but he could, on occasion, be as musical as Poe, as facile as Simms, as eloquent as Timrod, and as lush as Lanier. Poe, Simms, and Timrod are better poets than Hayne, if we select their best work to compare with Hayne's. This is not necessarily the case with Lanier, for his best work is in many ways very much like Hayne's in fulfillment and finish. Still, Hayne's canon is rounded in ways that Poe's, Simms's, Timrod's, or Lanier's is not. Its dimensions reflect the full scope of the way in which Hayne strove for expression in a spectrum of poetic types and structures and suggest therefore a range and completeness that is missing in the output of these other nineteenth-century southern poets of consequence. Nevertheless, the body of his work, it should be remembered, is not so vast as that of Simms. In the final analysis, however, Hayne's best poems have not stood the test of time as well as those of his chief rivals, nor are they now likely to supplant them in anthologies or in the minds of the academic public.

Aside from that of his southern contemporaries, Hayne's poetry should be considered with that of Thomas Bailey Aldrich, George Henry **Boker**, Edmund Clarence Stedman, Richard Henry Stoddard, and Bayard Taylor. Time has not been generous to any of these minor bards. To present tastes, their verse often exhibits the weakest features of nineteenth-century convention – ornate and artificial language, empty abstractions, unalloyed bookishness, and monotonous metrical regularity. This is not strange, for few of these poets dreamed that the fundamental changes being wrought by Walt **Whitman** and Emily **Dickinson** would modify or even one day supplant the poetic traditions they cherished and honored. Hayne, for example, expressed a widely held general view when he wrote of Whitman in March 1876: "One thing is certain: If Mr. Walt Whitman really is in any sense or to any degree, a genuine Poet; then, all the canons of poetic art must be reversed; and their most illustrious expounders be consigned to oblivion, from Job to Homer; from Homer to Horace; from Horace to Shakspeare [sic]; from Shakspeare to Tennyson." And as late as January 1892, Aldrich sounded a similar note on Dickinson in the *Atlantic*: "If Miss Dickinson's *disjecta membra* are poems, then Shakespeare's prolonged imposition should be exposed without further loss of time, and Lord Tennyson ought to be advised of the error of his ways before it is too late. But I do not hold the situation to be so desperate. Miss Dickinson's versicles have a queerness and a quaintness that have stirred a momentary curiosity in emotional bosoms. Oblivion lingers in the immediate neighborhood."

But such critical limitations should in no way detract from the valiant effort Hayne made to reach a national audience from the Georgia pine barrens nor from the long and dedicated devotion he paid to his muse amid discouraging conditions of poverty and ill health. It is obvious that he failed to write great poetry, but it is worth pondering how he managed to write poetry of any distinction at all.

Hayne himself recognized his limitations and accepted them. He knew early in his career that his song would not reach the heights where the "great Poets" sing, but he maintained in "Aspirations" (later "The Will and the Wing," 1854):

> Yet would I rather in the outward state
> Of Song's immortal temple lay me down,
> A beggar basking by that radiant gate
> Than bend beneath the haughtiest empire's crown!
>
> For sometimes, through the bars, my ravished eyes
> Have caught brief glimpses of a life divine,
> And seen a far, mysterious rapture rise
> Beyond the veil that guards the inmost shrine.

Nevertheless, he was exasperated with poetry from time to time because, as he wrote his old friend and fellow poet Margaret J. Preston in October 1875, he "must repeatedly" compose verses – "not *inspired* verses" – "but, (oh! shameful prostitution!!), rhymes for the trade, the hucksters in literary wares, for Poverty is a hard 'taskmaster.'" He concluded: "*Here* behold the *true* reason why I compose so *unevenly*!" Despite such reservations, he affirmed generally, echoing Samuel Taylor Coleridge, that "poetry was its *own* exceeding great reward," as he informed Mrs. Preston in July 1878. Such awareness and acceptance suggest Hayne's analytical acumen regarding his own work, but his dedication and modest achievement, far removed from the intellectual stimulus of a national literary center, demonstrate fully the plight of a poet and man of letters in the postwar south.

RAYBURN S. MOORE

Selected Works

Poems, Boston: Ticknor and Fields, 1855

Sonnets, and Other Poems, Charleston, South Carolina: Harper & Calvo, 1857

Avolio; A Legend of the Island of Cos. With Poems, Lyrical, Miscellaneous, and Dramatic, Boston: Ticknor and Fields, 1860

Legends and Lyrics, Philadelphia: Lippincott, 1872

The Mountain of the Lovers. With Poems of Nature and Tradition, New York: Hale & Son, 1875

Poems, Complete Edition, Boston: D. Lothrop, 1882

"Last Poems," uncollected poems, edited by Mary Middleton Michel Hayne and William Hamilton Hayne; manuscript in the Hayne Papers, Durham, North Carolina, Duke University, Perkins Library

A Collection of Hayne Letters, edited by Daniel M. McKeithan, Austin: University of Texas Press, 1944

The Correspondence of Bayard Taylor and Paul Hamilton Hayne, edited by Charles Duffy, Baton Rouge: Louisiana State University Press, 1945

"A Southern Genteelist: Letters of Paul Hamilton Hayne to Julia C. R. Dorr," edited by Charles Duffy, *South Carolina Historical and Genealogical Magazine* 52 (April 1951), pp. 67–73; 53 (January 1952), pp. 19–30

A Man of Letters in the Nineteenth-Century South: Selected Letters of Paul Hamilton Hayne, edited by Rayburn S. Moore, Baton Rouge: Louisiana State University Press, 1982

Further Reading

De Bellis, Jack, comp., *Sidney Lanier, Henry Timrod, and Paul Hamilton Hayne: A Reference Guide*, Boston: Hall, 1978

Hubbell, Jay B., ed., *The Last Years of Henry Timrod*, Durham, North Carolina: Duke University Press, 1941

———, *The South in American Literature, 1607–1900*, Durham, North Carolina: Duke University Press, 1954

Lanier, Sidney, *Works*, edited by Charles R. Anderson, et al., Centennial Edition, Baltimore, Maryland: Johns Hopkins Press, 1945, vols. 7–10

McKeithan, Daniel M., ed., *Selected Letters: John Garland James to Paul Hamilton Hayne and Mary Middleton Michel Hayne*, Austin: University of Texas Press, 1946

Moore, Rayburn S., *Paul Hamilton Hayne*, New York: Twayne, 1972

Parks, Edd Winfield, *Ante-Bellum Southern Literary Critics*, Athens: University of Georgia Press, 1962

Simms, William Gilmore, *The Letters*, edited by Mary C. Simms Oliphant, et al., Columbia: University of South Carolina Press, 1952–56, 1982, vols. 3–5

Josiah Gilbert Holland

(1819–1881)

Born in Belchertown, Massachusetts, on July 24, 1819, to Harrison and Anna (Gilbert) Holland, Josiah Gilbert Holland spent his boyhood and early manhood in various small towns and cities in western Massachusetts, a region then dominated by evangelical theology rooted in the work of Jonathan Edwards, whose career had been spent largely in Northampton, Massachusetts, three towns west of Holland's birthplace. Holland's boyhood reading included works by Edwards, Samuel Hopkins, and other Calvinist and evangelical theologians.

Holland was one of his region's principal delegates to the literary world – he preached and defended the morals and theology he had learned as a boy. But he was also a good storyteller, as is evident in "Bluebeard," originally published in his long narrative poem *Bitter-Sweet* (1858). Widely memorized by nineteenth-century school children, "Bluebeard" begins:

Centuries since there flourished a man,
(A cruel old Tartar as rich as the Khan,)
Whose castle was built on a splendid plan,
  With gardens and groves and plantations;
But his shaggy beard was as blue as the sky,
And he lived alone, for his neighbors were shy,
And had heard hard stories, by the by,
  About his domestic relations.

Bluebeard marries a woman named Fatima, and at first their marriage is happy. But then, when he is called away for a few days, he leaves the keys to the castle with her with the warning never "to enter the Chamber of Blue." Being "curiously inclined," she disobeys and finds a floor "red with the bloody tide / From headless women, laid side by side, / The wives of her lord and master!" Horrified, she drops the key in their blood and then finds that the stains cannot be washed off. Bluebeard returns, sees the key, and, enraged, threatens to behead her. As he draws his sword and swings it through the air, her brothers burst suddenly into the room and "[run] him through." Inheriting her husband's fortune, Fatima provides her "unfortunate" predecessors with proper burials, cheers "the hearts of the suffering poor," and gives her tenantry "an acre of land around each door / And a cow and a couple of sheep, or more."

This is all of the poem that students generally memorized, but there is another, rather long section that follows in which the moral implications of "Bluebeard" are discussed. "Bluebeard," we are told, illustrates the workings of justice and, in Fatima's conduct after her husband's death, the nature of kindness. One sees "The glory and the grace of life, / And love's surpassing sweetness," while looking "down with mercy's eye / On sin's accurst abuses."

The author of this curious mixture of violence and piety was celebrated particularly for his lofty moral instruction. After his death in 1881, one journal commented that his books would continue to have an audience because of "their moral teachings." In fact, much of Holland's work was still in print in the 1920s, but its lingering popularity, one suspects, may have had as much to do with a continuing taste for sentimentality and melodrama as with a desire for moral instruction.

Holland was not only a celebrated poet but a popular novelist as well. He was known for *The Bay-Path* (1857), an often reprinted historical novel set in colonial Massachusetts, and for various regionalist works such an *Arthur Bonnicastle* (1873), which anticipated the local-color fiction of Sarah Orne Jewett, Mary E. Wilkins Freeman, and other New England writers. His well-researched *History of Western Massachusetts* (1855) is still an important resource for regional historians. He also published children's books and a biography of Abraham Lincoln (1865) and was a respected literary critic, an essayist, a journalist, and a skilled editor of various newspapers and magazines, including *Scribner's Monthly*. He was the founding editor of the *Century Magazine*, the first issue of which was in press at the time of his death in 1881.

Aside from his novels, Holland was best known for his long narrative poems, including *Kathrina* (1867), *The Marble Prophecy* (1872; LOA, 1: 711), *The Mistress of the Manse* (1874), and *Bitter-Sweet*. He also published several shorter, rather sentimental poems such as "Sleeping and Dreaming," in which an older man dreams of himself as a youth:

My youth is round me, and the silent tomb
  Has burst to set its fairest prisoner free,
And I await her in the dewy gloom
  Of the old trysting tree.

I mark the flutter of her snowy dress,
  I hear the tripping of her fairy feet,
And now, pressed closely in a pure caress,
  With ardent joy we meet.

Holland's verse is rarely original in diction or in sensibility, but he cleverly manipulated the poetic conventions of his time. As Henry Houston Peckham observed in 1940, Holland was the "supreme apostle to the naïve," yet he also wrote with such evident sincerity and simplicity that he attracted the attention and admiration of his near-contemporary Emily **Dickinson**.

Holland was one of Dickinson's few literary correspondents, and there is no evidence that she ever had anything but generous regard for him. Writing to his widow shortly after his death, Dickinson said, for example, that she had "rarely seen so sincere a modesty on a mature Cheek" as she had when, many years earlier, Holland had offered a prayer at the Dickinson home. Holland in person was as supremely honest and plainspoken as he was in his writings; one might disagree with his views, but one could not deny his integrity and goodwill.

Dickinson and Holland were born in neighboring communities, and if she had little sympathy for his religious values, at least she knew well where he had found them. Belchertown, like Dickinson's Amherst, was a country village in which the Congregational church was the center of the community's social, cultural, and religious life. Holland's parents sent their son to high school in Northampton, where he lived with Judge Charles Augustus Dewey, one of the region's most prominent and wealthy citizens. After working briefly as a penmanship teacher, Holland studied medicine under physicians in Northampton and at the Berkshire Medical College. Graduating in 1843, he moved to Springfield, a few miles south of Northampton, but failed to develop a substantial practice. Three years later he established a newspaper, the *Bay State Weekly*. When that project also failed, he taught briefly at a business school in Richmond, Virginia, and then served as superintendent of schools in Vicksburg, Mississippi. Neither of these jobs proved satisfactory, and in 1849, he was back in Springfield.

Before Holland left for Richmond, he married into one of Springfield's more distinguished families, the Chapins, and so was now expected to provide a regular income and a good social position. He found both by becoming assistant editor to Samuel Bowles at the *Springfield Republican*, which at the time was one of the most respected newspapers in the country. Holland resigned as an editor in 1857 but continued as a principal contributor. By this time, he had established a national reputation as a writer and was able to support his family with income from lecture tours and popular books of essays, poetry, and fiction.

In 1870, Holland became the editor of *Scribner's Monthly*, which he made an important venue for Henry James, Edward Eggleston, Rebecca Harding Davis, and other realists whose work was radically outside his own sentimental and genteel tastes. Peckham, who finds little to praise in Holland's writings, concludes that as an editor he demonstrated "astonishingly good taste." If Holland's work as an editor seems progressive for his time, however, his critical opinions remained conservative. The editor who encouraged James could also, as Peckham notes, write in an essay that "of one thing, we may be reasonably sure, viz. that when the genuine geniuses of this period shall be appreciated at their full value ... their countrymen will have ceased discussing Poe and Thoreau and Walt Whitman."

It may be that Holland understood James no more than he understood Edgar Allan **Poe**, Walt **Whitman**, or Henry David **Thoreau**. Indeed, he grouped James and William Dean **Howells** as writers concerned with "the lighter social topics and types." As Peckham writes, James was simply "too subtle for the comprehension of so naïve a spirit as Josiah Holland."

Holland may have been a tolerant editor in part because he simply did not recognize how thoroughly the young writers he encouraged were dismantling the very moral order and literary values his own work attempted to sustain.

Whatever else one may think of Holland, his sincerity and candor were authentic, and his ability to convey them in his work constitutes his particular achievement. He is by any measure a genteel poet who preached values and manners to which few would now assent, and yet, one cannot but admire the enormous conviction his work conveys. That conviction, in turn, was shared by readers who, in spite of the Civil War and massive political corruption, tried to maintain the simple morality and assurance of an earlier world. *Bitter-Sweet* was published in 1858 as the nation hurried toward war, but its essential lesson is that anger and strife may be nothing more than the result of misunderstanding. In effect, Holland says, things will generally work out for the best if we can learn not to judge too harshly but to live in an optimistic, cheerful fashion. Under this genteel vision, even "Bluebeard" – "this wild tale of cruelty" – could prove itself to be "Love's gentle teacher."

EDWARD HALSEY FOSTER

Selected Works
Bitter-Sweet, New York, 1858
Kathrina, New York, 1867
The Marble Prophecy, New York, 1872
The Mistress of the Manse, New York, 1874
The Puritan's Guest, and Other Poems, New York, 1877

Further Reading
Lyman, P. W., *Josiah Gilbert Holland: A Memorial Address*, n.p., 1881
Peckham, Henry Houston, *Josiah Gilbert Holland in Relation to His Times*, Philadelphia, Pennsylvania, 1940
Plunkett, H. M., Mrs., *Josiah Gilbert Holland*, New York, 1894
Sewall, Richard B., *The Life of Emily Dickinson*, New York: Farrar, Straus and Giroux, 1987
Ward, Theodora Van Wagenen, *Emily Dickinson's Letters to Dr. and Mrs. Josiah Gilbert Holland*, Cambridge, Massachusetts, 1951

Oliver Wendell Holmes

(1809–1894)

Few mid–nineteenth-century writers in the United States felt more keenly the agonistic impulses of the age than did Oliver Wendell Holmes. His orientation in the empirical world of medicine provided him with a privileged position for registering the magnitude and consequences of an intellectual revolution that appeared to many to destroy the meaning of civilization and history. Yet Holmes did not despair; nor did he attempt, like so many of his contemporaries, to find emotional stasis in a tragic vision of life or in a retreat to the solipsistic ironies of nihilism. Instead, fortified by the comfort of a teacup and the matter-of-fact of a stethoscope – sufficient weapons, it would appear – he stood up to the conflicts of his age. When, at the end, he came to write his own epitaph – "Teacher of Anatomy, Essayist, and Poet" (the words that would adorn a tablet dedicated to his memory in King's Chapel, Boston) – he placed science and medicine before literature, and the prose essay before verse, therein establishing a priority of meanings and values that those who would remember him primarily as a poet cannot ignore.

Verse writing was important to Holmes; after all, he wrote a great deal of it and earned by it considerable affection and acclaim from his contemporaries. But even in his best poems, he rarely aimed very far or deep into the matter of things. Like the lesser poets of old, he did not strive to build great "temples of songs" filled "with the images and symbols which move us almost to adoration." Rather, he was content to "fill a panel or gild a cornice here and there, and make our hearts glad with glimpses of beauty" and our souls touched by the curious pathos of human venality. Holmes mostly wrote in a humorous key – not the discordant laughter of the frontier and the tall tale, but rather the urbane voice of one who believed in the sanctity of civilization but who at the same time was incapable of imagining a humankind able to achieve such an ideal, even in so desirable a place as Boston and its environs.

Born on August 29, 1809, in Cambridge, Massachusetts, on the edge of Harvard Yard, Holmes grew up in a community that was already noted for its hospitality to new thought and liberal intellectual fashions. But in his own father's household, adherence to the old, Calvinistic doctrines of New England's Puritan past – predestination, the total depravity of human nature, and original sin – was insisted upon. These were teachings that the son eventually rejected, although not without considerable emotional and intellectual consequences. The lessons of the old catechism – particularly its notion of sin, which presumed the hopelessly depraved actions of all men and women who did not accept the saving grace of Christ – "shocked and disgusted" Holmes's instincts "beyond endurance." "To grow up in a narrow creed and to grow out of it is a tremendous trial of one's nature," he later confessed. But those who survive the loss of their fathers' beliefs are often energized by the ordeal. Their lives are afterward defined by the need to reimagine the meaning of the world and to find in their works and days new truths and mythologies, those intellectual and emotional solutions that should provide the basis for social improvement and psychological integrity. Holmes was at least fortunate in that it was only his father's austere, Calvinistic ideas that he came in time to hate; for the man, a sweet-tempered Congregational minister called to the difficult task of preaching a doctrine that had become for many in eastern Massachusetts an irrelevant anachronism, the boy had deep affection and regard.

It was a learned, bookish household, although admittedly in an old-fashioned way, and among the arid landscape of his father's library, made up mostly of solemn histories and collections of sermons and theological tracts, young Holmes found occasional recesses of pleasure. He recalled that he eagerly read "everything but what tasted too strong of 'Thou shall' and 'Thou shalt not' – 'Be good and you will be happy.'" It was in his father's treasured collection of eighteenth-century British poets that the son found the greatest enjoyment and inspiration. He avidly read Oliver Goldsmith, Thomas Campbell, and Alexander Pope, especially the latter's translation of Homer, a work that sounded with splendid resonance in young Holmes's ear and stimulated his imagination. Throughout his long literary life, Holmes remained in his poetic sensibilities sympathetic to neoclassical forms, especially the "square-toed" heroic couplet, as he was wont to refer to it. During his 60-odd years of verse-making, which lasted through several international revolutions in poetic rules, Holmes never abandoned his trust in the efficacy of the formal measures of eighteenth-century verse, which he had learned as a child. He honored this faith in these lines, written in 1883:

> Full well I know the strong heroic line
> Has lost its fashion since I made it mine;
> But there are tricks old singers will not learn,
> And this grave measure still must serve my turn. . . .
> And so the hand that takes the lyre for you
> Plays the old tune on strings that once were new.
> Nor let the rhymester of the hour deride
> The straight-backed measure with its stately stride;
> It gave the mighty voice of Dryden scope;
> It sheathed the steel-bright epigrams of Pope;
> In Goldsmith's verse it learned a sweeter strain;
> Byron and Campbell wore its clanking chain;
> I smile to listen while the critic's scorn
> Flouts the proud purple kings have nobly worn.

Following preparation at Phillips Academy, Holmes attended Harvard College, graduating in 1829. He entered Harvard Law School, but within a few months his interests had shifted to the study of medicine. Opportunities for formal training in this field in the United States of the 1830s were fairly elementary, and Holmes's ambitions eventually led him to seek instruction at the prestigious École de Médicine in Paris under the tutelage of Pierre Charles Alexandre Louis, one of the pioneers of modern medical practice. Upon his return to New England, Holmes was awarded a doctorate of medicine from Harvard in 1836, the same year that his first volume, *Poems*, was published. Here, Holmes collected the verse he had written and published during the previous decade and, for the first time, formally attached his name to several popular poems that had frequently been copied by editors of anthologies and gift books. Among these poems were the immensely popular "Old Ironsides" (LOA, 1: 556), a rousing tribute to the Revolutionary War frigate *Constitution*, which was scheduled to be dismantled, as well as "The Last Leaf," a favorite poem of Abraham Lincoln's and a work that struck even the generally unsympathetic Edgar Allan **Poe** as possessing extraordinary merit. In the preface to the slender volume, Holmes confessed that since he was now engaged in other duties, he would have little opportunity to come before the public again as a poet. This prediction, like most of those that we make in life, speaks more accurately about the amazingly contradictory desires in our ambitions than it does about any certain sense of the future. Holmes enjoyed his role as a poet, and he enjoyed even more the public's enjoyment of his poetry.

While still a student at Harvard, Holmes had found that his poetic talents stood him in good stead with his fellows. Although a vocation in the literary arts would have been unthinkable for a young man of Holmes's temperament and worldly ambitions, his social class considered an aptitude for the writing of polite verse a virtue, a sign of a well-educated man. Holmes valued poetry primarily as a public act. Writing poetry was a way of establishing in the language of the culture a sense of community and sacred comradeship and of correcting public opinion through humor and satire. While the temptation merely to please his audience was great for Holmes, he never wished to forget his presupposition that the poet also should use his art to promote human understanding and to interpret the spiritual lessons of modern science.

Nearly half of Holmes's nearly 400 published poems were written "to order," performances dictated by particular events or celebratory occasions. These included the 44 sets of verses he wrote between 1851 and 1889 on the annual reunion of his Harvard class of 1829, as well as hymns and songs written to be delivered at the dedications of monuments and public buildings, to greet distinguished visitors, and to celebrate every imaginable sort of anniversary – of births, historic events, foundings of medical societies, social organizations, and public institutions. In 1872, he complained to his friend Thomas Wentworth Higginson: "I have . . . so belabored my own countrymen of every degree with occasional verses that I must have coupled 'name' and 'fame' together scores of times, and made 'story' and 'glory' as intimate as if they had been born twins." On one occasion – in public, of course – he playfully rehearsed in verse the many letters he had received over the years that asked him "to stand and deliver" the proper poetic sentiments for some gala feast or event:

The act of feeding, as you understand,
Is but a fraction of the work in hand;
Its nobler half is that ethereal meat
The papers call 'the intellectual treat;' . . .
Yours is the art, by native genius taught,
To clothe in eloquence the naked thought;
Yours is the skill its music to prolong
Through the sweet effluence of mellifluous song;
Yours the quaint trick to cram the pithy line
That cracks so crisply over bubbling wine.

The persona that he wished most to project in his work re-
flected the side of himself that he found to be most "like other persons." Holmes believed that he could write liberally of his own interests, "not because they are personal, but because they are human, and are born of just such experiences as those who hear or read what I say are like to have had in greater or less measure. I find myself so much like other people that I often wonder at the coincidence" (see also "Sympathies" [LOA, 1: 567]). One might even without fear tell one's secrets in verse: "Rhythm and rhyme and the harmonies of musical language, the play of fancy, the fire of imagination, the flashes of passion, so hide the nakedness of a heart laid open, that hardly any confession, transfigured in the luminous halo of poetry, is reproached as self-exposure." This is not to suggest that Holmes is in any manner of speaking a modern confessional poet; far from it. Through verse, he believed, idiosyncratic impulses might be transformed into universal meanings. As much as Ralph Waldo **Emerson**, Holmes believed the poet to be representative, although the self thereby revealed is far more public in its social dimensions than that imagined by his Concord neighbor. Not an Emersonian "transparent eye-ball," but "A Boswell, writing out himself!" is Holmes's seer, caught up in the midst of humankind's immense interconnections with one another.

Social caste for Holmes was always an important matter, and in large part his poetry was crafted to insure his place in the Boston society that he valued so much. Although one should never underestimate Holmes's irony and humor, there exists in many of his casual opinions – those habits of mind by which we make our way through the ordinary business of living in society – something akin to snobbishness and, worse, a superior and frivolous attitude toward matters that others viewed as deadly serious. Like his friend Nathaniel **Hawthorne**, Holmes remained aloof from the many reform movements that in retrospect characterize the age, including the abolition of slavery, the great political struggle that defined for many of his friends and literary associates the moral meaning of the times. In this, as well as in most other matters political, Holmes appears to many to be firmly allied with the conservative spirit of the nineteenth century. He valued an aristocracy of talent and proven ability, and he believed that the conditions of American civilization in his time were such as to insure the greatest possibility for this natural elite to win its rightful place in society.

His scientific rationalism, however, along with his temperamental aversion to all extreme positions and finalities of argument, also caused Holmes to oppose political (as well as metaphysical) radicalism in all of its many forms and disguises. If by "conservatism" one means an intellectual skepticism when it comes fully to comprehending humankind in its social organizations, then the term does have some meaning in describing Holmes's political attitudes. But Holmes was in no way a reactionary, and he made an effort to disassociate himself from "the party that resists all change." He valued civilized society not because it upheld the truth, the status quo, but because it provided a relatively safe arena for discussion, for diverse engagements, and for sincere exchanges of opinions and ideas. For Holmes, society was not something fixed and static, but fluid and evolving. And the poet was one of those who helped define the terms of that evolution.

Holmes quickly established himself as a leader in the field of medicine in the United States; he won important prizes and international acclaim for his clinical essays, including the important treatises *Homeopathy and Its Kindred Delusions* (1842) and *The Contagiousness of Puerperal Fever* (1843). Both of these early works, as well as his later scientific writings, reveal qualities of mind that set him apart from the New England literary contemporaries with whom he is so often grouped, the "Fireside" or "School Room" poets. Although never in any true sense an experimental scientist, Holmes was nevertheless thoroughly committed to an epistemological position that favored the empirical over the intuitive and that privileged the observed facts of one's experiences, however contradictory they might appear, over the ordering simplicities of tradition, as well as those of abstract thought and theory. Holmes later confessed that, when asked to contribute to the *Atlantic Monthly*, he felt himself "outside of the charmed circle drawn around the scholars and poets of Cambridge and Concord," for his time had been given mostly to his medical studies and duties. He was first and last a man of science, and his imagination was defined by the discipline to which he so passionately dedicated his life. In particular, he had little sympathy with the radical idealism espoused by the apostles of New England transcendentalism. For instance, in thoroughly scientific spirit, Holmes once declared: "There is no bridge my mind can throw from the 'immaterial' cause to the 'material' effect." He realized better than most of his contemporaries that science, as opposed to the sciences, is not a set of laws, but merely a method, an attitude toward reality that is empirical and inductive. Holmes's own explanation, as usual, is excellent: "Where facts are numerous, and unquestionable, and unequivocal in their significance, theory must follow them as it best may, keeping time with their step, and not go before them, marching to the sound of its own drum and trumpet."

In 1847, Holmes was awarded a professorial chair – which he humorously referred to as a "settee" – in anatomy at Harvard, a position that he held for 35 years (in 1870, his professorship was extended to include physiology). One of the most advanced thinkers of his age, Holmes also was one of the great scientific educators of the nineteenth century, not just in the Harvard lecture room (although his reputation there lived long into the next century), but also in his popular essays and poems. Holmes should figure prominently in any account of the great transformation of American intellectual society during the mid-nineteenth century, which shifted the broad cultural outlook from one based upon a theological view of the world to one founded upon a belief in scientific reasoning and detachment. Holmes was a major voice in the popularization of Darwinian evolution, and deserves considerable credit for the fact that this theoretical rethinking of the universe and humanity's relationship to creation met with relatively little intellectual opposition in the United States during the two decades following the Civil War. "Modern science," Holmes warned the largely middle-class readership of the *Atlantic Monthly*, "so changes the views of the universe that many of its long-unchallenged legends become no more than nursery tales." Although viewed by some as limiting, the doctrine of evolution was, for Holmes, liberating; as he argued, evolution changes "the whole relations of man to the creative power. It substitutes infinite hope in the place of infinite despair for the vast majority of mankind." The "secret of the profound interest" in

Darwinism, he claims in an ameliorating spirit, is the fact that "it restores 'Nature' to its place as a true divine manifestation. . . . If development upward is the general law of the race; if we have grown by natural evolution out of the cave-man, and even less human forms of life, we have everything to hope from the future." In his writings, he also redefines sin, which was a debilitating concept for human progress in his father's Calvinistic creed. Like physical disease, sin can be viewed as a vital process: it is thus "a function, and not an entity," something that is not to be condemned, but rather studied as an important dimension of anthropology. According to Holmes, only when the intellectual culture of the New World is rid of the anachronistic dogmas brought to these shores by his Puritan forebears will humankind realize its true relationship to the world: "Then shall the nature which had lain blanched and broken rise in its full stature and native hues in the sunshine. Then shall God's minstrels build their nests in the hearts of a newborn humanity."

Considering Holmes's repeated attempts to synthesize the scientific spirit of his age with a religious sentiment that transcended sect and creed, it is not surprising that he wrote several of the most durable of nineteenth-century religious poems and hymns. For example, in these striking lines from "The Living Temple" (originally called "The Anatomist's Hymn"; LOA, 1: 558), he discovers God's glory in the physiological structure of the human brain:

> Then mark the cloven sphere that holds
> All thought in its mysterious folds,
> That feels sensation's faintest thrill
> And flashes forth the sovereign will;
> Think on the stormy world that dwells
> Locked in its dim and clustering cells!
> The lightning gleams of power it sheds
> Along its hollow glassy threads!

Even more impressive is "The Chambered Nautilus" (LOA, 1: 557), no doubt Holmes's most popular poem, which along with a handful of other nineteenth-century works such as Emerson's "Threnody" (LOA, 1: 311) and William Cullen **Bryant's** "Thanatopsis" (LOA, 1: 122), spoke profoundly to the spiritual yearnings of many sincere readers. When this poem first appeared in *The Autocrat of the Breakfast-Table* (1858), it was introduced by "the Autocrat" to his auditors with a reference to Peter Mark Roget's *Animal and Vegetable Physiology Considered with Reference to Natural Theology* (1834) – a work that Roget, uses the shell of the nautilus to illustrate the "Unity of Design" in God's creation. For Roget, a scientific deist who insisted upon finding design in all manner of things, including human language, pieces of evidence such as the nautilus shell, with its "series of enlarging compartments successively dwelt in by the animal that inhabits the shell,"

> lead to the general conclusion that unity of design and identity of operation pervade the whole of nature; and they clearly point to one Great and only Cause of all things, arrayed in the attributes of infinite power, wisdom, and benevolence, whose mighty works extend throughout the boundless regions of space, and whose comprehensive plans embrace eternity.

Roget's description of the marine animal provided Holmes

(and his readers) with details that the latter needed merely to translate metaphorically in his poem. Regarding the nautilus' mode of movement, Roget recorded what was at the time regarded as scientific fact, but within a few years was discovered to be without foundation:

> The shell of the Argonaut is exceedingly thin, and almost pellucid, probably for the sake of lightness, for it is intended to be used as a boat. For the purposes of enabling the animal to avail itself of the impulses of the air, while it is thus floating on the waters, nature has furnished it with a thin membrane, which she has attached to two of the tentacula; so that it can be spread out like a sail to catch the light winds which waft the animal forwards on its course. While its diminutive bark is thus scudding on the surface of the deep, the assiduous navigator does not neglect to ply its tentacula as oars on either side, to direct, as well as accelerate its motion. No sooner does the breeze freshen, and the sea become ruffled, than the animal hastens to take down its sail, and quickly withdrawing its tentacula within its shell, renders itself specifically heavier than the water, and sinks immediately into more tranquil regions beneath the surface.

Equally suggestive, in terms of Holmes's imagery in the poem, is Roget's description of the shell's physical formation:

> The animal at certain periods of its growth, finding itself cramped in the narrow part of the spire, draws up that portion of the mantle which occupied it, thus leaving a vacant spect. The surface of the mantle which has receded immediately begins to secrete calcareous matter, which is deposited in the form of a partition, stretching completely across the area of the cavity. As the animal proceeds to increase in size, and to occupy a wider portion of the external shell, the same necessity soon recurs, and the same expedient is again resorted to. It withdraws its mantle from the narrowed into the wider part of the shell; and then forms a second partition, at a little distance from the first, corresponding to the space left by the receding of the mantle. This process is repeated at regular intervals, and produces the multitude of chambers contained in polythalamous shells, of which the living animal occupies only the largest, or that which continues open.

From a technical point of view, Holmes was unusually bold in his solution to the prosodic problem that "The Chambered Nautilus" posed for its maker. The combination in each stanza of three slow and stately pentameter lines, with a frequent occurrence of anapests, and three short, trimeter lines, followed by a final alexandrine, produces a cadence that led one critic to wonder if the rhythm of the poem were not meant "to symbolize the crenulated and scalloped shell of the chambered nautilus." Upon reading the poem, John Greenleaf **Whittier** remarked that Holmes's verses were "booked for immortality." Holmes himself was filled, he later recalled, "with a better feeling – the highest state of mental exaltation and the most crystalline clairvoyance, as it seemed to me, that had ever been granted to me."

Holmes also was able to keep open the possibility of belief in an age of increasing doubt. For him, accepting our human limitations to perceive or possess the absolute did not mean spiritual defeat or necessarily lead to despair, but rather made belief dynamic and progressive. "To fear science or knowledge, lest it disturb our old beliefs, is to fear the influx of the Divine wisdom into the souls of our fellow-men," he wrote in 1861; "for what is science but the piecemeal *revelation*, – uncovering, – of the plan of creation, by the agency of those chosen prophets of nature whom God has illuminated from the central light of truth for that single purpose?" These same sentiments – optimistically relativistic and engagingly dialectical – appear in "The Young Astronomer's Poem," which forms part of Holmes's longer work "Wind-Clouds and Star-Drifts" (1872):

> My life shall be a challenge, not a truce!
> This is my homage to the mightier powers,
> To ask my boldest question, undismayed
> By muttered threats that some hysteric sense
> Of wrong or insult will convulse the throne
> Where wisdom reigns supreme; and if I err,
> They all must err who have to feel their way
> As bats that fly at noon; for what are we
> But creatures of that night, dragged forth by day,
> Who needs must stumble, and with stammering steps
> Spell out their paths in syllables of pain?

Conventional minds in the nineteenth century probably regarded such thought as heretical, as indeed it was by the light of convention. Since so few have taken the trouble to consider his works, conventional criticism in the twentieth century has dismissed Oliver Wendell Holmes. But if we wish ever to discover again those wonderfully discordant harmonies that make human knowledge whole and to bridge that chasm that has too long separated the realm of science and the realm of the imagination, then we may find it to our advantage to go back and read again the essays and poems of this remarkable scientist-litterateur.

THOMAS WORTHAM

Selected Works

The Works of Oliver Wendell Holmes, Standard Library edition, 13 vols., Boston and New York: Houghton Mifflin, 1892

Life and Letters, edited by John T. Morse, Boston: Houghton Mifflin, 1896

Oliver Wendell Holmes: Representative Selections, edited by S. I. Hayakawa and Howard Mumford Jones, New York: American Book, 1939

The Complete Poetical Works of Oliver Wendell Holmes, edited by Eleanor M. Tilton, Cambridge Edition, Boston: Houghton Mifflin, 1975

Further Reading

Arms, George Warren, *The Fields Were Green: A New View of Bryant, Whittier, Holmes, Lowell, and Longfellow*, Stanford, California: Stanford University Press, 1953

Boswell, Jeanetta, *The Schoolroom Poets: A Bibliography of Bryant, Holmes, Longfellow, Lowell, and Whittier*, Metuchen, New Jersey, and London: Scarecrow, 1983

Currier, Thomas Franklin, *A Bibliography of Oliver Wendell Holmes*, edited by Eleanor M. Tilton for the Bibliographical

Society of America, New York: New York University Press,
  1953
Gibian, Peter, *Collisions of Discourse: Oliver Wendell Holmes
  in the Conversation of His Culture*, New York: Cambridge
  University Press, 1996
Howe, M. A. De Wolfe, *Holmes of the Breakfast-Table*,
  London and New York: Oxford University Press, 1939

Hoyt, Edwin Palmer, *The Improper Bostonian: Dr. Oliver
  Wendell Holmes*, New York: Morrow, 1979
Small, Miriam Rossiter, *Oliver Wendell Holmes*, New York:
  Twayne, 1962
Tilton, Eleanor M., *Amiable Autocrat: A Biography of Dr.
  Oliver Wendell Holmes*, New York: Henry Schuman,
  1947

George Moses Horton

(c. 1797–c. 1883)

An enslaved cowherder and field hand, George Moses Horton published three books of poetry in his home state of North Carolina. Horton was the first African American in the south to publish poetry, although the northern slaves Lucy Terry, Jupiter Hammon, and Phillis Wheatley had published poems earlier in the eighteenth century.

Starting when he was around 20, Horton walked on Sundays the eight miles from his master's farm to the University of North Carolina campus and sold fruit and vegetables. This was a standard Sabbath-day activity for selected slaves living near Chapel Hill. Before long, Horton was also selling love poems, mostly acrostics to southern belles, that students commissioned him to compose during the week. He would dictate the poems to the buyers the following Sunday and earn 25 to 75 cents per composition at a time when 50 cents could buy four pounds of butter or six dozen eggs, and when a university student typically had a spending allowance of one dollar a week. The verses were sentimental and nonspecific save for the beginning letters of the lines; the first six lines of an acrostic written to Sophia Alexander are representative:

> Selected lady belle of beauty blessed
> Of course i Laud thee far above the rest
> Pleasd with thy grace i can neglect thee never
> How can i fail to sing of thee forever
> i never never can the weight remove
> And shut my eyes against the torch of love.

By writing such poems and accompanying letters for courting young men and by working odd jobs around the campus, Horton arranged to live in Chapel Hill intermittently between 1832 and 1865; he paid his master 25 (and later 50 cents) for each day that he was free of farm duties.

The ironies of a system that provided quasi-freedom to an African American man capable of catering to capitalist desires (providing love poems and letters for university students and a weekly income to his master) emerge in both the process leading to Horton's publications and the messages found in his poetry. First, Horton taught himself to read in an era before education was compulsory for any American children, and in an environment where his master did not even educate his own children "at any high rate." In his autobiography, which prefaces *Poetical Works* (1845), Horton relates that he learned the alphabet by listening to other children recite it and that he then learned to read by spending his Sundays with an old speller and his mother's Wesleyan hymnal. Years later, he was taught to write by a professor's wife, Caroline Lee Whiting Hentz. Hentz was a poet, novelist, and playwright who in 1828 enabled the publication of Horton's poems "On Liberty and Slavery" (LOA, 1: 221), "Slavery," and "On Poetry and Musick" in her hometown newspaper, the *Lancaster Gazette*.

Later that year, in the hopes of accruing donations to purchase Horton's freedom, New York's *Freedom's Journal* (the first American newspaper edited by persons of color) printed his "Gratitude," a poem similar in content to "On Hearing of the Intention of a Gentleman to Purchase the Poet's Freedom"

(1829; LOA, 1: 222). "On Hearing . . ." compares "some philanthropic souls" who "strove to break the slavish bar" with a series of seemingly pleasant images; at the same time, Horton announces that he sends these people "floods of gratitude," since they proved that "on the dusky verge of deep despair, / Eternal Providence was with me there." The words are benign on one level, but on a more subtle level "floods" can drown, and Horton notes that the supposedly provided hope from "Providence" was "falsely promised." He further qualifies his praise by marking the tyrannical control, cruel tantalization, and emotionally dismal condition that these philanthropists bring upon him. Whether or not the editors and readers of *Freedom's Journal* recognized Horton's contradictions, this northern effort to gain funds for his manumission failed.

Hentz later became an apologist for slavery, but for the meantime, she continued to support her "cause." She helped Horton find local donors for the publication of his first collection, *The Hope of Liberty* (1829), whose profits were to finance his passage to Liberia. Joseph Gales – a regional secretary of the American Colonization Society and the editor of the *Raleigh Register*, which had published some of Horton's poetry – agreed to print the text. However, the necessary funds apparently never accrued. Although Horton did not profit financially from this publication, it nonetheless disseminated his works. Lewis Gunn in Philadelphia reprinted the text as *Poems by a Slave* (1837), and Isaac Knapp in Boston appended that text to *A Memoir and Poems of Phillis Wheatley, a North African Slave* (1838). Horton was unaware of and did not benefit directly from these reprints; his freedom would come only with the end of the Civil War. Although the Hentzes moved in 1830, Horton continued to have the support of community figures such as University of North Carolina president Joseph Caldwell, Chapel Hill physician Pleasant Henderson, and even North Carolina Governor John Owen.

A constant means of support also came from those who first discovered Horton's poetical talents – the university students. They purchased his poems, financially backed the publication of his first two books, and responded to his dormitory mendicancy. In addition to money and an audience, these young men gave Horton clothes and books. Among the texts he received were reference works such as Lindley Murray's *English Grammar* and copies of Samuel Johnson's, John Walker's, and Thomas Sheridan's dictionaries. These works – along with collections of poetry by Homer, Virgil, William Shakespeare, John Milton, and Lord Byron – certainly were tools for his poetic productions. Drawing upon these poetic models, Horton moved from hymnlike verse and explored such forms as the ballad, blank verse, and decasyllabic couplets. In "To Eliza," which appears in *The Hope of Liberty* and concerns lost love, Horton even closes his poem by quoting two of Byron's lines: "Fare thee well! – and if for ever, / Still for ever fare thee well!" Building upon these foundations, Horton eventually experimented with style and tone to create playful folk poems like "The Creditor to His Proud Debtor" (1845) and "Troubled with the Itch and Rubbing with Sulphur" (1865) and patriotic pieces such as "Gen. Grant – the Hero of the War" (1865). Students' texts that may have influenced Horton in other ways included Richard Snowden's *The American Revolution*, which addressed the spirit of freedom, and *The Columbian Orator*, which contained antislavery sentiments, and which also was instrumental in Frederick Douglass's development.

The fact that Horton could become established as a Chapel Hill curio and "cause" depended upon a remarkable confluence of events. Of course, Horton's life would have been far different had his master, William Horton, not moved from his Northampton farm (about 100 miles distant) to a farm in Chatham County and had his son James, who inherited Horton, not sent him to sell farm products in Chapel Hill. The time also proved as important as the place. The North Carolina cultural climate, however, was altered as a result of both Jacksonian democracy and more radical interpretations of this democracy, such as David C. Walker's *Appeal to the Colored Citizens of the World* (1829), which was published only months after *The Hope of Liberty*. Walker's three further calls for slave revolts in 1830, Nat Turner's Virginia insurrection in 1831, and ensuing North Carolina legislation that outlawed the teaching of black literacy may have intensified Horton's social and artistic difficulties.

On the whole, however, Horton was still supported by the southern academic community that later would fire Professor Benjamin Sherwood Hedrick and burn his effigy when he announced that he would vote for John C. Frémont, the Republican candidate for president. Around 1832, however, Horton even had enough personal incentives and financial patronage to move to Chapel Hill and to pay his master for his absence. Thus, it appears that any decrease in Horton's popularity related more to the diminished novelty of his daily presence than to fear of his darker skin or of his potentially subversive aims. For there was no sudden stop to requests that this black man write sentimental pieces for white women.

The death of Caldwell (the university president) in 1835 did bring some more changes for Horton, however. While Professor William Mercer Green stepped in as Horton's advocate and secured the publication of his poems "Ode to Liberty" and "Lines to My —" in the prestigious *Southern Literary Messenger* in 1843, a more prominent figure on campus proved less helpful. David Lowry Swain, the new university president, refused to subsidize Horton in the ways that Caldwell had. While Swain's name does appear among the sponsors of *Poetical Works*, evidence suggests that he misled Horton on multiple occasions. For instance, a letter that Horton wrote in 1844 to William Lloyd Garrison, editor of the abolitionist *Liberator*, and a letter he wrote in 1852 to Horace Greeley, editor of the *New York Daily Tribune*, were later found in Swain's university files. It appears that Horton had entrusted Swain to dispatch his correspondence, but that Swain had filed the letters instead.

In the 1840s and 1850s, when black writers in the north were forming literary communities and becoming increasingly productive and vocal, Horton was alone in Chapel Hill. His life and works reveal that same contradictory "synthesis of clown, contented slave, and victim" that Frances Smith Foster notes in the narratives of some escaped slaves. Horton appears to have experienced a sense of W. E. B. Du Bois's "double-consciousness," or seeing one's self through the other's eyes, similar to that which northern blacks experienced. Critics like

Blyden Jackson, Arthur P. Davis, and Joyce Ann Joyce, however, underestimate Horton's achievement when they present him as one to whom "the writing of poetry, whatever its nature or subject, was an inescapable accompaniment to the very act of breathing" or as a poet who was "accommodating to . . . a way of life that was cruelly exploitative and inexcusably demeaning." While Horton's life does support the position Alice Walker presents in "In Search of Our Mothers' Gardens" (1984) – namely, that no oppression can eliminate the creative potential of a mind – merely to marvel at his creativity and to dismiss any deeper significance in his art leaves unexplored a world of oppositional tensions.

The poems in *The Hope of Liberty* and *Poetical Works*, and the 92 new poems among the 133 poems in *Naked Genius* (1865), juxtapose heaven and earth, transcendence and immanence, acquiescence and resistance, hope and despair, idealism and realism, joy and pain, and misogyny and respect for women. This mixture shows Horton's capacity to be both comprehensive and evasive and to express his ideas within the given limitations of his situation. Sondra O'Neale and – to a somewhat lesser degree – W. Edward Farrison provide illuminating readings of his poems that illustrate these tensions (*Obsidian* 7 [1981], *College Language Association Journal* 14 [1971], respectively). An idea that has not yet been explored is how well Horton's poetry anticipates William Dean **Howells's** summation that the national literature should concentrate on "the more smiling aspects of life, which are the more American." Horton understood that his audience would expect to find these "smiling aspects of life" in his poetry.

In his first collection, for instance, Horton often uses the words "smile," "smiles," and "smiling." The undertones of these usages, however, undermine the smiles. "On Liberty and Slavery" begins with an honest complaint that the enslaved person is "deprived of all created bliss." Horton does downplay his harsh critique of slavery with the sing-song rhythm of the poem and with the quick move (after the opening three quatrains) to seven more quatrains that build a crescendo to "Liberty" and its "cheerful . . . joys" and "smiles." Such dizzying shifts, however, also sarcastically comment on his society's contradictory ideals and practices. "On Summer" implements a similar method of subversion with the word "smiling." Horton opens by showing a busy world working under the oppressive heat and sun and by telling children to "carefully avoid the snare, / which lurks beneath the smiling scene." After presenting this potential allegory of slavery and making it clear that things are not what they seem, he moves to more pleasant images, notes that there are "plenty smiles on every tree," and implores that his audience "with rapture view the smiling fields." The juxtaposition of "snare" and "rapture" with the "smiling scene" underscores Horton's critique of America's tendency to focus on "the more smiling aspects of life." The juxtaposition in "To Eliza" is less interrupted: "Although I smile, / I grieve." Again the poet is cunning, as the poem itself is about lost love and closes (as noted) with two lines from the renowned Byron. In his poetry, then, Horton proves subtly subversive.

In *Poetical Works*, Horton's attacks on the institution of slavery again emerge when he addresses issues that confront slave families. In the preface, he notes that he is the sixth of his mother's 10 children, the oldest boy, and the first child by his mother's second husband. While he provides a few details about his mother and siblings, he offers no specifics regarding his father. We do not even know if Horton knew his father. The situation may have been similar for his own children, Free and Rhody Snipes. In the 1830s or the 1840s, Horton had married a slave of Franklin Snipes. While poems in *Naked Genius*, such as "Snaps for Dinner, Snaps for Breakfast and Snaps for Supper," "Connubial Felicity," and "The Treacherous Woman," portray the negatives of marriage, poems in *Poetical Works* such as "Farewell to Frances" and "Division of an Estate" show the painful forced separations of slave families. In short, Horton and other slaves faced numerous gaps and uncertainties in contextualizing their identities.

At the end of the Civil War, after meeting Captain Will H. S. Banks of the Ninth Michigan Cavalry in Raleigh and procuring his help in publishing *Naked Genius*, Horton settled in Philadelphia in 1866. Records exist of Horton's unsuccessful attempt to gain publishing funds from the Banneker Institute there. And University of North Carolina geology professor Collier Cobb records a meeting with Horton in Philadelphia in 1883 (*North Carolina Review* [1909]); just as his exact birth date was not recorded, however, the precise place and date of Horton's death remain unknown. The final irony in Horton's life was that his career went into eclipse after he gained his freedom.

DESHAE E. LOTT

Selected Works
The Hope of Liberty: Containing a Number of Poetical Pieces, Raleigh, North Carolina: J. Gales, 1829

The Poetical Works of George M. Horton, the Colored Bard of North Carolina, Hillsborough, North Carolina: D. H. Heartt, 1845
Naked Genius, edited by Will H. S. Banks, Raleigh, North Carolina: William B. Smith, 1865

Further Reading
Davis, Arthur P., and Joyce Ann Joyce, eds., *Selected African-American Writing from 1760 to 1910*, New York: Bantam, 1995
Foster, Frances Smith, *Witnessing Slavery: The Development of Ante-bellum Slave Narratives*, Westport, Connecticut: Greenwood, 1979
Jackson, Blyden, *A History of Afro-American Literature*, vol. 1, Baton Rouge: Louisiana State University Press, 1989
Loggins, Vernon, *The Negro Author: His Development in America*, New York: Columbia University Press, 1931
———, *The Negro Author in America*, New York: Kennikat, 1964
Richmond, Merle A., *Bid the Vassal Soar*, Washington, D.C.: Howard University Press, 1974
Sherman, Joan R., *Invisible Poets: Afro-Americans of the Nineteenth Century*, Urbana: University of Illinois Press, 1974
———, ed., *African American Poetry of the Nineteenth Century*, Urbana: University of Illinois Press, 1992
Walser, Richard, *The Black Poet*, New York: Philosophical Library, 1966

Richard Hovey

(1864–1900)

Born in Normal, Illinois, the son of educator and Civil War General Charles Edward Hovey and Hariette Farnham Spofford Hovey, Richard Hovey grew up in North Amherst, Massachusetts, and in Washington, D.C., before receiving his formal education at Dartmouth College. He also did some theological study at the General Theological Seminary of the Episcopal Church in New York City. His first volume, *Poems* (1880), was published privately. His meeting with Canadian poet Bliss Carman (1861–1929) led to his introduction to Dante translator and literary scholar Thomas William Parsons, to whom he dedicated the memorial poem *Seaward* (1893). His walking tours with Carman in the late 1880s produced the collaboration on three volumes of "Vagabondia" or "tramp" verse: *Songs from Vagabondia* (1894), *More Songs from Vagabondia* (1896), and the posthumous *Last Songs from Vagabondia* (1900). In 1890, he met his future wife, Henrietta Knapp Russell, then the wife of actor Edmund Russell. She introduced Hovey to the philosophy of "Delsartism" (so named for a minor nineteenth-century French aesthetic philosopher), and traveled with him to Europe. During his European sojourns in the early 1890s, Hovey met many distinguished literary and artistic figures of the day, including Oscar Wilde, Stéphane Mallarmé, Paul Verlaine, James McNeill Whistler, and Madame Blavatsky. On his return to America, Hovey translated the plays of Symbolist playwright Maurice Maeterlinck. His volume *Along the Trail* (1898) contained verses in support of the Spanish-American War. That same year, he took up a lectureship at Barnard College. He died in 1900 following minor abdominal surgery. His posthumous collection of early college poetry, *Dartmouth Lyrics* (1924), did much to spread his reputation as a "bard" of that particular institution.

In their three collaborative volumes of "Vagabondia" poems, Hovey and Carman demonstrated a zealousness for nature that can easily be compared to that depicted in William Wordsworth's and Samuel Taylor Coleridge's *Lyrical Ballads* (1798). Hovey's and Carman's zealotry, however, was mixed with touches of the North American frontier enthusiasm found in the poetry of Bret **Harte**. The two poets' friendship, which celebrated wine, women, song, and the open road, broke important ground by linking the idea of romantic "wandering" (the same sense of here-ness and there-ness rooted in eighteenth-century British verse by William Collins and James Beattie and perhaps linked to the smaller medieval dream-vision quests depicted in William Langland's and the Pearl Poet's works) to the simple joys of vagrancy or "tramping," which was later celebrated by such twentieth-century notables as W. H. Davies, Robert Service, and even Samuel Beckett.

Richard Hovey met Bliss Carman and Thomas Meteyard (the third and minor player in their vagabond triumvirate, who illustrated the three volumes) in 1887. Hovey was enrolled in a theological program at a New York college, and Carman was studying philosophy at Harvard. William R. Linneman has suggested that Hovey started to formulate his ideas of "vagabondism" during his student days at Dartmouth (1881–85). Publication of the poem "Bohemia" in the student publication *Dartmouth* (retitled "Vagabondia" and recycled as the opening poem of *Songs from Vagabondia*), moreover, signaled a profound desire for unrestrained "Houp-la" and a casting-off of "the way of the Pharisee." Both Carman and Hovey may have perceived the writing of the poems in this first volume of the series as a muted poetic revolution, a Rousseau-like shedding of chains that propelled their poetic personae into the realm of liberated free spirits. "Off with the fetters / That chafe and restrain! / Off with the chain!" Hovey proudly announces in the first lines of "Vagabondia."

Songs from Vagabondia flies in the face of academic poetry. It contains poems that ramble from meter to meter and that find their end rhymes with a freewheeling sense of laughable joyousness. In one of Carman's earliest letters to Hovey, in November 1889, he acknowledges that their poetry was to be poetic work in pursuit of youthful freedom and boisterous celebration: "Still, one can strive to attain: the thing is to be able to see even dimly what we ought to strive to attain to." The point, they believed, was that poetry should openly pursue the "pleasure principle" – that poetry was a means of liberty rather than an exercise in boundaries. As in other "tramp" poetry, particularly that of Davies and Service, which celebrates a lifestyle of moral unaccountability and free movement, there is the overwhelming sense that Hovey's and Carman's poetry is self-consciously oral, audience-oriented, and purposely rough and irregular in structure so as to defy any serious attempts at scholarly explanation. So conscious were they that *Songs from Vagabondia* should flout academic poetic conventions that Carman even feared that reviews would hamper his ability to pursue a teaching position within the academy. Paradoxically, a number of the poems, "The Mocking-Bird" (LOA, 2: 564) included, carry a didactic element. Such poems are constantly instructing readers to listen, to watch, and to pay attention in order to put themselves in touch with nature, so that the role of the poet is that of a teacher, not of the academic arts, but of survival and natural harmony: "*I will make it all clear; / I will let you know.*"

Well within the academic tradition, however, the collaboration on *Songs from Vagabondia* appears to have had a long period of gestation. Shortly after their meeting, Hovey and Carman, accompanied by Meteyard, embarked on a walking tour of New England where, in the words of "Vagabondia," they endured "Laughable hardship" coupled with the "Glory of bardship." But the poems, however jovial and lively, were not immediate responses to life on the open road. According to John Coldwell Adams's biography of Carman's cousin, Canadian poet Sir Charles G. D. Roberts (*Sir Charles God Damn* [1986]), most of the "vagabond" verses from *Songs from Vagabondia* were composed during the summer of 1891 and succeeding summers at Roberts's retreat, known as Kingscroft. Roberts is honored in *Songs from Vagabondia* by "A Toast," which celebrates the arts of drinking and womanizing.

Roberts's view of the proceedings, which included daily poetry writing contests reminiscent of those held between Percy Bysshe Shelley and Lord Byron in Italy, suggests that Hovey's impending marriage to Henrietta Russell may have impelled him to record his youthful vernal wanderings with Meteyard and Carman. Hovey's nostalgia for revel and wine may, in fact, have been a response to the threat of domesticity.

In "Spring Song," Carman indulges in a whiff of sexuality. The poem is perhaps a nod to the hormones of young men who are caught up in the earthiness of the annual seasonal rites of passage:

> Only make me over, April,
> When the sap begins to stir!
> Make me man or make me woman,
> Make me oaf or ape or human,
> Cup of flower or cone of fir;
> Make me anything but neuter
> When the sap begins to stir!

The acknowledgment of sensual carnality carries with it hints of Ovidian metamorphoses (such as Hermaphroditus's) and suggests that the nature into which these vagabonds find themselves willingly cast is an animate one. The poem's vision of nature is Arcadia without the responsibility of sheep; lush and oversexed, it is a classical landscape not of ancient Greece but of nineteenth-century salon painting. The poem thus envisions a Land of Cockaigne that is full of "the old immortal indolence of life" and backgrounded by the music of Pan-like birds who sing as if their song was scored by Edvard Grieg's Gyntian interludes or Charles Gounod's Faustian intermezzos ("Like a whim of Grieg's or Gounod's"). In this rather operatic context, Carman and Hovey reinvent and redefine classical Arcadia, sans the typical elegy-inducing, short-lived shepherd, in terms of New England pastoralism. In "The Faun: An Argument," they offer a vision of paradise without peril:

> Let them in the charnel-houses pass their lives
> And seek in death life's secret! And let
> Those hard-faced worldlings prematurely old
> Gnaw their thin lips with vain desire . . .
> . . . They shall not find the way of Arcady,
> The old home of the awful heart-dear Mother,
> Whereto child-dreams and long rememberings lull us,
> Far from the cares that overlay and smother
> The memories of old woodland out-door mirth
> In the dim first life-burst centuries ago,
> The sense of freedom and nearness to Earth.

In short, this new world, deathless and beyond the grasp of the weary world, would be a paradisal place – a naturist's delight without care, meal schedules, or even clothing: "For I am weary of clothes and cooks."

The standard for all measures in this earthly paradise of "Vagabondia" is platonic friendship. The world of *Songs from Vagabondia* constitutes a mutual admiration society. The poems are peppered with references to the writers, with "Dick-on" as the code word for Hovey and the easy pun of "Bliss" or the more obscure "kin" (short for "Blisskin," with which Carman signed his letters to Hovey) referring to the Canadian. Meteyard and Roberts have brief walk-ons in "Vagabondia" as

"Tom" and "Karl." In "Joys of the Open Road," Carman offers an interesting insight into his perception of Hovey ("Black Richard") as a reticent, low-key personality who is exactly the sort of companion required for a long journey:

> Asking nothing, revealing naught,
> But miming words from fund of thought,
>
> A keeper of silence eloquent
> Needy, yet royally well content,
>
> Of the mettled breed, yet abhorring strife,
> And full of the mellow juice of life,
>
> A taster of wine, with an eye for a maid,
> Never too bold, and never afraid,
>
> Never heart-whole, never heart-sick,
> These are the thing I worship in Dick.

As Hovey writes in the famous prospect poem "Evening on the Potomac" (LOA, 2: 561), Carman is the "Faun brother in the ferny glen." (Canadian poet Earle Birney writes of a visit by Carman to the University of British Columbia in 1923. The poet was lost in the woods near Vancouver for 10 hours and had to be rescued by a search party. Asked why he had wandered off, Carman replied, "I wanted to be alone among the trees to commune with nature.") Carman's personality appears to have been that of the archetypal bon vivant, a celebrant in the shared revel in language whose attributes are slyly noted in a linguistic double-play on Carman's name that also pays homage to his recurring image of "wind" in Carman's successful volume *Low Tide at Grand Pré*:

> Free to rejoice
> In the blisses of beauties!
> Free as the voice
> Of the wind as it passes!
> Free as the bird
> In the weft of the grasses!
> Free as the word
> Of the sun to the sea –
> Free!

What appears to be missing from this picture of male bonding and mutual admiration is any hint of homosexual attraction; in fact, the poem constantly refers to the pursuit of available women as a law of Vagabondia. The implications of "immorality," cited by some critics on the publication of *Songs from Vagabondia*, seem to extend only into the realms of intemperance and loitering. For instance, the final poem of the collection, "Comrades," opens, "Comrades, pour the wine to-night." Hovey, in particular, may have been conscious of the possible misconstructions that such a collaboration might suggest.

Between 1891 and 1893, just as Hovey was preparing his poems for *Songs from Vagabondia*, he and Henrietta Russell (partly to hide the illegitimate birth of their son) spent time in Paris, where he became an acquaintance of Verlaine, whose career had been ruined through misrepresentations of his relationship with Arthur Rimbaud (see "Verlaine" [LOA, 2: 565]).

At the same time, the Verlaine-Rimbaud collaboration may have provided Hovey with the impetus to coauthor the "Vagabondia" series with Carman. In the end, *Songs from Vagabondia* and the succeeding *More Songs* and *Last Songs* are little more than the record of two young poets who are having a good time and reinventing themselves as ne'er-do-wells and socially peripheral bohemians with collegian bravado and energy.

The sophomore exuberance with which Carman and Hovey celebrate youthfulness draws upon a romantic assertion that life belongs to the young and that age is the enemy of all things. On a melancholy note, the penultimate poem in the collection, "Designation," almost anticipates a rock-and-roll sentiment that it is better to burn out than fade away:

> When I am only fit to go to bed,
> Or hobble out to sit within the sun,
> Ring down the curtain, say the play is done,
> And the last petals of the poppy shed.
>
> I do not want to live when I am old,
> I have not use for things I cannot love.

Both Carman and Hovey share the love of their own youth. *Songs from Vagabondia* is the product of coincidence in that two poets, almost of equal age and of seemingly compatible if not equal temperament, discovered each other at the right moment, when both had embraced similar, if not parallel, philosophies. Hovey's poetry was informed by a belief in "Delsartism," a tripartite philosophy that sought a balance among mind, body, and spirit; Carman's verse owed a great deal to his belief in "Unitrinianism," which sought to foster serenity and peace of mind through the equilibrium of the physical, emotional, and mental parts of the human composition.

The latter two volumes in the "Vagabondia" series were successful largely as a result of the popularity of *Songs from Vagabondia*, and repeated many of the earlier work's sentiments and themes: happy-go-lucky wandering, free-spirited drinking, and the youthful pursuit of beautiful women. To many readers, however, that first collection must have seemed strangely familiar for inexplicable reasons. Quite self-consciously, Carman and Hovey modeled the book on Wordsworth and Coleridge's *Lyrical Ballads*, perhaps the supreme example of a successful collaborative poetic effort.

The most powerful poem in the collection, Hovey's "Evening on the Potomac," is modeled on Wordsworth's "Tintern Abbey": it has irregular rhythms, offhand rhyme schemes, and a reverence for the restorative powers – in this case, that of love – that can be gleaned from observations on prospects. In another homage to Wordsworth, Hovey personifies Washington, D.C., as a "beautiful Girl-City," which serves as an oblique tribute to the English laureate's sonnet "Composed Upon Westminster Bridge," where London connotes the ethos of the age. For Hovey, Washington is an "Eldorado of the templed clouds," part Troynovant, part whited sephulchre, and part madding crowd, all of which is juxtaposed against the imperishable value of friendship – his friendship with Carman, his "Faun brother."

Indeed, Hovey's friendship with Carman may have indirectly influenced the work of Robert Frost in its intertwined thematics of male bonding and artistic endeavor. Frost, who met Hovey at Barnard College, referred to the elder poet as "Seaward" (recalling his elegy to Thomas W. Parsons) and was well acquainted with the "Vagabondia" poems, which may have played a part in Frost's collaboration on similar themes (tramping, friendship, nature worship) with English poet Edward Thomas. A further link between Frost and Hovey lies in the fact that while Frost was in England visiting Thomas, British tramp poet W. H. Davies was a frequent guest at the Thomas residence. Davies's favorite volume of poetry was *Songs from Vagabondia*, a book that he read while recovering from a leg amputation on his way to join the Klondike gold rush and that inspired his decision to become a poet. Like Robert Service – who subscribed to the oral tradition of the popular ballad, the pleasure principle in poetic composition, and the ideal union of humanity and nature through a balance of thought, body, and spirit – Davies appears to have learned a great deal from his reading of Hovey's and Carman's poetry.

Likewise, Wallace Stevens owed a debt to the "Vagabondia" poems. As Joan Richardson notes, Stevens "borrowed" a series of thematic and sonic references from "Quince to Lilac: To G. H." from *More Songs from Vagabondia* for his "Peter Quince at the Clavier." What fascinated Stevens in the poetry of Carman and Hovey was the "rustic" voice that often approximated prose – an idea that shows just how much they, in turn, owed to John Keats and his assertion that good poetry resembles prose. As Richardson points out, however, Stevens borrowed from Carman and Hovey (almost a "theft" in T. S. Eliot's complimentary sense) in the belief that the *Vagabondia* poems were not firmly entrenched in the contemporary canon and were, so to speak, musically inaudible and referentially invisible to most of his readers. On the other hand, the fact that Stevens did borrow from their work suggests that Carman and Hovey succeeded in achieving their end of creating casually "important" poems, "poet poems," worthy of being reworked and alluded to in a high-brow fashion. The impetus behind the *Vagabondia* poems was, after all, literary rather than popular. In sum, the phenomenon of "tramp" poetry in the late nineteenth century, not only in America but in England, can trace its roots through this intricate series of connections and influences to the underrated work of Richard Hovey and Bliss Carman.

BRUCE MEYER

Selected Works

Seaward: An Elegy on the Death of Thomas William Parsons, Boston: D. Lothrop, 1893

Songs from Vagabondia, Boston: Copeland & Day, 1894

More Songs from Vagabondia, Boston: Copeland & Day, 1896

Along the Trail, Boston: Small & Maynard, 1898

The Birth of Galahad, Boston: Small & Maynard, 1898

Taliesin: A Masque, Boston: Small & Maynard, 1899

Last Songs from Vagabondia, Boston: Small & Maynard, 1900

The Holy Graal and Other Fragments, New York: Duffield, 1907

Dartmouth Lyrics, Boston: Small & Maynard, 1924

Letters of Bliss Carman, edited by H. Pearson Gundy, Montreal, Quebec: McGill-Queen's University Press, 1981

Further Reading

Linneman, William R., *Richard Hovey*, Boston: Twayne, 1976

Lynch, Gerald, ed., *Bliss Carman: A Reappraisal*, Ottawa, Ontario: University of Ottawa Press, 1990

Macdonald, Alland Houston, *Carman: Quest and Revolt*, St. John's, Newfoundland: Jesperson, 1985

Richardson, Joan, *Wallace Stevens: A Biography of the Early Years, 1879–1923*, New York: Beech Tree/William Morrow, 1986

Stephens, Donald, *Bliss Carman*, Boston: Twayne, 1966

Julia Ward Howe

(1819–1910)

There are many selves of Julia Ward Howe we no longer know. Howe suggests three versions in "The Lyric I," a poem introducing her second collection, *Words for the Hour* (1857). The fact-collecting empiricist, the reader of German Romanticism, and the day-to-day pragmatist might each represent a different type in Howe's upper-class circle of antebellum Boston acquaintances. Subsequent stanzas, however, foreground contrasts among Howe's selves that seem closer to the bone: "The philosophic I, is not / The I that any man may meet / . . . Or hold to greetings in the street." Moreover, she frets,

The I that cannot choose but stand
Great rights and wrongings to assert,
Is not the I that wastes the meal,
And leaves hiatus in the shirt.

The poet sums up the state of her plural, fragmented self: "There is a difference in our I – s [i.e., I's]."

A book in one hand while the other is burning meals or holes under a hot iron – an absentminded postmodern might find something familiar in Howe's two or more personae in the same skin. A further bit of wit in her multiple self-exposure also implies Howe's affinity for transcendentalist wordplay, as she figures herself to be "the lyric I, / The poet's *eye* that finely rolls, / And holds convertible domain." The poet's eye, language, and the material demands of her circumstances convert not only the domain surveyed, but again and again the demeanor of Julia Ward Howe: Romantic poet, wit, scholar, philosopher, reformer, and absentminded domestic.

If we know Howe at all today, it is not as any of these personae, but as the sentimental lyricist of the Union army's Civil War rallying cry, "Battle-Hymn of the Republic" (LOA, 1: 709). We do not know Howe as either the rebellious wife or the erotic temptress, two notorious personae who appeared in her anonymously published first collection of poems, *Passion Flowers* (1854). When twentieth-century criticism established an American literary canon, it excluded a host of poets who, like Howe, did not practice their craft according to criteria preferred by modernists. It is therefore difficult to appreciate Howe's verse even when events of her life come to light. As Cheryl Walker laments, on behalf of many lost nineteenth-century women poets, "We don't know how to read their poems."

From her birth in 1819 in New York City until she was 23, Julia Ward lived in her banker father's wealthy household as the headstrong first of three daughters, the middle child of five, who was bent on living up to the "wild" reputation of her red hair. The poet's mother died when she was small, and her father in his grief turned to a severe evangelical version of Episcopalian piety. When Howe was 16, her female seminary education, common for daughters of well-placed families, was replaced by exacting private tutors at home, and Julia's social circle became limited to her father's extended family. Happily, this circle was a merry, inquisitive clan.

She was closest in temperament to her brilliant, mercurial older brother, Sam, who encouraged her to read widely from the library he collected during his studies at Columbia and lat-

er in Europe. Coming across Goethe's *Faust* among Sam's books, the poet's father once admonished her, "I hope you have not been reading this wicked book." Long before his scolding, she had probably read it in the original German. In this enclosed world, Julia later wrote, she sometimes "seemed to myself like a young damsel of olden time, shut up within an enchanted castle."

At 11, the budding poet handed in verses instead of a prose essay assigned by one of her schoolmarms who did not encourage her literary ambitions. Somewhere along the line, the girl read Hugh Blair's *Lectures on Rhetoric and Belles Lettres*, a course of study designed to popularize both sensationalist psychology and eighteenth-century rhetorical methods for use in public oratory and in the study of literary models for writing. Many years later, Howe recalled that "Blair's 'Rhetoric,' with its many quotations from the poets, was a delight to me." Although their father forbade attendance at public productions, Sam and Julia composed and produced plays in verse for family gatherings, and Sam encouraged her to submit poems for publication. Several of them appeared in the New York *American* when she was 14.

One does not need to accept faculty psychology to understand the explosive potential of Blair's "useful" deployment of written discourse, including poetry, for isolated, gifted young Julia Ward or for hundreds of antebellum women like her. Of today's boom in powerful verse by women, Florence Howe has observed: "Perhaps at no time since the early nineteenth century have poets so consciously spoken to help change the world." Because most twentieth-century scholarly discussions lack a sense of poetry as rhetorical, however, critics have ignored a scheme like Blair's rhetoric, which recommended to poets interruptions of the text, such as apostrophe, for representing feelings. This rhetorical view of poetry also advocated dialogue and direct address for dramatic and literary effect.

Howe sensed early on that, especially for women, verse could become, as Emily **Dickinson** would write, a "letter to the World / That never wrote to me" (LOA, 2: 259). Blair assumes that "you" and "I" inhabit a community of "hearers, as all men in general," an assertion that echoes in postmodern linguists Emile Benveniste's and Julia Kristeva's insights on the dialogic work of language. Emboldened by Blair's sanction and by the poetic possibilities early nineteenth-century literary culture afforded, a multitude of quite various, unexpected writers assumed the stance of poet in order to address all of "you." With increasing literacy, moreover, this generalized audience was less and less the exclusive domain of white men. The poet's persona of the day was a markedly passionate first-person "I," particularly concerning abolitionism. But like its audience, this persona was increasingly ambiguous in gender and identity as more and more women figured themselves to be writers.

The "Battle-Hymn of the Republic" exemplifies the force of poetry as rhetoric. Like Frances **Harper**, John Greenleaf **Whittier,** and many other antebellum poets, Howe felt herself called to shape abolitionist sentiment. Her last rousing stanza activates cultural codes of orthodox evangelical discourse for the Union cause:

> In the beauty of the lilies Christ was born across the sea,
> With a glory in his bosom that transfigures you and me:
> As he died to make men holy, let us die to make men
>   free,
>   While God is marching on.

Pronouns in the second line invoke listeners or readers with a generalized "you" and urge them to identify with the poet in common religious devotion. Next, poet and reader collapse into the plural pronoun "us," and when they are placed in parallel syntax, they are called to identify with Christ and his crucifixion, and thus to face a redemptive martyrdom to free black slaves. The poet's apostrophe constitutes a reading subject ready to march in Lincoln's army.

Although Howe received only five dollars for the "Battle-Hymn" from the *Atlantic Monthly* in 1862, many read the poem and it was widely sung. Toward the end of her life, Howe capitalized on the song's success and on its forceful persona – the one from "The Lyric I" who could not "choose but stand / Great rights and wrongings to assert" – by reciting it and relating in print and in public appearances the story of how its words came to her. One morning in November 1861, the poet claimed that she "sprang out of bed" to scribble its five stanzas "in the dimness . . . almost without looking at the paper." Like many a woman writer, she then crept back to bed in an attempt not to wake the baby or its father sleeping in the same room. Soldiers' campfires in her lines also recall the view at dusk of fields outside of Washington, D.C., which Howe saw while riding the train that took her to the capital; the image also drew force from a review of the Grand Army of the Potomac she had taken with other dignitaries. The family had been staying some weeks in Washington, D.C., while Howe's husband, Samuel, famous for his work in hospital reform, served on a Union sanitary commission. Sung to the tune of "John Brown's Body," the hymn grew enormously popular among Northern regiments. It was said that the first time President Lincoln heard the "Battle-Hymn," tears ran down his face and he shouted, "Sing it again!" Seven years later, Ralph Waldo **Emerson** wrote in his journal, "I honor the author of the Battle Hymn. . . . We have no such poetess in New England."

Looking back in her later years, Howe emphasized the inspiring reformer who wrote the "Battle-Hymn," a persona expedient to a woman who, after her husband's death, wrote, traveled, and lectured for a living. Two full chapters of her *Reminiscences* (1899) foreground the fervent days when the lyrics were written. In this book, she connects that abolitionist poet to the person who would later promote women's clubs as an arena of women's influence and oratory, to the woman who preached pacifism in late nineteenth-century New England and British Unitarian congregations, and to the lobbyist who continued to stump for women's suffrage to the end of her life in 1910.

In *Reminiscences*, Howe obscures reference to the erotic poet of *Passion Flowers*. Her daughters, however, were not shy about associating Howe with her first collection, and they assigned its title to a chapter of the biography they published six years after her death. Howe herself asserts that "the most important among my 'Passion Flowers'" were the volume's overt-ly political poems addressing European "events of 1848" that absorbed American intellectuals: "the heroic efforts of Italian patriots to deliver their country from foreign oppression, the struggle of Hungary to maintain her ancient immunities." Not eros but sober, reformist sympathy was the core of the persona Howe preferred to assume late in life.

But causes of a righteous crusader do not represent or account for the complexities of this poet, even in her last years. When she was 80, the same year that *Reminiscences* appeared, Howe's fourth volume of poetry, *From Sunset Ridge*, was published. This collection begins with the "Battle-Hymn" and other patriotic verses and includes sedate commemorative poems for Lincoln, James Russell **Lowell**, William Cullen **Bryant**, and Henry Ward Beecher. Yet the volume also reprints a steamy sequence called "Her Verses: A Lyrical Romance" from *Words for the Hour*, which some critics deemed the best of her five collections, "a book that palpitated, such red heart's blood coursed through the lines."

Although in later years, she encouraged comparisons of her physical appearance to that of Queen Victoria, Howe also enjoyed shocking Boston, as when in the 1880s she received Oscar Wilde in her home and at the Howe family retreat in Newport. He accepted one of her invitations by declaring that "when you are present the air is cosmopolitan and the room seems full of brilliant people; you are one of those rare persons who give one the sense of creating history as they live." A young niece who lived with the elderly Howe one winter seconded Wilde's estimate of her aunt's energetic influence: to Daisy Terry, she was "the best of company, witty and wise, merry and many-sided."

Just how successful Howe's campaign to bequeath to posterity the respectable, maternal reformer was may be judged by Madeleine B. Stern's incredulity, in 1978, that Howe had once been regarded by critics as "the most notable woman of letters" in premodern America. "It is more accurate," Stern asserted, "to regard her as the 'Dearest Old Lady in America.'" But in fact, taking up the "Battle-Hymn" or considering her verse *beyond* it can suggest quite different versions of Julia Ward Howe. One perceptive early response came from Nathaniel **Hawthorne**, who wrote from England in 1854 to thank his publisher Ticknor for sending him *Passion Flowers*: "Those are admirable poems of Mrs. Howe's, but the devil must be in the woman to publish them. . . . However, I, for one, am much obliged to the lady, and esteem her beyond all comparison the first of American poetesses. What does her husband think of it?"

Samuel Gridley Howe did not think much of it. And when he did, he was angry. *Passion Flowers* was published during her tenth year of marriage, when Julia was about to have the fifth of six children. The poet had realized a long time before, however, that this was a great mismatch. The man she fell in love with was a handsome hero of Greek uprisings, an intimate of outspoken abolitionist legislator Charles Sumner, and the founder of Boston's Perkins' Institute for the Blind. But Dr. Howe had no interest in the books Julia read or in the verse she wrote to make sense and fun out of life. During their 1843 honeymoon voyage on the *Brittannia*, for example, the new bride had even sponsored a parodic tribute to Queen Victoria in the ladies' cabin, complete with doggerel written to praise the stewardess. Before the European tour was over, however, the despairing poet wrote, "Hope died as I was led / Unto my marriage bed." It was perfectly clear to Julia that her husband shunned both bookish pursuits and the society she had come to relish after her father's death in 1839. With the 1854 publication of *Passion Flowers*, as Hawthorne noted, the rift became an open secret.

Some lines in the book attack a contentious male authority. One begins, "When I and Theologus cannot agree, / Should I give up the point, pray you, or he?" Obviously, the one to give in should not be the woman, the hostess of "little feasts / To pitiful witiful birdlings and beasts." In "My Last Dance" (LOA, 1: 708), a not very repentant matron justifies to a male critic her joining the dancers at a party by explaining that it was the "madd'ning tumult" that swept her unwittingly into "the shock of circling forms / Linked each to other." In "The Mill-Stream," an angry man tries to dam up the roiling feminine current of a river that at last tears his house apart. Although the collection was anonymous, everyone knew immediately that Howe had written *Passion Flowers*. She confided in a letter to her sister Annie how upset the reclusive doctor was to have his wife acknowledged as its author. "We have been very unhappy. The book, you see, was a blow to him, and some foolish and impertinent people have hinted that the Miller was meant for himself – this has made him almost crazy. . . . We have had the devil's own time of it."

Passion Flowers, moreover, addresses male readers who are clearly not the poet's husband. A host of friends, including her "Master," are thanked in the volume's "Salutatory" poem for their loving support of her work. In a more daring poem, "Mother Mind," the writer again uses the title "Master" to refer to one who beckons her at night by "his whisper and his nod." She then gives birth to "children of my soul." Her brainchildren are verses he will consecrate, she says, by "Baptismal rites they claim of thee." Some other man seems to be her reader in "The Royal Guest." Here, the woman poet claims, "I am shrewd with other men, / With thee I'm slow and difficult of speech." If words fail her, the woman's passion does not: "My lip will falter," she boldly states, "but my prisoned heart / Springs forth to measure its faint pulse with thine."

This book's most powerful section is a dialogue in three poems. A flirtatious feminine persona in the poem "Coquette et Froide" evokes the cautious interest of a masculine voice from a second poem "Coquette et Tendre." Because he hesitates, the woman apologizes in the last poem, "Answer," but she continues the intimate exchange and finally pouts:

> Is our jesting, then so fateful?
>   I'll be colder, if I must;
> Do not chide that I am grateful,
>   Dare not mock my childish trust.

There are overtly political verses in *Passion Flowers*: poems about Europe, Italy, and abolition. There are also some poems about her children and their nurse. One poem, "Sybyl," is a tribute to a brilliant woman friend, perhaps Margaret **Fuller**, whose biography Howe published in 1883. But the volume as a whole is directed at men: male guests who did not disdain her parties as Howe's father and her husband did, male readers more like her brother and his friends, and those exacting tutors who encouraged the poet to study and to write.

These men made way for a woman writer to enter nineteenth-century literary discourse, and thereafter American literature would never be the same. Looking back 55 years later at her first volume of poetry, Howe could then safely make explicit a rhetorical goal of *Passion Flowers*, although she mutes its sexual overtones: "It was a timid performance upon a slender reed, but the great performers in the noble orchestra of writers answered to its appeal, which won me a seat in their ranks." In the autobiography, Howe emphasized her Victorian performance as "Dearest Old Lady in America," and this aspect has come to dominate our memory of her. But the figure masks, among Howe's many other personae, the earlier erotic poet who with her "Passion Flowers" enticed "Master" readers and writers of poetry to share center stage. "There is a difference in our I – s," the difficult and complex poet insisted, and that difference can be powerful and productive. Those who read her rich and varied poetic works will find traces of Julia Ward Howe's other seductive selves.

WENDY DASLER JOHNSON

Selected Work

Passion Flowers, Boston: Ticknor and Fields, 1854
Words for the Hour, Boston: Ticknor and Fields, 1857
Later Lyrics, Boston: J. E. Tilton, 1866
Modern Society, Boston: Roberts Brothers, 1881
Margaret Fuller (Marchessa Ossoli), 1883; reprinted, Westport, Connecticut: Greenwood, 1970
From Sunset Ridge: Poems Old and New, Boston: Houghton Mifflin, 1898
Reminiscences, Boston: Houghton Mifflin, 1899
At Sunset, edited by Laura E. Richards, Boston: Houghton Mifflin, 1910
Julia Ward Howe and the Woman Suffrage Movement, edited by Florence Howe Hall, Boston: Dana Estes, 1913

Further Reading

Clifford, Deborah Pickman, *Mine Eyes Have Seen the Glory*, Boston: Little Brown, 1979
Tharp, Louise Hall, *Three Saints and a Sinner: Julia Ward Howe, Louisa, Annie and Sam Ward*, Boston: Little Brown, 1956
Walker, Cheryl, *The Nightingale's Burden*, Bloomington: Indiana University Press, 1982

William Dean Howells

(1837–1920)

When William Dean Howells died on May 11, 1920, the nation looked back to assess the 60-year career of America's leading man of letters. Dozens of obituaries and appreciations appeared in the months that followed. Along with his still-remembered contributions to American literature – as a novelist and literary craftsman, as an editor and patron of young writers, and as a critic and champion of realism – they also celebrated Howells the poet. It seems surprising today that the man so firmly associated with fiction and criticism should also have had a substantial reputation as a poet. But in the estimation of his contemporaries, Howells the poet lagged only a step or two behind Howells the novelist. His poems continued to be anthologized long after their initial publication, even as recently as 1953.

In fact, Howells's earliest ambition had been to make his literary mark as a poet. His first book was a collection of verse, and he continued to write poems throughout his life, publishing his last one in 1916. His poetic works include four collections of poetry, a long narrative poem separately published, five verse dramas, poems collected in a miscellany of prose and verse, and more than three dozen uncollected poems. He never wholly abandoned verse. He might put poetry aside for a space of years to focus more of his creative energies on prose, but he invariably wrote poetry again. Each of Howells's poetic phases has its distinctive features, for poetry served different purposes for Howells throughout his career.

Born in Martins Ferry, Ohio, on March 1, 1837, William Dean Howells was the second son of William Cooper Howells and Mary Dean Howells. His formal schooling was sporadic and all but irrelevant, for his real education took place at the typecase and the bookcase. From the age of six, Howells helped set type on the various newspapers put out by his father, a Swedenborgian printer and sometime Whig political correspondent. The literary conversation at the printshop was lively and, supplemented by Howells's enthusiastic reading in the family's small library, instilled in the boy an early and fixed ambition to make his life a literary one. In *My Literary Passions* (1895), Howells records the influence of Alexander Pope and Sir Walter Scott, Henry Wadsworth **Longfellow** and Alfred, Lord Tennyson, William Shakespeare and, especially, Heinrich Heine on the young poet-in-training. His earliest writing imitated his current favorites in verse and prose.

His first publication was "Old Winter, loose thy hold on us," a short and predictable nature poem that his father submitted to the *Ohio State Journal*, which printed it a few weeks after Howells's fifteenth birthday. The thrill of seeing his poem copied into other newspapers reinforced the boy's ambitions. Soon he was submitting poems, sketches, and translations from Spanish and German to newspapers and journals of ever increasing importance. By the late 1850s, his primary model for poetry was Heine. His first submission to the almighty *Atlantic Monthly* was "Andenken," a poem so Heinesque that the journal's editor, James Russell **Lowell**, spent months checking Heine's works to satisfy himself that the poem was not plagiarized.

Heine's influence was a mixed blessing for Howells, as for others of Howells's generation. The German poet did show him how to discard the formal constraints of the Augustans. Heine opened up the realm of poetry to more natural language and to the rhythms of common speech. At the same time, Heine's works drew Howells to his poetic persona, that of the sensitive genius who is suffocating and stagnating in the provinces. In his late adolescence, Howells would find himself similarly itching to get away from small-town Jefferson, Ohio, and even from the state capital, Columbus. The image of the poet as a misunderstood titan who suffered at the hands of an insensitive and cloddish society naturally appealed to the sensitive young man who had been the bookish boy in a village of the western reserve. In a mocking little rhyme of this period, Howells pictured himself as the singing robin and "The Poet's Friends" as "wise-looking, stupid" cattle who "never understand a word."

The romantic self-absorption he found in Heine served Howells less well. Already prone to introspection, Howells wallowed in sentiment and wrote brooding poems about lost loves, vain longings, and bitter sorrows – few of which had any basis in his own experience. The exaggerated emotionality of these poems, however, was tempered by the greatest gift that Heine offered Howells: an ironic voice. Howells's self-mockery undercut his own sentimentality even as he posed as a tragic figure. This ironic vision would stay with Howells long after he had disburdened himself of Heine's other legacies. A delicate irony would become the hallmark of his prose style, and it would stamp his later poetry as well.

By his early twenties, Howells had amassed a sufficient number of melancholy lyrics and bittersweet nature poems for about half a book. He collaborated with his friend and fellow Ohioan, John James **Piatt**, on *Poems of Two Friends*, which came out in time for Christmas of 1859. The 30 poems in Howells's part of the book had been written between the ages of 17 and 22, and more than half of them had been previously published. In spite of Howells's later recollection that the volume "became instantly and lastingly unknown to fame," it was reviewed in two of the most prominent journals of the day. Henry Clapp, who had already accepted several of Howells's poems for the *Saturday Press*, declared him "a man of genius" with a "brilliant future." Howells's Heine-influenced cynicism found a ready audience among the iconoclasts of Clapp's Bohemian circle, and although the editor also acknowledged that Howells's genius may not have been of the highest order, he welcomed the young poet into the literary fraternity of New York. At the *Atlantic*, Lowell noticed the book and praised its "fresh and authentic power." In a later review in 1866, he recalled that "sentiment predominated over reflection" in the poems, but he dismissed this tone as a proper product of youth. Nonetheless, Howells's "matured style" in these poems attracted him for its "subtilty of sentiment and delicacy of expression." Others noticed the influence of Heine, but not always favorably. Moncure D. Conway, editor of the Cincinnati *Dial*, observed Howells's "almost Heinesque familiarity with high things," but advised the poet to "take the anti-publication pledge for a year or so" in order to rid himself of all models that might tempt him away from the honest expression of experience. Gail Hamilton, the saucy critic of the *National Era*, poked fun at the two poets' pose of unfulfilled yearning; she speculated that far from being sensitive, broken-hearted aesthetes, they were "a pair of stout-limbed, ruddy-cheeked, corn-fed country boys."

Hamilton's criticism hit home with Howells, perhaps because he knew, as he says in "Rapture," just how often his verses "fable[d] anguish." With such titles as "Gone," "Dead," "Drowned," or "Drifting Away," the poems frequently lament a dear dead past that will come no more. They shed lonely tears over betrayal in love. They speak of a life filled with tragedy and loss. Too many of these poems, however, contain a note of forced melancholy that is inconsistent with the poet's youth. Howells's stylistic skills, what Conway called his "felicities of expression," seem at first to have outstripped his subject matter. In his early twenties, he had the means to write poetry, but nothing much to write about. Nothing, that is, that his then present notions of literature would consider suitable for poetic expression. Those notions, however, were changing.

Interspersed among the tragic lamentations are a few poems that hint at more homely themes. Most notable is "The Movers," a "sketch" about a family taking a last fond look at their old homestead. After the parents reflect on joys and sorrows of their everyday lives, they "[turn] their dim eyes to the Westward" and move on. This poem and a few others celebrate Howells's native landscape instead of opting for some pseudo-Germanic setting. Perhaps these were the poems Lowell was responding to when he struck a note that would be often repeated: according to Lowell, Howells's early poems exhibit a "thorough Western flavor," for the poet himself is "a product of the rough-and-ready West."

It was as a western product that Howells presented himself to the eastern literary establishment when he made his fabled journey to New York and Boston later in 1860. A few years later, his work would be accorded a place in a collection of *Poets and Poetry of the West*, edited by William T. Coggeshall (1864). And it was a young western poet who traveled to Europe in December 1861 to begin a four-year stint as American consul to Venice, a political appointment garnered in exchange for Howells having written a campaign biography of Abraham Lincoln. The man who returned from Venice in August 1865 with a wife and baby daughter, however, would no longer have the same aspirations, nor the same vision of literature.

Almost exactly a year after Will Howells had arrived in Europe, Elinor Mead landed in Liverpool to marry him. The two had met when she visited Columbus two years earlier, and by the summer of 1860, they were all but officially engaged. On his trip east, Howells stopped in Brattleboro, Vermont, to meet her rather extraordinary family. Related on her mother's side to John Humphrey Noyes, founder of the Oneida Community, and to Rutherford B. Hayes, Elinor could claim a place in the intellectual aristocracy of New England by heredity as well as on her own merits. She also had the same artistic talent that enabled her brothers to make their mark on the American creative scene: Larkin Mead was a sculptor and William Rutherford Mead was an architect. With a keen intellect, an artistic sensibility, and a good sense of humor, she was the ide-

al mate for Howells. They were married in Paris on Christmas Eve, 1862, and their first daughter, Winifred, was born just shy of a year later.

Life as a husband and a father changed Howells, as one might expect. Just as he began to think more seriously about earning an adequate livelihood through his writing, however, he found it all but impossible to get his poems published. The market for his sort of poetry had seemingly dried up, perhaps because Heinesque poems of jilted lovers had no audience in Civil War America. Alongside his poetry, he had always written prose: sketches, book reviews, political correspondence, and travel pieces. Now, he found he could easily sell his work in these genres, while his poetry was rejected by one editor after another.

The moment that he would later term "The Turning Point of My Life" came when Lowell accepted his essay "Recent Italian Comedy" for the *North American Review*. Lowell told Howells that his travel sketches (then appearing in the Boston *Advertiser*) and his literary criticism "fill a gap. . . . *They are the thing itself*." The older poet's letter confirmed what Howells had already begun to suspect. He would recall that "there was not so much a fatal turning in the way as an opening, a widening of the perspective in a quarter where there had indeed been scope." At this moment in time, he gave prose a chance, yet without abandoning a poetic model. Ultimately, he would come to believe that the finest writing resembled Heine's *Reisebilder*, "where the page of prose, always tremulous with inner music, breaks now and again into open rhyme." He may still have written the occasional poem when he returned to New York as a freelance critic, but he soon had more pressing literary work.

In 1866, Howells became assistant editor of the *Atlantic Monthly* when he was hired by James T. Fields to bring a new generation of talent to the journal's pages. Howells's editorial position might seem to have offered the opportunity to publish his beloved poems, but he took advantage of the connection only half a dozen times. Instead, he immersed himself in prose and began his fight for realism. Even before he became editor-in-chief in 1871, he was responsible for seeking out new writers, accepting or rejecting submissions, negotiating with contributors, and reviewing new books. Concurrently with his editorial duties during his 15 years with the *Atlantic*, Howells produced three travel books, three volumes of short sketches, a campaign biography of Hayes, three plays, and five novels, not to mention countless essays and reviews for other journals. He also issued his second collection of verse, entitled simply *Poems* (1873), and became the father of two more children, John Mead in 1868 and Mildred in 1872.

Howells's national reputation as a writer began almost immediately upon his return to America, when he published *Venetian Life* (1866) and *Italian Journeys* (1867). Lowell had not erred in his praise of the freshness of Howells's Italian pieces, and it was travel writing that gave Howells entry into the house of fiction. While abroad, he had developed his already keen habit of observation and turned his attention to everyday people. Returning home, he focused his eye for the ordinary on his Cambridge neighbors in *Suburban Sketches* (1871). The next year, he blended travel writing and fiction by moving newlyweds Basil and Isabel March through the American landscape on their way to Niagara in *Their Wedding Jour-*

ney (1872). Howells's career as a novelist was finally under way, and he would develop his powers in *A Chance Acquaintance* (1873), *A Foregone Conclusion* (1874), *The Lady of the Aroostook* (1879), and *The Undiscovered Country* (1880). After leaving the *Atlantic* editor's chair in 1881, he produced his masterpieces of realism: *A Modern Instance* (1882), *The Rise of Silas Lapham* (1885), *Indian Summer* (1886), and *A Hazard of New Fortunes* (1890).

In the midst of this flurry of creative activity, he published three volumes of verse: the narrative poem *No Love Lost: A Romance of Travel* (1869) and the 1873 collection *Poems*, which he also reissued in 1886 as an "enlarged edition" by including "No Love Lost" and three additional poems. Never one to let any of his literary efforts go to waste, Howells had been steadily disposing of his old poems wherever he could sell them since his "turning point" in Venice. Only a handful of verses appeared in the *Atlantic*, but others went to *Harper's*, *Galaxy*, *Commonwealth*, and the *Nation*. Eventually, Howells could boast that "every scrap of meter was marketed." Shrewd businessman that he was, he made his poems pay over and over again by reprinting them in collections.

The 1873 collection by no means represents the Howells of the 1870s, but re-presents the Heinesque Howells of the fifties and early sixties. Of the 47 poems in the volume, nearly all were originally published before the poet turned 30. Some poems were culled from the journals, other poem from his father's *Ashtabula Sentinel* and the Ohio newspapers of his youth, and 10 poems from *Poems of Two Friends*. Typical of the poems in this collection is "Forlorn" (LOA, 2: 351), a tale in 26 stanzas of a man haunted by longing for his lost love. He searches for her everywhere and finds her "shadowy presence" among the objects of the lonely house: the now silent piano, an open volume of love poems, and her shawl upon the floor. The rhyme and meter are precise and complicated, the diction is stilted ("closéd doors" and "quenchéd" roses), and a tragic sensibility is everywhere in evidence. Howells recounts the poem's publication history in *Literary Friends and Acquaintance* (1900), and here, too, the poem can stand for many others in the 1873 collection. It was written before Howells left for Venice, and he tried to publish it first with the *Atlantic* and *Harper's Monthly*, with no success. After he established himself in Italy, the poem made the rounds of the English magazines, including G. H. Lewes's *Fortnightly Review*, again unsuccessfully. When it was finally accepted, the editor died and the magazine likewise expired before the poem could see print. Once back in America, Howells offered it to the *Nation*, the newspaper he had just left to take up his post at the *Atlantic*, and it was at last "marketed."

By far the bulk of the poems in the collection treat the youthful Howells's favorite subjects: death and loss, loneliness and unrequited passion, memory and aging, the delicious torment of love, and the poet's cruel alienation from the mass of men. A sprinkling of nature poems offer some relief, although the verses concerning autumn predictably gravitate toward the theme of loss. "In Earliest Spring" (LOA, 2: 360) strikes a more optimistic note, as the poet tries to capture his sense of kinship with nature. He feels his own excitement rising as March's frostiness proves unable to stifle the gathering pulse of spring, "as if in the brier, / Leafless there by my door, trembled a sense of the rose."

Howells had not been unmindful of the war being waged in America while he sat comfortably in Venice, and a few poems address the great event of his generation. "The Pilot's Story" won him some acclaim in 1860, and Howells placed it first in the 1873 collection, perhaps as a reminder to the reader of his intellectual if not actual participation in the Union cause. The poem narrates the tale of a slave whose master loses her in a game of monte as they are traveling to St. Louis to reunite with their child; rather than become the property of the riverboat card sharp, the distraught mother leaps overboard and is crushed by the paddlewheel. "The Battle in the Clouds" memorializes the soldiers who "routed Freedom's foe" at the battle of Lookout Mountain, while "For One of the Killed" predicts "Glory and endless years" for those who died in battle. These later efforts, while certainly heartfelt, lack any strong sense of personal or emotional involvement in the war's events.

A much truer poem of mourning and loss is Howells's "Elegy on John Butler Howells," written in Venice in the days following news of his favorite brother's death from diphtheria at age 18. After movingly recalling his farewell three years earlier, when John was still little more than a child, and remembering boyhood days when he played with his baby brother, Howells imagines the familiar graveyard back home and pictures his sisters by John's grave. In the final section, the poet implores God not to let this loss cause him to "falter in belief," for that would be the "sorest grief." The fear of a loss of faith that flickered momentarily in 1864 would flame forth again three decades later.

The few poems that draw on Howells's European sojourn include "The Royal Portraits" (LOA, 2: 356) and "Louis Lebeau's Conversion." Musing on the portraits of the king and queen in the palace at Ludwigshof, the poet weaves a tale of suspected infidelity and murder that could have come from the pen of Edgar Allan **Poe**. Running beneath the surface is an undercurrent of democratic disgust at the corruption of the hereditary monarchies of Europe. According to the poet, the queen, a fabulous beauty who "might have been false," died suspiciously young, while the king died many years later, "Rotten with license, and lust, and pride." Although his features are unattractive – his face "fat and red," his neck "thick and coarse" – there can be no doubt that the king was

> One of the heaven-anointed sort
> Who ruled his people with iron sway,
>   And knew that, through good and evil report,
> God meant him to rule and them to obey.

In "Louis Lebeau's Conversion," Howells moves beyond ironic commentary on the morals of monarchs to a direct comparison of the religions of the old and new worlds. Moving among the crowd in Venice, the poet breathes air "full of Old World sadness" and remembers, by contrast, the "free, wild life in Ohio, / When the land was new." According to the poet, the outdoor camp meetings where the light filters through elms and maples outshines the stained glass windows of churches, and the scent of the hemlocks and pines surpass any censer the Catholic church could provide. It is here in the new world that the reprobate Louis finds his salvation, not in the churches of his French ancestors.

Apart from the interest this volume of poems may have for a postmodernist study of the aesthetic of appropriation, there would be little diminution in America's poetic achievement were this collection utterly forgotten. The influence of Heine and Longfellow all but swamp whatever individuality the young poet brought to his verse of this era. The poems disclose, as Oscar Firkins remarks, "youth, experiment, and insecurity." It would be 20 years before Howells was secure enough to speak in his own voice when he turned to verse.

In the two decades between *Poems* (1873) and *Stops of Various Quills* (1895), Howells became a major force in the shaping of American literature. He continued as editor of the *Atlantic* until 1881, when he resigned in order to devote his energies to his fiction. Before the decade was over, however, he would be back in the critic's chair, writing a monthly column for *Harper's*. From 1886 until 1892, Howells sat in "The Editor's Study" and fought relentlessly for his realistic principles. He introduced audiences to the European writers he admired – Leo Tolstoy, Fyodor Dostoyevski, Ivan Turgenev, Boyeson, Bjørnstjerne Bjørnson, and Henrik Ibsen – and to the American voices that needed to be heard. Dozens of women writers counted Howells as an ally: Sarah Orne **Jewett**, Mary E. Wilkins Freeman, Murfree, Charlotte Gilman, Rose Terry **Cooke**, and Constance Fenimore **Woolson**, to name just a few. He weathered attacks from both sides of the Atlantic for his stubborn insistence on the superiority of realism to romance. Although he wrote little poetry in this period, he read much verse and commented upon it in his columns. These were the years in which he recognized the startlingly new achievement of Emily **Dickinson** and assisted into print Stephen **Crane** and Paul Laurence **Dunbar**.

These were also the years that saw an erosion of Howells's faith in American society, which corresponded with his increased sense of skepticism and doubt. Howells's "whole pattern of ethical ideals was redirected and his moral sensibility etched deeper and much darker," according to Edwin Cady, while "his creative impulses shaped themselves to increasingly tragic conclusions." Howells's reading of Tolstoy had reawakened the ideals taught him by his Utopian father and imbued him with the conviction that each man is complicit in the fate of the whole race. Subsequently, he could not fail to wonder at the future of an America where the chasm between social classes widened more each year. The more than 10,000 strikes in 1886 focused Howells's attention on the friction between labor and capital, and he turned his novelistic pen to economic themes.

He also watched closely as America responded to the riots in Chicago's Haymarket Square in May of the same year, in which eight policemen were killed. When eight anarchists were convicted of murder, regardless of their alibis and purely on the basis of their opinions, Howells took a public stand. In a letter to the New York *Tribune*, he urged readers to ask the governor of Illinois to commute the anarchists' death sentences. He publicly abhorred "the principle of punishing [men] because of their frantic opinions, for a crime which they were not shown to have committed." Howells found himself almost completely alone in his opposition, and public opinion ran heatedly against him; his appeal nearly cost him the audience for his novels that he had built up over 15 years. The miscarriage of American justice and the bloodlust of the American public left Howells sick at heart and longing for a quiet, humble life where he could "be socially identified with the principles of progress and sympathy for the struggling mass." For the rest of his life, he would flirt with various forms of socialism and extend his doctrine of "complicity" to one of "solidarity."

The civic tragedy unfolding across America only added to Howells's personal tragedies of this period. In December 1886, malaria claimed the life of his favorite sister, Victoria. The most talented of his siblings, she had sympathized with and nurtured his early literary ambitions. Meanwhile, his eldest daughter, Winifred, who had been slowly wasting away since 1880, died in March 1889 of an unknown malady. She, too, had shown precocious literary promise, publishing poems as early as age 15. At 17, she began showing the first signs of her mysterious illness, which John Crowley suggests may have been anorexia. Her rallies and relapses exhausted the emotional resources of both her parents, and they eventually committed her to the rest and force-feeding regimen of S. Weir Mitchell. After her sudden death and the discovery that her disease was organic, not psychological, Howells and his wife tormented themselves with guilt and regret. Elinor collapsed under the emotional burden and became an invalid for most of her remaining years, which only added to Howells's suffering and sense of loss.

The events that brought tragedy and disillusionment into Howells's life, however, also brought back poetry. This time, the emotions would be genuine; the regretful sorrow was no longer a poetic posture. The six years after Winnie's death saw Howells's first real outpouring of verse in 20 years, and he published 39 poems in *Harper's Monthly*. In 1895, he added four more poems and published the collection as *Stops of Various Quills*, which was illustrated by his friend Howard Pyle. This volume is perhaps the single book that most obviously dispels the persistent notion that Howells was a fatheaded optimist and always looked at the smiling aspects of life.

More succinct and powerful than many of his novels, these poems express religious doubt, loss of hope, and despair over society's choices and economic inequalities. There are poems, too, of intensely personal questioning and guilt, poems that examine the value of success, and poems that explore the meaning of age in ways appropriate to a man nearing 60. The poems have a new look as well, which perhaps reflects the influence of Dickinson and Crane (whose poetry Howells was reading in manuscript at the time); short, epigrammatic bursts of emotion couched in natural diction replace the lyrics of Heine or the hexameters of Longfellow. It is almost as though the novelist who saw the big picture has yielded to the poet who glimpses but fragments. Instead of narratives, there are dreams, visions, and impressions.

Leading off the collection is "November" (LOA, 2: 361), subtitled "Impression." In a single 11-line sentence, the poet likens the crimson berries in an autumnal garden to the drops his heart bleeds when he recalls how the beauty and ruin of fall once made him glad, while he now finds it "now so intolerably sad." What saves this from becoming just another lament about aging is that the gladness came not just in his own childhood but in "my children's childhood," that is, in maturity as well. It is not the loss of childhood alone that has tinted autumn with sadness, but somehow also the loss of his children's childhood, and, indeed, his children themselves. Other poems in the volume allude to Winnie's death and conclude that "nothing can be what it used to be / . . . in the deathless days before she died" ("Change").

The major thrust of the volume is not mourning, but a deep and abiding sense of doubt. Howells questions the meaning of human suffering and finds he can no longer rely for answers on the faith that had guided his life for 60 years. In the ironically titled "Hope," he evokes the traditional image of heaven only to undercut it; his bold affirmation that "I shall see arise / Another world" at his journey's end gives way to what could stand as a refrain for the whole book: "Perhaps – perhaps – perhaps!"

A strong strain of self-rebuke runs through many of the poems, as Howells takes the measure of his own egotism and hypocrisy. The most stunning of these is "Calvary":

> If He could doubt on His triumphant cross,
> How much more I, in the defeat and loss
> Of seeing all my selfish dreams fulfilled,
> Of having lived the very life I willed,
> Of being all that I desired to be?
> My God, my God! Why hast thou forsaken me?

Howells had indeed realized all the aspirations of his youthful ego, but the poem implies that success has left him empty and abandoned. Aware of his tendency to be too hard on himself, he pleads in the poem "Conscience": "Judge me not as I judge myself, O Lord! / Show me some mercy, or I may not live."

As critical as he is of himself, Howells also uses these poems to criticize the social injustices everywhere around him. A cluster of poems at the heart of the book concerns class disparities and resonates with Howells's political beliefs. The two-part poem "Society" first presents a vision of the wealthy at play in a glorious field of flowers; upon closer inspection, however, the poet notices that the revelers tread "now upon an old man's head / And now upon a baby's gasping face, / Or mother's bosom." Although the gruesome dance continues, the occasional arm is lifted from the masses, "As if to strike in madness, or implore / For mercy." Another "Vision" contrasts the wide and airy banquet hall of the slumlord with the "squalid home" of his tenant: "The one bare chamber, where his work-worn wife / Above the stove and wash-tub passed her life, / Next the sty where they slept with all their brood."

The sordid realities of poverty found ample place in Howells's poems. He unflinchingly presents images of the working poor in such poems as "The King Dines." On a bench in Boston Common sit two ordinary laborers, "The woman's mouth purple with cold and pain," in the November rain. While she stares unseeing at the passersby, her partner dines:

> The man feeding out of the newspaper
> Wrapped round the broken victuals brought with her,
> And gnawing at a bent bone like a dog,
> Following its curve hungrily with his teeth,
> And his head twisted sidewise . . .

A related impression, "Labor and Capital," contrasts the plump, well-shod horses that pull the company's wagon with the "hunched" figure of the driver: "All hugged together / Against the pitiless weather, / In an old cardigan jacket and a cap / Of mangy fur. . . ." This toadlike creature, stiff with cold and blinking away frozen tears, is "The Company's man."

Sometimes the contrast between rich and poor is conducted more subtly. "Material of a Story" is related in something akin to Howells the novelist's ironic vein. In 54 lines of iambic pentameter, Howells presents a snippet of dialogue between a writer and his clergyman friend as they meet on a railway platform. The clergyman tells the story of a parishioner, an ex-con who has served time for a "heinous crime": "He said he had not done / The thing. They all say that. You cannot tell. / He might not have been guilty of it." It seems the man cannot stay in one place for more than a week because stasis reminds him too keenly of his imprisonment. The two friends both judge the affair "tragical," especially now that the man is dead. The clergyman finishes the story:

> "At the end
> It came out that his mother was alive –
> An outcast – and she asked our leave to attend
> The ceremony, and then asked us to give
> The silver coffin plate, carved with his name,
> And the flowers, to her." "That was touching. She
> Had some good left her in her infamy."
> "Why, I don't know! I think she sold the things,
> Together with a neck-pin and some rings
> That he had left, and drank. . . . But as to blame . . .
> Good-morning to you!" and my friend stepped down
> At the street crossing. I went on up town.

Serene in their ability to judge the poor "wretch," the complacent characters lump him and his mother together with all the other poor as "them." Howells does not exempt himself from the critique, as he proceeds "up town" to a better life. The stark and natural dialogue, with its broken lines and irregular rhyme scheme, reveals a poet comfortable with his own idiom, one who no longer needed to imitate the heroic couplets of his youthful idols.

In these poems, Howells also probed the basis of his faith in the context of some of the major intellectual developments of the last quarter of the century. In "Heredity," he ponders the ethical dilemma posed by Darwinism, but is finally unconvinced by the moral exculpation offered by the notion of genetic inheritance. The closest he gets to an affirmation of faith comes in "Statistics," a poem informed by the new science of sociology:

> So many men, on such a date of May,
> Despaired and took their hopeless lives away
> In such an area, year after year;
> In such another place, it would appear
> The assassinations averaged so and so,
> Through August after August, scarce below
> A given range . . .

Other crimes and tragedies have their own stoic tallies, and the "dark prophet" of science extrapolates from these figures to predict society's future. The numbers would seem to suggest that "We but return / Upon our steps, although they seem so free. / The thing that has been is that which shall be." The poet, however, sees some progress for the human race. The path is not circular, but spiral. It rises somehow beneath our feet. "Your facts are facts," he concludes, "yet somewhere there is God." As affirmations go, this is pale indeed: God is only "somewhere," location unknown.

The final poem in *Stops of Various Quills* gives us a benchmark for Howells's spiritual state as the century came to a close. In "What shall it profit?" he asks whether it is worthwhile to give up faith.

> If I lay waste and wither up with doubt
> The blessed fields of heaven where once my faith
> Possessed itself serenely safe from death;
> If I deny the things past finding out;
> Or if I orphan my own soul of One
> That seemed a Father, and make void the place
> Within me where He dwelt in power and grace,
> What do I gain by that I have undone?

No longer can he "serenely" trust the principles that had shaped his earlier life. Knowing that there are certain things "past finding out," he settles instead into agnosticism. It took ample courage just to doubt the beliefs that had gotten him this far in life. Nonetheless, Howells is not ready for atheism or open rebellion against faith. He would leave it for the younger generation of Crane and Ambrose **Bierce** to trumpet religious denial in their works.

Howells's new poetry of doubt struck a chord with many of his contemporaries. William James wrote to him after reading some of the poems in *Harper's*: "[I] don't know when I have had a greater pleasure – if pleasure is the word for so solid a sense of gratitude." Among the several editors who asked, Edmund Clarence **Stedman** received permission to reprint some of the poems in an anthology of American verse. Stedman considered the poems Howells's "most original" and went on to say, "Those strains are *de profundis*, and as I read them, . . . they sound in truth like a cry to the shore." Both Stedman and James sensed that Howells was voicing the fears of a generation that was hovering on the brink of a new century and uncertain where the years would lead. Howells wrote Stedman that he considered these the poems in which "I came fullest to my poetic consciousness." The form was tight, the voice was true, and the emotional intensity was earned rather than borrowed. As William James put it, "They are well forged – no fumbling and no spatter."

After venting his sorrow and doubt in the torrent of poems written during what he called the "dark time," Howells ebbed away from poetry for a while. Although he published verses sporadically for the next two decades, the flood had passed. Yet his pen was busier than ever. He wrote several regular columns for various magazines, sometimes simultaneously: he produced "Life and Letters" for *Harper's Weekly* (1895–98), "American Letter" for *Literature* (1898), "Diversions of the Higher Journalist" for *Harper's Weekly* (1903), and, most important, "The Editor's Easy Chair" for *Harper's Monthly* (1900–20). These columns allowed him to ruminate on the state of the world of letters and the world at large. In addition to reviewing hundreds of books, he discussed such things as international copyright laws, American imperialism, the death penalty, and the war in Europe.

It is his criticism of this period that most interests the literary scholar today. Howells was always alert to new voices in literature and he gave encouragement to a wide range of authors of succeeding generations. He heralded the fiction of Frank Norris, Crane, Harold Frederic, Hamlin **Garland**, Edith **Wharton**, and Charles Chesnutt; he promoted the plays of Ibsen, Sir Arthur Wing Pinero, George Bernard Shaw, and Henry Arthur Jones; and he drew attention to the poetry of Crane,

Edwin **Markham**, Paul Lawrence **Dunbar**, Edgar Lee Masters, Edwin Arlington **Robinson**, Amy Lowell, and Robert Frost.

When Howells found himself writing obituaries of the many friends he had outlived, his thoughts gravitated to the models of his youth and the authors of his own era. *My Literary Passions* (1895) and *Literary Friends and Acquaintance* (1900) offer reminiscences and appreciations, while *My Mark Twain* (1910) assesses the art and life of one of his closest friends. His final critical essay, left unfinished at his death, was a last look at the career of his other comrade, Henry James. Howells's output of fiction also continued almost unabated throughout the first two decades of the twentieth century. Although he still produced nearly one volume of fiction per year, only three novels approach the level of his best work. *The Landlord at Lion's Head* (1897), *The Son of Royal Langbrith* (1904), and *The Leatherwood God* (1916) all show that Howells's command of his craft was undiminished, even though their tone is darker and more cynical than his better-known novels of the 1880s. He also returned to the travel writing that had made his literary reputation in the 1860s. Howells traveled with his daughter Mildred almost constantly after his wife Elinor's death in 1910, and he used his sojourns as a source for half a dozen volumes.

Even amid all this activity in prose, the poet did not disappear. The final volume in which Howells collected his poems was *The Daughter of the Storage* (1916), a miscellany of fiction and poetry. Only five of the 19 pieces are verse, but those show Howells in yet another poetic phase. The novelist and the poet seem to have joined forces, and the resulting poems display a light touch with humor and dialogue and a clear hand at sketching character and voice. Unlike the epigrammatic verses of the 1873 volume, these works are all long poems with capacious pentameter or hexameter lines. In the book, there are three narratives, one monologue, and one dialogue; the poems are usually written in unobtrusive couplets, but some are unrhymed. In addition, all are written in a simple conversational style that will remind modern readers of Robert Frost. In fact, Frost would later pay tribute to Howells's "beautiful blank verse" and his ability to capture the natural tones of speech. "No one," he remarked to Hamlin Garland, "ever had a more observing ear or clearer imagination for the tones of those voices. No one ever brought them more freshly to book."

The voice of the narrator carries both the humor and the pathos of "Breakfast is My Best Meal," a splendid sketch of a simple country man uncomfortable in his hard-earned wealth. He compares the continental breakfast of the spa at Carlsbad, where he has come for his health, with the hearty breakfasts formerly cooked for him by his mother, his wife, and his daughter. The biscuits, the sugar-cured hams, the corn cakes, the steaks, the sausages – all represent the love and care that were lavished upon him by the women in his life. By contrast, the "little mis'able cup / Of this here weak-kneed coffee" only points up how bereft he is in his old age, when he has outlived all but his wealth and his grandchildren.

Two other poems narrate stories that hark back to the subject matter of Howells's earliest verses. "Captain Dunleavy's Last Trip" tells of an old riverboat captain who leaves the river after a mental lapse nearly causes him to crash the ship. "The Face at the Window" relates the tragic story of a seafaring family: when the father's two sons die while at sea with him, his love for the wife and daughters that he left behind enables his spirit to appear at their window weeks before he actually returns home. Although the territory may be familiar, the treatment is quite different. Both stories are framed narratives that include commentary on the tale-telling itself. At the end of his story of Captain Dunleavy, the tale-teller is asked by an obtuse dowager, "And what was it, / Captain, that kept him from going back and being a pilot?" He responds, "*I don't hardly believe that I could explain it exactly.*" The Captain cannot do more than he has done by telling the story itself; it must stand on its own, without explication. Narration becomes even more explicitly the subject of "The Face at the Window." Here, a group of city swells gathers at the Christmas fireside of a country estate, and one young man entreats the host for a story "in proper keeping / With the locality and hour and mood. / . . . Nothing remote, / But something with the actual Yankee note / Of here and now in it!" In spite of interruptions from the guests, the host narrates a suitable local color story, and then tries to avoid comment upon it. But the young people persist in appraising the story's technique and the narrator's invention. "How perfectly New England!" one exclaims, "How could you think of anything so true?" The host offers a perfectly Howellsian response: "Only the fact could make my story true."

Similarly, "Black Cross Farm" revisits subjects familiar to Howells's early poetry by treating the mournful silence of an abandoned house. But this house contains a mystery – a black cross nailed across the hay mow of the barn. The city narrator and his companion try to solve the riddle, but finally decide that it is better to leave it as an enigma. Edwin Cady points out that the poem resembles works by Frost and Robinson in its sense of alienation and in its bewilderment at the loss of New England's past. According to Cady, the acceptance of indeterminacy and the agnosticism of "Black Cross Farm" qualify Howells for a "place in the modern tradition of poetry."

Throughout the poems of this collection, the realist's sensibility prevails in Howells's eye for detail and his treatment of character and incident. One contemporary reviewer referred to the poems as "stories of every-day life," a catchphrase Howells himself had used time and again in his pleas for realistic fiction. Moreover, the form of the poetry does not get in the way, as it had in his earlier work. The lines read as easily and as naturally as Howells's finest prose, with unobtrusive rhymes providing a soft pulse in the background. In these simple, unadorned verses Howells almost achieved his ideal of literature: "the page of prose, always tremulous with inner music, breaks now and again into open rhyme."

Too often, Howells has been dismissed as a simple-minded optimist out of touch with the harsher aspects of American culture. One look at his poetry should convince any serious reader to revise this image of him. At no time did he write simple, frothy verses. Even his earliest poems contain a layer (perhaps too thick) of dark irony. But any assessment of Howells's achievement as a poet must be based on the poems he wrote after 1886, not the imitative verse of his adolescence.

Moreover, we must take into account the various phases of his work as a poet. The youthful romantic ironist used poetry as his way out of Ohio and into the glamorous world of literature. The businessman who marketed his shopworn verses in 1873 and again in 1886 deployed poetry as little more than a source of revenue. The agonized doubter of the 1890s wrote poetry to express his deepest fears and his most profound sorrows. The novelist who turned to narrative poetry in old age finally integrated his storyteller's art with his poetic soul. None of these several poets is finally a great poet (although there certainly are some great poems), and Howells's rank as a poet will never equal his rank as a novelist. But while he is by no means first-rate, he is an important and interesting minor figure in the story of American poetry. His contemporaries were right to have remembered William Dean Howells as a poet.

JULIE BATES DOCK

Selected Works

Poems of Two Friends, Columbus, Ohio: Follett, Foster, 1860
No Love Lost: A Romance of Travel, New York: Putnam, 1869
Poems, Boston: James R. Osgood, 1873
Poems, enl. ed., Boston: Ticknor, 1886
Stops of Various Quills, New York: Harper and Brothers, 1895
The Daughter of the Storage and Other Things in Prose and Verse, New York: Harper and Brothers, 1916
The Complete Plays of William Dean Howells, edited by Walter J. Meserve, New York: New York University Press, 1960
Life in Letters of William Dean Howells, edited by Mildred Howells, 2 vols., New York: Russell and Russell, 1968
Selected Letters of W. D. Howells, general editors George Arms, Richard H. Ballinger, and Christoph K. Lohmann, 6 vols., Boston: Twayne, 1979–83

Further Reading

Brenni, Vito J., *William Dean Howells: A Bibliography*, Metuchen, New Jersey: Scarecrow, 1973
Cady, Edwin H., *The Road to Realism: The Early Years of William Dean Howells, 1837–1885*, and *The Realist at War: The Mature Years of William Dean Howells, 1885–1920*, Syracuse, New York: Syracuse University Press, 1956–58
Crowley, John W., *The Black Heart's Truth: The Early Career of W. D. Howells*, Chapel Hill: University of North Carolina Press, 1985
The Mask of Fiction: Essays on W. D. Howells, Amherst: University of Massachusetts Press, 1989
Firkins, Oscar, *William Dean Howells: A Study*, Cambridge, Massachusetts: Harvard University Press, 1924
Gibson, William M., and George Arms, *A Bibliography of William Dean Howells*, New York: New York Public Library, 1948
Lynn, Kenneth S., *William Dean Howells: An American Life*, New York: Harcourt Brace Jovanovich, 1970
Merrill, Ginette de B., and George Arms, eds., *If Not Literature: Letters of Elinor Mead Howells*, Columbus: Ohio State University Press, 1988

William Reed Huntington

(1838–1909)

Huntington was born on September 20, 1838, the son of physician Elisha Huntington and Hannah Hinckley Huntington, in Lowell, Massachusetts. He received his degree from Harvard, where he was class poet in 1859. He then studied for the ministry, which was his lifelong profession. He wrote poetry primarily for his own enjoyment, although his poems were occasionally published in magazines. The larger portion of Huntington's publications stemmed from his ministry. He was rector of All Saints Church in Worcester, Massachusetts, from 1862 to 1883. He then assumed the rectorship of Grace Church in New York City, where he remained a prominent member of the city's religious and cultural life. Throughout this time, he wrote both prose and poetry. He revised the Book of Common Prayer and published several sermons, most notably *The Eagle and the Stars* and *Woman's Service of Christ*. His most productive prose period occurred in the 1890s, with such ecclesiastical works as *The Causes of the Soul*, *The Spiritual House*, and *A National Church*. Late in life, he published two volumes of memoirs.

Charles Lewis Slattery, a friend and colleague, called Huntington "one of the most versatile men of his time." Slattery remembers him as a lively wit, a skillful and brilliant debater, and an able preacher, whose sermons contained little of the fire and brimstone of traditional preaching. In private conversation, freed from the constraints of his very public profession, Huntington weighed his words less scrupulously and allowed his natural humor to surface. Huntington became a mentor for both younger preachers like Slattery and parishioners, while at the same time constantly writing polemical works, attending church conventions, and writing verse.

Upon his death in 1909, Huntington was one of the most conspicuous men in New York. Slattery offers testimonials to his kind, self-effacing nature: "To his thoroughness was added another quality which is a gift from God: he did the ordinary things of life in a new way, so that one felt that distinction had been conferred upon the commonplace, and all life was illumined." A sampling of Huntington's sermons places him staunchly among conservatives. With few exceptions, his opinions on social questions generally reflect the established order. For instance, he firmly believed that the government had the right to limit religious freedom to established Christian churches only. He held a low opinion of Mormons and took several opportunities to express his contempt for Islam, because both religions permitted polygamy. And although he was a pioneer of sorts in re-establishing women as deaconesses of the Episcopal church, he made it clear that in his opinion this "equality" in no way changed the "primal order," in which men ranked first unequivocally.

The Eagle and the Stars argues a conservative view against the separation of church and state. It asserts that since the United States was founded primarily by Christians, it could, and should, enact legislation to make both polygamy and divorce illegal. In this sermon, Huntington decries the secularization of the state, which permits the existence of nontraditional family structures: according to Huntington, the country instead needs "a definite scheme of morals, to the rejection of all other schemes plainly in conflict with the selected one." Although his case is carefully built, it amounts to an argument based upon social tradition: since the nation was founded by monogamous Puritans, it has the right to choose Christianity as the national religion. While conceding that Islamic nations survived and flourished under circumstances of polygamy, Huntington also insists that Islam is a threat to Christianity: the Mohammedan structure "developed, in its early days, sufficient racial strength to become a menace to Europe and well nigh to compass the overthrow of Christendom."

Even though *Woman's Service of Christ* (1887) appears supportive of women's rights, in it Huntington refuses to align himself with the women's movement. Rather, he claims that Christ "elevated, purified [and] ennobled" woman's position by "reassert[ing] the original equality of the sexes without disturbing their order." Although a woman was the first witness to Christ's resurrection, Huntington argues, no women were included in the original apostolate. Deliberating on "how far we may, as a Reformed church, safely go in this direction of giving women work," Huntington states that deaconess is the highest position that should be allowed to women, because such a position permits expressions of gratitude to God through good works without upsetting the natural order established at the Creation.

These sermons and other didactic writings form the bulk of Huntington's published work, except for the collection *Sonnets and a Dream*. His verse emerged sporadically in such magazines as *Century*, *Harper's*, *The Outlook*, and *The Spectator*, until the collection appeared in 1899, with a second edition in 1903 and a third shortly thereafter. The most recent edition reprints the original collection as part of the Romantic Tradition in Literature series, with Harold Bloom as the advising editor (1972). Most of Huntington's poetry takes the form of Italian sonnets, with notable exceptions like "The Child's Supremacy: A Dream."

Sonnets and a Dream organizes the 27 sonnets into thematic sequences: "Sonnets of Earth and Sky," "Sonnets of Country," "Sonnets of Doubt and Faith," and "Sonnets of Friendship." Huntington thus follows in the footsteps of Sir Philip Sidney and Edmund Spenser, although his sequences are much shorter, ranging from only two to 11 poems per sequence. Not surprisingly, all four sequences reflect religious themes. Each identifies a common observation of the world – from nature, a social situation, an experience of the poet's own life, or a biblical event – in the first eight lines, and the final six proposes a religious meditation or an act of faith as commentary.

The sonnets of "Earth and Sky" follow the Romantic tradition and take their impetus from the world of nature. "Tellus," the first, is one of Huntington's most frequently anthologized poems. Its title is derived from the Latin noun meaning "earth" or "soil," and references ancient divinities of Earth (Tellus Mater, Telluno). Since his focal point is earth's position among the planets of our solar system, Huntington also employs the play on "tell us," which evokes questions of universal design and the Maker's reasoning in placing humanity upon this instead of some other planet. All of the imagery depicts earth as a lifelong prison: "In what sad land among the scattered stars / Wrought she the ill which now for ever scars / By bitter consequence each victory won?" The turn addresses the "dearest friend," Christ, who was also imprisoned here until his death and resurrection. If Christ could confine himself to the shackles of earthly existence, the poem suggests, humanity ought to endure the present life by meditating on the ultimate promise of heaven. The sacrificed Christ's "tranquil presence shames our discontent."

"The Cold Meteorite" (LOA, 2: 379) also invokes the concept of sacrifice in Christ's name. In this poem, a comet achieves its most graceful and beautiful existence in the act of death. The speaker describes the comet's course as a "short-lived splendor" and a "journey ill-begun" and misinterprets its foreshortened life as "dishonored, cold, undone." When the comet speaks for itself in the sestet, however, it clarifies this misapprehension. The warmth of its transcendence into a "burning sacrifice" more than offsets the "frigid dignity" of a longer but less meaningful life:

> "... far better 't is to die
> "The death that flashes gladness, than alone,
> "In frigid dignity, to live on high;
> "Better in burning sacrifice be thrown
> "Against the world to perish, than the sky
> "To circle endlessly a barren stone."

Any sacrifice demanded by religious faith is inconsequential compared to that of the comet, which willingly forfeits life to become a cold meteorite at God's command.

"Love's Orbit" compares the natural motion of the earth with the monotonous round of day-to-day existence. Huntington contends here that the continuous flow of seasons, responsibilities, and social obligations may blind humanity to its goal: heaven. Thus, the very regularity of our secular lives creates a spiritual lethargy hazardous to the growth and health of the soul. According to the poet, we must take our cue from the behavior of the earth, which "reseek[s] the prizes won, / Afresh begin[s] the task so oft begun / Joyous she hears the starter's trumpet sound." Within the grind of daily existence, one can yet profess faith through renewal and rededication to God, and thus "in very sameness find delight."

In the final sonnet of this series, Huntington reasserts the classic "argument from design" – from the systematic order visible in the universe – to prove the presence of a deity. His affirmation of God's existence and control over the complex pattern of the universe renews his faith.

> ... Henceforth I cleave
> More firmly to the Credo; and my vow
> With readier footstep to thine altar bring,
> As one who counts it freedom to believe.

The order of the sonnets in this sequence moves toward ever larger conceptions: humanity's place on earth; earth's position in the solar system (the streaking meteorite, the planetary orbits); and finally, the design of the universe itself.

The sequences on "Doubt and Faith" and "Friendship" lack such careful organization; they are loosely grouped and without a central principle. In the former, the poet either supplies interpretations of biblical readings, using each sonnet's turn as an opportunity for commentary, or relates a personal experience that recalls an element of faith or Christian duty to him. The homey, informal "Visiting God," for example, reports the experience of testing a child's catechism. In this poem, the young girl's misstatement of "visit" for the term "call on" incites the poet to reassess his own quality of prayer, which he now sees as an opportunity to "visit" with God without fear. In "Lowlands" (LOA, 2: 379), the last poem of the "Doubt and Faith" sequence, Huntington emphasizes the contrast between mountain and lowland in comparing the spiritual to the secular life. Meditation upon the spiritual may create "discordance in the world below," yet be essential to spiritual growth. Most often, however, humanity moves in the "valley" and must content itself with mere glimpses of God's "converse sweet."

The "Sonnets of Friendship" appear to have been written later in the poet's life, because several refer to the deaths of friends or loved ones and become occasions for revitalizing his faith in the prospect of eternal life. In the paired sonnets "From Green Mountain" (LOA, 2: 380), the first describes a morning view from a height, as the speaker, awed by the play of light and shadow on the sea, contrasts his vantage point with that of the sailors on the shore below. The speaker revels in being "happier placed," but his advantage is short-lived: in the second sonnet, the afternoon sun burns off the mist, and "those below see clear, as we had done." The light of God's grace shines equally upon all "enfranchised spirits" and permits all to envision "both sides of things," the earthly and the divine, while "Spirits in shadow see but one."

Although Huntington's viewpoint is conservative and his themes show little variation, he works well within the stringent, formal specifications of the sonnet and demonstrates a mastery of sequence in "Sonnets of Earth and Sky." His poetry emulates the Romantics who observe the natural world as a method of finding faith, but he departs from William Wordsworth and John Keats in one fundamental way. Where they believed that nature was the ultimate expression of God, Huntington saw it as a separate wonder through which the Creator inspired awe and commanded obedience.

JANICE MCINTIRE-STRASBURG

Selected Works

Sonnets and a Dream, edited by Harold Bloom, New York: Arno Press, 1972

Further Reading

Slattery, Charles Lewis, *Certain American Faces*, New York: Dutton, 1918

Helen Hunt Jackson

(1830–1885)

In Jackson's poetry, the most powerful moments are allegorical. That is, they depend upon a philosophical understanding of human experience in which one story, whose particulars are homely, human, and transient, stands in for a second story. For Jackson, this second story's claims aspire to the claims of religion and give access to what is eternal, immutable, and thus not at risk. Consider, for instance, Jackson's poem "Danger":

> With what a childish and short-sighted sense
> Fear seeks for safety; reckons up the days
> Of danger and escape, the hours and ways
> Of death; it breathless flies the pestilence;
> It walls itself in towers of defense;
> By land, by sea, against the storm it lays
> Down barriers; then, comforted, it says:
> "This spot, this hour is safe." Oh, vain pretence!
> Man born of man knows nothing when he goes;
> The winds blow where they list, and will disclose
> To no man which brings safety, which brings risk.
> The mighty are brought low by many a thing
> Too small to name. Beneath the daisy's disk
> Lies hid the pebble for the fatal sling.

This poem conveys the essence of Jackson's formal talent (which was considerable), epitomizes the direction in which her imagination typically went (which was allegorical), and further demonstrates the nature of her mind (which was orderly, conservative, and Puritan-Victorian in the broadest sense).

Let us explore each of these points in turn. First, this sonnet is a superb example of Jackson's control of language and form. Among nineteenth-century sonnets it could hardly be bettered for sheer musicality. Although much more could be said, let me point merely to the intricacy with which the poet has interwoven the short *i* and *e* sounds with the long *a* and *i* sounds and cross-laced them with the recurrent *s*. Unlike the majority of minor poets of her time, Jackson also ingeniously varies the length of each thought so that final emphasis falls at various places in the line. Her use of enjambment lends considerable speed to the progress of the octave, a sense of speed only slightly retarded by the long *o*'s in the sestet. After a dazzling series of tricks with turns in the rhyme scheme – *abbaabbaccdede* – the poem ends neatly, as though a gymnast, having entertained us with a series of adept maneuvers, completes the exercise with a forward somersault and ends up balanced firmly on her feet and smiling. Indeed, Jackson's skill is often on display in her final lines. Her powerful conclusions undoubtedly influenced succeeding generations of poets – from Louise Imogen **Guiney**, Lizette Woodworth **Reese**, and Edith Thomas to Louise Bogan and Edna St. Vincent Millay. Such skill inspired Ralph Waldo **Emerson** to call her the best among contemporary woman poets. Thomas Wentworth Higginson, for his part, praised her as "the most brilliant, impetuous, and thoroughly individual woman of her time."

From both Emerson and Higginson, Jackson had learned a great deal. Higginson taught her to use common words, to pay attention to grammar, to avoid at all costs a sense of straining after effects and flowery diction, and to revise relentlessly. From Emerson, she drew her understanding of the usefulness of allegory, as one can readily see by focusing briefly on his poem "Days" (LOA, 1: 324) for purposes of comparison:

> Daughters of Time, the hypocritic Days,
> Muffled and dumb like barefoot dervishes,
> And marching single in an endless file,
> Bring diadems and fagots in their hands.
> To each they offer gifts after his will,
> Bread, kingdoms, stars, and sky that holds them all.
> I, in my pleachéd garden, watched the pomp,
> Forgot my morning wishes, hastily
> Took a few herbs and apples, and the Day
> Turned and departed silent. I, too late,
> Under her solemn fillet saw the scorn.

Like "Days," Jackson's "Danger" presents a philosophical statement about the nature of human existence by means of a story that represents another story. Like Emerson, Jackson makes the point that the choices we think we are making are frequently spurious. We scuttle about but find out too late that we failed to live as we should. Of the two poets, however, Jackson's view is the more conservative. Emerson suggests that we might make better choices if we took the time to live more fully and completely. By contrast, Jackson virtually paraphrases Jonathan Edwards's Puritan sermon "Sinners in the Hands of an Angry God," in which he catalogs the strategies with which human beings delude themselves that they are protected: "This spot, this hour is safe." Both Jackson and Edwards point to the foolishness of such efforts, although Jackson ends her poem with a reference to David and Goliath, which in turn implies that one effect of not knowing the consequences of our actions might be the unexpected triumph of the small over the great.

Although this idea was not close to Edwards's heart, it *was* dear to Jackson, who took considerable trouble to help those (including Emily **Dickinson**) whose position in the world was not what she felt it should or could be. Thus, when I say that she was "Puritan-Victorian in the broadest sense," I do not mean that she favored imperialism, subscribed to a dogmatic Christianity, was fastidious, or advocated repression. She was Victorian in that she exhibited strong beliefs in political reform and social justice, some of the characteristics that Walter Houghton has argued are particularly associated with the Victorians. She was Puritan-Victorian because she believed in solid moral values, hard work, and the subjugation of human life to a transcendental order. Her politics were conservative in the American sense. That is, she wished to carry forward what she felt were America's basic democratic principles. She therefore understood the value of freedom for blacks (see her poem "Freedom") and demanded justice for Native Americans (see *A Century of Dishonor* and *Ramona*). As Susan Coultrap-McQuin has shown recently in her study of Jackson's publishing career, Jackson also believed strongly in individualism and a free market.

Nevertheless, Jackson's belief in individualism and self-development did not coincide with feminism. She opposed the movement for women's rights. In 1873, she called the movement "an evil fashion of speech which says it is narrowing and [a] narrow life that a woman leads who cares only for her husband and children; that a higher, more imperative thing is that she herself be developed to her utmost." After the death of her first husband in 1863, Jackson did lead a very independent life herself, but she continued to believe that a wife's first and holiest responsibility was to her family. Her views about abolition, Native Americans, the importance of privacy, individualism, morality, and woman's place were also conventional in the sense that they were widely shared by those like her: cosmopolitan and professionally successful white women writers, most of whom were born in New England and, like Jackson, inherited a strong sense of Puritan values.

Although for a woman poet Jackson's values were not unusual, her literary talent and particularly her allegorical bent were. In general, women poets did not follow the lead of William Cullen **Bryant** and Emerson and move toward allegory but preferred lyric symbolism or less-ambitious forms of narrative verse. One might make an argument that Jackson's skill and preference for allegory were the result of her individual experiences, which interacted with social and cultural factors to produce Jackson's peculiar poetic strengths. To begin with, Helen Maria Fiske was born on October 15, 1830, into a comparatively privileged family. Her father was a classics professor at Amherst College. Helen was willful, hated discipline, and cast off her parents' gloomy Calvinism; nevertheless, she absorbed vital influences from her early life and family. Her father's interest in moral philosophy and her mother's predilection for vivid storytelling both may have given her a tendency to think in allegorical terms from an early age. The consequences of her youthful rebelliousness might also be seen in her later independence and political activism, but her values would always reflect her conservative New England upbringing.

More important, the numerous losses she suffered may have influenced her turn toward allegory. Helen's mother died in 1844; her father died three years later. This in itself was not as unusual then as it would be today, and Helen subsequently came to terms with her grief and married Lieutenant Edward Bissel Hunt – a mathematical physicist – in 1852. She lived happily as a wife and mother for 11 years. But her early bereavements were soon followed by others. Her first child, Murray, died of a brain tumor at the age of one, which left the poet utterly devastated for a time. Then her husband was killed in a freak accident in 1863. If this were not enough, her only surviving son, Rennie, who had become his mother's dearest compensation, died of diphtheria a year and a half later. "And I alone am left, who avail nothing," she wrote to a friend. No wonder her mind filled with thoughts of "danger" and the instability of human life. Later, she would write powerfully about loss and grief in the poem "The Prince Is Dead."

Helen Hunt's career as a poet began in the aftermath of these losses. Although she was now a widow, she was financially independent and could turn her attention to literature. Instrumental in her success were the social connections she had made while she was still married to Lieutenant Hunt. She knew the famous New York hostess (and poet) Anne Lynch Botta, at whose parties more than one career was launched. (Jackson later wrote a sonnet "To A. C. L. B.," which paid tribute to

Botta's hospitality.) In addition to many women of interest, Emerson, Higginson, and Parke Godwin all attended these entertainments; it was to Godwin of the New York *Evening Post* that Helen Hunt sent her first poem. She also apprenticed herself to Higginson, who helped her learn to write poetry that would please those who were in charge of the world of publishing.

Until 1879, when she took up the cause of the American Indians, however, Helen preferred to publish her work under some form of pseudonym or acronym rather than using her full name. *Verses* appeared in 1870 as the work of "H. H." She also deployed the pseudonyms Marah, Rip Van Winkle, and Saxe Holm – the latter adopted for short stories. During the 1870s, she encouraged her old friend Emily Dickinson and, in 1878, actually printed one poem by the Amherst recluse in *A Masque of Poets*, where the names of the authors were kept secret. In addition to short stories, she published one novel, *Mercy Philbrick's Choice*, in 1876, and another, *Hetty's Strange History*, in 1877, both anonymously.

During this time, the narrative impulse was taking hold even in her poetry. In 1874, she brought out as a separate work a long narrative poem that told of two Thai women mentioned in the memoirs of the governess to the Siamese court, Anna Leonowyns (this work later became the basis for *The King and I*). Jackson's poem, *The Story of Boon*, spun a tragic tale full of adulterous longings, betrayal, torture, and wifely faith. In addition, she composed a delightful "Ballad of the Gold Country," which juxtaposed the mad search for gold with the much wiser planting of vineyards in the far west. Again, in Jackson's works, material desires prove unstable, while faith puts down deep roots.

Although her career began in New England and would always reflect its values, Jackson is mainly remembered as a western writer. She journeyed to Colorado to recover from a case of septic sore throat in 1873. There, she met her second husband – a banker, William Sharpless Jackson, who had made a fortune in railroads. They married in 1875 and settled in Colorado. Jackson paid tribute to the landscape she loved in her poem "Cheyenne Mountain" (LOA, 2: 226), but she and her husband did not confine themselves to Colorado Springs. They traveled throughout the southwest. In 1879, Jackson became interested in the plight of the Ponca Indians and published a thoroughly researched account of government treaty violations with various tribes, *A Century of Dishonor* (1881). Her 1884 novel of romance and injustice, *Ramona*, became a bestseller and has given her lasting fame; it has since been made into several movies and is still widely available in print. For her works in support of Indian causes, Jackson was finally willing to use her full name. After she died of cancer on August 12, 1885, her writing continued to appear and find readers. In addition to reprints of *Ramona*, *Sonnets and Lyrics* came out in 1886 and her collected *Poems* arrived in 1891. To Higginson, Dickinson praised Jackson's poetry as "stronger than any written by women since Mrs. Browning – with the exception of Mrs. Lewes [George Eliot]."

Some of Jackson's poetry is not allegorical but instead develops a single image (usually drawn from nature) to suggest latent emotional content. Thus, "Poppies on the Wheat" (LOA, 2: 223) – a poem imitated by Jackson's protégée Edith Thomas – begins with these lines:

Along Ancona's hills the shimmering heat,
A tropic tide of air with ebb and flow
Bathes all the fields of wheat until they glow
Like flashing seas of green, which toss and beat
Around the vines. The poppies lithe and fleet
Seem running, fiery torchmen, to and fro
To mark the shore.

Like "Danger" this sonnet performs tricks with conventional sonnet rhyme schemes. Here, Jackson limits herself to three rhymes instead of the Shakespearean seven, *abbaabbaccacaa*, and achieves something of a tour de force. (One can see why she felt that "anything requiring as much labor to finish as a carefully constructed sonnet" should be valued more highly than a more discursive poem.)

The red and green color imagery in "Poppies on the Wheat" looks forward to late–nineteenth-century symbolist and naturalist experiments with color. One can also see color imagery of this sort in "Her Eyes," where the eyes of a friend are compared to water:

When, in deep nook
Of some green field, the water of a brook
Makes lingering, whirling eddy in its way
Round soft drowned leaves; and in a flash of sun
They turn to gold, until the ripples run
Now brown, now yellow, changing as by some
Swift spell.

The heaping up of images of gold in "September" – "O golden month!" (see also another poem entitled "September" [LOA, 2: 225]) – and again at the beginning of "A Ballad of the Gold Country" might be compared to color experiments undertaken by Stephen **Crane** and Frank Norris, among prose writers, or by the imagist poets Amy Lowell and H.D. (Hilda Doolittle).

Unlike these modernist works, however, poems that nineteenth-century readers particularly admired were more often conventionally allegorical. Higginson thought "Acquainted with Grief" one of Jackson's best works, and there is something haunting about this picture of the personified Grief as a loyal friend who will always stick by. It ends:

She to the gazing world must bear
  Our crowns of triumph, if we bid;
Loyal and mute, our colors wear,
  Sign of her own forever hid.

Smile to our smile, song to our song,
  With songs and smiles our roses fling,
Till men turn round in every throng,
  To note such joyous pleasuring.

And ask, next morn, with eyes that lend
  A fervor to the words they say,
"What is her name, that radiant friend
  Who walked beside you yesterday?"

Jackson wrote a good many poems about friendship – including "Her Eyes," "My Lighthouses" (LOA, 2: 222), "Found Frozen," and "My New Friend" – but "Acquainted with Grief" follows the allegorical pattern most fully. The partnership with Grief is here presented as a form of compensation after repeated losses. Grief, like religion, is what one is left with after all the intermediate strategies for living have proven ineffective.

"Coronation" was probably Jackson's most popular poem. Not only does it exemplify the poet's success with allegory, it illustrates her commitment to ending her poems powerfully. It also conveys her democratic spirituality, which was akin in some respects to Walt **Whitman's**. The poem laughs at class issues by providing a folkloric union between a beggar and a king. At a secondary level, however, time is the feature of life being overcome in the poem. Not only does the moment of encounter occur in a magical synchrony – "the drowsy snare" of noon – but the world into which the beggar and king are liberated is also one that eludes the destructive effects of time. When we first meet the king, he is "Watching the hour-glass sifting down / Too slow its shining sand." We might reasonably construct from these lines an expectation that once the king lays by his crown, his dull life will be replaced by a richer encounter with history. But this expectation is not fulfilled. The guards do return to human time once "the crafty noon" unweaves "its yellow nets of sun." Upon the king's gate, moreover, time does leave its signature: "the moss grew gray." But beggar and king are "free" not to pursue their quest but free of that quest, of time, itself. Previously, time was inscribed on the king's face as suffering written in crimson lines, but once he teams up with the beggar, he asks for the other king:

The beggar laughed. Free winds in haste
  Were wiping from the king's hot brow
The crimson lines the crown had traced.
  "This is his presence now."

Jackson's allegorical tendency reflects a desire to escape the destructive effects of human time and to find a realm – democratic, artistic, and transcendent – in which absolute contingency might melt into something truly empowering. Full presence? Yet here we need to remember the critique of allegory provided by twentieth-century theorists such as Walter Benjamin and Georg Lukács. They argue that the allegorical impulse, although seeking to redeem life from its situation of suffering, actually projects a sense of ultimate contingency by making all the particulars of life available for representation. Benjamin writes: "What ruins are in the physical world, allegories are in the world of the mind." "The laugh that free men know" thus cannot be validated by allegorical art because what we desire to enter (the realm of freedom) is forever subjugated in allegory to a realm of abstract necessity that is timeless but, for that same reason, barren as well. Indeed, only the mystic – whose concerns are not human, democratic, or artistic but nonhuman, teleological, and absolute – can find satisfaction in a world of allegory.

Helen Hunt Jackson was not a mystic. Not only had she no adult ties with official religion, she seems to have envisioned the divine realm only as a sort of utopian alternative to the inadequacy of human life. It was this inadequacy that concerned her most; it troubled her personally because it subjected her to the deaths of those she loved and concerned her politically because it forced her to confront perfidy, racism, and injustice. The last poem in her final collection, "The Song He Never Wrote," offers tantalizing reflections on several of these issues. Here, the poet is pictured as haunted by an ignis fatuus (will-o'-the-wisp):

A gleam of wings forever flaming,
  Never folded in nest or cote;
Secrets of joy, past name or naming;
  Measures of bliss past dole or rote;

Echoes of music, always flying,
  Always echo, never the note;
Pulses of life, past life, past dying, –
  All these in the song he never wrote.

This poem is itself another allegory, but at the same time it suggests a critique of allegory. The desire for completion presents itself as "always echo, never the note," and, indeed, it is only *after* death, when once again heaven emerges as the recompense for the inadequacy of earthly life, that such a song, fully adequate to human desire, is conceived of as genuinely possible. In the final stanzas, we can see both the hunger for ultimate satisfaction that produces the vision of the afterlife and the poet's sense that none of the allegories s/he has produced have consummated that desire for the Real.

Higher the singer rose and higher,
  Heavens, in spaces, sank like bars;
Great joy within him glowed like fire,
  He tossed his arms among the stars, –

"This is the life, past life, past dying;
  I am I, and I live the life:
Shame on the thought of mortal crying!
  Shame on its petty toil and strife!

"Why did I halt, and weakly tremble?"
  Even in heaven the memory smote, –
"Fool to be dumb, and to dissemble!
  Alas for the song I never wrote!"

The songs that Jackson wrote have not endured. Although Edmund Clarence **Stedman's** landmark *American Anthology 1787–1900* acknowledged Jackson as one of our finest American women poets, her poetry had disappeared from anthologies by the 1920s. Thus, she has been remembered primarily as a defender of Indian causes and as the author of *Ramona*. Feminist critics have returned to Jackson's poetry as well as to a greater range of her prose, but until the publication of *American Women Poets of the Nineteenth Century* (Rutgers University Press, 1992), very few of her poems were available in paperback. Jackson's poetry is certainly worth reading, although its pleasures derive principally from studying it in relation to its late nineteenth-century American contexts. She was energetic and skillful, supportive of younger writers, especially women, and passionate about social justice. That she mainly favored a form inadequate to her desires should not blind us to her strengths, which were both personal and poetic. Helen Hunt Jackson began her poetic career as a form of therapy, but she ended it having produced a number of highly effective poems.

CHERYL WALKER

Selected Works
Verses, by "H.H.," Boston: Roberts Brothers, 1870, 1873
The Story of Boon, Boston: Roberts Brothers, 1874
Sonnets and Lyrics, Boston: Roberts Brothers, 1886
Poems, Boston: Roberts Brothers, 1892
Poems by Helen Jackson, Boston: Little, Brown, 1898

Further Reading
Banning, Evelyn I., *Helen Hunt Jackson*, New York: Vanguard, 1973
Coultrap-McQuin, Susan, *Doing Literary Business: American Women Writers in the Nineteenth Century*, Chapel Hill: Universityof North Carolina Press, 1990
Dobson, Joanne, *Dickinson and the Strategies of Reticence*, Bloomington: Indiana University Press, 1989
Higginson, T. W., *Contemporaries*, Boston: Houghton Mifflin, 1899
Odell, Ruth, *Helen Hunt Jackson*, New York: Appleton-Century, 1939
Sewall, Richard B., *The Life of Emily Dickinson*, vol. 2, New York: Farrar, Straus, 1974
Walker, Cheryl, *The Nightingale's Burden*, Bloomington: Indiana University Press, 1982
Whitaker, Rosemary, *Helen Hunt Jackson*, Boise, Idaho: Boise State University Press, 1987

Sarah Orne Jewett

(1849–1909)

Born in South Berwick, Maine, Jewett was a local-color writer whose short stories remain among the best in the English language. The local-color school, which also included Harriet Beecher Stowe, Rose Terry **Cooke**, Elizabeth Stuart Phelps Ward, and Mary E. Wilkins Freeman, made a valuable contribution to women's literary traditions by creating a countertradition to the sentimental/domestic convention that dominated women's writing throughout most of the nineteenth century. An outgrowth of Romanticism, local-color writing was a reaction to industrialization, mass communication, and transportation. Using regional peculiarities in dialect, clothes, setting, customs, and characters, these women sought to preserve their heritage through their writing.

At the request of her family, Mark A. De Wolfe Howe collected 19 of Jewett's poems and published them in *Verses* (1916), seven years after her death. Although the collection was intended only for distribution among her friends, a centennial edition was published in 1949. In the introduction, Burton W. Trafton Jr. describes Jewett's poems as "homely . . . often lacking the precision of her prose" and questions whether she ever intended that they be collected. Nonetheless, he also finds a kind of beauty in them. Richard Cary supplements Trafton's strictures:

> *Verses* is not a distinguished volume. . . . There is little more than rhymed platitude. She extracts her topics from the moving stream of experience but treats them with equanimous superficiality. She avoids complexity in language and density in figures. Her meters are pedestrian. In an early letter to Scudder [editor of the *Atlantic Monthly*] she expresses doubt about her poetizing; her intuition was true.

Jewett's biographer, John Eldridge Frost, supports Cary's position and adds that "A large number of the verses were inspired by incidents in Miss Jewett's life: her father's death; an evening stroll in the garden; a visit to Powderhouse Hill; a Sunday morning passed at home; and visits to the Isles of Shoals, Bethlehem, Pennsylvania, and Dunlace Castle." "The Gloucester Mother," "Discontent," and "A Child's Grave" are her best-known poems.

In the autobiographical essay, "Looking Back on Girlhood," Jewett explains how she began writing verses as a young girl, only to find prose writing more appealing as she grew older:

> I was still a child when I began to write down the things I was thinking about, but at first I always made rhymes and found prose so difficult that a school composition was a terror to me, and I do not even remember writing one that was worth anything. But in the course of time rhymes themselves became difficult and prose more and more enticing, and I began my work in life, most happy in finding that I was to write of those country characters and rural landscapes to which I myself belonged, and which I had been taught to love with all my heart.

When Jewett began writing *Deephaven* in 1877, she realized what her goal in life would be. She was about 15 when the first summer tourists began visiting Berwick, and it upset her to see how they made fun of the country people who meant so much to her: "I determined to teach the world that country people were not the awkward, ignorant set those people seemed to think. I wanted the world to know their grand simple lives." It was also at this point that she realized how much her father, Dr. Theodore Herman Jewett, had influenced her. According to Jewett, his voice kept ringing in her ears as she tried to recapture some detail he had pointed out. He had given her what most writers never attain – a thorough love and knowledge of, and kinship with, the environment:

> I had no consciousness of watching or listening, or indeed of any special interest in the country interiors. In fact, when the time came that my own world of imaginations was more real to me than any other, I was sometimes perplexed at my father's directing my attention to certain points of interest in the character or surroundings of our acquaintances.
>
> I cannot help believing that he recognized, long before I did myself, in what direction the current of purpose in my life was setting. Now as I write my sketches of country life, I remember again and again the wise things he said, and the sights he made me see.

As she became more confident in herself as a writer, his advice was imprinted on her mind: "Don't try to write 'about' people and things, tell them just as they are!" Acknowledging her indebtedness, she dedicated *Country By-Ways* to him: "The best and wisest man I ever knew; who taught me many lessons and showed me many things as we went together along the Country By-Ways."

In "At Home from Church" (LOA, 2: 465), we can sense the deep appreciation and the reverence that Jewett felt for nature. She did not have a similar regard for organized religion. John E. Frost explains that Jewett was not a natural churchgoer, and, in a letter to Annie Fields, Jewett once confessed that she had just attended church because she had been remiss and had not been "preached at for some months." This sort of attitude was prevalent among nineteenth-century women, many of whom were critical of the religious doctrine of damnation, which was left over from its Calvinist teachings. Margaret Roman writes: "When [Jewett] attended services, it was frequently in body only. More often, like her characters, she preferred to read the Bible by her bed, in the privacy of her home, where she could foster her faith rather than convert to patriarchal demands." Thus, it is easy to understand how Jewett could feel "shut out" (in the words of the poem) both literally and figuratively from the religious community. Instead, her communion was with nature, and with a higher being through nature's beauty. Her reference to lilacs reflects her great love of flowers; she commented to a reporter in 1895: "I was born here [South Berwick] and I hope to die here leaving the lilac bushes still green, and all the chairs in their places." The beauty in this poem, therefore, stems from the poet's delight in the natural world and in the surrounding landscape, both of which she learned from her father. She is acutely aware of the birds and the bees, and the quiet hush that envelops the early Sunday morning. As her reverie fades, she is consciously aware, not of the religious significance of the event, but "only of a voice that sings" in all its glory.

In "A Country Boy in Winter" (LOA, 2: 466), we also see several themes familiar from Jewett's prose. Eugene Pool discusses the difficulty Jewett had in making the transition from childhood to adulthood: "Her life . . . seems to have been an uneasy middle road between childhood and adulthood, whether or not she was aware of it (although she certainly seems to be conscious of some tension)." This ambivalence is also evident in several letters. Jewett once confessed to Horace Scudder, "I'm not a bit grown up if I am twenty and I like my children's books just as well as ever I did, and I read them just the same. . . . It's a dreadful thing to have been born lazy." To William Dean **Howells**, she revealed her disillusionment with the hometown she dearly loved: "Berwick has grown quite uninteresting to me for once in its life, and everybody is distressingly grown – and I have 'nobody to play with.' I have been writing some children's stories for the *Independent*, and the state of my mind is shadowed forth in the last one, 'Half-done Polly,' which is severely moral." Perhaps the most revealing statement of all can be seen in a letter she wrote to Annie Fields when she was 48: "This is my birthday and I am always nine years old."

"A Country Boy in Winter" allows us to experience Jewett's childlike exuberance and her love of outdoor life. Jewett had a fun-loving, free childhood, and Frost describes her as having been "rebellious." She always loved sports and was much more interested in so-called boys' hobbies than in those traditionally associated with girls. Never one to be confined to the indoors, she loved coasting, skating, snow shoveling, fishing, rowing, diving, and horseback riding. According to Roman, "To play sports with a boy's enthusiasm and to adopt a boy's interests was to chose freedom over enclosure. Enthusiastic boys were forgiven their indiscretions in favor of the growth that must not be thwarted."

It is interesting, then, to note that the didacticism Roman cites in her children's stories can be seen in "A Country Boy in Winter" as well: "Despite her unhampered attitude as a child, Jewett seems to praise in her children's stories the very values she downplayed." We see the young boy in the poem anxious to grow up, do a man's work, and become a useful, productive member of society. This same attitude is expressed by Jewett in a letter to Scudder:

> I am getting quite ambitious and really feel that writing is my work – my business, perhaps; and it is so much better than making a mere amusement of it as I used. I am really trying to be very much in earnest and to do the best I can, and I even find I have achieved a small reputation already. I am glad to have something to do in the world and something which may prove very helpful and useful in the world if I care to make it so, which I certainly do.

The boy in the poem expresses his desire to grow up and "get all through with school." Jewett herself was never fond of formal education, preferring to accompany her father as he made his rounds to his patients. Richard Cary describes her schooling as "haphazard" and notes that while she displayed a natural inclination for writing, there was "no spark of superior scholarship" evident. Jewett attended the Berwick Academy from 1861 to 1865, where, according to Cary, she "went to classes desultorily for four years." Thus, as Cary states, "she seems never to have applied herself diligently to studies nor to have relished the shackles of schoolroom discipline." She was, however, a voracious reader who gained much of her knowledge of the world from the great writers. The references to other young "fellows talk[ing] about New York" and to the boy's desire to "stay at home" is another example of Jewett's moralizing. It is also likely that the last reference alludes to Jewett herself, for although she traveled extensively and lived part of the year in Boston, her home and friends in South Berwick always remained close to her heart.

The deep interest in local color after the Civil War aided the cause of women writers immensely. As Perry Westbrook states: "Obviously the village environment was one that women authors who were acquainted with rural New England would be best qualified to interpret." Josephine Donovan agrees:

> Many young men had been killed in the Civil War, or had left to seek their fortunes in the West or in urban centers. This meant that the world left behind was, so to speak, a world controlled by the mothers and their values. The New England local colorists depicted this matriarchal world positively and lauded its nourishment of strong women characters and their traditions of women's culture, such as herbology and witchcraft. The imaginative vision construed from this world provided an important counterweight to industrial capitalism and to Calvinism, . . . perceived by these writers as male systems.

Many people in the nation realized that there was much of the old life worth preserving and that some women writers were the ones best suited for the task.

The feeling of isolation expressed so profoundly in "A Caged Bird" (LOA, 2: 467) reflects the condition of women in the rural New England, a condition that Jewett also depicted in her fiction. Ann Douglas argues that the lives of the local colorists as a group "bear out . . . a pattern of retreat, whether enforced or voluntary, on the social, economic, and sexual levels," and that this "same note of attenuation, even impoverishment . . . is sustained also in their actual work." Opposed to the domestic/sentimental vision of the world as a place of abundance, the local colorists' "imaginary territory is dominated by the laws of scarcity: the wherewithal of life has somehow been withheld and the inhabitants quite literally must get bread from stones." Like the sentimentalists, the local colorists valued feminine virtue, but they no longer believed in its ability to sustain life: "Their theme is no longer . . . that of female superiority. It is not that their women are not superior to their men, . . . but the important and painful fact which their literature underscores is that women, whether superior or inferior, are superfluous as individuals, and strangely superannuated as a sex" (*Women's Studies* [1972]).

But in Jewett's fiction – and in poems like "A Caged Bird" – women do have each other and the comfort and security that friendship and a community provide. Jewett told Charles Eliot

Norton that she was most grateful for "the friends I love better as every year goes by" and said to his daughter Sally that "there is something transfiguring in the best of friendship." As Donovan glosses this phrase, Jewett meant that friendship "gives us 'shining hours' that sustain us when we descend 'from the mountain . . . into the fret of everyday life.' Such moments of transcendence validate our daily tasks and give us the courage to persevere." It is easy to see why Jewett concludes "A Caged Bird" with the idea that all we need in this world is "one true friend [who] green leaves can reach / From out some fairer, wider place, / And understand our wistful speech!"

James T. Fields, the most notable publisher in mid-nineteenth-century America, was editor of the *Atlantic* in the 1860s, and his and Annie Fields's residence at 148 Charles Street in Boston was the center of literary activity. In F. O. Matthiessen's terms, their home was "the nearest approach ever made to an American salon." After Fields's death, according to Frost, Jewett brought "sympathy, interest, enthusiasm, and – comparatively speaking – youth" to Annie Fields's home; in the process, Jewett expanded her own horizons. As it became more difficult for the two women to escape their literary reputations, they sought peace and solitude in an old Moravian settlement in Bethlehem, Pennsylvania, which is probably described in "The Widows' House" (LOA, 2: 469) – a place, as Jewett elsewhere said, "so small that you could have walked around it in an afternoon if one side of it wasn't bounded by heaven." Nina Auerbach contends that where all-male communities possess grandeur and magnitude and aim to leave their imprint on the world, communities of women have no such lofty aspirations: "In almost all instances, the male quest is exchanged for rootedness – a school, a village, a city of their own." In local-color fiction, this "rootedness" is centered on the home, but, according to Douglas, this home (unlike that represented in domestic fiction) is "at once a rocklike prison and a frail refuge from a world more frightening than any prison." According to Jewett, while women may not be locked in their homes, they can be forgotten there, isolated from society, and left to fend for themselves.

For Jewett, the maternal instinct that the sentimentalists revered now seemed inconsistent or inapplicable, because the women who were most typical in local-color fiction had undergone a significant metamorphosis: they had aged. Jewett always revered old age, especially old women; Willa Cather recalled Jewett's telling her that "her head was full of old houses and old women, and when an old house and old woman came together in her brain with a click, she knew that a story was under way." One such story, her best-known novel, *The Country of the Pointed Firs*, has such lasting value for Cather that she singled it out as a masterpiece: "If I were asked to name three American books which have the possibility of a long, long life, I would say at once, 'The Scarlet Letter,' 'Huckleberry Finn' and 'The Country of the Pointed Firs.' I can think of no others that confront time and change so securely." Most critics agree that Sarah Orne Jewett did far more to capture a chosen time and place and the personalities of her region than any of her contemporaries.

GAIL C. KEATING

Selected Works

Letters of Sarah Orne Jewett, edited by Annie Fields, Boston: Houghton Mifflin, 1911

Verses, Boston: Merrymount, 1916

Letters of Sarah Orne Jewett, edited by Richard Cary, Waterville, Maine: Colby College Press, 1967

Further Reading

Auerbach, Nina, *Communities of Women*, Cambridge, Massachusetts: Harvard University Press, 1978

Baym, Nina, *Women's Fiction*, Ithaca, New York: Cornell University Press, 1978

Cary, Richard, ed., *Appreciation of Sarah Orne Jewett*, Waterville, Maine: Colby College Press, 1973

_____, *Sarah Orne Jewett*, New York: Twayne, 1962

Donovan, Josephine, *New England Local Color Literature*, New York: Ungar, 1983

_____, *Sarah Orne Jewett*, New York: Ungar, 1980

Frost, John Eldridge, *Sarah Orne Jewett*, Kittery Point, Maine: Gundalow Club, 1960

Matthiessen, F. O., *Sarah Orne Jewett*, Boston: Houghton Mifflin, 1929

Nagel, Gwen L., ed., *Critical Essays on Sarah Orne Jewett*, Boston: G.K. Hall, 1984

Nagel, Gwen L., and James Nagel, *Sarah Orne Jewett: A Reference Guide*, Boston: G.K. Hall, 1978

Roman, Margaret, *Sarah Orne Jewett: Reconstructing Gender*, Tuscaloosa:University of Alabama Press, 1992

Westbrook, Perry D., *Acres of Flint: Writers of Rural New England 1870–1900*, Washington, D.C.: Scarecrow, 1951

Frances Anne Kemble

(1809–1893)

Kemble was born in London on November 27, 1809, and lived through most of the nineteenth century. As an actress, writer, and celebrity, she was well-acquainted with writers and philosophers on both sides of the Atlantic. Part of the third generation of a famous theatrical family, Kemble was the granddaughter of actor-manager Roger Kemble, the daughter of actors Marie Thérèse De Camp and Charles Kemble, and the niece of the celebrated tragedian Sarah Siddons and actor-theater manager John Philip Kemble. Because the Kembles wanted their daughter to receive an education that would allow her to move in the proper social circles, the young girl was sent to France, where she spent several years in a Paris boarding school. This separation from her family, especially her mother, was traumatic and may account for the frequent theme of leaving people and places in Kemble's poems.

It was perhaps during her school years that Kemble began her lifelong habit of reading – as Henry James once noted – everything except the daily paper. She evidently avoided the newspaper because it contained only mundane things, whereas Kemble sought to devote herself to the higher things in life. Dante (read in the original), John Milton, and William Shakespeare were Kemble's early staples. She also was a student of the Bible and studied it assiduously; however, it seems to have had little consequence for her poetry. Although avoiding Dante's and Milton's religious themes, Kemble borrowed the passion and the rhythm of their language. Her poems are spiritual, but celebrate nature rather than God. Kemble may have also used religion to tame or at least to balance her passionate nature, which appears to have been stirred to near frenzy by the works of the Romantics. Lord Byron, Percy Bysshe Shelley, John Keats, and William Wordsworth won out in this internal struggle, at least in her poetry.

Kemble confessed to having read Byron on the sly; she hid his poetry under a pillow because "the wicked poet" was not considered suitable reading for impressionable young ladies. Her early poems are evidence of how Kemble was "liable to the infection of the potent, proud, desponding bitterness of his writings"; she identified with the misunderstood, exiled poet. Later in life, although she still appreciated the "might, majesty and loveliness" of his poems, she also felt they contained too much "ego." Although Kemble has often been compared with Byron, her poetry and life also trace the path set by Wordsworth. She had a deep reverence for nature – mountains, rivers, and flowers – and, like Wordsworth, she felt an informing spirit in the world of nature. She also lived a long life, overcoming rather than giving in to travesties. In the end, Kemble proved more resilient than Byron, her earlier role model.

No doubt influenced by the Romantics, Kemble knew already by the age of 13 that she wanted to be a writer. To her, a writer's life was one where she could roam the mountainsides and capture the beauty of nature in her journal. Completing her first project, *Francis the First*, in 1829, Kemble wanted to have it published, as Byron's own verse plays had been. After reading *Francis*, Elizabeth Barrett Browning commented: "It seems to me a very clever and indeed surprising production as from the pen of a young person. . . . The dialogue is sometimes very spirited, and ably done – but the poetry is seldom good as poetry – and scarcely ever original or harmonious. There are, however, beautiful passages." Browning also noted that the play might not have been published if it had been written by someone without Kemble's family connections. This evaluation was echoed by the readers and reviewers of her later work. When the play was staged at Covent Garden in 1832, it received only a lukewarm reception.

Kemble did not care for what the critics said about her work; it was the act of writing, of recording her emotions, that had meaning for her. She may have taken at face value Wordsworth's definition of poetry as a "spontaneous overflow of powerful feelings." For whenever Kemble felt powerful emotions, she released them either in tears or in communications to friends. Since she moved in the same literary circles as Wordsworth, she met the surviving Romantic poet several times while she was in London. Kemble eventually claimed the acquaintance and friendship of many of the century's greatest creative minds and captivated them with her keen wit, intelligence, and candor. Given the impressive list of visitors who came to her parents' home, this ability to converse with ease and frankness came naturally to Kemble. Her brother John, who was a member of the Cambridge Apostles, brought home friends such as Arthur Henry Hallam, Alfred, Lord Tennyson, and Edward FitzGerald. She also met William Makepeace Thackeray, Thomas Carlyle, Sir Walter Scott, and Washington Irving.

By 1829, Charles Kemble, who had taken on the management of the Covent Garden Theater, began experiencing financial problems. In order to save the theater and to help her family, Kemble took to the stage and made her debut as Shakespeare's Juliet. Her portrayal of the tragic young lover was so moving that Thackeray later claimed to have fallen in love with her. She won immediate acclaim, a rare accomplishment for an actress so young. Her success on the stage helped to keep her family from financial ruin, but not completely out of risk, so Charles Kemble soon booked performances in America, where there was a demand for English culture. Thus, in 1832, accompanied by her Aunt Dall (Adelaide De Camp), Kemble went with her father on an American tour. Not surprisingly, she was unhappy about leaving home for two years, but she also became tired of being an actress. Although she enjoyed the attention and the parties, Kemble only acted out of necessity, for she still cherished her original dream of becoming a writer.

It was on this tour that Kemble met the Philadelphian Pierce Butler, who, as a nineteenth-century "stage-door Johnny," romantically wooed her. The courtship caused a minor scandal in Philadelphia society because Butler, with his social standing, ancestry, and family wealth, was ardently pursuing an actress. Kemble married Butler in 1834 and happily retired from the stage. It was not, however, a blissful union, because Kemble believed marriage should be a partnership based on equality. She was used to everyday freedoms such as horseback riding, hiking, and fishing; and although Butler knew of this side of Kemble, he soon tried to mold her into a more conventional, sub-servient wife.

One of the first of their many conflicts centered on the publication of Kemble's *Journal* (1835). She originally agreed to publish her memoirs so that her Aunt Dall would have a nest egg; when this aunt died, Kemble decided to go ahead with the publication and to give the proceeds to her Aunt Victoire. Although Butler did not encourage the project, he did have the foresight to anticipate the reception to Kemble's frank observations of her first years in America, which she had compiled from letters she had written to her English friends. In his self-conceived romantic role as his wife's protector, Butler edited the manuscript and erased both names and potentially offending passages. Not especially known for her tactfulness, Kemble took a candid and critical view of American hotels, railways, servants, food, and everyday life, and these views met with an angry reception from Americans who did not appreciate her pointing out their social and cultural flaws.

Kemble's less-controversial first book of poetry was published in 1844. Again, she turned to publication because of a need: to buy back a horse that Butler had sold to stop her from riding alone. The volume contained 94 lyrics, songs, odes, and sonnets – all written over a period of 20 years. Noting the understandable influence of Shakespeare, the critic Leota Driver considered the sonnets Kemble's best poetic effort. As audiences in America and England knew, Kemble was emotionally attuned to the Bard's lines. Her poetry is lyrical and descriptive; like Shakespeare, she uses language that is simple, yet rich with metaphor. But where Shakespeare's lines entice the reader into reflecting on larger issues such as time, change, and love, Kemble's verses are more a reflection of her private feelings. When describing Kemble's poetry, James wrote that it was "all passionate and melancholy and less prized . . . perfectly individual and really lyrical." She never hid the fact that her poems were autobiographical, and perhaps that was some of their appeal for readers curious to identify people and events in the life of such a famous actress. In the tradition of the poetry of her time, however, Kemble rarely identified a person outright. Biographer Dorothy Marshall speculates that poems filled with heartbreak, such as "To ——," were written in response to a romance with a fellow actor. Kemble expressed her sense of disillusionment and betrayal in lines such as "I would I knew the lady of thy heart," or:

> False love! in thy despite,
>   I will be with thee then.
> When in the world of dreams thy spirit strays,
> Seeking, in vain, the peace it finds not here.

Some of these poems of lost or false love may have been written when Kemble found out about Butler's extramarital affairs.

James noted that "her writing . . . had the same free sincerity as her conversation. She wrote exactly as she talked, observing, asserting, complaining, confiding, contradicting, crying out and bounding off, away." This conversational style resembles that of Wordsworth, who claimed that there was little essential difference between poetry and prose and that both forms grow out of common experience. Nature fills most of Kemble's poems, and is imaged in the different seasons, mountains, flowers, and the sky in the evening or at dawn. Her most recurrent symbol is water: rivers, waterfalls, lakes, and foun-

tains. For Kemble, water imagery represented life and destiny. She sometimes adorned her poems with Greek gods like the Muses, or with sprites, elves, and fairies. These references and her oft-stated feelings of dejection and melancholy caused Robert Browning to dismiss her work as "album writing about 'sprites,' and lily 'bell' and wishes – now to be dead and now alive." The pessimistic themes that Browning referred to come through strongly in lines such as: "Oh, weary, weary world! How full thou art in sin, of sorrow, and all evil things." In "The Vision of Life," Kemble personifies death as always present:

> Death and I,
> On a hill so high,
> Stood side by side
> And we saw below;
> Running to and fro,
> All things that be in the world so wide.

With death as a companion, Kemble depicted the world as consisting of "laughter and wailing" as well as "prayer and railing"; however, her overall view of the world was that of chaos, darkness, and tears.

Her poetry also reflected the style, voice, and imagery of writers that she read. "The Vision of Life" brings to mind the work of Emily **Dickinson**, and it is possible that the similarity derives from their common interest in Ralph Waldo **Emerson** and Wordsworth. Although both women produced poems of intensity and spontaneity, however, Kemble's were more personal reflections, and Dickinson's more visionary. Kemble's later poems never lost the trademark of suffering, but they did become more optimistic. Life was still a struggle, but there was hope. This change may be attributed to the influence of the transcendentalists, who she first encountered while visiting the novelist Catharine Maria Sedgwick. With their ties to Wordsworth's ideas, the transcendentalists complemented the way Kemble chose to live her own life; they also emphasized the importance of nature, self-reliance, and individualism.

The shift in Kemble's mood might also be attributed to a mellowing in her later years. Her life, after all, had not been totally tragic. She reconciled with her daughters, visited and was visited by friends, and ultimately led the life of a writer. One idiosyncrasy that separates Kemble from most writers, however, was her refusal to revise. James tactfully recorded that her poems were "so off-hand as to be rough." It was as if she lived her life without a second thought and had wanted her writing to reflect that. Despite the uneven quality of her poems, the expression of emotion remains their core strength. In the aptly titled "Impromptu" (LOA, 1: 586), Kemble tells the reader that she writes so much because she is so sad:

> You say you're glad I write – oh, say not so!
>   My fount of song, dear friend, 's a bitter well;
> And when the numbers freely from it flow,
>   'Tis that my heart, and eyes, o'erflow as well.

Kemble wanted her reader to know that all her words – in her letters, poems, and journals – were inspired by suffering. This particular poem was most likely dashed off in response to a friend's compliment on her ability to write and publish, and therefore, to obtain money when it was most needed. As the second stanza makes explicit, her poetic "numbers" were not like those of Thomas Moore or Anacreon, stemming from the spirit of Bacchus, but flowed instead upon a "sullen stream of tears." "Impromptu" was probably one of her earlier poems to plead with readers to understand the travail and despondency that drove her to write.

One prime cause of Kemble's unhappiness was parting from close friends and beloved places, and she always wrote as if she were leaving for the final time, never to return. "To the Wissahiccon" (LOA, 1: 585), which refers to a stream in southeastern Pennsylvania, exemplifies how Kemble used nature imagery to represent people and to reflect her sadness. It opens with a statement of farewell: "My feet shall tread no more thy mossy side." Like many of Wordsworth's works, the speaker in this poem walks through nature. The poem also prominently features water imagery: "*Pleasant Water*," "the sea that parts thy home and mine," and "Child of pure mountain springs" serve as examples. Although saying good-bye to the "dark green cedar" and the "stony rifts of granite gray" that sparkle "like diamond rocks in the sun's ray," the speaker ends with the familiar Romantic notion of revisitation in memory: "My spirit shall through many a summer's day / Return, among thy peaceful woods to stray."

Kemble is best known for her *Journal of a Residence on a Georgia Plantation* (1863), which contains vivid descriptions and observations of life on Butler's Sea Islands plantation. Her revulsion to slavery and her abolitionist stirrings came naturally to someone who valued personal freedom so highly, and as the wife of a domineering man, Kemble also felt a kinship with the slaves. Her opinions matched those of William Ellery Channing, the influential New England liberal, and were mostly likely shaped through their discussions. Interestingly enough, only two of her poems address the subject of slavery.

After her much-publicized divorce in 1849, which resulted in Butler's being awarded custody of their two daughters, Kemble was forced to find a way to support herself. She again turned to her dramatic ability and gave solo readings of Shakespeare's works. Her audience included the likes of Dickinson, Louisa May Alcott, the Brownings, Walt **Whitman**, and Emerson. Henry Wadsworth **Longfellow** was so moved by one of Kemble's performances that he wrote a sonnet about her. The success of her readings allowed Kemble to buy a home in the Berkshires – which became her equivalent of the Romantics' Lake District – and to join the Lenox community of intellectuals. The readings also enabled her to make pilgrimages to the Swiss Alps. When she could no longer hike, she was carried up into the Alps; when she no longer had the stamina to be carried, Kemble spent hours gazing at the sublime mountains from her window.

In 1859, a revised edition of Kemble's poems was published with 68 new poems, which had been written earlier during a year she had spent in Italy (on this sojourn, she also produced the journal entries that formed the basis of *A Year of Consolation* [1847]). Another edition of poems appeared in 1883, with 25 new poems replacing most of the poems in the original 1844 edition. Robert Browning wrote: "I had no conception Mrs. Butler could have written anything so mournfully mediocre . . . to go as near flattery as I can. With the exception of three or four pieces respectable from their apparent earnestness . . . [they are] descriptions without color, songs without tune." But neither criticism nor advancing age kept Kemble from writing. She produced many other works, including further memoirs, *Notes Upon Some of Shakespeare's Plays* (1882), her first novel, *Long Ago and Far Away* (1889), and essays and poems in leading periodicals.

During these later years, Kemble continued to entertain friends. James wrote that "her talk reflected a thousand vanished and present things . . . swarmed with people and with criticism of people, with the ghosts of a dead society." This ability to stimulate and infuse the works of others may have been Kemble's greatest contribution to literature, and although she was convinced that her grandson, Owen Wister, would never be a "man of books," she provided him entrée to the world of artists; at least one reviewer paid tribute to Kemble by stating that Wister, author of the 1902 bestseller *The Virginian*, had "inherited her genius."

Having contributed much to the century in which she lived, Kemble died on January 15, 1893. As a poet, she has faded from the limelight and appears only in the rare anthology. James conveyed her talent best when he wrote: "What she had in verse was not only the lyric impulse but the genuine lyric need; poetry, for her, was one of those moral conveniences . . . which she took where she found them. She made a very honest use of it, inasmuch as it expressed for her what nothing else could express – the inexpugnable, the fundamental, the boundless and generous sadness which lay beneath her vitality."

MARK P. BRODIE
KATHLEEN MOTOIKE

Selected Works
Poems, London: John Penington, 1844

Further Reading
Bobbe, Dorothy, *Fanny Kemble*, New York: Grosset & Dunlap, 1931
Driver, Leota S., *Fanny Kemble,* New York: Negro University Press, 1969
Fox-Genovese, Elizabeth, *Within the Plantation Household: Black and White Women of the Old South*, Chapel Hill: University of North Carolina Press, 1988
Furnas, Joseph Chamberlain, *Fanny Kemble: Leading Lady of the Nineteenth-Century Stage*, New York: Dial, 1982
James, Henry, *Literary Criticism: Essays on Literature, American Writers, English Writers*, New York: Library of America, 1984
Marshall, Dorothy, *Fanny Kemble*, New York: St. Martin's, 1978
Pope-Hennessy, Una Birch, *Three English Women in America*, London: E. Benn, 1929
Rushmore, Robert, *Fanny Kemble*, New York: Crowell-Collier, 1970
Seymour, Miranda, *A Ring of Conspirators: Henry James and His Literary Circle*, Boston: Houghton Mifflin, 1988
Wright, Constance, *Fanny Kemble and the Lovely Land*, New York: Dodd, 1972

Sidney Lanier

(1842–1881)

Best-known for his musical verse, Lanier is the only notable American poet who was also an accomplished professional musician. (Edgar Allan **Poe** and Walt **Whitman** also composed musically inspired verse, but they were not performing artists.) This fact is critical to an appreciation of Lanier's poetry, which developed from traditional nineteenth-century verse forms into a highly individual and innovative form that was unique for its musical qualities, which in turn derived from Lanier's personal, firsthand experience. Comparing his early, rather naive lyrics with a mature, multi-textured poem such as "Sunrise" will reveal how dynamically Lanier's style changed over the years. And the major cause of this change was his exposure to the avant-garde music of the day – works by composers including Richard Wagner, Franz Liszt, and Hector Berlioz. Lanier's earliest poetic works, such as "Little Ella" (which he set to music), are tied to a more simple song concept, while his later works reflect a more complex symphonic synthesis of lines, voices, and tones.

Considering Lanier's background, his successes in the worlds of both music and literature are quite amazing. He was without formal musical training, yet he became the principal flutist in a first-rate orchestra. He was also a respected literary scholar and popular teacher. And although he died young, at age 39, he lived long enough to see his poetry receive national acclaim.

Even as a youth in his native Macon, Georgia, Lanier showed a remarkable love and aptitude for music, but it was not considered seemly for a gentleman of the southern tradition to become a professional musician; musical talent was looked upon only as a social grace. Lanier graduated in 1860 from Oglethorpe University in Milledgeville, Georgia; he later referred to his education as "farcical" because of its limited and parochial nature. But he was enthralled with the scholar's life and hoped that he might pursue further study in Europe. His family assumed, however, that he would adhere to the traditions of his social class and follow his father into the legal profession. Both of these ideas were cut short by the beginning of the Civil War. Lanier joined the Macon Volunteers in 1861, serving in the signal corps and then on a blockade runner until he was captured and imprisoned at a federal camp at Point Lookout, Maryland. At this camp, he contracted tuberculosis, from which he died in 1881.

Upon Lanier's return to Macon after his release in a prisoner exchange, he found that his world had been completely altered. His mother died of tuberculosis shortly after his return. Lanier was in poor health, and his dreams of study in Europe were crushed by his family's new financial hardships. He worked as a hotel clerk, tutor, and headmaster. He then entered his father's law firm, but found all of these endeavors unrewarding. He also wrote some lyrical verse and a Civil War novel (*Tiger-Lilies*, 1867), but illness, unstimulating work, and economic struggle made the period a most depressing one for Lanier. The only happy note during this period was his wedding to Mary Day of Macon in 1867; judging from their correspondence and other materials, they enjoyed a very strong marriage. Mary Day Lanier always supported her husband's aspirations, even to the extent of raising their children alone in Macon for several years while he went to Baltimore, Maryland to pursue his dream of a life in the arts. Eventually, in 1876, she and their three sons – a fourth would be born in 1880 – joined him there. The couple's extensive and detailed correspondence reveals not only their personal reflections but a comparison of the postwar south and the cultural life of the more affluent Baltimore.

Lanier spent precious and frustrating years trying to resolve the conflict between what his tradition expected of him and his own wishes. This tension in his personal life appears as one of the major themes in his work: the conflict between the spiritual – art – and materialism – trade. This conflict is best expressed in his long poem *The Symphony*.

Lanier went to New York several times to transact business and to seek medical help; while in the city, he attended many concerts. For a while, in 1872, he lived in San Antonio, Texas, hoping that the drier climate would relieve his respiratory problems. San Antonio's large German community impressed Lanier with their active love of music, and he joined some of their musical groups as a flutist. For the first time in his life, he felt encouraged and successful as a musician. With the understanding of his father and the support of his wife, Lanier made the break with tradition and Georgia and moved north in the fall of 1873 in an attempt to gain entry into artistic circles. As he wrote to his brother Clifford, "An impulse, simply irresistible, drives me into the world of poetry and music."

First, he went to New York, seeking an orchestral position. From all accounts, he was a virtuoso flutist with incredible natural skill. But he may have underestimated the competition he would face from conservatory-trained musicians in the nation's largest city. He had hoped to join the orchestra led by Theodore Thomas – New York's premier ensemble – but this was not possible. But New York did influence the direction of his artistic life, for there, in 1870, he heard the music of Richard Wagner for the first time. Lanier was aware of Wagner's controversial reputation and admired him as a representative of the German culture that he himself had so long respected. After hearing Wagner's music, he wrote to Mary: "Ah, how they have belied Wagner! I heard Theo. Thomas' Orchestra play his overture to *Tannhäuser*. The 'Music of the Future' is surely thy music and my music. . . . The sequences flowed along, one after the other, as if all the great and noble deeds of time had formed a procession and marched in review before one's *ears*, instead of one's eyes. . . . I would I might lead a so magnificent file of glories into Heaven!"

Lanier's 1877 poem "To Richard Wagner" (LOA, 2: 423) depicts the bright cast of "Valkyries, heroes, Rhinemaids, giants, gods" that illuminate a modern world dominated by the grime of trade. Through his music and its connection to "old Romance," Lanier feels, present society can be illuminated: "O Wagner, westward bring thy heavenly art." Lanier idolized Wagner, notes Aubrey Harrison Starke, as the "musical prophet of a new age, an age of industry, more noble than an age of Trade, in which work should be performed to the sublime strains of divine music. . . . In *Tannhäuser* especially, with its theme of the life-long antagonism of good and evil, [Lanier] found an opera dear to his soul, the work of a brother artist." One of Lanier's many unfinished projects was a translation of Wagner's libretti for the *Ring* cycle.

Lanier's hope of a great musical career in New York remained unfulfilled, and there is no evidence that he was able even to meet Theodore Thomas. Instead, he appeared at a benefit concert in Brooklyn for the Church of the Reformation in November 1873. He played a nocturne by Guilio Briccialdi, variations on "the Blue Bells of Scotland," and his own composition *Black-birds*. This recital was considered important enough to be covered by the Brooklyn *Eagle* and the *New York Times*, which noted Lanier's "debut" and called his piece a "poetic fantasie upon the strain of the Southern blackbird, which it transforms into wild, sweet music; . . . as a composition it is of classic purity, and decided originality."

But Lanier's true recognition was waiting for him in Baltimore, which was then establishing itself as a growing cultural center. When he stopped there briefly to visit a friend, Henry Wysham, also a lawyer and flutist, Wysham arranged for Lanier to meet and play for Asger Hamerik, the Danish-born conductor of the orchestra of the new Peabody Conservatory of Music. After hearing Lanier play from *Black-birds*, Hamerik immediately offered him the coveted position of first flute. Lanier accepted, and this event marked the turning point of his career. At this moment in time, music became the chief motivating force in his life. Poetry was relegated to a minor activity, and Starke points out that none of Lanier's published poems seem to date from 1872 or 1873. In May 1873, Lanier wrote to his friend and fellow southerner, poet Paul Hamilton **Hayne**: "so much of my life consists of music . . . whatever turn I have for Art, is purely musical; poetry being, with me, a mere tangent into which I shoot sometimes. I could play passably on several instruments before I could write legibly: and since then the very deepest of my life has been filled with music, which I have studied and cultivated far more than poetry."

Lanier's internal crisis was resolved: in the fall of 1873, he decided to make Baltimore his home and music his life. Baltimore offered a congenial society dedicated to the enjoyment of the arts, and the European cultural ambience that Lanier had dreamed of as a student – camaraderie, enthusiasm, and *Gemütlichkeit*. In addition to formal concerts at the Peabody Institute, Concordia Hall, Lehmann's Hall, the Academy of Music, and Ford's Grand Opera House, there were recitals and "Sängerfeste" throughout the year. Musical organizations included the Rossini Musical Association, the Haydn Musical Association, the Baltimore Glee Club, and four large German choral groups. Finally, here was a society in which Lanier could comfortably express his artistic aspirations; moreover, here were people who appreciated him. Lanier was no amateur among professionals, however; reviews of the time consistently lauded his musical skill, and the conservatory faculty treated him as an equal and invited him to play in chamber ensembles and to join them for concert tours. Lanier joined several clubs and musical organizations; and in 1876, when he was elected a member of the prestigious Wednesday Club, he chose to be associated with its musical rather than its literary section. At this point, when it seemed he might be at the beginning of a bright career, he had only eight years to live.

The first decade of conductor Hamerik's leadership – when Lanier was a member of the orchestra – witnessed many of the new "programmatic" musical compositions in which ideas, stories, or emotions were conveyed in tone. Lanier found this thrilling, for it complemented his idea that poetry ought to convey images through sound as much as through specific words. The influence of such programme-music is very much evident in his own verse. His early poems are stylistically simple and follow the *abab* song concept. But his more mature works such as "The Marshes of Glynn" (LOA. 2: 412), which mark him as a literary innovator, blend various voices, lines, and tones; they are more symphonic and are rich in imagery and in deliberately crafted patterns of sound.

In the mid-1870s, although he maintained his schedule as a performing musician, and even composed a number of art songs and flute studies, Lanier began to devote more effort to writing poetry. This verse was increasingly and profoundly influenced by the music that he heard every day at rehearsals: works by composers such as Wagner, Liszt, and Berlioz. Many of Liszt's "symphonic poems" were based upon works of Lord Byron, Friedrich Schiller, and Alphonse de Lamartine. The *Symphonie Fantastique* of Berlioz, who had been Hamerik's teacher, was one of the Peabody orchestra's most popular pieces. This symphony, which tells an entire story through musical motifs, greatly appealed to Lanier's interest in creating forms of expression that united the arts. Just as he thrilled to these examples of poetic music, so he would create musical poetry.

Lanier's national reputation as a poet began in 1874 with the publication of "Corn" in *Lippincott's* magazine. This long poem is Lanier's first verse that is not dominated by the more limiting song concept, and here his gifts as a creator of synesthetic poetry are evident. The opening lines, for example, create the image, in both words and sounds, of the rustlings of nature:

> To-day the woods are trembling through and through
> With shimmering forms, that flash before my view,
> Then melt in green as dawn-stars melt in blue.
>   The leaves that wave against my cheek caress
>   Like women's hands; the embracing boughs express
>   A subtlety of mighty tenderness;
> The copse-depths into little noises start,
> That sound anon like beatings of a heart,
> Anon like talk 'twixt lips not far apart.

Lanier's most successful musical verse is inspired by nature: "Corn," "Song of the Chattahoochee" (LOA, 2: 420), "The Marshes of Glynn," and "Sunrise" (LOA, 2: 403). In these works, the words blend to form something more than poetry – a realm of sound. In his poetry, Lanier is a musical composer, for solo voice, but he also returns to the original function of poetry as a spoken art. Because he designed his poetry to be heard, its effects are more sensuous than intellectual. A parallel act would be reading a musical score and simultaneously hearing an orchestral piece playing in one's head. Few individuals can experience music in this way; the rest of us must actually hear the music being played before we can appreciate the interplay of sounds and themes. To achieve its maximum effect, therefore, Lanier's poetry must be read aloud.

Lippincott's now gave Lanier nationwide exposure, and as a result he was asked by the Atlantic Coast Railroad to write a rail travelers' guide to Florida. The assignment paid generously, and Lanier did it, but he was upset that he had to accept such work to put bread on the table. His great loves, poetry and music, unfortunately did not pay very well, and he had to think of the welfare of his wife and sons. He was often forced to waste precious time and strength and to suffer wounded artistic pride by writing "potboilers" – such as a series for Scribner's of classic tales retold for younger readers.

An assignment of infinitely higher status came from the U.S. Centennial Commission – to write the words of a cantata for the opening day ceremonies of the national exhibition at Fairmount Park in Philadelphia. The *Centennial Meditation of Columbia*, with music by Dudley Buck of Connecticut (an artistic collaboration chosen to symbolize the reconciliation of north and south), was performed in May 1876. For Lanier, this work represented the culmination of his idea of a total aesthetic experience in which words and music were mutually suggestive of each other's meaning. In this year, also, Mary Day Lanier moved to Baltimore with their sons, as Lanier's more secure financial situation made it possible for the family to live together at last.

By 1877, Lanier's activities had become predominantly literary. The only volume of Lanier's poetry to be published during his lifetime appeared during this year, which also saw the appearance of his most popularly acclaimed poem, "Song of the Chattahoochee." Lanier told his father that he had "some suspicion that it is the best poem I ever wrote." It describes the course of the Chattahoochee River from northern Georgia to the Gulf of Mexico. Typically, the poem – as with all of Lanier's nature works – is not merely descriptive, but is a metaphor of life. The call of "the voices of Duty" is more powerful than any distraction along the way. The source of the poem's magic lies in the singing quality of the verse. The steady rhythm, the echoing refrain, and the onomatopoeia all contribute to a rich sensation of sound. Indeed, the musical qualities put the poem in danger of being recited or read in a singsong fashion, which would destroy much of the effect Lanier was trying to create. The poem has been often likened to Alfred, Lord Tennyson's "The Brook" (which Lanier knew), and Philip Graham has compared its musical effects with those of Coleridge's "Song of Glycine" and finds them similar in "tone-color" (*University of Texas Studies in English* 17 [1937]). Actually, the work "Song of the Chattahoochee" most parallels a musical composition written at about the same time, the tone-poem *The Moldau (Vltava)* by the Czech composer Bedřich Smetana (although there is no evidence that Lanier knew this work). This piece also traces, in sound, the progress of a great river from a mountain stream to a broad waterway; indeed, comparing "Song of the Chattahoochee" with *The Moldau* will strengthen an appreciation of both musical poetry and poetic music.

An even clearer artistic parallel exists between Lanier's "The Marshes of Glynn" and Berlioz's *Symphonie Fantastique*. While both works are dreamlike, they are, of course, completely different visions; Berlioz's symphony is a hellish portrayal of an opium-induced nightmare, while Lanier's poem is a meditation on the peace that man can find in nature. But in the progression of symphonic "movements" and in the use of a recurrent motif, the works have strong structural links. For in-

stance, Berlioz employs a repeated musical theme, and Lanier uses the phrase "the length and the breadth and the sweep of the marshes of Glynn." Lanier also varies the meters of the poem, but they blend smoothly, with lines flowing into one another – the poem's short, strong, emphatic lines contrast with its longer, more mellifluous ones:

> Inward and outward to northward and southward the beach-
> lines linger and curl
> As a silver-wrought garment that clings to and follows
> the firm sweet limbs of a girl.

Lanier's last completed poem, "Sunrise," is also a tone poem that thematically complements "The Marshes of Glynn." Along with "The Cloud" (LOA, 2: 409), "Marsh Song – At Sunset" (LOA, 2: 411), "Between Dawn and Sunrise," "A Sunrise Song," and "To the Sun," Lanier intended "Sunrise" to be included in a projected volume titled "Hymns of the Marshes." The shorter lyrics demonstrate Lanier's penchant for seeing the ocean and marshes as a cavalcade of life and literary allusion. But "Sunrise" is the most sustained, sophisticated, and mature statement. The poet wakes to a dawn that promises a communion between his soul and the sun. There is both a premonition of and an acceptance of death. The poem is carefully structured, with Lanier using his strongest devices – the images of nature and the sounds of music – to convey his themes. The poem's short introductory and concluding sections enclose four longer sections. The first three sections represent different "voices" of nature – the woods, the marsh, and the sea – and the fourth is a hymn to the sun. Much like a string quartet in which each instrument has its own themes and then blends with the others to create the sound of a complete ensemble, the poem's distinct voices or lines eventually unite in a harmonious whole at the end. The poem begins and ends with sleep; but the return to sleep at the conclusion will be truly restful for the poet since he has come to a deeper understanding of the universe during the day. Lanier's musical search for the ethereal in nature – which he undertook in the compositions *Black-birds* and *Wind-Song* – has now culminated in an achievement of combined musical sound and intellectual meaning.

Although Lanier's major achievement during his last years was his sustained nature poetry, he continued to write short lyric pieces. But these were more sophisticated than his early song-influenced pieces; these later verses were even more lyrical as a result of his expanded musical experience. A prime example is "A Ballad of Trees and the Master" (LOA, 2: 425), which he wrote in 1880 and originally intended to be placed within "Sunrise." It is a religious poem – Lanier was a man of deep faith – that depicts Jesus in an olive grove. The subject matter, along with the internal rhymes and gentle meter, made this lyric a favorite among American composers in the early 1900s.

Lanier had extended his scholarly interests while in Baltimore and had delivered a very popular series of private lectures, or "parlor classes." Subsequently, he was asked, in 1878, to give a series of lectures on Shakespeare at the Peabody Institute. One of Lanier's dearest hopes was to teach at The Johns Hopkins University, which had just been established in Baltimore in 1876. After proving himself to the Johns Hopkins administration many times over, he was finally invited to join the faculty in the spring of 1879. By this time, his reputation as a lecturer was such that twice as many tickets were requested for his first presentation as were available.

At last, Lanier was fulfilled in the academic life that he had desired since his college days, but unfortunately he had only a little time left to enjoy it. By early 1881, he was quite weak and was forced to deliver his lectures from a chair. In the summer, with his family, Lanier went to western North Carolina, hoping to find relief in the cool air of the mountains. He died there on September 7, 1881; his grave in Baltimore is marked with an inscription from "Sunrise": "I am lit with the Sun." Despite setbacks, which included professional frustrations and increasingly poor health, Lanier remained an optimistic man. He was a cheerful companion who, from all evidence, enriched the lives of his colleagues and friends. He was devoted to his family, loved the arts, and envisioned the arts as beacons to light the path of all humankind. Even in his last days, he was ever hopeful and planning new artistic projects and books.

Despite Lanier's many accomplishments and the great surges of popularity and even adulation that he enjoyed in this country, he has never been granted more than minor literary status by critics. He was not part of any literary "set," nor did he strive to emulate other poets of his day; as a writer, he was truly independent. Although his career was brief, there is still a prodigious literary output to consider seriously for a number of reasons: his poetry delights the imagination and senses, and his prose (particularly the essays and letters) gives us a rich picture of American intellectual and artistic life in the decade and a half following the Civil War. It is as though Lanier was driven to accomplish an incredible amount in a short time. During his Baltimore period, he lectured on Shakespeare and on the English novel; held the honored position of first flute in the Peabody Conservatory orchestra; composed music for flute, voice, and piano; published an acclaimed book on English prosody (*The Science of English Verse*, 1880), as well as many essays on literature and music; wrote many lovely musical compositions; and produced some of the most stylistically original poetry in American literature.

The worlds of poetry and music inspired his strongest efforts and generated works of lasting significance. He envisioned music as symbolic of human harmony, and this belief is epitomized in his oft-quoted line: "Music is Love in search of a word" (from "The Symphony"). He was also deeply concerned with the power of nature, the progressive energy of science, religious faith, and the interrelationship of the arts. His mature poems – most notably "The Symphony," "The Marshes of Glynn," and "Sunrise" – are designed for their sound as much as for their literal meaning. Ironically, music bestowed upon Lanier's verse the qualities that cause it to be both admired and criticized. Music gave it inspiration, rich texture, and rhythm, but a number of critics have pointed out that this texture is *too* rich, "overwritten," or "lush." To use a phrase from "Sunrise," his poetry is sometimes "Over-sated with beauty." Perhaps, if he had been granted more time, he would have been able to tame his "luxuriance," as his contemporary and friend Bayard **Taylor** had suggested. Still, Lanier's creation of synesthetic verses that merge sound and idea into very musical poetry ultimately has secured his reputation.

As with any artist who dies prematurely, there is the problem of attempting to assess an unfulfilled career. Lanier wrote most of his major poetry later in life and was still honing his innovative poetic techniques at the time of his death. As a consequence, much must be left to speculation. What is certain is that Lanier left a remarkable body of work that continues to reward readers. His experiments in the layering and mingling of sound make him one of the most original of American poets. Like the marshes he loved so much, his verses are "beautiful-braided and woven / With intricate shades." And his life continues to inspire contemporary scholars and writers, including science-fiction author Piers Anthony (Lanier is featured in his 1969 *Macroscope*) and poet Andrew Hudgins, whose 1988 verse narrative *After the Lost War* takes on the voice of Lanier and retells the poet's struggles to stay alive during the war and after. Lanier remains a symbol of American individuality and courage, a man who chose not to be an artistic follower, but an explorer and discoverer.

JANE S. GABIN

Selected Works

Centennial Edition of the Works of Sidney Lanier, edited by Charles R. Anderson, et al., 10 vols., Baltimore, Maryland: Johns Hopkins University Press, 1945

Further Reading

Bode, Carl, *Antebellum Culture*, Carbondale: Southern Illinois University Press, 1970

Brown, Calvin S., *Music and Literature*, Athens: University of Georgia Press, 1948

De Bellis, Jack, *Sidney Lanier*, New York: Twayne, 1972

———, *Sidney Lanier, Henry Timrod, and Paul Hamilton Hayne: A Reference Guide*, Boston: G.K. Hall, 1978

Gabin, Jane S., *A Living Minstrelsy: The Poetry and Music of Sidney Lanier*, Macon, Georgia: Mercer University Press, 1985

———, *Southern Excursions: Essays on Mark Twain and Others*, Baton Rouge: Louisiana State University Press, 1971

Lenhart, Charmenz S., *Musical Influence on American Poetry*, Athens: University of Georgia Press, 1956

Mims, Edwin, *Sidney Lanier*, New York: Houghton Mifflin, 1905

Rubin, Louis D., Jr., *William Elliott Shoots a Bear: Essays on the Southern Literary Imagination*, Baton Rouge: Louisiana State University Press, 1976

Starke, Aubrey H., *Sidney Lanier*, Chapel Hill: University of North Carolina Press, 1933, reprinted 1964

Emma Lazarus

(1849–1887)

When Emma Lazarus died in 1887, her place in American letters seemed assured. A celebrated author of poetry, translations, and prose, she had won the acclaim of many leading literary figures. Today, however, Lazarus is known only as the writer who penned the words "Give me your tired, your poor, / Your huddled masses yearning to breathe free" ("The New Colossus," LOA, 2 :457), which are inscribed at the base of the Statue of Liberty. Her other works have been relegated to the margins of literary study. Long out of print, her books are nearly inaccessible, and only a handful or scholars are familiar with her oeuvre. But along with that of many other nineteenth-century women poets, Lazarus's work is currently being reclaimed, and her contribution to American literature revalued.

Lazarus spent the 38 years of her life in an America that underwent vast political upheaval but produced little substantive change in the codes that governed women's lives. Starting in 1845, the United States expanded to include California, Oregon, Texas, New Mexico, Alaska, and the southern portion of what is now Arizona, under the doctrine of manifest destiny. With these additions, the country increased its domain by about two-thirds and gained access to the Pacific Ocean. One year before Lazarus's birth, gold was discovered in California, and the cross-continental movement continued as more citizens heeded Horace Greeley's gendered advice, "Go West, young man." It was also in 1848 that the first women's rights convention was held in Seneca Falls, New York. During Lazarus's lifetime, immigration increased dramatically, with the Jewish population alone growing sixfold, from 50,000 in 1850 to 300,000 in 1880. In her brief span, Lazarus lived through the Civil War, the assassinations of Presidents Lincoln (1865) and Garfield (1881), and the tumultuous aftereffects of these events.

It was during these years of turmoil that Emma Lazarus came of age as both a woman and a poet. The society in which she wrote was largely antagonistic toward women who desired to participate in activities beyond the domestic sphere. Lazarus herself, moreover, was caught in a double-bind created by two overlapping concepts of ideal womanhood: the "true woman," a product of the dominant Christian culture that privileged attributes of piety, purity, submissiveness, and domesticity; and the "mother in Israel," a product of patriarchal Judaic culture. Drawing on Old Testament figures such as Deborah, the figure of the mother in Israel exemplified some of the cardinal virtues of the true woman but diverged from the latter figure in important ways. While the true woman strove to provide a haven for her husband in order to shield him from temptation, the mother in Israel was charged to provide a sanctuary in which her husband could study and practice his religion uninterrupted. Whereas the true woman's duty involved mainly her family, the duty of the mother in Israel extended beyond her family to the Jewish nation: she was called upon to keep the flame of Judaism burning in the hearts of her husband and children. Men and women who accepted these sanctioned feminine ideals were secure in the beliefs that women were dependent creatures and inferior to men and that God had not meant for women to participate in such "male" activities as public speaking, signing legal documents, or voting. Thus, women had practically no public voice – except when, like Lazarus, they could reach a larger audience through the written word.

Born on July 22, 1849, in New York, the fourth daughter of a wealthy Jewish family, Lazarus received an unusual private education. Unlike most nineteenth-century women authors, who had little formal training and wrote as a way to support their families, she had the education and the leisure to hone her poetic skills. Moses Lazarus, an enlightened father, supported and encouraged his talented daughter in her intellectual pursuits. The young Emma was trained in the classics and studied Italian, French, and German. Subsequently, her father underwrote the publication of her first book of poetry when she was 17, *Poems and Translations: Written Between the Ages of Fourteen and Sixteen* (1867–68).

Nonetheless, Lazarus was still a product of her times. According to her sister Josephine, who wrote the introduction to Lazarus's posthumously published collected poems, *The Poems of Emma Lazarus* (1889), she was "a true woman, too distinctly feminine to wish to be exceptional, or to stand alone and apart, even by virtue of superiority." To the degree that it implies a Christian model of womanhood, Josephine Lazarus's use of the phrase "true woman" in conjunction with her Zionist sister is unintentionally ironic. Josephine characterizes the poet as shy, retiring, and uninterested in the value general readers and critics placed on her work. As Dan Vogel has pointed out, however, Lazarus's actions contradict her sister's sentimental words. She traveled, began correspondences with renowned authors, and sent them poems, asking for their critiques (which she often ignored).

One of Lazarus's most famous exchanges was with Ralph Waldo **Emerson**, whom she met in 1868. She admired the "Sage of Concord" and sent him a copy of her first book, which in turn initiated their correspondence. Clearly involved in a mentoring relationship, Lazarus took much of Emerson's advice to heart. A sonnet that demonstrates his influence on the young poet is "Long Island Sound" (LOA, 2: 461), which transfigures the commonplace and lends freshness to nature imagery. Her training and her gift, however, could not be grafted onto Emerson's philosophy. Much of Lazarus's early work draws on her training in classical, continental, and British literature for both form and content. For three years, however, Emerson tried to make of Lazarus the kind of poet he wished her to be. He praised her poems but also offered suggestions for revision, sometimes going so far as to rewrite lines. Lazarus dutifully tried to incorporate his changes, while independently continuing to write on subjects that were anathemas to him. For instance, he disapproved of her rewriting of classical myths and tried to dissuade her from such endeavors: "Though you can throw yourself so heartily into the old world of Memory, the high success must ever be to penetrate unto and show the celestial element in the despised Present."

Nonetheless, Lazarus refused to give up her interest in "the old world of Memory" and, in fact, dedicated her retelling of the Admetus/Alcestis myth to Emerson. He reluctantly accepted the dedication, but their working relationship seems to have ended. She no longer sent him poems, and their diminishing correspondence became perfunctory. Three years after the publication of her second book, *Admetus and Other Poems* (1871), Emerson put together the anthology *Parnassus*; not one of Lazarus's poems was included. Stung by his rejection, she fired off a letter to him saying, "I felt as if I had won for myself by my own efforts a place in any collection of American poets, and I find myself treated with absolute contempt in the very quarter where I had been encouraged to build my fondest hopes."

These interactions deserve comment for the light they shed not only on Lazarus's poetic career but also on her personality. Shy and retiring young women do not send unsolicited manuscripts to established writers of Emerson's stature; women who are supposedly disinterested in their reception would not care whether their poems appeared in anthologies; certainly, such women also would not write hurt, angry letters taking the editor to task. These are not the actions of a deferential "true woman." Eventually, and in spite of past differences, Lazarus was invited to spend a week with the Emersons at Concord, and their friendship was re-established.

As a Jew and an American woman, Lazarus was constrained by both contemporary models of womanhood. In fact, one of her poems, "Echoes" (LOA, 2: 457), explicitly deals with the plight of the woman poet in America, and it met with the same fate from many male critics that, say, Anne Bradstreet's "Prologue" did more than 200 years earlier. On the surface, both poems seem to denigrate woman's capacity to write about anything but sentimental, domestic issues. Feminist critics, however, have noted the irony of Bradstreet's opening lines: "To sing of wars, of captains, and of kings, / Of cities founded, commonwealths begun, / For my mean pen are too superior things." Lazarus picks up the same theme and tone:

> Late-born and woman-souled I dare not hope,
> The freshness of the elder lays, the might
> Of manly, modern passion shall alight
> Upon my Muse's lips, nor may I cope
> (Who veiled and screened by womanhood must grope)
> With the world's strong-armed warriors and recite
> The dangers, wounds, and triumphs of the fight.

The poem concludes with the persona offering "elf-music," since that is the only expression of poetic gifts allowed to women. A poem like "Echoes" subtly portrays the poet as a subversive (if also necessarily "veiled") critic of "true women" who are too weak and fragile to attempt "men's topics." Long before "Echoes" appeared, however, Lazarus had been rewriting myths and translating poems dealing with quite "unwomanly" subjects. If any doubt remains, certainly her last two books of poetry belie such self-effacement. There is no "elf-music" in *Songs of a Semite* (1882) or *By the Waters of Babylon* (1887).

In fact, much of her work published after 1881 focuses on strong, "manly" subjects that were supposedly outside a woman's purview. That year marked a turning point in Lazarus's career. Renewed persecution of Jews in Russia and Poland caused untold suffering, and the pogroms forced many Russian and Eastern European Jews to flee to America. In Lazarus scholarship, one of the most heated controversies cen-

ters on the pogroms' effect on the poet's Jewish identity. Some critics assert that until the pogroms occurred, Lazarus had no Jewish consciousness. Others maintain that the outrages of 1881 caused her to refocus her attention from the thirteenth- and fourteenth-century persecutions of the Jews to the present. Morris Schappes casts matters in historical and demographic terms; until the pogroms and massive immigration began, no need existed for fiery poems that called her coreligionists to action: "In this context, her interest in Jewry was extensive but placid. She felt herself confronted with no *problems* that she and other Jews had to solve. No action was required. Her sympathies were all with the oppressed, whose history she was reading, but it was a passive sympathy because she saw no present issue." The pogroms, which began in 1879, gained terrible force by 1881. At this time, Lazarus revalued her Jewish heritage, became politically active, and began the drive for a Jewish homeland. Lazarus emerged as a leading spokesperson for the plight of the Jews and worked to raise the consciousness of American Jews about the circumstances of their brothers and sisters. A regular visitor to Ward's Island, a major immigration center, she witnessed firsthand the inhumanity to Jewish men, women, and children perpetrated by those in power abroad. Active in fundraising and in writing polemics for the *American Hebrew*, she also wrote and translated numerous poems that centered on the continuing persecution of world Jewry.

Many scholars believe that Lazarus's strongest work emerged in this period. The explicitly titled *Songs of a Semite* leaves no doubt that by 1882, she had embraced the Jewish cause. She worked indefatigably, writing a series of essays in 1882–83 that was posthumously published in 1900 as *Epistles to the Hebrews*. She also undertook the study of the Hebrew language to understand more thoroughly the nuances of Jewish thought. One of the first modern American Zionists, Lazarus called for a Jewish homeland for all Jews – except those living in the United States. The latter, she believed, had no need for a separate Jewish state since they were citizens of a country that offered both protection from persecution and redress if it occurred.

Interestingly, Lazarus wrote the poem for which she is famous as part of a fundraising effort. Congress had allocated money for the erection of Frédéric Bartholdi's statue but had not provided funding for a pedestal on which to place it. A committee of concerned citizens contacted Lazarus and other famous authors, asking for manuscripts that they could auction during the Bartholdi Statue Pedestal Art Loan Exhibition. Although "The New Colossus" has drawn a mixed critical reaction, in December 1883 James Russell **Lowell** wrote to Lazarus in praise of it:

> I must write again to say how much I like your sonnet about the statue – much better than I like the Statue itself. But your sonnet gives its subject a *raison d'être* which it wanted before much as it wants a pedestal. You have set it on a noble one, saying admirably just the right word to be said, an achievement more arduous than that of the sculptor.

Lazarus had experimented with some of the words, ideas, and phrasing of her poem in honor of the statue in an earlier effort, "1492" (LOA, 2: 464). This poem calls the year of the title "two-faced . . . Mother of Change and Fate," because it saw both the expulsion of Jews from Spain and Columbus's encounter with the American continent, which she viewed as offering an escape hatch for European Jews: "Hounded from sea to sea, from state to state, / The West refused them, the East abhorred. / No anchorage the known world could afford." The words "Ho, all who weary, enter here!" anticipate those of "The New Colossus," as does the idea of the lamp of truth in "Gifts" and "In Exile" (LOA, 2: 462). In "The New Colossus," Lazarus figures the United States as "Mother of Exiles," the all-embracing maternal figure who turns no one away, and the poem also contrasts the classical statue overlooking the waterway to Rhodes to the very different figure overlooking New York harbor whose "beacon-hand / Glows world-wide welcome." At the dedication of the statue, Lazarus's poem was recited; later, the words were engraved on the pedestal. To greet twentieth-century exiles who arrive by air, the last few lines now appear on a wall at Kennedy International Airport in New York.

That the United States became, for many Jews who had fled persecution, just the haven Lazarus envisions is suggested by "In Exile." The poem is based on a letter from a Russian refugee living in Texas, who wrote, "Since that day till now our life is one unbroken paradise. We live a true brotherly life. Every evening after supper we take a seat under the mighty oak and sing our songs." The first two stanzas of "In Exile" provide a portrait of pastoral life at twilight. The third stanza then compares these exiles with "the hounded stag that has escaped the pack," "the unimprisoned bird," the "martyr, granted respite," and "the death-doomed victim pardoned from his cell." Lazarus cites "the joy these exiles gain, – / Life's sharpest rapture is surcease of pain."

Lazarus's interest in current events, however, was not limited to those involving the Jewish people. Two poems, "1856" and "1879," commemorate the birth and death of Napoleon III's son, the Prince Imperial. In addition, "April 27th, 1865" and "The Mother's Prayer" focus on the assassination of Abraham Lincoln; the first is written from the point of view of John Wilkes Booth, the second from that of Booth's mother. Although these poems clearly condemn the murder of the president, they also evince sympathy for the wounded and hunted Booth who was desperately seeking shelter after the assassination. "Sic Semper Libertoribus," written upon the death of Alexander II of Russia in March 1881, and "Sunrise," dealing with the murder of President Garfield in September 1881, center on the loss of assassinated leaders.

A lifelong admirer of Heine, Lazarus translated portions of his oeuvre and felt a mystical kinship with him. After all, he, too, was a Jew holding a secular worldview, one who also admired the figures of classical mythology. This kinship appears in "Venus of the Louvre" (LOA, 2: 458), which is based on Heine's last visit to the statue:

> . . . at her feet a pale, death-stricken Jew,
> Her life adorer, sobbed farewell to love.
> Here *Heine* wept! Here still he weeps anew,
> Nor ever shall his sorrow lift or move,
> While mourns one ardent heart, one poet-brain,
> For vanished Hellas and Hebraic pain.

Lazarus demonstrates her abiding interest in classical mythology in the unusual poem "The Cranes of Ibycus" (LOA,

2: 458), which also refers to the legend of Faust and Helen. Briefly, the myth involves a man who is accosted and murdered by robbers. In his last moments, he observes a flock of cranes flying overhead and cries out to them to avenge his death. Later, while attending the theater in Corinth, the robbers see a flock of cranes in the distance; one of the robbers guiltily exclaims, "Lo the avengers of Ibycus," and thus identifies himself to the audience as the murderer. As Vogel points out, "the cranes of Ibycus became to Lazarus symbolic of divine inspiration." Lazarus's first poem to be anthologized, "The Cranes of Ibycus" appeared in Edmund Clarence **Stedman's** *Poets of America* in 1885.

Lazarus's poems include a group of sonnets that attempt to cross the boundary between music and poetry. Influenced by the composers Robert Schumann and Frédéric Chopin, these sonnets, Vogel asserts, "represent a notion in Lazarus' mind that music is translatable into poems." One cycle consists of eight sections that correspond to Schumann's *Phantasiestücke*; it is titled "Symphonic Studies (After Robert Schumann)." The poems appeared in *Lippincott's* in 1878. Another cycle, the terza rima "Phantasies (After Robert Schumann)" (LOA, 2:456), shows the imprint of her tutelage under Emerson, who believed that natural facts symbolize spiritual facts. Lazarus proclaims:

> Familiar things stand not for what they are:
>
> What they suggest, foreshadow, or recall
> The spirit is alert to apprehend,
> Imparting somewhat of herself to all.

What follows is a catalog of concertized, commonplace sounds that come close to imitating music; the poem recalls Edgar Allan **Poe's** "Tintinnabulation."

Lazarus also ventured into the writing of verse dramas, including *The Spagnoletto* and *Dance to Death*. The first, a three-act drama based on the life of José de Ribera, the Spanish baroque painter, presents a melodramatic tale of greed, seduction, disinheritance, and death. The *Dance to Death*, a dramatization of Richard Reinhard's prose narrative, *Der Tanz zum Tode* (1877), details the martyrdom of the Jews of Nordhausen, Germany, in May 1349. Lazarus dedicates this poem to George Eliot "for elevating and ennobling the spirit of Jewish nationality" in *Daniel Deronda*.

Diagnosed with cancer, Lazarus struggled to continue writing and even traveled abroad during the last year of her life. Replicating Heine's visit to the statue of Venus in the Louvre, she made her own pilgrimage to the "goddess without arms / Who could not help." On November 19, 1887, the voice of this champion of the oppressed was silenced.

CHERI LOUISE ROSS

Selected Works

Poems and Translations, New York: H. O. Houghton, 1866
Admetus and Other Poems, New York: Hurd and Houghton, 1871
Alide: An Episode of Goethe's Life, Philadelphia: J. B. Lippincott, 1874
Poems and Ballads of Heinrich Heine, translator, New York: R. Worthington, 1881
Songs of a Semite: The Dance to Death and Other Poems, New York: American Hebrew, 1882

By the Waters of Babylon: "Little Poems in Prose," New York: American Hebrew, 1887

The Poems of Emma Lazarus, 2 vols., New York: Houghton Mifflin, 1889

Emma Lazarus: Selections from Her Poetry and Prose, edited by Morris U. Schappes, New York: Cooperative Book League, 1944

Letters of Emma Lazarus, edited by Morris U. Schappes, New York: New York Public Library, 1949

Further Reading

Angoff, Charles, *Emma Lazarus: Poet, Jewish Activist, Pioneer Activist,* New York: Jewish Historical Society of New York, 1979

Harap, Louis, *The Image of the Jew in American Literature,* Philadelphia: Jewish Publication Society of America, 1974

Jacob, H. E., *The World of Emma Lazarus,* New York: Schocken, 1943

Lichtenstein, Diane, *Writing Their Nations: The Tradition of Nineteenth-Century American Jewish Women Writers,* Bloomington: Indiana University Press, 1992

Rusk, Ralph I., *Letters to Emma Lazarus in the Columbia University Library,* New York: Columbia University Press, 1939

Vogel, Dan, *Emma Lazarus,* Boston: Twayne, 1980

Wagenknecht, Edward, *Daughters of the Covenant: Portraits of Six Jewish Women,* Amherst: University of Massachusetts Press, 1983

James Mathewes Legaré

(1823–1859)

Along with Henry **Timrod** and Paul Hamilton **Hayne**, Legaré was one of the second-generation Charleston poets who matured during the literary reign of William Gilmore **Simms**. Although he was nearly forgotten in the aftermath of the Civil War, his carefully crafted poems about the South Carolina woodlands have secured for him a firm position among the minor southern poets of his day.

Legaré (pronounced luh-GREE) was born on November 26, 1823 to a prominent Charleston family, which included his distant cousin Hugh Swinton Legaré, the editor of the *Southern Review,* and the attorney general in President John Tyler's cabinet. The poet's father, John D. Legaré, founded and edited the *Southern Agriculturalist* before building and operating a health resort in southwestern Virginia. In 1838, J. D. Legaré returned to Charleston and opened an agricultural store. James Legaré attended the College of Charleston. He received his diploma in 1842, and then moved north for a year at St. Mary's College in Baltimore. Near the nation's capital, he regularly visited Hugh S. Legaré, who was by this time serving as interim secretary of state. Hugh's death in June 1843, occasioned one of Legaré's better-known poems, the elegy "On the Death of a Kinsman," which laments the great man's "Icarus like" fall:

I see an Eagle winging to the sun –
Who sayeth him nay?
He glanceth down from where his wing hath won:
His heart is stout, his flight is scarce begun, –
O hopes of clay!

While in Baltimore, Legaré published his first poems pseudonymously in Simms's magazine *The Magnolia.* He also concocted an elaborate hoax, which worked up a bogus Legaré genealogy that dated back to A.D. 912. A few months after his return to Charleston in 1843, he buried the false document so that a servant would find it; upon its discovery, news of the Legaré's "noble" roots created a minor sensation and made newspapers as far away as Boston before the hoax was uncovered.

In Charleston, Legaré obtained a position in the legal office of James Louis Petigru, a prominent attorney who later employed both Timrod and Hayne. At this time, he published a poem – a sentimental tribute entitled "My Sister" – that was the first to appear under his own name. After a series of lung hemorrhages, Legaré journeyed to northern Georgia, where he visited Toccoa and Tallulah Falls, both of which he later celebrated in verse. He continued to write steadily, publishing several lyrics in Simms's *Southern and Western Monthly Magazine and Review* and a longer narrative poem, "Du Saye: A Legend of the Congaree," in Simms's 1845 gift miscellany, *The Charleston Book.* Set against the backdrop of Francis Marion's Revolutionary War skirmishes – material Simms had also used for his verse and prose – "Du Saye" recounts the title character's attempt to rescue his bride from Tarleton's Redcoats, who had interrupted the couple's wedding to take her prisoner. Although much of the poem is marred by affectation and awkward syntax, certain passages show the hand of a true poet. The battle scene in which the Swamp Fox (Marion) vainly tries to rescue the beleaguered couple, for example, skillfully blends impressionistic imagery with a confident use of strong meter, evocative vowel patterns, and slant rhyme:

And all is rage, revenge, and fear,
And shout and answering groan;
Down trampling hoof, and flash and shout,
And shot at random thrown:
Till to the river's blood-tracked beach
The remnant faint is borne.

In 1846, with his financial assets dwindling, J. D. Legaré moved his family to Aiken, South Carolina, just across the Georgia border from Augusta. His son James's fragile health – he died of tuberculosis at the age of 35 – was one motivating factor, as the dry, mosquito-free environment of Aiken was considered salubrious. There, Legaré supported himself by painting, writing for magazines, and even opening (for a year) a finishing school for local girls. With his father, he attempted to begin a literary digest and enrolled support from, among others, former vice president John C. Calhoun. Like many of his projects, the digest never materialized. In 1848, Legaré was confirmed as an Episcopalian at Saint Thaddeus' Church, where he remained a devout communicant and eventually served as senior warden. In the same year, William D. Ticknor of Boston brought out, at the author's expense, Legaré's only volume of poetry, *Orta-Undis and Other Poems,* whose Latin title means "sprung from waves." Although reviews were generally positive, Legaré quickly became dissatisfied with the work and claimed in a letter to Thomas Powell that "with the exception of scarce three poems I am ashamed of the contents already, although it has been out little more than eighteen months or so."

In March 1850, Legaré married Anne C. Andrews of Augusta, Georgia. He continued to write verse, although he began to concentrate his literary efforts on fiction. He published romantic adventure stories, often set in exotic locales, in many of the day's leading magazines. Curtis Carroll Davis, Legaré's biographer, is on the mark when he claims that Legaré's fiction is "by today's standards, third-rate at best." Legaré planned and abandoned other projects, among them a "History of the conquest and civil wars of the Pacific Islands." For this project, he wrote a letter to Henry Wadsworth **Longfellow** and asked for aid in research. In 1852, Legaré set up adjacent to his parent's house a shop in which he developed several inventions. Although his efforts in perfecting a perpetual motion machine were predictably futile, he enjoyed some success with improved colored tiles, a cheaper glazier's putty, and plastic cotton, a chemically treated cotton compound that was easily molded, yet hard and durable after it had dried. He was at work on a more efficient dual-air engine when his health declined. He died on May 30, 1859, and was buried in Saint Thaddeus' churchyard in Aiken.

Although Legaré's poetry broke no new ground, Jay B. Hubbell is justified in claiming that his poems "reveal a more careful and competent workmanship than those of all but three or four of his Southern contemporaries." For example, "Tallulah" (LOA, 2: 134), which Ludwig Lewisohn singled out as an example of the "originality of technique which he alone possesses of all the minor Carolina writers of verse," shows the poet dexterously handling a complicated seven-line stanza: an *xabbcca* rhyme scheme with alternating tetrameter, dimeter, and trimeter lines. The envelope rhyme and driving rhythm – accentuated by the concluding trochees in lines 1, 3, 4, 5, and 6 – owe something to Edgar Allan **Poe's** "The Raven" (LOA, 1: 535). Legaré admired the older poet; in an 1849 letter to the editor of the *Southern Literary Messenger*, John R. Thompson, Legaré said that Poe's "poems rank first among my pet books, those almost-sacred few kept on a small shelf apart from mere library volumes." Unlike its companion piece, "Toccoa," in which the falls assume a feminine benevolence, "Tallulah" (whose Cherokee name Legaré gives as "the terrible") shows the waterfall taking on an ominous "giant shape":

> Vast and ponderous, of granite,
> Cloud enwrapt his features were.
> In his great calm eyes emotion
> Glimmered none; and like an ocean
> Billowy, tangled,
> Foam bespangled
> Backward streamed his hair.

The syntactical irregularity of this stanza – in prose, the first two lines would be "His vast and ponderous granite features were cloud enwrapt" – is characteristic of Legaré's verse. Occasionally, this technique appears as an affectation, but when used skillfully, as it is here, it effectively foregrounds the tangibility and vitality of Legaré's poetic language.

Like many of his Southern contemporaries (Simms, Timrod, and Hayne) and successors (Sidney **Lanier** and Madison **Cawein**), Legaré is acutely perceptive of the natural world and often blurs the boundary between speaker and scene. In such cases, the speaker's emotional projection onto the nonsentient world invokes the pathetic fallacy; this invocation – along with the poet's often overt didacticism – may account for Legaré's neglect by scholars of southern literature during the age of critics John Crowe Ransom and Allen Tate. Usually, nature is benevolent in Legaré's works, and even in such a poem as "Tallulah," the chthonic "phantom" recedes into a providential realm where "Higher power / Guards each flower." Like Simms, Legaré has a naturalist's eye; Davis has noted his frequent references to birds (the owl, mockingbird, crow, and wood dove), trees (the pine, oak, cypress, and willow), and flowers (the rose, haw blossom, yellow jasmine, laurel, and lily). "The manuscript of Nature's book / Is open spread to every eye," he writes in "The Book of Nature"; Legaré reads it well:

> The solemn brotherhood of pines,
> Like monks slow chaunting in the choir,
> *Nos miserere*: Cypress nuns
> In sad attire.

Unlike his transcendentalist contemporaries, however, Legaré infuses nature with a thoroughly Christian component and counsels his readers in the poem's final stanza to "Believe that God, in fruit or bloom, / Works out some good." Owing to his classical education, figures from Greek mythology are likely to appear as well.

The echoes of Renaissance humanism in "The Book of Nature" resonate in Legaré's love poetry, although less successfully. "Last Gift" employs Petrarchan conventions that Shakespeare found tired, and the love poems as a group suffer from the over-abstraction and idealization of the beloved. They do, however, suggest genuine emotion; we have little reason to doubt Legaré's claim – in response to critics' charges of affectation – that "I write only when touched to the soul or moved by some more transient emotion – and all I say is verily out of my heart." Too often, however, emotion out of the poet's heart rushes headlong to the printed page, and we are left with stanzas like: "Thy hair is brown, thy eyes are gray, / And many tender things they say; / (Sweet eyes, thus speak to me alway!)." Generally, Legaré's poems of conjugal and platonic love (the stanza above comes from "To My Very Dear Sister") lack the technical finish and the concrete quality that distinguish his nature poems.

"To a Lily" (LOA, 2: 133), which weaves a nature motif into a love poem, is a notable exception. Legaré's most often anthologized poem, "To a Lily" communicates a more muted, deeper emotion by constructing a celebration in absentia. Although the beloved's role as audience has been assumed by the flower, she nonetheless remains the recipient of the poet's praise:

> Go bow thy head in gentle spite,
> Thou lily white.
> For she who spies thee waving here,
> With thee in beauty can compare
> As day with night.

Like his unorthodox syntax, the two-stress line seen here is a Legaré trademark, a type of line that he often uses to avoid the too predictable, dog-trot rhythm that plagues his weaker verse. Like "Tallulah," "To a Lily" is formally sophisticated. The initial couplet of each stanza, with their end rhymes separated by only two stresses, might degenerate into a rather mechanical pattern if the primary caesura were not placed alternately after the fourth, third, fourth, and second foot. Similarly, the frequently enjambed lines suggest rhythms that a more strictly enforced pattern would eliminate. The fourth and final stanza combines almost absurd projection and injunction with hyperbolic praise, but within a measured cadence that formalizes and sustains the emotion:

> Inconsolate, bloom not again
> Thou rival vain
> Of her whose charms have thine outdone:
> Whose purity might spot the sun,
> And make thy leaf a stain.

Although Legaré is at his best working with short lyrics, he also wrote several longer poems. Despite its rather heavy-handed moralizing, "Ornithologoi" ("bird voices") contains passages that effectively capture the birds' "Sounds full of mystery." "Ahab-Mahommed" tells the story of a king who shares his last loaf of bread with an angel disguised as a beggar, even though the king's palace is being besieged by Medes. Although the didacticism is again obtrusive (the angel responds to this act of mercy by dispersing the enemy), the poem's rich verbal texture suggests its exotic Oriental setting: "From the high ceiling, perfume breathing, hung / Lamps rich, pomegranate-shaped, and golden-swung." "Thanatokallos" ("beauty in death"), Legaré's only poem in blank verse, is a Christian rewriting of William Cullen **Bryant's** "Thanatopsis" (LOA, 1: 122). In a letter to Evert and George Duyckinck, Legaré lamented that although he admired the "nobleness of ['Thanatopsis'] *as a poem*," he found it unfortunate "that so masterly a poet should have taught so sad a doctrine." The speaker of "Thanatokallos" rejects mourning rituals that "invest / A deathbed with a horror not its own": "I think we faint and weep more than is manly; / I think we more mistrust, than Christians should." Later in the poem, a widow is urged to "Thank GOD instead / That he who was so dear to thee, released / From sin and care, at length has found great peace." The blank verse of the poem, as well as the cadences and parallel phrasings taken from the King James Bible, are well-suited to the Christian stoicism Legaré counsels.

Conspicuous by their absence in Legaré's verse are any treatments of slavery or secession. On the former issue, Legaré was reticent and mentioned it only once in the writings that have come down to us. In an 1853 letter to Longfellow, with whom he carried on a long and cordial correspondence, Legaré calls slavery "a vile but hopelessly necessary American institution." With regard to secession, he was more vocal, decrying in a letter to John R. Thompson, "Heaven help us . . . in case of a Disunion!" Several of his short stories mention secession. Most notably, the narrator of "Pedro de Padilh" castigates those "military young men" who call for "a dissolution of the Union." With respect to these issues, Legaré is quite the opposite of his contemporaries Simms and Timrod, for whom the defense of the south and southern ways became dominant poetic themes in the years leading up to the Civil War. Nevertheless, it is as a member of this group that Legaré should continue to be read; the wholesome commerce with nature that finds powerful expression in his work is the enduring theme of the southern poetry of the period.

SCOTT ROMINE

Selected Works
Orta-Undis and Other Poems, Boston: W. D. Ticknor, 1848

Further Reading
Davis, Curtis Carroll, *That Ambitious Mr. Legaré*, Columbia: University of South Carolina Press, 1971
Rubin, Louis D., et al., eds., *The History of Southern Literature*, Baton Rouge: Louisiana State University Press, 1985

Charles Godfrey Leland

(1824–1903)

Leland would not choose for us to remember him as a poet. Instead, he would likely direct our attention to his accomplishments as a linguist, translator, or promoter of the practical arts in education. Yet, ironically, it is as a poet that twentieth-century readers most often encounter him. Leland considered his greatest accomplishment to be the discovery and recording of Shelta, a little-known tinker's language akin to Romany or Gypsy discourse. That he should instead remain associated with his garrulous, beer-drinking creation Hans Breitmann would not surprise him, however; it was as such that he was most commonly identified in his lifetime. In 1894, he wrote to a friend from Florence: "I don't dislike my *Breitmann Ballads* – indeed I love many of them – but I am sometimes highly pained when I find that people know nothing else about me." And although there is a great deal more to know, we come back to the character of Hans Breitmann, which was Leland's most enduring contribution to nineteenth-century literature. Despite his creator's many protests to the contrary, however, Breitmann is more than Leland's imaginary projection. He is a picaro who shares many of Leland's own life experiences. By doing so, Hans allows the poet to mark the passage of his own existence and chronicle fictional resolutions to the conflicts Leland found nearly insurmountable – namely, the animosities sparked by the Civil War and his own urge to counteract the mutability that otherwise rendered him powerless.

Leland could never satisfactorily account for Breitmann's popularity. He explained in the introduction to an 1871 collection that the "lyrics were written for a laugh – without anticipating publication." Yet speculation about that popularity reveals much, not only about Leland as a poet but about the American society for which he wrote. Ravaged by sectional tension and sobered by its consequences, Civil War America found little to ease its beleaguered existence. Hans Breitmann stumbled unwittingly into the country's troubled midst. As Elizabeth Robins Pennell, Leland's niece and biographer, pointed out, Hans could "make people laugh at a moment when laughter was not easy." While Hans, too, was depicted as fighting for the Union and fully understanding the tragedy of civil war, he also was "enough of a foreigner to carry the country's burden lightly." To credit Leland with recognizing the country's need for relief and consciously setting out to meet that need is to overestimate his perceptive ability. Yet the poet did capitalize on his discovery in order to create a comical character who was larger than life.

The scope of Leland's poetry, however, extends beyond the dialect of that alternately philosophical and intoxicated German American, Hans Breitmann. Leland's complete works remain uncollected; much of his poetry is scattered throughout the periodicals of his day, buried within his writing in other genres, or lost to public view because it appears only in first editions that are now difficult to obtain. Yet a survey of that verse reveals that in addition to comic poetry, he wrote a spate of conventional nineteenth-century stanzas, as well as hauntingly Edgar Allan **Poe**-like verses that exhibit, like Poe's works, a fascination with dreamlike states and death. Further, Leland did not always temper his Civil War poetry with the comic overtones of Hans Breitmann. Violent imagery characterizes much of the verse from this period, and Leland intended that a great deal of this poetry, along with the essays he was then publishing, should be an instrument to bolster flagging Union morale. In that respect, then, Leland becomes a Union counterpart to Henry **Timrod**, the widely touted poet of the Confederacy. Thus, the range of Leland's work is more varied and more significant than either Leland or the critics of two different centuries have suspected.

Charles Godfrey Leland was born on August 15, 1824 in Philadelphia, Pennsylvania, to Charlotte Godfrey Leland and Charles Leland. His father was a prominent local merchant and, reputedly, the descendant of Henry Leland, a Puritan who settled in Massachusetts in 1636. According to Leland himself, many of his exotic interests in later life came from the experiences of his early youth. His nurse, for instance, was a Dutch woman named Van der Poel who was rumored to be a sorceress. She performed a ritual on the infant Leland that used incantations to secure his "rising in life." Sorceress or no, Van der Poel's powers had little effect on Leland's scholastic performance; he was never an outstanding student. He received his education primarily in Philadelphia and briefly attended Bronson **Alcott's** experimental school in 1835. In his own words, however, that experience "was indeed going from the frying-pan into the very fire, so far as curing idleness and desultory habits and a tendency to romance and wild speculation was concerned. For Mr. Alcott was the most eccentric man who ever took it on himself to train and form the youthful mind." Leland early discovered a penchant for reading, which was offset by a hopeless ineptitude in mathematics. He recalled reading William Shakespeare as early as age six or seven, and by 1840, he had read extensively in Edmund Spenser, Thomas Carlyle, Baruch Spinoza, Friedrich Schelling, Immanuel Kant, and Johann Fichte, in addition to reading American authors like James Fenimore Cooper, Washington Irving, and Ralph Waldo **Emerson**. He developed among his adolescent tastes a particular interest in the supernatural. The result of this varied literary diet was that his horizons broadened beyond Philadelphia and his intellect quickened, but, as Pennell reports, his studies "carried him far from the practical world in which his father wanted to see him shine. And worst of all, it made him appear 'peculiar,' 'eccentric,' in the Philadelphia of the thirties and forties." Sadly, Leland felt for most of his life that he had disappointed his father, although he provides no concrete evidence in his *Memoirs* to support that claim. Instead, he records what appears in its harshest interpretation to have been paternal resignation to his son's interests. Leland notes, for instance, that his father often brought him books and even purchased for him a share in the Philadelphia Library.

Leland wrote poetry as early as age 10 or 11, and he first published his work shortly before his sixteenth birthday. Two of his poems appeared in a July 1840 issue of Philadelphia's *Daily Chronicle and General Advertiser;* both poems are fairly conventional in theme, form, and tone. Lamenting separation from a lost love, one poem asks, "Oh! will those happy hours return, / When we shall love as once before, / When I shall clasp thee to my breast, / And live with thee for evermore?" Entering Princeton in 1842, Leland already had a book-length publication to his credit: *The May Breezes*, a translation of German songs. At Princeton, Leland wrote regularly for the *Nassau Monthly*, often using the pen name "Carlos." His first article was an essay on the history of English poetry; he subsequently wrote on "European Prose Fiction," "Science and Poetry," the "History of Secret Societies," and "National Songs." He also published a number of poems in the college paper, most of them in the vein of earlier efforts. The poet was expelled briefly from college for participating in a minor freshman rebellion, but was soon allowed to return and graduated next-to-last in his class in 1845. Nonetheless, Leland was chosen to write the valedictory poem, although he did not read it at commencement. Pennell suspects that "youthful pride" prevented him from participating in the ceremony, while Leland recalled that he declined the honor because he felt himself unworthy.

Retrospectively, Leland lamented that his sheltered upbringing had left him upon graduation "morally where most boys in the United States are at twelve or thirteen." After graduation, he embarked with his cousin Samuel Godfrey on a European tour, which he took partly for his health (which remained delicate) and partly to continue his studies. His father later told him there was "an expression of innocence or goodness and gentleness [in his eyes] which he never saw again." Samuel went home after a short time, but Leland remained until 1848 and traveled throughout most of Europe. In 1846, he matriculated at the University of Heidelberg, and in 1847, he began attending the University of Munich. His immersion in German culture had begun.

That Leland viewed Germans humorously from his first exposure is evident in his letters. In 1846, he wrote to William Tiffany: "These young men fight about four duels, more or less, daily, and average each from 18 to 30 schoppens of beer daily." His letters home also show a marked preference for Germany over any other country. In October 1847, he wrote to his mother from Paris in highly poetic language: "German life was a solemn, somber twilight meditation among gray ruins and under the rustling boughs. Oh thou my soul, say whither art thou fleeting!" In both literature and life, Leland often found his refuge in German culture and thought.

His greatest adventure abroad – later his fondest European memory – awaited him in France. The year 1848 found him living in Paris, taking classes at the Sorbonne, and residing in the Hotel de Luxembourg, the setting of Irving's ghoulish "Adventure of the German Student" and the secret headquarters for the revolution that was then under way. Leland himself sallied forth to assist in defending the barricades erected in the student district, where he made, in Pennell's words, "a striking figure, with his rakish student cap set on one side of his long hair, a monocle in one eye, a red sash about his waist, a dirk and pistol for arms, so tall [6' 4"] he towered high above the mob." Hans Breitmann himself seldom attempted a more dramatic pose.

Not surprisingly, Leland's return to Philadelphia later in 1848 was anticlimactic. In October, he entered the Philadelphia law offices of John Cadwalader. A fellow law student described

him as "full of German life, and German mysticism, and European ideas of life." Although in 1851 Leland passed the bar examination and opened his own law office in Philadelphia, he quickly realized that he was unsuited to the profession. In his first six months, he had only two clients and claimed a profit of 15 dollars. Unfulfilled both financially and intellectually, Leland began to look elsewhere for a vocation.

The literary world had already provided him with several opportunities to establish his presence. In 1849, he began writing pieces with some regularity for *Sartain's Union Magazine*, Philadelphia's *Drawing-Room Journal* (as "the Chevalier"), *The Pennsylvanian* (as "Chrysa Dora"), and, occasionally, the *Knickerbocker*. In 1852, he moved to New York to pursue a career in journalism, and by January 1853, he had become the associate editor of Barnum's *Illustrated News*. Rufus Griswold was then editor, and he and Leland became good friends, despite the fact that Leland burned some disparaging material Griswold was collecting for a book on Poe. Regardless of that episode, Leland always maintained that Griswold was much less to blame for Poe's tarnished reputation than many people understood him to be. By 1854, Griswold had found other interests, and Leland, weary with managing the *Illustrated News* essentially alone, returned to Philadelphia.

Yet Leland's experience in New York had convinced him that his future lay in writing and editing. In 1855, he conclusively demonstrated his viability in these areas when he became the assistant editor of Philadelphia's *Evening Bulletin*. At this paper, Leland contributed daily to a column, wrote book reviews, and used the editorial page to speak out against religious intolerance and in favor of abolition – until the *Bulletin*'s owner put a stop to his forcefully expressed opinions. Also in 1855, Leland published several book-length works, including a translation of Heine's *Pictures of Travel*. Leland also introduced his first consistent comic persona when "The Observations of Mace Sloper, Esq." became a regular feature in the *Knickerbocker* between 1855 and 1861. Mace commented on a range of political and social issues during that time; he frequently imitated the commentaries of his fellow citizens by using New England and African American dialects. His "Observations" are often humorous; for instance, in a February 1856 column, Mace discusses the potential usefulness of advertising for a mate and then experiments by advertising himself. Clearly, Leland's interest in formulating a comic persona began well in advance of Hans Breitmann's birth.

Leland's major accomplishment in 1855 was publishing the eclectic *Meister Karl's Sketch-Book*, a compilation of short essays and poems, many of which had already appeared in the *Knickerbocker* between 1849 and 1851. He received a letter from Irving praising the book, but it did not sell particularly well and was not reissued until 1872, in the wake of Hans Breitmann's popularity. Yet this distinctively arranged collection deserves more than passing notice, especially because Griswold chose poems from it to represent Leland's work in *The Poets and Poetry of America* (1855). "The Three Friends," for example, appears in both volumes. In Meister Karl's book, the poem complements a discussion of "Ghost-Land" and reflects Leland's lifelong fascination with the mysterious and the occult. The poem also contains Poe-like imagery, while the poet renders his comments in a playful, half-serious tone that is the hallmark of Leland's comic verse. In the poem, the speaker meets the ghosts of two of his deceased friends every midnight: "The first with gnomes in the Underland is leading a lordly life, / And the second has married a mermaiden – a beautiful water-wife." The poem's concluding couplets reflect a typically unconventional twist to Leland's poetry. The persona declares that "whether I sink in the foaming flood, or swing in the triple tree, / Or die in my grave as a Christian should, is much the same to me." Leland periodically returned to ghostly imagery. "The Weed," which appeared in the November 1861 *Knickerbocker*, relates the story of lovers separated by death. They are reunited when the dead male's toppling gravestone crushes his mourning companion, so that "clothed in marble fair and white / The bride by her bridegroom passes the night."

Yet in selecting verses from *Meister Karl's Sketch-Book*, Griswold often does his friend and the reader a disservice, for much of these poems' meanings derive from their context within the *Sketch-Book*. "A Dream of Love," for instance, appears untitled in the *Sketch-Book* as part of a satirical discussion of what Meister Karl terms the "'Come-to-thy-lattice-love' school of poetry." Meister Karl explains that the poem was "written while under the influence of a heart-rending attack of Window Love" and then launches into the lines "Methought I lay, beside the dark blue Rhine, / In that old tower where once Sir Roland dwelt." That element of parody does not translate to the poem's isolated reprinting in Griswold's collection. There, the poem becomes merely conventional verse, although it offers an unusual concluding twist when the persona reveals that the vision of the woman in the window was but a dream. The persona dramatically implores his love's sympathy with the lines: "If thus, *in sleep*, love's pangs assail my soul, / Think lady, *what my waking hours must be*." The carefree tone of Meister Karl's observations is absent from Griswold's reprinting, and since Griswold's collection was far more widely read than *Meister Karl's Sketch-Book*, Griswold's editorial choices colored most readers' impressions of Leland's work. One stanza from "Manes" captures the nonchalance of Leland's original collection:

I have learned to love Lucy,
    Though faded she be:
If my next love be lovely,
    The better for me;
By the end of next summer,
    I'll swear on my oath,
It was best after all
    To have flirted with both.

Reprinted by Griswold with the singsong verse length regularized, much of the effect is lost. Yet the conclusion of that stanza hints at the juxtaposition of mutability and humor that courses beneath much of Hans Breitmann's verse as well:

But kind or uncivil
    Ill-natured or gay,
They'll [the women] blow to the devil,
    And vanish away.

A feature article about Leland in the February 1856 *Knickerbocker* declares of the *Sketch-Book*: "the boundaries between the real and the spiritual are completely broken down." In Leland's view, the spiritual infused the real. To separate the two was impossible; their union in his verse and in his life reveals both his indebtedness to German philosophy and the importance of this early volume for Leland.

Leland's stint with the *Bulletin* quickly came to an end, but his involvement with journalism did not. He began editing *Graham's Magazine* in 1857. Leland recalled filling this magazine "recklessly with all or any kind of literary matter as best I could." His most famous poem, "Hans Breitmann's Barty," was intended merely as filler for the May 1857 column "Editor's Easy Talk." The poem begins thus:

Hans Breitmann gife a barty,
    Dey had biano-blayin
I felled in lofe mit a Merican frau,
    Her name vas Madilda Yane
She hat haar as prown ash a pretzel,
    Her eyes vas himmel-plue,
Und ven dey looket indo mine,
    Dey shplit mine heart in two.

Hans goes on to chronicle the raucous festivities in which "We all cot troonk ash bigs" ("got drunk as pigs"). The poem includes lines that became infamous in Leland's time: "Hans Breitmann gife a barty – / Where ish dat barty now!" Leland wrote in his *Memoirs*: "I little dreamed that in days to come I should be asked in Egypt, and on the blue Mediterranean, and in every country in Europe if I was its author."

Leland's journalistic interests kept him in New York for most of 1857. There, he wrote at least 200 articles for Appleton's *Cyclopaedia* and worked as a foreign editor for the *New York Times*. Along with R. H. Stoddard, T. B. Aldrich, and Artemus Ward, Leland briefly edited the humorously satirical *Vanity Fair* in 1860. By the end of that year, however, his impassioned views of the impending war had become so extreme that they alienated the publication's owner. Leland then became editor and half-owner of the *Knickerbocker*, which evolved into a Republican mouthpiece with a nearly fanatical tone. Writings in the *Knickerbocker*, for example, predicted great prosperity for the North in an effort to stem the tide of pessimism threatening to overtake the Yankee war machine.

The hold of the *Knickerbocker* on public attention was fairly weak, however, and so when an overtly political publication called the *Continental Monthly* began in Boston, Leland moved there to devote his literary skills to the war effort. In "What To Do with the Darkies" (January 1862), he argued that since emigration plans to deport African Americans had begun to appear impractical, the U.S. government should designate South Carolina as the homeland for freed slaves: "as South Carolina was especially the State which brought about this war, for the express purpose of making the black man the basis of its society, there would be a wonderful and fearful propriety in carrying out that theory . . . even to perfection [by] making the negro not only the basis of society, but *all* society there whatever." For Leland, the central issue of the war was the preservation of the Union. A unified, central government rather than an "aggregate of smaller republics" was the conflict's goal; emancipation was not a desired outcome of the war. Rather, the people should empower a centralized government to resolve "the negro question" as "its first manifestation of strength" in the war's wake ("Our War"). Echoing Jefferson in

Notes on the State of Virginia (1785), Leland asked, "Do we not see, feel, and understand what sort of *white men* are developed by slavery, and do we intend to keep up such a race among us?" Not surprisingly, then, he promoted the slogan "Emancipation for the sake of the White Man." He maintained throughout his writing that the South's awareness of its inherent inferiority to the North contributed significantly to the origin of the war.

Leland's poetry from this period is similarly extremist and at times nearly visionary; it casts the Union cause as analogous to a holy crusade. "Cavalry Song" (*Knickerbocker*, August 1861), for instance, opens with these lines:

> Weaponed well to war we ride,
> With sabres ringing by our side –
> The warning knell of death to all
> Who hold the holiest cause in thrall:
>   The sacred Right
>   Which grows to Might,
> The dawn which dawns in blood-red light.

Leland also uses biblical imagery to depict the justness of Union convictions; he "Who braves the battle wins the bride" refers not only to material victory but to the Northern honor of serving as the bride of Christ. Despite its Christian overtones, however, the poem's imagery is violent. Leland describes

> The sabre, as it quits the sheath,
> And beams with the lurid light of death,
>   And the deadly glance
>   Of the glittering lance,
> And the taper-lights of the battle-dance.

Similarly, "The Knight and the Dragon" (*Knickerbocker*, October 1861) portrays the North as a knight who slays the Southern dragon and is then able to shed permanently his armor and reveal "Those fair limbs of ivory – purest beauty," which suggest a nearly holy radiance.

The imagery in Leland's later *Continental Monthly* war poetry is even more striking and violent. In "The Wolf Hunt" (November 1862), he again makes the Confederacy into a villain and casts the Union as an almost unwitting participant in the conflict. "Thank God for All" (December 1862) provides a litany of the ways in which the South has besmirched America's honor. In poems like "'What Will You Do With Us?'" (February 1862), the speaker suggests that a benevolent North is pursuing its inevitable victory. Yet more convincing are poems such as "'Ten to One on It'" (April 1862), in which the persona vows that

> When peace shall have come, and war be fled,
> And its hate be the tale of time long sped,
> That where there is work or thought for men,
> One Yankee is equal to Dirt-eaters ten.

Most striking of all Leland's Civil War poetry is "Bone Ornaments" (*Continental Monthly*, July 1862):

> Silent the lady sat alone:
> In her ears were rings of dead men's bone;
> The brooch on her breast shone white and fine,
> 'Twas the polished joint of a Yankee's spine;
> And the well-carved handle of her fan,

Was the finger-bone of a Lincoln man.
> She turned aside a flower to cull,
> From a vase which was made of a human skull;
> For to make her forget the loss of her slaves,
> Her lovers had rifled dead men's graves.
> Do you think I'm describing a witch or a ghoul?
> There are no such things – and I'm not a fool;
> Nor did she reside in Ashantee;
> No – the lady fair was an F. F. V. [First Family of Virginia]

A more unsettling image in Civil War poetry would be difficult to find. Recognizing the power of the pen as the strongest weapon in defending this cause, Leland wrote incessantly throughout the first years of the war; in these works, intense personal conviction usurped his comic personae.

Leland's war poetry is comparable to Henry Timrod's in significant and interesting ways. Readers often perceive Timrod's poetry as poignant because they know, even as they read the hopeful lines of "Ethnogenesis" (LOA, 2: 203), that the aspirations and visions that he records will be defeated. Yet although they may not discover in Leland's canon any poem as touching as this or Timrod's "Ode," the spoils of victory are seldom as haunting as the specters of defeat. Leland gives us his image of the South in "Bone Ornaments," however, and it is as unforgettable and powerful as Timrod's stooping angels. Certainly, his contemporaries thought so. In 1867, Harvard granted Leland an honorary degree "for literary service rendered to the country during the War," an accolade enjoyed by few of his countrymen.

In response to Lee's march into Pennsylvania in 1863, Leland decided to serve the Union physically rather than literarily and enrolled as a private in the army. Both he and his brother Henry were nearly involved in the Battle of Gettysburg, but their unit was finally held in reserve because it contained only raw recruits. After Union troops rebuffed Lee's advance, Leland left the army and, ironically, made his way into the south. He prospected briefly for oil in Tennessee, a dangerous mission since rebel guerrillas controlled much of the countryside. Finding no oil, he traveled to West Virginia, where he took a job renewing leases on oil and coal lands. Despite the fact that in 1862 he had become a member of Boston's literary Saturday Club, he reflected that "literature was dead in me." The war's casualties were indeed many.

Yet in 1866, he returned to journalism, as managing editor of the *Philadelphia Press*. Leland also received letters from James Russell **Lowell** and Oliver Wendell **Holmes** that urged him to collect his Breitmann poems, and *Hans Breitmann's Barty* appeared in 1868. The slapdash composition style of the title piece characterizes the other poems as well. The "Ballad" (LOA, 2: 146) of the maiden "Vot hadn't got nodings on," for example, Leland composed on a train in 1864. He originally included "Wein Geist" (LOA, 2: 147) in a letter to illustrate that writing in rhyme is easier than writing in prose. In fact, Leland wrote most of these poems with no greater purpose than to spice up his regular correspondence with fellow journalist Charles Astor Bristed. He retained no copies, and he said that after composing these early Breitmann poems, he "utterly *forgot* them."

Leland had never intended to collect the Breitmann verse,

and he remained, even as it went to press, uncertain of the venture's success. Nonetheless, eight separate editions reached print, either legally or illegally, over the next two years in America and in England, culminating in *Hans Breitmann's Ballads* in 1870. In 1871, Leland published two new sequences, *Hans Breitmann as an Uhlan* and *Hans Breitmann in Europe*. Hans appeared in cartoons in London newspapers like *Punch* and the *Standard*; an English weekly called *Hans Breitmann* also sprang up in 1871, as did a Breitmann brand of cigars. William Dean **Howells** speculated in the October 1868 *Atlantic Monthly* that Leland had expended Hans's usefulness, but no less a commentator than Leslie Stephen preferred Breitmann to both Lowell's Hosea Biglow and Artemus Ward's writings in his 1870 review of "American Humour" (*British Quarterly Review* 52 [1870]). Hans had become a nineteenth-century icon whose popularity carried him into the twentieth; by 1914, 26 authorized editions of Breitmann verse were in print.

Hans's popularity puzzled Leland, and it may also confuse today's readers. Certainly the character is humorous, especially as he relates his adventures in broken English that actually varies between poems, just as a real immigrant's speech often reveals inconsistent pronunciation. Yet, as Pennell points out, Hans's German-American dialect alone fails to provide a complete explanation of the poetry's success. The key lies, rather, in the figure's ability to cross sectional lines and ethnic divisions in order to amuse not only genuine Yankees, but the immigrant section of the population, as well as the Confederate readers who watched Breitmann come face to face with the Confederacy in the course of his Civil War adventures. By sheer accident, Leland happened upon a figure that had universal appeal.

An interesting split exists between the venomous magazine poetry that Leland wrote during the Civil War and his more benign treatment in the postwar Breitmann verse. In "Breitmann in Battle," for instance, Hans discovers his long-lost son is a soldier in a rebel unit, and the two enjoy a happy reunion "'Away down Sout' in Tixey.'" And when Breitmann visits Kansas, he learns that "De whiskey keg's de only dings / Dat's bleedin' der to-day" ("Breitmann in Kansas"). We know so little about the order of composition for much of his poetry that Leland may have in fact sent Breitmann into combat before composing "Bone Ornaments." At any rate, we may speculate that Hans's humor served his creator as it did his audience, as a balm for the country's sectional wound. The North and the South come back together in "Breitmann in Battle," even though reunion in actuality was still fraught with distrust and uncertainty.

Other Breitmann poems are less topical but reveal a great deal about Hans's popularity and his acceptance of the mutability that forms a necessary part of life. Two of Hans's greatest passions are unquestionably pursuing women and drinking beer. "Die Schoene Wittwe," for example, is an account of his wooing "Dat pooty liddle vidow / Vot we dosh'nt vish to name." Those passions merge in "Wein Geist," a poem in which Hans describes a drunken spree that leads him to grab a female passerby "Und giss her like efery dings." When a night watchman attempts to arrest his progress, "I oop mit mein oomberella, / Und schlog him ober de kop." But as in Breitmann's "Barty," this sheer abandon must come to an end, just

as the lost love that apparently sparked the bout of drinking did. Those facts lead Hans to observe that

> De blaetter are raushlin' o'er me,
>   Und efery leaf ish a fay,
> Und dey vait dill de windsbraut comet,
>   To pear dem in Fall afay.

The things that Hans values are transitory; seldom do poems about women and beer juxtapose so deftly the obviously humorous and the inescapably serious elements of the human condition.

Leland concedes the vanity of worldly things nowhere more clearly than in "Schnitzerl's Philosopede," an excellent example of his macaronic verse; Latin words and phrases appear throughout, particularly when the voice speaks from heaven. Given that the poem's questions of great import arise from the consideration of a bicycle, this work is certainly comically melodramatic. The persona wonders in light of Schnitzerl's demise:

> Oh vot ish all dis eart'ly pliss?
>   Oh, vot ish man's soocksess?
> Oh, vot ish various kinds of dings?
>   Und vot ish hobbiness?

And while Leland may well be treating such philosophical speculation satirically, "Schnitzerl's Philosopede" remains a poem about human efforts and the projects of a man's lifetime. The efforts of humanity, aimed in whatever direction, reach for "hobbiness" (happiness) but inevitably meet with this mortal fate. For Hans and for the reader, humor provides the cushion that softens the blow.

Much of the Breitmann verse is genuinely funny, and searching for greater meaning often clouds the enjoyment Leland intended it to provide. In "Breitmann in Politics," for example (see LOA, 2: 149), the words "soundt oopon der coose" form what is essentially a nonsense phrase that allows Breitmann and Leland to poke fun at politics in a world where voters know so little about the candidates that a member of the opposing campaign – one *Mishder Hiram Twine* – can pose as the other candidate and steal away votes. In the introduction to the 1871 *Ballads*, Leland describes Hans as a devotee of "entire skepticism or indifference." Hans demonstrates such an attitude in the stanzas of "Breitmann in Politics" by blithely submitting to the political machinations of the schemers who surround him. Yet it is his very indifference that lends the verse much of its humor. Not only are politics unimportant but they are comical, and the earnestness displayed by the poem's political figures only underscores the futility of their efforts when compared with Hans's lackadaisical approach.

Beginning with the 1871 volumes, Hans becomes less a sheerly comic figure and more of a picaro whose adventures bind him intimately to Leland in ways that the author himself may not have realized. Breitmann becomes an alter-ego of sorts for Leland; they share the same experiences, but Breitmann suffers none of the consequences – he does not remain an aging man surveying the adventure of this youth, as Leland does. Breitmann, too, traipses about Europe. In recounting Hans's adventures, Leland invariably returns to his own life-changing experiences, particularly those of his 1840s European tour. A *carpe diem* attitude characterizes the speaker's outlook in "Breitmann in Paris" (LOA, 2: 151): "Oonendless wisdom ish but dis: / To go it vhile you're yung!" And while Hans may doubt the promise of the next world, he never doubts the allure of this one:

> Und should dey toorn ids gas-light off,
>   Und nefer leafe a shbark,
> Sdill I'd find my vay to Heafen – or –
>   Dy lips, lofe, in de dark.

In "Breitmann in La Sorbonne" Hans is visiting the school on the twenty-second anniversary of his having studied there, approximately the same span of time since Leland himself would have been in Paris. Both author and persona wonder, "Oh, where ish all de characders, / Dat I hafe known since denn?" Neither receives an answer, but certainly Leland would have found that silence more troubling than would Breitmann. Perhaps Leland recalls his fondest memory in "Breitmann in Forty-Eight." Here, he describes Breitmann's appearance as "Like a trunken wild Don Quixote," which in turn recalls the actions of the student-poet during the French uprising of 1848. The hand that helps to build the barricades, moreover, is "de same Hans Breitmann's hand / Vitch now dese verses write." Breitmann lives immutably the youth otherwise lost to the poet. And Leland, despite his periodic frustration with the public for being unable to distinguish between Hans and himself, remained fascinated by the character and returned to him for *Breitmann in the Tyrol* (1894) and for *Flaxius* (1903), which places Breitmann in South Africa. Pennell even found uncompleted sketches for further Breitmann adventures among her uncle's papers following his death. Clearly Leland, too, had succumbed to Hans's spell.

Certainly, Hans's success contributed to Leland's financial security, as did the inheritance that he received following his father's death in 1867. Recognizing an opportunity to pursue his literary interests more freely, he resigned his position at the *Philadelphia Press* in 1869 and returned to Europe, where he lived and worked for the next 10 years. Although he headquartered himself in England, Leland traveled to places as far away and exotic as Russia and Egypt; the latter trip inspired *The Egyptian Sketch Book* (1873). Leland also developed during this second trip abroad an interest that would consume him for the rest of his life. He became a Romany Rye – a non-Gypsy who loves the culture and masters its language. Leland recorded voluminous notes about the Gypsy language and culture, and Pennell speculates that "Gypsying" was Leland's "most serious pursuit." That pursuit resulted in a number of literary efforts, including *The English Gypsies* (1873), *The Gypsies* (1882), and *Gypsy Sorcery and Fortune-Telling* (1891). Along with E. H. Palmer and Janet Tuckey, Leland also wrote a volume of poetry about Gypsy life called *English-Gipsy Songs* (1875); the poems appear in both standard English and Romany.

Leland did publish several other volumes of poetry in his lifetime, but none of them was either publicly or critically acclaimed. *The Music Lesson of Confucius* appeared in 1872, but it did not sell particularly well. Pennell attributes its failure to the public's unwillingness to accept serious poetry from a man that it had already classified as a humorist. The volume includes some poems reprinted from *Legends of the Birds* (1864) and contains the only collection (albeit incomplete) of Leland's Civil War poetry outside of magazines and newspapers. One of his final volumes of poetry, *Songs of the Sea and Lays of the Land* (1895), begins with a number of interconnected poems that are related as though they are ghoulish legends and songs being traded by seamen at an inn. The verse is often light and frequently uses comic rhyme. Leland similarly fills the "Lays of the Land" section with ballads, comic stories, and legendary accounts. A rhythmically typical stanza appears in the poem "Arizona John":

> John Lyons, late of Tombstone, had but just put in a
>   blast,
> When he saw four buck Apaches approximatin' fast
> Upon their headlong horses in a rackaloose career,
> And every one preceded by a long projectin' spear.

The rhythm gallops, but none of Leland's characters ever came to life as authentically as did Hans Breitmann.

Leland died in Florence in 1903, having made Europe his home after his final return there in 1884. Hans Breitmann enjoyed the status of favorite son on two continents, and while Leland remained as mystified by the character's success as he ever had been, creator and character peacefully coexisted. Leland published his *Memoirs* in 1902, but Hans had already offered glimpses into Leland's life by way of his adventures. Twentieth-century readers discover in Breitmann, then, not only a beer drinker and a philosopher in humorous tandem, but insight into the life of Charles Godfrey Leland and the America in which he wrote.

KATHRYN B. MCKEE

Selected Works

The Poetry and Mystery of Dreams, Philadelphia: E. H. Butler, 1855
Legends of the Birds, Philadelphia, Frederick Leypoldt, 1864
Hans Breitmann's Party, Philadelphia: T. B. Peterson, 1868
Hans Breitmann About Town and Other New Ballads, Philadelphia: T. B. Peterson, 1869
Hans Breitmann in Politics, Philadelphia: Lippincott, 1869; London: Trübner, 1869
Hans Breitmann und His Philosopede, New York: Jesse Haney, 1869
Hans Breitmann in Church, Philadelphia: T. B. Peterson, 1870
The Breitmann Ballads, Philadelphia: T. B. Peterson, 1871; London: Trübner, 1871
Hans Breitmann as an Uhlan, Philadelphia: T. B. Peterson, 1871; London: Trübner, 1871
The Music-Lesson of Confucius, Boston: James R. Osgood, 1872; London: Trübner, 1872
Memoirs, 2 vols., New York: D. Appleton, 1893; London: William Heinemann, 1893
Hans Breitmann in Germany Tyrol, London: T. Fisher Unwin, 1894
Songs of the Sea and Lays of the Land, London: Adam and Charles Black, 1895
Flaxius: Leaves from the Life of an Immortal, London: Philip Wellby, 1902

Hans Breitmann's Ballads, introduction by Elizabeth Robins Pennell, Boston: Houghton Mifflin, 1914; reprinted, Dover, 1965

Further Reading

Brooks, Van Wyck, *The Dream of Arcadia*, New York: E. P. Dutton, 1958

———, *Fenollosa and His Circle*, New York: E. P. Dutton, 1962

Jackson, Joseph, *A Bibliography of the Works of Charles G. Leland*, Philadelphia: privately printed, 1927

Literary Landmarks of Philadelphia, Philadelphia: McKay, 1939

Oberholtzer, Ellis P., *The Literary History of Philadelphia*, Philadelphia: Jacobs, 1906

Pennell, Elizabeth Robins, *Charles Godfrey Leland: A Biography*, 2 vols., Boston: Houghton Mifflin, 1906

George Cabot Lodge

(1873–1909)

Contemporary scholars of American literature have been expending enormous amounts of energy rediscovering, rereading, and reevaluating authors who have been marginalized or excluded from the canon. Writers are commended to our attention for a number of reasons. Some were popular in their day and spoke to audiences about things that were perceived to matter. Others never found their audience, but still spoke words that are important for the attempt or for their historical significance. Such a man is George Cabot Lodge.

Born in Boston to Anna Cabot Mills Davis Lodge and Henry Cabot Lodge on October 10, 1873, Lodge moved to Washington, D.C., in 1887, the year after his father was elected to Congress. He entered Harvard in 1891, and he published his first poem in the *Harvard Monthly* the year that he graduated. He immediately moved to Paris, where he studied French literature at the Sorbonne. After a year, Lodge moved to Berlin to study German philosophy. This venture, too, was short-lived. He returned to the United States in 1897, and then became his father's private secretary. Through this position, he came into contact with some of his father's friends who would serve him in good stead, including Theodore Roosevelt and Henry **Adams**. His father agreed to fund the publication of Lodge's first book of poetry, *The Song of the Wave* (1898), while Lodge served in the Spanish-American War as a gunnery officer aboard the *Dixie,* a ship captained by his uncle.

At this time, Lodge began to develop a theory of aesthetics and morality that reacted strongly to the social Darwinism that he saw in the culture around him. This theory, which he called "conservative Christian anarchy," informs his poetry, especially when he writes about the status of the poet in society. For Lodge, the poet, or the anarchist, must revolt against society and eventually be crushed by it. Through this seemingly futile process, the poet may perhaps sound a clarion call to others willing to stand against society and realize their full humanity. This elite would then create a new society, which would be founded on the idea of the self found in work by Walt **Whitman** and the transcendentalists. The degeneration of the human race would be halted through this rejoicing in the individual self.

Lodge married Elizabeth Frelinghuysen Davis in 1900. Their first child, Henry Cabot Lodge Jr., was born in 1902. That same year saw the publication of Lodge's second volume, *Poems 1899–1902.* His second son, John David Lodge, was born in 1903. Lodge's verse drama *Cain* was published in 1904, and *The Great Adventure*, his third volume of poetry, the following year. *Herakles*, another verse drama and his most powerful work, was published in 1908, the same year in which he was elected to the National Institute of Arts and Letters. Lodge died of ptomaine poisoning on August 21, 1909. *The Soul's Inheritance and Other Poems* was published posthumously in 1909. His collected works appeared in 1911.

Lodge never enjoyed a great following, and his slight popularity waned after his death. However, Henry James respected his work, Edith **Wharton** was moved to write a remembrance of him, and Henry Adams wrote his biography. Of course, his closest friend, Trumbull **Stickney**, also appreciated his talents.

Lodge had met Stickney at Harvard, and upon the latter's death in 1904, he had collaborated with William Vaughn **Moody** to edit Stickney's collected poetry. Although their editorial relationship was tempestuous, critics have addressed these three men as inheritors of "the genteel tradition," or as "the Harvard poets." The latter grouping sometimes includes George **Santayana**, Lodge's philosophy professor at the college.

Lodge can be seen as one of the liminal figures in American literature. He wrote at the tail end of the Romantic tradition and attempted to rebel against it, but his poetry also shows an effort to achieve a clarity of poetic image akin to that later propounded by T. E. Hulme. In many of Lodge's poems, precise images abut ethereal "poetic" diction. This Janus-like disposition makes it difficult to categorize his poetry.

Section I of "Tuckanuck" (LOA, 2: 630), from *The Song of the Wave*, introduces the themes that interested Lodge throughout his short poetic career. Tuckanuck, or Tuckernuck, is a small island off the coast of Nantucket, Massachusetts. William Sturgis Bigelow, Lodge's father's oldest friend, owned a retreat there, where Lodge spent his summers. In this males-only setting, in which he drank, dined as an epicurean, and was attended by servants, Lodge learned a derivative Buddhism that Bigelow had brought back from the Orient. The tension between the pantheism of the sonnet's second quatrain and the recognition of the *maya* – or illusion – of the world in the succeeding couplet demonstrates the stress not only of the paradoxical life on Tuckernuck, but also of the commingling of eastern and western worlds.

The persona places himself on the beach at Tuckernuck in the sonnet's first quatrain. He has already accepted the Buddhist life of the overcoming of the will and is "content to live the patient day." The "wind sea-laden," with its inversion, the "glittering gold of naked sand," and "The eternity of blue sea" are examples of the rather nebulous poetic rhetoric that clings to Lodge's verse. The verbs in this quatrain are weak and conjure up a languorous afternoon in which the persona does not act but merely observes nature acting around him.

The second quatrain creates a grand cosmic scheme from this little piece of nature. The persona moves beyond himself, taking the reader into his confidence and offering a way of life that hardly seems justified by the inactivity of the first quatrain. Again, the verbs show a denial of motion. Humanity has "no need to pray," for the "holy voices of the sea and air" do that for us. But are these things real? The prayer they speak is a dream. Indeed, in an interesting turn on the Buddhist belief that the earth is an illusory world, or *maya*, that must be lived in but never engaged, the poem depicts all of nature dreaming. Here, the persona does not rise above the world, for he sees it as a dream; the world itself dreams away its tears. Humanity is bound to no religious duty, because the world does it for us. Again, the abnegation of responsibility results in an even greater inactivity.

The persona and reader now move toward activity, "row[ing] across the waters' fluent gold," but Lodge's imprecise images impede this movement. Is this "age" that "seems blessèd" the age that we live in? Is it the old age of the person and reader? Or perhaps the old age of the world, which the poem mentions subsequently? Even the next action, the taking "from Nature's open palm," is mitigated; we do not grab forcefully but take "softly." Finally, persona and reader are subsumed into the activity of the earth. We "dream an Eastern dream," which is punctuated by the cries of the homing gulls, and again, there are questions of interpretation: do we dream, as Lodge did, of Buddhism filtered through the western philosophical tradition, especially Arthur Schopenhauer? What we end with is Lodge's aspiration to be a poet of ideas, not images.

The other three sections of "Tuckanuck" continue in this vein. They owe a philosophical debt not only to Schopenhauer and Friedrich Nietzsche, but also to sources as disparate as Plato's *Republic*, Augustine, and the medieval Scholastic philosophers. None of these poems are inherently satisfying, for they do not cohere into a unit but are like variations upon a theme that is too large for them to handle. In these sections, Lodge attempts to address the passage of time and eternity while clinging to an idea of the cyclical nature of time. He also concerns himself with the transmigration of souls, the dream of earthly existence, and the *ubi sunt* (they are where?) topos of the Germanic/Old English tradition.

The way in which Lodge integrated his fin de siècle philosophies and his ambitious themes makes us realize that he was a poet with promising skills. "Tuckanuck," however, was the apprentice work of a man who barely outlived his apprenticeship. As his career progressed, Lodge moved toward a fuller realization of these themes. At least in this poem, unfortunately, his images and emotionalism get in the way of his material.

"Pastoral" (LOA, 2: 630) is rather somber, as if Lodge is playing with the form. Expecting simplicity of thought and action in a rustic setting, we find instead a deep meditation on the vagaries of human existence and a longing for passage to another plane of existence. Lodge's play with musical imagery is handled well, and the paradox of the music of silence is especially fine. Again, however, the syntax is convoluted, and the poem's "content" is too dense for clarity.

The first lines speak of the setting, and although they claim that it has restorative powers for the soul, they also paint an unremittingly pessimistic picture of earthly existence, as in the arresting image of men who are "quenched like dewdrops in the sun." The next line, with its "haggard women" who "reach to God and weep," plays upon the lamentation tradition with an unusual force. Lodge continues with a catalog of earthly frustrations – projects that end badly or are left abandoned – but claims that these are nonetheless given by the world to "grace the splendid hope our youth imbued." The poem then turns upon itself and goes beyond the standard bucolic fare to explore an indifferent universe and this sylvan glade's participation in that universe: there is no safe haven in this life, even if it may at first glance appear so.

What does remain for humanity is to move forward to death, to the extinguishing of the soul. Only then shall we experience the full harmony of life. Lodge's conclusion is mature enough to acknowledge that worldly pain somehow participates in and enhances otherworldly music. It is not difficult to trace his ideas to pessimistic philosophies in the air at the time, but Lodge's allusion to the Pythagorean notion of the soul's afterlife communion with a force larger than itself suggests a sophistication of thought that bodes well for the depth of his future poetry.

In "Fall" (LOA, 2: 631), Lodge again attempts to be a nature poet, but nature calls him beyond his putative subject to more human themes. The persona tells the reader to "be content," for "Thy heart can ask no more" than the image of autumn framed by "our door that opens wide" – a device that neatly calls to mind Lodge's concern for the ordering of nature through art. What the reader and the persona perceive of nature is constrained by humanity's creations. Even the light that spans the world is constrained by the roof and floor of the dwelling the "door" opens.

This limiting is a reciprocal relationship between nature and artifice; for instance, the persona speaks not of the pine trees, but of the "horizon of the pines." This horizon "holds our world within its shadowy shore," for nature both bounds and is bound by our creations. Humanity perceives nature through the figure in the doorway, the liminal figure of beauty. Beauty participates both in the creations of humanity and in the creations of nature. But nature is self-contained, while humanity must come to nature by moving through beauty.

Instead of taking that step across the threshold, Lodge presents an allusion to John Donne's "The Good Morrow" with "Thine eyes in mine!" This allusion opens up the possibility of experiencing beauty without venturing into nature. We must see the reader's eye as a doorway akin to the doorway onto nature. In both cases, beauty sits on the threshold and is always a part of the experience of forward movement. The movement into nature is aligned with the movement into another person; both yield the same results. Succeeding images explore the cyclical character of the natural world and the unrelenting motion of time that is essential to the death and rebirth of the world. But Lodge and the reader "need not fear / The ceaseless pageantry of death and birth," for they have stopped time for themselves.

Lodge then begins to address his allusion to Donne. Donne's conceit was to compare lovers' eyes to two hemispheres. These hemispheres were "Without sharp north, without declining west." The lovers, then, possessed a love without decay, without diminution. Their love will enable them to live forever, for the lovers are mixed perfectly and possess the quintessence of love. Lodge ignores an ironic reading of this poem and chooses only to handle the conceit as it stands, without wordplay and sexual innuendo. He also offers a reference to "The Sun Rising," Donne's companion poem to "The Good Morrow." Lodge and the reader have tasted perfection (which is only possible if time does not move), even "if to-morrow's sun / Should find us fallen with the summer's rose." For Lodge, the gaze can encase moments in eternity. It does not stop time, but rather moves ahead of it. The persona and reader have touched the *Ipsum Esse*, being itself. In the western philosophical tradition, this is communion with the Godhead after death. But Lodge, influenced by the east, proclaims it "the soul's oblivion." The pains of earthly existence are transformed into art through this foretaste of the soul's rest. In the midst of this reverie, nature and time continue apace. Flowers bloom, the dawn gives way to morning (and eventual nightfall), and the season attacks both nature and humanity in its relentless pursuit.

Lodge is not concerned with the traditional form of the pastoral here, but this does not mean that he is uninterested in established poetic models. He shows a predilection for old forms, as evidenced by the inclusion of 44 sonnets in *The Song of the Wave*. "On an Æolian Harp," a representative sample, is also fairly typical of his thoughts on the crafting of poetry. The octave describes the harp, long a symbol of the poet's art. The sestet addresses the motivation for and subject matter of the songs that the harp produces. The first quatrain describes the sound of the harp and the proper presentation of poetry. Lodge infuses his description with melancholia, however, as if the harp played only in minor keys. For Lodge, poetry should be "wild," "strange," and "touched" – suggesting some sort of loss, diminishment, or suffering.

The second quatrain moves beyond humanity to something larger than mere mortality. Again, the picture of life is dour, with its "world-wide monotones that toll" and its "solution" that lies "past the mind's control." The traditional juxtaposition of head and heart is abandoned, however, for the heart is also too full of misery to grapple with the problems of existence. Lodge once again expresses his debt to Schopenhauer's pessimism, although he does not go so far as to advocate acquiescence in the universal will, which for Lodge may not even be, as it is for Schopenhauer, a blind striving force. According to Lodge, this acquiesence may actually be malevolent toward humanity. Certainly, something should be held accountable for the suffering that Lodge wallows in.

The sestet offers a solution. What is it that makes life so rough? Perhaps influenced by Santayana's thoughts on memory, Lodge holds this faculty to be the cause of humanity's woes. It is memory that creates the minor key of the harp, as if all the sorrows of the past must be recounted and relived in the present. But poetry allows us some hope in the midst of this despair. The sad "lapsing chords" of the harp call forth a more primitive memory, that "Of other lives, like some unceasing dream." This progression of life to life, filled with forgetfulness that can be overcome only through the music of the harp, is another of Lodge's amalgams of Platonic notions, Schopenhauer, and Buddhism.

Like Schopenhauer, Lodge advocates will-less perception. Like the Buddhist, moreover, he urges that we remove ourselves from the desires and anxieties of the world. Music allows humanity to do so, for it expresses the will directly. But even music is tainted with the sorrow of past experiences. For Schopenhauer and Lodge, music is nonehteless an aid to a state of enlightenment, for it enables the self to view life as a dream. Life's petty indignities and failures, sorrows and setbacks, are of no consequence, no matter how our memory presents them to us.

Lodge's second volume, *Poems 1899–1902*, was, like his first book, received tepidly by the critics. The consensus was that he did not address the shortcomings of his insubstantial images and ideas, which were too big for his forms. Again, most agreed that the poems showed promise, but the mere foretaste of great poetry is less to be forgiven in a second book than in a first. In this collection, Lodge began to extend his range, writing many longer poems in Whitmanesque rhythm and structure. He also produced 22 more sonnets and a few odes, which again showed his interest in traditional forms.

In "Strong saturation of sea!" (LOA, 2: 632), Lodge moves away from a meditation upon the human condition and, in a more mature vein, personalizes the experience of the poem. At once, we can see the power that this brings to his verse; however, he has not become a cheerier poet. The first quatrain imputes the pain of existence even to nature, for the sea moans its "litanies of pain." But Lodge loses hold of this image when he describes it as "the music of a wild refrain / Heard thro' the midnight of a feudal town!" Again, his ideas are too big for the words that seek to contain them. The second quatrain, too, is fraught with wan and pedestrian images of nightfall, save for the fine oxymoron where the "evening lights intensely wane."

The sestet takes this vague pain of the earth and personalizes it as a "formless fear" in the mind of the persona. The persona's thoughts return to a favorite theme for Lodge, the passage of time into eternity. But the guarded optimism of "On an Æolian Harp," where the past can be redeemed through will-less perception, is lost here; even memory cannot retrieve "life's lost, irrevocable hours." The "litanies of pain" and the intensely waning lights emerge as Lodge's "passionate fancies of a formless fear." In this poem, the pain of existence is not to be avoided, for the pain of the earth is the pain of the poet. Here, we see Lodge's conservative Christian anarchy at work: Christlike, the poet must take upon himself this pain and bear it in hopes of creating a new human order.

This goal of a new human order is brought out more forcefully in Lodge's verse dramas. Both *Cain* and *Herakles* show the individual at odds with the society that subjugates him. These are certainly Lodge's most ambitious works, as the verse drama enabled him to give full voice to ideas that were so cramped in other forms. Critics praised Lodge's daring, although noting that, as in his other poetry, his language sometimes did not live up to his ideas.

In a bold reading of Genesis, Lodge posits in *Cain* that the title character slew his brother not because of jealousy, but because Cain could not bear to see a race of callow men engendered by his brother. In this account, Cain recognizes the divinity of his own nature and does not wish to see the promulgation of subservience to any other God. Adam and Abel thus represent the cowed society that does not recognize its own worth independent of its fealty to God, while Cain and Eve possess the inner strength to stand on their own, with their own morality and self-justification. Lodge's distaste for the imposition of morality upon an individual obviously owes much to his reading of Nietzsche's *On the Genealogy of Morals*, but Lodge here also strikes at one of the core myths of western civilization. He saw this assault as a necessary step in the conversion of an elite class that would form a new human society. Although society is represented by only four characters in this play, there is a breadth here, a grappling with universal issues that makes the work both expansive and enlightening.

The plot of *Herakles* is similar. Lodge never intended this work for a large audience, for he had been discouraged by reviews and public reception and recognized the futility of writing for popular acclaim. Instead, he wrote *Herakles* for a select group of friends who might understand the complexities of his thought. Again, Lodge reworked a myth, choosing this time from the classical corpus. Herakles seeks his own self-divinity, and it comes at a terrible price. He must reject many temptations, especially those of worldly power and submission to it. He recognizes that he must distance himself from society and does so through the murder of his children. Subseqently, he attempts to acquit himself before the remainder of his family and moves forward to free Prometheus. It is only through this last, most heinous act that he becomes free enough to assay his heroic labors. While the most stunning scene here is the killing of his children, the most important for Lodge was Herakles's freeing of Prometheus. He does this not by force, but by making Prometheus realize that the chains binding him are only the products of his own mind. Through this perception of the truth, Prometheus becomes not only free but, like Herakles, an archetype of the conservative Christian anarchist. *Herakles* contains the summation of Lodge's philosophy, in a scope large enough for him, and presents some of his finest poetic and dramatic moments. Lodge saw it as his defining work and gave it a care that is sometimes missing from his other productions.

Lodge's final selection in the LOA anthology, "Lower New York" (LOA, 2: 633), was uncollected at his death, but his father placed it with *The Soul's Inheritance* in the collected works. These two sonnets are Lodge's answer to William Wordsworth's "Composed Upon Westminster Bridge": "Earth has not anything to show more fair. / This City now doth, like a garment, wear / The beauty of the morning." Lodge creates a bleak urban landscape that is familiar to readers who know the modernists, although he was writing before they flourished. The first sonnet begins painlessly and presents a spectacle of a dense slumber that is thrown over humanity's creations. But the image of "windows, blank as sightless eyes" is a harbinger of the despair to follow. The "haughty skies" are far removed from the futile strivings and innumerable miseries of humanity. Even the constant process of change, both natural and manmade, is without purpose. The sestet explains why death is no longer a refuge, for this city is already "a vast necropolis of souls!" The suspension of time and life that occurs here is not, as it was in "Fall," a thing of beauty, but rather a weary stillness that is "more dead than death." What we call life is nothing more than the empty and aimless thoughts of "an idiot's mind."

The second sonnet pounds home the emotion of the first. Dawn does not bring comfort, but rather a "sordid and pale" illumination. The image of the exhausted reveler, falling into oblivion rather than sleep, is simlilar to Eliot's "patient etherized upon a table." Humanity has lost not only things of the soul, but also all hope. The scene is so consuming, so dire, that it is difficult to imagine that different scenarios exist anywhere on earth. Lodge closes the door on any escape to his earlier "Eastern dream," for the tide does not flow outward, to deliverance or diversion, but turns in upon itself in self-destruction.

Lodge's command of emotions here is masterful. He channels his rage against society into language that fixes it resolutely. The energy and force of his images do not dissipate, and so the poem avoids the vagueness and ambiguity of his other works. His images have depth and resonance, declaiming with such force that we are taken aback. There is an urgency, as if the meaninglessness of the universe has finally overtaken Lodge, and he must write it out. The fascination with the city, as well as the foreshadowing of modernist concerns and im-

ages, shows that Lodge may have been moving in a new direction, one that faced the squalor of the modern world and denied the refuge of aesthetics or religion. As John W. Crowley has said of this late poem and its promise: "It is possible that the Imagist Movement, barely stirring in 1909, might have provided Lodge with a fresh poetics and thus have allowed him to escape the poetic genteel tradition."

Had Lodge lived in an earlier period, no doubt many would have dubbed him a "poetaster." And it is true that his family's influential position, as well as his father's friends, did much to further his poetic career. But all of this must be disregarded as we encounter the poems. They are not all of equal value, but they do show him as a transitional figure who attempted to address philosophical concerns in his poetic works. Unfortunately, the constraints of his language sometimes make a jumble of such efforts. Nevertheless, we must see him as more than a dilettante, as more than a Romantic orphan and a precursor to the moderns. He may not stand as tall as those who came before and after him, but he stands on his own two feet, his head filled with strong ideas that sometimes did not quite translate themselves into concrete images.

JOE PELLEGRINO

Selected Works

The Song of the Wave and Other Poems, New York: Scribner's, 1898

Poems (1899–1902), New York: Cameron and Blake, 1902

Cain: A Drama, Boston: Houghton Mifflin, 1904

The Great Adventure, Boston: Houghton Mifflin, 1905

Herakles, Boston: Houghton Mifflin, 1908

The Soul's Inheritance and Other Poems, Boston: Houghton Mifflin, 1909

Poems and Dramas of George Cabot Lodge, introduction by Theodore Roosevelt, 2 vols., Boston: Houghton Mifflin, 1911

Poems and Dramas of George Cabot Lodge, 2 vols., London: Heinemann, 1912

The Song of the Wave and Other Poems; reprinted, Upper Saddle River, New Jersey: Gregg, 1970

George Cabot Lodge: Selected Fiction and Verse, edited by John W. Crowley, St. Paul, Minnesota: John Colet, 1976

Further Reading

Adams, Henry, *The Life of George Cabot Lodge*, introduction by Edmund Wilson, Boston: Houghton Mifflin, 1911

Crowley, John W., *George Cabot Lodge*, Boston: Twayne, 1976

Frederick, William Conner, *Cosmic Optimism*, Gainesville: University of Florida Press, 1949

Jones, Howard Mumford, *The Bright Medusa*, Urbana: University of Illinois Press, 1952

Wharton, Edith, *A Backward Glance*, New York: Appleton-Century, 1934

Ziff, Larzer, *The American 1890s: Life and Times of a Lost Generation*, New York: Viking, 1966

Henry Wadsworth Longfellow

(1807–1882)

The brightest star in the American literary firmament when he died at his home in Cambridge, Massachusetts, in 1882, Longfellow has lately fallen into the black hole of critical neglect. His reputation has been in slow eclipse for the past century; his verse has been increasingly scorned for its sentimentality and conventionality and damned with faint praise if praised at all. In 1926, Herbert S. Gorman mocked Longfellow, with his "eminently 'safe' observation of life," as "a sort of American Queen Victoria." In 1929, on the basis of a celebrated experiment in practical criticism, I. A. Richards reported that more than 90 percent of his Cambridge students intensely disliked Longfellow's poetry – by far the most unfavorable ranking among all the poets in the test group. In 1932, Ludwig Lewisohn asked, if only rhetorically, "Who, except wretched schoolchildren, now reads Longfellow?" Such once-popular texts as *The Song of Hiawatha* (see LOA, 1: 399) and *The Courtship of Miles Standish* have been reviled in recent years as pale imitations of European models and as derivative monuments to bad taste that seem to epitomize all that was wrong with the genteel tradition in American letters.

Yet Longfellow was also among the most erudite Americans of his day. Born in 1807, in Portland, Maine, a town he apotheosized in "My Lost Youth" (1855; LOA, 1: 406), he was educated at Portland Academy and Bowdoin College, where he numbered among his classmates both Franklin Pierce, a future president, and Nathaniel **Hawthorne**. A gifted scholar and linguist, he studied at Göttingen University in Germany (in 1828–29), toured Europe four times (in 1826–29, 1835–36, 1842, and 1868–69), taught modern languages at Bowdoin (1829–35) and Harvard (1836–54), and translated poetry from no less than eight languages into English.

Still, the suspicion persists among many modern readers that Longfellow wore his learning lightly. Some of his best-known ballads and lyrics, such as "The Children's Hour" (1859; LOA, 1: 409) and "Paul Revere's Ride" (1860; LOA, 1: 418) from *Tales of a Wayside Inn,* seem febrile and glib, if facile and delicate versifications. Both his "Hymn to the Night" (1839; LOA, 1: 372), with its personification of night as a woman with "trailing garments" sweeping through her "celestial walls," and his sonnet "Autumn" (1845; LOA, 1: 390), with its personification of the season as a royal personage whose progress is heralded by "great gales incessant fanned," are virtually textbook illustrations of the pathetic fallacy. The 12 stanzas of "The Poet's Calendar" (1880; LOA, 1: 443), each one devoted to a single month, reads like the sort of hackneyed exercise that one of Tom Sawyer's classmates would have recited on examination evening at Master Dobbins's school. As one of the so-called Fireside or Schoolroom Poets, Longfellow was, especially in his mature years, a sort of unofficial American poet laureate. He dutifully turned out lyrics on such occasions as the death of Hawthorne in 1864, the seventieth birthday of John Greenleaf **Whittier** in 1877, and the assassination of President James A. Garfield in 1881. Styled a poet of domesticity, he became one of the most imitated lyricists of the century, flattered (as it were) by poets as different as

Horatio Alger Jr., Bret **Harte**, Gerard Manly Hopkins, Theodor Fontane, and Charles Baudelaire. No less a luminary than Robert Frost borrowed the title of his collection *A Boy's Will* from the refrain of "My Lost Youth." Longfellow was, in all, a more public figure than even the boisterous and ebullient Walt **Whitman**. Whereas the Good Gray Poet "insisted on the extent of our newness," as Angus Fletcher has explained, "Longfellow insisted on the depth of our oldness" (*Raritan* 10:4 [1991]). Longfellow strenuously opposed the call for an indigenous national literature, not because he was a provincial, but because he believed that the American literary tradition would combine the best elements of many European traditions and would be a composite or even cosmopolitan blend of their "peculiarities." For most of the next century, his argument seemed to prevail.

For most of the next century, too, he seemed to be the very type of professional man of letters who appraised his readers with a practiced eye and pitched his poems to appeal to the broadest possible audience. In 1873, for example, the *New York Ledger*, a popular weekly paper, paid him 3,000 dollars for his holiday idyl "The Hanging of the Crane." The same year, Longfellow celebrated the masters of English verse – those poets, as he wrote in "The Day is Done" (1844; LOA, 1: 383), "Whose distant footsteps echo / Through the corridors of Time" – in a series of sonnets entitled "Chaucer" (LOA, 1: 428), "Shakespeare," "Milton," and "Keats." In the first, he hailed the author of *The Canterbury Tales* as "the poet of the dawn" whose pages evoke "the crowing cock," the song of "lark and linnet," and the "odors of ploughed field or flowery mead." In the second, he portrayed the Bard as "the Poet paramount, / Whom all the Muses loved." In his private and academic life, however, Longfellow had little to say about the pre-Elizabethans in general and Chaucer in particular; and in 1840, he offered this judgment of Shakespeare's sonnets in his journal: "Either I was not wholly awake to their beauties, or those beauties have been exaggerated." That is, Longfellow seems to have written the sonnet sequence with a calculating eye upon the reputations of the poets that he honored in order to tap the esteem in which they were held. His public critical judgments were in most cases as conventional as his poetry.

His least satisfactory verses, at least from a modern perspective, are those that feature didactic exhortations. Longfellow believed, as he wrote in 1849, that the role of the poet was "to charm, to strengthen, and to teach." "The Village Blacksmith" (1839; LOA, 1: 375), for example, celebrates the honorable smith who, against the bucolic backdrop of rustic New England, steadily labors at his "flaming forge." This alliterative phrase recurs in the final stanza with its explicit lesson:

> Thus at the flaming forge of life
>   Our fortunes must be wrought;
> Thus on its sounding anvil shaped
>   Each burning deed and thought!

William Dean **Howells** later allowed that these final lines "make [the poem] a homily" and might easily have been omitted. Similarly, in "A Psalm of Life" (1838; LOA, 1: 370), the poet protests in sing-song stanzas of iambic tetrameters that "Life is real!" and "Life is earnest!" and admonishes his auditors to "be up and doing" and to "Let the dead Past bury its dead!" Hyatt Waggoner, who refers derisively to Longfellow's "generally fatal lack of intelligence," contends that the "Psalm," with its "absolute incoherence" of imagery, may be one of "the worst famous poems ever written." The poet asserts that life is worth living, although he seems to have forgotten why. Indeed, in stanza four he admits that "our hearts, though stout and brave, / Still, like muffled drums, are beating / Funeral marches to the grave." Stanza seven reports that "We can make our lives sublime, / And, departing, leave behind us / Footprints on the sands of time" – but, as Waggoner pointedly asks, "How long will footprints left in sand last?" Ironically, Longfellow answered such questions in "The Tide Rises, the Tide Falls" (1879; LOA, 1: 442): "The little waves, with their soft, white hands, / Efface the footprints in the sands."

Longfellow returned to the same valedictory theme in such popular lyrics as "The Day is Done," "Afternoon in February" (1845; LOA, 1: 386), "Curfew" (1845; LOA, 1: 388), "The Bridge" (LOA, 1: 386), "The Fire of Drift-Wood" (1848; LOA, 1: 391), and "My Lost Youth," as well as in his last completed poem, "The Bells of San Blas" (1882; LOA, 1: 447), with its renewed admonition to let the dead past bury its dead:

O Bells of San Blas, in vain
Ye call back the Past again!
    The Past is deaf to your prayer:
Out of the shadows of night
The world rolls into light;
    It is daybreak everywhere.

All in all, as Waggoner charged with understandable hyperbole, "Longfellow had just one thing to say, and he tried as best he could to deny it: that time is inherently and inevitably man's enemy, bringing only loss and nothingness." He was "a very sad poet who became not simply banal but incoherent and confused when he tried to cheer himself or others."

Longfellow's experiments in the standard ballad form were in general no more successful than his best-known lyrics. These experiments were often designed to extrapolate moral lessons from events such as the shipwreck near Marblehead, Massachusetts, in December 1839, which inspired "The Wreck of the Hesperus" (1839; LOA, 1: 373), and the discovery of a corroded suit of armor near Newport, Rhode Island, in 1840, which inspired "The Skeleton in Armour" (1840; LOA, 1: 377). "I have broken ground in a new field," the poet wrote a friend in January 1840, "namely, *Ballads*; beginning with the '*Wreck of the Schooner Hesperus.*' . . . I think I shall write more. The *National Ballad* is a virgin soil here in New England; and there are great materials. Besides, I have a great notion of working upon *people's* feelings." "The Wreck of the Hesperus," which is composed of 22 conventional stanzas, warns of the consequences of intellectual arrogance. After ignoring storm warnings with "a scornful laugh," the skipper wrecks the ship and kills himself, his entire crew, and his doting blue-eyed daughter. Longfellow received all of 25 dollars for it when it was first printed in the *New World* in January 1840. Although undeniably popular, this poem betrays the

same didactic tone that mars many of Longfellow's lyrics. "It is prolix, sentimental, unconvincing," and one of the most often-parodied of Longfellow's poems, according to Cecil B. Williams.

Longfellow's eight antislavery poems were nearly as clumsily polemical as his "psalms of life" and ballads were overtly didactic. The former were "written in a kindly – not a vindictive spirit," Longfellow maintained, because he thought that "Denunciation of Slave-holders would do more harm than good." Although he opposed slavery, he declined an invitation to campaign for Congress under the Liberty Party banner. His response to the crisis of the Union was, as John Seelye has remarked, "armchairism and fireside poetics epitomized" (*Virginia Quarterly Review* 60 [1984]). "The Warning" (1842; LOA, 1: 381) is, in fact, little more than a blatant admonition to white readers to beware the grim consequences of slave rebellions should justice be long delayed. The poem, that is, exploits readers' fears instead of pricking their consciences:

There is a poor, blind Samson in this land,
    Shorn of his strength, and bound in bonds of steel,
Who may, in some grim revel, raise his hand,
    And shake the pillars of this Commonweal,
Till the vast Temple of our liberties
A shapeless mass of wreck and rubbish lies.

Longfellow's quarrel with the peculiar institution finally seems more pragmatic than altruistic. Similarly, the poet voiced a proper Unitarian disgust for anti-Semitism in "The Jewish Cemetery at Newport" (1852; LOA, 1: 397), a meditation on the "sepulchral stones" with their names of "foreign accent." Only in the middle stanza, however, does Longfellow reach the crux of the issue:

How came they here? What burst of Christian hate,
    What persecution, merciless and blind,
Drove o'er the sea – that desert desolate –
    These Ishmaels and Hagars of mankind?

As George Monteiro has concluded, such poems expressed genuine sympathy for the plight of the oppressed, but they "exhibited none of the incendiary and righteous anger" voiced in the antislavery verse of writers like Whittier.

Hardly more satisfactory are Longfellow's several allegories on poetry and the role and function of the poet. In the very early "The Spirit of Poetry" (1825; LOA, 1: 369), for example, Longfellow personifies poetic inspiration as the voice of a woodland nymph who whispers in "the nice and delicate ear of thought," shouts in the "sylvan pomp of woods," and sings in "the rich music of a summer bird." "Seaweed" (1844; LOA, 1: 384) compares vegetation that washes up on shore with verse that floats to consciousness in storms of passion, although Longfellow revises the trope in the final stanza to stress how poems, once "in books recorded," are "like hoarded / Household words" and "no more depart." Rudolph von Abele dismisses the "pseudo-platonic 'inspiration' theory" of art, with its "anti-intellectual implications," that Longfellow propounded in this poem (*American Literature* 24 [1952]). Even the late "Kéramos" (1877; LOA, 1: 429), which compares the potter or ceramic artist at his wheel to the poet at his craft, seems clichéd in its affirmation of the task of the artist. Consider this stanza:

Turn, turn, my wheel! All life is brief;
What now is bud will soon be leaf,
    What now is leaf will soon decay;
The wind blows east, the wind blows west;
The blue eggs in the robin's nest
    Will soon have wings and beak and breast,
        And flutter and fly away.

Not only do these lines support Waggoner's thesis about Longfellow's poems – that they seem obsessed with the inexorable passage of time in the manner of a warmed-over Percy Bysshe Shelley – the stanza limps badly at its fourth line, which seems inserted for no better reason than to provide a rhyme for the words "nest" and "breast" in the next two lines. To be sure, the poet asserts in the final stanzas that "Art is the child of Nature" and that the artist ought to mirror or mimic nature, but he then qualifies these related points by admitting that the "majestic loveliness" of nature should be "Chastened and softened and subdued / Into a more attractive grace, / And with a human sense imbued." What seems at first to be a defense of poetic realism à la Whitman thus becomes a clichéd defense of idealism and didacticism in the arts. In all, as George Arms has opined, Longfellow's "poems on poetry do not go much beyond a genteel or romantic Platonism in their concept of the origin or function of art."

Still, despite the stodgy moralism of many of his most popular ballads and lyrics, some of Longfellow's poetry may be defended in the same way that Mark Twain excused Richard Wagner's music: it "isn't as bad as it sounds." Hawthorne once remarked that, at their best, "nothing equal" to Longfellow's poems "was ever written in this world." Newton Arvin asserted that Longfellow's verse, when successful, has "a kind of grave, slow-paced, mellifluous quality, like a slightly monotonous but not unmusical chant, which is genuinely expressive of its mournful and minor theme." Fletcher has recently argued that Longfellow was "a master of traditional lyric forms" and that some of his "ballads still rouse the blood." Arms, however, has correctly diagnosed the structural problem inherent in Longfellow's exhortatory verse. Typically, as in the three stanzas of "Snow-Flakes" (LOA, 1: 423), Longfellow begins with a physical description of a scene ("Silent, and soft, and slow / Descends the snow"), explores an analogy or relation between the scene and an emotion it evokes ("The troubled sky reveals / The grief it feels"), and concludes with an explicit lesson or moral statement ("This is the poem of the air," "This is the secret of despair"). In his didactic verse, in effect, Longfellow was ever the patient teacher, the reader the submissive student.

Fortunately, the very form or formula of the Italian sonnet, with its octave and sestet, required Longfellow to adopt a simpler, less directive two-stage movement. In "Mezzo Cammin" (1842; LOA, 1: 382), he laments past failures and blasted ambitions before turning in his last lines to a vision of the unrealized future, the "cataract of Death far thundering from the heights." Similarly, in "The Evening Star" (1845; LOA, 1: 390), the poet first addresses "the painted oriel of the West" in the heavens, which he then compares in the sestet to his beloved, his "morning and . . . evening star of love." In "The Harvest Moon" (1876; LOA, 1: 441), he depicts a pastoral scene of woodland villages illumined by the autumn night-sky before declaring that such "external shows / Of Nature have

their image in the mind" – that is, in Emersonian parlance, that "Nature is the symbol of spirit." In "Venice" (1876; LOA, 1: 440), he reminisces about the ethereal "phantom city" on the Adriatic, which he expects one day to "vanish like the fleets / Seen in mirage." And in "Night" (1879; LOA, 1: 442), the poet, who observed in his journal that in dreams "all things are possible," silhouettes the ideal world that dreamers occupy and the "better life" they lead across the boundary of sleep.

Occasionally, Longfellow was able to transcend the rigid conventions that normally governed his didactic verse. As Arms demonstrates, the elegiac "The Tide Rises, the Tide Falls" and "Aftermath" (1873; LOA, 1: 426), with its poignant evocation of harvest-time, are both heavily weighted with symbolic freight that functions "only in the stage of scene" and that does not "enter the second stage of analogy or the third of statement at all." In the dramatic monologue "Belisarius" (1875; LOA, 1: 427), Longfellow assumes the perspective of the aged sixth-century general, the leading military figure during the reign of the Byzantine emperor Justinian I, whose career was chronicled by the historian Procopius of Caesurea. While still in his twenties, Belisarius had won renown for pressing the emperor's cause on the Mesopotamian or eastern front in A.D. 530. Or, as Longfellow writes:

It was for him I chased
The Persians o'er wild and waste,
    As General of the East;
Night after night I lay
In their camps of yesterday;
    Their forage was my feast.

In 533, Belisarius reconquered the Roman territories in northern Africa that had been occupied by the Vandals. As Longfellow recounts:

For him, with sails of red,
And torches at mast-head,
    Piloting the great fleet,
I swept the Afric coasts
And scattered the Vandal hosts,
    Like dust in a windy street.

In 535, Belisarius began a torturous campaign to reclaim Italy from Sicily north from the Goths, which ended with their surrender in 540. As Longfellow says:

For him I won again
The Ausonian realm and reign,
    Rome and Parthenope;
And all the land was mine
From the summits of Apennine
    To the shores of either sea.

Still later, in 559, Belisarius was summoned from retirement by Justinian to organize the defense of Constantinople from the Huns:

For him, in my feeble age,
I dared the battle's rage,
    To save Byzantium's state,
When the tents of Zabergan,
Like snow-drifts overran
    The road to the Golden Gate.

Despite his long years of service to the emperor, however, Belisarius was stripped of authority. His wealth also was confiscated in 562 as a result of palace intrigue. According to legend, moreover, he was blinded on orders from the ungrateful Justinian and forced to beg for his livelihood in the streets of Constantinople during the final months of his life. Again, as Longfellow writes:

> And for this, for this, behold!
> Infirm and blind and old,
>   With gray, uncovered head,
> Beneath the very arch
> Of my triumphal march,
>   I stand and beg my bread!

A radical departure from Longfellow's normal didacticism, "Belisarius" is at least vaguely reminiscent of the dramatic monologues of Robert Browning, whose lyrics Longfellow admired.

Especially in his private verse, when Longfellow was relieved of the public poet's obligation to exhort or instruct his readers, he proved an able craftsman. The point is best illustrated by his sorrowful sonnet "The Cross of Snow" (LOA, 1: 441), which remained unpublished until after his death, and which eloquently belies his reputation as a sentimental poet incapable of profound emotion. In July 1861, his wife, Fanny Appleton Longfellow, had died when her muslin dress caught on fire in a household accident. The poet extinguished the flames that killed her by enveloping her in a rug; in the process, he so severely burned his hands and face that he was unable to attend her funeral four days later. (He wore a beard in later life to cover the scarring.) His modern reputation for shallow sentimentality notwithstanding, Longfellow was deeply affected by her death. As he wrote to his sister-in-law the next month, "How I am alive after what my eyes have seen, I know not." According to Samuel Longfellow's biography of his brother, when a visitor "expressed the hope that he might be enabled to 'bear his cross' with patience," the poet replied: "*Bear* the cross, yes; but what if one is stretched upon it!" The anecdote may suggest the donnée of the poem. At any rate, on the eighteenth anniversary of her death, in 1879, the still-grieving Longfellow wrote these lines in solemn and private commemoration of her passing:

> In the long, sleepless watches of the night,
>   A gentle face – the face of one long dead –
>   Looks at me from the wall, where round its head
>   The night-lamp casts a halo of pale light.
> Here in this room she died; and soul more white
>   Never through martyrdom of fire was led
>   To its repose; nor can in books be read
>   The legend of a life more benedight.
> There is a mountain in the distant West
>   That, sun-defying, in its deep ravines
>   Displays a cross of snow upon its side.
> Such is the cross I wear upon my breast
>   These eighteen years, through all the changing scenes
>   And seasons, changeless since the day she died.

With her halo of light and snow-white soul, the saintly Fanny seems vividly present to her husband in the glare of a sleepless night. The final lines of the sonnet, with its familiar two-stage

movement, contrast the martyrdom of fire that killed his wife with the poet's own martyrdom of ice, the glacierlike pathos with which he has mourned her over the years.

Longfellow's several long narrative poems are, on the whole, more qualified successes. *The Song of Hiawatha* (1855), published in the same year as the original edition of Whitman's *Leaves of Grass*, romanticizes the Indians, as Waggoner alleged: "Hiawatha and his associates are sometimes made to seem more like Victorian Bostonians" than Native Americans. The poet himself regarded his Indian hero as "a kind of American Prometheus," or noble savage. Although it was enormously popular in the nineteenth century, the poem is, at best, ethnographically uninformed and heavily dependent on H. R. Schoolcraft's writings on Indian mythology. Longfellow also borrowed the poem's eight-syllable trochaic verse from the unrhymed Finnish epic *Kalevala*, a choice that led later to trumped-up charges of plagiarism. Despite its flaws, the narrative continues to attract attention among comparativists. The epic idyl *Evangeline* (1847; see LOA, 1:393), written in the dactylic hexameters of classical Greek and Latin poetry, recounts the constancy of a pair of star-crossed Acadian lovers who were cruelly separated when British troops resettled the residents of Nova Scotia as a war measure in 1755. The gentle Evangeline proves the "beauty and strength of a woman's devotion" in her persistent quest for her betrothed Gabriel. She seeks him on the prairies, in the bayous of Louisiana, and even as far west as the Ozark Mountains, barely missing him on several occasions. "Thus did the long sad years glide on, and in seasons and places / Divers and distant far was seen the wandering maiden." In these cantos, according to Seelye, Evangeline is "a personification of alienation, the embowered yet accursed American Eve" who has been expelled from the paradise of Acadia. Similarly, Fletcher asserted that the poem is "a version of the Old Testament story of the Babylonian exile of the Jews." At length, Evangeline abandons the search to spend her last years as a Sister of Mercy, in which role she one day providentially discovers the aged Gabriel on his deathbed:

> Vainly he strove to rise; and Evangeline, kneeling beside
>   him,
> Kissed his dying lips, and laid his head on her bosom.
> Sweet was the light of his eyes; but it suddenly sank into
>   darkness,
> As when a lamp is blown out by a gust of wind at a
>   casement.

"It is impossible in this unsentimental age to imagine or understand" how *Evangeline* was received by Longfellow's contemporaries, Cecil B. Williams fairly allowed, "though even the cynical modern reader is likely to find an indefinable charm" in the poem. Certainly, it had the effect of cementing Longfellow's nineteenth-century reputation, for better or worse. As Theodore Parker then noted in his review of *Evangeline*, "American readers may well thank the author for a poem, so wholly American in its incidents, its geography, and its setting."

During the early years of his literary career, Longfellow was devoted to the study of Scandinavian and Romance languages. In fact, his translations from foreign sources during this period far outweigh the bulk of his original poems. As early as 1833, while still in his mid-twenties, he formally expressed his ideas on the topic: "The great art of translating well lies in the power of rendering literally the words of a foreign author while at the same time we preserve the spirit of the original." He later added that: "Most readers have not the slightest notion of the thought and creative power that goes into a translation." If his ostensibly original poetry was flawed by its overreliance on European sources, he turned this defect to his advantage in his translations. "As a translator, he was generally admitted to have no superior in the English tongue; his skill was unvarying and absolutely reliable," stated his friend Thomas Wentworth Higginson. According to Fletcher, Longfellow "educated the American reading public" and "he managed to do so because his translations are works of the most exquisite technical skill." Thus, Fletcher claimed, Longfellow "did nothing less than make literary Europe available to his readers." Even *Evangeline*, with its motif of exile and displacement, "is less an expression of tolerance toward immigrant peoples than a reflection of his own deep commitment to European culture," Seelye asserted. The poem is "a thoroughly derivative work, from its Goethean overtones to its perverse hexameters."

Longfellow's translations were, moreover, instrumental to his intellectual and artistic maturation. As his friend Horace Scudder once testified, "translating played an important part in the development of Mr. Longfellow's powers." The poet collected many of his early translations in the anthology *The Poets and Poetry of Europe* (1845), which was hugely popular and critically acclaimed. The volume, which includes translated texts by nearly 400 poets in 10 modern languages, introduced thousands of American readers to the non-English verse of Europe. No work like it had yet appeared in either America or England. Its sweep extended from the Middle Ages and early Italian poetry to the mid–nineteenth century and the verse of Heine. The original edition ran to 776 double-columned pages; in a second edition issued in 1870, Longfellow appended a 340-page supplement. He continued to pursue his interest in translation literally until his death. His bibliography for 1882 contains no fewer than 400 translated works. Yet the mature poet, acutely sensitive to the pitfalls of his profession, understood that translations are always at best approximations. In "Prelude to the Translations" (1870), he compares lyrics turned into another language to treasures "deep buried in seasands" and asks rhetorically whether they should not remain "locked in their iron chest." Ironically, although his own verse is disappearing from anthologies of American literature, his translations warrant wider celebrity.

More immediately to the point, while still in his thirties, Longfellow proposed to translate the whole of the *Divina Commedia*, which he pronounced a "sacred song" in his sonnet "Dante" (1845). He first made a stab at translating excerpts from the epic for his students at Bowdoin. After moving to Harvard, he worked haphazardly on the project for several months and completed work on 16 cantos of terza rima by 1843. He returned to it 18 years later, after his retirement from Harvard and the death of Fanny Longfellow. Over the years, Longfellow increasingly stressed accuracy and fidelity to the original text no less than elegance and grace of translation. "The business of the translator is to report what his author says, not to explain what he means," he remarked in his notebook. The chief merit of his translation of the *Divina Commedia*, he elsewhere suggested, "is that it is exactly what Dante says, and not what the translator imagines he might have said if he had been an Englishman." Still, Howells, for one, complained that Longfellow had translated the *Divina Commedia* "into the English dictionary rather than the English language." If Alexander Pope had made Homer ride a hobbyhorse, then surely Longfellow set Dante astride one. Edmund Clarence **Stedman** averred that "the three divisions seem leveled, so to speak, to the grade of the Purgatorio, midway between the zenith and nadir of Dante's song." Nevertheless, Longfellow's late version of the *Divina Commedia* was the highlight of his translating career. Despite its defects, it remains one of the standard English versions of Dante more than a century after its publication.

For the record, too, Fanny Longfellow figures as a type of Beatrice in the sonnet-sequence "Divina Commedia" (1867; LOA, 1:424), which prefaced the poet's three-volume translation of the epic. The fourth of the self-admonitory sonnets, which prefaced the *Purgatorio*, contains this riveting image, which is all the more striking given the cause of his wife's death:

> With snow-white veil and garments as of flame,
>   She stands before thee, who so long ago
>   Filled thy young heart with passion and the woe
> From which thy song and all its splendors came.

The next lines comprise a gloss of sorts on "The Cross of Snow" and invert its image of the stoic, cold-hearted poet:

> And while with stern rebuke she speaks thy name,
>   The ice about thy heart melts as the snow
>   On mountain heights, and in swift overflow
> Comes gushing from thy lips in sobs of shame.

In the fifth sonnet, which prefaced the *Paradiso*, Beatrice "again at Dante's side / No more rebukes, but smiles her words of praise." It was a consummation devoutly to be wished.

Although Longfellow will doubtless never again enjoy the high estate he was accorded in the late nineteenth century, neither does he deserve the derision he suffered in the heyday of the New Criticism. As Odell Shepard asserted in 1934, "The retreat from Longfellow, which has recently become almost a stampede, has been caused by nothing connected with the art of poetry." He has been caricatured as a Johnny-one-note of sentimental verse, but Longfellow was actually a virtuoso of sorts, adept at a variety of verse forms. Even at the height of his career, he would not rest on his laurels; as he wrote in the posthumously published "Michel Angelo": "I never am content, / But always see the labor of my hand / Fall short of my conception." Longfellow judiciously assessed the worth of his poems even as he shrewdly negotiated their price. In the end, Howells pronounced perhaps the most fitting epitaph on Longfellow's achievement in 1907: "No poet uttered more perfectly what was characteristically best in his own time."

GARY SCHARNHORST

Selected Works
The Complete Poetical Works of Longfellow, edited by
    Horace E. Scudder, Boston: Houghton Mifflin, 1893;
    reprinted as *The Poetical Works of Longfellow*, with new
    introduction by George Monteiro, 1975

Henry Wadsworth Longfellow: Representative Selections, edited by Odell Shepard, New York: American Book, 1934

The Letters of Henry Wadsworth Longfellow, edited by Andrew Hilen, 6 vols., Cambridge: Belknap, 1966

Further Reading

Arms, George, *The Fields Were Green: A New View of Bryant, Whittier, Holmes, Lowell, and Longfellow*, Palo Alto, California: Stanford University Press, 1953

Arvin, Newton, *Longfellow: His Life and Work*, Boston: Little, Brown, 1962

Higginson, T. W., *Henry Wadsworth Longfellow*, Boston and New York: Houghton Mifflin, 1902

Hilen, Andrew R., *Longfellow and Scandinavia*, New Haven, Connecticut: Yale University Press, 1947

Johnson, Carl L., *Professor Longfellow of Harvard*, Eugene: University of Oregon Press, 1944

Longfellow, Samuel, *Life of Henry Wadsworth Longfellow*, 2 vols., Boston and New York: Houghton Mifflin, 1886

Norton, Charles Eliot, *Henry Wadsworth Longfellow*, Boston: Houghton Mifflin, 1907

Pearce, Roy Harvey, *The Continuity of American Poetry*, Princeton, New Jersey: Princeton University Press, 1961

Richards, I. A., *Practical Criticism*, New York: Harcourt, Brace, 1929

Thompson, Lawrance, *Young Longfellow*, New York: Macmillan, 1938

Wagenknecht, Edward, *Henry Wadsworth Longfellow: His Poetry and Prose*, New York: Ungar, 1986

_____, *Henry Wadsworth Longfellow: Portrait of an American Humanist*, New York: Oxford University Press, 1966

Waggoner, Hyatt H., *American Poets from the Puritans to the Present*, Boston: Houghton Mifflin, 1968

Williams, Cecil B., *Henry Wadsworth Longfellow*, New York: Twayne, 1964

James Russell Lowell

(1819–1891)

Since virtually nothing of Lowell's poetry remains familiar to the reader of nineteenth-century American literature, we are pleasantly surprised to learn that he penned the famous line "And what is so rare as a day in June?" It is a striking thought, until we muse upon it, and then we note that Lowell's rhetorical question gets its force mainly from a sprightly rhythm. Lowell seldom allows imagistic, or more broadly imaginative invention to interfere with the construction of the elegant, well-formed phrase and sentence. There are numerous poems such as "An Indian-Summer Reverie" and "Beaver Brook," where the descriptive style of eighteenth-century topographical poetry achieves considerable picturesque charm, but often the poetry seems to miss a much wanted intensity. Lowell uses neo-classic and Romantic personifications to fill this need, but for some reason, the poetry pulls back from the claims of emotional conviction. Indeed, the surcharged flatness and the frequent attempt to break into a natural vigor are in themselves revealing phenomena, since by all accounts his contemporaries found him a lively speaker, a quick and pungent thinker, and a critic of strong, incisive, and discriminating taste. It is as if Lowell knew all about poetic flatness, and must have known how to avoid it. He was certainly well aware of the prevailing tendency of his own times to indulge in empty religious pieties, in what has been aptly called "the trivial sublime." As a critic, he always rejected sentimentality, recognizing it as a danger to art. He appreciated the worldly English authors, and against all platitudes appears forewarned and forearmed. We therefore wonder at any lack of memorable work to be found in the complete oeuvre. But Lowell suffers from a typical professorial weakness. While he knows how poetry *should* be written, he cannot let his own poetry come into being outside or beyond the bounds of his well-schooled academic knowledge of literature. Exactly how this constraint upon imagination, this defect of freedom occurs, and how Lowell occasionally broke free of it, are things worth considering, since they involve American literature throughout the nineteenth century. The poet and the professor may well be at odds with each other. Certainly in him the original wages a bold, if at times uneven war against the conventional.

James Russell Lowell was born to a noted New England family in 1819, the same year that Walt **Whitman** and Herman **Melville** were born. Lowell's father, Charles, was a well-known Boston minister; his mystical mother, Harriet Brackett Spence Lowell, descended from Orkney Island Scots. The family house in Cambridge, Massachusetts – Elmwood – remained home to the poet, with certain interruptions, for most of his life. He was early a great reader, devouring Dante, Tasso, Edmund Spenser, William Shakespeare, John Milton, and the Romantics. At Harvard, he became a poet, a bon vivant, and something of a satirist. He began in the late 1830s to think increasingly about the evils of slavery, views that sharply intensified when, on December 2, 1839, he married Maria White, an ardent abolitionist. Lowell took a law degree eventually, but by 1840 was beginning to publish his poetry in the *Southern Literary Messenger* and *Graham's Magazine*, to be followed by

contributions to other journals of the time. He also wrote appreciative criticism of Elizabethan drama and essays on miscellaneous domestic topics: "Getting Up," "Married Men," and the like, topics that in later life gave way to lengthy critical essays on major literary figures.

Launched into a somewhat desultory career – Roy Harvey Pearce was to call him a "chameleon-like figure" – Lowell experienced the literary life on several fronts. In 1842, he started *The Pioneer*, his own first impressive editorial venture which, although it did not financially succeed, showed the talent that would eventually lead him to be the first editor of the *Atlantic Monthly*. In *The Pioneer* were published Edgar Allan **Poe**, Nathaniel **Hawthorne**, Elizabeth Barrett (Browning), William Wetmore **Story**, John **Neal**, and Jones **Very**, among other luminaries. Joy and sadness mingled in the Lowells' marriage for, in 1847, their beloved daughter Blanche died, leaving her bereft father to mourn her in pathetic verses such as "She came and went," "The Changeling," and "The First Snowfall."

But Lowell's great year, 1848, was to see him publish his Arthurian "Vision of Sir Launfal," the *Fable for Critics*, and the first series of the *Biglow Papers* (see LOA, 1: 684–694 for excerpts of each). He soon issued a second book of lyrics, chief among them his 1844 poem "The Present Crisis" (see LOA, 1: 683), a pseudo-sublime, overwrought, but nonetheless heartfelt hymn to the need for abolition. All through this decade and well into the next, Lowell joined forces with the antislavery crusade, writing frequently and forcefully in its cause.

Maria White **Lowell** had never enjoyed robust health. Childbearing probably killed her, with its physical dangers and the loss of one child after another. On October 27, 1853, she died, despite a trip abroad for her health. In later years, Lowell was again to return to Europe on extended diplomatic missions to Spain and Britain, and he always maintained his sense of a transatlantic cultural mission. Having edited the *Atlantic* and later the *North American Review*, he achieved a very high profile in the production of mid-century American literature. Longer poems followed, most notably the "Commemoration Ode" of 1865 (LOA, 1: 696), "The Cathedral" of 1870 (inspired by a visit to Chartres), the memorial ode to Louis Agassiz (1874), "Ode Read at the One Hundredth Anniversary of the Fight at Concord Bridge" (1875), "An Ode for the Fourth of July" (1876), rounding with the volume of collected verses, *Heartsease and Rue* (1888). Throughout this period, Lowell wrote periodical essays. It was a full literary life, not least because in 1856 Lowell had succeeded Henry Wadsworth **Longfellow** in the professorship of modern languages at Harvard, a post he held for many years, whose tenure coincided with his happy second marriage to Frances Dunlap, his wife until her death in 1885. The poet in these years also served as minister to the Court of St. James (Great Britain), where his humor, erudition, and conversational charm won many friends.

In 1889, Lowell delivered a lecture, "The Study of Modern Languages," to the Modern Language Association, and the following year saw the completion of a 10-volume Riverside edition of his works. On August 12, 1891, he died in the old home, Elmwood. His life was literary from start to finish. It was, despite its political activity, deeply academic. Lowell was the brilliant, many-sided professorial poet and polemicist. To young writers like William Dean **Howells,** he was a hero, a man of exceptional powers and range. Robert Lowell – his great-grand-nephew – accounted him "a bubbling stylist . . . the first American literary critic with anything resembling the reading, wit, and worldliness of Matthew Arnold."

Lowell certainly did not fail to practice within a wide range of verse. He wrote songs and sonnets, formal odes, verse satires, elegies and neomedieval ballads, didactic visions, a major verse-essay in criticism, conversation poems, and long meditative rhapsodies such as "The Cathedral." As compared with the poetry being written in the United States at the time, all these verses are competently written, and any poet could learn from their apparent finish. Yet the body of the verse remains oddly miscellaneous, unduly occasional, and so, too, is its character, line by line, stanza by stanza. Lowell quite lacked the ability to form large structures of poetic discourse. At any moment one expects to turn the corner into a coherent structure; the poetic argument just about gets started, but then it dies, through inward prolixity. More than once the poet accuses himself of rambling and digressing. It is no accident that throughout his life Lowell was always much admired as an after-dinner speaker. The fact that he and his contemporaries expected from him great things is, however, not simply to be understood in terms of Lowell's own deficiencies as poet, as rather in the circumstance that he shared a deep defect of his whole society. His world was miscellaneous in ways that could hardly be avoided, except by extreme measures such as those of the masters of the American Renaissance – just think of Emily **Dickinson,** Whitman, and Melville – or by a natural genius for platitude, as in the case of Longfellow. The latter seems to play a much more powerful part in the drama of the genteel tradition, and in American letters generally, than has been noted. Perhaps Longfellow was Lowell's poetic precursor, more powerful than John Keats or Samuel Taylor Coleridge or Thomas Gray; if so, Longfellow's tone of relentlesss *control* would have been enough to set Lowell against his own more sprightly genius. Certainly, Longfellow lowered the level of textural density, surprise, and excitement, and if he was Lowell's poetic mentor (besides preceding him in the modern languages professorship at Harvard), Longfellow here as elsewhere settled that genteel American poetry would get strength by forming down, instead of up. There was always the troubling example of Whitman, whose "yawp," the Cambridge literati agreed, was "barbaric."

The question then had to be: could poetry express America without becoming barbaric? Longfellow's transatlantic sensibility suggested that American poets might continue onward from their English models by translating European literary culture – literally, as with his Dante translations, and figuratively by adopting and adapting old European models. This literary program looked backward, unlike Whitman's, which looked forward to the expanding context of an immigrant, as opposed to colonial, culture. The "fireside" vision also rejected the radical experimentalism of Edgar Allan Poe. Gentility required that the poet maintain his connection to the mother country, and yet resist a perfervid Puritanism and its stereotypes.

Lowell's output belongs to this translative enterprise, with one important exception, *The Biglow Papers*. A close look indicates how Lowell fails, and how he succeeds, in bringing the Old and New Worlds together. Cambridge and Boston of the nineteenth century shared English values, and, besides the common law, this sharing mostly depended upon a shared literary language. Coleridge, who used a pre-Romantic art of sublime personification, meant much as a model and influence to Lowell, who could write, in "An Incident in a Railroad Car":

> O mighty brother-soul of man,
>   Where'er thou art, in low or high,
> Thy skyey arches with exulting span
>   O'er-roof infinity!

Or, in "Columbus": "– Life, the one block / Of marble that's vouchsafed wherefrom to carve / Our great thoughts," etc. Or, in his "Ode to France":

> With eye averted, and an anguished frown,
>   Loathingly glides the Muse through
>   scenes of strife,
> Where, like the heart of Vengeance up
>   and down,
>   Throbs in its framework the blood-
>   muffled knife . . . etc., etc.

Or, typically, to the daughter of an American expatriate painter, herself an artist of picturesque landscapes:

SONNET
To Fanny Alexander

> Unconscious as the sunshine, simply sweet
> And generous as that, thou dost not close
> Thyself in art, as life were but a rose
> To rumple bee-like with luxurious feet;
> Thy higher mind therein finds sure retreat,
> But not from care of common hopes and woes;
> Thee the dark chamber, thee the unfriended, knows,
> Although no babbling crowds thy praise repeat:
> Consummate artist, who life's landscape bleak
> Hast brimmed with sun to many a clouded eye,
> Touched to a brighter hue the beggar's cheek,
> Hung over orphaned lives a gracious sky,
> And traced for eyes, that else would vainly seek,
> Fair pictures of an angel drawing nigh!

One could ask, what poetic vice is draining these poems of their energy? Surely Lowell's flaw is the combination of entirely conventional images with a somewhat laboring intelligence that seeks, by working or carving the imagery, to give it formal rigor. Lowell mistakes prosaic control over analogy and its parts for poetry's essential demand: a radical rejection of various allegorical devices, including "mechanical" analogies and tedious personifications of earnest sincerity. So, decently, laboriously, he works his personifications and *wills* his poems. Personification, which for pre-Romantics had been the archetypally passionate figure, readily here becomes routine. For instance, adverting to the profession of soldiering, Lowell ascribes to General Grant the power to "saddle opportunity," much as Fanny Alexander ministered to Italian beggars by painting them in charming poses, hanging "over orphaned lives a gracious sky." Everywhere in Lowell, one finds this tendency to paint idealized "pictures," as when he identifies the mental strength of Louis Agassiz, the scientist, with two old poets, "Deep-chested [George] Chapman and firm-footed Ben [Jonson]." The associations, the allusions, the images, and the tone *all* derive from a bookish sense of reality. Lowell does not sense the moral and aesthetic muddle arising when he depicts the dead Agassiz as "Loosed from the stiffening uniform of fame." Nor does it help to defend this image on "realistic" grounds by referring to the weight of heavy Victorian uniforms. The "uniform of fame" is a failed personification; it is ruined by the very thing that is intended to make it graphic, the allegorizing adjective "stiffening." In the error of such a seemingly minor misstep lies almost the whole story of the battle of American poets to free themselves of European domination. They mistook machinery for the divine mania Plato had assumed the poet would pray for. It would take a major detour away from conventional poetic manners for Lowell to escape his own accomplished routines.

In all this, one cannot avoid speculating about the repressive character of New England values, always tinged and controlled by the fact that men were idealized as "friends" or demonized as foes, while women, in this confining system, were ideally depicted as angels, as were their daughters. If one married, as Lowell did, a creature "pure and spirit-like . . . half of earth and *more* than half of Heaven," not only was one wedded to an illogical first step, one was also doomed to a round of inescapable ensuing domestic piety, and, as poet, one perforce would need resolute, subtle resistance to Puritan versions of this piety.

The Victorian myth of domestic (and domesticating) harmony, the view of wives and little children as angels, the denial of sexual conflicts and incompatibilities, and the canting enthusiasm for idealized homes – all these examples of "family values" served to glue the bourgeois family together as a social idea. They also, unhappily, poisoned the heart of poetry, which requires, not sincerity, but a widened experience. The ideal bourgeois home whose ultimate economic base – say the factories in Lowell, Massachusetts – must be hidden to public view rarely provides a fundamental expressive tension the poetry needs. (Henry James wrote often of this material drag.) Lowell may speak of his wife Maria's "strange earnestness," but cannot bring her into contact with the public world, where, in Longfellow's platitude, "Life is real! Life is earnest!" (see LOA, 1: 370). Her ardent abolitionist views are socially required to be divorced from the activism of Margaret **Fuller**, whom Lowell satirically attacked in his *Fable for Critics*. Maria Lowell was a poet herself, but, according to her cultural assignment as "angel of the hearth," she belonged to the home, blocked by her domestic duties from activity in the public world. Meanwhile, the physical hazards of being a mother could not be accorded a public voice. (For another account of the Lowells' marriage, see the essay on Maria White Lowell in this volume.)

On the husband's side, such divisions also imply that a vigorous, unsentimental man like Lowell would be forced to speak, questing the truth, in formal or official terms. Yet one finds throughout his verse a desire to sharpen ideas into news-like images – so he associates Agassiz with the scientific image of the telegraph ("The electric nerve, whose instantaneous

thrill / Makes next-door gossips of the antipodes . . ."). The poetry suggests a restless mind reminiscent of Thomas Browne's. The Harvard that Lowell watched change from "seminary" to university was alive with the knowledge of an increasingly technological world, and a decreasing belief in what Lowell regarded as the outmoded text-mongering of the "second generation" Puritans. These Puritans may have provided one myth of the American self, but during Lowell's lifetime this myth began to resemble, in its more obsessive typological details, what he said of Cotton Mather – a "pedantic nightmare." We need to recall this cosmopolitan response to the Mather who seems to students of Sacvan Bercovitch and David Levin to be a complex and powerful visionary. But Lowell is looking for a more worldly vision, or one less dependent upon textual pieties. He craved secularity.

What is most striking about Lowell, as public poet, is the fact that *as a matter of principle* he understood the hard, gritty nature of real poetry (a roughness that, as we have seen, would always in him be at war with polite personifications and locutions). The fact that poetry demands unguarded imagination, and a grip upon imperfect truths, was not lost on Lowell the critic. His *Fable for Critics*, which delights in cheerful academic doggerel, gives energetic proof that he could always or almost always discern the "real thing" in others' poetry, as Byron had in *English Bards and Scotch Reviewers*, to which the *Fable* was often compared. Lowell's problem was to find this real thing for himself, when, leaving criticism aside, he wrote his own poetry. Before the Civil War, he turned to an ingenious and successful solution – satires, pastorals, and lyrics written in a marked substandard dialect. Only in this way was he, remarkably, able to find a true poetic voice, in public terms, although at a considerable cost.

Here we glimpse the fundamental struggle of American poets of the period, which was in large part to escape the woeful machinery of the Puritan myth, to escape precisely what recent typological critics have argued was the great creatively determining force. Biblical typology, unfortunately, is the bad cholesterol of the American literary language. Typological scholars have found it in the American literary bloodstream, which does not argue that it is good for poetry; if anything, it just means that, like scientists who have to fight against the errors of so-called creationists, poets have had to fight against religious stereotypes. To break free of the allegorization of history, American literature, for Lowell as for other celebrated American authors, required a measured *rejection* of stereotyping Puritan typology. Puritans, Puritanism, and their modern exegetes tend to inhibit, control, trammel, and stifle the aesthetic drive that art – as such – seeks to engage. Typology, when it becomes a complex consensus-building procedure, is virtually an aesthetic curse, as those who found ways to escape it, notably Ralph Waldo **Emerson**, Melville, Hawthorne, Whitman, and Dickinson, knew so well. Fundamentalist critics who assemble collages of intertextual typological tags, refuse deliberately, it would seem, to perceive that the great American writers have universally rejected or resisted the Puritan legacy to which they fell heir. At the very least, these authors try to subvert the pedantic conformity of the Puritan hermeneutic, and this especially is the case with the most accomplished escape artist, Nathaniel Hawthorne. Typology is like advertising; it stereotypes, and poetry – for various reasons that have to do with the necessary primacy, for the poet, of poetics over rhetoric – must continually war against the blandishments – the simplistic spiels – the typologist purveys. Behind this assertion, of course, there lies a whole debate about the fate of art and poetry in our time, a period of knee-jerk allegorization, not least in relation to the earlier quest for a poetic American independence. Poetry is not a form of sophisticated Bible-thumping. Poets, authors like Hawthorne and Melville, clearly sense that they are in conflict with biblical determinisms of all sorts; nor does it help, as just said, to sophisticate the current version of Puritan hermeneutics. We are not surprised to find that a distrust of typology and a distaste for its anesthetic effects mark the opinions and practices of James Russell Lowell, the student of secularity and of Dante, in the sense of the poet of the secular world seen with religiously informed vision, Erich Auerbach's Dante in *Mimesis*. Lowell's enthusiasm for Dante, shared so widely in his literary New England, marks a dedication to classical aspirations.

Not unexpectedly, Lowell achieved one central evasion of the old typology by making use of neoclassic public conventions. His famed "Commemoration Ode," delivered at Harvard on July 21, 1865, expressing a characteristic tone of resigned expectation, brought true elegiac grandeur to its theme. Cadenced paragraphs deriving from the Pindaric tradition, well known to Lowell, as we learn from his 1868 critical essay on Dryden, gave to the memorial occasion its required neoclassic decorum. For various extraneous reasons, the "Ode" was not a great success on delivery, yet Lowell's method makes eminent rhetorical sense. A poem modern readers may find empty was still a poem that, in its time, enlisted the participation of its willing audience. Here, as elsewhere, Lowell emerges in the role of a *performing* poet, in Richard Poirier's sense. It may be too easy to show the unearned poetic conceits of such a performative poem – to show, for instance, that Lowell too smoothly likens his own stanzas to the "squadron-strophes" of military units, "Live battle-odes whose lines were steel and fire." Nevertheless, precisely these emblematic tokens work well for public performance. They are, oratorically, pre-sold. And the same may be said of all Lowell's conventional appeals to "God's pure altar" and to the promise of martyred young men on both sides of the conflict. Despite its austere elegiac eloquence, however, the "Ode" curiously lacks invention, perhaps because in such formal exercises the poet did not feel free to build the poem around a strong and supple armature.

In the "Commemoration Ode" and similar large poems, then, Lowell rises rhetorically, rather than poetically, to his occasion. Hence, to succeed in finding his authentic public voice, Lowell had still to find a style, a mode, a genre, and a poetic space where he could reject the impulse toward rhetorical convention. This deflating, original mode he had already discovered almost, it would seem, by accident. In 1846, he wrote a dialect satire on the question of America's role in making the Mexican War, which Lowell regarded primarily as a vicious excuse to enlarge southern slaveholding territories. A series of verse-letters, with pseudo-editorial "reviews" and prose comments, followed between 1853 and the final collected edition of 1866; the whole comprised the 20 separate *Biglow Papers*.

Complex emotions and critically poised opinions, such as his attitudes regarding abolition, were always to mark Lowell the public poet. Driven to express his powerfully abolitionist views, he found one of his truly public escapes from themes of domestic propriety, from lyrics that were labeled "Sentiments." He discovered a satirical voice in the New England dialect verses of his creation, Hosea Biglow, whose works, along with those of a few other New England characters, appeared in the two series of *Biglow Papers*. As with other occasional literature, it is not easy to define the exact poetic status of Lowell's creations. Roy Harvey Pearce has observed that they are almost not poems, since "they center on issues, problems, ideologies, and they are essentially argumentative." Their language is always seeking to escape an exegetical obsession with typological inevitabilities.

The Biglow Papers are written in dialect almost as hard for us to read today as the Scots poems of Robert Burns, about whom Lowell wrote one of his most powerful poems, "An Incident in a Railroad Car." Dialect provides a radical relief from prescribed formalities; Lowell could be free, down-to-earth, graphic, sharp, humorous, and even evocative. He could speak a language nourished by the soul and life of an older New England. This speech did not endorse Puritan commentary (whose legacy he satirized through his amiable, digressive Dr. Homer Wilbur). Rather, the dialect verses and interspersed prose commentaries of *The Biglow Papers* expressed a native linguistic vigor that it was Lowell's genius to have appreciated and employed.

For these satires, Lowell invented the upcountry New England voice of a sturdy freedom-lover, a "natural man" as Pearce calls him, Hosea Biglow, along with the voices of a few other moralists locally defined by their dialect. Like Twain later and humorous prose writers before, Lowell used American humor to express complex social attitudes, especially those of northerners toward southerners. Over a period of 20 years, he introduced a small cast of speakers who, while not always sharply dramatized, nevertheless gave voice to his libertarian convictions. Most deeply, Lowell wanted to get beyond the *isms*; in *A Fable for Critics*, he accused himself of toting "a whole bale of *isms* tied together with rhyme" and of rattling away "till he's old as Methusalem, / At the head of a march to the last new Jerusalem." Local color now broke away from the *isms*. Lowell had found a linguistic equivalent of the political independence that he wished all citizens to enjoy.

In the sixth episode of the second series of *Biglow Papers*, "Sunthin' in the Pastoral Line," Hosea Biglow makes his usual picturesque plea for justice and good sense. Rough, lively, rhymed couplets project a pastoral voice (Lowell wrote appreciatively of Spenser's *Shepheardes Calender*). Perhaps because dialect sets him free, Lowell brings the ghost of Hosea's Puritan ancestor into the poem, in a dream. This spectral event utterly rejects the usual pious, angelic tonality. The old Puritan ancestor and young Hosea trade folk wisdom back and forth, which evokes a native New England tradition of free speech. Commonsensical Hosea tells reformers that they should not "start Millenium too quick," while the Pilgrim Father in his steeple-hat and tall boots insists that against tyranny and slavery, as before against King Charles's tyranny, one was forced to "strike soon." The old man's impatient fury is so strident that when he brings his foot down hard on the ground, it "give me such a startle that I woke." Out of the quaint, unsophisticated truthfulness of dialect speech, Lowell crafts a language that has the power to wake its reader, as the old Puritan woke young

Hosea. As with Hawthorne, the critique of Puritanism here does *not* constitute an endorsement of Puritan interpretation. The exemplary power of Puritan heroism is not lost; but the potential pedantry of bibliolatry is not allowed to be equated with that heroism. The beauty of Lowell's method in these poems and their seriocomic commentaries from the Reverend Homer Wilbur is that, through a fresh language of protest, he could give his poetry something it usually lacked, an energetic coherence and a truthfulness to the tragicomic human condition.

To the second series of *Biglow Papers,* Lowell added an elaborate introduction in which he stepped out of his fictional personae in order to speak for himself. The introduction vindicates a program of literary understanding that deserves comment, so powerful is its general significance for American literature of the period.

The ending of the *Fable for Critics* (1848) had already framed the later introduction. In the *Fable,* having limned portraits of several major American authors, such as Emerson, James Fenimore Cooper, William Cullen **Bryant**, Hawthorne, Fuller ("Miranda," a slighting, hostile caricature), Poe (who was outraged by his portrait: "Three fifths of him genius and two fifths sheer fudge"), and even Lowell himself, he concluded his critical catalog by attacking the widespread American belief that democracy should guarantee the existence of dozens, even hundreds, of Shakespeares and Miltons. The *Fable* mocks this deluded disbelief in the special, the rare, the naturally elite, and the properly inspired character of genuine art. Lowell was an ardent supporter of the political ideals of the Constitution – he fought slavery, he attacked political chicanery, and he always praised the ideal of civil and political equality before the law – but he did not accept the notion that artistic, or creative, genius was evenly spread out over the whole democratic populace, like jam on a piece of Wonder Bread. In the final section of the *Fable,* he attacked the stereotyped leveling of talent; he understood that artistic power, unlike selling power, is rare.

This position left him, however, with a fundamental question about the role of the people in the development of a rich and vibrant culture. At least in regard to literature, his introduction to the *Biglow Papers* suggested that unless poets understand the true nature of a powerful poetic language, their quest for democratic diffusion of genius would remain merely deluded.

His aim in the introduction is to spell out the powers of an appropriate poetic vernacular. This he located, among other places, in the living language of people he knew: old-time "up-country" New Englanders. "To me the dialect was native, was spoken all about me when a boy . . . when I write in it, it is as in a mother tongue, and I am carried back far beyond any studies of it to long-ago noonings in my father's hayfields, and to the talk of Sam and Job over their jug of *blackstrap* under the shadow of the ash-tree which still dapples the grass whence they have gone so long." The introduction dwells at length on the technical difficulties of notating the pronunciation of the old-time Yankee talk, as upon the lexicon of the dialect or, as he preferred to call it, the lingo. A picture of his own and his contemporaries' artistic situation emerges from the detailed discussion. He shows, in effect, that his own formal verses, the bulk of his work in poetry, necessarily would fail to reach an effective energy, despite all of his best efforts to bring life into

the personifications that were intended to dramatize the flow of ideas. With the lingo of Hosea Biglow and his friends, by contrast, the poet found that he could express what he called "homely common-sense vivified and heated by conscience." Here, "true humor is never divorced from moral conviction," but, by the same token, morals could not decline into moralism, but were saved by humorous inflections, humorous perspectives. Birdofredum Sawin, another "Biglow" character, can genially show us that the American obsession with manifest destiny could be seen as a mania of "national recklessness."

The aesthetic here looks to an ideal of simplicity. "Very few American writers or speakers wield their native tongue with a directness, precision, and force that are common as the day in the mother country," yet the introduction points to Lincoln's Gettysburg Address to exemplify the ideal, "a truly masculine English, classic because it was of no special period, and level at once to the highest and lowest of his countrymen." Lowell the critic knew how hard it would be for American writers to achieve biblical or Shakespearean range, but he nevertheless understood one major obstacle to such imaginative power – conventional or stereotyping jargon.

Lowell tells us that for several years he had been setting down a list of "poisonous" locutions, whose "insensibly cumulative" effect resulted, the introduction states, from the inevitable illiteracy of "a people whose chief reading is the daily paper." Already, the destructive results of media-manipulation were evident to a critical mind. Like George Orwell after him, Lowell could tabulate the most egregious, mindless linguistic inflation – the bureacratic tendency – in parallel columns of the old style and its modern equivalent.

Old Style

Was hanged.	Man fell.
When the halter was put round his neck.	A horse and wagon ran against.
A great crowd came to see.	The frightened horse.
Great fire.	Sent for the doctor.
The fire spread.	The mayor of the city in a short speech welcomed.
House burned.	I shall say a few words.
The fire was got under.	Began his answer.
	Asked him to dine.
	A bystander advised.
	He died.

New Style

Was launched into eternity.
When the fatal noose was adjusted about the neck of the unfortunate victim of his ownunbridled passions.
A vast concourse was assembled to witness.
Disastrous conflagration.
The conflagration extended its devastating career.
Edifice consumed.
The progress of the devouring element was arrested.
Individual was precipitated.
A valuable horse attached to a vehicle driven by J.S., in the employment of J.B., collided with.
The infuriated animal.
Called into requisition the services of the family physician.

> The chief magistrate of the metropolis, in well-chosen
> and eloquent language, frequently interrupted by the
> plaudits of the surging multitude, officially tendered
> the hospitalities.
> I shall, with your permission, beg leave to offer some
> brief observations.
> Commenced his rejoinder.
> Tendered him a banquet.
> One of those omnipresent characters who, as if in
> pursuance of some previous arrangement, are certain
> to be encountered in the vicinity when an accident
> occurs, venture the suggestion.
> He deceased, he passed out of existence, his spirit
> quitted its earthly habitation, winged its way to
> eternity, shook off its burden, etc.

Lowell identifies the cause of this dreadful Orwellian jargon with the rise of a "universal" pedagogy that is trying to get all Americans to "talk like books." He cannot deal with the problem of upward mobility for an immigrant population. It may seem odd for such a bookish author as Lowell, a man who by 1864 claimed to have read through Dante 22 times, to be attacking bookishness and to propose returning to a country lingo. But Lowell perceives that the ministrations of the "Universal Schoolmaster" are a two-edged sword. They widen literacy but do so at the cost of bureaucratic abstraction, the political vice of an essential dishonesty, memorably analyzed by Orwell in "Politics and the English Language." Lowell's introduction continues:

> No language, after it has faded into *diction*, none that
> cannot suck up the feeding juices secreted for it in the
> rich mother-earth of common folk, can bring forth a
> sound and lusty book. True vigor and heartiness of
> phrase do not pass from page to page, but from man to
> man, where the brain is kindled and the lips suppled by
> downright living interests and by passion in its very
> throe. Language is the soil of thought, and our own es-
> pecially is a rich leaf-mould, the slow deposit of ages, the
> shed foliage of feeling, fancy, and imagination, which
> has suffered an earth-change, that the vocal forest, as
> Howell [a seventeenth-century character-writer] called
> it, may clothe itself anew with living green. There is
> death in the dictionary; and, where language is too strict-
> ly limited by convention, the ground for expression to
> grow in is limited also; and we get a potted literature,
> Chinese dwarfs instead of healthy trees.

There is nothing antiquarian or genteel about Lowell's aesthetic of vernacular experiment. "It is certain that poets and peasants please us in the same way by translating words back again to their primal freshness and infusing them with a delightful strangeness which is anything but alienation." This pastoral, like William Empson's variants in *Some Versions of Pastoral*, implies a widening of the social range of reference of literature. As a proper Bostonian, the professor-poet may not be able to accept the crude New York style of Whitman's democratic plenitude and expansionism; but there is still room here for the idea of the expansion of a poetic lexicon, and within his own terms Lowell is far from narrow elitist dogmatism. He would be willing to pay the price of a narrowness in aesthetic effect,

for, to be sure, dialect literature is always going to limit its audience among so-called polite readers. Yet the willingness to be a humorist is a democratic willingness, and he belongs to a great American tradition in that respect.

Finally, the defense of humor and simplicity in the introduction to *The Biglow Papers*, the satire and play of these poems themselves, and Lowell's almost wild excesses of personification and materializing figures ("saddle opportunity," "stiffening uniform") in many of his formal poems, all indicate that for poets the mere language available is far more important than any ideological components. Ideology and its encoding relate to each other ambiguously, nor can semiotics easily define this relation. Nevertheless, we can say that for most people ideology controls language; for the poet, language, mere vocal and scripted wording, is given precedence. Lowell, we must always remember, was not only a great Anglophile; like his immediate circle of friends, he was an Italophile, a student and disciple of Dante's treatise *De vulgari eloquentia*. Even a great cause like abolition inspires the poet, as poet, to look for what might be truly called freedom of speech.

Looking over his output as a whole, one must say that Lowell was a creative influence upon others, poets and general readers alike. If, as Emerson once said, he had to prime the pump of his inspiration, he was still one of the finest poets of our nineteenth century. His sense of poetic performance is exemplary, if conventional. His mastery of a humoristic lingo is without equal, until we reach Mark Twain. And his literary range, as poet and essayist and political writer and notable editor, is far beyond that of any but a few writers of his time.

Writing in 1897, Henry James called Lowell a fighter, "the American of his time most saturated with literature and most directed to criticism." For James, this "intellectual experience" was part of a general struggle to achieve sharply intelligent expression. From this perspective, one can only suppose that recent political trends have severed many Americans from the full scope of their national literature, which needed and still needs to connect with intellectual refinement. Henry James, perhaps our greatest literary critic, wrote four separate pieces on Lowell. Today, in our decreasingly subtle literary climate, there seems slight grasp of the question implied by James's positive estimate. It is as if a stable, moderate, and highly literate intellectual culture – Lowell's New England – is either invisible or disturbing to readers at the end of the twentieth century. A remark of T. S. Eliot, in his 1953 lecture "American Literature and the American Language," suggests the seemingly elusive character of Lowell's world for the late-twentieth-century reader: "The literature of nineteenth century New England, however, is patently marked by something more than the several personalities of its authors: it has its own particular *civilized* landscape and the ethos of a local society of English origin with its own distinct traits." Yet even granting what appears to be the remoteness of this "civilized landscape," scholars will surely in due course come to appreciate the achievement of its authors. Along with the other eminent Fireside Poets, despite their prodigious literary presence in their own time and for many subsequent years, Lowell and the group are accorded a mere dozen pages or so – insightful though they be – out of 1200 pages in a representative reference work, the *Columbia Literary History of the United States* (1988). Twelve out of 1200! This lack of balance will inevitably right itself as we come to understand the aesthetic demands of middle-class America, without, however, turning poetry and the other arts into mere symptoms of ideology and cultural production. Lowell, as author, deserves a better press than he has received in recent histories. Few are the poets who could have written the final lines of *The Biglow Papers*, which evoke the carnage of the Civil War. William Dean Howells recalled how the audience fell silent, when Lowell spoke:

> I seem to hear a whisperin' in the air
> A sighin' like, of unconsoled despair,
>   Thet comes from nowhere an' from everywhere. . . .

ANGUS FLETCHER

Selected Works

The Writings of James Russell Lowell in Prose and Poetry, Riverside Edition, 10 vols., Boston: Houghton Mifflin, 1890

The Writings of James Russell Lowell in Prose and Poetry, vol. 11, edited by Charles Eliot Norton, *Latest Literary Essays and Addresses*, Boston: Houghton, Mifflin, 1892

Letters of James Russell Lowell, edited by Charles Eliot Norton, 2 vols., Boston: Houghton Mifflin, 1893

The Complete Poetical Works of James Russell Lowell, Cambridge Edition, edited by H. E. Scudder, Boston: Houghton Mifflin, 1897

New Letters of James Russell Lowell, edited by Mark A. DeWolfe Howe, New York: Harper & Brothers, 1932

The Scholar Friends: Letters of Francis Child and James Russell Lowell, edited by M. A. DeWolfe Howe and G. W. Cottrell, Cambridge, Massachusetts: Harvard University Press, 1952

James Russell Lowell's The Biglow Papers, First Series, edited by Thomas Wortham, DeKalb: Northern Illinois University Press, 1977

Further Reading

Amory, Cleveland, *The Proper Bostonians*, New York: Dutton, 1947

Duberman, Martin, *James Russell Lowell*, Boston: Houghton Mifflin, 1966

Edel, Leon, ed., *Henry James: Literary Criticism, Essays on Literature, American Writers, English Writers*, New York: Library of America, 1984

Eliot, Thomas Stearns, *To Criticize the Critic: Eights Essays on Literature and Education*, New York: Farrar, Straus & Giroux, 1965

Elliott, Emory, et al., eds., *Columbia Literary History of the United States*, New York: Columbia University Press, 1988

Greenslet, Ferris, *The Lowells and Their Seven Worlds*, Boston: Houghton Mifflin, 1946

Hale, Edward Everett, *James Russell Lowell and His Friends*, introduction by Lewis P. Simpson, New York: Chelsea House, 1980

Levin, David, *Cotton Mather: The Young Life of the Lord's Remembrancer (1663–1703)*, Cambridge, Massachusetts: Harvard University Press, 1978

McGlinchee, Claire, *James Russell Lowell*, New York: Twayne, 1967

Pearce, Roy Harvey, *The Continuity of American Poetry*, Princeton, New Jersey: Princeton University Press, 1961

Tucker, Martin, ed., *Moulton's Library of Literary Criticism of English and American Authors*, New York: Ungar, 1966; abridged ed., vol. 4

Wagenknecht, Edward, *James Russell Lowell: Portrait of a Many-sided Man*, New York: Oxford University Press, 1971

Weeks, Edward, *The Lowells and Their Institute*, Boston: Atlantic Little Brown, 1966

Maria White Lowell

(1821–1853)

Maria Lowell, the first wife of James Russell **Lowell**, was not a prolific poet, and her collected poems – published together with letters and a biography by Brown University in 1936 – occupy only 46 pages of that volume. Among those verses, however, five poems continue to interest readers who are no longer enthralled by the tender religious sentiments that made Maria White Lowell's poems about the deaths of children – "The Alpine Sheep" and "The Morning-Glory," for instance – so popular during her lifetime. Although these two poems were the most reprinted of her poems in the nineteenth century, "Africa," "The Slave-Mother," "Rouen, Place de la Pucelle" (LOA, 2: 117), "The Sick-Room," and "An Opium Fantasy" (LOA, 2: 118) are of greater interest today, for they illustrate the poet's unusual range; the last two are particularly arresting for their moments of Dickinsonian metaphor.

What one discovers, upon reviewing the case of Maria White Lowell, is that a mid–nineteenth-century white woman of intelligence and talent might, under certain circumstances, read interesting books, have a good marriage, write original poems, publish, give birth, and continue to prosper creatively. Her biography brings into focus the limits of the theory that all nineteenth-century women were rendered miserable and mute by the pressures of patriarchy. But Lowell's case cannot be generalized, since her relationship with her husband was extraordinary for any time, and her life, cut short by tuberculosis when the poet was only 32, was too brief to yield clear evidence of more than partial exemption.

What *were* the "circumstances" that fostered Maria White's career? Although she was the fifth of nine children born to Abijah White and Anna Maria Howard White, Maria grew up in Watertown, Massachusetts, in comparative comfort. Two of her older siblings had already died by the time that she was born, but her father was hale and hearty, well-off financially, and highly respected in the community. Indeed, Maria was descended on both sides from New England settlers who came to the New World in the seventeenth century. On her mother's side, she was distantly related to Anne Hutchinson.

Her education began with her parents, who had a library full of "delightful" books. Mrs. White was a popular hostess. Friends came to borrow the books and to discuss social reforms. Mrs. White herself was one of the founders of a "humane society." Maria's father, as James Russell Lowell described him, was "the most perfect specimen of a bluff, honest, hospitable, country squire you can imagine." Maria's early childhood, therefore, was pleasant, and parental encouragement was followed up by a governess who stressed the arts, especially the drawing at which Maria excelled. Then (somewhat oddly) Maria was sent to the Ursuline Convent in Boston, where a number of prominent Protestants sent their daughters. According to Maria's biographer Hope Jillson Vernon, life at the convent was comparatively ascetic, with long periods of enforced silence, readings from the *Lives of the Saints*, and a very limited diet. Maria was liberated when the convent was burned in 1834 during an upsurge of anti-Catholic sentiment. Later works such as "The Legend of the Brown Rosarie," however,

show that she continued to be attracted to Catholic themes and symbols.

What she did between the time that she was 13 and the beginning of Margaret **Fuller's** "Conversations" in Elizabeth Peabody's room in West Street we do not know, but at the age of 18 she was ready to take her place among the cultured and cultivated group of women who assembled there to discuss topics such as the origins of the cosmos, the functions of the will and understanding, and Romantic theories of genius. Maria was infused with the reformist spirit of her day and became an ardent spokeswoman for both temperance and abolition. Her colleagues in the weekly discussion group included prominent women such as Anna Shaw, Caroline Sturgis, Lydia Maria Child, Sophia Hawthorne, and Lydia Emerson. Led by Fuller and Peabody, an early feminist, these women were unusually well-read, and many of them were fired with the spirit of "newness" that Romanticism brought to America.

Maria White was probably luckiest in having a peer group that allowed her to combine her intellectual and social interests. The women at Fuller's seminars were mostly older than Maria; many of them were already married. But in her older brother William, Maria had another valuable resource. Although she herself was not sent to college, William – then at Harvard – brought his friends and his ideas home to share. Known as "the Band," this group of young people became an important part of Maria's education. She read what they were reading (Goethe, for instance), and with them she discussed art, politics, poetry, ethics, religion, and philosophy. In fact, in important ways Maria had as good an education as many of the young men of her class and time, because the young people of both sexes with whom she argued were motivated by a sincere desire to master the ideas of the past and to think afresh. Many of the men who belonged to her set – such as William Wetmore **Story** – later became famous as artists, jurists, physicians, or writers.

It was through her brother William that Maria met James Russell Lowell in 1839. Lowell was himself born into a distinguished family; his grandfather had been the author of the words in the Massachusetts Bill of Rights (1774): "all men are born free and equal." His father, the Reverend Charles Lowell, was an author, a Fellow of Harvard College, and the pastor of the West Congregational Church of Boston for 55 years. After Maria and James married in 1844, Charles took his son's wife very much to his heart, and in fact the couple lived mostly with him, his then mentally ill wife (James's mother), and his eccentric sister.

James and Maria never had much money. His father's estate had been reduced to almost nothing by the mismanagement of a brother, and Maria's inheritance from her father (who died in 1845) was mostly in land, although it did assure them of 500 dollars a year in income. Despite their lack of funds, the couple was by all accounts extraordinarily happy. James was a talented and intelligent young man, but he needed a strong presence in his life to bring his talents to some point. Maria was that presence, as Maria's friend Sophia was in Nathaniel **Hawthorne's** life. Both James and Maria were admirers of Ralph

Waldo **Emerson**, but when James early in their relationship expressed the view that one should always follow one's proclivities and that he himself intended to dedicate his life to "self-culture," she replied scornfully that the highest form of self-reliance involves (as, indeed, Emerson himself said) an understanding of one's relations to others.

It would be a mistake, however, to characterize Maria as a dominant personality. She was usually described as noble and mystical, never as strident, and she often comported herself in a perfectly conventional manner with regard to her husband: doting upon him, keeping modestly in the background in company, making clothes for him, and championing his work. Of the two of them, James was the one who seemed more interested in reconfiguring the sex roles. For instance, he admitted to having a "feminine" side. He also departed from the purer transcendentalists in believing the heart should rule the intellect, and he argued for women's involvement in the public arena, especially as leaders of reform. When the babies came, James was more than happy to take his turn caring for them, and he expressed the hope that his daughter would be "a great strong, vulgar, mud-pudding-baking, tree-climbing little wench." According to Edward Wagenknecht, his attitude toward sex in his marriage was full of romantic exaltation. Even after his wife became pregnant, he wrote, "I never go to our bed with less reverence and less joy than to our bridal bed and I believe it will be so to the end of my days."

James helped Maria publish her poems and maintained in one letter that she was becoming a better poet than he. Her first poems were published in a journal that he was then editing called *The Pioneer*. After that, a number of her works were printed in the *Broadway Journal* and the abolitionist *Liberty Bell*, since, with Maria's strong commitment, both of the Lowells were active in the movement to free the slaves. James even made sure "by way of salt" (as he put it) that some of Maria's poems got in Rufus Griswold's anthology *Female Poets of America*.

Maria's career would surely have developed further and eventuated in the publication of a book of poetry had she not fallen prey to tuberculosis. Her lungs were never strong, and even at the time of her marriage it was clear that she had health problems. Nevertheless, she gave birth to four children between 1845 and 1850. She was writing and publishing steadily (although not prolifically) during this period. But three of the four babies died, and each death took a terrible toll on both parents. Of the first three, who were girls, only Mabel survived. Then Walter was born in 1850, and the couple decided to sell some land and go to Europe. But in Rome, Walter, too (who seemed so like his father), died at a year and a half. Maria never recovered. In 1853, three of her European poems – "Necklaces," "The Grave of Keats," and "Rouen, Place de la Pucelle" – were published in *Putnam's Monthly*, which was then edited by James's friend Charles F. Briggs, but on October 27, 1853, Maria White Lowell died at Elmwood, the family home in Cambridge, Massachusetts.

James's letters and journal entries show clearly that his grief was overwhelming, and he apparently had recurring suicidal fantasies. Slowly, he began to recover, but he never ceased to think fondly of Maria, although he eventually married again. In 1855, James brought out a private edition of Maria's poems and distributed the 50 copies among his friends. Toward the end of his life, he set about to publish a much expanded edition, including manuscript works, but the project died with him in 1891.

In 1907, Houghton Mifflin republished 330 copies of the 1855 edition of Maria's poems. Her work would then probably have disappeared entirely had it not been for her rediscovery by her husband's second cousin, Amy Lowell. After reading "An Opium Fantasy" out loud to her guests, she is said to have exclaimed: "That is *poetry*! It is better than anything her husband ever wrote, and he always said that she was a better poet than he." One of the guests was S. Foster Damon who, in 1936, wrote an introduction to the first and only publication of the complete poems of Maria White Lowell. Damon praised "An Opium Fantasy" but was even more enthusiastic about "Africa," which, he said, "has a massiveness of conception and a grandeur of expression beyond anything else she accomplished." In fact, Damon called it "the only Abolitionist poem I know that rises above oratory and propaganda into pure literature." The poem, which images Africa as a regal mother lamenting the loss of her children, concludes:

"There came a change. They took my free,
My careless ones, and the great sea
Blew back their endless sighs to me:

"With earthquake shudderings oft the mould
Would gape; I saw keen spears of gold
Thrusting red hearts down, not yet cold,

"But throbbing wildly; dreadful groans
Stole upward through Earth's ribbed stones,
And crept along through all my zones.
. . . .
"So I sit dreary, desolate,
Till the slow-moving hand of Fate
Shall lift me from my sunken state."

Her great lips closed upon her moan;
Silently sate she on her throne,
Rigid and black, as carved in stone.

Maria Lowell wrote much that will strike a modern reader as merely conventional. Her imagination was thoroughly infused with Romantic ideas, and many of her conceptions involve dreams and the supernatural. Yet it is a mistake to assume that these conceits were merely literary devices, since both she and her husband believed that they were visited by emissaries from the beyond. After Maria's death, James claimed that he saw her holding their son and speaking to him across the gulf of time. Although Maria had a mischievous streak, most contemporary accounts of her emphasize her almost mystical presence. She was strikingly beautiful and, like Sarah Helen **Whitman**, had extraordinarily large and limpid eyes. Perhaps she used drugs, but we have no clear evidence of this beyond the quite convincing portrait of a drug trance that she provides in "An Opium Fantasy":

Soft hangs the opiate in the brain,
And lulling soothes the edge of pain,
Till harshest sound, far off or near,
Sings floating in its mellow sphere.

What wakes me from my heavy dream?
  Or am I still asleep?
These long and soft vibrations seem
  A slumberous charm to keep.

The graceful play, a moment stopped,
  Distance again unrolls,
Like silver balls, that, softly dropped,
  Ring into golden bowls.

The surrealistic quality of the images here was hardly duplicated in her time, either by others or by herself. One can see why her work, and especially this poem, inspired Amy Lowell's admiration, since Amy, the leader of Imagism in this country, often tried for similar effects. Maria Lowell was not the only nineteenth-century American woman poet to write about drug experiences, however. Rose Terry **Cooke's** "Poppies" and Mary Tucker Lambert's "The Opium-Eater" also seek to evoke the amorphous exhilaration produced by opium use.

S. Foster Damon calls "The Sick-Room" "Dickinson before Dickinson: it is a cry of despair from the invalid, who senses the spring flooding the world outside her chill bedroom, while her life wastes away like the wood on her hearth – wood that also once responded to the coming of spring." Similar poems were written by Lydia **Sigourney**, Lucretia Davidson (who also died of tuberculosis), and Emma Embury, whose "The Garden" provides insight into the final years of that poet's invalidism. But Maria Lowell's poem is particularly memorable for its evocation of the contrast between the indoor and outdoor states of mind produced by the coming of spring.

Thou wilt not enter the chamber,
  The door stands open in vain;
Thou art pluming the wands of cherry
  To lattice the window pane.

Thou flushest the sunken orchard
  With the lift of thy rosy wing;
The peach will not part with her sunrise
  Though great noon-bells should ring.

The phrase "Those great noon-bells" is indeed reminiscent of Emily **Dickinson's** work, as is the reference to "Thy punctual feet, O Spring!" Less Dickinsonian and more particularly the art of Maria Lowell is the vision of spring "pluming the wands of cherry," and thus reinforcing the window pane/pain. The sunrise color on the peach, which mixes pinks and yellows, also reflects Maria's Mediterranean tastes.

In addition to using a more complex meter than the poems addressed above, "Rouen, Place de la Pucelle" captures the pure virginal sensibility of the poet, her Christian outlook, and her clear-eyed sense of dedication. Briggs once referred to Maria's outlook as somewhat naive, but in response James insisted that his Maria was less innocent than Briggs thought and not to be summed up by the word "transcendental." "The Slave-Mother" is testimony to this view; it foreshadows Toni Morrison's *Beloved* in its suggestion that a slave mother might prefer death for her daughter to a life of horror. "Africa," like *Uncle Tom's Cabin*, calls Africans "the children of the world" but conveys a much more clearly historicized sense of the sophistication of African culture than Harriet Beecher Stowe's work.

In sum, it seems fair to say that Maria White Lowell was both a woman of her time and a particularly fine example of her culture. The testimonies to her personal force and charm are many; for instance, the novelist Fredrika Bremer found her deeper and more genuinely philosophical than her husband. Her poetry does not surpass that written by all other American women poets of her day (as James thought it did), but it certainly contains moments of brilliance and an overall spirit of generosity that is quite in keeping with her family inheritance, her Romantic education, her marriage, and her unusual gifts. Although Maria died young, she lived fully and, until the last years, happily, unlike most of her sister poets who were not so blessed.

CHERYL WALKER

Selected Works
The Poems of Maria Lowell, edited by Hope Jillson Vernon, intro. S. Foster Damon, Providence: Brown University Press, 1936
American Women Poets of the Nineteenth Century, edited by Cheryl Walker, New Brunswick, New Jersey: Rutgers University Press, 1992

Further Reading
Duberman, Martin, *James Russell Lowell*, Boston: Houghton Mifflin, 1966
Wagenknecht, Edward, *James Russell Lowell: Portrait of a Many-Sided Man*, New York: Oxford University Press, 1971

Edwin Markham

(1852–1940)

Markham was born Charles Edward Anson Markham on April 23, 1852, in Oregon City, Oregon. Shortly after Markham's birth, his father Samuel divorced Elizabeth Winchell Markham, apparently because he suspected that the child was not his own. Elizabeth, a cold, sourly religious woman eager for money, moved with her son to the Suisan Hills Valley, northeast of San Francisco, California, and settled on a ranch in a barren one-room house. Markham wove a romantic tale about the early days of his youth and the vigorous life that he lived on the ranch with his mother. In reality, however, it was a hard, unpleasant existence out of which he managed to develop an interest in learning and books despite his mother's cruelty and indifference. He was by nature a dreamer and tended to mix idealized fantasies with the facts of his life.

Markham eventually ran away from home in April 1867, and he attended California College in Vacaville and the State Normal School at San Jose. He taught school for many years in several California cities, including Los Berros, Colonna, and Oakland. His first marriage ended in divorce, and after the death of his second wife, he married Anna Catherine Murphy, with whom he had a son. Throughout his life, many women were attracted to him, and he engaged in numerous discreet infatuations. One woman in particular, Florence Hamilton from Wellesley Hills, Massachusetts, whom he met late in life, developed into something of a disciple. Much to the chagrin of Anna Markham, Hamilton provided the poet with a home away from home and energetic assistance in organizing his papers, projects, and engagements.

Besides the Bible, Markham drew intellectual and spiritual inspiration from the ideas and lives of many people. Among them were the writings of the Unitarian clergyman William Ellery Channing (uncle of William Ellery **Channing** the poet), whose teachings gave Markham a sense of peace and stability. Thomas Lake Harris, a spiritualist and Swedenborgian who founded a transcendentalist community at Fountain Grove in Santa Rosa, also helped Markham understand God and the Scriptures. For a time Markham lived nearby Joaquin **Miller**, the California adventurer and poet, and admired him as a romantic troubadour, humanitarian, and literary man of action. Among other contemporaries from whom he drew inspiration were Ambrose **Bierce**, Charles Warren Stoddard, and Hamlin **Garland**.

Markham's literary career began early, and his first efforts were undistinguished pro-labor and socialist verses that provided him only regional recognition and had a limited impact. Sometime after 1886, after considering several possible name changes, he settled on Edwin Markham. In 1893, he visited Chicago, Boston, and New York City and made his first literary contacts with editors and writers from outside of California. His verses began to appear in increasing numbers in such periodicals as *Scribner's*, *Century*, and the *Atlantic Monthly*. He was committed to developing as a poet and worked hard in search of a vehicle for his vision and an avenue that would gain him the national recognition that he desired. Both finally came to him with the publication of "The Man with the Hoe" (LOA, 2: 496) in January 1899 in the San Francisco *Examiner*.

"The Man with the Hoe" stirred the nation and captured the attention of millions of Americans. Its appearance in *The Examiner* was the result of fortunate circumstances. Markham was intending to submit the poem to *Scribner's Magazine*, but took it with him to a New Year's Eve party. He recited the poem for the assembled guests, one of whom was Bailey Millard, the editor of *The Examiner*. Millard was deeply moved not only by the content of the poem but also by Markham's intensely dramatic reading of it, and so he decided to publish it.

The poem was picked up and reprinted in newspapers across the country. Editorials and public commentaries about it appeared everywhere. William James called it "magnificent and impressive in the highest degree." Hamlin Garland described it as "a great thing and a beautiful thing, in the sense that a strain from Wagner is great and beautiful." Clergymen used the poem in their sermons. Platform orators, college professors, debating societies, political leaders, and sociologists admired it and discussed it for its achievement in capturing the mood and beliefs of the American people. Almost a year later the poem was still in the news, and William Jennings Bryan, the premier spokesperson for the sort of reformism expressed in the poem, wrote, "It is a sermon addressed to the heart. It voices humanity's protest against inhuman greed. There is a majestic sweep to the argument; some of the lines pierce like arrows."

But those who supported the American status quo took exception to the poem. They felt it was a fallacious attack upon the American farmer, one that fostered pessimism and divisiveness in the ranks of the laboring classes. Many parodies of the poem appeared, with such titles as "The Man with the Load," "The Man with the Lawn-Mower," "The Man with the Hump," and "The Woman Under the Heel of the Man with the Hoe." A railroad millionaire offered a reward for the best poem written in answer to "The Man with the Hoe." He was hoping for an answer that made field labor appear attractive.

The poem itself was inspired by a reproduction of Jean-François Millet's painting *The Man with the Hoe*, which Markham saw in *Scribner's Magazine* in 1886. The memory of the painting haunted Markham for years and helped produce his vision of "the slow but awful degradation of man through endless, hopeless, and joyless labor." The poem is in the tradition of a jeremiad and is written in blank verse. The principal poetic device used in each of its five stanzas is the rhetorical question. Saddened with a vision of the worker crushed by physically abusive, mind-numbing labor, the poet implicitly asks: is this what the handiwork of God was meant to become? What powers on earth require humans to surrender their God-given rights to freedom, beauty, and creativity for the crushing burdens of endless, empty labor? The answer is that "the world's blind greed" is to blame for these "immemorial infamies, / Perfidious wrongs, immedicable woes." In the last two stanzas, Markham directly addresses those responsible.

"O masters, lords and rulers in all lands," he writes, how will you right the wrongs you have done to poor, suffering humanity? Further, he asks, what will you do "when whirlwinds of rebellion shake the world?"

"The Man with the Hoe" is a vivid portrait of the wrongs inflicted upon the working classes by the selfishness and indifference of the powerful and wealthy. It is also a call to reform society before a revolution of the working class brings fearful destruction. The poem effectively captured the feelings and thoughts of many regarding the exploited classes and helped revitalize the efforts of those engaged in labor reform and antitrust movements at the turn of the century. The sensation caused by the poem also catapulted Markham into the public arena. He became a much sought-after public speaker, and Doubleday McClure eagerly brought out Markham's first book of poetry in May 1899, *The Man with the Hoe and Other Poems*. Shortly thereafter, in order to take full advantage of all the opportunities suddenly available to him as a man of letters, Markham moved his home permanently to New York City.

Other noteworthy poems from his first volume are "A Leaf from the Devil's Jest-Book" (LOA, 2: 497), "After Reading Shakspere" (LOA, 2: 498), and "In Death Valley" (LOA, 2: 498). The first poem is similar in its reformist theme to "The Man with the Hoe" but is written in the traditional form of a Petrarchan sonnet. In the octave Markham sympathetically portrays the sweatshop seamstresses bound to their menial and thankless labors on behalf of the rich: "chained and bent, / They stitch for the lady, tyrannous and proud – / For her a wedding-gown, for them a shroud." In the sestet he envisions their lives as wasted in meaningless activity and poses a rhetorical question, which suggests that all our beliefs and philosophies are useless if the lives of these workers are thrown away for the vanities of a few:

> And what's the worth of all our ancient creeds,
>   If here at the end of ages this is all –
>   A white face floating in the whirling ball,
> A dead face plashing in the river reeds?

"After Reading Shakspere" is another Petrarchan sonnet, which reflects the aesthetic concern of Markham, the artist, who admires the works produced by fancy but wonders who will lead us to higher truths through the power of imagination. In Coleridgean terms, fancy is the logical, associative, and aggregative part of the mind. For instance, fancy helps to produce good science, as when "Men weigh the moons that flood with eerie light / The dusky vales of Saturn." As Markham asks, however, where is the living poet nourished by what Coleridge calls the creative and original imagination, which can lead us to the truths about the gods themselves and "follow on the awful sweep / Of Neptune through the dim and dreadful deep?"

The blank-verse poem "In Death Valley" returns to the theme of human greed. Looking at the barren landscape of Death Valley, the poet contemplates the moody ruins of ghost towns and mines that were abandoned after the days of the California gold rush: "And from the stillness of the down-crushed walls / One pillar rose up dark against the moon." Stains of blood on rocks still remain, the results "of a vast unknown Calamity." The poet perceives among the ruins "a nameless Presence everywhere," that all-pervading sense of evil of which one becomes conscious of wherever human tragedy has occurred. According to the poem, the "ancestral grief" is the fallen, sinful nature of humankind at the root of the violence among those early Death Valley miners who greedily pursued wealth and advantage.

For the next 40 years, Markham was an extremely visible literary figure in America. In addition to numerous lecture tours and speaking invitations, Markham regularly published poetry and prose in the leading periodicals, edited several anthologies of English and American poetry, published five more books of his own verse, and became a friend to many of the leading literary and society people of the time. He remained a supporter of progressive politics and continued his interest in the reformist movement. In 1914, he collaborated with several others in the writing of *Children of Bondage*, an influential piece of muckraking that helped to establish laws governing child labor practices.

As he aged, Markham became something of an institution. Birthday celebrations for him were regularly arranged. He was influential in the establishment of the Poetry Society of America and became its reigning figure. He was named "dean of American poetry" in the popular press and poet laureate of the state of Oregon. In a competition to find the best poem to commemorate Abraham Lincoln, Markham's was selected, and he was invited to read the poem in Washington, D.C., at the dedication of the Lincoln Memorial in 1922. He developed a skill for writing occasional verse and was frequently asked to compose poems to commemorate historical and cultural events such as the Dreyfus case, the Spanish-American War, and the Emerson centennial. There came invitations to return for visits to California, and Markham eventually witnessed the establishment of the Edwin Markham Landmark Association, which preserved the house in which he wrote "The Man with the Hoe."

His opinions regarding the new poets were not positive. For example, in one of his anthologies of contemporary poetry, he published nothing of Edgar Lee Masters, Edna St. Vincent Millay, T. S. Eliot, Ezra Pound, or Hart Crane. As a reader and writer, he preferred "older" poets such as William Wordsworth, Robert Browning, and a very limited amount of Walt **Whitman**. He liked poetry that elevated the soul, promoted the positive feelings of brotherhood and idealism, and showed a respectful attitude toward the subjects of sex and the cosmos.

Edwin Markham died in New York City on March 7, 1940, at the age of 88. The single largest collection of his manuscripts and papers is housed in the Horrmann Library of Wagner College, on Staten Island. The *Markham Review* appeared in 1968 under the sponsorship of Wagner College. Initially, it was a scholarly publication devoted to Edwin Markham and his age. In a short time it moved to publishing interdisciplinary articles on all aspects of American culture. It ceased publication in 1990.

PAUL J. FERLAZZO

Selected Works

The Man with the Hoe and Other Poems, New York: Doubleday and McClure, 1899
Lincoln and Other Poems, New York: McClure, Phillips, 1901

The Shoes of Happiness and Other Poems, New York: Doubleday and Doran, 1915

Gates of Paradise and Other Poems, Garden City, New York: Doubleday, Page, 1920

New Poems: Eighty Songs at Eighty, Garden City: Doubleday, Page, 1932

The Star of Araby, Stapleton, New York: J. Willig, 1937

Poems of Edwin Markham, edited by Charles L. Wallis, New York: Harper and Brothers, 1950

The Ballad of the Gallows Bird, Yellow Springs, Ohio: Antioch, 1967

Further Reading

Durham, J., *The Man with the Book: Companion to "The Man with the Hoe,"* Niles, California: Niles Herald, 1901

Filler, Louis, *The Unknown Edwin Markham: His Mystery and Its Significance*, Yellow Springs, Ohio: Antioch, 1966

Shields, Sophie K., *Edwin Markham: A Bibliography*, Staten Island, New York: Wagner College, 1952

Stidger, William L., *Edwin Markham*, New York, Cincinnati, and Chicago: Abingdon, 1933

Sullivan, Mark, *Our Times 1900–1925*, New York: Scribner's, 1927

Cornelius Mathews

(1814?–1889)

"The Poet" is the last of the verses that Cornelius Mathews included in *Poems on Man* (1843), and in the first stanza he announces his purpose to "embrace the father and the child, / The toiler, reaper, sufferer, rough or mild." Vigorously nationalistic, republican, and democratic in it aims, the collection has a breadth and sympathies that only palely foreshadow Walt **Whitman's** in *Leaves of Grass*, but Mathews's work at least approaches the same spirit. We even hear anticipations of Whitman's "I give the sign of democracy . . . / Through me many long dumb voices" in Mathews's stated intention that the poet should speak of "Mirth" and "sadness":

> Gather all kindreds of this boundless realm
> To speak a common tongue in thee! Be thou –
> Heart, pulse, and voice, whether pent hate o'erwhelm
> The stormy speech or young love whisper low.

(These lines are from the last and only stanza of "The Poet" that is presented in Edmund Clarence **Stedman** and E. M. Hutchinson's 10-volume *A Library of American Literature* [1889]). The poet, in brief, is "teacher" and "seer."

"The Sculptor" (LOA, 1: 668) reveals another dimension of Mathews the author: the artist who desires to express himself in more telling, resonant, and enduring forms. The language at the poem's beginning is tight and self-conscious, which creates a halting staccato rhythm. Perhaps the problem lies with the subject itself: Mathews is describing period sculpture's unrelentingly realistic, reductive process, which he seeks to apply to the serious writer's crafting of words. According to Mathews, the sculptor evokes realities by reaching into the past for "Chieftain and soldier, senator and sage" and breathing life into them so that they become "Benignant, wise and brave again!" These "crowned heroes of the early age" are clearly related to Mathews's own mythological and primitive hero Bokulla and his monstrous adversary Behemoth in *Behemoth: A Legend of the Mound-Builders* (1839). What Mathews is focusing on in his poems, therefore, is not the deep European past, but the aboriginal American past, similar to the history that he explores in *Behemoth*, as well as in *Big Abel* (1845) – and, indeed, in much of his work of the 1840s and 1850s.

In creating the conventional romantic tensions between the civilized and the primitive/pastoral, Mathews is clearly voicing period concerns. And as is frequently the case, although he is often at best skeptical about the benefits that accrue to the Native Americans during the United States westward expansion, he comes down on the side of the expanding, white civilization. These are the same conflicts we hear in Washington Irving, whose *Knickerbocker's History* satirizes the purposes and pretensions of the Dutch model of white colonialism, and whose "The Author's Account of Himself" (in *The Sketch-Book*) celebrates the cultural superiority of western Europe by insisting that the artist, as word sculptor, needs the Old World materials and will perish if limited to those available in his native land – despite the bounties nature has bestowed upon it.

The subjects and concerns that Mathews presents in works from *Poems on Man* such as "The Sculptor," "The Journalist" (LOA, 1: 669), and "The Masses" (LOA, 1: 670) are typical of those to which he addressed himself in most of his writings from the late 1830s to 1850, his belletristic period. We might take the full title of *Poems on Man in His Various Aspects under the American Republic* at its word, since all but five of the volume's 19 poems focus on occupations. Again, these poems are Whitmanesque in spirit and intention perhaps, but certainly not in their manner, style, or poetic power. The subjects of the child and the father, which begin the volume, evoke the family structure at the base of the social and political one; the teacher and the citizen exemplify the sense of civic responsibility that holds together *res publica* (the commonwealth); we might perhaps also include here the statesman, who is distinguished from the politician by a higher ideal of leadership. The rest of his poetic subjects treat various other occupations.

An aggressive literary nationalist, Mathews worked in virtually all genres: principally novels and short fiction, but also sketches, drama, nonfictional prose, and poetry. Poetry, however, was the form in which he published least – just the two small volumes *Poems on Man* and *Wakondah; The Master of Life* (1841). His subjects ranged from the aboriginal, prehistoric American continent to contemporary politics and manners, especially those in New York City, his home from early in life. As Mathews stated in his address at the famous 1842 dinner welcoming Charles Dickens to New York, the United States should promote "works of genius, the growth of our own soil, colored by our own skies, and showing something of the influences of a new community." The poems printed in the Library of America anthology and the others in *Poems on Man* attempt to let speak, or to speak for, some of the "thousand voices [that] now slumber in our vales, amid our cities, and along our hillsides." Trying to capture the vigor of American life, Mathews worked under the assumption – again, embraced by radical contemporaries – that American subjects were the only legitimate ones for the American author to explore. Nearly contemporary with Ralph Waldo **Emerson**, who complained that the English dramatic poets had "Shakespeareized . . . for two hundred years," and anticipating by more than a decade the nationalism of his literary companion Herman **Melville** (see Melville's "Hawthorne and His Mosses"), Mathews early dedicated himself to the cause of the Young America group. This nationalism fueled his social, political, and literary views and led him to the extreme right wing where, at least during the mid-1850s, he became active in the Native American or Know-Nothing Party at one of the high points of its popularity. (According to a June 1855 number of the New York *Tribune*, Mathews was serving as vice president of the New York–based group and had addressed them on Independence Day.) The Know-Nothing Party unleashed its intolerant chauvinism on new immigrants such as the Irish, who would change the complexion of the country's citizenry during Mathews's own lifetime.

Mathews's career declined from an early desire to be a literary artist to that for which he settled: work as a journalist and, more important, a journalistic editor trying to reach mass audiences. In 1840, he joined Evert A. Duyckinck, his close friend, colleague, and collaborator, to start *Arcturus: A Journal of Books and Opinion*, which was well received by Edgar Allan **Poe** and other literati but had a life of only a year and a half. As the decade unfolded, Mathews either planned or embarked on other journals: *The Millions*, which perhaps suggested the money that he and Duyckinck hoped to make by reaching a new mass audience created partly by advances in printing technology; *Yankee Doodle* (1846–47), which was modeled on *Punch* and is best remembered for having published minor satires by Melville; *Literary World*, owned and edited principally by Evert and George Duyckinck; *Holden's Dollar Magazine*, another joint venture with the Duyckincks; and the *New-Yorker*, with which Mathews was involved from 1858 to 1876.

Like "The Sculptor," "The Journalist" suggests Mathews's literary hopes in the worlds of art and popular literature. "Filled with the people's breath of potency," the journalist feels the pulse of the times: the ugly realities of the "dark-dyed spirit" and also "the gold-bright seeds of loved and loving truth!" Mathews here expresses the republican journalist's idealism under a constitution that guarantees freedom of speech and the press; the journalist reports it all, the message of the "angel," as well as that of he "who stuns, with dusk-red words of hate, his ear" so that the "mighty power to boundless wrath enrages." Moreover, while contemporaries such as Emerson and Emily **Dickinson** may have chanted the integration of railroad engines into the landscape, of industrial power's machinery into the American garden, Mathews's journalist sings only the "little curlew" (a kind of woodcock). The poem concludes with a return to the nautical metaphor of the first stanza, and, Whitmanesque in its hospitality to the conventionally unpoetic, the journalistic quality of the young writer's vision reaches toward the potency assured by objectivity and fairness.

In "The Masses," celebration of Jacksonian democracy is predicated on the young nation's constitutional republicanism. The poem's opening stanza is one of Mathews's best because there is none of the syntactical awkwardness that is painfully evident in the restricting self-consciousness of much of his poetry. The people's power "swells" as much in "The Masses" as in the voices that he attempts to capture. Potency and the threat of even greater power loom through the first stanza as the "fields of men, like lions, shake their fells / Of savage hair." The message offered is again perfectly Young American: the "heart of right" "secret and still and force-defying" allows the people to govern themselves and their nation in a fashion as orderly and gentle as though they were "as little children at a singing-school." The third and final stanza, however, threatens intimidating, unleashed power; it calls to mind the refrain, "Beware the People weeping / When they bare the iron hand," in Melville's "The Martyr" (1866), or the ardent writing of the American Revolution, an event that was always present for these grandchildren of the war's patriots. Goaded by violations

of their republican rights, the "arms uplifted for the deathward blow," these patriots will indeed rise up and prevail, letting "shine again God's rightful sun!" In a sense, this poem's republicanism and democratic sentiments may be taken as the thematic and ideological underpinning of *Poems on Man*.

Mathews became increasingly disillusioned about the promise of American life, which perhaps accounts for his turn to the editing of sometimes satirical humor papers in the 1850s. Also, both before and after publishing *Poems on Man*, he attacked political corruption in *The Motley Book* (1838), *The Career of Puffer Hopkins* (1842), and the play *Calmstorm, the Reformer* (1853). Mathews was neither a distinguished literary artist nor one of America's best poets. But he was a major voice in the dialogues surrounding some of his period's most important issues and developments. He ought to receive more and better consideration than he has been given, even by most of his contemporaries, whose wrath he perhaps brought on himself by his own confrontational, frequently strident, and even nasty behavior. Certainly, his writing itself deserves more attention, having been eclipsed by consideration of his roles in the time's ideological contests.

DONALD YANNELLA

Selected Works

Wakondah; The Master of Life, New York: George L. Curry, 1841
Poems on Man in His Various Aspects Under the American Republic, New York and London: Wiley & Putnam, 1843; rev. ed., New York: Paine & Burgess, 1846
The Various Writings of Cornelius Mathews, New York: Harper & Brothers, 1863

Further Reading

Bryant, John, ed., *A Companion to Melville Studies*, Westport, Connecticut: Greenwood, 1986, pp. 63–81
Chielens, Edward E., ed., *American Literary Magazines: The Eighteenth and Nineteenth Centuries*, Westport, Connecticut: Greenwood, 1986, pp. 451–456
Meserve, Walter J., *Heralds of Promise: The Drama of the American People During the Age of Jackson, 1829–1849*, New York: Greenwood, 1986
Miller, Perry, *The Raven and the Whale: The War of Words and Wits in the Era of Poe and Melville*, New York: Harcourt, Brace, 1956
Moss, Sidney P., *Poe's Major Crisis: His Libel Suit and New York's Literary World*, Durham, North Carolina: Duke University Press, 1970
Stafford, John, *The Literary Criticism of "Young America": A Study in the Relationship of Politics and Literature*, Berkeley: University of California Press, 1952
Stein, Allen F., *Cornelius Mathews*, New York: Twayne, 1974

Herman Melville

(1819–1891)

Many think of Melville as an exuberant romancer who was out of his element in verse. Certainly, there are at least formal and tonal differences between his romantic prose and pre- or post-romantic verse. From the beginning of his writing career, however, both his personal letters and his conspicuously literary and philosophical characters indicate that he preferred to see himself as poet, seer, soothsayer, and passional rhapsode, even though between 1839 and 1857 he published mainly narrative prose, much of it presented as based upon his experiences as a sailor – *Typee* (1846), *Omoo* (1847), *Mardi* (1849), *Redburn* (1849), *White-Jacket* (1850), *Moby-Dick* (1851), *Pierre* (1852), *Israel Potter* (1855), *The Piazza Tales* (1856), and *The Confidence-Man* (1857).

In his own day, moreover, as well as later, portions of that prose are most highly valued when most "poetic" – insistent in their cadencings, figurally venturesome, and ambitiously extravagant in their turnings of word, phrase, and notion. Then and since, of course, such passages also have been regularly derided by some for their creator's egregious violations of established borders between prose and verse, elegant and tortuous language, and decorous reason and unseemly enthusiasm – that is, for baroque, romantic, or transcendental transgressions like those occasionally charged against such exuberant high-planes drifters as Rabelais, William Shakespeare, Sir Thomas Browne, Robert Burton, John Milton, Thomas Carlyle, and Ralph Waldo **Emerson**, Melville's main troop among other writers of the purplish page. Battered by uncomprehending but passionately righteous reviewers, Melville himself may have begun to wonder whether his verbal flights were likely to get him anywhere he wanted to go.

Whatever the case, by 1857, he got to the end either of his patience with insufficient commercial success or of what he could still imagine bearable or worth doing in more-or-less popular prose. Thereafter, he devoted himself mostly to becoming a poet in verse. He did not succeed in getting his 1860 *Poems* accepted, but over the following 30 years, he published four volumes (the last two privately distributed) – *Battle-Pieces and Aspects of the War* (1866), *Clarel: A Poem and Pilgrimage in the Holy Land* (1876), *John Marr and Other Sailors* (1888), and *Timoleon Etc.* (1891) – about 750 pages worth that he partly or wholly subsidized putting into print. He also wrote another 100 pages of verse that he did not live long enough to shepherd into type. (Melville poems not quoted in full below may be found in the Library of America anthology, in the final LOA Melville volume, and, with extensive lists of variants, notes, and textual analysis, in volumes 11 and 13 of the Northwestern-Newberry *Writings of Herman Melville*, as well as in earlier collections by Howard P. Vincent, Hennig Cohen, and Robert Penn Warren.)

Unless some new document shows up – a table of contents, say, in Melville's or his wife Elizabeth's hand – we will have to go on not knowing what was in the 1860 volume that he wanted titled simply *Poems*. And therefore, we will also have to go on not knowing what kind of poet in verse he was initially. A memorandum to his brother Allan regarding this first volume

implies that it had no unifying topic, theme, or kind of poem, but was divided into self-contained sections that Melville called "books" – sections that were only to be numbered, however, not publicly called "books," lest that word suggest a unity and coherence of overall content or approach that he did not wish to imply. Selecting only from poems that may survive, in some form, from that time, we could guess that he may have offered in those "books" self-contained sections of verse devoted to rural, horticultural, travel, artifactual, historical, or even maritime matters – to show the range of what a true sea-poet could sound like, the one with his name proudly displayed on the title page.

So that we might get a better sense of how, if at all, he developed as versifier and supposer of poetic fictions, we would like to be sure that particular poems were or were not preserved, substantially unaltered, from 1860 – those, for example, that appear in the "Fruit of Travel Long Ago" section of *Timoleon*, which was printed at the end of his life. Many readers have inferred those poems "must date from" 1860 because most evoke scenes and responses Melville made at least brief note of in the journal of his 1856–57 tour of the Levant and Europe. Such inferring, however, indicates even as it tries to ignore several considerations.

First, except as their publication defines when some of Melville's poems were finished, we know of only a handful of them for which we can be sure of either initial or final dates of composition and revision. Second, claiming that Melville's 1891 crop was actually planted in 1856–57, ripened and harvested in 1860, and then stored in his poetic fruit cellar for 30 years is not supported by any unequivocal external evidence. Third, according to the implied logic that Melville wrote his poems closer in time than not to the personal and historical experiences they reflect or refract, many more poems might be hypothesized as first conceived and composed "early" rather than "late": (1) others associable with the 1856–57 tour or its aftermath, including many of the remaining poems in *Timoleon* and two that Melville left in manuscript, later printed as "At the Hostelry" and "Naples in the Time of Bomba"; (2) the rural poems presumably grounded in the years at Arrowhead, his home in the Berkshires; (3) many of the sea and sailor poems that the old salt also considered, in 1886–87, grouping with a fair number of the rural poems under a title like *Meadows and Seas*, before he decided to put the former into *John Marr and Other Sailors* and the latter into a volume that he did not get into print but provisionally titled *Weeds and Wildings Chiefly: With a Rose or Two*; (4) the rose poems that ended up appended to *Weeds and Wildings*, but that, for all we know to the contrary, could have preceded and artfully inspired Melville's becoming something of a rose grower if not quite a rose farmer in later life. Finally, however, the whole dating and development matter might be largely moot, both in general and in particular cases, if almost all the surviving poems are as much revised and effectually transformed into different works at indeterminate times, as many can be shown to be. Perhaps any such revised works should be regarded as both "early" and "late"? Maybe we need know only that all the poems that remain to us were judged worthy to survive the ceremonial bonfires hinted at in "Immolated" and starkly implied by the Berkshire Atheneum manuscript in Melville's hand of "In a Nutshell," on the verso of which he inscribed in large green letters before canceling and thereby commuting the sentence: "Burn!"

Partly because "In a Nutshell" is a marginal survivor, in fact, it offers some usable openings into an account of what Melville makes of the opportunities offered by verse. Can he finally not bear to burn it because it pithily sums up as well as wittily ensongs his bemused view, in and after *The Confidence-Man*, of some of this life's fundamental constraints? (Not even such an evidently simple poem, of course, may enable us to be in agreement as to how to take it – or whether to take it at all – let alone how to construe such further and passionate circumstances as its being consigned to destruction, then reprieved.) Why should this poem (not) be torched?

> Take a reef, take a reef
> In your wisdom: be brief.
> Well then – well-a-day!
> Wag the world how it may,
> The knaves will be tricking
> And fools still be kicking
> And Grief, the sad thief
> Will forever Joy's pocket be picking!

Melville might well be agitated to incinerate it when it temporarily seems too pat and pattering, too pointed, clear, simple, or conclusive, and thus unqualified to be considered suitably complex, shaded, inconclusive, open-ended, or engaging art. Especially its evident grim finality of claim might fleetingly bother him, if here he remains as he appears elsewhere – in, for example, *Moby-Dick*, *Pierre*, and "The Conflict of Convictions" (LOA, 2: 3) – both attracted to and repelled by such sobering conclusiveness. Like many an over-stimulated romantic, Melville can greatly desire the conceptual or emotional order and equilibrium allegedly bestowed by what are usually called settled views. But he can just as greatly fear that resigned or despairing conclusions (no matter how "realistic") may prove delusory or, worse, beget stasis, immobility, hopelessness, or perhaps even bring on – by bespeaking – that nothingness possibly revealed by going beyond what then may be suspected as only the *fictions* of change and learning. To keep hope alive – that hope the speaker in "Immolated" identifies as his "bride" and "mother to" his poems – what threatens it must be sacrificed, whether that threat be perceived as overwhelming conclusions, too excessive jingling of an irreducible jangling, too much preachment, or some other danger.

What changes his mind? Perhaps he sees as we may that the poem is not unequivocally or sourly preachy-teachy after all, that it does not so easily as might be feared reduce to lecture or crypto-sermon, and that by being cast into a compressed two-voiced play of mind its otherwise gloom-begetting conclusiveness is dramatized and thereby freed from the taint of unmediated authorial propositionality, which any creator of fictions may aptly dread (and which speakers in both "Montaigne and His Kitten" and "Rip Van Winkle's Lilac" express themselves leery of).

The poem's quick-wittiness is part, too, of what renders it as suppositional as any other comic fiction, and thereby enables its supposer provisionally to scratch an itch to believe in some simplifying conclusiveness, if only for relief from the unending complex uncertainty that occasionally makes his skin crawl. He may, that is, also (again?) or instead see that the poem's ostensible lightness of treatment does not make it too slight for consideration by the serious, even as it provisionally brightens and lightens (as witty fictions are supposed to) the dark heaviness that might else descend. He may even conclude that any verse cannot be bad or prosodically inestimable that serves up, almost liltingly, such take-'em-or-leave-'em hors d'oeuvres rather than a stomach-turning pot of message.

Some of the songs in *Mardi* and inset lyrics in *Clarel*, as well as portions of "Naples in the Time of Bomba" and passages in other works, show that Melville had a certain interest in as well as taste and talent for light verse, popular poetry, and song. A considerable part of the charm of all three for him may have been what he regarded as the possibilities they offered for temporary, unreflecting celebration as relief from oppressive cerebration and depression. Consider the evident light-minded or mind-less stance of "Merry Ditty of the Sad Man":

> Let us all take to singing
> Who feel the life-thong;
> Let us all take to singing,
> And this be the song –
>   Nothing like singing
>   When blue-devils throng!
>
> Along, come along:
> Nothing like singing
> (The rhyme keep a'ringing)
> Just nothing like singing,
> No, nothing for sorrow but song!

This "ditty," however, suggests what much other evidence implies: that as poet, and perhaps also as person – despite his announced inclinings toward simplicity, good feeling, and geniality – Melville was not able or willing to stray very far from what always threatened to make him blue: mindful "pondering" (as he called it), even brooding over cosmic and existential inequities, incongruities, incommensurables, or dilemmas. For instance, the rueful irony of "Fruit and Flower Painter" implies much about what he took to be unavoidable and saddening conditions for the (nineteenth-century?) artist who would otherwise seek to avoid "deceiving" if she could but choose not to respond to popular and commercial demands.

> She dens in a garret
>   As void as a drum;
> In lieu of plum-pudding –
>   She paints the plum!
>
>   No use in my grieving,
>   The shops I must suit:
>   Broken hearts are but potsherds –
>   Paint flowers and fruit!
>
> How whistles her garret,
>   A seine for the snows:
> She hums *Si fortuna*,
>   And – paints the rose!

December is howling,
But feign it a flute:
Help on the deceiving –
Paint flowers and fruit!

The conventionally blithe song meter (as in, say, Blake's *Songs*) plays sardonic counterpoint to the imagined-depressing situation of the artist who must not represent things as they actually appear but pretend wintry wind's howling is flute music.

These comparatively simple poems, which Melville did not put into print, may suffice also to suggest what emerges more insistently from an attentive reading of his first published volume, the Civil War verse in *Battle-Pieces*. On important matters, he was almost reflexively of more than one mind. That is, he found it desirable, even necessary to represent the attitudes of differing minds – not because he was himself naively uncertain or personally confused or uncommitted in his ordinary understanding, but because he saw, heard, and comprehended very well how various and often conflicting are the possible passions, motives, interests, explanations, values, and convictions that actual people voice. Various, too, are the resources of meter, rhyme, diction, and syntax that he marshaled to convey the sense and feel of different voices. Both of these points, in fact, are illustrated in "A Utilitarian View of the Monitor's Fight" (LOA, 2: 8), the third of three poems that constitute dramatically different responses to the first clash of the ironclads.

Plain be the phrase, yet apt the verse,
More ponderous than nimble;
For since grimed War here laid aside
His Orient pomp, 'twould ill befit
Overmuch to ply
The rhyme's barbaric cymbal.

Hail to victory without the gaud
Of glory; zeal that needs no fans
Of banners; plain mechanic power
Plied cogently in War now placed –
Where War belongs –
Among the trades and artisans.

Yet this was battle, and intense –
Beyond the strife of fleets heroic;
Deadlier, closer, calm 'mid storm;
No passion; all went on by crank,
Pivot, and screw,
And calculations of caloric.

Needless to dwell; the story's known.
The ringing of those plates on plates
Still ringeth round the world –
The clangor of that blacksmiths' fray.
The anvil-din
Resounds this message from the Fates:

War yet shall be, and to the end;
But war-paint shows the streaks of weather;
War yet shall be, but warriors
Are now but operatives; War's made
Less grand than Peace,
And a singe runs through lace and feather.

It may not be clear until the poem's last nine or 10 lines that its speaker (call him Melville at your own risk) is not himself a utilitarian but a poet who would be, if he but could be, a thoroughgoing anti-utilitarian. That he has, at least for the present, become a utilitarian empathizer if not sympathizer is indicated first by the title, but next by the expressive form and blunt sense of line one and the parsimonious rhyming of all stanzas, then by the honest admissions of stanza three with its (again brilliantly) expressive last three lines, and finally by the rueful but realistic last stanza – lines that strongly imply the speaker's aversion to both the spectacle and the significance of "that blacksmiths' fray," but cannot help hypothesizing (even if we take this for nostalgic-heroic grumbling) that a strangely useful result may prove a greater good for the greater number: that as a result of "warriors" becoming "but operatives" "War's made / Less grand than Peace."

A couple of letters he wrote to civil warriors after a visit to the front, as well as other evidence, suggest that it is quite possible the actual historical Melville did not believe for more than an artistic moment that war had been rendered "Less grand than Peace" (whatever the tonality we may attribute to that poetic hypothesis). The relevant point here, however, is that because Melville or his speaker cannot help but see how efficiently deadly modern machine war can be, effective expression of an almost inadvertent but real empathy for a utilitarian view is there in the poem. (For a different account of this poem, see the essay on Henry Howard **Brownell** in this volume.)

Similarly, in "The Frenzy in the Wake," there is powerful empathy and sympathy expressed for an imaginably vengeful Southern response to Sherman's march to the sea, and in "The Temeraire / (Supposed to have been suggested to an Englishman of the old order by the fight of the Monitor and Merrimac)" (LOA, 2: 6), a British aristocrat is imagined an apt persona for expressing, as Melville makes clear in his note to the poem, a "mind seeking for some one craft to stand for the poetic ideal of those great historic wooden warships, whose gradual displacement is lamented." Another such lamenter of the ironclad's rendering the wooden warship obsolete is the speaker in "The Cumberland." And a mourner in a related cause is the persona whose speaking is characterized in the subtitle of "The Old Stone Fleet / An Old Sailor's Lament."

Now all such grievers (although evidently not aggrieved Southerners) might be taken as but disguised stand-ins for the Melville who concludes in the "Supplement" to *Battle-Pieces* that "the glory of the war falls short of its pathos." But other poems in the volume, some not informed by pathos, similarly indicate how we are to take them dramatistically by offering explicit or implicit clues in their titles, subtitles, text, verse forms, or generic markers.

Most obvious are the signals given at the beginning of poems indicating that the poems are to be taken as dramatic monologues of one kind or another: "Stonewall Jackson / (Ascribed to a Virginian)"; "Battle of Stone River, Tennessee / A View from Oxford Cloisters"; "Running the Batteries / As observed from the Anchorage above Vicksburgh"; "The Fall of Richmond / The tidings received in the Northern Metropolis"; "A Canticle / Significant of the national exaltation of enthusiasm at the close of the War"; "The Martyr / Indicative of the passion of the people on the 15th of April, 1865"; "Presentation to the Authorities, / by Privates, of Colors captured in Battles ending in the Surrender of Lee"; "The Returned Volunteer to his Rifle"; and, most extensively, heading up the last poem in the volume (in case you have missed the point so far), "A Meditation / Attributed to a Northerner after attending the last of two funerals from the same homestead – those of a National and a Confederate officer (brothers), his kinsmen, who had died from the effects of wounds received in the closing battles."

More implicit but still unmistakable indications mark the dramatistic nature not only of "The House-top: A Night Piece" (a blank verse soliloquy that suggests itself as a solo scene in what the last paragraph of the "Supplement" calls "the terrible historic tragedy of our time"; LOA, 2: 10), but also "The Conflict of Convictions," "Donelson," "The Armies of the Wilderness," and "Lee in the Capitol" – the last four featuring typographically and otherwise differentiated voices obviously at odds.

At least three other tacitly dramatized voices in *Battle-Pieces* are those of figures we may provisionally call the Singer of Heroes, the Memorialist or Inscriber, and the Sage or Good Grave Poet. What we call them matters less here than recognizing their presence and function in "the symmetry of this book," as Melville refers to it in the first sentence of the "Supplement." So far, the commentators have centered on and preferred such vatic, soothsaying expressions of the Good Grave Poet as "The Portent" (LOA, 2: 2), "Misgivings" (LOA, 2: 2), "Apathy and Enthusiasm," "The March into Virginia," and "Dupont's Round Fight," and have identified those expressions as barely covert propositions made by the authentic, sincere Melville. On the same or similar grounds, those commentators have preferred trying to locate which of the voices is inferably Melville's in what they only reluctantly, if at all, admit to be dramatistic poems: "Malvern Hill" (LOA, 2: 9), "The Conflict of Convictions," "The Armies of the Wilderness," and "The Frenzy in the Wake."

They evidently have considerable difficulty with the sounding verses of the Singer of Heroes: "Lyon," "The Cumberland," "The Victor of Antietam," "Sheridan at Cedar Creek," "A Dirge for McPherson," and "The March to the Sea." The consensus thinking is probably close to: no truly self-respecting Melville could be guilty of such jingoistic jingling. Most of the productions of the Memorialist/Inscriber – mainly those in the section in *Battle-Pieces* titled "Verses Inscriptive and Memorial" – are also condemned to summary dismissal. A couple of the memorial verses are regularly exempted – "A Requiem / for Soldiers Lost in Ocean Transports" (LOA, 2: 16) and "Commemorative of a Naval Victory" – but the general judgment is that the rest must be regarded as mere padding-out of the volume or as Melville's cravenly giving in to expediency and trying to throw a few sops to popular taste and expectation.

One need not quarrel with the consensus hunch that some definable attitudes, responses, and deeper surmises of the actual Melville are discoverable in the poems. The only need is to notice, first, that his attitudes and responses are discoverable in more places and in greater abundance, if in more confounding variety and forms, than has so far generally been acknowledged. Melville is everywhere in the poems, not just in the few a critic selects. What in part follows from that noticing, as already indicated, is that Melville's primary mode and method in the poems are to be conceived as suppositional and dramatistic rather than propositional and propagandistic.

If there be any doubt on this point, Melville makes his suppositional approach clear when in the "Supplement" he says that he risks compromising the artistic "symmetry of this book" by putting himself forward, even in dignified propositional prose, as a patriotic good citizen who is attempting to persuade his countrymen of the justice and reasonableness of "a claim overriding all literary scruples." If his distinction there seems not sufficiently unambiguous, his subsequent assertion of dramatic intent and method should suffice to convince about both points, inasmuch as dramatism entails suppositionality. A third of the way into his 12-page essay, which urges national reconciliation and noble forgiveness of eligible Southerners, he confesses that "in looking over the battle-pieces in the foregoing collection, I have been tempted to withdraw or modify some of them, fearful lest in presenting, though but dramatically and by way of a poetic record, the passions and epithets of civil war, I might be contributing to a bitterness which every sensible American must wish at an end."

What are some consequences of recognizing the Melville of the poems as dramatic supposer rather than programmatic proposer? First can be an increased understanding or readiness to understand how the whole volume works to define a range of possible versions of and responses to the conflicts embodied in and engendered by the Civil War. Second can be an increased comprehension of and informed tolerance (if nothing else) for those parts of the whole – especially the songs and the inscriptive and memorial verses – that express responses troubling to the ordinary modern reader, who tends to have been conditioned to discount if not totally to distrust the uttering of such dangerous feelings, which bubble up in patriotic fervor and outright grieving, as well as the utterers themselves, the Public Singers and Memorializers. The corollary here is that the informed reader may be able to read, say, "Sheridan at Cedar Creek" and not make the categorical mistake of expecting a celebratory ballad to be a high lyric, elegy, or ode.

A third consequence of understanding the poems as set out dramatistically and suppositionally can be to question any simplistic identifying of Melville with any one of his speakers or personae. The tacit persona of the Sage or Good Grave Poet gains rather than loses from being taken as the seriously pondering but vulnerable hypothesizer that he must perforce be in Melville's idea of the fundamental nature of things, where (this again from the "Supplement") "to treat of human actions is to deal wholly with second causes" – and therefore to be, no matter how certain in conviction, nonetheless always in ultimate doubt, perpetually in question. Melville also gains in both literary and human stature once we are better able to take the Sage's poetic surmisings, figurings, and alludings as sensitive best guesses, eloquent hunches, and apt invokings of traditional associations rather than as covert lectures or crypto-sermons by a solemn pontificator.

The Good Grave Poet, in fact, and most obviously in his performing as elegist, enables Melville to distance himself from, defend against, and still sharpen his and our sense of the pangs of loss, uncertainty, or dread. Look but once at "The Portent," "Shiloh" (LOA, 2: 9), "Malvern Hill," "A Requiem: for Soldiers Lost in Ocean Transports," or "On the Slain Collegians," and you may see only image, figure, a skeleton of meaning, a tracing of predecessors, or a pattering of meter and rhyme – all impressive enough in themselves, but, as you may respond at first, a bit too formal, stiff. Look again, however, and take the trouble to feel what the forms both ceremonially clothe and reveal as otherwise ultimately naked, unaccommodated. Chances are that you will then begin also to experience more of the galvanizing currents that flow through these poems, as well as appreciate how the formal devisings of the Good Grave Poet insulate just enough to allow touching and feeling without too much shocking.

"On the Slain Collegians" is a perfect example of Melville at his formal and affective best. Almost alone, it suggests why and how he will eventually be read as a continuer and improviser of the poetic traditions and conventions that he purposefully works in – here, those of the commemorative and elegiac ode. Not only is the poem's language suitably dignified, elevated, and abstract – thereby suggestively increasing the meaning and importance of what some might otherwise take to be routine slaughter – but its central allusions are aptly classical. John Heath-Stubbs (in *The Ode*) helps to gloss the most significant of these allusions by pointing out that "Pindar's first Pythian ode . . . celebrates the power of music and the lyre of Apollo, patron deity of the Pythian games, which commemorated the god's victory over the monstrous snake Python," and that a passage from that first Pythian ode is incorporated in two works Melville knew well: Thomas Gray's ode "The Progress of Poesy" and Matthew Arnold's closet drama, *Empedocles on Etna*. Part of the force of the poem is generated by a specific historic tragedy, but much of the rest is created by connecting to that tragedy the even more extensively historical mass and momentum of elegy and ode as forms that work to contain as well as to recreate feeling.

> Youth is the time when hearts are large,
>   And stirring wars
> Appeal to the spirit which appeals in turn
>   To the blade it draws.
> If woman incite, and duty show
>   (Though made the mask of Cain),
> Or whether it be Truth's sacred cause,
>   Who can aloof remain
> That shares youth's ardor, uncooled by the snow
>   Of wisdom or sordid gain?
>
> The liberal arts and nurture sweet
> Which give his gentleness to man –
>   Train him to honor, lend him grace
> Through bright examples meet –
> That culture which makes never wan
> With underminings deep, but holds
>   The surface still, its fitting place,
>   And so gives sunniness to the face
> And bravery to the heart; what troops
>   Of generous boys in happiness thus bred –
>   Saturnians through life's Tempe led,
> Went from the North and came from the South,
> With golden mottoes in the mouth,
>   To lie down midway on a bloody bed.
>
> Woe for the homes of the North,
> And woe for the seats of the South:
> All who felt life's spring in prime,

And were swept by the wind of their place and time –
   All lavish hearts, on whichever side,
Of birth urbane or courage high,
Armed them for the stirring wars –
Armed them – some to die.
      Apollo-like in pride,
Each would slay his Python – caught
The maxims in his temple taught –
   Aflame with sympathies whose blaze
Perforce enwrapped him – social laws,
   Friendship and kin, and by-gone days –
Vows, kisses – every heart unmoors,
And launches into the seas of wars.
What could they else – North or South?
Each went forth with blessings given
By priests and mothers in the name of Heaven;
      And honor in both was chief.
Warred one for Right, and one for Wrong?
So put it; but they both were young –
Each grape to his cluster clung,
All their elegies are sung.

The anguish of maternal hearts
   Must search for balm divine;
But well the striplings bore their fated parts
   (The heavens all parts assign) –
Never felt life's care or cloy.
Each bloomed and died an unabated Boy;
Nor dreamed what death was – thought it mere
Sliding into some vernal sphere.
They knew the joy, but leaped the grief,
Like plans that flower ere comes the leaf –
Which storms lay low in kindly doom,
And kill them in their flush of bloom.

Of course, one must have no absolute objection to regarding the Good Grave Poet and "Melville" as more or less interchangeable, so long as that "Melville" be understood as supposer and dramatizer of ideas rather than as proponent of one or some over others (which latter the actual-factual Melville may well have been on occasion). The advantages of conceiving a functional distinction between the private person and the public poet appear time after time as we read through the rest of the poems, and nowhere more, perhaps, than in coming to terms with *Clarel* (see LOA, 2: 17). At 18,000 lines, this metrical romance or "whatnot" (Melville's word), ostensibly about a theology student whose faith has wobbled, is by far Melville's longest and most complex poetic effort. So complex is it that many have found it impenetrable. It is not, but for many it must seem so, because it explicitly and implicitly provides more questions all along than it has any ability or intention to answer. It is, in fact, a monument of as well as to unanswered and unanswerable questions, and is relentlessly conditional to the last line of its "Epilogue." Furthermore, as a poem that dramatizes a great range of religious, philosophical, scientific, historical, social, and political ideas, attitudes, motives, and traditions, it may require more knowledge or interest in the matters that it treats than most modern readers have to start with or are willing to work up. That may "intimidate or allure" – as Melville wrote to an English admirer, James Bill-son, in 1884 – after he had represented the poem as "eminently adapted for unpopularity."

Should you even bother to get interested? Hard to tell. Ed Dorn, the contemporary poet of *Gunslinger*, is reported to have claimed that "the great unread *Clarel* will prove, in this century, to be The Great American Poem." If you go there, as the travel pages say, your necessary guide must be Walter Bezanson, either in the 1960 Hendricks House edition or in the 1991 Northwestern-Newberry improved and updated edition. Otherwise, the best travelers' advisory may just be to begin at the beginning and go as fast as you wish or as slowly as you must – reading aloud when you can, especially when the idiom or syntax baffles you.

For most of this poem, Melville uses the four-stress line that he favors elsewhere (perhaps for its speed and liveliness, or perhaps because he had read in several places, including Hazlitt, that the pentameter line had become weak and boring). He rhymes and half-rhymes this four-stress line in several patterns throughout verse paragraphs of varying length. With the justificatory example in mind of Edmund Spenser but also the practice of Thomas Chatterton and James Macpherson and a few others given to purposeful "old-ageifying," Melville devises or improvises for *Clarel* a special language, the tacit rules of which allow but do not require: idiomatic inversion, truncation, and other variation; liberal substitution of archaic diction and neologisms for words and usages more current in the nineteenth century; and elevation of concern and consideration expressed in high-toned phrasing evidently meant to sound more or less Elizabethan-Jacobean – that is, reminiscent of both a timeworn translation of Scripture or ancient epic and Shakespeare (who, for Melville, was as good as a writer of holy books; "the divine William," he called him).

Perhaps even such a sober summary as this makes *Clarel* sound like a cracked or crazed project. Many have said as much. But the poem has gradually attracted admirers, and may gather more fans as the centuries wear on. Melville was pretty clearly not writing for his own time, narrowly construed, but for all time. If it took a tortuous syntax to tender a tough topic, so be it. Melville had never willingly considered himself as among the plain-style underwriters who take as an artistic virtue the concealing and effectual disavowing of art. As he looked back at a revered Spenser of 300 years before, he could imagine himself being looked back at with similar reverence in the twenty-second century. If he antiqued and otherwise tried to make his language time-proof according to models fashioned of old, such stylizing and formalizing would both elevate his words above the ordinary and insulate them from the common fate of linguistic change. Some such theory – coupled with his continuing fondness for old words and old books – impelled him.

The result, of course, although heroically ambitious, is not, except allusively, Spenserian, Shakespearean, epic, or scriptural in any usual sense. If anything – and perhaps it was conceived and consciously crafted to be – the poem may be counter-scriptural, an example of what a gospel written by a Melville in the nineteenth century would have to sound like: by turns bemused, exhilarated, dismayed, amused, knotted, gnarled, stewing and fuming, and half-choked with yearning, bafflement, frustration, and resentments justified and groundless – but always high-mindedly dedicated to order, plan, significance, the ideal, compassion for victims, and scorn of the superficial.

Beyond the tangled tunes and dangling vines of darkest *Clarel* lie the poems Melville in his later years tried out in various arrangements before settling upon those of *John Marr* and *Timoleon*, as well as virtually finishing that of *Weeds and Wildings Chiefly*. A few of these poems are preceded by prose accounts, which make explicit the setting and circumstances of what would otherwise be dramatic monologues only tacitly.

Whether pieces in these collections were originally conceived much earlier or not, the surviving manuscripts of many of them, as well as of those that Melville left undesignated for any planned volume when he died, show something of his habits of revision. Most evident and possibly significant of those habits was his tendency to expand and complicate by adding further specification to narrative accounts in prose or verse. As Harrison Hayford and Merton M. Sealts show, *Billy Budd, Sailor* grew in successive stages from a prose headnote to "Billy in the Darbies" (LOA, 2: 85) and is the most dramatic example of how Melville could become progressively engaged and challenged to say more. "Rip Van Winkle's Lilac" and "Bridegroom Dick" offer other examples of the same general process. The prose headnote to "John Marr" (see LOA, 2: 47) may also have been generated thus. The brief prose introduction to "Tom Deadlight" (LOA, 2: 49) probably shows the simple form of contextualizing from which the more complex forms grew.

Some suggestive evidence in the manuscripts, moreover, indicates that Melville might occasionally have revised in such a way that lines he had earlier used became inappropriate to the changing figure of a poem, and thus had to be used elsewhere if at all. This may well have happened, for example, when the last two lines of "In a Garret" were salvaged for recycling from their earlier function as the first two lines in an intermediate version of "Art" (LOA, 2: 72). (If so, "In a Garret" becomes one of the few poems we may more defensibly label "late.")

And other revisions can tantalize if not clearly reveal much. At one point, Melville considered changing the first line of "Monody" (LOA, 2: 71) – "To have known him, to have loved him" – to read, "To have known her, to have loved her." If "Monody" be other than an elegant exercise in a traditional genre, would such a revision have served truth better (if we may assume an actual person – and not necessarily Nathaniel **Hawthorne**, as most reflexively imagine – as the poem's object), or would it have served to universalize the treatment, as well as to offer a false trail to any sensationalists looking for a quick fix?

Melville's manuscript and proof revisions also tend to qualify, if not outright call into question, the general impression that he is an inept metrist. By now it is probably acknowledged that he resourcefully, frequently, and skillfully varies his rhyming and stanza patterns; and sophisticates will scoff at the claim, disproved by ancient and honorable poetic practice in English, that he should not be suffered to offer half-rhymes or rhymes based on a regional pronunciation (still heard in New York and environs) that, for example, makes out the words "law" and "war" as identical in their endings. In Melville's times and ours, both amateur readers of poetry and many who should know better have imagined that he ought to be a more perfect syllable-counter and not vary his feet so much, although the truth remains that he is (again, in an ancient and honorable tradition) an accentual-syllabic poet who is usually more concerned with the count of beats or stresses than with the number of syllables in a line.

He can write perfectly flowing lines when he wants to be smooth and regular in both stress and syllable count. But just as he seldom uses the five-beat line except for emphasis, closure, or especially appropriate situations – probably to avoid the monotony of over-familiar regularity – he is often reluctant to let a reader get too comfortable about the number of syllables to expect in a line otherwise sufficiently regulated by a predictable – although also variable – number of beats. Also, especially in verses presented as songs or songlike (and, again, with ancient and honorable . . .), he feels free to mix duple with triple feet. ("Tom Deadlight" and "The Maldive Shark" [LOA, 2: 57] offer differing effects here.) So when he comes to revise, he shows himself willing to vary not only wording but also syllable count and foot configuration, but hardly ever the number of previously stipulated beats.

To some this has implied what in fact may be true – that Melville is more concerned to get the words right than to maintain regularity of scansion. To many his verse often feels "rough" or "gnarly" – and that may be as Melville intended and felt on his nerve ends. One family story has it that he would on occasion declaim some of his verses with a pounding emphasis that the teller found excessive. A granddaughter guessed that when she heard him "pacing back and forth for a long time" in his study overhead, he "must have been walking off energy, instead of turning to writing as a safety valve for smoldering fires." There is little but this kind of family rumor to support the speculation, by some, that Melville was often so throbbing with one passion or another that he took to poetry both as substitute for pistol and ball and as a means simultaneously to administer and feel the beatings that he feared otherwise proscribed by "fate and ban."

Whatever the truth may be here, and family tales aside, one of Melville's motives to write poetry is everywhere evident. He was a poet because he did not know the truth, and he never quite wriggled free from having to ask the questions. Those who cannot bear to believe that he remained in fundamental doubt need to be very selective in picking out what they represent as his answers. Some who prefer an upbeat old man like to hang their hopes for a finally accepting or resigned Melville on the last of the short poems called "Pebbles" with which he ended *John Marr*:

> Healed of my hurt, I laud the inhuman Sea –
> Yea, bless the Angels Four that there convene;
> For healed I am even by their pitiless breath
> Distilled in wholesome dew named rosmarine.

This is a fine poem, and not least in illustrating how resourceful Melville could be in five-beat lines. The only and considerable problem is that at least two or three of the other "Pebbles," as well as "The Maldive Shark," "The Berg" (LOA, 2: 59), and a dozen others, call the solution or resolution of that final figure into question. Here, for example, is the second "Pebble":

> Old are the creeds, but stale the schools
>   Revamped as the mode may veer.
> But Orm from the schools to the beaches strays,
> And, finding a Conch hoar with time, he delays
>   And reverent lifts it to ear.

> That Voice, pitched in far monotone,
>   Shall it swerve? shall it deviate ever?
> The Seas have inspired it, and Truth –
>   Truth, varying from sameness never.

The pounding of one's heart echoed in a shell as an evidence of unvarying truth? And could a "healed" Melville persistently "laud" a shark gnawing at his nether parts? Has Herman gone soft? Questionable.

ROBERT C. RYAN

Selected Works

Battle-Pieces and Aspects of the War, New York: Harper & Brothers, 1866

Clarel: A Poem and Pilgrimage in the Holy Land, New York: G. P. Putnam's Sons, 1876

John Marr and Other Sailors, with Some Sea-Pieces, New York: De Vinne, 1888

Timoleon Etc., New York: Caxton, 1891

Collected Poems, edited by Howard P. Vincent, Chicago: Packard; Hendricks House, 1947

Clarel, edited by Walter Bezanson, New York: Hendricks, 1960

Billy Budd, Sailor, edited by Harrison Hayford and Merton M. Sealts Jr., Chicago: University of Chicago Press, 1962

The Battle-Pieces of Herman Melville, edited by Hennig Cohen, New York: Thomas Yoseloff, 1964

Selected Poems of Herman Melville, edited by Hennig Cohen, Garden City, New York: Doubleday, Anchor, 1964

Selected Poems of Herman Melville, edited by Robert Penn Warren, New York: Random House, 1970

Battle-Pieces, edited by Sidney Kaplan, Amherst: University of Massachusetts Press, 1972

Journals, edited by Howard C. Horsford, with Lynn Horth, vol. 15 of the Northwestern-Newberry *Writings of Herman Melville*, Evanston, Illinois, and Chicago: Northwestern University Press and The Newberry Library, 1989

Clarel, edited by Harrison Hayford, et al., vol. 13 of the Northwestern-Newberry *Writings of Herman Melville*, Evanston, Illinois, and Chicago: Northwestern University Press and The Newberry Library, 1991

Correspondence, edited by Lynn Horth, vol. 14 of the Northwestern-Newberry *Writings of Herman Melville*, Evanston, Illinois, and Chicago: Northwestern University Press and The Newberry Library, 1993

Published Poems, edited by Robert C. Ryan, vol. 11 of the Northwestern-Newberry *Writings of Herman Melville*, Evanston, Illinois, and Chicago: Northwestern University Press and The Newberry Library, 1995

Further Reading

Bryant, John, ed., *A Companion to Melville Studies*, Westport, Connecticut: Greenwood, 1986

Donoghue, Denis, *Connoisseurs of Chaos: Ideas of Order in Modern American Poetry*, New York: Columbia University Press, 1965; reprinted, 1984

Howard, Leon, *Herman Melville: A Biography*, Berkeley: University of California Press, 1951

Leyda, Jay, *The Melville Log: A Documentary Life of Herman Melville*, 2 vols., New York: Harcourt, Brace, 1951;

reprinted, with new supplementary chapter, New York: Gordian, 1969

Melville's Reading: A Check-List of Books Owned and Borrowed, Madison: University of Wisconsin Press, 1966, rev. and enl. ed., Columbia: University of South Carolina Press, 1988

Metcalf, Eleanor Melville, *Herman Melville: Cycle and Epicycle*, Cambridge, Massachusetts: Harvard University Press, 1953

Miller, Edwin Haviland, *Melville: A Biography*, New York: Persea, 1975

Rogin, Michael Paul, *Subversive Genealogy: The Politics and Art of Herman Melville*, Berkeley: University of California Press, 1983

Sealts, Merton M., Jr., *Melville as Lecturer*, Cambridge, Massachusetts: Harvard University Press, 1957

Shurr, William H., *The Mystery of Iniquity: Melville as Poet, 1857–1891*, Lexington: University Press of Kentucky, 1972

Stein, William Bysshe, *The Poetry of Melville's Late Years: Time, History, Myth, and Religion*, Albany: State University of New York Press, 1970

Adah Isaacs Menken

(1835?–1868)

When *Infelicia*, Menken's only book of poems, appeared in 1868, it was savaged by the critics and left to die. Menken herself, world famous as the uninhibited star of the play *Mazeppa*, and for her well-publicized affairs with Alexandre Dumas and Algernon Swinburne, was already dead, having passed away in Paris two weeks earlier. Despite the critics and the lack of an author to publicize it, however, *Infelicia* did not expire but went through at least four editions in the nineteenth century. It has lingered ever since as a literary curiosity, a kind of nineteenth-century feminist *Howl*.

Who was Adah Isaacs Menken, and why – as the title of her book suggests – was she unhappy? The answers to these questions are fairly complex. Although most sources agree that Menken was born on June 15, 1835, for many years her early life was almost a complete mystery. Each time that she was asked about her childhood, she gave a different report. The states of Ohio, Tennessee, Louisiana, and Texas were all suggested as sites for her upbringing. One British writer even claimed to have known Menken as the daughter of a London, England, clothier. Her parentage also was a point of dispute, which led to speculations about her religious and racial background. Allen Lesser claims that she was "born a Jewess"; Joan R. Sherman, however, says Menken was "probably" the daughter of Auguste Theodore, "a free man of color." Both of these suggestions lay the foundations for particular interpretations of Menken's life, but both have recently been proved wrong. By consulting previously unexamined records, John Cofran – Menken's current biographer, to whom this essay is indebted – has definitively settled the parentage question. Cofran discovered Menken to have been born Ada C. McCord, the daughter of Richard McCord, an Irish merchant from Memphis, and his wife, Catherine (*Theatre Survey* 31 [1990]).

Following her father's death and her mother's remarriage, Menken went with her family to New Orleans, Louisiana, where, shortly afterward, her stepfather also died. The loss of these two men and the move from Tennessee to Louisiana, all of which happened before she was 15, may have contributed to the emotional blind spot that caused Menken to be so evasive about her childhood. Certainly, one of the central themes in her life and in her poetry is the unreliability of love.

In New Orleans, Menken began working in the theater and writing poetry. In 1856, she married the first of four husbands, Alexander Isaac Menken (she later added the *s* to his middle name), the son of a Jewish businessman from Cincinnati, Ohio. With her husband as her manager, Menken performed in a variety of plays and gave literary readings to generally good reviews in major southern cities. In Louisville, Kentucky, she performed with Edwin Booth. In Nashville, Tennessee, she appeared as Lady Macbeth opposite James E. Murdoch, and although she forgot her lines and had to be coached through the part, the audience loved her good looks and reckless energy.

It was during this time that Menken, taking advantage of her dark eyes and dark flowing hair, invented her Jewish roots. She hinted to her husband about her Jewish past and started seriously studying Hebrew and the Bible. In part, this was an attempt to make herself more acceptable to her wealthy in-laws in Cincinnati, where the young couple now went, but it also suggests Menken's desire for the kind of deep family security that she never had. Although Menken moved on to other husbands and a more flamboyant life, she never abandoned the Jewish faith. While in Cincinnati, she began writing poetry in earnest. The *Israelite*, the local Jewish newspaper, regularly published Menken's poems and articles dealing with Jewish issues.

In July 1859, Adah and Alexander Menken were issued a rabbinical diploma of divorce, and she left the midwest to continue her stage career in New York City. At Pfaff's beer cellar on Broadway, she met Walt **Whitman**, Ada Clare, and other New York bohemians. Until then Menken had tended to write poetry in traditional forms, but under Whitman's influence she increasingly composed in a more confessional free-verse style. Soon after arriving in New York, she established a relationship with the *Sunday Mercury*, which, over the next year, published 25 of the 31 poems that were later collected in *Infelicia*. In "Swimming Against the Current," a front-page article Menken wrote for the June 10 *Sunday Mercury*, she astutely assessed Whitman's genius and importance:

> Look at Walter Whitman, the American philosopher, who is centuries ahead of his contemporaries, who, in smiling carelessness, analyzes the elements of which society is composed, compares them with the history of past events, and ascertains the results which the same causes always produced and must produce. . . . He hears the Divine voice calling him to caution mankind against this or that evil; and wields his pen, exerts his energies, for the cause of liberty and humanity!
>
> But he is too far ahead of his contemporaries; they cannot comprehend him yet; he swims against the stream, and finds no company. The passengers in their floating boats, call him a fanatic, a visionary, a demagogue, a good-natured fool, etc., etc. Still he heeds them not: his mental conviction will not permit him to heed them.

Then, in a neat turn, Menken closes by comparing the ultimate triumph of Whitman and Whitman-like messiahs to the eventual triumph of Israel:

> Thus Israel will rise to perpetual glory! So the house of Jacob will be rescued from the grave, and a proud monument assigned us in the history of the world. So Judea will triumph after darkness and ignorance will be utterly dispelled by the radiant sun of divine truth! For thus Israel has swam against the current for thirty centuries and more! Thus it has struggled and combatted against the corruptions of all ages in history; thus is Israel the savior, the Messiah of nations!

By linking Whitman's poetic revolution to the rise of Israel, Menken stakes out territory that she herself hoped to occupy.

Poems like "Hear, O Israel!" and "Judith" (LOA, 2: 335), the latter published as "The End" in the *Sunday Mercury*, contain an interesting combination of elements drawn from Whitman and Scripture.

In September 1859, Menken married the American heavyweight titleholder, John C. Heenan. It was a romance made for the press, especially when Alexander Menken publicly accused his former wife of bigamy. Sidestepping the question of the rabbinical divorce, he asserted that no legal papers had been filed. The vicious publicity that ensued is not surprising. Ada was outspoken and beautiful, and all women in the theater were suspected of having loose morals. The scandal helped drive the Heenans apart. At the end of 1860, disowned by her second husband, Menken hit bottom and briefly contemplated suicide. The poems she published in the *Sunday Mercury* at this time, with Whitmanesque titles like "Drifts That Bar My Door," are awash with emotional anguish.

In June 1861, Menken was in Albany, New York, preparing for a New York City comeback. The play that she hoped would return her to the limelight was the Byronic melodrama *Mazeppa*. In the play's central scene, the hero, a young Polish nobleman, is lashed to a horse that charges up a zigzag ramp, which leads offstage. Taking her cue from the folktale in which Mazeppa is stripped before being tied to the horse, Menken, playing the male lead, chose to wear only a flesh-colored body stocking and a flimsy tunic for the ride. The result was sold-out performances and theatrical history. The newspapers disapproved of the "naked hussy on horseback," but the people came in droves. On opening night in New York City, a month before the battle at Bull Run, nine Union generals turned up for the show. To dispel rumors of her Confederate sympathies, Menken distributed her poem "Pro Patria" to the audience.

In 1863, Menken took *Mazeppa* to California with her third husband, Robert Henry Newell, better known as the humorist Orpheus C. Kerr. San Francisco, still mourning the loss of Lola Montez, who had died there two years earlier, welcomed the actress with open arms. The *Golden Era* writers, including Bret **Harte**, Joaquin **Miller**, Charles Warren Stoddard, Mark Twain, and Artemus Ward, were fascinated. "Every curve of her limbs was as appealing as a line in a Persian love song," Stoddard enthused; Twain called her a fellow "literary cuss." Menken published several poems and another article lauding Whitman in the *Golden Era*.

The next year found Menken, alone once more, creating a sensation with *Mazeppa* at Astley's Amphitheatre in London. Many Victorian critics sneered, but again the public was enthralled. The story is told that when Charles Dickens tried to get in he was offered – and refused – a standing-room ticket. Another failed marriage, this time to gambler James Barkley, was followed in 1866 by what was perhaps Menken's crowning success, a sold-out run of *Les Pirates de la Savanne* in Paris, where she was befriended by George Sand and had a much-publicized affair with Alexandre Dumas, who was almost twice her age. When she returned to Astley's in 1867, however, the glow suddenly seemed gone. London was tired of *Mazeppa*, and "the Royal Menken" struggled to fill theaters. A liaison with Swinburne provided a romantic distraction, but her stage career languished. Invited back to Paris, an exhausted and seriously ill Menken collapsed during rehearsals and died in her hotel room from what later was diagnosed as cancer. She

was just 33. On August 10, after Kaddish was recited for her, Menken was buried in the Jewish section of Père-Lachaise Cemetery.

A year before her death, Menken had begun gathering, selecting, and editing the poems for *Infelicia*, the book that she hoped would secure her literary fame. It contains roughly half of her poetic output. Technically, *Infelicia* sprawls. Menken's work ranges from "Aspiration," a fairly tight irregular sonnet that was praised by Dante Gabriel Rossetti, to "Genius," a loose, essayistic prose poem, which begins with the declaration "Genius is power" and concludes with a bombastic eight-line rhymed stanza. Its title, aphoristic style, and mix of formal and colloquial diction give "Genius" an Emersonian ring: "To be popular is to be endorsed in the To-day and forgotten in the To-morrow. / It is the mess of pottage that alienates the birthright." Almost a third of the poems in *Infelicia* are in traditional poetic forms; the rest are in free verse that is occasionally studded with couplets and quatrains. Since the poems were written over a period of approximately 10 years, and in locations from San Francisco to Paris, the variety is not surprising.

Thematically, the book is about Menken and about the unhappiness life and love brought her. The final stanza of "Infelix," the last poem, puts it succinctly:

> Myself! alas for theme so poor
>   A theme but rich in Fear;
> I stand a wreck on error's shore,
> A spectre not within the door,
> A houseless shadow evermore,
>   An exile lingering here.

Here, the poet's unhappiness, while profound, is contained by the meter; elsewhere in the book the emotional agony takes control. "Resurgam," the first poem in the book, begins:

> Yes, yes, dear love! I am dead!
>   Dead to you!
>   Dead to the world!
>   Dead for ever!
> It was one young night in May.
> The stars were strangled and the moon was blind with
>   the flying clouds of a black despair.

Section IV of "Drifts That Bar My Door" begins: "Life is a lie, and Love a cheat. / There is a graveyard in my poor heart – dark, heaped-up / graves from which no flowers spring." In taking herself as her theme, Menken may have been drawing from Whitman, but where Whitman presents himself as a representative man, "one of the roughs, a kosmos," Menken personalizes her suffering, thereby giving her poetry its confessional quality. It is instructive to compare the opening lines of what Whitman later titled "Song of Myself" (LOA, 1: 720) with the first lines of Menken's poem "Myself":

> I celebrate myself,
> And what I assume you shall assume,
> For every atom belonging to me as good belongs to you.
>
> I loafe and invite my soul,
> I lean and loafe at my ease. . . . observing a spear of
>   summer grass.
>   (Whitman, 1855)

Away down into the shadowy depths of the Real I once
     lived.
I thought that to seem was to be.
But the waters of Marah were beautiful, yet they were
     bitter.
I waited, and hoped, and prayed;
Counting the heart-throbs and tears that answered
     them.

                    (Menken, 1868)

Both poems have strong first-person narrators, but where
Whitman establishes a speaker and a listener – "you" – in the
present, Menken is concerned only with herself in the past.
Whitman looks outward and celebrates; Menken looks inward
and mourns. Like Whitman, who identified himself with his
book, Menken seems to have thought of *Infelicia* as autobiography. She often signed her letters "Infelix," and she originally
had planned to use this as the book's title.

"Judith," one of the strongest poems in *Infelicia*, is worth
examining in detail to see many of the characteristics of
Menken's poetry. Judith is the heroine of a popular Jewish tale
that is recounted in the Apocryphal book bearing her name. In
this tale, Judith delivers her city from Holofernes, general of
the Assyrian king Nebuchadrezzar, by putting on her finest
clothing, seducing Holofernes, and cutting off his head while
he sleeps. Inspired by her deed, her countrymen rush from the
city and rout the invading army. On the surface, Menken's
poem narrates Judith's dramatic monologue as she prepares to
enter the enemy camp, but underneath this narrative the poem
is something more.

Menken's use of free verse in "Judith" reveals her debt to
the Bible and Whitman. The incantatory rhythms and the imperatives ("stand back," "creep back," "slouch back," and
"forget not") have a biblical force; the long lines, organic form,
and prophet-like narrator are, in large part, adapted from
Leaves of Grass, as is the catalog technique that Menken deploys effectively at the end of the poem's first section:

    Power that will unseal the thunders!
    Power that will give voice to graves!
      Graves of the living;
      Graves of the dying;
      Graves of the sinning;
      Graves of the loving;
      Graves of despairing;
    And oh! graves of the deserted!

The sensual, sadistic imagery of the third section (see LOA, 2:
336–7), which shocked contemporary readers, may also owe
something to Whitman's sexual frankness in *Leaves of Grass*.

But if stylistically "Judith" owes much to the Bible and
Leaves of Grass, its theme and emotional intensity are pure
Menken. Menken takes the tale of Judith and makes it her
own. She is not simply dramatizing an event from Jewish history but is identifying with Judith and invoking her help. At the
time "Judith" was published, Menken was struggling to preserve her reputation against the charges of bigamy and sexual

promiscuity. Heenan's cool indifference and final desertion
shattered and then enraged Menken. The rage in the poem is
not Judith's rage against Nebuchadrezzar's army, but Menken's
rage against her slanderers and against Heenan. The opening
quotation from Revelation makes clear that Judith's battle-ax
is a metaphor for Menken's verbal sword. Just as Judith triumphed over Holofernes, so Menken will prevail over Heenan
and her public humiliation. The last lines, "Oh forget not that
I am Judith! / And I know where sleeps Holofernes," are a clear
warning: Menken is out for revenge.

Taking this reading one step further, it is possible to see "Judith" as a nineteenth-century feminist call to arms. The biblical
story, which recounts the way in which an Assyrian general is
vanquished by a beautiful Jewess who is conscious of the power of her beauty, teaches a lesson. Women should not passively
surrender to social pressures but should actively use all of their
resources to achieve their goals. Judith's combination of
strength, courage, and defiance is also a model for women who
have suffered at the hands of men. Although much of *Infelicia*
concerns Menken's personal struggles, she was aware that her
situation was not unusual and that many of her female contemporaries experienced pain, injustice, and frustration when
they tried to develop an identity and sexuality outside traditionally accepted roles.

Infelicia is often said to contain some of the earliest examples of Whitman's influence on American poetry. Although this
may be true, Menken's poems do more than imitate Whitman's
prosody. Like Whitman, Menken was swimming against the
current, but largely because Menken was an ambitious, intelligent woman in a man's world, the problems that she encountered and wrote about were very different from Whitman's.
Infelicia is not an easy book to read. Taken individually, the
"wild soul-poems," as she called them, often seem raw and inchoate. Taken as a whole, however, the book's cry of loneliness
and anguish has a compelling intensity. As a poetic record of
Menken's controversial and meteoric career, *Infelicia* shows
the emotional price that she paid for fame.

                                        DORSEY KLEITZ

Selected Work
Infelicia, London, Paris, and New York: n.p., 1868

Further Reading
Franklin, Walker, *San Francisco's Literary Frontier*, rev. ed.,
     Seattle and London: University of Washington Press, 1969
Lesser, Allen, *Enchanting Rebel: The Secret of Adah Isaacs
     Menken*, Philadelphia: Ruttle, Shaw & Wetherill, 1947
Lewis, Paul [Noel Bertram Gerson], *Queen of the Plaza: A
     Biography of Adah Isaacs Menken*, New York: Funk and
     Wagnalls, 1964
Mankowitz, Wolf, *Mazeppa, the Lives, Loves, and Legends of
     Adah Isaacs Menken: A Biographical Quest*, New York:
     Stein and Day, 1982
Sherman, Joan R., ed., *Collected Black Women's Poetry*, vol.
     1, New York and Oxford: Oxford University Press, 1988

Stuart Fitz-Randolph Merrill

(1863–1915)

It is not often that diverse writers like Stéphane Mallarmé, Walt **Whitman**, Oscar Wilde, and Edward Bellamy can be placed into the same sentence, but then it is not often that one runs across a poet like Stuart Fitz-Randolph Merrill, transient New Yorker and longtime Parisian, symbolist and socialist, critic and translator. Frequently remembered as a second-rate French symbolist poet, Merrill deserves more than the passing dismissals that he has often received. Merrill was born on Long Island, New York, but spent most of his childhood and college days in France, where his teachers included Mallarmé. Even as an adult, his residence in America was more or less confined to an interlude that he called "my five eternal years in New York." Merrill's publications from this early, American stage include his first volume of French poetry, *Les Gammes* (The Scales, 1887); journalistic pieces in New York papers such as the *Times*, the *Post*, and others; and two poems in English, "Ballade of the Chinese Lover" (LOA, 2: 556) and "Ballade of the Outcasts" (LOA, 2: 557). (A volume of symbolist prose poems translated into English, four volumes of poetry in French, and numerous French articles and reviews would follow in later years.)

Perhaps the best way to contextualize "Ballade of the Chinese Lover" and "Ballade of the Outcasts" is to provide the reactions that two contemporaries had to Merrill's French poetry. The American critic Vance Thompson described Merrill as a carefree, thoughtless rhymester, "captivated by the facility with which French verse may be written by an accomplished amateur." Thompson cataloged Merrill's early subject matter (doubt and autumn rain, scepters and torches, and Wagnerian subjects like Parsifal and the Valkyries), while lampooning the results as "all kinds of verse – most of it curiously like real poetry." To support this contention, Thompson quoted from a poem not unlike "Ballade of the Chinese Lover," which was heavy with moonlight and musical references, and with rhyme, repetition, and refrain.

The French critic Remy De Gourmont offered a more measured, if less humorous, evaluation. Although noting that Merrill's second volume, *Les Fastes* (The Lucky Ones, 1891), was "doubtless . . . bedecked with too many rings and rubies [and] embroidered with too much gold," De Gourmont saw in it and in Merrill's third volume, *Les Petits Poèmes d'Automne* (Little Autumn Poems, 1895), an emergent diversity in technique, from "Parnassian stiffness" to the "*verso suelto* [free verse] of the new schools." Besides this movement toward the controversial vers libre (free verse), De Gourmont also saw, in Merrill's tone and content, a struggle between "a very spirited temperament and a very gentle heart . . . the violence of the brasses [and] the murmurings of viols."

While the two "ballades" might fall into De Gourmont's "stiff" category, his instrumental metaphors serve to highlight the difference between "Ballade of the Chinese Lover" and "Ballade of the Outcasts" – between the "viols" of dreamy, aesthetic introversion and the "brasses" of awakened social extroversion. "Ballade of the Outcasts" is unusual for Merrill's early work, since his humanitarian concerns tended mainly to

appear in *Une Voix dans la foule* (A Voice in the Crowd, 1909) and after. By then, he had shifted away from the intricate effacements of Mallarmé toward the prophet-like approach of Whitman: "Modern society is a poem badly written; it is a matter of correcting it."

The conclusion of Merrill's "Chanson de Paques" (Easter Song) describes a strategy applicable to many symbolist poems, including "Ballade of the Chinese Lover": "Love, cover my eyes to guide me in your way." In the latter poem, that is, Merrill evokes an ideal through indefinite references; this strategy recalls Mallarmé's aim for an effect "all music, essence, and softness: the flower which is absent from all bouquets." In his own "Credo," Merrill had offered a similar definition of the poet's task – "from forms of imperfect life, he should recreate perfect life" – and "Ballade of the Chinese Lover" employs several tactics associated with this symbolist idealism. First, Merrill describes something proximate to an object as a means of evoking that object. He calls attention to a peach tree, for example, through the blooms that rest on it. Other examples include Li's body and face, evoked through her "willowy waist" and "spangled veils"; Li's hands, conjured up by her "jasper nails"; and the tea fleet, with its wake and "moonlit trails."

In this poem, Merrill also uses the order of reading and syntactical ambiguities to create the fuzziness of semantic indecision: both the peach blooms and the nightingales initially seem to sprout from "porcelain towers," for example. Parenthetical phrases delay and diffuse concrete action across the time of reading, as when the relative speed of the barge ("fast") is withheld, thereby forcing the reader to *reconceive* the already nebulous peach-and-porcelain shoreline. As suggested already by its opening lines ("Down the waves . . . / In a gilded barge . . ."), the poem offers the reader a drifting syntax for a drifting journey.

"Ballade of the Chinese Lover" also covers the reader's eyes in order to open his or her ears. One could say that Merrill avoids the need to provide concrete lines of visual description by substituting the diffusive vibrations of aural ones. The "loud" nightingales, for instance, are described only through their song; the speaker and Li are described primarily by what comes out of their mouths. The barge's interior consists only of the "clang" of brazen kettledrums, the "weary wails" of flutes, Li's songs, the "hoarse . . . hails" of the pilot, and the narrator's tales.

By building a world around sound – including the synesthetic "dim gongs" and "silvery twang" – Merrill attempts to intensify a sense of both transience and permanence in the "Envoy" section that concludes the poem. Thanks to a syntactical ambiguity, one cannot tell whether the speaker praises Li before or after his "fantasy fails." On the one hand, the speaker puts the question of duration in terms of his echoing voice: the fantasy will last long enough for Li's "praises" to "ring" over the fields; then the aural world of the poem disappears and the fantasy ends. On the other hand, the speaker seems to bid Li farewell, promising to ring her praises later. In this case, sound becomes the medium for translating the fantasy into reality, and Merrill is attempting to give the fantasy lasting value through its sonorous imagery. Or, as Merrill said early in his career to his fellow French American poet Francis Vielé-Griffin, "To express the idea by words, to suggest emotion by the music of these words, – such are, I think, the alpha and the omega of our doctrine."

Presenting the audience with unfamiliar place-names (Han-Yang, Woo-Hoo, and Yang-tse-Kiang) is another way for Merrill to be specific without being concrete: the distance to "far Tchin-Ting" is not intended to be measured in miles. Merrill writes for a United States readership, and some of these readers would have been willing, even eager, to accept the poem's exoticized version of China as a distant setting for titillating fantasy – a setting "swooned" over by the "winds of spring."

"Ballade of the Outcasts" also positions the reader at a kind of distance, although here that distance is more a matter of the *emotional* and *class* differences between the speakers and the implied reader. By making the vagabonds, courtesans, and innocents describe themselves as "the hated of all men," and by having them ostensibly address "Kings whom Mammon sways," Merrill attempts to make the speakers as difficult to access as the scene of "Ballade of the Chinese Lover." Both "ballades" seek to create a vagueness in their subjects – the "Chinese Lover" exoticizes China and the "Outcasts" places the speakers "in some dark den" "beyond the town's lamp-litten haze." Both poems also invoke an element of nostalgia, of irrevocable temporal distance: Merrill seems to wish for the days of sailing junks, as opposed to New York's increasingly steam-powered harbors, and for the times of kings who could be deemed responsible for problems, as opposed to the circular finger-pointing typical of modern political machines or growing big business. Although the nostalgic events of "Ballade of the Chinese Lover" appear ready to fade into ethereal echoes by the end of the poem, however, the "Envoy of the Outcasts" also looks toward a future where hunger, inflexible morality, and outcast status become occasions for a call to arms rather than causes of death.

"Ballade of the Outcasts" originally appeared in *The Nationalist*, a magazine founded in the late 1880s to promote the ideas contained in Edward Bellamy's utopian novel *Looking Backward*. For a few years, the magazine was the organ of a series of "Bellamy Clubs" that sprang up across the country. A founding member and organizer of the first New York Nationalist Club, Merrill sought to apply evolutionary concepts to economic situations. In a burst of what now seems unbelievable optimism – shared by Bellamy and many early American socialists – Merrill came to the conclusion that rampant economic competition would eventually force cooperation to replace competition. In an article in *The Nationalist*, he wrote that "private interest will no more be hostile to public interest, but they will become identified, and as in a huge partnership, the purest altruism will prove the truest egoism." According to Merrill, capital and labor would inevitably cooperate; the only question that remained was how violent the transition would be: "but lest it work itself out in the tears and blood of future generations, it behooves all good men and true to go forth as prophets and apostles – prophets of the inevitable, apostles of all possible peace." "Ballade of the Outcasts" is such a prophecy: its threatening end is meant to scare the "Kings whom Mammon sways" into accepting the inevitable rather than con-

testing it. Perhaps the poem was also meant to spur action toward "all possible peace" among any proletarian eavesdroppers who might have been reading this upper-crust magazine.

In the course of this polemicizing, Merrill attempted to turn isolationist patriotism on its head by defining the evolution toward greater cooperation as "nationalism," and then praising the achievements of nationhood in the context of a progression that would obliterate the very nationhood he praised. "The ultimate term in this process of political evolution will be Internationalism, when the socialistic principle of co-operation shall have definitely superseded the anarchistic principle of competition." Merrill's belief in internationalism was among the reasons he left the United States for good: anti-immigrant sentiments had discouraged him. And although Merrill lived to see the outbreak of World War I, he did not live to see its conclusion. Vielé-Griffin said of Merrill's reaction to the hostilities, "the horrible butchery of the present hour surprised him in the midst of his dream."

But Merrill, although a product of his optimistic time, was not sleeping easily. Merrill's attitudes toward social reform shifted near the end of his life, and he seemed to recognize that his vision of evolution would require stronger measures than exhortation. In a 1906 letter, Merrill adopted a more militant attitude. Instead of returning to the United States, as his friends had wished, Merrill had just visited the city of Schweinfurt, Germany:

> I felt the same chill in my brain and heart during my five eternal years in New York. Humanity is going through a nightmare. Take Schweinfurt. . . . It is now a hideous, melancholy and unwholesome city, with a minority filling their money bags and a majority stupefied by work and drink and voting like sheep for the Socialist ticket instead of giving what is left in their veins of good red blood for the violent betterment of their condition.

Such a stance is also reflected in Merrill's late poetry. In "Apocalypse," the second part of a prose poem "Merveilles" (Miracles), which was published in the posthumous *Prose et Verse* (Prose and Verse), there are kings not unlike those from the "Envoy" of "Ballade of the Outcasts." "Their throats flayed with laughter," the drunken kings from "Apocalypse" are accompanied by queens whose heads are "reeling under the weight of their ancient crowns." The decadent royalty watch as bodies drift down a river; the bodies are of those who sought "by way of a pity contrary to that of God or the gods, to proclaim to the peoples grown pale through ancient sin the new good that the Book contains." Instead of constituting the poem itself, as in "Ballade of the Outcasts," the warning to reform is described as almost unsent in "Apocalypse": the bodies in the river were prophets struck down by angels for trying to bring news before the appointed time. "Ballade of the Outcasts" suggests the possibility that "Kings" can change, but in "Apocalypse," Merrill's prophetic message tells of ruling classes amid revolution and without recourse to hope. Notice in the latter poem that the presumably divinely approved invasion is presented through sound (far-off thunder), even as the belated, earthly warning of the overly optimistic prophets is described through silence (that of their dead bodies):

at the sight of those corpses which pass by palely on the

tide, and hearing the thunder of the barbarian cavalcade, [the drunken Kings and foolish Queens] desperately begin to weep in the irremediable night; and their fingers suddenly raised seemed to wish to pull from the sky its last remaining stars.

John Andrew Frey has criticized symbolist writing in general and Merrill's "Le Palais Desert" (The Deserted Palace) in particular for medieval imagery:

The whole representation of the Middle Ages, the captive princess, the enchanted castles, fairies, ghosts, and knight-errants . . . is oriented towards a sensualism. One is reminded of Swinburne making use of the Pre-Raphaelities in England. . . . It is the cloaking of earthly desires in a mantle of aristocracy, of manor houses, gilded ladies, estates swarming with peacocks and swans, of boat and garden parties, and the perpetual games of love.

In Merrill's case, however, imagery oriented toward idealized sensualism and mantled aristocracy can also be used to attack that orientation, and a stock of images and conventions can be turned to new purposes. The aristocratic princess of "Ballade of the Chinese Lover" can become the beleaguered kings of "Ballade of the Outcasts," or even the damned and despairing royalty of "Apocalypse."

The latter two poems are a long way from "Je Suis ce Roi des Anciens Temps" (I Am that King from Ancient Days), one of Merrill's more frequently reprinted poems from *Les Petits Poèmes d'Automne*. The speaker is a water-wandering ghost who, a bit mad, hunts for lost gold amid the waves; his fleet and once glorious city lie sunken below. In this poem, the predicament of royalty, while ostensibly glum, is nonetheless made a bit whimsical: confident that his sign will be traced in the sky, the King is not worried about being forgotten, and his narration almost seems a wistful trip down memory lane.

The figures of the vagabond and the courtesan also recur in Merrill's work. The vagabond can be found in "Visitation de l'amour" (Visitation of Love) and "Le Vagabond"; the courtesan can be seen in "La Nuit, un Cri, du Sang" (Night, a Cry, from the Blood). In fact, De Gourmont's criticism of the overly embroidered and bejeweled *Les Fastes* referred both to the poems and the "royal courtesans" depicted in them. But, as with his representations of royalty, the figure of courtesan gets refigured over Merrill's career, moving from an image of idealized self-indulgence to an accusatory warning against moral rigidity and economic ignorance. In "La Nuit, un Cri, du Sang," the courtesan is an impoverished old prostitute. The poem begins with the cry of her voice as she is murdered, her green belly split open on a dark winter street. The Bible-reading speaker who hears her cry sits safely inside his house, protected by a circle of lamplight and warm fire. Near the end of the poem, there is another cry, this time one of vengeance, which issues from a mixture of mud and blood in the gutter, not far from a group of uncaring theatergoers. The reader learns of the dubious "sanctity" of those who would help the prostitute: while she is alive, no one offers her more than candles to save her damned soul; when she is dead, the churchgoers make sarcastic offers of flirtation over her body to the pealing of Easter bells. Far from nostalgically wishing for the days when Jesus hallowed Magdalen, as do the courtesans of "Ballade of the Outcasts," the drinking, smoking subject of "La Nuit, un Cri, du Sang" takes matters into her own hands:

Nothing made her happy like taking a kid,
Crushing it against the pocket of venom that was her belly,
And returning it poisoned to its family
While singing to herself: "Yet another bourgeois done for!"

Merrill gives the negative view of religiosity here an interesting twist. When he places the "Alleluia!" that ends the poem apart from the rest of the poem, it is hard to tell whether it is a recapitulation of another, inappropriate "Alleluia!" ("*Alleluia . . . Une pauvre putain est morte!*" [Alleluia . . . A poor whore is dead!]) or a reaction to the threat of vengeance contained in the cry of the blood. The placement combines a sarcastic reference to the uncaring morality of the heavens with a sincere celebration of the cry for revenge against them.

In "La Nuit, un Cri, du Sang," Merrill attempted to unite his decadent aesthetics and socialist concerns in a prophecy of social vengeance. As a translator, he had long facilitated an intercontinental exchange of aesthetic and decadent writing. During Oscar Wilde's first stay in Paris, Merrill had, along with others, helped him to touch up the French in the stage version of *Salomé*, and he wrote several articles condemning the viciousness of the attacks that Wilde endured. Merrill also translated several of Yeats's early poems into French, along with work by William Morris, Ernest Dowson, and Arthur Symons. Last but not least, Merrill helped bring symbolist work to America through his series of prose poem translations, *Pastels in Prose* (1890).

In the end, however, Merrill kept himself at a distance from those he sought to help through his aesthetic and social contributions, as well as from those he condemned. Even as he attacked the moralists in "Oscar Wilde," for instance, Merrill adopted aesthetic priorities and sought to distinguish between Wilde's life and his work in order to save the latter. Vincent O'Sullivan describes a Merrill who refused to remain friends with Wilde upon his release from prison and return to Paris.

In one of his early pieces for the *New York Times*, Merrill wrote about a notorious Paris tavern, describing its transformation from a den of criminals to a highly publicized tourist trap and turning up his nose at the low conversations within. At the same time, however, as a literary man he saw it as a place to mine for material: the conversation is "made up of words that smell of the gutter. . . . Yet so rich is it . . . [that] it is a fascinating subject of study to literary men. This explains why, now and then, a poet or novelist of some distinction may be met at Père Lunette's jotting down notes amidst the pandemonium." Some sense of distance between Merrill and the objects of his sympathy never left him. In the late letter (1906) cited above, he expressed a contemptuous superiority that parallels the stance of the *Times* piece: "I am more and more convinced that what we must fight with all our might and power of hatred is the religious and patriotic spirit. Of course, our chief aids in our work of destruction and renovation will be the vulgar, base, stupid mob. But can't you write a sublime poem on a scrap of filthy paper?"

GERARD DEFOE

Selected Works

Bithell, Jethro, *Contemporary French Poetry*, New York: Walter Scott, n.d.

Payne, John, trans., *Flowers of France: The Latter Days*, London: Villon Society, 1913

Lewissohn, Ludwig, trans., *The Poets of Modern France*, 1918; reprinted, Port Washington, New York: Kennikat, 1970

Houston, John Porter, and Mona Tobin Houston, trans., *An Anthology of French Symbolist Poetry*, Bloomington: Indiana University Press, 1980

Mangravite, Andrew, et al., trans., *Atlas Arkhive Book Two: An Anthology of French Symbolist and Decadent Writing Based on The Book of Masks*, London: Atlas, 1994

Further Reading

De Gourmont, Remy, *The Book of Masks*, translated by Jack Lewis, Boston: John W. Luce, 1921

Frey, John Andrew, *Motif Symbolism in the Disciples of Mallarmé*, Washington, D.C.: Catholic University of America Press, 1957

Hartman, Elwood, "Minor Writers," in *French Literary Wagnerism*, New York: Garland, 1988

Henry, Marjorie Louise, *Stuart Merrill: La Contribution d'un Américain au Symbolisme Français*, Paris: Librairie Ancienne Honoré Champion, 1927; reprinted, Geneva, Switzerland: Slatkine, 1978

Thompson, Vance, *French Portraits: Being the Appreciations of the Writers of Young France*, Boston: Richard G. Badger, 1900

Joaquin Miller (Cincinnatus Hiner)

(1839–1913)

"Joaquin" Miller's role as poet was, in a sense, more important than his poetry. During the last third of the nineteenth century, he indeed created popular verse, but he also conceived and enacted a conspicuous and influential image of both the west and the western writer. His fame as an author and a public figure has become difficult to imagine or overestimate. His poetry is infrequently reprinted or anthologized, however, because his reputation has declined so much in the twentieth century. Yet in the 1870s, he was spoken of by astute critics as one of America's preeminent poets.

Even Miller's own beginnings became a source for his later myth-making and self-promotion. He was born, he reported, in a covered wagon that was headed west (although at the time near Liberty, in eastern Indiana). For the next dozen years, his restless and usually unsuccessful father, Hulings Miller, moved the family from one small Indiana town to another in search of a satisfactory occupation; Miller's father was, variously, a merchant, a schoolteacher, a farmer, and a magistrate. Young Miller's time on the newly opened Miami lands and his reading of the exploits of John C. Frémont and other western heroes fostered interests that he later put to literary use. The truly significant moment and movement of his childhood, Miller wrote in his autobiography, came in 1852, when the family set forth upon the Oregon Trail to possible "action, adventure, glory and great deeds away out yonder under the path of the setting sun." Nurtured by legend, and coming from the midwest, Miller was enabled to view the far west as not just a place but a time, a future of idealized possibility.

By recounting often embellished stories of his various western careers, Miller created his own legend. Leaving his family behind in Oregon, he joined adventurer and storyteller "Mountain Joe" DeBloney at a mining claim in northern California. The winter of 1856–57 and other periods were spent among Native Americans, whose cause he espoused in the prose works *Life Amongst the Modocs* (1873) and *Shadows of Shasta* (1881). Although at times he was forced by circumstances to participate in skirmishes against Native Americans, Miller formed a romantic liaison with a woman named Paquita, with whom he had a daughter, Cali-Shasta. Miller's newly adopted western name, Joaquin, came to seem appropriate after his run-ins with the law for stealing a horse (or mule), breaking out of jail, and wounding a sheriff. (The colorful Joaquin Murietta was a Mexican bandit and Robin Hood figure whom Miller defended in print; accounts vary as to whether he chose the name himself or was furnished it as a pen name by fellow author Ina Coolbrith.) Returning to Oregon, Miller briefly studied law, taught school, and worked as a surveyor before becoming a pony-express rider for a company in which he held a half-interest. With profits from mining and from selling the pony-express business to Wells Fargo, he invested in and edited the short-lived Eugene City *Democratic Register* in 1862. The *Eugene City Review*, a literary paper written almost wholly by Miller, also survived for only a few months. His marriage to Oregon poet "Minnie Myrtle" (Theresa Dyer) began with the couple's unsuccessful attempt to make a literary living in San Francisco, California, the thriving cultural center of the West Coast. Miller then seemed to settle down, as a husband, father, lawyer, and judge (1866–69) of Grant County, Oregon, but dissatisfactions with Canyon City, Oregon, and family life and disagreements with his wife led to a divorce.

The true making of Joaquin Miller as poet came in 1870, when he committed himself to an artistic life and set forth for the literary capital of London, England. He gained instant fame – and a publisher – as a flamboyant, wild, and supposedly authentic westerner, bedecked in cape and sombrero, chatting with Browning and the Pre-Raphaelites. His short *Pacific Poems* was revised and expanded as *Songs of the Sierras* (1871); surely if briefly, it became one of the period's most popular volumes of verse. Miller had become – improbably, at first glance, in England – the "Poet of the Sierras," the "Byron of Oregon," and the "Buffalo Bill of Poesy." *Songs of the Sierras* set the pattern for his later poetry in its use of romanticized western life and landscape, its evocation of idealized love, and its often imitative and awkward if sonorous versifying. Neither change nor improvement marked his later and less widely read books. Popular writers like Miller and Bret **Harte** were among the first to produce striking portraits of the west for eastern and European audiences. These audiences, however, were too far removed to play representation off against reality and to see that these western writers' depictions were quite stereotyped and exaggerated. Having mined the west for materials, in the familiar pattern of Mark Twain (another one-time San Francisco writer), these writers thus cashed in their literary gold in the cultural centers of the east and Europe, which set the terms of artistic, social, and economic success. Joaquin Miller, dubbed a "splendid poseur" by one of his biographers, certainly and histrionically presented himself as the poet of the west. At the same time, he apprehended and rendered his native subjects in the mode of an ill-defined and belated European romanticism that owed much to Lord Byron and Algernon Swinburne. Miller's literary theory held that "there are things that are sacred from severe prose" and that poetry is a passion that defies reason. His romanticism was far from either the avant-garde or Walt **Whitman** (although Whitman did have some praise for him), and his verse also seems estranged from the natural manner that would have been appropriate to some of his early-American themes. For Miller, however, excess and vague emotional effusion inhered not only in his subjects, but in the genre of poetry itself.

Songs of the Sierras is typical in its prosody and its telling of tender tales of love. Set against a backdrop of mountain, canyon, desert, prairie, or even jungle (most of the poems are not set in the Sierras), the poems are often maudlin and melodramatic treatments of tragic relationships between male protagonists and dark-hued women. The narratives characteristically contrast cultures and both evoke and exaggerate the exotic. For instance, the title character of "The Arizonian" woos and wins a "brown maiden," whom he leaves behind in order to return east to his first (white) love. But the latter woman has long since wed, which leaves the Arizonian with-

out mate or place. He ends up as a lonely and melancholy ancient mariner who is impelled to tell of his adventures in verse
sometimes as pathetic as his plight: "I am burnt by the sun, I
am browned by the sea; / I am white of my beard, and am bald,
may be." Miller turns to Central America in "With Walker in
Nicaragua" (although he had been neither with the American
military insurgent William Walker nor in Nicaragua). Heroic
skirmishes alternate with endless descriptions of jungle foliage
that encroach on ancient ruins. The narrator's faintly Mayan,
bronzed maiden drowns as she frantically swims after his departing ship. Verisimilitude, never a strength of Miller's, is
lacking in his depictions of Walker's actual enterprise, the traditions of native cultures, and love in the real world.

"The Last Taschastas" combines the theme of violation of
Native American lands and peoples with often violent action;
the poem also staunchly identifies with the lone Native survivor:

Through the land where we for ages
Laid the bravest, dearest dead,
Grinds the savage white man's ploughshare,
Grinding sire's bones for bread –
We shall give them blood instead.

(Helen Hunt **Jackson's** popular 1884 novel *Ramona* was far
from the only fictionalized passionate plea for the rights of the
"vanishing American." Here, with notable aplomb, Miller describes the white man as "the savage," and *Life Amongst the
Modocs* records – if in fictionalized fashion – the outcome of
his and DeBloney's proposal to found a Native American republic in northern California.) The quintet, from part two of
"Taschastas," also illustrates Miller's typical verse forms,
which are varied but always far from free verse. The stanza
rhymes in *abcbb* form, and the three rhyming lines are seven
rather than eight syllables in length; generally iambic, the meter is characterized by elision and other variations as well.
Many modern readers are put off by Miller's unevenness, his
infelicitous forcing of rhymes, his use of archaic and poetic diction even when he describes the mundane, and his distortion of
idiomatic and natural word order to maintain prescribed
rhyme schemes and sing-song effects. The unfortunate opening
of "The Tale of the Tall Alcalde" brings together many of these
faults:

Where mountains repose in their blueness,
Where the sun first lands in his newness,
And marshals his beams and his lances,
Ere down to the vale he advances . . .

And so forth. In this village of Renalda, the alcalde tells his tale
of lovers who are star-crossed by the cross-cultural. Considered
a renegade for siding with the Native Americans, the alcalde is
nursed through battle injuries by the self-sacrificing woman
who buys his safety with her virtue. All that remains for her, of
course, is melodramatically to stab herself but to live on in the
alcalde's story. Other settings of *Songs of the Sierras* range
from the plains of the popular "Kit Carson's Ride" to the Mexico of the verse drama "Inez" and the Britain of the poetic tribute "Burns and Byron."

After his initial acclaim, Miller went on to write a variety of
genres: the novel (*First Fam'lies of the Sierras* and *The One
Fair Woman*, set in the west and in Europe, respectively), dra-

ma (*The Danites in the Sierras* and *Forty-Nine*), and memoir
(*Shadows of Shasta* and *Memorie and Rime*). But he achieved
his literary reputation mainly as a poet and produced a succession of volumes much in the manner of *Songs of the Sierras*:
Songs of the Sun-lands (1873), *Songs of Italy* (1878), *Songs of
Far-away Lands* (1878), *Songs of the Mexican Seas* (1887),
and *Songs of the Soul* (1896). (Along with "songs," "pictures"
was another mannered Miller locution for "poems.") His long
narrative poems include *The Ship in the Desert* (1875) and
Light (1907). Miller's many – and many times – facile lyrics
and narratives are uneven in quality and often exhibit his particular failings as a poet.

Yet a few of his poems are sustained efforts of some power.
His celebration of Abelard and Eloise and love's lament, "In
Père La Chaise" (LOA, 2: 372), becomes an indictment of the
modern, the commercial, and the worldly minded. If the sentiment seems quaint, sentimental, and hackneyed, light years
from Whitman's paean to a locomotive, individual lines stand
out as Hardyesque in their starkness, like those that describe
lovers who "weep like silent, unobtrusive rain." Furthermore,
the enlightened cultural relativism of "Africa" (LOA, 2: 370)
seems especially surprising from a writer who, as editor of the
Democratic Register and the *Eugene City Review*, made himself unpopular by backing the Confederacy during the Civil
War. (Miller thought the Union was the aggressor, although evidently he was not pro-slavery.) Miller's words, ironically, assert the glories and antiquity of the continent while suggesting
that the message of Africa itself cannot be read because of prejudice and ignorance. Although he self-reflexively calls attention to his own poem, he also presents himself as a "no man"
who "dares to dignify / In elevated song." A tidy trope turns
about readers' expectations by making the fetters metaphorical
and placing them on the former masters: "The chains / That
held her race but yesterday / Hold still the hands of men." (A
negative construction of this passage would note that while
outsiders may be "no man," Africans rather than women seem
altogether excluded from the category "man.") In the alliterative "At Our Golden Gate" (LOA, 2: 373) as well, the deeds of
"Cowed, weak landsmen such as we" are not commensurate
with American promise or with old-time British derring-do –
this despite the locale's being a gateway into the nation, golden
(suggestive of a golden age), and "ours."

A more heartening tone and often memorable images predominate, however, in Miller's popular verse about the land of
his heritage and heart, the west. His parents' generation had
gone west as participants in a grand pioneering enterprise,
Miller wrote, just as he "blazed out the trail for great minds
over this field." Witness far and away his best-known poem,
"Columbus" (LOA, 2: 375). This poem has been read, recited,
and memorized by several generations of American schoolchildren as a general affirmation of moral uplift in the manner
of Henry Wadsworth **Longfellow's** "Excelsior." Columbus's
reiterated response to every occasion and difficulty is "Sail
on!" Although "he gained a world," Miller writes, Columbus
"gave that world / Its grandest lesson: 'On! sail on!'" The
poem also augments Miller's usual definition of the west by
making all of fifteenth-century America "the west," the undiscovered country of possibility, "Time's burst of dawn." The
terms here, considered logically, seem not to be contradictory
only because of the symbology that Miller and others have as-

sociated with the west. In other words, the region must be a place unachieved, held always in abeyance. Even when a world is gained, the impulse to go on to the new defines the very concept of the frontier; if a world is gained, it cannot be, ipso facto, the west. Not just at the beginning, but also at the end of Twain's novel, Huck Finn is also "lighting out." In the title of a Whitman poem, the persona faces west from (even) California's shores. Miller chose the site for The Hights, his home in the hills above Oakland, California, from 1887 until his death, partly on the requirement that he have a vista of the sun setting over the Pacific Ocean. At the Hights, he constructed monuments to Frémont, Robert Browning, and Moses. And his own most fabled adventure came in 1897, when Miller pushed on to a final frontier by joining the gold seekers on their trek to Alaska and the Yukon and Klondike territories as a newspaper correspondent.

Joaquin Miller's importance, finally, lies in his contribution to the myths of the American west that have affected national values, ways of thought, and both popular and "serious" literature, film, and television. He wrote of the region "to show to the world her vastness, her riches, her resources, her valor and her dignity, her poetry and her grandeur." Neither complex nor profound as a poet, he evokes depths (intentionally or not) in those passages that portray a west rendered universal, in a sense, by its disjunction from simple and naive optimism – that identify the west not only with beginnings but also with endings, the sunset and gathering darkness. Miller's vocabulary bespeaks a consciousness of implications when he writes, in *Overland in a Covered Wagon*, that "the little story of our pilgrimage is simply that of thousands and hundreds of thousands who peopled the ultimate west." The ultimate west: if too often Miller mildly muses musically of majestic mountains, he is also capable of the stirring strength of "Sierra" (LOA, 2: 369). The rampart of the High Sierra becomes the goal and resting place: "white pyramids of Faith, where man is free." "Serene and satisfied! supreme! white, lone / As God, they loom above cloud-banners furled; / They look as cold as kings upon a throne." "High held above a tossed and tumbled sea," the Sierras serve, too, as inspiration to "bearded prophets" who will one day "fill the hills and thrill with song the heed-ing throng." It is Miller's mystic monolith, Mount Shasta, unique even among the many imposing peaks of the range, that stands above human contention as the embodiment of the final myth in *Life Amongst the Modocs* ("As lone as God, and white as a winter moon") and in *Overland in a Covered Wagon* ("alone as God upon the great white throne"). (Miller typically repeated his own effective or favorite phrases.) Not just the local surviving Native Americans, called by Miller "the last of the children of Shasta," but all of us dwell in the shadows of Shasta.

BENJAMIN S. LAWSON

Selected Works

Songs of the Sierras, London: Longman, Green, Reader, and Dyer, 1871; Boston: Roberts Brothers, 1871
Pacific Poems, London: Whittingham and Wilkins, 1871
Songs of the Sun-lands, Boston: Roberts Brothers, 1873
Songs of Italy, Boston: Roberts Brothers, 1878
Memorie and Rime, New York: Funk and Wagnalls, 1884
Songs of the Mexican Seas, Boston: Roberts Brothers, 1887
Songs of the Soul, San Francisco: Whittaker and Ray, 1896
Joaquin Miller's Poems, 6 vols., San Francisco: Whittaker and Ray, 1910

Further Reading

Frost, O. W., *Joaquin Miller*, New Haven, Connecticut: Twayne, 1967
Lawson, Benjamin S., *Joaquin Miller*, Boise, Idaho: Boise State University Western Writers Series, 1980
Marberry, M. Marion, *Splendid Poseur: Joaquin Miller – American Poet*, New York: Thomas Y. Crowell, 1953
Peterson, Martin S., *Joaquin Miller: Literary Frontiersman*, Palo Alto, California: Stanford University Press, 1937
Starr, Kevin, *Americans and the California Dream, 1850–1915*, New York: Oxford University Press, 1973
Wagner, Harr, *Joaquin Miller and His Other Self*, San Francisco: Harr Wagner, 1929
Walker, Franklin, *San Francisco's Literary Frontier*, New York: Knopf, 1939

Harriet Monroe

(1860–1936)

Harriet Monroe occupies an ironic place in the history of American poetry. She is best known as the founder and editor of *Poetry: A Magazine of Verse,* and is credited by many literary historians with opening the road to modern poetry. Monroe's purpose for the magazine was to provide a forum for poets who were experimenting with verse and were denied publication by other magazines. Yet although Monroe was devoted to the avant-garde, her own poetry, although at times experimental in form, tended toward an optimistic faith in America and its technological inventions that was more reminiscent of the nineteenth century.

Monroe's subject matter is varied and exhibits a special interest in frontiers and things new. In an editorial in the May 1913 issue of *Poetry*, Monroe states that, rather than writing or printing poetry in the dead cadences of tradition, she desires "the free foot in the wilderness" and "the upward flight of danger in a monoplane." "Tradition, however grand and old," she says, "ceases to be of use the moment its walls are strong enough to break a butterfly's wing, or keep a fairy immured." Although Monroe generally did not wander far from the wall of tradition (she published Joyce Kilmer after all), she definitely was looking away from it. Her poetry expresses an excitement for literal frontiers such as the American southwest and figurative frontiers in science and technology.

Harriet Monroe was born on December 23, 1860, in Chicago, Illinois, the second daughter of Henry Stanton Monroe, a Chicago lawyer, and Martha Mitchell Monroe. For her schooling, she went to the Moseley Public Grammar School, and then to the Dearborn Seminary. At 17, she attended the Georgetown Convent of the Visitation in Washington, D.C., where, according to her autobiography, *A Poet's Life* (1938), "verse writing was a regular exercise . . . as necessary an accomplishment for a lady as playing the piano, speaking French, or painting rigid flowers on satin boxes." After graduating, Monroe returned to Chicago, where she then had to turn to making a living; after the Chicago fire of 1871, the once affluent Monroe family was no longer so. For the most part, she earned money by writing, serving as art critic for the *Chicago Tribune*, and freelancing for other papers, while also lecturing and teaching. Monroe is most remembered, however, for founding *Poetry* in 1912 and editing it until her death in 1936.

Early in life, Monroe struggled to find space for her own poetry. Her first published poem was "With Shelley's Poems" (see "To W. S. M." [LOA, 2: 529]), which she enclosed in the flyleaf of a volume of Percy Bysshe Shelley's that was given to her brother, William. The sonnet, published in the *Atlantic* in 1889, exemplifies a certain late-nineteenth-century verse style – a kind of poetry Monroe was later to work against. Using traditional poetic diction and form, and showing the strong influence of William Shakespeare and the British romantics, the sonnet is a call for her brother to be transported by Shelley's poems, which in turn suggests Monroe's faith in the saving power of poetry and in its importance to the contemporary world. Although her views of poetic form changed drastically over the years, her belief in the need for poetry never diminished.

It was in part this belief and in part her desire that Chicago be seen as something other than a "pork-packing" capital that led Monroe to write *The Columbian Ode*. The poem was commissioned by The Columbian Exposition of 1892, which was held in Chicago in honor of the four hundredth anniversary of Columbus's arrival in the New World. Monroe was outraged that while the exposition represented and, indeed, celebrated the plastic arts, it ignored poetry. She submitted a proposal to the organizing committee and claimed the resulting commission as a victory not only for herself but for poetry. *The Columbian Ode* won an important victory in court, too, when a newspaper printed an advance copy without Monroe's permission. Monroe sued for copyright infringement, won 5,000 dollars in damages, and established a precedent for the protection of writers' works.

The ode is, in Monroe's words, a "psalm of joy" that pictures the United States ("Columbia") as the "Leader of nations through the autumnal gales / That wait to mock the strong and wreck the free." Democracy combined with technology, the poem declares, will cure all social ills:

> Then shall want's call to crime resound no more
> Across her teeming fields; and pain shall sleep,
> Soothed by brave science with her magic lore;
> And war no more shall bid the nations weep.

In her autobiography, Monroe reflects on the optimism of the ode: "As we look back today upon the deadliest of all wars [World War I], and forward to prophecy of wars still deadlier, the finale of my poem is smeared by dark ironies. But at the time it expressed a feeling almost universal in the hearts of men and rising to rhapsody in the preparations for our world festival of peace and joy." *The Columbian Ode*, in other words, spoke more to the spirit of the exposition than to the spirit of the world.

Monroe's hope for and fascination with technology show most clearly in her "machine" poems such as "The Turbine" and "A Power Plant," which were published in the 1914 volume *You and I*. In *A Poet's Life*, Monroe says that she had "always been interested in machines, and in the marvelous and really affectionate dexterity of the born machinist; and ["The Turbine"] tries to show how such a man humanizes his huge creature of steel and makes it the point of departure for his imaginative and spiritual life." (Monroe's brother-in-law, John Wellborn Root, was a pioneering skyscraper architect, and her brother William was a builder of power plants.) In "The Turbine," which could almost be construed as a modern love song, the speaker describes the relationship as making the man simultaneously master of and slave to the turbine; the latter guise is evoked in the lines:

> Perhaps she feels
> An ache deep down – that agonizing stab

Of grit grating her bearings; then her voice
Changes its tune, it wails and calls to me
To soothe her anguish, and I run,
Her slave.

But later the same soothing hand is master and beats "back the chaos, hold[s] in leash / Destructive furies" and "rescue[s] her" from malfunctioning. The duality of this power relation poses no problem because such technology leads the speaker

Far out into the workshop of the worlds.
There I can feel those infinite energies
Our little earth just gnaws at through the ether,
And see the light our sunshine hides.

America's technology will also allow it to lead the world into tomorrow's peace and prosperity. The same sort of optimism also informs "The Graf Zeppelin," in which one of the speakers remarks, "It's great to be alive today, you know, / With all these wonders going on." With the faith Monroe had in American democracy, she saw these inventions and machines as bringing the world closer to peace.

Monroe shows an expansiveness in subject matter and form that may point toward the modernists, but her formal experiments are generally conservative. She was particularly proud of "The Hotel," regarding it as a prose poem and placing it at the beginning of two collections, *You and I* and *Chosen Poems* (1935). Her autobiography proudly explains that she wrote the poem in free verse "five or six years before Ezra Pound and the imagists . . . began in *Poetry* their campaign for a loosening of metrical rules." The poem depends on 23 "sentences" of description, which focus upon components of the Waldorf-Astoria Hotel in New York City. None of the sentences, however, contains a finite verb in a main clause, so the effect is that of a descriptive list.

Although "The Hotel" functions in part as a metrical experiment, its subject matter is not radical or ground breaking. As in much of her verse, Monroe takes the standpoint of an observer. She begins with the main rooms and moves her focus to the people:

The stout and gorgeous dowagers in lacy white and
    lilac, bedizened with many jewels, with smart little
    scarlet or azure hats on their gray-streaked hair.
The business men in trim and spotless suits, who walk
    in and out with eager steps, or sit at the desks and
    tables, or watching the shining women.

As the speaker gradually looks beneath this surface, the poem loses some of its shiny veneer:

The people inside of the clothes, the bodies white and
    young, bodies fat and bulging, bodies wrinkled and
    wan, all alike veiled by fine fabrics, sheltered by walls
    and roofs, shut in from the sun and stars.
The souls inside of the bodies – the naked souls; souls
    wizened and weal, or proud and brave; all
    imprisoned in flesh, wrapped in woven stuffs,
    enclosed in thick and painted masonry, shut away
    with many shadows from the shining truth.

From here, the final stanzas, which may be as dark as any Monroe ever wrote, look fully, not at an inevitable flowering of peace and plenty, but at God "veiled and wrapped and imprisoned and shadowed in fold on fold and flesh and fabrics and mockeries." Yet Monroe resurrects hope at the poem's conclusion, which pictures God as "ever alive, struggling and rising again, seeking the light, freeing the world."

"The Difference," the title poem of Monroe's third volume (1924), shows another slight change in her optimism. In the preface to this volume, Monroe comments on the way in which her optimism has diminished since the time at which she wrote *The Columbian Ode*; she states that she is "less hopeful today than thirty years ago of a world 'Laden with joy for all her thronging souls.'" Despite this disclaimer, the poems in this volume and in *Chosen Poems* are far from dismal. Although they do acknowledge social problems like war and unemployment, there remains a quiet optimism that the world will not always be so.

In "The Difference," Monroe self-consciously attempts to trace how the world has changed over the last century. The poem, which consists of two monologues entitled "1823" and "1923," shows Monroe's continuing fascination with material progress and her optimism about peace. The contrast between "1823" and "1923," however, does not simply present the way in which the world's manner of doing business has changed, from reliance on horses ("put on thy riding-skirt and saddle the mare") to reliance on cars ("absurdly driven by exploding little drops of oil"). The two sections also embody the change from traditional to free verse. "1823" uses archaisms and a loose blank verse to present a monologue in which a mother bids her daughter to go to the village on numerous errands. The voice betrays a regret that tea and silk come from non-Christian China, as well as a mixed feeling about the fact that the cloth is woven in Christian France, "If papists [i.e., Catholics] indeed be Christians in God's sight."

With the freer verse in "1923" comes also a voice with a freer attitude, which seeks to encompass all the world in "A world set free." For example, this second monologue shows discomfort with African colonialism: "The Congo must send us rubber – / Let us hope it costs no lives / As in good King Leopold's day!" This monologue focuses upon the way in which trade has changed the world and brought countries in close contact with one another, but the monologue also indicates that such changes have not necessarily brought peace. As Monroe comments in the preface, "A century ago each man's world was small, each neighborhood supplied most of its own needs; and even statesmen could measure up to national crises. Today each man's world is enormously enlarged, each village makes demands to the ends of the earth, and governmental issues seem to outgrow the capacity of the individual human brain." The poem looks critically at how machines have "invaded" the world and asks,

Will some Man of the crowd,
Some seer and lover, Lift this mess of a world –
This boiling cauldron –
From the ancient abominable fires,
And set it to cool in the winds of Time,
And mold it to beauty again.

Despite the bleak picture it paints, the poem nonetheless ends with a partially qualified optimism:

It might be done,
Little one!
There is power enough, light enough, wealth enough –
If we work together,
And waste not,
Haste not.
Is there love enough,
Little one?

Monroe does not question the world's capacity to overcome obstacles, but asks whether the world is willing to do what needs to be done.

Poems such as "Supernal Dialogue" and "Ten Years Old" also betray a less than absolute faith in humankind. "The Man of Science Speaks," published in *Chosen Poems*, most clearly declares Monroe's conviction of the superiority of science over a religious faith in matters that cannot be empirically proven. Although a reader today may be tempted to view the poem ironically, the poem itself suggests no ironic intentions. The man of science, the speaker of the poem, bases his talk on a system of oppositions; each stanza proclaims that science is true, firm, and ever expanding, while non-science is speculative, weak, and static. The "you" in the poem appears to be anyone who does not follow the "religion" of science:

While you speculate in vain,
Making little gods, forsooth,
We fathom infinities –
Mathematics *is* truth.

In most of her own poems, as well as in those by others that she published in *Poetry*, Monroe sought to articulate what she called a "stimulus toward a new revelation," and she continued the quest up to her death. In the fall of 1936, she attended the fourteenth International Congress of P. E. N. Clubs in Buenos Aires, Argentina, for which she had written a brief speech on the future of poetry. On the journey home, she went to visit Inca ruins in Peru, where she died of a cerebral hemorrhage on September 26, 1936. Harriet Monroe is best remembered for bringing experimental poetry into print in the United States. Her own verse, although frequently neither as experimental nor as rigorous as that which she published, shows American poetry in the midst of a vibrant transition.

MOLLY M. MUNRO

Selected Works

Valeria and Other Poems, Chicago: printed for the author, 1891

Commemoration Ode, Chicago: printed for the author by Rand McNally, 1892; reprinted as *The Columbian Ode*, Chicago: W. I. Way, 1893

The Passing Show: Five Modern Plays in Verse, Boston and New York: Houghton Mifflin, 1903

The Dance of the Seasons, Chicago: Ralph Fletcher Seymour, 1911

You and I, New York: Macmillan, 1914

The New Poetry: An Anthology, edited by Harriet Monroe and Alice Corbin Henderson, New York: Macmillan, 1917; rev. and enl. as *The New Poetry: An Anthology of Twentieth Century Verse in English*, New York: Macmillan, 1923; rev. and enl., 1932

The Difference and Other Poems, Chicago: Covici-McGee, 1924

Poets and Their Art, New York: Macmillan, 1926; rev. and enl., 1932

Chosen Poems: A Selection from My Books of Verse, New York: Macmillan, 1935

A Poet's Life: Seventy Years in a Changing World, New York: Macmillan, 1938

Further Reading

Cahill, Daniel J., *Harriet Monroe*, New York: Twayne, 1973

William Vaughn Moody

(1869–1910)

Moody embodied both the literary promise and the short-comings of fin de siècle American poetry. Regarded by his contemporaries as a major figure in both poetry and drama, Moody is little read today. His poetry is that of a talented individual who struggled, with occasional success, to create vital work from within the assumptions of the genteel tradition. Moody's career deserves attention because of noteworthy individual poems and because, through these isolated successes, he highlights lines of continuity, which link American poetry from the death of Walt **Whitman** in 1892 to the first issue of *Poetry: A Magazine of Verse* (1912). His most memorable achievements are his political poems and works influenced by the symbolist movement.

The son of a riverboat captain, Moody was born on July 8, 1869, in Spencer, Indiana, and grew up in New Albany, Indiana, across the Ohio River from Louisville, Kentucky. Raised as a Methodist, his religious faith was shaken by the deaths, during his teen years, of an older sister and both his parents. Moody gave to his remaining sisters the small amount of money that he inherited, but his poverty did not prevent him from pursuing higher education. He initially planned to teach in a country school so that he could earn enough money to attend university; however, Charles Rowley of Poughkeepsie, New York, asked him to serve as a tutor for his son, who was preparing for entrance examinations at Yale University. This arrangement enabled Moody to attend Riverview Academy in New York, where he occasionally helped with the teaching while earning the highest record ever achieved by a student at the school.

In 1889, Moody enrolled at Harvard University (with a scholarship) during a time of rapid transformation of the college, when the free elective system championed by President Charles William Eliot encouraged a lively, and occasionally contentious, atmosphere. Moody quickly gained the attention of the literati and was invited to join the staff of the *Harvard Monthly*. During his college years, he contributed a number of poems to this magazine, including "By the Evening Sea" (the first version of "The Departure"), and served for a time as one of the editors. Through his work on the *Monthly*, he absorbed the literary atmosphere of turn of the century Cambridge, Massachusetts. Harvard in these years was not merely repressive (as some caricatures have suggested) but instead an intriguing mixture of the languid and the vital, the parochial and the broadly cultured. When Moody served as an assistant to Lewis Gates, the famed writing instructor, for example, Gates was guiding such diverse talents as Josephine Preston Peabody and Frank Norris, that is, both a polished poet of genteel verse and a rough-edged, abundantly talented naturalist whose fascination with primitivistic characters prefigured one strain of modernism.

After Moody received his bachelors and masters degrees from Harvard (with a thesis on Sir Philip Sidney), he joined the faculty of Harvard's English department in 1894. A few poets had found livelihoods in academe before Moody – Henry Wadsworth **Longfellow** and James Russell **Lowell**, for example – but Moody would become one of the more prominent figures in a newly emergent class of academic artists, including George **Santayana**, Hugh McCulloch, and George Pierce Baker at Harvard, and George Rice Carpenter and Brander Matthews at Columbia University.

To help his family financially, Moody left Harvard in 1895 for the recently founded University of Chicago, where he joined Robert Herrick and an old friend from his Harvard days, Robert Morss Lovett. Moody became part of a faculty that also included such luminaries as John Dewey and Thorstein Veblen. Although the university's faculty was distinguished, Moody found Chicago itself to be raw and uncouth. Yet as time wore on, he grew to have a greater appreciation for the city's possibilities: "I have become a prowler in slums . . . a rapt visitor at Salvation Army gatherings, a hanger-about stage-doors, a talk-provoker at quick-lunch counters (locally known as snatcheries), a Lovelace of the public parks, a patient scavenger of the odds and ends of street adventure."

Moody strove to remain abreast of contemporary poetic and cultural developments, and he possessed other qualities as well that might have contributed to the making of a major poet. He was thoroughly acquainted with the English literary tradition, which enabled him to compose two-thirds of the noteworthy *History of English Literature* that he co-produced with Lovett. Moreover, his thought was marked by discriminating intelligence and a deep concern with social and political issues. Yet as R. P. Blackmur remarked of Moody's poetry, "it is astonishing that a man who wrote so well, and so vigorously, and had such good subjects, should not have written more maturely." Despite Moody's vigor and intelligence, he too often allowed himself to react to life in ways that were predetermined by standard fin de siècle models of literary experience. He only belatedly – and then only intermittently – recognized that ordinary people and ways need not be divorced from aspirations for beauty and truth and that art need not detach itself from immediate experience. One problem was that few major peers sustained or challenged Moody. The best American talent in these years gravitated toward fiction, and the best of the poets, including Stephen **Crane**, were peripheral figures who were hardly recognized by the major magazines and publishers. The poets celebrated at the time – Edmund Clarence **Stedman**, Thomas Bailey Aldrich, and Richard Henry Stoddard – now seem hardly better than competent versifiers.

Moody's poetry emulates the great English romantics and Victorians, whose ambitious scope he admired. Yearning to be a major poet himself, Moody sought important themes, which he treated in an elevated (when not bombastic) style. Admittedly, his work was vulnerable to attack for being pretentious, and at times even false. Edwin Arlington **Robinson** complained: "I beseech you to agree with [me] in showering all sorts of damnation on your occasional, inconsistent and obnoxious use of archaic monstrosities like 'lifteth,' 'doth,' etc.' I may be narrow and unreasonable on this point, but I am pretty confident that in ten years from now this sort of thing will not be tolerated." On this issue, Moody remained shortsighted.

He opposed all those, he told his friend Daniel Gregory Mason, who are "not tolerant enough of the instinct for conquest in language, the attempt to push out its boundaries, to win for it continually some new swiftness, some rare compression, to distill from it a more opaline drop. Isn't it possible, too, to be pedantic in the demand for simplicity?"

Moody's career shows only a faltering drift toward respect for the vulgar, and he never really overcame his decorous inhibitions and his love for ostentatious phrasing. Even when he claimed to stretch the boundaries of poetic language, he displayed cautious and fairly conservative impulses. Thus, despite his professed admiration for Whitman, he rejected what he called the "Whitmanic verse-mode" in favor of traditional forms and meters. During his professorial years, Moody regularly edited works of English authors (John Bunyan and John Milton, for example), and his immersion in the English literary tradition made difficult for him to move toward the American vernacular and away from the traditional forms of English poetry.

The half-dozen years following his move to Chicago in 1895 were productive ones for Moody. He placed individual poems in magazines with national circulations, edited various textbooks, and published *The Masque of Judgment* (1900), a long poetic drama in five acts. (The drama is most interesting as an early expression of his career-long commitment to the idea of the importance of passion and human will.) The crowning achievement of these years was the publication in 1901 of Moody's *Poems*, an event regarded by his contemporaries – poets and reviewers alike – as a major breakthrough.

Moody's poems had been written over a 10-year period, although little sense of progression is suggested by the book's arrangement. Half of the poems were written in 1900, when Moody was on leave from the University of Chicago. Although the book lacks a strong sense of structure, certain groupings are clear: the opening two poems, "Gloucester Moors" (LOA, 2: 574) and "Good Friday Night," treat the theme of brotherhood in radically different contexts, and the brotherhood theme continues in the Whitman-inspired "Road Hymn for the Start." Similarity of subject matter also prompted Moody to yoke together the next three poems: "An Ode in Time of Hesitation" (LOA, 2: 576), "The Quarry," and "On a Soldier Fallen in the Philippines." These political works are followed by fairly extensive monologues, "Jetsam" and "Until the Troubling of the Waters," and then by poems that reflect the influence of Darwinian thinking on Moody, "The Brute" and "The Menagerie." The volume concludes with various short lyrics and quest poems, which primarily address the themes of love and art.

Moody's opening poem, "Gloucester Moors," begins as a nature lyric but turns from pleasant reflections to sustained social protest. The first three stanzas, set on an open moor one mile from the coast and the port town of Gloucester, praise the natural scene. Yet the poet's reveries are jarred when he thinks of a ship that is controlled by a few officers who sit "gorged at mess" while the toiling crew keeps it afloat (and while slaves are kept in the hold). A contrast – simple but powerful – is drawn between the poet's peaceful, rewarding life on land and the troubled life on the sea. The poet conveys a sense of personal guilt when he considers his relatively fortunate position in a society largely given to exploitation. He muses that the entire earth is like a ship at sea, with the sun as "her masthead light" and the moon as "a pinnace frail," and he wonders whether caprice or human purpose guides the ship. While the smaller boats make their way into port and gain safety and rewards, the poet suggests, the larger ship of society lacks such purposeful movement. The poem, one of Moody's best-known works, displays to good effect his lyrical gift, love of nature, and social conscience.

The political urgency dominating the latter part of "Gloucester Moors" informs all of Moody's "Ode in a Time of Hesitation." The "Ode," written during the Spanish-American War, is an ambitious public poem that castigates America's ignoble acts in the Philippines by using the Civil War – or, better, a carefully selected incident from the Civil War – as a point of comparison. Many U. S. citizens originally took a sanguine view of the Spanish-American War, regarding it as an effort to oppose Spanish imperialism. But such an interpretation became hard to sustain when American troops remained in Cuba, and when Philippine fighters turned against the Americans who they first saw as liberators. The fighting dominated the news in 1899 and 1900. Even as expansionist politicians argued for annexation of the Philippines, opponents of the war, including many of Moody's friends, called for recognition of Philippine independence and deplored the cruelties reportedly committed by American soldiers.

The "Ode" is a jeremiad of sorts, expressing anger at ideals violated and celebrating ideals still to be fulfilled. For Moody, the "Ode" was composed in a time of "hesitation" because he saw the United States hovering between a commitment to previous high ideals of the past and debased goals that might mar the future. (He was especially bothered by the market-based rationale for imperialism: a common argument put forth by senators such as Albert Beveridge was that annexed lands were necessary to provide markets for surplus goods.) Unfortunately, Moody's poem now seems self-conscious and over-inflated in its rhetoric. This is regrettable because he had found a subject with both scope and importance and about which he felt deeply.

> Lies! lies! It cannot be! The wars we wage
> Are noble, and our battles still are won
> By justice for us, ere we lift the gage.
> We have not sold our loftiest heritage.
> The proud republic hath not stooped to cheat
> And scramble in the market-place of war;
> Her forehead weareth yet its solemn star.
> Here is her witness: this, her perfect son,
> This delicate and proud New England soul
> Who leads despisèd men, with just-unshackled feet,
> Up the large ways where death and glory meet,
> To show all peoples that our shame is done,
> That once more we are clean and spirit-whole.

The Civil War hero Robert Gould Shaw – leader of the first regiment of free black soldiers in the Civil War – bears the weight of Moody's positive message. Along with 27 of his soldiers, Shaw died during the siege of Fort Wagner off the South Carolina coast. (The marvelous Shaw Memorial by Augustus Saint-Gaudens, in Boston, Massachusetts, served to inspire Moody, as it would later poets.) Moody's point in contrasting the past and present gains impact because of the irony of the phrase "despisèd men, with just-unshackled feet," which refers both to the slaves who had served with Shaw and the Filipinos who had recently been freed from the Spaniards only to be subjected to the Americans. The indictments of the poem are so powerful, however, that they more than offset its optimistic assertions.

In writing "An Ode in Time of Hesitation," Moody invoked a widely divergent group of poetic models, including Milton and American poets such as James Russell Lowell, John Greenleaf **Whittier**, and Whitman. In Lowell's "Memoriae Positum" and his "Ode Recited at the Harvard Commemoration" (LOA, 1: 696), the black soldiers of the Civil War are notable only by their absence. In contrast – and to his credit – Moody features the black soldiers, although he does not succeed altogether in avoiding racial clichés (including a suggestion that African Americans are dull-witted). Nonetheless, he generally emphasizes the nobility of the black soldier:

They swept, and died like freemen on the height,
Like freemen, and like men of noble breed;
And when the battle fell away at night
By hasty and contemptuous hands were thrust
Obscurely in a common grave with him
The fair-haired keeper of their love and trust.
Now limb doth mingle with dissolvèd limb
In nature's busy old democracy
To flush the mountain laurel when she blows
Sweet by the southern sea,
And heart with crumbled heart climbs in the rose: –

In Moody's poem as a whole, the assertive moral tone is reminiscent of Whittier, and the faith in an ultimate comradeship recalls Whitman. The technique of fusing private meditation with public purpose, for example, seems to follow the example of Whitman's "When Lilacs Last in the Dooryard Bloom'd" (LOA, 1: 895). Moreover, like Whitman, Moody's vision moves gradually outward to offer a striking panorama of the way in which the entire American continent reawakens with the arrival of spring. By depicting Shaw as an unambiguously positive figure, Moody produces a portrait less complex than Whitman's treatment (through absence) of Abraham Lincoln or Robert Lowell's later treatment of Shaw. Lowell's memorable "For the Union Dead" expresses an awareness, lacking in Moody's poem, that Shaw's "angry wrenlike vigilance" signals some inflexibility and that the poetic speaker might be complicit with the evils that he condemns.

"The Quarry," another of Moody's political poems, is couched as an allegory. He applauds, in this instance, American foreign policy, especially what he saw as an effective American action in China to offset the greed of European powers bent on stripping China of wealth following the Boxer Rebellion. From Moody's perspective, Secretary of State John **Hay**, by means of his "Open Door Policy," had kept the imperial powers of France, England, Germany, Russia, and Japan from partitioning and plundering China. Moody held that Hay was attempting to reform China without destroying its essential character. Of course, within the poem there is a question, captured in the pun on "trade-wind," about whether the eagle wants to claim its share of the spoils. This question implies that America's handling of the Chinese crisis may well be similar to its handling of the Philippines, if America's foreign policy is oriented crassly toward commercial purposes. The poet registers surprise when the eagle, rather than attacking the elephant, turns against the attackers. Moody treats this matter briefly and then has the eagle fly off, "Crying a word I could not understand." This curious closing suggests that Moody could muster only partial belief in this particular political affirmation.

"On a Soldier Fallen in the Philippines" is obvious and melodramatic, and thus less successful as a political poem. It stands as Moody's most embittered attempt to shape politics through poetry. Each stanza exploits the irony of the soldier's courage (even to the point of sacrificing his life) in a highly dubious cause. The ultimate irony is that the heroic status of the soldier can be maintained only if he forever misunderstands the nature of the war in which he fights: "Let him never dream that his bullet's scream went wide of its island mark, / Home to the heart of his darling land where she stumbled and sinned in the dark."

Moody's work in the symbolist vein, although interesting, lacks the power generally seen in his political poetry. "Jetsam," originally written between 1895 and 1897 and set in Chicago, is one of Moody's important early achievements in the symbolist manner. In these blank-verse lines, he blends experimental technique with more traditional uses of narration and meditation. "Jetsam" moves in surprising and nonrational ways, although one can detect a deep logic of association that underlies the development. In his creation of ineffable meanings, Moody probably did more than any other American poet before 1912 to absorb the spirit of the symbolist movement. The poem, less orderly than most nineteenth-century dramatic monologues, anticipates the abrupt shifts and fragmentary nature of T. S. Eliot's "Love Song of J. Alfred Prufrock." "Jetsam" advances a few discernible ideas but is mainly devoted to creating an aura of suggestiveness. The poem is especially striking for its treatment of sordid urban settings. Lines such as "The river lay / Coiled in its factory filth and few lean trees" compare favorably with modernist visions of the nightmare city.

"Harmonics" (LOA, 2: 583) and "The Departure" (LOA, 2: 584), two of the more noteworthy poems in Moody's volume, are related works that offer contrasting views of a single topic. "Harmonics" is a rare example of student work that Moody continued to value (and reprint) as his career progressed. Here the experience of love serves to intensify the poet's sense of creativity. In "Harmonics" the artist's self-satisfaction is shaken by the old man who bends over the younger musician to draw music from his harp string. Appearing in the octave of "Harmonics," the Jacob's ladder image shows Moody's ability to give a fresh turn to a familiar figure of speech.

"The Departure," Moody's 1901 revision of "By the Evening Sea," is a double sonnet reminiscent of Rossetti's work. The poem – another work exploring the importance of human love in prompting artistic creation – concludes darkly as the ship sails away adorned with beauty but apparently bound for an encounter with death. The speaker is left "alone in my great need, / One foot upon the thin horn of my lyre / And all its strings crushed in the dripping weed." The two sonnets making up "The Departure" function allegorically. The first develops a scene in which the enervated poet ponders the departure of attractive women who, with flowers in their hair, take a boat propelled by saffron sails into the evening sea. The second sonnet presents a picture in its opening lines, which then evaporates in the final six. This tableau depicts four women:

> One gazed steadfast into the dying west
> With lips apart to greet the evening star;
> And one with eyes that caught the strife and jar
> Of the sea's heart, followed the sunward breast
> Of a lone gull; from a slow harp one drew
> Blind music like a laugh or like a wail;
> And in the uncertain shadow of the sail
> One wove a crown of berries and of yew.
> Yet even as I said with dull desire,
> "All these were mine, and one was mine indeed,"
> The smoky music burst into a fire,
> And I was left alone in my great need,
> One foot upon the thin horn of my lyre
> And all its strings crushed in the dripping weed.

Moody's treatment of the "smoky music" conveys a sense of promise, but hope for fulfilled desire vanishes in the destruction that brings the poem to closure.

Erotic frustration is also the concern of "The Bracelet of Grass" (LOA, 2: 583). The "throbs of storm" from the "ardent west" initially seem to match the passion of the lovers. But the mood shifts when the "lips of thunder muttered harm." The sudden storm breaks the illusion of shared love and "ravishe[s] all the radiancies / From her deep eyes of brown." In this poem, as with "Jetsam," one sees the influence of the symbolists' methods on Moody's work. Through curious indirection, Moody strives to express the inexpressible in the closing lines of "The Bracelet of Grass":

> We gazed from shelter on the storm,
> And through our hearts swept ghostly pain
> To see the shards of day sweep past,
> Broken, and none might mend again.
> Broken, that none shall ever mend;
> Loosened, that none shall ever tie.
> O the wind and the wind, will it never end?
> O the sweeping past of the ruined sky!

The sudden, powerful, and passing nature of the storm leads the poet to think of the impermanence of human love.

By 1902, Moody had largely given up teaching, although he remained listed on the faculty roster at the University of Chicago until 1907. In the years following the publication of *Poems*, Moody gave himself increasingly to drama. It has been argued that Moody's talent flourished in the larger structures of literature, which allowed him ample room for fully developing the complex issues that he wished to treat. Proponents of this view hold that Moody's best medium was the drama. Yet his verse dramas, *The Fire-Bringer* (1904) and the unfinished "Death of Eve," are hardly more than uninspired melodramas. On the other hand, his prose play *The Great Divide* (originally produced in 1906 as *A Sabine Woman*) was a notable success – both with popular and critical audiences. The play involves a love triangle and successfully exploits the contrast between the residual Puritanism of eastern characters and the more open and individualistic ways of the west.

In 1908, Moody was awarded an honorary doctorate from Yale University and, in the same year, was elected to the American Academy of Arts and Letters. Yet ominous signs marked his life as well. He contracted typhoid fever and recovered only after several months of care from his longtime friend Harriet Tilden Brainard. Moody and Brainard (who was 11 years older than the poet) were married on May 7, 1909, but Moody quickly began displaying the symptoms that would lead doctors to undertake two brain operations. Brainard and friends of the poet decided to forego a risky third operation, and Moody died in Colorado Springs on October 17, 1910.

KENNETH M. PRICE

Selected Works

A History of English Literature, co-authored by Robert Morss Lovett, New York: Scribner's, 1902

The Poems and Plays of William Vaughn Moody, 1912; reprinted, New York: AMS, 1969

Some Letters of William Vaughn Moody, edited by Daniel Gregory Mason, 1913; reprinted, New York: AMS, 1969

Further Reading

Brown, Maurice F., *Estranging Dawn: The Life and Works of William Vaughn Moody*, Carbondale: Southern Illinois University Press, 1973

Halpern, Martin, *William Vaughn Moody*, New York: Twayne, 1964

Henry, David D., *William Vaughn Moody: A Study*, Boston: Bruce Humphries, 1934

Perkins, David, *A History of Modern Poetry: From the 1890s to the High Modernist Mode*, Cambridge, Massachusetts: Belknap Press of the Harvard University Press, 1976

Waggoner, Hyatt H., *American Poets: From the Puritans to the Present*, Baton Rouge: Louisiana State University Press, 1968

Ziff, Larzer, *The American 1890s: Life and Times of a Lost Generation*, New York: Viking, 1966

John Neal

(1793–1876)

When the poet John **Pierpont**, author of the highly acclaimed *Airs of Palestine* (1816; see LOA, 1: 63), had finished reading *Battle of Niagara* (1818), written by his friend and former business partner John Neal, he wrote to his wife that Neal's work "contains more of the greatness and madness of poetry than *any* other poem that was ever written in America." Edgar Allen **Poe** wrote in 1840: "I should be inclined to rank John Neal first, or at all events second, among our men of indisputable genius."

Power and originality mark Neal's works, which were always written at incredible speed. The author of 14 novels and several dramas and long poems, the self-proclaimed rival of James Fenimore Cooper in the early 1820s, and a prolific journalist and editor, Neal reached his most lasting literary achievement in a handful of short stories, which critics have ranked with the productions of Nathaniel **Hawthorne**, Poe, and Herman **Melville**. A strong influence on Hawthorne and Walt **Whitman**, Neal was an ardent literary nationalist and a supporter of native talent who, as a magazine editor, encouraged young Poe and had a hand in launching many other literary careers, including those of his lifelong friends Henry Wadsworth **Longfellow**, John Greenleaf **Whittier**, and Elizabeth Oakes Smith. He produced the first American art criticism, and was the first serious criticism of American literature to be published in Britain. Neal introduced gymnastics into the United States, championed Bentham's utilitarianism, and threw himself into legal and social reform movements. A nationally known writer and lecturer on women's rights, he was one of the earliest advocates of woman suffrage in America. Today, two fine biographies (by Benjamin Lease and Donald A. Sears) on Neal are in print, several monographs have also appeared, and two entries about Neal exist in the *Dictionary of Literary Biography* (Sears, in volume 59, provides the best brief overview of Neal's life and works). But Neal is still far from receiving the recognition that he deserves as one of the landmarks of nineteenth-century American culture.

When *Niagara* appeared, John Neal was a law student in Baltimore, Maryland. Following a failed career as a merchant, he was an aspiring author. He contributed to *The Portico*, the monthly magazine of the Delphian Club, of which he was a founding member, and published his first novel, *Keep Cool*, in 1817. The Delphians were Neal's literary peers and critics. An all-male literary and debating club of just nine members, they awarded each other "clubicular" names (Neal's was "Jehu O'Cataract") and mock-academic titles (Neal became "Professor of Jocology"). For *The Portico*, Neal had written a long essay-review of Lord Byron's works; in Byron, Neal recognized a kindred spirit who also defied a hostile world. The Byronic hero was to become a staple of Neal's fiction. Neal was also a literary nationalist: "The time will arrive," he predicted in *Keep Cool*, "when the production of American science and genius, will bear some proportion to the scale of their inspiration."

At this time, Neal was developing a romantic theory of aesthetics influenced by the writings of A. W. Schlegel, which had also been discussed in the Delphian Club. According to Lease, Neal was

> primarily concerned with effect, with the varied responses of readers to varied literary stimuli: Man's faculties, according to Neal (and most of his contemporaries), consist of the *brain*, the *blood*, and the *heart*. Brain writings are excluded from the scope of true literature because they are the products of artificial effort and skill. The blood is aroused to sublimity by those mysterious, grand, indistinct manifestations of nature which suggest the unknown and unknowable. The heart is stirred to sympathy by the vivid, realistic, unadorned manifestation of another heart. The central problem of authorship, according to Neal, is concerned with the ways in which the writer incorporates into his work qualities analogous to those in nature.

For Neal, poetry of the blood and heart seeks to elicit emotional responses from its readers by appealing to the poetry in themselves. Poetry is thus a spontaneous expression of natural eloquence, whether in rhyme, prose, music, or visual representation. It is based on passion and appeals to a sympathetic response in the reader. As the hero Edward Molton in Neal's 1823 novel *Randolph* puts it, poetry is "whatever affects, touches, or disturbs the animal or moral sense of man." Neal predicted that the poetry of the blood, which relies on the most dramatic and stirring, often supernatural, effects, would eventually be superseded by a literature of the heart, whose primary expression would be the natural simplicity of spontaneous talk. Here is a second distinction: "poetry is the natural language of every human heart, when it is roused – or inflamed, or agitated, or affected: . . . prose, on the contrary, is the natural language of the human heart, on all other occasions." Yet that distinction is ultimately not one of form, as Neal further observes, for the poetry of the future will emancipate itself from rhyme and meter:

> A great revolution is at hand. – *Prose will take precedence of poetry*: or rather *poetry* will disencumber itself of rhyme and measure; and talk in prose – with a sort of rhythm, I admit – for there never was an eloquent sentence, written or spoken since the creation of the world, without a rhythm and cadence in it – a musick of its own – it is a part of the nature of eloquence, to be poetical and melodious. Yes, I repeat it – *Poetical thought, written like prose, will yet supersede poetry*, in the affection and reverence of the age.

As Lease has pointed out, the "new prose-poetry" prescribed and practiced by Neal "boldly prophesies the organicism of Emerson and Whitman."

After *Keep Cool*, Neal wrote two Byronic poems of the blood, *The Battle of Niagara* (LOA, 1: 113), with which the rest of this essay will be chiefly concerned (1818; 2nd ed. 1819), and *Otho: A Tragedy, in Five Acts* (1819). He wrote both of these works amidst the pressure of legal studies and literary hackwork. In 1822–23, he composed and published a series of four novels at the same white heat at which he had begun writing in his early Delphian period. Of these, *Logan*, *Randolph*, and *Errata* are prose poems of human passion. Neal's retrospective characterization of *Logan* applies to all three: "a wild, passionate, extravagant affair, with some . . . of the most eloquent and fervid writing I was ever guilty of."

Much the same can be said of *Battle of Niagara, A Poem, Without Notes; and Goldau, or The Maniac Harper* – which bears as its motto a line from Canto II, "Eagles! and Stars! and Rainbows!" and which is advertised as "By Jehu O'Cataract, Author of Keep Cool, etc." The poem consists of 854 lines and is divided into a long introduction and five cantos. In a brief prose preface, the author explains that he "attempted to do justice to . . . American scenery and American character, not versify the minutiae of battles," because he has "not attempted to write a *history* but a *poem*." In the poem, consequently, the historical events surrounding the Battle of Lundy's Lane (July 25, 1814), which ended the United States invasion of Canada, are only a pretext for unfolding the sublimity of the landscape and the sky, and the drama of human emotions in battle. Indeed, as Francesca Orestano has observed:

> The forces engaged on the battleground are essentially the atmospheric agents, pervasively present and endowed with the power to unify the otherwise scattered warfare. The soldiers are portrayed, or rather caught, as if appearing through momentary apertures in the elements. Light controls sight, frames description and ultimately conveys meaning to the landscape. . . . This medium, therefore, is endowed with a creative, mythopoetic power and has a moral role.

The introduction opens with a night vision that includes the essential elements of the poem: the grandeur of the continent, armies preparing for battle, and the American eagle soaring above. A "minstrel" apostrophizes the majesty of nature, which invites humans to feel the possibility of freedom: "All – all of this is Freedom's song, / And all that winds and waves prolong, / Are anthems rolled to Liberty!" The continent invites human action on a grand scale, and the country awaits a poet to sing of its deeds – a clarion call for a national literature.

Canto I begins with "There's a fierce gray Bird" – a passage that was to remain popular for much of the nineteenth century. The eagle's perspective is the long-distance view from which the first appearance of humans is viewed. Men come and go in quick succession until only the image of their heroic leader remains. As the day wanes, horsemen are seen again, descending from the mountain, and disappearing again, until night brings a battle scene, which is followed by the apparently victorious troops' return to "Freedom's camp."

Canto II celebrates the wilderness of Lake Ontario and metonymically identifies the lake region with its native inhabitants: "Be ever thus Ontario! – and be free: / The home of wild men, and of Liberty." The arrival of the white man will tame them both: each will be

> A naked monarch – sullen stern, and rude,
> Amid a robed and plumed multitude:
> Sublime and motionless – but impotent –
> Stripped of his arrows, and with bow unbent.

By contrast, the present "monarch" of the wilderness is godlike:

> For man is there sublime – he is a god!
> Great Nature's master-piece! like him who trod
> The banks of paradise, and stood alone,
> The wonder of the skies – erect upon his throne.

This godlike creature is then identified with the Greek Apollo – not in his incarnation as "the airy god of moulded light" but as "that angry god, in blazing light / Bursting from space!"

In her excellent discussion of *The Battle of Niagara*, Orestano has explained the sleight of hand by which Neal has made the American eagle a symbol of both the wilderness and the forces that seek to open it up to settlement – a means "by which the native inhabitant of Ontario, although doomed to extinction, becomes an incarnation of the spirit of the place." As Orestano further argues, "there is what we might call a transcendental migration, by which the Indian . . . becomes the American incarnation of the Greek god Apollo" – who, however, "must undergo a transformation before he can climb the American Pantheon":

> Not that Apollo – not resembling him,
> Of silver brow, and woman's nerveless limb:
> But man! – all man! – the monarch of the wild!
> Not the faint spirit – that corrupting smil'd
> On soft voluptuous Greece – But Nature's child . . .

In making this transatlantic migration, Orestano observes, the god must be regendered to become "the manly symbol of the American wilderness, which is equated with 'Freedom' and the 'sublime.'" That wilderness becomes the ground on which Neal claims that art is to be revitalized and liberated from the constraints of ancient rules, in order to secure the artistic independence of the new nation. Drawing on Neal's long introduction to the second edition of *Niagara*, Orestano concludes:

> Against the well-established, formalized and formalist idea of the classic, [Neal] maintains that what is classic founds its claim to universal excellency upon freedom from the sweeping rules of the classical tradition and, therefore, upon originality, individuality, particularity, and fragmentation; in short, upon a manifest relationship with the American landscape with its social, cultural, and historical meanings.

Those meanings, however, are still emerging during Neal's lifetime and in Neal's poem. Can the wilderness survive only in art? As improved "taste" replaces wild "nature," the manifest "destiny" of the new civilization seems to be problematic:

> Leave such cold bosoms, Nature, to their fate:
> And be thou grand – luxuriant – desolate –
> As it best pleaseth thee. These wretched fools
> Would have Creation work by lines and rules.
> Their's [*sic*] is the destiny – be theirs the curse,
> In their improvements still – to mount from bad to
>   worse.

On the other hand, the possible relationships between whites and Native Americans include not only hostility but also alliances and joint victory in the cause of "Freedom." In Canto II, a white soldier and his Indian ally meet, silently:

That glance! that white man's glance – the Indian feels
What none but Nature's savage man conceals –
The swell of sympathy – of brotherhood
In danger and in death – in solitude.

Here speaks the Neal who was a lifelong champion of the Indian and the author of such superb Indian stories as "Otter-Bag, the Oneida Chief" and "David Whicher." The enemy of the two allies in *Niagara* is the British force – which, despite Neal's nationalism, also comes in for its share of both heroism and suffering. Without taking sides, the poem balances the ultimate futility of war against the nobility of humans engaged in it: "A gun is heard! O, can it be indeed / That on a night, like this, brave men may bleed!" Canto V presents the results of the slaughter in the morning light; the instruments of martial music now must serve to maintain discipline, or else all survivors would "call for mercy, loud; and never cease / Their supplications, till the God of Heaven / Had offered them some sign that murder was forgiven." The pacifism of Neal's Quaker upbringing, so troubling to him in his youth and so firmly rejected in his later life, shines through in these lines. *Niagara* concludes its cavalcade of painterly scenes not with a celebration of national glory, but with its price: the wife of a dead warrior leaning over his corpse.

Despite his rejection of rigid rules, Neal acknowledged that art is not "natural" but arranged. As he points out in his introduction to the second edition of *Niagara*, "The language of poetry – the descriptions of poetry – are *not* those of nature. . . . It is all hyperbole – more highly coloured – and better grouped than Nature." The successful marriage of spontaneous originality and artfulness, then, is the goal of Neal's poetic production, however fitfully it was accomplished. In his 1825 "American Writers" series, Neal describes his past efforts as follows: "Works abounding throughout, in absurdity, intemperance, affectation, extravagance. . . . A few passages are equal to any poetry, that ever was written – to my knowledge."

Hard to argue with that. Neal's work awaits the attention of new readers.

FRITZ FLEISCHMANN

Portions of this essay have appeared in Fritz Fleischmann, *A Right View of the Subject: Feminism in the Works of Charles Brockden Brown and John Neal* (Erlangen, Germany: Palm & Enke, 1983). Reproduction here is by permission of the editors of Erlanger Studien.

Selected Works

Battle of Niagara: A Poem, without Notes; and Goldau, or the Maniac Harper, Baltimore, Maryland: N. G. Maxwell, 1818; 2nd ed., 1819

Wandering Recollections of a Somewhat Busy Life: An Autobiography, Boston: Roberts Brothers, 1869

American Writers: A Series of Papers Contributed to Blackwood's Magazine (1824–1825) by John Neal, edited by Fred Lewis Pattee, Durham, North Carolina: Duke University Press, 1937

Observations on American Art: Selections from the Writings of John Neal (1793–1876), edited by Harold E. Dickson, State College: Pennsylvania State University Press, 1943

The Genius of John Neal: Selections from His Writings, edited by and introduction by Benjamin Lease and Hans-Joachim Lang, Frankfurt am Main, Germany: Peter Lang, 1978

Further Reading

Fleischmann, Fritz, *A Right View of the Subject: Feminism in the Works of Charles Brockden Brown and John Neal*, Erlangen, Germany: Palm & Enke, 1983

Gidley, Mick, and Robert Lawson-Peebles, eds., *Views of American Landscapes*, Cambridge: Cambridge University Press, 1989, pp. 129–145

Lease, Benjamin, *That Wild Fellow John Neal and the American Literary Revolution*, Chicago: University of Chicago Press, 1972

Meindl, Dieter, and Friedrich W. Horlacher, eds., *Mythos und Aufklärung in der amerikanischen Literatur / Myth and Enlightenment in American Literature*, Erlangen, Germany: Universitätsbund Erlangen-Nürnberg, 1985, pp. 161–176

Orestano, Francesca, *Dal Neoclassico al Classico: John Neal e la Coscienza Letteraria Americana*, Palermo, Italy: Istituto di Lingue e Letterature Straniere, 1990

Sears, Donald A., *John Neal*, Boston: Twayne, 1978

Nineteenth-Century Versions of American Indian Poetry

Introducing the text of a Powhatan song in his *Historie of Travell into Virginia Britania* (1612), William Strachey offers what may be the first literary account in English of Native American cultural performance: "They have likewise their *errotica carmina*, or amorous dittyes in their language, which they will sing tunable ynough: [and] they have contryved a kynd of angry song against us in their homely rhymes, which concludeth with a kynd of Petition unto their *Okeus*, and to all the host of their Idolls, to plague [us]." Confident in his ability to make sense of the Powhatans, Strachey immediately recognizes "rhymes" in their singing, however "homely," and a literary genre, however low. Yet he also quietly admits to a degree of incomprehension. By inventing "a kynd of angry song" and by making "a kynd of Petition," the Powhatans elude his ability to describe them precisely; Strachey's word *kynd* hints at the dimensions of the Powhatans's cultural difference.

This tension – between an immediate presumption of the Powhatans' intelligibility and a persistent, if underarticulated sense of their strangeness – becomes a central tension, historically, in the reception of certain Native American cultural forms. In referring the Powhatan performances to the familiar, Strachey might be said to inaugurate the idea of a North American Indian poetry, whereby, up to the present moment, such forms have been represented and understood *as literature*. In suggesting that such performances may be unlike anything he knows, he anticipates much later attempts, mainly by professional anthropologists, to describe Native cultures on terms closer to their own.

Nothing in the wide array of indigenous forms that becomes "American Indian Poetry" at the hands of missionaries, travelers, litterateurs, and anthropologists over the course of the nineteenth century was intended for the kinds of literary interpretation we produce in relation to works by poets such as Emily **Dickinson** or John Greenleaf **Whittier**. While a few of these Native originals were preserved in original language texts, and many were associated with mnemonic pictographs, none was created within a print culture, or meant primarily for pleasure. Although a few were the recent creations of individual "poets," most were traditional. Some were secret and archaic, instruments of power subject to the control of a specific individual or set of initiates; others, like the Minnetare songs (LOA, 2: 679) that Lewis Henry Morgan recorded in the 1860s, were quite literally owned ("it is not uncommon to give a horse for [one]," Morgan notes in his *Indian Journals, 1859–62*). Almost all were associated with a particular activity (healing, gambling, or waging war), or time of day or year, or ceremony, from which they would not have been thought detachable. Each performance was bound up with its occasion.

The distinct orders of reality that find expression in Native performance modes beg questions of the non-Native interpreter who have considered such performances primitive. In the case of a typical song of the Kwakiutl winter ceremonial, for example – a "Hāmats'a Song of the Koskimo" (LOA, 2: 737), translated by Franz Boas – it is the world from which the song must have emerged that seems most in need of clarification:

You will be known all over the world; you will be
  known all over the world, as far as the edge of the
  world, you great one who safely returned from the
  spirits.
You will be known all over the world; you will be
  known all over the world, as far as the edge of the
  world. You went to BaxbakuālanuXsī'waē, and there
  you ate first dried human flesh.
You were led to his cannibal pole in the place of honor
  of his house, and his house is our world.
You were led to his cannibal pole, which is the milky
  way of our world.
You were led to his cannibal pole at the right-hand side
  of our world.

In what sort of cosmos does the singer of this song find himself or herself? Would this have constituted Kwakiutl reality, or some special condition of reality? Who is – indeed, how does one pronounce – BaxbakuālanuXsī'waē, and in what way is he associated with cannibalism? What exactly is a "cannibal pole," and why is it on the right-hand side of things?

In order to begin to get one's bearings in relation to this single song, one has to reconstruct and figure out an entire discursive world. This task would include reading the dense and complex work from which the song is taken (Boas's 1897 monograph "The Social Organization and the Secret Societies of the Kwakiutl Indians"), other songs, and other ethnographic accounts. In the course of this reconstruction-prior-to-criticism, metacritical questions, just as fundamental, might emerge as well: is close exegetical attention an appropriate way of engaging with such a text? In what sense can or should one interpret it? What sort of discipline would it take to come to know it?

Given the differences that exist between Kwakiutl culture and that of the Passamaquoddy, or the Choctaw, or the Navajo, is it even useful to speak of Native performance as such? Some literary students of Native cultures, such as Gretchen Bataille, confidently assert that "American Indian literature ranks with other great literary traditions of the past and present," but with what kind of instruments have such comparative judgments been made (*MELUS* 6 [1979])? Native American languages, as Daniel Garrison Brinton lamented in the late nineteenth century, are "one of the most neglected branches of learning." Echoing Brinton more than a century later, Karl Kroeber remarks with some frustration (see also Laura Coltelli) on the difficulty of addressing Native literatures in an adequately informed way:

One wants the comparatist to be competent in the language of a text foreign to that in which he writes precisely so that his critical translation will be cogent. But nobody can know more than a mere handful of languages. How, then, can a comparatist deal with the multiplicity and diversity of non-Western literatures? How can I begin to train students in the study of traditional Native American literatures when I cannot possibly know more than an infinitesimal number of the languages involved?

"The loss of a language," Wallace Stevens writes in *Adagia*, "creates confusion or dumbness." The task of recovering from this confusion – of learning how to describe and ask questions of Native forms while recognizing the fullness of their differences – has been subject, at least since the emergence of professional anthropology in the United States in the late 1870s, to an ever-increasing degree of rigor and specialization. With the authority granted by this disciplinary history, an anthropologist could argue that Native song belongs only to a tiny elite of scholars and to Native Americans themselves (who might in turn resent the scholars' encroachments). To approach Native texts with nothing more than a literary sensibility – without a knowledge of their original languages or of broader cultural vocabularies – would be to risk sheer impertinence, whether dilettantish or conscientious. Readers who took such an approach would look like they had an interest in strangeness for its own sake or for the sake of a token inclusiveness.

Some modes of anthropology, certainly, have been insufficiently interested in the complex stylistic features of Native performance. Despite all of their apparent linguistic sophistication, for example, Boas's versions of Kwakiutl song do little to register anything like performative élan, or the turn of voice and gesture. (A number of recent translators – among them Dell Hymes, Elaine Jahner, Howard Norman, Inés Talamantez, Denis Tedlock, and Paul Zolbrod – are attempting to recover this often neglected sense of oral style.) And anthropologists over the last couple of decades have begun to argue about the importance of texts and textual interpretation in their work, in a way that should at least complicate anthropology's claims that it has the primary responsibility, among the western disciplines, for addressing indigenous cultural production.

The most salient reason for deferring questions of disciplinary priority over the so-called traditional Native literatures, however, lies in the idiosyncratic and unreliable character of the *texts* that make up these literatures. In many cases, the oral performance modes of the nineteenth century are simply no longer vital or recoupable, or are at least much changed; their historical reception, which is diminishing and distorting sometimes beyond recognition, is all that remains. Where a continuous and stable performance tradition still exists, why bother with faded and curious representations of it? Indeed, a provisional imagination of traditions now lost, "upstreamed," as ethnohistorians would say, from more recent analogues, matters as much as the idea of fact matters in history: to draw attention to the contingencies of mediation and to give reasons for preferring some versions of history to others. As it is now available to us, however, the Native song and chant of the nineteenth century is a hybrid, para-literary genre in its own right – a record of the Anglo-Indian encounter that reveals as much about an evolving Euroamerican discourse on the Native as it does about the ostensible originals. At once literary and ethnographic, the intensely mediated nature of this record warrants a newly interdisciplinary kind of response – an *ethnocriticism* (to borrow Arnold Krupat's term) that would see traditional Native texts as a new set of objects, with demands that have been incompletely met by literary criticism, ethnohistory, or a functionalist anthropology alone.

The Delaware *Walam Olum* (LOA, 2: 699) could reasonably be included in a selection of nineteenth-century versions of American Indian poetry: as a significant fake (see the textual note in LOA, 2: 997–98). Ostensibly an ancient historical epic (and published as such as recently as 1993, with the endorsement of the Grand Chief of the Delaware Nation Grand Council), this text recounts the Creation to the arrival of Europeans in America. On linguistic grounds, however, the text appears to have been written much later. Its curious provenance, involving a shadowy "Dr. Ward," suggests the literary convention of the found manuscript, and its plot, which is replete with Old Testament parallels, would seem all too neatly to prove the "Lost Tribes of Israel" theory of Indian origins that was still current in 1820, the year of its supposed discovery. As what is probably the deliberate forgery of a Native American text, the *Walam Olum* has few counterparts. (Daniel Garrison Brinton unwittingly published one song – the work of two Frenchmen who had invented an entire tribal literature – in his 1882 *Aboriginal American Authors and Their Productions*, but he later caught his mistake; in *The Path on the Rainbow*, a still-reprinted anthology of 1914, this particular song is nonetheless singled out for praise as "intrinsically American.") Whether the apparently *legitimate* examples of American Indian poetry produced through the middle of the nineteenth century reveal works that are more original than the fabricated epic is open to question, however. The ideals of accuracy and disinterestedness in ethnographic representation begin to emerge only with the rise of anthropology as a profession, and even then inconsistently. Before this period, Native performance is invariably represented in ways that seem to owe as much to a preexisting discourse on the Indian, or to notions of the literary, as to the qualities of a particular Native original.

Lewis Cass, writing for the *Columbian Star* on April 20, 1822, offers a brief example of Miami song: "I will kill – I will kill – the Big Knives, I will kill" (LOA, 2: 662). While this text may or may not be faithful to a source now lost – there is little evidence either way – it would certainly have conformed to Cass's larger judgments about Native Americans. A defender, against substantial contemporary opposition, of the right of "the Big Knives," or white Americans, to effect a policy of Indian removal, Cass elsewhere argues that Indians bear a "natural hostility to, and even *hatred* of the whites," which arises out of a "natural jealousy" of their superior power. Provoked only by this jealousy, Cass argues, they attack frontier settlements (*United States Review and Literary Gazette* 2 [1827]). Cass's choice of this particular song, at least, out of an undoubtedly broader Miami repertoire, seems to reflect and confirm a preconceived idea of Indian savagery.

Cass appeals explicitly to an idea of the savage in order to criticize the writings of a contemporary translator of Native song, John Heckewelder. "Even without . . . an acquaintance [with actual Indians], with only a common apprehension of what would be the probable character of a *wild* man, most readers would set down many of his representations as absurd," Cass writes. Heckewelder's "Song of the Lenape Warriors Going Against the Enemy" (LOA, 2: 661) does give a more likable and complex picture of Indian subjectivity than "I will kill – I will kill – the Big Knives, I will kill," yet it may be the product of a set of preconceptions nonetheless. First printed in his *History, Manners, and Customs of the Indian Nations* (1819), a few years before the Cass text, it begins:

O poor me!
Who am going out to fight the enemy,
And know not whether I shall return again,
To enjoy the embraces of my children
And my wife.
O poor creature!
Whose life is not in his own hands,
Who has no power over his own body,
But tries to do his duty
For the welfare of his nation.
O! thou Great Spirit above!
Take pity on my children
And on my wife!

Cass, a frontier legislator, finds in Miami song a kind of savagery that would justify Indian removal. Heckewelder, a Moravian missionary, presents an Indian capable of the tenderest piety, domestic feeling, and civic pride – sensibilities that would argue not only for the Indian's full humanity but for his susceptibility to and worthiness of conversion.

Despite these apparent overdeterminations, both authors offer a kind of detail in their accounts that cannot be explained away as the product of an "anti-Indian" or "pro-Indian" ideology. In places they write as if, uncertain of what they knew, they had committed themselves simply to record everything. Heckewelder notes, for example, that the Lenape sing "in short lines or sentences, not always the whole at one time . . . as time permits and as the occasion or their feelings prompt them"; Cass remarks on the Indian use of "metaphorical expression" and, indeed, produced a lengthy questionnaire for Indian agents, *Inquiries Respecting the History, Traditions, Languages, Manners, Customs, Religions, &c. of the Indians, Living within the United States* (1823). Part of questionnaire asks, in a way that would seem irrelevant to a goal of clearing the land for white settlement, "do they relate stories, or indulge in any work of the imagination? Have they any poetry? If so, is it poetry with measured verse, or without? Have they any rhymes?"

These questions may contain their own answers, yet they at least suggest Cass's affiliation with later scientific anthropology. While he refers to Indian song and chant as "oral poetry," he offers examples far less to gratify his readers' aesthetic senses than to inform them of facts. Indeed, as William M. Clements usefully observes, it may be that *because* Cass and his contemporaries had few literary ambitions for Native materials, their translations are more accurate than those produced over the next three or four decades. If the idea of literary quality – of rhyme and measured verse – had entered their minds, it might have entirely obscured indigenous stylistic features.

American Indian poetry as such – as a specifically literary genre – appears to emerge alongside the American Renaissance, and most prominently at the hands of Henry Rowe Schoolcraft, whose six-volume *Historical and Statistical Information Respecting the History, Conditions and Prospects of the Indian Tribes of the United States* (1851–57) includes the first significant collection of Native American lyric ever published, although this collection is scattered among the myriad sections and subsections of Schoolcraft's work. Hired by Cass as a geologist on an expedition to the upper Mississippi River, Schoolcraft became, with Cass's help, an Indian agent for the tribes around Lake Superior. Schoolcraft married Jane Johnson, the European-educated granddaughter of an Ojibwa chief; she and her family, in the 1820s, provided him with his first translations of Native texts. By mid–century, Schoolcraft had recognized the literary opportunities such texts afforded, and his own reworkings of them had found a sympathetic audience.

As early as 1815, lamenting the absence of an American national literature and seeking a basis on which to found one, Walter Channing turned to indigenous tradition. "In the oral literature of the Indian," he writes, "even when rendered in a language enfeebled by excessive cultivation, every one has found genuine originality." While Channing stops short of suggesting that European Americans might look toward this oral literature as a source for their own work, others eventually followed his lead. Henry Wadsworth **Longfellow** not only versified one of Schoolcraft's Indian songs but borrowed considerably from the legends in Schoolcraft's *Algic Researches* (1839) for his *Song of Hiawatha* (1855; see LOA, 1: 399). (For a different account of Schoolcraft's efforts, see the essay on Henry Wadsworth Longfellow in this volume.) Walt **Whitman**, apparently unaware of Schoolcraft, had expressed the want of a figure like him in the late 1840s, in the Brooklyn *Daily Eagle*. His sentiments were by no means uncommon for the period:

It were a lucky thing could some itinerant author be found, willing to travel through wood and forest, over prairie and swamp, along the borders of rivers, and upon the bosom of lakes – in short, amid any and every part of what is now the margin of our cultivated American territory at the west and north and gather up the stories of settlers, and the remnants of Indian legends which abound among them. Such would be the true and legitimate romance of this continent.

Schoolcraft not only encouraged this gathering up of Native "remnants" and their literary appropriation but worked himself to "improve" upon texts he had collected, usually from third parties. It has become almost a commonplace in recent essays on the translation of Native American song, following A. Grove Day, to refer to Schoolcraft's dual translation of an Ojibwa "Chant to the Fire-Fly" (LOA, 2: 678) as an example of such improvement: a "literal" version purports to offer ethnographic fact, while a "literary" one reflects a new aesthetic appreciation for the oral production of the Indian. An even more striking example of such reworking can be found in what begins as an untitled Ojibwa war song, "taken from Tsheetsheegwyung, a young Chippewa warrior, of *La Pointe*, in Lake Superior, and translated by Mr. George Johnston." As first printed in Schoolcraft's *Travels in the Central Portions of the Mississippi Valley* (1825), one of its stanzas reads:

They cross the enemies' line – the birds!
    They cross the enemies' line!
The birds – the birds, – the ravenous birds!
    They cross the enemies' line, &c.

The subsequent history of this text shows not only the danger of looking to American Indian poetry for what it would reveal of its sources but some of the values involved in mid–nineteenth-century text-making. Schoolcraft introduces the song at first as "poetry, if it be not too violent an application of the term." Like his mentor Cass, he is unwilling to grant much appeal to Native texts in themselves. He does see them, however, as eminently improvable and as possessed of a kind of curious interest; so he tinkers. Printing another "literal" translation in *Oneóta* (1845), he suppresses repetition and pares down lines – "The birds of the brave take a flight round the sky," for one, becomes "The birds – circling" (LOA, 2: 671). In *Indian Melodies* (1830), he so embellishes his source that it becomes, like *The Song of Hiawatha*, a poem with an Indian theme more than an Indian poem:

> They cross the line . . . they cross the line, the birds they
>   cross the line,
> Foreboding to our foes defeat, all by the prophet's sign;
> And we will up and follow thence, and we will up and
>   fight,
> And die as erst our fathers died, combatting for our
>   right.
>   Our fathers' might,
>   Ye bards recite,
> Raise high the battle cry;
>   For we will go
>   To meet our foe,
> And like our fathers die.

In the 1840s, Schoolcraft persuaded the poet Charles Fenno Hoffman to offer yet another version:

> Bird, in thine airy rings
> Over the foeman's line,
>   Why do thy flapping wings
>   Nearer me thus incline?
>   Blood of the Dauntless brings
> Courage, oh Bird to thine!
>   *Baim-wä-wä!*

That most readers today would probably prefer the literal translations to Hoffman's on literary grounds alone is part of one of the larger ironies in the reception history of Indian poetry: that the semblance of accuracy in itself has been aestheticized at the expense of the seemingly too smooth. The rougher versions, however, are not necessarily more true than the smoother ones. Nevertheless, since Schoolcraft and Hoffman had no knowledge of the Ojibwa language, one can guess that their second- and third-hand revisions, however successful as English verse, were diminishing rather than elucidating. Yet translators began to emerge later in the century who ably balanced their knowledge of Native cultures with an ideal of literate English translation.

Washington Matthews provides a case in point. Stacks upon stacks of notecards, among his papers, testify to the years of amateur labor he devoted to the Navajo language. He *also* wrote to Edmund Clarence **Stedman**, editor of *An American Anthology* (1900), hoping (unsuccessfully) to find a place there for Navajo poetry; his translations, free but faithful, have a spare kind of eloquence. One example, the "Song of the Stricken Twins" (LOA, 2: 750), comes from a myth associated with a variant of the Navajo night chant:

> From the white plain where stands the water,
>   From there we come,
> Bereft of eyes, one bears another.
>   From there we come.
> Bereft of limbs, one bears another.

> From there we come.
> Where healing herbs grow by the waters,
>   From there we come.
> With these your eyes you shall recover.
>   From there we come.

> From meadows green where ponds are scattered,
>   From there we come.
> Bereft of limbs, one bears another.
>   From there we come.
> Bereft of eyes, one bears another.
>   From there we come.
> By ponds where healing herbs are growing,
>   From there we come.
> With these your limbs you shall recover.
>   From there we come.
> With these your eyes you shall recover.
>   From there we come.

One fairly recent example of the reception of Native American texts from within the perspective of western literary history can be found in Andrew Welsh's *Roots of Lyric* (1978). Crediting Native song forms with an unencumbered expressiveness akin to that of western poetry at its oral beginnings, Welsh characterizes the songs of the pan-tribal Ghost Dance religion (among other Native texts) as Ur-forms of the lyric, which are possessed of "communal rhythms" and "deeply rooted in the communal consciousness" in a way that "the most sophisticated poetic traditions" only rarely can be. Like Alice Fletcher, who describes Omaha song in *Study of Omaha Indian Music* (1893) as "nascent poetry," he assimilates Ghost Dance songs to the *primitive*, in the best sense of that term. Reoriented in relation to an evolutionary narrative of western literary history, their non-westernness is made to seem *pre*-western, their most conspicuous quality a freedom from the anxious, belated self-consciousness of modern literary culture.

To a point, the characterization makes sense: Native song and chant probably have more in common with the *Iliad* than with Henry James's *The Golden Bowl*. Yet, if critics dwell on the "earliness" of such forms, they tend to obscure the historical character of Native song and chant. In spite of the still-prevalent romantic association of Native cultures with an immemorial wisdom (as if they were our ancients) – and acknowledging the differences between a western historicism and indigenous ways of accounting for being-in-time – the content of songs and chants recorded in the nineteenth century remains unaffected by European invasion only in the rarest of cases. Most, like the "angry song" Strachey encountered at the outset of English colonization, already register the pressures of a post-contact order, however seamlessly they may have integrated these pressures into an indigenous worldview.

Within its own cultural situation, the Ghost Dance figures more like a last embellishment than a point of bright origin. Conceived in the extreme conditions created by westward expansion, its songs express a yearning, by turns apocalyptic and elegiac, for the restoration of a pre-European world and yoke together a host of distinct cultural traditions, including non-Native traditions, in an uneasy pastiche. Aimed at cultural revitalization, and in part effective as such, they reveal the syncretizing disintegration of the cultures from which they emerged. "Jesus has taken pity on us," one announces (in James Mooney's version, from the Kiowa, of 1896; LOA, 2: 735):

> God has had pity on us,
> God has had pity on us.
> Jesus has taken pity on us,
> Jesus has taken pity on us.
> He teaches me a song,
> He teaches me a song.
> My song is a good one,
> My song is a good one.

Relating his or her vision from within a trance state, the singer affirms this song as "a good one" to indicate the redemptive quality of the world to come. The fact that Ghost Dance songs have achieved a kind of canonical status among nineteenth-century Native texts, however, may have more to do with the way they exemplify certain literary-ethnographic conventions about the nature of Native utterance. Most prominently, their invocation of the idea of a happy beyond, especially from the midst of circumstances so acute, is elegiac in a way that fits the convention of the dying or vanishing Indian, a still-current convention that was already well-established when John Eliot published *Dying Speeches of Several Indians* in 1685. They also concentrate long-standing associations of Native speech with a natural, even a preternatural eloquence. Performed (if one credits the trance state) without artifice or self-consciousness, even without human agency, they appeal to a literary longing, especially pronounced under romanticism, for unmediated vision and more-than-human voice.

This longing produces some wildly generous or at least seemingly generous ethnographic representations in the nineteenth century, and may partly account for the century's proliferation of Indian poems. In his *Song of Myself,* for one, Whitman includes a "friendly and flowing savage" whose orphic persuasiveness is independent even of language – it is "wafted with the odor of his body or breath," and "fl[ies] out of the glance of his eyes." Caleb Atwater, in a chapter of *Remarks Made on a Tour to Prairie du Chien* (1831) on "Indian Poetry," claims that savages "*As a people* . . . are more poetical than civilized men" (emphasis added). Since the Indian under the mid–nineteenth-century discourse of noble savagism was poetical without even speaking, it is no wonder that the Native texts of the period were treated more as pretexts than in their difficult particularity. Looking at a typical example of Indian poetry, James S. Brisbin finds a poetry of nature – winds with voices and articulate trees. His description in "The Poetry of the Indians" (*Harper's,* 1887) of a singer-orator runs from actual topics (war, love) and definite stylistic features (meter, monosyllables) to "unseen yet beautiful spirits," which transcend both.

> War, love, and the chase burst from his lips in weird music, but it is impossible to reduce to metre and connect the flashes of his genius. His monosyllables, his eye, the nod of his head and the waving of hands – all these are potential in his song, and mean more than mere words. Viewed in this light, the winds have voices, the leaves of the trees utter a language, and even the earth is animated with a crowd of unseen yet beautiful spirits.

As right and as prescient as this passage may be in its refusal to accept "mere words" alone as bearers of meaning – at a time

when essential oral features of Native performance were regularly reduced and discounted – it turns on notions of orphic "potential" and Indian naturalness that are indebted more to Whitman and to the noble savages represented in books, it seems, than to the real eloquence of any native performer. More often than not, when later nineteenth-century fieldworkers actually listened to Native song, their reactions were mixed. Albert S. Gatschet's comments on the Klamath Incantation songs (LOA, 2: 711) that he collected in Oregon in the late 1870s are not atypical:

> The chorus varies the melody somewhat each time, but this musical variation is so slight and insignificant that the general impression of monotony is not dispelled by it. Quite a number of these songs have very pretty melodies, but by long repetition even these of course must produce tediousness and disgust; other songs have weird and strange tunes, others are quaint, but almost repulsive by their shrill accents.

It would not be too difficult to dismiss Gatschet's response here as an instance of cultural chauvinism – looking for "pretty melodies," he is fairly predictably let down. Yet this stubborn unreceptivity cannot be much worse than Brisbin's more sophisticated and appealing general praise, which the latter offered from an armchair. Klamath chant may simply have been unassimilable, even unpleasant, to a western aesthetic sense of the nineteenth century (and it might be premature to assume that we have since been enlightened). Pleasantness was not what Klamath chant was about in any case: it was meant to heal, not to entertain.

The preliterary nature of Native performance did not guarantee that its *intended* auditors experienced it as a pleasure, or in an authentic or immediate way. Quite a few examples of it, in fact, were esoteric, archaic, or difficult – even subject to exegetical dispute. Stephen Powers writes of the Konkow ceremonies that he witnessed in California in the 1870s: "a number of the words either belong to an occult, priestly language, or are so antiquated that the modern Indians . . . are unable to agree absolutely on their meanings." The singers of the Navajo Atsá'lei Song (LOA, 2: 749), which Washington Matthews translated around the turn of the century, approached their work with something like a hard professionalism, not an effortless orphic genius. As Matthews explains in "The Night Chant: A Navaho Ceremony" (1902):

> Although it consists mostly of meaningless syllables, [the song] is perhaps the most important of the whole ceremony. The singers are drilled long and thoroughly in private before they are allowed to sing in public. It is said that if a single syllable is omitted or misplaced, the ceremony terminates at once; all the preceding work of nine days' duration is considered valueless and the participants and spectators may return, at once, to their homes. Visiting chanters, and others who know the song well, having sung it at other celebrations of the rite, listen attentively and, if they note an error, proclaim it.

One never awakens, among Native Americans at least, to find a dream of natural eloquence come true: only to other sets of forms and conventions that are hard to see. If, working within these forms, a Native performer had risen to a moment of real eloquence, authentic on its own terms – *eloquence* not necessarily being one of these – even professional non-Native observers would likely not have noticed it, because they probably would not have known what to look for.

As such, when Leslie Silko refers to the collection of Native texts as a kind of theft (*The Remembered Earth*, edited by Geary Hobson, University of New Mexico Press, 1981), she at once incisively locates this activity in its imperialist context, but she also may be protesting too much:

> [A] racist assumption still abounding is that the prayers, chants, and stories weaseled out by the early white ethnographers, which are now collected in ethnological journals, are public property. Presently, a number of Native American communities are attempting to recover religious objects and other property taken from them in the early 1900's that are now placed in museums. Certainly, the songs and stories which were taken by the ethnographers are no different.

In the exhibition cases of the Museum of the American Indian in New York, red circles mark the places of religious objects returned to the descendants of their original owners – or at least their withdrawal from public view. Should a similar degree of reticence and respect be extended to traditional Native texts? Some were highly sacred, certainly – even meant to be kept secret.

Indeed, removed from the horizons of their original reception, these texts became part of a discourse of savagism inextricably linked to the westward consolidation of American empire. Most of these texts were produced by agents or agencies of the federal government that was dispossessing Native Americans: Schoolcraft's magnum opus (*Historical and Statistical Information . . .*) was made to congressional order, as was the Bureau of American Ethnology, the institution responsible for the large majority of the nineteenth-century texts now extant. Most ethnographers *also* collected objects for national museums; and while a few acted as advocates for Native peoples against official Indian policy – like James Mooney, who successfully protected the peyote rite as a religion – the rest tended in the manner of the times to act upon the hope that their objects of study might someday be assimilated.

It is not at all clear, however, that Native texts were ever efficiently "taken" in the first place, in spite of numerous attempts. Even the phonographs fieldworkers had begun to use around the turn of the century – the most advanced technology of ethnographic collection then available – lacked the magic entirely to carry away, to translate what was vital in what they recorded. The approximations that *were* taken, while they may satisfy the thief with an approximate appreciation and understanding of their owners, offer nothing immanent, nothing like the familiarity and self-possession with which Native Americans continue to perform their cultural inheritance.

MATTHEW PARR

Selected Works
Astrov, Margot, ed., *The Winged Serpent: An Anthology of American Indian Prose and Poetry*, New York: John Day, 1946

Bierhorst, John, ed., *Four Masterworks of American Indian Literature*, Tucson: University of Arizona Press, 1984
———, ed., *In the Trail of the Wind: American Indian Poems and Ritual Orations*, New York: Farrar, Straus and Giroux, 1971
Boas, Franz, *Report of the U.S. National Museum for 1895*, 1897
Cronyn, George, ed., *The Path on the Rainbow*, New York: Liveright, 1918
Curtis, Natalie, *The Indians' Book: Songs and Legends of the American Indians*, New York: Harper, 1907
Day, A. Grove, ed., *The Sky Clears*, Lincoln: University of Nebraska Press, 1951
Gatschet, Albert S., *Contributions to North American Ethnology*, 1890
Heckewelder, John, *History, Manners, and Customs of the Indian Nations Who Once Inhabited Pennsylvania and the Neighbouring States*, Philadelphia: Publication Fund of the Historical Society of Pennsylvania, 1876
Matthews, Washington, *Memoirs of the American Museum of Natural History 6* (1902)
Mooney, James, *Fourteenth Annual Report of the Bureau of Ethnology*, Washington, D.C.: Government Printing Office, 1896
Morgan, Lewis Henry, *The Indian Journals, 1859–62*, edited by Leslie A. White, Ann Arbor: University of Michigan Press, 1959
Sanders, Thomas, ed., *Literature of the American Indian*, New York: Glencoe, 1973
Swann, Brian, *Song of the Sky: Versions of Native American Songs and Poems*, n.p.: Four Zoas Night House, 1985
Velie, Alan R., ed., *American Indian Literature: An Anthology*, Norman: University of Oklahoma Press, 1979

Further Reading
Allen, Paula Gunn, ed., *Studies in American Indian Literature: Critical Essays and Course Designs*, New York: Modern Language Association, 1983
Bieder, Robert E., *Science Encounters the Indian, 1820–80*, Norman: University of Oklahoma Press, 1986
Brinton, Daniel Garrison, *Essays of an Americanist*, Philadelphia: Porter and Coates, 1890
Chapman, Abraham, ed., *The Literature of the American Indians: Views and Interpretations*, New York: New American Library, 1975
Clements, William M., and Frances M. Malpezzi, comps., *Native American Folklore, 1879–1979: An Annotated Bibliography*, Athens, Ohio: Swallow, 1984
Coltelli, Laura, ed., *Native American Literature*, Pisa, Italy: Servizio Editoriale Universitario, 1989
Dippie, Brian W., *The Vanishing American: White Attitudes and U.S. Indian Policy*, Middletown, Connecticut: Wesleyan University Press, 1982
———, *Catlin and His Contemporaries: The Politics of Patronage*, Lincoln: University of Nebraska Press, 1990
Hinsley, Curtis M., *Savages and Scientists: The Smithsonian Institution and the Development of American Anthropology, 1846–1910*, Washington, D.C.: Smithsonian Institution Press, 1981

Hymes, Dell, *"In vain I tried to tell you": Essays in Native American Ethnopoetics*, Philadelphia: University of Pennsylvania Press, 1981

Judd, Neil M., *The Bureau of American Ethnology: A Partial History*, Norman: University of Oklahoma Press, 1967

Kroeber, Karl, ed., *Traditional Literatures of the American Indian: Texts and Interpretations*, Lincoln: University of Nebraska Press, 1981

Krupat, Arnold, *Ethnocriticism: Ethnography, History, Literature*, Berkeley: University of California Press, 1992

Lee, Dorothy Sara, *Native North American Music and Oral Data*, Bloomington: Indiana University Press, 1979

Moses, L. G., *The Indian Man: A Biography of James Mooney*, Urbana: University of Illinois Press, 1984

Pearce, Roy Harvey, *Savagism and Civilization*, Berkeley: University of California Press, 1988

Ramsey, Jarold, *Reading the Fire: Essays in the Traditional Indian Literatures of the Far West*, Lincoln: University of Nebraska Press, 1983

Ruoff, A. LaVonne Brown, *American Indian Literatures*, New York: Modern Language Association, 1990

————, and Jerry W. Ward Jr., eds., *Redefining American Literary History*, New York: Modern Language Association, 1990

Strachey, William, *The Historie of Travell into Virginia Britania*, edited by Louis B. Wright and Virginia Freund, London: Hakluyt Society, 1953

Swann, Brian, ed., *On the Translation of Native American Literatures*, Washington, D.C.: Smithsonian Institution Press, 1992

Swann, Brian, ed., *Smoothing the Ground: Essays on Native American Oral Literature*, Berkeley: University California Press, 1983

————, and Arnold Krupat, eds., *Recovering the Word: Essays on Native American Literature*, Berkeley: University of California Press, 1987

Tedlock, Dennis, *The Spoken Word and the Work of Interpretation*, Philadelphia: University of Pennsylvania Press, 1983

Wiget, Andrew, ed., *Critical Essays on Native American Literature*, Boston: G. K. Hall, 1985

Native American Literature, Boston: Twayne, 1985

James Kirke Paulding

(1778–1860)

Pausing halfway through his second and last long poem, *The Backwoodsman* (1818; LOA, 1: 38), James Kirke Paulding reflects upon his compatriots' infamous indifference to the arts:

> 'Tis true – and yet 'tis no pity that 'tis true,
> Many fine things they neither felt nor knew.
> Unlike the sons of Europe's happier clime,
> They never died to music's melting chime,
> Or groan'd, as if in agonizing pain,
> At some enervate, whining, sickly strain.

Paulding's defense of his fellow Americans' resistance to culture seems a strategy of self-protection, for he also repeatedly confesses himself concerned about the reception of his poetic "experiment" with American materials and manners. Consistent with his notoriously nationalistic aesthetics and politics, best elaborated in such later essays as "On the Influence of Foreign Literature" and "The Wreck of Genius" (1820), Paulding juxtaposes his own poetic practice against what he calls the "sickly strain[s]" of European verse. And yet, like William Shakespeare's Polonius – whose "'tis true 'tis pity; / And pity 'tis 'tis true" that he recasts in the lines above – Paulding haplessly waxes poetic, commending but unable to satisfy a taste, like Queen Gertrude's, for "more matter with less art." Increasingly self-conscious about working in such an uncharacteristically "high" mode of heroic poetry as he does in *The Backwoodsman*, he is also steeling himself here against anticipated criticism by acknowledging and justifying his audience's indifference to literary labors like his.

And criticism was forthcoming. Upon publication, *The Backwoodsman* was recognized, judged, and generally condemned as one of the less successful epics of the early national period. The reviewer for the *Port Folio* remarked, in January 1819, "in such an utter absence of any thing like a hero or even a suitable scene . . . it required uncommon nerves and powerful motives to publish an epic lay." Poet and critic Fitz-Greene **Halleck** complained in *Fanny* (1819): "Homer was well enough; but would he ever / Have written, think ye, the Backwoodsman? Never." Paulding took this condemnation hard. Much was at stake: writing the poem had served to confirm his sense of vocation (at the rather late age of 40), and, breaking with his custom, he had published it under his own name. The thrashing that he and his poem received led him to forswear publishing poetry in a January 1820 letter to Washington Irving; although Paulding did not actually stop writing poetry, he never attempted anything so ambitious again. According to his son, William Irving Paulding, his father continued to revise his poem throughout his life, but he never published a further edition and did not include the poem, in any form, in the 15 volumes of his collected works (1835–39).

Paulding's critics, however, were right to insist that *The Backwoodsman* is best evaluated and understood in the context of the period's other epic efforts. Born during the American Revolution (August 22, 1778) and living until the eve of the Civil War (April 6, 1860), Paulding belonged to a generation of American writers who were burdened by an inordinate sense of their mission to manufacture a republic *in* and *of* letters. Between the American Revolution and the Civil War, many authors aspired to fulfill Bishop Berkeley's prophecy (in "Verses on the Prospect of Planting Arts and Learning in America," 1752) of "another golden age" in America. Central to this project was the epic, which was considered the record and means of nation making. As John P. McWilliams argues in his 1989 study of the transformation of the American epic between 1770 and 1860, this generation believed that "an American epic would be incontestable proof of cultural maturity." The "good and great" did, indeed, as Berkeley predicted, "inspir[e] epic rage" in the "wisest heads" and "noblest hearts"; most famous among these New World epics were Timothy Dwight's *The Conquest of Canaan* (1785) and Joel **Barlow's** *The Columbiad* (1787/1807; LOA, 1: 12).

Paulding attributes Americans' disregard for these belletristic travails to their fervent republicanism: "Nor would they mourn Apollo sent away, / More than the loss of Freedom's glorious day." He illustrates this point in *The Backwoodsman* with a scornful allusion to a much-admired work of classical statuary, the *Belvedere Torso* (a badly damaged, seated figure generally claimed during this period to represent Hercules):

> Among them was no driv'ling princely race,
> Who'd beggar half a state, to buy a vase,
> Or starve a province nobly to reclaim,
> From mother Earth, a thing without a name,
> Some mutilated trunk decay'd and worn,
> Of head bereft, of legs and arms all shorn,
> Worthless, except to puzzle learned brains,
> And cause a world of most laborious pains,
> To find if this same headless, limbless thing,
> A worthless godhead was, or worthless king.

Paulding's curious trope of the "mutilated trunk" works in several dimensions at once to focus our view of his poetry and poetics. Most obviously, the reference particularizes Paulding's disdain for his fellow American artists' emulation of classical models; just as Dwight, Barlow, and many other poets imitated classical epics, painters Benjamin West and John Singleton Copley copied the figural styles of classical statuary, and sculptors studied plaster casts at the New York and Pennsylvania Academies of Fine Arts.

Paulding's political empathy with his audience, however, vies with his uncomfortable awareness that he has perhaps made an inappropriate, even un-American, choice of form in his own epic. Even his most sympathetic reviewer, in the *American Monthly Magazine and Critical Review* (January 1819), took exception to Paulding's "taste" in choice of genre: poetry's "fire is damped," the reviewer suggests, "and her pencil languishes in the portraiture of ordinary forms and character. . . . She subsists by inequality, and has nothing to do with republicanism." Paulding's reference to the *Torso* registers just such a critique of heroic literature. Further, his emphasis on the figure's suggestion of violence – "of head bereft, of legs and arms all shorn" – echoes the early national period's revulsion against the brutality of the world represented in Greek art and literature. Recalling Charles Brockden Brown's criticism, cited by McWilliams, that "Homer was a man of a barbarous age, and a rude nation [when] . . . war and depradation made up the business and delight of mankind," Paulding preludes a later battle scene in *The Backwoodsman* with the complaint, "Why then should I luxuriate in gore / . . . We are no vampyres thus to live on gore."

Less obviously, the "mutilated trunk" also seems a fitting trope for Paulding's own poem. The *Torso* figures his ambivalence about his epic enterprise, but this same ambivalence *dis*figures ("mutilates") his poem. Critics of both his time and ours have perceived that *The Backwoodsman* founders upon the problem of creating an epic hero for a republican age. The cited passage comes at the end of the third book, which brings to a close Paulding's earnest effort to render an epic account of his titular hero, the backwoodsman Basil. In the next three books, the poet, with no advance notice, turns the poem over to a fictionalized account of the Shawnee Prophet, Tecumseh's brother Tens-qua-qa-wa. The sudden shift of focus did not escape the censure of the *Port Folio* reviewer, who snaps, "We were indeed much at a loss in what light to view the latter part, as it has not the slightest connexion with the former, except what the bookbinder has created." Like the "mutilated trunk," the broken-backed poem "puzzle[d] learned brains." And it continues to do so. *The Backwoodsman*, in fact, remains compelling reading precisely because of its falterings and failings of conception and execution. To look closely at the poem is to learn something about why and how epic efforts failed during this period. *The Backwoodsman* plainly displays the fits of artistic ambivalence and the imaginative impasses that led to the generic seizure and, eventually, the generic transformation that McWilliams chronicles in *The American Epic*.

To begin with, the poem's six books, which contain over 1650 heroic couplets, seem to reproduce exactly what the poet's own invocation indicts: the "servile, imitative rhyme" with which the "Neglected Muse! of this our western clime" conveys her "stifled energies" and "repress[es] the brave decisive flight" of the American poet's imagination. Further, Paulding's portrait of the "Thrice happy" poet "who first shall strike the lyre / With homebred feeling, and with homebred fire" evokes exactly the derivative and anachronistic model of the minstrel poet that he had parodied five years earlier in his other long poem, *The Lay of the Scottish Fiddle* (1813), a send-up of Sir Walter Scott's *The Lay of the Last Minstrel* (1805). In his burlesque account of the British siege of Havre de Grace during the War of 1812, Paulding lampoons Scott's characteristic poetic devices and techniques ("acquaintance with local scenery and tradition," "fondness for quoting old ballads," and self-plagiarism) and criticizes the codes of chivalric heroism that had been given new currency by Scott's work.

Paulding's antipathy to Scott, as well as his virulent anti-British feeling, had its roots in his early childhood experiences during the Revolutionary War in the lower Hudson River Valley's neutral territory. William Paulding claimed that his father's "very birth (his mother was a refugee from her home by reason of British hostility) was almost a pledge of inherited enmity." The financial ruin of Paulding's father after the new government declined to reimburse him for supplies that he provided to starving Continental troops (see Paulding's auto-

biographical story, "Dyspepsy," in *The Tales of the Good Woman*, 1829), and his cousin John Paulding's role in capturing Major John Andre, Benedict Arnold's British coconspirator (see Paulding's depictions of the much-maligned "pride of yeoman bold" in Book II of *The Backwoodsman* and in the novel *The Old Continental*, 1846), made powerful impressions on the young man. An active participant in the "Paper War" with England during the early part of the nineteenth century – his anti-British satires include *The Diverting History of John Bull and Brother Jonathan* (1812) and *The United States and England* (1815) – Paulding was awarded a political appointment as secretary of the Board of Navy Commissioners in 1824 during James Madison's administration; this appointment, in turn, led to further appointments as Navy Agent for New York under President James Monroe and as secretary of the Navy under President Martin Van Buren.

Like Washington Irving, Paulding was at his best as a satirist and iconoclast. Halleck confessed himself disappointed that Paulding did not stick to wielding the "battle axe of satire." (Serving later as a judge for actor James Hackett's 1830 playwriting contest, Halleck awarded first prize to Paulding's comedy *The Lion of the West*; the "lion," Nimrod Wildfire, is a Davy Crockett-like, comic version of the distinctly humorless backwoodsman Basil.) The degree to which his contemporaries were accustomed to considering Paulding a satirist is clear in their befuddlement at the uncharacteristically sober *Backwoodsman*. When Joseph Rodman **Drake** dubbed Paulding the "Pride of the Backwood! / The poet of cabbages, log huts, and gin" in "To John Minshull" (1819), he was fixating on a rare instance when the high seriousness of the poem is interrupted by a mock-epic impulse. Paulding's paean to a "stately cabbage waxing fat each day" is reminiscent of Joel Barlow's "The Hasty Pudding" (1796): Paulding's cabbage-hero "in a sav'ry sourkrout finds its end / From which detested dish, me Heaven defend!"

Most of all, however, it is the problem of the poem's hero that marks and measures the failure of *The Backwoodsman* to be what it set out to be. Even Paulding's description of his "humble theme" – the westward migration and settlement of a "hardy swain," Basil – seems to hearken back to earlier, English poetic conceptions of the rustic or often pseudo-rustic character. By contrast, the type-name given in the poem's title was of recent (1774) and American coinage. The discrepancy between the "swain" of the invocation and the "backwoodsman" of the title alerts us to the poem's most telling insufficiency: the reader never gains a clear view of its purported subject.

Basil only figures at all in the first three of the poem's six books, and even then he remains undeveloped, generalized, and representative; he is given no past, no surname, no physical description, or no speech. Book I most closely chronicles Basil's trials: experiencing a classic conflict between his impulse, as Huck Finn would say, to "light out for the Territory" and his domestic obligations (represented by his "fruitful wife"), Basil falls ill. Restored to health by the coming of spring, he packs up home and family, bids good-bye to friends, and heads for the backwoods. But only a little way into Book II, the poet tells us that he will not "stay to tell / What little rubs, or small mishaps befell" Basil; all in all, the hero is mentioned only nine times in more than 600 lines. In Book III, of roughly the same length, there are only four direct references to Basil.

More often in these first three books, Basil is cast as a passive observer of a sublime natural world that is consistently more active and animated than he. Nature, the agent of his healing in Book I, becomes the central subject of Book II. The energy and event of nature are consistently emphasized in Paulding's language. Nature is either personified – the mountain has a "brow," the "blue ey'd day" opens its "eyelids," the forest is "crown'd," the river "pursues" its way, and the "rabble insect crew" is "liveried" – or described as material treasure – the sky is "fring'd with burnish'd gold," the insects crawl "upon the jewell'd earth," and the stars "gem the sky." Two particular allusions reveal some of what is at stake in Paulding's renderings of nature. Basil wakes early one morning to find the "world . . . faded like a vision from his sight" and "one endless chaos spread before his eyes." A sole mountain peak penetrates the mist, and the poet remarks the similarity between this scene and that in which "the wandering grandsire of our race / On Ararat had found a resting place." The distinctive aspect of Paulding's reference to virtuous Noah's inheritance of a post-Flood world is its proleptic construction: he schedules the deluge *after* the sighting of Ararat. Basil and his family are also kept safe from a flood's rise, and when nature's wrath is over, they descend to cross the Ohio River, the last border between "the prowling savage and the Christian man." The scene anticipates William Cullen **Bryant's** "The Prairies" (1834; LOA, 1: 162) in its fantasy of an already accomplished ethnic cleansing that has cleared the way for the white settlers.

This premature bequest of an emptied and purified world is countered by the peril of temptation inherent in nature. Playing with the language of Shakespeare's *Antony and Cleopatra* (II.ii.192–206), Paulding compares the purple clouds at sunset to Cleopatra's gaudy bark:

With swelling purple sail, they rapid glide,
Gay as the barque, where Egypt's wanton queen
Reclining on the shaded deck was seen,
At which as gaz'd the uxorious Roman fool,
The subject world slipt from his dotard rule.

"Such an eve," the poet cautions, "might almost tempt an angel Heaven to leave": succumb to the spell of nature's splendor, and you will lose your virtue, or worse, like Antony, you will lose your empire, your "subject world," and perhaps your very sense of self.

Paulding's attempt to develop a clear picture of Basil falters as the more sinister side of nature comes into focus. Oblique, obscure references to the "serpent of this blooming paradise" and the "rash, malignant, reas'ning worm" reveal his fearful recognition of the potential degeneration of his backwoodsman hero. Rather than depict that transformation, as St. Jean de Crèvecoeur does in *Letters from an American Farmer* (1782), Paulding distracts the reader with a full and frightful portrait of the figure that has loomed over Basil's project of migration from the very start: the displaced Native American.

By Book IV, Basil has disappeared altogether, and is replaced by the far more vivid Prophet Tens-qua-qa-wa. The poem chronicles, in effect, two separate heroic actions, and the dramatic power of the second threatens to eclipse the quiet triumph of the first. Whereas Basil never utters a single word, the Prophet speaks over one-fifth of the lines of Books IV–VI, and his words are unfiltered by the poet's analysis. Speaking eloquent volumes, the Prophet is even given the last word in his long debate with a passing "aged pilgrim" who is trying to justify the ways of white men and their god. Although repeatedly described as "maniac," "madbrained," "benighted," and possessed by his "one bloody theme" of vengeance, the Prophet clearly proved a more compelling character than Basil in the eyes of the poem's first readers. The *American Monthly* reviewer observed, "We cannot but think the native sagacity of [the Prophet] appears to considerable advantage," and the *Port Folio* reviewer carried his point further:

The Indian who is introduced subsequently, was not quite so mad as the poet would have us believe, when, in his ravings, he complains that the white men intrude upon his domains, and by force or fraud eject him from his native woods. This "honest" Basil, this "learned Basil," thus turns out to be no better than a common *squatter*, and we are therefore no longer surprised at the rapid strides which he made in the road to wealth.

Such criticism of the "prevailing ideology of progress" was, claims McWilliams, a frequent consequence of depictions of American Indians as classical heroes who fought for land and liberty. But such dissent was not part of Paulding's plan; in a letter to Richard Henry **Wilde** of August 1830, he fully endorsed the Jacksonian policy of Indian removal. He seems rather to be compelled by the intrinsic epic force of the Shawnee Prophet's character and situation; according to an April 1818 letter to Irving, part of his original project was to "introduce the Indian character and manners." In realizing the Prophet, moreover, he was unhampered by any scruples about propagating anachronistic or elitist codes of martial heroism; such codes were integral to the culture of his chosen subject, as many of his contemporaries observed. When he first saw the *Apollo Belvedere* in Rome in 1759, painter Benjamin West exclaimed, "How like a Mohawk Warrior!" And, as Donald Foerster notes, Thomas Jefferson thought that the conduct of Homer's heroes effectively explained the actions of Native American warriors.

In the first three books of his heroic poem, Paulding clearly sets out to subvert epic conventions – he does not depict allegorical personifications, divine machinery, councils, underworlds, feasts, or catalogs, and he chooses a pointedly common hero. (His reviewers noted, and took exception to, the latter representational strategy, but it is perhaps going too far to claim, as McWilliams does, that Paulding's first three books evidence a "tentative groping toward the 1855 preface to *Leaves of Grass*," the locus of the first truly democratized theory of epic heroism.) In the second three books, Paulding's republican resistance to epic takes a different turn. He allies the epic tradition with the heroic codes of Native American culture, and then suggests that, because the former is obsolete, the latter is duly fated and white settlers are justified in wiping out the resisting aborigines.

Paulding is not without anxiety, however, about the poetic and political implications of his choices in these last three books. Accordingly, he first devotes a significant portion of the opening of Book VI to counterpointing the Prophet's Achilles-like heroism; a "nobler heroism" is modeled by the actions of those men "too lowly for the records of high Fame." Second, he invents the figure of the Renegade, the Prophet's British ally. This character, the very epitome of Crèvecoeur's barbarized frontiersman, serves to draw off and demonize the feral tendency of the backwoodsman hero.

In fact, the character of the Renegade provides a key to understanding a certain obfuscation or evasion that motivates the diptych structure of the whole poem. As noted by the *Port Folio* reviewer, there is a decided duplicity in Paulding's compositional choice to report the war for the land *after* the successful settlement. Further, by exiling Basil completely from the scene of bloodshed that secures his possession, Paulding keeps his hero innocent of the incriminating means of his gain. The poet returns, almost absentmindedly, one last time to Basil to record the character's prosperity:

> Let me waste one line to sing the lot
> Of one whom I in truth had half forgot.
> Old BASIL – for his head is now grown gray –
> Waxes in wealth and honours every day;
> Judge, general, congressman, and half a score
> Of goodly offices, and titles more
> Reward his worth, while like a prince he lives,
> And what he gains from heav'n to mortals gives.

These reports of Basil's worldly success come after a hiatus of almost 100 pages, during which the battles that secured his property and position are reported in full, gory detail. The backwoodsman was last depicted at the end of Book III as the village patriarch/storyteller who recounted tales of national heroes ("virtuous" Nathanael Greene, Francis Marion, and Benjamin Franklin) and also of those "nameless men" whom "stately Hist'ry deems beneath her pen." Basil is committed to circulating the same stories of common heroism that Paulding favors, but like his creator, he succumbs to the power of the more conventional strains of heroic narrative. Basil "lov'd the best to tell" of George Washington; the language of his account anticipates the formulas of Paulding's 1835 biography of the first president, "a hero of a new species." In the end, Basil is more clearly realized as epic teller than as epic hero.

Although Paulding claims that "not such [as Apollo or Hercules] were these, whose story I unfold," he has been drawn, helplessly, like Basil and like many of his generation, to the two sufficient heroic models of his time: Washington and the Native American tribal leader. The structure of his *Backwoodsman*

demonstrates his at least subconscious awareness that the triumph of the first (and of his soldier-settler Basil) depended on the destruction of the second. His inversion of the proper order of events – depicting the battle after the settlement – marks his attempt to elide that truth, but the remarkable image of the "mutilated trunk" of the *Belvedere Torso* again provides a figure that helps us fix Paulding's confounded poetic art. First and foremost, the broken *Torso* vividly illustrates his conscious shattering of traditional means of heroic representation. Second, itself "a thing without a name," the statue simulates Basil's celebration of "nameless men" as well as Paulding's memorialization of the "nameless forms" of the settlers who were sacrificed in battles for western territories. Last, and less consciously, the same dismembered heroic figure suggestively types both of the poem's protagonists: the incompletely realized Basil of the first half, and the dispossessed and eventually destroyed Indian prophet of the second.

LUCY RINEHART

Selected Works
The Lay of the Scottish Fiddle, New York and Philadelphia: Inskeep and Bradford, 1813
The Backwoodsman, Philadelphia: Thomas, 1818
Salmagundi, Second Series, by Launcelot Langstaff, Esq., 3 vols., Philadelphia and New York: Thomas, 1819–1820; rev. ed., 2 vols., New York: Harper and Brothers, 1835
The Letters of James Kirke Paulding, edited by Ralph Aderman, Madison: University of Wisconsin Press, 1962

Further Reading
Foerster, Donald M., *The Fortunes of Epic Poetry: A Study in English and American Criticism, 1750–1950*, New York: Catholic University of America Press, 1962
Herold, Amos L., *James Kirke Paulding: Versatile American*, New York: Columbia University Press, 1926
McWilliams, John P., *The American Epic: Transforming a Genre, 1770–1860*, Cambridge: Cambridge University Press, 1989
Paulding, William Irving, *The Literary Life of James K. Paulding*, New York: Scribner, 1867
Ratner, Lorman, *James Kirke Paulding: The Last Republican*, Westport, Connecticut: Greenwood, 1992
Reynolds, Larry, *James Kirke Paulding*, Boston: Twayne, 1984

James Gates Percival

(1795–1856)

James Russell **Lowell** observed that James Gates Percival was like a mad refrigerator salesman who "went on doggedly, making refrigerators of every possible pattern," even though he knew his neighbors would not buy all "twenty thousand of them" merely because he "had been at the trouble of making them." In this, one of many abuses in his review essay on Julius Ward's biography of Percival (*North American Review*, January 1867), Lowell primarily evokes Percival as a mass producer of bad poetry, who was honored because the young, post–Revolutionary War country needed a major poetic voice. In Lowell's eyes, however, Percival's figurative role as refrigerator huckster unconsciously slips over into his being the refrigerator itself. The "best" of Percival's writings reveal his "coldness": "If there be here and there a semblance of pale fire, it is but the reflection of moonshine upon ice."

Percival's life lends itself to various interpretations of this coldness: Lowell attacked it, whereas Henry Legler saw Percival as the American nineteenth century's counterbalance to Edgar Allan **Poe**, with Percival as a madman who froze into sober normality rather than sliding into drugged depravity. In this view, the common denominator remains a certain madness, and indeed Percival's career, like Poe's, invites both a psychopathic reading and a comparison with Baudelairean modernity.

Born in 1795, Percival suffered from typhoid, which left his speech impaired. In spite of public literary success in the poetry collections *Clio No. 1*, *Clio No. 2*, and *Prometheus, Part II, with Other Poems* of 1822, his private voice did not keep pace. A proposal of marriage in 1820 was rejected. Between 1824 and 1825, he withdrew from various Phi Beta Kappa poetry positions and an editorship with the American Athenaeum. Employed by the state of Connecticut as a geologist, he could not produce a report contracted in 1835 until 1842. When it appeared, it was, in the words of geology historian George Merrill, "beyond question one of the least readable issued by any state," because it devolved into "lithology" rather than "geology," a naming of rocks, not an overview of rock formations.

Disappointment about his inability to speak effectively, from his offer of marriage to his inventory of rocks, became one theme of Percival's life, as did his continual insistence on being heard. He began studying multiple languages, composed poems in German, and became an associate of Noah Webster's on *An American Dictionary of the English Language* in 1828. The clash between wanting to speak and fearing to speak cuts across his career, as do the inevitable conflicts of failed and successful expressions. Quoting the *Atlantic Monthly* of July 1859, Harry R. Warfel poignantly describes Percival at his death in 1856 as sitting "noiseless" in a library of "ten thousand books" (*Dictionary of American Biography*). The vignette cannot help recall Lowell's retrospective of Percival as the voice that the new republic needed but that was somehow bound not to speak.

The question is what the calmness, coldness, and noiselessness mean for this refrigerator poet. Perhaps the clearest idea comes from the poetic genre painting that most overlaps with earth science, Percival's other extensive occupation. Percival wrote many poems set on the sea floor such as "The Coral Grove" (LOA, 1: 219) and "Voyage of Life," meteorological poems like "The Spirit of the Air" and "Heaven," and such tellurian and vulcanist reveries as "A Picture" ("There is a fountain of the purest wave") and "Catania." If a quality in these poems associates Percival's "lithological" interest in naming stones with the more nearly modern icy diamonds of Baudelaire and Mallarmé – or, for that matter, with the empty, ethereal ionospheres found in such authors – these poems would seem to provide the link.

Certainly, these poems bear out the lithology that historians of geology lament and endow it with a symbolist chilliness, as in this description of a stream bottom from "A Picture":

> Its flow is over pebbles and bright sands,
> Which, from the curling waters flashing out,
> Inlay the channel with mosaic, where
> The white flint shines like pearl, the agate glows
> With playful tints, dove-like or pavonine,
> Catching new splendor from the wave; the while
> Smooth-rounded stones, deep blue and ebony,
> And slaty flakes of red and russet-brown,
> Lie darker in their brightness, as when gems
> Sparkle from out the chilly night of caves.

The reader can see here the attention to viewing particulars of stone, which exasperated readers of Percival's survey work for the state of Connecticut, as well as the poetic sense in which precise scientific naming overlaps with a revel in the gorgeousness of language.

The interest in language, however, goes beyond a relish in the sound of words and latinate elegances like "pavonine." Percival locates his "picture" of the stream in the cultural enterprise of art, with the stream bed as inlaid "mosaic"; in another stanza, the stream bed is "tapestried." Furthermore, the close of the passage just cited betrays an interest in the sinister, dangerous origin of verbal art, these "gems" issuing "from out the chilly night of caves." This description is, of course, an analogy, but the reader earlier learns that the stream has literally come from a "spring . . . hidden in a silent cave, / The shrine of darkness and of loneliness." Its development from "silence" to "chiming, like [a] tender voice" makes the stream a metaphor for language's birth and progress through culture. This language stream, however, never ceases to recall and recreate in analogy its origin in the "darker," "chilly night" of "lonely" silence.

Such a view of language as originating at a danger point takes various metaphoric forms in other poems. In the description of Mount Etna in "Catania," "the volcan's jaws" produce "a sullen roar" as from "the mountain's womb," a prenatal, dangerous vocalizing. In the meteorological "Spirit of the Air," it looks at first as if Percival comes close to another poetic position that Lowell deplored: imitating Percy Bysshe Shelley on poetic creativity. Percival, however, tries to describe poetic language in comparison not with Shelley's "wild West Wind" but with the mechanism behind it, whose first function is to "blow the trumpet of assault" "upon the pinions of the storm."

Images of Etna's pyroclastic roaring or the wind's hurricane force might suggest that for Percival language's danger lies in its power, but the opposite seems to be the case. Although the threat is evoked, superficially, in an analogy suggesting destructiveness, the root fear seems to be more one of language's impotence. In "A Picture," the stream is troublesome because it recalls the noiselessness of its beginnings; Etna disturbs because it suggests vocal noise in utero, where no such sounds could occur. In trying to do Shelley one better by imagining not the wind but the wind's own mechanism, the title's "Spirit of the Air," Percival assumes an empty persona: "I sit alone, / Shrouding behind a veil of night my form." He is not the air but "the spirit of the viewless air"; "Where'er the viewless waves of ether flow, / . . . I am there," a presence reduced beyond wind, even beyond "ether," a near nothing.

To Percival, language reduces to a fearful nothing because it is at heart analogical, a medium ultimately estranged from its intended object. In his opening prose statement to "Heaven," Percival claims to be explicating the mythological perception of the sky, but before ever discussing the air at all he makes a comparison to "the twinkling glance of waves." Turning his eyes upward, he sees "clouds of opal, laced / With gold," which in turn recalls the mineralogical specificity of "A Picture." The speaker can look up only by looking down, and the conventionally light clouds turn to stone.

To perform the tasks of speech, Percival implies, language must celebrate the ability to describe things as what they are not. At the same time, the users of this language realize an ominous lack of fit between what they say and what they intend. Later in "Heaven," Percival describes forms "covered . . . with dim transparency," and the metaphor draws attention to its own inadequacy. "Transparency" does not "cover"; by nature it is not "dim." Thus, the whole description operates only on an analogical basis and, thereby, paradoxically produces no "transparency" of reference.

In this account, language is attractive because of its precise ability to refer, as in a taxonomy of minerals, and fearful because of the suspicion that even this precision rests on an empty, imprecise analogy. "Storm," "eruption," "war," and the various other threats in Percival's poems thus do not actually represent the imitation of Shelley that Lowell has in mind. If they are imitations of Shelley at all, the metaphors more closely recall Shelley as later twentieth-century readings have treated him, as a trafficker in a poetic language that he simultaneously exposes as empty. Language threatens because it is not threatening enough. The calm that Percival seeks and that Lowell castigates as refrigeration ultimately signifies the threat of language's meaninglessness, a final silence to any poem.

Percival's poetry attempts to balance and reconcile the power that language should be with the empty calm that it finally is. Perhaps the best attempt to reconcile these two parts of Percival's linguistic and poetic awareness comes in "The Coral Grove," which is a celebration of an ambiguous calm. The explicit atmosphere of the coral grove is one of peace. All is

> . . . safe, when the wrathful spirit of storms,
> Has made the top of the wave his own:
> And when the ship from his fury flies,

> Where the myriad voice of ocean roar,
> When the wind-god frowns in the murky skies,
> And demons are waiting the wreck on shore.

This peacefulness, however, only reveals itself when we sort through the poem's various uses of the word "wave." In this passage, "the wave" seems to have levels, with a "top" that is violent and a lower part that is calm and "safe." This implication would seem to characterize the poem's opening line as well: "Deep in the wave is a coral grove." Reading "wave" in this way makes it a metonymy for "ocean"; literal waves do not roll on the sea bottom. But the poem also uses "wave" in the literal sense when it says, "The water is calm and still below, / For the winds and the waves are absent there." The grove thus exists both "in" a "wave" and not in a "wave." The tranquillity is both a part of surface energy and removed from it. What one description calls the grove's location, another description says is "absent."

The violence of this tranquil setting becomes jarringly clear in the sudden martial imagery that is so characteristic of Percival's poetry: here, seaweed appears "like a banner bathed in slaughter." Moreover, the danger implicated in this calm can be related or linked to problems of analogical language and to the difficulty of describing things directly. On the seabed, "The floor is of sand, like the mountain drift," and the "tufts of ocean, / Are bending like corn on the upland lea." If "Heaven" can describe what is high only by looking low, "The Coral Grove" can describe what is low only by looking high. This lithological morphologist, whose enterprise consists in discerning "slaty flakes of red and russet-brown," must be aware of even subtler misnamings in the poem, like references to the coral as "rocks" and "bowers of stone."

As the use of the word "wave" makes clear, such misnamings or blurred namings can be complex and ominous. Read in the context of other Percival poems, the vitreous "bright and changeful beauty" of the coral grove may not seem genuine. Often when the sea opens itself transparently in Percival's poetry, the view is more like the uncanny vision of Samuel Taylor Coleridge's Ancient Mariner or Poe's "MS Found in a Bottle," as in Percival's "Voyage of Life": "The crystal flood / Opened its awful depths beneath, – so clear / The bark seemed hanging in [a] midway space."

This "awful," empty "space," in which the poet hangs suspended in supernatural vertigo, suggests the state of his powers of language. For all its gorgeousness, "The Coral Grove" appears to be constructed in the same hollow medium that Percival is trying to balance out with the referring language of his geological career. Particularly striking for their vacuousness are the poem's third and fourth lines, "the sea-flower spreads its leaves of blue, / That never are wet with falling dew." Of course they are not wet with "dew," but the traditional trope of privileged existence nears silliness here. Permanently immersed, the "flowers" are more constantly sodden than their upland counterparts, to whom the sea blooms are supposed to pose some idealized contrast. Like the reference in "A Picture" to being "covered" with "transparency," this remark has an existence only in language and calls attention to its own semantic irrelevance.

The "calm" at the core of Percival's art reveals itself as a grim desideratum: "calm" is an item of poetic reverence, but the word also migrates close to the emptiness of the referring language that makes Percival frantic and un-"calm" to begin with. The cycle then, of course, continues. The poet seeks "calm" as a traditional ideal of verbal art, only in the process to reveal again to himself that this ideal works only as a verbal token. The attempt in "The Coral Grove" to balance language's referential impotence with a counter-ideal of language's referring power is as successful in this poem as the venture ever becomes: "wave" is simultaneously hollow metonymy and literal force. The success, however, noticeably remains precarious.

Among Percival's more unusual poems is an untitled composition that begins "A lake once lay," which goes even beyond the transparent ocean metaphors of Coleridge and Poe, as well as those of Percival's other verse. Here, the water is not transparent; it is simply gone. This paean to a dry lake, however, retains emptily the metaphors of analogous realms that characterize "The Coral Grove" and Percival's other geological poems. The speaker recalls that when the lake contained water, "a forest of verdure seemed waving below." By disappearing, the water has made this metaphor real: the dry lakebed now contains bushes, weeds, ferns, and other plants that had simply seemed to be there before. The great irony from a language standpoint is that by becoming real, analogy has become dissatisfying. Comparison works only by assuming its own inadequacy. When Percival's speaker finds real bushes where figurative bushes were before, "from my dream of delight, like a sleeper at night, / I awoke and found me alone." For Percival, reality without metaphor becomes a dismal awakening, but life with metaphor confesses to being mere "dream."

Admittedly, Percival is not Baudelaire, and Percival's critique of language has not attained a state that he could probably describe. Both "A lake once lay" and "Voyage of Life" end with the sort of moral tags about lost innocence that some-times disconcert, for parallel reasons, in Emily **Dickinson**. The critic outside these poems, however, sees the moral tag as subsumed under the criticisms about language that the poems imply. Percival should be the voice of the new republic, but he cannot physically speak very well, cannot effectively propose marriage, and cannot write so that a particularizing mineralogy can become a publicly recognized, meaningful geology. The crazed refrigerator merchant has become his own cold product and knows the peril of this cold calm.

WILLIAM CRISMAN

Selected Works

Poems, New Haven, Connecticut: n.p., 1821
Clio, No. 1, Charleston, South Carolina: S. Babcock, 1822
Clio, No. 2, New Haven, Connecticut: S. Converse, 1822
Prometheus, Part II, with Other Poems, New Haven, Connecticut: n.p., 1822
Works, New York: Charles Wiley, 1823
Clio, No. 3, New York: G. and C. Carvill, 1827
The Dream of a Day, and Other Poems, New Haven, Connecticut: S. Babcock, 1843
The Poetical Works of James Gates Percival, 2 vols., Boston: Ticknor and Fields, 1859

Further Reading

Legler, Henry E., *James Gates Percival: An Anecdotal Sketch and Bibliography*, Milwaukee, Wisconsin: Mequeon Club, 1901
Merrill, George P., *The First One Hundred Years of American Geology*, 1924; reprinted, New York and London: Hafner, 1969
Ward, Julius H., *The Life and Letters of James Gates Percival*, Boston: Ticknor and Fields, 1866

John James Piatt

(1835–1917)

Sarah Morgan Bryan Piatt

(1836–1919)

Although referred to in their lifetimes as the "American Brownings," there was no happy match of talent between John James and Sarah Morgan Piatt. He is a minor literary figure, whose surest claim to fame lies in whom he knew, not in what he wrote. Despite her faults, she is among the most substantive poets of her day. Sadly, but not surprisingly – to those familiar with the history of women's writing – it is the lesser author, John James, who is usually remembered, largely, it seems, because of his early collaboration with fellow Ohioan William Dean **Howells**. Sarah, whom most people, including Howells, considered by far the superior poet, has been well and truly forgotten. Complex, multifaceted, and ironic, she has come down in literary history (when she is mentioned at all) primarily as a wife and mother, and as a poet whose works, to quote *Notable American Women*, "reflect joy in her home and family and deep devotion between husband and wife." Identified thus, as one more nineteenth-century "sweet singer," she has been effectively erased.

The Piatts' story is one of brief literary success followed by years of agonizing personal and professional setbacks. Neither success nor setbacks were predictable on the basis of family and education alone. John James, or J. J., as he signed himself, was born on March 1, 1835, in James' Mills, Indiana, a town located close to the Ohio border. He came from a large, well-established family of Huguenot extraction that settled in New Jersey in the eighteenth century. It was a matter of some family pride that four Piatts, including J. J.'s great-grandfather William, served with distinction in the Continental Army during the Revolutionary War.

By the mid–nineteenth century, some midwestern Piatts were well-off and well-connected. Most important for J. J. and Sarah was his flamboyant second cousin, Colonel Donn Piatt, of Mac-a-Chee Castle, West Liberty, Ohio, a sometime judge, soldier, newspaper publisher, politician, litterateur, and ardent defender of the Union cause. Apparently more open to the savage moods in Sarah's poetry than the determinedly genteel J. J., whose editing of his wife's work is nothing if not problematic, Donn published many of her strongest poems in his Washington, D.C., weekly newspaper, *The Capital* (1871–80). Among these were a good two dozen poems on feminist or political issues that her husband never saw fit to reprint in her books. Of lesser note was Donn's cousin, John Bear Piatt, a farmer and J. J.'s father.

Incurably restless, or perhaps – like his son later – simply unsuccessful at whatever he tried, John Bear moved from place to place on the frontier, settling in Indiana, Ohio, Illinois, and, finally, Montana, his last known whereabouts. He – or his wife, Emily (Scott) Piatt – was sufficiently enlightened, however, to ensure that the children had a good education. J. J. attended grammar schools in Indiana and Ohio, and spent one

year, or possibly two, at Kenyon College, alma mater to such noteworthies as Stanley Matthews, associate justice of the Supreme Court, and President Rutherford B. Hayes.

No farmer – or politician, for that matter – J. J. wrote his first publishable poetry while he worked on his father's farm in Prairie Bird, Illinois, in the mid-1850s. By 1859, he was on the editorial staff of the *Louisville Journal*, and he had enough poems – 49 in all – to coauthor a slim volume of verse with Howells, *Poems of Two Friends* (1860). The two Ohioans first met as apprentices in the printing office of the *Ohio State Journal*, which was published by J. J.'s maternal uncle, Charles Scott. They renewed acquaintance in 1859, not long before J. J.'s "The Morning Street" appeared in the *Atlantic Monthly*. Although some of Piatt's later volumes were better received than this early venture, the "dreamy" or romantic quality of his writing never substantially altered. He could not have known it at the time, but between the excitement of the *Atlantic* publication – a truly significant breakthrough for a young midwesterner – and his first book, J. J. had reached the apex of his career.

Born on August 11, 1836, in Fayette County near Lexington, Kentucky, Sarah Morgan Bryan was, judging by her roots, even better situated to receive good fortune than J. J. The great-grandniece of Daniel Boone, she was connected on both sides to some of Kentucky's oldest pioneer families: through her father, Talbot Nelson Bryan, to the Boones and the Bryans, and through her mother, Mary Spiers, to the Stocktons and the Simpsons. Sarah's childhood, however, was severely disrupted by her mother's death in 1844. Not only did she lose a "tender mother" – as J. J. described her to James Russell **Lowell** in 1863 – but in keeping with the custom of the time, Sarah and her two siblings were dispersed among female relatives. Sarah and her younger sister went to their maternal grandmother's plantation near Lexington. After their grandmother's death, the two girls lived briefly with friends and then with their father and his wealthy new wife on their stepmother's plantation in Versailles, Kentucky.

This last arrangement did not work, and Sarah and her sister were finally settled with their paternal aunt, Annie Boone, of New Castle, Kentucky. Mrs. Boone sent Sarah to Henry Female College in New Castle to complete her education. Sarah came away from her schooling with a thorough knowledge of the Greek classics and William Shakespeare, and a deep love for the British romantic poets, in particular Lord Byron, Percy Bysshe Shelley, and Samuel Taylor Coleridge. Whatever wounds the various displacements of her childhood inflicted, she did not show them, at least not at this time.

Born, as she says in the poem "A Child's Party" (1895), to the "blue-blood," witty, and well-read, Sarah seemed destined, despite the traumas of her childhood, to do well. George D.

Prentice, the influential publisher of the *Louisville Journal*, adored her. Convinced that if she was "entirely true to [her]self," she would one day be "the first poet of [her] sex in the United States," he published over 50 of her juvenilia in the *Journal* between 1857 and 1861. Unlike J. J.'s early verses, however, the bulk of Sarah's first published poetry is not indicative of her mature work. As Prentice recognized, she still had a great deal more growing to do, and, far more important, she did it.

It was under the auspices of Prentice that Sarah and J. J. met in the late 1850s. To all concerned it must have seemed an ideal match when, on June 18, 1861, they were married in Annie Boone's home in New Castle. In addition to having a first book, J. J. had obtained a patronage position in the Office of the Treasury in Washington, D.C., so his career appeared well started and his financial prospects seemed secure. Sarah, blessed with talent that overflowed the measure, was marrying a man who would sympathetically support her writing and take her north as the south slipped from sectionalism to war. What no one could know was that the two most shaping experiences of Sarah Piatt's life, war and marriage, were still before her, whereas for her husband, rooted as he was in the romantic aspirations and pioneer fantasies of his childhood and adolescence, his shaping experiences were already part of the past.

To understand the peculiar contribution of J. J. Piatt to American poetry, one must look where his father did, to the frontier, and to the confused ambivalence and nostalgia its settling provoked in those most intimately affected by it – the sons of pioneers. To understand Sarah's contribution, one must look to the Civil War, and to the impact it had on her sense of herself as a woman, wife, mother, and member of nineteenth-century American society. For both poets, that is, issues related to national destiny were vital to their strongest work. But where the good Victorian J. J. sought, despite personal reservations, to submerge the specific in the universal, sacrificing his voice to the cultural ideology he purveyed, Sarah found – or created – her voice quite oppositely, by making lived experience the basis for her poetry. Angry, bitter, but ever acute, she used her response to the war – and to its personal and social horrors – as the foundation for a new poetic, one as devoted to the hard edges of reality as her husband's poetic was devoted to dream.

This difference in poetic is best approached by beginning with J. J.'s "Farther" (1872; LOA, 2: 328), which typifies the strengths and weaknesses of his oeuvre:

Far-off a young State rises, full of might:
  I paint its brave escutcheon. Near at hand
  See the log cabin in the rough clearing stand;
A woman by its door, with steadfast sight,
Trustful, looks Westward, where, uplifted bright,
  Some city's Apparition, weird and grand,
  In dazzling quiet fronts the lonely land,
With vast and marvelous structures wrought of light,
Motionless on the burning cloud afar: –
  The haunting vision of a time to be,
After the heroic age is ended here,
Built on the boundless, still horizon's bar
  By the low sun, his gorgeous prophecy
Lighting the doorway of the pioneer!

Like a number of other poems J. J. wrote, including "Fires in Illinois" – originally "Prairie-Fires" in 1860, revised in 1866 (LOA, 2: 329) – and "To the Statue on the Capitol" (1872; LOA, 2: 328), "Farther" is a visionary poem that is spoken by one who stands outside the events that he describes. Together, these poems celebrate the United States that was and will be, the land where that familiar threesome of the "lonely" ("Farther"), the "savage" ("Statue"), and the "boundless" ("Farther," "Statue," and "Fires") have been made amenable to civilized life. "Vast and marvelous structures wrought of light" ("Farther"), whose presence is marked by "numberless . . . / . . . windows [that] shine below" ("Fires") or, alternatively, by "boundless fields of harvest" ("Statue"), have now occupied the wilderness – America's limitlessness transformed into apparently unbounded good.

In all three poems – although by no means in all of J. J.'s poetry on pioneer experience – the speaker sounds unambivalently positive about the exchange. Indeed, when comparing the United States to Europe, where "lost Republics" and "ruin'd cities" are the order of the day ("Statue"), he sounds downright exultant. Like the eagle adorning the statue's crest, the United States is riding high. And in 1872, it was. With the country reunified after the Civil War and the Indian wars all but over, it was poised on the brink of an imperialist expansion that would someday help make it one of the greatest military powers in history.

Yet, as "Farther" hints, and other Piatt poems on western experience develop ("The Lost Farm" [1872], for example, and "The Pioneer's Chimney" [1866]), there is also a loss within this transformation, a loss that helps explain both the persistent undercutting melancholy in J. J.'s poetry and his tendency to vagueness and mendacity. For the frontier that evoked these visions of an all-conquering future has itself been conquered, and the "heroic age" is over. For a second-generation westerner like Piatt, who was intensely aware of his own belatedness but who wished nonetheless to record "authentic" pioneer experience, this loss presented certain difficulties. For not only did he lack the authority of the experience that he wished to inscribe, but, as the vagueness and conventionality of the three poems testify, he also lacked a vital language in which to inscribe that experience.

In an 1868 review of Piatt's *Western Windows and Other Poems*, Lowell states the problem nicely by laying down the rules by which the young western poet might hope to succeed. Contrary to "the dreams of our earliest horoscope-mongers," he declares – taking a swipe at Walt **Whitman**, among others – when "young Lochinvar comes out of the West," he will not be "shaggy . . . brown-fisted, careless of proprieties [and] unhampered by tradition," nor will he display "the rude vigor that is supposed to be his birthright." He will "aim . . . at elegance and refinement" instead and seek "his ideal somewhere outside of the life that [lies] immediately around him." For to the young poet "culture will seem the ideal thing, and, in a country without a past, tradition will charm all the more that it speaks with a foreign accent." He will, in short, come imitating the accent of his Europe-imbued (eastern) betters. The question was, could he keep his vigor – rude or otherwise – while doing so, and the answer, in J. J.'s case at least, was no, he could not.

In J. J., as in most genteel poets of the period, the ideality or "culture" for which Lowell calls was less likely to produce poetry of "universal" appeal than it was to encourage writing that was facile, derivative, and poetically limp. As George **Santayana** put it, the genteel tradition resulted in poems "without sensuous beauty, splendor, passion, or volume." Stated in more modern terms, it produced poems that took no risks – in J. J.'s case, the risk of saying things not as they "ought to be," but, as he knew from his own less-than-ideal experience, as they were.

In "Over in Kentucky" (1874), Sarah Piatt has her speaker's young daughter call Cincinnati, Ohio, where Sarah and J. J. spent most of their married lives, "the smokiest city in the world." By the 1870s, when "Farther" was published, this "marvelous structur[e] wrought of light" was a steam- and coal-driven industrial and commercial complex that abutted the Ohio River, which was thoroughly polluted with urban waste. As Gail Hamilton (Mary Abigail Dodge) noted in a wickedly funny review of *Poems of Two Friends*, in *The National Era*, it was a city better known for its hams, "the very apotheosis of swine, the peotry [punning on "Piatt-ry"] of pork," than for its poets. Cincinnati was a crassly money-oriented city, where, according to another one of Sarah's poems ("A Neighbourhood Incident," 1888), homeless people froze to death in the cliffs below the Piatts' home in North Bend. The frontier had passed a good 60 to 80 years before, along with the Indians who had inhabited the region but had been evicted by J. J.'s immediate ancestors.

Yet only in the early "Taking the Night-Train" (1860, revised 1866; LOA, 2: 331) does J. J. come close to dealing honestly with the sense of alienation and dislocation engendered in him by this other west – not the long-lost west of shaggy men and "rude vigor" or its idealized refigurement, created for genteel eastern consumption, but the west that his fathers had actually made. In this poem, J. J. confronts directly his terror at being one anonymous face among many and sends up a cri de coeur from the neediness that would haunt him all his life and make him dependent on the support of others, most especially his wife:

> From great hotels the stranger throng is streaming,
>   The hurrying wheels in many a street are loud;
> Within the depot, in the gaslight gleaming,
>   A glare of faces, stands the waiting crowd.
>
> The whistle screams; the wheels are rumbling slowly,
>   The path before us glides into the light:
> Behind, the city sinks in silence wholly;
>   The panting engine leaps into the night.
>
> I seem to see each street a mystery growing,
>   In mist of dreamland – vague, forgotten air:
> Does no sweet soul, awaking, feel me going?
>   Loves no dear heart, in dreams, to keep me there?

The streaming throng, the hurrying wheels, the glare of faces, the screaming whistle, and the lonely man wanting love and afraid that he may never find it – this is the stuff of so-called modern life. It was also the stuff out of which life in J. J.'s urban midwest was made. But it was not the sort of stuff most readers in the east, or the west, were eager to read about when they turned from the lurid headlines of their daily newspapers (which Sarah, like Herman **Melville** before her, would exploit in her poems) to what they thought of as belles lettres. Here, as

Lowell rightly recognized, they wanted "the ideal thing" – a portrait of the region and of pioneer character that was "unmistakably Western" yet could be assimilated to the gentility to which they aspired. Such, according to Lowell, was the "true poetic insight which *creates the ideal under the common and familiar*" (italics added), but it was also "insight" that poeticized the truth.

The mower in Ohio who stoically accepts his sons' deaths in the Civil War and goes on haying; "the old democrat in the west" who once voted for Andrew Jackson but who now, proudly, casts his ballot for the Republican Lincoln; and the pioneer who mortgages his cabin to help his son, only to lose his life's work and his life in the end – whether as winners or noble losers, these were the kinds of "manly" yet "common" men (to use one of J. J.'s favorite epithets) with whom readers wished to identify the west, as experience and character. The poems in which these figures appear – "The Mower in Ohio," "Riding to Vote," and "The Pioneer's Chimney," first published in 1866 in *Poems in Sunshine and Firelight* – constituted those that were most frequently associated with Piatt's name and most regularly reprinted in his books.

That the author who celebrated these stock figures of republican virtue was being just as derivative and facile in them as in his more blatantly imitative romantic exercises does not seem to have occurred to even so perspicacious a critic as Howells. Like the hundreds of idealized paintings on the opening of the west by Albert Bierstadt and others, Piatt's poems on pioneer men and frontier experience were not meant to represent "reality." Dedicated to defining the nation's identity and, not coincidentally, its ideal of manhood, they are ideological fictions, political dreams. Yet, because they spoke to what readers wanted to believe, they seemed even to Howells "simple," "touching," "genuine," "natural" and "real." As such, they helped soothe the wounds and silence the doubts of those, J. J. Piatt included, who otherwise might have wondered at what price, besides the wilderness itself, the wilderness had been lost.

In "The Grave at Frankfort" (1872), Sarah Piatt, the great-granddaughter of pioneers, and a woman not easily given to denial, totes up some of the cost in a poem that reads almost as a rebuttal of J. J.'s "Farther." Perhaps because she was somewhat further removed from pioneer experience, or because her youthful experiences on slaveholding plantations had, as she makes clear in "A Child's Party," given her "true . . . insight" into the un-ideal aspects of America's past, Sarah was much less sanguine than her husband about her country's history. And her assessment of its future is more chilling than anything J. J., or, indeed, most poets of her age, offered.

Like her husband's "Farther," Sarah's is a visionary poem, but she did not design it to soothe. Rather, in keeping with the terrible urgency of its thought, it is wiry and tough. And it is marked by an abrasive allusiveness that typifies her mature style, a style that, as her critics frequently observed, was nothing if not subtle, complex, and demanding of the reader. Her critics also duly noted the supposedly baleful influence of Robert Browning, to whom she had turned in her maturity, upon her mature style.

Like J. J., Sarah uses the image of the pioneer cabin to focus her comment on the direction the country is taking and on the relationship between this direction and the nation's past.

But the figure whom she places on the threshold, as it were, symbolically to link the past to what it will become, is not a steadfast, idealized, and improbable "pioneer woman." It is a concrete historical personage, her "old, rude kinsman" Daniel Boone, and the ambivalence that the speaker exhibits toward him is the ambivalence of a woman who has learned the hard way that the demonic and the charismatic are not so far apart – that the ability to lead does not necessarily lead to good. Despite his posthumous role as the avatar of quintessential American manhood, and despite her own recognition of his superiority to men like Ulysses S. Grant, whom Sarah frankly and unequivocally detested (see "Shoulder-Rank," 1871), Piatt does not treat her "grand old kinsman," as J. J. calls Boone in "The Birthdays" (1864), as a "Ulysses of the Indian wild." To her, he is at best Byron's "backwoods general" and, at most, a man with a gun.

> I turned and threw my rose upon the mound
>   Beneath whose grass my old, rude kinsman lies,
> And thought had from his Dark and Bloody Ground
>   The blood secured in the shape of flowers to rise.
>
> I left his dust to dew and dimness then,
>   Who did not need the glitter of mock stars
> To show his homely generalship* to men
>   And light his shoulders through his troubled wars.
>
> I passed his rustling wild-cane, reached the gate,
>   And heard the city's noisy murmurings;
> Forgot the simple hero of my State,
>   Looked in the gaslight, thought of other things.
>
> Ah, that was many withered springs ago;
>   Yet once, last winter, in the whirl of snows,
> A vague half-fever, or, for aught I know,
>   A wish to touch the hand that gave my rose,
>
> Showed me a hunter of the wooded West,
>   With dog and gun, beside his cabin door;
> And, in the strange fringed garments on his breast,
>   I recognized at once the rose he wore!
>
> * "General Boone, backwoodsman of Kentucky." –
>   Byron [poet's note]

It hardly needs saying that "The Grave at Frankfort" lacks the smoothness that makes J. J.'s poetry – like so much genteel verse – easy reading. "Grave" is a knotted poem linguistically, imagistically, and intellectually. Like much of Sarah's Civil War poetry, including "Giving Back the Flower" (1867; LOA, 2: 349), "One from the Dead" (1871), and "A Ghost at the Opera" (1879), it depends for its meaning and effect upon a romantic narrative whose basic constituents it never fully discloses. Indeed, although this narrative is the backbone of her Civil War poetry, these constituents, including such fundamentals as the number of the speaker's lovers and their regional identity, north or south, are never unequivocally established in her work. Equally difficult, "Grave" takes place in multiple time-frames whose parallelism is only hinted at through the reiterated reference to the rose. And, finally, the poem itself refuses closure. Ending without ending, it deprives us of that sense of completedness that we normally expect as our reward for reading. Here, we are left with an enigmatic flower instead.

It is the flower – sometimes a "blush rose," sometimes a "rose geranium," and sometimes, as in "Giving Back the Flower," merely a bud – that identifies "The Grave at Frankfort" as a Civil War poem and that relates it to other Piatt poems in which her speaker explores the significance of her relationship to her (now dead) lover(s). For this is the rose that "he" gave her before he went off to die of a wound – need I say it? – in the breast. Through the rose, the Civil War enters the poem and the implied reference helps to shape the poem's meaning. But the reader must tease out this meaning from hints that the speaker provides. In contrast to J. J.'s "Farther," nothing is presented as a transparent sign or as an "escutcheon" whose significance it is the poet's task and privilege authoritatively to explain.

Rather, what Sarah Piatt offers here is the enigmatic surface of history itself and an alternative and far more painful way to arrive at the meaning embedded within it. For J. J., as for most genteel poets, meaning was, as we have seen, wrought by "insight" in the commonplace. For all her presumptive historicity, therefore, the figure of the pioneer woman at her cabin door has no concrete reality or significance in herself. She is what the poet makes her: a symbol of the destiny to which the nation is drawn. Read in this way, history conforms to and, not coincidentally, confirms orthodox belief. Politics is buried in "art," and historical meaning and national ideology are inseparably wedded.

In "The Grave at Frankfort," a poem as concrete and specific as its graveyard setting, Sarah Piatt rips all this apart. Although she knowingly plays on Boone's role as an ideological signifier, her reading is not ideological but, in Erich Auerbach's sense of the term, figural. Boone is what he is; but he is also something more: a shadow, or sign, of what is to come. Read thus, a pattern of prefiguration and fulfillment can be seen to control the poem and to link its two initial time-frames – Boone's time, and the soldier-lover's. For the promise made in her kinsman's long and vicious Indian wars – or "troubles," as they were called – and inscribed in the (inaccurately derived) Indian etymology of Kentucky's name was fulfilled when America's young men turned their guns against themselves: then, not just Kentucky, but all of the United States, became a "Dark and Bloody Ground." This – not some "marvelous structur[e] wrought of light" – was the country's "prophesied" destiny, the future that was folded into the past and that time has now revealed. For such a future, Boone, the backwoods "general," is indeed the logical true sign, a warning of what was to come.

The bitterness expressed through this reading of national destiny is compounded – as in much of Piatt's best work – by her speaker's ironic awareness of her own substantial complicity in the evil she describes. In "The Grave at Frankfort," the "rose" of (woman's) love does not secure peace. Rather, the figure of hunter/Indian-fighter, Boone, swallows the rose up, converting it into the wound from which the speaker's lover dies. As Oliver Wendell **Holmes** recognized in his energetic call-to-arms, "Never or Now," a woman's rose is, finally, just one more incentive to use when urging young men to go out and die. In this context, the flower's color, not its traditional function as a symbol for love and peace, is valorized. Far more than its symbolic associations, its color bespeaks the flower's "true" significance in the web of social meaning that war, history, and politics weave:

> Break from the arms that would fondly caress you!
>   Hark! 't is the bugle-blast, sabres are drawn!
> Mothers shall pray for you, fathers shall bless you,
>   Maidens shall weep for you when you are gone!
>
> Never or now! cries the blood of a nation,
>   Poured on the turf where the red rose should bloom;
> Now is the day and the hour of salvation, –
>   Never or now! peals the trumpet of doom!

Coming from a border state, Sarah Piatt knew that the mere fact of being situated in the North or the South made no difference. Male or female made no difference either. Whatever the side in the war, the rhetoric did not change, nor did the response that men and women had to it. Roses, like everything else, were part of the language (and ideology) that lured men to war and that led women to cheer them on. As he stands with his dog and his gun at his cabin door, Daniel Boone this "simple Hero of [his] State," appears to be proud of what he wrought. But to his great-grandniece, the pioneer vision that he embodied not only legitimated but glorified killing in the name of manly identity and nationhood. However charismatic in itself, it led nowhere but to the corpse-filled ditches of Antietam and Chancellorsville, to noisy, smoke-filled cities, and to the vague half-fevers that beset a woman who was desperate for a kind of love and a kind of world in which roses could not be twisted into signifiers of our wounds.

I believe that Sarah Piatt's complex response to the Civil War was due, at least in part, to the part of her childhood that she spent on slaveholding plantations. There she learned early of her own complicity in evil, and in many poems her speaker expresses guilt for crimes that she committed before she could even have known they were crimes. "I . . . think of it with shame," the voice in " A Child's Party" says of cruel words that she spoke to a "dusky playmate," a slave child, on her grandmother's plantation.

But, as the enormous stylistic and thematic difference between her antebellum and postbellum poetry indicates, whatever guilt Sarah felt was crystallized by the Civil War. The war cast its shadow on all that she wrote thereafter, and in these writings she not only resisted the cultural values that justified this elemental exercise in fratricide but also those upon which her own experiences as a wife and, eventually, as a mother were based. Turning from poems on war to poems on marriage and poems on (not to) children, Piatt – the mother of six sons and one daughter (one other child died immediately after birth) – explored the extent to which both mothers and their progeny are corrupted by the society in which they live. Repeatedly, the speaker of these poems expresses her dismay at the way in which this corruption is inscripted into the inequitable power distributions of marriage and into the gender roles that children are encouraged to assume: boys learn from their earliest toys and books that it is glorious "to fight" ("Their Heroic Lesson," 1888; "A Sea-Gull Wounded," 1895), and girls learn to dress and bury their dolls in the same way that they will be dressed and "buried" some day ("The Funeral of a Doll," 1874; "The Coming Out of Her Doll," 1888).

And it is this bourgeois woman speaker's knowledge of her own complicity in evil – as a child, wife, mother, lover, and citizen – that makes Sarah Piatt's poetry unique and uniquely valuable in both the canons of nineteenth-century verse and Anglo-American women's poetry in general. Far from restricting herself to "joy in her home and family, and deep devotion between husband and wife," Piatt is one of the great singers of domestic and social infelicity: of wives who long for lovers from the dead, of women who lack the courage to act on their political convictions, of husbands who are utterly indifferent to, or oblivious of, the social and personal misery around them, and of children whose very games inculcate the morbid and destructive values of the society in which they live (see, for example, "Giving Back the Flower," "The Palace-Burner" [1874], "His Mother's Way" [1888], and "Playing Beggars" [1871], respectively). Like Melville, and like a number of the period's female prose ironists such as Fanny Fern, Caroline Kirkland, Rebecca Harding Davis, and Gail Hamilton, Sarah Piatt was fully in touch with the all-too-concrete unpleasant "realities" that her culture wished to deny, and sometimes subtly, sometimes blatantly, she made them fundamental to what she wrote.

Given her husband's profound commitment to nineteenth-century mythic verities, from the "pioneer spirit" to the concept of woman as ministering angel, Sarah Piatt's writing also marked the yawning gulf between J. J. and herself. Time and again, one feels, as with "Farther" and "The Grave at Frankfort," that her poems answer his back: his naïveté and neediness is rebutted by her bitter, sophisticated awareness; her doubt and despair confound his faith in "the ideal." Her best poetry is merciless on these scores, a constant ironic deconstruction of everything that J. J. and much of genteel society claimed to believe. Responding to the times, she grew and he refused to grow, clinging to the past instead (see my article in *American Literary History* 7 [1995]).

But Lowell was right, of course. Such deconstructive cynicism was not what appealed to most late-nineteenth-century readers. As is clear from reviews, although her strength and originality were readily acknowledged, her volumes did not please. If her husband bored readers with too much warmed-over Victoriana, she disturbed them too much. Even when she wrote of children – her "infantile undertakers," Howells called them in his troubled review of *Poems in Company of Children* (1878) – too many of her themes were harsh, and her manner of treating them often was too difficult and uncompromising. As a *Scribner's* reviewer forthrightly complained (1880), she demanded "more intelligence than is possessed by one reader in a hundred." And what her readers did not have, they could not give.

It may have been such criticism that led J. J., to whom Sarah yielded complete control of her publishing, to keep so many of her strongest and most important poems such as "Giving Back the Flower" and "The Grave at Frankfort" out of her books. Or it may simply have been that, given his own taste, he neither cared for nor understood such poems. Certainly, his selection of "representative" poems for Edmund Clarence **Stedman's** *An American Anthology* suggests that he preferred her weaker works. Whatever the reason, the result is that one can read all of her books, even the best of them – *A*

Woman's Poems (1871), *Voyage to the Fortunate Isles* (1874), *That New World* (1877), and *Dramatic Persons and Moods* (1879) – and, despite all the criticism contemporary critics lavished on them, never get a clear idea of how powerful and scathing a poet that she is. Too many weaker poems where she seems, at least, to be more conventional, get in the way, while many of the most important poems, those that cue you on how the rest should be read, are quite simply missing, – a risky business at best for a poet so dependent on irony to make her meaning.

Since she let J. J. handle most of her contacts with the outside world, including most of her publishing correspondence, it is impossible to say whether she cared about or approved of what he did. Given J. J.'s officiousness when it came to publishing, she may have preferred letting him have his way rather than disturbing the family peace in such matters. Both his letters and the few of hers that exist establish that this was her practice in other areas. Or, as Prentice claims, she may indeed have had no interest in the *ignis fatuus* (will-o'-the-wisp) of fame. Certainly, unlike J. J., she made no attempt to chase after fame. Just getting the poems off her chest may have been enough.

But it is also possible that she could not let herself care. Saddled as she was with seven children and a husband who alienated even their closest friends, which in turn damaged both their careers, the miracle is that she produced at all, let alone at the quality she achieves. To have fought J. J. for the control of each book (17 titles, but substantively, perhaps seven volumes) may have been physically and emotionally beyond her. Like other American women poets in similar situations – Lydia Huntley **Sigourney**, for example – she seems to have affected not to take her poetry seriously instead. When first one child (1874) and then another (1884) died in freak childhood accidents, she did not completely recover. According to the Irish author Katherine Tynan, whose memoir of the Piatts in Ireland is the best piece on them, Sarah spent much of her time by 1887 "in a passionate companionship with her dead children." She may, however, have preferred such companionship to J. J.'s, whose "bad taste" and "gloomy" company, as Howells complained in 1870, seem, judging by Tynan's report, not to have improved with age.

Despite his 11-year tenure abroad (1882–93), nine years of it as U.S. Consul in Cork (not a desirable posting), J. J.'s bureaucratic career did not flourish. Nor did his writing, which dried up long before he stopped publishing books (16 titles, but substantively, perhaps three volumes). After *Landmarks and Other Poems* (1872), all of his books, whatever their titles, are composed largely of old work. During the last three decades of their life together, he and Sarah sank slowly and inexorably into genteel poverty as he failed to get one job after another, although never for want of trying. He eked out a living for them both by freelance work, book sales, and help from friends, especially Howells. After a carriage accident in 1914, he was completely disabled, mentally and physically, and he became dependent upon Sarah for everything until his death in Avondale, Ohio, in 1917.

Sarah died two years later in 1919 in Caldwell, New Jersey, at the home of her youngest son, Cecil, one of only two known surviving children. Despite everything, she kept writing through a good part of these years (1894–1919). A small handful of her finest poems come from this period, none more moving than her last published poem, the only sheerly beautiful poem that she ever wrote. "A Daffodil" was printed in the *Independent* in 1911 – a poem in which Piatt celebrates, appropriately enough, beauty's power to lighten even the darkest of hells:

> Look! – all the vales of all the world are bright
>   With you, as that of Enna was of old!
> One sees the flutter of her apron light,
>   All overflowing with your dew-dim gold!
>
> Oh, shining memory of Persephone!
>   Loosed from the dark of Dis, in this her time,
> The sadder for its sweetness, does not she
>   Out of her under-realm, rejoicing, climb?
>
> And should the Shadow-King, in anger, miss
>   His fair, young, wandering Queen, as well he might,
> Then let her take the lord of Hades this –
>   For his dark crown – this flower of living light!

Sarah Piatt was 75 when this poem appeared. In a photograph taken at about the same time, she looks beaten. But her eyes are sharp. Tired beyond telling, her face still possesses strength, intelligence, and character to spare. These qualities – not a love of beauty – were the richest and most lasting sources of her art. They brought sadness, not sweetness, to her work, as they did to her life. But in their own way, they, too, brought light.

PAULA BERNAT BENNETT

Selected Works
John James Piatt
Poems of Two Friends, with W. D. Howells, Columbus, Ohio: Follett, Foster, 1860
Poems in Sunshine and Firelight, Cincinnati, Ohio: R. W. Carroll, 1866
Western Windows, Cincinnati, Ohio: R. W. Carroll, 1868
Landmarks and Other Poems, New York: Hurd and Houghton, 1872
Sarah Morgan Bryan Piatt
A Woman's Poems, Boston: Osgood, 1871
The Voyage to the Fortunate Isles, Boston: Osgood, 1874
That New World, Boston: Osgood, 1877
Dramatic Persons and Moods, Boston: Houghton, Osgood, 1880
The Witch in the Glass, Boston: Houghton, 1888
Child's World Ballads, Westminster: Constable, 1895
John and Sarah Piatt
The Nests of Washington, New York: Walter Low, 1864

Further Reading
Coyle, William, ed., *Ohio Authors and Their Books*, Cleveland, Ohio: World, 1962
Howells, William Dean, *Literary Friends and Acquaintance*, edited by David F. Hiatt, Bloomington: University of Indiana Press, 1968
Stoddard, R. H., *Poets' Homes: Pen and Pencil Sketches of*

American Poets and Their Homes, Boston: D. Lothrop, 1877

Townsend, John Wilson, *Kentucky in American Letters: 1784–1917*, 2 vols., Cedar Rapids, Iowa: Torch, 1913

Tynan, Katherine, *Memories*, London: Eveleigh Nash & Grayson, 1924

———, *Twenty-Five Years: Reminiscences*, London: Smith, Elder, 1912

Venable, Emerson, *Poets of Ohio*, Cincinnati, Ohio: Stewart and Kidd, 1912

Watts, Emily Stipes, *The Poetry of American Women from 1632 to 1943*, Austin and London: University of Texas Press, 1978

Willard, Frances, and Margaret A. Livermore, eds., *American Women: Fifteen Hundred Biographies*, 2 vols., New York: Mast, Crowell and Kirkpatrick, 1897

John Pierpont

(1785–1866)

An emotional Protestantism, a belief in political liberty and progress, and a yearning, self-propelled aesthetic sensibility – all these have frequently been adduced as signs or at least as symptoms of the American temperament. But seldom have these traits been so seamlessly linked in an American literary career as in that of John Pierpont.

Born in 1785 in Litchfield, Connecticut, Pierpont was old enough by a considerable margin to have served in the War of 1812 (which, in fact, as a New England Federalist, he largely opposed). Yet he was sufficiently long-lived to do government service on the Union side in the Civil War; he died in 1866, in Washington, D.C. Pierpont's career spanned the nation's most tumultuous decades. He was never a professional writer; writing was something he did either to make money to support other enterprises or to display or embody emotions that he could not put across in the prose discourses associated with his vocation as a Unitarian minister. Yet Pierpont's verse is nothing if not creative. Although it might not seem formally innovative, or likely to stand out among contemporary productions for novelty or daring, Pierpont's poetry nonetheless possesses a distinct and individual voice.

Pierpont's poetic debut occurred in 1812 with "The Portrait," a political poem that reflected his Federalist sentiments and adopted the style of his remote kinsman Timothy Dwight. But "Airs of Palestine" (LOA, 1: 63) was Pierpont's first poem to attract wide notice. Although its treatment of biblical themes proceeds in a fashion that can be seen as a product of its American origin, its inspiration is largely European. In the narrative epics of English poets such as Robert Southey, and in the more contemplative romantic biblicism of French lyric poets such as Gérard de Nerval, there existed a mode of biblical reference that, although ostensibly and often genuinely pious, participated more generally in a sort of "Orientalism." This tendency delighted in the color and panoply of biblical settings as a part of a general romantic ethos, yet at the same time literalized the biblical landscape by placing it in its real, near eastern geographical setting; this strategy, in turn, avoided the kind of transposition into European landscapes that had been previously customary.

Pierpont launches his poetic argument in "Airs of Palestine" by enumerating a series of European sites only to dismiss them in favor of biblical ones. Greek mythological sites such as Parnassus and Tempe are canvassed, with an overall descriptiveness that is spotted with moments of lushness and delicacy, as in the mention of Tempe's "flowers, / forever verdant." Their juxtaposition to the "Lonelier, lovelier path . . . where Gilead sheds her balm" and the other Palestinian sites and fanes evoked by Pierpont is meant to suggest a spiritual contrast, not just a geographical one: he announces his poem as possessing a higher, sacred purpose. Palestine is not the place so much as the state of mind of the poet. This Miltonic move, however, is considerably complicated by Pierpont's own American geographical and temporal placement, as is indicated at the poem's very beginning.

Even before the choice of a biblical setting, "Airs of Palestine" opens with a panoramic survey of landscape. Yet it is not a specific landscape, but a kind of meta-landscape, or, more aptly, the idea of landscape in general. The "opening prospect" that Pierpont invites his reader to view is outside of the specific classical or biblical options and clearly alludes to the American distance from the inherited pasts evoked by the poet. From this American vantage point, the poet's question, "Where lies our path? – though many a vista call, / We may admire, but cannot tread them all," becomes an inquiry into the multiple cultural traditions that are possible sources for American inheritance. The classical and biblical pasts are the most obvious ones, but Pierpont is clearly alive to other possibilities, as his sympathy for African Americans attests. In choosing Palestine over Greece, Pierpont is expressing an emotional and spiritual preference. But he is also calling to the audience's attention a certain American cultural relation to the biblical landscape.

The linkage between America and Palestine, as landscapes, is especially complicated. In Puritan accounts of America as the New Jerusalem, the Palestinian landscape is used simply as a typological premise whereby the American scene can be imagined as sacred. But in much nineteenth-century literature, the America-Palestine link becomes more reciprocal. The paramount example is in Herman **Melville's** poem *Clarel* (LOA, 2: 17), which tells the story of a set of American pilgrims in Palestine. One of the conceptual structures of *Clarel* derives from Melville's habit of envisioning Palestinian settings in light of American ones, particularly the Hudson Valley or the Catskills. This is a complete reversal of the New Jerusalem trope, in that America is now vehicle, not tenor, of the typological comparison; in other words, Palestine now supplies the literal base, America the metaphoric flavor. This procedure complicates the themes that arise from the landscape as well. The New Jerusalem cannot be trumpeted so certainly in light of the sheer physical persistence of the old Jerusalem. These geographic reversals, and the pleasures derived from them, resound through Pierpont's poem.

In "Airs of Palestine," the exotic biblical landscape and the picturesque vistas of Pierpont's own American northeast are constantly merging. The mountains of his Palestine are not beacons of majesty piercing a gaunt and thirsty desert, but are laden with lush, fertile verdancy:

> I love to wet my foot in Hermon's dews;
> I love the promptings of Isaiah's muse:
> In Carmel's holy grots, I'll court repose,
> And deck my mossy couch, with Sharon's deathless
>   rose.

These glades and flowers are as much American as Palestinian. Sharon and Carmel were names of places in ancient Israel; yet they are also the names of American towns where moss grew and flowers bloomed even as Pierpont wrote. (There happen to be a Sharon and a Carmel within 50 miles of Pierpont's birthplace in Litchfield.) Pierpont, who wrote "Airs of Palestine" years before actually visiting Palestine, may well have had those American sites in mind rather than the biblical originals that are his manifest subject. Indeed, the American landscape, fashioned by its colonizers in the image of their biblical dreams, took on the hallowed aura of its original and became as fit an open-air theater for sacred poetry as any exotic Near Eastern milieu.

Considering the poem's overtly meditative nature, there is, indeed, a lot of drama in "Airs of Palestine." Herod's massacre of the innocents is vividly and rather luridly evoked. Yet even here, the contemplative filter of the American landscape obtrudes; the nineteenth-century pilgrim recalls Herod's atrocities while "falling leaves flit o'er Ohio's flood." The reader at this point reevaluates the title: does "Airs of Palestine" mean "airs describing Palestine" or "poems giving the air of Palestine"? Attending closely to Pierpont's subtle interchanges between scriptural reference and natural experience provides a fresh and invigorating sense of what it must have been like to be an American reader of sacred works in the early nineteenth century.

The latter portions of the poem seem less to describe one particular place than to offer an arena for a roving lyricism that is prepared to take on virtually any subject and imbue it with an air of Palestine. With a Unitarian faith in the omnipresence of God's will, Pierpont permits divinity to infiltrate the mixed elements of the universe. His reference to an Italian boatman who throws his arms "round Vallombrosa" is an obvious attempt to evoke a Miltonic spirit of universality and deep Protestant piety, and the boatman's act initiates the most sustained lyrical sequence in the poem. The ecstasy of Pierpont's verse often seems to call attention to its own verbal celebration "above" the scene it depicts:

Hush'd by her silver sceptre, zephyrs sleep
On dewy leaves, that overhang the deep,
Nor dare to whisper through the boughs, nor stir
The valley's willow, nor the mountain's fir,
Nor make the pale and breathless aspen quiver,
Nor brush, with ruffling wing, that glassy river.

As in the case of William Cullen **Bryant**, it can be said with only some simplification that Pierpont uses neoclassical forms to express a definitely romantic content. His rhymes are generous and expressive, rejoicing in their power to create rhythm and excitement. Whatever the bounds in which his quite conventional heroic couplets held him, rhyme in "Airs of Palestine" is not just a background mechanism but a medium for a pervasive melody and musicality. In the poem, Pierpont describes a kaleidoscopic series of natural delights and spectacles and concludes that these sights and sounds, Palestinian in meaning if not in provenance, are all "music to Religion's ear." The power of the poet to hear God in nature engenders not just an aura of the sacred but a spiritual intensity that is almost electric.

"Airs of Palestine," although Pierpont's most ambitious work, is not characteristic of his mainstream poetic career. Most of his mature productions came out of his work as a Unitarian minister. These poems included some hymns, like the popular "O, Bow Thine Ear, Eternal One" (1823), and this soft, elevated doxology of the same year:

All glory in Thy wondrous name
Father of mercy, God of love

Exalted be the Lord, the Lamb
And thus we praise the heavenly Dove.

This attempt to provide a Unitarian equivalent to the credo of the established churches was among Pierpont's most widely broadcast compositions during his lifetime. He directed his spirituality to the outside world, however, more concertedly than he did toward churchly worship. A strong political activist who sought public office on two occasions (as a Liberty and then as a Free Soil candidate), Pierpont was an unshrinking advocate for both the temperance and abolitionist movements. No serene Brahmin, Pierpont loved the rough-and-tumble of partisan politics. In "A Word from a Petitioner" (LOA, 1: 66), Pierpont mounts a vigorous argument in favor of the American democratic system. In a riddling manner, he describes a "weapon" that is silent but "executes a freeman's will / As lightning does the will of God"; this weapon turns out to be a ballot-box. The ballot-box is pictured here as the great equalizer that, with an almost impersonal power, will weed out the right from the wrong, the virtuous from the corrupt. Its power is a permanent rebuke to those who would falsely assume the prerogatives of concentrated power. "The men that thicken in your rear, – / Kings though ye be, – may not be scorned. / Look to your move! your stake! – YE'RE WARNED!"

His colloquial diction and his innovations with punctuation and capitals illustrate that the meditative vein was not Pierpont's sole poetic option. His pride in the American commonwealth, exemplified in other poems such as the historical "Warren's Address at the Battle of Bunker Hill" (long a favorite in nineteenth-century elementary school curricula), resonates through all of his political verse, even when, as in his antislavery poems, he savagely castigates American society's own mockery of its stated ideals. Pierpont's works manifest a Whitmanian confidence in the potential of the democratic polity to augment its good fortune and to represent the truth; yet having participated in the political process, Pierpont was more attuned to democratic actuality than was Walt **Whitman's** visionary consciousness. Whitman, needless to say, possessed a more capacious vision of democracy, but Pierpont's faith in the American democratic system was unequaled; according to Pierpont, the ballot-box guaranteed that the truth will out and that the righteous will emerge victorious. This fervently libertarian belief was to be interpreted quite differently by his grandson, J. Pierpont Morgan.

The heart of Pierpont's political poetry, however, is his abolitionist verse. In the twentieth century, critics such as the Southern Agrarians would allege that abolitionism was somehow antiliterary, that its moralism and commitment to the idea of truth and righteousness fell short of aesthetic standards in a way that the moral ambiguity and political coalition-building of a writer like Nathaniel **Hawthorne** did not. More like Harriet Beecher Stowe than like Hawthorne, Pierpont had confidence that eloquent, moving poetry could help in the struggle to blot out the greatest inequity – to his fiercely religious mind, the greatest sin – that America would ever know. Pierpont's dedication, oratorical and otherwise, to the fight against slavery combined with his anti-temperance crusading to affront his colleagues and neighbors even in New England; he had to change parishes twice in a short number of years. "The Fugitive Slave's Apostrophe to the North Star" (LOA, 1: 67) displays the grandeur and the outrage of his abolitionist verse. Complex in its discursive operation, it is a monologue spoken by a slave who has escaped from the south and is hoping to flee to Canada, where he will be forever out of the reach of the federal authorities, who were constrained by what Pierpont considered an evil law to return slaves to their white owners. The slave addresses the North Star, which guides him to Canada, in a romantic trope of apostrophe: ironically, as Pierpont's subject-matter became more public, he adopted a quality of lyric introversion that would typically be more associated with a poem like "Airs of Palestine," whereas that earlier poem, however rhapsodic its vistas, remains external and meditative.

The apostrophized object is less an object than the negation of the uncertainty and anguish of the person addressing it. Whereas the slave is tired, afraid, oppressed, and outraged, the North Star, like the ballot-box in the earlier poem, presents an imperturbable impartiality that will sort out the inequities of the world and guide the benighted toward justice: "Thy light and truth shall set me free; – / Thy light, that no poor slave deceiveth; / Thy truth, that all my soul believeth."

The North Star is a pure polarity, a moral compass set out against the earthbound dross of political injustice. Making no attempt to mimic the "actual" speech rhythms of the fugitive slave (indeed, archaisms such as "thy" and "believeth" render the poem's language outside of nineteenth-century American living speech), Pierpont mounts a deliberately rhetorical and stagy argument that emphasizes the universal elements of the slave's situation in a way that would have maximum appeal to an educated, white readership. The slave's ordeal is linked to an ancient lineage of pathos, both historical and literary, represented by Pierpont's elevated diction and philosophy. Yet Pierpont does not for a moment deny that African Americans suffered very specific indignities and harbored concrete grievances against a system that spoke of liberty and justice but was so horribly inhumane.

Pierpont's Christianity intersects with his presentation of the fugitive slave in interesting ways. The slave makes an explicit typological parallel between the star "that over Bethlehem's manger glowed" and the star that guides people to freedom:

Wise were the men who followed thus
    The star that sets man free from sin!
Star of the North! Thou art to us, –
    Who're slaves because we wear a skin
Dark as is night's protecting wing, –
Thou art to us a holy thing.

Here, the North Star is the sign of a providential progress. But the same linkage to the biblical star that authorizes this symbolism also destabilizes it. The shift from an east-west to a north-south axis stresses the purely natural and astronomical nature of the North Star's illumination; its light is not a token of divine intervention, although Pierpont would surely assume that its representation of justice would meet with divine approval. Not explicitly invoking a biblical God who transcends the awesome majesty of the stars, Pierpont associates justice with a naturally premised order rather than with a supernatural mercy. The change of direction from east to north also has relevance to American politics in Pierpont's time. The slave's flight to the north runs against the providential direction of American history, the east-west course of manifest destiny. Pierpont combines relief and hope at the liberation of individual slaves with the shame that it is, paradoxically, the remaining North American colonies of Britain, the whipping-boy of American literary nationalists, that offer unimpinged liberty to African Americans. That the yearned-for home of freedom is Canada, not the fabled western prairies (themselves agonized sites of conflict over slavery's extension), contributes a bitter taste to Pierpont's celebrations of American liberty. The slave's praise of "England's Queen and English law" for extending sanctuary to him comments ironically on the fact that America's elected representatives and idealistic constitution have thus far failed in their mission.

Pierpont, again like Stowe, is as obviously orthodox in his Christian belief as he is staunch in his liberal political views. Yet, like Stowe in *Uncle Tom's Cabin* and *The Pearl of Orr's Island*, Pierpont, through a kind of "free reference," permits himself to unhinge Christian typological truisms and unsettle them by applying them to new situations where they assume and provoke different meanings. Pierpont's abolitionist discourse is thus hardly univocal and moralistic but filled with motility and transposition even as it heartily cries for the atrocity of slavery to be ended once and for all, for the American shame to be thoroughly repudiated. Pierpont's antislavery convictions never dimmed; indeed, well into his seventies, he insisted upon serving as a chaplain in the Civil War. Only the infirmity of age, which would lead to his death in 1866, prevented him from carrying out this duty.

It is one of the dominating circumstances of American literary studies that those writers who have traditionally been most valued by literary critics have stood (or, more truly, have been interpreted as standing) athwart the main currents of American political development, preferring a tragic sense of life and an aesthetic pathos to the workaday melodies of democracy and equality. Pierpont's strength as a poet lies in the way that he combines aesthetic beauty and liberal assertiveness. For him, democracy and poetry are not opponents, but partners.

NICHOLAS BIRNS

Selected Works
Airs of Palestine, 2nd ed., Boston: Wells and Lilly, 1817
The Anti-Slavery Poems, Upper Saddle River, New Jersey: Literature House/Gregg, 1978

Further Reading
Ahlstrom, Sydney, and Jonathan S. Cary, *American Reformation: A Documentary History of American Unitarianism*, Middletown, Connecticut: Wesleyan University Press, 1985
Davis, Moshe, *America and the Holy Land*, Westport, Connecticut: Praeger, 1995
Frothingham, Octavius Brooks, *Boston Unitarianism, 1820–1850*, New York: Putnam, 1890
Lader, Lawrence, *The Bold Brahmins*, New York: Dutton, 1961

McKivigan, John R., *The War Against Proslavery Religion: Abolitionism and the Northern Churches, 1830–1865*, Ithaca, New York: Cornell University Press, 1984

Moffat, R. Burnham, *Pierpont Genealogies: From Norman Times to 1913*, New York: Middleditch, 1913

Spiller, Robert, et al., *Literary History of the United States*, New York: Macmillan, 1974

Wright, Conrad, *American Unitarianism: 1805–1865*, Boston: Northeastern University Press, 1989

———, *The Liberal Christians*, Boston: Beacon, 1970

Edward Coote Pinkney

(1802–1828)

Pinkney was born in London, England, the son of William Pinkney, a United States commissioner there and, subsequently, minister plenipotentiary to the Court of St. James (1807–11), and Ann Maria Rodgers Pinkney, the sister of Commodore John Rodgers of the United States Navy. Pinkney was educated in England, and upon the return of the family to Maryland in June 1811, he attended St. Mary's College in Baltimore, Maryland, as a day student. In November 1815, he was appointed a midshipman in the United States Navy, presumably with the help of his uncle, Commodore Rodgers. He served on active duty until 1822, although he did not resign his commission until 1824, and participated in action against pirates; on one occasion, he was cited for bravery. Pinkney got into several scrapes over matters concerning his honor, and, in May 1820, was court-martialed and reprimanded for "disrespect to a superior officer." He published his first poem, "Serenade" (LOA, 1: 248), in January 1823, and shortly thereafter *Rodolph: A Fragment*.

The following autumn, Pinkney, outraged by some uncomplimentary remarks about his father in John **Neal's** *Randolph* (1823), challenged Neal to a duel, and when Neal refused to fight, Pinkney distributed handbills about the city characterizing Neal as one "unpossessed of courage to make satisfaction for the insolence of his folly." After resigning from the navy in September 1824, Pinkney was admitted to the bar and began to practice law in Baltimore. In the same year he married Georgiana McCausland, the daughter of a well-known businessman and the inspiration for some of his verses; a collection of these lyrics and other pieces came out the following year as *Poems*. Concurrently, he was appointed professor of rhetoric and belles-lettres at the University of Maryland, but when the law and teaching failed to provide a living, Pinkney went to Mexico to seek a commission in the Mexican navy under Commodore Porter. Upon failing to receive an appointment there, he returned to Baltimore in poor health and, in December 1827, became editor of the *Marylander*, a newspaper founded by supporters of John Quincy **Adams**. During the next four months, Pinkney devoted himself to the publication of editorials that attacked Andrew Jackson and that supported Adams, but his health was permanently damaged during his trip to Mexico, and he died on April 11, 1828, six months before his twenty-sixth birthday.

Pinkney's life, then, was as brief as Keats's, but his literary career was less productive. He published his first poem and his first book (actually a pamphlet) at the age of 20 and his last poem at the age of 25. His longest poem, *Rodolph*, is actually a "fragment" of only two parts and 23 stanzas. Many of his lyrics are short; they often treat themes of love and time and praise women and their beauty. A number of these are addressed to Mary Hawkins, who failed to return his love, and to Georgiana McCausland, during their courtship. They remind readers of works by the seventeenth-century Cavalier poets, but as T. O. Mabbott and Frank L. Pleadwell have pointed out, they actually owe more to Lord Byron, Sir Walter Scott, William Wordsworth, and Thomas Moore.

Such poems as "Serenade," "A Health" (LOA, 1: 248), and "On Parting" (LOA, 1: 249) suggest the qualities of melody, wit, and urbanity that we associate with the seventeenth-century lyrics that poets addressed to ladies. Pinkney's first published piece, "Serenade," addressed to Mary Hawkins, demonstrates well his promise and accomplishment along these lines, as its final stanza indicates:

Look out upon the stars, my love,
And shame them with thine eyes,
On which, than on the lights above,
There hang more destinies.
Night's beauty is the harmony
Of blending shades and lights;
Then, Lady, up, – look out, and be
A sister to the night! –

Reminiscent in theme, tone, and imagery (especially hyperbole) of Romeo's approach to Juliet and of Ben Jonson's "Drink to Me Only with Thine Eyes," the poem nevertheless stands on its own and is remarkable not only for its early appearance in Pinkney's career but also for its achievement at this early stage in the development of American poetry. The lyrics of Philip **Freneau** and William Cullen **Bryant** were its chief rivals in 1823.

"A Health" (1824), Pinkney's best-known poem then and now, adumbrates the qualities found in "Serenade" but is more serious in tone and intention, as its purported address to his wife may suggest. In the tradition of complimenting a lady's health and beauty, the poem takes its place with the best of its kind in Anglo-American song.

I fill this cup to one made up of loveliness alone,
A woman, of her gentle sex the seeming paragon;
To whom the better elements and kindly stars have
    given,
A form so fair, that, like the air, 'tis less of earth than
    heaven.

Having established the lady as a "paragon," the speaker proceeds to characterize her affectations, feelings, and passions as they are imaged in her "bright face" and "voice." He concludes:

I filled this cup to one made up of loveliness alone,
A woman, of her gentle sex the seeming paragon –
Her health! and would on earth there stood some more
    of such a frame,
That life might be all poetry, and weariness a name.

As is well known, Edgar Allan **Poe** thought highly of this poem for its "brilliancy and spirit" and for "the poetic elevation which it induces" ("The Poetic Principle," 1847), and twentieth-century critics – Mabbott, Jay B. Hubbell, and C. Michael Smith (*Fifty Southern Writers before 1900* [1987]), among them – have praised it as well.

"On Parting" (1823), on the other hand, displays a kind of reflective vein that is Wordsworthian. Its tone and mood are also suggested in "The Widow's Song" (1825; LOA, 1: 249) – "I burn no incense, hang no wreath, / On this, thine early tomb" – and in "Song" (1825):

> We break the glass, whose sacred wine
> To some beloved health we drain,
> Lest future pledges, less divine,
> Should e'er the hallowed toy profane.

And the ironies inherent in "thoughts" and "fears" are well expressed in "Evergreens" (1825):

> Thus thoughts that frown upon our mirth
>   Will smile upon our sorrow,
> And many dark fears of to-day
>   May be bright hopes to-morrow.

Another poem that Pinkney addressed to his wife, "To [Georgiana]" (1823), is explicitly linked "With Wordsworth's 'She was a Phantom of Delight'" – a "portrait of thee," of which the speaker claims:

> Time may mar
> All meaner sculpture of my mind,
> But in its darkness, like a star,
> Thy semblance shall remain enshrined.
> Nor would I that the sullen thing
> Its place in being should resign,
> While, like a casket rich with gems,
> It treasures forms so fair as thine.

A slightly longer poem, "Italy" (1824; LOA, 1: 243), reveals not only the narrator's feeling for his "Beloved" but expresses a similar emotion for "the land which lovers ought to choose" – Italy – "that delightful spot" where "nature is delicate and graceful" and "the speaking ruins in that gentle clime / Have but been hallowed by the hand of Time."

An even longer and more forceful poem, "The Voyager's Song" (1825; LOA, 1: 244), is Pinkney's most successful ode. Composed of six 10-line stanzas, each with a truncated last line and a rhyme scheme of *ababccdede*, the lyric is a kind of dramatic monologue in which Ponce de León exhorts his followers to seek Bimini, where the fountain of youth may be found. In words not unlike those Alfred, Lord Tennyson's Ulysses (1842) uses to rally his men to "seek a newer world" and to "sail beyond the sunset, and the baths / of all the western stars," de León speaks to his men:

> Onward, my friends, to that bright, florid isle,
> The jewel of a smooth and silver sea,
> With springs on which perennial summers smile
> A power of causing immortality.

The great theme, of course, is the overcoming of time by means of the "wondrous waters" with their promise of "perpetual life." Along the way, the speaker turns from his men to address "Miranda" – the beautiful one who represents the "brave new world" mentioned by Prospero's daughter Miranda in Shakespeare's *The Tempest* – and contemplates the future with her:

> The envious years, which steal our pleasures, thou
> May'st call at once, like magic memory, back,

And, as they pass o'er thine unwithering brow,
Efface their footsteps ere they form a track.
Thy bloom with wilful weeping never stain,
Perpetual life must not belong to pain.
For me, – this world hath not yet been a place
Conscious of joys so great as will be mine,
Because the light has kissed no face
Forever fair as thine.

Pinkney's longest poem, *Rodolph*, was published first as a pamphlet in 1823 and in a revised but still incomplete form in 1825. It contains 554 lines in a style made popular by Scott, Byron, and Moore. Rhyme schemes vary from stanza to stanza, but the couplet dominates throughout. Offering a narrative of lawless love and murder in the Byronic tradition, Pinkney focuses on the psychological state of his hero and displays his own intellectual interests and learning in allusions and references to a wide range of ancient and modern lore. But the poem remains, after all, a "fragment" and not as important an achievement as his short poems.

These lyrics constitute a body of work that entitles Pinkney to consideration as a significant poet of the 1820s. "Serenade," "A Health," "Evergreens," "Song" ("We break the Glass"), "The Widow's Song," and a few others are close to a perfection of their kind and establish a voice inimitably Pinkney's own. Admittedly, his corpus is small – the poems cover only 98 pages in the Mabbott and Pleadwell edition of the *Life and Works* (1926) – but Pinkney, after all, died at the age of 25, and during this brief span spent much of his time in the navy and in the practice of law and in journalism. A minor poet he may be. An inheritor of unfulfilled renown he obviously is. But his best work is finely crafted, intriguing, and worthy of serious consideration, especially in a day when craftsmanship and artistry are frequently unappreciated and undervalued.

RAYBURN S. MOORE

Selected Works

"Serenade" ("Look Out Upon the Stars, My Love"), Baltimore, Maryland: John Cole, 1823
Rodolph: A Fragment, Baltimore, Maryland: Joseph Robinson, 1823
Poems, Baltimore, Maryland: Joseph Robinson, 1825; reprinted, New York: Arno Press, 1838, 1844, 1972
The Life and Works of Edward Coote Pinkney, edited by Thomas Ollive Mabbott and Frank Lester Pleadwell, New York: Macmillan, 1926

Further Reading

Duyckinck, Evert A., and George L. Duyckinck, eds., *Cyclopedia of American Literature*, vol. 2, New York: Charles Scribner, 1856, pp. 338–341
Hubbell, Jay B., *The South in American Literature, 1607–1900*, Durham, North Carolina: Duke University Press, 1954
Rubin, Louis D., Jr., et al., *The History of Southern Literature*, Baton Rouge: Louisiana State University Press, 1985

Edgar Allan Poe

(1809–1849)

"With me poetry has been not a purpose, but a passion," wrote Edgar Allan Poe in the preface to his volume *The Raven and Other Poems* (1845). Yet, apart from some juvenilia and fugitive verses, his poetic legacy consists of only some 70 poems. Poe's extensive oeuvre is comprised of his tales of detection, exploration, and horror; two novellas; political satires; philosophical colloquies; a cosmological prose poem over 100 pages long; critical essays on poetics; over 300 reviews of contemporary books of all kinds, from the fiction of Washington Irving, Nathaniel **Hawthorne**, and Charles Dickens and the poems of Elizabeth Barrett Browning and Henry Wadsworth **Longfellow** to ephemeral verses by Elizabeth Oakes Smith and S. Anna Lewis; the introduction to a book on shellfish; a series of character sketches of the literati based on analyses of their handwriting; "Marginalia," his notes on a miscellany of literary topics; and other journalism. In this life of busy hackwork for magazines, Poe managed to perfect two forms of fiction – the mystery and the horror tale – that have made him have a greater influence on the popular culture of our century than any other writer of the nineteenth century. His essays on poetics – written "not above the popular, nor below the critical taste" – defined the art and the work of the poet, influencing the French symbolists and, through them, T. S. Eliot, Wallace Stevens, and other modernist poets.

Compared to the voluminous work of Walt **Whitman**, or the 1,775 lyrics left us by Emily **Dickinson**, Poe's output makes a meager offering. His verse has been attacked for its mechanical meters, inflated diction, and other infelicities, yet few poets of his century beside those just named have been as widely read in our time as Poe, or have contributed to our national culture such unforgettable poems as "To Helen" (LOA, 1: 522), "Israfel" (LOA, 1: 523), "The City in the Sea" (LOA, 1: 525), "The Raven" (LOA, 1: 535), "Ulalume" (LOA, 1: 540), "The Bells" (LOA, 1: 543), and "Annabel Lee" (LOA, 1: 550). To these, among Poe's essential poems, let us add "Romance" (LOA, 1: 520), "Alone" (LOA, 1: 522), "To Science" (LOA, 1: 508), and "Lenore" (LOA, 1: 532). A careful reading will show that while consistency of theme striates all of these, in mode, in form, and in diction they are by no means alike, although Poe's unmistakable handprint marks every line.

The author of these works was born in Boston, Massachusetts, on January 19, 1809, to Elisabeth Arnold Poe, a British-born actress of great beauty, charm, and popularity, and David Poe, son of a Revolutionary quartermaster general from Baltimore, Maryland. David Poe also trod the boards, but with so little talent as to be derided in the press. Edgar had a brother, William Henry, and a sister, Rosalie; when Edgar was a year old, his father, drinking heavily, deserted the family. Elizabeth Poe went on tour with little Eddie in her care; his siblings were raised by relatives in Baltimore. When Edgar was two, his mother, at liberty in Richmond, Virginia, fell ill with consumption and died a lingering death in a boardinghouse, attended by sympathetic Richmond matrons. One of these, Frances Allan, herself childless, took in the orphaned boy.

Her husband, John Allan, was an ambitious, self-righteous tobacco merchant who took his family along when he went on business to London, 1815–20. While there Edgar attended a school in Stoke Newington (described in his tale "William Wilson"). By 1825, Allan, inheriting a legacy, was a wealthy man, and, although he was never adopted, Edgar grew up in expectation of becoming Allan's heir. Allan, however, required that Edgar take part in his business and had a utilitarian contempt for the boy's literary ambitions and strivings. Their relationship was filled with tension, exacerbated after Mrs. Allan's death (also from consumption) and John Allan's remarriage. Allan sent Edgar to the newly established University of Virginia on a paltry allowance; there, surrounded by the profligate sons of wealthy planters, Poe ran up gambling debts and tailors' bills that Allan refused to pay. Returning to Richmond, Poe quarreled with Allan and left home in 1827. Henceforth, he lived a precarious life. He made his way to Boston, where he published his first book, *Tamerlane and Other Poems. By a Bostonian.* This volume, containing the title poem, a narrative of 400 lines, and nine lyrics, created no stir whatever. Its penniless author enlisted in the U. S. Army, signing on as "Edgar A. Perry" since a gentleman would not serve as an enlisted man. In 1830, with the intercession of John Allan, Poe qualified for the U. S. Military Academy at West Point under his own name, but after serving a year he appealed to Allan to secure his release; when Allan refused, Poe got himself dismissed for neglect of duty. Nonetheless, he dedicated his volume *Poems,* by "Edgar A. Poe" (1831), "To the U.S. Corps of Cadets," and a decade later he canvassed his one-time classmates in the corps for contributions to support a magazine of his own – a project in which he was never successful.

After West Point, Poe moved in with his aunt, Maria Clemm, and her eight-year-old daughter Virginia in Baltimore. When his cousin Virginia turned 14, Poe married her. She and Mrs. Clemm (whom he called "Ma") comprised Poe's only stable family, whom he tried to support on the meager salary of a magazine editor, which was augmented by small payments for poems, stories, and essays. Poe was an editor, successively, of the *Southern Literary Messenger* in Richmond, 1835–36; *Burton's Gentleman's Magazine*, Philadelphia, 1839–40; *Graham's Magazine*, 1841–42; the *New York Evening Mirror*, 1844–45; and, on borrowed money, he became editor and proprietor of the *Broadway Journal*, 1845–46. These brief tenures reflect Poe's "tetchy" disposition, his quarreling with employers over salary and editorial decisions, and his drinking (Poe alternated periods of sobriety with disabling binges). Despite these spells of insensibility and their consequences, he produced a prodigious amount of work and was a very successful editor; he increased the subscription list of his employers' journals with his exacting literary reviews and by offering readers prizes for the solution of cryptograms. (The author of "The Gold Bug" was fascinated with secret writings and codes.)

Virginia Poe, trained as a singer, spat blood one day – the first sign of the consumption from which, after a lingering illness, she died at age 23, in 1847. Poe, ill himself, depressed, half-mad with grief and loneliness, courted several literary women simultaneously, including a childhood sweetheart in Richmond whom he visited in hopes of arranging a marriage. Unsuccessful, on his way back to New York he stopped in Baltimore and was found delirious in a gutter under conditions still unexplained. Taken to a hospital, he died four days later, on October 7, 1849.

According to Poe biographers from Marie Bonaparte to Kenneth Silverman, the key events in this sad life were the successive wasting illnesses and deaths of Poe's mother, stepmother, and wife. The agonizing deaths of the women from whom he sought security and comfort surely marked his imagination in ways reflected in his tales and poems – particularly his poems; his fiction has a wider range of theme and feeling, including satires, hoaxes offered as aggression against his readers, and, in his tales of detection, ratiocinative plots for which there is little room in his verses.

In Poe's first volume of poems, *Tamerlane*, published when he was 18, the concluding poem, "The Lake" (LOA, 1: 507 for a later variant), demonstrates not only his precocious facility but a strangeness, an original conception of theme. The genre to which "The Lake" belongs is the nature poem, much practiced by such American followers of William Wordsworth as William Cullen **Bryant** (as in "Inscription for the Entrance to a Wood" [LOA, 1: 126]), Ralph Waldo **Emerson** ("Musketaquid" [LOA, 1: 308], "The Rhodora" [LOA 1: 272], "Woodnotes" [LOA, 1: 275], and "Monadnoc" [LOA, 1: 280]), and Longfellow ("Autumn" [LOA, 1: 390] and "Snow-Flakes" [LOA, 1: 423]). In such poems, the poet feels identified with the spirit of nature, a source of benignity and beauty. But the young Poe chooses to memorialize "a wild lake, with black rock bound":

> My infant spirit would awake
> To the terror of the lone lake.
> Yet that terror was not fright –
> But a tremulous delight.
> And a feeling undefined
> Springing from a darken'd mind.
> Death was in that poisoned wave
> And in its gulf a fitting grave
> For him who thence could solace bring
> To his lone imagining –
> Whose solitary soul could make
> An Eden of that dim lake.

Poe's originality is still more striking in his sonnet "To Science," the introductory poem to the verse epic "Al Aaraaf" (LOA, 1: 508), from which his second volume, published in 1829, derived its title.

> Science! True daughter of Old Time thou art!
>   Who alterest all things with thy peering eyes.
> Why preyest thou thus upon the poet's heart,
>   Vulture, whose wings are dull realities?

Readers are prone to assume that Poe is attacking science, the Cartesian tradition, and intellectual analysis, since the "dull realities" that hold science aloft are the enemies of imagination and prevent the poet from "his wandering / To seek for treasure in the jewelled skies." This antipathetic force has "driven the Hamadryad from the wood / To seek a shelter in some happier star." All this is so, but overlooks a major symbol contributing to the sonnet's meaning. The image of a vulture or condor, as Richard Wilbur pointed out in his introduction to the Laurel edition of Poe's *Poems* (1959), recurs often in Poe's writings and always represents the destructiveness of time, the ultimate enemy of our happiness. The vulture or condor feeds on carrion, which is to imply that it destroys mortality, and mortality, because imprisoned in the realm of time, is inexorably subject to change, death, and decay. But the poetic imagination would soar free of this subjection to contemplate and express unchanging perfection, beauty, which is found on "some happier star." As the next poem makes clear, that star is Al Aaraaf. In this poem, the formal execution is impressive, as Poe combines with the rhyme scheme of the Shakespearean sonnet the development of theme characteristic of the Petrarchan form.

Poe's non-adoptive foster father, John Allan, had no clue to the scope or relevance of his contrary young charge's ambition. Allan was not the man to infer from young Edgar's seven-mile swim in the James River, in emulation of, or rivalry with, Lord Byron's swimming the Hellespont, how grandiose were his literary aims. At 20, Poe had conceived, and in "Al Aaraaf" (LOA, 1: 508–19) attempted to embody, a cosmology, a philosophical aesthetic that enshrined imagination and gave it dominion over a realm untouched by the baseness of human passions or experience of the time-bound world. The 422 lines of this poem (just a dozen shorter than *The Waste Land*) show Poe's borrowings from John Milton and from Thomas Moore's then popular *Lalla Rookh* – strange juxtaposition! – in a plot of his own devising. Poe, an omnivorous reader, seized on an encyclopedia account of the observations of the Danish astronomer Tycho Brahe, who in 1572–74 recorded the sudden appearance and subsequent fading away of a bright star – what we now know to have been a supernova – in the constellation Cassiopeia. Poe also read, in George Sale's translation of the Koran (1734), a passage describing "Al Araf" as a sort of limbo between heaven and hell where reside those "whose good and evil works are so equal that they . . . deserve neither reward nor punishment and will, on the last day be admitted to paradise, after they perform an act of adoration." Poe boldly transformed this description, locating Al Aaraaf on Tycho Brahe's star now vanished from human sight, and making it the realm of Nesace, the spirit of beauty. Here, on this happier star that is foretold in his sonnet, passion, such as that between the demispirits Ianthe and Angelo (Michelangelo Buonarroti), has no place. "They fell: for Heaven to them no hope imparts, / Who hear not for the beating of their hearts." What they "hear not" is the harmony of the spheres whose avatar is described thus:

> Ligeia! wherever
>   Thy image may be,
> No magic shall sever
>   Thy music from thee.

Later, in his essay "The Philosophy of Composition" (1846), Poe decided that a true poem must be readable at a single sitting and should not exceed the length of 100 lines, which tacitly admits that "Al Aaraaf" failed by his own measure. What it succeeds in doing, however, is in making specific the aim that Poe's poems will attempt to fulfill. This aim is to enact the autonomy of the imagination in its own self-generated and self-contained universe of dreams, where beauty is its subject and the baseness of the world, subject to the decay of time, is left behind by the poet's vision of a happier star.

At this point, it is useful to consider "The Philosophy of Composition," the essay that purports to explain how Poe wrote "The Raven" (1845), since it so clearly states the principles enacted by his other poems. The reason for limiting the poem to 100 lines is that its objective is the excitation of the reader's soul, an effect a longer poem can only intermittently achieve. Everything in the poem must contribute to this effect – rhythm, sound, rhyme, and especially subject. The optimum subject for producing this effect is the most melancholy, the emotion educed by the contemplation of the death of a beautiful woman. Poe reasons back from the text of "The Raven" to the putative choices by which he claims it was written. Although the poem is driven by an unassuageable emotion, Poe claims that its composition resulted from a series of interlocked conscious choices. Over these details we need not pause, but the importance of this essay lies in its portrayal of the poetic act of creation not as a spontaneous overflowing of inspiration but as the conscious embodiment in verse by a craftsman of his predetermined ideas. Poe's presentation of the poet as maker, rather than, as with other romantics, as finder, greatly influenced French and American poetry and criticism.

Poe's reasoning, or, as he called that faculty, his ratiocinative mind, represents one aspect of his sensibility – the opposite, as it were, of his romanticism, with its emphasis on both the exploration of extreme psychological states of terror and guilt, and the transcendence of such emotions in ideality. Poe takes certain aspects of romanticism to their limits – his tales of terror and poems of being haunted by lost loves probe and dramatize these states of feeling with a specificity and depth beyond their appearances in the poems of Samuel Taylor Coleridge or in earlier Gothic novels such as Horace Walpole's *The Castle of Otranto*. At the same time, Poe inherits the Enlightenment's rage for order and systematization. His psyche is deeply divided; he adopts the eighteenth century's facultative psychology, which separates intellect, emotion, and moral sense. In his critical writings, he proclaims that poetry must deal only with beauty, not with truth or virtue, which are subjects fit for prose. Thus, he fixes, as with an exclusionary lens, upon only one side of Coleridge's aesthetic and debars from poetry almost all the *materia poetica* as the rest of the world apprehends it.

Despite, or because of, these divisions in his mind and psyche, Poe at the same time is driven by a need to unify all that his philosophy proclaims is divided. In his tales of detection and the best of his critical essays and reviews, his mind quite brilliantly analyzes and constructs an intellectually comprehensible order. His criticism was the first in America that was rigorously devoted to enforcing literary standards.

Two brief lyrics define the poet's fate and his role. "Alone" (LOA, 1: 522), inscribed in the album of a woman friend but not collected by Poe or published until 1875, 26 years after his death, described the poet's sense of his separation from humanity. "From childhood's hour I have not been / As others were," nor has he "seen / As others saw."

I could not bring
My passions from a common spring –

. . . .
And all I lov'd – *I* lov'd alone –
Then – in my childhood – in the dawn
Of a most stormy life – was drawn
From ev'ry depth of good and ill
The mystery which binds me still –
From the torrent, or the fountain –
From the red cliff of the mountain –
. . . .
From the thunder, and the storm –
And the cloud that took the form
(When the rest of Heaven was blue)
Of a demon in my view –

This demon is the spirit compelling the poet to write down his vision. It will be seen that the particulars of nature enumerated here are listed only to be disregarded; his demon will compel him to obliterate the tactile world.

Like Poe's sonnet "To Science," his poem "Romance" (LOA, 1: 520) was prefaced to "Al Aaraaf." This lyric also dwells on his fated childhood, in which "Romance, who loves to nod and sing, / With drowsy head and folded wing" taught the poet his alphabet and earliest word. Romance appears to him "a painted paroquet" – this spirit of poetry is itself an image, not a real speaking bird. As in "To Science," the poet is menaced by a rival bird, "eternal Condor years" that "So shake the very Heaven on high / With tumult" that the poet has "no time for idle cares." Yet when a calmer hour invites him "with lyre and rhyme / To while away" his time in "forbidden things," his heart would feel it "to be a crime / Unless it trembled with the strings." Here, the poet's heart is transfigured as an aeolian harp, an image Poe will use again in "Israfel" (LOA, 1: 523).

That poem is prefaced by a motto that Poe attributed to the Koran (it is actually from the commentary of its translator, Sale): "And the angel Israfel, whose heart-strings are a lute, and who has the sweetest voice of all God's creatures."

In Heaven a spirit doth dwell
    "Whose heart-strings are a lute;"
None sing so wildly well
As the angel Israfel,
And the giddy stars (so legends tell)
Ceasing their hymns, attend the spell
    Of his voice, all mute.

Poe boldly elaborates a passage from the end of Moore's *Lalla Rookh* describing "Israfil, the Angel," of whose song "none knew whether / The voice or lute was most divine, / So wondrously they went together." Mythologizing Moore's subject, Poe has his Israfel sing "ecstasies above" since heaven is his, while we mortals must make our songs in this world where "the shadow of thy perfect bliss / Is the sunshine of ours." The earthbound celebrant of the angel's heavenly song concludes,

If I could dwell
Where Israfel
    Hath dwelt, and he where I,
He might not sing so wildly well
    A mortal melody,
While a bolder note than this might swell
    From my lyre within the sky.

Poe's aesthetic inevitably burdened many of his lines with abstract diction, but several of his lyrics are distinguished, as we have seen, by their combinations of clarity, concision, and verbal music. The cameo masterpiece among Poe's poems is "To Helen" (LOA, 1: 522). Two cruxes in the text may require explanation. In line two, "those Nicéan barks of yore" alludes to the Grecian vessels sailing home after the Trojan War ("Nicéan" is Poe's spelling of Nikean, dedicated to Nike, goddess of victory); and "thy hyacinth hair" in line seven describes not a color but a hairdo – set in tight curls, like the petals of a hyacinth. With those puzzles clarified, we can see that the poem offers a four-stage description of Helen. First, she is the beautiful woman for whose sake the war was fought and for whom "the weary, way-worn wanderer" returns "to his own native shore." In the course of his journey ("On desperate seas long wont to roam"), her features and her "Naiad airs" have brought him "home / To the glory that was Greece, / And the grandeur that was Rome" – which is to say, Helen, now a Naiad or spirit, has returned her worshipper to his native shore, the world of classical perfection. In the final stanza, however, she is transformed yet again; now "in yon brilliant window-niche / How statue-like" she stands, as though an image of the Virgin in a cathedral. There, in her final transformation, she holds aloft "the agate lamp," which reveals her as "Psyche, from the regions which / Are Holy-Land!" Thus, Poe has his reader ascend with him a Platonic ladder of love, moving from love of the beauty of a woman to its culmination in which she personifies Psyche, his soul; and the "native shore" to which he, following her, has returned is not Achaia, not Greece or Rome, but "Holy-Land." Here, the philosophical idealism so copiously expounded in "Al Aaraaf" is condensed into 15 lines that move with surety, swiftness, and grace unparalleled elsewhere in Poe's canon, as if these strophes were indeed struck upon the lyre of Israfel.

In "Fairy-Land" (LOA, 1: 520), "The Valley of Unrest" (LOA, 1: 524), "The City in the Sea" (LOA, 1: 525), and "Dream-Land" (LOA, 1: 533), Poe attempts to have his soul approach the Eden or Holy Land that are envisaged in other poems by obliterating the base life that he would escape. In "The City in the Sea," there are "shrines and palaces and towers" that "resemble nothing that is ours"; in this city of the dead, "On the long night-time of that town," light comes not from heaven but "from out the lurid sea," streaming up domes, spires, fanes, and walls –

> Up many and many a marvellous shrine
> Whose wreathéd friezes intertwine
> The viol, the violet, and the vine.

In other words, the realms of music, natural beauty, and intoxication in which we seek in art similitudes of the beauty of nature, are all subsumed by the weird supernal light from below.

> So blend the turrets and shadows there
> That all seem pendulous in air,
> While from a proud tower in the town
> Death looks gigantically down.

These lines, with their reverberating grandiloquence, create an effect at once compelling, disturbing, and mysterious. As the city sinks beneath the sea, "Down, down that town shall settle hence. / Hell rising from a thousand thrones, / Shall do it reverence."

Although this must be a city of ghosts, none is to be seen; the exact significance of the apocalyptic tableau is masked in the indefinable terror that it evokes. Elsewhere, in my 1972 study, I have attempted to define this terror:

> Poe is describing, with his customary energy and invention, the most dramatic moment in all human perception: the End of Everything. For some poets the most dramatic moment is the union of the soul with nature, for others the juncture of soul with soul in the physical union of love. For Poe it is the death of the universe. (Hoffman, 58)

In "Dream-Land" Poe sets out to annihilate the real world, describing "bottomless vales and boundless floods," formless chasms and caves, and "mountains toppling evermore / Into seas without a shore" – a lengthy catalog of self-destructing natural features, passage through which leads "the spirit that walks in shadow" to "an Eldorado" that can be beheld only "through darkened glasses."

> By a route obscure and lonely,
> Haunted by ill angels only,
> Where an Eidolon, named NIGHT,
> On a black throne reigns upright,
> I have reached these lands but newly
> From an ultimate dim Thule –
> From a wild weird clime that lieth, sublime,
> Out of SPACE – out of TIME.

Cognate with this theme are two poems that Poe inserts in his most famous short stories as epitomes of the stories' meaning: "The Haunted Palace" (LOA, 1: 529), from "The Fall of the House of Usher," and "The Conqueror Worm" (LOA, 1: 531), from "Ligeia." In the latter tale, the nameless narrator has married the lady Ligeia, who, like her namesake in "Al Aaraaf," represents the harmony of the universe: all wisdom issues from her eyes. He worships her, but Ligeia sickens and dies, and the narrator, wild with grief, after a time remarries. His second wife is Rowena, whom he installs in a bedchamber of psychedelic terrors, for he hates her. While he is in an opium trance, she, too, sickens and dies – and in her death throes is transformed into Ligeia. The poem "The Conqueror Worm" is spoken by Ligeia. She envisages our life as a play that is watched in a theater by angels – a play with "much of Madness, and more of Sin, / And Horror the soul of the plot." In this spectacle, mimes, puppets, and phantoms "Flapping from out their Condor wings / Invisible Wo[e]" act out a "motley drama" that appalls even the visiting angels, who,

> all pallid and wan,
> Uprising, unveiling, affirm
> That the play is the tragedy, "Man,"
> And its hero the Conqueror Worm.

The poem is vivid, but not nearly as effective as the tale of "Ligeia."

Death triumphs in "The Conqueror Worm," but in "The Haunted Palace" we find an allegory of a mind going mad. The palace is the head, "In the monarch Thought's dominion," where wanderers "through two luminous windows [the eyes], saw / Spirits moving musically, / To a lute's well-tunéd law."

This is a scene such as Israfel might sing – the harmony is celebrated by

> A troop of Echoes whose sweet duty
>   Was but to sing,
> In voices of surpassing beauty,
>   The wit and wisdom of their king.

> But evil things, in robes of sorrow,
>   Assailed the monarch's high estate.

"Vast forms that move fantastically / To a discordant melody" displace the Echoes, while "A hideous throng rush out forever."

This song is prophetically sung by Roderick Usher, as one of his artworks (he composes a guitar rhapsody and a symbolic painting, too), while his sister languishes in the tomb in which he has buried her alive. From the tomb she will emerge, to fall upon him as the house falls, and all disappear in the dark tarn that bears the reflection of the affrighted House of Usher. The whole tale is a fable of dissolution, of a mind, of a soul, of a family, and of a world: the end of everything.

It will be inferred from these bald plot summaries that both tales involve, as Poe said a poem must, the deaths of beautiful women. This, the most melancholy of themes, is the burden of Poe's literary ballads, "Lenore," "The Raven," "Ulalume," and "For Annie" (LOA, 1: 546). These are the poems most responsible for Poe's unending popularity. Among them are those that have attracted the most denigration, even derision, for their inflated and pretentious diction, their mind-deadening repetitions, and their commitment to draconian rhyme-schemes and mechanical meters. Although these characteristics are indeed true, a defense of Poe's practice is in order.

By definition, a ballad is a narrative in verse, intended to be sung and characterized by rhyme, strong metrical stresses, and, often, refrains. The literary ballad imitates folk balladry but inevitably differs from such originals in its more complex structure and in diction that has not worn smooth through generations of oral transmission. In the case of Poe's ballads, it must be emphasized that they are designed to illustrate the sort of verbal music that he invokes in several of the poems discussed above, although the taste of his time was more tolerant than ours of the incessant rhyming and unvaried meters that he uses. Further, Poe's ballads are intended to be recited aloud rather than read silently to oneself, and each is spoken by an invented character – Guy De Vere, the bereaved lover in "Lenore" and, it is probable, also in "The Raven"; the mourner is not named in "Ulalume" or "For Annie." Therefore, these ballads should be interpreted as dramatic monologues. The seeming excrescences of style in fact dramatize the mental state of the speakers. Thus, the rhodomontade of "Ulalume," with its manic repetitions, its inch-by-inch progression, and its wildly inflated diction, represents the grief-maddened quest of its speaker. He unwittingly seeks, on All Souls' Night, the tomb of his lost love Ulalume. He wanders past "this dank tarn of Auber" (the line invokes the composer of a then-familiar orchestral suite, "Le Lac des Fées") and "this ghoul-haunted woodland of Weir" (a painter of the Hudson River school). So the tomb of his lost love is in a ghoul-haunted fairyland, which is depicted only in the imaginings of artists. In this poem, as in "Lenore" and "The Raven" – to say nothing of "The Bells" –

Poe is virtuosic in creating compulsive structures of rhythm, rhyme, and interior rhyme, which all conspire to compel the reader's attention. Poe means to lull the reader's cognitive mind, to make it unresisting in the presence of meanings suggested in the poems by images and symbols. Thus, in "The Raven" (LOA, 1: 535), the bereaved scholar in his study contrives a series of queries that can be answered only by the ominous bird's single-word vocabulary, "nevermore." Such sounds as "the silken, sad uncertain rustling of each purple curtain" draw a spell across our conscious minds, which in turn makes us accept as true the unlikely scenario, accept as inevitable its development and denouement:

> And the Raven, never flitting, still is sitting, *still* is
>   sitting
> On the pallid bust of Pallas just above my chamber
>   door;
> And his eyes have all the seeming of a demon's that is
>   dreaming,
> And the lamp-light o'er him streaming throws his
>   shadow on the floor;
> And my soul from out that shadow that lies floating on
>   the floor
>   Shall be lifted – nevermore!

In "For Annie" and "Annabel Lee," the hysterical magniloquence of the foregoing ballads gives way to a lyrical style that invokes surcease – in "For Annie," from "the fever called 'Living,'" and, in "Annabel Lee," from an incurable nostalgia, an unassuageable longing for his lost love.

With a score of poems and half a dozen essays, Poe left his mark upon the poetry of the succeeding century and a half, for he provided the theoretical grounding and justification for the symbolist and modernist movements. Isolating the aesthetic impulse from the pursuit of morality or truth, Poe enshrined imagination and made of poetry (and, by implication, all other arts) a self-creating, self-sufficing empery; he empowers the poet, who, by his fealty to the laws by which his art produces its desired effects, elevates the souls of his readers while expressing the inescapable depths of his own. Poe's aesthetic requires the imagined annihilation of the physical world and the suppression or evasion of human passion; otherwise, the poet remains a prisoner of the destructive element, time. Thus, Poe strove to strike upon his lyre the hymns of angels. As Richard Wilbur concludes, "There has never been a grander conception of poetry, nor a more impoverished one."

Poe's poetry is but a portion of his oeuvre; in fiction he could admit into the materials of his art a range of feeling and experience that his aesthetic banished from his poems. The underlying assumptions on which all his writings rest are fully explicated in his astonishing long prose poem, *Eureka*, a treatise based on the most advanced astronomical knowledge of the time, which presents the universe as "a plot of God." Poe's work is at once complex and consistent. Indeed, although he "could not bring / [his] passions from a common spring," Poe's work explores dark recesses and illuminates transcendent ideals widely shared. The very extremities of his sensibility, arising from a life of peculiarly individual circumstances and sufferings, give his writings universal relevance.

DANIEL HOFFMAN

Selected Works

Poe (complete poems), introduction by Richard Wilbur, New York: Laurel Poetry Series, Dell, 1959

The Poems of Edgar Allan Poe, edited by Floyd Stovall, Charlottesville: University Press of Virginia, 1965

The Poems of Edgar Allan Poe, edited by Thomas Ollive Mabbott, Cambridge, Massachusetts: Belknap, 1969

Edgar Allan Poe: Poetry and Tales, edited by Patrick Quinn, New York: Library of America, 1984

Edgar Allan Poe: Essays and Reviews, edited by G. R. Thompson, New York: Library of America, 1984

Further Reading

Bonaparte, Marie, *The Life and Works of Edgar Allan Poe, A Psycho-Analytic Interpretation*, London: Imago, 1933

Booth, Bradford Allen, and Claude E. Jones, *A Concordance of the Poetical Works of Edgar Allan Poe*, Baltimore, Maryland: Johns Hopkins University Press, 1941

Budd, Louis J., and Edwin H. Cady, eds., *On Poe: The Best from 'American Literature'*, Durham, North Carolina: Duke University Press, 1993

Carlson, Eric W., ed., *Critical Essays on Edgar Allan Poe*, Boston: G. K. Hall, 1987

———, *The Recognition of Edgar Allan Poe*, Ann Arbor: University of Michigan Press, 1966

Dameron, J. Lasley, and I. B. Cauthen, *Edgar Allan Poe: A Bibliography of Criticism, 1827–1967*, Charlottesville: University Press of Virginia, 1974

Davidson, Edward H., *Poe, A Critical Study*, Cambridge, Massachusetts: Belknap, 1966

Hoffman, Daniel, *Poe Poe Poe Poe Poe Poe Poe*, Garden City, New York: Doubleday, 1972; reprinted, New York: Marlowe, 1990

Hyneman, Esther F., *Edgar Allan Poe: An Annotated Bibliography of Books and Articles, 1827–1973*, Boston: G. K. Hall, 1974

Jackson, Dwight Thomas, and David K. Jackson, *The Poe Log: A Documentary Life of Edgar Allan Poe 1809–1849*, Boston: G. K. Hall, 1987

Meyers, Jeffrey, *Edgar Allan Poe, His Life and Legacy*, New York: Scribner's, 1992

Quinn, Arthur Hobson, *Edgar Allan Poe: A Critical Biography*, New York: D. Appleton-Century, 1941

Regan, Robert, ed., *Poe: A Collection of Critical Essays*, Englewood Cliffs, New Jersey: Prentice-Hall, 1967

Silverman, Kenneth, *Edgar A. Poe: Mournful and Never-Ending Remembrance*, New York: HarperCollins, 1991

Stovall, Floyd, *Edgar Poe the Poet*, Charlottesville: University Press of Virginia, 1969

Walker, I. M., *Edgar Allan Poe, The Critical Heritage*, London and New York: Routledge and Kegan Paul, 1986

Wilbur, Richard, *Responses, Prose Pieces, 1953–1976*, New York: Harcourt Brace Jovanovich, 1976

Wiley, Elizabeth, *Concordance to the Poetry of Edgar Allan Poe*, Selingsgrove, Pennsylvania: Susquehanna University Press, 1989

Wright, George T., ed., *Seven American Literary Stylists from Poe to Mailer*, Minneapolis: University of Minnesota Press, 1973

Popular Poetry

Popular American poetry of the nineteenth century is a part of the history of popular and mass culture. To propose a working description of popular poetry that draws on its status as a category of popular culture: popular poems are commercial productions intended to reach as large an audience as possible. In form and message, popular poetry must appeal to and express widely shared tastes and assumptions. The popular success of a poem depends on its being readily understood and on its delivering to the audience meanings and values that they already hold – capturing in repeatable form a structure of feeling that is already among them. Conventional formulas for heightening the surprise of recognition when the familiar is unfolded are thus of far more value to popular poetry than formal originality. Popular poetry also responds to the conditions of its reproduction and distribution; for instance, such poems tend to be short since, in print, they may be filler for a few inches of column space, and in recitation they must not be so long as to overwhelm the audience's comprehension. Like popular culture generally, popular verse may proffer homogenized, mainstream themes that override or subsume minority cultural motifs. But popular verse does not always simply consent to the dominant cultural myths; it can also enact resistance, facilitate shifts in the relations among different group interests, and produce emerging structures of feeling.

Popular culture can be described in rough schematic terms as the large middle ground between folk culture and elite culture. Interrelated conditions allowed and shaped the emergence of this middle ground in Britain, parts of Europe, and the American states from the mid–eighteenth through the nineteenth century: democratization, urbanization, industrialization, improvements in transportation and print technology, the growth of commerce, increasing literacy, and the rising hegemony of the middle class. Popular culture differs from folk culture in that folk art is generally associated with rural or village life. Until it is appropriated for popular or elite cultural purposes, moreover, folk art circulates with little reliance on technological reproduction or distribution. Folk poetry, for example, typically circulates orally, through recitations or songs. Popular art, in contrast, arises in urban environments, for print media, exhibitions, and performance sites take up the task of constructing communities and shaping localized knowledge for displaced, mobile populations. People must have money in order to consume popular culture – it exists within commerce; and, for an audience to exist for popular literary forms, the literacy level must be high. Although the folk artist typically is anonymous, the artist's name (like the designer tag today on retail clothes) may be a significant part of the commercial value of a popular work. Popular art differs from high art in that high art, as it came to be defined from the late eighteenth century through the modernist era, aspires to hold itself above the commercial market, responds mainly to technical standards drawn from the history of an art medium, and seeks innovations that recognize and transcend those standards. Although high art often strives for immortality through the expression of a unique consciousness, popular art succeeds only by capturing current widespread sentiment. The aims of high art are allied to conditions of aristocratic leisure and self-cultivation that popular art, ever on the market, cannot afford to target. Although skill is important to popular art, the rules for producing it shift with the demands of present-day consumers rather than resting on a canonized tradition.

This schematization spelled out, a caveat must be added: to set these definitions within a specific historical setting complicates the picture. Over the course of the nineteenth century, as the increasingly centralized media and entertainment industries interacted with the growth of education, complex layers of low-, middle-, and high-brow culture developed in the United States – layers that formed around ideologies of class, region, gender, and ethnicity. The examples of popular nineteenth-century American poems that are discussed later in this essay show the categories of folk, popular, and elite culture blending into each other. Folk blends into popular, for instance, in the anonymity of newspaper poems. Scholarship on women who published anonymously has claimed this practice as evidence that women writers needed to mask their gender, but men, too, often published anonymously or under pseudonyms; the issues surrounding this practice, therefore, seem to go well beyond gender to the preservation of a folk-cultural mask within popular media. Often – as was the case with Edgar Allan **Poe's** "The Raven" (LOA, 1: 535) – the author's name appeared in print only after the initial reception of a poem assured its success as a popular cultural production.

As for the blending of popular and elite, arguably, any artist working within the social conditions that produce popular culture must contend with the popular. These same conditions released high art from dependency on aristocratic patronage; this process, in turn, opened questions about the relationship between the artist (as an exemplary self) and the sociopolitical world, which romantic theorists addressed in recasting the idea of high art. Although the idea that poetry should be autonomous – unentangled with social purposes – gained increasing advocacy throughout the nineteenth century, many serious British and American poets wrote in the didactic vein of popular verse, and clear distinctions between the ways elite and popular poetry circulated in the period were slow to develop. As eminent a poet as Henry Wadsworth **Longfellow** sold his poems to magazines, even though he did not need the money; William Cullen **Bryant** also supported himself comfortably on sales of poems.

Walt **Whitman** and Emily **Dickinson**, the two American poets whose canonicity is now most firmly established, offer polar examples of struggle with the popular market. Promoting himself as the very embodiment of the popular, Whitman sought to evade the press's gatekeeping function by self-publishing. Although much of *Leaves of Grass* imagines a mass audience, however, few of Whitman's poems achieved popularity. One notable exception is "O Captain! My Captain!" (LOA, 1: 904), for which Whitman adapted a conventional form, imitating the three-question formula of Felicia Hemans's enduringly popular poem "Casabianca." In contrast, Dickinson quickly withdrew from efforts to publish. Since she seems to represent high art's total separation from the social world, her large body of brilliant verse has made her a valuable figure to the tradition of elite art that developed alongside popular culture. Yet her thousands of ballad stanzas show Dickinson in constant engagement with popular cultural forms.

Perhaps the most vivid illustration of a career that mingles popular and elite aesthetic values is that of Poe, who precariously straddled the widening gap between the need to make money at literature and the aspiration to formulate a high aesthetic code free of didacticism. In "The Philosophy of Composition," an essay ostensibly explaining his stunningly popular "The Raven," Poe states his aim of pleasing both the public and the critics. The poem itself can be read as an allegory of the morbid uncertainties of meaning accruing to language that is mechanically reproduced. In his lecture "The Poetic Principle," moreover, Poe renders romantic idealism as poetic dogma and presents as examples a mixture of romantic poems and popular magazine verse. That Poe, through the French symbolist poets, was a precursor of modernism suggests how central the struggle to resist, absorb, and transform attributes of popular culture was to the continuing reformulation of elite art throughout and after the nineteenth century. Conversely, many writers of popular verse contended with and drew on the standards of elite poetics.

The conditions necessary to the emergence of a popular culture originated as prominent trends in the United States by around 1830, taking their most dramatic turns after the Civil War. The number of urban centers with populations over 25,000 increased more than 30-fold, from four to 124, between 1810 and 1890. Urban populations in the 1830s were largely uprooted rural people who migrated to the cities, leaving behind subsistence farming to join the wage-earning workforce. To these in-migrations of American rural people were added waves of urban immigrants from northern and western Europe from 1845 to 1860 and from 1865 to 1885, with immigration from southern and eastern Europe increasing after the mid-1880s. After the Civil War, corporate capitalism burgeoned as huge corporate monopolies formed, supported by the large urban labor supply, new technology (the telegraph, the telephone, the elevator, the pneumatic tube, and the typewriter, among others), and the continued development of systems of transport, manufacture, and finance. The growth of business opened white-collar as well as blue-collar occupations, and working city dwellers, whose on-the-job hours decreased to yield more leisure time over the latter third of the century, were consumers as well as workers. From 1865 to 1900, the advertising industry became professionalized and multiplied its output tenfold. By the end of the century, mass culture promoted national interests alongside the values of achievement and consumerism associated with corporate capitalism – a combination that effectively overshadowed local interests and agrarian and petit-bourgeois values.

Two developments in United States culture will especially help to situate the examples of popular poetry that are discussed below: the growth of newspapers which, together with magazines, were popular verse's major route to its consumers, and the elocution movement, which circulated poetry through schools and the popular lecture circuits. With a literacy rate of around 90 percent of white adults in the early nineteenth century, the United States was a leading country in the development of newspapers. Early in the century, most of these newspapers were unstable business enterprises. Circulations were small, subscriptions too costly for most readers, and editorial policies generally followed the pattern of journals and addressed audiences constituted by specific religious, political, or intellectual interests. Advances in print technology from the 1830s on made newspapers cheap to produce, and the news content of papers began to reflect the idea of a general readership. Cheap papers that printed general news brought folk themes to the city in the form of stories about local events that helped to create a new sense of community and a shared wisdom about the dangers and opportunities of city life. Newspapers were a focus of immigrants' lives for these reasons and because they offered practice in English literacy. During the Civil War, daily newspapers became the vehicle of war news, and with the antebellum industrial boom came a concurrent boom in newspaper circulation. The first mass-circulation urban newspapers were established in the 1880s and 1890s.

The cultural significance of the elocution movement has not recently been critically analyzed, but its impact on the formation of nineteenth-century popular culture must have been considerable. The movement arose in eighteenth-century Britain in response to mounting criticisms of classical rhetoric, the gist of which was that the principles concerned with knowing and arranging the subject matter of an oration were epistemologically wrong for a modern scientific, Protestant setting. Although some rhetoricians worked to defend these classical principles, others abandoned them and, using the classical principles of vocalization and delivery style that had escaped criticism, developed the elocution movement by 1770. The movement took hold quickly in the American colonies and remained influential well into the twentieth century, despite its being decried as unscholarly and artificial. Elocution handbooks published throughout this period spelled out detailed rules for varying the voice, enunciation, posture, and gesture to create nuanced emotional effects consistent with the content of a recitation. These books also offered practice pieces – collections whose range of inclusions flattened distinctions among historical and cultural settings, as well as among various categories of public declamation, dramatic storytelling, and poetry.

The cultural uses of elocution clearly correspond with some of the social issues surrounding democratization and urbanization. The movement's adaptation of elite learning as a method for training individuals how to speak influentially was compatible with a democratic class structure. As eighteenth-century dictionary writers worked toward a standardized written language, elocutionists sought to standardize both the pronunciation of spoken language and its expressive qualities. At stake was not just the elimination of accents and dialects but the production of a common set of bodily signs that represented shared feelings and a merged internal and external language, which in turn signified the speaker's earnest commitment to truth. At a time when theorists of reading worried about the gap between the inward thought and outward appearance of silent readers, elocution made reading synonymous with reading aloud to an audience; in effect, elocution reinvested practices of oral cultural transmission into print culture as a hedge against the slippage of textual meaning. Oratory was a function belonging traditionally to the clergy, the law, and politics; by installing it as part of public education, the elocution movement in the United States merged sacred, judicial, and legislative functions into the role of every educated citizen. In the first half of the century, elocution thus played a role in the efforts to cultivate and standardize the individual American citizen and to counteract fears about the mindlessness of the democratic masses. Later in the century, however, elocution became an occupation, and the elocutionist was as much an entertainer as a didact. The object of elocution, as it was described in an 1893 guide to careers for women, was to seize and embody the spirit of the author; rather than being, like the orator, an authority herself, the woman elocutionist was a medium for translating authoritative texts into a reproduced material presence.

This essay does not attempt a comprehensive taxonomy of nineteenth-century American popular poetry; instead, it turns now to 11 examples. Many others could have been chosen – for example, "Ben Bolt" by Thomas Dunn English (1843; LOA, 1: 718); "Rock Me to Sleep" by Elizabeth Akers Allen (1860; LOA, 2: 321); "Curfew Must Not Ring To-Night" by Rose Hartwick Thorpe (1887; LOA, 2: 483); or selections from poets known for their careers as a whole, such as Lydia Huntley **Sigourney**, John Greenleaf **Whittier**, Frances Ellen Watkins **Harper**, Ella Wheeler **Wilcox**, and James Whitcomb **Riley**. The most serious limitation of the sampling below is that it includes no poems by women. A rationale for this omission is that many popular women poets are represented in separate entries in this volume of essays, which in turn reflects the wider movement in current scholarship to recuperate their work. It must be noted here, however, that the sociohistorical developments described above as shaping the growth of popular culture in nineteenth-century America were precisely the conditions that opened poetic production to women and other social groups for whom elite education and patronage were inaccessible; thus, understanding the demands and opportunities presented by popular cultural production is important in evaluating the cultural role of women's poetry. Further, gender is a defining category that weaves through the delineation of cultural layers, although which gender is assigned to which layer shifts in relation to changing social purposes.

The poems discussed below sketch out three of the many themes taken up in nineteenth-century American popular poetry. These three themes fall into a chronological sequence, with a few poems standing out as marking distinctive transitions. The first theme, nostalgia for a rural life associated with childhood, is represented by "The Bucket" by Samuel Woodworth (1818; LOA, 1: 70) and "The Oak" by George Pope Morris (1837; LOA, 1: 251); "A Visit from St. Nicholas" by Clement Clarke Moore (1823; LOA, 1: 44) veers remarkably from this theme to a kind of suburbanism, which is at home with tropes that foreshadow the growth of commercial culture. Next are poems about the Civil War, all concerned with undoing difference or opposition: "Sheridan's Ride" by Thomas Buchanan Read (1865; LOA, 2: 127), "Bivouac of the Dead" by Father Abram Ryan (LOA, 2: 377), and "The Blue and the Gray" by Francis Miles Finch (LOA, 2: 181). "Sheridan's Ride" is exceptional in that its figures seem to naturalize the spread of technology as a heroic force that brings order and morale to a nation in chaos. The last five poems form a somewhat forced category – nonsense, children's, and ludicrous verse – whose common thread is a departure from the declamatory social messages of the earlier poems into the play of language and image; these popular poems of the 1880s and 1890s move toward

the autonomous aestheticism of "art for art's sake." Ernest L. Thayer's mock-encomium "Casey at the Bat" (1888; LOA, 2: 588) serves as a mediating example between poetry of the war and nonsense verse; Charles Carryl's "A Nautical Ballad" (1884; LOA, 2: 401) and Eugene Field's "Wynken, Blynken, and Nod" (1889; LOA, 2: 477) and "The Duel" (1894; LOA, 2: 476) are children's poems; and Frank Gelett Burgess's "The Purple Cow" (1895; LOA, 2: 573), perhaps the most disruptive of these special cases, ends the sample. This selection moves westward, beginning in tough New England soil and ending in San Francisco's bohemia; it also moves from a print culture still deeply tied to oral culture to a print culture engrossed with its special capabilities as a visual medium. The career of "The Purple Cow" suggests, however, that oral transmission returns from its displacement with a vengeance.

"The Bucket," later retitled "The Old Oaken Bucket," was first printed in June 1818 in *The Republican Chronicle*, one of the many newspapers that appeared and disappeared in American cities early in the nineteenth century. The poem's author was the newspaper's publisher, Samuel Woodworth, who headed more than his share of short-lived publications. Woodworth grew up with little schooling in austere Massachusetts farm country, showed an early penchant for poetry, and left the farm at age 15 to apprentice as a printer. In 1809, he settled in New York, where publishing repeatedly sank him into poverty, which was relieved by modest successes in theater, military history, and patriotic-lyric writing. Woodworth's first collected poems bear the title *Melodies, Duets, Trios, Songs, and Ballads, Pastoral, Amatory, Sentimental, Patriotic, Religious, and Miscellaneous, Together with Metrical Epistles, Tales and Recitations* (1826) – verse for every occasion and mode of delivery. Some poems, including "The Bucket," appear with the names of melodies to which they can be sung, and the index lists people for whom the poems were written; this additional material gives the impression that publication was a supplement to face-to-face transmission, not an end in itself. Nostalgia for rural life is the obvious substance of the much-anthologized "Bucket"; but the poem offers a caution against underestimating the serious intent of popular verse. Woodworth was a follower of the mystic Emanuel Swedenborg, and the bucket may well be a Swedenborgian receptacle – a dead object capable of containing life, which is love emanating from God. With three stanzas and three thrice-repeated descriptions of its contemplative object, "The Bucket" also invokes Swedenborg's matrix of triple structures: divine mind, spiritual world, and natural world; end, cause, and effect; love, wisdom, and use.

"The Oak" by George Pope Morris (once Woodworth's partner) had a career that could serve as the standard for a popular poem's history. First published anonymously in a city newspaper, the poem appeared next in a slim volume bearing the author's name (*The Deserted Bride and Other Poems*, 1838); eventually, the poem's original title yielded to a rhetorically richer one ("Woodman, Spare That Tree"). For over a century, it circulated in poetry anthologies, songbooks, elocution manuals, and school grammars. "Woodman" was not its author's only popular success; his longtime partner, Nathaniel Parker **Willis**, remarked that Morris could, "at any time, obtain fifty dollars for a song unread [i.e., by the editor]." Supporters and detractors alike saw Morris as a feminine, domestic poet: "his fame is certain to endure," ran one review, "while the Anglo-Saxon Woman has a hearthstone over which to repeat her most cherished household words." Morris's now most renowned literary act was publishing Poe's "The Raven." But before that climactic moment, he spent 20 years cultivating the corps of writers – including Fitz-Greene **Halleck** and Joseph Rodman **Drake** – that became known as the Knickerbocker School. This context, rather than the hearth, is where "Woodman" belongs. The Knickerbockers' world was one where rural and cosmopolitan blended, where the loss of the Dutch past met the gains of pluralism and indigenous American culture. The story Morris told about how "The Oak" came to be written places its origins in the Hudson Valley during a transitional time. He was sitting with a friend under a tree in the woods near Bloomingdale, New York, when a man came to chop it down. Since Morris's friend had played under the tree as a child, he offered the man 10 dollars not to cut it down and had a bond drawn up protecting the tree – in effect paying to have a piece of nature withheld from commerce as a monument to a personal past. With this part of the story left out of the poem, the theme was transposable to a multitude of conservative-minded agendas, even finding its way into an argument in the British House of Commons.

If Woodworth's and Morris's poems searched the rural past for values in which to anchor modern life, Clement Clarke Moore, who also moved between the city and its rural environs, created a set of images that anticipated the future of mass culture. Moore composed "A Visit from St. Nicholas" in 1822 for his family (he had 11 children) and never made money on it. A visitor to the family estate in Chelsea, New York (now part of Manhattan), sent the verses to the newspapers in 1823, and for 21 years they appeared in broadsides and periodicals without the author's name. It was during this time, as Moore's poem circulated with increasing popularity, that Christmas took form in the United States; the first state declared it a holiday in 1836, with most states following in the 1850s and 1860s. Moore's poem does little more than sketch St. Nicholas, but it is a sketch comparable in its cultural significance to Walt Disney's transformation of folklore into cartoons. Nicholas was a fourth-century Christian bishop, the patron saint of children, merchants, and sailors, who was associated with commerce and gift-giving. Moore's portrait of the saint as a fur-clad elf proved a flexible vehicle for consolidating European traditions into a winter festival that overrode whatever cultural force the Puritans' antipathy to saints, play, and revelry may still have retained. Particularly important to Moore's poem were the remnants of Dutch cultural traditions: the Dutch celebrated St. Nicholas day on December 6, and honored him as patron of the New York City area. Dutch and German influences linger, too, in the names of the reindeer Donder and Blitzen (Thunder and Lightning). Moore transformed the early Turkish Christian saint into a prosperous tradesman dressed for the North Atlantic cold and embellished with epic similes that associate him with nature in early winter. What traces remain of the Old Country saint who judged children, or the carnivalesque Lord of Misrule, Moore renders domestic and unfallen; it is as if Moore is declaring consumerism an innocent state. "A Visit from St. Nicholas" precedes the height of British and American children's literature by several decades – and the children's role in the poem consists entirely of dreaming of sugarplums. Moore's vision of sooty St. Nicholas and his team of reindeer is the privileged vision of the family patriarch. Childhood had not yet, for Moore, become the autonomous zone of imaginative play that it would become for later writers; we catch the "Visit" narrator in an early stage of projecting that zone. As for his vision, it is nothing less than the casting of a secularized and dehistoricized icon of prosperity out of the American melting pot's assorted religious and folk traditions.

Abram Joseph Ryan's "Lines Respectfully Inscribed to the Ladies' Memorial Association of Fredericksburg, Va.," sometimes titled "The Bivouac of the Dead" (1866), and Francis M. Finch's "The Blue and the Gray" (1867) both refer to burial sites where unidentified casualties of the Civil War were gathered. The contrasts between these two commemorations suggest that Finch's poem retorts to the sentiment of Ryan's by asserting the north's ascendant authority over even the jurisdiction of death. Ryan, a Catholic priest who served as a Confederate chaplain, unifies the dead under a patriotism for a nation that no longer exists. Ryan's effort thus asserts the sacred legitimacy of the Confederacy even as it is buried. The central rhetorical movement of the poem, however, exists elsewhere; the poem directs the audience to bury soldiers of all ranks together. The funeral trope of equality in death lends itself here to mass burial of the agrarian class system, "from cabin to lordly hall." Finch was a lawyer in Ithaca, New York, where he eventually served as a judge. He wrote "The Blue and the Gray" after reading in a New York newspaper that a group of women in Columbus, Mississippi, "strewed flowers alike on the graves of the Confederate and of the National soldiers." The poem, first published in the upper-brow *Atlantic Monthly*, was hailed for its efficacy in healing the wounds between north and south: "all the orations and sermons and appeals for the restoration of kindly feeling between the two sections," one comment ran, "have been exceeded in real effect upon the national heart by this simple poem." Despite this comment's associating the poem with folk feeling rather than public rhetoric, Finch makes subtle rhetorical use of a varying refrain, which links the colors of the Union and the Confederacy with images that combine difference and similarity and, in the fifth stanza, that melt difference away: "Wet with the rain, the Blue; / Wet with the rain, the Gray." Like Father Ryan, Finch plays on the social indifference of death, but he adds a dimension that suggests a role for feminized conciliatory gestures in closing the cycles of war. The dead are "waiting the judgment day" – laying the two armies to rest, the poem defers judgment of the war's agents to God and instead extends condescension toward the women of Columbus, Mississippi, judging their heroism equal to the soldiers'. The women's act of honoring the Union dead merges with nature's action in minimizing the differences between the antagonists. Yet the difference returns: "They banish our anger forever" – the war over, us-versus-them persists as a lever for the victors to use in adjudicating the terms of reconciliation.

"Sheridan's Ride" commemorates a battle, not a burial place, yet it resembles Ryan's and Finch's poems in its concern with difference – in this case, the gap between two locations. Poet-painter Thomas Buchanan Read wrote "Sheridan's Ride" for recitation by his friend James Edward Murdoch, a leading American elocutionist; both men, like Whitman, nursed wounded Union soldiers during the Civil War. The poem celebrates the battle of Cedar Creek on October 19, 1863, a victory that earned Philip Henry Sheridan the title of major general. Sheridan was 20 miles north of Cedar Creek in Winchester, Virginia, when the battle began; Read's poem dramatizes the closing of the distance between the chaotic "red sea" of battle and the leader whose presence in the end organizes the demoralized, straggling troops into a "whole great army." Earning a reputation for fearlessness and strategic skill, Sheridan went on to lead the devastation of the Shenandoah Valley and, in March 1865, the north's final victory. Recited in hospitals and theaters soon after the war ended, this story could well be taken to encapsulate the Union's achievement in the war as a whole. Read's countdown of the miles – from 20 to 15 to 10 to five – undoubtedly was central to the poem's success in dramatic presentation. Peculiarly, the key stanzas ending with the countdown take the speaker into the horse's consciousness, not the rider's. This is particularly striking for an elocution piece, for the elocutionist's task was to embody the soul represented in a piece. Read deflects the performer's and the audience's identification from the paragon of military nerve to a supporting character, the horse, which appears like an omen and moves like a steamship, its heart one with its rider's. The horse is thus already presented as an industrialized form of nature, and its course is swift and inevitable: this role, the role of the masses engaged with the continuing defeat of agrarianism, is what the poem celebrates, not the military hero.

Written over 20 years after the end of the Civil War, "Casey at the Bat" owes much of its wild success to a resolution of suspense that reverses the resolution contained in "Sheridan's Ride"; the hero arrives, but he brings bathos rather than order to a crowd in distress. The audience's enthusiasm for Casey's failure suggests that, with the advance of modernity and corporate capitalism, the hero who saves the day may have lost his credibility, may even have become an object of scorn. "Casey" made print as a part of the early years of William Randolph Hearst's newspaper empire. The Harvard career of the author, Ernest L. Thayer, included editing the *Lampoon* with the assistance of George **Santayana**, who later recalled Thayer's sense of the ludicrous: "his wit was . . . curious and whimsical, as if he saw the broken edges of things that appear whole. There was some obscurity in his play with words, and a feeling (which I shared) that the absurd side of things is pathetic." Hearst, the *Lampoon*'s business manager, was expelled for practical jokes, and he then went to work operating the *San Francisco Examiner* so that it promoted his father's political career. Thayer became a reporter and balladeer (under his Harvard pen name "Phin") for his classmate's paper. "Casey," printed in the Sunday *Examiner* on June 3, 1888, was the only of Thayer's ballads to capture the popular imagination, and it had professional help. About six months after the poem appeared, Broadway actor William De Witt Hopper, anticipating an audience stocked with ballplayers, consulted a literary friend about something special to recite. The friend gave him a clipping of "Casey." In his memoirs, Hopper reported that the audience shouted with glee at the end of the recitation. Over the next half-century he would perform the poem some 10,000 times. Hopper's recitations stimulated the start of an abundant publication history: across the country newspapers and magazines reprinted "Casey at the Bat" with multiple alterations and without, at first, the author's real name. Throughout the twentieth century, scores of public speaking handbooks and poetry anthologies included "Casey," and takeoffs have proliferated in print and film. Few need reminding what happens in Thayer's poem: The Mudville team is down 4 to 2 with two outs in the last inning. Inferior players manage to fill two bases, and then Casey comes to bat. He spurns two pitches that the umpire judges good, and then he faces the last pitch like a warrior poised for the kill – and strikes out. Hopper explained his audiences' enthusiasm for the poem in terms of the deflation of Casey's gigantic potency with the bat: "the contrast between the terrible threat of his swing and the futility of the result is a banquet for the malicious, which includes us all."

"A Nautical Ballad" first appeared embedded in a children's story, *Davy and the Goblin, or What Followed Reading Alice's Adventures in Wonderland*, which was serialized, richly illustrated, in *St. Nicholas Magazine* in 1884. The author was a New York stockbroker, Charles E. Carryl, who started his business career at barely 16 years of age. Besides Lewis Carroll, Carryl's inspiration was his young son, Guy Wetmore Carryl, who in adulthood authored his own parodies (e.g., *Far from the Madding Girls*). Published in book form in 1885, *Davy and the Goblin* was hailed as a work that broke new ground for American letters. "A Nautical Ballad" has had a peregrinating career on its own, appearing in collections of nautical, juvenile, and light verse through the 1980s. Typical of popular poems, it has changed guises, kept or dropped revisions, gone under alternate titles ("A Capital Ship" and "The Walloping Window Blind"), and appeared in songbooks with a folk melody (and an all-purpose nautical chorus: "Then blow, ye winds, heigh-ho"). "A Nautical Ballad" is an insouciant tale of shipwreck. Unfazed by treacherous weather, the crew passes time playing, being tickled, and punishing the cook for the sickening food. Inexplicably, they abandon ship on the Gulliby Isles. A diet of rubagub bark proves malnutritious, so when a junk appears, the crew take it by tricking the Chinese sailors into sampling the indigenous fare. As the illustrations for a book version of the poem (1963) make evident, the ship "the Walloping Window-blind" is a regressed world of hierarchically ordered, nationally chauvinist male enterprise (the terrible cook is Dutch). One suspects Carryl of retroactively inventing his curtailed childhood: in *Davy and the Goblin* he mourns the flight of "blithesome youth" and works to abolish the difference between youth and age in the face of wonder. Oddly for a poem with so much oral play in its language, "A Nautical Ballad" (like the rest of *Davy and the Goblin*) is full of horrible food: for Carryl, consumption seems much more problematic than it was for Moore's sugarplum dreamers. No relief is in sight until the end of Davy's "believing journey" when his grandmother calls him to dinner. But will she serve him a royal meal like the Window-Blind captain's or "a number of tons of hot-cross buns, / Chopped up with sugar and glue"?

Eugene Field's contributions to popular poetry reflect several trends in late-nineteenth-century American cultural production. First, there is the increasing importance of the west as a source of popular culture. Field, born in St. Louis, Missouri, was a columnist for the Chicago *Morning News* when he privately published his first volume, A *Little Book of Western Verse*. Second, Field's best-remembered poems, "Wynken, Blyken, and Nod" and "The Gingham Dog and the Calico Cat," were for children. Built of whimsy and nonsense, these poems, like Carryl's, turn away from the rural nostalgia of earlier popular poets and link childhood not to rustic settings but to an autonomous sphere of fantasy, where images and words play by their own rules. Yet "Wynken, Blynken, and Nod," which first appeared in Field's newspaper column on March 11, 1889, slyly refers to the Knickerbocker School's involvement with the Dutch past while amusing itself with the linguistic peculiarities of midwestern European ethnic groups (Field played with and even invented dialects in his column). Wynken – one of a child's two dreaming eyes – is kindred to Washington Irving's great sleeper Rip Van Winkle; and lest we miss the reference, Field put his three fishers in a Dutch wooden shoe. The dream resembles one of Jesus' first miracles: three fisher-disciples, Simon Peter, James, and John, draw in so many fish by casting their nets where Jesus tells them to that their boat nearly sinks. In Field's turmoil-free version, it is the fish themselves – the stars – that invite the three fishers to cast their nets. Besides pure fantasy, the lullaby suggests an innocent dream of a purely gratifying consumerism – one that transcends oral consumption by depicting an aestheticized, celestial sea of sparkling "beautiful things." In "The Gingham Dog and the Calico Cat," Field transposes the conventions of the gossip column into children's verse in which household objects behave like fetishized commodities that act out social malaise. Citing two informants, a Dutch clock and a Chinese plate, Field describes the shocking mutual destruction of two stuffed animals. Besides high-society gossip, the poem recalls the popular imagination's earlier preoccupation with a "family row," the Civil War. Situating historical conflict in a childhood fantasy places it in a near-irretrievable past and reduces it to an absurdity that even a child can see through. "Now what do you really think of that!" the poem exclaims, having provided no motive for the fight except that the animals stayed up too late.

"The Purple Cow" bounded into the American imagination in the first issue of *The Lark* (May 1895), a San Francisco little magazine. *The Lark* rode the tide of a craze for specialty periodicals ("fadazines"), a movement of smallness situated, like today's fanzines, both within and against mass culture. More than any other poem discussed here, "The Purple Cow" seems authorless, and its publication history looks irrelevant to its part in American culture. Yet it had an author, Frank Gelett Burgess; and the publishers of *The Lark* – Burgess and Bruce Porter – invested the cow's appearance with a highly self-conscious mission: to capture the new spirit of self-expression that they felt other little magazines failed to capture and to baffle philistinism while demolishing decadence with California non-

chalance. Aiming for total originality, Burgess and Porter "ransacked" Chinatown in search of paper and chose a cheap bamboo stock yellowed by mildew. The cow quatrain was printed sideways on a page bearing this title: "THE PURPLE COW's Projected Feast: / Reflections on a Mythic Beast, / Who's quite Remarkable, at Least." Burgess's silhouetted illustration suggests an alternate myth of humanity's fall: an agonized naked man faces a leaping cow with nothing but a loveknot-shaped tree between them. The cow has minotaur-like horns, her tongue curls out, and her bug-eyes fix on the man – her "projected feast." Another cow appears on the previous page of *The Lark* in a child's drawing illustrating an article by Burgess on primitive art. This drawing, too, renders the agrarian world strange: a farmer and a rectangular dog "wander back from their labors, leaving the giant cow alone upon the horizon, the day is over – finally, irrevocably," Burgess says. This context, as well as that provided by *The Burgess Nonsense Book* (1901), reinforces an observation about influences converging in "The Purple Cow": minstrelsy, an orientalist avant-gardism, and a terror of powerful female figures. What, then, possessed Burgess to write another quatrain – "The Purple Cow: Suite" (LOA, 2: 573) – threatening to kill anyone who recited "The Purple Cow"? His essay *Are You a Bromide?* (1906) offers a likely answer. Everything Bohemian, Radical, Interesting, and Gothic is a Sulphite; everything else is a Bromide. Oral transmission of "The Purple Cow" separated it from its Sulphitic print origin and turned it into a Bromide.

JANET GRAY

Selected Works
Burgess, Gelett, *Burgess Unabridged: A New Dictionary of Words You Have Always Needed*, Hamden, Connecticut: Archon, 1986
Gardner, Martin, ed., *The Annotated Casey at the Bat: A Collection of Ballads About the Mighty Casey*, Chicago: University of Chicago Press, 1984
Geist, Christopher D., and Jack Nachbar, eds., *The Popular Culture Reader*, Bowling Green, Ohio: Bowling Green University Popular Press, 1983

Further Reading
Inge, M. Thomas, ed., *Handbook of American Popular Literature*, New York: Greenwood, 1988

Alexander Posey

(1873–1908)

In 1903, Alexander Lawrence Posey wrote to his friend Frederick Barde:

> Old Walt Whitman has wound himself into my affections as thoroughly as "Bobbie" Burns. He celebrates any old thing regardless of how it sounds and jars the over-sensitive and civilized nature of man and maid. But his "yawps" are interwoven with finely spun sentiment and philosophy and there is in him on the whole more gold than dross.

When he made the statement, the young Tuskegee writer had given up poetry for journalism. His admiration of Walt **Whitman** suggests his awareness of new directions in American poetry; his equal affection for Robert Burns, on the other hand, helps explain his general failure as a poet and, perhaps, his reasons for giving up the writing of serious poetry and turning, instead, to humor.

Given the time and circumstances of his birth and early life, it is remarkable that Posey became a poet at all. He was born on August 3, 1873, in a remote section of the Creek Nation known as the Tulledega Hills, about 15 miles west of Eufaula (in what is now Oklahoma). His mother was Chickasaw-Creek, and through her he acquired his membership in Tuskegee tribal town and in the wind clan. His father, although white, had lived in the Creek Nation since his childhood and was a member, probably by adoption, of Broken Arrow tribal town. The young Posey spent his childhood in the Tulledega Hills, where the family engaged in subsistence farming and grazing; he roamed the region, closely observing the flora and fauna and learning to appreciate the natural beauty of the hills. Although he ultimately became fluent in English, he did not speak it until his father forced him to do so at age 14. About that time, the elder Posey decided that his children needed an education, and Alex, the oldest, was sent to the Creek national boarding school at Eufaula, where he remained until 1889. That year, he was chosen as one of the students whom the Creek Nation sponsored to attend the Indian University at Bacone, near Muskogee (Oklahoma).

At Bacone, where Posey remained until 1894, he fell under the influences that shaped his poetic efforts. He studied history, the sciences, philosophy, classical languages, and, most important, English and American literature. He became fond of reading the poets, from the late eighteenth century poets to his contemporaries. From the earlier periods, he enjoyed Robert Burns, Percy Bysshe Shelley, Alfred, Lord Tennyson, William Cullen **Bryant**, Henry Wadsworth **Longfellow**, James Russell **Lowell**, John Greenleaf **Whittier**, and Whitman. Among contemporary writers he read James Whitcomb **Riley**, Rudyard Kipling, Thomas Bailey Aldrich, Joaquim **Miller**, Bret **Harte**, and countless newspaper versifiers. Such writers provided Posey's models, and, in subsequent years, his romanticism and sentimentality were reinforced by his isolation in the Indian Territory and by close friends who shared his tastes in verse.

Although Posey had written a handful of poems before he left Bacone, his time of greatest production was 1897 through 1900. His lifestyle during this period provided time for literary pursuits. He was elected to the Creek National Council in 1895 and, late that year, was appointed superintendent of the Creek Orphan Asylum at Okmulgee, where he remained two years. He then served as superintendent of public instruction for the Creek Nation and, in 1898, moved to the small town of Stidham, near which he controlled a large acreage on the Creek national public domain, which he rented to tenant farmers. In 1899, he was appointed superintendent of the Creek boarding school at Eufaula and, the next year, superintendent of the boarding school at Wetumka. Posey handled his administrative duties in a relaxed fashion. He left many of the details to his wife, Minnie Harris Posey, who made it her responsibility to leave him as much undisturbed time as possible for reading, thinking, and writing. This period of his life was quite productive, especially his year as a gentleman farmer at Stidham; he read voraciously and wrote extensively. In all, he left in print or manuscript more than 200 poems, including occasional and humorous pieces and works that celebrated love, nature, rural life, and great men.

Posey's poems vary widely in quality, as can be seen by comparing those from the 1897–90 period. Many, such as "What My Soul Would Be," "Nature's Blessings," "When Love Is Dead," and "Life's Mystery," are abstract and sentimental. Others such as "Ensapahutche" are little more than experiments in rhyming. Still others such as "Morning" and "Sunset" are simply expanded images. Among the most successful poems are those celebrating nature – his most common theme – for which he drew inspiration from the Tulledega Hills, where he frequently returned as an adult. Some poems celebrate animal life, such as "Bob White" and "The Mocking Bird"; others, the onset of night or the seasons, such as "Nightfall" (LOA, 2: 629), "July" (LOA, 2: 628), "Midsummer" (LOA, 2: 628), and "Autumn" (LOA, 2: 629); still others, the landscape, such as "Tulledega" and "Song of the Oktahutchee" (LOA, 2: 627).

Posey's poetry also reflects the dramatic changes that were taking place on the landscape of the Creek Nation. During the 1890s, the Creek Nation's status as a domestic dependent nation was undermined. Thousands of non-Creeks entered the nation and rented or squatted, and federal legislation was passed to force the nation to dissolve, give up the common tribal title to the land, and allot parcels to individual Creeks. Posey embraced these changes as "progress." His poetry thus most often reflects a landscape that is becoming more and more domestic, perhaps even pastoral. A good example is "Song of the Oktahutchee," about the North Canadian River, which flows through the Tulledega Hills. It concludes, "Towns nestle in the vales I wander thro'; / And quails are whistling in the waving grain, / And herds are scattered o'er the verdant plain." Here is his vision of the twentieth-century Creek Nation. Still, Posey recognized the cost of progress to nature, to the less progressive Creeks (in "The Coyote" and "On the Capture and Imprisonment of Crazy Snake"), and even to himself. When the "noise of strife" in the new society became too burdensome, he sought refuge in the wilder reaches of the Tulledega Hills.

In form, as in subject, Posey's work varies in quality. He most often imitated his models. His ideas are usually couched in conventional verse forms: couplets, triplets, variations on ballad stanza, blank verse, and sonnets. Yet there are apparent experiments in versification. "Autumn," for instance, a poem about the sounds and colors that mark the onset of the season, is written in unrhymed trochaic trimeter. "July" has a more complex form: lines containing four stresses and beginning and ending with unstressed syllables alternate with lines containing five stresses and beginning and ending with stressed syllables. The language of Posey's work is at times comprised of conventional, even hackneyed, poetic diction. Yet there are often startling images; in "To a Hummingbird," for example, the bird is compared to "some frenzied poet's thought, / That God embodied and forgot," and in "Nightfall," a large bright star is the pin that holds night's robe, and the new moon is like a scimitar thrown into the night sky. Posey also experimented with dialect. During his poetic period, he counted Burns as his favorite poet, whom he admired for his use of dialect. He was also familiar with the dialect works of such contemporaries as Riley and Paul Laurence **Dunbar**. In "Wildcat Bill," he experimented with the white cowboy lingo, and in "Happy Times for Me and Sal," the dialect of rural white farm folk. It was not until "Hotgun on the Death of Yadeka Harjo," however, that he successfully matched subject and language; in his Creek English dialect, Hotgun reflects on the passing of the old-time Creeks and contemplates his own death. Throughout the poem, Posey maintains control of language and tone as he does nowhere else, and it stands today as his best poem.

During the period of his most intense poetic production, Posey seems to have been overwhelmed by poetry and the idea of being a poet. He actively sought inspiration in the Tulledegas. He reacted spontaneously to their beauty, as he apparently thought a romantic poet should, and the result was often sentimentality and didacticism. Descriptions of him as a dreamy, distant youth during this period suggest that there may have been something of a pose in his presentation of himself as a poet. By 1900, he was approaching 30; with his youth behind him, he took stock of himself and decided to give up poetry for other literary pursuits.

That year, he refused to seek a wider market for his poetry. From his college days onward, his poems had appeared frequently in Indian Territory publications. In 1900, newspapers in the midwest and the east reprinted some of his works and asked for additional submissions. He told the *Philadelphia Press* in November that he considered himself a western poet who might not be appreciated by eastern readers because his works were tied too closely to the landscapes of the Creek Nation. He reflected Ralph Waldo **Emerson's** belief in the purity of the language that is rooted in nature when he said:

The Indian talks in poetry; poetry is his vernacular, not necessarily the stilted poetry of books, but the free and untrammeled poetry of nature, the poetry of the fields, the sky, the river, the sun and the stars. In his own tongue it is not difficult for the Indian to compose, he does it instinctively; but in attempting to write in English he is handicapped. Words seem hard, form mechanical, and it is to these things that I attribute the failure of the civilized Indian to win fame in poetry.

By the time Posey made this statement, he had practically ceased writing serious poetry. Few of the poems that he had written during the preceding three years had been published; he had apparently sent few of them out. Posey was a far better reader than writer of poetry. He must have realized that most of his poetry was imitative, that little of it succeeded. In arriving at an understanding of Whitman's achievement, he must have seen the weaknesses in his own work.

For whatever reason Posey gave up poetry, after 1900 he turned to prose. In early 1902, he bought the *Indian Journal*, a weekly newspaper at Eufaula. Later that year, he created the persona Fus Fixico, whose dialect letters to the editor satirized social, political, and economic conditions in the Indian Territory. Posey continued the letters after he left journalism in 1904 to work for the Dawes Commission, whose task was to oversee the dissolution of the tribal titles and the allotment of Indian lands in the Indian Territory. Posey worked for the commission until 1907, served briefly as a real estate agent, and, shortly before his death in 1908, resumed the editorship of the *Indian Journal*. The Fus Fixico letters, which appeared throughout this period, established his reputation as a humorist, won him more recognition than his poetry had, and stand today as his greatest literary achievement. During this time, Posey wrote only a little verse, most of it was humorous, including some limericks and political doggerel.

In early 1908, Posey had material ambitions based on the speculation in land and oil rights that attended the founding of the state of Oklahoma. He had plans as well to revise some of his earlier works and to establish a writer's colony in the Tulledega Hills. However, in late May, he drowned while attempting to cross the flooding Oktahutchee, which, ironically, he had celebrated in song.

DANIEL F. LITTLEFIELD JR.

Selected Works

The Poems of Alexander Lawrence Posey, Topeka, Kansas: Crane, 1910

Further Reading

Littlefield, Daniel F., Jr., *Alex Posey: Creek Poet, Journalist, and Humorist*, Lincoln: University of Nebraska Press, 1992
_____, and James W. Parins, *A Biobibliography of Native American Writers, 1772–1924*, Metuchen, New Jersey: Scarecrow, 1981

Lizette Woodworth Reese

(1856–1935)

"The Victorians had a full cup and it spilled over," wrote Lizette Woodworth Reese in her memoir *A Victorian Village* (1929). "I think this is the reason that their faults, worst amongst which were their over-elaboration and sentimentality, are so apparent." As that critical but affectionate line suggests, the memoir is in no way an excoriation of Victorianism; Reese looks back fondly on a childhood spent in the village of Waverly, Maryland, "a green, quiet place, well-beloved and long-remembered," at a time when "we were as sure of God as we were of the sun." Yet throughout her long career as a poet, the succinct, packed poetic language that she created constitutes an argument against the Victorian mode of "over-elaboration and sentimentality." A gifted and careful practitioner of poetic craft, Reese represents a transition from nineteenth-century to modernist poetry; this transition, however, is marked more by subtle thematic and formal innovation than by the ruptures proclaimed by louder voices like Ezra Pound or Amy Lowell.

We can see a summation of Reese's anti-sentimental argument in the poem "Scarcity," which was published in the collection *White April* (1930) five years before her death. Written in four compact four-line stanzas, the poem celebrates in both form and theme a paradoxically fertile deprivation. "Scarcity saves the world," announces the first stanza, "And by that it is fed / Then give it hunger, God / Not bread." The second stanza goes on to extol the power of littleness and scarcity:

> Scarce things are comely things;
> In little there is power;
> November measures best
> Each vanishing flower.

The third stanza introduces the idea that this principle of prodigious, empowering, and "comely" scarcity also underpins art:

> If you dig a well,
> If you sing a song
> By what you do without,
> You make it strong.

The final stanza drives home this connection between the speaker's philosophy of life and her approach to art:

> And life as well as art,
> By scarceness grows, not surfeit.
> Theirs must be
> The hunger of the rose.

In its untouchable, "hungry" beauty, the rose is a potent symbol of Reese's anti-sentimental poetic discipline. She uses the rose to convey not beauty itself, but the strictness with which the artist must approach beauty. In "Revelation," a poem about the responsibilities of the poetic vocation (also from *White April*), Reese refers to "the unescapable rose," which challenges the poet's ability to "grow high." She must "prove myself worth and more" the simple things from which her poetry springs: "This awful sky, the rose, / These doubled acres at

my door." The speaker emphasizes the role of the poet as a conduit of simplicity and wonder: ". . . I am a thing / Of strange and humble eyes."

"The hunger of the rose" well describes not just Reese's poetics but the outlines of her modest life as well. She was born on January 7, 1856, with her twin sister, Sophia, the first of five children of David Reese and Louisa Gabler. Both parents had immigrated as children: her father was Welsh, her mother German. Waverly, a few miles outside of Baltimore, was Reese's home all of her life. Her mother and her German grandparents, with whom the family lived while David Reese fought with the Confederate Army in the Civil War, taught Reese German as well as English. Never marrying, she began a teaching career at age 17 that lasted until she was 65. Her bilingual upbringing enabled her to teach at Baltimore's English-German School (half a day in each language) for 21 years, and she also taught at Baltimore's Colored High School for "four years that were among the happiest of my life." All the while she produced the spare, exquisite poetry that made her in her day a well-known figure, the recipient of a steady stream of honors and awards. She was hailed as one of the best sonnet writers in the English language, the "spiritual godmother" of Edna St. Vincent Millay and Elinor Wylie, and a precursor of the imagists.

In all, she produced 11 volumes of poetry, beginning with *A Branch of May*, which was published in a subscription edition in 1874. A review copy that she sent to Edmund Clarence **Stedman**, "the dean of American poetry," was enthusiastically received, and Stedman became a supportive friend who introduced Reese to the literary circles of the day. By 1891, 42 new poems were added to *A Branch of May* and published by Houghton Mifflin as *A Handful of Lavender*, followed by *A Quiet Road* in 1896. For the next 13 years, Reese slowed down her production, publishing an occasional poem in periodicals such as *Scribner's* or the *Atlantic*. Another book did not come out until *A Wayside Lute* in 1909, and there was another long gap before *Spicewood* in 1920. The demands of making a living as a schoolteacher seem to have been the crucial factor in this decreased output: after her retirement in 1921, nine of her 14 books appeared. In all, according to Robert T. Jones's study, she wrote between 300 and 500 poems – a big but not a huge number, which accounts in some measure for the precariousness of her reputation. Yet if it took time away from her writing, Reese's teaching fostered and nourished her spirit, and she expressed not regret but gratitude for the years given over to it: "I shall always be deeply thankful for having been a working woman among other working women for so long, for having been part of the common lot." After Reese's death in 1935, her reputation went into eclipse, and although she makes an occasional appearance in anthologies and critical considerations of American poetry, her name is today mostly unknown outside of Baltimore, where she is remembered in monuments and plaques.

The sparse critical treatment that Reese has received has been uneven. Critics often approach Reese as part of a group of poets, and whether the group is disparaged, as in Roy Harvey

Pearce's account of turn-of-the-century poets' "depressing" lack of talent, or lionized, as in Alicia Ostriker's grouping of early modernist women poets who "subvert masculine authority," critics generally do not give full measure to her singular style. Reese's anomalous critical status is best captured by Hyatt S. Waggoner's *American Poets from the Puritans to the Present*: he notes, in the preface, that he "would very much have liked to discuss the unique virtues" of Reese (the only name given of certain "ignored or forgotten poets"), but she is nonetheless not included in the survey. Like Waggoner, critics tend to like Reese's poetry very much, even to rave about it, but do not pursue their interest very far. Perhaps the facility of her craft makes her a "poet's poet," one who often inspires praise rather than analysis. H. L. Mencken, a notorious hater of poetry who was surprised to find himself greatly moved by Reese's work, wrote to her about the poem "Tears" that he was "almost afraid to mention that sonnet in print, for when I do I cease to be a critic and become a rhapsodist!"

To all appearances, Reese's poetry does not have a political agenda or reveal much of a worldly political awareness. Reconstruction and the Jim Crow South, the rise of feminism, World War I – none of these make their way into her poetry. Instead, her poems describe a placid southern village life that is tied to the rhythms of nature, the seasons, emotions, family life, and Christian faith. Like Emily **Dickinson**, the poet whom she most resembles, Reese mined insights from the "small" world of everyday experience, what she called "commonness." She was steadfast in her dedication to poetry as first and foremost an aesthetic experience, and her aesthetic was in many ways quite traditional. The ruptured aesthetic of modernism she held to be a mere failure to see beauty. "From this lack of discrimination, of the deep, discerning eye, arises the very modern apotheosis of the ugly," she wrote in *A Victorian Village*. "Ugliness is put on a pedestal. Words are wrenched out of their usual context and applied to subjects for which they are most inadequate. It is playing on a cracked instrument. For when a verse is ended, should it not leave behind it a sense, if only a faint one, of loveliness?" Although Reese praised the free-verse movement for its healthy spirit of revolt, she rejected the idea that verse can be completely unfettered: "The term free verse was untenable, for verse, like all Art, is under the law; its only liberty comes from that. But the movement, when it had spent its initial force, had succeeded in shaking up and revigorating [*sic*] the traditionalists; this was worth every blow struck in the battle."

Reese's quarrel with the modernist aesthetic, however, does not run as deep as her comments about the "modern apotheosis of ugliness" imply. Although harmonious, beautiful language was the raison d'être of her poetry, it is not ugliness per se that she turned away from; in a modern way, her poems often look unflinchingly at hard, ugly reality. At the same time, Reese's terse language and spare, precise imagery place her squarely within the emerging minimalist style that was codified by Pound as imagism. The transition to minimalism reverberated throughout American literature around the turn of the century, and Reese was not alone among women poets in rejecting Victorian sentimentalism in order to forge something new. As Paula Bennett has shown, not only Dickinson but numerous women in the latter nineteenth century wrote nature poetry that moved away from the "religiously based domestic and cul-

tural values" of "high sentimentalism" toward "greater concrete detail, more ambiguous and flexible stylistic expression, and . . . a much wider – and more disturbing – range of themes," thus laying the groundwork for the imagism that Pound "invented" in 1912 (*Legacy* 9, no. 2).

Reese is often at her most "modern" when working within and breathing new life into established genres and modes. Her gift for concision and appreciation of "scarcity," for example, give an epigrammatic quality to much of her verse, and, in fact, she wrote several epigrams. *A Branch of May* contains two bold, two-line poems that Reese placed together both there and in *Selected Poems*:

"Doubt"
Creeds grow so thick along the way
Their boughs hide God; I cannot pray.

"Truth"
The old faiths light their candles all about,
But burly truth comes by and blows them out.

The pared-down form of the poems conveys well the speaker's sentiment: truth and faith are not found in clutter and overabundance, in "thick" creeds whose "boughs hide God" or in faiths strewn "all about." Yet in "Truth," there is a pleasing surprise in the adjective "burly," which suggests that truth is not simple, gentle, or graceful. "Burly truth" has a robustness and, in its evocation of "hurly-burly," a hint of unpredictability and danger that offsets the delicate diction of the poem and saves it from preciousness. Similarly, the stark clause "I cannot pray" that ends "Doubt," set as it is following a semicolon in the middle of a perfectly metrical line, has a firmness and finality to it. This boldness, paradoxically, turns what could be a lament for lost faith into resolution and sureness. The speaker may be put off by the accumulated "thickness" of organized religion, but she is certain that the problem lies neither with God nor with herself.

As "Doubt" and "Truth" reveal, Reese uses the epigram as a sort of guerrilla attack on sentimentality. In both form and theme, her epigrams crystallize the alternative that she offers to sentimentality's dilatory aesthetic. For Reese, on the one hand, emotion must be clarified and stripped down to its essential components; on the other hand, oversimplification of painful or confusing feelings is also a sentimental trap. In the four-line "Death's Guerdon" (LOA, 2: 520), Reese's precise language takes to task vague, prettified emotions:

Secure in death he keeps the hearts he had;
    Two women have forgot the bitter truth;
To one he is but her sweet little lad;
    To one the husband of her youth.

No individual word or phrase stands out; the plain language conveys the banality of the two women's turning away from "the bitter truth." Nonetheless, the speaker subtly conjures the disturbing, complicated reality these women have "forgot." In the idea that he "keeps the hearts he had," she reveals a hint of anger at the "he" in question, who has reaped this "guerdon," or reward. The word "had," emphasized by its placement, registers a hint of force or thoughtlessness: did he merely possess the hearts or did he use them for his own purposes? The speaker's strong feeling is carefully contained by the precise rhymes and the neatness of the final two lines, each of which begins "To one." Yet slight metrical irregularities give away some of her turbulence.

Alongside the epigram's demand for terseness, the sonnet's requirement of dilation within strict boundaries gives Reese more ground to develop her anti-sentimental poetic argument. "April in Town" (LOA, 2: 518), from *A Handful of Lavender*, uses not only the sonnet form but a favorite trope of Reese's that reworks a common sentimental topic and that also anticipates T. S. Eliot: the use of April to convey a complicated mood of beautiful yet excruciating redemption. (In the later sonnet "White April," the painful quality is magnified, as the speaker, "dripping with April, April to the heart," must "run back to the house and bolt the door.") In "April in Town," Reese evokes a wet spring afternoon in a bustling town by packing as much imagery and meaning as possible within exacting boundaries. The result is a response to nature whose strikingly modern spareness plays off the sonnet form in interesting ways. The octave, rhymed according to the challenging *abbaabba* scheme, describes a riot of activity, as a rainfall "That just now drove its wild ranks down the street" passes through town at sunset. A series of striking noun-verb combinations captures a sense of vigorous but controlled action: "Spouts brawl, boughs drip and cease and drip again, / Bricks gleam." To this visual and aural record, the speaker adds a pleasing smell: "Innumerable odors fine and fleet / Are blown this way from blossoming lawn and lane." The sestet adds new images: "Wet roofs show black against a tender sky," while almond bushes "show all their draggled white." The poem ends with a human presence, "a troop of laborers" who pass "slowly by" all this natural beauty as if to consecrate it: "One bears a daffodil, and seems to bear / A new-lit candle through the fading light."

If Reese rejected the faults of Victorianism outright, Romanticism provided her with a more suitable starting place; indeed, she is best considered as an heir of Romantic poetry. "April in Town" exemplifies a productive tension between Romantic and modern poetic sensibilities (also evident in the sonnet "One Night" [LOA, 2: 517]). The way in which the speaker describes a transcendent experience in nature and conveys an almost sacramental response to the natural scene seems Romantic. Yet the focus remains on the objects that she describes rather than on her feelings about them, which we must intuit. There is no comment on or generalization from the experience; the poet's lens stays firmly fixed on, in Pound's famous phrase, "the thing in itself." However, the poem is clearly reaching for some feeling of transcendence, particularly in the final line – albeit a transcendence based not so much on the "communal values" of sentimentalism as on something more ambiguous and personal. We can discern a religious sensibility at work, but one that insists on setting its own agenda. The taut discipline of language also allows "April in Town" to venture onto potentially sentimental ground (even ending with flower imagery) without falling into triteness or exaggeration. A powerful yet carefully controlled emotionalism comes through.

The sonnet "Tears," first published in *Scribner's* in 1899 to enormous acclaim and reprinted many times throughout Reese's life, crystallizes an elegiac mood that runs throughout her work.

When I consider Life and its few years –
A wisp of fog betwixt us and the sun;
A call to battle, and the battle done
Ere the last echo dies within our ears;
A rose choked in the grass; an hour of fears;
The burst of music down an unlistening street –
I wonder at the idleness of tears.
Ye old, old dead and ye of yesternight,
Chieftains, and bards, and keepers of the sheep,
By every cup of sorrow that you had,
Loose me from tears, and make me see aright
How each hath back what once he stayed to weep;
Homer his sight, David his little lad!

As elegy, the poem succeeds beautifully, working its way from a state of listless grief to an affirmation of redemption and compensation for loss. Yet the pervasive plangent mood and the sophisticated qualifications of the final affirmation lift the poem above run-of-the-mill work. After alluding to Milton's famous sonnet "When I consider how my light is spent," the octave establishes a haunting feeling of sadness that borders on a modernist anomie, as the speaker runs through a series of images of loss and alienation: "A wisp of fog betwixt us and the sun," "A rose choked in the grass; an hour of fears," and the most striking image, a "burst of music down an unlistening street." In the smooth final line of the octave, "I wonder at the idleness of tears," she hints that there might be some meaning behind all of this. Why bother to grieve, she asks, given the relentlessness of loss in the "few years" of life we are given?

In the sestet, the speaker asks for help from the "old, old dead and ye of yesternight" to "make me see aright" the traditional Christian view of redemption and reconciliation, that all will be restored and rectified. The standard consolation message – in the end "each hath back what once he stayed to weep" – rounds out the poem by means of an example of recovered loss – "Homer his sight" – that resonates with the early allusion to Milton's blindness. Yet the poem delivers a sense of struggle and striving rather than complacency. The speaker does not declare herself "over it" but rather *asks* to be "loosed from tears," as if she knows it is actually impossible. The sestet resolves the poem not in easy pieties, but rather with a complex awareness of the difficulty of belief in an alienated, fallen world of which tears and grief are integral parts. As the final stanza of "In Time of Grief" (LOA, 2: 518) makes starkly clear, Reese is not so much interested in mastering or even overcoming her grief as in naming it and finding a way to turn it into poetry:

I knew not Grief would go from me,
And naught of it be plain,
Except how keen the box can be
After a fall of rain.

Reese relied on the sonnet's formal strictness to harness emotion, especially in her few personal sonnets. In perhaps her most nakedly personal poem, "To Myself," written in 1918, the speaker finally confesses to herself the shameful "old secret" – a lover's devastating rejection – that has hid her from herself and forced her to play roles in public. The power of the speaker's emotion lies like a coiled spring pressing back against the sonnet's pressures. The sonnet form also plays off a certain modern sensibility at work in the poem: the oddness of a sonnet, traditionally a form written to a beloved or to a generalized audience, that is addressed to the poet's own self (with the splitting-off of identity thus implied) gives the poem an intense, heady mood. In the octave, the speaker announces to herself in a direct, colloquial voice that she is tired of her somehow untrue, variable persona: "Girl, I am tired of blowing hot and cold; / Of being that with that, and this with this." The next lines use Reese's more characteristic formal language to add a natural image; she is sick of being "A loosened leaf no bough would ever miss / At the wind's whim betwixt the earth and sky." Also sick "Of wearing masks," she goes on to describe the new policy of self-revelation that she wants to follow: "Oh, I would rend them all / Into the dust that by my door is blown." The desire to expose the secret becomes the desire to be her true self and to experience the cathartic relief that this moment of honesty would bring: "Of my old secret bare me to the bone, / Myself at last, none other!" The line goes on to prepare us for the sestet, in which the confession comes:

> . . . I would call:
> "I had a lover once. This is the face
> He lauded April-high and April-deep
> As fair a flower as hers of Camelot
> And yet he loved it but an April's space.
> This is myself indeed. Now hear me weep.
> I had a lover once, but he forgot."

Yet for all its emphasis on catharsis, the release that the poem seems to work toward is mediated in ways that the choice of the sonnet form presages. Most notably, the confession is put into the conditional tense: she "would rend" her masks, she "would call" out her confession. It remains ambiguous whether her desire to discard the masks that she has worn and to let go of the shame that has caused her to nurture the old secret would mean "calling" to others or only, as the title says, to herself. The choice to put the entire sestet, the revelation, in quotation marks intensifies its force as "reality," as the speaker's own, most personal words, but it is still unclear who she is willing to let hear them and on what terms.

The anti-sentimental agenda of the poem also remains striking. The speaker undoes the lover's sentimental narrative: we know the romantic message that he intended by "lauding" her face "April-high and April-deep," but we also know that for Reese, April has its bite, and the line "And yet he loved it but an April's space" brings his sentimental rhetoric crashing back to earth. The last line, "I had a lover once, but he forgot," also lends the poem an anti-sentimental but emotional force. Ironically, Reese adds emotional weight through language that downplays emotion. No complex drama here; the lover hurt

her in a banal way that becomes all the more potent for the unflinchingness of her description. As Hemingway and other fiction writers were discovering at about the same time, a sly simplicity of language actually magnifies feeling rather than negating emotion.

Yet for all her prescience, ultimately it is not just as a bridge to modernism that we should read Reese. Reese is a transitional figure whose work has an uncommon integrity to it. The pleasure of entering her poetic world comes from the rare combinations of qualities that coexist harmoniously there: obliqueness alongside precision, passion alongside reticence, and strangeness alongside "commonness."

MARIA RUSSO

Selected Works

A Branch of May, Baltimore, Maryland: Cushing and Bailey, 1887; Portland, Maine: Thomas B. Mosher, 1909
A Handful of Lavender, Cambridge, Massachusetts: Houghton Mifflin, 1896; Portland, Maine: Thomas B. Mosher, 1919
A Quiet Road, Cambridge, Massachusetts: Houghton Mifflin, 1896, Portland, Maine: Thomas B. Mosher, 1916; reprinted, 1924
A Wayside Lute, Portland, Maine: Thomas B. Mosher, 1916; reprinted, 1922, 1929
Spicewood, Baltimore, Maryland: Norman Remington, 1920
Wild Cherry, Baltimore, Maryland: Norman Remington, 1923
The Selected Poems of Lizette Woodworth Reese, New York: George H. Doran, 1926
Little Henrietta, New York: George H. Doran, 1927
A Victorian Village, New York: Farrar & Rinehart, 1929
White April, New York: Farrar & Rinehart, 1930
The York Road, New York: Farrar & Rinehart, 1933
Pastures, New York: Farrar & Rinehart, 1933
The Old House in the Country, New York: Farrar & Rinehart, 1936

Further Reading

Jones, Robert T., *In Praise of Common Things: Lizette Woodworth Reese Revisited*, Westport, Connecticut: Greenwood, 1992
Ostriker, Alicia, *Stealing the Language: The Emergence of Women's Poetry in America*, Boston: Beacon, 1986
Pearce, Roy Harvey, *The Continuity of American Poetry*, Princeton, New Jersey: Princeton University Press, 1961
Walker, Cheryl, *The Nightingale's Burden: Women Poets and American Culture Before 1900*, Bloomington: Indiana University Press, 1982

John Rollin Ridge

(1827–1867)

When John Rollin Ridge was born on March 19, 1827, in the Cherokee Nation, his people were in a state of turmoil. Like other American Indian groups in the southeast at the time, the Cherokees were being pressured by white settlers and the federal government to leave their lands and to immigrate to territories in the west that had not as yet been reached by the advancing frontier. Ridge was born into an important Cherokee family; both his father and grandfather, John and Major Ridge, were leaders in the tribe, and they, like the majority of the Nation, at first opposed leaving their lands in Georgia and moving to the wilds of the west. As time went on, however, they and other educated Cherokees began to regard resistance to removal as futile. They entered into negotiations with the federal government, made the best bargain they thought that they could, and, in 1835, signed a treaty that ceded their lands in the east for land in what is now Oklahoma. This began the time in Cherokee history known as the Trail of Tears (1838–39), during which U.S. troops forcibly removed the majority of the tribe. Most of the latter did not agree with the treaty, and in 1839 Ridge's father was dragged from his bed and brutally assassinated in front of Rollin and the rest of the family; his grandfather was killed on the same day. Clearly, the rest of Ridge's life bore the impress of these events.

John Rollin Ridge was educated in Arkansas, where the family fled after the assassinations, and later in Massachusetts. His education was a rich one, especially in literature and history. He began writing poetry and essays as a young man, even as he settled down to a life as a farmer and rancher on the border between Arkansas and the Cherokee Nation. He married a white woman, Elizabeth Wilson, and looked forward to a life in which he would rebuild the social and economic prominence that his family had lost since his father's death. In 1849, however, Cherokee affairs again intruded. He was involved in a fight over a horse with David Kell, a man from the Cherokee faction that was still hostile to his family. Ridge shot and killed his adversary, but he was then forced to flee. Early the next year, he joined a wagon train for California, never to return to the Cherokee Nation.

In California, Ridge tried gold mining. Finding this hard and unprofitable work, he soon found employment as a writer. He was first a reporter from the Gold Rush towns, and then he served as an editor of several of the newspapers that were springing up in northern California. All this time, he was writing poetry and publishing it in newspapers and in San Francisco literary journals. His reputation as a writer grew and was greatly enhanced in 1854, when he published *The Life and Adventures of Joaquín Murieta, the Celebrated California Bandit.* Ridge's book is considered to be the first novel written in California. This romance was read widely, as were subsequent pirated editions. In the years immediately preceding and during the Civil War, he allied himself with the anti-abolitionist Democrats and editorialized in his party's favor. After the war, he participated in the peace settlement between the Cherokee Nation and the United States. Ridge died in 1867.

The largest part of Ridge's poetry was written in Arkansas and during the early years in California. In later years, his writing consisted mainly of news and editorials as well as essays, although he did write some poetry during the late 1850s and 1860s. The earlier poetry is romantic, often autobiographical and personal. The later verse reflects Ridge's journalistic and political interests, for it is almost wholly based on historical subjects.

Many of Ridge's early works deal with nature and his reaction to the natural environment. Ridge's experiences with the environment often take on the spiritual or transcendental qualities seen in the works of other writers of the time. These special or enlightening encounters with nature are most often represented as the result of the poet's imaginative powers.

A good example is "To a Star Seen at Twilight," which is important for its assertion of the power of imagination and the role of the artist. It also is a declaration of Ridge's public persona. In the first section, the persona describes a solitary star in the twilight sky, "companionless in light," peerless and aloof. Separate from earth, the star is part of another reality; it seems to have an eternity and immutability not found in mortal realms. After the persona describes the star, he begins to meditate on the similarity between his own spirit and the distant object. Both are isolated and far from the rest of their kind. But there the similarity ends. The spirit of the persona, anchored by his own mortality, cannot match the star's pureness and nobility. Although his spirit can soar, can partake of the transcendental experience, it cannot sustain the vision, cannot as yet enter the eternal world permanently, as the star does.

Next, Ridge makes a statement about his own poetic vision and, by implication, about the ability of all poets. He wishes that all people could "in their bosoms drink / Thy loveliness and light like me." Poets are special and can make their mystical perceptions visible to common people. The poet's role, for Ridge, is to use his special power to translate his own experiences, transcendental and otherwise, to his readers. The poet recreates, as far as possible, his own special insights into the universe that surrounds us all. Thus, Ridge establishes himself as one of the seers, one of the priests of nature. In the poem's final section, the persona exults in the star's isolation: "Thou are the throne / Of thy own spirit, star! . . . / 'Tis great to be alone!"

Many of Ridge's poetic works echo those by other nineteenth-century writers. An example is "A Night Scene," which is reminiscent of the odes of John Keats. It follows the structure of the Keatsian ode and contains some rather standard romantic metaphors that are found throughout the poetry of William Wordsworth, Percy Bysshe Shelley, and Lord Byron.

As the poem opens, the persona waits for that Wordsworthian "impulse from the vernal wood":

I sit
And muse alone – the time and the place are fit –
And summon spirits from the blue profound
That answer me and through my vision flit.

His vision has not yet come, but in the next stanza it appears in the guise of a maiden, "a beauteous being" "with hair night-hued, and brow and bosom white." She seems to float in the soft light and shadows of evening, and for the moment all is still. Then he hears a heavenly sound whose "tones are filling up the air, / That brings them, with the star-light blended now, / And wavelet murmuring from below." The maiden's voice and harp are making this nightingale song, and the music lures him to her. He knows there is an abyss between them, yet still he reaches out for that momentary glimpse, that fleeting perception of immortality: "But o'er that gulf my spirit loves to lean." With his "spirit bride," he senses a connection with the divine, if only in promise; but the tryst is futile, and it is not long before he is called back to his own reality. The poem ends on a plaintive note:

> Fair words, like ripples o'er the watery deep
> When breezes softly o'er the surface play,
> In circles one by one ye stretch away,
> Till, lost to human vision's wildest sweep
> Our souls are left to darkness and dismay.

The poem follows a familiar romantic three-part movement. It opens with the persona "outside" the state of vision, isolated in his own humanity, but clearly reaching beyond himself. In the second part comes the connection of the persona and the object. But this coming together is temporary, and in the third part, the persona finds himself alone again and musing on the experience. Ridge's diction and imagery are typically romantic as well. Obvious examples can be seen in his use of the "watery deep" to convey the vast immutability of eternity and the references to the breezes that play both on the surface of the water and on the human soul. The form the vision takes, too, is important and recalls the ghostly maidens in poems by Edgar Allan **Poe**, Shelley, Keats, and others.

Ridge's most famous poem, "Mount Shasta" (LOA, 2: 183), closely resembles Shelley's "Mont Blanc" in theme, natural description, diction, and even meter. Both poems are written in blank verse with indiscriminate rhyme. The diction in many cases is strikingly similar. For example, Ridge's "vast Reflector in / The dome of heaven" resembles Shelley's "infinite dome / Of Heaven." Shasta as a "monarch mountain" and an "Imperial midst the lesser heights" compares with Mont Blanc, which towers above "Its subject mountains." The American poem, like the English one, deals with the perception of eternity in the face of the all-consuming flux of time. The mountain peaks in both cases symbolize the ultimate reality that stands behind and occasionally intrudes into the transient and mortal world. Mount Shasta is seen as "the great material symbol of eternal / Things!" in much the same way as the Alpine pinnacle is depicted as the immutable in a changing universe.

By contrast, many of Ridge's early poems deal with love. Some are conventional, describing unspecified women, but others are clearly autobiographical and personal. "To Lizzie" – a poem addressed to his wife, Elizabeth Wilson, and written on his trek across the plains to California – shows that Ridge recognized, valued, and missed her calming influence, especially after he was forced to leave her behind in Arkansas. The poem also expresses Ridge's image of himself as a Cain figure, a defiant exile who roams the world alone far from home. His self-image is revealed in another poem that is perhaps a romanticized version of his and Lizzie's courtship (she, like

Ridge's mother, was white). "The Stolen White Girl" (LOA, 2: 188) tells of a "wild half-breed" who takes a beautiful white girl captive, not by means of the usual weapons and bonds, but by his own attractiveness. If the poem does present the self-portrait that it seems to, Ridge saw himself as a romantic hero – a dashing, passionate adventurer.

In "The Harp of Broken Strings," written shortly after Ridge's arrival in California, several themes emerge, the chief one being isolation. Following again the romantic exile motif, the poem's narrator describes himself as "a stranger in a stranger land." He also recognizes his own psychic instability when he says that he takes a perverse delight in his misery. His only solace seems to be his ability to conjure up the image of his beloved, although this "delight," too, is often darkly tinged. But also implied here is the threat of losing this imaginative power – another romantic staple – since his harp bears broken strings, which suggests the loss of youth, potential, and opportunity.

"The Still Small Voice" is another poem written in the romantic tradition, in which Ridge assesses his situation as an outcast. Here, he comments on the twin forces of fate and history that he believes govern his life. The narrator asserts that wherever he goes, whatever he does, he hears a voice within him saying, "Too late! too late! the doom is set, the die is cast." His every action, he believes, has been ordained in the past; his present and future are ruled by his history. Applied to Ridge's own life, this theory is correct. His preoccupation with revenge, his ambition to become a successful man, and his chronic financial instability all had their genesis in two key events in Ridge's past: the assassination of John and Major Ridge and the related killing of David Kell. In this poem, as in "The Harp of Broken Strings," the narrator seems to relish his despondency and the hopelessness of his situation; perhaps, like a Byronic hero, he considers that he is being given special attention by fate.

"A Cherokee Love Song" (LOA, 2: 185) and "Song – Sweet Indian Maid" are traditional invitational poems in which the speaker urges his love to escape with him into a bower of bliss. In "Song – Sweet Indian Maid," the narrator asks an Indian woman to accompany him on a river journey to an island that he knows, where they will be alone and may do as they please. A similar situation exists in "A Cherokee Love Song," but this time the woman invited on the canoe trip is white. As in the other poem, nature is cooperative here and, as the narrator points out, even approves of the tryst. It is interesting to note that in the posthumous volume of his poetry – edited by his wife – "A Cherokee Love Song," which feature a white heroine, is included, although the other "Song" is not. As in the other love verse, the invitational poems use traditional language, imagery, conceits, exaggeration, and structure. They reflect the poetic tradition of both the past, especially that of English romanticism, and of nineteenth-century America.

In his later years, Ridge wrote little verse, but what he did produce was decidedly different from his early work. His significant later works include "The Atlantic Cable," "California," and two works called simply "Poem" (LOA, 2: 189). All deal with Ridge's view of history and his belief in the confident nineteenth-century idea of progress. In this view, in its several components: Societies, races, and nations are caught up in the inevitable march of progress and constantly evolve toward higher and higher levels. The march is not merely technological; human intelligence and even human spirituality move upward. Implicitly, various contemporary societies, races, and nations have reached different plateaus on the evolutionary scale, because of environment and other factors. Some of the hunter-gatherer societies have barely begun the climb of progress. The western nations, including the United States, are at the cutting edge of the evolutionary process. Ridge's theory could seemingly be supported empirically, by looking at the advances made every day in the developed countries – the Atlantic Cable was a notable example – and comparing this activity with the apparent stagnation of societies perceived to be less advanced.

Among the many implications of such a system is that the "advanced" nations are morally obligated to spread their ideas and methods to the "benighted" peoples of the world. A corollary is that less advanced people should accept these offerings wholeheartedly and learn to live like their more civilized counterparts. The message for American Indians was obvious. By the time Ridge wrote these poems, he believed that his family had made the transition in only three generations from a primitive aboriginal existence to a modern civilized one. His own experience and success as a writer helped to encourage this view.

JAMES W. PARINS

Selected Works
Poems, San Francisco: Henry Payot, 1868

James Whitcomb Riley

(1849–1916)

There is a photograph of the poet at age 22 in Marcus Dickey's *The Youth of James Whitcomb Riley*. Riley has an elegant mustache, lightly turned up at the end; hair indifferently combed; liquid eyes; and a flowing tie over his white shirt. Clearly, an artist or an artist in embryo. Riley was born in Greenfield, Indiana, on October 7, 1849, the son of a lawyer who named him after Governor Whitcomb and who hoped the boy would follow in his footsteps. He briefly worked in his father's office, but he had no taste for law and his relationship with his father was always a prickly one – particularly after the death of his mother in 1870. During the 1870s, he worked as an itinerant sign painter, traveled briefly with a medicine show, and tried to find his footing as a poet. He had a reputation for conviviality, playfulness, and japery, but he was also given to depression and to drink. Shadow and shine, to use a favorite phrase of his, marked much of his verse.

Riley was a newspaper poet at the time, and that was a special breed of versifier. Most papers accepted contributions, many of them execrable, for which there was usually no pay. Other papers picked up the best verses, of which Riley's – however conventional – were an example. He began to be known to other newspaper poets and to editors, many of whom wrote verse themselves, but it was his ambition during the 1870s to break out of his poetic ghetto and to be accepted by the magazines in the east. This did not happen until late in the 1880s, and by that time he had written most of his interesting verse, as well as a great deal of relentlessly ordinary poetry. In 1879, he went to work for the *Indianapolis Journal* and stayed there until 1888. These were his most prolific years, and his position at the paper gave him a base and a loyal following. In 1883, he published his first book, ostensibly by "Benj. F. Johnson, of Boone," *"The Old Swimmin'-Hole" and 'Leven More Poems*, a collection of dialect poems, which was followed by a host of volumes averaging one a year.

After some disastrous early attempts at public readings, he found his platform voice and manner in the 1880s. In a period in which performing poets, humorists, and lecturers crisscrossed the country, he became a welcome addition to programs and often appeared with other celebrated speakers. He did a double with Bill Nye from 1886 to 1890 (they published a shared collection, *Nye and Riley's Railway Guide*, in 1888), when, as the *Louisville Courier-Journal* (February 2) said, "The Poet Breaks with Bill Nye to Go in with John Barleycorn." Dried out from his alcohol binge, Riley continued to tour until 1894 and to read on special occasions after that. He did not simply read his poetry and his prose platform pieces; he acted them, assuming the character of his speakers. In "How to Tell a Story," Mark Twain says that Riley's telling of "The Wounded Soldier," in which he spoke as a "dull-witted old farmer" who got everything wrong, is "about the funniest thing I have ever listened to." Eugene V. Debs, five times Socialist candidate for president, said of Riley's reading of "When the Frost Is on the Punkin" (LOA, 2: 473): "his impersonation of the old farmer was perfect. Riley himself completely vanished and reappeared in the role of the homespun tiller of the

soil. As a mimic he was incomparable" (*Pearson's Magazine*, March 1917). These testimonials to Riley as a performance artist are important for readers of the LOA anthology to consider because so much of his verse – and not simply that in dialect – was intended to be read aloud. Riley often seems dead on the page, but spoken aloud, the poems come to life.

Increasingly, with the Raggedy Man poems and, more obviously, the pieces written for *A Child-World* (1897), Riley became celebrated as a children's poet, and the baby talk that had always figured discreetly in his work began to overflow it. "W'y, one time wuz a little-weenty dirl" begins "Maymie's Story of Red Riding-Hood." Although it is a revision of a comic piece from 1878, this poem is obviously far removed from Riley's oddly erotic "Red Riding-Hood" of 1875, which imagines the girl "out in the gloomy old forest of Life! / And a Heart, ravenous, trails in the wood / For the meal have he must, – Red Riding-Hood!" In the 1890s, his platform career largely behind him, Riley wrote fewer poems, choosing to recycle, reshuffle, and rework earlier material to fill the annual volumes that he usually prepared for the Christmas trade. Take "Out to Old Aunt Mary's," for instance. When it was first published in 1884, it was a fairly lean nostalgia poem with five stanzas of reminiscence and a requisite sixth for the old woman's death; when it was redone in 1904 as one of a group of single-poem volumes with Howard Chandler Christy's illustrations, it had grown to 20 stanzas and foundered like an overfed swimmer in deep water.

It was just at this point in time, as Riley misused his own early work, that the romantic figure who opened this essay finally disappeared into the slightly elfin banker depicted by John Singer Sargent in his much-reproduced portrait of the poet. Riley had turned into an institution. He somewhat belatedly became comfortable with the eastern establishment. He was given honorary degrees by Yale University (1902) and the University of Pennsylvania (1904), and he became the first poet to receive the Gold Medal of the American Academy of Arts and Letters. He died in 1916, full of honors, lay in state under the Indiana State House dome, and – although he apparently wanted to be buried simply in Greenfield – ended up under a pseudo-Greek grandiosity at the highest point in Indianapolis' fashionable Crown Hill Cemetery. Scattered in more modest graves farther down the hillside lay lesser luminaries like President Benjamin Harrison, Vice President Charles W. Fairbanks, and Indiana's Civil War governor, Oliver P. Morton. The young Riley could have got some comic mileage from that setting.

A look at the topic indexes in *The Complete Works of James Whitcomb Riley* (1913) indicates that he worked poetic grounds that were familiar to most popular poets. For instance, the topics "Nature Poems" and "Poems of Sentiment" have predictable subheads – "Love," "Friendship," "Reflection," "The Old Days," "Home," "Patriotism," and "Bereavement." Not that more serious poets have not treated similar themes; after all, both W. H. Auden's "In Memory of W. B. Yeats" and Emmeline Grangerford's "Ode to Stephen Dowling Bots, Dec'd" (LOA, 2: 338), courtesy of Twain, might be called bereavement poems. Run-of-the-mill popular poets tended to treat such material either humorously or sentimentally and to use doggerel rhythms and easy or easily strained rhymes. What separated Riley from his lesser colleagues was his attempt to achieve something more than a newspaper throwaway. He saw himself as a vehicle through which poems could find their way to the page (see the strange prose piece "Tale of a Spider" for a metaphorical treatment of poetic afflatus); unfortunately for Riley, however, his poetic gems did not simply flow onto the page. Although it may not always be evident when one examines his choice of words and meter, he did work over his verse diligently. "It's like grinding sausage-meat with bones in it," he told Debs. "I felt when I got through with that job as if I had given birth to a rough-shod colt."

He worked in rhyme, of course, and usually in couplets or quatrains. Sometimes he tried set forms like the sonnet, but usually the length of stanza and line was decided by the subject matter, the genre (comic or sentimental/serious), and the persistent voice that wants to speak the poem aloud. The poems often contain surprising metaphors (the tired farmer in "A Summer's Day" wishes that he "could spred / Out like molasses on the bed, / And jest drip off the aidges in / The dreams that never comes ag'in"), strange twists of thought, and jokes that are not simply jokes (the old man in the third of the "Songs Tuneless" remembers men, like him, "who boasted here and there, / They would have died for the fair thing / They after murdered, marrying").

One of the most persistent themes for Riley is nostalgia for a rosily remembered past, when "The world was having a jollier time / Than it ever will have again." These lines are from the first poem in Collected Works, "A Backward Look," written when Riley was only 20, and broadly speaking, both the subject and the narrator are borrowed conventions. What makes the poem, however, is the specificity of the recollected details. There are foolish bits like "the selfsame clock that ticked / From the close of dusk to the burst of morn," as though it did not keep time during the day, but for the rest – particularly the children's games – the poem is properly evocative. In some ways, this poem is more effective than the much neater "The Days Gone By" (LOA, 2: 472), which was written when Riley was in his thirties and presumably almost ready for a backward look; the later poem calls up generalized nature references (apples, rye, robin, and quail) that are more labels than tangible, audible things, and are less beguiling than the chorus to that other Indiana treasure, Paul Dresser's "On the Banks of the Wabash":

Oh, the moonlight's fair tonight along the Wabash,
From the fields there comes a breath of new mown hay,
Thro' the sycamores the candle lights are gleaming,
On the banks of the Wabash, far away.

The quality in "Days" lies in its verbal devices such as its discreet alliterations: "the splashing of the swimmer," "faith in fairies," and "simple, soul-reposing." Another line includes the *tripped-dipped* rhyme with an interior assonantal echo: "ripples . . . lipped." Or, better yet, the poem's last line has both alliteration and internal rhyme: "In the golden olden glory of the days gone by." However appealing this wordplay, nostalgia poems are more effective when the re-creation of the past is full of concrete details, as in "A Backward Look," the first stanza of

"Little Orphant Annie" (LOA, 2: 474), in which Annie's chores are specified, and "The Old Swimmin'-Hole" (LOA, 2: 471), which borrowed "the swimming-hole" from the much earlier "A Backward Look" and set it to dialect.

There is more to "The Old Swimmin'-Hole" than a recollection of happier days. As in so many of Riley's nostalgia poems, the speaker not only wants to escape the present into memory, but he wants to escape from consciousness altogether: "And I wish in my sorrow I could strip to the soul, / And dive off in my grave like the old swimmin'-hole." In a letter of March 1883 to his friend and fellow poet James Newton Matthews, Riley complained, as he often did, that Edgar Allan **Poe** "seems, always, to me, unhappy, and his influence always cheerless." Perhaps Poe was his whipping boy because Riley remembered sadly the notoriety that he himself achieved in 1877 when, as a prank and to prove that he was the equal of the magazine poets, he published a fake "lost" Poe poem, an event that led to his being fired from the *Anderson Democrat* and to a two-month drunk. Poe aside, Riley came increasingly to believe in happy poems for happy people. He admitted to Matthews, "All melancholy themes are pets of mine – positively; but I am growing to avoid them as much as possible." What this attitude ignores is that popular poetry has always had a lugubrious note to it, a fact that is obvious to anyone who has read *Percy's Reliques* or listened to country music. Riley knew it, too. His work is full of dead mothers, dead babies, dead friends, lost love, lost childhood, and lost innocence. A note in *Collected Works* identifies "Dot Leedle Boy" (1874), a heartbreaker of a German dialect Christmas poem about a dead child, as one of Riley's "earliest recitations and from the first one of his most popular numbers." More interesting is "Joney," a sad-heroic-death or they're-sorry-now poem in which the protagonist, so often mocked because of his looks, dies saving 13 "childern drowndin'." The first and last stanzas end with: "Purty is as purty does!"

Riley is quoted at length in a sketch of his life in the *Collected Works*: "In my readings, I had an opportunity to study and find out for myself what the public wants, and afterward I would endeavor to use the knowledge gained in my writing. The public desires nothing but what is absolutely natural, and so perfectly natural as to be fairly artless. It can not tolerate affectation, and it takes little interest in the classical production. It demands simple sentiments that come direct from the heart." Depending on one's opinions about art and commerce, Riley was either a crass purveyor who sold out to the market or an artist who perfected his work – like the Marx Brothers, who tried out the famous stateroom scene in live performance before it was filmed for *A Night at the Opera*. Although Riley does not say so at this point, clearly the most popular items in his nonclassical production are the dialect poems – both on stage when Riley performed them and in reprint after reprint ever since. I am not thinking here of works like "Dot Leedle Boy," because, despite its initial success, the German dialect in it ("He vas yoost a leedle baby") – like Riley's Irish, Scottish, and black dialects and his baby talk – is about as genuine as Chico Marx's Italian. About his Hoosier dialect and the possibility of using dialect in non-comic poetry, however, Riley was very serious. In the lecture "Dialect in Literature," he argues the legitimacy of dialect and harks back to Geoffrey Chaucer. Elsewhere, he is a bit more venomous. He deplores the fact that editors tended to see dialect verse simply as humorous. Case in point: when *Century Magazine* accepted "Nothin' to Say" in 1883, the editor apologized for returning a serious poem at the same time: "we thus seem to put a premium on humorous work." The piece was not published until 1887, and when later that year in New York Riley read "Nothin' to Say" before a gathering of literary lights who knew the work, if at all, only from the pages of the *Century*, his reading – or so Richard Crowder reports in his biography of Riley – "was so delicate and touching that the audience was overcome."

One of the reasons that dialect verse was automatically taken as humorous was the success of the great misspellers. In his stage introduction to his reading of "Old-Fashioned Roses," Riley defended dialect verse from its debasement at the hands of "the rhyming punsters and poetical thugs of our 'Comic Weeklies.'" This was a general rather than a specific denunciation. In his memorial poem to Josh Billings, a friend from the platform circuit who had been an early admirer of Riley, the poet dwelt on the comedian's virtues without mentioning that Billings was one of the most famous of the misspellers; in a plug for Riley as a performer, Billings wrote, "He is phunnier than tung kan tell."

Riley prized himself on the accuracy of his ear, on the correct reproduction of Hoosier rural speech. A note to "What Smith Knew about Farming" in the *Collected Works* says, "Mr. Riley has made a deliberate use of both 'o" and 'of' in this and other dialect poems. In this detail as in all others he has carefully followed the dictates of spoken dialect as he has learned it." There remain occasional words that seem a touch too grand for his rural characters, but – despite the cavils of some dialect experts – the rhythm and the indicated pronunciation seem right enough. Besides, in "Dialect in Literature" and in praising writer-performers that he admired, like Mark Twain and George Washington Cable, Riley says that "all true dialect-writers . . . are also endowed with native histrionic capabilities." He wished to be counted in that company, and so he should be.

GERALD WEALES

Selected Works

The Complete Works of James Whitcomb Riley, edited by Edmund Henry Eitel, 6 vols., Indianapolis, Indiana: Bobbs-Merrill, 1913

Letters of James Whitcomb Riley, edited by William Lyon Phelps, Indianapolis, Indiana: Bobbs-Merrill, 1930

The Best of James Whitcomb Riley, edited by Donald C. Manlove, Bloomington: Indiana University Press, 1982

Further Reading

Crowder, Richard, *Those Innocent Years*, Indianapolis, Indiana: Bobbs-Merrill, 1957

Dickey, Marcus, *The Youth of James Whitcomb Riley*, Indianapolis, Indiana: Bobbs-Merrill, 1919

———, *The Maturity of James Whitcomb Riley*, Indianapolis, Indiana: Bobbs-Merrill, 1922

Russo, Anthony J., and Dorothy E. Russo, *A Bibliography of James Whitcomb Riley*, Indianapolis: Indiana Historical Society, 1944; reprinted, New York: Haskell Booksellers, 1972

Edwin Arlington Robinson

(1869–1935)

Born in Head Tide, Maine, on December 22, 1869, Robinson clearly has the characteristics in poetic taxonomy to be classified as a "transitional poet." That is, he was born sufficiently early in the nineteenth century, and was sufficiently influenced by predilection and training to seem, by virtue of his poetic form, to be a traditional nineteenth-century poet. Yet because of his dark temperament, which was shaped by the hardness of his life and times, and because of his tautness of language within the form, there is something very modern, distinctly post-nineteenth-century, about his poetry.

Gardiner, Maine, where Robinson was moved as a baby with his family and where he lived until he was in his late twenties, became the model for the Tilbury Town of his best-known – and some of his best – poems. There, in Gardiner, under the mentorship of his doctor friend Alanson T. Shumann, a local versifier who railed against the inadequacies and inanities of poetry in his time, Robinson decided to become a poet. And, of course, since Gardiner was the place that Robinson understood, it was Gardiner and the people he knew there that he transmogrified into his poetic world, the sad, dead-end world of Tilbury Town, with its down-and-outers and its lost romantics who finally surrendered to suicide or alcohol.

For Robinson, there were plenty of people from Gardiner whom he could use as models for the figures in his poems, including ample varieties of failure from his own family. Among these was his bankrupt father, who died during the two years that young Robinson spent at Harvard University, which in turn left the young man in a desperate financial situation. One elder brother abused alcohol, another morphine. Small wonder that although Robinson was attracted to the forms and romantic escapes of his New England poetic predecessors – Henry Wadsworth **Longfellow**, Oliver Wendell **Holmes**, and John Greenleaf **Whittier** – and William Cullen **Bryant**, uncertainty and pessimism smoldered within the traditional forms of his own poems. Given Robinson's thoughtful, introspective personality; the dysfunctionality of his family; and his acute perception of the historical forces at work in his time – the unbridled industrialism, mendacity, expansionism, and greed; the spiritual downdraft created in the wake of Darwinism's sweeping-away the religious verities of the past – it could not have been otherwise.

From the outset Robinson's work demonstrated his power to infuse the old forms – notably the aging sonnet, which by the late nineteenth century had acquired some wrinkles and liver spots – with a new vitality. Even in his first collection of poems, *The Torrent and the Night Before*, a thin volume that he published privately in 1896, when he was in his late twenties, he showed the potent tension that was to run through much of his work between, on the one hand, his modernist condemnation of the effete and materialistic age and, on the other, the unquenchable Emersonian spark of optimism that he frequently tried to ignite into flame despite the overall darkness of his poems. Thus, in the sonnet "George Crabbe" (LOA, 2: 597), Robinson praises that English poet (1754–1832) for the energy that pulses through his poems of English rural life, which he

contrasts to what he sees as the hollowness, "the shame / And emptiness of what our souls reveal," of life in fin de siècle America. Always alert to the mistaking of shadow for substance, he indicts his society for "kneel[ing] / To consecrate the flicker, not the flame." In "Credo," from that same volume, he laments the loss of bearings in "The black and awful chaos of the night," in a world in which it has become impossible to navigate with "no star / In all the shrouded heavens anywhere." Yet even in this lightless emptiness, his senses – sharpened by his hope for the understanding of some benevolent principle in the universe, and of self – detect an almost indecipherable message of hope. It comes from so far away that he "can hear it only as a bar / Of lost imperial music," but it is there, this "far-sent message of the years," and it is nothing less than "the coming of the Light."

The possibility of rescue from the spiritual void of the times is suggested even in a grieving lover's apparent contemplation of suicide, the often-anthologized "Luke Havergal" (LOA, 2: 592), also from his first collection. Although the bereaved Havergal is told to go to "the western gate" (presumably death) to be reunited with his lost love, where "the dark will end the dark, if anything," it is possible to read the poem as a contending against darkness and at least a kind of victory over it. Whatever the interpretation of "Luke Havergal," in the body of his poetry Robinson never misplaced for long the essential optimism – the belief in the possibility of redemption – that was at his center, however much he was haunted by the blindness and pettiness of his fellow human beings. Ultimately, he always cherished the belief in a being, an intelligence, or a force beyond and greater than humanity – the awareness of which humanity ignored or forgot at its peril.

Robinson's debut volume showed great promise in its reinvigoration of the sonnet form, but it was justly criticized for a tendency toward didacticism and abstraction. He took the criticism seriously when he moved to New York City in 1897 and made the city his home; there, he succeeded in growing measurably as a poet. That year, he published his second collection, *The Children of the Night*, in which he introduced the people of Tilbury Town, people who lived in the realm of his imagination but sounded like – and, sad to say, acted like – his father, brothers, and the other denizens of Gardiner, Maine, whom he had known, sometimes all too well. Louise Bogan later honored *The Children of the Night* as a landmark accomplishment, "one of the hinges upon which American poetry was able to turn from the sentimentality of the nineties toward modern veracity and psychological truth."

In New York, Robinson, understanding the need to put didacticism behind him, had a productive period and worked on a number of longer poems, including *Captain Craig*. He began to have dire money troubles, however, and soon, saddled with the addictive personality that ran in his family, he would have worse than money problems. For most of 1898 he was forced to return to Maine, and for about the first half of the following year he had to take a job as secretary to Harvard's president, Charles W. Eliot, a position that Robinson heartily despised.

On returning to New York he had difficulty earning enough money on which to live. The manuscript of *Captain Craig* was ready, but Robinson could not find a publisher for it until Houghton Mifflin accepted it. They did so, however, only on the stressful condition that Robinson's friends underwrite the costs of publication. The book came out in 1903, but things got worse for Robinson. He had to take a job as a time-checker of laborers who worked on the construction of the New York subway system, but physical and mental fatigue, and the gaseous, fetid atmosphere of the newly dug tunnels broke him down, and he turned to alcohol to get through his depression. Only with difficulty did he manage to control the resulting disease.

In 1905, friends rode to his rescue. One of them, William E. Butler, found a place for Robinson in the advertising department of Butler's Boston store and saw to it that Robinson would have a good deal of time to write poetry. Then, in that same year, something wonderful happened to Robinson: his friend Henry Richards, a teacher at the Groton School in Groton, Connecticut, whose family had financially backed the publication of *Captain Craig*, showed *The Children of the Night* to one of his students, Kermit Roosevelt, whose father happened to be President Theodore Roosevelt. The boy passed the poems on to his father, who was much taken with them and arranged for a political appointment for the poet as a special treasury agent at the New York Customs Service. Not satisfied with providing this act of mercy to Robinson, the president wrote a glowing review for *The Outlook* that instantaneously enlarged and enhanced Robinson's literary reputation. Robinson was not slow to recognize what Teddy Roosevelt had done for him, and he did not forget it; later, he recalled in a letter to Kermit that his father had "fished me out of hell by the hair of the head."

Although the president's kindness did not make Robinson financially independent or worry-free, it forever changed his life for the better. *Captain Craig* did not attract much critical or public attention, but the poet's work at the Customs Service permitted him time to work on a number of writing projects. These projects included a new volume of poems, *The Town Down the River* (1910), and some plays, which Robinson hoped would earn him more money than his poetry was bringing in, including *Van Zorn* (originally titled *Ferguson's Ivory Tower*), the one-act play *Terra Firma*, and *The Porcupine*. Robinson undertook to help support his brother Herman's family, as well as himself, on his income from the subway construction job, so the loss of the sinecure when President Roosevelt departed from office in 1909 was certainly a blow. Robinson tried writing more drama over the next couple of years, but he had to declare in March 1913 that these attempts, primarily motivated by the need to make money, had led to the writing of "the damndest rubbish that you ever heard of." He now resolved to commit himself to poetry.

In 1911, Robinson began migrating to the MacDowell Colony, a fine – and subsidized – retreat for writers in Peterborough, New Hampshire; this was a creative enterprise that he had the good sense to continue to take advantage of until his death from pancreatic cancer in 1935. The summer sojourns at MacDowell, together with a bequest from a friend in 1914, a trust fund established for him by friends in 1917, and free lodging given to him by friends in New York finally allowed him to live the last couple of decades of his life in the kind of material certainty – although surely not opulence – about which many a poor poet has dreamed.

Some of the reasons for Robinson's continuing applause from twentieth-century critics may be largely technical – based on his revivification of the sonnet and his use of accurate dialect, for example. Another important reason for his ongoing popularity among general readers of American poetry is, undoubtedly, the gallery of believable, often sympathetic failures that he created to inhabit his Tilbury Town. Why he chose failure as a theme – or why failure chose him – is a matter of conjecture. He had certainly seen enough of it in his father's financial catastrophe, in the addictive illnesses of his brothers, and in his literary misfires and his own economic woes through many years of his life. Moreover, though he sustained a transcendental intuition of some cosmic, mystical being and some hope that should never be abandoned, a somber side to his personality made him wary of the joy of living.

The title characters of his poetic sketches are distinctly, and often disturbingly, human – unhappy, without insight into the conditions of their lives, and sometimes rueful of unfulfilled promise. They are lost because they do not know where to look for themselves, or because they have been looking but have circled back in the dark to where they began. In Miniver Cheevy (in *The Town Down the River*), Robinson created one of the most poignant romantic failures in literature in the person of a man who, disenchanted with the present, yearns for a romantic past that never was as admirable as he likes to imagine it, a man who devotes himself to the pursuit of the very money, the very materialistic aim, that he tells himself is loathsome. Here, as elsewhere in his work, Robinson's sardonic wit is at work; although Cheevy has never seen a Medici, "He would have sinned incessantly / Could he have been one." Yet there is no gladness in the laughter that Robinson evokes, only nervousness. Bewick Finzer (in the same collection) so thoroughly identifies himself with money that when his money goes, his sense of self goes with it, and he is destroyed; he becomes an unhinging reminder to his townspeople of the similarity of their own lives to his. He is to them, "Familiar as an old mistake, / And futile as regret." Eben Flood (in *Avon's Harvest*, 1921) is one of the most memorable characters in Robinson's Tilbury Town gallery. Like many of Robinson's creations, he lacks sufficient core to withstand life's buffeting without blowing away in the wind. Flood is a pitiable man who has outlived all of his friends except the jug, the sole companion in his bid to escape from an empty existence in his dwelling place above the town.

The character sketches of the lost are many. In "Eros Turannos" (in *The Man Against the Sky*, 1916), the wife is chained to her morally corrupt husband in a house "where passion lived and died," because she is too proud and fears too much to escape and achieve her independence. "Karma" (in *Dionysus in Doubt*, 1925) underscores the moral bankruptcy of American society, as Robinson perceived it. It tells of a businessman who has financially ruined a friend and expiates his sin by donating to a sidewalk Santa Claus "from the fullness of his heart . . . / A dime for Jesus who had died for men." It is clear that Robinson had his own vision of the category of human beings that T. S. Eliot called "the hollow men." There are many of them in his 1925 collection. In "Cassandra," the prophetess rails against a society that has given up ethics and morality for materialism and hollow patriotism. She harangues the people as if they were willing to listen:

> Your Dollar, Dove and Eagle make
> A Trinity that even you
> Rate higher than you rate yourselves;
> It pays, it flatters and it's new.

But, of course, the modern Cassandra is mocked and her warning ignored as arrogantly – and as perilously – as that of the ancient one: "None heeded, and few heard."

Small wonder, given Robinson's dismal worldview – despite his hope for a mystical universal force – that death looked awfully fetching sometimes, as it is presented not only in "Luke Havergal" but in "Richard Cory" (in *The Children of the Night*; LOA, 2: 594) and in "How Annandale Went Out" (in *The Town Down the River*). A paragon of material success, Richard Cory is admired and envied by his townspeople. But for an unspoken reason – presumably the empty place at his center – one "calm summer night" Cory went "home and put a bullet through his head." That ought to shake up a society that has no better hero, nothing better to idolize. Perhaps Robinson had in mind as a remedy for the modern world's ills the solution of the unhappy physician in "How Annandale Went Out" – euthanasia.

In a sense, "Miniver Cheevy" may have been as autobiographical as any of Robinson's poems, not only because of the shared alcoholism of poet and character but because of their shared romanticism. Robinson used the poem to show the ridiculousness of preferring medieval to modern warfare (suits of armor to modern uniforms), and of longing for the good old days, which were not really very good, but long for them he himself did in some part of his imagination. For much of his artistic life, in fact, in three volumes that he published over a decade – *Merlin: A Poem* (1917), *Lancelot: A Poem* (1920), and *Tristram* (1927) – Robinson found occasion to retreat into Arthurian legend. Once he arrived there, however, like Mark Twain and other anti-romantic romantics, he found it less than entirely attractive, certainly less marvelous than Cheevy, that "child of scorn," found it. Writing *Merlin* during the accumulating horrors of World War I, Robinson commented that in the poem "Arthur and his empire serve as an object lesson to coming generations that nothing can stand on a rotten foundation." He was clearheaded enough to use the legend effectively, at least at times, as a symbolic structure on which to build another one of his cases against the loss of values in modern life. The poem contains an apocalypse that is all too appropriate to the modern world and to the soulless technology of its warfare, as the magician sees "a crumbling sky / Of black and crimson, with a crimson cloud / That crumbled into nothing." And the poem ends with this nightmare of even more emptiness: "Colder blew the wind /Across the world, and on it heavier lay / The shadow and the burden of the night / And there was darkness over Camelot."

If anything, the second volume of the trilogy, *Lancelot*, is even gloomier. Merlin's hopeless vision comes true, and Lancelot has only that nightmarish landscape of fire and ice to traverse. "There was nothing," Robinson's terse summary of Lancelot's world, is the emblem of the poet's own hollow world of materialism and the senseless slaughter of the First World War. But Robinson cannot live with such an unalleviat-

ed apocalyptic vision. The Cheevy in him, the romantic, opens the curtain a crack in the last line and allows that "in the darkness came the Light." Alas, the "Light" at the end of *Lancelot* is far too contrived, unprepared for; it is a very little whistle in a very heavy, cold, lonely darkness.

Nor is the "Light" that Robinson conjures at the finish of the trilogy, at the end of the *Tristram* volume, more convincing. Isolt of Brittany has lost Tristram, her adored husband, to Isolt of Ireland and deeply grieves. She gazes longingly out to sea for the man, the ideal, now gone from her forever, and at this moment her desolation is ameliorated by an intimation of the "Light," in this case "white birds flying, / Flying, and always flying, and still flying, / And the white sunlight flashing on the sea." The desperation of Isolt's situation scarcely justifies the hope symbolized by the birds and the sunlight, so in the end Isolt may be seen as a figuration of Robinson himself – attempting to light a match against the dark whirlwind of his vision.

Another of Robinson's frequently anthologized poems, "The Man Against the Sky" (the title poem of the 1916 collection), does no better than the Arthurian trilogy at justifying his wishful thinking about a mysterious entity outside of human ken that could yet straighten out the mess that humanity has made of its affairs. This poem is surprisingly – and unduly – long for a poet like Robinson, who has a deserved reputation as a man of few words. It runs to 314 lines, which seek to make some sense of a world that often, especially at the time of World War I (although the war is not directly mentioned), seemed senseless. The work speculates upon the possible states of mind of a symbolic, universal man who is silhouetted against a sky at sunset and is viewed "before the chaos and the glare / As if he were the last god going home / Unto his last desire."

The image of that man seen against the sky of fading day occasions a contemplation of humanity's place in the universe and, in particular, of five possible philosophical approaches to that question. Robinson presents these possibilities in descending order from total religious acceptance to the total abnegation of religion in favor of a consuming materialism – in the poem's terms, from "a faith unshaken"; to "easy trust assumed of easy trials"; to "sick negation born of weak denials"; to "crazed abhorrence of an old condition"; to the lowest circle of Robinson's philosophical hell, "blind attention of a brief ambition," his nomenclature for surrender to self-absorption and materialism. The descent of humankind, the poem asserts, has been gradual, and, in latter times, it has been deepened by a tyrant that humanity mistakenly believes it has created and controls – "infant Science," which "makes a pleasant face / And waves again that hollow toy, the Race." In a reference to Nahum 3:17, a biblical prophecy of the ruin of Nineveh, Robinson warns that with the rejection of religious faith in favor of secularism and materialism, modern technological man may perceive himself to be "so great / That satraps would have shivered at his frown." Robinson also cautions, however, that the self-satisfied would do well to remember that "Nahum's great grasshoppers were such at these, / Sun-scattered and soon lost."

But as in the volumes of his Arthurian trilogy, Robinson could not tolerate the emotional bleakness of such an ending, as artistically powerful as that ending would have been. After what may be the true end of the poem, he is driven to go on, to aver – and to reassure himself – that humanity must believe in that something beyond itself that sustained Robinson; ultimately, he simply could not bear the notion that only clay-footed humanity and death exist on earth. And so, he almost cries out the conundrum at the end:

> If after all that we have lived and thought,
> All comes to Nought, –
> If there be nothing after Now,
> And we be nothing anyhow,
> And we know that, – why live?
> 'Twere sure but weaklings' vain distress
> To suffer dungeons where so many doors
> Will open on the cold eternal shores
> That look sheer down
> To the dark tideless floods of Nothingness
> Where all who know may drown.

As strong and direct an assertion of Robinson's sense of the meaning of life and of God comes in *King Jasper*, another book-length poem, which he completed only days before his death in 1935, and which was published later that year. In this allegory on the dangers of materialism (he named the poem for the Jasper County mine, the failure of which had dropped his father into bankruptcy), he reveals the essential mistrust of collective humanity that likely inspired his need of God. With acerbic irony, he points out that

> . . . No God,
> No Law, no purpose, could have hatched for sport
> Out of warm water and slime, a war for life
> That was unnecessary, and far better
> Had never been – if man, as we behold him,
> Is all it means.

A lifetime of misanthropy – his mistrust of the human race, for all of his close friendships with individual members of it – was confirmed now in the 1930s, with the Great Depression plaguing the western world and with fascism on the rise in Europe. He observes in *King Jasper* that "Today the devil is more than God. Tomorrow / He will be more, and more." Uncertain, as always, of precisely what "God" signifies, to him it is nonetheless the only concept that offers any hope for relief from intolerable meaninglessness:

> I don't say what God is, but it's a name
> That somehow answers us when we are driven
> To feel and think how little we have to do
> With what we are.

Edwin Arlington Robinson's desperate reaching for redemption, although not, perhaps, *artistically* satisfying, does not diminish his importance – both technical and substantive – as a late-nineteenth and early-twentieth-century American poet. Indeed, the spectacle of this modern man searching in pain for the antidote to modern life may well be a crucial element of his importance, the strongest part of the connection readers feel to him.

ALAN SHUCARD

Selected Works

The Torrent and the Night Before, privately published, Cambridge, Massachusetts: Riverside, 1896

The Children of the Night, Boston and New York: Richard G. Badger, 1897

Captain Craig, Boston and New York: Houghton Mifflin, 1902

The Town Down the River: A Book of Poems, New York: Scribner's, 1910

Van Zorn: A Comedy in Three Acts, New York: Macmillan, 1914

The Porcupine: A Drama in Three Acts, New York: Macmillan, 1915

The Man Against the Sky: A Book of Poems, New York: Macmillan, 1916

Merlin: A Poem, New York: Macmillan, 1917

Lancelot: A Poem, New York: Thomas Seltzer, 1920

The Three Taverns: A Book of Poems, New York: Macmillan, 1920

Avon's Harvest, New York: Macmillan, 1921

Collected Poems, New York: Macmillan, 1921

Roman Bartholow, New York: Macmillan, 1923

The Man Who Died Twice, New York: Macmillan, 1924

Dionysus in Doubt: A Book of Poems, New York: Macmillan, 1925

Tristram, New York: Macmillan, 1927

Collected Poems, 5 vols., New York: Macmillan, 1927

Sonnets: 1889–1927, New York: Macmillan, 1928

Cavender's House, New York: Macmillan, 1929

Collected Poems, New York: Macmillan, 1929

The Glory of the Nightingales, New York: Macmillan, 1930

Selected Poems, with a preface by Bliss Perry, New York: Macmillan, 1931

Matthias at the Door, New York: Macmillan, 1931

Nicodemus: A Book of Poems, New York: Macmillan, 1932

Talafer, New York: Macmillan, 1933

Amaranth, New York: Macmillan, 1934

King Jasper, New York: Macmillan, 1935

Selected Letters of Edwin Arlington Robinson, introduction by Ridgely Torrence, New York: Macmillan, 1940

Letters of Edwin Arlington Robinson to Howard G. Schmitt, edited by Carl J. Weber, Waterville, Maine: Colby College Library, 1943

Untriangulated Stars: Letters of Edwin Arlington Robinson to Harry DeForest Smith, edited by Denham Sutcliffe, Cambridge, Massachusetts: Harvard University Press, 1947

Edwin Arlington Robinson's Letters to Edith Brower, edited by Richard Cary, Cambridge, Massachusetts: Belknap, 1968

Further Reading

Anderson, Wallace L., *Edwin Arlington Robinson: A Critical Introduction*, Cambridge, Massachusetts: Harvard University Press, 1968

Bloom, Harold, *Edwin Arlington Robinson*, New York: Chelsea, 1988

Barnard, Ellsworth, *Edwin Arlington Robinson: A Critical Study*, New York: Macmillan, 1952

Cestre, Charles, *Edwin Arlington Robinson*, New York: Macmillan, 1930

Coxe, Louis, *Robinson*, Minneapolis: University of Minnesota Press, 1962

Fussell, Edwin S., *Edwin Arlington Robinson: The Literary Background of a Traditional Poet*, Berkeley: University of California Press, 1954

Hagedorn, Hermann, *Edwin Arlington Robinson*, New York: Macmillan, 1938

Kaplan, Estelle, *Philosophy in the Poetry of Edwin Arlington Robinson*, New York: Columbia University Press, 1940

Neff, Emery, *Edwin Arlington Robinson*, New York: Sloane Associates, 1948

Shucard, Alan, Fred Moramarco, and William Sullivan, *Modern American Poetry 1865–1920*, Boston: Twayne, 1989

Smith, Chard Powers, *Where the Light Falls: A Portrait of Edwin Arlington Robinson*, New York: Macmillan, 1965

Stanford, Donald C., *Revolution and Convention in Modern Poetry: Studies in Ezra Pound, T. S. Eliot, Wallace Stevens, Edwin Arlington Robinson, and Yvor Winters*, Newark and London: University of Delaware Press, 1983

Winters, Yvor, *Edwin Arlington Robinson*, Norfolk, Connecticut: New Directions, 1946

George Santayana

(1863–1952)

Although his poetry does not compare either in scope or in depth with his philosophical writings, Santayana began his career as a poet. When he virtually ceased writing poetry in his late thirties, he had amassed a volume of work notable for its craft and philosophical insight. Santayana's poetry, which he described as "simply my philosophy in the making," explores the breakdown of traditional faith and the search for a philosophical alternative.

Jorge Agustín Nicolás Ruiz de Santayana was born in Madrid, Spain, on December 16, 1863, to Spanish parents. He remained a Spanish subject all his life. Before her marriage to Santayana's father, Agustín Ruiz de Santayana, Josephina Borrás Santayana had been the wife and then widow of an American, George Sturgis. She separated from her second husband, and along with her three children from the previous marriage, she moved to Boston, Massachusetts, when Santayana was five. Santayana himself followed her three years later, in 1872, to receive a better education than was available to him in Spain. At the age of 10, he entered the Boston Latin School, where six years later he read one of his first poetic efforts, "Day and Night," on Prize Day. Although it must be categorized as juvenilia, the poem is an impressive effort for a 16-year-old, and certain lines prefigure his mature poetic voice: "The earth by day is prodigal of charms, / And the blue waters are another sky."

In 1882, Santayana entered Harvard University, where, as a student, instructor, and then professor, he would remain until 1912. After he arrived at Harvard, he soon moved among the leading intellectual circles, drawing cartoons for the *Harvard Lampoon* and taking classes from Josiah Royce and William James. He helped to found the *Harvard Monthly*, which published his poetry alongside that of William Vaughn **Moody** and Bliss Carman (see Richard **Hovey**). After his freshman year, he visited Spain, where he saw his father for the first time in 10 years. William H. Holzberger claims that during his trip to Spain, Santayana began to "think of himself as a Spaniard in exile," a feeling that imbues many of the poems that he wrote during the ensuing decade. In "Avila," the poet surveys the "fragrant moor" of the Spanish countryside and concludes, "Nor world nor desert hath a home for thee." His fifth Sapphic ode, a panegyric to the Mediterranean Sea, employs a similar nostalgic tone. After describing the wonder of the northmen at encountering the "eternal / Solace of mortals," the poet affirms, "The more should I, O fatal sea, before thee / Of alien words make echoes to thy music." In addition to his love of Mediterranean culture, Santayana was skeptical of American materialism, as his second ode suggests: "My heart rebels against my generation, / That talks of freedom and is slave to riches." Although uncomfortable in America, he had no career prospects in his native land. His return to Spain impractical, he remained at Harvard to receive the best education America had to offer a budding poet and philosopher.

After his graduation in 1886, Santayana traveled to Europe on a Walker fellowship and studied philosophy at Berlin. A year later, he returned to Cambridge to write his dissertation on the German philosopher Lotze. After receiving his doctorate in 1889, he began his teaching career at Harvard as an instructor in the philosophy department. He dismayed his colleagues and university officials by spending his time on poetry rather than writing serious philosophy or serving on university committees. He was extremely popular with undergraduates, however, holding meetings in his room where he and a small group would read and discuss poetry. In October 1893, his close friend Warwick Potter, a recent Harvard graduate, died of cholera, which he contracted after a serious bout of seasickness. His death occasioned four elegiac sonnets collectively entitled "To W. P." Santayana was deeply shaken by Potter's death, which precipitated what he later called in his autobiography a "philosophical metanoia." In "To W. P.," however, the tone is far from grief-stricken. Although the poet claims that "With you a part of me hath passed away" and that he has "grown much older in a day," he aesthetically rationalizes the death: "Your virgin body gave its gentle breath / Untainted to the gods. Why should we grieve, / But that we merit not your holy death?" Like Housman in "To an Athlete Dying Young," Santayana affirms the beauty of an early death: "The bough that falls with all its trophies hung / Falls not too soon, but lays it flower-crowned head / Most royal in the dust."

"To W. P." is typical of Santayana's verse in its muted emotion. Although he denounced romantic excesses and professed the need for classical restraint in art throughout his career, there may be more personal reasons for his distrust of unchecked passion. His most recent biographer, John McCormick, has convincingly argued that Santayana's sexual preference was for "homosexual over heterosexual attachment." In 1929, Santayana remarked to his friend, Daniel Cory, that he supposed "Housman was really what people nowadays call 'homosexual,'" and then he confided, "I think I must have been that way in my Harvard days – although I was unconscious of it at the time." Robert K. Martin claims that a number of Santayana's published love sonnets were directed to Potter, and McCormick finds overt homoerotic elements in several sonnets that remained unpublished in Santayana's lifetime. One reason for Santayana's poetic restraint may have been the suppression of an emotion that was simply unmentionable in the Harvard community of the time.

During the early years of the 1890s, Santayana continued to publish verse in the *Harvard Monthly*, and in 1894, he published *Sonnets and Other Verses* with Stone and Kimball, a publishing house founded by two recent Harvard graduates. The volume contained his first sonnet sequence of 20 poems, "To W. P.," five odes, and various other poems. It received favorable reviews, and Santayana soon found himself the toast of a salon of faculty wives headed by Nancy Toy, the wife of theologian Crawford H. Toy. His poetry, however, along with his exotic dress, did little to endear him to the Harvard administration, who felt that he should spend his time more productively. In 1895, Santayana wrote Stone and Kimball, who were planning on reissuing his volume, and asked if he could include some additional sonnets. They agreed, and the 1896 revised edition of *Sonnets and Other Verses* contained the second sonnet sequence of 30 Petrarchan love poems. Santayana published his first philosophical work, *The Sense of Beauty*, the same year. Apparently satisfied with their young instructor, the Harvard administration promoted Santayana to the rank of assistant professor in 1898. He also continued to write poetry, publishing the blank verse drama *Lucifer: A Theological Tragedy* in 1899. Holzberger claims that in this volume, Santayana is closest to the other Harvard poets of the time, including Moody, George Cabot **Lodge**, and Trumbull **Stickney**, a group whose work is dominated by myth. The volume was not received well, although Santayana continued to think highly of it.

By 1900, Santayana had written the vast majority of the poetry that he would ever publish. As his biographer George W. Howgate writes, "In 1900 Santayana was known to his reading public as a young poet who dabbled in philosophy; in 1910 he was a moral philosopher who had once been a poet." Although he published *A Hermit of Carmel and Other Poems* in 1901, his main interest now lay in philosophy. He published *Interpretations of Poetry and Religion* in 1900, and he spent the early years of the new century writing the five-volume *Life of Reason* (1905–06). Santayana continued to be a brilliant and popular teacher, a facet of his career that was itself a major contribution to American poetry. From among those he taught or knew as students at Harvard, one could compile a "Who's Who" of modern American poetry, including such figures as Wallace Stevens, T. S. Eliot, Conrad Aiken, and Robert Frost. Although both Eliot and Stevens would eventually reject the philosophical position that Santayana articulated in *Interpretations of Poetry and Religion*, Santayana's thought was a seminal influence on the younger poets. In his preface, Santayana claims that

> religious doctrines would do well to withdraw their pretension to be dealing with matters of fact. . . . The excellence of religion is due to an idealization of experience which, while making religion noble if treated as poetry, makes it necessarily false if treated as science. Its function is rather to draw from reality materials for an image of that ideal to which reality ought to conform.

Santayana's equation of poetry and religion prefigures Stevens's conception of a "supreme fiction," although Stevens would modify Santayana's exclusion of facts in the realm of ideals. Although Santayana asserted that "brute fact" provides merely "a starting point for a creative movement of the imagination," Stevens would wrestle more fitfully with the dialectic between fact and imagination. On the other hand, Eliot's eventual return to Christian orthodoxy signaled a rejection of what he considered an effete theory of religion. If Santayana, as Robert Lowell's poem claims, "found / the Church too good to be believed," Eliot saw a deeper necessity for religious faith.

In 1912, Santayana's mother died, leaving him with a modest inheritance. Never fully at home in his adopted land, he decided to resign his Harvard professorship. At the age of 48, he returned to Europe. While living in England during the war years, he rejected a position at Oxford University that Robert Bridges offered to arrange. He traveled extensively throughout Europe, eventually settling in Rome in 1924. He wrote steadily, publishing several philosophical works, including *Skepti-*

cism and Animal Faith (1923). Although he published a judicious selection of his poems in 1922, his tone in the preface is that of an ex-poet. He claims that he has "committed his rash act once for all" and apologizes for the new edition "to my best critics and friends, who have always warned me that I am no poet." His self-effacement notwithstanding, the volume received favorable reviews. In 1927, Santayana published *The Realm of Essence*, the first of four volumes contained in *The Realms of Being*, which also included *The Realm of Matter* (1930), *The Realm of Truth* (1938), and *The Realm of Spirit* (1940). In 1935, he published his only novel, *The Last Puritan*. Set on an American college campus, the novel provides a critique of American Puritanism and philistinism. Selected by the Book-of-the-Month Club, it was both a popular and a critical success. During World War II, he began writing his three-volume autobiography, *Persons and Places*, the last volume of which was published in 1953. Santayana did not live to see it in print. On September 26 of the previous year, he had died of stomach cancer in Rome.

Stylistically, Santayana was skilled but not innovative. His diction is heavily Latinate and often archaic. He explains in the 1922 preface that poetic diction is elevated "just because it is consecrated and archaic; a pomp as of a religious procession, without which certain intuitions would lose all their grace and dignity." This overlay of artifice – embodied in the O's, Thou's, and ere's that sprinkle his verse – appears unnecessarily stylized at times, although it often skillfully invokes a poetic tradition. In the second sonnet sequence, for example, the overt archaisms provide a suggestive texture that underlies the poet's manipulation of Petrarchan conventions. Although he participates in certain poetic traditions, however, he fails to assert himself as an individual talent. His perspicuous critique of his own verse in the 1922 preface includes the claim that he lacks

> that magic and pregnancy of phrase – really the creation of a fresh idiom – which marks the high lights of poetry. Even if my temperament had been naturally warmer, the fact that the English language (and I can write no other with assurance) was not my mother tongue would itself preclude any inspired use of it on my part; its roots do not quite reach to my centre.

McCormick argues that the distance between poet and language created a "distrust for the spontaneity in diction," which resulted in Santayana's reliance on dated poetic conventions. Other commentators have found that, although the interaction with tradition is a more positive one, his poetry is, as John Lachs puts it, too "conceptually heavy."

Certainly, Santayana breaks Goethe's maxim that a poet must know all philosophy but keep it out of his poetry. His method of composition calls to mind the methodology of Ciceronian rhetoric. As he explained in a 1938 letter, quoted in Holzberger:

> The recipe for the dish is, first, to have a clear thought expressible in prose, which carries with it, in your mind, a definite emotion, and second to heighten or leaven it with meter, alliteration, and allusions to kindred matters, so that an educated man (like the author) can vibrate largely and sympathetically to the whole thing.

Modern critics are likely to dismiss a poet who claims that his poetry "heightens" a "clear thought expressible in prose." Although a categorical denouncement on these grounds would be imprudent, it is true that in a number of his weaker poems, the meaning seems tangential to the poem itself. For Santayana, poetry was not so much a mode of experience as a vehicle of expression, and as a result, his verse often lacks the enriching ambiguity and viscerally affective quality of first-rate poetry, a fault that he shares with other philosopher-poets. As Archibald MacLeish noted, Santayana's "glimpses of reality are labored into closely articulated epigrams, and his phrases of wonder or of doubt or grief are inevitable unities, perfect to the uses of his will" (*American Criticism 1926*, William A. Drake, ed. [1926]). Many commentators have seen his turn from poetry to philosophy as a movement toward a more congenial mode of expression, although, ironically, he has sometimes been criticized, notably by Bertrand Russell, as being too poetical a philosopher.

Yet, if Santayana was not a major poet, he was a skilled craftsman with a firm grasp of poetic form. He wrote the majority of his poetry in iambic pentameter, and he was capable of inflecting his meter to suggest tonal shifts. In his extensive analysis of Santayana's prosody, Howgate shows that strict iambic meter generally connotes an "emphatic assertiveness," but metrical variations, particularly trochaic inversions, often suggest a "softening of poetic texture" associated with more contemplative, wistful moods. Santayana's sonnets, in both the two sequences and in his miscellaneous sonnets, are all variations of the Italian form. In *The Sense of Beauty*, Santayana writes that the "sonnet in which the thought is not distributed appropriately to the structure of the verse has no excuse for being a sonnet," and his sonnets exhibit a close connection between structure and sense. At times, however, the structure becomes mechanical, which results in a form that overwhelms organic expression.

Although he scoffed at critics who he thought paid too much attention to his technique, Santayana was capable of technical sophistication. "Cape Cod" (LOA, 2: 552), with its consonantal and vocalic interconnections within its three-line stanzas, shows the poet at the height of his craft. Written after a visit to the summer home of one his undergraduate friends, the poem suggests Santayana's homesickness for his native land:

> The low sandy beach and the thin scrub pine,
> The wide reach of bay and the long sky line, –
> O, I am far from home!
>
> The salt, salt smell of the thick sea air,
> And the smooth round stones that the ebbtides wear, –
> When will the good ship come?

The couplet is comprised of a six-stress line, each with two groupings of three consecutive stresses separated by two unstressed syllables. The integrity of the groupings is strengthened by the internal consonantal repetition between lines: beach/bay, scrub/sky, smell/smooth, and thick/that. In addition, the stanzas are interconnected through end rhyme in the final line.

The tension between the poetic couplet and the relatively discursive third line suggests a division between an overly cerebral speaker and his natural surroundings. W. B. Yeats once wrote that "when the tide of life sinks low, there are pictures. . . . The pictures make us sorrowful. We share the poet's separation from what he describes." At the same time, the outer landscape mirrors the inner, a connection strengthened by the speaker's use of prosopopoeia (the ebbtides "wear" stones) and the pathetic fallacy ("the wretched stumps"). Yet the landscape, although it may offer an objective correlative for the speaker's mood, can never offer answers to the questions he poses:

> The wretched stumps all charred and burned,
> And the deep soft rut where the cartwheel turned, –
> Why is the world so old?
> . . . .
> And among the dark pines, and along the flat shore,
> O the wind, and the wind, for evermore!
> What will become of man?

Although highly praised by Moody, "Cape Cod" was not one of Santayana's favorite poems. Perhaps he found fault in the conceptual thinness of the poem, which presents a scene and poses questions but offers no answers. Deeply committed to philosophical investigation, Santayana would likely have viewed a poem of mood and imagery as an evasion of more serious issues.

This critique could hardly be leveled at the majority of Santayana's poetry, which confronts the philosophical burdens of secular existence. The first sonnet sequence – probably his best work overall – traces the poet's rejection of the Christian faith and his subsequent quest for an alternative within the natural world. The 20-sonnet sequence progresses through various states of despair, elation, and reasoned insight in response to the passing of the old dispensation. Sonnet I functions as an epitome for the entire sequence, which progresses through mood rather than narrative. In it, the poet relates that during his youth, he "worshipped at the piteous height / Where God vouchsafed the death of man to share," but he has since renounced Christianity for the "Eternal Mother" of the natural world, to whom his supplication is directed: "let the sun and sea / Heal me, and keep me in thy dwelling place." Sonnet III (LOA, 2: 546), which Santayana claimed was the first poem written in the sequence, warns against a constraining rationality:

> O world, thou choosest not the better part!
> It is not wisdom to be only wise,
> And on the inward vision close the eyes,
> But it is wisdom to believe the heart.

In the introduction to the 1922 *Poems*, Santayana claims that the "verses of a philosopher will be essentially epigrams," an accurate description of the initial quatrain. (When he signed books, Santayana often added the line "It is not wisdom to be only wise" below his signature.) The development of the poem, however, transcends this label. The second quatrain grounds the epigram by portraying Columbus as a man who, through trusting "the soul's invincible surmise," "found a world" without a chart. The spatial imagery continues in the sestet: "Our knowledge is a torch of smoky pine / That lights the pathway but one step ahead / Across a void of mystery and dread." The poet equates "knowledge" with the wisdom that, paradoxically, is not wisdom. True wisdom requires "the tender light of faith," "By which alone the mortal heart is led / Unto the thinking of the thought divine." Prefiguring Stevens, Santayana equates religion with a mode of thought. Although Christianity may be incompatible with rational inquiry, the function of religion as an imaginative interaction with the world is, for Santayana, not a dated concept. On the contrary, the death of God necessitates a new mode of religious experience, one compatible with the life of reason. Within this frame of reference, a return to archaic paganism, although attractive, will not suffice. Sonnet IV recounts the poet's nostalgia for pagan times. Even though he wishes that he had been "born in nature's day," however, he realizes now, as humanity must "groan beneath the weight of boasted gain," that "No unsung bacchanal can charm our ears," just as "No hope of heaven" can "hush the importunity of pain."

Having rationally discarded both Christian and pagan belief, the poet attempts in Sonnet V (LOA, 2: 546) to find an epistemological bedrock, a Cartesian cogito from whence to rebuild his world. Such a position, however, proves illusive; in comparing dream and waking consciousness, the poet cannot confidently answer his question, "Of my two lives which should I call the dream?" Equating his dream with subjective experience, the poet questions its ability to stand the light of day:

Even such a dream I dream, and know full well
My waking passeth like a midnight spell,
But know not if my dreaming breaketh through
Into the deeps of heaven and of hell.
I know but this of all I would I knew:
Truth is a dream, unless my dream is true.

The demanding syntax here exemplifies the rhetoricity of Santayana's verse. Some critics have found fault with this aspect of his work, although few would go so far as to agree with Jessie Rittenhouse's claim that the poems "creak and totter on the stilts of rhetoric." Unsatisfied with purely objective knowledge, the poet asserts that truth is dependent on his dream, which is comparable to the "inward vision" of Sonnet III.

The remainder of the sequence uses this type of vision to reestablish communion with the natural world. In Sonnet XVI, the poet claims that "heaven shines as if the gods were there," an image that calls to mind another poem that posits a secular heaven, Stevens's "Sunday Morning," in which the speaker claims that the sky will be "much friendlier then than now," "Not this dividing and indifferent blue." In thus asserting the efficacy of the imagination to reclaim nature, Santayana seeks to rectify the divisions between, on the one hand, humanity and the spiritual realm, and, on the other, humanity and the natural world. As the poet affirms in the concluding sonnet: "The soul is not on earth an alien thing / That hath her life's rich sources otherwhere; / She is a parcel of the sacred air."

Whereas the first sonnet sequence locates the Platonic ideal within nature, the second sequence more clearly marks the boundary between the realm of matter and the realm of essence. Comprised of 30 sonnets numbered from XXI to L, the second sequence invokes the Petrarchan tradition of love poetry to comment on more contemporary philosophical issues. This sequence also prefigures the philosophical stance of *Interpretations of Poetry and Religion* (1900), in which Santayana would argue the necessity of "recognizing facts as facts and accepting ideals as ideals." Holzberger writes that "the poet uses the traditional language and images of love to render the sentiment of renunciation of worldly things in order to possess them ideally." This divorce between reality and the ideal necessitates a revision in the traditional Petrarchan doctrine. In "Platonic Love in Some Italian Poets," Santayana argues that Petrarch is too obsessed with Laura, and thus lacks the "tendency to impersonality . . . essential to the ideal." Ascension to the ideal requires a renunciation of the particular, for "while the object of love is any particular thing, it excludes all others; but it includes all others as soon as it becomes a general ideal." This concept is in harmony with Santayana's conception of religion. According to Santayana, although religion could no longer claim to be grounded in reality, it retained an "excellence . . . due to an idealization of experience."

The sequence begins with the poet's praise of Platonic love, which "moveth the celestial spheres / In endless yearning for the Changeless One." Yet although the poet concludes Sonnet XXII by affirming that "In love's eternal orbit keeps the soul," he begins the next sonnet by describing a different kind of love:

But is this love, that in my hollow breast
Gnaws like a silent poison, till I faint?
Is this the vision that the haggard saint
Fed with his vigils, till he found his rest?

Mired in a physical passion that separates him from the ideal, the poet despairingly demands, "Is this the heaven, poets, that ye paint?" The pessimistic outlook continues in Sonnet XXV (LOA, 2: 547), where a suggestive texturing of analogy provides a counterpart to the poet's mood of resigned despair:

As in the midst of battle there is room
For thoughts of love, and in foul sin for mirth;
As gossips whisper of a trinket's worth
Spied by the death-bed's flickering candle-gloom;
As in the crevices of Caesar's tomb
The sweet herbs flourish on a little earth:
So in this great disaster of our birth
We can be happy, and forget our doom.

The first two lines draw rather uninspired parallels, but the following images are more intriguing. Although the parallel phrasing – typical of Santayana's verse – suggests a logical progression, the logic is dependent on the poet's mood of despair. The herbs flourishing on the tomb of Caesar could easily function as an image of renewal, but the image of the gossips' momentary diversion from incipient death relies on the poet's equation of death with doom for its rhetorical impact. The gloomy tone continues in the sestet, where morning "hides the truth" and evening "gently woos us to employ / Our grief in idle catches." Such illusory optimism is consigned to the realm of youth, "Till from that summer's trance we wake, to find / Despair before us, vanity behind." The depth of despair comes in Sonnet XXVI, which concludes with the poet's plea for an early death.

In the ensuing sonnets, however, the poet finds some consolation through the idealization of his beloved. In seeking to attain the woman, he aspires "to perfect good" by "Accounting little what all flesh desires." In Sonnet XXXI, the love becomes all-encompassing: "Thus in my love all loves are reconciled / That purest be, and in my prayer the right / Of brother, lover, friend, and eremite." By Sonnet XLIII (LOA, 2: 547), the poet's apotheosis of the woman has become reciprocal; she, like the goddess Diana, will "lead her lovers into higher ways." The consummation of the love is not physical, but spiritual; her presence brings "the light of heaven / And a lost music I remember well." The increasing idealization and distancing of the woman parallel her increasing ability to sustain the poet in his mortal lot, a movement that reaches its apogee in Sonnet XLVIII (LOA, 2: 548). The octave of this sonnet recounts the story of Helen's brothers, Castor, who was mortal, and Pollux, who was immortal. In the mythical story, Castor dies and Pollux refuses the immortality then unavailable to his brother. Zeus then transforms them into the constellation Gemini:

> They would have lived and died alternately,
> Breathing each other's warm transmuted breath,
> Had not high Zeus, who justly ordereth,
> Made them twin stars to shine eternally.

The sestet applies, perhaps too mathematically, the myth to the poet's situation. Like Castor, the poet's "heart was dying," only to be saved by the absent beloved, whose "flame of youth" inspires the poet so that "My life is now thy beauty and thy truth." Although the beloved "wouldst come down, forsaking paradise," the poet, "by Heaven's ruth" will "go to burn beside thee in the skies." The distance between lover and beloved fits the idealization and abstraction that Santayana associates with the Platonic tradition of Renaissance love poetry, but a number of elements suggest that the poem could have originated in homosexual affection. First of all, the myth involves not a man and a woman, but two men, whose fraternal loyalty might serve to figure other intense bonds. Second, the elegiac tone is unmistakable. The poet's claim that his life is "now thy beauty and thy truth" recalls the second sonnet of "To W. P.," in which the poet's life is "rich" with the virtues of dead youth. Yet whatever its origin, the poet's love is efficacious in removing him from the tribulations of earthly existence. As he affirms in the final line of the sequence, "One love sufficeth an eternity."

Whereas in the second sonnet sequence, Santayana employs a poetic tradition to explore more general philosophical issues, he also used poetry to explore the philosophy of art itself. He wrote numerous ecphrastic poems that take a spatial work of art as a poetic point of departure. In *Reason in Art*, the fourth volume of *The Life of Reason*, Santayana writes that a man's "habits and pursuits leave their mark on whatever he touches. His habitat must needs bear many a trace of his presence, from which intelligent observers might infer something about his life and action." His ecphrastic poems usually involve the discovery of a material object that expresses intent – what Santayana classifies as art – and a subsequent inference on the part of poet as to that intent.

The sonnet "On a Piece of Tapestry" (LOA, 2: 548) is a typical example. As it begins, the poet contemplates the work of art:

> Hold high the woof, dear friends, that we may see
> The cunning mixture of its colours rare.
> Nothing in nature purposely is fair, –
> Her beauties in their freedoms disagree.

Standing in opposition to nature's disorder, the tapestry is what Santayana calls a "humanized" or "rationalized" object, one that communicates intention. In the tapestry, the "vivid dyes" are "mellowed" to the tint that "the sense will bear," thus permitting an act of communication via the material alteration of nature. This "remodelling of the outer world," Santayana writes in *Reason in Art*, molds "outer things into sympathy with inner values, establishes a ground whence values may continually spring up; . . . the sign that once expresses an idea will serve to recall it in the future." This formulation, which prefigures Eliot's objective correlative, emphasizes the materiality of the communicative ground; art cannot exist as a passive medium through which ideas are preserved. Thus, as the sonnet progresses, the tapestry's material features, especially its rich colors, are foregrounded, until the concluding lines reveal another order of meaning within that color and texture: "While silver threads with golden intertwine, / To catch the glimmer of a fickle sheen, – / All the long labour of some captive queen." The speaker here attributes a human quality, fickleness, to the tapestry, thus claiming it as a "humanized" repository of reason. Although the reader is never shown what the tapestry represents, the poet is able to infer that it is the "long labour of some captive queen."

Santayana's ecphrastic poems often describe a specific work of art as a way of examining the creation and efficacy of art itself. "On an Unfinished Statue" (LOA, 2: 552) takes an unfinished sculpture of Michelangelo as an impetus for a didactic meditation. Pondering the relationship between the material of art, characterized as "beauty's tomb," and the Platonic form that would give it shape, the poet laments that the union was not achieved:

> Fair homeless spirit, harbinger of bliss,
>   It wooed dead matter that they both might live,
> But dreamful earth still slumbered through the kiss
>   And missed the blessing heaven stooped to give.

Artistic sensitivity to the realm of spirit requires a "docile" soul; the "chisel shaking in the pulse of lust" cannot "find the perfect line, immortal, pure." The "distracted hand" must leave "the baffling stone, / And on that clay, thy fickle heart, begin." The artist must "tame the body," a process that itself is a "patient art," before commerce with the realm of spirit can occur. "Before a Statue of Achilles" (LOA, 2: 549), a three-sonnet sequence, describes a more successful work of art. Like John Keats's Grecian urn, the statue statically fixes an "immutable," "immortal form no worm shall gnaw." The second sonnet begins by describing, in images emphasizing motion, the birth and boyhood of Achilles. Yet now that "Thessaly forgets thee," the statue remains to allow "new generations" to keep "Thy laurels fresh." In the last sonnet, the poet gazes on the statue, just as the sculptor gazed on Achilles. Yet although the sculptor "cast his wonder in heroic mold," the poet can only unhappily "behold" the resulting work of art, which captures better than the poet is able "what serene and whole / In nature lives, nor can in marble die."

Like the speaker of "Before a Statue of Achilles," Santayana knew art well enough to realize that he left no immortal verse. Although few would deny that his turn to philosophy was in the end a fortuitous decision, it is interesting to speculate about the way in which his career as a poet would have evolved had he not abandoned his Muse. What little poetry he wrote after the turn of the century employs a less archaic idiom, and the poetic environment would have encouraged a more experimental style. Yet even if he failed to become a major poet, his poetry retains for the modern reader an interest in its own right. Santayana claimed that a man need not "pose as a poetic genius, and yet his verses . . . may form a part, even a subordinate part, of the expression of his mind." With a mind as rich as Santayana's, even a partial expression is worthy of close scrutiny.

SCOTT ROMINE

Selected Works

The Sense of Beauty: Being the Outlines of Aesthetic Theory, New York: Scribner's, 1896

Interpretations of Poetry and Religion, New York: Scribner's, 1900

Reason in Art, New York: Scribner's, 1905

Poems, London: Constable, 1922

The Philosophy of George Santayana, edited by Paul A. Schilpp, Evanston, Illinois: Northwestern University Press, 1940

The Complete Poems of George Santayana, edited by and introduction by William G. Holzberger, Lewisburg, Pennsylvania: Bucknell University Press, 1979

Further Reading

Cory, Daniel, *Santayana: The Later Years: A Portrait with Letters*, New York: Braziller, 1963

Howgate, George W., *George Santayana*, Philadelphia: University of Pennsylvania Press, 1938

Lachs, John, *George Santayana*, Boston: Twayne, 1988

Martin, Robert K., *The Homosexual Tradition in American Poetry*, Austin: University of Texas Press, 1979

McCormick, John, *George Santayana: A Biography*, New York: Knopf, 1987

Rittenhouse, Jessie Belle, *The Younger American Poets*, Boston: Little, Brown, 1904

Epes Sargent

(1813–1880)

Epes Sargent, son of Epes Sargent and Hannah Dane Coffin, was born on September 27, 1813, in Gloucester, Massachusetts. (The family name of Epes was pronounced "eeps.") Epes's father was a descendant of William Sargent, who had received a grant of land in Gloucester in 1678. Other early ancestors of the family were Governor John Winthrop and Governor Joseph Dudley. Epes's father was a Gloucester shipmaster. Hannah was his second wife. In 1818, the family moved to Roxbury, Massachusetts, where Epes's father had a relatively unsuccessful career as a merchant; eventually he returned to the sea. Initially, Epes was sent to school in Hingham, Massachusetts. In 1823, at the age of nine, he entered the Boston Latin School. His education was interrupted for several months while he traveled with his father to Russia. In St. Petersburg, he visited the palace often, enjoying the paintings in the Hermitage and exploring the luxurious apartments. While in Russia, he attracted the attention of Baron Stieglitz, the famous financier. The baron offered to educate Epes with his son and to provide a place for him in his counting room with an opportunity for advancement, but the offer was declined. Epes returned to the Boston Latin School, where he helped begin the school's *Literary Journal*, which printed materials describing his Russian experiences. This youthful literary engagement provides early evidence of Epes's commitment to writing and editing, which would last a lifetime.

In 1829, Sargent graduated from the Boston Latin School. Admitted to Harvard's freshman class, he contributed to the *Collegian*, a campus literary publication said to have been established by his elder brother, the successful politician and journalist John Osborne Sargent, and to which Oliver Wendell **Holmes** and others contributed. Although Epes did not graduate from Harvard, some years later he was asked to return to read his poetry before the Phi Beta Kappa Society of that institution.

In his twenties, Sargent found work first on the editorial staff of the Boston *Daily Advertiser* and subsequently on that of the Boston *Daily Atlas*. While with the *Atlas*, he also served as its Washington, D.C., correspondent. Reporting the news of Washington, D.C., gave him access to the politically powerful; he also was friends with John C. Calhoun, William Preston, Daniel Webster, and Henry Clay. (He was later to write a biography of Clay [1842], of which Horace Greeley wrote that he had "reason to believe that Mr. Clay himself gave preference, among all the narratives of his life, to that of Epes Sargent.") After leaving the *Atlas*, Sargent tried his hand at various literary forms. For a time he worked with S. G. Goodrich in the preparation of the popular *Peter Parley* books. In 1836, he wrote for Josephine Clifton a five-act play, *The Bride of Genoa*, which was successfully produced at the Tremont Theater. Subsequently, it was acted by Charlotte Cushman at the Park Theater. The next year he produced the tragedy *Velasco* for Ellen Tree. The play was produced in several theaters, had a modest success in London, and drew favorable comments from Thomas Noon Talfourd, playwright of the critically admired *Ion*. Edgar Allan **Poe** found *Velasco* "a tragedy full of beauty as a poem" that was at least as good as other American tragedies; but in the larger context of world literature, he found the play wanting and speculated that it was not suitable for "representation."

In 1838, Sargent's elder brother departed for New York, and in 1839, he followed, having been invited by George Pope Morris to take charge of the New York *Mirror*. Eventually he left the *Mirror* and went to work with Park Benjamin on another newspaper, the *New World*. During his New York years, he started his own literary magazine, *Sargent's New Monthly Magazine* (January–June 1843). Poe wrote of this magazine that it "had the misfortune of falling between two stools, never having been able to make up its mind whether to be popular with the three or dignified with the five dollar journals. It was a 'happy *medium*' between the two classes, and met the fate of all happy *media* in dying, as well through lack of foes as of friends." Following the failure of the magazine, Sargent continued to edit and write. In 1844, the collection *The Light of the Lighthouse and Other Poems* was published in New York. (Poe scholars will be interested in Gerald E. Gerber's suggestion that several poems in this collection were possible influences on "The Raven" [LOA, 1: 535]; *Poe Studies* 19 [1986].) In 1846, he originated and served as editor on the seven-volume *Modern Standard Drama*, the rights to which he subsequently sold. During this time he was a member of the Union Club and became a founder of the New York Club.

In 1847, Sargent returned to Boston, to become the editor of the *Evening Transcript*. He established himself in Roxbury, and in May 1848, he married Elizabeth W. Weld of Roxbury. He remained editor of the *Transcript* until 1853, when he left to devote himself to writing plays, poems, novels, textbooks, and miscellaneous pieces. He also was often on call as a popular public speaker.

Sargent's *Songs of the Sea, with Other Poems* (1847) included a number of poems published in the earlier collection and elsewhere; several of them were based on incidents during a voyage to Cuba. Demand justified a second printing of the collection in 1849. Several lyrics in the collection lent themselves to song and were soon set to music and performed with considerable success, the most memorable being "A Life on the Ocean Wave." Poe, however, did not share this general opinion: "Mr. Sargent is fond of sea pieces, and paints them with skill, flooding them with that warmth and geniality which are their character and their due. 'A Life on the Ocean Wave' has attained great popularity, but is by no means so good as the less lyrical compositions."

In Poe's judgment, some of the best of Sargent's poems appeared in the subsection of *Songs of the Sea* entitled "Shells and Seaweeds" – a 16-sonnet cycle that records the voyage of a young man who had not been to sea in six years. In the first two sonnets he considers his "fatherland," where many "a sacred spire and happy home" may be seen. He also remarks, however, that labor has raised "a canopy of smoke" above these happy sights, a slightly negative observation in the light of the cycle's frequent references to the pleasure of clear air and cooling breezes. The initial mood of excitement is quickly lost in the threat described by Sonnet III, "The Gale." A great storm reminds the young man that his voyage, which is increasingly emblematic of life's voyage, is not without its perils; however, the next morning is marked by clearing and a return of the sun. This return of peace is treated symbolically as a type or emblem of the restorative power of "Hope," which drives away the "hour of gloom" endured by a "sorrow-clouded soul." The storm, followed by a peaceful interlude in the voyage, encourages in the young man a degree of pensiveness. In Sonnet V, "To a Land Bird," he observes a bird flying near the ship that is not properly a sea bird and derives a moral lesson from its struggle to survive in a foreign element. The bird represents the sensitive soul that is battered by competitive forces, the "selfish strife" of nineteenth-century society. Salvation from this strife rests with "Chance" – the chance that a "zephyr" will arrive in time to waft those who struggle to "their own home of peace, across the world's dull track." The alternative is a ceaseless struggle to the death.

Readers may find it instructive to compare this sonnet with another poem in *Songs of the Sea*, "Rockall" (LOA, 1: 644). The tone of "Rockall" is much more in keeping with the treatment of "indomitable will" in the popular poetry of the period. A great, isolated rock in mid-ocean inspires the poet to think that he might emulate its resistance to the elements: "O, might I stand as steadfast and as free / 'Mid the fierce strife and tumult of the world." He would defy the world's mutability: "then might frown / The clouds of fate around me! Firm in faith, / Pointing serenely to that better world, / Where there is peace, would I abide the storm." The militancy of this poem contrasts strikingly with the gentler lyricism of "Shells and Seaweeds," perhaps because the subject of the latter is clearly a youth rather than a mature man.

In Sonnet VI of the cycle, "A Thought of the Past," the young man's restless mind, perhaps stimulated by the increasing heat of the tropics and his recent considerations of struggle and mortality, dreams of an cool, idyllic childhood: "Old memories, bursting from Time's icy seal, / Rushed, like sun-stricken fountains, on my mind." This sonnet curiously recalls the language and theme of William Wordsworth's famous Immortality Ode, although its resolution lacks the consolation of Wordsworth's poem, concluding as it does with the young man weeping at his loss of childhood innocence and joys.

The journey continues in this verse cycle, the weather becomes increasingly warm, and the ship is becalmed. The young man yearns for a cooling breeze: "Though wrapped in all the storm-clouds of the North / Yet, from thy home of ice, come forth, O breeze, / come forth." He fantasizes about being once again on shore and resting in the shade near a cooling stream, hidden by shadows "through which the sultry Noon / Might stoop in vain its fiery beams to send." The only escape from the heat comes in the night, when the air cools slightly and a light breeze rises. The isolation, the dangers, and the oppressive heat of the journey move the young man to a yet more

pointed consideration of his own mortality in one of the finer sonnets of the cycle. In Sonnet XI, "The Planet Jupiter" (LOA, 1: 643), he describes his fascination with that planet and the tenacity with which he has watched for it during the long nights. For him, the planet has become not only a means of orienting himself on his sea journey but a symbol of the transcendent, a "ray / From the Eternal Source of life and light!" In a moment of faith, he expresses the desire that this same light will provide a beacon at his hour of death: "Shine but as now upon my dying eyes, / And Hope, from earth to thee, from thee to Heaven shall rise!"

The following sonnet, "To Egeria," bears on a similar theme of transcendence. The poem centers on the young man's sense of the immanence of the goddess Egeria in the seascape; the conceptual movement here, as in the "Jupiter" sonnet, is toward rebirth. All the subtle suggestions of the goddess's presence in the world that the young man perceives are accepted as hints of a hoped-for theophany; these ephemeral glimpses of the goddess in the world are but "the bright prefiguration of her who waits, / With snow-white veil and wreath, beside the Future's gates!" These thoughts of despair, mortality, and futurity recede into the background in the following three sonnets, whose context is the safe arrival of the ship in a Cuban harbor. Of these three, only Sonnet XIV, "The Sea-Breeze at Matanzas" (LOA, 1: 643), reprises in secular terms the hope and desire for rebirth explored in "Jupiter" and "Egeria." The concluding couplet has a disturbing resonance with the concern for struggle and mortality in the earlier poems, however, since it suggests a possible comparison with the familiar lair of mermaids, who are known for drawing men to their homes where they drown: "ocean solitudes, and caves, / Luminous, vast, and cool, far down beneath the waves." This image reinforces the idea of recovery from torpor, but it also echoes commonplace descriptions of the mermaids' dangerous dwelling.

The last sonnet, "Weighing Anchor," looks back on this ambiguous image of both life and death by first calling attention to the vibrant growth of the tropics – the orange groves, coffee fields, and "bright" and "bountiful fruits" – and then by associating these attractions with death: "But here the noontide Pestilence recruits / (Stern minister!) Death's ever-gathering ranks." The young man then turns his eyes from the outward vision of the lush tropical life to an inward vision of his homeland, and he recalls "the cedar on its brown hills, ribbed with rocks." The cedar becomes an emblem of freedom and endurance, "rough without, all fragrance at / the core," a freedom gained by striking down roots through rocky soil, resisting the storms that twist the rough bark, and maintaining at the core an integrity, a "fragrance," of which few may be aware.

Sargent continued to the end of his life writing poems and books, editing textbooks, and making a name for himself as an educator. His health declined; his death on December 30, 1880, in Boston, came from a painful and disfiguring cancer of the mouth. For his contemporaries, the image that he left behind was that of a gentlemanly, generous, and dapper man of letters, who was untiring in his devotion to the literary arts.

GLENN M. REED

Selected Works

Velasco: A Tragedy in Five Acts, New York: Harper, 1839

The Light of the Lighthouse and Other Poems, New York: James Mowatt, 1844

Songs of the Sea, with Other Poems, Boston: James Munroe, 1847

The Woman Who Dared, Boston: Roberts Brothers, 1870

Further Reading

Harrison, James A., *The Complete Works of Edgar Allan Poe*, vol. 15, New York: AMS, 1965, pp. 91–93, 252–253

Kunitz, Stanley J., and Howard Haycraft, eds., *American Authors: 1600–1900*, New York: Wilson, 1938

Clinton Scollard

(1860–1932)

Clinton Scollard's bibliography shows us a poet who published profusely throughout his life, but critical studies of the man simply do not exist. The closest we come to thorough analyses of Scollard's poetry are in a chapter of *The Younger American Poets*, written by his second wife, the poet Jessie B. Rittenhouse, and in her remembrance of him in the introduction to his *The Singing Heart*. Her first attempt, made around the midpoint of Scollard's publishing history, is remarkably free of the usual flaws inherent in any work on a living author. The latter attempt, which is as kind as a spouse may be to her mate's art, nevertheless remains the only summation of Scollard's career that is currently available. When mentioned in literary histories, Scollard is usually lumped together, in a fleeting reference, with other minor poets who flourished at the turn of the century.

Born in Clinton, New York, near Syracuse, Scollard overcame a debilitating childhood illness to become a strong athlete in his youth. He also showed great interest in observing nature, a habit that would serve him well in his poetry. As an undergraduate at Hamilton College, he was a pitcher for the baseball team, and is credited with introducing the curve ball to college athletics. He also excelled at public speaking, giving the commencement address at his graduation. After college, he taught English at Brooklyn Polytechnic Institute, but his health soon forced him to leave this post. He traveled for a year – to Florida, Arizona, and California – and it was at this time that he developed his poetic skills. His early efforts, as with many other young poets of the time, were based on French forms. Even in his first collection, *Pictures in Song* (1884), we can see his amazing technical skill and his facility with form and rhyme. Scollard entered Harvard University for a graduate degree in graphics, and while he was there he became fast friends with other poets, notably Frank Dempster Sherman and Bliss Carman (see Richard **Hovey**).

Scollard stayed in Cambridge after his graduation to prepare his second volume, *With Reed and Lyre* (1886), for publication. It is from this volume that "As I Came Down from Lebanon" (LOA, 2: 524) is taken. This poem is Scollard's most widely recognized work, and it was included in most American anthologies for the next 50 years. During 1886, his work began to be accepted by the important literary journals: the *Atlantic Monthly*, *Harper's*, *Scribner's*, and *Century*. He also struck up a great friendship with the transcendentalist Christopher Pearse **Cranch**, who was by then an old man. After a year of special study in Cambridge, England, another tour abroad (this time in the Near East) gave Scollard what was to be his most important well of experiences for his poetry. His third volume, *Old and New World Lyrics* (1888), did not incorporate these foreign incidents, but his next one, *Songs of Sunrise Lands* (1892), is almost completely informed by his experiences during this year of travel.

During this period, Scollard also assumed the duties of associate professor of English at Hamilton College. In 1890, he married Georgia Brown, who 10 years later bore their only child, Elisabeth, herself a poet. In 1896, Scollard gave up his position at Hamilton to devote himself to writing, but he returned in 1911 for one more year as the chair of the English department. During this time away from the college, Scollard produced not only poetry, but also six novels, four of them historical novels set in Italy. His most important volume of verse in this period was *Blank Verse Pastels* (1907). This collection contained both blank and free verse, years before the latter was made fashionable by modernism. After 1912, Scollard gave up both fiction and teaching for good and turned his full attention to poetry. He was no longer interested in creating large volumes of verse; instead, he produced pamphlets on concentrated themes, mainly for his friends. *Lyrics of Summer*, *Lyrics of Life*, and *Lyrics of Florida* are typical of his later output. After a divorce, Scollard married Rittenhouse in 1924. He died of heart disease in 1932.

Although it would be stretching the truth to say that Scollard was greatly admired for his poetry, he was nevertheless well-respected, with more than 100 poems published in magazines. However, Scollard recognized his strengths and weaknesses as a poet and addressed them squarely. His title for an uncompleted autobiography, "The Adventures of a Minor Poet," aptly sums up his self-knowledge. He knew himself to be a fine craftsman who was able to fashion delicate lyrics that sacrificed contemplative weight for perfection in form. His verse delights in the natural world, in small incidents that are honed to perfection. It is easy to view him as a Robert Frost without the philosophy.

Scollard's most persistent thematic concern, a thread that connects not only his landscapes, but also his lyrics and even his fiction, is memory. He relied heavily upon his memory for subject matter in his travel poems, and he was much more comfortable writing about a personal or cultural past than about the present. Other poems bear out this fascination with the past. His volumes of war poetry, *Vale of Shadows*, *Let the Flag Wave*, and *War Voices and Memories*, are filled with patriotic verse that call upon good citizens to do their part for the war effort, as was the fashion of the time. As these poems call for a defense of cultural values held dear, they owe much to the cultural memories that carried those values. Scollard's historical novels also obviously declare their attention to memory in their genre and subject matter.

"As I Came Down from Lebanon" illustrates this fascination with memory. Arising from his memory of a trip to the Middle East, the poem itself is a downward spiral that marks the passage of time. The first stanza places us in a personal gyre, for the persona comes "winding, wandering slowly down / Through mountain passes bleak and brown." The stanza also sets up a temporal spiral, for the day is "well-nigh done." The description of the city, worked out in more detail in the following two stanzas, prepares us for introduction to a culture that has remained unchanged for centuries, ever dwelling within the spiral of cultural history. Finally, the first and last lines that bracket each stanza, reiterating the title, forcefully remind us that Scollard has caught us in these descents and that we may not lose our memory of these passages.

The second stanza describes the land lying below the persona's mountain descent. By a type of pathetic fallacy, even the landscape participates: like the sheikhs who populate it, the landscape gives off an air of inactivity, as if entropy has the persona and all that he describes in its grasp. The river moves lugubriously, like "lava in the dying glow" of the day. The image patterns set up in the first stanza are repeated, as the persona is drawn ever deeper into this recess of communal, cultural memory.

The inhabitants of the landscape are further detailed in the third stanza. Here, the stasis of the scene, although not abandoned, is at least not placed in the forefront. Instead, Scollard emphasizes the idea of the Other. All those who dwell here are Other, not only to the persona, but also to each other. The poem shows the Magi and the Moslem in opposition and completely segregates the occupants of the seraglios, who act only as inert voyeurs of this scene. All these people participate in the entropy of the city and, therefore, of the culture. Indeed, the only action is the Effendi's sipping of sherbet as he observes the stasis around him.

The diurnal imagery is revisited in the final stanza, and nature moves once again to participate in this descent into memory. Here, the "flaming flower of daytime" finally dies. The twilight is once again static, as the speaker revels in the finery of "Night, arrayed as is a bride" awaiting "some great king." But night itself is filled with a memory of the day, for the image of the shining moon depends upon the reflection of the sun, and this moon shines "like a keen Damascus blade." The land seems depopulated now, as befits a region in which nature moves relentlessly in her cycles, indifferent to human concerns.

Scollard's attention to detail is as much a part of this poem as his attention to memory. In the opening stanza, he appeals to the senses of sight and hearing. The city is "like an opal, set / In emerald." The minarets, "Afire with radiant beams of sun," produce the synesthetic colors of "orange, fig and lime." And all is surrounded by the "melodious chime" of the songbirds. The middle two stanzas are alive with smells and tastes such as the olives and "precious spices," the Effendi's sherbet, and the roses on the seraglio balconies. The final stanza returns to the sense of sight. Night, the king's bride, is clothed in "purple and the finest gold." Like a flower, night does not steal upon the scene but blooms over it. And the Damascus blade tells not only the brightness of the moon, but also its shape.

Scollard again utilizes personal and cultural memories in "A Bit of Marble" (LOA, 2: 525). Although based on a trip to Greece, this poem moves beyond the memory of a concrete event to discuss the nature of poetry itself. Because Greece was seen as the cradle of western civilization, Scollard is able to exploit the entire cultural memory of the Athenian age in this short lyric. In the first stanza, he addresses a small piece of the ruins of the Acropolis. We see the glory that was Greece, for Athens still "proudly rears / Its temple-crowned Acropolis," but we are also reminded of the decay of time and the salvation of memory, for this Acropolis is "hoar with years." Corporate memory is the fundamental principle of civilization, but it is not enough to counteract the gyre of the years.

The second stanza places the sculptor before us: he who carved this bit of marble "fine and small" like a jewel. Scollard imagines it to be part of a grander scheme, "A part of base, or column grand / Or capital." He then places this diminished bit of ruin in juxtaposition with the larger purpose for which it was intended. What we possess are merely the remnants of a greater age, and yet a deeper meaning resides in this remnant. This classical notion informs the entire poem, for it forms an analogy with the work of the poet in the final stanza.

Here, Scollard breaks the frame by inserting himself ("Regarding it, I mind me") and moving us to a present continuous with the remembered past. Importantly, his prescription for poetry contains as its base (or column grand, or capital) the "ardor" of the poet. Only in the passion of the maker is memory forged into something valuable. This passion then creates a poem from the "firm Pentelic snow / Of lofty thought." Pentelicus is a mountain in southeastern Greece, near Athens, where the marble for the Acropolis supposedly was mined. Ironically, despite what Scollard sees in this bit of marble, he claims no such hardness or defense against decay for his poetry. His poems are created from snow, not marble. Although fashioned from lofty thought, they will not withstand the passage of time. In looking backward to a golden age, Scollard assesses not only his own poetry, but his entire culture. If even such glorious civilizations as the Greeks' eventually decay to small fragments, what is to be the fate of his culture?

Personal and cultural memories, then, are the snow out of which Scollard constructs his poems, but the process of writing itself contains a more significant form of memory. Throughout his career, Scollard was noted for his able versification. He was not an innovator in either form or content, but he was a perfecter of the received tradition. In the final analysis, this talent, his ability to polish his lyrics to such a degree that they became jewel-like, makes him important. And it is this facility with form that constitutes his most enduring use of memory. Scollard's contribution to poetry in America, and his skillful use of deep traditions to create a body of work, should not be neglected.

JOE PELLEGRINO

Selected Works

Pictures in Song, New York: G. P. Putnam's Sons, 1884
Songs of Sunrise Lands, Boston: Houghton Mifflin, 1892
Skenandoa, Cambridge, Massachusetts: Harvard University Press, 1896
Lyrics of the Dawn, Clinton, New York: n.p., 1902
Odes and Elegies, Clinton, New York: Browning, 1905
Blank Verse Pastels, Clinton, New York: Browning, 1907
The Singing Heart, Asbury Park, New Jersey: Pennypacker, 1910
Poems, Boston: Houghton Mifflin, 1914
War Voices and Memories, New York: White, 1920
The Singing Heart: Selected Lyrics and Other Poems of Clinton Scollard, edited by Jessie B. Rittenhouse, New York: Macmillan, 1934

Further Reading

Rittenhouse, Jesse B., *The Younger American Poets*, Boston: Little, Brown, 1904
Shepard, William Pierce, *Clinton Scollard: An Address Delivered at the Funeral in the Chapel of Hamilton College*, Clinton, New York: Hamilton College Library, 1932

Lydia Huntley Sigourney

(1791–1865)

"If there is any kitchen in Parnassus," Lydia Sigourney wrote in her posthumously published autobiography, *Letters of Life*, "my Muse has surely officiated there as a woman of all work, an aproned waiter." During her 50-year career, Sigourney published 15 volumes of poetry, a novel, works of history, children's books, conduct manuals, and hundreds of magazine articles. Both as an ideologue of domesticity and as a sentimental celebrity, she has since served to focus the embarrassment of modern readers who are unnerved by antebellum taste and doctrine. Following the lead of her urbanely disdainful biographer Gordon Haight, in a telling confusion of social class with literary merit, critics have read Sigourney's "aproned" muse as a sign of her own low evaluation of her writing. Yet this vivid and approachable muse wittily comments not on the aesthetic value of Sigourney's work but rather on the conditions of its production, as well as on the figure of the muse itself. If Lord Byron's mock invocation in *Don Juan*, "Hail, Muse, etcetera," suggests a modern poet who is too busy, savvy, and earthbound to court the muse, Sigourney's parody makes the muse herself the busy one. Shoulder to shoulder with her muse, Sigourney transfers the source of poetry from the leisure of divine ether to the everyday labors and obligations of a flesh and blood, hard-working woman. As a consequence of this democratic-romantic aesthetic, she addresses and welcomes a new audience that had long been excluded – by gender, class, or level of literacy – from the elite precincts of lyric poetry.

Sigourney's own labors as a writer made her the most popular poet in America before Henry Wadsworth **Longfellow**. Then as now celebrity had its price. The poet's muse-as-maid joke in *Letters of Life* follows an eight-page sampling of what strangers routinely demanded of her: to write, for example, "A poem proposed on the feather of a blue-bird picked up by the road-side." Judith Fetterley has observed that Sigourney "made the career of poet to some degree an extension of the service role conventionally assigned to women"; emphasizing Sigourney's historical sensibility, Nina Baym sees her as a "republican public mother," who was heir to classical republicanism's Spartan maternal ideal. Indeed, Sigourney's audience seems to have regarded her writing as a public resource, her labor as a public service; fellow citizens, her readers felt they had a claim on her.

It was a claim that her husband deeply resented. Charles Sigourney's faith was vested in the culturally sanctioned misogynist association of female publicity with promiscuity. On these grounds, as Ann Douglas has discussed, he upbraided his wife for what he called her "lust of praise, which like the appetite of the cormorant is not to be satisfied," and for her "unconquerable passion of displaying herself." To publish is hence to advertise narcissism, exhibitionism, and a predatory sexual appetite. But Charles Sigourney's greatest grievance was economic as well as sexual: "Who wants, or would value, a wife who is to be the public property of the whole community?" Lydia Sigourney may have judged that a piece of property might be better husbanded by the joint-stock company of the American public than by the leanly proscriptive Mr. Sigourney. In any event, her marriage in 1819, at the age of 28, interrupted but did not halt her increasingly public writing career.

The heroine of her novel, *Lucy Howard's Journal* (1857), is born with the century, and her experiences are meant to be representative. Lydia Howard Huntley Sigourney (New Englanders accent the first syllable of Sigourney) was in many respects a child not of the century, but of the new republic. Born in Norwich, Connecticut, on September 1, 1791, she was the only child of Ezekiel Huntley, a Revolutionary War veteran, and his second wife, Zerviah Wentworth Huntley. Her father was the gardener for Mrs. Jerusha Lathrop, a wealthy and socially prominent widow, and the Huntleys rented out part of Mrs. Lathrop's house. The doting companionship of the childless widow was an important source of affection, education, and social advancement for the precocious Lydia. Between district schools, tutors, boarding school, and, always, Mrs. Lathrop's library, she was well-educated in the classics and in both the sentimental and Augustan traditions of the eighteenth century. With the help of Lathrop connections with the Wadsworth family in Hartford, Connecticut, Lydia Huntley established a school in Hartford and, with Daniel Wadsworth as patron, anonymously published her first book, a miscellany of verse and prose, *Moral Pieces*, in 1815. In Hartford, she met and married the widower Charles Sigourney, 13 years her senior and father of three children. He prospered, for a time, in the hardware trade, but as business suffered, the income from his wife's writing career, however mortifying, became more and more useful. Lydia Sigourney lost three children at birth or in infancy; in 1827, she gave birth to Mary, who survived her, and in 1831, to Andrew, who died of tuberculosis in 1852. Aside from her writing career, the poet was involved in many charitable causes, cared for her parents as well as her children, and corresponded with intimate friends, fans, and professional contacts in as many as 2,000 letters a year.

Lydia Sigourney was a celebrity and a celebrant of the new republic's newly literate classes. Like many members of the first post-Revolutionary generation, she was conscious of literacy itself as a force in her life. Reading, she remarked in her autobiography, had become "almost in babyhood, a necessity of existence." Recollections of bookish experiences – reading Edward Young's *Night Thoughts* to Mrs. Lathrop, stealing away to an attic nest with Ann Radcliffe's *Mysteries of Udolpho*, and writing her first novel at the age of eight – form a significant passage in her memoir. The experiences of reading and writing were not limited, in Sigourney's mental world, to what we usually think of as texts: books, letters, and journals. Writing, in particular, was for her a trope for every kind of public influence. In the popular *Letters to Mothers* (1838), she advises readers that "Every trace that we grave upon [the infant soul], will stand forth at the [last] judgment; when the 'books are opened'": "Write what you will, upon the printless tablet, with your wand of love." The writerly nature of this relationship benefits both the child and the mother, who has now risen in "the scale of being" and will "no longer be noteless and unrecorded, passing away without name or memorial among the people." When mother writes on the blank page of the child, she secures not only the child's moral future, but her own newly noted, recorded, and named history. Given the textuality of the mother-child union, poetry naturally "comes forth as the usher and ally of the mother."

Sigourney's poetry speaks not only for mothers, but also for many conventionally silenced and powerless people, in whose very passivity she locates a concentrated moral force much like the power of scriptural texts. In this poetic universe, children, the dead and the dying, the deaf and dumb, African American slaves, and Native Americans all share an enforced passivity and an equal portion of spiritualized power. For Sigourney, spiritual and ethical reform occurs without anyone's seeming to stir; she would have agreed with William Wordsworth's dictum that the "moving accident is not my trade." Indeed, action itself in the world of Sigourney's writings is almost always pernicious. She explicitly and bitterly indicts the silencers of slaves and Indians; she regarded both slavery and the genocide of the indigenous peoples as national shames. In her first book exclusively devoted to poetry, the five-canto *Traits of the Aborigines of America* (1822), she sketches the savage traits of the conquerors. The natural history title plays upon the root of "trait" in *tractus*, "land"; the word's double meaning combines notions of ownership and inherent attributes, while carrying the further signification of "written trace." A sense of the Native American's prior claims to the land as well as to the moral high ground pervades this poetry.

The Indian, like the mother writing on the child, influences the world through a process of inscribing or "stamping." The anonymous epigraph to "Indian Names" (LOA, I: 111), one of Sigourney's most accomplished poems on this subject, provides the poem's argument: "How can the red men be forgotten, while so many of our states and territories, bays, lakes and rivers, are indelibly stamped by names of their giving?" Like both textual and maternal power, the power of the Indian resides in endurance and ubiquity. But although books circulate through the marketplace and the mother distributes her influence through her children, the Indian broadcasts his power through nature itself. In this American Eden, the Indian is the name-giving Adam; and like Adam, the Indian is evicted from his paradise. But beyond this, the analogy must fail, for Sigourney clearly identifies the agents, far from divinely sanctioned, of the Indian's expulsion.

Sigourney's "Ye," the white reader being addressed by the poem, avoids using active verbs with identifiable agents in relation to the fate of the Indians: "Ye say they all have passed away," "That their light canoes have vanished," "That 'mid the forests . . . / There rings no hunter shout," and that "their cone-like cabins / . . . / Have fled away like withered leaves / Before the autumn gale." Against this feeble discourse of avoidance, Sigourney posits an epic Indian language that is inscribed on and spoken by nature: "their name is on your waters, / Ye may not wash it out," and "Your everlasting rivers speak / Their dialect of yore." The Indian, like John Keats, has left a name "writ in water," fleeting and insubstantial, but powerful, too, which partakes of uncanniness and enchantment. For the Indian's name is alchemically bonded to the water itself: "Ye may not wash it out." Here, evoking Lady

Macbeth, Sigourney directly implicates her readership in guilty action.

This five-stanza poem, which Sigourney often republished, may seem only to pose her tragically fatalistic view of the Indian against her culture's smugly fatalistic one. But when this poem appeared in *Poems* in 1834, two stanzas added at the end substantially raised the volume of its outrage:

> Ye call these red-browed brethren
>   The insects of an hour,
> Crushed like the noteless worm amid
>   The regions of their power;
> Ye drive them from their father's lands,
>   Ye break of faith the seal,
> But can ye from the court of Heaven
>   Exclude their last appeal?
>
> Ye see their unresisting tribes,
>   With toilsome step and slow,
> On through the trackless desert pass,
>   A caravan of woe;
> Think ye the Eternal's ear is deaf?
>   His sleepless vision dim?
> Think ye the *soul's blood* may not cry
>   From that far land to him?

Sigourney here provides a definite locus for the agency lacking – and implicitly disavowed – in the previous stanzas. The Indian's "caravan of woe" issues not from a natural process or a generalized fate: "*Ye* drive them from their father's lands / *Ye* break of faith the seal" (my emphasis). Far from urging Christian resignation on the Indians, her forensic rhetoric presses an attack on the Christianity of the white community. Late in life, she wrote that *Traits of the Aborigines* was "singularly unpopular, there existing in the community no reciprocity in the subject." In this atmosphere, sentimental appeals would be unavailing; Sigourney appeals instead to her community's guilty and self-interested fear of God's wrath. The Indians are present in her courtroom, too, but only as ghastly, disembodied voices: their "last appeal" comes in the crying of their "*soul's blood*." To ennoble and spiritualize these Indians, Sigourney has had to separate them from their bodies. Here is the double-bind of the doctrine of influence: in order to acquire the power of text, one has to become, as it were, a dead letter. Paradoxically, therefore, Sigourney replicates her culture's nostalgic and pastoral view of the Indian, while at the same time excoriating that culture for its demonizing and demonic politics.

In her Indian poems, Sigourney positions herself as a national conscience, and in many other poems she functions as an affirming national bard. Heir to eighteenth-century British satiric, elegiac, and sentimental traditions, as well as to American republican and patriotic rhetoric, Sigourney demonstrates a correspondingly broad poetic range. Satires, epics, ballads, and odes are some of her genres. Some of her topics include local topographies; national and private occasions; historical, mythic, and biblical events; patriotic heroes; and local worthies. Given the variety of genres and themes available to her, it is striking that roughly a third of her poems are elegies; many others have an elegiac tone. Nina Baym, revising a critical tradition that scorns at Sigourney's elegizing, suggests that these elegies function much like modern obituaries and should be regarded as public poetry. Memorial in spirit rather than philosophical or metaphysical, these poems follow Wordsworth's principles for the epitaph, which, unlike the traditional elegy, avoids "transports of mind, or . . . quick turns of conflicting passion." Sigourney's elegies thus establish a place within the realm of lyric poetry to commemorate, in monuments of text, signal events in the life of the ordinary citizen. Situated halfway between "Lycidas" and "the short and simple annals of the poor" (as in Gray's famous "Elegy"), Sigourney's elegies memorialize neighbors, students, and local notables, conferring on these middle-class figures the aura of literary immortality – or, at the very least, an aura of gentility that literacy and literature, in this era, emblematized.

Sigourney functions as a kind of town crier of gentility and literacy, a latter-day Prometheus, who brings not letters, but the privileges of literacy, to a new democratic audience. Her role as poet thus incorporates aspects that in traditional cultures are the domain of oral performers; her elegies not only record brief life histories, but also perform the ministerial work of professional mourner and public consoler. Sixty-two elegies are arranged chronologically in *Man of Uz* (1862), and 135 pages of *Letters to My Pupils* (1851) are devoted to elegiac prose and verses that memorialize the students that Sigourney calls "My Dead." This constant presence and plain face of death in Sigourney's work may make our sensibility cringe, as it did some of her waggish contemporaries. But it was the role of antebellum women to care for the sick and to prepare the dead for burial, and Sigourney added the task of memorializing to these duties. That many of these poems are written about children reminds us that only very recently in western history has the death of a child been statistically "unnatural." And although parents have always mourned their children, the central position of the child that the nineteenth century inherited from Enlightenment and republican pedagogy made these losses public as well as private catastrophes.

In "Death of an Infant," one of Sigourney's most famous and most frequently anthologized poems, the figure of death is modeled on Milton's violent and cowardly interloper, Satan: "Death found strange beauty on that polish'd brow, / And dash'd it out." But at the infant's smile, "So fix'd, so holy," "Death gazed, and left it there": "He dar'd not steal / The signet-ring of Heaven." In her final image, Sigourney again deploys the textualizing notion of enstamping or inscribing. Here, the dead child's smile becomes the "signet-ring" with which heaven itself stamps its mark and its influence on all who witness the child's face.

In *Select Poems* (1841), Sigourney notes that this poem had been "inserted by mistake, in one of the American editions of the late Mrs. Hemans." Felicia Hemans, one of the most popular poets in England ("Casabianca," "The Homes of England"), was also avidly read in America. In recognition of both Sigourney's appeal and her many imitations of the English poet, she was known as "the American Hemans." Sigourney's footnote turns the editorial slip to good use. Although asserting her own authorship of this famous poem, she siphons off an endorsement as well; ostensibly still on the topic of authorship, she writes: "Should other testimony [to the poem's authorship] be necessary, it may be mentioned that a letter from Mrs. Hemans,

to a friend in this country, pointing out some poems in that volume which pleased her, designated, among others, this 'Death of an Infant.'" The mistake of Hemans's editors suggests that as commodities put before the public the poems of these two women were interchangeable, a recognition, as we might now say, that the two poets performed similar cultural work.

Like her reputation for a morbid sentimentality, Sigourney's self-promotion has embarrassed and alienated twentieth-century critics. But the problem that critics have had with her careerism differs little from the problem that Charles Sigourney had with her career. We might, instead, read in Sigourney's career a story of the changing conditions of and possibilities for women's writing between the early republic and the antebellum period; with the values absorbed in Mrs. Lathrop's household, the poet participated in the newly forming mass culture. Sigourney's sense of the world as text allowed her to circulate freely in the world, both virtually, through the wide distribution of her writings in books, magazines, and annuals, and actually, as her celebrity opened doors for Sigourney herself in America and Europe. She learned from the British Romantics, from Hemans as well as from Wordsworth, not only styles of poetry – she wrote "lyrical ballads" and meditations on nature as well – but a notion of the poet as a professional and as a public figure. Lydia Sigourney adapted the British model to the more democratic and fluid needs of her devoted American readers by inviting them into the world of literacy and literature. With the tools of the incipient mass culture at her disposal, she created a text-based community of citizen-readers, with herself at its center, as bard and scribe, teacher and mother, conscience, counselor, and consoler.

PATRICIA CRAIN

Selected Works

Moral Pieces, in Prose and Verse, Hartford, Connecticut: Sheldon & Goodwin, 1815

Poems, Boston: S. G. Goodrich, 1827

Poems, Philadelphia: Key & Biddle, 1834

Zinzendorff, and Other Poems, New York: Leavitt, Lord, 1835

Pocahontas, and Other Poems, New York: Harper and Brothers, 1841

A Book for Girls, in Prose and Poetry, New York: Turner & Hayden, 1843

Illustrated Poems, Philadelphia: Carey & Hart, 1849

The Western Home, and Other Poems, Philadelphia: Parry and McMillan, 1854

Past Meridian, New York: D. Appleton, 1854; Boston: J. P. Jewett, 1854

The Man of Uz, and Other Poems, Hartford, Connecticut: Williams, Wiley & Waterman, 1862

Letters of Life, New York: D. Appleton, 1866

American Women Poets of the Nineteenth Century, edited by Cheryl Walker, New Brunswick, New Jersey: Rutgers University Press, 1992

Further Reading

Baym, Nina, *Feminism and American Literary History*, New Brunswick, New Jersey: Rutgers University Press, 1992

Douglas, Ann, *The Feminization of American Culture*, New York: Knopf, 1977

Fetterley, Judith, *Provisions: A Reader from 19th-Century American Women*, Bloomington: Indiana University Press, 1985

Haight, Gordon, *Mrs. Sigourney: The Sweet Singer of Hartford*, New Haven, Connecticut: Yale University Press, 1930

Walker, Cheryl, *The Nightingale's Burden*, Bloomington: Indiana University Press, 1982

Watts, Emily Stipes, *The Poetry of American Women from 1632 to 1945*, Austin: University of Texas Press, 1977

Edward Rowland Sill

(1841–1887)

W. B. Yeats once wrote that we make of the quarrel with others rhetoric, while poetry comes from the quarrel with ourselves. The poetry of Edward Rowland Sill seems to bear out Yeats's observation. Sill's dilemmas were the same as those that perplexed other nineteenth-century poets: how to reconcile faith and science, how to believe in progress in the face of spiritual decay, and how to balance the vacillating feelings of optimism and reactionary pessimism. Sill's influences were English and continental writers who also thought poetry a fit mode for intellectual musings, most notably Alfred, Lord Tennyson, Matthew Arnold, and William Wordsworth. Sill did not belong to any movement in American literature, but was a maverick, writing according to his own idea of poetry's purposes and proper subject matter. Very few of his poems were published during Sill's lifetime, and then they were often published anonymously.

Only two books of poetry – *The Hermitage and Other Poems* (1867) and *The Venus of Milo and Other Poems*, which Sill had privately printed in Berkeley, California, in 1883 – appeared during his lifetime. *The Venus of Milo* was printed in a limited edition and distributed mostly to his friends. He also sent a copy to Arnold. *The Hermitage* was reissued posthumously in 1889 by Houghton Mifflin. Sill also published poetry, sometimes anonymously, in such venues as the *Yale Literary Magazine*, the *New York Evening Mail* (where he worked for a short time), *Atlantic Monthly*, *Overland Monthly*, and *Century*. Sill's collected poetry was published posthumously as *Poems* by Houghton Mifflin in 1887 and reissued in 1902 and 1906.

In "The Principles of Criticism," published in the *Atlantic Monthly* in November 1885, Sill contended that he could not talk only about poetry because all of the arts answer the same need in humankind: they quicken "our interest in some crisis of human destiny" and awaken "feelings and ideas that are vital with tendencies toward more and still more of attainment and being." In distinguishing between beauty, which awakens "the higher activities of our inner nature," and prettiness, which only pleases the senses, Sill does not mean that all art must express beauty but that whatever it expresses must be full of a passionate intensity, not mere empty decoration. For this reason, Sill thought that "poetry is the highest form of literary art," because it has "the fullest expressive power . . . it not only expresses thought, like prose, but feeling also." Still, it was possible to misuse verse – "the musical form" – by expressing "dry, cold ideas, or . . . vague feeling, unlighted by thought." For Sill, "The verse form is most fitly used . . . for the expression of thought and feeling together, of thought, in other words, which is aglow with feeling, and feeling which is illuminated by thought." Poetry was a spiritual force that expressed "more fully than any other form has been found able to do the soul of the writer to the soul of the reader." The essence of poetry for Sill was that it conveyed thoughts about the human experience, "faint reverberations of whole aeons of human, and perhaps of animal, experience."

Alfred Riggs Ferguson, a late biographer, explained that Sill thought the vocation of poetry sacred because he believed that the poet served as an interpreter between humanity and God in confronting serious issues. Sill does fault some contemporary verse for being "mere music, – flowing rhythm, and sounding rhymes, and a pretty babble of insignificant 'words, words, words.'" For Sill, however, an evocative "atmosphere of feeling" is nonetheless important to a successful poem, provided that it is accompanied by significant content: the "mere perception of some external object is not literature." A book thus becomes literature only when the writer "builds himself into the work, expressing inner states of thought, feeling, or purpose either of its own individuality or, best of all, of the universal human being."

In another essay, "The Clang-Tint of Words" (1886), Sill uses "clang-tint" to signify a word's connotations along with its sound qualities – its "atmospheric effect." Each word has "its own enveloping suggestiveness," which is essential for a successful poem. A poet must "use language with an exact sense of definitions" but also with a kind of instinctive sense of a word's ability to evoke a certain mood. Even though Sill read much French poetry and used phrases that sound very *symboliste*, however, it is Wordsworth who served as his exemplar of the poet who employed clang-tint most brilliantly. According to Sill, Wordsworth chooses his words for their ideas and associations, never using "unmeant 'poetic words,'" which are "ear-marks of insincerity and of the mere ambition to write something." Like the famous Romantic, Sill believed that the words for poetry must be chosen from common language rather than special poetic diction, and he argued that the poet must make his choices by intuition and instinctive sensitivity. The vocabulary must create a mood in the audience and "stir in us those truths, emotions, impulses that are wrought into our inmost being by the long race experience."

For Sill, as for Tennyson and Arnold, truths wrought into one's inmost being suddenly seemed less than sure. What had once seemed certain had become questionable, and what once was sacred had become the domain of scientific inquiry. In the same period that Sill entered Yale University in 1857, Darwin published *The Origin of the Species*, which effectively exploded the sacred myth of creation and made scientific positivism a religion for many Victorian intellectuals. Like Tennyson, the major influence during Sill's Yale years, Sill was a romantic who found himself in a world where cause and effect, the prime movers of scientific rationalism, were challenging traditional bases for belief. As a consequence, Sill wondered what place the human spirit held in the new paradigm. Since his romantic outlook dictated that the human spirit was divine, vast, and capable of unlimited potential, he could not accept the limitations placed on it by the scientific outlook. In one of Sill's best early poems, "Man, the Spirit" (1865), we hear him railing against the twin forces of science and progress:

What has this new, pert century done for man,
That it affords to sneer at all before,
Because it rides its aimless jaunts by steam
And blabs its trivial talk by telegraph?

Worried that materialism was blinding humankind to the truer, richer horizons belonging to self-exploration, Sill decides that people would be better off "if the mind could sometimes be content / To cease from its male madness, its desire / To radiate outward," could look inward for meaning and truth.

"Truth at Last" (LOA, 2: 399) clarifies what Sill meant by truth and why it is essential to a well-lived, meaningful existence. Imagining the last moments of life, the moment of truth, of the famed Swiss mountaineer Johann Bennen, who died in an avalanche, Sill wonders if Bennen hoped until the end and died hoping that he and his party would be saved: " Or did he think, even till they plunged and fell, / Some miracle would stop them?" In the poem, Bennen heroically accepts that he will die, and he does so gracefully after "Stretching his arms out toward his native vale / As if in mute, unspeakable farewell." The vignette epitomizes what Sill thought truth to be – an instant of spiritual perfection and enlightenment when an individual sees "Clear-eyed the future as he sees the past, / From doubt, or fear, or hope's illusion free."

Truth is also a concern in "The Fool's Prayer" (LOA, 2: 397), first printed in the *Atlantic Monthly* in January 1879 and long popular among audiences who had probably never even heard of Sill. In the poem, "truth and right" are analogous to heaven. The speaker is a king's jester – a fool – whom the king has asked to "make for us a prayer," as the feasting is done and the bored king seeks "some new sport to banish care." The vision humanity strives toward, according to the fool's prayer, is "the onward sweep / Of truth and right" so that it may find heaven on earth. "'Tis not by guilt" that we keep truth at bay, but by "our follies" and "our blunders," which cause us to fall in shame "Before the eyes of heaven." Stupidity is the sin for which the fool asks forgiveness, because it is possible to avoid stupid actions. Everyone has innate shortcomings, and "Our faults no tenderness should ask, / The chastening stripes must cleanse them all." The fool clarifies what constitutes an unforgivable, because unnecessary, blunder:

> "The ill-timed truth we might have kept –
>   Who knows how sharp it pierced and stung?
> The word we had not sense to say –
>   Who knows how grandly it had rung?"

Sill chose the archaic setting because he liked the archetype of the fool who embodies wisdom in simplicity, thinking aloud before God about the problems of foolishness and truth. As for the reason that "We hold the earth from heaven away": "'Earth bears no balsam for mistakes; / Men crown the knave, and scourge the tool / That did his will." After the fool's prayer, the king experiences an epiphany, realizing that he is no different from any other man; during a melancholy walk in his gardens, he prays, "Be merciful to me, a fool!" As this insight is common to all people, the poem finally offers a democratic vision of humanity.

"Opportunity" (LOA, 2: 398) further explores the concept of equality by showing that it is not an individual's station in life that determines success, but self-application. First published in the *Californian* in November 1880, this poem was also widely known to American readers into the early twentieth century. "Opportunity" is set in an archaic dreamscape where a battle is raging, and gains its tension by contrasting the actions of a "craven" with those of a king.

The craven stands at the battle's edge, blaming his inability to fight on his blunt sword: "[He] thought, 'Had I a sword of keener steel – / That blue blade that the king's son bears, – but this / Blunt thing – !' he snapt and flung it from his hand." After the craven has "crept away and left the field," the king's son, who is wounded and has lost his sword, stumbles upon the broken sword, and with a battle cry "Lifted afresh he hewed his enemy down, / And saved a great cause that heroic day." Sill makes the point that it is not the trappings of wealth or royalty that give the prince courage and let him save the day; it is simply a matter of integrity and strength of character. In the spirit of democracy and Emersonian self-reliance – if also following **Emerson's** curious use of regal metaphors to convey that spirit – the poem implies that one person will be a craven and another a king because of individual choices, not because of one's place in society's class structure.

"California Winter" (LOA, 2: 399), first published in the *Californian* in January 1882, is a nature poem that builds on the contrast between a New England winter and a California one. A quick biographical sketch demonstrates why this regional contrast would have engaged the poet. Sill was born and spent his boyhood in Windsor, Connecticut (passing his teen years in Ohio), but after graduating from Yale in 1861, and with no firm plans for the future, he moved to California, living in Sacramento and, from 1862 until 1866, in Folsom. After losing at love, Sill moved to Cambridge, Massachusetts, for a few months. He then went to the home of an uncle – who had been his legal guardian after the early deaths of both parents – in Cuyahoga Falls, Ohio. There, Sill married his cousin, Elizabeth Sill. In 1871, the two settled in Oakland, California, until 1883 when Elizabeth's father fell ill, which forced their return to Cuyahoga Falls, where Sill lived until his death in 1887.

"California Winter" is one of Sill's stronger poems. It is written in plain language, its images are pungent and fresh, and it shows Sill's tenderness for each place – New England and California – without heavy sentiment. He begins, cleverly, by making it sound as if he will denigrate the California winter in favor of a nostalgic memory of the hard winters in New England: "This is not winter: where is the crisp air, / And snow upon the roof, and frozen ponds, / And the star-fire that tips the icicle?" The California rose is "pale and odorless," probably because it grows in a land "That has not dreamed of such a thing as spring." The first three stanzas make it seem that California does not have winter, only a poor excuse for it: "It is a land without a fireside," after all. During a New England snowstorm, "Heaven is not far away," "And many things their resurrection wait." With the fourth stanza, however, Sill provocatively counters the poem's beginning: "Yet even here / We are not quite forgotten by the Hours." Then comes the revelation that the California winter awaits resurrection, too. Although New England has snows that blanket the earth, making it "like a sepulchre," California has a "strong south wind" and "the singing rain" that "Enwraps the drowsy world." Sill offers a comforting image of the way in which spring is born after the winter rain cleanses the world and then recedes: "some night, / Its flowing folds invisibly withdraw, / Lo! the new life in all created things." In "California Winter," Sill nicely sustains the musical and imagist qualities of his verse.

A major weakness in Sill's work is that it is erratic; he needed a good editor. Not only are there well-crafted poems like

"California Winter," but there exist some deadly ones as well, like "A Fable" or "The First Cause." Sill is inconsistent even within poems, as in "Man, the Spirit," which flows brilliantly in one section but limps along in another. The poet possessed the gift of inspiration, but as he wrote in a December 1887 letter to a colleague in California, he abhorred editorial work: "It has been my case, always, that a thing once written is dismissed from my mind with a kind of cold dislike. I never liked my children, so to speak. . . . I hate every bit of verse I write, as soon as it is printed, and would gladly never see it again." Sill's distaste for revision is a shame because his superior poems sing, evoking goddesses, as in "Semele," and creating provocative metaphors, as in "Man, the Spirit." For such accomplishments, Edward Rowland Sill deserves to be remembered in American literary history.

SUSAN JOHNSTON GRAF

Selected Works

The Hermitage and Later Poems, Boston and New York: Houghton Mifflin, 1867

The Poetical Works of Edward Rowland Sill, edited by William Belmont Parker, Boston and New York: Houghton Mifflin, 1867, reprinted 1906

The Prose of Edward Rowland Sill, Boston and New York: Houghton Mifflin, 1900

Around the Horn: A Journal, edited by Stanley T. Williams and Barbara D. Simison, New Haven, Connecticut: Yale University Press, 1944

Further Reading

Ferguson, Alfred Riggs, *Edward Rowland Sill: The Twilight Poet*, The Hague, The Netherlands: Martinus Nijhoff, 1955

Parker, William Belmont, *Edward Rowland Sill: His Life and Work*, Boston and New York: Houghton Mifflin, 1915

William Gilmore Simms

(1806–1870)

Born in Charleston, South Carolina, Simms was the son of Scotch-Irish merchant William Gilmore Simms and a Virginian mother, Harriet Ann Augusta Singleton. Failing in business, his wife deceased, Simms's father left the boy in the hands of his maternal grandmother. Mrs. Gates, who had lived through the British occupation of Charleston, entertained her grandson with oral histories. The tradition of family storytelling, the impetus for the later development of most southern literature, accounts in part for the narrative instinct in Simms. His grandmother's stories also evidently fed the intense nationalism in Simms that would one day draw him to the Young America Movement.

Charleston became an especially strong shaping force on Simms's personality and work. With 16 churches, two banks, a literary and philosophical society, and three daily newspapers, the city of 2,500 inhabitants was the most important cultural center in the southeastern United States. Because of its colonial ties to various members of the English aristocracy, Charleston was also the most aristocratic city in the south. The city's sociological dynamic thus required some difficult but not impossible rites of passage for the son of a failed merchant who had left the town, calling it a "city of tombs," to make his future in Mississippi.

Although William P. Trent's 1892 biography of Simms remains a major source, his reconstructionist thesis that Simms would have been a more successful writer had he lived outside the south merely reflects the biographer's deterministic creed and political orientation. In 1818, Simms's father went to court to win custody of the child from Mrs. Gates; given a choice by the court, Simms chose to remain in Charleston, a city that, as John McCardell notes, he clearly saw as maternal. More often than not, Charleston and South Carolina figure as nurturing forces in Simms's work (*Intellectual Life in Antebellum Charleston*, Michael O'Brien and David Moltke-Hansen, eds. [1986]). Simms especially loved the landscape of his native state, the low-country forests, the savannahs, and the primeval Spanish moss that lends mystery to both the coastland and the seasons. William Cullen **Bryant**, who visited Simms at his second wife's family plantation – Woodlands, just south of Charleston – noted that his host had "made large and striking use of the imagery supplied by the peculiar scenery of this region." Simms's second marriage, in 1836 – his first wife had died in 1832 – brought him into the plantation aristocracy, an admission to privilege that complemented his interest in agrarian ideals.

At age 18, Simms had left the apothecary shop where he had been apprenticed by his grandmother. Admitted to the bar at age 21 in April 1827, Simms, like the southern lawyer-writer John Pendleton Kennedy, grew more and more attracted to belletristic writing. Simms had already read poetry by Lord Byron, Sir Walter Scott, William Wordsworth, Thomas Moore, and John Keats. Although he is primarily remembered as a novelist and romancer of South Carolina life and history, as in *Woodcraft*, *The Yemassee*, and *Eutaw*, Simms began his career as a poet in 1825 with a monody on the death of General

Charles Cotesworth Pinckney. By September of that year, the Charleston *Courier* observed that copies of the poem were sold out, which in turn attests to Simms's very early positive reception as a poet in his own community.

Simms became, as Edd Winfield Parks early observed, the literary successor to fellow South Carolinian Hugh Swinton Legaré, and, as a poet-critic, he encouraged younger Southern poets like Henry **Timrod**, Paul Hamilton **Hayne**, and James Mathewes **Legaré**. Jay Hubbell asserts that Simms was nationally known and had more readers in the north than in the south before 1860, when his strict constructionist views regarding states' rights alienated him from his northern readers. Simms's developing "southernness" was owing in part, ironically, to his sympathies with the northern-based Young America Movement. Like Walt **Whitman**, who also belonged to this nationalistic group, Simms exploited the indigenous and, in his poetry and prose, reacted against British and New England domination of art. As a nationalistic poet, he saw Henry Wadsworth **Longfellow**, for example, as highly skilled but highly imitative. In his dedication in *The Wigwam and the Cabin* (1856), he lodged the argument, one applicable to most of the popular American art of the day, that being sectional and indigenous was being national. In his indigenous work he is, as Hubbell observes, every bit as "national" a poet as Longfellow or Henry David **Thoreau**.

In terms of his poetic reputation, Simms passed, according to James Kibler, through three distinct phases. The early phase marked a rapid rise to fame, during which he won the admiration of both Bryant and Evert Duyckinck; moreover, discerning periodicals like the *North American Review* and the *Knickerbocker* gave him favorable reviews. After the Civil War, however, Simms, because of his political sympathies, was largely ignored or disparaged by his critics. His reputation was further eclipsed by "New South" writers like Joel Chandler Harris and George Washington Cable and American nationals like Twain, William Dean **Howells**, or Henry James, alongside whom Simms seemed strangely old-fashioned. Contemporary scholars, however, view him as an important writer of the Old South and a largely unappreciated poet.

Like his English Romantic counterparts Keats and Samuel Taylor Coleridge, Simms held the figure of the poet in high regard. Indeed, he always saw himself as a maker or "feigner," a belletristic man. Part of his esteem for poets and poetry was rooted in the Young America Movement of the 1840s, which held that "poetry" included all literary genres, even novels, and that poets working valiantly at poetry that expressed a Jacksonian viewpoint would create a truly American national art that was both poetic and useful. Certainly, as Kibler has noted, Simms's achievements in American Romanticism and transcendentalism equal those of Bryant.

The Simms canon contains more than 1,830 poems, less than half of which ever appeared in book form. The greater body of his material still remains scattered throughout literary periodicals. Anthologists since Simms's day have given representation to both Ralph Waldo **Emerson** and Bryant as poets but have ignored Simms altogether. More recent anthologies include his "The Grapevine Swing" and "The Edge of the Swamp" simply because Bryant included them in *Selections from the American Poets* (1840), but neither poem belongs to Simms's best work.

The range of Simms's poetic forms is extensive, for he makes use of ballads, odes, political and social satire, humorous verse, psychological studies, dramatic monologues, love songs, sonnets, occasional verse, and epigrams; his poetic range is also suggested by one of his titles: *Poems: Dramatic. Descriptive. Legendary, and Contemplative.* The Spenserian stanza, ottava rima, blank verse, heroic couplets, and ballad meter are his favored versifications. Contrary to arguments in some anthology introductions, Simms labored over revisions to his poems. His biographer, Trent, overemphasizing a comment from Hayne, popularized the portrait of a poet who spent little or no time on revisions. But Kibler presents Simms as a truly professional poet who frequently revised poems even after publication and who cut and pasted revised poems and emendations in his scrapbooks.

Simms began his poetic career indebted to the Greek and Latin poets and the English Romantics; much of his earliest poetry was either imitative or derivative. The more passionate nature of Keats, Percy Bysshe Shelley, and Byron especially won his admiration. To follow James Hoge, Byron clearly influenced Simms's use of picturesque language, his melancholic protest against the inroads of time, his enthusiasm for political freedom, and his fondness for the themes of isolation and loneliness, as in *Areytos, or Songs of the South* (*Essays in Literature* 2 [1975]). Byron was at his greatest popularity in America just as Simms was approaching manhood, and the political alienation and estrangement of southerners from the national scene may have intensified Simms's acceptance of Byronic themes.

Like Wordsworth and Coleridge, moreover, Simms was often more philosophical than poetic in his nonlyrical verse. Like Wordsworth, Simms in such poems as "By the Swannanoa" (LOA, 1: 365) or "The New Moon" (LOA, 1: 368) is "man speaking to men," sharing his own personal relation to the cosmos. As Kibler notes, Simms greatly admired Coleridge's capacity for psychology, his use of the intellectual and the spiritual in his poetry, and his ability to demonstrate facts amid appearances – to reconcile the apparent opposites in human perception.

As an American Romantic, Simms is more akin to Whitman, for his poetry is replete with qualities that we associate with Whitman: "largeness" and "coarseness," a fondness for the riches of the earth, and an apparently unrestrained expression. Like Whitman, whom he preceded, Simms is at his best in the out-of-doors – the fields, swamps, and trails of America. And, transcendental at heart, he is at his worst when he enters the drawing-room to write "with his pen and not his heart," to use John Erskine's phrase.

As a Romantic poet at mid-century, and like other contemporary American poets, Simms longed to separate himself from "coarse leveling," to quote McCardell, yet to play a "guiding usually restraining role in managing and directing change." The result of this longing, always frustrating, was intellectual ambivalence, the creation of an artist isolato who nevertheless served a "central social and political view." As a distinctly "southern" poet, Simms demonstrates the odd combination of attitudes that make up such an entity. First is his love of the earth, his tie to the land, as seen in "By the Swannanoa." Frequently, this tie to the earth bespeaks the southern desire for a continuity that admits change but that also values the stability of an acute awareness of the past and of one's traditions. This awareness, in turn, enables an individual to see himself clearly, to exist within a context. (Kibler observes that Simms creates a brooding sense of the past that is both "mysterious and unfathomable.") Most modern in Simms's southern view is his antipathy toward the development of a rootless, mechanical, nonspiritual society, a view that places him in the lineage of Edgar Allan **Poe**, Sidney **Lanier**, Donald Davidson, and Allen Tate. Simms's pessimism, his developing cynicism in old age, also brings him one step closer to the Victorian temperament of Robert Browning or Matthew Arnold.

The major subject of Simms's poetry is nature. Within his nature poetry (as Kibler also records), Simms demonstrates three basic techniques for the Romantic reconciliation of opposites; such reconciliation also was a major concern for both Coleridge and Emerson in their poetry and criticism. In his poetry, Simms often links nature to the state of mind and the disposition of the perceiver. Thus, the physical landscape becomes reconciled to a spiritual or psychological world. Nature thereby becomes emblematic or symbolic, revealing to the poet a truth in a manner recalling Wordsworth's notion that we "half perceive, half create." The subjects of "By the Swannanoa" and "The New Moon" become, for example, emblem/symbol; this strategy suggests that Simms is best judged in the tradition of Anne Dudley Bradstreet, Edward Taylor, Philip **Freneau**, and Bryant, all of whom viewed landscape as a metaphor or sign for the sometimes perilous journey through life. Running waters such as streams and rivers, in particular, become the image of rites of passage in Simms's work, which is not altogether different from the way poets like Emily **Dickinson** and Robert Frost configure roads, paths, and journeys. Such moving waters in Simms, Kibler rightly asserts, suggest both continuity and timelessness, the données of southern writing. The great poet reads the book of nature, in the Emersonian sense, to demonstrate universal analogies leading to the discovery of eternal truths.

Conversely, for nature to draw new life from the perceiver, the poet must always be a personality – complete, whole, healthy – never a scientist, a rationalist (see Kibler, "Perceiver and Perceived"). In this regard, Simms seems to agree with Coleridge's view in "Dejection: An Ode" that "we receive but what we give, / And in our life alone does nature live." Thus, the poet establishes his relationship with nature, for he becomes both giver (through his "fancy") to nature and receiver from nature. A poem like "The Lost Pleiad" (LOA, 1: 363) reveals this intense spiritual and intellectual relationship with nature when the poet is able to read the emblem of the sky. A mutual compatibility between poet and nature is established when the poet superimposes some part of himself over the object that he perceives. When the relationship is harmonious, the ideal is, momentarily at least, attained. In Simms's poetry, the landscape is both mirror and metaphor for the speaker's mood, disposition, and acumen.

Simms was an unusually spiritual man. As he moved closer to the middle of the nineteenth century and then into the period following the Civil War, he saw modern humanity as having limited itself to responding only to the physical, the literal, and the material. Seeing his fellow Americans as coming from the philosophic tradition of John Locke and René Descartes, Thomas Jefferson and Benjamin Franklin, Simms believed that his contemporaries saw nature only as a created, mechanical object. In the landscape poetry, his purpose is to rekindle in his readers a spiritual relationship with the natural world, a notion shared by Emerson and Thoreau. Viewing fancy as a literal/mechanical perception of the world and imagination as a spiritual insight or vision, Simms concluded, like Whitman, that the truly national poet was the poet of the imagination.

"The Lost Pleiad," according to the poet, was first published when he was 19-years old. As Simms subsequently noted in *Areytos* (1860), the initial version needed both elaboration and substantial development of the major themes. The lyric poem, always his most popular mode, is characterized by its musical, highly imaginative, and intensely subjective character, which is fused into one overall impression, as the poet mirrors himself in the sky. That the poem was first published when Simms was 19 suggests the possibility that intense emotional pressures were playing on him at the time of its composition. It was in his eighteenth year, we recall, that he was forced by court decree to decide upon his own fate, and anxiety over an unknown future evidently weighed him down. On October 19, 1826, just after publication of the poem, Simms resolved his angst when he married his first wife, Anna Malcolm Giles.

"The Lost Pleiad" also reminds us of Simms's love of music. Parlor music was very popular in the south, particularly among the affluent, and it moved Simms to this early experiment in verse. Indeed, the final published appearance of the poem in 1860 in *Areytos* suggests that Simms himself linked "The Lost Pleiad" to the plaintive, melodic songs of the Old South. The musical nature of the collection as a whole implies that Simms is best read in the context of fellow poets Edward Coote **Pinkney**, Philip Pendleton **Cooke**, Richard Henry **Wilde**, and Poe, all of whom championed the musical development of beauty.

The poem exhibits a peculiar combination of classic and Romantic modes that coexist in the Byronic expressions of loss and alienation. Drawn, in his fondness for classicism, to the legend of the lost Pleiades – in Greek myth, the seven daughters of Atlas and Pleione are saved from the pursuing Orion by Zeus, who turns them into a constellation – Simms views the Pleiades, as did the Greeks, as omen, sign, or emblem. Appearing to mark the May harvest, disappearing, and then reappearing to mark the November time for plowing and harvesting, the Pleiades symbolize the poet's need for guidance, for faith in life. Although Simms knew little or no Greek (his Latin was proficient), he may well have stumbled upon a reference to the origin of the word *pleiades* in the Greek *plein*, which means "to sail." The latter word also recalls the Greek belief that the appearance of the constellation signified safe passage for the Mediterranean sailor. If Simms was familiar with the etymology, then the lost Pleiades become fittingly symbolic for the themes of perilous passage and universal pilgrimage. Melancholic over the continuing absence of the sign from above, the poet concludes "The Lost Pleiad" somewhat didactically:

The dearest hope is that which first is lost,
The tenderest flower is soonest nipt by frost –

Are not the shortest-lived, the loveliest –
And like the wandering orb that leaves the sky,
Look they not brightest, when about to fly,
The desolate spot they blest?

The transience of ideal beauty and the consequences of time are given full play in Simms's use of the metaphor of the frost that bites.

Simms's concept, moreover, of the faithful mariner who holds "his course alone" or the "Chaldean" (Babylonian) shepherd who searches for the light that warns him home from the hills of his grazing mountain flock in stanzas II–IV, suggests the need, universal in nature, for spiritual guidance through life. His sense of the necessity to function harmoniously within a universal, natural, or spiritual context is also one of his most southern themes. In Simms's awareness of the sea, which itself constitutes a major ingredient in the ever-present natural beauty surrounding Charleston and low-country South Carolina, is an intense recognition of the restlessness of humanity, of change and continuity, and of anxiety about the voyage of life that lies before each of us. In this regard, Simms's poem takes on much of the spirit of Arnold's "Dover Beach" (composed 1851).

The unique 1860 version of "The Lost Pleiad" appearing in *Areytos* demonstrates that Simms sought to amplify, to develop further, and to objectify the abstract and scantily developed concerns of the 1829 version. In stanza III, for example, he parallels Arnold in both voice and vision when he states, "We are as men at sea, by tempests tost, / Looking out vainly for the one true star." In the true Victorian temper he concludes: "We snatch the flower above the precipice, / And fall in snatching. Our footsteps miss, / While our hands clutch, and, with the treasure won, / We are undone!"

Simms was a prolific landscape poet and may (as Kibler notes) have written more poems about the landscape than any other American poet. Through camping trips and flatboat travel, he was well-acquainted with the topography of his country. He was also well read in the naturalists, especially William Bartram, whom he loved, and Joel Roberts Poinsett (1779–1851). Generally speaking, however, his landscape poetry moves from the purely descriptive to depictions of the spiritual union of humanity, nature, and God.

First published in March 1843 in *Magnolia*, "By the Swannanoa" reveals Simms's sense of such profound natural affinities. *Grouped Thoughts and Scattered Fancies* (1845), in which this poem was collected, also demonstrates the poet's desire to free himself from the traditional, purely mechanical rhyme of the Italian sonnet. Rather than limiting himself to two rhymes in the quatrain, for example, Simms employs four, whereas he limits himself to three rhymes in the concluding sestet.

Sound and sense are particularly harmonious in the poem; the enjambment of the first line and the very long last line of the poem remain noteworthy in this regard. A highly romantic, virtually fluid view of the South Carolina landscape, the poem employs the Swannanoa as a sparkling, lively, flashing, murmuring symbol of nature speaking to the heart of humanity. The mountains stand in marked contrast as though awaiting "some high ambassador from foreign ground," which suggests, perhaps, the powerful song of nature. Not unlike Coleridge in "Kubla Kahn," Simms implies in the expansive final line the extent to which appearance and reality can be resolved by a poetic, seerlike vision when he images the Swannanoa "Now foaming white o'er rocks, now glimpsing soft through groves."

A part of the English tradition of graveyard poetry, "The City of the Silent" (LOA, 1: 365), like Bryant's "Thanatopsis" (LOA, 1: 122), is, at times, directly or indirectly concerned with the inscrutability of death, varying burial customs, and faith. Unlike the better-known "Thanatopsis," Simms's poem suggests a faith in spirit that transcends the fear of death. Simms composed the poem for the dedication, on November 19, 1850, of Charleston's new Magnolia Cemetery. The poem was popular with the audience at the dedication, and Simms subsequently reissued it in pamphlet form with explanatory notes composed by his friend James Warley Miles. A hybrid of classic and Romantic attitudes, the 650-line poem consistently employs the heroic couplet; perhaps it owed its form to the formality of the occasion. Recognizing the largely Augustan taste of his native South Carolina, Simms begins the poem with an allusion to the "ruder pomp" of Abyssinian (i.e., Ethiopian) burial rites. In emphasizing the physical and omitting the spirit, the Abyssinians, like the Egyptians, sought to preserve the physical corpus with "costly balms" and exposed the corpse to public view. Such older civilizations, in that display "raised on high pillars," mocked "Life with Death, and Time with Fate." Developing a contrast, the poet contends the Etrurians (i.e., the Etruscans of central Italy) moved forward with "sepulchre[s] designed" to suggest faith in the unknown. Thus, the Etrurians "still survive the worship they believed; / That left to Rome their gods, without their faith / And live in marble though they sleep in death."

Alluding to Gonfaloniere Avotta's archaeological account of opening the grave of the Etrurian monarch, the "Lucumo," Simms notes the beauty of discovery, that first vision, through a crevice of the tomb, of the corpus before it is exposed to air and light. Such a view provides a "life-seeming state of ancient days." Most importantly, Simms observes of these burial rites, one reads a "wondrous story, which reveals a faith / That sees the soul escaped, surviving death." Reflecting the moral imperative of contemporary Victorianism, Simms states that our burial traditions, like those of the Etrurians, "sought an upward goal, / And challenged wings for the immortal soul!"

"The New Moon," first published in 1853, is characteristic of the collection in which it appeared, *Poems: Descriptive, Dramatic, Legendary and Contemplative*, which in turn clearly bears the influence of Shelley, Coleridge, and Byron. The sense of alienation in this particular poem aligns it more clearly with Byron, the favorite Romantic of most southern poets of the day. Representative of Simms's landscape poetry and similar to "By the Swannanoa," this apostrophe to the new moon reflects the speaker's state of mind, which works to enrich nature with dreamy contemplation. Simms's experimentation with verse, iambs, and trochees here suggests his desire to free his voice for poetic revelation, to authenticate the feeling of an insight born of a moment of reflection.

Addressing in lines 1–4 the moon as Diana, Roman goddess of the hunt, well-known for her modesty, ease, and sponta-neous oneness with the natural world, the poet asks that the goddess above bring her light (metaphorically, her "arrow") to remove the cloud (metaphorically, her "shroud") and to dissipate the obscurity about him. Simms's use of "shroud" implies a belief that death/pain often encapsulates life/health. The dark, enveloping night figures the melancholy of the speaker. With the first appearance of the light, the rivulets themselves break forth in song as though blessed; water in this poem once more symbolizes rebirth and cleansing. As in the Swannanoa poem, the moving waters suggest change, life, movement, and, especially, the stirring of the poet's soul to renewal and health. Diana, ever-watchful huntress, has sent her arrow to pierce the cloud/shroud of darkness, thus making, as in the Pleiades poem, a saner pathway for the persona through life.

Simms remains a major figure in the writing of the Old South. Classically trained but romantically disposed, he was the leader of the Charleston coterie that included both Timrod and Hayne. In the American canon, his work constitutes an important addition to the Romantic, often transcendental landscape poetry of Poe, Emerson, Thoreau, Longfellow, Whitman, and Dickinson. He deserves far greater attention than he has received.

GEORGE C. LONGEST

Selected Works

Pseudonymous Poetry of William Gilmore Simms, edited by James E. Kibler Jr., Athens: University of Georgia Press, 1976

Selected Poems of William Gilmore Simms, edited by James E. Kibler Jr., Athens: University of Georgia Press, 1990

Further Reading

Bryant, William Cullen, *Little Journeys to the Homes of American Authors*, edited by Elbert Hubbard, New York: Putnam, 1896

Butterworth, Keen, and James E. Kibler Jr., *William Gilmore Simms: A Reference Guide*, Boston: G. K. Hall, 1980

Duyckinck, Evert, and George L. Duyckinck, *Cyclopedia of American Literature*, vol. II, Philadelphia: W. M. Rutter, 1875, pp. 256–260

Erskine, John, *Leading American Novelists*, New York: Books for Libraries Press, 1910

Guilds, John Caldwell, ed., *"Long Years of Neglect": The Work and Reputation of William Gilmore Simms*, Fayetteville: University of Arkansas Press, 1988

Hubbell, Jay B., *The South in American Literature*, Durham, North Carolina: Duke University Press, 1954

Parks, Edd Winfield, *Southern Poets*, New York: American Book, 1936

Quinn, Arthur Hobson, *American Fiction: An Historical and Critical Survey*, New York: Appleton-Century-Crofts, 1936

Trent, William P., *William Gilmore Simms*, Boston and New York: Houghton Mifflin, 1892

Wimsatt, Mary Ann, *The Major Fiction of William Gilmore Simms: Cultural Traditions and Literary Form*, Baton Rouge: Louisiana State University Press, 1989

Songs and Ballads

The popular songs and ballads of nineteenth-century America were as diverse as the country itself and derived from as many sources. They included work songs, religious hymns, stage and show tunes, play-party songs, and folk-lyrics; they were written by well-known composers like Stephen Collins Foster and Daniel Emmett and put together by numerous anonymous folk performers; they came from the north, from the Appalachian Highlands, from the deep south, and from the western frontier. Given this inherent complexity, any attempt to describe the terrain of nineteenth-century American song will inevitably be partial and somewhat arbitrary.

It is useful to distinguish at first between "true" folk songs, composed and transmitted orally and only later recorded by collection, and popular songs, written and published with sheet music or in songbooks, but even this distinction has its limitations. Versions of folk songs often found their way into print in songsters and broadsheets, while published songs, to the extent they were "popular," had their life in the oral culture of the country.

As America was a land of immigrants, so American popular music was funded by many national traditions, and although the Library of America selection is limited to the English language, we should not forget that American popular song also includes French language ballads from Louisiana, Spanish *corridos* (popular ballads) and *decimas* from the southwest, German songs from Pennsylvania, and songs in many other languages from other national traditions, not to mention the songs of Native Americans. American songs in English, however, emerge from two basic families: the British and the West African. The earliest English, Scotch, and Irish immigrants brought their ballads with them, as well as a musical style based on solo performance and an emphasis on words rather than music or rhythm. On the other hand, although very little of real African song survived in America, a distinctly African pattern of leader and chorus, call and response, and a privileging of rhythmic complication both continued to inform songs in the African American tradition.

The earliest songs of America were direct imports from Europe; ancient British ballads were preserved in oral culture in isolated parts of the new continent, and even today there are more traditional songs in circulation in the United States than survive in the British Isles. "The House Carpenter," "Barbara Allen," "Lord Randal," "The Daemon Lover," "The Gypsy Laddie," "Pretty Polly," and "The Farmer's Curst Wife," among many others, continued in wide distribution in all parts of the continent into the twentieth century. Traditional ballads did, however, undergo a transformation in their new environment: the role of supernatural and magical elements tended to be diminished, and incidents of incest and kin-murder were often edited out.

Indigenous American compositions began to appear gradually, in response to specifically American experiences. In the post-Revolutionary and Federal periods and in the early years of the nineteenth century, much popular music composed in the United States had a patriotic color. In 1798, for example, "Hail, Columbia" became an overnight success; other popular songs around the turn of the century included "Adams & Washington," "The Ladies Patriotic Song," and "Adams and Liberty." The last named, set to the music of an old English drinking song, "To Anacreon in Heaven," achieved immortality a few years later when Francis Scott Key, after watching the bombardment of Fort McHenry by the British in 1814, composed a new set of patriotic words and a new title, "The Star Spangled Banner" (LOA, 1: 46).

One of the most fertile sources of American folk songs in the nineteenth century was work. American sailors, in particular, developed a large body of chanteys, especially after the War of 1812. With the rise of the British Merchant Marine and the growth of competition from its rapidly-expanding American counterpart, the leisurely atmosphere of the eighteenth-century ship was replaced with a new order of demanding labor, which was paced and relieved by the singing of chanteys. Generally the chanteys took the call-and-response form, with the strongest singer providing the verses while the rest of the crew answered with a refrain. In addition to tunes composed on board, sailors frequently adapted songs long known on land and made them their own. The famous "Shenandoah" (LOA, 2: 807) is a typical example. Generally thought to have originated with Canadian or American voyageurs, it became especially popular with American sailors around the time of the Civil War, when it was sung as a capstan chantey; the song helped sailors pace the turning of the capstan while raising the anchor.

Meanwhile, the interior of the continent was being opened as well. In 1825, the Erie Canal, connecting Albany and Buffalo, New York, was completed, making the midwest accessible to trade and migration, and it quickly became one of the busiest waterways in the country. "The Erie Canal" ("Low Bridge, Everybody Down"; LOA, 2: 790) is only one of many songs that originated with the barge haulers and that reflected the slow trek from the Hudson to the Great Lakes.

But the Erie Canal was dwarfed by the great engineering project of nineteenth-century America, the building of the railroad. The completion, on May 10, 1869, of coast-to-coast communications with the meeting of the Union Pacific line (proceeding west from Omaha, Nebraska) and the Central Pacific line (building east from Sacramento, California) climaxed the first phase, but this was only the beginning. With the end of the Civil War, the nation's energies were devoted to covering the continent with a network of rail; where in 1865 there had been only 35,000 miles of track, by 1890 there existed over 125,000. This great enterprise required hecatombs of laborers, and much of this demand was supplied by immigrants, in particular Irish immigrants. Between 1820 and 1856, Ireland was the leading source of new arrivals to the United States, especially in the years following the first potato crop failure in 1846. A large number of these immigrants went into the labor-hungry railroads; by 1870, 25 percent of all railroad employees (excluding clerks), were Irish. Not surprisingly then, folk songs based on the experience of the railroad construction gangs tend to have an Irish tinge. "Paddy Works on the Erie" ("Working on the Railway"; LOA 2: 823), dating probably from the 1850s or early 1860s, is a typical example.

In the south, the railroad work gangs were more frequently black, and it is to this population that we owe what has been called America's greatest ballad, "John Henry" (LOA, 2: 782). Although it was not collected until the second decade of the twentieth century, it soon became one of the most researched of American songs, and its inspiration has been reliably identified as the arduous construction of the Big Bend Tunnel on the C & O line in West Virginia in the early 1870s. Whether there actually was a John Henry working there will never be known, but researchers found many people who claimed to remember the indomitable steel-driver and his exploit very well. Contemporary records indicate that his feat was by no means incredible. But more important than the possible historicity of the character of John Henry is his mythical role as an archetypal, larger-than-life black hero, an embodiment of unyielding prowess and virile self-confidence for black work and chain gangs who labored to exhaustion.

Other groups had their own songs, like the lumberjacks ("The Jam on Gerry's Rocks" and "Canada-I-O") and miners ("The Avondale Mine Disaster" and "The Dreary Black Hills"). The miseries of migratory farm labor, for example, are depicted in "The State of Arkansas" (LOA, 2: 814). Such songs of regional satire were common, and this comic song became widely popular in nineteenth-century America, for Arkansas had already become firmly established nationally as the butt of much humor, as in the famous comedy dialogue "The Arkansas Traveller."

Americans have always had as great a thirst for what we may call play songs as for those inspired by work. Throughout the length of the western frontier, from Michigan to Texas, from Kentucky to Nebraska, scattered settlements were isolated from the rest of the world and forced to depend on themselves for music and entertainment. The notion of "dancing," however, continued to be regarded with an inherited Puritan suspicion; the result was the rise of a distinctive American institution, the play-party. At a play-party, young people of both sexes could meet and engage in simple figures and steps similar to, and often derived from, children's games, while all the time maintaining the pretense that they were not "dancing." Instrumental accompaniment was generally forbidden – the fiddle was regarded as the devil's tool – but the participants provided their own musical rhythms, singing songs like "Skip to My Lou," "Coffee Grows on White Oak Trees," and "Shoot the Buffalo."

In those parts of the frontier where religious constraints were less strong, however, undisguised frolics, hoedowns, and "infares" were held without apology. Music was permitted, and, indeed, expected, whether provided by a fiddler or banjo-player, or by the participants themselves, who sang "mouth-music." Any lyrics would take second place to the raucous dance tunes, and would normally be interjected at intervals by a practiced caller for humorous purposes. Frolic songs and dance calls, like "Shady Grove" (LOA, 2: 805), "Cumberland Gap" (LOA, 2: 761), "Cripple Creek" (LOA, 2: 760), and "Old Joe Clark" (LOA, 2: 796), typically took the form of long strings of brief comic stanzas with little narrative or other connection to the song, stanzas seemingly suggested only by the title of the dance tune. The length of the song was determined by that of the dance, and it is fair to say that these songs provided the only examples of extensive improvisation in non-Afro-American folk music. One consequence of these songs' popularity was the development of a class of skilled and semiprofessional musicians and singers, which laid the foundation for the endurance and growth of what would come to be identified as "country music."

The great western migration produced a large number of songs, beginning with the Gold Rush of 1849 and the cross-continental surge that it inspired. In January 1848, Captain John A. Sutter discovered gold while building a mill on a branch of the American River in California; when the news reached the east and a notice was published in the Baltimore Sun in September, it set off a stampede. By 1850, there were 100,000 new settlers in California. And the lucky strikes continued; in the first year 5 million dollars worth of gold had been mined; by 1853, over $63 million. The mining camps attracted many entertainers who toured the territory, often performing songs based on the miners' own experiences. John A. Stone, a former prospector who himself had made the overland trek in the 1850s, composed the largest number and most popular of the gold rush songs. After he made his fortune in 1853, he took to touring the camps under the pseudonym "Old Put"; leading a troupe called the Sierra Nevada Rangers, he performed his own compositions. In 1855, he published his first collection, The Original California Songster, which contained the quintessential ballad of the overlander, "Sweet Betsey From Pike" (LOA, 2: 817). This song was set to a popular English tune, "Vilikins and His Dinah." "The Days of '49" (LOA, 2: 762) is another typical prospector's lament. It was written by Charley Rhodes, probably in the late 1850s, although it was not published until 1876. Perhaps the best-known song set in the California gold fields, however, was written long after the original rush was over and was already a sentimental memory. "Clementine" (LOA, 2: 796) appeared as a college or popular song in 1884, with words and music credited to the otherwise unknown Percy Montrose.

A somewhat later phase of the movement west is reflected in what might be called songs of settlement. With the passage of the Homestead Act of 1862, most areas of land in Kansas, Iowa, and Nebraska were opened to occupancy; for a fee of 18 dollars, any citizen who agreed to reside for five years could receive a tract of 160 acres. Acquiring the land was, of course, only the beginning, and the daily tribulation of early life on the frontier is expressed in songs like "Starving to Death on a Government Claim" (LOA, 2: 812). A more sanguine view was offered as well, especially in what is undoubtedly the most famous settler's song of all, "A Home on the Range" (LOA, 2: 776). It was considered an anonymous folk song at the time of its collection, but in the course of a copyright suit in the mid-1930s, when the song was one of the most popular tunes on the radio, it was discovered to have been composed by Brewster Higley, an amateur poet and homesteader who lived near Smith Center, Kansas, in 1873.

But by far the most interesting and celebrated character in the western drama was the cowboy. The preeminent place of the cowboy in the American imagination is matched by the enduring popularity of his songs; indeed, cowboy songs were the first to be collected extensively, mostly by John A. Lomax in the first decade of the century, and the first to lead scholars to suggest that there was still a large body of unrecorded folk music in oral circulation in America.

The earliest cowboys were a colony of Americans in what is now southern Texas, who had settled there in 1821 at the invitation of the Mexican government. The San Antonio valley became the center of a cattle industry based on the Texas Longhorn, a cross-breed of English and Mexican strains. Between 1836, when Texas gained its independence, and the Civil War, ranching expanded rapidly in response to the growing North American market for beef. The outbreak of hostilities between the Union and the Confederacy brought an economic contraction to the industry, but trade began to flourish again, especially after the establishment of a railhead at Abilene, Kansas, which made it possible to ship cattle directly to Chicago, Illinois. In the 1860s, "cowboy" was still synonymous with Texan, but the extermination of the buffalo in little more than a decade opened the great plains for domestic breeds, and cattle and cattlemen swarmed over the new territories.

In spite of its romanticization, the life of the cowboy was hard, lonely, and frequently violent, and cowboy songs reflect a wistful, and often wry, awareness of its hardships. The tunes were frequently borrowed from long familiar songs and ballads, but the result was generally so thoroughly adapted to its new environment that it became unique. Such well-known western songs as "Bury Me Not in the Lone Prairie" and "The Cowboy's Lament" (LOA, 2: 758), for instance, both derive from earlier British models. "The Cowboy's Lament" is a distant descendant of an eighteenth-century broadside ballad, "The Unfortunate Rake," but although the hero of the original is dying of syphilis, in the cowboy's version he meets a more violent end. "Red River Valley" (LOA, 2: 801) is another melody that is best known as a cowboy song, but the song seems to have migrated to its home in the American west. Evidence suggests that the original setting was the Red River in western Canada, not that in Texas, and that the song expressed the love of a half-breed maiden for a British soldier who was sent west during the Red River Rebellion of the Metis led by Louis Riel in 1869.

The long overland cattle drives, when the herds were taken to railheads or northern pastures, produced a large number of well-known tunes. These are true work songs, sung by the cowhands to while away hot days in the saddle or, as some claim, to soothe restive steers at night. They tend to take the form of potentially endless accumulations of short stanzas that alternate with refrains derived from cattle cries: typical examples are "The Old Chisholm Trail," named for the most famous of several cattle trails that led from southern Texas to Abilene, "Git Along Little Dogies" (LOA, 2: 822), and "Rye Whisky" (LOA, 2: 803), which celebrated the pleasures waiting at the end of the drive.

According to one scholar, religious songs account for more than half of all indigenous American compositions. With the establishment of religious freedom after the American Revolution, dissenting Protestant sects began to expand rapidly, especially on the southern and western frontiers. Between 1783 and 1800, for example, the Baptists quadrupled their membership. The Great Revival that spread from Kentucky through the south and west in the early century resulted in huge open-air camp meetings, which often consisted of days of preaching, praying, and singing. The growth of these religious groups led to the development of new religious songs; these works generally refitted familiar folk songs with spiritual lyrics. These new

songs were often collected into "shape note" hymn books, in which, as the name indicates, different notes were printed as distinctive shapes for the musically illiterate. The first half of the nineteenth century saw an explosion of popular hymn books, including, to name just a few, Davisson's *Kentucky Harmony* (1816), Carden's *Missouri Harmony* (Abraham Lincoln's songbook), Moore's *Columbian Harmony*, "Singin' Billy" Walker's *The Southern Harmony* – claimed to have sold 600,000 copies – and White's *The Sacred Harp* (1844).

The camp meetings were often interracial, and one feature of nineteenth-century spiritual folk song was the complicated interaction of black and white traditions. Many Afro-American spirituals resemble tunes from white hymnodies, and typical Afro-American musical features such as musical repetition and frequent refrains appear in white religious songs. "Lonesome Valley" (LOA, 2: 789) and "Old Time Religion" (LOA, 2: 799) are just two of many songs whose origin is uncertain, and which appear in collections of both black spirituals and white hymnbooks.

Especially interesting sources of religious songs were the small but astonishingly creative Shaker communities. The great period of Shaker song composition began with the peculiar spiritual revival, called "Mother Ann's Work," that started in 1837 and lasted for more than a decade. During this period, a large number of "gift" or "vision" songs were supposedly received spontaneously by inspired individuals – often during a trance or visionary state – and recorded on the spot by a second person. Authority was variously ascribed, often to Mother Ann Lee, founder of the church, or to other deceased elders, but also to a varied company of celebrities, including George Washington, Christopher Columbus, Napoleon, and many others, all of whom had supposedly converted to the faith after death. "Simple Gifts" (LOA, 2: 808) is a late and well-known product of this period of spiritual ferment.

But religious songs existed alongside another set of songs in the oral tradition that expressed a very different fascination, ballads celebrating notorious outlaws and deeds of violence. Naturally, these were most common in the wide-open west; "Jesse James" (LOA, 2: 777), composed soon after James's murder in 1872, is only one example of the peculiar cultural process by which cultural memory and popular song converted criminals such as Jesse James, Billy the Kid, Sam Bass, and many others, into sentimental heroes. African American "bad men" remembered in song were more often presented in a grittier and less sentimental fashion. "John Hardy" (LOA, 2: 781), for example, based on an actual murderer executed in 1894, is a kind of inverted "John Henry" (LOA, 2: 782). In some versions of the former ballad, which depict a desperado contemptuous of any authority, the two figures are confused. A similar figure appears in the many versions of the widely known ballad "Stagolee" or "Stackerlee" or "Stackalee" (LOA, 2: 809), which seems to have originated in Memphis, Tennessee.

Another popular variety of ballads was inspired by a fascination with the crime rather than the criminal. Lurid murder stories, especially stories of young women killed by their false lovers, had always been appealing to ballad makers, and are frequent in British collections. In the United States, according to one expert, fully half the ballads composed by white singers are devoted to this theme. American versions, like "On the Banks of the Ohio," "Pearl Bryan," or "McAfee's Confession," tend to be more subjective and pathetic than their British predecessors, as well as more circumspect about the nature of the relation between the lovers. "Naomi Wise" – or "Poor Naomi" (LOA, 2: 800) – evidently based on the 1808 murder of Naomi Wise by one Jonathan Lewis, who drowned her in the Deep River in North Carolina, is a typical and well-known example.

Afro-American murder ballads generally spend less time on the horror of the crime and show more sympathy for the plight of the murderer, as in the many versions of "Frankie and Albert" (LOA, 2: 769), or "Frankie and Johnnie," which has retained its popularity throughout the twentieth century. It has been connected to various actual nineteenth-century murders, most commonly that of Allen Britt by Frankie Baker in St. Louis, Missouri, in 1899.

The most important theatrical source of songs in nineteenth-century America was probably the immensely popular minstrel show phenomenon. By the mid to late 1820s, the blackface stereotype had become a standard fixture on the American comic stage. In 1828, Thomas Dartmouth ("Daddy") Rice became a sensation with his portrayal of "Jim Crow," which was supposedly based on an old black hostler that Rice had seen dancing a peculiar shuffling step and singing an accompanying song as he brushed down the horses. Rice took his act across the United States and to England, becoming the most recognized American comedian of his time. The minstrel show proper emerged after an economic downturn in 1842 made theater work hard to find, which in turn induced performers to combine their acts. In 1843, Daniel Decatur Emmett and three New York musicians formed the first minstrel group, the Virginia Minstrels, and other groups soon followed, including the New Orleans Minstrels (1843), the Kitchen Minstrels (1844), the Christie Minstrels (1846) – which first established the standard three-part form of "olio" or variety show, free form fantasy, and burlesque – the White Minstrels (1846), the Ordway Minstrels (1850), and the famous Bryant Minstrels (1857).

To be sure, the songs had for the most part little to do with authentic Afro-American culture and were based largely on English models. But at their most interesting, these songs showed some evidence of the rhythmic complexities and syncopations typical of Afro-American musical style. As well, the shows provided the first large dependable market for indigenous popular American songs and inspired a large body of work. Emmett was the greatest of the composer-performers, and he claimed credit for many songs that became standards, including "Old Dan Tucker," "De Boatman's Song" or "Boatman's Dance" (LOA, 1: 647), and "Dixie" (see "Dixie's Land," LOA, 1: 646). It is not certain whether he wrote "The Blue Tail Fly" (1844; LOA, 2: 778), but it was one of the Virginia Minstrels' numbers; it became popular among abolitionists for its satire on "Ole Massa," and is reported to have been the favorite minstrel melody of Lincoln, who called it that "buzzing song." Another popular composer-performer was Charlie "Cool" White, who performed with his Virginian Serenaders, and whose 1844 song "Lubly Fan Will You Come Out Tonight?" soon became famous, after several adaptations to performing locale, as "Buffalo Gals" (LOA, 2: 757).

But the most famous composer of minstrel songs was not a performer. Stephen Collins Foster, the greatest American popular song writer of his time, was born in Pittsburgh, Pennsylva-

nia, in 1826. Between 1844, when he published his first song, "Open the Lattice, Love," and his death 20 years later, he wrote more than 200 songs; many of these songs, especially in the early phase of his career, were intended for the minstrel theater. In 1847–48, for example, he produced "Lou'siana Belle," "Away Down South," "Old Uncle Ned," and finally "Oh! Susanna" (LOA, 2: 174), which brought him immediate fame, though not fortune, given Foster's inexperience and the casual nature of contemporary copyright law.

Foster was ambivalent about his association with the minstrel stage, and at the same time as he was writing his dialect blackface numbers he also was turning out a series of household songs destined for the parlor piano. Around 1850, he initiated a new form, the "plantation melody," which took the Old South as its subject matter, but which, unlike the minstrel songs, avoided specific reference to black life and shunned dialect entirely. The simplicity and melodiousness of Foster's household songs made them extremely popular; by the early 1850s, several had sold more than 100,000 copies, which enabled Foster to become the first American composer to live entirely on his sales. Part of the songs' appeal was the nostalgic and sentimental tone, which was a staple of antebellum popular music. Americans seemed fascinated by a vision of an idyllic lost past, and this backward-looking obsession is evident even in the titles of some of Foster's most beloved melodies: "Old Folks at Home" (1851; LOA, 2: 172), "My Old Kentucky Home, Good Night!" (1853; LOA, 2: 173), and "My Old Dog Tray" (1853).

After the minstrels, the most popular musical performers in the United States at mid-century were singing families, beginning with the Austrian-born Rainers in the late 1830s. The success of their tours inspired imitators, the most successful being the Hutchinsons. The large Hutchinson family had long been favorite amateur local singers in Milford, New Hampshire; in 1839, four of the brothers (later joined by a sister) decided to form a professional touring group. In a short time, they became the most popular singing family of their age, in the United States and abroad, and in 1844 they performed before President John Tyler. As their success grew, so did the size of the group, until they finally divided into several troupes, as various of the original members split off with his own "tribe."

The Hutchinsons were significant in their time not only as entertainers but as champions of social and political causes as well. Although most of their songs, like "The Old Sexton," "The Lament of the Blind Orphan Girl," or "The Snowstorm," displayed the highly sentimental style of the period, many had a distinctly didactic purpose, too. One of their earliest sensations was a very theatrical presentation of "The Maniac," by Henry Russell, a melodramatic depiction of the horrors of contemporary insane asylums. Later they took up temperance ("King Alcohol" and "Cold Water"), women's suffrage, abuses of Native Americans ("The Indian's Lament"), and abolition ("The Bereaved Slave Mother" and "Gone, Sold and Gone").

Topical songs began to appear in larger numbers in the midcentury. Abolitionist songs, in particular, proliferated as the antislavery movement gained ground and political passions became more heated in the years leading up to the Civil War. Poems denouncing the institution were composed and set to familiar tunes such as "Auld Lang Syne" and "Oh! Susanna" by, for example, the prominent abolitionist William Lloyd Garrison. New songs were composed as well; many of these were published in the 1851 collection *The Anti-Slavery Harp*.

But the political event that was by far the greatest stimulus to composition was the Civil War, which, it has been claimed, generated more popular music than anything else in the nation's history. The conflict broke out just as the market for printed sheet music and piano scores had begun to expand, so that not only were many new songs composed about the conflict, but songs such as "Dixie," "The Battle Cry of Freedom," and "The Bonnie Blue Flag" had a significant effect on shaping public opinions. Already in mid-1860, the New Orleans, Louisiana, publisher P. P. Werlein had brought out "Minute Men, Form; the Anthem of the South," which contained lyrics calling on southerners to stand up to the "enemy"; northerners were, not surprisingly, somewhat offended. Among the many songwriters who responded to the sudden demand were, in the north, Foster ("We Are Coming, Father Abraham"), George Frederick Root ("The Battle Cry of Freedom" and "Just Before the Battle, Mother"), and Henry Clay Work ("Marching Through Georgia"; LOA, 2: 324), and in the south, John Hill Hewitt ("All Quiet Along the Potomac") and James Ryder Randall ("Maryland"; LOA, 2: 390). Musical sides, however, were hard to maintain; ironically, the song that became the anthem of the Confederacy, "Dixie," was not written by a southerner. It was Daniel Emmett, an ardent Union supporter, who took credit for the piece; his claims have been disputed, however, and some researchers have even argued that he learned it from a black family who lived in Ohio.

But one of the earliest and undoubtedly the most influential Civil War song was not the work of a professional composer: "John Brown's Body" (LOA, 2: 780). The most surprising thing about the song in its original version is that the eponymous hero was in fact not the John Brown of Harpers Ferry, Virginia, fame, but Sergeant John Brown of the 2nd Battalion, Boston Light Infantry. In early May 1861, the battalion choral society, of which Brown was a member, put together a comic song set to the music of an early and long familiar hymn, "Say, brothers will you meet us," and within a few months the new song became a sensation. Naturally, the hero was assumed to be the more famous John Brown, and the popularity of the song easily led to the polarizing impression on both sides of the conflict that the Union was already committed to the cause of abolition a year and a half before the Emancipation Proclamation.

There were several attempts in the early months of the war to provide more exalted words for what had become the anthem of the Union troops. The first to succeed was that of Julia Ward **Howe**, the wife of a prominent New England reformer and an author of some reputation for her essays and poems. In December 1861, she was visiting a Union army camp near Washington, D.C., when a small skirmish broke out and a detachment of troops marched by, singing "John Brown." Another member of her party suggested that she try her hand at composing new lyrics for the song, and the next morning, in a fit of inspiration, Howe wrote down the poem that became the definitive expression of the Union's apocalyptic conception of its divinely sanctioned mission, "Battle-Hymn of the Republic" (LOA, 1: 709).

After the war, public and social topics largely disappeared from popular song. The minstrel show continued to be as popular as it had been before 1859, but its character began gradually to change. One innovation was the appearance for the first time of Afro-American minstrel groups, sometimes themselves in blackface. Indeed, the last important minstrel tunesmith, and the first successful black American composer, was James A. Bland, author of more than 700 songs, including such standards as "Carry Me Back to Old Virginny" (1878; LOA, 2: 516) and "Oh, Dem Golden Slippers!" (1879; LOA, 2: 515). The influence of new black spiritual groups such as the very popular Fisk University Jubilee Singers was felt as well. But the minstrel show as a whole was becoming less centered on African American characters and plantation themes and was gradually turning into something closer to a variety show. Finally, in the later decades of the century, it was superseded by vaudeville, which looked in spirit and style not to the old American south, but to the new ethnically mixed culture of the booming American urban centers, the culture that would give a distinctive new form and sound to the popular music of the twentieth century.

DAVID H. EVANS

(See also, John Howard Payne, "Home, Sweet Home!" [LOA, 1: 110]; George Pope Morris, "The Oak" [LOA, 1: 251]; Lydia Maria Child, "The New-England Boy's Song about Thanksgiving Day" [LOA, 1: 252]; Edmund Hamilton Sears, "'It came upon the midnight clear'" [LOA, 1: 588]; Thomas Dunn English, "Ben Bolt" [LOA, 1: 718]; John Henry Hopkins Jr., "Three Kings of Orient" [LOA, 2: 98]; Robert Lowry, "Beautiful River" [LOA, 2: 176]; Phillips Brooks, "O Little Town of Bethlehem" [LOA, 2: 339]; George Washington Cable, "Creole Slave Songs" [LOA, 2: 447–450]; Katharine Lee Bates, "America the Beautiful" [LOA, 2: 522], **Nineteenth-Century Versions of American Indian Poetry, Popular Poetry, Spirituals**)

Further Reading

Andrews, Edward D., *The Gift To Be Simple: Songs, Dances and Rituals of the American Shakers*, 1940; reprinted, New York: Dover, 1962

Brink, Carol, *Harps in the Wind: The Story of the Singing Hutchinsons*, 1947; reprinted, New York: Da Capo, 1980

Chase, Gilbert, *America's Music: From the Pilgrims to the Present*, rev. 3rd ed., Urbana: University of Illinois Press, 1987

Courlander, Harold, *Negro Folk Music, U.S.A.*, New York: Columbia University Press, 1963

Epstein, Dena J., *Sinful Tunes and Spirituals: Black Folk Music to the Civil War*, Urbana: University of Illinois Press, 1977

Heaps Willard A., and Porter W. Heaps, *The Singing Sixties: The Spirit of Civil War Days Drawn from the Music of the Times*, Norman: University of Oklahoma Press, 1960

Hitchcock, H. Wiley, *Music in the United States: A Historical Introduction*, 2nd ed., Englewood Cliffs, New Jersey: Prentice-Hall, 1974

Howard, John Trasker, *Stephen Foster, America's Troubadour*, New York: Thomas Y. Crowell, 1953

Jackson, George Pullen, *White Spirituals in the Southern*

Uplands: The Story of the Fasola Folk, Their Songs, Singings, and "Buckwheat Notes," 1933; reprinted, New York: Dover, 1965

Jackson, Richard, comp., *Popular Songs of Nineteenth-Century America: Complete Original Sheet Music for 64 Songs*, New York: Dover, 1976

Lomax, Alan, *The Folk Songs of North America in the English Language*, Garden City, New York: Doubleday, 1960

Lomax, John A., and Alan Lomax, *Folk Song: U.S.A.*, New York: Meredith, 1947

Lott, Eric, *Love and Theft: Blackface Minstrelsy and the American Working Class*, New York: Oxford University Press, 1993

Nathan, Hans, *Dan Emmett and the Rise of Early Negro Minstrelsy*, Norman: University of Oklahoma Press, 1962

Silber, Irwin, ed., *Songs of the Civil War*, New York: Columbia University Press, 1960

Spaeth, Sigmund, *A History of Popular Music in America*, New York: Random House, 1948

Stevenson, Robert, *Protestant Church Music in America: A Short Survey of Men and Movements from 1564 to the Present*, New York: Norton, 1966

Toll, Robert C., *Blacking Up: The Minstrel Show in Nineteenth-Century America*, New York: Oxford University Press, 1974

Yerbury, Grace D., *Song in America: From Early Times to About 1850*, Metuchen, New Jersey: Scarecrow, 1971

Spirituals

Like the biblical Psalms they so closely resemble, the African American spirituals of the nineteenth century are essentially folk-verses or poems that follow a closely knit pattern of design and thematic structure. They are derived from both English revival music and verse, and the cultural habits of mind of the slaves who were brought from Africa. This fusion of cultural horizons combines with the dramatic moment of black spiritual composition to provide American music with one of its most moving and inspirational forms. This essay will trace the evolution of the antebellum spiritual, and it will discuss the Library of America selections for thematic and formal elements.

The Grove Dictionary of Music defines the African American spiritual as "a type of folksong which originated in American revivalist activity between 1740 and the close of the 19th century. The term is derived from the biblical "spiritual songs" (Colossians 3:16), a designation used in early publications to distinguish the texts from metrical psalms and hymns of traditional church usage." The spiritual song does indeed belong to revivalist literature, or to the "revivalist liturgy," and it is primarily distinguished from the more traditional hymns of the Protestant church by its emphasis on repetition and parallelism in the structure of verses and refrains and by its highly emotional and dramatic content, with a pervasive focus on eschatology, millennial fulfillment, and the drama of entering the next life, or "Crossing Over Jordan." More than anything else, African American spirituals are unique for their emotionally dramatic force, a vitality and spiritually profound feeling that has been recognized by countless journal writers and audiences who have personally witnessed the singing of black spirituals. For example, the escaped slave Frederick Douglass recalled the emotional power of listening to slave singing when he was a child. A passage from his *Narrative of the Life of an American Slave* (1845) clearly suggests this spontaneous overflow of powerful feeling:

> The slaves selected to go to the Great House Farm for the monthly allowance for themselves and their fellow slaves, were peculiarly enthusiastic. While on their way, they would make the dense old woods, for miles around, reverberate with their wild songs, revealing at once the highest joy and the deepest sadness. They would compose and sing as they went along, consulting neither time nor tune. The thought that came up, came out – if not in the word in the sound – and as frequently in the one as in the other. They would sometimes sing the most pathetic sentiment in the most rapturous tone, and the most rapturous sentiment in the most pathetic tone. Into all of their songs they would manage to weave something of the Great House Farm. Especially would they do this when leaving home. They would then sing most exultingly the following words: – "I am going away to the Great House Farm!, O yea! O, yea!, O." This they would sing, as a chorus, to words which to many would seem unmeaning jargon but which, nevertheless, were full of meaning to themselves. *I have sometimes thought that the mere hearing of those songs would do more to impress some minds of the horrible character of slavery, than the reading of whole volumes of philosophy on the subject could do.* [emphasis added]

But Douglass and other slave auditors were not the only ones moved by the pathos and integrity of the black spiritual of the antebellum south. Mary Chesnut was a white South Carolinian whose journal has been frequently cited to represent the values and attitudes of antebellum southerners, and her description of spiritual singing invokes a stereotype for performance that later influenced minstrel show parodies and imitations of black spiritual singing. Modern studies show how often the auditors would remark on the character of the African American while recollecting. Dena Epstein, a leading authority on the subject of spirituals, quotes an entry from Chesnut's diary for October 13, 1861, which describes a service that she attended with her husband's family at a black church on their plantation, Mulberry, near Camden, South Carolina:

> [There was] a very large black congregation. . . . Jim Nelson, the driver . . . a full-blooded African, was asked to lead in prayer. He became wildly excited, on his knees, facing us with his eyes shut. He clapped his hands at the end of every sentence, and his voice rose to the pitch of a shrill shriek, yet was strangely clear and musical, occasionally in a plaintive minor key that went to your heart. Sometimes it rang out like a trumpet. I *wept bitterly*. It was all sound, however, and emotional pathos. . . . The words had no meaning at all. It was the devotional passion of voice and manner which was so magnetic. The Negroes sobbed and shouted and swayed backward and forward, some with aprons to their eyes, most of them clapping their hands and responding in shrill tones: "Yes, God!!" "Jesus!!" "Saviour!" "Bless de Lord, amen," etc. *It was a little too exciting for me. I would very much have liked to shout, too.* Jim Nelson when he rose from his knees trembled and shook as one in a palsy, and from his eyes you could see the ecstasy had not left him yet. He could not stand at all, and sank back on his bench. . . . Suddenly, as I sat wondering what next, they broke out into one of those soul-stirring Negro camp meeting hymns. *To me this is the saddest of all earthly music, weird and depressing beyond my powers to describe.*

In both the Douglass and the Chesnut accounts, emotive power is paramount. The experiential dimension of the spiritual overshadows all content and thematic or ideological value. Contemporary accounts are filled with recollections of spiritual singing, and some provide analytical and critical perspective on the music in addition to recalling the emotional moment, which almost all do. Epstein also cites a Methodist minister from Maryland, John D. Long, who wrote in 1857: "The prayer-meetings of the slaves are conducted in the following manner: the colored exhorter or leader calls on two or three in succession to pray, filling up the intervals with singing tunes and words composed by themselves." And another account that Epstein cites from Macon, Georgia, dated 1858, shows how a liturgical pattern is present even in the most highly emotional spirituals: "Their hymns or religious chants, might furnish a curious book. The words are generally very few, and repeated over and over again; and the lines, though very unequal, are sung with a natural cadence that impresses the ear quite agreeably. Most of them relate to the moment of death, and in some of them are simple and poetic images which are often touching."

Some of these contemporary accounts work very well to provide modern readers with a realistic understanding of the origins and early performance of black spiritual music. However, some others exceed descriptive reporting and offer commentary on the African American character, which has led to stereotyping, to parodic imitation in minstrel shows, and even to the kind of stereotyping that appears in significant works of literature such as Harriet Beecher Stowe's *Uncle Tom's Cabin* (1852). Epstein records that in 1851, a Reverend C. F. Sturgis, of Greensboro, Alabama, described black religious singing this way: "The negro is a great singer, and he sings religious songs in preference to any other; indeed, unless now and then a comic song, often, as I suspect, falsely attributed to them, they sing but few others. They sing at their work, at their homes, on the highway, and in the streets; and, in the large majority of cases, their songs have a decidedly religious character. How common to see an old woman at her work, *'lining out'* a hymn to herself, and then singing it in a spirit of rapt abstraction from earth and all earthly things."

This liturgical form, the "lining out" widely used in Puritan New England for the antiphonal saying of the Psalms (before music was officially condoned by the religious authorities), is of course a very traditional practice in American Protestant churches, dating from the earliest New England congregations. But the African American practices were a constant fascination to white writers, who viewed the religious rituals and accompanying music sympathetically if paternalistically. Thomas Jefferson remarks on the culture of spirituals in his *Notes on the State of Virginia*, and one of Dena Epstein's sources, Sir Charles Lyell, an English visitor, wrote: "Of dancing and music the Negroes are passionately fond." She also cites the account of Fanny **Kemble**, who wrote of a slave funeral that she witnessed in 1838: "Yesterday evening the burial of the poor man Shadrach took place. . . . The coffin was laid on treadles in front of the cooper's cottage, and a large assemblage of the people had gathered round, many of the men carrying pinewood torches. . . . Presently, the whole congregation uplifted their voices in a hymn, the first high wailing notes of which – sung all in unison, in the midst of these unwonted surroundings – *sent a thrill through all my nerves*."

Funerals became a focal point for African American ritual and religious musical expression. It is well known that jazz originated in the funeral processional music of the deep south, particularly New Orleans, Louisiana, and that en route to the burial a type of lamentation or dirge music would be performed by ambulatory musicians, particularly on trumpet, trombone, clarinet, and drums, sometimes accompanied by harmonica. After the burial, the musical mood would shift to joy, a celebration of the release of the soul from bondage to the body, and rhythmic expressions such as "When the Saints Go

Marching In" would characterize the return from the cemetery. These songs were often accompanied by dancing, and eventually the music became a pervasive form of African American expression, with characteristic subsets of the dirge or the lament (the blues) and the abandonment of structured form in the joyful improvisations of the most creative American minds.

Rhythm appeal is essential to jazz; without it, the music would languish and die. And this legacy of feeling is essential to an understanding of African American spiritual music as well. Without the most prominent emotional expression, the formal elements would have little value except as historical phenomena. Instead, spirituals and funeral music evolved into twentieth-century gospel music, although both the ballad tradition and the joyful ejaculations of abandoned improvisation in contemporary gospel music owe much to the original spiritual forms, which blended Protestant hymnody and African rhythms. The funerals particularly impressed auditors such as Frederick Law Olmsted (also quoted in Epstein), the famous landscape-architect who toured the south in 1853 and kept an elaborate journal:

> On a Sunday afternoon I met a negro funeral procession, and followed after it to the place of burial. . . . The hearse halted at a desolate place, where a dozen colored people were already engaged in heaping the earth over the grave of a child, and singing a wild kind of chant. After the sermon, an old negro raised a hymn, which soon became a confused chant – the leader singing a few words alone, and the company then either repeating them after him or making a response to them, in the manner of sailors heaving at the windlass. [The allusion to the sea chantey invokes another genre of work song from the nineteenth century.] I could understand but very few of the words. The music was wild and barbarous, but not without a plaintive melody. A new leader took the place of the old man, when his breath gave out (he had sung very hard, with much bending of the body and gesticulation), and continued until the grave was filled, and a mound raised over it.

Olmsted's observations are extremely important, for the journal that he kept was published and provided northern readers with vivid accounts of life among the slave population of Virginia. Specifically, he described in great detail the auction of slaves in Richmond in 1853, a scene in which several African families were broken up to suit the economic convenience of the buyers and sellers.

A cultural analysis of the place of spirituals in American musical and religious history inevitably discovers examples of the stereotyping of black character already cited. Stowe's *Uncle Tom's Cabin* invokes precisely this kind of character formation to elicit sympathy from the reader and to create a kind of audience identification. Curiously, Stowe neglected the musical traditions of her black characters, which had the force of associating the African American slave with the most emotional phenomena in American history, the experiential religious movements known as the Great Awakening of the mid-eighteenth century and the Second Great Awakening of the early nineteenth century. At the heart of this association is "slave song," the rhetorically powerful musical expression through which the oppressed slave was regularly and repeatedly identified with the suffering Israelites in ancient Egyptian bondage. Music, more than slave narratives or slave speech-making on the abolitionist circuit, was pervasive in the culture, since even illiterate slaves (teaching a slave to read and write was forbidden by law in most southern states, as Frederick Douglass's *Narrative* makes very clear) were able to respond in unison to the "lining out" of spirituals. In 1847, a minister named James Waddell Alexander (quoted in Epstein) wrote an account of slave singing:

> The fondness of the black race for music is proverbial. It is rare to meet with a negro who does not sing. . . . We have listened to a great variety of sacred music . . . but if we were summoned to declare which of all seemed most like the praises of God, we should reply, the united voices of a thousand slaves. . . . As the Southern servants can seldom read, and, therefore, have no use for hymn books, the memory must be the sole depository of their sacred song. It is known that they largely frequent the assemblies of illiterate and enthusiastic persons, and catch up snatches of hymns, which are full of error, if not of absurd irreverance.

The white minister's objections to the textual inaccuracies of black spiritual singing is often accompanied by graphic depictions of the body language that the singers used to accompany their verbal and musical expressions. Despite the enthusiasms of the First and Second Awakenings in New England, the phenomenon of whole congregations shouting and moving rhythmically in response to chant struck many white observers as irrational ranting. It is, however, to their accounts of these performances that we owe much of what we know about the earliest spirituals and religious rites.

What remains, then, is an analysis of the texts found in the Library of America volume (LOA, 2: 757–824) in relation to some of the prominent themes of spiritual verse, such as eschatological warnings, hope for a future deliverance from suffering, and the subject of mortality and death. We should also interpret these significant cultural artifacts not only as artistic expressions of a prominent American population, but also as cultural representations of an historical American moment, the antebellum culture of the slaves in the plantation south.

Franklin Frazier, in *The Negro Church in America*, observes that the acceptance of Christianity by the African slaves was "governed by a desire to fulfill psychological and social needs." Herskovits Melville, in *The Myth of the Negro Past*, echoes this sentiment by remarking that the slaves "used religion as an outlet for the release of emotions and frustrations because they were unable to express themselves through political action or other means." The future-oriented theology of Christianity, with its vivid and pervasive contrast between the blessings of the afterlife for God's chosen people and the sufferings and distress of this fallen world, appealed particularly to an enslaved multitude who were able to identify with the plight of ancient Israel.

Most of the images in African American spirituals thus come from the Old, not the New Testament. In many spirituals, Moses figures as a kind of messianic cultural leader for all oppressed peoples, and the emotional qualities of performance were always accompanied by reference to the Old Testament sufferings of Israel in ways that made the slave's sufferings a credible recapitulation of Israel's experience. If the Old Testament Israel could anticipate the New Testament Incarnation, could not the slave experience foreshadow the Second Coming of Christ and the Millennium, when suffering would end and slavery would be abolished for an eternity of freedom? Epstein cites the account of a former slave and that of a minister named Robert Mallard as examples of this enthusiasm for the coming of the spirit.

> The way in which we worshipped is almost indescribable. The singing was accompanied by a certain ecstasy of motion, clapping of hands, tossing of heads, which would continue with a cessation of about half an hour; one would lead off in a kind of recitative style, others joining in the chorus. . . .

> Hearing singing in the neighborhood of the hotel, I went to the church from which it proceeded. . . . I stood at the door and looked in – and such confusion of sights and sounds! The Negroes were holding a revival meeting. Some were standing, others sitting, others moving from one seat to another, several exhorting along the aisles. The whole congregation kept up one loud monotonous strain, interrupted by various sounds: groans and screams and clapping hands. One woman specially under the influence of the excitement went across the church in a quick succession of leaps; now down on her knees with a sharp crack that smote upon my ear the full length of the church, then up again; now with her arms about some brother or sister, and again tossing them wildly in the air and clapping her hands together and accompanying the whole by a series of short, sharp shrieks. . . . Considering the mere excitement manifested in these disorderly ways, I could but ask: What religion is there here? . . . Some allowance, of course, must be made for the excitability of the Negro temperament.

The stereotyping previously cited is often present in these accounts of hearing and witnessing African American worship. Nevertheless, the enthusiasm they describe should also be considered in the context of the religious beliefs governing some of the worship and certainly in the context of the ideology governing the spirituals themselves.

It is well known that the spirituals of nineteenth-century America, the most significant historical moment of their evolution, were developed by fusing the "white spirituals" of eighteenth-century English evangelism with the rites, the rituals, and, occasionally, the themes of African American folklore and religious traditions. Musically and literally, they take the form of a folk hymn (as defined by Lowens, "basically a secular folktune which happens to be sung to a religious text") or of a religious ballad. Religious ballads and folk hymns in the Protestant tradition were the first spirituals to appear in the English colonies, at the time of the Great Awakening and Jonathan Edwards's "New Light" movement in New England. Later in the century, as the enthusiasm generated earlier in New England moved into the southern colonies, the music associated with evangelical enthusiasm moved, too, so that the more rural populations of the deep south and Appalachia inherited not only the doctrines of the Methodist and Baptist churches, but also the musical traditions of "white spirituals."

Publication of these musical texts began as early as the 1740s, and by century's end, we find Joshua Smith's popular *Divine Hymns or Spiritual Songs for the Use of Religious Assemblies and Private Christians* (1784). The Grove Dictionary makes clear that it was Jeremiah Ingalls who, in 1805, provided *The Christian Harmony*, a work that, following the earlier analyses of Andrew Law and William Billings, attempted to set forth the texts and the music. There are literally dozens of collections and studies of these "white spirituals," including *Spiritual Folk-Songs of Early America* (1937), *Down-East Spirituals* (1943), and *Another Sheaf of White Spirituals* (1952), all of which provide the modern reader with examples of the genre. Again, the Grove Dictionary establishes a connection to the past by showing that Ingalls and John Wyeth "provided conclusive evidence that the early converts drew on their knowledge of folk and popular tunes to give musical expression to their new religious feeling" (see Ingalls and Wyeth, *Repository of Sacred Music* [1813]). As the evangelical movement grew in strength, it appropriated tunes and musical forms from folk melodies but infused them with lyrics drawn from scriptural interpretation and prophetic language. It is this fusion that characterizes the African American spiritual, whose singing and performance also mirrors African ritual and tradition. Although the African American spiritual is closely related to the "white spiritual," however, it has unique qualities that have warranted its historical study in a separate tradition of scholarship.

In the first place, slaveholders in the nineteenth century were apprehensive of the psychological power of black spiritualism, and they often suppressed the dissemination of religious musical literature or the evangelical singing of hymns – moving accounts of their performance notwithstanding. In addition, there were few worship services where blacks and whites shared the pews or the pulpit; social customs and often the laws forbade integrated services, and, therefore, separate worship led to separate traditions of liturgy and form. Camp meetings, however, were common to both groups, and often the music of one camp would influence that of the other. Grove notes that "the repetition, tag lines, and refrains provided for 'call and response' performances between evangelist and people. The most popular forms were four-line arrangements of AAAB, and the couplet with tag line. The texts of the camp-meeting spiritual appeared in pocket songsters without music."

African American spirituals were thus first noted by visitors like Fanny Kemble and Frederick Law Olmsted, whose journals and diaries called attention to this moving form of human expression that transcended the oppression of the enslaved state. They were eventually gathered, like the "white spiritual songs," into collections by music-history editors. Just after the Civil War, W. F. Allen, C. P. Ware, and L. M. Garrison published *Slave Songs of the United States*. The end of the war commenced a prolific period of collecting and editing slave materials, although paradoxically the Emancipation Proclamation brought an abrupt end to the publication of slave narratives, whose purpose had been to end the "peculiar institution." During and after Reconstruction, public interest turned to African American music and culture, and between 1925 and 1927, James Weldon Johnson published *The Book of American Negro Spirituals*, which today remains the standard collection of the genre. Other studies and works include H. W. Odum and G. B. Johnson, *The Negro and His Songs* (1925), N. I. White,

American Negro Folk-songs (1925), R. N. Dett, *The Dett Collection of Negro Spirituals* (1936), J. W. Work, *American Negro Songs* (1940), and L. A. Parrish, *Slave Songs of the Georgia Sea Islands* (1942). These pioneering works have been in some respects superseded, but they remain standard texts and authorities.

However, as the preceding discussion has shown, it was in the *hearing* of spiritual music that one experienced the intense passion of the singer's feeling. These same decades saw lecture halls of the United States and Europe fill with groups of singers who performed the slave songs, and the Fisk Jubilee Singers became one of the best-known groups who regularly performed the songs of former slaves. Founded as a student singing group at Fisk University in Nashville, Tennessee, it quickly became a world-class performance group; it was later joined in prominence by the Hampton Singers from the Hampton Institute in Virginia. Individual performers who became associated with the spirituals included Roland Hayes, Paul Robeson, William Grant Still, and James Weldon Johnson. These early singers relied heavily on the spirituals inherited from slave times; but the genre quickly dissolved into new forms of African American music, including the deeply religious gospel singing that superseded the straight spiritual in the twentieth century. Gospel is, like the spirituals, rhythmic. However, it incorporates a more secular kind of jazz-based musical rhythm that allows more departures into the music for its own sake than the structured texts of the spirituals. It is to the *texts* themselves, found in the Library of America edition, that we now turn.

A number of fundamental, religious themes pervade these spirituals: 1) deliverance from the perils of earthly life; 2) water images, depicting both the destructive power of water and its saving, cleansing power; 3) the preservation of God's saints, His "chosen people," a distinction that the American slaves are represented to have in common with the New England Puritans and the Israelites of the Old Testament; 4) the designation of certain leaders to be recapitulations of the Old Testament concept of heroism (e.g., Abraham Lincoln as Moses); and 5) the suggestion that Old Testament typological figures like Moses and Joshua have a direct association with the saving power of Christ. This last feature, of course, is a sophisticated Judeo-Christian trope that was regularly used to demonstrate the long history of God's preservation of His "chosen people." The New England Puritans rewrote their history as a record that recapitulated the experience of Old Israel. Thus, if Old Israel had prefigured the Incarnation of the New Testament and Christ's first coming, could not the cyclical recapitulation of this experience, through parallels drawn by those seventeenth-century Puritans to the Old Testament record, prefigure the Second Coming and the Millennium? This argument was used extensively by Increase and Cotton Mather, in sermons like *Ichabod, or the Glory Has Departed* (1702) and the *Magnalia Christi Americana* (1702), and during the Great Awakening of the 1730s, Jonathan Edwards and his "New Light" followers predicted the coming of the Millennium through a similar system of finding "types" in their contemporary experience that adumbrated the Second Coming.

Although the spirituals contained in this volume do not exhibit a sophisticated theological exegesis of scriptural patterns in relation to contemporary nineteenth-century slave experience, it is clear from their allusions that the typological system was well understood and accepted as a way of providing hope to the downtrodden, suffering slave population. "Let My People Go" (LOA, 2: 786) is a well-known verse that is also called "Go Down, Moses," later the title of a William Faulkner novel. The theological parallels are self-evident:

When Israel was in Egypt's land,
O let my people go!
Oppressed so hard they could not stand,
O let my people go!

O go down, Moses
Away down to Egypt's land,
And Tell King Pharaoh,
To let my people go!

The "Moses" figure here is a larger-than-life hero, perhaps Abraham Lincoln, and the deep south – always feared among slaves who were "sold down the river" – is, of course, Egypt. These parallels are more than mere illustrations for effect; they give the experience of nineteenth-century American slaves the authority of Scripture history. Two specific principles are established in this spiritual: first, that God is the providential leader of his suffering chosen people, in this case, the slaves; second, that a Mosaic leader will eventually lead the slaves-as-chosen out of Egyptian captivity and into the "Promised Land" of deliverance.

These themes are repeated in "Joshua Fit de Battle ob Jerico" (LOA, 2: 785), which treats the recorded historical experience of Joshua, one of Moses' successors, a militaristic hero whose achievements are contained in the long Old Testament narrative that bears his name. We know much more about Joshua's record of achievement than we do, say, about Samson, who was also a judge of Israel and was inserted into the Old Testament narrative in only three books. However, because the record concerning Joshua is confined to his leadership qualities and military record, where the narrative of Samson is highly personal and shows his many human failings, the latter's story is better known. The story of Joshua is one of victory over the enemies of God, which white American slaveholders were clearly perceived to be, not only in the spiritual literature, but also in slave narratives. In the spiritual, Joshua is only a name – his personal qualities are not mentioned. Rather, he is compared to Gideon, another military leader of ancient Israel, who falls short in comparison, as does King Saul, the first King of Israel and another type of religious leader altogether:

You may talk about yo' king ob Gideon,
You may talk about yo' man ob Saul,
Dere's none like good old Joshua
At de battle ob Jerico.

The refrain illustrates Joshua's singular achievement:

Joshua fit de battle ob Jerico
Jerico, Jerico,
Joshua fit de battle ob Jerico,
An' de walls come tumblin' down.

The "falling" of Jericho's walls was, in fact, not an overwhelming military victory. Rather, it was depicted as a devastating psychological triumph in which the Israelites figured as actors in a divine drama that was produced, directed, and staged by God. Joshua, like his peers, was only a participant in the event. His military achievements, sacking the city and enslaving its inhabitants, only came later. The spiritual, like the Old Testament narrative, thus celebrates the achievements of Providence as much as those of Israel's leader. For it was Providence that offered hope to the suffering slaves.

The water imagery offers a rich configuration of tropes for the spiritual writers. "One More River" (LOA, 2: 800) clearly associates the crossing of the river Jordan with death, and, of course, this is an ancient idea that was also popular in Greek mythology (e.g., the crossing of the river Acheron into the afterlife).

O Jordan bank was a great old bank!
Dere ain't but one more river to cross.
We have some valiant soldier here,
Dere ain't but one more river to cross.

The path to the "final crossing" is straight and narrow, like John Bunyan's allegorical pilgrimage in *The Pilgrim's Progress*: "Dere's a hill on my leff, and he catch on my right, / Dere ain't but one more river to cross." Water here is literally perceived as the dividing line between life and death, and crossing the Jordan river becomes a transfiguring event or episode to be anticipated by every believer. In "Michael Row the Boat Ashore" (LOA, 2: 793), the theme is repeated:

Boastin' talk will sink your soul,
Hallelujah!
Brudder, lend a helpin' hand,
Hallelujah!
Sister, help for trim dat boat,
Hallelujah!
Jordan stream is wide and deep,
Hallelujah!
Jesus stand on t'oder side,
Hallelujah!

The "reward" for crossing over Jordan is union with Jesus, the Savior or Messiah figure. Following the tradition that Noah established in saving a select few of God's elect saints, Jesus is typologically associated with Moses, Aaron, and Joshua of the Old Testament. There is clear doubt in the mind of the spiritual narrator about the fate of slaveowners – "I wonder if my maussa deh" – but he has little doubt that other relatives will make it into heaven: "My fader gone to unknown land." The water is both saving and destroying, as it has been for Noah and the Flood victims. "Riber run and darkness comin' . . . / Sinner row to save your soul."

The theme of "crossing" and the river's power is also present in "Roll, Jordan, Roll" (LOA, 2: 803), which associates behavior on this earth with the rewards of the next: "O, let no false or spiteful word / Be found upon your tongue; / Roll, Jordan," etc. Again, the "crossing" theme pervades the well-known spiritual "Deep River" (LOA, 2: 765). This spiritual describes the narrator's home as thet promised land that lies across the Jordan River ("*Deep river, / My home is over Jordan*"), and the chorus refrain yearns for deliverance from the perils of this earthly existence into the new, Millennial paradise: "*Lord, I want to cross over into camp ground*," and "I'll go into heaven, and take my seat, / Cast my crown at Jesus' feet." All of these metaphors of deliverance pervade spiritual literature, and together they form a vision of the future that is optimistic, in contrast to the suffering and anguish of earthly existence.

Death, then, provides deliverance and release, and is not to be feared. Like the New England Puritans, and like the Christian tradition since St. Paul's original interpretations of the Gospels, the spiritual narrators contrasted the sufferings of earthly existence with the eternal blessings of the next life. Anne Bradstreet states the theme eloquently in a 1669 poem, "As Weary Pilgrim," by showing that

All cares and fears he bids farewell
And means in safety now to dwell.
A pilgrim I, on earth perplexed
With sins, with cares and sorrows vext
By age and pains brought to decay
And my clay house mouldring away.
Oh, how I long to be at rest
And soar on high among the blest.
This body shall in silence sleep,
Mine eyes no more shall ever weep,
No Fainting fits shall me assail,
Nor grinding pains my body frail,
With cares and fears ne'er cumb'red be
Nor losses know, nor sorrows see.
What though my flesh shall there consume,
It is the bed Christ did perfume.

Among the spiritual selections in the Library of America volume, the one containing the most specific allusions to this eschatology is "Swing Low, Sweet Chariot" (LOA, 2: 818). Here, death is clearly perceived as a release, and, in one of the most common tropes in all spiritual literature, "home" is depicted as the life after death. The narrator's visionary perception of future events remains optimistic and fulfilling:

I looked over Jordan [i.e., beyond death], and what did
    I see,
Coming for to carry me home?
A band of angels coming after me,
Coming for to carry me home.

This optimistic theme is carried in one of the most warm and melodic of all spiritual tunes, and the power of the vision is unrelenting:

The brightest day that ever I saw,
Coming for to carry me home,
When Jesus wash'd my sins away,
Coming for to carry me home.

This theme is repeated in "Steal Away" (LOA, 2: 816), in such lines as "*Steal away, steal away, steal away to Jesus! / Steal away, steal away home, / I hain't got long to stay here.*" A specific reference in this spiritual suggests the last days:

Tombstones are bursting,
    Poor sinners stand trembling [awaiting Judgment];
The trumpet sounds it in my soul:
    I hain't got long to stay here.

The pervasive optimism of the vision of the next life is echoed in "My Lord, What a Morning" (LOA, 2: 794), where the Jubilee of Christ's Second Coming and millennial rule are suggested in lines like:

You'll hear de trumpet sound,
    To wake de nations underground,
Look in my God's right hand,
    When de stars begin to fall.
You'll hear de sinner moan,
    To wake de nations underground . . .

Here, the thousand years of peace and prosperity promised to God's elect saints in the Book of Revelation have some specific signs of the Second Coming, such as the sounding of the trumpet, the raising of the dead, and the judging of humankind. Although spirituals do not develop an intricate theology of millennial eschatology – that is, the thousand-year reign of Christ and his saints at the end of human time – they do allude to these phenomena often and suggest a thorough acquaintance with the doctrines of millennialism.

Finally, the sufferings of slaves were often justified as an accepted donnée of the human condition, that postlapsarian state in which all humans inevitably exist. Although slavery was a "peculiar institution" inflicted by Europeans on African Americans, the Christianized slave accepted the doctrine of the Judeo-Christian tradition that all suffering was somehow the result of human error, and thus deserved. Deliverance was to come through grace, through a gift of God to his repentant sinners, who in turn must transform their spirit to become elect saints. This theme is contained in several of the spirituals, particularly "We Are Climbing Jacob's Ladder," a highly melodic spiritual that was used as the theme music for Ken Burns's *Civil War* series on PBS. The title alludes to a long-known Christian tradition, that the sinner must "climb" through stages of growth from earth to heaven, from Babylon to Jerusalem, surviving tests along the way, as Christian in *The Pilgrim's Progress* was forced to resist temptations of earthly life in his pilgrimage to heaven. The locus classicus of this idea is in the *Ladder of Divine Ascent* by the medieval writer St. John Climacus, but it is an idea that pervaded Christian folklore. "Climbing Jacob's Ladder" refers to the dream of Jacob and his vision at Bethel, and the military nature of the Christian life is contained in the refrain, "Soldiers of the Cross." As the Protestant hymn "Onward Christian soldiers" states, the progress of the soul from earth to heaven provides tests of the saints often figured as confrontations with enemies, for example, Canaanites, slaveholders, or the North American Indian opponents of "manifest destiny." The alignment of "suffering saints" and enemy oppressors was thus generalized and relative, and the Old Testament configuration of Israel as God's chosen people on a divine mission made the slave spirituals a natural recapitulation of these ideas.

What remains is to ask a final question, one that has been rhetorically posed by scholars of the spiritual: "Did the African slave make his spiritual from his own ingredients, culled from Africa and/or America, or did he make it from ready-made white spirituals and hymns?" It should be clear from the argument here that the nineteenth-century spirituals were a mixture of both traditions and that the slave writers have left us with a deeply moving musical account of their experience.

MASON I. LOWANCE JR.

(See also **Songs and Ballads**)

Selected Works

Allen, W. F., C. P. Ware, and L. M. Garrison, *Slave Songs of the United States*, New York, 1867; reprinted, 1971

Dett, R. N., *The Dett Collection of Negro Spirituals*, Chicago, 1936

Johnson, J. W., and J. R. Johnson, *The Book of American Negro Spirituals*, New York, 1925–27

Marsh, J. B. T., *The Story of the Jubilee Singers with Their Songs*, London, 1875

Odum, H. W., and G. B. Johnson, *The Negro and His Songs*, Chapel Hill, North Carolina, 1925

Parrish, L. A., *Slave Songs of the Georgia Sea Islands*, New York, 1942

Scarborough, D., *On the Trail of Negro Folk Songs*, Cambridge, Massachusetts, 1925

Seward, T. F., *Jubilee Songs as Sung by the Jubilee Singers of Fisk University*, 1872

White, N. I., *American Negro Folk Songs*, Cambridge, Massachusetts, 1928

Work, J. W., *American Negro Songs*, New York, 1940

Further Reading

Andrews, William, *To Tell a Free Story: The First Century of African-American Autobiography*, Urbana: University of Illinois Press, 1988

Bibb, Henry, *The Narrative of the Life and Adventures of Henry Bibb*, New York, 1849

Bryant, William Cullen, *Travels, Addresses, and Comments*, vol. 2 of *Prose Writings*, edited by Parke Godwin, New York: D. Appleton, 1889

Chesnut, Mary Boykin, *A Diary from Dixie*, Boston: Houghton Mifflin, 1949

Child, Lydia Maria, *An Appeal in Favor of That Class of Americans Called Africans*, New York: J. S. Taylor, 1836

Courlander, Harold, *Negro Folk Music, U.S.A.*, New York: Columbia University Press, 1963

Douglass, Frederick, *Narrative of the Life of Frederick Douglass, an American Slave*, edited by Benjamin Quarles, Cambridge, Massachusetts: Harvard University Press, 1960

Epstein, Dena, *Sinful Times and Spirituals: Black Folk Music to the Civil War*, Urbana: University of Illinois Press, 1977

Jacobs, Harriet, *Linda: Incidents in the Life of a Slave Girl*, edited by Jean Fagin Yellen, Cambridge, Massachusetts: Harvard University Press, 1985

Lehmann, Theodore, *Negro Spirituals: Geschichte und Theologie*, Berlin: Eckart-Verlag, 1965

Olmsted, Frederick, *The Cotton Kingdom*, edited by Arthur Schlesinger, New York: Knopf, 1953

Stearns, Marshall, and Jean Stearns, *Jazz Dance: The Story of American Vernacular Dance*, New York: Macmillan, 1968

Stowe, Harriett Beecher, *Uncle Tom's Cabin*, edited by Ann Douglas, New York: Penguin, 1985

Edmund Clarence Stedman

(1833–1908)

In a brief autobiographical anecdote, Harriet **Monroe** captured the essence of the modernist disdain for E. C. Stedman and the worn-out idealism that he championed as a poet and critic. While attending a dinner party at Stedman's New York home in 1888, Monroe engaged in a friendly argument with Henry Harland over the relative merits of Percy Bysshe Shelley and Robert Browning. Their host, acknowledged by all present as the foremost arbiter of American taste in poetry, overheard the lively debate and rushed across the room to lend his support to Monroe, who was standing up for Shelley. Adopting the polite but authoritative tone that marked his reign as dean of American critics, Stedman pronounced Browning the inferior poet, because "Shelley soared higher into the Empyrean."

Probably no one laughed at this profound – and, to modern ears, profoundly ridiculous – critical judgment. Monroe had won the debate, and if she found Stedman's inspired defense of her position a bit silly, she had the good sense not to reveal the fact. By 1912, however, four years after Stedman's death, Harriet Monroe was moving in other literary circles and debating the merits of Shelley and Browning with young writers like Ezra Pound, for whom Stedman's idealization of poetry represented the worst vestige of a bankrupt genteel tradition. Writing with her own measure of cultural authority as editor of *Poetry* magazine, Monroe explained that the greatest obstacle to experimental verse in America was a brand of aesthetic idealism epitomized by Stedman's desire to locate poetic value in the empyrean, wherever that imaginary region might lie. Her radical little journal insisted that such an indistinct critical terminology should no longer dominate the discussion of American verse; that poetry, as Pound put it, should be at least as well written as prose; and that modern verse should no longer be measured with a critical altimeter, according to the simplistic credo: the higher it soars, the better it is.

According to his mother's recollection, Edmund Clarence Stedman was quite literally born a poet on October 8, 1833. In a family memoir, she proudly recalled that "as soon as he could speak, he lisped in rhyme." Perhaps it was this early affinity for rhyme that fueled his lifelong dislike of free verse and other prosaic tendencies on poetry. After being thrown out of Yale University for his association with an itinerant acting troupe, Stedman worked as a journalist and editor in Connecticut and New York City, eventually serving as a Civil War correspondent for the New York *World*. Two years before Appomattox, he moved from the battlefields to Wall Street, where he found the time to pursue his literary interests while working as a broker and member of the New York Stock Exchange. Providing an unlikely bridge between "Philistia and Bohemia," as Harriet Monroe put it, Stedman produced a number of hybrid literary curiosities such as his dreamy lyric "Pan in Wall Street" and a sober history of the stock exchange.

Although he was troubled by ill health and fits of hypochondria throughout his adult life, Stedman produced a number of respectable volumes of poetry and a staggering succession of major critical works, including two seminal anthologies. Stedman's poems were collected in 1908, the year of his death, and were promptly forgotten by all but a few friends, but his critical works – especially *Victorian Poets* (1875), *Poets of America* (1885), and *The Nature and Elements of Poetry* (1892) – still define an important chapter in American literary history. Ultimately, it was as a critic, rather than as a poet, that he most clearly articulated the genteel argument in a heated debate over cultural authority in late-nineteenth-century America.

Stedman arrived on the New York literary scene in 1859, when the *Tribune* published his popular satirical poem, "The Diamond Wedding," but it was not until the latter part of the century that the views he espoused began to dominate literary opinion in America. Disturbed by the nation's post–Civil War drift from familiar bearings, Stedman and a group of highly influential companions proposed to make poetry – or "ideal effort," as they preferred to call it – a last refuge for the beleaguered imagination. Richard Henry Stoddard, Bayard **Taylor**, George **Boker**, and Thomas Bailey Aldrich, with Stedman leading the phalanx, intended to present a unified stand against crass materialism and its literary manifestations in journalism and realist fiction. Let the muckrakers and novelists quibble about today's injustices and tomorrow's reforms, the group agreed. Only the poet, according to Stedman's somewhat diluted Emersonian idealization, soars into the empyrean on wings of imagination. In making such dramatic claims for the nature and role of poetry, as Harriet Monroe clearly understood, Stedman and his circle inadvertently trivialized their beloved medium and presented themselves as hopelessly out of touch with the demands of American life at the end of the nineteenth century. Determined to revive what they took to be a classical understanding of poetry as the repository of spiritual truth, they purged their writing of anything that might have made it relevant to the experiences of readers who lived in an increasingly urban and industrial culture.

For all their dislike of worldly entanglements, members of the group were uniquely positioned to influence a wide readership with their opinions about poetry, and they rarely missed an opportunity to enforce their taste on the reading public. In an era when few publishers were interested in gambling on new volumes of poetry, the major periodicals became virtually the only literary organs accessible to serious poets who wished to see their work in print. And to appear in the major periodicals, one had first to reckon with a genteel tribunal that included such figures as Aldrich at the *Atlantic* and Richard Watson **Gilder** at *Century* magazine. These men were Stedman's close friends, and through their editorial influence and his own tireless work as a poet, anthologist, and critic, he emerged as the chief spokesman for a retrenchment of genteel literary values at the end of the nineteenth century. In his flaccid verse and his largely impressionistic works of criticism, he articulated the era's standards for "good" poetry, by which he meant an elite, highly formal, cosmopolitan, and essentially eastern brand of verse. Writing of his contemporaries with admirable tact but without equivocation, he denounced poetry that was, in his opinion, homespun, vulgar, or eccentric.

At least, this is modernism's unflattering portrait of E. C. Stedman, the stubborn formalist and reactionary who fought to retard the inevitable emergence of a modern consciousness in American poetry. The portrait handed down by Harriet Monroe and others has some validity, but it is important to recognize that the image of a bumbling genteel despot is, to some extent, a modernist fiction, which was born in part from a deep resentment. Poets like Pound and T. S. Eliot had every reason to lash out at Stedman and his genteel phalanx, for the latter group's tight control of the literary periodicals and of public opinion during the late nineteenth century muted dissenting voices and denied younger writers any share of cultural authority in the ongoing discourse of, and about, American poetry. But after wresting control for themselves, members of Pound's generation exaggerated their scorn for Stedman's circle, and thus, distorted an important continuity in the development of modern verse.

In fact, Stedman's was the first voice from within the heavily fortified citadel of high culture in America to call eloquently for a new poetry, a poetry that he saw foreshadowed in the rhapsodies of Walt **Whitman** and in the psychological complexity of Edgar Allan **Poe**. At a time when few important critics were willing to take these writers seriously, Stedman championed Whitman and Poe for their refusal to run in the old grooves of didacticism and moral platitude, and for their insistence on the aural nature of poetry. Deeming his own period a "twilight interval" in the development of American verse, Stedman seems to have been vaguely aware of the dead-end of genteel aesthetics, and – despite his feverish idealism – he expended much of his critical energy outlining a rough and useful course for the emerging generation to follow. Although he never quite anticipated Pound's celebrated dictum, "make it new," Stedman insisted over and over that the first phase of a distinctively American poetry was finished and that another was about to begin. He had no interest in repeating the past, and his candid assessment of his own mediocre contemporaries must have looked, at least implicitly, like an invitation to test the limits of genteel authority. His antididactic, anticapitalist, and antibourgeois aesthetics led him to the unfortunate conclusion that the future for poetry lay in the irrelevant zone that he called the empyrean, but the fact remains that Stedman's genteel program brought him perilously close to embracing, in Frank Lentricchia's words, "most of the canonical modernist literary and social biases." Perhaps he would not have recognized Eliot's J. Alfred Prufrock as an appropriate poetic subject, and certainly Eliot's language would have struck Stedman as melodically deficient; yet behind the image of a patient etherized upon a table lies a modernist critique of alienation and reification – a critique whose origins are inseparable from the self-defeating genteel aesthetics of social disengagement.

Stedman's reading of Whitman neatly illustrates his divided allegiance in regards to, on the one hand, a nascent modern sensibility and, on the other, a genteel conception of art and nature. In his chapter on Whitman in *Poets of America*, he praises the author of *Leaves of Grass* as a "full-throated poet" who is engaged in a monumental "revolt against the artifice of current life and sentiment." The genteel critic seems almost ready to join the bohemian poet in revolt when he explains that, for Whitman, "it was necessary to celebrate the body with special unction, since, with respect to the physical basis of life, our so-

cial weakness and hypocrisy are most extreme." Stedman goes on to offer an unexpectedly evenhanded defense of Whitman's sensuality:

> Not only should the generative functions be proclaimed, but, also, – "to show that there is in nature nothing mean or base," – the side of our life which is hidden, because it is of earth, earthy, should be plainly recognized . . . and out of rankness and coarseness, a new virility be bred, an impotent and squeamish race at last be made whole.

This is not the sort of thing that one expects to hear from the doyen of genteel opinion, but Stedman's aesthetic – like Whitman's – called for "a new virility," an end to the domination of poetry by the "wigged and gowned" leisure classes, and an end to "pedantry and dullness." Marking his distance from an earlier phase of American poetry, a period characterized, he claims, by its excess of "effeminate sentiment," Stedman sounds, ironically, like a young Wallace Stevens, who himself challenged his culture's effete conception of poetry (embodied for Stevens by Stedman himself) in "Sunday Morning." Convinced that his own era represented "an interregnum," "a lull in the force and efficacy of American song," Stedman believed that he recognized the sound of a new and promising poetry in the "fresh breeze from old Paumanok," and he encouraged young poets to listen.

Stedman's sense of Whitman's modernity and his surprising identification with elements of Whitman's sensual aesthetic involved a courageous insight. But that insight was clouded by Stedman's equally strong and perfectly contradictory commitment to a genteel aesthetic. Having praised Whitman's discovery of "a new virility" lurking "in the side of our life which is hidden," Stedman goes on to impose prudish limits on the process of exposing that side of life. He applauds Whitman's naturalism but points out that nature "covers her slime, her muck, her ruins, with garments that to us are beautiful." Whitman, it turns out, violates nature with his celebration of that which nature would conceal. This insight leads Stedman, who seemed on the verge of formulating a program for modern poetry, back to the essence of genteel aesthetics. Agreeing with Alexandre Dumas, *père*, that "the Underside of things should be avoided in art," he explains that, "the delight of Art is to heighten [nature's] beguilement, and, far from making her ranker than she is, to portray what she might be in ideal combinations." Whitman's mistake, Stedman concludes, was to draw away "the final veil."

As Stedman surely understood, this amounts to saying that poets ought to be more interested in veils that in what they conceal, a notion that perfectly illustrates the self-defeating logic of the genteel aesthetic. After calling for an end to artifice and affectation in new American poetry, here Stedman argues against a vision that penetrates too far, which in turn relegates poetry once again to the trivial task of adornment. In his important study of Victorian poets, he criticized British writers for their overuse of decoration as a way of compensating for a deficiency of natural passion; unlike Whitman, however, he retained a lingering belief that the proper subject of "ideal effort," or poetry, is an ornamental naturalistic veil, and thus Stedman was never able to commit himself entirely to a poetry of vision.

The germs of a modernist discourse that are everywhere audible in Stedman's critical prose rarely surface in his poetry, where he dwells constantly on the notion of art as a means of disengagement from the world. He insisted that the poetry of the future would be something other than mere decorative speech, but his own verse appears almost stubbornly irrelevant. His ideal poet in "Corda Concordia" is a hermit with no real passion for nature or solitude.

> In scorn of meaner use,
>   Anon, the young recluse
> Built his hut beside the woodland lake,
>   And set the world far off,
>   Though with no will to scoff,
> Thus from the Earth's near breast fresh life to take.
>   Against her bosom, heart to heart,
> All Nature's sweets he ravished for his Art.

Whitman would have laughed at this asexual image of the poet ravishing nature, and Henry David **Thoreau** might have commented that there is nothing very principled about this hermit's decision to "set the world far off, / Though with no will to scoff." Perhaps the most interesting line is the first ("In scorn of meaner use"), where Stedman seems to opt against the usefulness of poets and poetry – an incredible trivialization of the medium that he worked so hard to popularize. In lieu of utility, Stedman resorts to his favorite hyperbole as a way to dignify the poet, who soars like the Shelley of Stedman's 1888 dinner party,

> with tuneful sounds that wing
> The upper air a few perchance have known,
>   The stormless empyrean, where
> In strength and joy a few more unaware.

The comparison is unfair, but it is worth pointing out that Whitman's vision always focuses downward on the stormy earth, while Stedman, when his eyes are open at all, gazes longingly at a "stormless empyrean." This distinction, however, should not stand as the final word on Stedman's literary achievement. Moving unpredictably between the roles of nurturing elder and genteel censor, he occupied an undeniably paradoxical relation to the era's "younger celebrants" of verse, whose "impassioned song" interrupts the otherwise staid rhythms of Stedman's "Prelude to *An American Anthology*"

(LOA, 2: 327). Although usually considered a reactionary conservative and an obstacle to experimental writing, he is perhaps better understood as a bridge between two American generations, that of William Cullen **Bryant**, John Greenleaf **Whittier**, Ralph Waldo **Emerson**, and Henry Wadsworth **Longfellow**, and that of Pound, Eliot, William Carlos Williams, and Stevens. Stedman had the prescience and the intellectual honesty to describe his career as just such a bridge when he deemed his era an "interregnum." In denying his important service to modernism, literary history has fashioned this interregnum as a break in the continuity of American poetry, yet a more considered reading of Stedman's career must acknowledge his role, for all its contradictions, in promoting a new poetry for the modern period.

HENRY B. WONHAM

Selected Works

Victorian Poets, Boston: J. R. Osgood, 1875
Poets of America, Boston: Houghton Mifflin, 1885
The Nature and Elements of Poetry, Boston: Houghton Mifflin, 1892
A Victorian Anthology: 1837–1895, Boston: Houghton Mifflin, 1895
An American Anthology: 1787–1900, Boston: Houghton Mifflin, 1900
The Poems of Edmund Clarence Stedman, Boston: Houghton Mifflin, 1908
Genius and Other Essays, New York: Moffat, Yard, 1911

Further Reading

Lentricchia, Frank, *Ariel and the Police*, Madison: University of Wisconsin Press, 1988
Pearce, Roy Harvey, *The Continuity of American Poetry*, Princeton, New Jersey: Princeton University Press, 1961
Perkins, David, *A History of Modern Poetry: From the 1890s to the High Modernist Mode*, Cambridge, Massachusetts: Harvard University Press, 1976
Spiller, Robert E., ed., *The Literary History of the United States*, 3 vols., New York: Macmillan, 1960
Stedman, Laura, and George M. Gould, *Life and Letters of Edmund Clarence Stedman*, 2 vols., New York: Moffat, Yard, 1910

Trumbull Stickney

(1874–1904)

Trumbull Stickney died young, at age 30, leaving behind him a largely ignored book of verse and some remarkable poems in manuscript. His work was kept alive, after his death, by other poets. The edition that his Harvard University friends William Vaughn **Moody** and George Cabot **Lodge**, both poets themselves, prepared in 1905 was crucial. But the remarkably sensitive selection of Stickney's work by Conrad Aiken in successive versions of his Modern Library anthology of twentieth-century American poetry was very important indeed. Aiken invoked Stickney as "a forerunner," and as "the natural link between Emily Dickinson and the real twentieth-century 'thing.'" Edmund Wilson wrote a short but intense essay on him in 1940; but interestingly enough, it was in England, in 1968, that there first appeared a good collection of over 70 of Stickney's poems, both published and from manuscript, four years before the only American text of his work.

Joseph Trumbull Stickney came from an expatriate New England family. Born in Geneva, Switzerland, he grew up, like someone in a Henry James story, in London, Italy, and Switzerland. He studied classics – and perhaps became romantically involved with an older woman – at Harvard (graduating six years before Wallace Stevens); he returned to France to study at the Sorbonne, where he took the first doctorate in Greek ever awarded to an American. The final year of his life was spent in teaching Greek at Harvard and in suffering the pain of a brain tumor, from which he died in October 1904. His Harvard was that of George **Santayana**; his émigré Europe that of his friends Henry **Adams** and Bernard Berenson. His poems – save for his verse drama, *Prometheus Pyrphoros*, and some dramatic fragments all sonnets and strophic lyrics full of a revised romantic Hellenism and a formal sense stronger than their rhetoric – needed half-apologizing for under the strictures of modernism. But in the light of American poetry's coming to terms with its romantic origins in the later part of this century, his work appears more central than before.

Stickney's vision was transformed by the actual landscape of Greece, which he visited, for the only time, in the next-to-last summer of his life. The rugged Arcadian mountain scenery (not the Virgilian mythological Arcadia), read through post-Wordsworthian filters, becomes for him a vision that cries out for meditation, in an ironically anti-Wordsworthian turn. Thus, for example, his fine poem on Mount Lykaion (LOA, 2: 654), the great mountain in the northern Peloponnesus sacred to Zeus as wolf, starts out with one kind of fiction – the columns and eagles that he read about in Pausanias, the second-century A.D. historian (who, by the way, was himself reporting hearsay). But then the poem moves into another mode:

> Alone on Lykaion since man hath been
> Stand on the height two columns, where at rest
> Two eagles hewn of gold sit looking East
> Forever; and the sun goes up between.
> Far down around the mountain's oval green
> An order keeps the falling stones abreast.
> Below within the chaos last and least

> A river like a curl of light is seen.
> Beyond the river lies the even sea,
> Beyond the sea another ghost of sky, –
> O God, support the sickness of my eye
> Lest the far space and long antiquity
> Suck out my heart, and on this awful ground
> The great wind kill my little shell with sound.

The monumental columns (traces of "long antiquity") exist only in text; but in the eye's plain experience, the "far space," the nest of Emersonian circles – river, sea, and sky – figures the dissolving limits of transcendence. And the combined voices of poetic past and physical present seem louder than can be borne. The eye's "sickness" here – that clouding of the eyeball's (again Emersonian) transparency – brings an imaginative health, however, in poems like "Near Helicon" (LOA, 2: 655), another of his late "Sonnets from Greece." Here, the overpowering ghosts of William Wordsworth and John Keats, haunting the sonnet for Stickney as much as the mythology of the landscape haunts its visual presence for him, emerge in order in the sestet:

> To me my troubled life doth now appear
> Like scarce distinguishable summits hung
> Around the blue horizon: places where
> Not even a traveller purposeth to steer, –
> Whereof a migrant bird in passing sung,
> And the girl closed her window not to hear.

Helicon, sacred to Apollo, is the dancing-place of the Muses, but the mythology is closed off here by the actual landscape.

Stickney never simply replays Romantic motifs. He is always aware of how late he has come to Greece, to poetry, indeed to his own American imagination. Consider how he muses on the columns of the temple of Poseidon at Sounion, near Athens, built in propitiation of the sea-god who lost out as patron to Athena, but whose powerful presence is attested to by all capes and small islands. (On one of these columns, incidentally, Lord Byron carved his name, which can still be read.) The figure that Stickney makes of these columns partakes of the same sort of revision of that ubiquitous Romantic trope, the aeolian harp, in nineteenth-century German and American poetry. Starting with Coleridge's evocation of nature itself as "one organic harp, divinely framed," this imagery can be traced through Ralph Waldo **Emerson** and Henry David **Thoreau** (who wrote constantly in his journals of his "telegraph harp" – the wind making a literal aeolian harp out of telegraph wires) to Hart Crane's Brooklyn Bridge cables. In Stickney's "Sunium" (LOA, 2: 654), the columns are played upon both by the hand of the wind and by light itself, even as the strength of the traditional image is consumed by the very poetic light – that of the sun, and thus Apollo's – that has played upon it for over 150 years of metaphor:

> These are the strings of the Ægean lyre
> Across the sky and sea in glory hung:
> Columns of white thro' which the wind has flung
> The clouds and stars, and drawn the rain and fire.
> Their flutings now to fill the notes' desire

Are strained and dubious, yet in music young
They cast their full-blown answer far along
To where in sea the island hills expire.
How bravely from the quarry's earthen gloom
In snow they rose amid the blue to stand
Melodious and alone on Sunium!
They shall not wither back into the land.
The sun that harps them with his golden hand
Doth slowly with his hand of gold consume.

The columns' "flutings" are both the vertical striations (in the term's architectural sense) and the musical sounds, now of wind and string mixed. The powerful and elegant chiasmus of the ending ("harps . . . golden hand / . . . hand of gold consume") is by no means archaistically decorative, but itself sets up a momentary trope of reciprocity.

Nine years earlier, Stickney had merely copied Percy Bysshe Shelley's exhortation to the west wind ("Make me thy lyre, even as the forest is") in an untitled sonnet that also began with an allusion to Wordsworth's "Immortality Ode" ("though inland far we be"):

Tho' inland far with mountains prisoned round
Oppressed beneath a space of heavy skies,
Yet hear I oft the far-off water-cries
And vast vague voices which the winds confound.
While as a harp I sing, touched with the sound
Most secret to its soul, the visions rise
In stately dream . . .

And yet only a year after this, at the age of 21, he can undo another romantic myth – of the seashell as a sort of ear-mouth that speaks prophetically of the sea (Wordsworth and Walter Savage Landor had quarreled over which of them had introduced it to poetry). William Butler Yeats had, a decade before Stickney's poems, invoked this commonplace in "Go gather by the humming sea / Some twisted echo-harboring shell"; 30 years later, Hart Crane would invigorate it in "As steadily as a shell secretes / Its beating leagues of monotone." It is almost as if, in "On Some Shells Found Inland" (LOA, 2: 641), the young Stickney were lamenting, not just the shells' distance from the Yeatsian humming sea, but their meaningless status as relics of romantic poetry:

These are my murmur-laden shells that keep
A fresh voice tho' the years be very gray.
The wave that washed their lips and tuned their lay
Is gone, gone with the faded ocean sweep,
The royal tide, gray ebb and sunken neap
And purple midday, – gone! To this hot clay
Must sing my shells, where yet the primal day,
Its roar and rhythm and splendour will not sleep.
What hand shall join them to their proper sea
If all be gone? Shall they forever feel
Glories undone and worlds that cannot be? –
'Twere mercy to stamp out this agèd wrong,
Dash them to earth and crunch them with the heel
And make a dust of their seraphic song.

But these are not the speaking shells that the poet has himself borne inland. They engage a recapitulation of the eighteenth-century geological speculations, occasioned by thinking about seashells on inland mountaintops, that had such profound repercussions for nineteenth-century religious thought, specifically by casting doubt on the literal historicity of the Bible. For Stickney, the shells were emblems of poetic figuration that must be reconstituted, but he has not yet realized that the dust into which they are ground in despair must become part of a limestone, as it were, from which new emblems and new figurations can be carved.

The poems he wrote upon finally seeing the Greek landscape that had previously been the stuff of literature for him – poetic, and minutely scholarly text – keep breaking out into supplication. Like the last lines of "Mt. Lykaion," they ask for imaginative strength with which to cope with the relations between what he sees, has read, has heard, and both knows he feels and feels he knows. At the end of the first of three sonnets on Mount Ida (LOA, 2: 656–57), his prayer to the sacred place asking for poetic power is couched in terms hardly neoclassical, but in those of an American romantic Hellenism that in some ways parallels his friend Henry Adams's gothicism:

O Ida, snowy bride that God espoused
Unto that day that never wholly is,
Whiten thou the horizon of my eyes,
That when the momentary sea aroused
Flows up in earthquake, still thou mayest rise
Sacred above the quivering Cyclades.

To "whiten the horizon" of his vision – is this to "widen" it? or to narrow its focus for greater concentration? The grandeur of Friedrich Hölderlin's earlier construction of Greece involved complex religious displacements and transfers of belief. For Stickney, the matters of poetry, of work and métier (his classical scholarship), and of a first glimpse that is in itself an intricate re-vision, all add density to his American fascination with the meaning of landscape.

As Edmund Wilson indicated, the elegantly strong closure of sonnets like the one just quoted was characteristic of Stickney, and could tighten up the language at the end of the poem to a pitch that even a modernist taste could acknowledge. Thus, the image of Delos, the central island of the Cyclades invoked above, emerges exuberantly at the close of an untitled sonnet (LOA, 2: 641) that starts out portentously (watered-down Pater? watered-down Nietzsche?), moves through the beautiful image of the rainbow of promise as a lyre with broken strings, and breaks forth itself into a resonant final line:

Live blindly and upon the hour. The Lord,
Who was the Future, died full long ago.
Knowledge which is the Past is folly. Go,
Poor child, and be not to thyself abhorred.
Around thine earth sun-wingèd winds do blow
And planets roll; a meteor draws his sword;
The rainbow breaks his seven-coloured chord
And the long strips of river-silver flow:
Awake! Give thyself to the lovely hours.
Drinking their lips, catch thou the dream in flight
About their fragile hairs' aërial gold.
Thou art divine, thou livest, – as of old
Apollo springing naked to the light,
And all his island shivered into flowers.

And again, at the end of the sonnet "Tho' inland far," quoted above: "the mellow evening falls; / Alone upon the shore in the wet light / I stand and hear an infinite sea that calls." The rhythm of the penultimate line here, and the vowel-and-consonant patterns of lines 6–8 in the previously quoted sonnet, all manifest Stickney's remarkable ear for verse, which seems unmatched in its mode since Alfred, Lord Tennyson.

Throughout the brief history of Stickney's poetry, the imaginative movement was from text to place, from poetic topos to geographic location. But when the sense of place is fully achieved, it is never bare of historical significance, or of poetic illumination. Just as "the far space and long antiquity" doubles the visual present with the dimension of visionary myth – rather than merely historical time – to overpower the poet's sight on Mount Lykaion, so the wind blowing past his precursors – past Hölderlin, past Giacomo Leopardi and Ugo Foscolo – can be heard on nearby hills in his later lyrics.

Dying in his own late spring, Stickney never escaped from what he calls in one sonnet "the tone / Of memory's autumnal paradise." In another poem, his Decembering urban vision – trees and chimneys intermingled – focuses on an image of belatedly revived desire that seems self-descriptive of the "rich belated flower" of his own poetry. In "The melancholy year is dead with rain" (LOA, 2: 643), memory and desire are associated not with T. S. Eliot's relentlessly unhopeful April of "The Waste Land," but with the autumnal condition generally, and with the refrain of rainfall to which Stickney would return, as will be seen, at the end of his finest poem. But at the close of this sonnet what appears to blossom is his own poem:

> So in the last of autumn for a day
> Summer or summer's memory returns.
> So in a mountain desolation burns
> Some rich belated flower, and with the gray
> Sick weather, in the world of rotting ferns
> From out the dreadful stones it dies away.

(These ferns return again in the cycle of love poems called "Eride," when "Desire / Revives like ferns on a November fire.") Poetic as well as erotic desire is shadowed by the past for Stickney. A garden speaks of this in "An Athenian Garden" (LOA, 2: 653):

> The burned and dusty garden said:
> "My leaves are echoes, and thy earth
> Is packed with footsteps of the dead.
>
> "The strength of spring-time brought to birth
> Some needles on the crooked fir, –
> A rose, a laurel – little worth.
>
> "Come here, ye dreaming souls that err
> Among the immortals of the grave:
> My summer is your sepulchre."

Some of Stickney's more moving poems embrace topographical prospects, like those of American landscape painting of the later nineteenth century, framed with a touch of ironic distancing. "In Ampezzo" (LOA, 2: 635) is one of these: it starts out with a half-avowed echo of Milton's "Lycidas" ("Yet once more, O ye Laurels") to underscore its own derivative

hesitation, as if all the old poems, as well as the landscape, lay before him.

> Only once more and not again – the larches
> Shake to the wind their echo, "Not again," –
> We see, below the sky that over-arches
> Heavy and blue, the plain
>
> Between Tofana lying and Cristallo
> In meadowy earths above the ringing stream:
> Whence interchangeably desire may follow,
> Hesitant as in dream,
>
> At sunset, south, by lilac promontories
> Under green skies to Italy, or forth
> By calms of morning beyond Lavinores
> Tyrolward and to north . . .

Here, in the northern mountains of Cortina d'Ampezzo, is Stickney's inland scene again, in which he tracks the signs of the landscape to the sea, even as the echo of Milton's word "over-arched" (for the Tuscan shades in Book I of *Paradise Lost*) calls up a landscape far to the south. This poem ends quite beautifully in contemplation of the distance from its mountainous prospect to a sea itself enisled – never has its name been more literalized in its landed surroundings than in the short line of the penultimate strophe here:

> Just as here, past yon dumb and melancholy
> Sameness of ruin, while the mountains ail,
> Summer and sunset-coloured autumn slowly
> Dissipate down the vale;
>
> And all these lines along the sky that measure,
> Sorapis and the rocks of Mezzodì
> Crumble by foamy miles into the azure
> Mediterranean sea:
>
> Whereas to-day at sunrise, under brambles,
> A league above the moss and dying pines
> I picked this little – in my hand that trembles –
> Parcel of columbines.

The poet plucks the day, and the poem, from the moment of sunrise, which is also the dawning of the sea's ultimate hegemony.

The overambitious *Lieder* (song) style of "Eride" (from Eridanus – the river Po – made into a local river-muse, in grand poetic tradition: the actual muse may have been a Jewish girl whom the poet knew in Paris) colors another of these autumn visions, but in another sort of place. The opening of its fifth section (LOA, 2: 638) frames a moment typical of Stickney's best poetry, an instant in which the autumnal scene itself, rather than a self-assessing speaker, summons up the remembrance:

> Now in the palace gardens warm with age,
> On lawn and flower-bed this afternoon
> The thin November-coloured foliage
> Just as last year unfastens lilting down,
>
> And round the terrace in gray attitude
> The very statues are becoming sere

With long presentiment of solitude.
Most of the life that I have lived is here,

Here by the path and autumn's earthy grass
And chestnuts standing down the breadths of sky:
Indeed I know not how it came to pass,
The life I lived here so unhappily.

Palace gardens were the poet's playground as a child – he seems to be evoking the Luxembourg gardens – and the color of Paul Verlaine's *vieux parc, solitaire et glacé* (The old park, solitary and frosty), washed as it were into the engraving here, arises from childhood memories.

Another longer meditative poem is "Lakeward" (LOA, 2: 644), in which yet once more the young poet's Horatian control of his verse is patent, as in these stanzas that start out with a prospect of boulders that

Stand to the burning heaven upright and cold.
Then drawing lengthily along their shoulders
  Vapours of white and gold

Blow from the lowland upward; all the gloaming
Quivers with violet; here in the wedge
The tunnelled road goes narrow and outcoming
  Stealthily on the edge

Lies free. The outlines have a gentle meaning.
Willows and clematis, foliage and grain!
And the last mountain falls in terraces to the greening
  Infinite autumn plain.

The flow of syntax here through the line and stanza breaks (like that in lines 3–7 of "On Some Shells Found Inland," quoted earlier) and the interruptions of the eye's scanning process work together almost cinematographically. The "representative versification" (in Samuel Johnson's phrase) of the penultimate long line is also very fine indeed. But they are all suffused with the light of earlier poetry.

Stickney's ecphrastic sonnets come from Dante Gabriel Rossetti in some measure, rather than from Théophile Gautier or Charles Baudelaire. In his poem on a piece by Auguste Rodin called *L'Illusion, fille d'Icare* (Illusion, daughter of Icarus), his title (rather touchingly, given the vague strain of incestuous longing in many of his poems) misremembers Rodin's and substitutes perhaps the "sister lovely in my sight" of "Mnemosyne," to associate her with Illusion. The sonnet's "moment's monument," its brief memorial, is of a myth even more belated than John Keats's Psyche:

On Rodin's "L'Illusion, Sœur d'Icare"

She started up from where the lizard lies
Among the grasses' dewy hair, and flew
Thro' leagues of lower air until the blue
Was thin and pale and fair as Echo is.
Crying she made her upward flight. Her cries
Were naught, and naught made answer to her view.
The air lay in the light and slowly grew
A marvel of white void in her eyes.
She cried: her throat was dead. Deliriously

She looked, and lo! the Sun in master mirth
Glowed sharp, huge, cruel. Then brake her noble eye.
She fell, her white wings rocking down the abyss,
A ghost of ecstasy, backward to earth,
And shattered all her beauty in a kiss.
        (LOA, 2: 640)

The unrolling of the little narrative is continuous here through the sonnet's room, as contrasted with the way in which Yeats, in his famous "Leda and the Swan," revises the Rossettian pattern by confining his description of the scene to the octave, retreating into an intrepretive distance in the first half of the sestet, and, finally, distancing himself so totally that the verb tense changes to the preterite in the last three lines.

An untitled sonnet referred to as "On Sandro's Flora" (LOA, 2: 660), written in Paris in 1897 when Stickney was 23, is half-conscious of Rossetti's sonnet on the same picture. But Stickney focuses on one figure in the painting, on her half-smiling look, complicated by her palpably unspeaking closed mouth – and what he sees in her face seems to be his own doubt:

She is not happy as the Poets say,
And passing thro' her garden paradise
She scatters the divine wet flower that dies
For so much gathered in the luscious day.
Behind, the rioting Satyr has his play,
A wind lays near the Graces' draperies,
And the sweet Earth with inattentive eyes
Mildly remembers toward the growing day.
Her lips would sing but, fearing hazard, press
The music inward where her breath is caught.
She dances to an under-melting stream.
But dubious of this utter happiness
She dulls her simple ecstasy with thought,
And lacking Summer doubts herself a Dream.

In her meditative mood, Flora stands almost as a surrogate for the poet's own voice from outside the painting, which might break the composition of the scene that – in this poem – contains her. The "hazard" would be the effects of such an intrusive breaking. The partial ecphrasis of Sandro Botticelli's painting seems to reflect a somewhat faulty memory, for a nonexistent satyr is added. The poem's power to grasp Flora's inner state is modulated generally by unusual bits of diction – the earth remembering "toward the growing day," the flower dying "For so much gathered in the luscious day," and the "under-melting stream" (her unexpressed music – she is dancing not to her own singing, but to her internal, unvoiced song.) And Flora herself cannot remain untroubled even in her garden paradise. The whole vision is transitory, and whether his lady – the syntax goes both ways – "doubts herself" into a dream (of, say, absent summer) or doubts that she is herself a dream, a visionary form informing her proper bower, she is silent in thought.

Stickney's verse drama, *Prometheus Pyrphoros* ("Fire-bearer"), has some memorable moments; one is Prometheus's account of his ascent of Olympus as he "floundered up the dumb dead humid night," and another, later on, is a short song of Pandora's (LOA, 2: 649):

As an immortal nightingale
I sing behind the summer sky

Thro' leaves of starlight gold and pale
That shiver with my melody,
Along the wake of the full-moon
Far on to oceans, and beyond
Where the horizons vanish down
In darkness clear as diamond.

Even here, there occurs Stickney's characteristic moment of reading the signs in landscape to track them seaward.

Among the smaller fragments, some of which Lodge and Moody collected, are two that, slightly more than a decade after Stickney's death, might have been claimed by imagist aesthetics as complete little poems. One may be so by design (LOA, 2: 660); it is obviously supposed to be "from" a pastiche of Jacobean drama, which poets from Thomas Beddoes through Algernon Swinburne and Eliot had studied and adored. Indeed, to the antiromantic modernist, it reads like something Eliot might have quoted in an essay on John Webster:

Sir, say no more.
Within me 't is as if
The green and climbing eyesight of a cat
Crawled near my mind's poor birds.

The mediated but uncompromising assault of the cat's gaze fixes, in this powerful image, that only half-mad fear that one is going mad, a fear that marked some eighteenth-century British poets in particular. As such, the fragment seems a complete poem – a moment of Robert Browning, perhaps – and it may, indeed, have been written – like many of the epigraphs that George Eliot composed for her chapter headings – as a "fragment" to begin with.

More likely planned either as the opening of a quatrain, part of something longer in terza rima, or very possibly the start of a villanelle, this second example (LOA, 2: 660) nevertheless constitutes a perfect three-line poem, powerfully concise and finer than anything of its sort until early Stevens:

I hear a river thro' the valley wander
Whose water runs, the song alone remaining.
A rainbow stands and summer passes under.

This is a beautiful revision of Heraclitus's trope of time and river and banks, and it governs the other figures here – of water under the bridge of the rainbow, of the song or poetic discourse of the concrete but visionary stream. These are, in almost haiku-like fashion, quite disjunct; yet the connections of rhyme, and the phonological patterns within the last two lines, themselves form bridging structures.

In the lines about the Athenian garden, full of burnt-out summer, it is not ruins that are at issue, but Miltonic and Shelleyan leaves, echoes themselves of older metaphors – "barren leaves" in both Wordsworthian and Whitmanian senses. As we saw, those lines attempt to unroll some new metaphor of "birth" from "earth" in the terza rima, but the poem collapses at the end into a banal anecdote of children playing in the dust, "with pail and hoe": desert is momentarily redeemed as sandbox. Stickney was unable at the age of 30 to set these dead leaves "turning in the wind," as Stevens does in "Domination of Black" (1916), and thereby turning, troping again, the very tradition of the leaf-image (from Homer through Shelley and

Walt **Whitman**). But Stevens at 30 could probably not have written Stickney's absolute masterpiece, "Mnemosyne" (LOA, 2: 637), which he composed in his middle twenties.

Ultimately, this is his one major poem. In its very structure it so animates the sense of the past as to turn it in the wind of imagination, somehow to reinvent the concept of remembering. Sometimes one feels that only Marcel Proust lies between it and much of James Merrill. It also marks Stickney's most powerfully and fruitfully autumnal moment. Variants of the opening line – "It's autumn in the country I remember" – return throughout the poem to mediate between the unfolding tercets and to serve both as refrain for the preceding three lines and as subtitle for the following three. Janus-like, the line is lingeringly ambiguous in its syntax (*It is autumn now in the country that I remember?* or *I remember that it is autumn in the country?* or even *It is autumn in the country. I remember, for example . . .?*)

It's autumn in the country I remember.

How warm a wind blew here about the ways!
And shadows on the hillside lay to slumber
During the long sun-sweetened summer days.

It's cold abroad the country I remember.

The swallows veering skimmed the golden grain
At midday with a wing aslant and limber;
And yellow cattle browsed upon the plain.

It's empty down the country I remember.

I had a sister lovely in my sight:
He hair was dark, her eyes were very sombre;
We sang together in the woods at night.

It's lonely in the country I remember.

The babble of our children fills my ears,
And on our hearth I stare the perished ember
To flames that show all starry thro' my tears.

It's dark about the country I remember.

There are the mountains where I lived. The path
Is slushed with cattle-tracks and fallen timber,
The stumps are twisted by the tempests' wrath.

But that I knew these places are my own,
I'd ask how came such wretchedness to cumber
The earth, and I to people it alone.

It rains across the country I remember.

Masterful here are the modulations of the off-rhyming words in each tercet (save for the inevitably autumnal "ember" that, we also remember, composes the final syllables – here also impregnated with the autumnal – of "September," "November," and "December"). They are matched by the semantic variation of the predicates in the refrain, once *autumn* departs literally from the line (*autumn in . . . cold abroad . . . empty down . . . lonely in . . . dark about*). And after the poignant ellipsis of the refrain itself before the last tercet, it returns with the final *rains across* (the only time its verb is not merely the copula), filled as much with the wind and the rain of Feste's song at the end of *Twelfth Night* as of Verlaine's "*il pleure dans mon cœur. . . .*"(it is raining in my heart). The "sister lovely in my sight" is perhaps both biblical (from the Song of Songs – "my sister, my spouse") and Baudelairean ("*mon enfant, mon sœur*" [my child, my sister] of "*L'invitation au voyage*" [Invitation to the voyage]). But to "stare the perished ember / To flames" is a full revisionary resurrection of the scene that Shakespeare implicitly conjures up in his great autumnal sonnet 73 ("That time of year thou mayst in me behold") and that Gaston Bachelard so charmingly mythologized in *The Psychoanalysis of Fire*. The neoclassicism of the poem's title is totally transcended in that Mnemosyne – memory – the mother of the muses, has indeed begotten here a new muse, the ad hoc spirit of an autumnal poetry far removed from Keats's. This new muse presides over Stickney's strange sense of displaced landscape (the memory of a European-American oscillating back and forth); perhaps she is a female counterpart of the Roman god of autumn, Vertumnus, whose name is marked by *vertere* ("to turn") and whose nature is to turn the weather, the vegetation, the year itself. And *vertere* – which gives us "verse" – is the Latin counterpart of the Greek word that gives us the "trope," which is poetic life. In a poem like this a moment of glorious originality opens up.

It is impossible to say what kind of poet Stickney would have gone on to become, what the outbreak of World War I when he was 40 might have meant for him imaginatively, and so forth. His friends Moody and Lodge never showed the formidable skills and resonant ear that place Stickney, as belated Keatsian, somewhere between Rossetti and that usually unacknowledged disciple of Rossetti, Robert Frost. "Mnemosyne" concludes with a strong movement away from the internalization of landscape, and with the homely native image – "It rains across the country I remember" – derived from the immediate parks and gardens of European cities and palaces, but transformed into that central scene of American poetry, the landscape within which – but necessarily out of which – we all grow up.

JOHN HOLLANDER

Selected Works
The Poems of Trumbull Stickney, edited by George Cabot Lodge, William Vaughn Moody, and John Ellerton Lodge, Boston: Houghton Mifflin, 1905
Oxford Book of American Verse, edited by F. O. Matthiessen, New York: Oxford University Press, 1950
Homage to Trumbull Stickney, edited by and introduction by James Reeves and Seán Haldane, London: Heinemann, 1968
The Poems of Trumbull Stickney, edited by Amberys R. Whittle, New York: Farrar, Straus and Giroux, 1972

Further Reading
Haldane, Seán, *In the Fright of Time*, Ladysmith, Quebec: Ladysmith, 1970
Hollander, John, *Melodious Guile*, New Haven, Connecticut: Yale University Press, 1988

William Wetmore Story

(1819–1895)

Near the end of 1846, Henry Wadsworth **Longfellow** noted in his journal that "there is a great 'stampede' on Parnassus at the present moment, a furious rushing to and fro of the steeds of Apollo." Among the poets whom he records as issuing new collections "all in a month" were two well-known Boston, Massachusetts, names, Ralph Waldo **Emerson** and William Wetmore Story. Having delivered his poem "Nature and Art" before Harvard University's Phi Beta Kappa Society just two years before, Story was already revealing in his mannered style what a later generation was to observe in American poets writing at mid-century – that the fate of these Brahmin "steeds" depended much on whether they dug their imaginations into native soil and fortuitously adopted the forward-looking poetic vision of Emerson, or, as followers of Longfellow, whether they were led to near obscurity by revering a romanticized, classical past. Those verse-makers, like Story, who adhered to a highly formalized, impossibly idealized European tradition, came to be seen as mere "practitioners" of poetry rather than as artists immersed in the real substance of experience. In Story's case, no disciples emerged to challenge the fact of his ephemerality.

Yet if Story's verses often operated on mere form and a florid sentimentality that occasionally dismayed even the critics of his own day, he nonetheless at the time won a popular audience, especially in England. With Story, however, it is difficult to determine whether that appeal was based on the poems themselves, on his better-known reputation as a sculptor, or, as the son of the eminent Supreme Court justice Joseph Story, on the sheer respectability of his familial connections. As his reluctant biographer Henry James remarked, it is tempting to regard Story's happy success as "an affair of the general good-nature" on the part of the rarified world that had bred him. His first poems, mostly studies on classical or artistic themes, were amicably published in the *Boston Miscellany* by his friend and Harvard College classmate Nathan Hale, and in the *Pioneer* by another good friend, James Russell **Lowell**. And despite his undistinguished performance at Harvard, where classmates remembered him mainly for the artistic "cleverness" that he indiscriminately applied to drawing, music, poetry, and drama, he was early on handed a commission by the Cambridge dons for a statue of his father. This invitation, as James wryly notes, "preceded rather than followed any serious practice, on his part, of the sculptor's art."

Already well launched in a prosperous but unsatisfying law career, Story welcomed the commission as an excuse to flee New England for Europe (1847), where, he insisted, he would first study the great works of art before taking chisel to marble (his mother heralded the decision as an act of madness). Although his early sculptures demonstrate competence, the one of his father included, they failed to generate any larger excitement. Thus, adversely, he made a second attempt to find contentment in Boston, producing well-respected tracts on law and working on his literary writing. But unable to resist the romance of Italy and the lure of his own artistic leanings, impuls-

es easily indulged thanks to inherited wealth, Story resettled with his wife (Emelyn Eldredge) and his children (eventually four in number) in Rome, where he remained from 1856 until his death.

Story gained his first real artistic legitimacy with the acceptance of two statues for the 1862 London Exhibition. The public who enthusiastically viewed his *Cleopatra* could hardly have been more predisposed to such a reaction. The drama and seemingly raw sensuality of Story's much-admired poem, "Cleopatra" (LOA, 1: 677), published a few years earlier, promised a stimulating visual sequel. More significant, however, was the 1860 publication of *The Marble Faun*, in which Nathaniel **Hawthorne**, having visited Story's Roman studio when the *Cleopatra* was under way, had immortalized it. His fictional sculptor, Kenyon, is at work on his own Cleopatra, which Hawthorne describes as

> fierce, voluptuous, passionate, tender, wicked, terrible, and full of poisonous and rapturous enchantment – what, only a week or two before, had been a lump of wet clay from the Tiber . . . would be one of the images that men keep forever, finding a heat in them which does not cool down, throughout the centuries.

No work of art ever enjoyed better pre-event publicity.

Today, the aloof, highly chiseled sculpture seemingly contradicts not only Hawthorne's inflamed vision but, more curiously, Story's own fervid verses. Considered face to face, the marble and verse Cleopatras speak to each other of their creator's Victorian predilections and struggles. The figure of Cleopatra was a favored subject of Story's audience; made familiar by William Shakespeare, this figure still luxuriated in the regal, erotic exoticism of a remote time and place. Clearly, it is less the foreignness of Cleopatra's emotions that interested Story and his public (imported though they required them to be) than their unchecked nature. In the poem, a dramatic monologue, Story introduces the Egyptian queen in a highly charged state, which has been brought on by her craving for the absent Antony:

> Here, Charmian, take my bracelets,
>   They bar with a purple stain
> My arms; turn over my pillows –
>   They are hot where I have lain:
> Open the lattice wider,
>   A gauze o'er my bosom throw,
> And let me inhale the odours
>   That over the garden blow.
>
> I dreamed I was with my Antony,
>   And in his arms I lay . . .

Like the statue version, this Cleopatra remains in one spot (albeit restlessly) to think over her plight. What follows is a jungle-theme waking dream in which, as a tiger, she "knew but the law of my moods" as she greets her mate:

We toyed in the amber moonlight,
   Upon the warm flat sand,
And struck at each other our massive arms –
   How powerful he was and grand!
. . . .
Then like a storm he seized me,
   With a wild triumphant cry,
And we met, as two clouds in heaven
   When the thunders before them fly.
We grappled and struggled together,
   For his love like his rage was rude;
And his teeth in the swelling folds of my neck
   At times, in our play, drew blood.

Despite his efforts to enter Cleopatra's psyche, we can only conclude that Story remains helplessly trapped in his male perspective. The harsh critics of the 1920s and 1930s, although not noticing this particular narrative failure, found the poem lacking in other ways. Louis Untermeyer pronounced it a "poor piece of rhetoric" with a "trumped up" voluptuousness; Alfred Kreymborg claimed to hear in it "the sigh of a shop girl." However, the stanzas still convey a vivid psychological tale with a certain metrical music, and Story reaches well beyond the academic treatment such antique subjects were often assigned.

Story's marble rendering, in contrast, sits pensively, heavily draped except for one exposed breast; one hand lies across a thigh, the other, reinforcing the contemplative mood, supports her head. Despite the possibly provocative slant of her body, this subdued queen evinces none of the volatility of her poetic sister. She is, as James observed, "costumed," a concession to the mid-Victorian "felt 'demand' for drapery"; James was intrigued by the notion that even in his own day "there . . . was and is a presentable case (although never presented) against the nude, to which these arts are of necessity beholden." Although James allowed that the Cleopatra and other figures affirm that Story "loved the nude, as the artist . . . essentially and logically must," the sculptor nonetheless kept to the "safe side" of that tension.

Extending these ideas, Joy S. Kasson accounts for the marked difference between Story's statue and poem by suggesting that Story and his public could explore "the spectacle of woman's other face" more freely in words than in a visual medium. American ideal sculptors of this period, she explains, were faced with

> the problem of reconciling their attraction to dramatic narratives of female identity with their reluctance to consider openly the darker aspects of human, and especially female, nature. . . . Story evoked images of dangerous female passions only to affirm that they could be contained and controlled. . . . The melancholy Cleopatra is the dark lady tamed, constrained, neutralized.

In this vein, Story had found a fertile theme, one he would return to again and again. The title character of his metered "Cassandra," for instance, sees a Medea of wild emotions, although Story chooses only her brooding aspects to sculpt. At first, the seer asks:

. . . What does Medea there
In that dim chamber? See on her dark face

And serpent brow, rage, fury, love, despair!
What seeks she? . . .

A few lines later, Cassandra questions why, "Her brow shut down, her mouth irresolute, / Her thin hands twitching at her robes the while, / As with some fearful purpose does she stand?" In both art forms Medea deliberates, her expression "irresolute," and in both, as Frank R. DiFederico and Julia Markus point out, "we are to 'read' Medea's tale"; thus, the woman "as myth, personage, and personality is revealed to us" (*Browning Institute Studies* 1 [1973]).

But Story's ancient women enact an even deeper anxiety, one that Story felt keenly as a result of his preference for the romantic sensibility. His disposition and circumstance granted him little imaginative capacity to see beyond what had gone before. The current day, burdened artistically by what he viewed to be a golden legacy, could only come up wanting. As Story's Cleopatra laments, "this weak human life" of the present, "with its frivolous bloodless passions," hungered for a more vibrant existence. Moreover, following John Keats's model, Story sometimes found in art a taunt of life, as we see in his lyrical "Praxiteles and Phryne":

> "But there thy smile for centuries
>   On marble lips shall live, –
> For Art can grant what Love denies,
>   And fix the fugitive. . . ."

This poem was dedicated to his close friend Robert Browning, whose influence in the development of Story's aesthetic sensibility and achievements was significant, even though Browning's talents were of a different order. If Story managed to imbue his work with any psychological depth or insight, he is indebted to Browning for its presence.

Their relationship intensified when, during the period preceding Elizabeth Browning's death, the two families lived in daily proximity. Browning, who had not yet gained renown, published *Men and Women* in 1855, the collection of poems in which his use of dramatic monologue is most fully evolved. In 1856, Story embraced the same technique in his second collection of poems, where Cleopatra, Cassandra, and the like speak through its form. With both Browning and Story, we cannot overlook the function of the "speaker" in the dramatic monologue as a mask behind which to hide one's own insecurities. Furthermore, the psychological complexities that such a narrative device allows carried over into Story's sculpture, where, arguably, he was able to use it to greater effect. As DiFederico and Markus see it, Story's first successes, at the 1862 Exhibition, can be traced to Browning's presence and inspiration. His *Cleopatra* and *Libyan Sibyl* – and later, for instance, the *Medea*, *Salome*, and *Saul* – all display a dramatic change in style from his earlier, pallid statues.

When Story, in his poems, turns to more immediate themes his style relaxes, and we glimpse a rarer gift. His "Io Victis," an affecting hymn to fallen soldiers, imparts its simple somberness by use of a long line. It sings "Not the jubilant song of the victors,"

> But the hymn of the low and the humble, the weary, the
>   broken in heart,

Who strove and who failed, acting bravely a silent
and desperate part . . .

Among his lighter verses, which often err in pitch and drown in
their silliness, his "Snowdrop" sounds just the right tone for its
blithe spirit and conceit on the fickleness of women's love:

When, full of warm and eager love,
I clasp you in my fond embrace,
You gently push me back and say,
"Take care, my dear, you'll spoil my lace."

On the whole, Story's artistic proliferation, which included
prose and playwriting, earned him more detraction than praise
from his American observers. "The most remarkable fact concerning him is his versatility," quipped *The New York Times* in
1869. As James drolly put it, his multifariousness represented
"an irresponsible outpouring." Even Hawthorne, although citing his brilliance, still noted in him "a too facile power." And
Hawthorne's son, Julian, who witnessed the unfinished *Cleopatra* with his father, remarked later that the sculptor's fastidious-
ness meant he "could not trust a great idea to manage itself."
Story smarted from the general accusation of dilettantism,
which in turn led him to disparage his native land. "Since
George Third nobody ever treated it so," wrote an amused
Lowell to Emelyn Story in 1856. In this light, "A Contemporary
Criticism" (LOA, 1: 681), in which we hear the painter Raphael
answer a similar charge, seems to bear Story's self-defense:

. . . "You thought,"
He says, "that in too many arts I wrought;
And you advised me to stick close to one.
Thanks for your gracious counsel, all too kind;

And answering, if I chance to speak my mind
Too boldly, pardon. Yet it seems to me
All arts are one, – all branches on one tree."

RENEE TURSI

Selected Works
Nature and Art, Boston: Little, Brown, 1844
Graffiti D'Italia, London: Blackwood and Sons, 1868
Poems, Boston: Houghton Mifflin, 1886
Excursions in Art and Letters, 1891; reprinted, Boston:
   Houghton Mifflin, 1899
Browning to His American Friends, edited by Gertrude Reese
   Hudson, New York: Barnes and Noble, 1965

Further Reading
Hawthorne, Julian, *Hawthorne and His Circle*, New York,
   Harper, 1903
James, Henry, *William Wetmore Story and His Friends*,
   Boston: Houghton Mifflin, 1904
Kasson, Joy S., *Marble Queens and Captives: Women in
   Nineteenth-Century American Sculpture*, New Haven,
   Connecticut: Yale University Press, 1990
Kreymborg, Alfred, *A History of American Poetry: Our
   Singing Strength*, New York: Tudor, 1934
Phillips, Mary, *Reminiscences of William Wetmore Story*,
   New York: Rand, McNally, 1897
Tuttleton, James W., and Agostino Lombardo, eds., *The
   Sweetest Impression of Life: The James Family and Italy*,
   New York: New York University Press, 1990
Untermeyer, Louis, *American Poetry from the Beginning to
   Whitman*, New York: Harcourt, Brace, 1931

John Banister Tabb

(1845–1909)

Tabb was born at "The Forest," in Amelia County, Virginia, the third child and second son of Thomas Yelverton Tabb and Marianna Bertrand Archer Tabb. He studied with a private teacher, John L. Hood, until about 1859 when, as he recalled, an "affection of the eyes put an end to my studies." Tabb's poor eyesight prevented him from joining the Confederate army, but he was appointed clerk to Captain John Wilkinson aboard the blockade-runner *Robert E. Lee.* Tabb took one trip to England with Wilkinson, and he made the trip from Wilmington, North Carolina, to either Bermuda or Nassau at least 18 times. It is unknown whether Tabb was experimenting with verse during these wartime voyages, but he was beginning to view the world with poetic sensibilities.

His first sight of San Salvador in the Bahamas, for instance, provided imagery for a later poem. In "Off San Salvador," he depicts the island as "An emerald bar across the gold / Of sunset," and the setting sun would become one of his favorite images. He found transitional places and moments such as dusk especially attractive, for in them the poet could see his own world from a different perspective and catch a glimpse of another world. In the second stanza of "Off San Salvador," Tabb describes the corpse of a young seaman aboard the ship. Just as the beauty of the island had beckoned early explorers to its shores, a beckoning angel summons the young seaman's spirit to a more beautiful place.

In June 1864, Tabb was running dispatches between Bermuda and Wilmington on another vessel, the *Siren,* when it was captured by the Union's *Keystone State.* He was sent to Point Lookout, Maryland, where he was imprisoned for the next seven months and where, by a happy coincidence, he met fellow prisoner Sidney **Lanier.** One evening, Tabb, who had been ill, heard Lanier playing his flute and was drawn to the music; much later, he would write "Lanier's Flute":

> When palsied at the pool of thought
>   The Poet's words were found,
> Thy voice the healing Angel brought
>   To touch them into sound.

The two young men quickly began a friendship that would last until Lanier's death in 1881. Tabb's poems "To Sidney Lanier" and "At Lanier's Grave" commemorate his friend and his first important poetic influence.

After the war, Tabb studied music in Baltimore, Maryland, taught English, and planned to enter the Episcopal priesthood. While in Baltimore, he became acquainted with Father Alfred Curtis, an Episcopal priest who would soon convert to Catholicism. In the fall of 1870, Tabb traveled to Wisconsin to teach English at Racine College, but his sister Hallie's illness brought him back to Virginia in 1871. During the summer of the pivotal following year, he began writing serious verse, converted to Catholicism, was baptized, and decided to take holy orders. In November 1872, Tabb began studying at Saint Charles College, Ellicott City, Maryland, where he became a member of the faculty after completing his degree in 1875. Tabb's little textbook, *Bone Rules; or, Skeleton of English*

Grammar (1897), suggests that he had a delightful classroom manner. The book contains several grammatically flawed quatrains that his students used as exercises:

> "Lay still," his mother often said
> When Washington had went to bed.
> But little Georgie would reply:
> "I set up, but I cannot lie!"

Tabb's teaching responsibilities delayed his theological studies, but he eventually completed them at Saint Mary's Seminary in Baltimore and was ordained in December 1884. After his ordination, he returned to Saint Charles College, where he taught English until complete blindness overtook him near the end of his life. Although Tabb ended his days in Maryland, he remained fond of his native Virginia. In one poem, "In the Mountains of Virginia," he wrote:

> Nurtured upon my mother's knee,
>   From this her mountain-breast apart,
> Here nearer heaven I seem to be
>   And closer to her heart.

His fondness for the south is evident in a poem that he wrote during the last decade of his life, "Doing Well," which concludes: "But whether you send me to heaven or hell, / An unredeemed rebel I'll faithfully dwell."

Tabb's first published poem, "The Cloud," appeared in *Harper's Monthly* (July 1877). He received 15 dollars for it, and he then bought a new pair of shoes with the money. He was genuinely pleased with his first commercial success, remembering it in "A Confession," a quatrain he wrote 20 years later that reveals his lifelong fondness for puns:

> One day with foot upon the ground,
>   I stood among the crowd;
> The next, with sole renewed, I found
>   A footing on "The Cloud."

He published several other poems in magazines before his first volume, *Poems* (1882), appeared. The work was privately printed in Baltimore and attracted little attention. His second book of verse was *An Octave to Mary* (1893). Although neither of these volumes brought him much notice, his third book, *Poems* (1894), was a popular success. Published by Copeland and Day in Boston, *Poems* would go through 17 editions during the next quarter century, and it far exceeded the popularity of a contemporary Copeland and Day publication, Stephen **Crane's** *The Black Riders.* Tabb's *Lyrics* (1897) and *Later Lyrics* (1902) also went through many editions well into the second decade of the twentieth century, and a posthumous collection, *Later Poems,* appeared in 1910. Significantly, the last volume was published in New York by Mitchell Kennerley, who was making a reputation for himself by publishing avantgarde poets. A collected edition, *The Poetry of Father Tabb,* appeared in 1928; the poems that are discussed here can be found in this edition.

Nearly all of Tabb's poems are brief lyrics. His subjects often come from nature. Tabb was fascinated with the evanescence of nature's most delicate creations and inevitably compared his chosen subjects with the brevity of human life on earth. In "Wilted," for example, the poet addresses a "Little blossom" and recognizes that he and the flower were "born alike to die." The flower's wilted condition makes the poet realize that it has less time on earth than he does, but, he concludes, it will happily have "more Eternity." Tabb often saw the ways in which nature manifested God's handiwork. In "Autumn-Glow," Tabb paid tribute to the fall color and wondered, "If this the preface be of death / . . . / What wondrous art illumineth / The story still untold?" Despite his frequent description of the colors and beauty of nature, Tabb's favorite imagery remained the shadowy spaces between darkness and light.

His first published poem, "The Cloud," anticipates much of his subsequent work. As the poem begins, a cloud appears on the eastern horizon the moment before sunrise. The underside of the cloud reflects light from the yet-to-appear sun and anticipates the new day. After the sun has risen, the cloud's appearance changes completely: that part which first reflected the sunlight is now shaded. Not until the sun sets on the western horizon does the earth-facing side of the cloud once again reflect light. With darkness, the cloud completely disappears. The final stanza reveals that the cloud is a metaphor of the soul, which possesses no beauty in itself without divine light.

Another early poem, "The Bridge" (LOA, 2: 451), illustrates Tabb's original perspective. In the first stanza, the bridge is "majestic," but as the poem develops, the bridge loses its material qualities. Besides seeing the bridge horizontally – as something that connects two shores – Tabb observes it vertically. The river that flows beneath the bridge and the crowd that flows across it are perpendicular yet parallel streams. The people, a "motley throng" made up of "Hearts yet untaught of wrong" who "Mingle with souls accursed," cross the bridge unaware of one another. The bridge thus becomes a point of stability and serenity between the "twin currents."

As Tabb matured as a poet, he retained his fascination with shadowy in-between states and his original perspective, but his poems became increasingly more compact, with most presenting a single simile or metaphor within a few lines. The quatrain became his favorite form, although he frequently wrote sestets and sonnets. Much of his work anticipates that of the imagists, but Tabb, unlike later experimental poets, never relinquished his tight control of rhyme or meter. Like his earlier poems, Tabb's later works by and large remain in the timeless realm between heaven and earth.

Occasionally, however, Tabb wrote verses that reflected technological or political developments in late-nineteenth-century America. In "A Phonograph," Tabb compares this popular modern means of entertainment with the mockingbird, an icon of the southern poetic tradition since the colonial period. In "The United States to the Filipinos," Tabb provides a brief sardonic comment concerning U. S. foreign policy:

> We come to give you liberty
> To do whate'er *we* choose,
> Or clean extermination
> If you venture to refuse.

Such political comments were rare, however. Tabb preferred to linger between the flowers on earth and the stars in heaven.

Tabb's failing eyesight informs much of his verse. One poem, "The Shadow" (LOA, 2: 453), can be read as a comment about what he would lose with the loss of sight: the shadow is a "friend of fortune that once clung to me" who would leave him all alone in the darkness. With blindness, Tabb implies, instead of missing the light, he will miss the shadows, that is, the subtle gradations between light and darkness. The light, understood as divine light, will remain with him. Tabb's feeble eyesight and spiritual inclinations make it unsurprising that he would find a kindred spirit in John Milton, to whom he addressed the following quatrain (LOA, 2: 453):

> So fair thy vision that the night
> Abided with thee, lest the light,
> A flaming sword before thine eyes,
> Had shut thee out from Paradise.

Although Tabb's failing eyes made him empathize with Milton, his poetry has more of an affinity with the work of the English metaphysical poets, Robert Herrick and George Herbert. Tabb's greatest poetic influence, however, was Edgar Allan **Poe**. Tabb was disturbed by the Poe-bashing that took place among literary historians, and he wrote several poems condemning Poe's detractors and praising his verse. In "Poe's Critics," Tabb writes, "Each passing critic has his throw, / Nor sees, defeating his intent, / How lofty grows the monument."

The haunting quality of Tabb's imagery in "A Winter Twilight" (LOA, 2: 454) is reminiscent of Poe's "Ulalume" (LOA, 1: 540), which Tabb recognized as "unearthly *music* that haunts and appeals." In "A Winter Twilight," the sun setting across the snow looks "Blood-shotten through the bleak gigantic trees." The growing darkness creates fear and apprehension: "In every skulking shadow Fancy sees / The menace of an undiscovered foe." Twilight is like an isthmus, a "dim, mysterious land" that sets people's lives asunder. Once again, Tabb loses himself within those shadowy spaces between day and night.

Tabb uses sound imagery much in the same way as he does visual imagery, preferring utterances that are neither sound nor silence. In "Whisper" (LOA, 2: 453), Tabb personifies a whisper as a "timorous child" holding the hand of her sister, Silence. Tabb had a sensitivity toward children, and he often employs the child as a metaphor in his poetry. In this poem, the state of silence is a familiar, comfortable place, while sound is an alien world into which the child has never before ventured. Echoes were another noise in between sound and silence that Tabb found fascinating, and he uses echo metaphors in several poems. In one, entitled "Echo" (LOA, 2: 454), the echo is a "famished Prodigal," vainly seeking its father's door. In another ("Echoes," LOA, 2: 452), the echoes are "Hints of heavenly voices / . . . wooing hence to worlds beyond the shadowy zone." Tabb's epithet for the earth, "the shadowy zone," hints that life itself is a gray area, the shadowy part of existence between birth and everlasting life.

Although another title, "Evolution" (LOA, 2: 453), suggests prevalent scientific notions, Tabb's poem is not about Darwin's theories. Evolution was an attractive metaphor for Tabb because it suggested that every form of life was in an in-between stage of development: every creature had been one thing and was on its way to being another. Tabb takes quite a different stance toward evolution from that of Darwin, however. The poem consists of a series of prepositional phrases but no verbs, thus suggesting that earthly existence possesses a kind of static quality. The last phrase reads: "Out of the dead, cold ashes, / Life again." For Tabb, the most important step in humanity's evolution occurs in the passage from flesh to spirit.

Another quatrain, "Tenebrae" (LOA, 2: 455), literally suggests darkness, but the word specifically refers to a Catholic rite during Holy Week in which candles lighted at the beginning of the ceremony are extinguished one by one after each psalm is read to commemorate the darkness during the Crucifixion. Tabb, whose gradual blindness became complete during the last years of his life, could have made the quatrain his motto:

Whate'er my darkness be,
'T is not, O Lord, of Thee:
The light is Thine alone;
The shadows, all my own.

KEVIN J. HAYES

Selected Works

Poems, Baltimore, Maryland, 1882
Octave to Mary, Baltimore, Maryland, 1893
Poems, Boston: Copeland and Day, 1894
Lyrics, Boston: Copeland and Day, 1897
Child Verse; Poems Grave and Gay, Boston: Small, Maynard, 1899
Two Lyrics, Boston, 1900
Later Lyrics, London and New York: J. Lane, 1902
The Rosary in Rhyme, Boston: Small, Maynard, 1904
Selections from the Verses of John Banister Tabb, edited by Alice Meynell, London: Burns and Oates, 1907
Later Poems, New York: Mitchell Kennerley, 1910
Poetry of Father Tabb, edited by Francis Litz, New York: Dodd, Mead, 1928
John Bannister [sic] *Tabb on Emily Dickinson*, New York: Seven Gables Bookshop, 1950
Letters – Grave and Gay and Other Prose of John Banister Tabb, edited by Francis Litz, Washington, D.C.: Catholic University of America Press, 1950
Best Poems of John Banister Tabb, edited by Francis Litz, Westminster, Maryland: Newman, 1957

Further Reading

Blair, Gordon, *Father Tabb: Poet – Priest – Soldier – Wit*, Richmond, Virginia: Whittet and Shepperson, 1940
Litz, Francis, *Father Tabb: A Study of His Life and Works*, Baltimore, Maryland: Johns Hopkins Press, 1923
McDevitt, William, *My Father, Father Tabb, at Home and at College*, San Francisco: Recorder-Sunset, 1945
Tabb, Jennie Masters, *Father Tabb, His Life and Work*, Boston: Stratford, 1921

Bayard Taylor

(1825–1878)

Bayard Taylor's poetic reputation has fallen fast and far. Once ranked with the New England worthies – Oliver Wendell **Holmes**, Henry Wadsworth **Longfellow**, James Russell **Lowell**, and John Greenleaf **Whittier** – as one of the top poets in the United States, today Taylor is virtually unknown. Except for the occasional appearance of "Bedouin Song" (LOA, 2: 166) and his parodies in anthologies (see LOA, 2: 163–65), his poems attract no attention. The reasons for Taylor's eclipse are several, and examining them reveals much about the genteel taste of the second half of the nineteenth century.

Taylor was born in Kennett Square, Pennsylvania, on January 11, 1825, to a farming family with a Quaker background. Uninterested in working the land and unable to afford a college education, he set out to build a literary career. Encouraged by Rufus Griswold, then an editor at *Graham's Magazine*, Taylor gathered enough subscriptions to publish a short book of poems, and with the money that he earned and promises from newspapers to publish his letters, he set off for a two-year tramp around Europe. *Views A-Foot; or Europe Seen with Knapsack and Staff* (1846), the book resulting from Taylor's tour, went through six editions in the first year, won Longfellow's and Whittier's approval, and established the author, at age 21, as an important travel writer. Back in New York, Taylor cultivated friendships in the literary world and edited and wrote for various publications; he eventually began a lifelong association with Horace Greeley's *New York Tribune*. An assignment to cover the California gold rush was followed by a two-and-a-half-year trip to Africa, the Middle East, India, China, and Japan, the last of which he visited as a seaman and historian for Commodore Perry's expedition in the black ships. After returning to the United States, Taylor published two travel books and *Poems of the Orient* (1854), a best-selling collection of verse inspired by his visit to the Middle East.

By this time, the basic pattern of Taylor's life had been fixed. Periods of travel, either to generate material for articles or to lecture, were followed by time in New York and at Cedarcroft, the large estate that he built in Kennett Square, during which he would shape the articles into books and concentrate on creative projects – poetry and fiction. In 1870–71, Taylor's two-volume verse translation, in the original meters, of Goethe's *Faust* appeared to universal acclaim. Still read in Modern Library and Oxford World Classics editions, this is Taylor's most accomplished work, and for many years it was considered to be *the* English *Faust*. In its fluid faithfulness, it ranks above the other major translations undertaken by Taylor's American peers, such as Longfellow's *Divine Comedy* (1865–67) and William Cullen **Bryant's** *Iliad* (1870) and *Odyssey* (1871–72). Five years later, Taylor published *The Echo Club and Other Literary Diversions* (1876), a satirical volume of criticism and parody. Although the book initially received scant attention from the public, and Taylor himself did not seriously value it, over the years the agile parodies have continued to find readers.

In 1878, Taylor was appointed American minister to Berlin, a position that he had long coveted. Less than a year after his arrival in Germany, however, he died unexpectedly on December 19. Taylor's passing was mourned throughout America and celebrated in verse by the literary lights of his day. Before burial in Pennsylvania, his body lay in state in New York City Hall. When Taylor died at the age of 53, he had visited most of the countries in Europe, Asia, and the Middle East, and had published more than 50 books of travel, poetry, fiction, short stories, history, and translations.

Taylor's writing interests current critics because it gives us insight into the genteel tradition, the tradition in American literature informed by Victorian taste and values. Genteel standards stressed conventionality, correctness, and rigid moral and mental discipline; they generally opposed intellectual and artistic innovation, and – with the exception of sentimentality – emotional indulgence. The commercial and industrial middle class was growing during this era, and Taylor was especially popular among middle-class readers who aspired to a thoroughly genteel way of life. Possibly because of his own conservative Quaker background and his desire for respectability and economic security, Taylor wrote for this uncritical audience, implicitly accepting the limits of its narrow world.

Although Taylor was known during his lifetime as the premier American travel writer, his ambition was to be the premier American poet. Travel writing was his bread and butter, but poetry was his love. Taylor's poetic career can roughly be divided into an early period, when he concentrated on lyrical poems, ballads, and romances, and a later period, when he attempted longer, more complex pieces such as masques and verse dramas. A convenient dividing point is *The Poems of Bayard Taylor* (1864), a volume of Taylor's collected poems that Ticknor and Fields published in their prestigious Blue and Gold Series. Although much of the early work is imitative of poetry written by his more gifted contemporaries, *Poems of the Orient* is an interesting volume worth examining more closely.

In the nineteenth century, the Orient was roughly equivalent to what is now called the Middle East. Although this area had been the focus of western political and commercial activity during the late eighteenth century, it was not until Lord Byron published his oriental tales, including "The Giaor" (1813), "The Corsair," "The Bride of Abydos," and "Lara" (1814), and Thomas Moore's *Lalla Rookh* (1817) appeared that the Orient became a popular setting for western literature. During this period, orientalism caught on in earnest in Europe and the United States, affecting everything from architecture to literature. Taylor's visit to the Orient and his book of orientalist poems may have been sparked by a genuine concern for the Levant, but they should also be viewed in the context of the nineteenth-century fascination with this part of the world. Except for a trip deep into Sudan, Taylor's oriental travels were along routes already well-blazed by tourists. Indeed, for international travelers in the mid-1850s, visiting the Orient was second in popularity only to the European grand tour.

In publishing *Poems of the Orient*, then, Taylor was, in part, simply capitalizing on the western vogue for things oriental. This is not to say that the poems are without merit, for within the tradition of American orientalist poetry, which includes Ralph Waldo **Emerson's** "Days" (LOA, 1: 324) and Herman **Melville's** *Clarel* (LOA, 2: 17), they are some of the best. Taylor's Orient is by turns glowing and languorous, sensuous and austere. Richard Henry Stoddard, a close friend whose praise must be taken with a large grain of salt, claimed that Taylor had "captured the secret feeling of the East as no English-writing poet but Byron had." James Russell Lowell, another friend, told Taylor, "I cannot help twitching off my cap to fling it up with the rest." But unlike "Days" and *Clarel*, which transcend their oriental motifs to engage a reader's interest at the deepest level, Taylor's oriental poems rarely have more than a kind of picturesque romanticism.

"Bedouin Song," the most famous poem in the collection, is representative of the book's contents. Although this brief, three-stanza, three-refrain lyric shows technical skill in its metrical variation, it is not innovative. Percy Bysshe Shelley's influence on Taylor was pervasive, and "Bedouin Song" owes an obvious debt to his famous "Indian Serenade." Despite this, however, Taylor's poem has character and can stand on its own. The subject, passionate love tinged with religious fervor, was one of the quintessential subjects of orientalist verse. There were many nineteenth-century myths about the Orient; one of the most common was that it was a land of exotic love, a land where relations between the sexes were freer and less guilt-ridden than in the west. "Bedouin Song" is well within the realm of good taste, but the attraction it must have had to buttoned-up genteel readers looking for emotional release is clear. They could indulge their fantasies in the image of the exotic Arab galloping from the desert for a midnight rendezvous with a dark-eyed woman who is hidden behind a lattice window-screen. His passionate plea to her to

> Open the door of thy heart,
>   And open thy chamber door,
> And my kisses shall teach thy lips
>   The love that shall fade no more

gave readers exactly the illicit thrill that they expected from orientalist verse. That the fame of the poem was due largely to its love theme is reinforced by the change the title popularly underwent from "Bedouin Song" to "Bedouin Love Song." With this new title, the poem was set to music no less than five times and is still occasionally revived by university glee clubs.

A second orientalist fascination was religion. The Levant was the Holy Land – the birthplace of Judaism, Christianity, and Islam, the great religions of the west. Many nineteenth-century travelers went to the Levant as pilgrims to visit ancient holy sites. The refrain in "Bedouin Song," climaxing with the speaker's declaration that his love will last till "the leaves of the Judgment / Book unfold!" legitimizes his passion by placing it within the context of timeless religious faith. He is no Arab bounder; his love is as true and lasting as his religious devotion.

Turning to the poetry that Taylor published after 1864, three long works deserve brief notice: *The Masque of the Gods* (1872), *Lars: A Pastoral of Norway* (1873), and *Prince Deukalion, A Lyrical Drama* (1878). Taylor continued to write lyrics all his life, but now his main poetic interests involved drama and narrative. *The Masque of the Gods* was written in

four days, "almost at white heat," according to his second wife, Marie Hansen-Taylor, and owes much to the *Faust* translation that Taylor had recently completed. The idea of a late nineteenth-century American masque sounds both intriguing and novel. Unfortunately, in Taylor's case, it fails to intrigue and the novelty quickly wears thin. The drama centers on the development of human spiritual consciousness. In the last scene, when Man says that he does not understand the high-flown dialogue that he has been listening to, a "Voice from Space" closes the masque by melodramatically announcing, "Wait! Ye shall know." Holmes, Longfellow, and Whittier claimed to be delighted, but the public was baffled by Taylor's pretentiousness. *Lars: A Pastoral of Norway*, an ambitious blank-verse narrative, has aged better. Set in Norway and America, it, too, concerns spiritual development, but this time Taylor represents such concerns in the context of Quaker farm life, something with which he was familiar. The poem has several good sections, including a famous knife fight. After the book's publication, the author's Kennett Square neighbors held a town picnic to honor him for his accurate portrayal of Quaker thought and principle. With *Prince Deukalion*, a verse drama, Taylor was again reaching too far. The poem exhibits technical skill in its potpourri of metrical and stanza forms, but since the subject is the progress of man over a 2,000-year period, and the characters are all murky abstractions, only the intrepid read to the end. Taylor thought it his best work, and among the long poems it may be. Its lack of concreteness, however, is a major stumbling block. Taylor here is indebted once more to Shelley (*Prometheus Unbound*) and Goethe (*Faust*), influences which, in this case, overshadow the poem's originality.

In 1876, one of Taylor's most unusual books, *The Echo Club and Other Literary Diversions*, appeared. In *The Echo Club*, Taylor used satire and parody to turn his greatest fault, his tendency to imitate, into an asset. Originally published as written by a "Nameless Reporter" and serialized in the January–July 1872 issues of the *Atlantic Monthly*, *The Echo Club* is arranged as a series of eight "nights" when a group of literary men meet to write and discuss poetry in the back room of a New York beer cellar. During the first night they hit on the idea of forming a "club of Parodists, – of Echoes – of Iconoclasts." Each night as a means of entertainment, they draw names of famous poets from a hat and write parodies of their work. The names of the four parodists are given as The Ancient, Galahad, Zoilus, and The Gannet. Each has a different literary temperament, and much of the text is taken up with the clash of their opinions on poetry and poetic taste. Although Taylor, the "Reporter," is depicted as one of a "chorus" of three or four members who attend meetings but do not participate in the wrangling and writing, The Ancient seems to be the mouthpiece for his views.

On the first night they discuss their task. "To undertake parodies, as the word is generally comprehended," The Ancient says, "to make a close imitation of some particular poem, though it should be characteristic of the author, would be rather a flat business." He approves instead "something altogether more original and satisfactory, – a simple echo of the author's tone and manner." A diversion of this sort, he claims, is "a higher and finer recreation of the mind, than the mechanical setting of some given poem, line by line, to a ludicrous subject." As to the poets parodied, The Ancient suggests choosing ones with a "distinct individuality." "We can only make those the objects of our fun," he continues, "whose manner or dialect stamps itself so deeply into our minds that a new cast can be taken." For The Ancient, then, parody is a form of flattery.

With the guidelines drawn, the names of William Morris, Edgar Allan **Poe**, and Robert Browning are taken from the hat, and the poets begin their work. "The Promissory Note," a parody of Poe, and "Angelo Orders His Dinner," one of Browning, are especially good. The second night is devoted to John Keats, Emerson, Algernon Swinburne, Lydia **Sigourney**, and Edmund Clarence **Stedman**. The Keats parody, "Ode on a Jar of Pickles," and the Emerson parody, "All or Nothing" (LOA, 2: 163), a conflation of Emerson's "Each and All," "The Sphinx," and "Brahma" (LOA, 1: 254, 258, 319), are excellent. Taylor's Emerson is a sphinxlike guru offering snake-oil solutions to believers. Subjects of parodies on the third night are Thomas Holley **Chivers**, Barry Cornwall, Whittier, Dante Gabriel Rossetti, and Thomas Bailey Aldrich. The Whittier parody, "The Ballad of Hiram Hoover," and the Rossetti parody, "Cimabuella," are both well done. The fourth night covers Bryant, Holmes, Nathaniel Parker **Willis**, and Alfred, Lord Tennyson, who becomes the focus of much attention. The fifth night finishes Tennyson and also includes Henry Tuckerman, Longfellow, William Dean **Howells**, and Stoddard. The Howells parody, however, does not actually appear. As the editor of the *Atlantic*, Howells took the liberty of omitting the poem, dryly commenting in a footnote that he "trusts the propriety of doing so will require no explanation." On the sixth night the poets parodied are Lowell, Taylor himself, Elizabeth Barrett Browning, and George **Boker**.

Because the real importance of Taylor's *Poems of the Orient* is in its perfection of popular orientalist verse rather than in its originality, "Hadramaut" (LOA, 2: 164), the author's outlandish self-parody, is more a parody of orientalist poetic fashion than a parody of Taylor. Indeed, "Hadramaut" barely hits the mark, since the extravagant orientalist poems upon which it is based are so close to parody to begin with. The poets dealt with on the seventh night are Jean Ingelow, James B. Read, Julia Ward **Howe**, John James **Piatt**, Sarah Morgan **Piatt**, and William Winter. Because these are as yet young poets without strong voices, the parodies on the seventh night are meant to test – and prove – The Ancient's theory that a parody must be written against a writer with a "distinct individuality." Since three of the poets are female, it also provides an opportunity for comments on poetry by women. On the final night, the Echo Club returns to more solid ground by taking on the "dialect" group, which includes Walt **Whitman** (LOA, 2: 165), Bret **Harte**, John Hay, and Joaquin **Miller**. Of these, the Whitman parody, "Camerados," portraying Whitman as a hearty pied-piper followed by "cosmical multitudes," is the best.

Taylor's high reputation as a poet was due, in part, to the close friendships that he nurtured with the important writers of his day. Thus, as might be expected, the criticisms and parodies in *The Echo Club* are rather mild. Taylor knew better than to jeopardize his fame by giving his parodies more bite. Still, the poems are excellent examples of light verse. Howells, although unhappy with the machinery of the eight nights in the beer cellar, recognized the quality of the poems and claimed that they were "matchless pieces of fun," "the best parodies ever written." Time has largely upheld Howells's evaluation. Although parody was popular with a number of genteel writers, including Harte, Mark Twain (see LOA, 2: 338), and Phoebe **Cary**, none of them parodied as many poets and did it as successfully as Taylor did. Anthologies today continue to mine *The Echo Club* for its parodic gems.

The sad irony of *The Echo Club* is that although Taylor desperately wanted to be remembered for his serious work – especially for the long poems – it is his parodies that have survived. Taylor's skill as a parodist is not surprising, however, since he was an avid reader with a powerful memory. When he came to write his own verse, it was natural for him to compensate for his lack of originality by unconsciously "echoing" his reading. In his serious poems this is a fault, but for writing parodies it is a virtue. In *The Echo Club*, Taylor took advantage of his ability to imitate by consciously turning to parody.

In the context of Taylor's impulse to imitate, it could be argued that *Poems of the Orient* is also a book of imitations. Much orientalist verse played fast and loose with ideas of translation. Shelley's "Indian Serenade," for example, which inspired "Bedouin Song," is based on an original oriental love lyric. Even Emerson, despite his assertion that imitation is suicide, translated German versions of Persian poetry into English and then used these as models for several of his own poems. Read in this way, much in *Poems of the Orient* consists of imitation translations that are informed by nineteenth-century stereotypical views of the Orient.

Poems of the Orient and *The Echo Club*, although minor, are no small accomplishments and deserve a larger audience. Granted these books contain nothing timeless, but they are interesting documents in the poetic history of the United States. Taylor's orientalist poems are excellent examples of the influence that the Middle East had on the nineteenth-century imagination, and the parodies show the limited poetic talent of genteel America in its best light.

DORSEY KLEITZ

Selected Works

Ximena, or the Battle of the Sierra Morena, and Other Poems, Philadelphia: Herman Hooker, 1844
Rhymes of Travel, Ballads and Poems, New York: Putnam, 1849
A Book of Romances, Lyrics and Songs, Boston: Ticknor, Reed and Fields, 1851
Poems of the Orient, Boston: Ticknor and Fields, 1854
Poems of Home and Travel, Boston: Ticknor and Fields, 1855
The Poet's Journal, Boston: Ticknor and Fields, 1862
The Poems of Bayard Taylor, Blue and Gold ed., Boston: Ticknor and Fields, 1864
The Picture of St. John, Boston: Fields, Osgood, 1866
The Golden Wedding: A Masque, Philadelphia: Lippincott, 1868
The Ballad of Abraham Lincoln, Boston: Fields, Osgood, 1870
The Masque of the Gods, Boston: James R. Osgood, 1872
Lars: A Pastoral of Norway, Boston: James R. Osgood, 1873
The Prophet. A Tragedy, Boston: James R. Osgood, 1874

Home Pastorals, Ballads and Lyrics, Boston: James R. Osgood, 1875

The National Ode, Boston: William F. Gill, 1877

Prince Deukalion, A Lyrical Drama, Boston: Houghton, Osgood, 1878

Poetical Works of Bayard Taylor, Household ed., Boston: Houghton, Osgood, 1880

Dramatic Works of Bayard Taylor, Boston: Houghton Mifflin, 1880

Further Reading

Beatty, Richmond Croom, *Bayard Taylor: Laureate of the Gilded Age*, Norman: University of Oklahoma Press, 1936

Cary, Richard, *The Genteel Circle: Bayard Taylor and His New York Friends*, Ithaca, New York: Cornell University Press, 1952

Conwell, Russell H., *The Life, Travels, and Literary Career of Bayard Taylor*, Boston: B. B. Russell, 1879

Hansen-Taylor, Marie, and Horace E. Scudder, eds., *Life and Letters of Bayard Taylor*, 2 vols., Boston: Houghton, 1884

Haskell, Juliana, *Bayard Taylor's Translation of Goethe's Faust*, New York: Columbia University Press, 1908

Smyth, Albert H., *Bayard Taylor*, Boston and New York: Houghton Mifflin, 1896

Stedman, E. C., *Poets of America*, Boston and New York: Houghton Mifflin, 1885

Wermuth, Paul C., *Bayard Taylor*, New York: Twayne, 1973

Whittier, John G., *The Tent on the Beach and Other Poems*, Boston: Ticknor and Fields, 1868

Wilson, Douglas L., ed., *The Genteel Tradition, Nine Essays by George Santayana*, Cambridge, Massachusetts: Harvard University Press, 1967

Henry David Thoreau

(1817–1862)

Thoreau is so completely identified as the author of *Walden* that many readers are surprised to learn of the extent and range of his other literary productions. His writing was the lasting harvest of what Ralph Waldo **Emerson**, in his eulogy, called Thoreau's "simple and hidden life." His journal, which survives in 43 complete, bound manuscript volumes and four fragmentary ones, is the great evolving, organic work of his literary career. Most of what he published has its source in that journal, which served from 1837 until 1861 as a repository for observations that were shaped, combined, and augmented to create three books besides *Walden* and more than 25 essays. Like most of the transcendentalists, Thoreau wrote poems, too; he served his literary apprenticeship as a poet, composing almost three-quarters of his 200 poems – including all but one of those in the LOA anthology – before 1845, when he began writing his first book, *A Week on the Concord and Merrimack Rivers*.

Thoreau also was an accomplished naturalist who collected specimens for Louis Agassiz, the first professor of natural science at Harvard University. Bradford Torrey, in his introduction to the earliest complete edition of Thoreau's journal in 1906, expressed a misunderstanding of Thoreau's level of achievement: "Thoreau the naturalist appears in the journal, not as a master, but as a learner," he wrote, and this judgment has persisted. The voluminous manuscripts of Thoreau's incomplete phenological studies and late natural history writings have attracted the interest of only a few scholars persistent enough to take on the task of interpreting Thoreau's difficult handwriting and reconstructing the original order of hundreds of pages of material now held in a number of different libraries. But their studies reveal Thoreau's knowledge and skill and help to contradict the unfounded but tenacious cliché that Thoreau spent the years from the publication of *Walden* in 1854 until his death in 1862 in defeated disappointment.

The activities associated with his writing – observing the phenomena of nature, studying and copying from useful scientific, historical, and literary works, and keeping a journal – occupied Thoreau for some hours each day, but he still had to make a living. Between 1837 and 1848, he taught school for a time, lived for two extended periods in the Emerson household, and sometimes worked at odd jobs – painting, gardening, and hauling. Beginning in 1838, he also lectured several times a year at lyceums and in private homes from Maine to New Jersey. For a steady income, however, he relied for years on two sources in which his practical talent served him well: he worked in the family pencil-making and ground-lead business and developed new machines and methods that improved the products, and he surveyed for Concord, Masschusetts, and the surrounding towns, and for private landowners. By the time he died, in May 1862, he had overcome a reputation for quirky irresponsibility, which his individuality had earned him, and had been accepted as a respected citizen of Concord.

In summing up Thoreau's life, Emerson complained that Thoreau failed to achieve his full potential because he lacked ambition – "instead of engineering for all America, he was the captain of a huckleberry party." This opinion indicates how deeply Emerson misread his friend's intentions. The two had a close but difficult relationship, and Emerson, lionized in his own lifetime, probably never realized that Thoreau's accomplishments would one day be ranked with his own. With greater powers of narrative description than Emerson and from a position closer to the social margin than Emerson's, Thoreau both describes and represents the complex nature of American experience, balancing observation and reflection, detail and perspective, and local wisdom and universal truth, always probing the question, "How shall we live?"

Thoreau wrote most of his poems when he was between 21 and 28 years old, and although they contain the germs of themes and ideas and images that he later explored more successfully in prose, they reflect the experiences and occasions of his youth. He was born in July 1817 in Concord, where his father, John, was a shopkeeper. In October, he was christened David Henry, named for his father's younger brother, who had died the previous August. His sister Helen and brother John were older; Sophia was the youngest child. John Thoreau moved his family to Chelmsford and Boston, Massachusetts, following business opportunities; in 1823, the family moved back to Concord, where John joined a pencil-making concern established by his brother-in-law, Charles Dunbar, and another Concordian, Cyrus Stow. When Dunbar and Stow dropped out, John Thoreau continued the business, which eventually brought financial stability to the family. Thoreau's mother, Cynthia Dunbar, took in boarders for many years to help make ends meet.

David Henry was apparently a quiet, serious child; William Ellery **Channing**, Thoreau's walking companion, reports that Samuel Hoar, a local lawyer and U. S. Congressman, nicknamed him "the judge." Thoreau grew up in a large, lively household, which included the five other immediate family members, two or three boarders, and, starting in 1830, his uncle Charles Dunbar and his aunt Louisa Dunbar. When Thoreau was older, his father's sisters, Jane and Maria, were frequent visitors. Thoreau left no extended account of his childhood, but he occasionally alluded in his journal to a memorable event. In an entry written after August 6, 1845, for example, he associates his adult preference for Walden Pond's "sweet solitude" and "speaking silence" over the "tumultuous and varied city" with his recollection of a visit to the pond when he was five, "one of the most ancient scenes stamped on the tablets of my memory," a "woodland vision" that "for a long time made the drapery of my dreams" (note the use of this image in "Fog" [LOA, 1: 660]). Thoreau's older siblings were both schoolteachers; when it was decided that their brother should go to Harvard, as had his grandfather Dunbar before him, they contributed from their teaching salaries to help pay his expenses, about $179 a year (not a small sum at a time when a laborer earned about a dollar a day). Thoreau had spent 10 years in Concord schools – Miss Wheeler's infant school, the public grammar school, and the private Concord Academy – and took the Harvard entrance examinations at the then-standard age of 16. "Conditioned" in three subjects, he just managed to be admitted.

Harvard put heavy emphasis on the classics – Thoreau studied Latin and Greek grammar or composition for three of his four years. He also took courses in mathematics, English, and history; in several modern languages; and in mental, natural, and intellectual philosophy. Judged only by the numbers, Thoreau's record at Harvard was not outstanding – he graduated nineteenth in a class of almost 50 – but the system of grading rewarded rote learning and punished absences, and Thoreau was out for an entire term with what may have been his first bout with tuberculosis. He did do well enough both to earn monetary prizes for his grades in three of his four years at Harvard and to be awarded a small scholarship.

Thoreau was never happy about the teaching methods used at Harvard – Emerson is supposed to have remarked that most of the branches of learning were taught at Harvard, and Thoreau to have replied, "Yes, all of the branches and none of the roots" – but he began there a process of self-education that continued throughout the rest of his life. The skill he developed in both Greek and Latin and in modern languages allowed him to explore the classics of several cultures on his own. He learned Italian and Spanish, and he was able to read Goethe's works and the French Jesuits' accounts of their experiences in the New World in the languages in which they were written. He was introduced to English poetry, and he began to collect examples of poetic phrases that he admired. He started the habit of copying extracts from his reading into notebooks that became sources for quotations and information he would use in his writings. And as a Harvard graduate he earned access to and borrowing privileges from the Harvard Library; he took full advantage of this opportunity all his life.

Sometime after he graduated from Harvard in August 1837, probably about the time he began keeping a journal in October of that year, David Henry Thoreau became Henry David Thoreau. Up to then, he had composed a number of themes for his Harvard professors, written a few poems, and copied extracts and kept observations that were important to him in an "Index Rerum" (of which a few pages survive). Now, however, he was declaring himself to be a new man – a writer. For the rest of his life, he divided his energies between supporting himself and writing.

Thanks in part to a recommendation from the president of Harvard, Josiah Quincy, Thoreau's first job was a well-paying one at the district school in Concord. However, he kept it only two weeks: when he was instructed by one of the school committee to maintain stricter discipline in his classroom, he selected several students at random, feruled them, and quit. Thoreau looked unsuccessfully for another teaching job, then, in 1838, he started his own school, which soon was able to take over the Concord Academy's name. John joined him in 1839, and they operated the academy together until April 1841, when John became too ill with tuberculosis to continue. After the Concord Academy closed, Thoreau accepted an offer from Emerson, who lived across town, to stay with Emerson's family and earn his keep as a handyman and gardener while he concentrated on his writing. His two-and-a-half years based in the Emerson household gave him freedom to read, think, and write when he most needed it, resulting in the reorganization of his journal, the production of essays and poems, and the gathering and structuring of materials for *A Week on the Concord and Merrimack Rivers*.

All during the time he was teaching, Thoreau was also keeping a journal and composing poetry. In July 1840, he published an essay, "Aulus Persius Flaccus," and the poem "Sympathy" ("I am a parcel of vain strivings tied" [LOA, 1: 662]) in the first number of *The Dial*, the transcendentalist periodical edited by Emerson and Margaret **Fuller**; in January 1841, he published "Stanzas." Emerson, 14 years older than Thoreau and an important figure to him and to many younger writers and intellectuals, had become acquainted with Thoreau in the fall of 1837, and had soon become a friend and mentor. From 1839 until 1843, Emerson actively fostered Thoreau's efforts at poetry, praising his poems in letters and in his journal, transmitting copies of them to Fuller for *The Dial*, and preferring them to Thoreau's essays. Encouraged by this support from one who proclaimed poets to be divine liberators, Thoreau composed during these years more than half of the poems that survive.

All but one of the LOA poems date from this period. Ordered by date of composition, these are "Guido's Aurora" (probably 7/40; LOA, 1: 664), "I am a parcel of vain strivings tied" (1/16/41), "They who prepare my evening meal below" (4/4/41; LOA, 1: 660), "Dong, sounds the brass in the east" (5/9/41; LOA, 1: 661), "My life has been the poem I would have writ" (8/28/41; LOA, 1: 662), "Inspiration" (9–10/41; LOA, 1: 665), "Rumors from an Æolian Harp" (before 10/42; LOA, 1: 661), "Light-winged Smoke, Icarian bird" (before 4/43; LOA, 1: 663), "Fog" (4/11/43), and "On fields oer which the reaper's hand has passd" (8–9/43; LOA, 1: 660). "Music" probably was composed in the late summer of 1851, as part of a last small group of serious poems (LOA, 1: 664).

The selection of poems is representative of Thoreau's use of verse forms – he wrote about half of all of his poems in stanzas, usually quatrains, and about half in verse paragraphs – and they demonstrate his experimentation with both conventional poetic language and occasions and the situations and speech rhythms of everyday life. Because Thoreau was unsuccessful in achieving a satisfactory voice in poetry, all of his efforts seem more or less experimental: it is difficult to locate individual poems on a continuum of progress. In a general way, however, his poetry evolves in parallel with his journal descriptions, which move from the titled set-pieces of 1837, 1838, and 1839 – "Heroes," "Sphere Music," and "Alma Natura" – to more pointed comments on his reading and particularized observations of the people, places, and natural phenomena around him. "Guido's Aurora," which describes Guido Reni's fresco, a print of which Thoreau could have seen at Emerson's, is at one end of this spectrum, with its stylized descriptions of nature as mediated by another artist's vision ("prancing steeds," "curling waves," "slumbering sea"). Details in later poems show them to be grounded more firmly in Thoreau's direct experience – the sound of a cowbell in a copse where he picked flowers ("They who prepare . . ."), the stubble of harvested grain filling the October air ("On fields oer which . . ."), the protean forms of the river fog ("Fog").

These poems are representative, too, in that, as Thoreau writes in the second paragraph of *Walden*, "the I, or first person . . . [is] retained": more than three-quarters of his poems display the self-consciousness that helps to mark them as characteristically transcendentalist. The speaker's experience of inspiration or of another, higher state of being – the eternal, unchanging realm identified by the transcendentalists as the source of truth, goodness, and beauty, and considered by them to be immanent in and accessible to all, but more keenly present to the poet – is the subject of many of Thoreau's poems, and sound is often involved. In several of the LOA poems, sound is the immediate stimulus for this experience – the clangor of preparation in the kitchen, the ringing of a nearby steeple bell, the harmony of music. Receptivity is indicated by the willingness to listen – "if you hearken well" ("Rumors from an Æolian Harp") the spiritual kingdom indicated by the æolian harp will be revealed; to be blessed with inspiration, the poet gropes, "Listening behind me for my wit" ("Inspiration").

Inspiration as a concept is central to Thoreau's poetics, and "Inspiration" is central to the most significant group of interrelated poems that Thoreau composed, at Emerson's in the late summer and early fall of 1841. Thoreau had made the move to Emerson's an occasion to take stock of his literary accomplishments and to plan new projects. He reviewed his journal, which filled almost 1,000 pages and contained a number of his poems, and copied selections from it into new manuscript volumes. (Using an agricultural image that operates in several poems, including "I am a parcel of vain strivings tied" and "On fields oer which the reaper's hand has passd," Thoreau titled the first manuscript volume of selections "Gleanings – Or What Time Has Not Reaped Of My Journal"). He also planned what he described in his journal (September 4, 1841) as "a poem to be called Concord," an epic with a part for each important natural feature of the area, the village itself and its inhabitants, each time of day, and each season.

Writing to a friend several days later, Thoreau compared himself with the god of autumn, surrounded by the rustling leaves of paper that contain a new poetic composition. Inspired by what Emerson described to Fuller as "noble madness," Thoreau had begun his epic with five long poems about the act of creating poetry. These are "Inspiration," "Independence," "Cock-crowing," "The Soul's Season," and "The Fall of the Leaf" (texts for the latter four can be found in my "Thoreau's Watershed Season as a Poet," in *Studies in the American Renaissance 1990*, edited by Joel Myerson). Each of the first three poems deals with an aspect of the true poet's experience: the conditions under which the poet is inspired, the poet's spiritual freedom in a world of confining materiality, and the simple natural sounds that herald the onset of inspiration. "The Soul's Season" and "The Fall of the Leaf" link inspiration with autumn, implying a connection between artistic and seasonal maturity. Having completed these poems, Thoreau then arranged the rough drafts of stanzas from all of them to create the schema for a much longer poem that was designed to explore the relationship between the season of autumn and the poet's creative life.

He did not complete this project, however, and he published in full only "Independence," although several stanzas from "Inspiration" appear in *A Week*. At the moment of his greatest sustained work as a poet, he realized his own limits in the form and set these pieces aside. As early as August, he had expressed dissatisfaction with poets' inability to convey the essential wildness of nature: "The best poets, after all, exhibit only a tame and civil side of nature." Perhaps in August he still assumed that he could surpass the "best poets." By November, he had embarked on another new project – he was reading the poetry of earlier writers in order to make a selection for an anthology he was planning. Still dissatisfied with the limits of the genre, he could now compare what he had written at his most inspired with the classics of poetry in English and come to a clearer understanding of his own limits.

Thoreau continued to compose and publish verses during the next three years, but poetry figures less prominently in his journal and as a focus of his creative effort. His poetic ambitions must have been affected by the waning of Emerson's enthusiasm, which was evident in a journal entry of fall 1842. There, Emerson compares Thoreau's poems to a profusion of seashells spilled from boxes and crates; he indexed the passage as "H.D.T.s poetry; . . . mass a compensation for quality." His young poet full of promise had become a prolific writer of second-rate verse. After Emerson's early encouragement, this appraisal must have stung Thoreau, and may have been influential in what he described to Frank Sanborn as the destruction of "many of his early verses because Emerson criticised them." Sanborn suggests that many of these poems were extant in other versions and so survived, leading to speculation about what it was that Thoreau destroyed and when. Thoreau may have collected his poetry in a notebook or kept a gathering of leaves containing poems written out individually – Emerson's description suggests an accumulation of verses. This would help to explain the fact that poems are not included in the indexes Thoreau made to the journal volumes he filled from 1838 to 1844: his final versions were kept separate and perhaps indexed separately. And it would have been these final versions that he destroyed, individually or all at once.

Thoreau's move to Walden on July 4, 1845, marks the beginning of his apprenticeship in prose, which culminated four years later in *A Week*. He did not lose the labor he had put into poetry, however: he incorporated more than 60 poems into prose contexts, to intensify and dramatize his exposition and to give the prose depth, as does his quotation of the poetry of others. He reworked many of the poems that he used in *A Week*, often shaping them to interact with and gloss the prose. "Fog," which survives in four manuscript versions, is an example. The first version (LOA) is a series of loosely linked images, as casual and flowing as the fog itself. Lines and images drift in and out of later versions, but the one that appeared in *A Week* is crafted to serve a particular purpose. It functions as an apostrophe to the fog that is central to Thoreau's description of a foggy morning on the Merrimack River:

> Low-anchored cloud,
> Newfoundland air,
> Fountain-head and source of rivers,
> Dew cloth, dream drapery,
> And napkin spread by fays;
> Drifting meadow of the air,
> Where bloom the daisied banks and violets,
> And in whose fenny labyrinth
> The bittern booms and heron wades;
> Spirit of lakes and seas and rivers,
> Bear only perfumes and the scent
> Of healing herbs to just men's fields.

Of the few poems that Thoreau composed after 1850, the

most significant are a group of five that treat the theme of the duality of human existence and that describe a progression of responses to human limitations. "Music" concludes Thoreau's final arrangement of these five: the first four, in his order, are "Life," "The moon moves up her smooth and sheeny path," "I'm thankful that my life does not deceive," and "Manhood." These poems are not dated, but both textual and contextual evidence suggests that Thoreau wrote them in late summer 1851. The 23-year-old poet who expressed his youthful sense of fragility, uselessness, and despair in "I am a parcel of vain strivings tied" has given way in "Music" to a more experienced writer, author of one book and a number of essays, who is now accustomed to dealing with his limitations and has earned the circumscribed sense of hope with which the poem closes.

With the publication of *Walden*, Thoreau announced to the world that he had found his voice in prose: in *Walden* he finally fulfilled his plan for a "poem to be called Concord." The process by which he achieved this was complex and sometimes painful, much more rugged than Emerson's simplified version: "Finding he could write prose so well, . . . he soon gave up much verse-writing, in which he was not patient enough to make his lines smooth and flowing." In fact, Thoreau never lacked for patience, whether standing in a swamp studying the habits of the bullfrog or sitting at his desk revising *Walden* for the seventh time. But he did have a standard of perfection in writing, and he composed a couplet that pithily expresses his failure to meet that standard in his poetry: "My life has been the poem I would have writ, / But I could not both live and utter it" (LOA, 1: 662). He elaborates upon this observation in many places in his writing. In the journal entry for August 28, 1841, in which the observation first appeared, he preceded it with the sentence: "True verses are not counted on the poet's fingers – but on his heart strings." In *A Week*, he put it into another context:

> The true poem is not that which the public read. There is always a poem not printed on paper, coincident with the production of this, stereotyped in the poet's life. It is *what he has become through his work*. Not how is the idea expressed in stone, or on canvass or paper, is the question, but how far it has obtained form and expression in the life of the artist. His true work will not stand in any prince's gallery.
>
> My life has been the poem I would have writ,
> But I could not both live and utter it.

Thoreau worked all of his creative life to make his writing "a deed" as well as "the record of a deed." At first, he assumed that he would accomplish this complex goal in verse; gradually he turned away from verse, and in the light of his completed career, writing poems was less important as a product than as a discipline that prepared him to accomplish in prose the poet's task, as he described it in "Walking":

Where is the literature which gives expression to Nature? He would be a poet who could impress the winds and streams into his service, to speak for him; who nailed words to their primitive senses, as farmers drive down stakes in the spring, which the frost has heaved; who derived his words as often as he used them, – transplanted them to his page with earth adhering to their roots; whose words were so true and fresh and natural that they would appear to expand like the buds at the approach of spring, though they lay half smothered between two musty leaves in a library, – aye, to bloom and bear fruit there, after their kind, annually, for the faithful reader, in sympathy with surrounding Nature.

ELIZABETH HALL WITHERELL

Selected Works

Collected Poems of Henry D. Thoreau, enl. ed., edited by Carl Bode, Baltimore, Maryland: Johns Hopkins University Press, 1964

Further Reading

Buell, Lawrence, *The Environmental Imagination: Thoreau, Nature Writing, and the Formation of American Culture*, Cambridge, Massachusetts: Belknap, 1995

Cameron, Sharon, *Writing Nature: Henry Thoreau's Journal*, New York: Oxford University Press, 1985

Cavell, Stanley, *The Senses of* Walden, New York: Viking, 1972; rev. and enl. ed., San Francisco: North Point, 1981

Emerson, Ralph Waldo, *The Journals and Miscellaneous Notebooks of Ralph Waldo Emerson*, edited by William Gilman, Ralph H. Orth, et al., 16 vols., Cambridge, Massachusetts: Harvard University Press, 1960–1982

Harding, Walter, *The Days of Henry Thoreau*, New York, Knopf, 1965; enl. ed., Princeton, New Jersey: Princeton University Press, 1982

Myerson, Joel, ed., *The Cambridge Companion to Henry David Thoreau*, Cambridge: Cambridge University Press, 1995

Paul, Sherman, *The Shores of America: Thoreau's Inward Exploration*, Urbana: University of Illinois Press, 1958

Peck, H. Daniel, *Thoreau's Morning Work*, New Haven, Connecticut: Yale University Press, 1991

Richardson, Robert D., Jr., *Henry Thoreau: A Life of the Mind*, Berkeley: University of California Press, 1986

Sanborn, F. B., *The Life of Henry David Thoreau*, Boston: Houghton Mifflin, 1917

Sattelmeyer, Robert, *Thoreau's Reading: A Study in Intellectual History*, Princeton, New Jersey: Princeton University Press, 1988

Stowell, Richard, *A Thoreau Gazetteer*, edited by William L. Howarth, Princeton, New Jersey: Princeton University Press, 1970

Henry Timrod

(1828–1867)

Henry Timrod, the "laureate of the Confederacy," was the poetic oracle of the West's last feudal civilization. His death from tuberculosis and the effects of poverty shortly after the Confederate defeat fixed him in the mind of white southerners as a martyr to the lost cause; among northern cultural brokers he gained a reputation as a *poète maudit*, a talent unsupported by his native people, whose perverse commitments and unhealthy disposition contributed to his premature demise. Twentieth-century scholarship added two features to this portrait. Timrod was discovered to have been an ethical poet on the model of William Wordsworth, adducing spiritual truths inscribed in nature, and thus the southern antithesis of Edgar Allan **Poe**, "the aesthetician." Timrod was also found to have been a forceful critic, important in countering the lingering effects of neoclassicism represented quintessentially in the work of William John Grayson. Against neoclassicism's conception of poetry as a social instrument and a body of technique, Timrod advocated romanticism's conception of poetry as the means of cultural creation and legislation. There was an irony in Timrod's emergence as a champion of poetic romanticism, for he began his career as the most traditional of neoclassical poetasters, dispensing polite rhymes and verse compliments to young ladies. The mystery of Timrod's poetic vocation lies in its several transformations: from school wit in 1843 to polite neoclassicist in 1845, to "Aglaus" the minor nature poet in 1849, to "Henry Timrod" public poet in 1856, to national prophet of the Confederacy in 1861. What drove the restless self-transformations? What pattern of mutation and self-revelation emerges in the work?

Henry Timrod was born to William Henry and Thyrza Prince Timrod on December 8, 1828, the third of four children and the only male. His father, a bookbinder, was active in Charleston, South Carolina, civic affairs, presiding over an after-hours conversation circle in his shop, agitating against nullification (John Calhoun's doctrine that a state had the right to abrogate the federal union by withdrawing when other states violated the Constitutional covenant), and serving the interest of the city's German community ("Dimroth" was the original family name) in the German Friendly Society and the German Fusiliers. His mother, schooled in reading, writing, and keeping accounts by her Methodist father, was a capable woman. The family aspired to gentility. One expression of the family's ambitions was the effort to give Henry a gentleman's education. He learned rhetoric, history, logic, mathematics, ethics, and the ancient languages at Cotes Classical School in Charleston, perhaps the south's premier academy during the 1830s. His classmates included poet Paul Hamilton **Hayne** and Basil L. Gildersleeve, the Latinist. Cotes School did not nurture Timrod's love of belles lettres, however; the curriculum excluded contemporary English verse. Ancient epic, tragedy, and lyric monopolized study. Timrod imbibed his taste for English verse at home, where his father wrote and recited nature lyrics like those of Philip **Freneau** and neoclassical poems on affairs of state. A collection of some of these pieces was published in 1814 as *Poems, on Various Subjects*. William Henry was typical of genteel Charlestonians of the early nineteenth century in regarding letters as an adornment of polite character and a medium of promoting sociability. Writing was not seen as a priestly vocation, or even a profession. Local taste, as registered in the poetry columns of the city gazettes, ran to the sociable wits, Robert Burns, Lord Byron, and Thomas Moore, rather than to the ethical visionaries among the English romantics, Wordsworth, Samuel Taylor Coleridge, and Percy Bysshe Shelley.

Henry Timrod began writing verse as a student at Cotes. The surviving sample of his boyhood wit, "Not a Grin Was Seen," a sardonic meditation on the body of a dead tutor, suggests why belles lettres was discouraged there. The verses composed during Timrod's brief year and a half as an undergraduate at the University of Georgia (1845–46) display greater craft and a new subject, women. Certain of these verses were compliments intended for the autograph books of the young ladies of Athens. Others were more finished love lyrics. All were pieces marshaling a repertoire of petitions, arguments, wishes, and praises familiar to sociable poets since Edmund Waller introduced the polite manner into English poetry in the 1630s. The highest virtue in polite verse was polish – the elegance of poetic surface. The subjects, whether love, a lovely woman, or one's disappointments in wooing, served as pretexts for eloquent expression. When Timrod returned to Charleston in 1846, he forwarded the best of the lyrics to the poetry columns of the Charleston newspapers. There they were printed not because they exemplified certain emotions, but certain modes of expression. His craft was particularly apparent in his elastic meter. Contemporaries considered his language "chaste," that is, untroubled by exotic words or tortuous syntax. Yet compared to Thomas Moore, the paragon of the era's polished lyricists, Timrod's early verses seem awkward in their frequent positioning of the critical word in a line as the end rhyme:

> Now I know, cried I, delighted
>   By yon welcome sign,
> That she keeps the faith she plighted
>   And her heart's still mine.

The bulk of Timrod's production as a poetaster never saw print. It survives in scattered albums and the manuscript collection "Autographic Relics," which is owned by the Charleston Library Society.

Timrod became a poet in 1849. The circumstances attending his aesthetic self-renovation are difficult to reconstruct precisely. Sometime during 1848, Timrod ceased reading law with James L. Petigru, abandoning his aspirations to the bar. He formed an ambition to become a college lecturer in classics, a position for which neither his credentials nor his abilities qualified him. According to legend, he prepared a translation of Catullus (now lost, perhaps never completed) that would serve as his qualification for a collegiate post. The annotations on his Latin text of Catullus show that Timrod struggled to find a contemporary diction suited to the spirit of the original. This effort appears to have led him to study the works of the foremost living technician of English verse, Alfred, Lord Tennyson.

The encounter may have been traumatic. Timrod put aside his translation and abandoned the search for a lectureship. He hired himself out as a plantation tutor and began to publish his first verses under the name "Aglaus."

"Aglaus" first appeared in the pages of the *Southern Literary Messenger* in July 1849. Timrod took the cognomen from a minor Greek pastoral poet. "Aglaus" proclaimed himself to be the poet of the "lowly earth" who would disclose "truths as wide as nations, and as deep as love" by representing local landscapes. "Aglaus" would make of a southern rural and domestic circumstance a strength, for "humility is power" ("Sonnet: Poet! If on a lasting fame"). Yet only two of the poems composed between 1849 and 1854 managed the scope and passion for which "Aglaus" hoped in his explorations of nature, the hearth, and the human heart: "The Summer Bower" and "The Stream Is Flowing from the West." "The Summer Bower" rejected Wordsworth's doctrine of therapeutic nature. In this work, the poet, suffering from a nameless despondency, visits a favorite haven in the woods, hoping that the genius loci might overcome his discontent:

> Not a leaf
> Stirred with the whispering welcome which I sought,
> But in a close and humid atmosphere,
> Every fair plant and implicated bough
> Hung lax and lifeless.

Nature possesses no autonomous spirit that can overmaster the subjective dispositions of human beings: "For the pains, the fever, and the fret / Engendered of a weak, unquiet heart, / She hath no solace" (compare "Tintern Abbey": "the fretful stir / Unprofitable, and the fever of the world"). In this poem, one's subjectivity supplies the emotional content of experience. Consequently, dejection or any similar state of affective alienation cannot be overthrown. One reads in nature's "unreplying lineaments" only "rebukes" – imagined signs of rejection.

"The Stream Is Flowing from the West" reveals the muteness of natural objects when the poet attempts to employ them as vehicles of feeling. The eastward-flowing stream, despite its sunlit resplendency, cannot transmit the poet's love to a distant woman: "I leave no trace behind – / As little on the senseless stream / As on thy heart, or on thy mind." These poems on nature's resistance to the works of healing and of love showed "Aglaus" to be something other than a follower of Wordsworth. "Aglaus" viewed nature as neither an instrumentality nor a spiritual force; rather, it was that objective realm which registered the limits of a poet's subjective power.

During the 1850s, Timrod worked at a series of South Carolina estates as plantation tutor. Although unremunerative and often boring, this type of job had certain attractions – ample leisure time, proximity to nature, and off-seasons in Charleston. When in Charleston, Timrod met with the coterie that gathered around William Gilmore **Simms** at Russell's Bookshop. This company constituted the most important literary group in the south. The conversation ran to politics and letters, and the frequent arguments honed the critical faculties of the participants. Becoming a force in the debates at Russell's made Timrod something more than a fugitive presence in print; he became a major actor in literary affairs. His realization of his fully public status as a man of letters led him in 1856 to publish as "Henry Timrod" in the *Southern Literary Messen-*

ger. The creation of *Russell's Magazine* in 1857, a periodical produced by the bookshop coterie, gave Henry Timrod a home venue for his art.

Russell's Magazine aspired to a southern readership and invited submissions from the general public, yet it relied upon the bookshop coterie for much of its contents. Timrod regularly supplied poetry secure in the knowledge that the editor, his friend Hayne, would print it. Timrod exploited this security, publishing poem after poem that obsessively elaborated a personal myth of poetic vocation. A curious lapse of Timrod scholarship has been its inability to recognize this myth. The consequence of this failure has been the misrepresentation of Timrod as a poet of love and nature, a southern Wordsworth. He was none of these. Rather, he was a poet who identified poetic power with the sublimation of desire, and the task of poetry with supplanting by mythopoesis the natural world of growth and decay with a timeless realm of youthful glory. Timrod frequently presented his myth in the form of a dream. The myth's symbolic structure can be abstracted by procedures of formalist analysis.

The mythic dream: a young man suffers mental torment in a southern, sylvan landscape (as in "The Problem," "A Rhapsody of a Southern Winter Night," "To Whom," "Too Long, O Spirit of Storm," and "A Vision of Poesy"). He is approached by a girl of supernatural beauty ("A Rhapsody of a Southern Winter Night," "Praeceptor Amat," and "A Vision of Poesy"). One gives the other a flower ("On Pressing Some Flowers," "A Rhapsody of a Southern Winter Night," "The Messenger Rose," "Praeceptor Amat," "The Lily Confidante," "A Boquet," and "Dedication to Fairy"). The girl is revealed to be a supernal being – a fairy, an angel, or an ideal ("A Rhapsody of a Southern Winter Night," "Sonnet: At Last Beloved Nature," and "A Vision of Poesy"). The youth wishes to kiss the girl ("A Rhapsody of a Southern Winter Night," "To Whom," "To Thee," "Love's Logic," "A Trifle," and "A Vision of Poesy"). The supernal girl initiates the youth into love, hope, and joy ("Retirement" [LOA, 2: 202], "A Rhapsody of a Southern Winter Night," and "A Vision of Poesy"). This new sense of being is recognized as poetry ("A Rhapsody of a Southern Winter Night," "Dedication to Fairy," and "A Vision of Poesy"). Poetry makes an unseen glory appear in the world ("A Rhapsody on a Southern Winter Night" and "A Vision of Poesy").

The myth operates by a series of substitutions: poetry for kiss, kiss for flower, glorious nature for dejected nature, poet for youth, and fairy for girl. In most cases the mundane is supplanted by the supernal. "A Rhapsody of a Southern Winter Night" (1857) presents the symbolic argument most cogently. A youth suffers despondency while reading a book beneath an oak. His abjection is such that he lacks even the will to live manifested by "the humblest flower." He notices a tulip nearby:

> A little child,
> Most dear to me, looked through the fence and smiled
> A hint that I should pluck it for her sake.
> Ah, me! I trust I was not well awake –

In this indeterminate state the poet sees the child as a "pretty fay." The child's kiss disrupts an unfruitful mental dispute over the possibility of an epicurean existence of "sensuous rest."

The kiss gives the poet "a sense of joy so wild 't is almost pain." The sense of being loved transmutes the poet's sense of the earth and the heavens: "The heavens appear with added stars to-night, / And deeper depths, and more celestial height, / Than hath been reached except in dreams or death." The southern woods are transmuted into fairyland. The poem concludes with an invocation of the fairy host:

> Come, Fairy Shadows! or the morn is near,
> When to your sombre pine ye all must creep;
> Come, ye wild pilots of the darkness, ere
> My spirit sinks into the gulf of Sleep;
> Even now it circles round and round the deep –
> Appear! Appear!

The poet's task in the poems of 1856–59 is to cause a glory to appear in the world that is beyond nature's "fruitage and its green." The poet clothes creation "with a glory all unseen" ("A Vision of Poesy," 1859). The realm of fairy is thus constituted in the unseen glory that the poet makes appear. Poetry is the means by which fairy/glory comes to be seen. In "A Vision of Poesy," the fairy whose kiss transforms the dejected youth into the joyful poet is identified as "Poesy," the "angel of the earth." Her task is "to keep the world forever fresh and young." Against the transiency of the breeding, aging, and dying world, she projects a timeless image of youthful fullness and perfection – the flower in full bloom. For Timrod, the fairy's kiss takes the poet away from the world of common sexuality, where one meets, mates, begets, and dies. The poet must be a paragon of purity, with a "spirit cased / And mailed in a body clean and chaste." The sexual sublimations entailed in the fairy's kiss are symbolized in one of two ways in Timrod's poems: either the poet is presented as a youth "unto whom love was yet an innocent dream," or, more frequently, the poet is a young man who is kissed by a girl/fairy. The disparity of ages is correlated with the difference between mortality and immortality.

The psychological implications of Timrod's symbolism become interesting when one considers his "Praeceptor Amat," a long Browningesque character study. It tells of a tutor whose stiff manners disguise an infatuation with a young female student who brings a bouquet of flowers to class. A psychoanalytic critic might offer an explanation of the symbolism, indicating that the forbidden nature of Timrod's love for younger girls such as his student Felicia Robinson, and the social imperative to repress the desire to substitute the gift of flowers with the kiss, caused him to de-realize these counters in the guise of a spiritual covenant between the poet and the fairy. In the "Dedication Addressed to Fairy" that introduced *Poems* (1859), the one volume of verse collected during his lifetime, Timrod confesses the animating power of such causes:

> Do you recall – I know you do –
> A little gift once made to you –
> A simple basket filled with flowers,
> All favorites of our Southern bowers?
> . . . .
>   you could not then divine
> The promise in that gift of mine,
> In those bright blooms and odors sweet,
> I laid this volume at your feet.

> At yours, my child, who scarcely know
> How much to your dear self I owe, –
> Too young and innocent as yet
> To guess in what consists the debt.

> Therefore to you henceforth belong
> These Southern asphodels of song,
> Less my creations than your own,
> What praise they win is yours alone.

> For there no fancy finds a place
> But is an effluence of your grace; –
> And when my songs are sweetest, then,
> A Dream like you hath touched my pen.

Timrod here confesses that a gift of flowers turns into the gift of poetry and that a young girl's grace had motivated his dreaming. In a lyric entitled "Dreams" (LOA, 2: 201) Timrod says,

>   dreams in sooth,
> Come they in shape of demons, gods, or elves,
> Are allegories with deep hearts of truth
>   That tell us solemn secrets of ourselves.

The solemn secret that Timrod allegorizes is how the emotional force of his own unnatural susceptibility to girlish beauty is redirected into the creation of a poetry whose power strives to annihilate time and age, arresting the world in timeless youthful glory.

Timrod understood that his myth of poetic vocation was more than merely a figuration of his desire. Its symbolism drew upon archetypes traditionally employed in non-Christian western poetry to explain how a young man becomes wedded to inspiration. There were several specific antecedents for Timrod's symbolism. The dejected man in nature haunted the verse worlds of Shelley and Coleridge. The flower gift drew on a tradition dating back to Rufinus, the Roman lyricist. The supernal girl was a refraction of the Muse. The realm of fairy was that place beyond life and death where Poe communed with his departed lover. The transforming kiss was the central image of the Cavalier poets. The poet who speaks the unseen glory into being was a more modern version of Amphion. Timrod's myth resonated with elements of the western myth that spoke about how certain men redirect their sexual energies from procreation to poetry. Against this background, the distinctive features of Timrod's dream stand out, such as the disparities of age, knowledge, and condition between the fairy/angel and the poet; the effects of the poet's initiation into joy are registered in the renovation of southern nature, rather than the world at large, or society.

Timrod was sufficiently honest to confront the psychic costs of sublimating his desire for sexual transgression into a poetic *conjunctio oppositorum*. In his longest and most troubled composition, "A Vision of Poesy," Timrod supplied an epilogue to his myth. Prematurely aged, the poet lies dying. His morbid self-involvement has disgusted the woman he loves, vitiated his poetic powers, and caused the world to reject him. The angel of the earth, "Poesy," diagnoses the poet's failing: "It was thy own peculiar difference / That thou did'st seek; nor did'st thou care to find / Aught that would bring thee nearer to thy kind."

Poesy offers little consolation, and that little derives from daring to expose "truths that for man might else have slumbered long." These truths, one gathers, concern the perverse power of human subjectivity. Poesy confesses her hand in the distortion of the poet: "I chide, / Perchance, myself within thee, and the fate / To which thy power was solely consecrate." Because of the poet's perverse devotion to the angel, she claims him in the end for a life beyond death. Nevertheless, the effect of the poem is odd. The damaged poet dies with Poesy's faint praise lingering in his ears, as well as the sound of her ringing endorsement of another sort of poet, one who "would represent his race and speak for all." The dying poet's "truth" runs a distant third to Shelleyan power and Wordsworthian sympathy in the sweepstakes of immortality. Poesy declares,

> As that same law that moulds a plant, rounds
>   A drop of dew, so the great Poet spheres
> Worlds in himself; no selfish limit bounds
>   A sympathy that folds all characters,
> All ranks, all passions, and all life almost
>   In its wide circle.

Critics from Hayne onward have regarded "A Vision of Poesy" as an unsuccessful piece because of its interruptions and cross-purposes. They have worried about its domination of *Poems*, yet if one reads that volume as a work promulgating a myth of poetic vocation, "A Vision of Poesy" is the most necessary piece, for it is the poem that dramatizes the exhaustion of Timrod's narrative. With the death of the poet, the story of subjective compulsion ended for Timrod. He was freed to become the speaker for "his race." This resolution alone indicates why the dreamer of the flower, the kiss, and the fairy became the oracle of Confederate "Ethnogenesis."

Timrod's metamorphosis into a powerful civic poet was sudden and unexpected. Prior to writing "Ethnogenesis" (LOA, 2: 203) in February 1861, he had composed two verses on public occasions: "Hymn Sung at the Consecration of Magnolia Cemetary [sic], Charleston, S. C." (1851) and "Song Composed for Washington's Birthday, and Respectfully Inscribed to the Officers and Members of the Washington Light Infantry of Charleston, February, 1859." Both suffered from banal sentiment. Magnolia Cemetary was lauded for beautifying Death's "mansion." Washington's birthday was celebrated because "we are a mighty nation now / Because that child was born." When other poets north and south in 1859 were questioning how mighty the nation was, Timrod could blithely mouth a thoughtless phrase.

Politically, Timrod was not disposed toward southern secession. He had grown up in an anti-nullification household. The Russell's Bookshop circle, although greatly concerned with the cultural distinctiveness of the south, was no cabal of fire-eating secessionists. Timrod's southern identity was largely manifested in a sense of belonging to a southern landscape. The glades, trees, breezes, and flowers that inhabited Timrod's dream were southern. Even in "Ethnogenesis," the birth of confederate national identity is envisioned through natural imagery: a star is added to the firmament, the land is blessed with preeminent fruitfulness by the sun, and the nation is secured and comforted by countrysides of wheat and cotton. Yet there is no mistaking that Timrod presents a new myth here and projects a new speaker. "We" is the superintending pronoun of the poem, not

"I." Timrod has ceased being the poet of subjective truth, becoming instead the representative voice of his race, the race of white southerners.

"Ethnogenesis" was written during the meeting of the first southern congress in Montgomery, Alabama. Although intended for broadside publication, its fame was established by a private reading before an elite circle of southern leaders in Charleston. The hearers awarded Timrod a purse of gold for his efforts. A Pindaric ode, the poem has four sections, each presenting a discrete argument: section I describes nature's validation of southern distinction; section II offers apocalyptic assurance that the south will prevail in any battle with northerners, for the latter are allies of Satan, and the southerners possess the advantage of defending their own homes on familiar territory; section III provides a biblical sanction for the southern system and asserts judgment against the northern wage economy; and section IV projects the future prosperity of the southern nation, envisioning its benefit to the world. The poem was ingenious in a number of ways. It replied to the northern barrage of civic apocalyptic epitomized by "The Battle-Hymn of the Republic" (LOA, 1: 709) with a southern revelation that pointedly asked what righteousness attached to an economic system that left "the neighboring poor / To starve and shiver at the schemer's door." Furthermore, Timrod doubted the biblical faith of a region that had embraced "vague philosophies" such as Unitarianism and transcendentalism. Both points were well-taken: the former distilled the economic critiques of the northern system of Grayson and Trescott, the latter reiterated Simms's cultural critique of the north.

In retrospect, the oddest feature of "Ethnogenesis" was its confidence that cotton's economic power was such that the north would not risk war. Timrod's faith in cotton's power found its fullest expression in the second of his national odes, "The Cotton Boll" (LOA, 2: 206). Timrod's poem was the penultimate work in the central tradition of southern civic poetry, projecting the meaning of southern civilization in terms of the global effects of the staples it produced. Charles Woodmason's "Indico" (1758), James Grainger's *The Sugar Cane* (1764), and George Ogilvie's rice georgic *Carolina; or, The Planter* (1776) founded the tradition; Sidney **Lanier's** "The Waving of the Corn" (LOA, 2: 419) completed and overturned it. Timrod abided by the conventions of the genre, projecting cotton's power on a global scale, as an impetus of trade. Cotton's "mighty commerce"

> Goes out to every shore
> Of this broad earth, and throngs the sea with ships
> That bear no thunders; hushes hungry lips
>   In alien lands;
> Joins with a delicate web remotest strands;
> And gladdening rich and poor,
>   Doth gild Parisian domes,
> Or feed the cottage-smoke of English homes,
> And only bounds its blessings by mankind!

Alluding to the old mercantilist doctrine that commerce nurtures the "arts of peace," Timrod implied that northern malice, not cotton, was responsible for the bloodshed of the war.

One feature intrinsic to the staple-poem genre is missing in "The Cotton Boll," a consideration of the circumstances of the African American slave. Slaves appear only parenthetically in the ode, at the beginning of the verse in which the poet first examines the boll: "Small sphere! / (By dusky fingers brought this morning here / And shown with boastful smiles)." Here, marginalized and reduced by synecdoche, slaves nevertheless are present; they are invisible in the remainder of Timrod's poems. In "Ethnogenesis," their condition must be inferred to be the opposite of the poverty and exploitation of northern wage laborers. Nothing is said explicitly. There are none of the rosy representations of the conditions of slaves found in the ample proslavery polemic literature. For Timrod, the slave was a being inimical to poetry. In "The Cotton Boll," only beneficial whiteness and sanguinary redness can be discerned clearly.

The war for Timrod had little to do with slavery, and everything to do with the north's violation of the constitutional covenant and its subsequent aggression against southern lands. Timrod's war poetry, consequently, featured two moods: a righteous, patriotic fervor, found in poems such as "A Cry to Arms," "Carolina" (LOA, 2: 212), "Ripley," and "Address Delivered at the Opening of the New Theatre at Richmond," and anxiety at the effects of the northern war effort, seen in works like "Sonnet: I Know Not Why" (LOA, 2: 206), "Charleston" (LOA, 2: 215), "Christmas" (LOA, 2: 216), "Spring," and "The Unknown Dead." The latter series of poems has monopolized the attention of historians and critics. "Sonnet: I Know Not Why" and "Charleston" are poems dominated by a mood of uncertainty. In both, Timrod senses danger and the possibility of terror beneath the placid surface of Carolina locales. In the sonnet, the tidal marsh rustles "like whispers round the body of the dead!" Images of war and destruction impinge on places where the war has not yet touched. (Timrod had viewed the horrors of battle firsthand the previous summer when, as a reporter for the *Charleston Mercury*, he attached himself to the Confederate army during the retreat from Shiloh.) In "Charleston," the old city waits patiently for a violence whose incipience is registered in a host of subliminal signs. The visible landscape is not so meaningful as the invisible one that persons carry in their thoughts as they walk the city:

> And down the dunes a thousand guns lie couched,
>   Unseen, beside the flood –
> Like tigers in some Orient jungle crouched
>   That wait and watch for blood.

The poet surveys the city on a calm, warm day in November 1862, thinking how the coming winter would probably mark the decisive campaign against the city. Whether Charleston will survive unscathed until spring is uncertain. Despite the general preparedness of the population for battle, the poet feels trepidation concerning the outcome. "We know not; in the temple of the Fates / God has inscribed her doom." Gone is the certitude of divine sanction found in the national odes. Unspoken yet tacit in the poet's understanding is the knowledge that the city had fallen to the enemy in a previous war – the greatest disaster to befall the patriot cause in the American Revolution. Timrod asserts that the city waits "untroubled in her faith" biding "the triumph or the tomb." Yet the anxiety pervading the lines belies the poet's assertion of untroubled faith.

"Christmas," the finest of the war poems and the lyric that prompted Tennyson to proclaim Timrod the laureate of the Confederacy, was written and published a month after "Charleston." Like the other lyrics of anxiety, "Christmas" tells how the invisible horror of the war impinges and disrupts the visible world. Christmas in the first half of the poem is more an old English festival than a celebration of the Savior's birth. It is the time of "feast, and song, and dance, and antique sports, / And shout of happy children in the courts, / And tales of ghost and fay." Yet treating the holiday in such a manner might call up a more dreadful specter than those in ancient tales:

> Would not some pallid face
> Look in upon the banquet, calling up
> Dread shapes of battle in the wassail cup,
>   And trouble all the place?
>
> How could we bear the mirth,
> While some loved reveller of a year ago
> Keeps his mute Christmas now beneath the snow,
>   In cold Virginian earth?

To exorcise the spirit of the dead, the revel must cease, and the holiday be devoted to prayers addressed to the Prince of Peace. The final half of the poem consists in a prayerful meditation on peace, imagining it as a presence universally quieting the southern landscape:

> Peace in the quiet dales,
> Made rankly fertile by the blood of men;
> Peace in the woodland, and the lonely glen,
>   Peace in the peopled vales!

In the end, even the hearts of Timrod's readers are pacified.

"Spring" marks the end of winter of trepidation. The Confederacy and Charleston still stand intact. The Carolina countryside reenacts the process of regeneration. Yet the glories of nature cannot lay to rest the human sense of anxiety. The language of vernal rhapsody dissipates as the poet attends to "thoughts of war and crime":

> Yet not more surely shall the Spring awake
> The voice of wood and brake
> Then she shall rouse, for all her tranquil charms,
> A million men to arms.

Instead of the harbinger of life, Spring becomes the clarion of death, tempting a new cohort of recruits into peril with "her tranquil charms." It is, of course, humankind that thus inverts the meaning of the natural order. The lyric concludes with Spring holding up to God "her bloody daisies,"

> And calling with the voice of all her rills
> Upon the ancient hills,
> To fall and crush the tyrants and the slaves
> Who turn her meads to graves.

Spring petitions the God of nature to visit universal retribution upon those who spilled blood upon the earth. This apocalyptic wish invokes a total and universal judgment upon "tyrants and slaves" who wage war; no longer does Timrod envision a southern millennium of peace and prosperity.

From August 1863 until the end of the war, Timrod worked as a newspaperman, first as assistant editor of the *Mercury*, then, in January 1864, as associate editor of the Columbia *South Carolinian*. His absorption in the work of reportage and editorial writing drew him away from poetry. His marriage to Katie Goodwin in February 1864 settled somewhat his volatile emotional life, although the marriage did not prove completely felicitous. The birth of a son, Willie Timrod, on Christmas Eve, 1864, marked a solitary respite in what would be an almost unending series of travails troubling the poet's final years. The southern defeat and the collapse of its economy spelled the financial doom of the newspaper. Attempts at opening a school failed. In October 1865, the couple's infant son died. (The death inspired the most heartfelt of the small group of poems that Timrod composed in 1866, "Our Willie.") Attempts to earn money by placing poems with northern periodicals were frustrated. When a regular position with a Columbia newspaper became available in 1867, Timrod's tuberculosis had become so far advanced that he could not perform his duties. He died on October 7, 1867, abandoning agnosticism and embracing Christianity in his final illness.

Timrod was distinguished among American poets of the nineteenth century for the will to power manifested in his self-transformations. During the 20 years of his career as a poet, he repeatedly remade himself, seeking greater visionary power, capturing more difficult truths. He was at times a neoclassical poetaster, a minor pastoralist, a mythographer of poetic vocation, and a public oracle of a failed nation. In each role, his quest for poetic power had an atavistic direction. He tried to discover the power in old forms (the sonnet and the Pindaric ode particularly fascinated him), old realms of poetry (fairyland, the haunted wood, and the pastoral countryside), and old myths (the commission of the Muse and the glamour of a mortal by the fairy). Although a newspaperman, city dweller, and teacher, his poetry did not register the nineteenth-century world as Walt **Whitman's** did. Indeed, there is a sense in which Timrod's poems, even at their most political, spoke at a distance from the market, the factory, and the street. The commodity of cotton, as celebrated by Timrod, circulated through the world of trade with a sublime lubricity, unsullied by cash exchange. The slaves whose backs supported the south's agricultural civilization were all but invisible in Timrod's landscapes. Yet for all of Timrod's atavisms, myopias, and restrictions, the poetry of the 1850s and 1860s possesses an intensity, a disquiet that remains in memory. Haunted by the supernal girl or the spirit of the slaughtered youth, the poems document a southern world in which the relations between visible and invisible, man and woman, peace and war, and living and dead have fallen into crisis.

DAVID S. SHIELDS

Selected Works

Poems, Boston: Ticknor and Fields, 1859

The Poems of Henry Timrod, with a Sketch of the Poet's Life, edited by Paul Hamilton Hayne, New York: E. J. Hale, 1872

Poems of Henry Timrod: Memorial Edition, edited by W. A. Courtenay, introduction by John Pendleton Kennedy Bryan, Boston: Houghton Mifflin, 1899

The Uncollected Poems of Henry Timrod, edited by Guy Cardwell Jr., Athens: University of Georgia Press, 1942

The Essays of Henry Timrod, edited by Edd Winfield Parks, Athens: University of Georgia Press, 1942

The Collected Poems of Henry Timrod: A Variorum Edition, edited by Edd Winfield Parks and Aileen Wells Parks, Athens: University of Georgia Press, 1965

Further Reading

Hubbell, Jay B., *The Last Years of Henry Timrod, 1864–1867*, Durham, North Carolina: Duke University Press, 1941

Parks, Edd Winfield, *Henry Timrod*, New York: Twayne, 1964

Rubin, Louis D., Jr., *The Edge of the Swamp: A Study of the Literature of the Old South*, Baton Rouge: Louisiana State University Press, 1989

Frederick Ridgely Torrence

(1874–1950)

In November 1899, Small, Maynard and Company published *The House of a Hundred Lights*, Ridgely Torrence's first book of poetry. This volume, consisting of 100 quatrains, is very much a product of its time. Late-Victorian poetry, especially that of Algernon Swinburne and Oscar Wilde, emphasized hedonism and exoticism, for it was partly inspired by the success of Edward FitzGerald's translation of *The Rubáiyát of Omar Khayyám*. Torrence was seeking the same kind of success that FitzGerald had, and he began translating the writing of Bidpai, a third-century Indian whom he had read in a Persian translation. Like FitzGerald's *Rubáiyát*, Torrence's work was modernized for a contemporary audience, and it eventually became more Torrence than Bidpai.

Originally, the editors of Small, Maynard had rejected Torrence's manuscript, but this rejection became fortuitous for the young poet. Torrence decided to seek the opinion of a leading poet of his day, Edmund Clarence **Stedman**, who helped Torrence revise his work. Since most of the earlier work had been Torrence's anyway, he and Stedman dropped the claim that it was a translation. They also excised 20 verses and rearranged others; with Stedman's influence, the publisher accepted the collection. Also under the auspices of Stedman, to whom he dedicated the volume, Torrence met many other poets, including the then little-known Edwin Arlington **Robinson**, who became a close friend.

The House of a Hundred Lights is not Torrence's best work, but it brought him his first real recognition, recognition that he earnestly desired. Born on November 27, 1874, in Xenia, Ohio, Torrence was the oldest child of Findley David Torrence, a lumber dealer, and Mary Ridgely Torrence, and the grandson of John Torrence, who had helped found both Lexington, Kentucky, and Xenia. After a fairly conventional midwestern childhood (with two years spent in California), Torrence enrolled in Miami (Ohio) University in the fall of 1893. Two years later he transferred to Princeton University, but an illness prevented his return in 1896, and he eventually withdrew. Ridgely moved to New York City, determined to become a success and, after his unfortunate college experience, to win his parents' approval. His first jobs were in libraries, and it was from the head of the Oriental collection at the Astor that Torrence learned Persian. Before *The House of a Hundred Lights*, Torrence had published only six poems: five in college literary magazines and the sixth, "Astarte," in the *New England Magazine*. His father, disapproving of his son's literary aspirations, collected Torrence's early poems to use as evidence of his son's mental instability.

Although *The House of a Hundred Lights* is somewhat derivative, it received mostly positive reviews. One reviewer in *The Critic* stated that "it will be time to read it when you know Omar by heart." Others praised Torrence for the promise that he showed, and the New York *Tribune* asserted that his book had "the caustic cynicism, mingled with gallant faith and resignation" of both eastern and modern western poetry, as well as "a certain spirit of youth and courage, with a certain grace of form." W. N. Guthrie, in the *Sewanee Review*, wrote that

"Ohio is to be congratulated on this first good American epigrammatist."

It is this epigrammatic quality that prevents *The House of a Hundred Lights* from being a cohesive work. As Jessie B. Rittenhouse says in her essay on Torrence in *The Younger American Poets*, many of the quatrains could be moved without any apparent damage. The lack of cohesion occurs partly because of the obscurity of the speaker's identity. At first, an older sage seems to be advising a youth, because in the third verse "the Thinker" says, ironically, "'Doubt everything . . . have utter faith in me, – and doubt!'" The advice continues, and the speaker refers to his maiden daughter; then, in verse 51, apparently another speaker says:

> I did not hate the orator
> of many words for what he said:
> I only thought it just some old
> quaint game his tongue played with his head.

Having a comment by the youth at the midpoint of the poem shows that Torrence (with Stedman's help) had attempted some organization and coherence. It also suggests that the youth is unreceptive to the advice that he has been receiving. Yet many of the later quatrains focus on humanity's fate, a topic that seems incompatible with a youthful speaker. And there are other quatrains emphasizing egotism and irresponsibility that appear to be spoken by a youth. The alternating of these topics, along with subsequent shifts in tone, causes confusion about who is speaking, perhaps partly because Torrence was attempting to write with the wisdom of old age when he was only 25 and had not yet gained a broad outlook on life.

At the same time, the difference in the perspectives asociated with age and youth is the main theme of the work. The old know that life scars a person, while youths impetuously seek the fulfillment of desire. One form of desire is love, which the speaker begins discussing in verse 11. The next five verses tell the story of the maiden who beckons her lover to come while her parents sleep. The love of these two appears to be strong ("God gave them Youth, God gave them Love, / and even God can give no more"), but Torrence has already dismissed love as a source of happiness: "'Beware of Love; / behold, its end is Ash and Rue!'" This warning overshadows any happiness the young lovers may find. The speaker's pessimism continues as he describes women's vanity and the strength of their lies, concluding by equating love and death, which thus destroys any promise of happiness:

> The night passed and some youths caroused
> and some poor Fakir kept his fast:
> Some lovers kissed, some graves were dug,
> all the same night, and the night – passed.

Although the speaker appears to be wise, he also discusses the impossibility of gaining wisdom. As a youth, the speaker's "head was hollow, like / a gourd"; now he is "like / a reed, – wind-shaken – hollow still." He has not stored up any wisdom over the years, unless it is the realization that gleaning solace from life is impossible. Although the young attempt to live a carefree life, the speaker knows that life brings pain; trying to avoid it is like trying to "tilt up the sky / and yet . . . not to spill the stars" – one impossible task contingent on another. There are only two comforts in life, friendship and religion, which are combined in one of the most sentimental verses:

I give God praise because of right,
    and fear, for terrors that He sends;
But more than all, I give Him love
    because He gave to me – my friends.

Torrence argues that wealth cannot bring happiness either. No matter what one's station in life, death is the great leveler:

The same small windows light all lives
    whether they be of rich or poor:
A sigh, a laugh, some wine, a sleep,
    a tear, and then – the open door.

According to Torrence, even poets cannot gain immortality. What begins as a celebration of the poet's mounting "the Skies of Poesy" on the day of the vernal equinox quickly concludes that poetry has no effect on others. If a poet believes that his work will live forever, "Bethink thee, friend, what fine springs rise / impotently from the sea's bed." Even the first verse has an image of human insignificance and transience:

On the pond's face, the pelting rain
    made bubbles, and they broke again,
And reappeared and disappeared
    and, ah! I knew them – they were men.

The strength of *The House of a Hundred Lights* is Torrence's imagery; however, this strength is often undermined by the organization of the quatrains. For example, a verse comparing a woman's eyebrow to the new moon ("Night is a woman vaguely veiled") is inconsistently followed by one beginning, "I know a Thief who longs to steal / from the moon's granary on high." Ultimately, this lack of continuity and the work's epigrammatic quality both keep *The House of a Hundred Lights* from being a great accomplishment. With so many unconnected quatrains, Torrence cannot expand on his ideas. The verses tend toward flippancy and youthful coyness.

Only gradually would Torrence forsake this style of poetry, which was prevalent in the 1890s, and learn to write from more personal experiences. First, he tried his hand at verse drama, again influenced by other poets such as his friends William Vaughn **Moody** and Josephine Preston Peabody. These poets' dramas harkened back to the Elizabethan period rather than attempting to create a new kind of verse for modern America. Only Moody's effort in this vein was successful, with *The Masque of Judgment* (1900). Torrence's first attempt, *El Dorado*, a romantic drama of unrequited love set during a search for the legendary lost gold, was not published until August 1903, after numerous rejections. The critical reception was mixed, with *El Dorado* receiving praise for its poetry, but censure for its dramatic quality. Torrence's other foray into verse drama was *Abelard and Heloise* (1907), a medieval romance about the priest's struggle between his love for Heloise and his devotion to God. This second effort received greater acclaim than *El Dorado*, but neither verse drama was ever produced. With

both, Torrence was hampered by writing on subjects alien to his experience.

Torrence next turned to prose drama, a turn again influenced by Moody, who had achieved success with *The Great Divide* (1906). Torrence wrote two dramas in 1907, "The Madstone" and "The Thunder Pool," neither of which was published. Both use folklore from his native Ohio and deal with strong women who break with established social mores. The "madstone" of legend, when placed on a sick person, would draw out the infection and fall off: Torrence's madstone is Lestra Doane, who absorbs her husband's moral degeneracy but eventually leaves him because of this unhealthy relationship. The weakness of the play, as well as that of "The Thunder Pool," is that Torrence's explicit symbolism leaves nothing to the imagination.

Torrence's greatest success in drama, and his most important contribution to literature, would not come until 1917, when his *Plays for a Negro Theater* were published and produced. Before the performance – at New York's Garden Theatre on April 5, 1917 – of *Granny Maumee*, *The Rider of Dreams*, and *Simon the Cyrenian*, African Americans were portrayed as stereotypes on the stage, particularly in vaudeville, whereas Torrence's representations were grounded in hometown experiences. Having been a stop on the Underground Railroad, and with Wilberforce College nearby, Xenia had a sizable African American population, and Torrence himself had had African American friends as a boy. However, Torrence's inspiration may have been the success of Irish folk drama, which once again shows his reliance on other literary achievements.

In all three plays, Torrence suggests a revolt against African Americans' station in life. Granny Maumee, who practices voodoo, plots to kill the white man who sired a baby with her great-granddaughter, thus fouling the family's pure racial line. Furthermore, this man's grandfather had killed her son, Sam. In the second play, Madison, the "rider of dreams," in an attempt to become as rich as white folk, almost loses his wife's savings. In the last play, Simon the Cyrenian, Christ's crossbearer, could, and almost does, choose to lead the African slaves to riot against their Roman oppressors. In all three plays, however, these black characters return to their position within the supposedly "natural" order. Granny Maumee obeys her son's spirit, who tells her to "fuhgives uthehs," and then dies; Madison agrees to work as a music instructor after his landlord retrieves his wife's money; and Simon follows Christ's injunctions, choosing spiritual over temporal greatness. This last play may be Torrence's most important, because it suggests that black suffering will lead to a greater reward in the life to come. Despite the conservative resolution of these three plays, they set a precedent – along with works by Eugene O'Neill and Paul Green – for African Americans to perform serious drama.

Although Torrence made these forays into drama, he continued to write poetry throughout his life; however, he was to have only two more volumes. *Hesperides*, a collection of 20 poems, most of which had been previously published in magazines, appeared in 1925, while *Poems*, which had 34 poems, including all of those in *Hesperides*, appeared in 1941. This low output has led critics like Louis Untermeyer to question such a lack of achievement from the promising poet of 40 years before (*Saturday Review of Literature* 24 [1941]). In Torrence's defense, he also held editorial positions: first at *The Critic* (1903–1905) and then at *Cosmopolitan* for two years after that. His most important editorial post, however, was as poetry editor for *The New Republic* (1920–1933). He may have contributed more to poetry by supporting other poets and discovering new talent than by writing poetry himself. One poet he supported was Robert Frost, whom he first met in 1919 and who dedicated "A Passing Glimpse" to him.

Several of Torrence's other poems merit discussion. "The Lesser Children," first published in the *Atlantic* (September 1905), concerns man's exploitation of the natural world, in this case the slaughter of birds, the "lesser children." John Clum points out that for the first time here, Torrence stresses his subject over his style, but two aspects of style that contribute to the poem's success are his imagery and his irregular rhyme scheme. For example, when advising the birds to flee, he writes:

> Gather your broods about you and depart,
> Before the stony forward-pressing faces
> Into the lands bereft of any sound;
> The solemn and compassionate desert places.
> Give unto men no more the strong delight
> To know that underneath the frozen ground
> Dwells the warm life and all the quick, pure lore.
> Take from our eyes the glory of great flight.

Torrence's image of men as "stony forward-pressing faces" combines with his view that men hunt because of "ancestral urges out of old caves." His use of irregular rhyme, which can easily go unnoticed because of the many enjambed lines, contributes to the poem's continuity. Still, as first published, "The Lesser Children" is, according to Robinson, "a bit vague." Torrence's poems were often seen as obscure, but by the time he published *Poems*, he had revised and condensed this poem into a much more effective work.

The poem that Clum calls Torrence's first modern poem, "Three O'Clock (Morning)" (*Scribner's*, December 1908), is composed of three octaves and contains striking images of the desolation of life. Those people who are still out in early morning are "A whitened few [who] wane out like moons, / Ghastly, from some torn edge of shade." Torrence concludes that the years of our lives can pass by unnoticed: "The lights go out in red and gold, / But time goes out and gray." The grayness shows the lack of accomplishments that color life.

Two other important poems are "The Bird and the Tree" and "The Son." "The Bird and the Tree" involves an African American man, the "blackbird," who is about to be lynched by the Ku Klux Klan. Torrence successfully builds tension for the victim ("The minutes crawl by like last year's flies") and then gives a strong indictment of the Klan's prejudice and cowardice:

> Perhaps you'll meet again some place.
> Look for the mask upon the face:
> That's the way you'll know them there –
> A white mask to hide the face:

And you can halt and show them there
The things that they are deaf to now . . .

Not coincidentally, this poem appeared in 1915, during the same period that Torrence was working on his dramas of African American experience.

"The Son," a poem of 16 short lines, has a farm wife speak about the death of her son, whose loss has placed a greater burden on his aging parents. Not only did they have to harvest the crops alone, but they also may be nearing the end of their lives: "'The crop's all in, / We're about through now.'" Interestingly, Frost published "'Out, Out – ,'" a superior poem on a similar subject, only five months later. He may have been influenced by this poem; in fact, George Monteiro suggests that many of Frost's themes can be traced to "The Lesser Children" (*South Carolina Review* 15 [1982]).

Of the other poems that helped to establish Torrence's reputation, "Evensong," "Eye-Witness," and "The Singers in a Cloud" have been the most anthologized. All of these appear in *Hesperides* and *Poems*. After *Hesperides*, Torrence's production declined; he was not to publish another poem until "Outline" appeared in 1936. Most of the later poems deal with the coming of World War II and the wasteful deaths of the young men who fought in it. The final quatrain of "Men and Wheat" sums up Torrence's feelings about this war:

> The sheaves of men lie flat
> And are buried where they bleed.
> But what dread food is that?
> And what mouths does it feed?

Ridgely Torrence died on Christmas Day, 1950, in New York City. A revised edition of *Poems*, including two additional poems, was published in 1952. Although Torrence achieved only minor success, his work as a poetry editor, especially his encouragement of younger poets, deserves praise. At the same time, his poetry influenced others like Frost who achieved the greatness that he did not. Thus, Torrence can be seen as a secondary figure – in the best sense of the term – in the realm of American literature.

JOHN SAMONDS

Selected Works

The House of a Hundred Lights, Boston: Small, Maynard, 1900
El Dorado: A Tragedy, New York: John Lane, 1903
Abelard and Heloise, New York: Scribner's, 1907
Granny Maumee, The Rider of Dreams, Simon the Cyrenian: Plays for a Negro Theater, New York: Macmillan, 1917
Hesperides, New York: Macmillan, 1925
Poems, New York: Macmillan, 1941; enl., 1952

Further Reading

Clum, John M., *Ridgely Torrence*, New York: Twayne, 1972
Rittenhouse, Jessie B., *The Younger American Poets*, Boston: Little, Brown, 1904

John Townsend Trowbridge

(1827–1916)

Fully invested in the literary circles of his time, Trowbridge was both a prolific and a popular writer. He wrote short stories, children's stories, novels, and poetry, as well as numerous essays and reviews. Born in Ogden, New York, on September 18, 1827, Trowbridge published his first poems when he was 16; his first novel (*Father Brighthopes*) came 10 years later in 1853. In between, he lived in New York City and later Boston, Massachusetts. He also began publishing short stories and essays during this time, and in Boston he was editor for the *Yankee Nation* and then the *Boston Sentinel*. Trowbridge received widespread recognition for his antislavery novel *Neighbor Jackwood* (1857) and successfully adapted it to the stage in the same year. Also in 1857, he contributed the story "Pendlam: A Modern Reformer" to the first issue of the *Atlantic Monthly*. He was the youngest of the contributors.

Trowbridge's first wife, Cornelia Warren, died in 1864, after only four years of marriage. He moved with his two children to Arlington, Massachusetts, in 1865. After the popularity of *Neighbor Jackwood,* he was regularly asked to read his work in public. He was also commissioned to travel through the south after the Civil War, and he compiled his observations in *The South: A Tour of Its Battlefields and Ruined Cities* (1866). In 1865, Trowbridge became an editor of the new children's magazine *Our Young Folks*, and in 1870, he became the managing editor. He left the magazine when it was sold in 1873, and that same year he married Sarah Adelaide Newton, with whom he had three more children.

The critical reception of Trowbridge's writing was warm but seldom enthusiastic. A story here (e.g., "Coupon Bonds") and a poem there (e.g., "The Vagabonds") found hearty praise, but most of the praise received was accompanied by criticism. One article (1874) that found Trowbridge "a genius . . . thoroughly plastic and sympathetic" also noted that aside from a few "poems the best of their kind that have been produced in a long while," his "collected poems lack a sufficiently distinct flavor of their own." In 1890, William Dean **Howells** wrote in *Harper's New Monthly Magazine*: "though we have now passed the time in which our great cycle of poets flourished, we still have Holmes, Whittier, Lowell, Whitman, Trowbridge, and [R. H.] Stoddard among us."

Critical estimation of Trowbridge has not grown over time, but he enjoys a privileged place in scholarship as Walt **Whitman's** friend, observer, and critic. Of less importance is his acquaintance with Ralph Waldo **Emerson**, although it was Emerson whom Trowbridge admired more, with a respect not far removed from awe. In his autobiography, Trowbridge lists his evolving "literary passions," and above the likes of Lord Byron, Alfred, Lord Tennyson, Thomas Carlyle, and William Shakespeare, he places Emerson, "to whom my spiritual indebtedness was first and last the greatest." His initial encounter with Emerson and his subsequent voracious reading of him produced in Trowbridge something "more like the old-time religious conversion or change of heart than anything I had ever before experienced."

The primary role that Trowbridge plays for critics of Whitman is in the well-known debate over Emerson's influence on Whitman. Trowbridge asserted that Whitman admitted to having read Emerson before writing *Leaves of Grass* (see LOA, 1: 720ff.), and it is from Trowbridge that we have Whitman's now-famous homage, "'I was simmering, simmering, simmering; Emerson brought me to a boil.'" Whitman suggested later – after the pair's mutual admiration had waned – that he had not read Emerson at all before writing *Leaves of Grass*. Dismissing this contradiction, Trowbridge defended his claim to the Emersonian influence by noting that Whitman also said that "Leaves of Grass would not now be existing" without the experience of the Civil War, even though three editions of the work had been published before the war began. "After this," says Trowbridge, "we need not wonder that he forgot he had read Emerson before writing his first Leaves."

Trowbridge tries to play as fairly as he can with both Emerson and Whitman, in spite of (or perhaps because of) his greater admiration for Emerson. He defends Whitman's unauthorized publication of Emerson's letter of praise for the 1855 *Leaves* ("I greet you at the beginning of a great career") as an "instance of bad taste, but not of intentional bad faith," and he finds it curious that Emerson criticized Whitman's lack of form, given that Emerson's "chief defect as a writer seemed to be an imperfect mastery of form." On the other hand, Trowbridge published his "Reminiscences of Walt Whitman," with its arguments about Emerson's influence, in 1902, 10 years after Whitman's death, effectively leaving Whitman no opportunity for rebuttal.

Trowbridge is also important for his critical reaction to Whitman's poetry. M. Jimmie Killingsworth comments, "Critics who had not known him personally eventually perceived the Whitman of the 1870s and 1880s as a very different poet from the one he had been in the 1850s and early 1860s. Almost without exception, these modern readers preferred the earlier Whitman." Of the critics who knew Whitman personally, Trowbridge was one of the few who did not consider Whitman's later poetry the successful culmination of a lifelong process. Trowbridge recalls that upon reading the first edition of *Leaves of Grass*, he recognized "the tremendous original power of this new bard": "the freshness, as of nature itself, which breathed through the best of his songs or sayings, continued to hold their spell over me." However, like Emerson and many others, Trowbridge also "found in it much that impressed me as formless and needlessly offensive; and these faults were carried to extremes in the second and enlarged edition of 1856." After hearing Whitman read his Civil War poems (see LOA, 1: 887ff.), Trowbridge found them more like conventional poetry than his previous output, and in no way "comparable with the greatly moving passages in the earlier Leaves" (although he was pleased that the poems were "free from the old offenses against propriety"). Trowbridge catalogs the differences between the old and the new Whitman, finding that the newer poetry suffers from literary pretension. For instance, Trowbridge complains that the line "No poem proud I, chanting, bring to thee" – from the 1865 "Lo, Victress on the Peaks" –

would have been "I bring to you no proud poem" in 1855. Almost all of Whitman's alterations of the original *Leaves of Grass,* he argues, result in "a sacrifice of euphony or of atmosphere in the lines."

Trowbridge thus fronted a critical tradition that finds Whitman's later poetry less offensive, but also less vital. He did not articulate his reservations publicly until after Whitman had died, but he was openly critical of Whitman in private, drawing the charge of "apostasy" from loyalists. In spite of his sincere disapproval of Whitman's indecorous language, however, Trowbridge considered Whitman a friend and worked not only to get him a job with the State Department, but also to encourage publishers to reprint *Leaves of Grass.* Whitman himself had a higher estimation of Trowbridge than others in their circle: "The way Trowbridge stuck by me through thick and thin was beautiful to behold. He had objections to me always: has objections to-day: but he accepted me on general principles and has never, so far as I know, revised his original declaration in my favor."

Trowbridge's own writing was as conventional as Whitman's was not. In spite of his attraction to Whitman's "freshness," Trowbridge was never tempted to experiment in free verse, and, as one reviewer wrote, he was "never vulgar nor profane." Although his adherence to conventional form inevitably led Trowbridge to produce some mechanical poetry, he often twisted creatively within the constraints that he set for himself. "An Idyl of Harvest Time" (LOA, 2: 191) – which, along with the other poems in the Library of America edition, was included in *A Home Idyl* (1881) – strictly maintains an *aabb* rhyme scheme, but the poem also represents one of Trowbridge's slight nods to experimentation, for he writes in iambic heptameter, a rare length for a verse line.

Whatever else it may say about work, love, and harmony with nature, the poem is clearly meant as a directive to artists. The narrator is trying to paint the harvest scene before him but cannot get the effect he wants: "Could I but group those harvesters, paint sunshine on the grain!" Only once does he begin to respond personally and emotionally to the activity before him, to the happiness of the workers and the blossoming of love between the farmer's daughter and one of the fieldhands. Then,

> The picture grows, the landscape flows, and heart and
> fancy burn, –
> The figures start beneath my brush! (So you the rule
> may learn:
> Let thought be thrilled with sympathy, right touch and
> tone to give,
> And mix your colors with heart's blood, to make the
> canvas live.)

One of Trowbridge's romantic attitudes was a reaction against the overly intellectual artist – a belief that to exclude the emotional is to ignore a vast realm of human experience. The narrator here commands that the artist's observation of the world not be sterile, but "thrilled with sympathy," saturated with an emotional response that manifests itself in the work. By making his subject a painter, Trowbridge extends his statement to cover all artists. Trowbridge also de-emphasizes mechanical skill, which for him is, like intellectualism, sterile without emotion. As the poem ends, the narrator looks at the

painting after some months, and even though the craftsmanship is "Faulty and crude enough," the feeling that inspired the artwork transcends the technique, and "it wafts my soul away!"

The lesson is one that Trowbridge himself learned. His poem "The Vagabonds" is a long account, told by a traveler to a companion at a bar, of the destitute life and unhappy history of a beggar who travels "From door to door, with fiddle and dog." The poem enjoyed tremendous popularity and was read often in public; Trowbridge claims to have "heard of it in places as remote as Melbourne and Shanghai." As entries to the *Atlantic Monthly* were unsigned at the time, the fame of "The Vagabonds" failed to attach to Trowbridge himself for a while; in fact, his own sister wrote to him that its author must have "gone through some such terrible experience of intemperance and misery." Curiously enough, Trowbridge was unsure of the poem when he first wrote it, and he sent it to the *Atlantic Monthly* along with a more "sufficiently literary" poem, "By the River."

The difference between "The Vagabonds" and "By the River" is striking and telling. Trowbridge no doubt considered "By the River" more literary because it does not evoke a "real" world, a world with people and personal interactions. A long description of a peaceful river and wood, the poem is an extended metaphor, one that Trowbridge feels compelled to explain: "THE WORLD is the River that flickers by." "The Vagabonds," by contrast, is based on a memory from Paris of "a strolling showman with a troupe of six trained dogs," which Trowbridge reduced to one dog named Roger. The poem's power lies in the pathos of the beggar's stoic resignation to his miserable life, a pathos that would have suffered from any attempt to moralize beyond the beggar's closing prayer: "But soon we shall go where lodgings are free, / And the sleepers need neither victual nor drink: – / The sooner, the better for Roger and me!" Trowbridge did not realize it perhaps, but in writing this poem he was following the advice that he would later give in "An Idyl of Harvest Time": the more literary "By the River" is pure thought, but the more moving "The Vagabonds" lets "thought be thrilled with sympathy."

Trowbridge was tempted to moralize in both his fiction and his poetry, and he was often afraid that a piece could not make its point without an overt explanation. "Coupon Bonds," a short story successful enough that various attempts were made to turn it into a play, tells of an unhappy, miserly couple who are inadvertently led to do the right thing by the innocent maneuverings of their adopted son, Thaddeus. Their surly selfishness is replaced with the joy and satisfaction that accompany justice, but to reinforce the point, Trowbridge confronts his readers in the ending, which is unconventional but less literary in its purpose than corrective: "But [Thaddeus] did not know what made the Ducklows so much happier, so much gentler and kinder, than formerly. Do you?" Even "An Idyl of Harvest Time" must pause in the middle of the scene to provide a "rule" for artists to follow. Trowbridge's better writing avoids the temptation altogether, as exemplified by "The Vagabonds" and the later, and even more moving, "The Old Lobsterman" (LOA, 2: 197). This poem presents a man who has lost his family and who, after trying to lose himself by going to sea, returns to face his solitude, and, of course, himself:

He sleeps, he wakes; and this is his life.
Nor kindred nor friend in all the earth;
Nor laughter of child, nor gossip of wife;
Not even a cat to his silent hearth!
Only the sand-hills, wrinkled and hoar,
Bask in the sunset, round his door,
Where now I can see him sit, as gray
And weather-beaten and lonely as they.

Trowbridge has dropped largely from the public and academic eye. As much as he admired the unconventional that he found in Whitman and in Emerson, he never attempted it in his own fiction, and his poetry is uniformly traditional: an enabler of great works, he was not a writer of them. Thirteen years before his death in 1916, Trowbridge wrote *My Own Story*, in which he evaluated his place in literary history:

The fame of good fortune I cast my line for, which hope and imagination magnified to such alluring proportions, proved but modest prizes, when landed in the light of common day. . . . Instead of great epics and works of fiction that all the world would be waiting to acclaim, I have written some minor poems cared for by a few, half a dozen novels, and a large number of smaller books, that have been successful enough in their way.

MICHAEL R. LITTLE

Selected Works

My Own Story: With Recollections of Noted Persons, Boston and New York: Houghton Mifflin, 1903

The Poetical Works of John Townsend Trowbridge, Boston and New York: Houghton Mifflin, 1903

Further Reading

Killingsworth, M. Jimmie, *The Growth of 'Leaves of Grass': The Organic Tradition in Whitman Studies*, Columbia, South Carolina: Camden House, 1993

Quinn, Arthur Hobson, *American Fiction*, New York: Appleton-Century, 1936

Willard, Charles B., *Whitman's American Fame*, Providence, Rhode Island: Brown University, 1950

Frederick Goddard Tuckerman

(1821–1873)

"Tuckerman's sonnets rank with the noblest in the language and dignify America with poems not bettered in their kind by anyone of his time or since." This is the opinion of Witter Bynner, published in 1931. Thirty-four years later, Dennis Donoghue would hail Sonnet IX of Tuckerman's first series as "one of the best short poems in the language" and would call his ode "The Cricket" (LOA, 2: 113) "an exemplary American poem and one of the greatest poems of its tradition"; Yvor Winters would state even more emphatically that "The Cricket" is "the greatest poem in English of the century" and that "the amount of unforgettable poetry in the sonnets is large." These judgments come from three distinguished critics – the first and last of them also poets of some distinction – and the three are not alone in their high estimate of Frederick Goddard Tuckerman. Yet however numerous his "unforgettable" poems may be and however impressive his champions, Tuckerman remains an obscure, an almost entirely forgotten, figure.

Obscurity was not his birthright. Pull down the *Dictionary of American Biography* and you will discover that he is one of six nineteenth-century members of his family whose accomplishments won them places there: Joseph, his uncle, was a distinguished Unitarian clergyman and philanthropist; Joseph's son, Henry Theodore, was a prominent figure in New York's literary circles; a genus of the Compositae, *Tuckermania*, and a ravine on Mount Washington bear the name of Frederick's older brother Edward; their cousin Bayard was an editor, historian, and literary scholar of some reputation; and Frederick's son and namesake (medical degree from Harvard University; doctorate at the University of Heidelberg) published on comparative anatomy and a range of quite unrelated subjects. The *DAB* skipped over the brother between Edward and Frederick, Samuel Parkman, for several years the organist of New York's Trinity Church, but he does appear in *Grove's Dictionary*. And the *DAB* neglected their grandfather and father, Edwards both, mercantile Bostonians who established the family's considerable fortune. The men of the Tuckerman clan were an accomplished and – almost in spite of themselves – a conspicuous lot.

If one wanted to make a case for the usefulness of a leisure class, the Tuckermans would offer eloquent supporting evidence. A few made money; the rest, while spending that money unostentatiously, made contributions to art, science, religion, and the social good. Some piled academic degree upon academic degree; others dropped out early. It seems not to have mattered much: the dropouts published; the holders of professional degrees wandered into fields far from the ones they had prepared to enter. The unifying traits of the family were indefatigable labor and boundless curiosity: if one can speak of an "American Renaissance," here are its Renaissance men.

Frederick Goddard Tuckerman was born into this singular family on February 4, 1821. At 12, he was sent to Burlington, Vermont, to study in a school conducted by John Henry Hopkins, the first Episcopal bishop of Vermont. To complete his preparatory schooling, Tuckerman returned home and entered the Boston Latin School. Then he enrolled at Harvard, in the class of 1841. Jones **Very** was his tutor; Thomas Wentworth Higginson, later to be Emily **Dickinson's** "tutor," was a classmate. The atmosphere crackled with Ralph Waldo **Emerson's** new ideas. But at the end of his freshman year, Tuckerman dropped out. He blamed a problem with his eyes, but a passage from one of his sonnets (LOA, 2: 108) suggests other reasons:

> How oft in schoolboy-days, from the school's sway
> Have I run forth to Nature as to a friend, –
> With some pretext of o'erwrought sight, to spend
> My schooltime in green meadows far away!
> (II.xxix)

A year later, however, he returned to Harvard, this time to the law school. In 1842, he took a bachelor of laws degree. After another year's work in the law office of a family friend, he was admitted to the Suffolk County Bar. That marked the beginning and the termination of his career in the law.

He seems to have planned a trip to England in 1844, but he deferred it. Why he remained in America is unclear; indeed, everything about the next two and a half years remains unclear, but in February 1847, he bought a house in Greenfield, Massachusetts, and in June, the records of Greenfield's St. James's Episcopal Church indicate that he married Hannah (Anna) Lucinda Jones. The marriage record lists Tuckerman's occupation as "lawyer," but his surviving notebooks demonstrate that astronomy, meteorology, botany, and, preeminently, poetry were his true occupations. In the margins of a copy of Emerson's *Poems* (now in the University of Pennsylvania Library) he received in 1847 and annotated into the 1850s, Tuckerman entered quotations he saw as analogues – perhaps occasionally sources – for some of Emerson's lines: Edmund Spenser, Michael Drayton, William Shakespeare, Ben Jonson, George Chapman, George Herbert, John Milton, Abraham Cowley, Andrew Marvell, Oliver Goldsmith, Robert Burns, William Wordsworth, Samuel Taylor Coleridge, Walter Scott, Lord Byron, Percy Bysshe Shelley, William Cullen **Bryant**, Alfred, Lord Tennyson, and the ubiquitous "Festus" (P. J. Bailey) are among the poets cited, most of them quoted – and in most cases apparently from memory. These marginalia and those in other books that he owned bear witness to the depth and breadth of his study of the English poetic tradition.

The marriage was a happy one, although the death of the Tuckermans' first child, shortly after her birth in 1848, cast a shadow over their first years together. A son, Edward, was born in 1850. Tuckerman's wife and child remained in Greenfield when he traveled to England and Scotland for the summer of 1851. A daughter, Hannah, was born in 1853. A year later, Tuckerman and his wife, leaving the children in the care of her parents, traveled together to Scotland, England, Italy, Switzerland, and France. For the young poet, the most memorable occurrence of the six-month excursion came close to its end. In January 1855, he visited the Isle of Wight to pay his respects to Tennyson, a poet not known for his cordiality to strangers. Tuckerman's knowledge of the poet laureate's work made an immediate impression and won an invitation to dinner. After the evening meal, the two men retired to the study where, according to Tennyson's grandson, "over pipes and brandy and water, they talked and spouted poetry till far into the night, Alfred reclining at full length on the hearth rug. . . . Indeed, the two men found each other so congenial that the brief visit turned into a three-days' sojourn, and the young American went away with the manuscript of *Locksley Hall* in his pocket." We know that they talked about Tennyson's work and about Edgar Allan **Poe's** (Tuckerman engaged to send the great man some volumes of Poe); it seems clear that they also talked about some of Tuckerman's own work. The American left the Isle of Wight surer, it would appear, of his vocation as poet.

He had probably written many poems by then, but only eight had been published, starting with the two sonnets "November" and "April," which appeared in the *Literary World* in those months in 1849 and 1850. There are hints in both of these sonnets of the achievements that lay ahead for Tuckerman in that form, but most of the early poems are in other forms. "The Question" (LOA, 2: 101) is a splendid example of his dexterous management of a lithe and animated measure. Its meter, trochaic tetrameter (predominantly catalectic), calls to mind Milton's "L'Allegro" and parts of *Comus*, Poe's "A Dream within a Dream" and "The Valley of Unrest" (LOA, 1: 524), and, even more clearly, John Keats's "Bards of Passion and of Mirth," "Fancy," and the early lines to Georgiana Wylie, later his sister-in-law, which open:

> Hadst thou liv'd in days of old,
> O what wonders had been told
> Of thy lively countenance,
> And thy humid eyes that dance
> In the midst of their own brightness;
> In the very fane of lightness.

Light-footed, Keats's lines dance. And so do Tuckerman's:

> How shall I array my love?
> How should I arrange my fair?
> Leave her standing white and silent
> In the richness of her hair?
> Motion silent, beauty bare
> In the glory of her hair?
> Or for place and drapery
> Ravage land, and sack the sea?

The poet – the speaker – is a painter. He is to "arrange," to "array," the woman he proposes to depict in his portrait. He seeks the proper costume, the proper setting for the beauty he hopes to capture in his picture.

We can assign precise dates of composition to almost none of Tuckerman's poems, but we can confidently place "The Question" in his early period. I venture, moreover, that it dates from after his 1851 visit to Europe, and probably from after the 1854 visit. It is the poet's representation of himself as artist that leads me to that conclusion. New England was hardly destitute of European art in the 1850s, but Americans still traveled to Europe "to see the pictures." Tuckerman must have had many an opportunity in the galleries of Great Britain and the continent to contemplate the answer artist after artist provided to the question "How shall I array my love?" The painters of the past – Tintoretto, let us say, or Gainsborough – offered relevant answers, but the new painters attracting attention when

Tuckerman visited England in 1851 were the Pre-Raphaelites. John Everett Millais' *Mariana*, a response to Tennyson's poem, was on display at the Royal Academy that year. The Pre-Raphaelites were an even more conspicuous presence in the galleries of London, when Tuckerman next visited the city. In 1854, the Academy showed William Holman Hunt's *The Awakening Conscience*, another painting containing an homage to Tennyson. The subjects of these paintings would have sufficed to attract Tuckerman's attention, but the Pre-Raphaelites would have had a more general appeal for him: Millais, Hunt, and the third founder of the group, Dante Gabriel Rossetti, never hesitated to "Ravage land, and sack the sea" to array the models who were often, in point of fact, their loves. The lapidary catalog of "The Question" may tax the resources of the *Oxford English Dictionary* –

> Pearl, and priceless marbles bright, –
> Onyx, myrrhine, marcasite,
> And the jasper green! – nor these alone,
> But the famed Phengites stone, –

but it places every glittering image precisely where it belongs. And its breathless conclusion presses home its point: a beauty beyond all ornament fills the poet's vision.

> The river-riches of the sphere,
> All that the dark sea-bottoms bear,
> The wide earth's green convexity,
> The inexhaustible blue sky,
> Hold not a prize, so proud, so high,
> That it could grace her, gay or grand,
> By garden-gale and rose-breath fanned;
> Or as to-night I saw her stand
> Lovely in the meadow-land,
> With a clover in her hand.

Tuckerman visited England two decades too early to see Edward Burne-Jones's *King Cophetua and the Beggar Maid*, another Pre-Raphaelite picture after a Tennyson poem. The transcendent, unadorned simplicity of the figure of Burne-Jones's maid has something in common with the final image of Tuckerman's poem.

The image is the image of Hannah Tuckerman. On May 7, 1857, Hannah bore Tuckerman a second son, his namesake. Five days later, she died. The first phase of his poetic career died with her. He would never again enter Keats's "fane of lightness." The elegiac was henceforward to be his dominant – almost his exclusive – mode. His dominant form was to be the sonnet.

Descriptions of Tuckerman's sonnets habitually begin with the assertion that they are "unorthodox in structure" (Donald Barlow Stauffer). Tuckerman indeed rejected the orthodox rhyme-scheme of the Petrarchan and Shakespearean sonnets and their octave/sestet divisions, but so had Shelley ("Ozymandias," "England in 1819," and "Ode to the West Wind" are notable examples), and among Tuckerman's contemporaries in America, Washington **Allston**, James Gates **Percival**, William Gilmore **Simms**, and Frances Anne **Kemble** figure in the numerous company of poets who produced "unorthodox" sonnets. English and American sonneteers of the nineteenth century – and even the English sonneteers of the Renaissance – provide abundant precedents for Tuckerman's "unorthodox" sonnets. What sets Tuckerman apart from other sonneteers is that his practice was invariably "unorthodox." The octaves of "November" and "April," his first published poems, begin with the envelope quatrains of the Pertrarchan sonnet (*abba*), as if to announce "this is going to be a sonnet," but they substitute alternating rhymes in the next four lines (*acac, abab*); the rest of the rhyming is "orthodox." The first poem "turns" conventionally at the end of the eighth line; the second pauses there, as if feigning conformity to the textbook rule that Petrarchan sonnets "turn" at that point. The prosodic variations of these two poems are the same minor ones that Tuckerman would have encountered in the "unorthodox" sonnets of his American contemporaries. In 1850, however, he would have read a series of much more radically "unorthodox" sonnets by a British poet: "Sea-Side Sonnets" "by an Invalid," who signed himself or herself "L." They employ the singularly aberrant rhyme schemes Tuckerman would henceforth employ: they "turn," not at the octave/sestet division, but wherever meaning dictates, just as their rhyme patterns underscore meaning; they make effective use of slant rhyme, a device Tuckerman would come to employ frequently and tellingly; and six of them end, as seven of Tuckerman's sonnets from later dates end, in alexandrines. For every one of these features other antecedents could be found, but in the "Sea-Side Sonnets" they occur together. And we can be virtually certain that Tuckerman read these sonnets, which had originally appeared in the influential London magazine *Fraser's*, because they were reprinted in New York's *The Living Age* of October 19, 1850. That was the issue in which Tuckerman's "Mayflowers" appeared.

"Sea-Side Sonnets" may have influenced Tuckerman in another respect: they are a sequence; they aspire to be a single poem. Tuckerman wrote only three sonnets that are intended to stand alone, no more than one of them after he encountered the poems of the British "Invalid." The two sonnets beginning "The starry flower, the flowerlike stars that fade" (LOA, 2: 100) and "And so, as this great sphere now turning slow" (LOA, 2: 100) make one poem, not two. And the great enterprise of his middle years is a sequence, most of his critics agree, of 65 sonnets. In his original manuscript they were numbered as a single sequence, but when in 1860 he had a private edition of those sonnets and 34 of his other poems printed, he divided the sonnets into two parts, the first of 28 poems, the second of 37. All subsequent printings have followed the first in dividing the 65 sonnets into two series. The division is helpful: both the imagery and the theme of I.i and I.xxviii show that they bracket an integral sequence of poems. But II.i, if a beginning, is not a beginning *de novo*, and II.xxxvii, unnumbered in the manuscript, is a moving conclusion to the whole sequence of 65 sonnets – "These offspring of my sorrow," Tuckerman calls them there – and it answers the question posed in I.i: of what use can these expressions of a private grief be "if all the hearers fail" – if they find no understanding audience? Although there were to be three more printings of the *Poems* in Tuckerman's lifetime, the 1860 private printing contains all the poems that he was to publish. For his 1931 edition of *The Sonnets of Frederick Goddard Tuckerman*, Witter Bynner recovered the manuscripts of three later series of sonnets. His edition precedes the first two series with a portrait of Tuckerman and a title page, "SONNETS / 1854–1860," and the remaining three series with a

portrait of Hannah Tuckerman and another title page, "SONNETS / 1860–1872." N. Scott Momaday's 1965 edition, *The Complete Poems of Frederick Goddard Tuckerman*, provides a title page for each of the five series and appends the dates Bynner had given. How Tuckerman himself would have treated the five series if he had published all of them, we cannot be sure, but the editorial practice that has evolved obscures the integrity and the interrelatedness of the first two series. They constitute, in an important sense, one poem.

One very long poem. Poe may have been right for his own time; he is surely right for ours: "it is . . . clear that no very long poem will ever be popular again." Reading straight through Tennyson's *In Memoriam* or Ezra Pound's *Cantos* is an unappealing prospect for most of us. We settle for excerpts. At any rate, we start with excerpts. We shall, however, fail to sense Tennyson's full accomplishment – perhaps Pound's also – until we attack the "very long" poem as a whole. That is true also of Tuckerman's great sequence of 65 sonnets, but, like *In Memoriam* and the *Cantos*, the sequence will yield excerpts of great power and integrity. Yet reading individual sonnets and sequences of two or three sonnets will not merely obscure for us the power of the whole and of the individual sonnet in the context of the whole, it will also confront us with a special problem. John Berryman prefaced an edition of *The Dream Songs* with this: "The poem . . . is essentially about an imaginary character . . . who has suffered an irreversible loss and talks about himself sometimes in the first person, sometimes in the third, sometimes even in the second." Readers who had followed Berryman's sequence from the first "Dream Song" forward should have sensed that the "character" who speaks about himself, whatever the person, is the same character – and not really an "imaginary character" – but Berryman was convinced that some of his critics had missed that point. Tuckerman's sonnets are no more about an "imaginary character" than Berryman's *Dream Songs* are, nor do they make any such pretense, but the rest of Berryman's statement is true of both sets of poems. An "irreversible loss" is at the heart and center of Tuckerman's sequence of sonnets: the death of Hannah. The poet who has lost her speaks of himself "sometimes in the first person, sometimes in the third, sometimes even in the second." Reading the whole sequence makes that clear. In the thirty-fifth sonnet (II.vii; LOA, 2: 106), he presents himself as a Thoreauvian "florist" who had "held his eyes / Close to the ground." In the next sonnet that character speaks:

> asserting thought is free
> And wisest souls by their own action shine.
> "For beauty," he said, "is seen where'er we look,
> Growing alike in waste and guarded ground
> And like the May flower, gathered equally
> On desolate hills, where scantily the pine
> Drops his dry wisps about the barren rock,
> And in the angles of the fences found."
> (II.viii)

The "florist" seems a separate character – is, in a sense, a separate character, one who has lost a brother as the poet has lost a wife – but their grief makes them one:

> Undimmed the May went on with bird and bower;
> The summer filled and faded like a flower;

But rainy autumn and the red-turned leaf
Found us at tears and wept for company.
        (II.ix)

In the text of nature the "florist" and the poet seek to read consolation, but the text is blurred, opaque. No more Thoreauvian than Tuckerman, Emily Dickinson put it this way:

. . . nature is a stranger yet;
The ones that cite her most
Have never passed her haunted house,
Nor simplified her ghost.

To pity those that know her not
Is helped by the regret
That those who know her, know her less
The nearer her they get.
        (#1400)

In a moving group of sonnets in the first series, Tuckerman depicts the perplexing situation of all who seek to read the text of nature. At first, even the "Beds of the black pitchpine in dead leaves set" (I.vii; LOA, 2: 104) seem to offer a text of consolation, but our situation is that of mariners descending "some broad River" (LOA, 2: 104). "As the great Watercourse / Pushes his banks apart and seeks the sea," the "Benches of pine," the "flats of willow and low sycamores" disappear and the "wave" becomes our only "horizon":

So fades the portion of our early world.
Still on the ambit hangs the purple air;
Yet, while we lean to read the secret there,
The stream that by green shore-sides plashed and purled
Expands; the mountains melt to vapors rare,
And life alone circles out flat and bare.
        (I.viii)

The arresting metrical irregularity of that last line accents the absence of nature, the empty blankness of the text that the poet squints to read.

Yet wear we on, the deep light disallowed
That lit our youth; in years no longer young
We wander silently, and brood among
Dead graves, and tease the sunbreak and the cloud
For import . . .
        (I.ix)

So the next sonnet opens. It closes with the hope that the poet may at last suddenly "come into light," as Saul had done on the road to Damascus (Acts 9), "Struck to the knees . . . one arm against / The overbearing brightness," and "hear a voice" (I.ix).

In the sonnet that closes this sequence within the larger sequence, the poet experiences his vision, but it is not the regenerative vision of Saul. Saul had seen his Savior. The poet sees only himself in utter desolation – himself, although he speaks of "that man alone" in the third person. He stands in "An upper chamber in a darkened house" (LOA, 2: 105). He has suffered the vastation of spirit that the three preceding sonnets have prepared us to understand. If his epiphany is not like Saul's, he must nevertheless, like Saul, face it:

Nor can I drop my lids, nor shade my brows,
But there he stands beside the lifted sash;

And, with a swooning of the heart, I think
Where the black shingles slope to meet the boughs,
And – shattered on the roof like smallest snows –
The tiny petals of the mountain-ash.
        (I.x)

The lines conflate the poet, "I," and the mourning figure, "that man alone," while also conflating the seasons of his grief. The present is "the autumn" when "The cricket chides beneath the doorstep stone," seeking refuge from the chill of the fields, but it is fused both with the season of loss, the spring – when the "mountain-ash" scattered its blossoms on the "black shingles" of the roof of the "darkened house" – and with the winter of the spirit suggested by "smallest snows." In the text of nature neither poet nor reader can discover a message of consolation: the tiny petals are not scattered, they are "shattered" into indecipherability.

Tuckerman's great sonnet sequence accepts that indecipherability and accepts it without despair: if he cannot read the enigmatic text of nature, he can describe it with singular precision and responsiveness, and his description is, as it were, an affirmation of his affiliation with readers who share the same debility and desire. The sonnets of the three later series – we assume that they were written after 1860 because they were not included in the edition he published then and because three of them (IV.vi–viii; LOA, 2: 110–11) concern the Civil War – are not a part of the great sequence, but they continue and advance many of its themes. In common with the final sonnets of each of the first two series, the fifth closes with a prayer. Turning upon a phrase from Phil. 4.7, "The peace that passeth understanding," a phrase the poet would have heard often in a benediction of his Episcopal church, this last sonnet affords us what may be our final image of a courageous figure whose faith is unshaken, whose eloquence is undiminished.

That image also is inscribed in the most impressive of the poems that Tuckerman left in manuscript, "The Cricket." Of this poem, he left no fewer than five manuscripts, evidence, in spite of his having never published the poem, of his view of its place among his works. It may be later than the latest of the sonnets. We cannot be sure. "The Cricket" is the poem that Winters called "the greatest poem in English of the century." Great English odes abound in the nineteenth century. Wordsworth's "Intimations of Immortality," Keats's "Grecian Urn" and "Nightingale," and Walt **Whitman's** "Crossing Brooklyn Ferry" and "Out of the Cradle Endlessly Rocking" are among the poems in competition for the title that Winters so confidently bestowed upon "The Cricket." Winters, it should be noted, held a low opinion of all of those poems – and of virtually all romantic and Victorian poetry, English and American. But we must not discount his praise of "The Cricket" on that account. In the process of illustrating its "structure of controlled association" by comparing it to three of the most majestic poems of the early twentieth century, Wallace Stevens's "Sunday Morning" and Paul Valéry's "Le Cimetière marin" (The Graveyard by the Sea) and "Ébauche d'un serpent" (Outline of a Serpent), Winters could not resist the temptation of measuring it against those touchstones of modernism: "'The Cricket' is a greater poem than 'Sunday Morning' and is almost equal to either poem by Valéry." Lavish praise indeed. Tuckerman's great poem does have something in common with the high modernist odes Winters cites, but it has much more in common with the great odes of Wordsworth, Keats, and, coincidentally, we may suppose, Whitman. It is, far more than Winters was ready to acknowledge, a poem of its century, the century in which religious faith first seemed to falter and poets everywhere sought new bulwarks against oblivion. Keats's Nightingale was "not born for death": the bird's song "was heard / In ancient days by emperor and clown"; it had perhaps "found a path / Through the sad heart of Ruth, when, sick for home, / She stood in tears among the alien corn." The mockingbird of Whitman's "Out of the Cradle Endlessly Rocking" and the seagulls of his "Crossing Brooklyn Ferry," those "dumb, beautiful ministers," "furnish [their] parts toward eternity." The cricket seems a less entrancing "minister" – and it is hardly "dumb," silent – but in Tuckerman's ode it will become, like the nightingale, the mockingbird, and the seagull, an agent of transcendence that leads the imagination beyond the boundaries of our mortal life.

And it is a winning agent, this "little cooing cricket." Can we be expected to take the proposition advanced in the first strophe – that the cricket would suffer a "wrong" if it lacked a "bard" – quite seriously? I think not, but the ode's assertion that the "humming bee" and the "dogday locust" had had their bards is true enough: the bee had been celebrated by poets from Shakespeare ("Where the bee sucks, there suck I") to Emerson ("The Humble-Bee"; LOA, 1: 272); and if we may treat "locust" and "grasshopper" as interchangeable – the translators of the King James Bible offer some warrant for that – Richard Lovelace's "The Grasshopper" and Abraham Cowley's lovely translation from Anacreon, also titled "The Grasshopper," are among the celebrations of that insect. But the cricket had hardly suffered literary neglect either. Indeed, two well-known sonnets, written in friendly competition by Keats and Leigh Hunt, celebrate both the grasshopper and the cricket ("On the Grasshopper and the Cricket"; "To the Grasshopper and the Cricket"). Like a yet more famous cricket in Dickens's *The Cricket on the Hearth*, these were indoor crickets. So was William Cowper's:

> Little inmate, full of mirth,
> Chirping on my kitchen hearth;
> Wheresoe'er be thine abode,
> Always harbinger of good,
> Pay me for thy warm retreat,
> With a song more soft and sweet,
> In return thou shalt receive
> Such a strain as I can give.
> ("The Cricket")

The ode's suggestion that the cricket has lacked a literary champion is disingenuous – craftily disingenuous. It leads us to expect – it provides – an ingratiating, a disarming, touch of mirth.

The second strophe, however, takes a different turn. Its music is contrived to lull us into a trance-like state. The "dead fragrance" of the "dull hop" and the "poppy's dark refreshing flower" stun "the sense to slumber." They recall the "hemlock" and the "dull opiate" that cause the poet of Keats's "Ode to a Nightingale" to sink "Lethe-wards." The final line of the strophe – "Acres of cricks!" – may effect a reprise of the lighter mood of the first strophe, but it is only a momentary reprise.

The fourth strophe will again recall a strategy of Keats's ode. The living equivalent of his Grecian urn, Keats's nightingale transcends time: "The voice I hear this passing night was heard / In ancient days." Tuckerman's ode treats his cricket in a similar fashion: "So wert thou loved in that old graceful time / When Greece was fair, / While god or hero hearkened to thy chime." Both poets employ a range of allusions to enforce the idea of time transcended. The mythological and historical references in Keats's ode are easily accessible – although college texts continue to gloss references such as Flora, Hippocrene, Bacchus, and Ruth. The references in the fourth strophe of "The Cricket" confront the modern reader with more of a challenge. Caÿster is the ancient name of a river celebrated by Homer that empties into the Aegean near Ephesus; Eurotas is a Greek river that flowed past Sparta; Xenaphyle (or Xenaphilus) was a Pythagorean philosopher said to have written on music; Psammathe (or Psamathe), whose name in Greek denotes a sandy shore, is one of the 50 Nereides, the gentle attendants of the sea-goddess Thetis; and Plutarch (the source of other Tuckerman allusions) wrote of the death of Pan in *Why Oracles Are Silent*. If Tuckerman's poem reached any contemporaries who might have failed to recognize such apparently arcane allusions, however, they would not have had to "Ravage land, and sack the sea" to understand him: Caÿster, Eurotas, Xenaphilus, Psammathe, and, of course, Pan are glossed in the standard reference work of the time, Lempriere's *Bibliotheca Classica*. Tuckerman owned a copy. Tuckerman does not aim to mystify. He evokes appropriate images of Hellenic civilization to register the point that the cricket we hear was heard by Xenaphyle and Psammathe: the present is linked to the past, "The moments take hold of eternity."

Before he develops that linking of past and present, time and eternity, the poet explores in the third strophe the personal associations elicited by the cricket's music. Its rejoicing is "dear to the child"; but to the adult it brings the "burthen of the unresting Sea" and personal "remembrances of joy and pain," the very "joy and pain" the great sonnet sequence had recorded.

The poet of "Ode to a Nightingale" had been "half in love with easeful death"; the poet of "The Cricket" affirms the "joy and pain" of life. He may wish, the final strophe acknowledges, that "Like the Enchanter old" he could "hear articulate voices . . . / In cry of beast, or bird, or insect's hum," that he could decipher the text of nature, but he must "ignorantly hear." He accepts his limitation. And he may wish that he were gifted with a prophetic vision that would win him "at last some low applause," a responsive audience, but he is content finally that his song should, like the single cricket's song, become an indistinguishable part of a greater song, "Naught in innumerable numerousness."

> Even while we stop to wrangle or repine
>   Our lives are gone –
>   Like thinnest mist,
> Like yon escaping color in the tree;
> Rejoice! rejoice! whilst yet the hours exist –
> Rejoice or mourn, and let the world swing on
> Unmoved by cricket song of thee or me.

The world was to remain unmoved by Tuckerman's poetry, but we have no reason to believe that Tuckerman was moved by its neglect. The collection that he printed privately in 1860 and sent to distinguished literary figures was reissued in a trade edition in London in 1863, perhaps, as Bynner speculates, "the result of Tennyson's interest." Tuckerman made two slight changes for it, but he included no additional poems. That edition was reprinted in Boston, Massachusetts, without any changes or additions in 1864 and again in 1869. Perhaps those printings were the result of Emerson's interest. We have no evidence that Tuckerman took any interest in them. An enigma, but not a unique enigma: 14 miles away in Amherst, Emily Dickinson was producing a much larger oeuvre that was to remain almost entirely unpublished in her lifetime. Her letters show that she knew Tuckerman's botanist brother, his sister-in-law, and later his son and daughter-in-law. Can New England's two most extraordinary poets of the age have remained entirely ignorant of each other? No shred of evidence has emerged to enable us to answer that question, but the likely inference from the absence of any mention of him in her letters to his family is that, indeed, each was unaware of the other.

Frederick Goddard Tuckerman died in Greenfield on May 9, 1873. The world took little notice.

ROBERT REGAN

Selected Works

Poems, Boston: John Wilson, 1860
Poems, London: Smith, Elder, 1863
Poems, Boston: Ticknor and Fields, 1864
Poems, Boston: Little, Brown, 1869

The Sonnets of Frederick Goddard Tuckerman, edited by Witter Bynner, New York and London: Knopf, 1931
The Complete Poems of Frederick Goddard Tuckerman, edited by N. Scott Momaday, New York: Oxford University Press, 1965

Further Reading

Donoghue, Denis, *Connoisseurs of Chaos: Ideas of Order in Modern American Poetry*, New York: Macmillan, 1965
England, Eugene, *Beyond Romanticism: Tuckerman's Life and Poetry*, Provo, Utah: Brigham Young University, 1991
Ghodes, Clarence, ed., *Essays on American Literature in Honor of Jay B. Hubbell*, Durham, North Carolina: Duke University Press, 1967
Golden, Samuel A., *Frederick Goddard Tuckerman: An American Sonneteer*, New York: Twayne, 1966
Hagenbüchle, Roland, ed., *American Poetry Between Tradition and Modernism, 1865–1914*, Regensburg, Germany: Verlag Friedrich Pustet, 1984
Stauffer, Donald Barlow, *A Short History of American Poetry*, New York: Dutton, 1974
Wilson, Edmund, *Patriotic Gore: Studies in American Literature of the Civil War*, New York: Oxford University Press, 1962
Winters, Yvor, *Forms of Discovery: Critical and Historical Essays on the Forms of the Short Poem in English*, Denver, Colorado: Alan Swallow, 1967

George Boyer Vashon

(1824–1878)

Vashon was one of the most important African American men of letters of the nineteenth century. Born in Carlisle, Pennsylvania, he was the son of a prominent freeman, abolitionist, and anticolonialist, John Bethume Vashon. In Pittsburgh, Pennsylvania, George Vashon began in the public schools what was to become an illustrious academic career. A precocious young man, he followed his father's footsteps in antislavery advocacy and became the secretary of the Juvenile Anti-Slavery Society at age 14. By age 16, he was enrolled at Oberlin College in Oberlin, Ohio, and became its first African American graduate in 1844. At this point, the trajectory of his life was altered when his quest for learning and professional advancement was derailed by the most straightforward racism. After completing his graduate studies in law, he was denied the opportunity to take the bar examination in Pennsylvania in 1847.

In response to this disruption, he decided to go into exile in Haiti, arriving in the island nation in 1848. There, he began his career as a scholar, first teaching at the College Faustin in Port-au-Prince. We know little about his experiences on the island, little more than that he eventually returned to the United States in 1850 and practiced law in Syracuse, New York (after passing the bar exam to become the first African American lawyer in the state). In 1854, he resumed his scholarly career and became professor of belles-lettres and mathematics at New York Central College in McGrawville, New York. A marriage to Susan Paul Smith – and a family of seven children – followed, as did a return to Pittsburgh, where he became a prominent teacher and principal in the "colored" public schools. In 1864, there was another return to the scholarly life at Avery College.

In the final period of his life, he took on work as a solicitor for the Freedmen's Bureau (1867), which led to much travel in the south. There is speculation that he may have briefly taught at Alcorn State University in Lorman, Mississippi, during this period. As to the events of his life after his participation in the national convention of Colored Men of America in 1869, little is known. It is amazing to consider that, with the very full and sedulous life he led, Vashon was somehow able to write poetry. Even more strikingly, he was able, in "Vincent Ogé" (LOA, 2: 136), to complete a complex and weighty poetic treatment of a major revolutionary struggle, while attempting to get on in a culture that was skeptical of and had little use for intellectual endeavors by African Americans.

The version of "Vincent Ogé" that has come down to us – as originally published in Julia Griffiths's *Autographs for Freedom* (1854) – is more than 300 lines in length and is composed of eight uneven sections; an author's headnote, however, tells us that what we have are "fragments of a poem." It is unclear whether the headnote suggests that the poem is incomplete or, perhaps, that it constitutes a fragmentary treatment of an important and complicated theme. The poem does raise questions about positivist constructions of history, as it more straightforwardly sets out to commemorate the "revolt of the free persons of color, in the island of St. Domingo (now Hayti), in the years 1790–1." To suggest this theme of fragmentation and the un-

predictability of history, the poet later writes, "But ah! life is a changeful thing," but we cannot be sure whether Vashon's commitment is, as Joan Sherman suggests, "Heraclitian," or a product of the West African tendency to "deify accident," or, more simply, a good historical reading of the events of the Haitian revolution.

The eighteenth-century African American poet Phillis Wheatley pioneered in the early African American poetic genre of works that commemorated the lives of individuals. In "On the Death of the Rev. Mr. George Whitefield" and "To S. M., a Young African Painter, on Seeing His Works," she celebrates creativity or virtue when she identifies the individual subject of the poem as exemplary. Vashon's poem, however, is unique to nineteenth-century African American poetry in that, although it utilizes a "hero" or historical protagonist, it is not simply a praise poem. In another transgression of convention, neither is the poem especially interested in exploring the verities of Christian patience or forgiveness, and what Christian imagery it possesses seems demonstrably apocalyptic. The description of the process of revolution that leads to further revolution completely outweighs any direct exhortation of the special gifts of Ogé. Part of the poem's task seems to be the redefinition or re-evaluation of heroic action.

This is not to suggest that the specific selection of Ogé is without significance. Far more typical of nineteenth-century African American writing was an interest in Toussaint L'Ouverture, the more celebrated leader of the Haitian revolution. Ogé was a mulatto, educated in France, who returned to Saint Domingue (Haiti) in 1791 to participate in a rebellion that was meant to further mulatto claims to citizenship. As Vashon "shapes" Ogé, he becomes a romantic hero, more comfortable in contact with nature than with the political realities of rebellions and struggles for power. Ogé's was:

> . . . a mind that joyed
>   With nature in her every mood,
> Whether in sunshine unalloyed
>   With darkness, or in tempest rude
> And, by the dashing waterfall,
>   Or by the gently flowing river,
> Or listening to the thunder's call,
>   He'd joy away his life forever.

The deeper meaning of the poem is found in the careful use of historical analogy. Although Ogé's action is depicted as heroic – and the ultimate gains of the revolution, tangible and significant – readers were also aware of his horrific demise and of the difficult path toward freedom. With the horror of the Civil War less than a decade away, there is some aspect of "Vincent Ogé" that is best thought of as prophetic. More generally, the "analogical imagination" bridges the distance between the reader and this somewhat isolated set of historical events.

Ultimately, however, the indirect or diffuse nature of the poem's praise must lead us to center the relationship between narrative and history in a consideration of its meaning. Despite the poem's title, that is, the lack of *individual* dramatic action on the part of Ogé suggests that his presence might best be read as synecdochic. Although he stands for "nation," "justice," or "action" away from nature and toward an inevitable and unpredictable struggle with the forces of corruption, we are left to place ourselves not in relation to this historical figure, but to the processes in which he is caught. In other words, we are left to grapple with the *progress* the poem attempts to make.

The poem begins by expressing the analogic pattern that we note in regard to character. The "twilight's gift" makes possible the night's "deepest gloom." This relationship, Vashon suggests, parallels the experience of surviving slavery or the denial of citizenship.

> Such sight is like the struggle made
> When freedom bids unbare the blade,
> And calls from every mountain-glen –
>   From every hill – from every plain,
> Her chosen ones to stand like men,
>   And cleanse their souls from every stain
> Which wretches, steeped in crime and blood,
> Have cast upon the form of God.

This psychological analogy is followed by a description of the island that suggests a place anointed by the state ("coronet" and "diadem") and also by spiritual authority ("If Eden claimed a favored haunt"). The description suggests a further analogy in that it resonates with the setting evoked in Shakespeare's *The Tempest*; the analogy, however, points toward the lie of the Edenic isle, not a simplistic celebration of its "new world" possibilities. The introduction of Ogé, then, emphasizes the need to address the dissonance remaining in the series of analogies that have structured the poem:

> And Ogé stands mid this array
>   Of matchless beauty, but his brow
> Is brightened not by pleasure's play;
>   He stands unmoved – nay, saddened now,
> As doth the lorn and mateless bird
> That constant mourns, whilst all unheard,
> The breezes freighted with the strains
> Of other songsters sweep the plain, –
> That ne'er breathes forth a joyous note,
> Though odors on the zephyrs float –
> The tribute of a thousand bowers,
> Rich in their store of fragrant flowers.

In "traditional" poems of heroic action, the pain of dissonance or separation, or the awareness of hypocrisy, would be enough to call the protagonist either to cathartic action or to moral agency. But Vashon leads us to a consideration of the ways in which the news of revolution (in France) can lead to revolution (in Haiti), even as he suggests that such historical interconnectedness is ephemeral and transitory. Again, this skepticism or hesitation as to the possibility of Ogé's success disappoints readerly expectation as to the nature of this heroic epic. The "age of revolution" is problematized as a period in which repression "slumbers" as often as it is straightforwardly realized.

After a brief – and highly stylized – meditation on the nature of this repression, Ogé is finally placed center stage, although not without irony. Vashon's skepticism about the character of his poetic celebration is represented by the introduction

"And Ogé standeth in his hall; / But now he standeth not alone." The centering of the hero within the epic is immediately undone. The resolution of the dramatic tension is initiated quickly. The anonymous band directly comes to the realization that "when the heart is filled with grief, / For wrongs of all true souls accurst, / In action it must seek relief, / Or else, o'ercharged, it can but burst."

But one of the most interesting parts of the poem is the use of the female voice to confirm the ethics of the action. In particular, it is Ogé's mother who motivates the men. If the men should fail to be spurred to action by her action, she suggests that she will offer a prayer:

> "Passing from guilt to misery,
> May this for aye your portion be, –
> A life, dragged out beneath the rod –
> An end, abhorred of man and God –
> As monument, the chains you nurse –
> As epitaph, your mother's curse!"

This unusual exhortation recalls the dilemma faced by the escaped slave mother Sethe in Toni Morrison's *Beloved*. Indeed, the horrible fate of Ogé and the short-lived nature of the celebration of the revolution's successes – arguably only seven lines long – parallel the ambivalence or unresolved guilt that the presence of "Beloved" marks in Morrison's novel. It is not so much that the heroic action and moral agency of Ogé and others are undercut by "counter-revolution" and torture, but that the unpredictable character of such moral action is emphasized. What does remain clear is the incompatibility of slavery with a satisfactory human existence: "But alas! although many lie silent and slain, / More blest are they far than those clanking the chain, / In the hold of the tyrant, debarred from the day."

The artistic accomplishment of the poem is especially evident in its structural completeness. Vashon returns toward the end to the imagery of sunlight and to the analogic relationship between the experience of "light" and hope or sustenance. First we are told:

> Another day's bright sun has risen,
> And shines upon the insurgent's prison;
> Another night has slowly passed,
> And Ogé smiles, for 'tis the last
> He'll droop beneath the tyrant's power.

Moreover, the "revolutionaries" as a group are described as:

> – they who have stood
> Firmly and fast in hour of blood, –
> Who've seen the lights of hope all die,
> As stars fade from a morning sky, –
> They've gathered there, in that dark hour –
> The latest of the tyrant's power, –
> An hour that speaketh of the day
> Which never more shall pass away,
> The glorious day beyond the grave,
> Which knows no master – owns no slave.

Finally, and ironically, the poet notes that at the torture and murder of the martyrs:

> The sunbeams on the rack that play,
> For sudden terror flit away

From this dread work of war and death,
As angels do with quickened breath,
From some dark deed of deepest sin,
Ere they have drunk its spirit in.

The manipulation of the imagery of night and day, the symbolic use of light and dark, and the subsequent personification of light together make "Vincent Ogé" among the most sophisticated of early African American poems. The way in which the poem interrelates history, moral agency, and the natural world defines a complex romanticism that further complicates our understanding of "nature poetry" in the American Renaissance. If the poem concludes in a somewhat conventional fashion ("Thy coming fame, Ogé! is sure"), only the most cursory or facile reading would allow for any simplistic sense of triumph.

Does the poem mean to be expressly didactic about mid-nineteenth-century American life? Clearly one "message" concerns the nature of political and social action. It is, Vashon would have us remember, not without risk:

Though the hearts of those heroes all well could accord
With freedom's most noble and loftiest word;
Their virtuous strength availeth them naught
With the power and skill that the tyrant brought.

Ogé's fate, after all, is not especially glorious. However, we should not downplay that the poem does take heroic action seriously. Moreover, its publication in the United States in the 1850s was not without cultural significance. The example of Haiti was often used in discussions about the merits and limitations of various colonization and emigration schemes. Vashon was part of a generation of "sons of anticolonists and anti-immigrationists" who were more skeptical of the prospects for citizenship and justice for Africans in the United States. And the 1850s marked the most vigorous period of this debate. Still, there is little evidence that Vashon meant explicitly to participate in debates about the fate of Africans in America. Of course, on the other hand, the poem expressly condemns injustice (although not so much what we would call racism) and speaks to the situation of a nation heading for internecine struggle.

The most interesting questions left to us as readers are: where did Vashon learn this story? Moreover, in what ways might knowing about the tale's original production help us to understand the meaning of its retelling less than a decade before the beginning of the Civil War? Most obviously, we might look to Vashon's own Haitian experience, although the search for an answer must also consider the relationship between stories of martyrdom circulated within abolitionist circles and representations of heroism produced within the tradition of African American folklore. For it is within this space – between the message of an unpredictable and harsh universe and the message of political action – that the meaning of Vashon's "Vincent Ogé" seems to lie.

George Vashon did complete poems other than "Vincent Ogé," but none of these compare in ambition or complexity. We do have "A Life Day" (1867) and "Ode on the Proclamation of the Fifteenth Amendment" (1870), which further testify to Vashon's intellect and social concerns. Still, as a result of the success and distinctiveness of "Vincent Ogé," we are left to speculate about what other work may have been lost or never shared with the public. Might George Vashon have become a major nineteenth-century American poet if racial circumstances were different? Of course, we will never know. As it is, we are left to puzzle over the unique poetic accomplishment of his Haitian allegory and the greater puzzle of a culture without the means to acknowledge it.

JAMES C. HALL

Selected Works

African-American Poetry of the Nineteenth Century: An Anthology, edited by Joan Sherman, Urbana: University of Illinois Press, 1992

Brawley, Benjamin, *Early American Negro Writers*, Freeport, New York: Books for Libraries, 1968

Griffiths, Julia, *Autographs for Freedom*, Auburn, New York: Alden, Beardsley, 1854

Further Reading

Jackson, Blyden, *The History of Afro-American Literature*, vol. 1, Baton Rouge: Louisiana State University Press, 1989

James, C. L. R., *The Black Jacobins*, New York: Vintage, 1963

Loggins, Vernon, *The Negro Author: His Development in America to 1900*, New York: Columbia University Press, 1931

Quarles, Benjamin, *Black Abolitionists*, New York: Oxford University Press, 1969

Redding, Saunders, *To Make a Poet Black*, College Park, Maryland: McGrath, 1968

Redmond, Eugene, *Drumvoices: The Mission of Afro-American Poetry*, Garden City, New York: Anchor, 1976

Sherman, Joan, *Invisible Poets: Afro-Americans of the Nineteenth Century*, Urbana: University of Illinois Press, 1989

Jones Very

(1813–1880)

Very's literary production, more than that of most poets, ranges widely from the sublime to the pedestrian. Part of the explanation for this variation is biographical. Two facts that have not been generally recognized are basic to the understanding of Very's poetry: the poems he wrote during an approximately 18-month period in 1838–40 – mostly sonnets that were almost exclusively religious and characterized by a peculiar intensity – were composed under the direct influence of a recent overwhelming mystical experience; those composed earlier or later were not. Failure to appreciate this distinction has marred a good deal of the criticism of Very's poetry. Critics have frequently puzzled over inconsistencies between these "ecstatic" poems and those written earlier or later. But these differences should not be surprising, for in a very real sense it was not the same mind that produced the poems of the different periods.

Very was born, died, and lived almost all of his life in Salem, Massachusetts. The basic biographical facts are available in William I. Bartlett's *Jones Very: Emerson's "Brave Saint,"* and, with critical analysis, in Edwin Gittleman's *Jones Very: The Effective Years 1833–1840.* Shortly before he entered Harvard College in 1833, Very began publishing poems in a local newspaper. He continued writing poetry during his undergraduate years (1833–36) and while he studied at the Divinity School and served as a tutor in Greek at Harvard (1836–38). At the end of this period, he underwent a psychological/spiritual crisis, culminating in September 1838, that led to his dismissal by Harvard, resulted in a month-long stay in the nearby McLean Asylum, and radically changed the character of his poetry for a brief period of some 18 months.

While he was still a tutor, Very made the acquaintance of Ralph Waldo **Emerson**, whose *Nature* (1836) he had read and admired, and attended by invitation meetings of the Transcendental Club, where mysticism was one of the topics of discussion. In the summer of 1838, Emerson's Divinity School address urged each of the students to become a "new-born bard of the Holy Ghost"; two months later Jones Very seemed to be fulfilling this visionary ideal with a literalness that Emerson hardly expected. He announced to his Greek class that they should flee to the mountains, for the end was at hand, and went about delivering his "revelation" to students and professors at Harvard and friends and ministers in Salem. Furthermore, he began writing religious poetry of an extraordinary character. The poems were, he believed, the utterances of the Holy Spirit; he told Emerson that he valued them not because they were his, but because they were *not* his.

An ongoing debate over Very's poetry has considered his religious-philosophical orientation: was he Calvinist, Unitarian, or transcendentalist? Historically speaking, it is clear that Very was a transcendentalist, at least in the sense that for a period of some two years he was closely associated with the transcendental circle. Transcendentalism itself, however, was not a rigid monolithic philosophical system. It was a loose association of thinkers who espoused many differing and conflicting shades of religious and philosophical opinions but held in common a trust in man's intuitive powers as a source of truth. For a time, Very was part of that association, and he undeniably placed great faith in the voice within. For Very, however, the voice within was in a certain sense not the voice of his own self, for that self had been effaced to make place for the divine. Very's Unitarian connections were also strong; for nearly 40 years he was a licensed supply preacher in Unitarian churches. The Unitarians treated Very (for a few years before and for decades after his mystical period) as a Unitarian, and the transcendentalists treated him for a few years during the height of the movement as a transcendentalist. The groups were not mutually exclusive.

But during the most significant period of his poetic production, such categories are to a large extent irrelevant. During that time, Jones Very, believing himself to have experienced a spiritual rebirth and union with the divine, was essentially a mystic, a classification that cuts across lines of dogma. He was, of course, a Christian mystic, and the form that his mysticism took was no doubt influenced by the Calvinistic milieu of New England, as well as by more immediate Unitarian, and especially, transcendentalist influences at Harvard. His only extant direct statement on this experience (a letter to Henry W. Bellows, a recent graduate of the Harvard Divinity School) describes his having gone through several stages in reaching the state of complete union with God's will.

The poetry that resulted from this experience was highly admired by Emerson, and, at his urging and under his editorship, a small selection was published (along with three of Very's essays on epic poetry and on Shakespeare) in 1839 as *Essays and Poems.* Believing in the divine source of the poetry that came to him during this period, Very objected, in vain, to any correction or revision of his verse. He continued writing poetry in this extraordinary vein until early 1840, when he ceased writing for several months. When he resumed, the poetry was in a different key.

Thus, we can classify Very's poetry into three major periods, each differing significantly from the others: the early period, from 1833 to September 1838; the ecstatic period, from the fall of 1838 to early 1840; and the late period, comprising the remainder of his life. In the early period, he was an aspiring young poet writing on secular themes with a view to publication. The verse that he wrote between mid-1833, when he was 20 years old, and the late summer of 1838 is largely imitative of English late-neoclassical and Romantic poets, notably William Wordsworth, and it is often sentimental. The very earliest poems, often in the form of long blank verse meditations, and sometimes in heroic couplets or rhymed quatrains, give way toward the later part of the first period to the form that was to become his favorite, the sonnet. The poems of this early period reveal a self-conscious young poet struggling to find his voice. Except for certain poems ("Beauty" and "The Columbine") that were written late in the period, few of these works have much intrinsic aesthetic merit; they are interesting largely for what they reveal of Very's life and his poetic development.

At the point of Very's religious awakening in 1838, his poetry takes on a strikingly new character. The conventional, sentimental, and often forced nature poetry of the early period is suddenly supplanted by a poetry of exaltation. In "The New Birth" (LOA, 1: 629), Very both announces and demonstrates his new style, subject matter, and manner of composition. The poem begins by describing these changes:

'Tis a new life – thoughts move not as they did
With slow uncertain steps across my mind,
In thronging haste fast pressing on they bid
The portals open to the viewless wind.

Then it goes on to illustrate the new ecstatic intensity:

And from before man's vision melting fade
The heavens and earth – Their walls are falling now –
Fast crowding on each thought claims utterance strong,
Storm-lifted waves swift rushing to the shore
On from the sea they send their shouts along,
Back through the cave-worn rocks their thunders roar,
And I a child of God by Christ made free
Start from death's slumbers to eternity.

Very's mystical experience, which this poem attempts to communicate, has radically altered the nature of his poetry. The intensity of the poem's tone and its apocalyptic theme are significant departures.

"The New Birth" also marks a watershed in terms of the poet's habits of composition. The manuscripts that survive from this period show little if any revision and reflect the "thronging haste" and "fast crowding on" of thoughts and words described in this poem. In many cases, punctuation is entirely absent. (Quotations here follow Very's punctuation practice.) Sometimes a large number of sonnets, written in both small script and pencil, are crowded on a single sheet. This sort of composition was clearly not slow and laborious but spontaneous, at times an almost frenzied recording of the voice of the Muse, or, as Very would have it, the Spirit. Very's output during these months was remarkable for its volume. At one point, Elizabeth Palmer Peabody reported to Emerson that the poems flowed from Very at the rate of one or two per day. Within 18 months he had produced more than 300 poems.

It is the poems of the ecstatic period that have attracted most of the critical interest in Very; this poetry constitutes his distinctive contribution to American literature. Very's chief concern in these poems was more evangelistic than aesthetic: they are his attempts to deliver the message that came, in whatever way, to him. Yet Very's belief in the divine origin of his words accounts for both some of the strengths and some of the weaknesses of the poems. A number of them are little more than paraphrases of Scripture – the sayings of Jesus, often, put into verse. Stylistically, among the hallmarks of the poems of this period are a sense of urgency or, conversely, a tone of serene passiveness; a Walt **Whitman**-like expanding of the possibilities of poetic voice, which sometimes mingles the human and the divine; reliance on scriptural language; elliptical scriptural allusions, often multiple references in a single poem that have an associative rather than a logical connection; and certain recurrent patterns of imagery. A number of critics from Emerson forward have noted Very's lack of polish and craftsmanship in individual lines and the frequent failure of his poems to live up to their arresting openings. The note of egotism inherent in the poetry of one who

feels himself to be a special mouthpiece of God offends some readers. A concomitant note of paranoia also sometimes irritates, although the reader should bear in mind that Very was, indeed, persecuted by the Harvard authorities and by the Salem ministers for delivering his revelations.

But the special nature of this poetry is also responsible for the verse's breathless intensity. The compressions and potent images occurring in some of these poems have been compared with those found in the metaphysical poets. The opening lines of "The Resurrection" illustrate the sense of urgency that characterizes many of the ecstatic poems: "The dead! the dead! they throw their grave clothes by, / And burst the prisons where they long have lain." At its best, as in "The New Birth," "The Dead" (LOA, 1: 632), and "Hope," Very's poetry is a highly charged utterance; or, in another vein, as in "The Son" and "The Prayer" (LOA, 1: 638), it is striking in its depiction of a devout submissiveness of the soul to God.

The ecstatic poetry is the product of Very's mystical experience and reflects his concerns resulting from that experience. In certain of these poems, like "The New Birth" and "The New World" (LOA, 1: 634), the speaker attempts to describe the illuminative experience itself or to depict himself in his newly regenerated state, a condition of harmony with God and nature. "The Garden" (LOA, 1: 630) portrays this spiritually idyllic situation:

I saw the spot where our first parents dwelt;
And yet it wore to me no face of change,
For while amid its fields and groves I felt
As if I had not sinned, nor thought it strange.

Other poems of the same period, including "The Hand and the Foot" (LOA, 1: 636) and "In Him we live, & move, & have our being" (LOA, 1: 629), express the speaker's determination to submerge his own will and wait for God. "The Son" typifies the best of the poems that communicate the passive state of the regenerated soul:

Father! I wait thy word – the sun doth stand,
Beneath the mingling line of night and day,
A listening servant waiting thy command
To roll rejoycing on its silent way;
The tongue of time abides the appointed hour,
Till on our ear its solemn warnings fall;
The heavy cloud withholds the pelting shower,
Then every drop speeds onward at thy call;
The bird reposes on the yielding bough
With breast unswollen by the tide of song;
So does my spirit wait thy presence now
To pour thy praise in quickening life along
Chiding with voice divine man's lengthened sleep,
While round the Unuttered Word and Love their vigils
    keep.

Similarly, in "The Prayer," like "The Son" a frequently anthologized poem, the speaker waits passively if anxiously for the regenerating visit of God:

Wilt Thou not visit me?
The plant beside me feels thy gentle dew;
    And every blade of grass I see,
From thy deep earth its quickening moisture drew.

Because by its very nature mystical experience defies expression, mystics frequently resort to symbolic language in an effort to convey their experience as nearly as possible. Harry L. Jones has noted a number of symbolically functioning images and image clusters in Very's mystical poetry. Those associated with the reborn include day/dawn/morning/light, house/mansion, flowers, fruitful trees, food, and sight. In "Day," for example, the regenerated speaker identifies with the daylight that dispels the darkness of the earth:

> Great fellow of my being! woke with me
> Thou dost put on thy dazzling robes of light,
> And onward from the east go forth to free
> Thy children from the bondage of the night;
> I hail thee, pilgrim! on thy lonely way,
> Whose looks on all alike benignant shine;
> A child of light, like thee, I cannot stay,
> But on the world I bless must soon decline,
> Nor leave one ray to cheer the darkening mind
> That will not in the word of God its dayspring find.

But if the reborn being is in consonance with God and nature, such a soul feels alienated in a world largely peopled by the unborn masses. A number of poems dwell on this sense of estrangement from the human world. In "The Strangers" (LOA, 1: 639), the speaker complains that

> I see none whom I know, for they
>   See other things than him they meet;
> And though they stop me by the way,
>   'Tis still some other one to greet.

Very devotes still other poems to characterizing or addressing the unregenerate, associating them with images of dryness, deadness, darkness, iciness, and sterility; the imagery of "The Dead" is typical:

> I see them crowd on crowd they walk the earth
> Dry, leafless trees no Autumn wind laid bare;
> And in their nakedness find cause for mirth,
> And all unclad would winter's rudeness dare;
> No sap doth through their clattering branches flow,
> Whence springing leaves and blossoms bright appear;
> Their hearts the living God have ceased to know,
> Who gives the spring time to th'expectant year;
> They mimic life, as if from him to steal
> His glow of health to paint the livid cheek;
> They borrow words for thoughts they cannot feel,
> That with a seeming heart their tongue may speak;
> And in their show of life more dead they live
> Than those that to the earth with many tears they give.

Such scathing depictions of the unborn comprise some of Very's most successful poems.

The question of voice or persona in many of the ecstatic poems, first considered by Lawrence Buell, is one of the more intriguing raised in recent Very criticism. Very's assumption of the divine voice within certain of these poems is a truly daring poetic pose, so daring for its time that the poems of this sort remained unpublished during his lifetime and were not included in the two collections of his poems (one supposedly complete) published within six years after his death. The apparent voice of the Holy Spirit proclaims in "The Promise," "I come the rushing wind that shook the place / Where those once sat who spake with tongues of fire." Presumably, it is God the Father who announces in "The Message," "There is no voice but it is born of Me / I Am there is no other God beside." The Father likewise speaks in "The Creation":

> I said of old when darkness brooded long
> Upon the waste of waters Be thou light
> And forthwith sprang the sun rejoicing strong
> To chase away the mystery of the night.

In "I Am the Bread of Life," it is apparently the voice of the Son that declares, "I am thy life thou shalt upon me feed / And daily eat my flesh and drink my blood."

But the identification of the persona in these poems is not always so straightforward. In some of the ecstatic poems, it is impossible to resolve the voice into a single speaker. Buell cites the sonnet "Terror," which seems to begin with the voice of an observer of the apocalypse:

> There is no safety! fear has seized the proud;
> The swift run to and fro but cannot fly;
> Within the streets I hear no voices loud,
> They pass along with low, continuous cry.

But the speaker suddenly shifts in the last two lines to become God himself: "Repent! why do ye still uncertain stand, / The kingdom of My Son is nigh at hand."

A complex voice different from the two unresolved or separate voices in "The Terror" is present in several poems such as "My Meat and Drink," which reads equally well if the "I" is understood to be either that of the reborn or of Christ. In poems like this, it is useful to think in terms of a double or a *layered* voice. And a yet more intricate layering of voices occurs in "I am the Way":

> Thy way is simple for I am the light
> By which thou travelest on to meet thy God
> Brighter and brighter still shall be thy sight
> Till thou hast ended here the path I trod
> Before thee stretches far the thorny way
> Yet smoothed for thee by him who went before
> Go on it leads you to the perfect day
> The rest I to the patriarch Abraham swore
> Go on and I will guide you safely through
> For I have walked with suffering feet thy path
> Confide in me the Faithful and the True
> And thou shalt flee the approaching day of wrath
> Whose dawn e'en now the horizon's border shows
> And with its kindling fires prophetic glows.

In the first five lines the speaker appears unequivocally to be Christ. In line six, which refers to Christ in the third person, the speaker seems to be the voice of the regenerated preacher. A third voice materializes in line seven, that of God, who swore to Abraham. The effect achieved in such poems is the mingling of Very's own self with the divine through the medium of poetic voice.

Toward the end of the ecstatic period, Very was exploring verse forms (chiefly quatrains with alternating rhyme) other than the sonnet (in "The Cottage" [LOA, 1: 638], "The Strangers," "The Prayer," and "The Fox and the Bird," for example). The poetry of exaltation continued to be written until early 1840, when it suddenly ceased. Seven or eight months elapsed before there was another documented instance of Very's composing a poem. Of the 870 or so poems that Very produced during some 47 years of writing, more than one-third belong to the 18-month period from 1838–40.

The poetry of the last 40 years is anticlimactic. The religious, nature, and occasional poems typical of this period generally lack originality. They reflect the attitudes of an enlightened, orthodox Unitarian New Englander in the mid- to late nineteenth century. Nothing better illustrates this change than the way in which Very, in his later years, revised several poems from the preceding period. "The First shall be Last," first published in April 1839 at the height of the ecstatic period, bears many of the hallmarks of the verse of that period: the sense of urgency, the suggestion of the divinity of the speaker, the reliance on scriptural language, the elliptical nature of the scriptural allusions, and the associative rather than logical manner in which the allusions are connected. When Very recast the poem more than 30 years later as "Ye have hoarded up treasure in the last days. – James 5: 3," some sense of urgency was retained. The poem, moreover, continues to rely on scriptural language. But the message – a condemnation of the rich – is more obvious, and the frantic intensity of the early version, in which the speaker alludes to scriptures whose relevance is not always entirely apparent, has been lost. The changes to this poem typify the manner in which Very tamed a number of ecstatic poems later in his career.

This is not to say that the later poems are entirely without interest or merit. They have historical value in illuminating the views of an educated, informed, and articulate person such as Very on topics like evolution, slavery, war, and technology. In the late poems, Very expressed faith in human progress, not merely in scientific and technological advancement (which he does celebrate as tokens of that progress), but – despite such temporary setbacks as the Civil War – in moral nature as well. In several poems such as "Superfluities" and "Pompeii," he deplores the materialism of the age, although without the intensity that permeates his searing indictments of man's lack of spirituality in ecstatic poems such as "The Dead" and "The Graveyard." In keeping with his position as Unitarian preacher, however, he saw the Bible as the definitive source of truth. As he does in his sermons, Very frequently preaches in his poems (in, for example, "Man's Need of a Spiritual Birth") that humanity's spiritual existence should begin on earth, not in some future state. If the later poems lack intensity, however, they occasionally demonstrate an appealing sensitivity and simplicity, as in "The Hepatica in Winter" or "The Wild Rose of Plymouth" (LOA, 1: 640). In the latter the speaker sees in the ancient rose that has bloomed at Plymouth from time immemorial a link between himself and the Pilgrims, the Native Americans who preceded them, and future generations. The rose "Wreath[es] earth's children in one flowery chain / Of Love and Beauty."

In the late poems, there is generally little hint of the Spirit-filled enthusiast of 1838–40. Yet one of his most successful later poems, "On Finding the Truth," reflects wistfully upon his earlier illuminative experience:

With sweet surprise, as when one finds a flower,
Which in some lonely spot, unheeded, grows;

Such were my feelings, in the favored hour,
When Truth to me her beauty did disclose.
Quickened I gazed anew on heaven and earth,
For a new glory beamed from earth and sky;
All things around me shared the second birth,
Restored with me, and nevermore to die.
The happy habitants of other spheres,
As in times past, from heaven to earth came down;
Swift fled in converse sweet the unnumbered years,
And angel-help did human weakness crown!
The former things, with Time, had passed away,
And Man, and Nature lived again for aye.

The poem suggests that from a distance of some 15 years, although he was reticent about openly discussing it (the poem was not published until after his death), Very did not renounce but remembered with feeling the experience that had transformed his life and his poetry.

A persistent element in Very's poetry that has been a major topic of critical discussion is his use of nature. Some critics have found his attitude toward nature inconsistent. In fact, Very does hold different views of nature at different stages in his development, but he does not hold them simultaneously. In many of his earliest poems, nature is a source of joy and calm, an escape from the tribulations of life. In "The Sabbatia," the speaker imagines that this "pure, ideal flower" has appeared "To lead our thoughts to some serener clime, / Beyond the shadows and the storms of time." In other early poems, nature is associated with pleasant memories of childhood ("The Painted Columbine"). Many of the poems of this first period feature hummingbirds, robins, columbines, and other humble specimens of nature that the poet sentimentalizes. In "The Humming-Bird," he laments, "I cannot heal that green gold breast, / Where deep those cruel teeth have prest." And sometimes nature is put to the use of simple moralizing, as in "The Autumn Leaf," where the reader is instructed that "Heaven's teachings . . . / Though written on the leaves, and strown upon / The faithless winds . . . / Forever reach the heart that loves its God."

Near the end of the early period, Very produced some of his best pure nature poetry. The speaker in "The Tree" seeks no lesson from nature but simply rejoices in the beauty that he finds at every season:

I love thee when thy swelling buds appear,
And one by one their tender leaves unfold,
As if they knew that warmer suns were near
Nor longer sought to hide from winter's cold;
And when with darker growth thy leaves are seen
To veil from view the early robin's nest,
I love to lie beneath thy waving skreen [sic]
With limbs by summer's heat and toil opprest;
And when the autumn winds have stript thee bare,
And round thee lies the smooth untrodden snow,
When nought is thine that made thee once so fair,
I love to watch thy shadowy form below,
And through thy leafless arms to look above
On stars that brighter beam when most we need their
    love.

In "The Columbine," another poem written near the end of the first period, the speaker seems to achieve complete identification with the flower:

> Still, still my eye will gaze long-fixed on thee,
> Till I forget that I am called a man,
> And at thy side fast-rooted seem to be,
> And the breeze comes my cheek with thine to fan;
> . . . .
> And here we'll drink with thirsty pores the rain,
> And turn dew-sprinkled to the rising sun,
> And look when in the flaming west again
> His orb across the heaven its path has run;
> Here, left in darkness on the rocky steep,
> My weary eyes shall close like folding flowers in sleep.

In the ecstatic poetry of 1838–40, nature is used in two notable ways. First, consonance with nature becomes one of the marks of the reborn soul. In the sonnet "Nature" from this period, the regenerated speaker revels in this harmony:

> The bubbling brook doth leap when I come by,
> Because my feet find measure with its call;
> The birds know when the friend they love is nigh,
> For I am known to them both great and small;
> The flowers, which on the lovely hill-side grow,
> Expect me there, when Spring their bloom has given;
> And many a bush and tree my wanderings know,
> And e'en the clouds and silent stars of heaven.

The explanation for this accord between the speaker and the natural world is his regenerated spiritual state, as the poem elaborates:

> For he, who with his Maker walks aright,
> Shall be their lord, as Adam was before;
> His ear shall catch each sound with new delight,
> Each object wear the dress that then it wore;
> And he, as when erect in soul he stood,
> Hear from his Father's lips that all is good.

Second, and this is Very's most frequent use of nature in the ecstatic poems, he appropriates symbolic images from nature in order to depict the conditions of his mystically-oriented world. Thus, the unregenerate masses are associated with images of sterility, winter, and night; the reborn are identified with day, dawn, morning, and fruitfulness; and wind, breath, and rain are connected with the Holy Spirit. "The Latter Rain" (LOA, 1: 631), a typical instance of Very's successful appropriation of symbols from nature, combines a number of these images:

> The latter rain, it falls in anxious haste
> Upon the sun-dried fields and branches bare,
> Loosening with searching drops the rigid waste
> As if it would each root's lost strength repair;
> But not a blade grows green as in the spring,
> No swelling twig puts forth its thickening leaves;
> The robins only mid the harvests sing
> Pecking the grain that scatters from the sheaves;
> The rain falls still – the fruit all ripened drops,
> It pierces chestnut burr and walnut shell,
> The furrowed fields disclose the yellow crops,

> Each bursting pod of talents used can tell,
> And all that once received the early rain
> Declare to man it was not sent in vain.

The analogy is unstated but clear; only in line 12 does "bursting pod of talents used" imply a human correspondence. Another ecstatic poem, "The Earth" (LOA, 1: 633), bears comparison with the early poem, "The Columbine," in which the speaker identifies with the flower. In the ecstatic poem, the speaker's identification with the earth itself is much less conventional and is startling in its literalness:

> I would lie low, the ground on which men tread,
> Swept by thy spirit like the wind of heaven;
> An earth where gushing springs and corn for bread
> By me at every season should be given.

The poet here uses natural imagery with stunning effect to communicate the spiritual condition to which he aspires.

Less subtle than in "The Latter Rain" but like "The Earth" striking in its boldness and pertinence is Very's use of nature in "The Barberry Bush" for the revelation of his peculiar spiritual stance. He first describes the distinctive character of this fruit:

> The bush which bears most briars, and bitter fruit,
> Wait till the frost has turned its green leaves red,
> Its sweetened berries will thy palate suit,
> And thou may'st find, e'en there, a homely bread.

Then he draws the arresting parallel:

> But now I know, that other fruit, as sour,
> Grows on what now thou callest *Me*, and *You*;
> Yet, wilt thou wait the Autumn that I see,
> 'Twill sweeter taste than these red berries be.

In the poems of the post-ecstatic period, Very continues to use nature as a language in which to read moral and religious truths, but much less cryptically and subtly than in the ecstatic period. He finds predictable lessons in flowers, trees, and the cycle of the seasons, and he regularly observes that embodying such messages is a major function of nature, a vital source of truth for man. In "Autumn Flowers" (LOA, 1: 641), he sees flowers as "tokens . . . of an Exhaustless Love, / That ever to the end doth constant prove." Only rarely does he rise above this mundane level to write a nature poem with the delightful unpretentiousness of "The Hepatica in Winter:"

> Underneath its snowy bed,
> The hepatica lies dead!
> All its beauteous colors fled!
>
> No, not dead, but sleeping; Spring
> Shall again its beauty bring,
> And its beauty poets sing.
>
> There, protected from the cold,
> Doth the plant its life still hold,
> Woolly leaves the germ infold.
>
> In the bud a flower survives,
> Hidden from man's searching eyes;
> 'Tis not Beauty's self that dies!

Beauty still is born anew,
We again its tints shall view,
Rosy purple, deepest blue.

Very was surely in agreement with the theory of correspondence expressed in Emerson's *Nature*, the notion that nature reveals by analogy spiritual truth. In a few poems written late in the early period (the spring and summer of 1838), and in his ecstatic poems, the expression of this correspondence is likely to be compressed, charged, metaphorical, and integral to the poem's structure; in the early and late poems, it often appears as an obtrusive didacticism.

Very's poetry has periodically excited the interest of discriminating readers and critics. In his own day not only Emerson, but also Henry David **Thoreau**, Nathaniel **Hawthorne**, and William Cullen **Bryant** were his great admirers. Critic Yvor Winters's rediscovery of Very earlier in this century stimulated the modest critical interest that has been maintained over several decades. Today, with the frequent inclusion of Very's works in major anthologies, the favorable assessments of him in the *Columbia Literary History of the United States*, and the publication of a complete scholarly edition in which the poems are dated and chronologically arranged, Jones Very seems poised on the verge of a major reappraisal.

HELEN R. DEESE

Selected Works

Essays and Poems, edited by Ralph Waldo Emerson, Boston: Little and Brown, 1839
Poems by Jones Very, edited by William P. Andrews, Boston: Houghton Mifflin, 1883
Poems and Essays by Jones Very: Complete and Revised Edition, edited by James Freeman Clarke, Boston: Houghton Mifflin, 1886
Poems and Essays by Jones Very: James Freeman Clarke's Enlarged Collection of 1886 Re-edited with a Thematic and Topical Index, edited by Kenneth Walter Cameron, Hartford, Connecticut: Transcendental, 1965
Jones Very: Selected Poems, edited by Nathan Lyons, New Brunswick, New Jersey: Rutgers University Press, 1966
Jones Very: The Complete Poems, edited by Helen R. Deese, Athens and London: University of Georgia Press, 1993

Further Reading

Bartlett, William Irving, *Jones Very: Emerson's "Brave Saint,"* Durham, North Carolina: Duke University Press, 1942
Buell, Lawrence, *Literary Transcendentalism: Style and Vision in the American Renaissance*, Ithaca, New York: Cornell University Press, 1973
Gittleman, Edwin, *Jones Very: The Effective Years, 1833–1840*, New York: Columbia University Press, 1967
Lee, A. Robert, ed., *Nineteenth-Century American Poetry*, London: Vision, 1985, pp. 166–193
Myerson, Joel, ed., *Studies in the American Renaissance*, Charlottesville: University Press of Virginia, 1986, pp. 305–371
The Transcendentalists: A Review of Research and Criticism, New York: Modern Language Association of America, 1984, pp. 186–194
Winters, Yvor, *Maule's Curse*, Norfolk, Connecticut: New Directions, 1938, pp. 125–136

Edith Wharton

(1862–1937)

In a 1907 letter, Edith Wharton confesses, "I am abjectly humble about my poetry & not at all sure that I have ever risen even to . . . [the] delightful standard of 'creditable verse.'" A best-selling American novelist, acknowledged by many to be one of the early twentieth century's foremost prose writers, Wharton has found considerably less success in the pages of American poetry. Although her second novel, *The House of Mirth* (1905), won her international acclaim for its pointed scrutiny of the cruel excesses of New York's social elite, Wharton's early poetry seemed to turn an inexplicably blind eye to the social, industrial, and economic upheavals of the day. Indeed, if her signature traits – a keen sense of irony, a sharp-tongued wit, and a cool perspective on contemporary culture – propelled novels like *The Custom of the Country* (1913), *Summer* (1917), and *The Age of Innocence* (1920) to the forefront of American fiction, these qualities seem unaccountably absent from her early poetic forays into the relative arcana of Renaissance painting, Gothic architecture, and Greek mythology. Wharton's poetry, one reviewer complained in 1909, was "too sicklied o'er with the pale cast of thought, its artifice is too evident, its song (as far as it sings at all) does not well straight up from the heart."

Wharton's early critics evidently expected a poetry of sentiment, only to be disappointed by a poetry of intellect. Her first widely circulated collection, *Artemis to Actaeon and Other Verse* (1909), was commended for its "high seriousness," but the *Review of Reviews* faults the poet for what it terms the absence of "emotional appeal." And although her poetry was "very beautiful and perfect in its way," London's *Spectator* primly notes, the verse makes "its chief appeal to the intellect."

The demand that Wharton subordinate her voracious mind to the rigid societal requirements of properly "feminine" behavior did not begin with her critics. After meeting Wharton in Newport, Rhode Island, in 1893, the French writer Paul Bourget was moved to model his satiric depiction of the "intellectual tomboy" after his newfound acquaintance: "Before the intellectual girl one longs to cry – 'Oh, for one ignorance, one error, just a single one. May she make a blunder, may she prove not to know!' In vain. A mind may be mistaken, a mind may be ignorant, but never a thinking machine!" Wharton's reputation as a poet also suffered in part from the manichean categories of her day. Part sentimental Edna St. Vincent Millay and part empiricist Ezra Pound, the androgynous "intellectual tomboy" confounded gendered expectations. The work of critics Suzanne Clark, Sandra M. Gilbert, and Susan Gubar has shown that modernism developed within a specific rubric of sexual politics – one in which the modern was increasingly aligned with an anxious masculinity that fetishized "hard" intellectual facts, while the sentimental or non-modern was associated with the abject, the immature, and the feminine.

In a transitional poetic era that increasingly crystallized around gender-based notions of genre, Wharton's carefully constructed sonnets, her sometimes sadomasochistic dramatic monologues, and her densely allusive lyrics escaped easy categorization. Her poems could range from studiously rhymed narratives taken up with prosaic moments of domestic intimacy to violent experiments in modernist symbolism. Wharton's poetry was, to use her own word, "fugitive." She wrote so much and so frequently that she often lost track of her poems and had to recall copies from editors and friends. Yet her poems were also "fugitive" in a more substantive way: belying classification, they were consistent only with her restless need to try something different. As Elaine Showalter points out, Wharton was caught in "the historical transition from one house of American women's fiction to another, from the homosocial women's culture and literature of the nineteenth century to the heterosexual fiction of modernism." Similarly poised between two distinct moments in American poetry, Wharton's verse spoke to both: her poems were alternately acutely personal and broadly public, sentimental and symbolist, Victorian and modernist, and safely conventional and boldly experimentalist.

Despite the cool reception that Wharton met with at the hands of her critics, she persisted in writing and publishing a steady stream of poems throughout her 75-year lifetime. For young Edith Newbold Jones, growing up in "Old New York," poetry answered a very private need for order in a world that seemed threatening and confusing. As a child, Edith Jones frequently felt menaced by some unnameable lurking source of turmoil and emotional devastation. "The sense of bewilderment, of the need of guidance, the longing to understand *what it was all about*," Wharton later reports in her unfinished autobiography, "Life and I," "dogged her morbidly sensitive conscience. "My little corner of the cosmos seemed like a dark trackless region 'where ignorant armies clash by night,' & I was oppressed by the sense that I was too small & ignorant & alone ever to find my way about it." Barbara A. White has used this passage to make a compelling argument that Wharton was the victim of childhood incest at the hands of her adored father. Whether based on experience, imagination, or some combination of the two, incest would serve as a latent theme in most of her major fictions (*Edith Wharton Review* [1991]).

If Wharton repressed incidents of psychic trauma, poetry bridged the gap between a terrifying incestuous threat and the tender father whom she adored. Verse had a rhythmic consistency that imposed order on her jumbled thoughts. As she prowled the shelves of her father's library, young Edith discovered William Wordsworth ("without enthusiasm") and the poetry of Samuel Taylor Coleridge, which she devoured. "Let no one ask me why!" she recalls after a raptured reading of Coleridge's "Friend": "I can only suppose it answered to some hidden need to order my thoughts, & get things into some kind of logical relation to each other." To a little girl who felt herself to be mysteriously oppressed, poetry extended new imaginative vistas. "When I read my first poetry I felt that 'bliss was it in that dawn to be alive,'" Wharton later writes, ironically echoing the poet she had earlier dismissed. "Here were words transfigured, lifted from earth to heaven!" Poetry continued to inspire her with an almost religious reverence. Despite the success of her fiction, she confided to *Scribner's* editor William

Crary Brownell, "Poetry is to me so august a thing that I always feel that I should be struck by lightning when I sidle up to the shrine."

If poetry offered a creative territory at once sacred and secure, it also furnished a language that enabled safe passage into Wharton's secret netherworld of transgressive desires. Delighting in "the sensuous rapture produced by the sight & sound of the words," Wharton declares that these words "sang to me so bewitchingly that they almost lured me from the wholesome noonday air of childhood into some strange supernatural region, where the normal pleasures of my age seemed as insipid as the fruits of the earth to Persephone after she had eaten of the pomegranate seed." As Candace Waid has suggested, consuming the pomegranate seed was for Wharton an act fraught with sinful pleasure: if tasting the fruit fated Persephone to life in Hades, then consuming the pomegranate seed introduced the woman poet to both "the underworld of experience and the transgression of erotic knowledge." Indeed, if George Frederic Jones was the source of incestuous conflict in his daughter's life – at once, as she would write, a "warm-blooded temptation" and the cause of a "choking agony of terror" – then poetry was the pomegranate seed. Persephone-like, Wharton could have it both ways – spending part of her creative seasons "above ground" in the orderly world of convention, while dipping periodically into the appealing realm of subterranean chaos. Poetry temptingly linked the permissible and the forbidden.

Wharton clearly associated her love of poetry with her father. In *A Backward Glance* (1934), she sketches her "tall splendid" father as a man who was deeply moved by Thomas Babington Macaulay and Alfred, Lord Tennyson, but whose nascent "buds of fancy" were withered by his wife's "matter-of-factness." "I imagine there was a time when his rather rudimentary love of verse might have been developed," Wharton wistfully recalls, "had he had any one with whom to share it." Poetry enabled Wharton to be her father's imaginative partner, to speak to "the stifled cravings [that] had once germinated" in him. According to "Life and I," when George Jones first read the "Lays of Ancient Rome" to his daughter, she found "the movement of the metre . . . intoxicating: I can still feel the thump thump of my little heart as I listened to it!" Poetry was the genre of thresholds for Wharton, articulating the bewildering intersection between cadenced discipline and the transgressive opportunity to travel into places of erotic knowledge.

At the age of 10, Edith Jones began pilfering scraps of wrapping paper from around the house and furtively scribbling what she would later term "sentimental poems . . . & mawkish stories about little girls who 'got lost.'" For a child who herself felt nervously confused, these poems may have served a therapeutic need. Wharton's mother, however, evidently considered her daughter's work inspired. Showing what her daughter would later describe as "an odd inarticulate interest" in Edith's rhymes, Lucretia Jones began to collect the verses and transcribe them into a private notebook. By the fall of 1878, Lucretia Jones had arranged to have 29 poems privately published by a small Newport press. As R. W. B. Lewis has pointed out, the collection, entitled *Verses*, although technically competent, lacks the humor and originality that would ultimately become the hallmark of Wharton's fiction. Only a self-mocking inscription that the young poet scribbled into her own copy indicates

the untapped resources of Wharton's wit: "Who wrote these verses, she this volume owns. / Her unpoetic name is Edith Jones."

Verses piqued the interest of the *North American Review* editor and Newport neighbor Allen Thorndike Rice, who forwarded a handful of Edith's poems to Henry Wadsworth **Longfellow**. The famed American poet subsequently prevailed upon William Dean **Howells** to publish one poem in the *Atlantic Monthly*. Wharton later dismissed the whole incident as an embarrassing parental folly: "nothing of my oeuvre de jeunesse," she remarks, "showed the slightest spark of originality or talent."

Wharton in fact dated her first independent literary achievement to a poem that she submitted to the New York *World* in 1879. The poem, inspired by a newspaper item about a little boy who had committed suicide after being imprisoned overnight for a childish infraction, perfectly suited the adolescent writer's morbid temperament. Some years earlier, Edith's governess had given her a copy of John Quakenbos's *Practical Rhetoric*, a grammar book that not only taught her to appreciate the distinctions between English and Latin verse, but also warned her "not to speak of the oyster as a 'succulent bivalve.'" She responded to the gift with a mixture of anxiety and delight: "I knew now when I was writing in Iambic pentameter, & when a dactyl or a spondee fell from my pen. I was proud of this knowledge, & zealous to conform to the 'rules of English versification'; and yet – and yet – I couldn't see that Shakespeare or Milton had! This was almost as dark a problem as the Atonement – life & art seemed equally beset with difficulties for a little girl!" Fearing that the *World*'s editor would spot her metrical irregularities, she conscientiously enclosed a note justifying her submission: "I carefully explained that I 'knew the rules of English versification', but that I had put in the extra syllables *on purpose!*" The poem was duly published "in all of its native redundancy." Despite these early victories, however, Wharton would publish nothing for the next 10 years.

When she did return to writing four years after her marriage to Edward Wharton in 1885, Edith was anxious to play by what she called "the rules of the game," and she increasingly gravitated toward the conventional forms so esteemed by Mr. Quakenbo. Unlike the sprawling poetic meditations of her revered role-model, "the great Originator" Walt **Whitman**, Wharton's early poetry tended toward traditional forms and meters, taking Robert Browning, Tennyson, and Algernon Swinburne as models. Her first mature success, a dramatic monologue entitled "The Last Giustiniani" (LOA, 2: 535), appeared in *Scribner's* in October 1889. Covering the thematic territory that Henry James would explore with considerably less success in his ill-fated play *Guy Domville* (1895), Wharton sets the poem in eighteenth-century Italy, where the last surviving member of the Giustiniani family has learned that his fellow kinsmen have all died in defense of their native Venice. Forced to abjure his monastic vows and ensure the clan's survival, the last Giustiniani reluctantly takes a wife, relinquishing his life of celibacy. A great deal of trepidation, however, accompanies his decision: "I feared you!" he confesses to his bride. "I, indeed, / For whom all womanhood has been, forsooth, / Summed up in the sole Virgin of the Creed." Giustiniani's anxiety is symptomatic. Although patterned after Victorian models, the poem examines what would develop into a signature modernist preoccupation: the confrontation between male impotency and female sexual ascendancy.

"The twentieth century's most characteristic citizen," Sandra M. Gilbert and Susan Gubar observe, was the "anonymous dehumanized man, that impotent cypher." Wharton prefigures T. S. Eliot's J. Alfred Prufrock and Virginia Woolf's Mr. Ramsay in a hesitant monk who is forced into sexuality by a dynastic crisis. First in a long line of Wharton's equivocating male characters, Giustiniani suffers "A certain monkish warping of the blood" when he sees his approaching bride and "would have crept again / To the warped missal" of his isolated cell had his abbot not "snatched a sword / And girded me." Like Lawrence Selden in *The House of Mirth*, Newland Archer in *The Age of Innocence*, and Martin Boyne in *The Children* (1928), the poem's title character cannot come to terms with a "real" woman: his mental taxonomy – holy Virgin versus diabolical temptress – cannot allow for a woman who fits neither category. The threat of oligarchical male impotency, moreover, underscores the poem's class and racial concerns: Wharton's implicit anxiety that upper-class men will prove incapable of reproducing succeeding generations of "sweetness, whiteness, youth" compels her to force a rather abrupt resolution on a complex modernist problem: "Ah, then the monk's garb shrivelled from my heart," Giustiniani sighs with relief, "And left me man to face your womanhood."

Despite the mild success of "The Last Giustiniani," Scribner's refused one of Wharton's next poems and declined her ecstatic offer to produce an entire volume of verse. Rejection shattered Wharton's fragile self-confidence, and Edward L. Burlingame of Scribner's quickly wrote to reassure her. "You are entirely too tender-hearted to be an editor," Wharton responded in July 1897. "I saw no undue flippancy in your manner of refusing my little dialogue, & was only sorry that I couldn't think of just the right way of changing it." She returned to the "pure form" of the reliable sonnet, only to be overwhelmed with the sense of her own inadequacy. "What thing am I, that undismayed have sought / To pour my verse with trembling hand untaught / Into a shape so small yet so sublime?" she had meditated in her 1891 poem "The Sonnet":

> Because perfection haunts the hearts of men,
>   Because thy sacred chalice gathered up
>   The wine of Petrarch, Shakspere, Shelley – then
> Receive these tears of failure as they drop
>   (Sole vintage of my life), since I am fain
>   To pour them into a consecrated cup.

Wharton's disclaimer is at once conventional and candid. When Brownell of Scribner's asked her to reconsider her original offer to publish a volume of poetry, Wharton self-consciously declined: "There are degrees in prose & poetry – below a certain point – well, it simply isn't poetry; & I am not sure I've ever reached the 'poetry line.'"

Her struggle to reach that "line" was encumbered by her ongoing effort to find her own distinctive poetic voice. At once flexible and indecisive, she tried a number of possibilities, as two poems entitled "Life" indicate. The first, "a sonnet after Carducci" (LOA, 2: 537), appeared in *Scribner's* in 1893. In strict Petrarchan form, the poem mocks the self-important artist who "Muses which god he shall immortalize" in the marble of life – here humorously expressed in the elaborate alliteration "proud Parian's perpetuity." Yet the sonnet also criticizes the artist for being so withdrawn from the commonplace details of daily experience that he can only indulge in abstract "high visions" at the expense of concrete artistic production. In the end, the speaker prophetically warns, "the night cometh wherein none shall see."

Wharton would return to this issue with an erotic immediacy in a subsequent dramatic monologue entitled "Life," published in *Artemis to Actaeon* in 1909. The speaker of the poem, a reed, breathlessly begs Life to "lift me to thy lips, Life, and once more / Pour the wild music through me." In her groundbreaking analysis of this poem, Candace Waid suggests that Wharton associated art not only with erotic communion, but also with a specifically sadomasochistic form of gratification: the reed pants with pleasure, recalling how Life "Severed, and rapt me from my silent tribe, / Pierced, fashioned, lipped me, sounding for a voice." The reed enjoys even fuller ecstasy, however, when Life "in my live flank dug a finger-hole, / And wrung new music from it. Ah, the pain!" Wharton's fascination with the relationship between desire, physical violation, and immortality stemmed, Waid convincingly argues, from her longing to penetrate "the secrets of the female body" and to discover the mystery of fertility. A wounding eroticism violently pierces the bland facade of Wharton's previous sonnet: Life is no longer an inert piece of aestheticized marble, but an active agent of sexual transformation.

Wharton alternated between these two positions by seeking the safety of established forms while welcoming the titillating danger of "underworld" poetic experimentalism. She frequently stressed that a poet must master traditional forms before attempting new methods. Faulting her friend Sara Norton's poetry for its "bareness," Wharton argues that such economy is a privilege, not a right. "It is not *being simple* so much as being excessively subtle; & the less-practiced simplicity is apt to have too loose a 'weave,'" she explains. "Personally, I think a long apprenticeship should be given to form before it is thrown overboard."

Convinced that form was the necessary backbone for innovative content, Wharton did not hesitate to give her frank opinion of Corinne Roosevelt Robinson, Theodore Roosevelt's younger sister and a published poet. Wharton's critique is indicative of her demandingly intellectual approach to poetic economy:

> Technique can be cultivated, & chiefly, I think, by reading only the best & rarest things, until one instinctively rejects the easy, accommodating form, where the sentiment helps the verse to dissemble its deficiencies. The cultivation of rhythmical sense is all the more important because there develops with it, undoubtedly, an acuter sense for the right word, right in sound, significance, colour – & also in expressiveness. The whole thing – all the complex process – is really one, & once one begins to wait attentively on the mysteries of sound in verse, the need of the more expressive word, the more imaginative image, develops also, & one asks more of one's self, one seeks to extract more from each sensation & emotion, & to distil that "more" into fewer and intenser syllables.

Wharton understood form in rigorous architectural detail, as her studies of house and landscape design in *The Decoration* of Houses (1897) and *Italian Villas and Their Gardens* (1904) readily attest. Indeed, her 1893 double sonnet "Chartres" (LOA, 2: 539), written in slow iambic pentameter, imitates the scrupulous construction of the title's immense cathedral, here gothically transformed into a stone flower. Yet if the first stanza commemorates the cathedral, "Immense, august, like some Titanic bloom," it also mourns the decline of the church's spiritual importance in the modern world. "Withdrawn / From hot humanity's impatient woes," the church becomes "mute and cold," the "blank eyes" of its sculpted Virgin viewing only a "meagre remnant" of elderly worshipers. The second stanza, a deconstruction of the first, withdraws into the sublimity of "The roseate coldness of an Alp at dawn." Despite this romantic retreat, the cathedral's diminished role and its ironic detachment from what Wharton considered the mob of common humanity anticipates Eliot's modernist elegies on spiritual impoverishment and the ironic detachment of art.

Wharton included "Chartres" in *Artemis to Actaeon*, a heterogeneous volume that speaks through her many voices. Her implicit disdain for the self-congratulatory aesthete is evident, for example, in her double sonnet "Experience" (LOA, 2: 538), a poem that explains life through an extended market metaphor. The poem is grounded in the same sophisticated understanding of industrial capitalism that underpins both *The House of Mirth* and *The Custom of the Country*. The speaker mocks those who would seek to make an exchange-based bargain with Death: "shall our hopes and fears / Buy nothing of thee, Death? Behold our wares, / And sell us the one joy for which we wait." Immortality, however, cannot be "purchased cheap," and Death informs the speaker that years of hoarded experience merely "'purchase sleep.'" Interestingly, although the poem ostensibly critiques capitalist logic, the market ultimately prevails: life's currency cannot buy off Death, but it can successfully procure a reasonable "product" – rest. Commodities continue to be exchanged, Wharton assures us, even at the end of "life's small market."

Like her contemporaries Charlotte Perkins Gilman and Thorstein Veblen, Wharton also saw the market as institutionally gendered: women served as decorative commodities to be exchanged between men. In *The House of Mirth*, for instance, the financier Simon Rosedale prizes Lily Bart precisely because she is a "highly specialized product." Yet, as Wharton observed, such objectification was ultimately predicated on the elimination of female subjectivity altogether: a woman must forfeit at least part of her identity to become an exchangeable aesthetic commodity. Wharton was darkly fascinated by the power of the consuming male gaze to fetishize the female object of desire. In "The Tomb of Ilaria Giunigi" (LOA, 2: 541), a Petrarchan sonnet from *Artemis to Actaeon*, the male speaker commissions a tomb for his beloved departed wife. The sculpted burial case, however, bears such a striking resemblance to its model that the tomb itself eventually surpasses and supplants Ilaria Giunigi. Ilaria's soul, the ecstatic husband declares, has "cast the sweet robing of the flesh aside" and "Into these lovelier marble limbs it stole, / Regenerate in art's sunrise clear and wide." To the husband-speaker, the monument surpasses the original woman. Captured in a work of art, Ilaria is a "perfect image" for her husband to adore. Like Lawrence Selden, who fancies that he sees "the real Lily Bart" in the heroine's dead body, Ilaria Giunigi's widower finds his wife "lovelier" and more authentic in her

new marble robes. And like Selden, who hears from his dead lover "the word which made all clear," Giunigi commissions sculpted "lips that at love's call should answer 'Here!'"

Although Wharton generally sacrificed idealism to realism, the title poem of *Artemis to Actaeon* seeks to rectify the imbalances implicit in these gender arrangements. In Ovid's original narrative, Artemis, the virgin goddess of the hunt, punishes Actaeon, the mortal hunter, for spying on her while she bathes in a spring. Mortified by this transgression, Artemis transforms Actaeon into a stag and, in a sweepingly ironic move, dooms him forever to flee his fellow hunters. As Nancy J. Vickers has pointed out, the classical Petrarchan version of this myth denies Artemis a voice and subverts Actaeon's punishment: by lyrically praising his lady's beauty, Petrarch's speaker inverts the goddess' silencing intent. "A modern Actaeon affirming himself as poet cannot permit Ovid's angry goddess to speak her displeasure and deny his voice; his speech requires her silence." Rendering Artemis voiceless, according to Vickers, is "an emblematic gesture; it suppresses a voice, and it casts generations of would-be Lauras in a role predicated upon the muteness of its player" (*Writing and Sexual Difference*, edited by Elizabeth Abel [1982]).

Wharton's poem radically rewrites the Petrarchan model, positioning Artemis as the powerful narrator in a story of female desire and conquest: "Thou couldst not look on me and live," the goddess boldly declares. Lamenting the disadvantages of immortality, Artemis observes that deities are permitted "Man's wealth, man's servitude, but not himself!" The divine huntress longs for the day when a mortal man might

> with all-adventuring hand,
> Break rank, fling past the people and the priest,
> Up the last step, on to the inmost shrine,
> And there, the sacred curtain in his clutch,
> Drop dead of seeing – while the others prayed!

The "sacred curtain" could, of course, veil what Wharton called in her 1893 story "The Fullness of Life" "the innermost room, the holy of holies, [where] the soul sits alone and waits for a footstep that never comes." Or, more convincingly, the veil could screen the female "palpitating centre" that Wharton so graphically described in her unpublished pornographic fragment of father-daughter incest, "Beatrice Palmato."

In a scene that in many ways both anticipates and significantly reverses William Butler Yeats's "Leda and the Swan" (1924), Wharton describes a female divinity who sexually toys with her human inamorato: "I from afar / Beheld thee fashioned for one hour's high use, / Nor meant to slake oblivion drop by drop." Artemis determines that she will have this brash young man: "*Because I love thou shalt die!*" The moment of gazing is here figured as a moment of violent sexual communion, and Actaeon's punishment is thus simultaneously his reward. In the concluding moments of erotic metamorphosis, Artemis congratulates Actaeon for his daring decision to look beyond the "sacred curtain":

> And this was thine: to lose thyself in me,
> Relive in my renewal, and become
> The light of other lives, a quenchless torch
> Passed on from hand to hand, till men are dust
> And the last garland withers from my shrine.

Wharton not only restores Artemis's voice, but she also makes it possible for a woman to derive pleasure from the male gaze while not falling victim to its attendant objectification. Artemis serves as a powerful antidote to Lily Bart, her fictional predecessor. Because Lily cannot reconcile the various identities imputed to her by the novel's scrutinizing men, she commits suicide. By contrast, Wharton's goddess *herself* wields the potent gaze, transforming her mortal admirer into an eroticized male victim: indeed, like Lily Bart, who is "fashioned to adorn and delight," Actaeon is "fashioned for one hour's high use."

Wharton's grim assessment of American gender relations grew, in part, out of her own experience. Her unhappy marriage to Teddy Wharton culminated in divorce in 1913. In 1907, Wharton had met one catalyst for her divorce – an attractive American journalist named Morton Fullerton. Their love affair, which lasted from 1908 to 1910, proved to be both exhilarating and humiliating. Her passionate letters and private journals from this period attest to the emotionally consuming nature of the liaison. If Wharton's sexual awakening opened new emotional vistas, however, it also introduced an unaccustomed self-abasement: when Fullerton's attention began to flag, his lover struggled frantically to preserve their vanishing ardor. Numerous private poems written during this period, largely unpublished, are consumed with the ecstasy and pathos of her relationship with "M. F." In "Terminus," an unrhymed Whitmanesque lyric written after one particularly passionate night that the lovers spent together in London's Charing Cross Hotel, Wharton empathizes with other women who have spent similar nights in this prosaic bed, anticipating the same sad conclusion to a fleeting love affair:

> And thus some woman like me waking alone before
>   dawn,
> While her lover slept, as I woke and heard the calm stir
>   of your breathing,
> Some woman has heard as I heard the farewell shriek of
>   the trains
> Crying good-bye to the city and staggering out into
>   darkness,
> And shaken at the heart has thought: "So must we forth
>   in the darkness,
> Sped down the fixed rail of habit by the hand of
>   implacable fate – "

Wharton would translate the raw immediacy of "Terminus" into two poems in *Artemis to Actaeon*. "The Mortal Lease," an eight-part sonnet sequence, is the most obvious of the published Fullerton poems. Giving measured consideration to the futility of erotic love and the inevitability of death, the poem's speaker ultimately chooses to heed the Marvellian words of her persuasive lover and "live to-day":

> Yet for one rounded moment I will be
> No more to you than what my lips may give,
> And in the circle of your kisses live
> As in some island of a storm-blown sea,
> Where the cold surges of infinity
> Upon the outward reefs unheeded grieve,
> And the loud murmur of our blood shall weave
> Primeval silences round you and me.

A less conspicuous treatment of this theme appears in "Two Backgrounds" (LOA, 2: 540), a double sonnet loosely inspired by two Leonardo da Vinci paintings. The poem rigidly intellectualizes the more direct emotional issues at stake in "Terminus" and "The Mortal Lease." In the first sonnet, "La Vierge au Donateur," Wharton constructs, in her trademark architectural detail, a city ideally hospitable to romantic love:

> And in that narrow burgh, with equal mood,
> Two placid hearts, to all life's good resigned,
> Might, from the altar to the lych-gate, find
> Long years of peace and dreamless plenitude.

The second sonnet, however, revises the vision of the first. The bountiful gratification promised in "La Vierge" is translated into a torment of unsatisfied desire. The metropolis that previously enjoyed "fat plenty in her halls" is in "Mona Lisa" "Yon strange blue city," which "crowns a scarpèd steep / No mortal foot hath bloodlessly essayed." Those who have tried to reach the mystical azure land have met only with maddening failure. The land "Lit with wild lightnings from the heaven of pain" remains as far away at the end of the journey as it seemed at the beginning. A sadomasochistic "heaven of pain" displaces the promised fulfillment. The lovers, no longer blessed with "placid hearts," become "two souls, whom life's perversities / Had mocked with want in plenty, tears in mirth." Denied the rapture of "dreamless plenitude," they can only hope to "meet in dreams, ungarmented of earth, / And drain Joy's awful chalice to the lees." As Wharton had painfully learned from the Fullerton affair, the torments of unfulfilled desire invariably replaced the insubstantial promise of perfect bliss. Fullerton's erratic behavior had driven Wharton to distraction: "My life was better before I knew you," she wrote to him in 1910. "That is, for me, the sad conclusion of this sad year. And it is a bitter thing to say to the one being one has ever loved d'amour."

Wharton continued to write and publish poetry throughout the rest of her life; she compiled only one more collection, *Twelve Poems*, which appeared in 1926. Her love of France, the country that she adopted and made her home and her fierce disappointment at American reluctance to enter the Great War both inspired her to write a number of aesthetically marginal but starkly partisan verses. Of these, some were moving expressions of personal grief. Wharton dedicated a poem entitled "On Active Service" (1918), along with two wartime novels, *A Son at the Front* and *The Marne*, for example, to young Ronald Simmons, a fellow American in Paris who died while stationed in Marseilles. Simmons's death transformed the war from a national emergency into a personal tragedy: "He is dead that was alive. / How shall friendship understand?" Despite her numerous humanitarian activities, Wharton felt utterly hollowed by world conflict. As she observed to her friend Bernard Berenson, "So much of me is dead."

If the First World War became the watershed even for an emerging generation of American modernists, Wharton saw the war as a fulfillment of her own symbolist prophesies. Like Yeats, Pound, and later Eliot and H. D., Wharton's most gripping poetry turned away from the material world to discover a more compelling place in the landscape of the mind. Her neglected early example of imagism, "An Autumn Sunset" (1894; LOA, 2: 542), is a neo-symbolist excursion that not only echoes the intricate cosmology of Charles Baudelaire and Edgar Allan **Poe**, but also weirdly anticipates the coming international conflict. The setting sun in this two-part poem acts as an agent of "universal carnage," casting its rays on an increasingly violent scene in which storm clouds form "an advancing mob in sword-points penned." The image of the "wan Valkyrie," a Norse mythological handmaiden who was charged with choosing those to be slain in battle, who flies over "the ensanguined ruins of the fray" and carries the evening star "Above the waste of war . . . / . . . to search the faces of the dead," strangely prefigures Isaac Rosenberg's voracious Valkyries in "Daughters of War" (1917), whose necrophilic "passion for the sons of valour" leads unsuspecting soldiers into a woman-sponsored massacre. Wharton's Valkyrie, however, is less the instrument of destruction than the impassive author-observer, "searching" and recording the faces of the dead.

In the second part of the poem, the speaker imagines that the "wild black promontories" she sees on the horizon are really "outposts of some ancient land forlorn, / Uncomforted of morn, / Where old oblivions gather." In a faint echo of Poe's "The Raven" (LOA, 1: 535), these oblivions form a

> melancholy unconsoling fold
> Of all things that go utterly to death
> And mix no more, no more
> With life's perpetually awakening breath.

In this increasingly surreal interior world, the speaker foresees a deathly existence of numbing forgetfulness:

> Shall I not wander there, a shadow's shade,
> A spectre self-destroyed,
> So purged of all remembrance and sucked back
> Into the primal void,
> That should we on that shore phantasmal meet
> I should not know the coming of your feet?

Like Persephone, the poet-speaker is doomed to dwell in the oblivion of her own private waste land – a "primal void" that hearkens back to Baudelaire's "The Seven Old Men" ("Swarming city, city full of dreams / Where the specter in broad daylight accosts the passerby") and that anticipates the "forgetful snow" of Eliot's desolate terrain in *The Waste Land* (1922).

Of the various explanations for Wharton's exile from the canon of American poetry, the most compelling may be her own best asset. In an era of poetic manifestos, emerging "schools" and accompanying "isms," Wharton's poetry was elastic and unsettled; it resisted the implicit poetic requirements of decisiveness and consistency. Her restless imagination and her willingness to try new forms of expression – alternately classical, Victorian, Whitmanesque, and boldly modern – makes her a peculiarly appropriate archetype for the transitional years surrounding the turn of the century. Wharton's ambivalent and, at times, astonishingly visionary poetry belies categorization. Fascinated by the changing times, Edith Wharton offered an unruly chorus of competing voices to articulate the increasingly rich complexity of the modern experience.

JENNIE A. KASSANOFF

Selected Works

Verses, Newport, Rhode Island: C. E. Hammett, 1878

"The Sonnet," *Century* (November 1891), p. 113

Artemis to Actaeon and Other Verse, New York: Scribner's, 1909

"Belgium," in *Poems of the Great War*, edited by J. W. Cunliffe, New York: Macmillan, 1916

"On Active Service," *Scribner's* (November 1918), p. 619

Twelve Poems, London: Medici Society VII, 1926

Eternal Passion in English Poetry, edited by Wharton with Robert Norton, 1939; Freeport, New York: Books for Libraries, 1969

The Letters of Edith Wharton, edited by R. W. B. Lewis and Nancy Lewis, New York: Collier, 1988

"Life and I," in *Edith Wharton: Novellas and Other Writings*, edited by Cynthia Griffin Wolff, New York: Library of America, 1990

Henry James and Edith Wharton; Letters: 1900–1915, edited by Lyall H. Powers, New York: Scribner's, 1990

Further Reading

Ammons, Elizabeth, *Edith Wharton's Argument with America*, Athens: University of Georgia Press, 1980

Benstock, Shari, *No Gifts from Chance: A Biography of Edith Wharton*, New York: Scribner's, 1994

Bloom, Harold, ed., *Edith Wharton*, New York: Chelsea House, 1986

Clark, Suzanne, *Sentimental Modernism: Women Writers and the Revolution of the Word*, Bloomington: Indiana University Press, 1991

Erlich, Gloria C., *The Sexual Education of Edith Wharton*, Berkeley: University of California Press, 1992

Fryer, Judith, *Felicitous Space: The Imaginative Structures of Edith Wharton and Willa Cather*, Chapel Hill: University of North Carolina Press, 1986

Gilbert, Sandra M., and Susan Gubar, *No Man's Land: The Place of the Woman Writer in the Twentieth Century*, vol. 2, New Haven, Connecticut: Yale University Press, 1989

Goodman, Susan, *Edith Wharton's Women: Friends and Rivals*, Hanover, New Hampshire: University Press of New England, 1990

Lewis, R. W. B., *Edith Wharton: A Biography*, New York: Fromm International, 1985

Michaels, Walter Benn, *The Gold Standard and the Logic of Naturalism*, Berkeley: University of California Press, 1987

Showalter, Elaine, *Sister's Choice: Tradition and Change in American Women's Writing*, Oxford: Oxford University Press, 1991

Tuttleton, James W., Kristin O. Lauer, and Margaret P. Murray, eds., *Edith Wharton: The Contemporary Reviews*, Cambridge: Cambridge University Press, 1992

Waid, Candace, *Edith Wharton's Letters from the Underworld: Fictions of Women and Writing*, Chapel Hill: University of North Carolina Press, 1991

Woolf, Cynthia Griffin, *A Feast of Words: The Triumph of Edith Wharton*, Oxford: Oxford University Press, 1977

James Monroe Whitfield

(1822–1871)

We know little about the early life of the African American poet James Monroe Whitfield. Born on April 10, 1822, in New Hampshire, he was able to attend district schools, but how he acquired his sensitivity to world affairs and knowledge of world cultures and mythologies remains a mystery. Not only was he likely self-taught, he must have been vigorous in seeking outlets for his intellectual aspirations. He spent most of his adult life earning a living as a barber, largely in Buffalo, New York, and San Francisco, California, which seems incongruous with the urgency of his ambition and the scope of his artistic and political concerns.

In other ways, however, this incongruity is typical of the struggle of early African American artists. The practical problems of supporting oneself in a society hostile to one's existence took precedence over indulging oneself in a completely scholarly or artistic life. Indeed, Whitfield's most significant contribution to the canon of African American literature is his poetic dramatization of this struggle. In his important poem "The Misanthropist" (1853), Whitfield portrays African American poetic identity in the nineteenth century as a disturbing encounter of the mind with evil. Lest any reader be deceived that such an encounter might result in an easy transcendence of history, Whitfield makes clear the sense of personal and communal devastation that the artist is compelled to portray *and live*. Denied an adequate catharsis, a transformation of the human dilemma through artistic experience, by a social and political system that systematically denied the humanity of the African American artist despite his or her accomplishment, Whitfield sees the African American poet as condemned to become misanthropic, a "pariah" to his race.

The opening lines of the "The Misanthropist" are an ironic statement of artistic identity that prefigures the experience of many others to follow Whitfield: "In vain thou bid'st me strike the lyre, / And sing a song of mirth and glee, / Or, kindling with poetic fire, / Attempt some higher minstrelsy." Whitfield here indicates the impossibility of an African American poetic tradition, possessed of integrity, that could proceed without self-consciousness, or with purely celebratory aims. Indeed, "minstrelsy" both refers to a poetry that might be straightforwardly mimetic and registers a political economy that dictates certain relationships between African American artistry and white audiences. African American poets of the nineteenth century struggled against white skepticism as to whether they were capable of anything more than mimicry, while at the same time seeking to place themselves as individuals and artists in the struggle for race improvement.

The poem moves from this complex endeavor to a transformation of the American romantic tradition:

> From childhood, then, through many a shock,
> I've battled with the ills of life,
> Till, like a rude and rugged rock,
> My heart grew callous in the strife.
> When other children passed the hours
> In mirth, and play, and childish glee,

> Or gathering the summer flowers
> By gentle brook, or flowery lea,
> I sought the wild and rugged glen
> Where Nature, in her sternest mood,
> Far from the busy haunts of men,
> Frowned in darksome solitude.

Nature here is not Henry David **Thoreau's** site of introspection and even less Nathaniel **Hawthorne's** site of possibility. Whitfield's "embrace" of nature shares more with the dramatic escapes of the slave narratives in which the forest, the swamp, and the river are both co-conspirators in a battle with a corrupt civilization *and* a force that endangers the commitment to civilization, and thus, to humanity, itself. Whitfield's vision is a Blakean "song of experience," not so much a lament but an attempt to explain what the nature of the African American poetic calling might be.

Other early African American poets, from Phillis Wheatley to Paul Laurence **Dunbar**, also expressed the constraints and ironies of their poetic calling. It is Whitfield, however, who most fully complicated understandings of this vocation by introducing *desire* and *pleasure* into the interpretive process. Whitfield's poem allows for a different set of artistic motivations than those usually allowed the African American poet:

> Whene'er I turned in gentler mood
> To scan the old historic page,
> It was not where the wise and good,
> The Bard, the Statesman, or the Sage,
> Had drawn in lines of living light,
> Lessons of virtue, truth and right;
> But that which told of secret league,
> Where deep conspiracies were rife,
> And where, through foul and dark intrigue,
> Were sowed the seeds of deadly strife.

Whitfield's vision of the American scene would seem to challenge Hawthorne's assertion that American creativity was "lacking a shadow." And, more provocatively still, he describes the effect of his reading:

> For then my spirit seemed to soar
> Away to where such scenes were rife,
> And high above the battle's roar
> Sit as spectator of the strife –
> And in those scenes of war and woe,
> A fierce and fitful pleasure know.

This "fitful" pleasure is inevitably and inextricably related to artistic inspiration. The discovery of a relationship between "literature" and gratification, the representation of violence, conspiracy, and pleasure – even as ominous and foreboding as this last set of connections, in Whitfield's case, may be – can be seen as complex acknowledgments of the contradictions of the poetic life. The struggle for many – although not all – African American writers at mid-century was how to contribute practically to the concrete struggle for abolition and racial justice, while cultivating some nascent artistic sensibility. Exemplifying this writing at its best, Frederick Douglass refined new forms (such as the slave narrative) to do the necessary cultural and political work. Although only indirectly involved in this kind of formal innovation, Whitfield does complicate notions of motive and allegiance. At a minimum, contemporary readers should resist reading Whitfield as a propagandist or, equally demeaning, as a celebrant. The poetic identity that Whitfield has in mind is "A ghastly monument of wrath," the individual who must inevitably "live estranged from sympathy." He concludes:

> Buried in doubt, despair and gloom;
> To bare my breast to every blow,
> To know no friend, and fear no foe,
> Each generous impulse trod to dust,
> Each noble aspiration crushed,
> Each feeling struck with withering blight,
> With no regard for wrong or right,
> No fear of hell, no hope of heaven,
> Die all unwept and unforgiven,
> Content to know and dare the worst
> Which mankind's hate, and heaven's curse,
> Can heap upon my living head,
> Or cast around my memory dead;
> And let them on my tombstone trace,
> Here lies the Pariah of his race.

Whitfield overturns the "helplessness" of nineteenth-century African American poetry by naming his own dilemma.

Of course, readers should be amazed at the simple fact that an African American man in the mid–nineteenth century who, although intellectually gifted, had limited time and economic resources nonetheless produced long, literate, and psychologically complex poems. To ignore the ways in which Whitfield's accomplishments might challenge our understanding of early African American intellectual communities or American poetic achievement generally, however, would surely be an injustice. We would do well, moreover, to consider that Whitfield's construction of an African American poetic identity recalls the West African tradition of the griot, the village storyteller who was also the political conscience of the community. The tendency to romanticize this figure must be tempered by the reality that the community often rejected the implications of the tale, and the speaker found himself or herself literally or symbolically ostracized. To write effectively, Whitfield suggested, was to make a claim for a kind of outlaw status.

Elements of Whitfield's biography confirm this suspicion and concretely record his total commitment to such an artistic life. He entered into public life through his regular contributions to the *North Star* and *Frederick Douglass' Magazine* from 1849 to 1852, and, less regularly, through the mid-1850s. These proclamations of self – perhaps even private proclamations of independence, freedom, and equality – asserted the humanity of African Americans, the hypocrisy and immorality of the system of slavery, and the vision of an inevitably growing sense of black nationhood. After the publication of his collection of poems, *America; and Other Poems* (1853), he became increasingly contentious in asserting the fundamental injustice of black existence in America. In September 1853, he wrote in the *North Star* that the "American government, the American

churches, and the American people, are all engaged in one great conspiracy to crush us." Some months later, he continued, "A *black patriot* in this county must be more fool than knave. The fact is, I have no country, neither have you, and your assumption that you are an *integrant* part of *this* nation is not true." This corpus of work, although not extensive, establishes Whitfield, along with David Walker, Martin Delaney, and others, as a proto-nationalist. So committed was Whitfield to this black nationalist vision that he took on the very pragmatic task of investigating possible sites for a new homeland, a duty and a burden that took him to Central America in the later 1850s. With unprecedented confidence, Whitfield asserted that blacks would "develop a higher order of civilization and Christianity than the world has yet seen."

Although Whitfield forcefully articulated his skepticism that African Americans would ever become anything more than a pariah in the American mind, the appearance of his collection *America* in 1853 demands that we place him within the national context of that most crucial of decades in the development of the American literary tradition. The task here is not to make premature claims for Whitfield's artistry in relation to that of the central figures of the literary flowering of the 1850s, but we should consider the ways in which Whitfield's contribution clarifies our perception of the cultural context. Indeed, it is a commitment to describing context, to grounding literary activity, that jumps out at us as Whitfield's most enduring legacy. Poems like "How Long?," "Prayer of the Oppressed," "To Cinque," and "Stanzas for the First of August" are more than subtle reminders of the hypocrisy that separated the founding energy of the nation from the realities of mid-century African American life. In "How Long?" Whitfield writes:

> But when I turn the land to view,
>   Which claims, par excellence, to be
> The refuge of the brave and true,
>   The strongest bulwark of the free,
> The grand asylum for the poor
>   And trodden-down of every land,
> Where they may rest in peace secure,
>   Nor fear the oppressor's iron hand –
> Worse scenes of rapine, lust, and shame,
> Than e'er disgraced the Russian name,
> Worse than the Austrian ever saw,
> Are sanctioned here as righteous law.

In opposition to a faithful transcendentalism, Whitfield uncompromisingly articulates a historical realism. This reading of nation is supplemented by a series of poems that encourage a similar reading of character. "Delusive Hope" and "Yes, Strike Again That Sounding String," Joan Sherman argues, are "dark imprecations against a world 'disjoint and out of frame' in which men, women, religion, love, and the gentler aspects of nature seem . . . corrupt and meaningless." Even the Emersonian vision is transformed by Whitfield's poetry. In "Self-Reliance" – the most direct allusion in Whitfield's work to the American literary renaissance – he writes:

> I love the man whose lofty mind
>   On God and its own strength relies;
> Who seeks the welfare of his kind,
>   And dare be honest though he dies;

Who cares not for the world's applause,
  But, to his own fixed purpose true,
The path which God and nature's laws
  Point out, doth earnestly pursue.

Ralph Waldo **Emerson's** fundamental optimism, which encourages the individual spirit, is here replaced with Whitfield's skepticism, which encourages individual improvisation in the midst of an uncaring and hostile state. Whitfield works the same terrain as his white colleagues, yet the lens of race yields different insights.

The most provocative historical interpretation comes from considering Whitfield's "America" (LOA, 2: 120) alongside Walt **Whitman's** "Song of Myself" (LOA, 1: 720). Where *Leaves of Grass* chooses a synecdochic strategy for representing the relationship between nation and text, Whitfield uses direct address. The "I's" of Whitman's assault on poetic conformity are less tempered than the "I" in Whitfield's jeremiad. The celebratory tone of Whitman's epic meditation on American identity is matched in vigor by Whitfield's accusatory introduction:

America, it is to thee,
Thou boasted land of liberty, –
It is to thee I raise my song,
Thou land of blood, and crime, and wrong.

Ironically, the language of song is maintained here even as Whitfield immediately deflates the possibility of a straightforward celebration. By manipulating the language of "rights," consistent with the work of Douglass and Walker, Whitfield's poem becomes a reminder that America has not yet fulfilled its political promises of liberty to all. The "inherent rights of man" is a constant in Whitfield's poetic universe. By reminding his readers of the contribution of African American soldiers in the Revolutionary War ("Oh no; they fought, as they believed, / For the inherent rights of man; / But mark, how they have been deceived / By slavery's accursed plan"), he draws attention to America as a "lie." Although Whitman and Whitfield converge in places, Whitfield describes victimization and loss in the midst of poetic utterance, where Whitman sees possibility and transformation.

Ultimately, Whitfield's accomplishment in the poem lies in asserting the inconsistency of America's foundational statements about liberty and equality and in evoking the existential crisis that this hypocrisy initiates.

And manhood, too, with soul of fire,
And arm of strength, and smothered ire,
Stands pondering with brow of gloom,
Upon his dark unhappy doom,
Whether to plunge in battle's strife,
And buy his freedom with his life.

The poem considers this problem through the lens of Christian teachings about patience and forgiveness, while self-consciously making a "prayerful" call for God's intervention in history. The conclusion of the poem is striking:

But in the sacred name of peace,
  Of justice, virtue, love and truth,
We pray, and never mean to cease,
  Till weak old age and fiery youth
In freedom's cause their voices raise,

And burst the bonds of every slave;
Till, north and south, and east and west,
The wrongs we bear shall be redressed.

Remarkably, here as in "The Misanthropist," the poet chooses to sustain the psychological strain that leads to his sense of ostracization.

The meaning of "America" is to be found, however, not only within its didacticism. In other poems, Whitfield records careful meditations on celebrations, nature, and love. "To A. H." (LOA, 2: 124) is among Whitfield's best efforts in this regard. This love poem is an extended comparative study in which the object of the poet's affection is shown to be more beautiful than any figure from the classical pantheon. Although we are not informed as to the racial identity of "A. H.," it is reasonable to assume, based upon Whitfield's nationalist politics, that the object of desire is a woman of African descent. With this knowledge, the significance of this somewhat conventional paean of love is more pointed. Whitfield's appropriation of the imagery of classical culture overturns the ideological basis of slavery that denied both African beauty and humanity. Whitfield significantly extends this system of allusion to include references to middle eastern cultures and directly suggests a link between western classical culture and Africa: "Here Egypt's sages, skilled of yore / In Isis' dark mysterious rites, / Unveiled their find of mystic lore / To eager Grecian neophytes." Furthermore, the contemporary reader needs to keep in mind the revolutionary character of the assertion that an African American man might be "sadly musing." The impossibility of a contemplative life for African men and women was at the foundation of Enlightenment theories of race and race hierarchy, which were a fundamental part of the justification for slavery. Although Whitfield tended to perceive his life in terms of loss and missed opportunity, we are struck by the enormity of his accomplishment 10 years before emancipation.

Despite Whitfield's skepticism and dramatic attempts to seek out in Central America a possible black homeland, he became increasingly more at ease – in both personal life and writing – with his situation in the United States. On his return from his Central American travels, he settled in San Francisco in the early 1860s, where he continued work as a barber, became grand master of the Prince Hall Masons, and wrote occasional pieces, including poetry, for local papers like the *San Francisco Elevator*. We might assume that age had mellowed Whitfield, but this, too, might be an ignorance about history. More likely, it seems, the monumental character of the Civil War provided for Whitfield – as for Whitman – an entirely new framework within which to conceive of his art and artistic calling. His 1867 effort, a 400-line "Poem" that venerated the Emancipation Proclamation, is respectful in its survey of American history and appreciative of the Civil War struggle, but it does not hesitate to identify a new hypocrisy on the horizon, the lack of urgency concerning questions of African American civil rights in the aftermath of the war:

Yet once again our moral air
Is tainted by that poisonous breath,
Which Freedom's lungs can never bear,
Which surely ends in moral death.
. . . .
Proclaim the truth that equal laws

Can best sustain the righteous cause;
And let this nation henceforth be
In truth the country of the free.

The study of nineteenth-century African American poetry is in its infancy, so it seems premature to expend a great deal of energy in speculating on the aesthetic quality of the poems at hand. We can say that Whitfield can be favorably compared to other popular poets of his day and that the juxtaposition of his work with the giants of the American tradition reveals new insights. But there are extensive gaps in our knowledge about Whitfield, his audience, and his contemporaries. For now, we should ensure that his attempt to participate in mid-century poetic and political conversations is taken seriously and begin the evaluation of his ideas and art that should have taken place in his own time.

JAMES C. HALL

Selected Works
America and Other Poems, Buffalo, New York: J. S. Leavitt, 1853

Brawley, Benjamin, *Early American Negro Writers*, Freeport, New York: Books for Libraries, 1968
Sherman, Joan, ed., *African-American Poetry of the Nineteenth Century: An Anthology*, Urbana: University of Illinois Press, 1992

Further Reading
Jackson, Blyden, *The History of Afro-American Literature*, vol. 1, Baton Rouge: Louisiana State University Press, 1989
Loggins, Vernon, *The Negro Author: His Development in America to 1900*, New York: Columbia University Press, 1931
Redding, Saunders, *To Make a Poet Black*, 1938; College Park, Maryland: McGrath, 1968
Redmond, Eugene, *Drumvoices: The Mission of Afro-American Poetry*, Garden City, New York: Anchor, 1976
Sherman, Joan, *Invisible Poets: Afro-Americans of the Nineteenth Century*, Urbana: University of Illinois Press, 1974

Albery Allson Whitman

(1851–1901)

On "Colored American Day" at the Chicago, Illinois, World's Fair in 1873, Albery Allson Whitman stood on a stage alongside Frederick Douglass and other leading figures of African American political and cultural life in the nineteenth century. Although known more for his long narrative poems, Whitman chose to read a shorter piece that he had composed especially for the World's Fair, "The Freedman's Triumphant Song." In this poem, Whitman optimistically figures African Americans alongside whites in a vision of cooperation and sharing that was belied by the reality of increasing segregation, disenfranchisement, and lynching in late-nineteenth-century America. Yet Whitman's World's Fair reading, as Richard Barksdale and Keneth Kinnamon have pointed out, is a significant marker in the history of African American poetry; this event also indicates Whitman's high standing and recognition as one of the foremost voices of the race. Indeed, when "The Freedman's Triumphant Song" was published along with a poetic tribute to African American servicemen in a short book entitled *World's Fair Poem*, the frontispiece portrait of Whitman is captioned "Poet Laureate of the Afro American Race." Among nineteenth-century African American poets, only Frances Watkins **Harper** rivaled Whitman in prominence and accomplishment before Paul Laurence **Dunbar** began to publish his poems in the final decade of the century.

Whitman was born a slave on a farm near Munfordville, in Hart County, Kentucky, on May 30, 1851. His mother died just before the Emancipation Proclamation, and his father just after, leaving him an orphan at age 12. After the farmwork of his boyhood, Whitman worked as a laborer, attended school for seven scattered months, and taught school in Ohio and Kentucky. About 1870, Whitman enrolled at Wilberforce University. Although a student at Wilberforce for only six months, Whitman came under the influence of the university's president, the African Methodist Episcopal (A. M. E.) Bishop Daniel Alexander Payne, an important race leader. Bishop Payne became a lifelong mentor to Whitman, who retained an official connection with Wilberforce for a number of years following his student days. Whitman went on to become a very successful A. M. E. minister himself. Especially known for his effective preaching, Whitman served as pastor of churches in Ohio, Kansas, Texas, and Georgia, where, as pastor of Allen Temple in Atlanta, he died of pneumonia in June 1901.

Whitman's public speaking talents were also evident in frequent poetry readings at which he and his wife, Caddie, performed from an ever-increasing body of Whitman's own verse. Following his two early books, *Essay on the Ten Plagues and Miscellaneous Poems* (1871?), no copies of which are known to have survived, and *Leelah Misled* (1873), a narrative poem of romantic betrayal that portrays white characters, Whitman published his first well-known work, *Not a Man, and Yet a Man* (1877). A long narrative poem that shows the influence of Henry Wadsworth **Longfellow's** *The Song of Hiawatha* (1855; LOA, 1: 399) and other classic American and English works, *Not a Man, and Yet a Man* recounts events in the life of the slave Rodney. Rodney rescues his master's daughter from Indians, only to be sold into the deep south in order to forestall the developing love between Rodney and the young woman that he rescued. Rodney, who discovers a more genuine love in the far south with the Creole slave Leona, eventually joins Union forces in the Civil War to help overturn slavery. As does much of his more interesting work, *Not a Man, and Yet a Man* presents Whitman's imaginative development of multiethnic themes and characters whose actions are often set in the midst of important American historical events.

In the first edition of *Not a Man, and Yet a Man*, the long title poem is followed by a selection of shorter "Miscellaneous Poems," including "The Lute of Afric's Tribe" (LOA, 2: 491). Inscribed "To the memory of Dr. J. McSimpson, a colored Author of Anti-Slavery Ballads," the poem suggests the inhibition of African American expression in slavery time through an opening analogy to the "tuneless," captive Israel of the Old Testament. Released from the "iron clutch" of slavery, African American song will come forth, as signaled by the appearance of "Simpson, man of song and soul." Although focused on the period of slavery and emancipation, "The Lute of Afric's Tribe," especially in the line that recalls "When Wrong the gospel of endurance preached," resonates with the time of the poem's publication, when segregation and disenfranchisement were spreading, as well as with aspects of our own time today. Such resonance across eras is typical of Whitman at his best.

Whitman followed *Not a Man, and Yet a Man* with a second long narrative poem, *The Rape of Florida*. First published in 1884 and revised under the title *Twasinta's Seminoles* (LOA, 2: 487) a year later, this second major work is Whitman's best known. Judging from older commentary on the poem, *Twasinta's Seminoles* has long impressed readers with its ambitious display of 257 Spenserian stanzas. Whitman is thought to be the first African American poet to employ this challenging verse form. Today's reader might not be so much impressed by the complex versification of *Twasinta's Seminoles* as by its complex presentation of multiethnic American themes. Building on historical materials of the Florida Seminole Indian Wars, Whitman deploys characters of American Indian, African American, and Anglo-Saxon ethnicity in intricate and convincing interrelationships and actions in Florida and Mexico.

Twasinta's Seminoles presents Palmecho, Seminole chieftain, his daughter, Ewald, and Atlassa, a young Seminole leader and lover of Ewald. Although courageous fighters, the Seminoles suffer incursions by white American military forces. Following many events, including the betrayal and capture of Palmecho by whites at a "peace" conference in St. Augustine, the Seminoles along with allied Black Maroons are shipped in chains to Mexico. Blyden Jackson associates the concluding events of *Twasinta's Seminoles* with greater mythic and historical patterns when he observes that for Whitman the group of Seminoles and Black Maroons "that was forced to start life anew in Mexico, as Adam and Eve were forced to do . . . out of Eden, was not a party without hope. Neither should be the Negroes recently emancipated and still under heavy burdens in America." Carl L. Marshall demonstrates how *Twasinta's*

Seminoles, with its depiction of Seminoles and Black Maroons fighting for freedom against the duplicitous white American military forces, provides a significant basis for considering Whitman as an important writer of racial protest in post-Reconstruction America (*CLA Journal* [September 1975]).

If we turn to specific passages of *Twasinta's Seminoles* such as canto I, stanzas xv–xix, and canto II, stanzas iv–xii, we clearly see Whitman's sensitive and articulate response to and use of nature in his poetry. As Jackson notes, "We may wish to remember here Whitman's love of the country – of his external surroundings sheerly as substances of themselves – in the part of Kentucky where he was born and to parallel that love with the feeling for similar aspects of his environment so ardently enunciated by [William] Wordsworth in such poems as *The Prelude* and 'Tintern Abbey.'" Thus, the first canto suggests Whitman's recollection of cherished experiences in the country during his Kentucky boyhood. More importantly, for Whitman, as with Wordsworth and other romantic poets, essential truths are symbolized in nature. In Whitman's view, persons of all races enjoy a direct relationship with nature, a relationship unmediated by corrupt society with its false distinctions of race and class. Through direct observation of nature we may learn our essential freedom, as expressed in a memorable passage from canto II:

> I never was a slave – a robber took
> My substance – what of that? The *law* my rights –
> And that? I still was free and had my book –
> All nature.

Whitman's last major work, *An Idyl of the South* (1901; LOA, 2: 492), is presented in two parts: "The Octoroon" and "The Southland's Charms and Freedom's Magnitude." Both sections are written in ottava rima. Generally considered to be among the poet's best pieces, "The Octoroon" relates the tragic love affair of the beautiful young "octoroon" Lena and Sheldon Maury, the son of her master. Because Sheldon is sincere in his love for Lena and because he intends to marry her, his father, in order to preserve the southern color caste system, sells Lena to an older man who will presumably rape her and ultimately destroy her spirit. Lena escapes such a fate, but her ordeal exhausts her so much that she is at the point of death when Sheldon finally finds her. As Jackson suggests, in "The Octoroon" Whitman movingly dramatizes some of the terrible costs of that pillar of the color caste system, the ban on interracial marriage.

"The Southland's Charms and Freedom's Magnitude" offers a kind of retrospective meditation on and prophetic vision for the south and, by extension, America. Published in the last year of his life, this poem may be seen as the poet's final testimony. Through his "I" narrator, Whitman early on offers a reverie prompted by recollections of Civil War scenes: when in battle, "The Negro stood with Saxon side by side, / And face to face." Regretting, in some respects, the demise of the pre–Civil War south, the narrator expresses hopes for a new, industrialized south that will supplant romantic "old south" dreams: "we shall learn that toil excels our dreams, / That mills make better music than the streams!"

The theme of freedom pervades all of Whitman's work, and it is nowhere more evident than in "The Southland's Charms and Freedom's Magnitude," the closing stanzas of which give a unique prophetic vision of a possible future south – of a possible future America: "These all are prophecies of what shall be, / When Freedom's sons shall leave their brothers free." Anticipating in language and themes a later southern preacher and visionary, Martin Luther King Jr., Whitman opens the final, prophetic section of "The Southland's Charms" with the words, "I had a dream." In telling his dream, Whitman projects a future America that cares for all of its children,

> The nation held first claim in all the great
>   Concerns of health and training.
> . . . .
> And so, no children roamed the streets at will,
>   In hungry shoals.

In Whitman's vision for America, industry is prized yet regulated for the good of society: "I understood – / The State-fixed bounds for corporate Enterprise." Whitman concludes his "prophecies" with a vision that offers a worthy challenge for fulfillment today, a vision of a multiethnic, multicultural America, with "a populace / Unnumbered, drawn from ev'ry human race."

Appreciation of Whitman has been hindered by limitations of past criticism. In an early and influential study of African American literature, Vernon Loggins unfortunately tagged Whitman with the label "mockingbird" because the influence of earlier classic American and British poetry is discernible in his work. Many subsequent critics of Whitman have followed Loggins in focusing discussion on Whitman's tendency to utilize techniques, especially in his metrical patterns, of earlier poets. The issue of Whitman's "originality," especially when we consider how he, like most English-language poets in the nineteenth century, chose to write in traditional metrical forms, has led to sterile discussion. Of course, all writers reveal the "influence" of earlier practitioners of their chosen expressive modes, and most, in turn, go on to exert some influence themselves. The originality issue has distracted readers from Whitman's special vision, which he revealed in multiculturally and historically grounded themes that tell of an America that has the potential to discover its freedom, a freedom to remake itself through interaction of its diverse peoples.

Important recent commentary on Whitman includes Jackson's work, especially his generously conceived discussion of the poet in *A History of Afro-American Literature*; briefer, but also stimulating, is commentary by Anne E. Rowe. Present trends, including the renewed attention being given to traditional metrical verse and the increased interest in nineteenth-century African American poetry, as well as contemporary multiculturalism, which Whitman definitely anticipates, suggest a widening readership for his work in the future.

JAMES ROBERT PAYNE

Selected Works

World's Fair Poem, Atlanta, Georgia: Holsey Job Print, n.d.
Leelah Misled: A Poem, Elizabethtown, Kentucky: Richard LaRue, 1873
Not a Man, and Yet a Man, 1877; reprinted, Upper Saddle River, New Jersey: Literature House, 1970

The Rape of Florida, 1884; reprinted, Miami, Florida:
Mnemosyne, 1969; revised as *Twasinta's Seminoles; or,
Rape of Florida*, St. Louis, Missouri: Nixon-Jones, 1885
An Idyl of the South: An Epic Poem in Two Parts, New York:
Metaphysical, 1901

Further Reading
Barksdale, Richard, and Keneth Kinnamon, *Black Writers of
America*, New York: Macmillan, 1972
Jackson, Blyden, *A History of Afro-American Literature: The
Long Beginning, 1746–1895*, vol. 1, Baton Rouge:
Louisiana State University Press, 1989
Jackson, Blyden, and Louis D. Rubin Jr., *Black Poetry in
America: Two Essays in Historical Interpretation*, Baton
Rouge: Louisiana State University Press, 1974
Loggins, Vernon, *The Negro Author: His Development in
America to 1900*, 1931; reprinted, Port Washington, New
York: Kennikat, 1964
Redmond, Eugene B., *Drumvoices: The Mission of Afro-
American Poetry*, Garden City, New York:
Anchor/Doubleday, 1976
Rowe, Anne E., *The Idea of Florida in the American Literary
Imagination*, Baton Rouge: Louisiana State University Press,
1986
Sherman, Joan R., *Invisible Poets: Afro-Americans of the
Nineteenth Century*, 2nd ed., Urbana: University of Illinois
Press, 1989

Sarah Helen Whitman

(1803–1878)

Sarah Whitman was a writer who wore many hats. She was best known, among the cognoscenti, as a poet and frequenter of the most fashionable literary salons. But she was also a journalist who was interested in topics such as Ralph Waldo **Emerson**, Goethe, and spiritualism, and a respected translator of German poetry. In addition, she served as a mentor to several young writers, including such later luminaries as George William Curtis and John **Hay**.

But students of American literature usually remember Whitman as the first biographer and critic to defend Edgar Allan **Poe**, who had been posthumously maligned by Rufus Griswold's scurrilous reports. Whitman is studied today, when she is studied at all, as the object of Poe's thwarted romantic attentions: she is remembered, in fact, as "Poe's Helen."

Nineteenth-century anthologies provide a clue to this remodeling process, and to the use we have made of Poe's one-time love. In the 1840s, Griswold, Caroline May, and Thomas Buchanan Read found many Whitman poems worth collecting in their several anthologies of American women poets. Their choices included such sentimental efforts as "She Blooms No More," "David," "A Song of Spring," and "A September Evening, on the Banks of the Moshassuck," and the melancholic ruminations of "Thoughts of the Past," "The Past," and her early "Retrospection." But by the turn of the century, Edmund Clarence **Stedman** would represent Whitman's entire oeuvre with sonnets "from the series relating to Edgar Allan Poe." Anthologists of our own day have followed Stedman's lead, if not his tastes: few readers now look at the Whitman verses that Poe admired.

Comparisons with other women remembered in verse may spring to mind: like H. D., Whitman was well regarded by discriminating contemporaries; like Dorothy Wordsworth, she provided material for another's poetry. Until recently, H. D. and Wordsworth were only remembered as supplements to famous male poets (Ezra Pound and William Wordsworth, respectively); to date, Whitman still holds only that begrudging claim to fame.

Yet her contemporaries thought her verse possessed great merit, and Whitman was an established writer well before Poe paid her any addresses. She was not, to be sure, a household name: according to one admiring contemporary, Whitman's "skilful pen has won – not a wide popularity, but – an honourable reputation among the most able judges in matters of literary taste." Among the discerning, Whitman was well-liked for her youthful spirit, beauty of person, and ladylike charm; she also was noted for wearing pale, diaphanous garments. Indeed, Whitman, more than better-known contemporaries, embodied the "lady poet" of antebellum days, right down to a weak heart and fluttering fan. As such, she had a loyal, if select, following, including such prominent New York litterateurs as Elizabeth Oakes Smith, Maria J. McIntosh, Horace Greeley, and Anna Cora Mowatt.

Born and raised in Providence, Rhode Island, Sarah Helen Power spent her childhood in a feminine household; her father, a merchant, left for the West Indies in 1813, and did not return until almost two decades later. After attracting the eye of local lawyer John Winslow Whitman with her poetry, she married him in 1828. He must have encouraged her literary flair: she published her first poem, "Retrospection," in 1829, in Sarah Josepha Hale's *American Ladies' Magazine*. After John Whitman's death in 1833, the poet lived with her mother and sister in Providence.

By the late 1840s, Whitman had turned her hand to journalism and translation, although her specialty was exploring her own delicate sensibilities in poetry. In 1838, she read a prize poem to commemorate the opening of Shakespeare's Hall in Providence; at other times, she wrote poems inspired by various statuary, and a hymn for the consecration of a garden cemetery. Whitman, in short, was very much the sentimental writer, although not, like most of her contemporaries, apt to write biographical verse. Her favored venues were such genteel gatekeepers as Hale's *Godey's Lady's Book*, Nathaniel Parker **Willis's** *Home Journal*, and the *American Metropolitan Review*. Favored themes, in such periodical work, were nature studies, fairy tales, and odes to feminine beauty.

But Rufus Griswold, a prominent critic of the day, thought the more adventurous – and vaguely uncanny – "Hours of Life" Whitman's best work, although he called it "somewhat too mystical and metaphysical to be very popular." He could have been right: the best-selling novelist Susan Warner knew the popular taste and intensely disliked Whitman's poetry. Warner, Whitman's distant cousin, prayed for the poet's soul, thinking poetry dangerous; by contrast, George Ripley, who turned to literary criticism after the demise of Brook Farm, thought "Hours of Life" very fine. Another critic attracted to the "mystical and metaphysical" was Whitman's poetic contemporary, the man who sprang to national prominence with "The Raven" (LOA, 1: 535).

Through her friendships with Frances Osgood, Anne Lynch, and other popular poets, Whitman was aware of Poe even before his most famous poem appeared. In a letter written after Poe's death, Whitman recalled that her first impression of him, after reading a short story, was "a sensation of such intense horror that I dared neither look at anything he had written nor even utter his name." "By degrees," she added, "this terror took the character of fascination – I devoured with a half-reluctant and fearful avidity every line that fell from his pen." Poe knew Whitman's work, too, which she liked to sign "Helen," and admired it a good deal; in fact, both poets had asked friends about the other solely on the basis of published work. It may indicate the somewhat bohemian cast of antebellum literary circles that Whitman, apparently a perfect lady, made the first overtures to her soon-to-be suitor, in a rhyming – and highly allusive – valentine addressed simply to "The Raven." Because Poe was in disgrace at the time, Whitman's friends advised her not to publish her tribute. She complied but, taking matters into her own hands, sent the poem directly to Poe; he, widowed for just over a year, responded promptly.

After learning who had written the graceful homage, Poe sent Whitman a copy of his 1831 poem "To Helen" (LOA, 1:

468

522), which he had written to a boyhood love named Helen Stanard. Poe later told Whitman that the coincidence of names struck him with "an overwhelming sense of Fatality," "so conclusively, that a thrill of intense superstition ran at once through my frame." Because Poe did not sign his initial missive, Whitman had to learn from a visitor that the address on the envelope was in his hand.

From this thrilling, self-conscious beginning, the two poets' courtship progressed apace. It was broken off, amid doubts about Poe's drinking and perhaps the suspicion that he coveted Whitman's income, but it was resumed almost immediately, when Whitman decided that Poe could be saved. Finally, further gossip, or Whitman's own doubts, intruded again and caused her to break the engagement in late December 1848, less than a year after it had commenced.

According to a contemporary, poet Mary E. Hewitt, Poe had predicted that he and Whitman would never wed. By January 1849, he was writing to Annie Richmond that the love he had felt for Sarah Whitman was as nothing compared to "such as burns in my very soul for *you* – so pure – so unworldly – a love which would make *all* sacrifices for your sake." The last clause may also indicate that, in Poe's opinion, his ex-fiancée did not make enough allowances for her bedeviled suitor. Certainly, she did not intend to tolerate his drinking; she also quailed at confronting her mother, who controlled the widowed Whitman's finances.

In a letter to Hewitt written after Poe's death, Whitman attributed her refusal to wed to "a communication . . . handed me cautioning me against this imprudent marriage & informing me of many things in Mr. Poe's recent career with which I was previously unacquainted." One such caution was that Poe had broken his vow of temperance: "I bade him farewell with feelings of profound commiseration for his fate." Poe, she said, left her house with great bitterness, although his ire was directed against her family and not herself. To bolster her claims of disinterested benevolence, she recalled having written to a fellow-poet for news of Poe's "health & welfare" for some months into 1849; he died in July of that year. She also sent the five-stanza poem "Lines" to Poe's one-time journal, the *Southern Literary Messenger*, in the spring of 1849. "I bade thee stay," the poem states, "Too well I know / The fault was mine, mine only."

Whitman's continuing interest in her ex-suitor may mark the lure of forbidden fruit: later poems would depict Poe as mesmerizing, dangerously attractive, and deeply passionate. One calls Poe back to religious faith, although most depict him as serene in death. But Whitman's concern, and later poems, could also have resulted from a self-fashioning as the doomed love Annabel Lee (see LOA, 1: 550). Whitman's claim that she served as model for Poe's heroine has not persuaded scholars. But the desire to be, or to be thought, Poe's lost love changed the direction of Whitman's career. The first indication of this shift is her foray into biographical criticism, with the publication of *Edgar Poe and the Critics* in 1860. This small volume still merits scholarly attention: more than a rebuttal of Griswold's gossip, it offers a critically alert look at Poe's themes, images, and interests. A later manifestation is Whitman's voluminous correspondence with Poe biographers: in the last decades of her life she became, like the Misses Bordereau in Henry James's "The Aspern Papers," the keeper of a shrine and supposed source of authoritative knowledge about a beloved

writer. But it is even more important that Whitman's poetry also changed; indeed, her reincarnation as the dead Poe's last love seems to have granted her a newfound power to proclaim her thoughts.

Not that Whitman abandoned her previous interests: she could still write a poem on "Christmas Eve" for a friend's children, and "A Pat of Butter" reveals a whimsy not found in Poe. But Poe's affection for certain Whitman poems such as "To Arcturus" and the fateful valentine must have impressed her deeply: after the couple parted, Whitman's poetry, especially on Poe, began to sound like attempts to please, or even summon up, her demon lover.

One good place to see this process taking place is in the eight Whitman poems entitled "To ———." Barring the exception of a poem by the same title that addresses an unidentified "Eva," the "To ———" series seems firmly directed at the critic and poet who had praised Whitman's most mystical work, and from whom she had learned the ways of the dark romantic. In these Poe-like poems, phrases such as "The enchanted wood / Thrilled, as by some foreboding terror stirred" and "the night's phantasmal glories" mark a shift from her earlier themes and language; a poem that invokes "mouldering sepulchres and cypress bowers" sounds almost parodic. Descriptions of the loved one's beautiful eyes – "glorious," "unearthly," "starry," or "tender" – are also frequent, as are hints of tempestuous passions now cooled by death.

This may sound like a morbid absorption in the dead and absent. But in fact, read together, Whitman's work on Poe suggests the unsettling conclusion that, all things being equal, the narrating poet might be better off alone. Certainly, the collaboration was significant and fruitful: as noted, Whitman post-Poe was a different Whitman. And it would seem, from "To ———" (LOA, 1: 348), that Whitman appreciated the lesson: her mood, theme, and imagery all resemble Poe's, although Whitman's tone is less despairing than her lover's would have been.

Her relative contentment may reveal second thoughts on her short betrothal. Whitman must have known that her financial security would have been threatened by the impecunious Poe. But on a less mercenary note, she might also have perceived that, if she valued her art, Poe was most useful to her dead. One way to read this poem, then, is as a hint that Whitman found strength in refusing and then iconizing Poe.

The suggestion sounds harsh, but consider the cultural milieu. Emily Stipes Watts has argued that America's antebellum women poets "concentrated upon themes which concern women, children, their homes, and their local communities"; Cheryl Walker, who generally agrees, contends that women poets such as Whitman's friend Frances Osgood won approval by accepting male critics' bounds. Griswold admired Osgood, Walker notes, because this poet did not aspire "to travel beyond the legitimate sphere of woman's observation." The question, then, is what happened to those women who needed or wanted to travel outside "woman's sphere." Emily **Dickinson's** story tells us one way women poets entered new realms; Sarah Whitman may have found another.

For by riding on Poe's coattails, as it were, Whitman found a way to express ideas that were then deemed unfit for women, chief among them passion, sexual tension, and female power outside marital bliss. The strategy is subtle: on first reading, "To ———" sounds like standard gender-typing. Thus, the lover enjoys "sorceries," the role of "Destiny," and the might of the "wild enchantments" of love; the speaker, meanwhile, is a timid heart, trembling like insubstantial starlight, sheltered by the lover's magus-like strength until his untimely death. But look again: what this poem tells us is that the man is gone and the solitary woman speaks.

Yes, she misses her sorcerer; yes, she realizes she has lost the glory, kingdom, and power that illumined her days. But it seems clear that he has left her a priceless gift, which she seems strong enough to publish in his absence. If "thy song, thy fame," outstrip the speaker's own – well, she's still here, and writing about the loss, a star no longer afraid to be "O'er-fraught with light and splendor." It is even hinted that "pain could . . . dwell / Where thy bright presence cast its blissful spell"; apparently, attending a genius is no simple joy.

Painting herself the truest of true women, Whitman nonetheless manages to remind readers who is alive, who is dead, and who is in charge of managing Poe's posthumous career. Although she reaffirms the "separate spheres" ideology current in her day, Whitman notes that she has the upper hand, in language that ostensibly describes grief. In the same way, she tried to control the Poe industry, corresponding with virtually all nineteenth-century Poe biographers and writing a series of sonnets to the dead mentor that Stedman would choose to represent her life's work.

The point is not that Whitman ventriloquized her former love or cannibalized his corpus; on the contrary, the argument for her growth as a poet rests on the value judgment that her most powerful verse was written in the 1860s and 1870s, and had little to do with Poe's living presence. After making a name for herself as Poe's Helen, that is, she was able to speak with an authority other women poets lacked, in poems from the wryly questioning "Science" to the lovely "Night Wanes," and the magisterial "In Memoriam." She did not forget Poe: the late poem "The Portrait" calls up the best known Poe daguerreotypes in the reader's mind. But the virtue of the LOA selection lies in its recognition of a pivotal moment in Whitman's long career, the point at which she both recalled and moved beyond her storm-tossed discipleship to Poe. "To ———" is not the tribute of a mere hanger-on, or frustrated widow chasing celebrity. Instead, it suggests a writer who tried to break, ever so gently, with her era's gender boundaries or, better, to use them to her own ends.

BARBARA RYAN

Selected Works

Hours of Life and Other Poems, Providence, Rhode Island: George H. Whitney, 1853
Edgar Poe and His Critics, New York: Rudd & Carleton, 1860; reprinted, New Brunswick, New Jersey: Rutgers University Press, 1949
Poems, Boston: Houghton, Osgood, 1879

Further Reading

Miller, John Carl, *Poe's Helen Remembers*, Charlottesville: University of Virginia Press, 1979
Thomas, Dwight, and David K. Jackson, *The Poe Log*, Boston: G. K. Hall, 1987
Ticknor, Caroline, *Poe's Helen*, New York: Scribner's, 1916

Walt Whitman

(1819–1892)

Probably the most important question attending the study of *Leaves of Grass* is which edition to use. During Whitman's lifetime, there appeared six American editions (defined as having original pagination and the type redistributed from earlier editions) and almost as many issues (editions with supplementary material or poems). The most significant editions are the first (1855), the third (1860), and the sixth (1881/82). Critics are almost evenly divided as to whether Whitman's best work resides in the first and third editions or in the 1881/82 final arrangement, upon which the 1891/92 "Death-bed" and modern editions of *Leaves of Grass* are based. When the transcendentalist Ralph Waldo **Emerson** first read the 1855 edition, he wrote the poet a letter in which he greeted him "at the beginning of a great career." Yet Whitman was only half a transcendentalist because he celebrated the body, or nature, equally with the soul, or spirit. Later, after 1860 and the third edition of *Leaves*, Whitman became more spiritual and "transcendental" – only to have Emerson lose interest in his work.

Emerson mainly objected to Whitman's long catalogs, but he must have missed the spontaneity of the earlier poems, where consistency for consistency's sake was not Whitman's main concern. As the poet declared at the end of "Song of Myself," he often contradicted himself because he was "large" and contained "multitudes." Whitman's major disagreement with Emerson and the transcendentalists was that nature was not simply an emblem of God, or the Oversoul, but *part* of God. Yet Whitman was not a pantheist in making such an argument because he found God in the spirit as well as the flesh. He was no philosopher either, but a poet whose "conversation with nature," as Emerson described the bard's powers in "The Poet" (1844), alternated in intensity but never completely lost its mystic glow.

Doubtless, Whitman was aware of the changes that had taken place within his "vision" between 1855 and 1880, but he also knew that eclecticism would save his poetry for future readers and save his reputation from the charge of pantheism or of discipleship to Emerson. "As there are now several editions of L. of G., different texts and dates," he wrote on the copyright page to the 1891–92 issue of *Leaves of Grass*, "I wish to say that I prefer and recommend this present one, complete, for future printing, if there should be any." Some, including the poet himself, have suggested that the final 1881/82 arrangement was the result of a lifelong plan, in place from the first, to construct a literary "cathedral." Yet it is clear from this definitive arrangement that the only true or effective planning came in the ordering of the general sections.

The heart of the book is "Song of Myself" (LOA, 1: 720), but this personal epic is introduced by two groups of poems composed after 1855. The first section, called "Inscriptions," presents an overview of the various themes in *Leaves of Grass*, and the second, "Starting from Paumanok," provides the reader with perhaps a more literal or autobiographical version of "Song of Myself." "One's-Self I Sing," the first piece in "Inscriptions," opens not only that section but the entire volume in terms of its major themes. As a micro version of *Leaves*, it celebrates the "simple separate person," yet utters "the word Democratic, the word En-Masse." This reflects Emerson's idea of the poet as "Representative Man," whose inmost secrets are the secrets of all humankind. The second stanza establishes that the poet will sing "Of physiology from top to toe" and of equality between male and female. He intends to speak of both body and soul ("I say the Form complete is worthier far") and of modernity.

Whitman was a romantic poet in the sense that he sought to "transcend" the physical in his poetry, but he was also our first "modern" poet because he focused on the "emblem" of God, or nature, as something real in and of itself. Anticipating the modernist poets of this century, whose existentialist approach found value in nature, or "thingness," as William Carlos Williams called it, Whitman found "the body permanent . . . within [the corporeal] body." The quote comes from "Eidólons" (LOA, 1: 838), the most important poem in the "Inscriptions" section. The Greek word means spirit or phantom, and in Whitman's application it indicates the soul that lurks behind all appearances – "the hues and objects of the world, / The fields of art and learning, pleasure, sense." More than one scholar has speculated that Whitman's interest in the soul increased as his health declined. He may have picked up the title word (which Whitman pronounced with the emphasis on the second syllable) from P. G. Tait's *The Unseen Universe* (1875), where it is suggested that every organic object has a spirit or "eidolon." The idea is reminiscent of the spiritualist notion in the 1840s that there were too few bodies available for the number of souls, and thus they invaded tables and other inanimate objects. Whitman was probably no more committed to this theory than he was to phrenology (discussed below) but merely used both ideas to convey – phenomenologically perhaps – his original idea about the equality of body and soul.

"Starting from Paumanok," called "Proto-Leaf" when it opened the 1860 edition of *Leaves of Grass*, is a more direct and personal use of autobiography than "Song of Myself." The American Indian name for Long Island (literally "fish-shaped"), Paumanok was the place of the poet's birth, where he was "well-begotten, and rais'd by a perfect mother." It suggests the myth of a poet who has emerged with his vision of America after roaming the United States – "Solitary, singing in the West, I strike up for a New World." The historically minded reader will note in *Leaves of Grass* the poet's imagery, which relates directly to his background. "Leaves" in his title refers to the pages of a book, a term familiar to the printing trade of which the author had been a member. Striking up for a New World reflects the author's love of music and, especially, the opera (where the conductor in the pit would "strike up" his orchestra). Whereas the imagery is often an accurate indication of the person behind the poet, the narrative is largely fictional. Although the narrator in *Leaves of Grass* has traveled extensively throughout the United States, Whitman had visited very little of the country by the time of the definitive arrangement of *Leaves of Grass* in 1881/82. His sense of geography came mainly from his reading as a schoolteacher and journalist.

Nevertheless, the narrator of "Starting from Paumanok" is prepared to speak as his country's representative seer:

> Take my leaves America, take them South and take
>   them North,
> Make welcome for them everywhere, for they are your
>   own off-spring,
> Surround them East and West, for they would surround
>   you,
> And you precedents, connect lovingly with them, for
>   they connect lovingly with you.
> I conn'd old times,
> I sat studying at the feet of the great masters,
> Now if eligible O that the great masters might return
>   and study me.

Having studied for so long the American character and achievement, the poet will now make poems of its "materials," will "make the poems of my body and mortality." "Starting from Paumanok" names all the main themes of Whitman's book, now more extensively than suggested in the first poem in "Inscriptions." Echoing the transcendentalist idea that "no man has ever yet been half devout enough" with regard to his worth as a symbol of God, the poet promises to celebrate the "divine average." This involves, of course, a celebration of democracy, seen now spiritually as well as politically. Indeed, democracy is viewed sexually – as Whitman addresses the concept as "Ma femme!" Whitman may have used sexuality as a metaphor for equality, the complete "merge" of bodies and souls in the triumph of democracy. This includes not only equality of the male and female, but of "sexual organs and acts," along with other, more "mentionable" parts of nature, the present and the future, life and death. All are part of the great "ensemble": "Was somebody asking to see the soul? / See, your own shape and countenance, persons, substances, beasts, the trees, the running rivers, the rocks and sands." The poem concludes with a series of catalogs that suggests the diverse "unity" of America.

Although more than 20 poems precede it in the definitive edition, "Song of Myself" remains the "premier" poem in *Leaves of Grass* and the poet's most important work. Untitled in the 1855 edition, it became "Poem of Walt Whitman, an American" in the 1856 edition and simply "Walt Whitman" in 1860. It was not called "Song of Myself" until the edition of 1881–82. Imagine writing a poem and then giving it your own name for a title. Whitman's literary narcissism, it would appear, knew no bounds. Yet he assures the reader at the outset that his celebration of self is a representative act: "And what I assume you shall assume, / For every atom belonging to me as good belongs to you." "Song of Myself" is not a monologue, but half a dialogue between the "I" of the poem and the "you" of the reader. First of all, Whitman revived the use of the first person in literature, something Benjamin Franklin had done in his *Autobiography* and Henry David **Thoreau** had done in *his* autobiography, *Walden*. Second, he spoke directly to the reader, not merely in the company of an assumed reader. It is an "I"-"you" exchange in which the colloquial and even slang punctuate the rhythm of the poem: "For every atom belong to me as good belongs to you. / I loafe and invite my soul." Earlier, he ignores the proper idiom and "sing[s him]self." Along with the use of the adjective "good" in place of an adverb and

the slang term "loafe," Whitman's idiom suggests a poet who is of the people. He is also totally American: "My tongue, every atom of my blood, form'd from this soil, this air, / Born here of parents born here from parents the same, and their parents the same."

The key word in "Song of Myself" and the 1855 edition of *Leaves of Grass* is *freedom* – "nature without check with original energy." Anticipating Emily **Dickinson's** idea in the poem "I taste a liquor never brewed – " (LOA, 2: 231), Whitman is intoxicated with the senses, with being alive. He is fascinated, for example, with the "smoke of [his] own breath," his "respiration and inspiration, the beating of [his] heart, the passing of blood and air through [his] lungs." Like Emerson before him, Whitman requires no "miracles" other than those of nature itself. Unlike Emerson, he finds this nature much more than an emblem of the Oversoul. Emerson's other "disciple," Thoreau, simply liked the emblem too much but was otherwise as much of a transcendentalist as Emerson. In Whitman's case, the body or nature was no emblem but something just as "clear and sweet" as the soul. In what became section 5 of an originally unsectioned poem, the body and soul engage in what appears to be a sexual act. Yet it is important to note that the reader cannot completely follow the imagery. We might envision the scene to the point where the soul parts "the shirt from [the body's] bosom-bone," but the scene becomes unchartable in any recognizable reality when the soul also plunges its "tongue to [the body's] bare-stript heart." The sexual act, accordingly, produces not fleshly progeny but a mystical vision of the world, passing "all the argument of the earth." This is the central contradiction of "Song of Myself" – that the body is sometimes equal to the soul and at other times merely symbolic of it.

In the following section, the motif of the grass is explained as "the handkerchief of the Lord, / A scented gift and remembrancer designedly dropt, / Bearing the owner's name someway in the corners, that we may see and remark and say *Whose?*" In other words, the grass is likened to a handkerchief that is dropped to gain our attention. It is "a uniform hieroglyphic," a secret and sacred writing from God. It grows "among black folks as among white, / Kanuck, Tuckahoe, Congressman, Cuff, I give them the same, I receive them the same." The grass, uniformly green and "hopeful," suggests the cyclical nature of existence: "All goes onward and outward, nothing collapses, / And to die is different from what any one supposed, and luckier." In the next stanza, the poet announces that he has passed "death with the dying and birth with the new-wash'd babe, and am not contain'd between my hat and boots." Much later in the poem, he recalls how "cycles" of time had "ferried my cradle, rowing and rowing like cheerful boatmen." "Before I was born out of my mother," he continues, "generations guided me, / My embryo has never been torpid, nothing could overlay it."

Much like Herman **Melville's** *Moby-Dick* (1851), "Song of Myself" has generally eluded critics when it comes to classifying the poem. Not only is it finally debatable whether the poem is a lyric or an epic, but the question of structure has elicited no fewer than 20 well-known arguments. The best known, by Carl F. Strauch, appeared in the periodical *English Journal* in 1938. The most novel and imaginative (for its time, 1955) is by James E. Miller Jr. And perhaps the one that makes the fewest demands on the reader is by Gay Wilson Allen (in the original

Walt Whitman Handbook). Since the poem is not primarily logical, Allen notes, it resists all attempts to make it so. Rather, he suggests, the most useful analogy for its structure is the symphony: "A theme (i.e., an idea or a sentiment) is advanced briefly in one section and later developed in more detail in other sections, so that the movement is often more spiral, or even circular, than forward." With its overtures and interludes, this symphony of words builds on section 5 in the same fashion that Emerson's principal essays build on *Nature* (1836). Having established the idea that body and soul, or nature and spirit, are equal, Whitman proceeds to celebrate the "divine average" that peoples all of nature. His newspaper background suggested, no doubt, the catalogs that note everything from the "suicide sprawl[ing] on the bloody floor" to the "runaway slave." This poet relates to and speaks for everyone, even the sexually frustrated woman in section 11 of the poem. Here and in other early sections, he surveys scenes from the city, the country, and the west, announcing himself as "the caresser of life." Touch is very important to this poet, who refers to himself by name in what became section 24: "Walt Whitman, a kosmos, of Manhattan the son, / Turbulent, fleshy, sensual, eating, drinking and breeding." In fact, touch is *the* key to this poet between 1855 and 1860, and this is why nature is not limited to the status of mere (transcendental) emblem. The grass, of which this book offers many "leaves," is the most immediate evidence of our *physical* relationship with the spiritual. As the poet writes in one of the most spectacular passages in the poem:

> I believe a leaf of grass is no less than the journeywork
> of the stars,
> And the pismire is equally perfect, and a grain of sand,
> and the egg of a wren,
> And the tree-toad is a chef-d'oeuvre for the highest,
> And the running blackberry would adorn the parlors of
> heaven,
> And the narrowest hinge in my hand puts to scorn all
> machinery,
> And the cow crunching with depressed head surpasses
> any statue,
> And a mouse is miracle enough to stagger sextillions of
> infidels.

Although "Song of Myself" was the best of the 1855 edition of *Leaves of Grass*, the best of the 1856 edition was the "Sun-Down Poem," which became "Crossing Brooklyn Ferry" in 1860 (LOA, 1: 864). Whereas in the first poem, the poet addresses the reader ("you") directly, and thus, colloquially, the narrator of "Crossing Brooklyn Ferry" *becomes* the reader and vice versa. Indeed, one critic has remarked that students frequently have the eerie feeling that Whitman is peering over their shoulder as they read – which was precisely the effect sought after by the poet:

> It avails not, time nor place – distance avails not,
> I am with you, you men and women of a generation, or
> ever so many generations hence,
> Just as you feel when you look on the river and sky, so I
> felt,
> Just as any of you is one of a living crowd, I was one of
> a crowd,

> Just as you are refresh'd by the gladness of the river and
> the bright flow, I was refresh'd,
> Just as you stand and lean on the rail, yet hurry with
> the swift current, I stood yet was hurried,
> Just as you look on the numberless masts of ships and
> the thick-stemm'd pipes of steamboats, I look'd.

Time and space are relative and certainly subordinate to the fact that we are all spiritually unified in this "well-join'd scheme" called experience.

Whitman's first two editions did not sell well, mainly because of his unorthodox rhythm, or "free verse," and the quotidian nature of his subject matter. Emerson's nature had been symbolic; Henry Wadsworth **Longfellow's** "Nature" had been allegorical; Whitman's nature, however, was a bit too lusty and barbarous. His third edition contained two sections suggestive of the carnival of the flesh: "Children of Adam" and "Calamus."

The idea in the first series is that man is like Adam, waking up in the morning of the world to his sexuality – to "pent-up aching rivers, / From that of myself without which I were nothing, / From what I am determin'd to make illustrious, even if I stand sole among men" (LOA, 1: 841). And alone the poet was in this campaign against "infidelism about sex," as Whitman put the matter in his 1856 open letter to Emerson. When the two walked on Boston Common in 1860, as the third edition of *Leaves of Grass* was going through the press at the firm of Thayer and Eldridge, Emerson urged Whitman to omit the "Adam" poems (originally entitled "Enfans d'Adam") in order to allow the public a chance to see his originality. By 1860, the transcendentalist of *Nature* had become something of a realist and knew that their Victorian society would condemn such poems out of hand (one Boston newspaper, noting Emerson's earlier support of *Leaves of Grass*, thought that the third edition said one thing about both writers: temporary insanity). Whitman, on the other hand, was determined to have the body represented in its sexuality as well as other aspects. Otherwise, he thought, it would mean literary castration for his book.

Whitman had perhaps been encouraged by the pseudoscience of phrenology to view the body as the signature of a healthy soul. In "I Sing the Body Electric" (LOA, 1: 809), which was included in the first edition and called "Poem of the Body" in the second, the narrator asks: "Was it dreamed whether those who corrupted their own live bodies could conceal themselves?" The phrenology movement, especially in New York City in the 1850s as it was spearheaded by the firm of Fowler and Wells, was essentially a health movement. Earlier as a journalist, Whitman had urged his readers to adopt a better program of personal hygiene (e.g., bathing at least once a week), and he was very proud of his own physique and good health. In line with the statement in "Song of Myself" about the "procreant urge," Whitman felt that sexuality was as much a part of nature as anything else and ought not to be slighted:

> Have you ever loved the body of a woman?
> Have you very loved the body of a man?
> . . . .
> If any thing is sacred the human body is sacred.
> . . . .
> Hips, hip-sockets, hip-strength, inward and outward
> round, man-balls, man-root,

Strong set of thighs, well carrying the trunk above,
Leg-fibres, knee, knee-pan, upper-leg, under-leg.

The last three lines and the many that followed them were designated as obscene by the district attorney of Boston in 1881. But the main idea in "Children of Adam" is that man is born of woman to be reborn in the sexual act with a woman. When Thoreau read these poems, he said, "It is as if the beasts spoke." Yet he thought that the problem was not in the sexual allusion itself but in the minds of those whose society had demonized the sexual act. In "Spontaneous Me" (originally called "Bunch Poem" in reference to the seminal seed), Whitman went so far as to call the phallus a poem: "This poem drooping shy and unseen that I always carry, and that all men carry.'" No wonder Emerson tried to talk Whitman out of including these poems in *Leaves of Grass*. It was an age in which even piano legs were covered, and Whitman was talking about *sexual* organs!

After 1860, he softened the "Adam" theme somewhat with such poems as "I Heard You Solemn-Sweet Pipes of the Organ" (LOA, 1: 843), the revised "As Adam Early in the Morning" (LOA, 1: 843), and "Out of the Rolling Ocean the Crowd." The first may be based upon an actual sentiment or experience and is preoccupied more with love than sex. The second eventually served as an epilogue to the "Children of Adam" group by bringing it back to the allegory of the Garden of Eden (where Adam first awakes to his sexuality); here, too, the "body heat" of the sexual imagery is lower. The third is one of Whitman's true love poems – and possibly the best of the final arrangement of "Children of Adam." Composed in the early 1860s and transferred from the "Drum Taps" section in 1871, it may – like "I Heard You Solemn-Sweet Pipes of the Organ" – refer directly to personal experience. A close friend, Ellen O' Connor, stated that "Out of the Rolling Ocean the Crowd" was directed to a woman who had written Whitman letters of literary praise and possibly love; yet O' Connor herself was infatuated with the poet and may have fantasized the story of a heterosexual Whitman. The idea of the poem is more platonic than anything else and centers on the inseparability of two who have "look'd" upon one another:

Out of the rolling ocean the crowd came a drop gently
  to me,
Whispering *I love you, before long I die,*
I have travel'd a long way merely to look upon you to
  touch you,
For I could not die till I once look'd on you,
For I fear'd I might afterward lose you.
Now we have met, we have look'd, we are safe,
Return in peace to the ocean my love,
I too am part of that ocean my love, we are not so much
  separated,
Behold the great rondure, the cohesion of all, how
  perfect!

Whereas in "Children of Adam" Whitman celebrates the phrenological idea of "amativeness," or heterosexual love, "Calamus" focuses on "adhesiveness," or male friendship. According to the poet's testimony, this is not to be confused with homoerotic desire. When the British critic and poet John Addington Symonds inquired about the possibility, he was told bluntly that homosexuality was not part of its theme: "Ab't the

questions on Calamus pieces &c: they quite daze me. L. of G. is only to be rightly construed by and within its own atmosphere and essential character . . . that the calamus part has even allow'd the possibility of such a construction as mention'd is terrible" (August 19, 1890). There is, however, internal evidence that "Calamus" speaks of homosexuality and some external evidence that the poet feared his homosexuality would be found out, or that it would be concluded erroneously that he was a homosexual.

Although there is no convincing, prima facie evidence of Whitman's homosexuality, the "Calamus" poems are nevertheless today strong emotional evidence of that orientation. Whatever the case, the love poems are mainly here in "Calamus," not in "Children of Adam," where "libidinous joys only" are celebrated. Whitman's theme, as he announces in "In Paths Untrodden" (LOA, 1: 843), the opening poem of "Calamus," is "To tell of the secret of my nights and days, / To celebrate the need of comrades." This poem and those that follow (initially 45 poems, but reduced to 42 poems in 1867) reveal the poet as the "tenderest lover." "Calamus" refers to a calamus root, "the very large & aromatic grass, or rush, growing about waterponds in the valleys – spears about three feet high – often called 'sweet flag.'" The plant looks like a phallic symbol, but the only known Whitman reference to its shape is that the "recherche or ethereal sense [of sweet-flag], as used in my book, arises probably from the actual Calamus presenting the biggest & hardiest kind of spears of grass – and their fresh, acquatic, pungent bouquet." To Whitman, a spear of grass symbolized the unity and equality of all nature.

It has been said that the "Calamus" sequence resembles the drama of love and disappointment in William Shakespeare's sonnets; this comparison may be particularly apt because the "Calamus" poems (most clearly in the 1860 edition) resemble a dialogue or a lovers' quarrel in which the narrator seldom receives a satisfactory response. Moments of ecstasy give way to "hours discouraged, distracted," as the narrator sees his lover "content himself without me." Indeed, at one particularly stressed juncture it is declared that the elusive lover is "dead" – as far as the narrator is concerned. Probably the most famous poem in "Calamus" is "I Saw in Louisiana a Live-Oak Growing" (LOA, 1: 856), which has been taken as either a biographical statement of the poet's homosexuality or a broader statement about the glories and difficulties of maintaining friendships. According to Whitman, live oak leaves embody "the passion of friendship for man." Probably few other major American writers had more sexless friendships and fewer sexual ones. Whitman maintained platonic connections with both men and women – and tended to reflect his Neoplatonic age in preferring (or holding in higher regard) male relationships. The poem, then, if it is not an outright confession of homosexuality, is an ode to the difficulty and the resulting loneliness in male relationships:

I saw in Louisiana a live-oak growing,
All alone stood it and the moss hung down from the
  branches,
Without any companion it grew there uttering joyous
  leaves of dark green,
And its look, rude, unbending, lusty, made me think of
  myself,

But I wonder'd how it could utter joyous leaves
    standing alone there without its friend near, for I
    knew I could not,
And I broke off a twig with a certain number of leaves
    upon it, and twined around it a little moss,
And brought it away, and I have placed it in sight in my
    room,
It is not needed to remind me as of my own dear
    friends,
(For I believe lately I think of little else than of them,)
Yet it remains to me a curious token, it makes me think
    of manly love;
For all that, and though the live-oak glistens there in
    Louisiana solitary in a wide flat space,
Uttering joyous leaves all its life without a friend a lover
    near,
I know very well I could not.

Whitman may have been undergoing a personal crisis during or shortly before the writing of "Calamus," which was probably written in 1859. Two other "crisis" poems penned during this year were "Out of the Cradle Endlessly Rocking" (LOA, 1: 871) and "As I Ebb'd with the Ocean of Life" (LOA, 1: 877). These two poems make up the major part of the "Sea-Drift" section in the 1881–82 edition of *Leaves of Grass*. The term "crisis" does not refer exclusively to a personal crisis, but also to a literary one in which the power of poetry to overcome the fear of death is challenged. Entitled "A Child's Reminiscence" in 1859, when it first appeared in a magazine, and retitled "A Word Out of the Sea" in the 1860 edition of *Leaves of Grass*, it became "Out of the Cradle Endlessly Rocking" in 1871. The first title is more accurate: the poem is narrated by a man who has been stirred by a reminiscence of childhood. Arising one night to witness the separation of two lovers, "Two feather'd guests from Alabama," the man, now in mid-life, realizes the ruling principle of existence – the balance of life and death in every human or natural equation. Whitman the poet comes to an important juncture when he turns away from the celebration of freedom to the more sobered notion that the poet's duty is to sing of love and death: "Now in a moment I know what I am for, I awake, / And already a thousand singers, a thousand songs, clearer, louder and more sorrowful than yours, / A thousand warbling echoes have started to life within me, never to die." Indeed, the second title is also more accurate than the third, if not as elegant or original, because the poet hears, when he begs the sea for "a clue" ("the clue" in later editions) to understanding the enigma of life, "a word out of the sea." That word is death, chanted four times. The poet is truly "out of the rocked cradle," or "out of the cradle endlessly rocking," in the sense that the illusions of youth – indeed, the romantic illusions of literature – have now been seriously qualified.

The appearance of the poem in 1859 and in the 1860 edition coincides with the transition from the romantic or "transcendentalist" period to American literary realism. Here, we find the poet moving into this second major phase as a major poet. Whereas his themes in the first three editions of *Leaves of Grass* had been romantic, they would be "realistic" after the Civil War. This change, if not altogether effected in "Out of the Cradle" (where there remains hope for poetry to overcome or

compensate for the cycle of love and death), is clearly signaled in "As I Ebb'd with the Ocean of Life." As with "Out of the Cradle," the narrator of "As I Ebb'd" goes down to the seashore, but this time the "clue" that he receives from the sea is less reassuring of the poetic process. Walking the shores of Paumanok "with that electric self seeking types," he finds that poetry cannot not always fulfill its promise to rid empirical reasoning (the "Understanding" in transcendentalist parlance) of its fear of death and the accompanying lack of a meaningful and permanent identity:

O baffled, balk'd, bent to the very earth,
Oppress'd with myself that I have dared to open my
    mouth,
Aware now that amid all that blab whose echoes recoil
    upon me I have not once had the least idea who or
    what I am,
But that before all my arrogant poems the real Me
    stands yet untouch'd, untold, altogether unreach'd,
Withdrawn far, mocking me with mock-congratulatory
    signs and bows,
With peals of distant ironical laughter at every word I
    have written,
Pointing in silence to these songs, and then to the sand
    beneath.

Originally entitled "Bardic Symbols," the poem is not altogether a personal lament but a poetic or public one (in the sense that the poet is representative of the "public" or all humankind). All humanity is "baffled, balk'd, [and] bent to the very earth" in its attempt to transcend the limits of human knowledge.

Most of the poems discussed thus far appeared in the third edition of *Leaves of Grass*, which was published almost on the eve of the Civil War. Although it rapidly sold out its first issue of 1,000 copies, the 1860 edition was discontinued when the publishers filed for bankruptcy during the war. Whitman brought out no more books of poems until 1865, when *Drum-Taps* appeared, but he was writing those wartime poems from the very beginning of the war. One of the most famous of the early pieces is "Beat! Beat! Drums!" which encouraged (legend has it) two of the poet's younger brothers to enlist in the Union army. Note how the spondaic and anapestic measures reinforce the martial sound of an army on the march:

Beat! beat! drums! – blow! bugles! blow!
Through the windows – through doors – burst like a
    ruthless force,
Into the solemn church, and scatter the congregation,
Into the school where the scholar is studying;
Leave not the bridegroom quiet – no happiness must he
    have now with his bride,
Nor the peace farmer any peace, ploughing his field or
    gathering his grain,
So fierce you whirr and pound you drums – so shrill
    you bugles blow.

The point is that no one can go on with normal life once the war has begun and the integrity of the Union is threatened.

Whitman himself was brought out of New York City by his concern for his soldier-brother, George Washington Whitman. Once he found him, wounded but safe after the Battle of Fredericksburg in 1862, he could return no farther than Washington, D.C., where he secured a part-time job and began his famous hospital work, for which he was later called "The Wound Dresser" (also the title of one of the *Drum-Taps* pieces; LOA, 1: 891). When the war broke out in 1861, Whitman was in his forties, too old to fight and lacking the inclination for battle anyway. In "The Wound Dresser," this "old man bending" puts it best: "Arous'd and angry, I'd thought to beat the alarum, and urge relentless war, / But soon my fingers fail'd me, my face droop'd and I resign'd myself, / To sit by the wounded and soothe them, or silently watch the dead." Whitman spent the war years and the rest of the decade ministering to sick and wounded soldiers from both sides of the conflict. There were over 40 temporary hospitals in the nation's capital, and Whitman probably saw the inside of every one of them – assisting the physicians in amputations, bringing sweetmeats, candy, tobacco, and stationery to the ailing combatants, and writing letters home to their parents, sometimes to convey the sad news that their son had died. This is the substance of "Come Up from the Fields, Father" (LOA, 1: 887), in which Whitman fleshed out the scene that he knew his letters must have created. While the family "stand at home at the door he is dead already, / The only son is dead."

In *Drum-Taps,* Whitman's poetry shifted into a third and final phase, one in which the focus is not on the self or the self's function as a poet any longer, but on figures of courage and pathos: the common soldier, and the commander in chief of the Union, who would also pay the ultimate price for democracy. Aside from the bloody hospital and camp scenes, Whitman saw nothing of the actual war. Yet his vicarious participation was probably second to none. Not only did he live the war through his soldiers, but through his soldier-brother as well – who described battle in letters that Whitman got directly or through his mother in Brooklyn. In "Vigil Strange I Kept on the Field One Night" (LOA, 1: 889), the poet imagines himself speeding into battle, but that storyline soon gives way to the melancholy of losing a "dear comrade." In "A Sight in Camp in the Daybreak Gray and Dim," that young man "is the face of the Christ himself, / Dead and divine and brother of all, and here again he lies." In "As Toilsome I Wander'd Virginia's Woods" (LOA, 1: 890), his epitaph is *Bold, cautious, true, and my loving comrade.* These poems reveal the deep emotion and emotiveness of Whitman as he witnessed four years of war and wasted lives. He may have been excited in the beginning (as the introductory poems in *Drum-Taps* suggest), but he ultimately wearied of all the trauma and heartache. In "Reconciliation," a poem with which Whitman should have concluded the original *Drum-Taps,* it is observed that the war – with both its deeds of greatness and its episodes of death and destruction – must give way to the oblivion that seizes all human acts: "Beautiful that war and all its deeds of carnage must in time be utterly lost, / That the hands of the sisters Death and Night incessantly softly wash again, and ever again, this soil'd world." For war's reality had been the enemy ("a man divine as myself"), who is now dead and lying "white-faced and still in the coffin." All one can do at the end of war is to embrace the dead, for the *lives* of the enemy no longer give war any meaning: "[I] bend down and touch lightly with my lips the white face in the coffin." The antiwar idea is also present in "Dirge for Two Veterans" (LOA, 1: 894), where the dead are a son

and a father, "dropt together, and the double grave awaits them."

Not long after the assassination of President Lincoln on April 14, 1865, Whitman wrote his *Sequel to Drum-Taps.* Its 18 poems included four treating the slain leader, two of which are well-known, the first for being one of the poet's worst and the other for being one of the poet's very best. "O Captain! My Captain!" (LOA, 1: 904) is conventional in its meter, rhyme, and stanzaic structure, a feat quite unusual for Whitman. Its rhythm has a sing-song effect that probably undermines the authenticity of feeling that Whitman was trying to express. To the poet's annoyance, "O Captain! My Captain!" became his best known poem in the nineteenth century – indeed, the one that his family most appreciated. "I'm almost sorry," he told Horace Traubel, "I ever wrote the poem."

Many would argue that "When Lilacs Last in the Dooryard Bloom'd" (LOA, 1: 895) is Whitman's best poem (the other candidates for this most American of honors are "Song of Myself" and "Out of the Cradle Endlessly Rocking"). Perhaps the poem is Whitman's "greatest" in the sense that it brought about (however briefly) a reconstruction and a revision of his earlier poetic vision in which the representative self is always at the center of the universe. In becoming the "Wound Dresser," he had given up his earlier identity as "Walt Whitman, a kosmos," and become a "simple, separate person," a comrade to soldiers from both the north and south. In the poems of the first three editions of *Leaves of Grass* (before 1860), the focus is on the first person; in *Drum-Taps* it shifts to the third. This is not to say that all or even most of the poems are literally written in the third person, but that the mood and tone are now detached from the barbaric self of the earlier poetry. This shift from the one to the many prepared Whitman for his great elegy to Lincoln. Deeply impressed by the heroism of the soldiers to whom he had ministered in the hospitals, he came to focus that empathy on the commander in chief. "Lilacs" celebrates the plurality of the personal: out of the death of the multifaceted figure of the president had come the birth of a Lincoln enshrined as a symbol of America's greatness. The poems to the slain president were eventually placed in *Leaves of Grass* under the heading of "Memories of President Lincoln." Whitman realized that it was the memory of Lincoln that best represented and preserved America's "divine average." His elegy, therefore, calls attention not to the past or even to the life of its subject (indeed, the president is never named in the poem), but to Lincoln's life in our imagination, an image that makes the poem as perennial as the faithful blossom of the lilacs every spring.

There are three basic symbols in the poem. The first is the lilacs of spring, which represent the poet's enduring love of the president. (In one of his Lincoln lectures, Whitman remembered seeing lilacs in bloom when he first heard of Lincoln's assassination.) The fallen western star stands for the stricken leader, and the hermit thrush indicates the spiritual meaning of the president's death. As with any great work, of course, such an outline is reductive. Actually, these symbols overlap in complex ways – the lilacs also representing the cycle of life, the star as Lincoln's "life" after death, and the bird as an agent of resolution. As in John Milton's "Lycidas" or Percy Bysshe Shelley's "Adonais," the issue resolved is death – as the subject of the poem comes to stand for eternal life rather than death. Death becomes a *strong deliveress,* as it is in section 49 of "Song of

Myself ("To his work without flinching the accoucheur comes"); yet in "Lilacs" the agent of change, or subject of the poem, is not the speaker but the object of the speech act. As far as we know, Whitman had never met Lincoln, and this is probably why his personal admiration for the man was so easily changed into the public worship of the memory of the president. Lincoln was "assassinated," Whitman later wrote in *Specimen Days*, "but the Union is not assassinated." "O what shall I hang on the chamber walls? [he asks] . . . To adorn the burial-house of him I love?" Its walls, of course, will be covered with scenes of America and its perennial cycles of growth: "Pictures of growing spring and farms and homes," "the city at hand with dwellings so dense, and stacks of chimneys, / And all the scenes of life and the workshops, and the workmen homeward returning."

Although "The Sleepers" (LOA, 1: 799) appears late in the definitive arrangement of *Leaves of Grass*, it was one of the original 12 poems in the first edition. It may be that Whitman came to see the poem in the context of his "Lilacs" phase – where the observed takes precedence over the observer. The poet of "The Sleepers" wanders all night in his vision, going from "bedside to bedside, [sleeping] close with the other sleepers each in turn." Here, the poet is a representative *dreamer*, and sleep represents a freeing of the spirit to become fulfilled in the oneness of humankind: "I swear they are averaged now – one is no better than the other, / The night and sleep have liken'd them and restored them." Although "The Sleepers" is an enigmatic poem that continues to draw original criticism, there are many who fail to see it as a great poem. John Burroughs, one of the poet's closest friends, claimed not to understand the poem. Indeed, one might consider the scenes in the poem as consisting largely of "out-takes" from "Song of Myself," which may explain its apparent surrealism.

During the final years of his last poetic phase, in which Whitman had shifted from the self to the other, or from the one to the many, he also shifted from emphasis on the body to a focus on the soul. The poems from this chapter of Whitman's poetic progress were "pegged" for greatness – in the sense that Whitman now adopted a more traditional poetic approach in terms of themes. The theme of "Proud Music of the Storm" (LOA, 1: 922) is that poetry should discover a "new rhythmus" by "bridging the way from Life to Death." The early Walt Whitman had made poems out of the earth, so to speak; the later Whitman senses the overwhelming spirituality of the body that he had once held up as equal to the soul. Apprehension of this spirituality unifies the world community – another theme the poet develops, especially in "Passage to India" (LOA, 1: 928). "Proud Music" opens with descriptions of sea and prairie storms, which are "hidden orchestras" that blend "with Nature's rhythmus all the tongues of nations." The poem involves a dream in which the human voice or music is finally suspected of being the essence of the sounds that storms (and nature in general) make. This recognition introduces allusions to the music of different countries, until the narrator wakes from his dream at the opening of section 6 to find the "clew" he had sought for so long.

Not only do storms suggest the ultimate unity of humankind; technological feats do as well. In "Passage to India," the Suez Canal, the transcontinental railroad, and the transatlantic cable suggest a "passage to more than India!" It is

through contemplation of these physical events – just as the storms in "Proud Music" had suggested the spirituality of nature – that we can come to see that death is the way to life in the sense of finally coming face to face with God:

> Swiftly I shrivel at the thought of God,
> At Nature and its wonders, Time and Space and Death,
> But that I, turning, call to thee O soul, thou actual Me,
> And lo, thou gently masterest the orbs,
> Thou matest Time, smilest content at Death,
> And fillest, swellest full the vastnesses of Space.

To many critics, Whitman's final themes about death and the spirit suggest a forced Emersonianism in which nature is merely the emblem again. Back in "Song of Myself," nature had been much more *physical*. And death had been something to stand up to: "And as to you Death, and you bitter hug of mortality, it is idle to try to alarm me." Even God himself was to be addressed directly and, as it were, on a first-name basis: "Listener up there! what have you to confide to me? / Look in my face while I snuff the sidle of evening, / (Talk honestly, no one else hears you, and I stay only a minute longer.)" The directness of this poet's speech suggests a more spontaneous, vigorous, and sincere poet than does the chastened voice of "Passage to India": the poet "worthy that name" would violate even Emerson's definition of the poet as being Christ-like in the apprehension of his own divinity but not Christ himself – "the true son of God," as he is described in "Passage to India."

In this regard, the edition of *Leaves of Grass* that Whitman wanted us to read tends to parcel out his originality to the demands of traditional authorship as it focused on metaphysical themes. Not only were these themes seriously qualified or enhanced by the presence of the body in the early editions of *Leaves of Grass*, but the original language of the revised poems is often more evocative and genuine. This essay opened with the question of which edition to use. Its ambivalence on the question (with perhaps a slight preference for the early versions) suggests that readers of *Leaves of Grass* ought at least to avail themselves of both the first and sixth editions. The more serious student should also investigate the 1860 edition, and the professional reader of Whitman will, of course, use the three-volume variorum of the printed poems of *Leaves of Grass*.

JEROME LOVING

Selected Works

Leaves of Grass; The First (1855) Edition, edited by Malcolm Cowley, New York: Viking, 1959

Leaves of Grass; Facsimile Edition of the 1860 Text, edited by Roy Harvey Pearce, Ithaca, New York: Cornell University Press, 1961

Leaves of Grass; Comprehensive Reader's Edition, edited by Harold W. Blodgett and Sculley Bradley, New York: Norton, 1965

Leaves of Grass; A Textual Variorum of the Printed Poems, edited by Arthur Golden, et al., 3 vols., New York: New York University Press, 1980

Walt Whitman: Complete Poetry and Collected Prose, edited by Justin Kaplan, New York: Library of America, 1982

Leaves of Grass, edited by Jerome Loving, Oxford: Oxford University Press, 1990

Selected Letters of Walt Whitman, edited by Edwin Haviland Miller, Iowa City: University of Iowa Press, 1990

Further Reading

Allen, Gay Wilson, *The Whitman Handbook*, Chicago: Packard, 1946

_____, *The New Walt Whitman Handbook*, New York: New York University Press, 1975

_____, *The Solitary Singer. A Critical Biography of Walt Whitman*, New York: New York University Press, 1955

Aspiz, Harold, *Walt Whitman and the Body Beautiful*, Urbana: University of Illinois Press, 1980

Asselineau, Roger, *The Evolution of Walt Whitman*, 2 vols., Cambridge, Massachusetts: Harvard University Press, 1960, 1962

Erkkila, Betsy, *Whitman the Political Poet*, New York: Oxford University Press, 1988

Folsom, Ed, *Walt Whitman's Native Representations*, Cambridge: Cambridge University Press, 1994

Folsom, Ed, ed., *Walt Whitman: The Centennial Essays*, Iowa City: University of Iowa Press, 1994

Folsom, Ed, and Dan Campion, eds., *Walt Whitman: The Measure of His Song*, Minneapolis, Minnesota: Holy Cow!, 1981

Greenspan, Ezra, *Walt Whitman and the American Reader*, Cambridge: Cambridge University Press, 1990

Hollis, C. Carroll, *Language and Style in Leaves of Grass*, Baton Rouge: Louisiana State University Press, 1983

Hutchinson, George B., *The Ecstatic Whitman: Literary Shamanism and the Crisis of the Union*, Columbus: Ohio State University Press, 1986

Kaplan, Justin, *Walt Whitman: A Life*, New York: Simon and Schuster, 1980

Killingsworth, M. Jimmie, *Whitman's Poetry of the Body: Sexuality, Politics, and the Text*, Chapel Hill: University of North Carolina Press, 1989

Klammer, Martin, *Whitman, Slavery, and the Emergence of 'Leaves of Grass'*, University Park: Pennsylvania State University Press, 1995

Kuebrich, David, *Minor Prophecy: Walt Whitman's New American Religion*, Bloomington: Indiana University Press, 1989

Loving, Jerome, *Emerson, Whitman, and the American Muse*, Chapel Hill: University of North Carolina Press, 1982

Marki, Ivan, *The Trial of the Poet: An Interpretation of the First Edition of Leaves of Grass*, New York: Columbia University Press, 1976

Miller, Edwin Haviland, *Walt Whitman's Poetry: A Psychological Journey*, Boston: Houghton Mifflin, 1968

_____, *Walt Whitman's "Song of Myself": A Mosaic of Interpretations*, Iowa City: University of Iowa Press, 1989

Miller, James E., Jr., *The American Quest for a Supreme Fiction: Whitman's Legacy in the Personal Epic*, Chicago: University of Chicago Press, 1979

_____, *A Critical Guide to Leaves of Grass*, Chicago: University of Chicago Press, 1957

Myerson, Joel, ed., *Whitman in His Own Time: A Biographical Chronicle of His Life, Drawn from Recollections, Memoirs, and Interviews by Friends and Associates*, Detroit: Omnigraphics, 1991

Price, Kenneth M., *Whitman and Tradition: The Poet in His Century*, New Haven, Connecticut: Yale University Press, 1990

Sill, Geoffrey M., ed., *Walt Whitman of Mickle Street: A Centennial Collection*, Knoxville: University of Tennessee Press, 1994

Thomas, M. Wynn, *The Lunar Light of Whitman's Poetry*, Cambridge, Massachusetts: Harvard University Press, 1987

Woodress, James, ed., *Critical Essays on Walt Whitman*, Boston: G. K. Hall, 1983

Zweig, Paul, *Walt Whitman: The Making of a Poet*, New York: Basic, 1984

John Greenleaf Whittier

(1807–1892)

Whittier has the unique distinction in American literature of being both the best-loved poet of his day and the most politically active. Although Whittier's fellow "fireside poet" Henry Wadsworth **Longfellow** may have achieved a greater popularity in terms of book sales, it was the more accessible and less bookish Whittier who could earn both the respect of poets like Alfred, Lord Tennyson and Oliver Wendell **Holmes** and the affection of a wide range of general readers. Thousands of admirers overwhelmed the poet with letters of appreciation toward the end of his life. Whittier's poems touched the hearts of contemporary readers in a way that is perhaps difficult to understand today; one of his "fans" was the young Helen Keller, whose poignant letters expressed "how much your little blind friends love their sweet poet." Holmes wrote of a "free and sweet atmosphere" in Whittier's poems, which provides its readers with the "fragrance of a loving spirit"; at least one admirer, Dorothea Dix – a social reformer and superintendent of Civil War nurses – asked that a copy of Whittier's book of poems be buried with her. Whittier not only garnered such epithets as "Poet Laureate of the Nation," "Our Rustic New England Bard," and "the Poet of Hope and Immortality," but he also had both a college in Iowa and a city in California named after him.

Yet John Greenleaf Whittier was not always destined to be a celebrated poet: his early life was devoted more to political ambitions and causes than to poetry. One of the foremost voices in the abolitionist movement, he served as a delegate to the national Republican convention and to the inaugural meeting of the National Anti-Slavery Society, as a member of the Massachusetts legislature, as a political lobbyist in Boston and New York City, as secretary for various abolitionist societies, as an editor of *The Emancipator and Anti-Slavery Record*, and even as an unsuccessful candidate for the United States Congress, all by the age of 30. During this period he also published a substantial antislavery treatise, *Justice and Expediency* (1833), as well as an 1837 volume of poems devoted to the abolitionist cause. His political interests and activism continued throughout the late 1830s, 1840s, and 1850s: he edited the *Pennsylvania Freeman* in 1838, left the Whig Party in 1839 to become one of the founders of the Liberty Party, campaigned for various Liberty Party candidates and ran for Congress on the same party's ticket, toured the eastern United States with English abolitionist Joseph Sturge, published *Voices of Freedom* (1846), lobbied in Washington, D.C., against the admission of Texas as a slave state, worked for the antislavery cause with both the Free-Soil and Republican Parties, wrote for a decade as a corresponding editor to the *National Era* (the weekly publication of the National and Foreign Anti-Slavery Society), helped elect abolitionist candidate Charles Sumner to the U. S. Senate in 1850, wrote campaign songs for John C. Frémont's presidential bid of 1856, and corresponded with such important figures as Sumner, William Lloyd Garrison, Henry Clay, William Ellery Channing, Elizur Wright, John Quincy **Adams**, Lydia Maria Child, and Harriet Beecher Stowe.

But if Whittier's credentials as a political and personal force in the abolitionist movement are undisputed, his talents as a poet have been the matter of some disagreement. Although Whittier's contemporaries honored him as a "true poet" and an "inspiration to all that is highest and best" (Stowe), a poet whose "perfect chastity of thought and speech" provided "an uplifting moral power" (Garrison) and whose "perfect truthfulness of expression" accompanied an "exquisite expression of high poetical feeling" (James Russell **Lowell**), later estimates have been generally less positive. Hyatt Waggoner speaks for most twentieth-century critics when he writes that Whittier was a respected poet but not a great one: "his poetic ear was deficient, his moralizing often obtrusive, his language too often a jarring mixture of the rustic and the literary, his meters too often inappropriate to the subject." No other famous American poet of the nineteenth century, Waggoner argues, "offers greater obstacles to a just evaluation today."

In fact, much of Whittier's poetic output must be judged deficient not only in originality and aesthetic power, but in technique and conception as well. Whether or not Whittier's poetic abilities were as "meager" as Gay Wilson Allen claims, he was certainly not a great versifier (*Critical Essays on John Greenleaf Whittier*). His rhythms are not spontaneously lyrical, and for that reason many of his most successful poems are hymns, a form in which an unobtrusive regularity of meter is most effective. Whittier's lack of formal education may have contributed to a less sophisticated sense of prosody than that of contemporaries like William Cullen **Bryant**, Longfellow, Lowell, or Holmes. If Whittier's verses have often been the target of critical ridicule, it is because they tend in many cases to be old-fashioned, moralistic, and sentimental to an extent not matched by even the works of the other "fireside" poets. Lacking the poetic gifts of some of his contemporaries, Whittier relies heavily on moral didacticism and conviction of feeling. As others have noticed, his frequent use of the exclamation point indicates a lack of the kind of ambivalence, uncertainty, or philosophical and spiritual questioning that we associate with great poetry in the post-romantic era.

On the other hand, Whittier's poems often exemplify the kind of rustic simplicity and directness of expression that we associate with the lyrics of Robert Burns (one of Whittier's important early influences), and with the Quaker religion of Whittier and his family, rather than with the complex poetry of the romantic sublime. As a kind of New England primitive, Whittier differed not only from the British romantics, but from American contemporaries like Longfellow, Lowell, Ralph Waldo **Emerson**, Holmes, and even Bryant. Simple rural virtue, the love of nature, and the celebration of family and local community will carry an extended body of poetry such as Whittier's only so far, however; it is generally agreed that with the exception of a few truly powerful poems – "Snow-Bound" (LOA, 1: 476) foremost among them – most of Whittier's poetry is pleasant without being particularly memorable.

This assessment of the poet may in part be explained by a change in critical tastes. Whittier's own poetic sensibilities reflect literary judgments that by today's standards appear naive, if not misguided. As Waggoner points out, Whittier often appeared to value the sentimental verse of Lydia Child, Grace Greenwood, Alice and Phoebe **Cary**, and other women that he knew and promoted, more highly than the intellectually sophisticated and aesthetically challenging romantic poetry of John Keats, Percy Bysshe Shelley, and William Wordsworth. For Whittier, Waggoner claims, there is no significant aesthetic principle at work, only a moral one: poetry is message, and any pleasure that it produces has more to do with the sentiments that it expresses than with its style, form, or intellectual complexity. On the other hand, Whittier was not merely the homespun, untaught bard of Amesbury, Massachusetts, that many have believed him to be. Although he was hardly an "intellectual" in the sense that Longfellow was, he was widely read. A list of the authors that he mentions most frequently in his own writing includes not only those popular in his own day – William Shakespeare, John Bunyan, Walter Scott, Burns, Lord Byron, and Charles Dickens – but also an impressive group of the most important writers from the English and European literary traditions: Sir Philip Sidney, Edmund Spenser, Francis Bacon, George Herbert, Andrew Marvell, John Milton, Laurence Sterne, Edmund Burke, James Boswell, Thomas Gray, William Cowper, Wordsworth, Samuel Taylor Coleridge, Keats, Shelley, Matthew Arnold, Tennyson, Robert Browning, Thomas Carlyle, Thomas Babington Macaulay, Dante, Cervantes, and Lamartine. Although his critical tastes may differ from our own (and to some extent even from the more sophisticated tastes of his own day), he was capable of making informed literary judgments on writers like John Brainard, Holmes, Longfellow, and even William Blake. (For examples of Whittier's literary criticism, see *The Works of John Greenleaf Whittier*, vols. 6 and 7, and *Whittier on Writers and Writing: The Uncollected Critical Writings*.)

It may be the case, as some have claimed, that Whittier simply wrote too much and too quickly; at times, his letters suggest an almost casual attitude toward the details of poetic composition. It is certainly true that the idea behind the poem mattered more to Whittier than the brilliance of its execution; as one contemporary, Augustine Duganne, pointed out in a satirical jab at Whittier's careless verse:

> I prize the spirit which exalts thy strain,
> And joy when truth impels thy blows amain;
> But, really, friend! I cannot help suspecting
> Though writing's good, there's merit in correcting.

A century later, Howard Mumford Jones essentially concurred with this judgment, adding that Whittier had a "fatal inability to distinguish between having a poem to write and having to write a poem" (*Critical Essays on John Greenleaf Whittier*).

In recent years, Whittier's verse has suffered the same critical neglect as that of his poetic contemporaries, with the exceptions of Walt **Whitman**, Emily **Dickinson**, Emerson, and Edgar Allan **Poe**. Aside from a few scattered articles, virtually no new critical or biographical work has appeared on Whittier in the last 20 years. The question Perry Miller asked three decades ago is even more appropriate today: "has Whittier's stature so dwindled . . . that there is no longer anything worth saying about him?" Nonetheless, Miller provided one of the most interesting arguments for a continued interest in Whittier

as a literary and cultural figure. Whittier is in fact more interesting than the other "fireside" poets, Miller claims, because his life and work reflected unique tensions in his relationship to social and historical trends. Whittier had an essentially conservative disposition, for instance, that was incited only by the abolitionist cause. He underwent a "crisis" in his mid-twenties, according to Miller, which caused him both to embrace the antislavery movement that would occupy most of his attention for the next 15 years and to change from an ambitious, Byronic young man who wanted nothing more than political and poetic success to a mature and almost selflessly committed poet-reformer. By the end of 1833, Whittier had "found a resolution which gave him, for the rest of his life, a way of living with a self which he feared he might not otherwise control." In making his own career subservient to the abolitionist cause, he abandoned his burning desire for fame (*Critical Essays on John Greenleaf Whittier*).

Miller's may be the most polemical summation of Whittier's life, but others have provided further reasons to value his contributions to nineteenth-century poetic culture. Robert Penn Warren, whose book remains the most comprehensive discussion of Whittier's poetic career, traces his trajectory from a talented but fairly undistinguished young poet who "could only pile up words as a mason piles up bricks" to a mature poet who could achieve great richness of language and thought in works like "Snow-Bound" and "Telling the Bees" (LOA, 1: 468). For Warren, Whittier's best poems are those that reflect a nostalgia for childhood, a lost Eden. Howard Mumford Jones has also found distinctive qualities in Whittier's description of nature in New England, his presentation of character, his assertion of a deeply felt religious conviction, and his consciousness of the passage of time and the transience of human existence. Bernard Duffey has identified in Whittier's poems about family life an effective portrait of the family as the microcosm of the largely homogeneous America that was idealized in the nineteenth century. Alan Shucard, although regretting the jejune and "hopelessly sentimental" quality of much of Whittier's verse, finds in it an expression and idealization of "the common American life of mid-century." And Waggoner considers Whittier's masterpiece, "Snow-Bound," to be "the finest American pastoral poem before the pastorals of [Robert] Frost."

Since there is no definitive modern biography of Whittier, the details of his life must be culled from various sources: his collected letters; his prose writings; the testimony of early biographers like Francis Underwood, Samuel Pickard, George Rice Carpenter, and Thomas Wentworth Higginson; and general studies of the poet such as those of Warren, Edward Wagenknecht, and Lewis Leary. Whittier was born in December 1807, in Haverhill, Massachusetts, the second child and first son of John and Abigail Whittier. He spent his early years in the quiet seclusion of a Quaker farmhouse that was built by his ancestor Thomas Whittier, who had arrived in New England in 1638. The family had been Quakers for over 100 years by the time of Whittier's birth, and they lived frugally on what revenue could be generated from a 185-acre farm. As Warren notes, they were neither rich nor poor, and although they had a fairly limited library, they were by no means illiterate. As a boy, Whittier was exposed to various books, including the Bible (much of which he learned by heart), the works of William Penn and other Quaker authors, the writings of Bunyan, some works of history and travel, popular novels by Scott and others, and an anthology of English literature. By age 15, Whittier had discovered Burns, and by age 18, Byron; before his nineteenth birthday, he had published his first poem, "The Exile's Departure," in Garrison's *Free Press* of nearby Newburyport, Massachusetts. So impressed was Garrison with the young poet that he drove 14 miles to meet and congratulate Whittier in person. By the following year, Whittier had written some 50 poems, and he enrolled in the newly founded Haverhill Academy. After only two sessions, he had completed what would be his formal education and left school to become a full-time journalist and writer. While his poems began to be published in Boston, Hartford, Connecticut, and Philadelphia, Pennsylvania, Whittier took jobs editing various newspapers – the *American Manufacturer*, the *Haverhill Gazette*, and, in Hartford, the *New England Weekly Review*.

In 1831, Whittier published his first book, a mixture of prose and poetry entitled *Legends of New England*. Although he had already published as many as 200 poems by this time, the book was immature enough that he later sought to burn the remaining copies. Influenced by folk collections of John Brainard and Washington Irving, Whittier's collection was an attempt to encourage the preservation of the "traditionary lore" in which New England was so rich – "a thousand associations of superstition and manly daring and romantic adventure . . . connected with her green hills and her pleasant rivers" (Preface). Divided into seven prose sketches and 11 poems, the collection documented both historical and legendary incidents – including Indian warfare, a murder by pirates, and an attack by starving wolves – and anecdotes involving hunting, witchcraft, specter ships, and phantom warriors. Some of the poems, like the eerie ballad "The Black Fox," show the promise of things to come: a spare but effective style, a skill in storytelling, and an imaginative reach beyond the historical record or the hackneyed cliché. But much of the material is weak, especially when contrasted with Nathaniel **Hawthorne's** treatment of similar material in tales like "Young Goodman Brown."

By the early 1830s, Whittier had already displayed an interest in issues beyond the literary. In an 1828 letter to Garrison, he writes that he admires Garrison's efforts "against those fearful evils – Slavery, Intemperance, and War," but that, although wishing that he could join in the fight, his "noblest resolutions are continually bending to circumstances around me." The "circumstances" to which Whittier refers could have had to do with his failing health – a problem that plagued him throughout his life – with his poetic production, or with family matters (his father was to die only two years later). Much as he pursued his poetic career, other desires continued to emerge. In 1831, he wrote a revealing letter to Louisa Tuthill in which he appeared to be working through several issues: friendship and the possibility of real human contact in a world of "frozen decorum," the question of aesthetic beauty, and his own ambitions and disappointments. Although he claims to have experienced disappointment "in a thousand ways," he continues to "look forward with high anticipations":

I have placed the goal of my ambition high – but with the blessing of God, it shall be reached. The world has at last breathed into my bosom a portion of its own bitterness, and I now feel as if I could wrestle manfully in the strife

of men. If my life is spared, the world shall know me in a loftier capacity than as a writer of rhymes.

Whittier's prediction that he would enter the "strife of men" soon proved to be true. Although he complains in an April 1831 letter of a "band of negroes" who "paraded our streets, knocking down every white man who made his appearance," he also writes to Benjamin Lundy, publisher of an antislavery paper, in support of "the great object – emancipation of the slave." At the same time, he began in earnest to work toward a political career that would continue in some form throughout the decade.

The pursuit of a poetic career, still very much on Whittier's mind in the early 1830s, appears to have waned in importance after 1833, as he turned most of his attention to the issue of slavery. Several projects occupied his attention in 1831–32, including editing a daily paper in Cincinnati, Ohio, publishing a volume of poems (no such volume appeared until 1838), publishing a long narrative poem ("Moll Pitcher"), writing a series of prose sketches in the manner of Irving, writing a work of fiction concerning "the reconciliation of the North and the South" (never finished), and publishing a "Coleridge-like fragment" ("The Demon-Lady"). In a letter to Lydia **Sigourney**, the most popular female poet of her day, Whittier suspects his own limitations as a poet ("I have more philosophy than poetry in my composition") and attempts to explain the tensions between poetic writing and his other pursuits, namely politics:

The truth is, I love poetry, with a love as warm, as fervent, as sincere, as many of the more gifted worshippers at the temple of the Muses. I consider its gift as something holy and above the fashion of the world. . . . But I feel and know that "To other chords than mine belong / The breathing of immortal song." And, in consequence, I have been compelled to trust to other and less pleasant pursuits, for distinction and profit. Politics is the only field now open for me, and there is something inconsistent in the character of a poet and a modern politician.

Whittier makes clear that he will take fame wherever he can find it and that he may achieve it sooner through the world of politics than through that of literature:

I would have fame visit me *now*, or not at all. I would not choose between a nettle and a rose to grow over my grave. If I am worthy of fame, I would ask it now – now in the spring-time of my years – when I might share its smile with the friends whom I love, and by whom I am loved in return.

At the same time that he was struggling with decisions about the course of his career, he was dealing with romantic yearnings toward various women; but, as he wrote in one letter, he feared that his "doom [was] fixed – to live a bachelor."

In the spring of 1833, Whittier abandoned the majority of his literary and romantic pursuits and threw himself wholeheartedly into the abolitionist cause. Whether he was primed for such a philanthropic pursuit by his Quaker background or by feelings of frustration and disappointment about his personal aspirations, he was clearly ready to be engaged by something. It was a letter from Garrison asking Whittier to "enlist your talents, zeal and influence" that first galvanized the young poet to action, and by June of that year he had read every available publication dealing with colonization and slavery and had written and published at his own expense the long essay *Justice and Expediency: Or Slavery Considered with a View to Its Rightful and Effectual Remedy, Abolition.* As John Pickard points out, the publication of this polemical pamphlet essentially determined Whittier's subsequent career, since it made hopes of individual political success much less likely, while it also severely limited the number of journals that would publish his poetry (*Critical Essays on John Greenleaf Whittier*). Whittier's essay criticized the efforts of the Colonization Society and other non-abolitionist movements and demonstrated with logical precision that immediate abolition was the only reasonable alternative. Not until the eradication of the evil of slavery from the United States, Whittier argues at the conclusion of his essay, "shall it go well for America."

Virtually all of Whittier's activities for the next several years would in one way or another involve the slavery issue: letters to congressmen and other people of influence, poems on slavery, and direct political action. So strong was Whittier's commitment to the abolitionist cause that he even criticized Sarah and Angelina Grimké for writing articles on the rights of women at a time when he felt that their efforts would only detract from the central cause of freeing the slaves. Whittier's attitude toward his own poetry had also changed dramatically. Writing in an 1837 letter that it would be "a criminal waste of life" for him to devote himself to writing poetry rather than serving "the sacred interests of religion and humanity," Whittier concludes that "mere intellectual renown is valueless":

> Do the best that we can, in the matter of mere intellect, the Devil is wiser than any of us. The humblest and weakest follower of the meek and lowly Redeemer is more to be envied than a Voltaire, a Rousseau, or a Byron, and the lowliest teacher of that sublime philosophy which "the wisdom of the world accounteth foolishness" is wiser and better than those prodigies of intellect whose learning and acquirements only enable them . . . to descend wisely into hell.

Whittier's antislavery crusade of the 1830s certainly appeared to deepen the religious conviction that was already present in his earlier years: in another letter of 1837, he comments that "my mind has been a good deal exercised of late on the subject of religious observation." Whittier saw his religious duty not only as a justification for devoting himself to the eradication of slavery, but also as a motivation for his own more intimate relationship to spiritual forces: "I feel that there are too many things of the world between me and the realization of a quiet communion with God."

During the 1830s and 1840s, Whittier published a number of antislavery poems, which appeared both in *Poems Written During the Progress of the Abolition Question in the United States* (1837–38) and *Voices of Freedom* (1846). As could be imagined, these poems are uncompromisingly critical of slavery and its effects on individuals and social institutions; at times, they seem hyperbolic in their dramatic use of biblical language and imagery. Some are topical poems that were written either in response to or in commemoration of specific events; others take on the voice of individuals ("The Farewell of a Virginia Slave Mother to Her Daughters Sold into South-

ern Bondage"); others address historical topics ("Toussaint L'Ouverture"); and still others are more general commentaries on slavery or the abolitionist cause. In "The Slave-Ships," Whittier relates the historically true story of a French ship whose cargo of 160 slaves had contracted a terrible disease and thus had been thrown mercilessly "to the sharks." The poem ends with the ship, all its crew now blind from the spreading disease, having arrived in Guadeloupe without its freight. Whittier compares the "slaver's darkened eye" and the "blackness of his crime" with the natural paradise of the island, with its "blossom of the orange" and "palm-trees by the hillside." Whittier's poems are bolstered by a fervent and self-righteous Protestantism and a hymnlike conviction that lead many readers to dismiss them as hackneyed and one-dimensional attacks on slavery, which made little attempt to nuance what had become a very complex and divisive issue. As Roy Harvey Pearce has argued, the poems do not seek to explore the institution of slavery or even to explore with any depth the condition of slaves themselves. The poems simply "reinforce in memorable language a noble sentiment which already exists" and then "editorialize on it." In "The Christian Slave," Whittier writes of "that vile South Sodom first and best"; speaking of the hypocrisy of those who would raise their slaves as "good Christians" without teaching them the true meaning of Christ's message, Whittier concludes that Christianity's "rites will only swell his market price, / and rivet on his chain."

Whittier was not the only American of his day to argue the abolitionist cause in his poems: Longfellow published his own *Poems on Slavery* in 1842, and so many imitations of Whittier's antislavery verses appeared that he felt the need to complain, in an 1840 letter, about seeing "one's own ideas hunted down by one of these merciless Djezza Pachas in literature, maltreating and disguising them to suit his purposes, and then sending them into the world limping, eyeless, and tongueless."

In 1842, Whittier began what would prove to be perhaps his most important literary relationship: he wrote to the young publisher James T. Fields about the possibility of publishing a volume of his verses. Whittier's *Lays of My Home* appeared from Fields's firm the following year, and over the years the poet not only continued to publish with the firm (which became Ticknor and Fields in 1854), but also relied increasingly on Fields both as a publisher/editor and as a friend. *Lays of My Home*, as its title indicates, was a significant change from the abolitionist and political poetry of Whittier's years in Philadelphia (1838–39); now he could both celebrate the scenery of his native Massachusetts and elaborate the lore of his region. As Pickard writes, the volume represented Whittier's "first crucial step in establishing himself as a poet, rather than an abolitionist versifier or editor-reformer."

At about the same time, Whittier began corresponding with another man who would become one of the most important literary figures of his day, James Russell Lowell. Lowell had just published his first volume of poetry and would also become active in the antislavery movement. In one letter, Whittier complains that he is not able to do more literary writing of his own: "what with cares of all sorts on my hands . . . as well as the drawback of ill health . . . I can do little or nothing in the way of rhyme or reason." In addition to his many campaigning and lobbying efforts, Whittier was involved with two newspapers – the *Middlesex Standard* and the *Essex Transcript* – and he was bringing out a collection of prose pieces, *The Stranger in Low-ell* (1845), and an English edition of his poems. He nonetheless continued his efforts on behalf of the antislavery cause, even attempting to draft his fellow poet Longfellow as a Liberty Party candidate for Congress (a nomination that Longfellow ultimately declined).

The major event of the late 1840s for Whittier was his assumption of the position of corresponding editor of the *National Era*, a new abolitionist weekly published in Washington, D.C. From 1847 to 1857, Whittier published his poetry and prose there alongside works by Hawthorne and Stowe. Finally, a living wage for Whittier and his family was secured. He contributed numerous pieces to the *National Era,* including biographical sketches, fictional pieces, prose essays, antiquarian articles, and literary reviews of writers such as Longfellow, Holmes, Lowell, Bayard **Taylor**, Grace Greenwood, and Lucy Larcom. He also published several books of his own: *The Supernaturalism of New England* (1847), a book of tales that received lukewarm praise in a review by Hawthorne; an edition of collected poems, *Poems by John Greenleaf Whittier* (1849), for which he received the then considerable sum of 500 dollars plus royalties; the extended historical prose piece *Margaret Smith's Journal* (1849); *Old Portraits and Modern Sketches* (1850), primarily a study of seventeenth-century reformers; and *Songs of Labor, and Other Poems* (1850). In the "Dedication" to this last volume, Whittier vows to speak "The unsung beauty hid life's common things below" and to turn from "youth's enchanted forest" to the "sober after-growth" of "life's autumnal lea." His "simple lays of homely toil," he claims, must have the high moral purpose of elevating the act of physical labor to the level of prayer; he also expresses the somewhat naive hope that his poems may "gladden duty's ways" and provide the worker with "a manlier spirit of content." The book as a whole is a pre-Whitmanic celebration of the hard work of various kinds of laborers: shipbuilders, shoemakers, drovers, fishermen, cornhuskers, farmers, and lumbermen.

It was in the 1850s that Whittier made his first concerted effort to become the mature poet whose work would culminate in "Snow-Bound." The year 1850 saw the publication of "Ichabod!" (LOA, 1: 454), which Warren calls his "first really fine poem." The poem was a reaction to a speech by Daniel Webster, senator from Massachusetts, in favor of the Fugitive Slave Law, which had just been proposed by fellow senator Henry Clay. Expressing "the surprise and grief and forecast of evil consequences" that he felt upon hearing the speech (by a man he had formerly admired), Whittier makes a powerful attack on Webster through the use of the biblical allusion to Ichabod, the child who is named as a sign that the glory had departed from Israel (1 Sam. 4:21), as well as allusions to Milton's Satan ("A fallen angel's pride of thought, / still strong in chains") and to the story of Noah and his sons in Gen. 9:20–25 ("Walk backward, with averted gaze, / And hide the shame"). These allusions, along with the pounding rhythms and mercilessly condemning rhetoric, arguably make "Ichabod!" Whittier's most effective political poem. It had a considerable impact on contemporary readers who were sympathetic to the abolitionist cause, although Whittier himself later regretted its "severity of judgment" and printed another, softer poem about Webster alongside it. "Ichabod!" begins with the emphatic lines –

So fallen! so lost! the light withdrawn
    Which once he wore!
The glory from his gray hairs gone
    Forevermore!

The poem proceeds to argue for "pitying tears," rather than "scorn and wrath," as an appropriate response to Webster's actions.

Scorn! would the angels laugh, to mark
    A bright soul driven,
Fiend-goaded, down the endless dark,
    From hope to heaven!

Let not the land, once proud of him,
    Insult him now,
Nor brand with deeper shame his dim,
    Dishonored brow.

The poem concludes with a comparison of Webster to the drunk and naked Noah, whose youngest son Ham is branded for merely having looked at his shameful nakedness:

All else is gone; from those great eyes
    The soul has fled:
When faith is lost, when honor dies,
    The man is dead!

Then, pay the reverence of old days
    To his dead fame;
Walk backward, with averted gaze,
    And hide the shame!

In 1853, Whittier published another book of poems, *The Chapel of Hermits, and Other Poems*, and in 1856, yet another volume, *The Panorama and Other Poems*, appeared, followed quickly by the two-volume "Blue and Gold" edition of his *Poetical Works* (1857). Now Whittier was truly an established poet with a status not far below that of Bryant and Longfellow. By the mid-1850s, his poetry had made the turn from political and reformist verse to work of interest to a wider readership. This new work was concerned with rural life, and with New England history, legend, and scenery. Two of his most popular poems from this period, "Maud Muller" (1854; LOA, 1: 458) and "The Barefoot Boy" (1855; LOA, 1: 462), demonstrate this new sensibility. The first tells the story of a barefoot country girl and a judge from the city whose brief encounter leads them to think forever after that "It might have been." The poem, composed in tetrameter couplets, is both very simple and highly sentimental, yet it retains a degree of innocent charm. The second poem, equally simple, involves a nostalgia for the poet's childhood, as reexperienced vicariously through an idealized "barefoot boy, with cheek of tan." As Edward Wagenknecht has observed, the poem is somewhat Wordsworthian in its presentation of nature; despite its rather jejune quality, however, it contains descriptive passages of lyric richness that suggest a newfound delight in language:

I was rich in flowers and trees,
Humming-birds and honey-bees;
For my sport the squirrel played,
Plied the snouted mole his spade;
For my taste the blackberry cone

Purpled over hedge and stone;
. . . .
Mine the sand-rimmed pickerel pond,
Mine the walnut slopes beyond,
Mine, on bending orchard trees,
Apples of Hesperides!

This fecund period in Whittier's poetic life concluded with the 1860 publication of *Home Ballads and Poems*. By the start of the Civil War, he had written many of his best poems and achieved the status of the "Poet of New England," although true stardom was not to come his way until "Snow-Bound" six years later. Whittier was now publishing poems in the *Atlantic Monthly*, which was founded in 1857 by Francis Underwood and edited by Lowell. This magazine quickly became the pre-eminent literary journal of its day and published works by Longfellow, Holmes, Emerson, Lowell, Stowe, and other major figures. It was here that Whittier first published such famous poems as "Skipper Ireson's Ride" (LOA, 1: 465) and "Telling the Bees," which helped convince a large readership that he was more than the radical abolitionist or third-party reformer that they had previously known. "Skipper Ireson's Ride" (1857) is a poem on an historical topic that Pickard calls "the best American ballad of the nineteenth century." Based on a local folk song, the poem relates the story of an old Marblehead, Massachusetts, sailor, Floyd Ireson, who was tarred and feathered by a group of angry women after he had allegedly allowed a crew of fishermen to drown at sea. Here, Whittier combines a psychological study of social conflict with an evocation of legend and local color, even quoting in dialect the "refrain" of the women, which also constitutes the refrain of the ballad stanzas themselves: "'Here's Flud Oirson, fur his horrd horrt, / Torr'd and futherr'd an' corr'd in a corrt / By the women o' Mor-ble'ead!'"

"Telling the Bees" (1858) must be considered one of Whittier's finest poems. Based on a recollection of the poet's boyhood farm, it portrays the local custom of informing the bees of a death and dressing their hive in mourning so that they will not fly away to a new home. Whittier's mother had died in December of the previous year, and the poem not only thematizes the death of a loved one (a young woman named Mary), but also seems permeated with a nostalgic yearning for a past time unlike the "heavy and slow" progress of the present. The poem also contains a surprise ending, as the speaker belatedly discovers that it is Mary herself, and not the aged grandfather, who has died. The effectiveness of the poem is achieved through contrasts: the assurance and expectation of the young man – to whom nothing appears to have changed – with the brutal reality of the situation, and the external beauty and simplicity of nature with the fragility of human life and love. The tension builds gradually throughout the last five stanzas, until it is finally discovered by both speaker and reader that "Mistress Mary is dead and gone!"

Some other poems of these years also deserve notice. "First-Day Thoughts" (LOA, 1: 456) is a short but powerful meditation on the poet's relationship to his religious faith. Only in the silence of a Quaker meeting can the speaker hear "the still small voice which reached the prophet's ear." "The Last Walk in Autumn" is one of Whittier's better descriptive poems. The early stanzas in particular demonstrate Whittier's sensitivity to the landscape and changing seasons. At times, the poem's rhythm and tone seem to anticipate the nature poetry of Robert Frost:

I passed this way a year ago:
    The wind blew south; the noon of day
Was warm as June's; and save that snow
    Flecked the low mountains far away,
    And that the vernal-seeming breeze
    Mocked faded grass and leafless trees,
I might have dreamed of summer as I lay,
Watching the fallen leaves with the soft wind at play.

"The Haschish" (LOA, 1: 457), published in the first issue of the *Atlantic Monthly*, satirically links the drug's narcotic effects to the north's reliance on southern cotton. After a long catalog of the effects of "the Haschish plant" on various "Orient lands," Whittier turns to the various ways in which Americans succumb to the spell of cotton, "The Haschish of the West," even to the point of advocating slavery:

The preacher eats, and straight appears
His Bible in a new translation;
    Its angels negro overseers,
And Heaven itself a snug plantation!

In "The Panorama," another satirical poem of the period, Whittier directly criticizes those who would put the preservation of the Union above the abolition of slavery:

Such are the men who, with instinctive dread,
Whenever Freedom lifts her drooping head,
Make prophet-tripods of their office-stools,
And scare the nurseries and the village schools
With dire presage of ruin grim and great,
A broken Union and a foundered State!

"My Playmate" (LOA, 1: 470), one of Whittier's most attractive lyrics, is an elegiac remembrance of a young girl (a playmate of the speaker) who left her home, never to return. The poem, which presents a New England landscape in May, evokes the moment between childhood and adolescence when the "bashful boy" first experiences a budding of sexuality, which is expressed through the various manifestations of nature's springtime activity. Yet there is also an element of mystery to the poem: where has the girl gone, and why does the speaker still feel her absence so strongly? The ending of the poem demonstrates Whittier's use of a late-romantic idiom to express his feelings of loss:

The winds so sweet with birch and fern
    A sweeter memory blow;
And there in spring the veeries sing
    The song of long ago.

And still the pines of Ramoth wood
    Are moaning like the sea, –
The moaning of the sea of change
    Between myself and thee!

One biographical clue to the poem's feeling may lie in Whittier's own romantic life at the time. In the spring of 1859, Whittier had visited his longtime friend Elizabeth Lloyd Howell, now widowed, in Philadelphia. The relationship soon developed beyond the bounds of mere friendship, as Whittier wrote her letters that suggested romantic attachment, perhaps even the possibility of marriage. He writes her on May 18: "Elizabeth, I have been happy – far more so than I ever expected in this life. The sweet memory of the past few weeks makes me rich forever. What Providence has in store for the future I know not – I dare not hope scarcely – but the past is mine – may I not say ours – sacred and beautiful, a joy forever." This relationship was the closest that Whittier ever came to marriage, but by late summer he had ended any hope of a lasting relationship, whether because of Elizabeth's criticisms of Quakerism, the continuing poor health of both Whittier and his sister, or his fear of exchanging the familiar life of a bachelor for that of a married man.

In 1864, Whittier published *In War Time and Other Poems*, which contained the popular "Barbara Frietchie" (LOA, 1: 472). In this, Whittier's most famous ballad, he tells the supposedly true story of an elderly woman who waved the Union flag in the face of conquering rebel troops. The poem, written during the bloodiest days of the Civil War, presents both the heroism of the woman who is willing to sacrifice her own life for the flag, and the humanity of the Confederate leader Stonewall Jackson, whose "nobler nature" is stirred so much that he orders his troops not to fire on the woman or the banner she waves.

Throughout the 1860s and 1870s, Whittier continued to publish volumes of poetry at regular intervals. *Snow-Bound* (1866), to which we shall return, was his first real popular success, selling 20,000 copies in the first few months; *The Tent on the Beach and Other Poems* (1867), following on the success of *Snow-Bound*, did even better; and *Among the Hills, and Other Poems*, one of his strongest volumes, appeared in 1868. In 1870, Whittier published both *Ballads of New England* and *Miriam and Other Poems*; in 1872, *The Pennsylvania Pilgrim, and Other Poems*; in 1874, *Hazel-Blossoms*; and in 1878, *Vision of Echard, and Other Poems*. During this time he also published a two-volume collection of prose (1866), a one-volume collected edition of his poems, and a poetry anthology, *Songs of Three Centuries* (1876).

It is in Whittier's letters from the summer of 1865 that we first hear of a "winter idyll" to be called "Snow-Bound," which will be a "homely picture of old New England times." When the poem was published in a volume of 52 pages – "if it were not mine I should call it pretty good," Whittier commented – it was a success of a kind previously unknown to him: he received a first royalty check of 2,000 dollars, and he would ultimately receive 10,000 dollars on sales of the book. So successful was the book that his publisher, Thomas Fields, ordered an advance printing of 10,000 copies for Whittier's next volume, *The Tent on the Beach*. Just why "Snow-Bound" was such a popular poem is difficult to say: Pickard attributes it to "Whittier's assertion of family affections, his faith in the democratic heritage, and his evocative recreation of the farm world that produced him and thousands of other Americans." Revisiting an earlier world of pastoral beauty and innocence, inhabited by a secure family group with deep and simple Quaker beliefs, Whittier presents a scene that had iconic significance for many Americans. The poem portrays Whittier's family and a couple of guests in his boyhood home, sitting around the fire telling stories as the snowstorm rages outside the walls.

An essay of this scope can only point in the direction of possible readings of the poem. Warren provides an excellent one in which he argues that it was not only "a summarizing poem for Whittier," but a "summarizing moment for the country." With its new affluence, the nation could now afford to look back on what it saw as its more innocent past. Another valuable reading is that of Waggoner, who argues that Whittier's poem is not simple nostalgia, but nostalgia in tension with judgment. Here, Whittier ceases to be a Quaker, claims Waggoner, and becomes a poet who captures a secular spiritualism akin to that of Hawthorne and Herman **Melville**. For Pearce, it is the tension between fantasy and reality that makes "Snow-Bound" a great poem. Lewis Leary reads the poem as in part a meditation of the passage of time: the compacting of a lifetime of feeling into one evening around the fireside makes a pattern "in which chronology and theme are intricately woven." And Emily Miller Budick emphasizes the power of the imaginative faculty "as the force that can counter the de-imagizing threats of time and change" (*ESQ* 31 [1985]).

What Whittier had intended as a highly personal poem became a great commercial success as well; so surprised was the poet at the sudden popular reception of *Snow-Bound* and the succeeding volume that he compared himself to a P. T. Barnum, "swindling" the public: "Think of bagging in this Tent of ours an unsuspecting public at the rate of a thousand a day!" Whittier would never allow his popular success to go to his head; in fact, he was never completely comfortable either with the sometimes exhausting demands of his new popularity or with the scrutiny of his private life that it brought about. In one letter, he finds "the life of a hard-working farmer or mechanic altogether more enviable than that of a writer or politician," and in other letters he chastises would-be critics and biographers for descending into "small gossip about me." Whittier went so far as to destroy a large collection of letters that he had received from various people (fearing that "to leave them liable to publicity might be injurious or unpleasant to the writers and their friends"), and he even wrote of the hope that his own letters "to thousands of correspondents may be as carefully disposed of." Fortunately for us, this was not the case, and the three-volume edition of Whittier's letters, collected and annotated by Pickard, is an invaluable source of information about the poet's life.

Despite his popular success, few of the poems that Whittier wrote after "Snow-Bound" were of the quality of that or earlier poems of the 1850s and 1860s. The "Prelude" to *Among the Hills* (1869; LOA, 1: 495) is deservedly one of the most famous of the later works. This blank verse poem shows Whittier's mature style at its best. Here we see a greater command of the poetic medium than is usual in Whittier: a good sense of the possibilities of rhythms generated by caesura and enjambment, a succinctness of expression, an increased attention to the sound of language, and an almost sublime power of description in passages like the following:

> The locust by the wall
> Stabs the noon-silence with his sharp alarm.
> A single hay-cart down the dusty road
> Creaks slowly, with its driver fast asleep
> On the load's top. Against the neighboring hill,
> Huddled along the stone wall's shady side,

The sheep show white, as if a snow-drift still
Defied the dog-star. Through the open door
A drowsy smell of flowers – gray heliotrope,
And white sweet-clover, and shy mignonette –
Comes faintly in, and silent chorus lends
To the pervading symphony of peace.

Yet Whittier is also able to portray the "other side" of rural life, which was filled with "the grind of toil" and "starved amid the plenitude of nature":

Within, the cluttered kitchen-floor, unwashed
(Broom-clean I think they called it); the best room
Stifling with cellar damp, shut from the air
In hot midsummer, bootless, pictureless
Save the inevitable sampler hung
Over the fireplace, or a mourning-piece,
A green-haired woman, peony-cheeked, beneath
Impossible willows; the wide-throated hearth
Bristling with faded pine-boughs half concealing
The piled-up rubbish at the chimney's back;
And, in sad keeping with all things about them,
Shrill, querulous women, sour and sullen men,
Untidy, loveless, old before their time,
With scarce a human interest save their own
Monotonous round of small economies,
Or the poor scandal of the neighborhood.

This is a painful passage, and we can only imagine that it was a difficult one for Whittier to write. We have the impression, when faced with such passages, that Whittier might have been a far greater poet had he been willing to deal more often and more directly with the harshness of reality rather than sweetening it with oversentimentalized language and feeling. Whittier does end the poem on a hopeful note; with the "prophecy" that "manhood" will be raised above such a dismal state "through broader culture, finer manners, love, / and reverence," however, he finally dissipates much of the imaginative power that his poem might have had, for the ending is motivated by moral imperative rather than by artistic integrity.

As Whittier neared the end of his life, he spent much of his time responding to letters from readers and admirers: in his final four years alone he wrote more than 900 letters. He was still able to publish several more books of poetry – The King's Missive, and Other Poems (1881), The Bay of Seven Islands, and Other Poems (1883), Saint Gregory's Guest and Recent Poems (1886), and At Sundown (1890) – as well as overseeing the publication of the seven-volume Riverside Edition of his writings. One of Whittier's final poems, "Burning Drift-Wood" (1890; LOA, 1: 502), summarizes his own past and present while it looks toward his future. Borrowing a general motif from Longfellow's "The Fire of Drift-Wood" (LOA, 1: 391), Whittier's work is clearly a poem of old age, as he turns from the "fair, fond fancies dear to youth" to embrace "the sober grounds of truth." He distills his own experience, as he watches the piece of driftwood burning away before him, into two essential qualities – Love and Duty:

And of my ventures, those alone
    Which Love has freighted, safely sped,
Seeking a good beyond my own,
    By clear-eyed Duty piloted.

In this brief allegory, Whittier sums up a lifetime's work in poetry and politics, as well as a life of deeply felt spirituality and love for friends and family. Saddened by the deaths of his contemporaries Emerson and Longfellow a decade before, he had felt oppressed by a "feeling of loneliness and isolation." Now, he foresaw his own end, which he accepted with the belief that "Faith and Hope and Charity / Sit by my evening hearth-fire's blaze." His death, on September 7, 1892, also marked the close of an era in American literature: Lowell having died the year before, all of Whittier's poetic contemporaries, with the exception of Holmes, had passed away. Whittier left two valuable legacies that have yet to be fully appreciated: a group of the most eloquent writings against slavery in our literature and a body of verse that is – with the exception of those by Whitman and Dickinson – as significant as that of any nineteenth-century American poet.

CHRISTOPHER BEACH

Selected Works

The Works of John Greenleaf Whittier, 7 vols., Boston and New York: Houghton Mifflin, 1892
Legends of New England (1831), edited by John Pickard, Gainesville, Florida: Scholar's Facsimiles & Reprints, 1965
Whittier on Writers and Writing: The Uncollected Critical Writings, edited by Edwin Cady and Harry Clark, Syracuse, New York: Syracuse University Press, 1950
The Letters of John Greenleaf Whittier, 3 vols., edited by John Pickard, Cambridge, Massachusetts: Harvard University Press, 1975

Further Reading

Duffey, Bernard, Poetry in America: Expression and Its Values in the Times of Bryant, Whitman, and Pound, Durham, North Carolina: Duke University Press, 1978
Kribbs, Jayne K., ed., Critical Essays on John Greenleaf Whittier, Boston: G. K. Hall, 1980
Leary, Lewis, John Greenleaf Whittier, New York: Twayne, 1961
Pearce, Roy Harvey, The Continuity of American Poetry, Princeton, New Jersey: Princeton University Press, 1961
Shucard, Alan, American Poetry: The Puritans Through Walt Whitman, New York: Twayne, 1988
Wagenknecht, Edward, John Greenleaf Whittier: A Portrait in Paradox, New York: Oxford University Press, 1967
Waggoner, Hyatt, American Poets from the Puritans to the Present, Baton Rouge: Louisiana State University Press, 1968; 2nd ed., 1984
Warren, Robert Penn, John Greenleaf Whittier: An Appraisal and a Selection, Minneapolis: University of Minnesota Press, 1971

Carlos Wilcox

(1794–1827)

Carlos Wilcox was born on October 22, 1794, in Newport, New Hampshire, the eldest child of Ebenezer Wilcox, a prosperous farmer, and Thankful Stevens Wilcox, the well-educated and pious daughter of Josiah Stevens, a deacon and later preacher in Newport. As a small boy, Carlos was lively of body and mind. His mother later wrote of him: "As soon as he began to talk, I began to teach him to repeat the Lord's Prayer, the Assembly's Catechism, and devotional Hymns. He was very active, and appeared much delighted with receiving instruction. He early showed a great fondness for books." In 1798 or early 1799, the family moved to Orwell, in western Vermont, where his parents still lived at the time of Carlos's early death in 1827. In his ninth year he suffered a terrible accident, wounding himself in the knee with an ax. Infection set in, and Carlos spent many months in severe pain; he made his way to school on crutches, but he was never healthy or normally active after this childhood episode.

But his physical infirmity seemed to intensify his love of books and study. At 15, although now chronically afflicted with "cough and hectic fever," he entered newly established Middlebury College, Middlebury, Vermont, in September 1809, where he intended to pursue classical studies. As early as December, however, he experienced a powerful renewal or clarification of faith that changed the course of his life. He wrote to his parents at that time: "I believe I can say as much as this, that every thing appears different to me: the word of God, religious worship, Christian people, religious conferences, and prayer, which before appeared to be gloomy, now appear quite the reverse. It now seems to me that if there is any happiness in this life, it is in living near to God." He resolved to devote himself to the ministry. After graduating from Middlebury with highest honors in 1813 and spending a year in Georgia with his maternal uncle, Carlos began his studies at Andover Theological Seminary, Andover, Massachusetts, in 1814.

In the spring of the following year, he wrote the first small parts of the long poem ultimately called *The Age of Benevolence* (see LOA, 1: 119) and began to feel a tension between his religious calling and the desire to write verse. He seemed at times overwhelmed by melancholy or even depression. He wrote to a friend: "I dread the sight of my pen and half written sermon. . . . I have such a disheartening consciousness of my unfitness for the ministry, that I cannot engage in it. I have studied nothing but poetry, am fit for nothing but poetry." Ill health had also returned to plague him – one of the sources of his feeling unfit for the ministry – and he was often not able even to attend the many activities of Andover Seminary. By the summer of 1817, however, he had substantially completed his studies there and was contemplating his next step. He also felt, however, that the arduous life of the full-time ministry was perhaps beyond his powers. He wrote to his parents in June: "I am at present hardly fit for study, being very poor in flesh, and troubled with pain in my breast. . . . If I should enter the ministry, unless my constitution should first undergo a great and radical change, I should not expect to live many years."

He remained at Andover through 1817 and spent the following year at his parents' home in Vermont, in part to recover his health. There, he continued to work on *The Age of Benevolence*. By 1819, he felt sufficiently strong to search actively for a ministerial position. He visited and preached in various towns of western Connecticut, but received no call. Throughout most of 1820–21, he stayed with friends in Salisbury, East Haven, and New Haven, Connecticut, working on his poem and occasionally preaching. Early in 1822, Book I of *The Age of Benevolence* appeared; printed in New Haven in an edition of 1,000 copies, it sold out entirely. He continued occasional and part-time preaching throughout 1823, saying in a letter dated early in 1824, "I have been wandering to and fro, so long, that I am strongly averse to packing up my little all into my little trunk, and moving again, nobody knows where." In the summer of that year, he composed and delivered the Phi Beta Kappa poem "The Religion of Taste" at Yale College in New Haven, and in October he received at last a call to the full-time ministry at North Church in Hartford, Connecticut, where he was ordained in December 1824.

Here began the last few and harrowing years of his short life. As he had himself predicted, the labors of the ministry soon proved too much for his fragile physical constitution. Those palpitations of the heart that he had previously been able to control or subdue with a combination of rest and exercise now became chronic and unbearable. He found himself preaching sermons under the stress of such strong chest pains and rapid heartbeats that he nearly fainted away in the pulpit. The leaves of absence that his admiring congregation was glad to extend did not improve matters substantially; he was forced to resign his appointment in Hartford in the spring of 1826. He traveled and rested that summer, and by the end of the year he felt able to accept a second call to a smaller and older church of Danbury, Connecticut, where he was able to serve but a few months until his death on May 29, 1827. He was buried in Hartford.

Carlos Wilcox's published work as a poet is almost entirely contained within the two long poems, *The Age of Benevolence* (1822) and "The Religion of Taste" (1824). The title of the former was perhaps intended as a counterstatement to Thomas Paine's *The Age of Reason* (1794), a notorious work of the period that was often seen as an exposition not merely of rational and deistic Christianity, but of outright atheism. More certainly, Wilcox conceived *The Age of Benevolence* after the model of the English poet William Cowper's *The Task* (1785), a lengthy, discursive poem in six books. *The Task* encompasses many themes from the trivial and humorous to the sublime, including such subjects as "The Winter Walk at Noon" in Book VI, which mingles a radiant observation of nature with reflections on its Creator. Wilcox's admiration for and debt to Cowper is beyond dispute; his early admirer George Cheever says that had Wilcox lived to complete his work he would have become "the Cowper of New England." Cheever also praises Wilcox's dedication to a single, large work: "instead of devoting his mind to the composition of short, artificial pieces for the public eye, he started at once upon a wide and noble subject, with the outline in his mind of a magnificent moral poem."

That outline survives in Wilcox's *Remains*, which is still the chief source of information about him. According to this outline, the theme of Book I is "Benevolence the glory of Heaven"; Book II treats "Benevolence on earth the resemblance of Heaven"; Book III, "The Need of Benevolence" (the topics of "Profaneness, Sabbath-breaking, Intemperance, Slavery and War" are also listed); and Book IV, "The Rewards of Benevolence." For Book V, just the title is listed: "Triumph of Benevolence." Only Book I was completed and published (in 1822). For the other books, we have only those lines printed in the *Remains* volume; the volume's editor and publisher Edward Hopkins refers to them as "extracts" from the surviving manuscripts. Book I of "The Age of Benevolence" opens with epic grandeur and conveys at once the quality of Wilcox's optimism and his sincere Christian faith:

Of true benevolence, its charms divine,
With other motives to call forth its power,
And its grand triumphs, multiplied beyond
All former bounds, in this its golden age,
Humbly I sing, awed by the holy theme;
A theme exalted, though as yet unsung,
In beauty rich, of inspiration full,
And worthy of a nobler harp than that
From which heroic strains sublimely sound.

John Milton rather than Cowper seems the model here for tone and style (blank verse rather than couplets, inversions of word order, and the epic announcement of subject and singer), and Miltonic, too, is the insistence that the sublime theme is as yet "unsung," although of more intrinsic worth than the merely "heroic strains" of previous epic harps. An American note is struck, too, in the idea that the present day is the "golden age" of benevolence on earth, as the infant democracy of the United States, grounded in benevolent principles, begins its life.

Book I is the most sermonlike of the books, expounding a view of the world in much the way Alexander Pope does in "An Essay on Man," although with more emotion, less doctrine, and a more pronounced optimism. God's benevolence is to be seen in the beauties of nature, in the gift of His written book, in the whole historical scheme of redemption, and, above all, in the sacrifice of the cross. Because of that generous giving of immortal life, the soul can rise from the sullied earth to heavenly glory in a way that Wilcox's figure of the soul as a water-lily rising to the surface of a pond vividly suggests:

So from the filthy bottom of the pool,
Up through its waters, to the surface springs
The lily, and there blooms a perfect flower,
Of brilliant whiteness, beautifully pure.

In Book II, Wilcox's narrative and reflective voice returns to earth and creates those poetries of nature that have been most often prized by his anthologists. The poet himself, however, seems to regard the poetry of earth as a lesser thing than the poetry of heaven that he had produced in Book I, when he pictures himself as "thrown, / As from the glowing centre of the sun, / Down to earth's frozen and benighted pole." But the earth that he shows us is not "frozen and benighted." Rather, it is altogether too warm, sensuous, and appealing to the "pen-

sive mind," offering "A tenderness voluptuously soft" that can be "Fatal to active usefulness." For Wilcox, "active benevolence" is the true vocation of humankind on earth, not a mere luxuriating in earth's moods and beauties. Thus, the "sultry noon" passage in the LOA volume (lines 73–154 of Book II), although showing Wilcox's powers as a poet of nature to their best advantage, depicts the mind in one of its lesser phases, when it is merely "soothed" and "enervated" by the "thousand charms" of nature. Perhaps we see here the preacher and the poet at war in Wilcox, as we saw earlier in his letters. The poet in him cannot let the thousand charms of nature go; he produces an extraordinarily sustained, loving, and detailed picture, which moves from primarily visual images in the first half (field, stream, flock, thistle, and cloud) to primarily aural images in the second (where the occasional sounds of birds and insects only emphasize – by breaking in upon – the pervasive silence and peace of the scene). The overall theme of the passage is the peace that a benevolent creator provides his creatures; this theme also constitutes the subject of the ninth of Wilcox's published sermons (*Remains*, 337–352), which are based on the text from Matthew, "All ye that labor, I will give you rest."

Of Book III, "The Need of Benevolence," about 500 lines were completed. One long passage pictures Napoleon Bonaparte (under imprisonment on the island of Saint Helena at the time the lines were written) as the type of worldliness and tyranny, and it prays that he will find his God again in penitence and conversion. But Book III is dominated by Wilcox's vigorous and powerful indictment of slavery, which was written nearly 10 years before Garrison's American Anti-Slavery Society was founded in 1833. Cowper's antislavery poems and satires, published in 1793 and concerned with the British trade in African slaves in the West Indies, were probably an inspiration to Wilcox; as an American, however, he writes with vigor and eloquence about an abomination in his own land:

All are born free, and all with equal rights.
So speaks the charter of a nation proud
Of her unequall'd liberties and laws,
While in that nation, shameful to relate,
One man in five is born and dies a slave.
Is this my country? this that happy land,
The wonder and the envy of the world?
O for a mantle to conceal her shame!

The cruel yoke of enslavement cannot be softened; it must be removed. It is "Our duty to emancipate the whole": "But when and how may this be safely done? / Done it should be; with safety if it can, / With danger if it must." He refers at one point to his own personal observation of slavery – apparently during the year that he spent in Georgia – and is throughout in firm command of his subject, never speaking in hollow abstractions. He closes with a confident prediction that slavery in America will be ended, and he urges his own nation to lead others in a kind of blockade of Africa, which will prevent all "ruffian outlaws" from raiding her unoffending shores ever again.

Of Book IV, "The Rewards of Benevolence," only about 225 lines were completed. Some words of the "Argument" suggest the theme: "The body to share in the glory of heaven – its resurrection certain – a Spiritual body, incorruptible, glorious." The completed lines speak of "The liberated body, in the realms / Of perfect bliss" and later tell the story of "Horatio," a youth dying of consumption whose "fluttering spirit, struggling to get free" at last joins "with the blest / In chanting hallelujahs to the Lamb."

"The Religion of Taste" (1824) is Carlos Wilcox's only completed poem. It shows him abandoning the blank verse of *The Age of Benevolence* fragments for the tighter ordering of Spenserian stanzas. Hopkins tells us also that, after the success and public reading of "The Religion of Taste," Wilcox planned to recast all that he had so far written into Spenserian stanzas and to publish the whole in five cantos – of which "The Religion of Taste" would have been the second. As it stands, the poem articulates very well the tension between the poet and the preacher in Wilcox, the major but contradictory impulses of his talent and character.

It begins as an allegory modeled somewhat on James Thomson's "The Castle of Indolence" (1748), with "an Enchantress of romantic mood . . . Her name Imagination" inhabiting a castle "all of marble, smooth and white" in the middle of a wooded labyrinth. Here the souls of men may be entrapped, but as Wilcox says:

'Tis not for me, in weak revenge to war
With beauty's reign, or e'en to wish it less;
'Tis not for me, ungratefully to mar
Delight, so ready and so rich to bless . . .

Or, coming closer to the real point:

To love the beautiful is not to hate
The holy, nor to wander from the true;
Else why in Eden did its Lord create
Each green and shapely tree to please the view?

Yet there is a danger in the love of the beautiful, for it is not the same thing as the love of the holy, after all, and such souls as Lord Byron's or Jean-Jacques Rousseau's may linger in the former, becoming "Slaves of fine sense" merely. The religion of taste, focused on the rosebud, not upon the cross, can lead men far astray and even issue in false feeling, foul desires, profligacy, misanthropy, and atheism. The later stanzas are an exhortation to abandon the false religion of taste and to embrace the true one. By this point in the poem, Wilcox has abandoned the framework of allegory with which he began and has moved into an autobiographical mode suggestive of William Wordsworth. He tells of an overnight trip into the mountains of New Hampshire, where among the midnight peaks he had both dreaming and waking visions of the last day and of the true heaven. In the light of such intimations of immortality, all the pleasures of nature and of time seem mere beguilements.

Carlos Wilcox's early death and division of mind between poetry and preaching – and the emergence in the 1830s of such new and powerful voices as William Cullen **Bryant**, Edgar Allan **Poe**, John Greenleaf **Whittier**, and Henry Wadsworth **Longfellow** – caused a rapid, undeserved, and nearly total eclipse of his poetic reputation. Of these figures, Bryant alone was prominent before 1830, and the early anthologist George Cheever could say in successive sentences: "None can describe nature with a simpler and more affecting beauty than Bryant. None could draw an American landscape in truer colors, and throw more endearingly around it the charm of moral and devout reflection, than Wilcox." Cheever regards Richard Henry **Dana** Sr. as the chief poet of the land in 1829, with Bryant and Wilcox close behind. In Samuel Kettell's larger anthology, also published in 1829, Wilcox plays a much smaller part – a forecast of his shrinking reputation. The Duyckincks print 150 lines from "The Religion of Taste" in their *Cyclopaedia* of 1856, but Edmund Clarence **Stedman's** *An American Anthology* of 1900 does not include Wilcox at all. There is no entry for Carlos Wilcox in the *Dictionary of American Biography,* nor in *Who Was Who in America 1607–1985,* although he has held on to his nine-line entry in the *Oxford Companion to American Literature* from 1941 to 1983. He is not even mentioned in *The Columbia History of American Poetry* (1993), edited by Jay Parini, nor in earlier histories by Roy Harvey Pearce (1961), Hyatt H. Waggoner (1968), Donald B. Stauffer (1975), and Alan Shucard (1988). Wilcox, moreover, is not represented in current standard teaching anthologies. Inclusion in the LOA volume is a belated and well-deserved recognition of the poetic talent of this romantic, philosophical, religiously committed poet of the early republic. A modern edition is needed.

JAMES HAZEN

Selected Works

The Age of Benevolence, Book I, New Haven, Connecticut: A. H. Maltby, 1822
Remains of the Rev. Carlos Wilcox, edited by Edward Hopkins, Hartford, Connecticut: Edward Hopkins, 1828
The Poets of America, edited by George B. Cheever, New York: Hurst, n.d.
Cyclopaedia of American Literature, edited by Evert Duyckinck and George Duyckinck, vol. 1, New York, 1856; Philadelphia: Ruter, 1875; reprinted, Detroit, Michigan: Gale, 1965, pp. 897–899
Specimens of American Poetry, vol. 3, edited by Samuel Kettell, New York: Benjamin Blom, 1967

Further Reading

Brooks, Van Wyck, *The Flowering of New England 1815–1865*, New York: Dutton, 1937
Buell, Lawrence, *New England Literary Culture: From Revolution Through Renaissance*, London: Cambridge University Press, 1986
Pattee, Fred Lewis, *The First Century of American Literature, 1770–1870*, New York: Appleton, 1935
Spiller, Robert E., ed., *The Roots of National Culture: American Literature to 1830*, New York: Macmillan, 1938

Ella Wheeler Wilcox

(1850–1919)

"Solitude," Wilcox's most famous poem, begins: "Laugh and the world laughs with you, / Weep and you weep alone." Although most Americans recognize these lines, few can identify either the poem or the poet. Yet Ella Wheeler Wilcox occupied a prominent, if often disparaged, place in American letters during the Gilded Age and the Progressive era. She has the dubious honor of having been maligned by some of the foremost writers and scholars of the early twentieth century. Adjectives such as "facile," "fatuous," and "easy" were typically applied to her and point to a bias, especially with the advent of New Criticism, that favored the impersonal intellectualism of emergent male poets and that contributed to the disappearance of many nineteenth-century women writers from anthologies. In *Principles of Literary Criticism* (1925), I. A. Richards relies on the example of Wilcox's sonnet "Friendship After Love" (LOA, 2: 479) in a chapter entitled "Badness in Poetry." A thinly veiled attack on the sentimental and popular women's poetry that had gained such momentum in the second half of the nineteenth century, Richards's chapter seeks to distinguish between this low-brow, "bad" poetry and "valuable" poetry, which requires a higher stage in "the development of attitudes." He concedes that Wilcox's sonnet successfully communicates her ideas and produces "pleasure and admiration" in "a numerous class of readers"; nonetheless, he claims that it represents "stereotyped," "immature," and "conventional" attitudes. Other critics also cited Wilcox as the exemplar of the sentimental poetess. Alfred Kreymborg's *A History of American Poetry* (1934) refers to her as a "leader of fireside sentiment" whose poems offer a "facile optimism."

This association with sentimental poetry neatly removed Wilcox from the modernist canon. Yet, ironically, much of her most popular work does not conform to the model of the genteel poetess. She first achieved national recognition with *Poems of Passion* (1883), romantic love poems that critics labeled scandalous and immoral; later, she wrote *Poems of Progress* (1909), which supported the idea of labor unions and pled the cause of the working class; and, in her last years, she traveled through France during World War I, warning troops of the dangers of venereal disease by reciting her poem "Soldiers, Come Back Clean." Wilcox was extremely popular in her lifetime, in part because her work was so recognizable and accessible to the reading public. Her poems lack the formal innovation that characterizes much turn-of-the-century poetry. She favored sonnets and metrically regular lyrics with simple alternating rhyme schemes. Her poetry thus relies largely upon an emotional appeal and, like her famous sonnet "Solitude," offers moral lessons and platitudes. Yet her work also reflects interest in new ideas of the day. Along with her husband, Robert Wilcox (whom she married in 1884), the poet became fascinated by theosophy and "New Thought." The two studied with the Hindu mystic Swami Vivekananda and believed in reincarnation. (Wilcox's World War I travels were motivated by what she claimed was the voice of her dead husband.) She published a number of essay collections on the subject, including *The Heart of New Thought* (1902) and *New Thought and*

Common Sense and What Life Means to Me (1908), and many of her poems are littered with the language of spiritualism (see especially *Custer and Other Poems* [1895]).

More significant to her poetry was her strong interest in the "Woman Question," as also evidenced by the polemical tract *Men, Women and Emotions* (1896). Although the volume begins conventionally enough by asserting the importance of "teaching our girls how to be successful wives," Wilcox's lesson plan is radical. She maintains that "common sense" dictates an open acceptance of physical as well as spiritual attributes, and she repeatedly reminds readers that the young woman is a "growing animal" who requires an outlet for her sexual vitality. Wilcox notes disapprovingly that "our grandmothers and mothers never confessed to the possession of bodies and knew absolutely nothing about themselves physically." Her fourth book, *Poems of Passion*, demonstrates this belief in the importance of the physical aspect of romantic love. The poems seem innocuous to a late-twentieth-century reader, but at the time of publication they aroused a good deal of hostility. Believing the work immoral, her former publishers, Jansen and McClurg, rejected the manuscript. A local paper reported on the story with the headline "Too Loud for Chicago; The Scarlet City by the Lake Shocked by a Badger Girl [Wilcox was from Wisconsin] whose Verses Out-Swinburne Swinburne and Out-Whitman Whitman." The story was soon picked up nationally, and another house, W. B. Conkey & Company of Chicago, Illinois, exploited the publicity, selling over 60,000 copies of *Poems of Passion*.

For the rest of her career, Wilcox was known as "the Poetess of Passion," a label that her critics often used derisively. One of her most virulent critics, Neal Brown, spent an entire chapter in *Critical Confessions* (1899) lambasting Wilcox: "Of what avail is this lawless and wanton verse? It bears the stigmata of mental debauchery and hysteria and does not teach one valuable lesson." One particularly "lawless and wanton" poem, "Communism," offers an excellent example of Wilcox's treatment of love and sex. The poem plays on the conventional mind/heart dualism within a political metaphor: the heart is a communist threatening the political order in the court of "King Reason." Love's treason is to reverse the hierarchy and to identify reason as wicked and sinful for trying to control the passions:

> But Love is a spy who is plotting treason,
> In league with that warm, red rebel, the Heart.
> They whisper to me that the King is cruel,
> That his reign is wicked, his law a sin,
> And every word they utter is fuel
> To the flame that smolders within.

The poem is directed to a lover whom the speaker's reason tells her that she must forget. Yet she resists, and the poem is remarkable both for its depiction of physicality and for the speaker's unreserved sexual desire:

> And on nights like this, when my blood runs riot
> With the fever of youth and its mad desires,

490

When my brain in vain bids my heart be quiet,
When my breast seems the center of lava-fires,
Oh, then is the time when most I miss you,
And I swear by the stars and my soul and say
That I will have you, and hold you, and kiss you,
Though the whole world stands in the way.

Although passion remains potentially threatening, the speaker appears to exult in what she later calls this "insurrection of uncontrol." She also expresses a willfulness and determination that assume heroic proportions in the context of the political battle. Her vow to regain her lover ("And I swear by the stars and my soul") has a noble, almost transcendent quality: she will fight the wickedness of reason that would contain her passion. The poem thus implicitly exalts a most atypical nineteenth-century female lover, one characterized by an assertive, passionate nature. This quality becomes more explicit in the final lines: "Across the miles, does this wild war thrill you / That is raging in my soul?" The speaker slyly suggests that it is not her own passions that require release, but those of her lover. The description of her own emotional battle is merely a performance meant to excite this lover. When the speaker inquires whether her "wild war" has thrilled him, she ultimately undermines the sense of an ongoing battle with "King Reason." Clearly, the communist heart has already won the day and is now whispering its treason in the ear of the lover by way of the poem.

Representing women lovers with pulsing, breathing bodies, Wilcox's love poems stand in stark contrast to the popular women's poetry of the mid-nineteenth century. For such poets as Lydia **Sigourney**, Frances Osgood, and Elizabeth Oakes-Smith, modesty, refinement, and self-effacement were the prevailing qualities. In Oakes-Smith's "Let Me Be a Fantasy" – anthologized in Rufus Griswold's *The Female Poets of America* (1858), the next edition of which contained a number of Wilcox poems – the speaker identifies herself with conventional images of poetic craft such as the lute and the Aeolian harp. The intimate tone suggests a love lyric, one in which the speaker – really a disembodied voice – will be loved precisely because she is so delicate and modest that she seems nothing more than a fantasy:

Like the faint breathing of the distant lute . . .
    Heard in the hush of the evening still and low
For which we lingering listen though 'tis mute,
I would be unto thee and nothing more
    Oh nothing more.

Significantly, the speaker does not express her desire to be a poet, but to be the music produced by a poet.

Wilcox also treats the subject of a romanticized poetic identity in "Individuality" (also in *Poems of Passion*). The title itself suggests an assertiveness that differs greatly from Oakes-Smith's gentle entreaty. Wilcox's speaker demonstrates little modesty as she explicitly identifies herself as a poet and then explores the tension between this role and her role as a lover. In the first half of the poem, the speaker explains the depth and passion of her love by indicating what power her lover has over her life. The poem turns at its midpoint when she asserts: "And yet, and yet – one thing I keep from you." This "thing" is her "long pursued and worshiped art":

Thank God, you cannot grasp it; 'tis mine own.

Thank God, I say, for while I love you so,
With that vast love, as passionate as tender,
I feel an exultation, as I know
I have not made you a complete surrender.
Here is my body; bruise it, if you will,
And break my heart; I have that something still.

Here is a female poet who loves with her body as well as with her heart; moreover, it is a body over which she has utter control, since it is she who chooses to give it to her lover ("Here is my body"). Wilcox's use of "bruise" in such a literal connection with the body was unusual, and it would have been perceived as slightly vulgar. The assertion of self is powerful: rather than using her poetic gift as a means of offering herself up to her lover, as in the Oakes-Smith poem, the speaker exults in the ways that her art permits her to stand distinct and apart. It is her identity as poet that gives the speaker her sense of "individuality."

Wilcox is particularly interesting because, although easily disparaged, she is not easily dismissed. Critics and poets found her a useful foil against which to articulate their own poetics. Virginia Woolf, James Whitcomb **Riley**, William K. Wimsatt, and Louise Bogan all offered critiques of Wilcox, yet significantly, these often contradictory responses all share some notion of aesthetics that is informed by an embedded classism. Woolf and Riley pay little attention to Wilcox's poetry and are appalled by what they perceive as her vulgar materialism – her failure to conform to the image of either the "genius" or the "bluestocking." Wimsatt uses the carcass of her sonnet "Friendship After Love" as the site upon which to decimate I. A. Richards's methodology. Agreeing with Richards that, indeed, the work is bad, he takes issue with the grounds upon which Richards proclaims it bad. Bogan offers the most clear-eyed assessment of Wilcox in *Achievement in American Poetry, 1900–1950*. Although she decries nineteenth-century women's poetry for the way it "diluted" American verse, Bogan commends Wilcox for bringing "into popular love poetry the element of sin." Yet she concludes by dismissing Wilcox as the leader of a "thoroughly middle-class genre" that contributed to a "ridiculous record of sentimental feminine attitudinizing." Ultimately it was not Wilcox's sentimentality that most critics found so distressing, but her popularity. Richards is perhaps most explicit on this score. Comparing Wilcox's readers to admirers of John Keats, he offers the transparent analogy of the drinker who becomes more discriminating as his preference evolves from beer to brandy. Wilcox did, in fact, offer the public a product that was accessible and inexpensive, which they imbibed rapidly. She was a prolific writer, publishing over 40 volumes, including novels, poetry, and essays, and she achieved her greatest fame as a newspaper poet, contributing regularly to the Hearst syndicate.

Wilcox makes it clear that she is aware of her devalued status among the literati in her three autobiographical accounts (see bibliography); but she also suggests that although this is a source of dismay, she firmly believes in her own literary project. Raised on a small, impoverished Wisconsin farm by transplanted New Englanders, Wilcox was determined to improve her lot in life by becoming a writer. As a young woman she wrote feverishly, often producing several poems a day, flooding the local periodicals and newspapers with submissions. Her first volume, *Drops of Water* (1872), was primarily temperance poetry and marked the beginning of her interest in works that offered moral and practical advice. Wilcox was also interested in pleasing her public, and such verse was wildly popular in her day. Her aspirations derived largely from her poor childhood, and a resounding theme in her autobiographies is the great value that she places on financial success. In "Literary Confessions of a Western Poetess," she describes her response to her first publication: "I received my first cheque, and felt fully launched on the great sea of literature" (*Lippincotts Monthly Magazine*, May 1886). What is most striking and engaging about "Literary Confessions" is Wilcox's unabashed careerism, which is underscored by a pervasive sense of the inequity of America's class system. After attending the University of Wisconsin for a year, for instance, she returned home to pursue her writing career: "I felt the gulf between myself and the other girls whose gowns and privileges revealed to me for the first time, the different classes in American social life." This revelation finds voice in poems like "No Classes!" (LOA, 2: 479), which punctures the hypocritical "idle talk" and the pretensions to social equality involved in political and religious discourse ("'We are one family'"), and which admonishes readers: "It is the vain but natural human way / Of vaunting our weak selves, our pride, our worth!"

For Wilcox, poetry was never an end in itself, but also a means by which she could help her family and raise her own social status. The conclusion of "Literary Confessions" makes this point explicit when it invokes the period's leading arbiter of poetic taste, Edmund Clarence **Stedman**:

> I heard recently that Mr. Edmund Clarence Stedman honored me by the remark that he wished he could have had the literary training of me from my twelfth year; he would have made a better poet of me. I believe this to be true. He would have taught me that the manner of expression is as worthy of consideration as the thought to be expressed, – a fact I was sadly tardy in discovering. He would have caused me to contribute more to art, but, I fear, less to duty than I have done. I should have been a better poet, but a less useful financier and citizen. I should be remembered longer by critics, but less gratefully by those to whom I owe my existence.

Wilcox was not as naive as this quotation might suggest; she was aware of the way in which critics would receive these confessions. Relying on a religious metaphor that pokes fun at the current reverence for art with a capital *A*, she humorously addresses her "brethren and sistren" in art from the slightly sarcastic pose of "one who is partially reformed." She begs her readers to pray for her and admits, "I am afraid you will say I had no high ideals in art, – that I placed a purely commercial value on my gift: I am afraid it would be almost the truth if you should say it." Yet significantly, her next move is to complicate a value system in which the holy are those who disdain finan-

cial success. She describes an experience of religious ecstasy and transcendence in which she fervently thanks God, not for a conversion to ideal art, as her metaphor would lead us to expect, but "for the gift that enabled me to be such a help to my parents and that gave me such broadening pleasures and advantages in life."

As her playful jab at the "high ideals of art" suggests, Wilcox understood the tensions between a distinctly upper-class aestheticism and her notions of the function of art. In her autobiographies, she makes clear that given the choice between worshipping at the altar of art or paying the bills, she would always choose the latter. She had a profound sense of her own public image and included dramatically posed photographs of herself in almost every one of her books: Wilcox is the poor little farm girl who has made good, becoming a chic and cosmopolitan poet. But of course, this was a posture, the boundaries and limitations of which she was well aware. Critics have mistaken the posture for the woman and, in doing so, have failed to read Wilcox on her own terms. Ella Wheeler Wilcox did not suggest that beer is superior to brandy. She merely recognized the distinction between the two and made her own choice.

ALLISON GIFFEN

Selected Works

Poems of Passion, Chicago: W. B. Conkey, 1883
Maurine and Other Poems, Chicago: W. B. Conkey, 1888
Poems of Pleasure, 1888; reprinted, with additional poems, London: Gay & Bird, 1900
Custer and Other Poems, Chicago: W. B. Conkey, 1896
Three Women, Chicago: W. B. Conkey, 1897
The Story of a Literary Career, with Ella Giles Ruddy, Holyoke, Massachusetts: Elizabeth Towne, 1905
Poems of Progress, Chicago: W. B. Conkey, 1909
The Art of Being Alive, New York and London: Harper, 1914
The Worlds and I, New York: George H. Doran, 1918

Further Reading

Ballou, Jenny, *Period Piece: Ella Wheeler Wilcox and Her Times*, Boston: Houghton Mifflin, 1940
Brown, Neal, *Critical Confessions*, Wausau, Wisconsin: Philosophers, 1899
James, Edmund T., et al., eds., *Notable American Women, 1607–1950*, Cambridge, Massachusetts: Belknap, 1971; London: Oxford University Press, 1971
Richards, I. A., *Principles of Literary Criticism*, New York: Harcourt, Brace, Jovanovich, 1925
Walker, Cheryl, *The Nightingale's Burden*, Bloomington: Indiana University Press, 1982
Watts, Emily Stipes, *The Poetry of American Women from 1632–1945*, Austin: University of Texas Press, 1977
Woolf, Virginia, *Women and Writing*, edited by Michelle Barrett; reprinted, New York and London: Harcourt, Brace, Jovanovich, 1979

Richard Henry Wilde

(1789–1847)

Wilde was born in Dublin, Ireland, on September 24, 1789, the son of Mary Newett Wilde and Richard Wilde, an ironmonger and hardware merchant. He was the sixth of 12 children, four of whom died in infancy. Hoping for better living conditions, the Wildes left Ireland in 1796 and settled in Baltimore, Maryland. They gave up any thought of returning to their homeland when, during the Irish Rebellion of 1798, Richard Wilde's property in Dublin was confiscated. When Richard Henry Wilde was 11, he was forced to abandon his formal education in order to help in his father's store. Upon his father's death in 1802, he moved to Augusta, Georgia, a popular town for Irish immigrants, to work with his older brother. In 1803, Mary Wilde and the other children joined the two sons in Augusta, and she opened a clothing store. Although everyone worked hard, life was difficult, and the members of the family were always poor.

At 18, Richard Henry Wilde, while continuing as a store clerk, was permitted to read law books in the office of Joseph Hutchinson. After admittance to the bar in 1809, he became Hutchinson's law partner. In 1811, he was appointed attorney general of Georgia, and he held this position until 1813. Elected to the 14th Congress (1815–17) as a representative from Georgia, he served with such giants as John Randolph, John C. Calhoun, Henry Clay, and Daniel Webster. He was not reelected to the 15th Congress, but he ran again and served in the 20th through the 23rd (1827–35), coming close to being chosen Speaker of the House in 1834. In 1819, Wilde had married an Augusta widow, Caroline Buckle, the owner of a clothing store who had a daughter by her first marriage. Richard and Caroline Wilde had three sons, the first of whom died in early childhood. When Caroline died in 1827, Catherine, Wilde's unmarried sister, joined the household to supervise the upbringing of the two remaining sons.

In June 1835, Wilde, tiring of political life, left for Europe. After traveling through England, France, and Germany, he arrived in Italy in September 1835, and Florence became his home for the rest of the European trip; his family joined him in 1838. The years 1835–41 were the most glorious of his life: he moved in fashionable circles and knew well artists such as Horatio Greenough and Hiram Powers; he helped in the discovery of a portrait of Dante by Giotto; and, leaving commercial interests behind, he studied intensely Italian writers and translated some of their works. In *Hesperia* (see LOA, 1: 86), he writes:

My Italy! although of thine not born,
Nor worthy mine own land's maternal breast,
Thy child in heart I am . . .
Ay, Mother of my Soul!

But the Italian dream ended: Wilde, his sons, and sister were forced, by finances, to return to America in 1841. Augusta and the state of Georgia were in wretched economic conditions, and so the four moved in with Wilde's brother, Wilde returning to the practice of law. Considering political life again, he ran for the House of Representatives, but was defeated. In 1843,

he reluctantly concluded that he must leave Augusta if he expected to practice law on a more active scale. In early 1844, he headed for New Orleans, Louisiana, where he spent his last years. Competition was stiff in the Crescent City, but he enjoyed some noteworthy achievements: he acquired prominence in the legal profession and even argued before the Supreme Court, he had an active social life, he obtained a statue of Benjamin Franklin by Hiram Powers for the city, and he helped in founding the law school at Tulane University. During the humid summer months, the city was invaded by swarms of mosquitoes, and many people died from yellow fever; Wilde succumbed on September 10, 1847. He was buried in New Orleans, but in 1886, the remains were placed in Magnolia Cemetery, Augusta.

Wilde was described as polished and gentlemanly, with grace and elegance. An excellent orator, he made a handsome appearance with his long, flowing locks. Although he might assume the appearance of a brooding romantic in many of his poems, he was actually happy and cheerful, except in political debates, when he could become vitriolic. He delighted in social life, especially the companionship of women.

At an early age, he began to compose poems, and later he collected many of them in the manuscript "Poems: Fugitive and Occasional." Wilde's outstanding scholarly work is *Conjectures and Researches Concerning the Love, Madness and Imprisonment of Torquato Tasso*. An unpublished work in two parts, "The Italian Lyric Poets" (sometimes called "Specimens of Italian Lyric Poetry"), also written while Wilde was in Italy, contains biographical introductions to a number of Italian poets, together with 96 translations (the biographical introductions, now in the Library of Congress, have never been published). While in Italy, Wilde spent much time studying Dante. He read biographies of the poet, gained access to the appropriate archives, and perused manuscripts and printed books. He planned an elaborate work, "The Life and Times of Dante, with Sketches of the State of Florence and of His Friends and Enemies," but he completed only one of the projected two volumes (also housed in the Library of Congress).

Wilde's most famous poem, "The Lament of the Captive" (LOA, 1:85), was composed about 1813 or 1814 and published in 1819. The lines were written to honor the poet's brother, James Wilde, a member of the U. S. Army who went to Florida on an expedition against the Seminole Indians and was killed in a duel. The entire work consists of four fragments of a proposed epic and two lyric poems. The captive in the famous lines is Juan Ortiz, the last survivor of an expedition to Florida in 1528 led by Panfilo de Narvaez. An Indian, speaking in the fragment just before the poem, states that many years ago white men had arrived at the site, which God had given the Indians. There was a skirmish, and many were killed. The Indians had called the whites "brothers" but then discovered that they wished only to spoil the land. Eventually a single white man was left, a captive – good and true and beloved by the Indians. He taught the Indians many things, but his soul was sad because he longed for his native home.

The poem has three stanzas in iambic tetrameter. Each stanza begins with an extended simile taken from nature: (1) the summer rose – actually the daily or Florida rose – opens, fades, and perishes in less than 12 hours, and night weeps for the rose; (2) the autumn leaf falls and fades, and the tree mourns its loss; (3) the footprint left on Tampa's "desert strand" vanishes, and is mourned by the sea. Although all these elements of nature are mourned, no one mourns for the captive. The most highly acclaimed line in the poem – "On that lone shore loud moans the sea" – has only monosyllables, several long vowels, and liquids with no harsh consonant sounds, which give vivid expression to the melancholy theme. There was a long dispute about the authorship of the poem – including claims that it had been written by an Irishman, Patrick O'Kelly, or translated from the Greek of Alcaeus – but Wilde definitely wrote it. Set to music by Charles Thibault, Sidney **Lanier**, and Stephen Foster, the poem was very popular; with reference to its opening line ("My life is like the summer rose"), it was often parodied in works with such titles as "My Life is Like the Shattered Wreck," "My Life is Like a Wreath of Smoke," and "My Life is Like a Sickly Pear."

Another poem that has received much attention is "To the Mocking-Bird" (LOA, 1: 85), which was written in the romantic tradition of southern poetry. This variation on an Italian sonnet, published before 1836, was reprinted in *Hesperia* with notes about the mockingbird – "a great rogue even according to aboriginal testimony." Indian legend held that the mockingbird "stole the tongues of all the other birds while they slept, and hence the variety of his notes, which are an imitation of all." An Indian name for the bird can be translated as "trick-tongue." The poem presents the mockingbird as (in the terms of the notes) a "sentimental swindler, – a minion of the moon, – melancholy and gentlemanlike." It seems appropriate to invoke William Shakespeare to contrast these two moods: in the octave, the bird resembles the jester Yorick in *Hamlet*, a man "of infinite jest, of most excellent fancy," whose "flashes of merriment" could "set the table on a roar"; in the sestet, the bird resembles the sentimental, cynical Jaques in *As You Like It*, who speaks of a "motley fool" and can "suck melancholy out of a song as a weasel sucks eggs."

Wilde's crowning achievement was his extended *Hesperia*, which is part epic, part Byronesque narrative in the manner of *Childe Harold*, part autobiography, and part philosophic essay. Edited by his son, the work was published 20 years after Wilde's death. Following a dedication of four pages, there are four cantos in ottava rima: "Florida," "Virginia," "Acadia," and "Louisiana." According to the dedication, the title *Hesperia* "comes from *Hesperus*, a name given to Venus when the star of evening, and signifies a setting, or the West"; the Greeks called Italy Hesperia, but "since that time, the West has moved westward," and the name may now "be applied to America." The poem, then, celebrates America, and "our country's plains, lakes, rivers, woods, and skies." There is a magic in nature; in "hill, dale, brook, forest, lake"; in a "fertile, verdant, woodless, boundless plain"; or in barren places where "gigantic Sauri, lizards, bats, and fern" are embalmed together with "tortoise, bird, and shell." The poet – who calls himself Fitzhugh De Lancy, Esq. – is the "wreck of love and time," world-weary with a "stagnant" heart, someone for whom "there is no help, no hope, no cure"; he offers his thoughts in a

"rambling and incoherent" narrative. As he views the glories of America's natural settings, he is filled with "a thousand thoughts of joy and pain." The poem is dedicated to "La Signora Marchesa Manfredina di Cosenza," to whom there are frequent references:

> Upon that night we met! . . . The hour, the scene
> Remain forever graven on my heart,
> And ever since that meeting there hath been
> No life or joy for me but where thou art!

Aubrey H. Starke has speculated that the "Marchesa" was Mrs. Ellen White-Beatty. A celebrated beauty, she was the daughter of General John Adair and was married twice, first to Joseph M. White, Wilde's business partner, and then, upon his death, to Dr. Theophilus Beatty, a physician of New Orleans.

The work begins with "Florida" because the town of Saint Augustine "dates back to 1565" and Virginia did not boast of a permanent settlement until 1607. But each of the four geographical divisions in the poem includes "a large part of its ancient boundaries." "Florida," in consequence, addresses places that are now in Georgia or the Carolinas. De Lancy refers to someone who was a jurist and a politician – meaning Wilde himself – who had praised Saint Augustine elsewhere. Saint Augustine, the oldest city in the United States, was founded by Menendez de Aviles on the site of an old Indian village near Ponce de León's landing place. There are references in this canto to Saint Anastasia's isle; to the column of the Constitution, which was still standing in 1826 in the public square of Saint Augustine; to Santa Rosa Island; and to the "big spring" of Chippola, supposed by the Indians to be the fountain of everlasting youth, the purported object of Ponce de León's voyage. Wilde's theme is that of leave-taking – saying good-bye to a setting that has seduced him by its loveliness – but also that of time.

The latter theme is continued in the "Virginia" canto. The poet reflects that America may once have had giant mammoths and monsters, but "change blots out change." He refers to people important in the history of the state: George Washington, Thomas Jefferson, Patrick Henry, "Foremost of all who wrote, or spoke, or bled / To win their country's birthright, LIBERTY!" There are also references to places of interest: Mount Vernon, Monticello, the Shenandoah Valley, the Dismal Swamp, and Weyer's Cave. The description of Niagara in "Acadia" is memorable:

> Approach! look down the dizzy precipice,
> And gaze upon the yawning deep below:
> One step will plunge you into the abyss,
> And end at once, forever, mortal woe.

This section contains descriptions not only of places in present-day Canada, but also of present-day New England: the "green hills" of Vermont, the "snow-clad mountains" of New Hampshire, and Mount Auburn Cemetery in Cambridge, Massachusetts, which no other cemetery can match in "native beauty." An obelisk marks the "glorious bed of rest" of Joseph Warren, the "first officer of rank" who fell in the Revolutionary War; he was killed at Breed's Hill (Battle of Bunker Hill) in June 1775.

The fourth canto, "Louisiana," covers a vast space, going all the way to Kentucky, Tennessee, and Lake Superior. Of special interest is the Mississippi River, the "Father of Rivers," which glides "calm and pure" until it meets the Missouri River, with its "dirty, muddy, whitish color"; the Missouri is like "the Barbarian" attacking "his Roman prey." The Mississippi, "whirling and boiling, ceaseless in commotion," with its "amphibious beasts or hideous fish of prey," figures as the American Nile. Giacomo Constantino Beltrami (1779–1855), who "trod the wilderness" and furnished the account *Discovery of the Sources of the Mississippi* (1824), resembles the Scottish explorer James Bruce (1730–94), who wrote *Travels to Discover the Source of the Nile* (1790). The canto has references to the "Nimrod of the West," Daniel Boone, as well as to important places like St. Louis, Missouri, New Orleans, and Nauvoo. The latter, called the "modern saint and prophet's bower" and located in western Illinois on the Mississippi, was occupied by the Mormons under Joseph Smith until the group left for Utah in 1846.

References to Native Americans are frequent throughout *Hesperia*, but the most interesting occur in the last canto. The Indians have been "Sons of the Forest" and "Children of Nature." They have been kind and good – "strangers to falsehood, pity, mirth and fear" – and have welcomed the visiting white men. Of particular note is the story of the beautiful Ozolapaida, abducted by Ohatampa, who then killed her husband, Wihanoa-appa, and two of her brothers when they tried to free her. A terrible battle ensued between the Assiniboins and the Sioux. The canto concludes with an apostrophe to Ozolapaida, the "Helen of the West": "no Homer kept / The memory of thy charms, and so they slept."

Although Wilde is remembered today as the author of just one poem, "The Lament of the Captive," he remains of interest for other reasons as well. The child of an Irish immigrant, he rose to considerable prominence in American political life. He fits in very closely with the interests of romanticism, especially in his melancholy mood and his descriptions of nature. He devoted himself passionately to the life and works of Italian authors, and his *Hesperia* was one of the few full-length poems by early southern writers.

EDWARD L. TUCKER

Selected Works

Conjectures and Researches Concerning the Love, Madness and Imprisonment of Torquato Tasso, 2 vols., New York: Alexander V. Blake, 1842
Hesperia: A Poem, edited by William Cumming Wilde, Boston: Ticknor and Fields, 1867
The Italian Lyric Poets, in Edward L. Tucker, *Richard Henry Wilde: His Life and Selected Poems*, Athens: University of Georgia Press, 1966, pp. 200–249
Poems: Fugitive and Occasional, in Edward L. Tucker, *Richard Henry Wilde: His Life and Selected Poems*, Athens: University of Georgia Press, 1966, pp. 117–199

Further Reading

Barclay, Anthony, *Wilde's Summer Rose: or the Lament of the Captive. An Authentic Account of the Origin, Mystery and Explanation of Hon. R. H. Wilde's Alleged Plagiarism*, Savannah: Georgia Historical Society, 1871
Parks, Edd Winfield, *Ante-Bellum Southern Literary Critics*, Athens: University of Georgia Press, 1962, pp. 51–59
Tucker, Edward L., *Richard Henry Wilde: His Life and Selected Poems*, Athens: University of Georgia Press, 1966

Nathaniel Parker Willis

(1806–1867)

Today, Nathaniel Parker Willis is often remembered only as the notorious subject of nineteenth-century literary anecdote: he was parodied as Hyacinth Ellet in *Ruth Hall*, the roman à clef of his sister Fanny Fern, challenged to duels, and named as a defendant in the divorce case of actor Edwin Forrest. Instead of being ruined by the negative publicity surrounding these events, Willis flourished because he understood and anticipated the desires and interests of reading audiences. He astutely used the press to parlay his initial popularity as a writer of scriptural verse into a 45-year career as a cosmopolitan man of letters and arbiter of cultural taste. He wrote less poetry as his reputation grew, however, and what he did write became increasingly secular and complemented the sophisticated public persona that he cultivated. And, although he continued to reprint his poetry throughout his life, his later work was largely confined to his role as a magazinist and editor.

Willis was born in Portland, Maine, on January 20, 1806, the second of Nathaniel and Hannah Parker Willis's nine children. Nathaniel Willis was a journalist who founded the *Boston Recorder*, a religious newspaper, and the *Youth's Companion*, a juvenile magazine. The elder Willis was the first publisher of his son's poetry; "To My Mother" appeared in the *Boston Recorder* in February 1823, and "To My Father" soon followed. Sparked by the religious revivalism sweeping Andover, Massachusetts, Willis soon began writing religious verse, which his father also published in the *Boston Recorder*. While at Yale College in New Haven, Connecticut, where his Calvinist father sent him to escape the influence of the Unitarians, Willis wrote secular as well as religious verse and published it in the *Christian Examiner*, the *Connecticut Journal*, *The Boston Statesman*, and other journals. He also delivered the commencement poem when he graduated from Yale in 1827. By this time, Willis was one of the best known and most popular of the younger generation of poets in America. He capitalized on this popularity by publishing two volumes of collected poetry, *Sketches* (1827) and *Fugitive Poetry* (1829).

Willis worked for a number of literary publications throughout the 1820s and 1830s, sometimes as a correspondent, but more often as the editor. Many of these were short-lived ventures, but they helped establish his reputation as a man of letters. First, he edited Samuel Goodrich's periodical *The Legendary* (1828), which published such authors as Lydia **Sigourney** and Fitz-Greene **Halleck**, and then the 1829 edition of Goodrich's literary annual *The Token*, which again published Sigourney, as well as John **Neal** and Sarah Josepha Hale. Willis continued in journalism by founding the *American Monthly Magazine* in April 1829, which helped to crystallize his cosmopolitan persona; he adopted a gossipy, informal editorial pose in "The Editor's Table," which became a trademark of his career. His social life during this time, however, soon earned him the censure of the religious community in Boston, Massachusetts: the Park Street Church excommunicated him in April 1829 for attending the theater but failing to attend church.

After the financial collapse of the *American Monthly Maga-zine* in August 1831, Willis moved to New York City and began work for George Pope Morris's *New York Mirror*. He collaborated with Morris, with only a few brief interruptions, for the rest of his career. In October 1831, Willis began traveling in Europe and Asia Minor as a correspondent for the *Mirror*. The chatty, impressionistic style of his "letters" was intended to amuse. He wrote about museums, social life, and other writers, including James Fenimore Cooper. Willis later collected many of these sketches in *Pencillings by the Way* (1835). Although popular, a number of gossipy, indiscreet letters alienated various constituencies and led to a falling-out between Willis and Morris.

The years 1835–36 were very eventful ones. Willis had settled in England, where he married Mary Stace, an Englishwoman, in October 1835. Shortly after, he became involved in a highly publicized literary feud with Captain Frederick Marryat of the British journal *Metropolitan*. The feud originated when Morris published in the *Mirror* a letter in which Willis called Marryat's work "gross trash." Willis later claimed that this was meant to be a private letter, but the quarrel between the two men escalated when Marryat challenged Willis to a duel. Their respective friends eventually settled their disagreements, but the publication of their correspondence in the London *Times* brought Willis international notoriety.

In May 1836, Willis and his wife returned to America. Their first child was born dead in December 1840, prompting Willis to write "Thoughts While Making the Grave of a New Born Child." His daughter Imogen was born in June 1842. Mary Willis died in March 1845, while giving birth to a child who also died. Leaving Imogen to the care of Harriet Jacobs, who was employed by the Willis family as a nurse for more than 20 years (the Willis family is thinly disguised in Jacobs's *Incidents in the Life of a Slave Girl* as the "Bruce" family of New York), Willis traveled to Europe, where he became seriously ill. Henry A. Beers, author of the only full-length biography of Willis, claims that he was never very well after this time and that in later years Willis suffered from epilepsy, which grew increasingly debilitating. Willis did regain his health sufficiently to marry Cornelia Grinnell in 1846. They had five children: Grinnell, Lilian, Edith, Bailey, and another daughter who died soon after birth.

Still unreconciled with Morris, Willis's next major literary project was as a coeditor of *The Corsair*, beginning in March 1839. In protest against the lack of international copyright laws (which cost Willis a significant amount of money on the lucrative British market), Willis and his partner planned to pirate the works of British authors, and thereby, to profit themselves from the absence of legal restraints. As Beers notes, the recent introduction of transatlantic steamers made this project more feasible, as it was now possible to acquire quickly recent works from British presses. Despite this effort, *The Corsair* was never financially stable, and it ceased publication in March 1840.

In 1843, Willis renewed his friendship with Morris, and they began a series of joint publishing ventures. First, they founded the *New Mirror*, later retitled the *Evening Mirror*, which also employed Edgar Allan **Poe**. Willis became personal friends with Poe at this time, and they remained friends for the rest of Poe's life. Consequently, Poe generally wrote flattering reviews, including an essay in *Literati of New York City*, of Willis and his works. The various incarnations of the *Mirror* suffered from financial problems, however, so in 1846 Willis and Morris created yet another periodical, the weekly *Home Journal*. This journal targeted a female audience that was interested in society and fashion – areas Willis regarded as his forte. The *Home Journal* was the most long-lived and successful of the publications with which Willis was associated, and he edited and wrote for it until his death. Although it provided him with the steady income that his rapidly growing family required, his editorship occupied much of his time, and he published relatively little new poetry during the last 20 years of his life. Willis did, however, continue to publish works in a variety of other genres, including fiction, drama, and travel writing. He also wrote two romantic blank verse dramas, *Bianca Visconti; or The Heart Overtasked* (1839) and *Tortesa; or The Usurer Matched* (1839), both of which were staged in New York.

In 1850, Willis was involved in a serious scandal, which stemmed from the divorce case of the actor Edwin Forrest and his wife, Catherine Sinclair Forrest. Mrs. Forrest was friends with both Willis and his wife Cornelia, as well as with Willis's younger brother Richard. When Forrest filed for divorce, accusing his wife of adultery, the Willis family sided with Mrs. Forrest, and Willis even printed a defense of her in the *Home Journal*. An angry Forrest maliciously named both Willis and his brother Richard in the suit. Forrest later attacked Willis in New York, knocking him to the ground; lawsuits proliferated as Willis sued Forrest for assault, and Forrest countersued for libel. The divorce case was eventually decided in Mrs. Forrest's favor (although not finally settled until 1868), but it nonetheless brought Willis a great deal of notoriety and may have further weakened his health; certainly, it distracted his attention from his literary work.

In the early 1860s, Morris became increasingly unwell and was unable to continue managing the business operations of the *Home Journal*. More work fell to Willis, who was himself in poor health. Morris's death in 1864 increased the burdens on Willis, who was forced to retire in 1866 to Idlewild, New York, his country estate on the banks of the Hudson River. The renowned cosmopolitan man of letters died there on January 20, 1867, his sixty-first birthday.

Despite the sophistication that Willis cultivated, his rise to fame was predicated upon his reputation as a writer of sacred verse. While at Yale, Willis shrewdly created a public image of himself as a devout, pious poet. Although he wrote little religious poetry after 1830, he reprinted his early works again and again, seldom revising them, in attractive gift editions that were complete with engravings. Much of Willis's religious poetry falls under the subgenre of scriptural verse. His most popular religious poems are narrative verse paraphrases of well-known biblical passages. Totaling 19 poems, these scriptural verses are almost evenly divided between paraphrases of the Old and New Testaments. Matthew serves as the source for four poems, while II Samuel and Luke serve as the source for three each. The subject matter varies, but death, sacrifice, heal-

ing, and resurrection predominate. Willis's Old Testament poems such as "The Sacrifice of Abraham" and "Jephthah's Daughter" focus on the demands that religious faith places upon the individual. In contrast, the New Testament poems show a Jesus of mercy, as in "Healing the Daughter of Jairus" and "The Leper."

Despite their thematic differences, these poems all have dramatic atmospheres that Willis creates through scenic and descriptive embellishments. "Healing the Daughter of Jairus," for instance, expands 10 brief biblical verses from Mark into 135 lines. Romanticized descriptions, typical of nineteenth-century sentimental verse, predominate. "Spice-lamps" in "alabaster urns" dimly light the room, and "silken curtains" hang at the window. As Jairus watches the body of his beautiful daughter,

> The dark lids lifted from her languid eyes,
> And her slight fingers moved, and heavily
> She turn'd upon her pillow. He was there –
> The same lov'd, tireless watcher, and she look'd
> Into his face until her sight grew dim
> With the fast-falling tears.

The sanitized version of death that Willis describes here is peaceful and highly stylized; after her death, Jairus's daughter lies "Like a form / Of matchless sculpture in her sleep." Jesus appears only in the last 10 lines, commanding her to *Arise!* Her father has faith, and she awakes. Nonetheless, the poem focuses on the evocation of scene and emotion, rather than on theology, and this treatment of its source is typical of Willis's other scriptural verses.

Although Willis's biblical poems did not meet with great critical success (James Russell **Lowell**, among others, praised their piety rather than their poetic imagination), contemporary audiences found them immensely moving. As Beers explains, these poems "appealed to an intensely biblical and not very literary constituency; to a public familiar with the Old and New Testaments alike, and familiarized also with the life and scenery of the East through Bible commentaries and the lectures of missionaries who had traveled in Palestine." Further, such poetry was appropriate for younger readers as well as adults, and many in his audience would have deemed it suitable reading even for the Sabbath.

Willis's other sacred poems include "On Witnessing a Baptism," "The Sabbath," and "Homes for the Friendless." As in his scriptural poems, he emphasizes the role of emotion and sentiment in religion over doctrinal theology. The speaker of "On Witnessing a Baptism," for instance, compares the baptismal waters with a mother's tears and finds "That, to the eye of God, that mother's tears / would be a deeper covenant – which sin / And the temptations of the world, and death, / Would leave unbroken." Willis further sanctifies motherhood and redemptive maternal love in such poems as "The Mother to Her Child" and "Better Moments." His poem "Sonnet," which compares the sunset after a storm with the spiritual light that falls upon the dying Christian, is also worth noting because he seldom used the sonnet form.

Willis categorized many other poems as "reflective" – meaning that they were meditative, even devout, but not overtly religious. Prompted by the sight of a pigeon nest built in a bell tower, the speaker of "The Belfry Pigeon" reflects that "Whatever is rung on that noisy bell – / Chime of the hour or funeral knell – / The dove in the belfry must hear it well." Yet the bird's serenity symbolizes spiritual peace to the poet, who wishes

> that I could be
> A hermit in the crowd like thee!
> With wings to fly to wood and glen,
> Thy lot, like mine, is cast with men;
> . . . .
> But, unlike me, when day is o'er,
> Thou canst dismiss the world and soar.

"Psyche, Before the Tribunal of Venus" (LOA, 1: 352) uses Willis's more customary blank verse. Originally written for an engraving, this poem celebrates the beauty of the spirit over that of the outward form:

> – the glory of the human form
> Is but a perishing thing, and Love will droop
> When its brief grace hath faded; but the mind
> Perisheth not, and when the outward charm
> Hath had its brief existence, it awakes,
> And is the lovelier that it slept so long.

Outward beauty may initially overshadow the soul, but "the soul is better than its frame" and will triumph.

Two other important reflective poems are "January 1, 1828" and "January 1, 1829" (LOA, 1: 351), in which Willis reflects upon a past year. "January 1, 1828" is a conventional poem of praise, which concludes "'God hath been very good!'"; the poet tells his reader that "in the plenty of the feast, / And in the lifting of the cup, let Him / Have praises for the well-completed year." More interesting and more successful in conveying the reflective nature of winter itself is "January 1, 1829," which again ponders the work of God in creating the seasons. The poet finds that God deliberately gave winter "an unlovely aspect" and that winter "hath a meaning hid / Under the shadow of His hand." The lack of outside distractions forces one indoors and causes introspection, for winter "is a season for the quiet thought, / And the still reckoning with thyself":

> Life stands still
> And settles like a fountain, and the eye
> Sees clearly through its depths, and noteth all
> That stirr'd its troubled waters.

The end of the old year and the beginning of the new naturally coincide with the seasonal change, thus synchronizing the natural and social orders.

Although the majority of Willis's poetry has sacred or reflective overtones, a number of poems bear a decidedly Byronic influence, such as "Misanthropic Musings," an early, uncollected trilogy of misogynistic magazine poems. Their tone is brooding rather than reflective. The serious disdain for women is atypical of Willis's oeuvre, however, and perhaps for this reason these pieces remained uncollected. In his longer works, "Lady Jane; or, An Old Maid's Love" and "Melanie" (see LOA, 1: 353), the Byronic parallels become more obvious as Willis refers directly to the English poet. Modeled after *Don Juan* and written in ottava rima, "Lady Jane" strives for cosmopolitan wittiness as it tells the story of the 40-year-old Lady Jane, who falls in love for the first time with 22-year-old Jules Beaulevres. The narrator cleverly describes the circumstances of Lady Jane's first meeting with Jules: "And Jules, throughout, was beautifully tender – / Although he did not always comprehend her." Throughout "Lady Jane," Willis plays with compound and slant rhymes, but at times his wit is at odds with the poem's sentimentality.

A more successful, yet highly melodramatic, poem is "Melanie," which has six sections and is written in iambic tetrameter with a varying rhyme scheme. Despite the poem's length, the meter and rhyme allow Willis much more flexibility than he had in "Lady Jane," and the versification is appropriate to the serious subject matter. De Brevern, a melancholic Byronic narrator, reflects upon the disastrous history of his family – a past of "thwarted schemes" and the "ashes of a thousand dreams." For him, "Life had no joy, and scarce a pain, / Whose wells I had not tasted deep." The story he tells is that of his younger sister, Melanie, "the last of the De Brevern race," who falls in love with Angelo, a poor young Italian artist of unknown parentage. At the time of their wedding in St. Mona's, a praying nun catches sight of the narrator's face and interrupts the ceremony by shrieking: "De Brevern! . . . The bridegroom is thy blood – thy brother! / Rodolph De Brevern wrong'd his mother!" Melanie dies of shock at this revelation, and Angelo dies soon after of grief. Next to Melanie's grave, "Her lover – brother – sleeps as well!" The poem concludes with De Brevern's words: "Peace to the broken-hearted dead!" Although "Melanie" is melodramatic and clichéd in places, it is the best of Willis's long poems, and its versification shows considerably more polish than many of his other poems.

Willis also wrote lighter vers de société throughout his career. His use of different pseudonyms for different kinds of poetry again reveals an astute understanding of the reading public; he crafted an image to appeal to each audience. But eventually his reputation as a poet and man of letters became a source of professional jealousy among other magazinists. And because his social verse and his use of the pseudonym "Down Town Bard" furthered his image as a literary dandy, much contemporary criticism targeted his person: his appearance, propensity for dandyism, frivolity, and social aspirations. Lowell, for example, gently lampoons him in *A Fable for Critics* as "the topmost bright bubble on the wave of The Town." Yet these attacks served only to entrench Willis in this persona of the man of mode, and his verse celebrates this sophistication.

Like his Byronic verse, Willis's vers de société maintains an urbane veneer, but it is much lighter in tone and wittier. "Love in a Cottage" perhaps best demonstrates Willis's cosmopolitan sympathies; the narrator explains that although "they" idealize "love in a cottage" and the romance of bucolic settings, he prefers romance in the city:

> Your love in a cottage is hungry,
>   Your vine is a nest for flies –
> Your milkmaid shocks the Graces,
>   And simplicity talks of pies!
> You lie down to your shady slumber
>   And wake with a bug in your ear,
> Your damsel that walks in the morning
>   Is shod like a mountaineer.

Although Willis mocks those who romanticize the countryside, he equally romanticizes the gaiety of city life. In "City Lyrics" (LOA, 1: 359), the narrator describes the scenes of New York

City that one might encounter during a walk downtown for ices. Upon seeing St. Paul's, he explains, "Religion seems very ill-plann'd! / For one day we list to the pastor, / For six days we list to the band!" In the same key, his "city poems" often detail a brief, romanticized encounter between two city dwellers. In "To the Lady in the Chemisette with Black Buttons," the narrator sees a beautiful woman and concludes that "The world is full of meetings such as this – / A thrill, a voiceless challenge and reply – / And sudden partings after!" Ultimately, however, the imaginative process that the encounter sparks, rather than the encounter itself, is the more important. In a more serious poem of the city, "The Lady in the White Dress, Whom I Helped into the Omnibus" (LOA, 1: 360), the pure beauty of such anonymous women represents inspiration, like "bright lamps with loveliness alight – / And all may in their guiding beams rejoice." The conspicuous gallantry of these poems, so sharply counter to both the misogyny of the "Misanthropic Musings" trilogy and the cynicism of "Lady Jane," is more characteristic of Willis's work.

Although the city is filled with loveliness and gaiety, Willis also portrays it as a cold and indifferent place. In "The Pity of the Park Fountain," a hearse rolls silently past the fountain, which continues to flow "gaily," and the mindless, unceasing beauty of the fountain as it continues to "play on" mocks a girl who is "sick with the pangs of poverty." "Unseen Spirits" (LOA, 1: 358), one of Willis's most popular poems and Poe's personal favorite, illustrates the hypocrisy of city life. Unseen spirits escort two women who walk down Broadway at dusk, but the poem highlights the difference in their escorts. Alongside a wealthy, proud lady walk Peace and Honor, because "She kept with care her beauties rare / From lovers warm and true – / For her heart was cold to all but gold." The other, even more beautiful young woman walks instead "'Twixt Want and Scorn." Despite this woman's beauty,

> No mercy now can clear her brow
>   For this world's peace to pray;
> For, as love's wild prayer dissolved in air,
>   Her woman's heart gave way! –
> But the sin forgiven by Christ in heaven
>   By man is cursed alway!

Despite its glittering surface, the city judges harshly. The second woman has the warmth and passion that the first lady lacks, but the world scorns her. In spite of its heavy-handed allegory and awkward concluding rhyme, the poem manages to combine the city atmosphere of Willis's ephemeral social verse with the strong morality of his more popular religious verse. Further, the combination of internal and end rhymes creates a poem that can be easily memorized, which in turn very likely contributed to its popularity.

Willis's reputation declined after his death, although some of his scriptural poems continued to be reprinted into the early twentieth century. His work owed much of its popularity to the force of his personality and to the astute manner in which he marketed both himself and his writing. In a review essay in the *Atlantic Monthly* in 1884, when Willis's work had already begun to be forgotten, Edward F. Hayward explored Willis's former vogue and concluded that he "transcribe[d] the social economy of his time." Hayward's comments are even more apropos today, as modern readers must sometimes struggle to understand the popularity of Willis's work. Willis understood the literary marketplace and the tastes of the average reader as did few other writers of his time, and he capitalized on this understanding by offering lofty, stylized religious verse to a conservative northeastern audience during the early decades of the nineteenth century and supplying lighter social verse suited to the cosmopolitan sympathies of his later audience.

KAREN A. WEYLER

Selected Works
Fugitive Poetry, Boston: Peirce & Williams, 1829
Melanie and Other Poems, New York: Saunders and Otley, 1835
Poems of Passion, New York: Mirror Library, 1843
The Sacred Poems of N. P. Willis, New York: Mirror Library, 1843
Lady Jane and Humorous Poems, New York: Mirror Library, 1844
Poems of Early and After Years, Philadelphia: Carey and Hart, 1848
The Poems, Sacred, Passionate, and Humorous of Nathaniel Parker Willis, New York: Clark & Austin, 1844; rev. ed. 1860

Further Reading
Auser, Courtland P., *Nathaniel P. Willis*, New York: Twayne, 1969
Beers, Henry A., *Nathaniel Parker Willis*, Boston: Houghton Mifflin, 1885
Buell, Lawrence, *New England Literary Culture from Revolution Through Renaissance*, New York: Cambridge University Press, 1986
Poe, Edgar Allan, *Edgar Allan Poe, 1809–1849: Essays and Reviews*, New York: Library of America, 1984

Byron Forceythe Willson

(1837–1867)

Between his birth in Little Genesee, New York, on April 10, 1837, and his death in Alfred, New York, on February 2, 1867, Willson achieved extraordinary success as the author of "The Old Sergeant," one of the most sensational poems of the Civil War era. During the 1860s, he became an occasional contributor to major periodicals such as the *Atlantic Monthly* and an intimate associate of nineteenth-century American literature's most venerated figures, nearly all of whom considered him a rare talent and a poet of great promise. Although Willson would only publish a slim volume of verse during his lifetime, he was an eclectic poet whose art embodied a range of disparate interests seen in his culture.

Willson was the eldest son of very industrious parents. At various times his father, Hiram Willson, served as postmaster of Little Genesee (during the presidency of Andrew Jackson), operated a modestly successful lumber mill, worked as a teacher, and acted as superintendent of common schools in Alleghany County, New York. A native of Vermont who was raised in the Unitarian faith, Hiram Willson was also an early, although moderate, abolitionist. Willson's mother, Ann Calvin Ennis Willson, a Seventh-Day Baptist from Rhode Island, was a teacher as well, and together with her husband she provided their adolescent children with a proper liberal education at home, including an uncommonly thorough introduction to English literature.

In 1846, Willson's family left New York and moved westward. Traveling by raft, upon which Hiram erected a log cabin as a temporary residence, the Willson family drifted down the Alleghany and Ohio Rivers deep into the heart of the midwest, landing temporarily in Maysville, Kentucky. In 1847, they resumed their migration and eventually settled in Covington, Kentucky, situated on the high bluffs across the Ohio River from Cincinnati, Ohio. Over the next five years, Willson's father established himself as an active community leader, most notably in helping to found Covington's common school system. By 1852, however, the Willson family uprooted itself yet again, relocating downriver at New Albany, Indiana, opposite Louisville, Kentucky. There, Willson's father recommenced his lumber business, which over the next several years blossomed into a prosperous enterprise.

Willson entered early adulthood experiencing both remarkable personal achievement and tragedy. He enrolled at Antioch College in Ohio in his mid-teens, and after a fruitful year of study under the guidance of Horace Mann, he moved on to Harvard College. By this time, Willson had dropped his first name and began introducing himself to colleagues and professors as Forceythe. But his halcyon days in the east came to an end in 1856, when he received word that his mother had died. Then, after completing only a few semesters at Harvard, he began to show signs of tuberculosis, which soon forced him to withdraw from the college without taking a degree. Although doctors had given him only a few months to live, obliging him to return home to Indiana, Willson there experienced a near-miraculous recovery.

About this time, Willson developed a profound and lasting preoccupation with spiritualism, which was presumably kindled by a "spiritual excitement" in New Albany in 1858. Even Willson's father, a steadfast Unitarian who was skeptical of "spiritual manifestations," was fascinated by this local phenomenon and began investigating spiritualism himself. Willson read voluminously over the next several months and developed his own theories of spiritualism; he believed that at times the dead communicated with the living. He declared himself a medium and for the rest of his life earnestly maintained that he possessed clairvoyant power. He was said to have been able to identify the contents of a sealed envelope and to enumerate personal characteristics of the sender simply by placing the piece of mail against his forehead. One particularly engaging story survives in which Willson supposedly accurately determined the contents of an official letter from Washington, D.C., that his father had received some years earlier. The letter was from John C. Calhoun.

Hiram Willson died in 1859, leaving his children a comfortable fortune. As the eldest, Willson assumed legal guardianship and the day-to-day care of two brothers and a sister. By this time, Willson had begun to write poems, which were occasionally published in the *Louisville Journal*. Soon after the outbreak of the Civil War, he drafted several editorials for the *Journal* in support of the Union cause in Kentucky. Although philosophically an abolitionist (his father believed that emancipation with compensation to slaveowners was the only viable option), Willson was curiously moderate in tone and opinion as an editorialist, in effect accepting Kentucky's neutrality. During these years, however, he composed several poems that betray a far less restrained attitude.

"In State" (LOA, 2: 364), begun with the start of the Civil War but not finished until a few years later, expresses Willson's unequivocal contempt for the southern cause. In the opening lines, a nameless representative of the human race makes an impassioned plea to a divine being to portend the outcome of the war:

> O Keeper of the Sacred Key,
> And the Great Seal of Destiny,
> Whose eye is the blue canopy,
> Look down upon the warring world, and tell us what
> the end will be.

The divine being's reply, which comprises all but the first and the last of 28 stanzas, envisions the world amid the bleakness of winter, as he gradually fixes his gaze on America:

> "Lo, through the wintry atmosphere,
> On the white bosom of the sphere,
> A cluster of five lakes appear;
> And all the land looks like a couch, or warrior's shield,
> or sheeted bier."

The divinity then reports that stretched out across the snow-covered country is the slain body of a mythically colossal woman. She is the personification of a unified America, and her death symbolizes the larger effect of the Civil War. A few lines later, other Giants (personifying various foreign nations) pass by and observe the ghastly sight with an air of detached pity: "The sceptred Giants come and go, / And shake their shadowy crowns and say: 'We always feared it would be so!'" "In State" thus refers both to the death of the Union and the literal funereal atmosphere of the country during the war.

In the second section, the divine being reveals that the dead woman was the mother of two warring sons, one of whom is guilty of matricide:

"And lo, the children which she bred,
And more than all else cherishéd,
To make them true in heart and head,
Stand face to face, as mortal foes, with their swords
    crossed above the dead.

"Each hath a mighty stroke and stride:
One true – the more that he is tried;
The other dark and evil-eyed; –
And by the hands of one of them, his own dear mother
    surely died!"

Despite the thin veil of ambiguity, the "true" brother clearly represents the Union forces and the "dark and evil-eyed" brother symbolizes the Confederacy. An overt condemnation of the southern cause and a dismal view of the nation's fate, "In State" is the grimmest of Willson's Civil War poems.

On January 1, 1863, Willson anonymously published "The Old Sergeant," his greatest popular success, in the *Louisville Journal* (under the heading "The Carrier's New Year's Address"). Willson was at first reluctant to admit authorship, perhaps because the poem was based on an actual event involving a New Albany doctor named Austin who had served as a Federal assistant surgeon at the battle of Shiloh. This was, after all, a time when personal privacy was honored among acquaintances, especially in print. In any case, with "The Old Sergeant" Willson again demonstrated his unyielding promotion of the Union cause. The poem depicts a melodramatic dialogue between a field surgeon and a wounded officer who recounts his vision of visiting heaven, where he beheld the Union flag waving high atop New Jerusalem's "mighty tower." Newspapers around the country soon reprinted the anonymous poem, and it quickly became a national sensation. Despite his original apprehensions, Willson eventually saw the poem privately printed and bound in a patriotic red, white, and blue cover. "The Old Sergeant" no doubt received its highest acclaim when Oliver Wendell **Holmes**, deeming it "one of the most impressive poems in our literature, – I should be inclined to say in any literature," included it in his famous lecture tour on the poetry of the Civil War during the mid-1860s.

In the autumn of 1863, Willson married Elizabeth Conwell Smith, whom he had met in New Albany the year before, while she was attending a local college. In early 1864, the couple moved to Cambridge, Massachusetts, mainly to care for Willson's younger brother at Harvard. Willson bought an old mansion across the street from James Russell **Lowell's** residence and soon became intimately acquainted with Boston's literati, visiting frequently with Lowell, Henry Wadsworth **Longfellow**, William Dean **Howells**, and the Holmeses. These renowned writers welcomed Willson into their exclusive circle and offered their encouragement. Holmes even contacted Ralph Waldo **Emerson** in hopes of arranging an introduction for Willson, describing him to the sage of Concord as a shy young poet "as strange as Hawthorne."

Tragically, Willson's wife died suddenly in the autumn of 1864, and over the next few years his belief in spiritualism intensified. He routinely told friends of long visitations by his father and his wife. Indeed, Howells recounts in *Literary Friends and Acquaintance* (1900) one of Willson's tales told to him by Lowell, "who thought it almost the best ghost story he had ever heard": "The spirit of Willson's father appeared to him and stood before him. Willson was accustomed to apparitions, and so he said simply, 'Won't you sit down father?' The phantom put out his hand to lay hold of a chair-back as some people do in taking a seat, and his shadowy arm passed through the frame-work. 'Ah!' he said, 'I forgot that I was not substance.'" Holmes, who also admired such anecdotes of spiritual encounters, based his novel *The Guardian Angel* (1867) on one of Willson's stories.

Willson, too, transformed his curious consciousness into literary art. "The Voice," a poem originally published in the *Atlantic Monthly*, depicts the sort of supernatural meeting that he often described to others:

"Where art thou, blessed spirit, where,
Whose voice is dew upon the air?
I looked around me and above,
And cried aloud, 'Where art thou, Love?
Oh let me see thy living eye
And clasp thy living hand, or die!'
Again upon the atmosphere
The self-same words fell, '*I am here!*'

'Here? Thou art here, Love?' – '*I am here!*'
The echo died upon my ear!
I looked around me everywhere,
But ah! there was no mortal there!"

Willson published *The Old Sergeant and Other Poems*, his only book of verse, in November 1866 (the official year of publication is 1867). This diverse collection reflects well his eclectic personality; it includes not only Civil War verse and accounts of supernatural encounters, but also several romantic-pastoral poems. These quaint, light-hearted pieces, somewhat imitative of Emerson and Edgar Allan **Poe**, typically depict a fantastic Arcadian experience in nature. In "The Estray" (LOA, 2: 362), for instance, Willson presents an exchange – at once comical and mystical – concerning the momentary appearance of a fairylike creature:

"Now tell me, my merry woodman,
    Why standest so aghast?"
"My lord! – 't was a beautiful creature
    That hath but just gone past!"

"A creature – what kind of a creature?"
    "Nay now, but I do not know!"
"Humph – what did it make you think of?"
    "The sunshine on the snow."

"I shall overtake my horse then:"
    The woodman opened his eye: –

The gold fell all around him,
    And a rainbow spanned the sky.

In a similar vein, "To Hersa" (LOA, 2: 362) demonstrates a Keatsian sensibility: essentially an ode on musical beauty, the poem well illustrates Willson's debt to a more purely aesthetic strain of early nineteenth-century romanticism.

In the autumn of 1866, Willson left Cambridge and returned to New Albany to attend to family business. While in Indiana he experienced a relapse of tuberculosis. By early December he had recovered well enough to visit his brother and sister in Alfred, New York, but his condition deteriorated rapidly, and he died in February 1867, at the age of 29. His friend John James **Piatt** provided a vast store of biographical information on Willson in a memorial published in the *Atlantic Monthly* in March 1875. Although Forceythe Willson never achieved the lasting success of many of his contemporaries, his work offers modern readers insights into the curious times and interests of his mid-nineteenth-century culture.

JOSEPH CSICSILA

Selected Work

The Old Sergeant and Other Poems, Boston: Ticknor and Fields, 1867

Further Reading

Howells, William Dean, *Literary Friends and Acquaintance*, New York and London: Harper & Brothers, 1900

Constance Fenimore Woolson

(1840–1894)

"If I had told you my verses were by somebody instead of a nobody, you would have found wonderful beauties in them," complains an aspiring poet to a critical friend in Woolson's story "St. Clair Flats" (1873). Woolson knew that fame could make a difference, for a great American actress had secured the reputation of one of her own poems. "I do not think much of my 'Kentucky Belle' [1873]," she wrote, "but Charlotte Cushman's reading made it, and now that one little ballad is better known than anything I have written." Still, "St. Clair's Flats" suggests that even "a nobody" can write poetry that will one day be recognized. "All the critics in the world can neither make nor crush a true poet," the friend reassures the striving author. Yet, despite Woolson's ability to place her poems regularly in the nation's top literary magazines, she was never sure if she was "a true poet." Eventually she stopped publishing poems and concentrated upon the short stories and novels for which she is best known today.

Born on March 5, 1840, in Claremont, New Hampshire, Woolson in many ways fits the "composite biography" of the nineteenth-century female poet described by Cheryl Walker. She was white, born in New England, especially attached to her father, and possessed of a precocious talent; middle-class and well educated for a woman, she decided early not to marry, remained single, and died at age 53 – probably by suicide – in Venice, Italy, on January 24, 1894. Like other American women who became poets, Woolson struggled against poor mental and physical health. Although devoted to vigorous exercise, rowing or walking daily in good weather, she suffered recurring depression, as well as a painful inner ear disorder and, finally, deafness. Also like other women poets, Woolson depended upon male friends and literary advisers to establish herself as a writer. Edmund Clarence **Stedman**, William Dean **Howells**, and Henry James, among others, became friends and admirers of her work. Unlike the female poets Walker discusses, however, Woolson did not benefit from working with other women on behalf of social causes and did not form close relationships with other women artists. Finally, she differed from these artists because she did not ultimately make her mark as a poet. Her fiction includes two volumes of short stories, *Castle Nowhere* (1875) and *Rodman the Keeper* (1880), the novella *For the Major* (1883), and four novels: *Anne* (1882), *East Angels* (1886), *Jupiter Lights* (1889), and *Horace Chase* (1894). Two collections, *The Front Yard, and Other Italian Stories* (1895) and *Dorothy, and Other Italian Stories* (1896), came out after her death. A travel book, *Mentone, Cairo, and Corfu* (1896), was also published posthumously.

By birth and family background, Woolson was all her life attached to the northeast. Her father was descended from an old New England family, and her mother, the niece of one of America's most famous writers, James Fenimore Cooper, kept close ties with Cooperstown, New York. Shortly after her birth, however, Woolson's parents decided to move west after scarlet fever had devastated their young family. Three of her older sisters died when she was only three weeks old. She grew up in Cleveland, Ohio, then a frontier city. The Old Northwest

Territory, including upper Michigan and Mackinac Island, where her family vacationed, inspired her early verse and fiction. Her first effort, which seems not to have survived, was a poem in imitation of Henry Wadsworth **Longfellow's** *The Song of Hiawatha*. In 1870, she made her literary debut, publishing travel sketches in the *Cleveland Morning Herald*, which was owned by her sister's father-in-law. Her first published poem, the memorial tribute "Charles Dickens, Christmas, 1870," appeared in *Harper's Bazaar*.

Although now remembered as a writer of "local color" sketches and associated with the development of realism, in the first seven years of her career Woolson published as many poems as travel pieces and short stories. By 1877, she had in print 45 of the 60-odd poems now extant, and major magazines such as the *Atlantic Monthly, Galaxy,* and *Appleton's Journal* featured her poems. The long poem *Two Women. 1862*, a dramatic dialogue between a southern and a northern woman, was published serially in *Appleton's*; it then came out as a separate volume in 1877. However, many unpublished poems survive only because her niece, Clare Benedict, reprinted them in a memorial volume in 1930. We can be reasonably sure that many of these poems belong to the same decade of her greatest poetic output; "In Memoriam. G. S. B.," for example, was probably composed in 1871–72, not long after her sister's husband died in a train accident.

The majority of her poems were written during her mother's lifetime. Possibly the last poem that Woolson ever wrote is "Mentone" (1884), which was likely composed about six months after her mother's death in 1879. Woolson had left Florida for Europe, hoping that travel would combat the severe depression that was caused by this loss. In "Mentone," the speaker finds comfort on "this sunny shore," an evocation of the French Riviera that Woolson visited in 1880, but also a metaphor for life's transient joys. If God grants us only "a little space for love," it is also only "a little space to wait":

> Upon this sunny shore
> A little space to wait; the life-bowl broken,
> The silver cord unloosed . . .
> . . . .
> The hour is Thine, dear Lord; we ask no more,
> But wait Thy summons on the sunny shore.

Woolson's father had died 10 years before her mother, in 1869, making it more of a necessity than a luxury that she, as a middle-class woman, achieve a successful literary career; it may also be that his dying freed her to pursue an uncommon literary ambition. But the loss of her mother seems to have had the opposite effect – a severely disabling one – upon her poetry. However, Woolson may have abandoned poetry for more prosaic reasons; her fiction not only began to win acclaim, but also to sell. Whatever the reason, the poems that once came spontaneously seem to have ceased around 1880.

Like "Mentone," most of Woolson's poems have a direct connection to a place that she visited or lived in; her early poems invoke the Old Northwest and Ohio, and many later poems pay tribute to the American south, where Woolson so-journed with her widowed mother for six years. Mother and daughter made St. Augustine, Florida, their home base, but they traveled widely in the south. In Florida, the poet and critic Stedman befriended Woolson, and Paul Hamilton **Hayne**, the well-known southern poet, wrote to her to introduce himself; he praised her poems as "full of 'grit,' vigor, and almost manly verve." It was to Hayne that Woolson confessed in a letter, "I have not yet decided whether I can write verses or not. . . . Such as they are they come of themselves without the slightest effort; whereas my prose is always the result of long and careful thought" (Jay B. Hubbell, *New England Quarterly* 14 [1941]).

Woolson never consented to having her poems collected; while in Europe, she was approached by Appleton's and Harper's, but she declined "to allow the collection of all my scattered verses in a volume." In the same letter to her nephew, March 31, [1887?], she goes on to explain: "'Cora' having stolen 'K. Belle,' I doubt whether a re-issue on my part would be wise." This may refer to Cushman's having appropriated "Kentucky Belle" as one of her most frequently performed pieces, and Woolson's desire not to appear to "upstage" the memory of the actress, who had died in 1876. But there may be another reason; always uncertain about the ultimate value of her poetry, Woolson may have decided that it was best not to gather her "scattered verses." Her decision makes it difficult for contemporary students to read her poetry. Although Benedict republished quite a few of Woolson's poems, others are available only in nineteenth-century periodicals and newspapers. Those in *The Old Stone House* (1873), Woolson's first book, a prize-winning children's story about five cousins, which includes nonsense verse, are also not readily available because the volume has become a rare book.

The three Woolson poems in the Library of America anthology – "Love Unexpressed," "The Florida Beach," and "Detroit River" (LOA, 2: 393–396) – belong to her early career and are representative of her lyric voice. Walker argues that nineteenth-century women's poetry is "peculiarly autobiographical" because, like Philomela in the myth, these women writers wanted to convey female pain and desire in a culture that idealized women's silence: such "messages, for all they come veiled and 'slant,' are part of these poets' aims." Even by these standards of indirection, however, Woolson's poetic voice is peculiarly *un*autobiographical – even when she is writing about places rich in personal associations. In an age when the "woman question" was widely debated, Woolson's poetry typically addresses women's lives only in oblique ways. In a posthumously published poem, "Alas," "the wise" advise "the timid poet" that

> . . . "all the burning
> of thy inmost altar-fires
> Sing in glowing, cadenced verse;
> To the world's hot eager ear
> All thy deepest love rehearse."

But the poet answers, "But my heart I cannot / Share with all the world. Alas! Alas!" If this is meant to be a confession of Woolson's own reservations about baring her soul in verse, she blunts its force by turning it into a stiff allegory. Although the poem may imply a female subjectivity in the "timid" poet, its careful suppression of all marks of gender robs the poem of its power to protest, and reluctance to reveal the self seems reduced to a personality flaw. Rather than use the lyric form to confess private feelings, Woolson often chooses to project more personal emotions into characters who speak in dramatic monologues. The majority of Woolson's nondramatic poems mute the lyric "I" and foreground instead specific places or landscapes.

"The Florida Beach" appeared in *Galaxy* in October 1874, a year after her first trip to the south. "Love Unexpressed" (*Appleton's Journal*, March 9, 1872) and "Detroit River" were probably both written in 1872. "Detroit River," published posthumously, strongly echoes her travel sketch "American Cities. – Detroit," the lead article for *Appleton's Journal* (July 27, 1872). It seems to have been her usual practice to write poems on the spot, while her impressions were fresh. "The Detroit is one of the most beautiful rivers in America," Woolson declares in her sketch, adding that "it always looks brimful and ready to overflow its green banks." Similarly, the opening stanza of "Detroit River" creates an image of a "brimming river": "E'en one drop more, thou must o'erflow / The velvet land. . . ." The writer was also proud of the city's "claims to antiquity," noting that "the site was first visited by the French 10 years before the Puritans landed on Plymouth Rock." The poem evokes the French conquest of Native North America, which is now remembered only in place names:

> Insouciant French! your fathers sailed
> These Lakes as Kings; – but now their claims
> From Gaspé Bay to far La Pointe,
> Live only in the Gallic names.

Despite the impassioned closing address – "But haste not, river; – stay where I / Love thee, remember thee, evermore" – the lyric "I" remains oddly impersonal. As in many of her lyric poems, Woolson creates a voice that is stripped of anything that would locate it in a female body or a private history. By choosing an impersonal voice to speak of personal attachments, she is sometimes able to gain a disquieting power, as in "Love Unexpressed" (discussed below). Yet this strategy risks eviscerating the lyric.

Woolson wrote few lyrics about love, and most of them are more concerned with being blocked from feeling than with feeling passionately. She writes about love from a safe distance; it is always in the past, or in some hazy future. For example, both "We Shall Meet Them Again" and "The Haunting Face" (1873) take for their subject the past possibility of love, those "we might have loved." "Memory" (1873) appeals to the man or the woman who remembers, "'Once I was loved.'" Yet the speaker seems to draw sustenance from what could have been rather than to regret some actual loss:

> The weary heart would soon lie down and die
> Of its own sin and sorrow
> Could it not from this treasured memory
> Ever new courage borrow.

On such scanty evidence some critics have suggested that Woolson fell unhappily in love in her youth, but outside of an infatuation with a childhood friend who became a soldier in the Civil War, there does not seem to have been any love interest in Woolson's life. Her avoidance of intimacy may be more plausibly traced to childhood than to thwarted romantic love. Speculating that Woolson may have been haunted by a survivor's guilt – she was born in the wake of death and became the eldest child when three more of her sisters died, one shortly after marriage and the other in childbirth – Joan Myers Weimer suggests that she "came to associate marriage and childbearing with death" and, therefore, "avoided intimacy with men, whose love seemed to kill, or with women, who died and left her."

Cheryl B. Torsney suggests that Woolson's desire to pursue literature rather than marriage was also shaped by her being born into a transitional generation of American women – a "lost generation" who resisted the domesticity and self-sacrifice that determined their mothers' lives, but who nevertheless remained loyal to these values and unable to embrace the female independence that the "New Women" writers (e.g., Kate Chopin and Charlotte Perkins Gilman) championed at the turn of the century. Never truly settling anywhere but always longing for a real home in Florida, Woolson – Torsney argues – presaged "the rootlessness and the alienation thematized in modern literature rather than the ethos of women's community." As a professional writer, alone and often far from family, as well as under financial pressure, Woolson coped with conditions new to American women; the strain is evident, Torsney reminds us, in this generation in which female suicide first becomes a trend. Torsney argues that Woolson's marked copy of *The Teaching of Epictetus* provides strong evidence that she believed suicide was justified for those who were no longer able to lead a full and healthy life. Weimer agrees that there is a good reason to think that Woolson chose to jump to her death from a second-floor window in Venice when she was very ill. Based upon her study of eyewitness accounts of Woolson's symptoms, Weimer believes that she was suffering from "one of three things: gallstones, pancreatitis, or an intestinal blockage – all excruciating, all difficult to treat in the nineteenth-century, and all potentially fatal." She adds, "By jumping, she may have been saving herself from a prolonged agonizing death" (letter to author, August 4, 1993).

If Woolson did choose to take her own life, the choice was in keeping with the independence that characterized her life. Even Woolson's last letters to friends and family testify to her zest for new places and people, her wit, and what her niece called her "powers of enjoyment." To Woolson and many women of her generation, a literary career meant giving up the security of marriage, but for her the stresses of life as a woman artist still seem to have been preferable to the pitfalls of a Victorian marriage.

Woolson's "love" poems suggest her complex reactions to the demands of intimacy. In "Love Unexpressed," she comes closest to confronting the pain of suppressing feeling: the poem develops an image of a numb army, marching to the same "dreary music / Upon the self-same strains," but "Each longing, sighing, for the heavenly music / He never hears." Here, as elsewhere, the poet could just as easily be speaking about filial as about romantic love; nothing in the poem definitively establishes the gender of the speaker, although its central image – a plodding army – is drawn from the masculine sphere. Not a typical lover's lament, the poem treats the subject of withholding words of comfort, love, and praise in intimate relationships. The predicament that the poem poignantly elaborates is

that we are unable to break out of our isolation – to give what we ourselves most want to receive: "We shrink within ourselves in voiceless sorrow, / Leaving the words unsaid." The broken couplets seem to resolve this emotional double bind too neatly in the conventional consolation of the final lines:

> The only difference of the love in heaven
> > From love on earth below
> Is: Here we love and know not how to tell it,
> > And there we all shall know.

Yet the emphasis throughout on the "love on earth below" is in keeping with Woolson's preoccupation with the world. In this poem, as in her other poems that allude to a better hereafter, heaven is distant, and earthly suffering not easily dismissed. Like other Victorians, Woolson did not seriously doubt God's existence; at the same time, however, she did not see religious faith as solving the perplexities of human relations.

Woolson's Episcopalian orthodoxy gives way in her poetry to the belief that God is to be found in nature, a belief shared by two of her favorite American writers, Ralph Waldo **Emerson** and Henry David **Thoreau**, and one that had become a commonplace in American poetry by 1870. Poems such as "The Herald's Cry" (1872), "Two Ways" (1873), and "Indian Summer" (1874) connect the Christian God with the rebirth of nature. In "Two Ways," the embodiment of godhead, explicitly associated with the repeated line "The spring returneth ever," resembles Pan more than Christ. It is nature's seasonal renewal, not Christian doctrine, that inspires the persona to believe that "Even my dead are living and are glad / in some far spring!" In "The Herald's Cry," another poem performed by Cushman, Christ appears as a kind of New Year's knight.

But Woolson's most deeply felt lyrical poems are not her allegories of Christianity or of the seasons such as " The Herald's Cry," "October's Song" (1872), "February" (1873), and "March" (1873); rather, they are those poems that evoke particular landscapes such as "Mentone." "Pine-Barrens" (1874), for example, recalls the wild Florida Pine country where time and distance are erased in a landscape made of sky and trees. The poem concludes: "How little seem earth's sorrows, how far off the lost to-morrows, / How broad and free the Barrens lie, how very near to God!"

"The Florida Beach," one of Woolson's most striking poems, recreates a similarly distinctive landscape. But the mood has less to do with being near to God than to nature. Here is the ancient and mysterious beauty of the New World before it was discovered: wild ducks who "have not yet learned to fear" and mockingbirds who sing "in the low palmetto near." The beauty of the alligator and that of the dolphin are conjoined in this almost primeval landscape. The Florida beach becomes a magical crossroads where time operates differently; the poet imagines that she can "call across to Africa" and that the waves bring back an answer of "Antony! Antony!" On the edge of the "silvery" beach, the ancient world of Cleopatra's Nile does not seem distant, although the everyday "world is far away." Ships "that pass far out at sea" from Cuba and "tropic Carribee" have been sailing past the Spanish lighthouse for centuries, yet the Florida beach is curiously cut off from this workaday traffic since the ships are not visible from shore, and to those at sea the beach is marked only by a "distant gleam."

Weimer identifies the woman writer with the lighthouse

keeper in the poem, who is "visible, even essential, to an audience she cannot see from her position where land meets sea at the margins of culture." Walker might interpret this poem as a "sanctuary poem," common among nineteenth-century women who longed for a "private realm protected from incursions from the outside world." Yet what is most noteworthy in this poem, as in Woolson's other poetry, is the deliberate erasing of the poet's gender. Unlike women poets who enshrined the home as a female sanctuary, or who sought retreat in nature from a violent world, Woolson speaks in the name of a gender-inclusive "we," we humans who have built "our" driftwood fire on this hazy beach: "Ah, Destiny! Why must we ever go / Away from the Florida beach?" Moreover, the two distinct human figures here seem to be male: the lighthouse keeper and the "poet" who "called to Spain," possibly a reference to "The Secret of the Sea" (1850) by Longfellow. On the other hand, the poet speaks for "us," perhaps a group exploring Florida, but certainly an imagined group of readers, who will respond to the desire to linger on the beach. Men such as the keeper who "trims his light" bear the burdens of civilization. The poet, however, speaks for the rest of "us," who have the time to listen to what the waves say, yet understand that destiny, the drive to act in the world, must take us away from a more satisfying and immediate connection with the earth.

The achievement of Woolson's poem is that although it represents a magically beautiful and primordial place, a place where one can, for a moment, simply be, this place is not a site of sentimentalized innocence. The waves call to mind Eros – Antony and Cleopatra – while the seascape teems with strange sea life that is wholly apart from human passions. The "glass-like creatures that ride the waves / With azure sail and oar" are only humanized through a whimsical metaphor; the effect of the comparison is to make them more strange, somehow both boat and sailor at once. These and the other "wide-mouthed things from the deep sea caves / That melt away on the shore" remind us rather of human limits: their existence is beyond our ken. The birds, "who fly low, / As if to catch our speech," do not signal the dream of recapturing paradise where once humans and animals communicated in perfect harmony: the poet knows better. Instead, the poem recreates a space for meditation and dreams – the "as if" that is so necessary to humans but sets us apart from other creatures. Perhaps the poem's only comment upon being female is this: it conjures up a place where gender, for once, is not so terribly important.

The strategy of erasing gender by submerging the personal in the public "we" appears in Woolson's fiction as well as in her poetry. When a nineteenth-century female poet adopts this neutral tone of public address, it may be a means of claiming a wider literary territory, of attempting to speak for the culture, as a Longfellow or a William Cullen **Bryant** might. Yet a number of Woolson's poems overtly focus upon women. But even these poems bear witness to Woolson's avoidance of a literary voice marked as female. When a woman writer attempts to shed the particulars of her gender in the service of the "universal," however, she risks appearing to sanction the culture's misogyny. An early poem, "Commonplace" (1873), illustrates the problem. This poem, a dramatic monologue by a father in defense of his daughter, begins, "My little girl is commonplace, you say?" Yet the defense he offers is a strange one. A would-be writer himself, he appears to be admonishing a young man who finds his daughter too ordinary in her tastes and aspirations. He argues that it is better that she cannot appreciate works of daring souls:

> Then as to pictures, if her taste prefers
> That common picture of the "Huguenots,"
> Where the girl's heart – a tender heart like hers –
> Strives to defeat earth's greatest powers' great plots
> With her poor little kerchief, shall I change
> The print for Turner's riddles wild and strange?
> Or take her stories – simple tales which her leisure
>   hours beguile –
> And give her Browning's *Sordello*, a Herbert Spencer, a
>   Carlyle?

The poem seems to approve an old-fashioned view that a woman is "fitted for her present sphere" when she does not challenge her mind artistically and intellectually, but "prays on with faith half ignorant, half sublime." But the effect of a woman writer's assuming the persona of the father – moreover, a woman who has clearly read Robert Browning closely – creates the impression of ventriloquism and ironically points to the opposite conclusion: arrogant men are deciding what is proper for their daughters to know. It is hard to locate the female author's position in such a poem.

Some of Woolson's poems are openly critical of women. Like the "cherubic creatures" whose "dimity convictions" Emily **Dickinson** mocks, Woolson's targets in "The Greatest of All is Charity" (1873) are middle-class women who shut out poor women and prostitutes: "Your pitiless scorn keeps her back from your door, / Your pitiless hand keeps her down evermore, / Though the Saviour himself said, 'Go, sin no more' – ." Another poem in a more lighthearted mode, "An Intercepted Letter" (1878), adopts the persona of a well-to-do young woman visiting a fashionable resort. Not impressed by young men showing off their bodies in "bathing" costumes ("e'en the handsomest resemble / Swimming *dogs*"), the letter writer also satirizes the pretensions of women who try for the "close to nature" look, quoting mystic verses and trailing about the beach in "oriental" wraps and "simple knots of daisies." The greatest ridicule, however, is reserved for women such as "Mrs. Flodden-Tompkyns," who holds forth that "We human birds" must also make migrations "and throw ourselves on Mother Nature's Tawny breast." Upper-class female effusions over nature Woolson finds especially ludicrous. And other poems disturbingly register how deeply ingrained is misogyny, even within a highly self-conscious female poet. In "On a Homely Woman, Dead" (1876), the poet works on the premise that it is tragic for a woman to be born ugly.

Even the poem Woolson contributed to *The New Century for Woman* (May 20, 1876), a newspaper published by the Women's Centennial Committee at the International Exhibition in Philadelphia, Pennsylvania, displays the complexity of her attitudes toward women, especially women who write. Much as a male poet might, Woolson celebrates women by elevating one woman to a greatness that appears to transcend gender. Yet her sonnet to George Eliot also records her desire for solidarity with other women artists:

> O wondrous woman! shaping with thy pen
> As Michael Angelo did shape from stone,

Colossal forms of clear-cut outline, when
We dwell upon thy pages, not alone
The beauty of thy rose, we see, as finely traced
As roses drawn by other woman-hands
Who spend their lives in shaping them, but faced
We find ourselves with giant's work, that stands
Above us as a mountain lifts its brow,
Grand, unapproachable, yet clear in view
To lowliest eyes that upward look. O, how
Hast thou shed radiance as thy finger drew
Its shapes! A myriad women light have seen,
And courage taken, because *thou* hast been!

More a phenomenon – a giant, a mountain – than a literary sister, Eliot both inspires and forbids the approach of other women artists. Significantly, the only artist Woolson sees fit to compare her to is Michelangelo, a figure of masculine genius whose greatness, like William Shakespeare's, is incontestable. In the presence of Eliot's grand work, female artists are reduced to faceless, nameless hands; Eliot is able not only to trace roses (an image of female art), but also to create the "colossal forms" of great male artists. Woolson's most feminist poem, then, is characteristically double-edged: it celebrates a woman writer at the expense of other women, although it also asserts that women can equal the greatest achievements of men. Yet what is the relation between the female writer and the subject of this sonnet: is the writer herself another lowly, faceless woman unable to rise, or is she, like Eliot, capable of reaching the pinnacle? That a possible answer to this dilemma – founding an aesthetic upon a collective female identity – is only half recognized in the closing image of "myriad women" taking light and courage from other women should not make us judge Woolson too harshly. Very few women (or men) in the nineteenth century were able to suggest that the standards by which art was measured might be warped by male bias, a subject Woolson takes up later in a remarkable short story, "Miss Grief" (1880), which was reprinted in *Women Artists, Women Exiles.*

Woolson identified with women who aspired to produce lasting work, even if it offended conventional morality. Praising Eliot's *Adam Bede* to a close female friend, Woolson wrote, "Would you like to have a friend of yours the author of such a story? Dealing with such subjects? And yet it was a great book." She concluded, "I would rather be strong than beautiful, or even good, provided the 'good' must be dull." The majority of her poems, however, do not challenge traditional morality. For her most daring work, she seems to have needed the narrative distance between creator and character that is more typical of fiction than of lyric poetry. Not surprisingly, many poems take the form of dramatic monologues, often put in the mouth of characters remote from the poet's own life, such as the ex-Confederate soldier, the Ohio farm wife, or the father whose child is trapped in a fire. Some of these are among her most effective poems, but some are among her worst.

"Tom" (1876), according to John Dwight Kern, used to be a popular choice for declamation. Although one can see why the family dog's rescue of Robin from the fire would make good schoolroom melodrama, now it appears trite. "A Fire in the Forest" (1875) and "On the Border" (1876) both exploit sensational rescues, but the latter is offensive to modern tastes in its caricature of "Injuns." Still, the power of poems like "Tom" lies in Woolson's knack for creating a colloquial voice that tells a dramatic story – something Charlotte Cushman capitalized on when she used Woolson's poems as scripts for her readings. In "At the Smithy. (Pickens County, South Carolina, 1874)" (1874), an old man shoeing a Yankee's horse relates how all of his sons were killed in the war. "'Only the Brakesman'" (1876) dramatizes the shock of a working-class mother who learns that her only son has been killed in an accident. Cushman's favorite, "Kentucky Belle," features a farm wife, born in Tennessee, but living in Ohio during the Civil War. Although married to a Union man, she gives away her prized horse, "Kentucky Belle," to save the life of southern boy riding with Morgan's Raiders:

When Conrad came in the evening, the moon was
    shining high,
Baby and I were both crying, I couldn't tell him why!
But a battered suit of rebel grey was hanging against the
    wall,
And a thin old horse with drooping head stood in
    Kentucky's stall.

Woolson's most ambitious dramatic poem, *Two Women. 1862,* a long dialogue first published anonymously, also takes place during the border warfare of 1862. The poem centers on a confrontation between a northern "maiden" and a southern "lady" who turn out to be seeking the same wounded soldier. Strikingly, the poem reverses the stereotypical situation of the passionate, dark-haired woman – here, the southerner – losing out to the pure, fair-haired one: it is the name of the beautiful southerner, Helena, that the dying man speaks. Ironically, the northern girl – who comes off as an inexperienced prig – never learns this fact. Instead, she holds fast to her belief that "Willie" remained true to her. Although Helena in the end chooses not to disillusion her, at first she is furious when she realizes the girl sees her as an evil temptress:

    "Oh, the small,
Most small foundation for a vast conceit!
Is it a merit that you never learned
But one side of this life? . . .
    You never yearned
For freedom, born a slave! You never felt
The thrill of rapture, the wild ecstasy
Of mere existence that strong natures know . . ."

Although the dialogue is sometimes overblown, Woolson brings to life the tense encounter between the worldly young widow with a taste for horse racing and plays and the scandalized girl, who inwardly criticizes her opponent as "too brown." Although the author sides with passion, she portrays sympathetically the way in which fear and narcissism contend with better feelings in the girl's breast, as she prays for her rival in love, "Change her, Lord – make her good!" Her self-righteousness, however, proves chilling: unlike Helena, she would not wish to bring Willie back to life, certain that he is in a better place. This brand of piety, Woolson suggests, is self-deluded and self-serving. Helena's wild grief is proof of love; she rages at God, "who makes us at his will, and gives us hearts / Only to rend them in a hundred parts." Yet she bows in the end to God and convention; true to her dead love, she never marries and looks forward to their reunion in heaven. The "maiden," how-ever, soon marries. Ironically, their tug-of-war is not quite re-solved: the maiden also plans to rejoin Willie in heaven.

In a late story by Woolson, "At the Château of Corinne" (1887), a man severely criticizes a woman's poetry: "Its rhythm was crude and unmelodious; its coloring exaggerated." He ex-plains, "We do not expect great poems from women any more than we expect great pictures"; nevertheless, he objects to women's daring to try: "Thinking to soar, she invariably de-scends." In this scene, Woolson may be playing out her own harsh judgments of her early poems. But what she also drama-tizes here is the age's virulent prejudice against women writers. Literary genius was believed rare, if not impossible, in women (as Nina Baym and others have shown), and should a woman dare to follow her genius, Woolson speculates in "Miss Grief," her work would be judged as fatally flawed, somehow lacking. Despite the marks of genius that the male writer in that story discovers in an older woman's work, he also sees it as full of "barbarous shortcomings" that he fancies he can fix. That Woolson all too accurately diagnosed the mentality that she and other nineteenth-century women artists faced is suggested by the case of Emily Dickinson. Although her genius was even-tually recognized, her poetry, too, was first viewed as flawed and in such need of help that editors often freely tampered with her words.

Unlike Dickinson's, however, most of Woolson's poetry re-mains conventional, lacking the originality, subtlety, and dar-ing of her fiction. Her fiction explores such themes as violence against women, genteel hypocrisies, and female desire. Perhaps fiction freed her because she saw it as a genre that was more suited to telling other people's stories, rather than her own. Fic-tion thus may have appealed to her because it allowed her more scope than poetry to circumvent the age's gender expec-tations. Or, perhaps, as Joan Weimer has suggested, her poetry was "somehow written *for* her mother," and therefore her mother's death "meant the end of thinking and feeling in ap-proved ways" (letter to author, August 4, 1993). In any case, Woolson did not trust herself very much as a poet, and most of the time she chose standard subjects for poems. Like other American poets of her time, she observes nature closely in po-ems like "Cornfields" (1872), "Lake Erie in September"

(1872), and "Yellow Jessamine" (1874). Two unpublished po-ems, "Ferns" and "Fern Fragments," recently discovered by Torsney at Rollins College, show her devotion to botany (as in the rain forest of today, America's plant species were still being collected and identified in Woolson's time). Her poetry, too, re-veals a current of national pride; poems like "Gettysburg. 1876" and "Morris Island" (1876) memorialize American bat-tle scenes. And she shares with other Victorian poets a taste for the playful, which is evident even in a melancholy poem like "'Gentlemen Waife,'" which was written on the death of her pet dog. Despite its frequent conventionality, Woolson's poetry provides us with an uncommon record of a nineteenth-century woman writer in search of literary authority and power.

CAROLINE GEBHARD

Selected Work

Benedict, Clare, ed., *Five Generations (1785–1923)*, 3 vols., London: Ellis, 1930, 1932.

Further Reading

Kern, John D., *Constance Fenimore Woolson: Literary Pioneer*, Philadelphia: University of Pennsylvania Press, 1934

Moore, Rayburn S., *Constance Fenimore Woolson*, New York: Twayne, 1963

Torsney, Cheryl B., *Constance Fenimore Woolson: The Grief of Artistry*, Athens: University of Georgia Press, 1989

———, ed., *Critical Essays on Constance Fenimore Woolson*, New York: G. K. Hall, 1992

Walker, Cheryl, *American Women Poets of the Nineteenth Century: An Anthology*, New Brunswick, New Jersey: Rutgers University Press, 1992

———, *The Nightingale's Burden: Women Poets and American Culture Before 1900*, Bloomington: Indiana University Press, 1982

Weimer, Joan Myers, *Back Talk: Teaching Lost Selves to Speak*, New York: Random House, 1994

———, ed., *Women Artists, Women Exiles: "Miss Grief" and Other Stories*, New Brunswick, New Jersey: Rutgers University Press, 1988

NOTES ON CONTRIBUTORS

Aiken, David. Assistant Professor, Department of English, Charleston Southern University, South Carolina. Author of *Fire in the Cradle: A Literary History of Charleston* (1998). Editor of William Gilmore Simms's *The Golden Christmas* (1995) and *The Cassique of Kiawah* (1989). Contributor to *Southern Writers at Century's End* edited by James A. Perkins and Jeffrey Folks (1997), *Bibliography of American Fiction Through 1865* edited by Kent P. Ljungquist (1994), and to the journals *Arizona Quarterly, Thought, Mississippi Quarterly, The Simms Review, South Carolina Review, Habersham Review,* and *Southern Quarterly*. **Essay:** Dickson.

Barrett, Laura. Postdoctoral Fellow, Department of English, State University of New York, Stony Brook. Contributor to *Studies in the Novel* and *Western American Literature*. **Essay:** Charles Timothy Brooks.

Beach, Christopher. Assistant Professor, Department of English, University of California, Irvine. Author of *ABC of Influence: Ezra Pound and the Remaking of American Poetic Tradition* (1992) and *The Politics of Distinction: Whitman and the Discourses of Nineteenth-Century America* (1996). Editor of *Artifice and Indeterminacy: An Anthology of Contemporary Avant-Garde Poetics* (1998). **Essay:** Whittier.

Bennett, Paula Bernat. Associate Professor, Department of English, Southern Illinois University, Carbondale. Author of *My Life A Loaded Gun: Dickinson, Plath, Rich and Female Creativity* (1986) and *Emily Dickinson: Woman Poet* (1990). Editor of *Nineteenth-Century American Women Poets: An Anthology* (1997) and *Solitary Pleasures: The Literary, Historical and Artistic Discourses of Autoeroticism* (with Vernon Rosario II, 1995). Contributor to *Lesbian Texts and Contexts: Radical Re-Visions* edited by Karla Jay and Joanne Glasgow (1990), *Sexual Practice, Textual Theory: Lesbian Cultural Criticism* edited by Julia Penelope and Susan Wolfe (1993), and *Periodical Literature in Nineteenth-Century America* edited by Kenneth M. Price and Susan Belasco Smith (1995), and to the journals *Legacy, Signs, American Literary History,* and *PMLA*. **Essay:** John James Piatt and Sarah Morgan Bryan Piatt.

Birns, Nicholas. Member of the Faculty, New School for Social Research, New York. Book review editor of *Antipodes* and editor of *Powys Notes*. Contributor to *Arizona Quarterly, CLIO, Studies in Romanticism,* and *New York Times Book Review*. **Essays:** Halleck, Pierpont.

Boren, Lynda S. Independent Scholar, New Llano, Louisiana. Author of *Eurydice Reclaimed: Language, Gender, and Voice in Henry James* (1989). Coeditor of *Kate Chopin Reconsidered: Beyond the Bayou* (with Sara deSaussure Davis, 1992). Contributor to *American Studies, Mosaic, Centennial Review,* and *Dictionary of Literary Biography*. **Essay:** Blood.

Boyd, Melba Joyce. Chair, Department of Africana Studies, Wayne State University, Detroit, Michigan. Author of *Cat Eyes and Dead Wood* (1978), *Song for Maya* (1983), *Thirteen Frozen Flamingos* (1984), *The Inventory of Black Roses* (1989), *Letters to Che* (1996), and *Discarded Legacy: Politics and Po-*

etics in the Life of Frances E. W. Harper (1994). Writer, director, producer of the documentary *The Black Unicorn: Dudley Randall and Broadside Press* (1995). **Essay:** Harper.

Bray, Paul. Instructor, Santa Fe Community College, New Mexico. Contributor to *Raritan* and *Review of Contemporary Fiction*. **Essay:** Bryant.

Brodie, Mark P. Graduate Student, Department of English, Clemson University, South Carolina. Author of *Courting Disaster* (1998). **Essay:** Kemble.

Cantalupo, Barbara. Associate Professor, Department of English, Pennsylvania State University, Allentown Campus, Fogelsville. Editor of *Poe Studies Newsletter*. Contributor to *Companion to Poe Studies* edited by Eric Carlson (1996), *Jewish American Women Writers* edited by Ann Shapiro (1994), and to the journals *Poe Studies, ATQ, Studies in Jewish American Literature, Bestia, New Orleans Review,* and *Journal of Contemporary Thought*. **Essay:** Chivers.

Cooper, Allene. Lecturer, Arizona State University, Tempe. Contributor to *American Periodicals, Studies in Short Fiction,* and *Studies in American Humor*. **Essay:** Harte.

Crain, Patricia. Assistant Professor, English Department, Princeton University. Author of *The Story of A: The Poetics of Alphabetization in America* (forthcoming). **Essays:** Hawthorne, Sigourney.

Crisman, William. Associate Professor of English, Comparative Literature, and German, Pennsylvania State University, Altoona College. Author of *The Crises of "Language and Dead Signs" in Ludwig Tieck's Prose Fiction* (1997). Contributor to *The Romantic Movement: A Selective and Critical Bibliography* edited by David Erdman (1980–), *Subversive Sublimities: Undercurrents of German Enlightenment* edited by Eitel Timm (1992), *Encyclopedia of Romanticism: Culture in Britain, 1780s to 1830s* edited by Laura Dabundo (1992), and the journals *Studies in Romanticism, Journal of English and Germanic Philology, Keats-Shelley Journal, Wordsworth Circle, Studies in American Fiction, ATQ, Modern Language Quarterly, English Language Notes, Colloquia Germanica,* and *English Literary History*. **Essay:** Percival.

Csicsila, Joseph. Visiting Lecturer, Department of English, Eastern Michigan University, Ypsilanti. Contributor to *American Literary Realism, Studies in American Humor, Essays in Arts and Sciences, Critical Matrix: The Princeton Journal of Women, Gender, and Culture, Faulkner Journal,* and *David Mamet Review*. **Essay:** Willson.

Deese, Helen R. Professor of English, Tennessee Technological University, Cookeville. Editor of *Jones Very: The Complete Poems* (1993). Contributor to *Emersonian Circles: Essays in Honor of Joel Myerson* edited by Wesley T. Mott and Robert Burkholder (1996) and to the journals *American Literature, Harvard Library Bulletin, Studies in the American Renaissance, Documentary Editing,* and *ESQ*. **Essay:** Very.

DeFoe, Gerard. Ph.D. Candidate, Department of English, State University of New York at Stony Brook. **Essay:** Merrill.

Dock, Julie Bates. Independent Scholar, Torrance, California. Editor of *Charlotte Perkins Gilman's "The Yellow Wall-paper" and the History of Its Publication and Reception* (1998) and *The Press of Ideas: Readings for Writers on Print Culture and the Information Age* (1996). Contributor to *American Playwrights, 1880–1945* edited by William W. Demastes (1995) and to the journal *PMLA*. **Essay:** Howells.

Donahue, Joseph. Instructor, Department of English, University of Washington, Seattle. Coeditor of *Primary Trouble: An Anthology of Contemporary American Poetry* (with Leonard Schwartz and Edward Halsey Foster, 1976). **Essay:** Fenollosa.

Eppard, Philip B. Dean and Associate Professor, School of Information Science and Policy, University at Albany, State University of New York. Editor of *The American Archivist*. Coauthor of *Epitome of Bibliography of American Literature* (with Michael Winship and Rachel Howarth, 1995), *Bibliography of American Literature: A Selective Index* (with Michael Winship and Rachel Howarth, 1995), and *A Guide to the Atlantic Monthly Contributor's Club* (with George Monteiro, 1983). Editor of *Critical Essays on John O'Hara* (1994) and *First Printings of American Authors*, vol. 5 (1987). Contributor to *Bibliography of American Fiction 1866–1918* edited by James Nagel and Gwen L. Nagel (1993), *Bibliography of American Fiction 1919–1988* edited by Matthew J. Bruccoli and Judith S. Baughman (1991), *Critical Essays on Sarah Orne Jewett* edited by Gwen L. Nagel (1984), *American Women Writers: Bibliographical Essays* edited by Maurice Duke, Jackson R. Bryer, and M. Thomas Inge (1983), and *American Writers in Paris, 1920–1939* edited by Karen Rood (1980), and to the journals *American Literary Realism*, *Colby Quarterly*, *Documentary Editing*, *Resources for American Literary Study*, *Papers of the Bibliographical Society of America*, *Journal of Library History*, and *American Literature*. **Essay:** Hay.

Evans, David H. Postdoctoral Fellow, Calgary Institute for the Humanities, Alberta, Canada. Contributor to *Faulkner and the Natural World* edited by Ann Abadie (1998) and *Teaching Faulkner: Approaches and Contexts* edited Steven Hahn and Robert W. Hamblin (1998). **Essay:** Songs and Ballads.

Eversley, Shelly. Ph.D. Candidate, Department of English, The Johns Hopkins University, Baltimore, Maryland. **Essay:** Dunbar.

Farr, Judith. Professor of English and American Literature, Georgetown University, Washington, D.C. Author of *The Passion of Emily Dickinson* (1992), *The Life and Art of Elinor Wylie* (1983), and *I Never Came to You in White: A Novel* (1996). Editor of *Emily Dickinson: A Collection of Critical Essays* (1995). **Essay:** Dickinson.

Ferlazzo, Paul J. Professor, Department of English, Northern Arizona University, Flagstaff. Author of *Emily Dickinson* (1976). Editor of *Critical Essays on Emily Dickinson* (1984). Contributor to *Dictionary of Literary Biography* (1988), *The*

Transcendentalists: A Review of Research and Criticism edited by Joel Myerson (1984), and to the journals *American Quarterly*, *Whitman Review*, *Midamerica*, and *South Dakota Review*. **Essay:** Markham.

Fleischmann, Fritz. Professor of English, Babson College, Wellesley, Massachusetts. Author of *A Right View of the Subject: Feminism in the Works of Charles Brockden Brown and John Neal* (1983). Editor of *American Novelists Revisited: Essays in Feminist Criticism* (1982). Coeditor of *Women's Studies and Literature* (1987). Contributor to *American Reformers* edited by Alden Whitman (1985), *Myth and Enlightenment in American Literature* edited by Dieter Meindl et al. (1985), *Consumable Goods* edited by Kirk Vaughn (1987), *Classics in Cultural Criticism* edited by Hartmut Heuermann (1990), *Bibliography of United States Literature: Fiction to 1865* edited by Kent Ljungquist (1994), *Kindlers Neues Literaturlexicon*, *Dictionary of Literary Biography*, and *American National Biography*, and to the journals *New England Quarterly*, *Amerikastudien/American Studies*, and *Works and Days*. **Essay:** Neal.

Fletcher, Angus. Distinguished Professor of English, Lehman College and the Graduate School and University Center of the City University of New York. Author of *Allegory: The Theory of a Symbolic Mode* (1964), *The Transcendental Masque: An Essay on Milton's "Comus"* (1971), *The Prophetic Moment: An Essay on Spenser* (1971), and *Colors of the Mind: Conjectures on Thinking in Literature* (1991). Contributor to *New Perspectives on Coleridge and Wordsworth* edited by Geoffrey Hartman and Samuel Hynes (1972), *I. A. Richards: Essays in His Honor* edited by Reuben Brower et al. (1973), *Representing Kenneth Burke* edited by Hayden White and Margaret Brose (1982), *Textual Analysis: Some Readers Reading* edited by Mary Ann Caws (1986), *The Legacy of Northrop Frye* edited by Alvin Lee and Robert D. Denham (1994), *Shakespeare's Universe: Renaissance Ideas and Conventions* edited by John M. Mucciolo (1996) and to the journals *Representations*, *Critical Inquiry*, *Diacritics*, and *Raritan*. **Essay:** James Russell Lowell.

Foster, Edward Halsey. Professor of English and American Literature, Stevens Institute of Technology, Hoboken, New Jersey; President, Talisman House, Publishers. Author of *Catharine Maria Sedgwick* (1974), *The Civilized Wilderness: Backgrounds to American Romantic Literature, 1817–1860* (1975), *Josiah Gregg and Lewis Hector Garrard* (1977), *Susan and Anna Warner* (1978), *Richard Brautigan* (1983), *William Saroyan* (1984), *Jack Spicer* (1991), *William Saroyan: A Study of the Short Fiction* (1991), *Understanding the Beats* (1992), *The Space Between Her Bed and Clock* (1993), *The Understanding* (1994), *All Acts Are Simply Acts* (1995), *Understanding the Black Mountain Poets* (1995), and *Adrian as Song* (1996). Editor of *Cummington Poems* (1982) and *Postmodern Poetry* (1994). Coeditor of *Hoboken* (with Geoffrey W. Clark, 1976), *The New Freedoms* (with Vadim Mesyats, 1994), and *Primary Trouble: An Anthology of Contemporary American Poetry* (with Leonard Schwartz and Joseph Donahue, 1976). Contributor to *American Literature to 1900* edited by Lewis Leary (1980), *William Saroyan* edited by Leo Hamaliam

(1987), *Reference Guide to American Literature* edited by Daniel Fitzpatrick (1988), *The Birth-Mark: Unsettling the Wilderness in American Literary History* by Susan Howe (1993), and *Critical Essays on William Saroyan* edited by Harry Keyishian (1995), and to many journals. **Essays:** Bodman, Holland.

Gabin, Jane S. Assistant Director of Undergraduate Admissions, University of North Carolina at Chapel Hill. Author of *A Living Minstrelsy: The Poetry and Music of Sidney Lanier* (1985). Contributor to *Jewish Women in America* edited by Paula E. Hymanadn and Deborah Dash Moore (1998), *Fifty Southern Writers Before 1900* edited by Robert Bain and Joseph Flora (1987), and *Reference Guide to American Literature* edited by Daniel Kirkpatrick (1987). Reviewer for *Choice*. **Essay:** Lanier.

Gebhard, Caroline. Assistant Professor, Department of English and Foreign Languages, Tuskegee University, Alabama. Contributor to *Haunted Bodies: Rethinking the South Through Gender* edited by Susan V. Donaldson and Anne Goodwyn Jones (1997), *Narratives of Relocation/Dislocation: Women, America, and Movement* edited by Susan L. Roberson (1998), and to the journal *Tulsa Studies in Women's Literature*. **Essay:** Woolson.

Giffen, Allison. Assistant Professor, English Department, New Mexico State University, Las Cruces. Contributor to *Genre and Writing: Issues, Arguments, Alternatives* edited by Wendy Bishop and Hans Ostrom (1997), and *American Women Prose Writers to 1820* edited by Carla Mulford, Amy Winans, and Angela Vietto (1998), and to the journals *Early American Literature* and *Emily Dickinson Journal*. **Essay:** Ella Wheeler Wilcox.

Graf, Susan Johnston. Instructor in English, Pennsylvania State University, Mont Alto. **Essay:** Sill.

Gray, Janet. Poet and Independent Scholar. Author of *Flaming Tail Out of the Ground Near Your Farm (1987)* and *A Hundred Flowers* (1993). Editor of *She Wields a Pen: American Women Poets of the 19th Century* (1997). Contributor to *American Writers* (supplements III [1991], IV [1996]) and *Retrospective Supplement* edited by A. Walton Litz (1997), *Feminist Literary Theory: A Dictionary* edited by Beth Kowaleski-Wallace, *The Oxford Companion to Women's Writing in the United States* edited by Cathy Davidson (1994), and *Modern American Women Writers* edited by Elaine Showalter (1991) and to the journals *Critical Matrix, A/B: Auto/Biography Studies*, and *Princeton University Library Chronicle*. **Essay:** Popular Poetry.

Grenander, M. E. Distinguished Service Professor Emeritus, Department of English, The University at Albany, State University of New York. Author of *Ambrose Bierce* (1971). Editor of *Apollo Agonistes: The Humanities in a Computerized World* (1979) and *The Poems of Ambrose Bierce* (1985). Contributor to *Dictionary of Literary Biography* (1982, 1983, 1988), *Benét's Reader's Encyclopedia of American Literature* edited by George Perkins et al. (1991), and *Twentieth-Century Liter-*

ary Criticism edited by Laurie Di Mauro and Marie Lazzari (1994), and to the journals *PMLA, Nineteenth-Century Fiction, Western Humanities Review, College English, Early American Literature, American Literature, American Quarterly, Southern Quarterly, Modern Language Studies, Modern Fiction Studies*, and *American Literary Realism*. **Essay:** Bierce.

Hall, James C. Assistant Professor of African-American Studies and English, University of Illinois at Chicago. Coeditor of *Teaching a New Canon?: Students, Teachers, and Texts in the College Literature Classroom* (with Bruce Goebel). Contributor to *Approaches to Teaching Wright's "Native Son"* edited by James Miller (1997), and *Approaches to Teaching Morrison's "Song of Solomon" and Other Novels* edited by Kathryn Earle and Nellie McKay, and to the journals *African-American Review, Callaloo*, and *Langston Hughes Review*. **Essays:** Vashon, Whitfield.

Hall, Jonathan. Instructor in American Literature, Rutgers University, Newark, New Jersey. Contributor to *ATQ, ESQ, American Literature, Sou'wester, Another Chicago Magazine*, and *Hawaii Review*. **Essay:** Alice Cary and Phoebe Cary.

Hayes, Kevin J. Associate Professor of English, University of Central Oklahoma, Edmond. Author of *A Colonial Woman's Bookshelf* (1996), *Folklore and Book Culture* (1997), and *The Library of William Byrd of Westover* (1997). **Essay:** Tabb.

Hazen, James. Professor of English, University of Nevada, Las Vegas. Contributor to *Dictionary of Literary Biography* (1987), *Encyclopedia of American Humorists* edited by Stephen Gale (1988), and *History and Humanities* edited by Francis X. Hartigan (1989), and to the journals *Blake Studies, Texas Studies in Literature and Language, ATQ, Victorian Poetry, College Literature, The Pre-Raphaelite Review*, and *Essays in Graham Greene*. **Essay:** Carlos Wilcox.

Hoffman, Daniel. Poet in Residence and Felix E. Schelling Professor of English Emeritus, University of Pennsylvania, Philadelphia. Consultant in Poetry to The Library of Congress (1973–74). Author of 10 books of poems, including *Hang-Gliding from Helicon: New & Selected Poems, 1948–1988* (1988) and *Middens of the Tribe* (1995), and of *The Poetry of Stephen Crane* (1957), *Poe Poe Poe Poe Poe Poe Poe* (1972), *Form and Fable in American Fiction* (1961), *Faulkner's Country Matters* (1989), and *Words to Create a World* (1993). Editor of and contributor to *American Poetry and Poetics: Poems and Critical Documents from the Puritans to Robert Frost* (1962), *Harvard Guide to Contemporary American Writing* (1979), and *Ezra Pound and William Carlos Williams* (1983). **Essays:** Crane, Poe.

Hollander, John. Poet and Sterling Professor of English, Yale University, New Haven, Connecticut. Author of 15 books of poetry, including *Selected Poetry* (1993) and *Tesserae* (1993), and 7 critical studies, including *The Work of Poetry* (1997), *The Gazer's Spirit* (1995), and *Melodious Guile* (1988). Editor of *American Poetry: The Nineteenth Century* (Library of America, 1993) and coeditor of *The Oxford Anthology of English Literature* (with Sir Frank Kermode, 2 vols., 1972). **Essay:** Stickney.

Honaker, Lisa. Assistant Professor, Division of Arts and Humanities, Richard Stockton College, Pomona, New Jersey. Contributor to *Essays for the 80's* edited by William Vesterman (1986), and *Effective Writing for the College Curriculum* edited by William Vesterman and Robert Atwan (1987), and to the journals *Modern Fiction Studies* and *SITES*. Essay: Cranch.

Hunter, Doreen M. Professor of History, Department of History and Faculty of Women's Studies, Fort Lewis College, Durango, Colorado. Author of *Richard Henry Dana, Sr.* (1987). Contributor to *New England Quarterly* and *American Quarterly*. Essay: Dana.

Johnson, Wendy Dasler. Assistant Professor, Department of English, Washington State University, Vancouver. Essay: Howe.

Kane, Paul. Associate Professor of English, Vassar College, Poughkeepsie, New York. Author of *Australian Poetry: Romanticism and Negativity* (1996) and *The Farther Shore* (1989). Coeditor of *Ralph Waldo Emerson: Collected Poems and Translations* (with Harold Bloom, 1994). Editor of *Poetry of the American Renaissance: A Diverse Anthology from the Romantic Period* (1995). Essay: Emerson.

Kassanoff, Jennie A. Assistant Professor of English, Barnard College, New York. Contributor to *The Unruly Voice: Rediscovering Pauline Elizabeth Hopkins* edited by John Cullen Gruesser (1996), and *American Writers: Retrospective Supplement* edited by A. Walton Litz (1997), and to the journal *Arizona Quarterly*. Essay: Wharton.

Kasson, Joy S. Professor of American Studies and English, University of North Carolina at Chapel Hill. Author of *Artistic Voyagers: Europe and the American Imagination in the Works of Irving, Cooper, Hawthorne, Allston, and Cole* (1982) and *Marble Queens and Captives: Women in Nineteenth-Century American Sculpture* (1990). Editor of *Louisa May Alcott's Work* (1994). Contributor to *The Aesthetics of Sentiment* edited by Shirley Samuels (1992), and to the journals *American Quarterly, American Historical Review, Journal of Interdisciplinary History,* and *Journal of American History*. Essay: Cole.

Keating, Gail C. Assistant Professor of Women's Studies and English, Pennsylvania State University, Worthington Scranton Campus, Dunmore. Contributor to *Nineteenth Century American Women Writers: A Bio-Bibliographical Critical Sourcebook* edited by Denise Knight (1997), and to the journals *The Literary Griot: International Journal of Black Expressive Culture Studies* and *The International Journal of Aging and Human Development*. Essay: Jewett.

Kilcup, Karen L. Associate Professor of English, University of North Carolina at Greensboro. Author of *Robert Frost and Feminine Literary Traditions* (1998). Editor of *Nineteenth-Century American Women Writers: An Anthology* (1997) and *Nineteenth-Century American Women Writers: A Critical Reader* (1998). Contributor to *Tricksterism in Turn-of-the-Century American Literature: A Multicultural Perspective* edited by Elizabeth Ammons and A. White-Parks (1994), *A Noble*

and Dignified Stream: The Piscataqua Region in the Colonial Revival, 1860–1930 edited by Sarah M. Giffen and Kevin M. Murphy (1992), *Out of Bounds: Male Writers and Gender(ed) Criticism* edited by Laura Claridge and Elizabeth Langland (1990), *New Directions in American Humor Studies* edited by David E. E. Sloane (1998), and *Scribbling Women: Engendering and Expanding the Hawthorne Tradition* edited by John Idol and Melinda M. Ponder (1998), and to the journals *Legacy, ESQ, Colby Quarterly, Journal of Gender Studies* (UK), *Women and Language,* and *Studies in American Humor*. Essay: Rose Terry Cooke.

Kleitz, Dorsey. Associate Professor of English, Tokyo Woman's Christian University, Japan. Essays: Menken, Taylor.

Lawson, Benjamin S. Associate Professor of American Literature, Albany State College, Georgia. Author of *Rereading the Revolution: The Turn-of-the-Century American Revolutionary War Novel* (1998) and *Doors: Reflections on Life at an African-American College* (forthcoming). Contributor to *Twentieth-Century Literary Criticism* edited by Paula Kepos and Dennis Poupard (1989), *Intertextuality in Literature and Film* edited by Elaine D. Cancalon and Antoine Spacagna (1994), and *Impossibility Fiction: Alternativity, Extrapolation, Speculation* edited by Derek Littlewood and Peter Stockwell (1996), and to the journals *South Dakota Review, Extrapolation, Southern Literary Journal,* and *Liberian Studies Journal*. Essay: Miller.

Little, Michael R. Doctoral Student, Department of English, Texas A&M University, College Station. Contributor to *American National Biography* and *Contemporary Popular Writers*. Essay: Trowbridge.

Littlefield, Daniel F., Jr. Professor of English and Director, American Native Press Archives, University of Arkansas at Little Rock. Author of *Alex Posey: Creek Poet, Journalist, and Humorist* (1992). Editor of *The Fus Fixico Letters* (1993). Coeditor with James W. Parins of *Native American Writing in the Southeast* (1996), *Tales of the Bark Lodges* (1996), *Ke-maha, The Omaha Stories of Francis La Flesche* (1995), *A Biobibliography of Native American Writers, 1772–1924* (2 vols., 1983), and *American Indian and Alaska Native Newspapers and Periodicals, 1826–1985* (3 vols., 1986). Contributor to *American Studies, Studies in American Indian Literatures, American Indian Quarterly, Mississippi Quarterly, Southern Literary Journal,* and *Markham Review*. Essay: Posey.

Longest, George C. Associate Professor, Department of English, Virginia Commonwealth University, Richmond, Virginia. Author of *Genius in the Garden: Charles F. Gillette and Landscape Architecture in Virginia* (1992) and *Three Virginia Writers: Mary Johnston, Thomas Nelson Page, Amélie Rives Troubetzkoy* (1978). Editor Emeritus of *Resources for American Literary Study*. Coeditor of *Veins of Endurance: The Fiction of Ellen Glasgow* (with W. D. Taylor, 1998). Contributor to *Mississippi Quarterly*. Essay: Simms.

Lott, Deshae E. Ph.D. Candidate, Department of English, Texas A&M University, College Station. Essay: Horton.

Loving, Jerome. Professor of English, Texas A&M University, College Station. Author of *Emerson, Whitman, and the American Muse* (1982), *Emily Dickinson: The Poet on the Second Story* (1987), *Lost in the Customhouse: Authorship in the American Renaissance* (1993), and *Walt Whitman: The Song of Himself* (1998). Editor of *Leaves of Grass* (Oxford World Classics, 1990). **Essay:** Walt Whitman.

Lowance, Mason I., Jr. Professor of English, University of Massachusetts, Amherst. Author of *Increase Mather* (1974), *Massachusetts Broadsides of the American Revolution* (1976), *The Language of Canaan* (1980), *The Typological Writings of Jonathan Edwards* (1993), *The Stowe Debate: Rhetorical Strategies in "Uncle Tom's Cabin"* (1994), and *A House Divided: The American Antebellum Slavery Debate, 1776–1865* (forthcoming). Editor of *Early American Literature* and *Studies in Puritan American Spirituality*. Contributor to *American Literature, Early American Literature, New England Quarterly, William & Mary Quarterly, Arizona Quarterly, American Quarterly, American Historical Review,* and *Proceedings of the American Antiquarian Society.* **Essay:** Spirituals.

McCullough, Joseph B. Professor of English, University of Nevada, Las Vegas. Author of *Hamlin Garland* (1978). Editor of Hamlin Garland's *Tales From the Middle Border* (1990), *A Son of the Middle Border* (1995), and *Main-Travelled Roads* (1995). Coeditor of *The Bible According to Mark Twain: Writings on Heaven, Eden and the Flood* (with Howard Baetzhold, 1995; reprinted 1996) and *Selected Letters of Hamlin Garland* (with Keith Newlin, 1998). **Essay:** Garland.

McIntire-Strasburg, Janice. Lecturer, University of Nevada, Las Vegas. Contributor to *Notes on Modern Irish Literature, Thalia,* and *Mark Twain Forum.* **Essay:** Huntington.

McKee, Kathryn B. Assistant Professor of English and Southern Studies, University of Mississippi, Oxford. Contributor to *Mississippi Quarterly, Studies in the American Renaissance, American Transcendental Quarterly,* and *Southern Quarterly.* **Essay:** Leland.

Meyer, Bruce. Head, Creative Writing Program, School of Continuing Studies, University of Toronto, Canada. Author of *In Their Words: Interviews with Fourteen Canadian Writers* (1985), *Profiles in Canadian Literature: Leonard Cohen* (1986), *The Open Room* (1989), *Profiles in Canadian Literature: Frank Prewett* (1990), *Profiles in Canadian Literature: Robert Service* (1990), *Radio Silence* (1991), *Lives and Works: Interviews with Fourteen Canadian Writers* (1991), *Goodbye Mr. Spalding* (1996), and *The Presence* (1998). Editor of *Arrivals: Canadian Poetry in the Eighties* (1985), *The Selected Poems of Frank Prewett* (1987), *Separate Islands: Contemporary British and Irish Poetry* (1988), and *The Stories: Contemporary Short Fiction of the English Language* (1997). Contributor to *The Oxford Companion to Canadian Literature* edited by William Toye (1982), *Contemporary Poets* (1991), *Reader's Guide to Literature in English* edited by Mark Hawkins-Dady (1996), and *The Oxford Companion to Canadian Literature* (1997). **Essay:** Hovey.

Modey, Christine A. Ph.D. Candidate, Department of English, University of Delaware, Newark, Delaware. **Essay:** Canning.

Moore, Rayburn S. Professor Emeritus of English, University of Georgia, Athens. Author of *Constance Fenimore Woolson* (1963) and *Paul Hamilton Hayne* (1972). Editor of *For the Major and Selected Short Stories of Constance Fenimore Woolson* (1967), *A Man of Letters in the Nineteenth-Century South: Selected Letters of Paul Hamilton Hayne* (1982), *Selected Letters of Henry James to Edmund Gosse, 1882–1915* (1988), and *The Correspondence of Henry James and the House of Macmillan, 1877–1914* (1993). Coeditor of *The History of Southern Literature* (with Louis D. Rubin Jr. et al., 1985). Contributor to *Southern Literary Study: Problems and Possibilities* edited by Louis D. Rubin Jr. and C. Hugh Holman (1975), *Ante-Bellum Writers in New York and the South* edited by Joel Myerson (1979), *The Work and Reputation of William Gilmore Simms* edited by John C. Guilds (1988), and *Criticism on Constance Fenimore Woolson* edited by Cheryl B. Torsney (1992), and to the journals *American Literature, South Atlantic Quarterly, Mississippi Quarterly, Georgia Review, South Atlantic Review, American Literary Realism, American Quarterly, South Carolina Review, Southern Review, University of Mississippi Studies in English, Postscript, Henry James Review, Studies in the Novel,* and *Mark Twain Journal.* **Essays:** Hayne, Pinkney.

Motoike, Kathleen. Instructor of English, Santa Monica College and Glendale College, California. Contributor to *Crescent Review.* **Essay:** Kemble.

Munro, Molly M. Ph.D. Candidate, Department of English, University of North Carolina at Chapel Hill. **Essay:** Monroe.

Norko, Julie. Ph.D. Candidate, Department of English, University of North Carolina at Chapel Hill. Contributor to *American Transcendental Quarterly* and *Studies in the American Renaissance.* **Essay:** Freneau.

Packer, Barbara. Professor, Department of English, University of California at Los Angeles. Author of *Emerson's Fall* (1982) and *The Transcendentalists,* in *The Cambridge History of American Literature,* vol. II, edited by Sacvan Bercovitch (1994). Contributor to *The Columbia History of American Literature* edited by Emory Elliott (1988). **Essay:** Drake.

Parins, James W. Professor of English and Director, Native American Writers Archival Project, University of Arkansas at Little Rock. Author of *John Rollin Ridge* (1991). Coeditor with Daniel F. Littlefield Jr. of *Native American Writing in the Southeast* (1996), *Tales of the Bark Lodges* (1996), *Ke-ma-ha, The Omaha Stories of Francis La Flesche* (1995), *A Biobibliography of Native American Writers, 1772–1924* (2 vols., 1983), and *American Indian and Alaska Native Newspapers and Periodicals, 1826–1985* (3 vols., 1986). **Essay:** Ridge.

Parr, Matthew. Editor, The Library of America, New York. **Essays:** Bristol, Nineteenth-Century Versions of American Indian Poetry.

Payne, James Robert. Professor, Department of English, New Mexico State University, Las Cruces. Editor of *Multicultural*

Autobiography: American Lives (1992) and *Joseph Seamon Cotter, Jr.: Complete Poems* (1990). Contributor to *The Heath Anthology of American Literature* edited by Paul Lauter et al. (1997), *The Oxford Companion to African American Literature* edited by William L. Andrews et al. (1997), *Encyclopedia of English Studies and Language Arts* edited by Alan C. Purvis (1994), *Native American Women: A Biographical Dictionary* edited by Gretchen M. Bataille (1993), and *Afro-American Writers Before the Harlem Renaissance (DLB)* edited by Trudier Harris and Thadious M. Davis (1986), and to the journals *MELUS, A/B: Auto/Biography Studies, Quarterly Review of Film Studies, Explorations in Ethnic Studies, Markham Review, Henry James Review, American Literary Realism, World Literature Today, Resources for American Literary Study,* and *Rocky Mountain Review of Language and Literature.* **Essay:** Albery Allson Whitman.

Pellegrino, Joe. Assistant Professor, Department of English, Eastern Kentucky University, Richmond. Author of *American Artifacts: College Students' Perspectives on America* (1994) and *Seamus Heaney: A Critical Introduction* (1995). Contributor to *Biographical Dictionary of Transcendentalism* edited by Wesley Mott (1996), *The Robert Frost Encyclopedia* edited by Nancy L. Tuten and John Zubizarreta (1998), and to the journals *Robert Frost Review* and *Notes on Modern Irish Literature.* **Essays:** Lodge, Scollard.

Price, Kenneth M. Professor of English and American Studies, College of William & Mary, Williamsburg, Virginia. Author of *Whitman and Tradition: The Poet in His Century* (1990). Codirector of Walt Whitman Hypertext Archive (<http://jefferson.village.virginia.edu/whitman>; with Ed Folsom). Editor of *Walt Whitman: The Contemporary Reviews* (1995). Coeditor of *Walt Whitman: Major Authors on CD-ROM* (with Ed Folsom, 1977), *Critical Essays on James Weldon Johnson* (with Larry Oliver, 1997), *Periodical Literature in Nineteenth-Century America* (with Susan Belasco Smith, 1995), *Critical Essays on George Santayana* (with Robert Leitz, 1990), *Dear Brother Walt: The Letters of Thomas Jefferson Whitman* (with Dennis Berthold, 1984). Contributor to *American Literature, Texas Studies in Literature and Language, Resources for American Literary Study, ESQ,* and *Walt Whitman Quarterly Review.* **Essay:** Moody.

Reed, Glenn M. Associate Professor of English, Northern Arizona University, Flagstaff. Contributor to *Southern Studies.* **Essay:** Sargent.

Regan, Robert. Professor of English, University of Pennsylvania, Philadelphia. Author of *Unpromising Heroes: Mark Twain and His Characters* (1969). Editor of *Poe: A Collection of Critical Essays* (1967). Contributor to *American Bypaths* edited by Robert G. Collmer and Jack W. Herring (1980), *One Hundred Years of Huckleberry Finn* edited by Robert Sattelmeyer and J. Donald Crowley (1985), *Mark Twain Encyclopedia* edited by J. R. LeMaster and James D. Wilson (1994), and *Dickinson and Audience* edited by Martin Orzeck and Robert Weisbuch (1996), and to the journals *American Literature, American Studies, Delta, Mark Twain Journal, Nineteenth-Century Fic-*

tion, *Studies in American Humor,* and *Virginia Quarterly Review.* **Essay:** Tuckerman.

Remus, Jane. Independent Scholar, Hamden, Connecticut. **Essay:** Henry Adams.

Rinehart, Lucy. Assistant Professor, Department of English, DePaul University, Chicago, Illinois. Contributor to *American Drama* and *Resources in American Literary Study.* **Essays:** Boker, Paulding.

Romine, Scott. Assistant Professor of English, University of North Carolina at Greensboro. Contributor to *Style, Mississippi Quarterly, Southern Quarterly, Southern Literary Journal, South Atlantic Review, Arkansas Quarterly.* **Essays:** Legaré, Santayana.

Ross, Cheri Louise. Assistant Professor of Humanities, Pennsylvania State University, Harrisburg. Contributor to *CLA Journal, Journal of Popular Culture,* and *Journal of the Midwest Modern Language Association.* **Essay:** Lazarus.

Russo, Maria. Independent Scholar, New York. Contributor to *Lingua Franca.* **Essay:** Reese.

Ryan, Barbara. Assistant Professor of English, University of Missouri at Kansas City. **Essays:** Guiney, Sarah Helen Whitman.

Ryan, Robert C. Professor of English, Emeritus, Boston University, Massachusetts. Editor of the *Published Poems* volume in the Northwestern-Newberry *Writings of Herman Melville* (forthcoming). **Essay:** Melville.

Samonds, John. Instructor of English, Rhodes College, Memphis, Tennessee. Contributor to *Encyclopedia of Transcendentalism* and *Biographical Dictionary of Transcendentalism* edited by Wesley Mott (1996) and *The Robert Frost Encyclopedia* edited by Nancy L. Tuten and John Zubizarreta (1998). **Essay:** Torrence.

Scharnhorst, Gary. Professor of English, University of New Mexico, Albuquerque. Editor of *American Literary Realism* and *American Literary Scholarship.* Author of *Charlotte Perkins Gilman* (1985), *Nathaniel Hawthorne: An Annotated Bibliography* (1988), *Bret Harte* (1992), and *Henry David Thoreau: An Annotated Bibliography* (1992). Editor of *Critical Essays on the Adventures of Tom Sawyer* (1993) and *Selected Letters of Bret Harte* (1997). Contributor to *Nineteenth-Century Literature.* **Essay:** Longfellow.

Shields, David S. Professor of American Literature, The Citadel, Charleston, South Carolina. Author of *Civil Tongues and Polite Letters in British America* (1997) and *Oracles of Empire: Poetry, Politics and Commerce in British America 1690–1750* (1990). Coauthor of *The Cambridge History of America Literature, Volume One 1590–1820* edited by Sacvan Bercovitch (with Myra Jehlen, Emory Elliott, Robert Ferguson, and Michael T. Gilmore, 1994) and *The History of the Book in America, Volume One* edited by David D. Hall and Hugh

Amory (forthcoming). Contributor to *Everyday Life in the Early Republic* edited by Catherine E. Hutchins (1995), *A Mixed Race: Ethnicity in Early America* edited by Frank Shuffelton (1993), *The Meaning of South Carolina History: Essays in Honor of George C. Rogers, Jr.* edited by David R. Chesnutt and Clyde N. Wilson (1991), *Federal New York: A Symposium* (1990), *The Age of William III and Mary II; Power, Politics and Patronage 1688–1702* edited by Robert P. Maccubbin and Martha Hamilton-Philips (1989), *Like Seasoned Timber: New Essays on George Herbert* edited by Robert DiYanni (1988), *Deism, Masonry, and the Enlightenment* edited by J. A. Leo Lemay (1987), *Teaching Early American Literature* edited by Carla Mulford (1998), and *The Serpent in the Cup: Temperance in American Literature* edited by David S. Reynolds and Debra Rosenthal (1998), and to the journals *William & Mary Quarterly, Resources for American Literary Study, Proceedings of the American Antiquarian Society, American Literary History, Early American Literature, Princeton University Library Chronicle, Pennsylvania Magazine of History and Biography, Southern Literature,* and *American Literature*. **Essay:** Timrod.

Shucard, Alan. Professor, English Department, University of Wisconsin – Parkside, Kenosha, Wisconsin. Author of *American Poetry: The Puritans Through Walt Whitman* (1988, 1990), *Countee Cullen* (1984), *The Louse on the Head of a Yawning Lord* (1972), and *The Gorgon Bag* (1970). Coauthor of *Modern American Poetry, 1865–1950* (1989, 1990). Editor of Twayne's Critical History of Poetry Series (English Language Section): *Containing Multitudes: American Poetry 1950 to the Present* (1997) and *Nineteenth-Century English Poetry* (1994). Contributor to *Contemporary Novelists* (1972, 1973, 1975, 1996), *Contemporary Poets* (1975, 1996), *Writers in English* (1979), *Dictionary of Literary Biography* (1987), *Contemporary Authors* (1988), *Historical Dictionary of the Progressive Era* (1988), *The Reader's Guide to American Literature* (1991), *The Walt Whitman Encyclopedia* edited by J. R. LeMaster and D. Kummings (1998), and to the journals *Arizona Quarterly, English Quarterly, World Literature Written in English, Canadian Literature, CLIO, Mickle Street Review, American Literature, Beloit Poetry Journal, Kansas Quarterly, Great Lakes Review,* and *The Literary Review*. **Essay:** Robinson.

Steele, Jeffrey. Professor, Department of English, University of Wisconsin, Madison. Author of *Unfolding the Mind: The Unconscious in American Romanticism and Literary Theory* (1987) and *The Representation of the Self in the American Renaissance* (1987). Editor of *The Essential Margaret Fuller* (1992). Contributor to *Emerson: Prospect and Retrospect* edited by Joel Porte (1982), *Dictionary of Literary Biography*, vol. 71 (1988), *Influence and Intertextuality in Literary History* edited by Jay Clayton and Eric Rothstein (1991), *Dressing in Feathers: Images of Native Americans in Popular Culture* edited by S. Elizabeth Bird (1996), *Criticism and the Color-Line: Desegregating American Literary Studies* edited by Henry B. Wonham (1996), *An Emotional History of the United States* edited by Peter N. Stearns and Jan Lewis (1998), *The Cambridge Companion to Emerson* edited by Joel Porte (1999),

and *Approaches to Teaching the Narrative of the Life of Frederick Douglass* edited by James C. Hall (1999), and to the journals *Studies in the American Renaissance, New England Quarterly, University of Mississippi Studies in English, Walt Whitman Quarterly Review, Historia 16,* and *Wisconsin Academy Review*. **Essay:** Fuller.

Stein, Lorin. M.F.A. Candidate, The Writing Programs, The Johns Hopkins University, Baltimore, Maryland. **Essay:** Allston.

Taylor, Welford Dunaway. James A. Bostwick Professor of English, University of Richmond, Virginia. Author of *Amélie Rives (Princess Troubetzkoy)* (1973), *Sherwood Anderson* (1977), and *Robert Frost and J. J. Lankes: Riders on Pegasus* (1996). Editor of Sherwood Anderson's *The Buck Fever Papers* (1971), *The Newsprint Mask: The Tradition of the Fictional Journalist in America* (1990), and *Our American Cousin: The Play That Changed History. A Modern Reading Edition* [by Tom Taylor] (1990). Coeditor of *Southern Odyssey: Selected Writings by Sherwood Anderson* (with Charles E. Modlin, 1997). Contributor to *Sherwood Anderson: Centennial Studies* edited by Hilbert H. Campbell and Charles E. Modlin (1976) and *Sherwood Anderson: Dimensions of His Literary Art* edited by David D. Anderson (1976), and to the journals *Mississippi Quarterly, The Old Northwest, Antiquarian Book Monthly, Dartmouth College Library Bulletin, Virginia Cavalcade, Modern Language Journal, Gulliver,* and *Journal of Modern Literature*. **Essay:** Philip Pendleton Cooke.

Tucker, Edward L. Professor of English, Virginia Polytechnic Institute and State University, Blacksburg, Virginia. Author of *Richard Henry Wilde: His Life and Selected Poems* (1966) and *The Shaping of Longfellow's "John Endicott": A Textual History, Including Two Early Versions* (1985). Contributor to *ANQ, Georgia Historical Quarterly, Dickens Studies Annual, Resources for American Literary Study,* and other journals. **Essay:** Wilde.

Tursi, Renee. Ph.D. Candidate, Department of English and Comparative Literature. Columbia University, New York. Contributor to *Encyclopedia of African-American Culture and History* and *American Philosophical Society Yearbook*. **Essay:** Story.

Vance, Jane Gentry. Professor of English, University of Kentucky, Lexington. Author of *A Garden in Kentucky* (1995). Contributor to *American Women Writing Fiction: Memory, Identity, Family, Space* edited by Mickey Pearlman (1989), and to the journals *Southern Literary Journal, Mississippi Quarterly,* and *Kentucky Review*. **Essay:** Cawein.

Veitch, Jonathan. Chairman of Humanities, New School for Social Research, New York. Author of *American Superrealism: Nathanael West and the Politics of Representation in the 1930s* (1997) and *Mediating Modernity: The Construction of Hollywood in the American Imagination* (forthcoming). Contributor to *Contemporary Literature, Public Culture, The Journal of Film and Video,* and *CLIO*. **Essay:** Brownell.

Vickers, Anita M. Assistant Professor of English and Humanities, Pennsylvania State University, Capital College, Schuylkill. Contributor to *Cordially Yours, Brother Cadfael* edited by Anne K. Kaler (1998), *Great Women of Mystery* edited by Kathleen Gregory Klein (1994), *Masterplots II: African American Fiction* edited by Frank N. Magill (1994), and *Encyclopedia of United States Popular Culture* edited by Ray B. Browne and Pat Browne (1998), and to the journals *Modern Fiction Studies* and *CLA Journal*. **Essay:** Barlow.

Walker, Cheryl. Richard Armour Professor of Modern Languages, Scripps College, Claremont, California. Author of *The Nightingale's Burden: Women Poets and American Culture Before 1900* (1982) and *Indian Nation: Native American Literature and Nineteenth-Century Nationalisms* (1997). Editor of *American Women Poets of the Nineteenth Century* (1992). **Essays:** Jackson, Maria White Lowell.

Walker, Geofrilyn M. Department of English, College of William & Mary, Williamsburg, Virginia. **Essay:** Maria Gowen Brooks.

Walter, Krista. Instructor, Department of English, Loyola University of Chicago. Contributor to *American Transcendental Quarterly*. **Essay:** Channing.

Weales, Gerald. Professor of English Emeritus, University of Pennsylvania, Philadelphia. Author of *Canned Goods as Caviar: American Film Comedy of the 1930s* (1985), *Clifford Odets, Playwright* (1971, reprinted 1985), *The Jumping-Off Place: American Drama in the 1960s* (1969). Editor of *The Complete Plays of William Wycherley* (1966), *Death of a Salesman: Text and Criticism* (1967), and *The Crucible: Text and Criticism* (1971). Contributor to *The Achievement of Arthur Miller* edited by Steven R. Centola (1995), *Critical Essays on E. B. White* edited by Robert L. Root Jr. (1994), and *Public Issues, Private Tensions: Contemporary American Drama* edited by Matthew Charles Roudane (1993), and to the journals *Georgia Review*, *Gettysburg Review*, *Sewanee Review*, *American Theatre*, and *Virginia Quarterly Review*. **Essay:** Riley.

Weyler, Karen A. Visiting Assistant Professor, Department of English, Wake Forest University, Winston-Salem, North Carolina. Contributor to *Sex and Sexuality in Early America* edited by Merrill D. Smith and *Biographical Dictionary of Transcendentalism* edited by Wesley T. Mott (1996), and to the journals *Early American Literature*, *Studies in Short Fiction*, and *Southern Quarterly*. **Essays:** Chapman, Willis.

Witherell, Elizabeth Hall. Editor-in-Chief of *The Writings of Henry D. Thoreau*, Davidson Library, University of California, Santa Barbara. Coeditor of Henry D. Thoreau, *Journal 1: 1837–1844* (with William L. Howarth, Robert Sattelmeyer, and Thomas Blanding, 1981) and *A Week on the Concord and Merrimack Rivers* (with Carl F. Hovde and William L. Howarth, 1980). Contributor to *Studies in the American Re-*

naissance, *Prospects for American Literary Study* edited by Richard Kopley (1997), *The Cambridge Companion to Henry David Thoreau* edited by Joel Myerson (1995), *Thoreau's World and Ours* edited by Edmund A. Schofield and Robert C. Baron (1993), and *Thoreau Among Others: Essays in Honor of Walter Harding* edited by Rita K. Gollin and James B. Scholes (1983). **Essay:** Thoreau.

Wonham, Henry B. Assistant Professor, Department of English, University of Oregon, Eugene. Author of *Mark Twain and the Art of the Tall Tale* (1993). Editor of *Criticism and the Color Line: Desegregating American Literary Studies* (1996) and *Charles W. Chesnutt: A Study of the Short Fiction* (1998). Contributor to *Critical Essays on "The Adventures of Tom Sawyer"* edited by Gary Scharnhorst (1995), and to the journals *American Literature*, *American Quarterly*, *American Literary Realism*, *Arizona Quarterly*, *Studies in American Fiction*, *Twentieth-Century Literature*, and *Nineteenth-Century Literature*. **Essays:** Gilder, Stedman.

Woodall, Guy R. Professor Emeritus, Department of English, Tennessee Technological University, Cookeville. Contributor to *American National Biography* edited by John A. Garraty (1995), *Biographical Dictionary of Transcendentalism* edited by Wesley T. Mott (1996), *Dictionary of Literary Biography* (vol. 59) edited by John W. Rathbun and Monica Grecu (1987), *Proceedings of the Unitarian Universalist Historical Society* (vol. 21) edited by Conrad Wright (1989), *Studies in the American Renaissance* edited by Joel Myerson (1981, 1982, 1986, 1987, 1991), and *The Transcendentalists: A Review of Research and Criticism* edited by Joel Myerson (1984), and to the journals *American Notes & Queries*, *American Transcendental Quarterly*, *Bulletin of Bibliography & Magazine Notes*, *Concord Saunterer*, *Essays in English and American Literature*, *Journal of Newspaper and Periodical History*, *Maryland Historical Magazine*, *Pennsylvania Magazine of History and Biography*, *Restoration Quarterly*, *Studies in Bibliography*, *Resources for American Literary Studies*, and *Tennessee Studies in Literature*. **Essays:** John Quincy Adams, Alcott.

Wortham, Thomas. Professor and Chair, Department of English, University of California at Los Angeles. Editor of *James Russell Lowell's "The Biglow Papers" [First Series]: A Critical Edition* (1977), *Letters of W. D. Howells: 1892–1901* (1983), *The Early Prose Writings of William Dean Howells, 1853–1861* (1990), and *The Poems of Ralph Waldo Emerson* (forthcoming). Editor of *Nineteenth-Century Literature*. **Essay:** Holmes.

Yannella, Donald. Professor of English, Barat College, Lake Forest, Illinois. Author of *Ralph Waldo Emerson* (1982). Coauthor of *Herman Melville's Malcolm Letter: "Man's Final Lore"* (with Hennig Cohen, 1992). Contributor to *A Companion to Melville Studies* edited by John Bryant (1986), and to the journals *Melville Society Extracts*, *Studies in the American Renaissance*, *Studies in the Novel*, and *ATQ*. **Essay:** Mathews.

INDEXES

TITLE AND FIRST LINE INDEX

GENERAL INDEX

*Numbers in **bold** indicate subjects with their own entries.*